THE
READER'S
ADVISER

THE READER'S ADVISER

A LAYMAN'S GUIDE TO LITERATURE
12TH EDITION

Volume 2: The best in American and British
drama and world literature
in English translation

Edited by F. J. Sypher

R. R. BOWKER COMPANY
NEW YORK & LONDON, 1977

Published by R. R. Bowker Co.
1180 Avenue of the Americas, New York, N.Y. 10036
Copyright ©1977 by Xerox Corporation
All rights reserved
International Standard Book Number 0-8352-0852-4
International Standard Serial Number 0094-5943
Library of Congress Catalog Card Number 57-13277
Printed and bound in the United States of America

Contents

Preface

THE TWELFTH EDITION of *"The Reader's Adviser"* carries forward a volume which has proven its usefulness since 1921, when the first edition appeared. The present volume retains the main features of the eleventh edition, but differs from it in several respects.

The material covered in Volume One of the eleventh edition has been greatly expanded and now fills two volumes: the first, published in 1975, covers American and British fiction, poetry, essays, literary biography, and reference; the second, the present volume, covers American and British drama and world literature in English translation. As before, we have confined ourselves to listing books in English, in print, available in the United States. There are occasional exceptions to this rule, but they are few.

The chapters on American and British drama (Chapters 1–5) are arranged in essentially the same manner as before, but they have been carefully revised and expanded, with new introductions and many new biographical sketches, as well as listings for contemporary authors who have not appeared before in *"The Reader's Adviser."*

The greatest changes have been introduced in the remaining chapters—those on world literature in English translation (Chapters 6–19). Literatures previously treated in separate chapters—classical (now divided into Greek and Latin), French, German, and Russian—have been drastically revised, with new introductions, new commentaries on individual authors, and many new listings. The rest of world literature, formerly placed under the heading "Other Foreign Literature," is now, as a glance at the table of contents will show, represented by a number of independent chapters, each of them completely revised. Furthermore, the volume has been improved by the addition of a number of new chapters and sections within chapters on literatures which were not represented at all in the previous edition.

In Chapter 15, "Other European Literature," the existing sections have been thoroughly revised, and for the first time there are new sections on Albanian, Byelorussian, Bulgarian, Estonian, Latvian, and Ukrainian literature. Since many of the publications listed in this chapter are not distributed through regular commercial channels, there is much information here that is virtually unique to *"The Reader's Adviser."*

Similarly, Chapter 18, "Middle Eastern Literature," contains entirely new material and for the first time includes sections on ancient Near Eastern literature, Armenian literature, and Turkish literature. The detailed introduction to each section of Chapter 18 should give the reader some notion of how much material in these literatures, among the richest in the world, remains to be translated into English.

Chapter 19, "Asian Literature," has been skillfully and authoritatively expanded and revised. For the first time there are separate discussions and bibliographies for the literatures of Southeast Asian nations, Mongolia, and Tibet.

Although the volume is quite large as it stands, it is regrettable that there is so little available in translation for many of the literatures. It is to be hoped that the present work will not only introduce readers to new riches of world literature, but will also help make way for new translations. Each language has its own distinct voice and its own contribution to make. Insofar as we can hear these voices speak and respond to their forms of expression, we will come closer to that ideal condition of being citizens not of this or that nation, but citizens of the world.

It remains to thank all those who have worked on the volume. First of all, I must thank the contributing editors, whose conscientious efforts provided the essential material for this edition. I should also like to thank all those, too numerous to mention here, who gave advice on particular points in the progress of the work. Mrs. Julia Miele deserves special thanks for her close editorial checking and reading of the whole text. Finally, I must thank Mrs. Sarah L. Prakken, the general editor of *"The Reader's Adviser,"* for her patient and generous advice at every step in the preparation of the book.

F. J. Sypher

New York 1977

Contributing Editors

D. A. Dina Abramowicz, Yivo Institute for Jewish Research (*Yiddish Literature*)

E. J. A. Eileen Jorge Allman, Department of English, Herbert Lehman College of the City University of New York (*British Drama Early to 18th Century; Shakespeare*)

D. B. David Bady, Department of English, Herbert Lehman College of the City University of New York (*The Drama; Modern British Drama*)

H. B. Henryk Baran, Department of Russian, State University of New York at Albany (*Russian Literature*)

C. A. B. C. Arthur Brakel, Department of Hispanic and Italian Studies, State University of New York at Albany (*Portuguese Literature*)

M. C. Matei Calinescu, Department of Comparative Literature, Indiana University (*Rumanian Literature*)

F. G. G. Francis G. Gentry, Department of German, The University of Wisconsin (*German Literature*)

G. J. Glenderlyn Johnson, Schomburg Center for Research in Black Culture, Astor, Lenox and Tilden Foundations (*African Literature*)

G. K. Geoffrey Kabat, Ph.D., Columbia University (*Czechoslovak Literature; Hungarian Literature*)

E. K. Edward Kasinec, Ukrainian Institute, Harvard University (*Ukrainian Literature*)

V. K. Vitaut Kipel, Science and Technology Research Center, New York Public Library (*Byelorussian Literature*)

C. K. Christopher Kleinhenz, Department of French and Italian, The University of Wisconsin (*Italian Literature*)

J. K. K. Joan K. Krasner, formerly with Harvard-Yenching Library, Harvard University (*Asian Literature*)

E. K. Egbert Krispyn, Department of Germanic and Slavic Languages, The University of Georgia (*Netherlandic Literature*)

J. F. L. John Fiske Loud, Department of Modern Languages and Literatures, Texas Christian University (*Yugoslav Literature*)

J. R. L. J. Robert Loy, Department of Modern Languages, Brooklyn College of the City University of New York (*French Literature*)

C. A. M. Charles A. Moser, Department of Slavic Languages and Literatures, The George Washington University (*Bulgarian Literature*)

V. N. Valters Nollendorfs, Department of German, The University of Wisconsin (*Latvian Literature*)

L. L. O. Louis L. Orlin, Department of Near Eastern Studies, The University of Michigan (*Ancient Near Eastern Literature*)

D. H. P. David H. Partington, Middle Eastern Department, Harvard College Library (*Arabic Literature; Persian Literature; Turkish Literature*)

J. P. Jean Peters, Library, R. R. Bowker Co. (*World Literature*)

M. P. Mark Piel, Upsala College Library (*American Drama*)

xi

N.F.P. & Nadine F. Posner and Lawrence H. Schiffman, Department of Near
L.H.S.   Eastern Languages and Literatures, Hagop Kevorkian Center for
          Near Eastern Studies, New York University (*Hebrew Literature*)

P. R. P. Peter R. Prifti, Center for International Studies, Massachusetts Insti-
          tute of Technology (*Albanian Literature*)

A. R.   Aleksis Rannit, Department of Russian and East European Studies,
          Yale University (*Estonian Literature*)

R. Š.   Rimvydas Šilbajoris, Department of Slavic Languages, Ohio State Uni-
          versity (*Lithuanian Literature*)

C. S.   Carole Slade, Department of English, Bronx Community College of
          the City University of New York (*Spanish Literature; Latin American Lit-
          erature*)

E.C.K.S. Eleanor C. K. Sypher, Ph.D., Columbia University (*Classical Greek Liter-
          ature; Latin Literature*)

R. W. T. Robert W. Thomson, Department of Near Eastern Languages and Civ-
          ilizations, Harvard University (*Armenian Literature*)

P. W. W. Paul W. Wallace, Department of Classics, State University of New
          York at Albany (*Modern Greek Literature*)

D. K. W. Donald K. Watkins, Department of Germanic Languages and Litera-
          tures, The University of Kansas (*Scandinavian Literature*)

Abbreviations

abr.	abridged	*LJ*	*Library Journal*
annot.	annotated	ltd. ed.	limited edition
Am.	American	MLA	Modern Language Association
app.	appendix		
arr.	arranged	Mod.	Modern
assist.	assisted, assistance	mor.	morocco
bibliog.	bibliography	ms., mss.	manuscript(s)
bd.	bound	NYPL	New York Public Library *Branch Library Book News*, etc.
bdg.	binding		
Bk., Bks.	Book(s)		
Booklist	*Booklist and Subscription Books Bulletin*	*N.Y. Times*	*New York Times*
		orig.	original
c.	circa	o.p.	out of print
Chil.	Children's	pap.	paper
Class.	Classics	*PBIP*	*Paperbound Books in Print*
coll.	collected		
coll. ed.	collected edition	Perenn.	Perennial
comp.	compiled, compiler	Pock.	Pocket
d.	died	pref.	preface
Devot.	Devotional	pseud.	pseudonym
dist.	distributed	pt.	part
ed.	edited, editor, edition	ptg.	printing
Eng.	English	*PW*	*Publishers Weekly*
enl.	enlarged	*q.v.*	*quod vide* (which see)
Enrich.	Enrichment	repr.	reprint
fl.	flourished	rev. ed.	revised edition
fwd.	foreword	Riv.	Riverside
gen. eds.	general editors	sel.	selected
Gt.	Great	Ser.	Series
ill.	illustrated, illustrations	*SR*	*Saturday Review*
		Stand.	Standard
imit. lea.	imitation leather	suppl.,	supplement(s)
(in prep.)	in preparation	suppls.	
introd.	introduction	*TLS*, London	*Times Literary Supplement*
lea.	leather		
lg.-type ed.	large-type edition	trans.	translated, translator, translation
lib. ed	library edition		
Lib.	Library, Liberal	Univ.	University, Universal
Lit.	Literature	Vol., Vols.	Volume(s)

THE
READER'S
ADVISER

Chapter 1

The Drama

"From the smallest theater to the most eminent, the word 'Art' should be written in auditoriums and dressing rooms. . . . And distinction, discipline, and sacrifice and love."

—Federico García Lorca

In 1969 Richard Schechner, a respected drama critic, New York University professor, and former editor of *The Tulane Drama Review,* collected a company (The Performance Group), rented a garage in downtown New York, and began production of a violent, athletic, orgiastic floorshow roughly based on "The Bacchae" of Euripides, which he renamed "Dionysus in 69." Three years later Peter Brook, of the Royal Shakespeare Company, led an international troupe to the hills of Iran, where they performed a spectacle, "Orghast," in an unintelligible (but expressive) language which had been invented for them by the poet Ted Hughes. Theatre, in the late sixties and early seventies, has given every indication of turning physical and nonverbal.

But there has been no noticeable decline in drama publishing. Indeed, an inarticulate drama seems more dependent than ever on the medium of print (and photographic reproduction) to record its works. Both "Dionysus" and "Orghast," significantly, have had illustrated books devoted to them ("Dionysus in 69." Ed. by R. Schechner. *Farrar, Straus* Noonday $4.95; "Orghast at Persepolis." By A. C. H. Smith. 1972. *Viking* 1973 $8.75). The literature of the newest drama seems, paradoxically, to be returning to the situation of the twenties, when gorgeous picture books by Gordon Craig, Huntley Carter, and Sheldon Cheney commemorated the accomplishments of the "theatre arts."

There has also been an avalanche of theory and criticism justifying the new styles of performance. Both Brook and Schechner appear in the bibliography which follows with manifestoes for versions of an "open" theatre. But interestingly, the nonverbal revolution (or its excesses) seems to have sent other critics back for a serious reexamination of the literary foundations of modern drama. Richard Gilman and Eric Bentley and others have recently produced the best studies of Ibsen, Shaw, and Brecht we have seen for a decade.

Finally, while the theatre seems to have turned against language, the classroom has remained the reserve of the play as literature. There has been a remarkable growth in drama anthologies, mainly in soft-covered editions intended for college students. As a result the selection of plays easily available to the general reader has increased tremendously. Some of today's best drama criticism and theory is to be found in the introductions and commentaries which often accompany these plays (as in the important anthologies of Otto Reinert and Alvin Kernan).

The reference and guide books on Dramatic Technique listed below form a necessary backdrop for the Anthologies of Plays and the books on Dramatic Criticism and History. A brief listing of Oriental Drama follows the section on History and Criticism.

The *Drama Review* (formerly the *Tulane Drama Review*) provides excellent coverage of developments in world theater. *Caedmon* and *Spoken Arts* are among the recording companies carrying drama on records, which we do not attempt to cover here.

The Lively Arts—Dance, Opera, Cinema, Television, Mime and Marionettes—venture into areas outside the realm of Literature proper, the subject of the present volume of *"The Reader's Adviser,"* and so have been transferred to Volume 3.

See also bibliographic lists for all "Drama" chapters in this volume.

REFERENCE BOOKS

Anderson, Michael, and others. CROWELL'S HANDBOOK OF CONTEMPORARY DRAMA. *T. Y. Crowell* 1971 $10.00

Bowman, Walter Parker, and Robert Hamilton Ball. THEATRE LANGUAGE: A Dictionary of Terms in English of the Drama and Stage from Medieval to Modern Times. *Theatre Arts* 1961 $9.95 pap. $3.95. A highly recommended and important volume not only for theater and drama collections, but for reference collections of middle-to-large public and university libraries. Defines some 3,000 terms.

Finley, Robert, Ed. WHO'S WHO IN THE THEATRE: A Biographical Record of the Contemporary Stage Originally Compiled by John Parker. 1912. *Pitman* 15th ed. 1974 $32.50.

Gassner, John, and Edward Quinn, Eds. READER'S ENCYCLOPAEDIA OF WORLD DRAMA. *T. Y. Crowell* 1969 $15.00

Hartnoll, Phyllis, Ed. THE CONCISE OXFORD COMPANION TO THE THEATRE. *Oxford* 1972 pap. $5.95

THE OXFORD COMPANION TO THE THEATRE. *Oxford* 1951–1957 3rd ed. 1967 $17.50

"This is the most valuable reference tool yet to be published in the theatre world"—*(LJ)*. "A representative selection of what was most likely to interest the English-speaking reader was aimed at, and the emphasis throughout has been on the popular rather than on the literary theatre." Contains a bibliography and 150 illustrations of theaters and settings. The 1967 revision contains articles by 30 new contributors; all previous material has been updated or corrected.

MCGRAW-HILL ENCYCLOPAEDIA OF WORLD DRAMA. *McGraw-Hill* 4 vols. 1972 $129.00

Matlaw, Myron. MODERN WORLD DRAMA: An Encyclopaedia. *Dutton* 1972 $25.00

Melchinger, Siegfried. CONCISE ENCYCLOPEDIA OF MODERN DRAMA. Ed. by Henry Popkin; trans. by George Wellwarth *Horizon Press* 1965 $15.00

Contains 150 photos in a special section. "The text comprises a long introductory essay, a group of 'documents' on modern drama, a short but probing analytic glossary of dramatic theory, a table of first performances of major plays, and a biographical dictionary of 800 modern playwrights with outlines of the chief plays"—(David Glixon, in *SR*).

THE NEW YORK TIMES THEATRE REVIEWS, 1920–1972. *Arno* 9 vols. and 2 vol. index $895.00

Rae, Kenneth, and Richard Southern. AN INTERNATIONAL VOCABULARY OF TECHNICAL THEATRE TERMS. *Theatre Arts* $5.25. A total of 637 terms used in the English, American, German, Italian, French, Spanish, Dutch and Swedish theaters.

Rigdon, Walter, Comp. and Ed., and George Freedley, Ed. Consultant. THE BIOGRAPHICAL ENCYCLOPEDIA AND WHO'S WHO OF THE AMERICAN THEATRE. *James H. Heineman* 1966 $82.50

"Amazingly detailed records of 3,300 (European as well as American) actors, agents, producers, playwrights, costumers, scene designers, dancers, drama teachers and curators of theater archives. . . . Useful lists: every play put on in New York since 1900, American theater awards and winners; books about individual theater figures; complete play-bills of shows off-or-on Broadway since 1959; a necrology of 9,000 world-wide theater personnages; of New York theater buildings (annotated); spoken and musical play recordings; European premieres of American shows; and . . . identification of some 50 'theater organizations.' . . . Highly recommended"—*(LJ)*.

Schoolcraft, Ralph N. PERFORMING ARTS BOOKS IN PRINT. 1973. *Drama Bk. Specialists* $22.50

Shank, Theodore J., Ed. A DIGEST OF 500 PLAYS: Plot Outlines and Production Notes. 1963. *Macmillan* Collier Bks. 1966 pap. $1.95

Shipley, Joseph Twadell. GUIDE TO GREAT PLAYS. *Public Affairs Press* 1956 $15.00. Lists 660 plays of all countries and ages, with a synopsis for each.

Simon, Bernard, Ed., and Avivah Simon, Assoc. Ed. SIMON'S DIRECTORY OF THEATRICAL MATERIALS, SERVICES AND INFORMATION. Introd. by Norman S. Nadel *Package Publicity* 1966. 5th ed. 1974 $6.95

> "A classified guide, listing where to buy, rent, lease, find out everything needed for the production of stage attractions and the management of theatres."

Sprinchorn, Evert. TWENTIETH CENTURY PLAYS IN SYNOPSIS. *T. Y. Crowell* 1966 $6.95

> "Provides extensive act-by-act summaries of 133 plays ranging in date, origin, and manner from *Peter Pan* . . . to *The Blacks* and *Marat/Sade*. . . . The writing is practical, with no attempt at style. The format, however, is inviting"—(David Glixon, in *SR*).

Taylor, John Russell. THE PENGUIN DICTIONARY OF THE THEATER. *Penguin* (orig.) pap. $1.95; *Harper* Barnes & Noble 1967 $8.00

For indexes to plays in collections, see Chapter 3, Reference Books–Literature: Basic Indexes for Literature, Reader's Adviser, Vol. 1.

BIBLIOGRAPHIES

Adelman, Irving, and Rita Dworkin. MODERN DRAMA: A Checklist of Critical Literature on 20th Century Plays. *Scarecrow Press* 1967 $9.00

> A "valuable tool" essential for drama and theatre libraries—(*LJ*).

Baker, Blanche M. THEATRE AND ALLIED ARTS: A Guide to Books Dealing with the History, Criticism and Technique of the Drama and Theatre and Related Arts and Crafts. 1952. *Blom* 1966 $17.50

> The only comprehensive annotated bibliography dealing with all aspects of the theater. Based on the earlier "Dramatic Bibliography" (1933, o. p.), the material has been entirely reorganized and rewritten. About 6,000 volumes published between 1885 and 1950 have been included, with valuable annotations.

Berquist, G. William, Ed. THREE CENTURIES OF ENGLISH AND AMERICAN PLAYS: A Checklist; England: 1500–1800; United States: 1714–1830. *Hafner Service* 1963 $25.00

> One of the major bibliographical contributions in the dramatic theater field, it includes all the extant plays from England and America in the dates listed. It "is a basic reference tool for all drama, reference, and theater collections regardless of size and regardless of purchasing means"—(George Freedley, in *LJ*).

Breed, Paul F., and Florence M. Sniderman. DRAMATIC CRITICISM INDEX: Bibliography of Commentaries on Playwrights from Ibsen to the Avant-Garde. *Gale Research Co.* 1972 $20.00

Coleman, Arthur, and Gary Tyler. DRAMA CRITICISM. *Swallow* 2 vols. Vol. 1 A Checklist of Interpretation Since 1940 of English and American Plays $7.50 Vol. 2 A Checklist of Interpretation Since 1950 of Classical and Continental Plays $12.50

Connor, John M., and Billie M. Connor. OTTEMILLER'S INDEX TO PLAYS IN COLLECTIONS: An Author and Title Index to Plays Appearing in Collections Published between 1900 and Mid-1970. *Scarecrow Press* 1971 $11.00

Gohdes, Clarence. LITERATURE AND THEATER OF THE STATES AND REGIONS OF THE U.S.A.: An Historical Bibliography. *Duke Univ. Press* 1967 $10.00. A valuable checklist of books, chapters from books, pamphlets, periodical articles, anthologies and monographs.

Hunter, Frederick J., Ed. DRAMA BIBLIOGRAPHY: A Short-Title Guide to Extended Reading in Dramatic Art for the English-Speaking Audience and Students in Theatre. *Hall* 1971 $25.00

INDEX TO FULL LENGTH PLAYS. *Faxon* 3 vols. Vol. 1 1895–1925 ed. by Ruth G. Thomson (1956) Vol. 2 1926–1944 ed. by Ruth G. Thomson (1946) Vol. 3 1944–1964 ed. by Norma O. Ireland (1965) each $11.00

Keller, Dean H. INDEX TO PLAYS IN PERIODICALS. *Scarecrow* 1971 $15.00; Supplement 1973 $7.50

Limbacher, James L. THEATRICAL EVENTS: A Selected List of Musicals and Dramatic Performances on Long-Playing Records. *Pierian* 1975 (in prep.)

PLAY INDEX. *Wilson.* 1949–1952 ed. by Dorothy H. West and Dorothy M. Peake (1953) $8.00 1953–1960 ed. by Estelle A. Fidell and Dorothy M. Peake (1963) $11.00 1961–1967 ed. by Estelle A. Fidell (1968) $16.00 1968–1972 ed. by Estelle A. Fidell (1973) $20.00

Salem, James M. A GUIDE TO CRITICAL REVIEWS. *Scarecrow* Pt. 1 American Drama 1901–1969 (1966 2nd ed. 1973) $15.00 Pt. 2 The Musical from Rodgers and Hart to Lerner and Loewe (1967) $9.00 Pt. 3 British and Continental Drama from Ibsen to Pinter (1968) $7.00 Pt. 4 The Screenplay from the Jazz Singer to Dr. Strangelove (1971) 2 vols. $30.00

Samples, Gordon. THE DRAMA SCHOLAR'S INDEX TO PLAYS AND FILMSCRIPTS. *Scarecrow* 1974 $12.50

Silverman, Maxwell. CONTEMPORARY THEATRE ARCHITECTURE: An Illustrated Survey. With a Checklist of Publications 1946–1964 by Ned A. Bowman. Fwd. by George Freedley *N.Y. Public Lib.* 1966 $10.00

Silverman has provided an "admirably concise, yet comprehensive survey of recent trends both here and abroad"—(*LJ*).

Stratman, Carl Joseph. BIBLIOGRAPHY OF ENGLISH PRINTED TRAGEDY, 1565–1900. *Southern Illinois Univ. Press* 1966 $15.00

BIBLIOGRAPHY OF THE AMERICAN THEATRE, EXCLUDING NEW YORK CITY. *Loyola Univ. Press* 1965 $8.00

BRITAIN'S THEATRICAL PERIODICAL, 1720–1967: A Bibliography. 1962. (orig. title: "British Dramatic Periodicals, 1720–1960"). *N.Y. Public Lib.* 2nd rev. ed. 1972 $11.00

DRAMATIC PLAY LISTS, 1591–1963. *N.Y. Public Lib.* 1966 pap. $2.50

YEARBOOKS AND SURVEYS

THE BEST PLAYS OF 1894–1974 [THE BURNS MANTLE YEARBOOK]. Various editors. Consult publisher's catalog for annual volumes. *Dodd* 1920–

Published annually since 1920, this presents the "ten best plays of the year" produced in New York, with excerpts from the dialogue and summary of each plot, together with critical comments. A complete index of each volume is to be found under "Mantle, Burns, Editor" in the *Dodd, Mead* catalog in the current "Publishers' Trade List Annual." After Burns Mantle's death in 1948, John Arthur Chapman became editor of the retitled volumes, "Burns Mantle Best Plays." With the 1952–53 edition, Louis Kronenberger became the editor. Henry Hewes edited the 1961–63 volumes. Since the 1964–65 edition, the annual has been prepared by Otis Guernsey, editor of the *Dramatists Guild Quarterly.* (As of July, 1967, there were 48 such volumes available.) "Index to the Best Plays Series, 1899–1950," edited by John Chapman (1950, o. p.) is a master index, still valuable, of the 32 Burns Mantle volumes. Titles of all the plays and names of all authors, composers and others are listed alphabetically with reference to the annual volume and page number. Recent volumes also provide details about every play produced in New York (on and off Broadway), the season in London and the theater abroad, the season across the continental United States, the Shakespeare festivals, yearly awards; each contains "vital statistics of productions, prizes, people and publications" and a necrology. "The Index to the Best Plays Series: 1949–1960" (1962, o. p.) takes up where the 1899–1950 volume left off and is an invaluable tool. "The Best Plays of 1894–1899" links the last (1894) volume of G. C. Odell's "Annals of the New York Stage" (1927–1949. *AMS* 1970 15 vols. each $46.50, set $695.00) with the present series.

THE BEST PLAYS OF 1894–1899. Ed. by Burns Mantle *Bks. for Libraries* $14.50

THE BEST PLAYS OF 1899–1909. Ed. by Burns Mantle *Bks. for Libraries* $29.75

THE BEST PLAYS OF 1909–1919. Ed. by Burns Mantle *Bks. for Libraries* $27.50

THE BEST PLAYS OF 1919–20 to 1946–47. Ed. by Burns Mantle *Arno* each $20.00

THE BEST PLAYS OF 1947–48 TO 1951–52. Ed. by John Chapman *Arno* each $20.00

THE BEST PLAYS OF 1952–53 TO 1960–61. Ed. by Louis Kronenberger *Arno* each $20.00

THE BEST PLAYS OF 1961–62 TO 1962–63. Ed. by Henry Hewes *Arno* each $20.00

THE BEST PLAYS OF 1963–64. Ed. by Henry Hewes *Dodd* $15.00

THE BEST PLAYS OF 1964–65 TO 1973–74. Ed. by Otis L. Guernsey, Jr. *Dodd* each $15.00

Brockett, O., and R. Findlay. CENTURY OF INNOVATION: A History of European and American Theatre and Drama, 1870–1970. Theater and Drama Ser. *Prentice-Hall* 1973 $14.50

CELEBRITY SERVICE CONTACT BOOK. *Celebrity Service, Inc.* (171 W. 57 St., New York, N.Y. 10019) 1967 1974 $5.00. A directory of people in the acting and entertainment world and fields of allied interest.

Chapman, John Arthur. *See* THE BEST PLAYS, *above, and Chapter 5, American Drama, this volume.*

Gassner, John. MASTERS OF THE DRAMA. *Dover* 1940 1945 3rd rev. and enl. ed. 1953 $8.50
> A historical survey of drama from the time of primitive man to the present. "This valuable and readable standard reference work has now been expanded to include material on the contemporary drama both in America and Europe. . . . There is a fine bibliography, which has been brought up to date in this new edition"—*(Theatre Arts).*

Guernsey, Otis, Ed. *For his volumes of* THE BEST PLAYS *see above.*

Hewes, Henry, Ed. *For his volumes of* THE BEST PLAYS *see above.*

Kienzle, Siegfried. MODERN WORLD THEATRE: A Guide to Productions in Europe and the United States since 1945. Trans. by A. Henderson and E. Henderson. *Ungar* 1970 $12.50

Kronenberger, Louis, Ed. *For his volumes of* THE BEST PLAYS *see above.*

WHO'S WHERE. *Leo Shull Pubns.* $2.00. Tells who's where in show biz. Some 10,000 names, addresses and phone numbers.

ANTHOLOGIES OF PLAYS

Modern anthologies provide the text of the play, often with the addition of much critical and biographical material. The following list does not include anthologies of plays for schools. The catalogs of *Dramatists Play Service, Samuel French* and *Walter H. Baker* are a good source for these. Specialized anthologies of plays will be found in various chapters as indicated at the end of this section.

Allison, Alexander W., and others, Eds. MASTERPIECES OF THE DRAMA. *Macmillan* 1957 1966 3rd ed. 1974 pap. $5.95. Sophocles: Oedipus Rex; Euripides: Alcestis; Jonson: Volpone; Molière: The Miser; Sheridan: The Rivals; Ibsen: Hedda Gabler; Chekhov: The Cherry Orchard; Synge: Riders to the Sea; O'Casey: Juno and the Paycock; Lorca: The House of Bernarda Alba; Giraudoux: The Madwoman of Chaillot.

Barnet, Sylvan, Morton Berman, and William Burto. EIGHT GREAT COMEDIES. *New Am. Lib.* pap. $1.75. Aristophanes: The Clouds; Machiavelli: Mandragola; Shakespeare: Twelfth Night; Molière: The Miser; Gay: The Beggar's Opera; Wilde: The Importance of Being Earnest; Chekhov: Uncle Vanya; Shaw: Arms and the Man.

EIGHT GREAT TRAGEDIES. *New Am. Lib.* pap. $1.75. Aeschylus: Prometheus Bound; Sophocles: Oedipus the King; Euripides: Hippolytus; Shakespeare: King Lear; Ibsen: Ghosts; Strindberg: Miss Julie; Yeats: On Baile's Strand; O'Neill: Desire under the Elms.

Benedikt, Michael. THEATRE EXPERIMENT. *Doubleday* 1967 Anchor Bks. 1968 pap. $2.50. Seventeen American plays linked by style rather than subject. *See Chapter 5, American Drama, this volume, for further comment.*

Bentley, Eric. THE CLASSIC THEATRE. *Doubleday* Anchor Bks. 4 vols. Vol. 1 Six Italian Plays
(1958) Vol. 2 Five German Plays (1959) Vol. 3 Six Spanish Plays (1959) Vol. 4 Six
French Plays (1960) Vols. 1 and 4 $2.95 Vols. 2 and 3 $2.50; *Peter Smith* 3 vols. Vol. 1
$4.25 Vols. 2 and 3 each $4.50 set $13.25

Vol. 1 Machiavelli: The Mandrake; Beolco: Ruzzante Returns; Goldoni: Servant of Two Mas-
ters, Mirandolina; Gozzi: King Stag; Anon.: The Three Cuckolds. Vol. 2 Goethe: Egmont; Schil-
ler: Don Carlos, Mary Stuart; Kleist: Penthesilea, The Prince of Homburg. Vol. 3 Rojas: Celestina;
Cervantes: The Siege of Numantia; Lope de Vega: The Trickster of Seville; Calderon: Love after
Death, Life Is a Dream. Vol. 4 Corneille: The Cid; Molière: Misanthrope; Racine: Phaedra; Le
Sage: Turcaret; Marivaux: The False Confessions; Beaumarchais: Figaro's Marriage.

FROM THE MODERN REPERTOIRE. *Indiana Univ. Press* Series I 1949 $10.00 Series II 1952
$12.50 Series III 1956 $12.50 set $29.95

Ser. 1 Becque: La Parisienne; Brecht: The Threepenny Opera; Büchner: Danton's Death; Coc-
teau: The Infernal Machine; Musset: Fantasio; Eliot: Sweeny Agonistes; Lorca: The Love of Don
Perlimpin; Schnitzler: Round Dance; Sternheim: The Snob; Yeats: A Full Moon in March. Ser. 2
Brecht: Galileo; Cummings: him; Fergusson: The King and the Duke; Giraudoux: Electra;
Grabbe: Jest, Irony, and Satire; MacNeice: The Dark Tower; Mirabeau: The Epidemic; Obey:
Venus and Adonis; Ostrovsky: Easy Money; Wedekind: The Marquis of Keith. Ser. 3 Anouilh:
Cecile; Brecht: Saint Joan; Büchner: Leonce and Lena; Cocteau: Intimate Relations; Musset: A
Door Should Be Either Open or Shut; Jeffers: The Cretan Woman; Pinero: The Magistrate; Ro-
mains: Dr. Knock; Schnitzler: Anatol; Zola: Thérèse Racquin.

THE MODERN THEATRE: An Anthology. *Doubleday* Anchor Bks. 6 vols. of 5 plays each
1955 pap. vols. 1, 3, 4, 5, o.p. Vol. 2 $1.75; *Peter Smith* 6 vols. each $6.00

THE PLAY: A Critical Anthology. *Prentice-Hall* 1951 $5.95. Nine plays, ancient and mod-
ern, with notes.

Block, Haskell M., and Robert G. Shedd. MASTERS OF MODERN DRAMA. *Random* 1962
$15.75 text ed. $12.95. Forty-five modern plays, ranging from Ibsen's "Peer Gynt" to
Frisch's "Biedermann and the Firebugs."

Bloomfield, M. W., and R. C. Elliott. GREAT PLAYS: Sophocles to Brecht. *Holt* 1965 pap.
$6.75. Sophocles: Antigone; Shakespeare: Othello; Molière: The Misanthrope; Con-
greve: The Way of the World; Strindberg: Miss Julie; Ibsen: Hedda Gabler; Shaw:
Arms and the Man; Chekhov: Three Sisters; O'Neill: The Hairy Ape; Williams: The
Glass Menagerie; Brecht: The Caucasian Chalk Circle.

Booth, Michael. HISS THE VILLAIN: Six American and English Melodramas. *Blom* 1965
$8.75

Calderwood, James, and H. E. Toliver. FORMS OF DRAMA. *Prentice-Hall* 1969 $8.50

FORMS OF TRAGEDY. *Prentice-Hall* 1972 pap. $7.95

Caputi, Anthony. MASTERWORKS OF WORLD DRAMA IN SIX VOLUMES: Classical Greece to
the Nineteenth Century. *Heath* 1968 Vol. 1 Classical Greece pap. $3.95 Vol. 2 Rome
and the Middle Ages pap. (o.p.) Vol. 3 The Renaissance pap. $4.25 Vol. 4 Baroque
and Restoration Theater pap. $4.25 Vol. 5 The Eighteenth Century pap. $2.95 Vol. 6
Romanticism and Realism pap. $2.95

MODERN DRAMA. *Norton* 1966 pap. $3.25. Ibsen: The Wild Duck; Chekhov: Three Sis-
ters; Shaw: The Devil's Disciple; Strindberg: A Dream Play; O'Neill: Desire under
the Elms; Pirandello: Henry IV. Includes biographies, background, and critical information.

Cerf, Bennett. PLAYS OF OUR TIME. *Random* 1967 $10.00. Miller: Death of a Salesman;
Williams: A Street Car Named Desire; O'Neill: The Iceman Cometh; Inge: Come
Back, Little Sheba; Bolt: A Man for All Seasons; Hansberry: A Raisin in the Sun;
Osborne: Look Back in Anger; Shisgall: Luv; Heggen and Logan: Mr. Roberts.

(With Van H. Cartmell) TWENTY-FOUR FAVORITE ONE-ACT PLAYS. *Doubleday* 1958 $6.95
Dolphin Bks. 1963 pap. $2.50. The moderns, including Arthur Miller, Tennessee
Williams, Inge, Wilder and O'Neill.

Clark, Barrett Harper. WORLD DRAMA: An Anthology. *Dover* 1955 2 vols. each $4.00; *Peter Smith* 2 vols. $12.00. Vol. 1: Ancient Greece, Rome, India, China, Japan, Medieval Europe and England; Vol. 2: Italy, Spain, France, Germany, Denmark, Russia and Norway.

Clayes, Stanley, and David Spencer. CONTEMPORARY DRAMA: Thirteen Plays—American, English, Irish, European. *Scribner* 1962 2nd ed. 1970 pap. $3.95

Clurman, Harold. SEVEN PLAYS OF THE MODERN THEATRE. *Grove* 1962 pap. $4.95. Beckett: Waiting for Godot; Behan: The Quare Fellow; Delaney: A Taste of Honey; Gelber: The Connection; Genet: The Balcony; Ionesco: Rhinoceros; Pinter: The Birthday Party.

Cohn, Ruby, and Bernard Dukore. TWENTIETH CENTURY DRAMA: England, Ireland, The United States. *Random* 1966 pap. $5.25. Shaw: Major Barbara; Synge: The Playboy of the Western World; Yeats: The Only Jealousy of Emer; Eliot: Murder in the Cathedral; Odets: Awake and Sing; Wilder: Our Town; Williams: The Glass Menagerie; O'Neill: The Iceman Cometh; Osborne: Look Back in Anger; Pinter: The Dumb Waiter; Albee: The Zoo Story; Beckett: Embers.

Corrigan, Robert W., Ed. MASTERPIECES OF THE MODERN THEATER. *Macmillan* Collier Bks. 9 vols. 1967 pap. each $1.50. Modern English, German, Irish, Russian, Central European, Spanish, Scandinavian, French and Italian plays. Each volume is devoted to one area and includes a general introduction, notes and bibliography.

THE NEW THEATRE OF EUROPE. *Dell* Delta 4 vols. pap. each $2.25

Vol. 1 Bolt: A Man for All Seasons; Sartre: Anna Kleiber; Peryalis: Masks of Angels; Ghelderode: Pantagleize; Betti: Corruption in the Palace of Justice. Vol. 2 Brecht: Mother Courage; Fratti: The Cage, The Suicide; Grass: The Wicked Cooks; Schehade: Vasco. Vol. 3 Osborne: Inadmissible Evidence; Forssell: The Sunday Promenade; Dorst: The Curve; Guerdon: The Laundry. Vol. 4 (Ed. by Martin Esslin) Ginzburg: The Advertisement; Hochwaelder: The Raspberry Picker; Handke: Self-Censure; Bond: Saved; Grumbert: Tomorrow, From Any Window.

Cubeta, Paul M. MODERN DRAMA FOR ANALYSIS. *Holt* 1962 pap. $8.00. Shaw: Devil's Disciple; Ibsen: Rosmersholm; O'Neill: Desire under the Elms; Chekhov: The Cherry Orchard; Wilder: The Skin of Our Teeth; Williams: The Glass Menagerie; Eliot: Murder in the Cathedral; Miller: View from the Bridge; Anouilh: Becket; Albee: The Sand Box.

Dean, Leonard F. TWELVE GREAT PLAYS. *Harcourt* 1970 pap. $5.50. Aeschylus: Agamemnon; Sophocles: Oedipus Rex; Marlowe: The Jew of Malta; Shakespeare: Henry IV, Part One; Jonson: Alchemist; Molière: Tartuffe; Ibsen: Ghosts; Chekhov: The Cherry Orchard; Pirandello: Six Characters in Search of an Author; Brecht: The Caucasian Chalk Circle; Williams: The Glass Menagerie; Abse: The House of Cowards.

Dent, Anthony. INTERNATIONAL MODERN PLAYS. *Dutton* $3.95 pap. $1.85. Čapek: The Life of the Insects; Chiarelli: The Mask and the Face; Cocteau: The Infernal Machine; Hauptmann: Hannele; Strindberg: Miss Julie.

Dickinson, Thomas H. THE CHIEF CONTEMPORARY DRAMATISTS: Series Three. *Houghton* 1930 $11.50

Downer, Alan S. GREAT WORLD THEATER: An Introduction to Drama. *Harper* 1964 pap. $8.00. Euripides: The Bacchae; Sophocles: Antigone; Plautus: The Little Ghost; Shudraka: The Toy Cart; Anon.: Everyman; Webster: The Duchess of Malfi; Molière: The Misanthrope; Goldsmith: She Stoops to Conquer; Ibsen: The Master Builder; Chekhov: Three Sisters; Giraudoux: Tiger at the Gates; Miller: View from the Bridge; Wilder: The Skin of Our Teeth; Pirandello: Six Characters in Search of an Author.

Felheim, Marvin. COMEDY: Plays, Theory and Criticism. *Harcourt* 1966 pap. $4.95. Comedies by Aristophanes, Shakespeare, Molière, Sheridan, Chekhov, Shaw and Wilde, among others.

Felperin, Howard M. Dramatic Romance: Plays, Theory, Criticism. *Harcourt* 1973 pap. $4.95. Euripides: Alcestis; Shakespeare: The Tempest; Gay: The Beggar's Opera; Ibsen: When We Dead Awaken; Brecht: The Caucasian Chalk Circle; Eliot: The Cocktail Party. Includes important essays on a genre which has only recently begun to be taken seriously by critics.

Fitzjohn, Donald. English One-Act Plays of Today. Introd. by the compiler. *Oxford* English Association Ser. 1962 pap. $2.25. A collection of moderns including Rattigan, Fry, Priestley and John Mortimer; the two Americans are Susan Glaspell and Tennessee Williams.

Franklin, Clay. Mixed Company: An Assortment of Monologues. *French* 1959 $2.50. An excellent collection.

Gassner, John. A Treasury of the Theatre. *Holt* college ed. 2 vols. Vol. 1 From Aeschylus to Ostrovsky 3rd ed. $13.50 Vol. 2 From Henrik Ibsen to Eugene Ionesco 1950 4th ed. $14.00; *Simon & Schuster* 3 vols. Vol. 1 Aeschylus to Ostrovsky rev. ed. 1967 Vol. 2 Ibsen to Sartre Vol. 3 Wilde to Arthur Miller rev. ed. 1951 each $10.00 set $30.00. First published in 1935, ed. by Burns Mantle and John Gassner; one of the best collections available—in these revised and expanded forms.

Twenty Best European Plays on the American Stage, 1915–1955. *Crown* 1957 $9.95 text ed. $7.50

See also following section—Dramatic Criticism and History. For anthologies of American plays, see Chapter 5, American Drama, this volume.

Goldstone, R., and A. Lass. Mentor Book of Short Plays. *New American Lib.* pap. $1.25. Includes work by Wilde, Williams, Chekhov, Rostand, and Synge.

Houghton, Norris. The Golden Age. Masterpieces of Continental Drama Ser. *Dell* Laurel pap. $.95. Corneille: The Cid; Molière: The Misanthrope; Calderon: Life Is a Dream; Lope de Vega: The Sheep Well; Racine: Phaedra.

The Romantic Influence. Masterpieces of Continental Drama Ser. *Dell* Laurel pap. $1.25. Goethe: Faust, Part One; Schiller: Mary Stuart; Hugo: Hernani; Rostand: Cyrano.

Seeds of Modern Drama. Masterpieces of Modern Drama Ser. *Dell* Laurel pap. $1.25. Zola: Thérèse Racquin; Ibsen: An Enemy of the People; Strindberg: Miss Julie; Chekhov: The Sea Gull; Hauptmann: The Weavers.

Kernan, Alvin B. Character and Conflict: An Introduction to Drama. *Harcourt* 1969 pap. $6.95. Ibsen: Hedda Gabler; Anon.: Everyman; Brecht: Mother Courage and her Children; Wilder: The Skin of Our Teeth; Sophocles: Antigone; Strindberg: The Stronger; Chekhov: The Cherry Orchard; Synge: Riders to the Sea; Molière: The Misanthrope; Giraudoux: Tiger at the Gates; Arrabal: Picnic on the Battlefield. Elaborate critical commentaries accompany the first six plays.

Classics of the Modern Theater: Realism and After. *Harcourt* 1966 pap. (orig.) $6.50. Ibsen: Ghosts; Strindberg: The Father; Chekhov: The Cherry Orchard; Shaw: Arms and the Man; Pirandello: Six Characters in Search of an Author; Strindberg: The Ghost Sonata; Lorca: Blood Wedding; Brecht: Mother Courage and Her Six Children; Betti: Corruption in the Palace of Justice; Ionesco: The Chairs; Albee: The Zoo Story.

Kirby, Michael. Happenings: An Illustrated Anthology. *Dutton* 1965 pap. $1.95. Scripts and productions by Jim Dine, Red Grooms, Alan Kaprow, Claes Oldenburg and Robert Whitman.

"An important book for art and theater collections because it is the first full-scale study of the form, because it brings together 14 'scripts' which may be studied for their merit, and because Happenings are something that is happening"—(*LJ*).

Lahr, John. GROVE PRESS MODERN DRAMA: Six Plays by Baraka, Brecht, Feiffer, Genet, Ionesco, and Mrozek. *Grove* 1975 pap. $5.95. Brecht: The Caucasian Chalk Circle; Baraka: The Toilet; Feiffer: The White House Murder Case; Genet: The Blacks; Ionesco: Rhinoceros; Mrozek: Tango.

Modern Library. NEW VOICES IN THE AMERICAN THEATRE. Fwd. by Brooks Atkinson *Random* Modern Lib., 1955 $2.95. Six plays produced in New York 1947–54.

Moon, Samuel. ONE ACT: Short Plays of the Modern Theatre. *Grove* Black Cat Bks. 1960 pap. $2.45; *Peter Smith* $4.50. Strindberg, Yeats, Pirandello, Wilder, Saroyan, Williams, O'Casey, Anouilh, MacLeish, Miller and Ionesco.

Nathan, George Jean. WORLD'S GREAT PLAYS. 1957. *Grosset* Univ. Lib. pap. $2.50

PLAYBOOK: Five Plays for a New Theatre. *New Directions* 1956 $7.50. Plays by Lionel Abel, Robert Hivnor, Junji Kinoshita, James Merrill, I. A. Richards.

PLAYS FOR A NEW THEATER: Playbook 2. *New Directions* 1966 $7.50 pap. $2.95. Plays by Corrado Alvaro, Yvan Goll, John Hawkes, Robert Hivnor, Boris Vian.

Reinert, Otto. CLASSIC THROUGH MODERN DRAMA: An Introductory Anthology. *Little* 1970 pap. $6.95. Sophocles: Oedipus; Anon.: Everyman; Shakespeare: Hamlet; Molière: Tartuffe; Etherege: The Man of Mode; Ibsen: The Wild Duck; Shaw: Caesar and Cleopatra; Chekhov: The Three Sisters; Synge: Riders to the Sea; Strindberg: The Ghost Sonata; O'Neill: The Emperor Jones; Brecht: The Caucasian Chalk Circle; Albee: Who's Afraid of Virginia Woolf?; Jones: Dutchman; Weiss: Marat/ Sade.

DRAMA: An Introductory Anthology. *Little* alternate ed. 1961 pap. $5.95. Sophocles: Antigone; Shakespeare: Othello; Jonson: Alchemist; Molière: Misanthrope; Sheridan: The Rivals; Ibsen: Hedda Gabler; Strindberg: Miss Julie; Shaw: Caesar and Cleopatra; Chekhov: The Cherry Orchard; Synge: Playboy of the Western World; Pirandello: Six Characters in Search of an Author; Brecht: The Caucasian Chalk Circle; Albee: The American Dream.

MODERN DRAMA. *Little* alternate ed. 1966 pap. $5.50. Ibsen: The Wild Duck; Strindberg: The Father; Shaw: Caesar and Cleopatra; Chekhov: The Cherry Orchard; Synge: Playboy of the Western World; Yeats: The Hour Glass; Pirandello: Six Characters in Search of an Author; Ghelderode: Chronicles of Hell; Brecht: The Caucasian Chalk Circle; Williams: The Glass Menagerie; Albee: The Zoo Story.

SIX PLAYS: An Introductory Anthology. *Little* 1973 pap. $3.95. Sophocles: Antigone; Shakespeare: Othello; Molière: The Misanthrope; Ibsen: Hedda Gabler; Chekhov: The Cherry Orchard; Williams: The Glass Menagerie.

Richards, Stanley. THE BEST SHORT PLAYS, 1968. *Chilton* $6.95

THE BEST SHORT PLAYS, 1969. *Chilton* $6.95; *Avon* pap. $1.95

THE BEST SHORT PLAYS, 1970. *Chilton* $7.50; *Avon* pap. $3.95

THE BEST SHORT PLAYS, 1971. *Chilton* $7.50; *Avon* pap. $3.95

THE BEST SHORT PLAYS, 1972. *Chilton* $7.95; *Avon* pap. $3.95

THE BEST SHORT PLAYS, 1973. *Chilton* $8.95

THE BEST SHORT PLAYS, 1974. *Chilton* $8.95

SIX GREAT MODERN PLAYS. *Dell* 1956 pap. $1.25. Chekhov: Three Sisters; Ibsen: The Master Builder; Shaw: Mrs. Warren's Profession; O'Casey: Red Roses for Me; Miller: All My Sons; Williams: The Glass Menagerie.

Waith, Eugene M. THE DRAMATIC MOMENT. *Prentice-Hall* 1966 pap. $7.95. A collection that stresses the relation of plays to the theaters for which they were written.

Watson, E. Bradlee, and Benfield Pressey. CONTEMPORARY DRAMA: European, English, Irish and American Plays. *Scribner* 1941 $8.95. Some 37 plays with brief introductions, biographical notes and bibliographies.

CONTEMPORARY DRAMA: Eleven Plays. American, English, European. *Scribner* 1956 pap. $3.95. Plays by Shaw, Connelly, Wilder, Coward, Saroyan, Anouilh, Williams, Giraudoux, Hellman, Miller, Fry.

CONTEMPORARY DRAMA: Fifteen Plays. American, English, Irish, European. *Scribner* 1959 pap. $3.95. Plays by Ibsen, Wilde, Chekhov, Strindberg, Shaw, Synge, Pirandello, O'Neill, Lorca, Eliot, O'Casey, Wilder, Inge, Miller, Frings.

CONTEMPORARY DRAMA: Nine Plays. *Scribner* 1941 pap. $3.50. Plays by O'Neill, Rice, Sherwood, Howard, Galsworthy, Barrie, Maugham, Capek, Rostand.

Whitman, Charles H. SEVEN CONTEMPORARY PLAYS. *Houghton* 1931 $7.50

See also Chapter 2, British Drama: Early to 18th Century; Chapter 4, Modern British Drama; Chapter 5, American Drama, this volume.

DRAMATIC CRITICISM AND HISTORY

Abel, Lionel. METATHEATRE: A New View of Dramatic Form. 1963. *Farrar, Straus* (Hill & Wang) Dramabks. pap. $1.95. Perceptive essays on Greek tragedy, great dramatists, the Theater of the Absurd and other aspects of the modern stage.

Beaumont, Cyril. HISTORY OF HARLEQUIN. 1926. *Blom* 1965 $13.50

Beerbohm, Sir Max. AROUND THEATRES. 1924. *Greenwood* 1969 $20.75; *Taplinger* $7.95. In 1898 Beerbohm succeeded Shaw (*q.v.*) as dramatic critic of the English *Saturday Review,* where these contributions appeared for the next 12 years.

See also Chapter 15, Essays, Reader's Adviser, Vol. 1.

Bentley, Eric. IN SEARCH OF THEATRE. 1953. *Atheneum* pap. $4.95. A survey of dramatic and theatrical activity in America and Europe, 1945–1953. Includes essays on Shaw, Pirandello, Chekhov, Yeats, and Ibsen.

THE LIFE OF THE DRAMA. *Atheneum* 1964 $4.25

"A remarkable exploration of the roots and bases of dramatic art, the most far-reaching and revelatory we have had"—(*Book Week*).

THE PLAYWRIGHT AS THINKER. 1945. *Harcourt* 1967 pap. $3.15. A foundation of contemporary criticism of modern European drama. Bentley was for twenty years Brander Matthews Professor of Drama at Columbia, as well as a working critic (*New Republic*), director, and playwright.

THE THEATRE OF COMMITMENT AND OTHER ESSAYS ON DRAMA IN OUR SOCIETY. *Atheneum* 1967 $5.00. Articles and lectures from the past 14 years.

THE THEATRE OF WAR: Modern Drama from Ibsen to Brecht. *Viking* 1973 abr. ed. pap. $2.50. Essays on playwrights and single plays.

(Ed.) THE THEORY OF THE MODERN STAGE: An Introduction to Modern Theatre and Drama. 1968. *Penguin* pap. $2.45. An anthology of statements by "ten makers of modern theatre," accompanied by important critical and historical essays.

WHAT IS THEATRE? 1956. *Atheneum* pap. $4.95. Theatre reviews, 1952–56.

Bermel, Albert. CONTRADICTORY CHARACTERS: An Interpretation of the Modern Theatre. *Dutton* 1973 pap. $4.95

Blau, Herbert. IMPOSSIBLE THEATER. *Macmillan* Collier 1966 pap. $1.95. Contemporary productions discussed by an important director.

Bogard, Travis, and William I. Oliver, Eds. MODERN DRAMA: Essays in Criticism. *Oxford* Galaxy Bks. 1965 pap. $3.95

Brook, Peter. THE EMPTY SPACE. 1968. *Atheneum* $5.00; *Avon* 1969 pap. $1.65. Four perspectives on the pathologies and possibilities of contemporary conceptions of theatre (the "Deadly," the "Holy," the "Rough," the "Immediate").

Brooks, Cleanth, and R. B. Heilman. UNDERSTANDING DRAMA: Twelve Plays. (Enlarged volume of "Understanding Drama: Eight Plays" 1945 o.p.). *Holt* 1948 $10.50. Plays intensively examined by two major American critics. A pioneering textbook.

Brown, John Mason. DRAMATIS PERSONAE: A Retrospective Show. *Viking* 1963 Compass Bks. 1965 pap. $2.25

Brustein, Robert. SEASONS OF DISCONTENT: Dramatic Opinions 1959–1965. *Simon & Schuster* 1965 $5.95 pap. $1.95

"A collection of superb analytical reviews and essays, pointing angrily, but with stunning perception, at what has gone wrong today, particularly in American playwriting"—(*N.Y. Times*). Articles mainly from the *New Republic*.

THE THEATRE OF REVOLT: An Approach to the Modern Drama. *Little-Atlantic* 1964 pap. $2.45. Studies of Ibsen, Strindberg, Chekhov, Shaw, Brecht, Pirandello, O'Neill, Artaud and Genet illustrate Brustein's idea that "revolt is the energy which drives the modern theatre, just as faith drove the theatre of the past."

Butcher, S. H. ARISTOTLE'S THEORY OF POETRY AND FINE ART. *Dover* 1955 pap. $3.00. With a critical text and translation of The Poetics. A good English translation of *The Poetics,* with a thorough explanatory essay.

Calderwood, James L., and H. E. Toliver, Eds. PERSPECTIVES ON DRAMA. *Oxford* 1968 pap. $3.95

Cheney, Sheldon. STAGE DECORATION. 1928. *Blom* 1966 $15.75. The development of stage art from that of ancient Athens to 20th-century realism.

THE THEATRE: Three Thousand Years of Drama, Acting and Stagecraft. *McKay* 1930 new ed. 1972 $14.95. A standard reference guide with facts about playhouses, anecdotes of dramatists and actors.

Clark, Barrett H., Ed. EUROPEAN THEORIES OF THE DRAMA. 1916. *Crown* rev. ed. by Henry Popkin 1965 $7.50 text ed. $5.65. An anthology of dramatic theory and criticism from Aristotle to the present day. A most important collection of writings on dramatic technique with commentaries, biographies and bibliographies, with a valuable supplement on American drama.

Clurman, Harold. THE NAKED IMAGE: Observations on the Modern Theatre. *Macmillan* 1966 $6.50

Articles and reviews, mainly from *The Nation*. "Immensely valuable as the thoughtful, quietly stated and carefully considered views of a thorough professional"—(*Los Angeles Times*). "He . . . writes with clarity and strength, often with brilliance"—(*LJ*). Mr. Clurman has had an impressive career as a producer and director of numerous stage and movie productions and as the drama critic of *The Nation*.

Cole, Toby, Ed. PLAYWRIGHTS ON PLAYWRITING: The Meaning and Making of Modern Drama from Ibsen to Ionesco. *Farrar, Straus* (Hill & Wang) Dramabks. 1960 pap. $2.95

Corrigan, Robert, Ed. THE THEATRE IN SEARCH OF A FIX. *Delacorte* (dist. by Dial) 1973 $10.00; *Dell* Delta 1974 pap. $3.25. Essays on dramatic forms, themes, and contexts from ancient Greece to the present.

THEATRE IN THE TWENTIETH CENTURY. *Grove* Black Cat Bks. 1963 pap. $1.95. A collection of essays on the international drama scene by outstanding actors, directors, playwrights and critics.

(With James L. Robenberg, Eds.) CONTEXT AND CRAFT OF DRAMA: Critical Essays on the Nature of Drama and Theatre. *T. Y. Crowell* (Chandler Pub.) 1964 $6.25

Donoghue, Denis. THE THIRD VOICE: Modern British and American Verse Drama. *Princeton Univ. Press* 1959 $8.50 pap. $2.95

Downer, Alan S. THE BRITISH DRAMA: A Handbook and Brief Chronicle. *Irvington Pubns.* text ed. 1950 $19.50 pap. $8.95. An "extraordinary little book" which analyzes typical plays of every important period.

Driver, Tom F. ROMANTIC QUEST AND MODERN QUERY: History of the Modern Theater. 1970. *Delacorte* (dist. by Dial) $7.50; *Dell* Delta pap. $2.95. A study of nineteenth and twentieth century theatre.

Dukore, B. F. Ed. DRAMATIC THEORY AND CRITICISM. 1974. *Holt* $9.95. A collection of the major documents in dramatic theory from the Greeks to Grotowski. Also includes works by philosophers, psychologists, and social theorists.

Esslin, Martin. THE THEATRE OF THE ABSURD. *Doubleday* Anchor Bks. 1969 pap. $2.50; 1961 *Overlook Press* 1973 $12.50. An introduction to the work of Beckett, Adamov, Ionesco, Genet, Pinter, and other contemporary playwrights, with a discussion of their common idea of drama.

Fergusson, Francis. IDEA OF A THEATRE: A Study of Ten Plays; The Art of Drama in Changing Perspective. 1949. 1953 *Princeton Univ. Press* 1968 $10.00 pap. $2.45. An important work of modern criticism. Plays by Sophocles, Wagner, Racine, Shakespeare, and others read in the light of neo-Aristotelian theory.

Freedley, George, and John A. Reeves. A HISTORY OF THE THEATRE. *Crown* rev. ed. 1967 $10.00 text ed. $7.50

From pre-Greek days to modern American. "This newly revised and augmented edition brings the history of theater up to 1967, and adds much valuable new material to what has been probably the most comprehensive volume on world theater history"—(*LJ*).

Frenz, Horst. AMERICAN PLAYWRIGHTS ON DRAMA. *Farrar, Straus* (Hill & Wang) Dramabk. 1965 pap. $1.95. Fourteen playwrights, from O'Neill to Albee, write about drama and theatre.

Gassner, John. MASTERS OF THE DRAMA. *Dover* rev. ed. 1967 $8.50. A comprehensive history of world drama with plot summaries, details on about 800 theatrical personalities and analyses of dramatic trends and influences.

THE THEATRE IN OUR TIMES: A Survey of the Men, Materials and Movements in the Modern Theatre. *Crown* 1954 $7.50 pap. 1960 $2.95. A "unified, coherent, provocative review of developments in the American and European theater. Until his death in 1967, John Gassner, eminent writer and essayist on the theatre, was Sterling Professor of Drama at Yale.

(Ed.) IDEAS IN THE DRAMA. *Columbia* 1964 $7.00

"A scholarly, stimulating book consisting of talks by experts on the Greek theater and on Shaw, O'Neill, Brecht and Sartre, at conferences of the English Institute in 1962 and 1963"—(*N.Y. Times*).

(With Ralph G. Allen) THEATRE AND DRAMA IN THE MAKING. *Houghton* 2 vols. 1964 vol. 1 o.p. vol. 2 pap. $6.95

See also two preceding sections and Chapter 5, American Drama, this volume.

Gilder, Rosamond. ENTER THE ACTRESS. 1931. Essay Index Reprint Ser. *Bks. for Libraries* 1974 $14.95; *Theatre Arts* pap. $1.95. A history of women in the theater from ancient Greek to modern times.

Gilman, Richard. THE MAKING OF MODERN DRAMA. 1974. *Farrar, Straus* $8.95 pap. $2.95

"The best single study of the astonishing transformations dramatic art has undergone in the last century or so"—(*N.Y. Times Book Review*)

Granville-Barker, Harley. ON DRAMATIC METHOD. 1931. 1956 *Peter Smith* 1960 $4.00

Guthke, Karl S. MODERN TRAGICOMEDY: An Investigation into the Nature of the Genre. *Phila. Bk. Co.* 1966 pap. $3.95; *Peter Smith* $5.00

Hathorn, Richmond Y. TRAGEDY, MYTH AND MYSTERY. *Indiana Univ. Press* 1962 pap. $2.65; *Peter Smith* $4.75. With "vigor, wit, logic, insight, and vast but unobtrusive erudition," he analyzes 8 great myth-based dramas: "The Oresteia," "Antigone," "Oedipus Rex," "Hippolytus," "The Bacchae," "Hamlet," "King Lear," and "Murder in the Cathedral."

Herrick, Marvin Theodore. COMIC THEORY IN THE SIXTEENTH CENTURY. *Univ. of Illinois Press* 1964 pap. $1.75

TRAGICOMEDY: Its Origin and Development in Italy, France and England. *Univ. of Illinois Press* 1955 pap. 1962 $1.95. A "remarkable, comprehensive" historical study.

Houghton, Norris. THE EXPLODING STAGE: An Introduction to Twentieth Century Drama. 1971. *McKay* (Weybright & Talley). $6.95; *Dell* Delta pap. $2.75. Theatre history and theatrical criticism, meant as an introduction for the playgoer.

Hoy, Cyrus. THE HYACINTH ROOM: An Investigation Into the Nature of Comedy, Tragedy, and Tragicomedy. *Knopf* 1964 $6.95

Hunningher, Benjamin. THE ORIGIN OF THE THEATER. *Farrar, Straus* (Hill & Wang) Dramabk. $1.35. Challenges the theory that the modern theatre had its origins in church festivals.

Hyams, Barry, Ed. THEATRE II. Pref. by Alan Pryce-Jones *Farrar, Straus* (Hill & Wang) pap. $1.95

This "small anthology of writings on theatrical repertory by such writers as Alan Pryce-Jones, Henri Peyre, Lionel Abel, Nancy and Richard Meyer, Kenneth Tynan, . . . Sir Tyrone Guthrie, Herbert Blau and Harold Clurman [is an] excellent compendium"—(*LJ*).

Jones, Robert Edmond. DRAMATIC IMAGINATION: Reflections and Speculations on the Art of the Theatre. Introd. by John Mason Brown *Theatre Arts* 1956 $4.25. By the innovator in 20th-century theater design who died in 1954.

Jones, Willis Knapp. BEHIND SPANISH-AMERICAN FOOTLIGHTS. *Univ. of Texas Press* 1965 $11.50

"A clearly documented account . . . covering the theatrical efforts of 19 countries over 475 years. . . . The most comprehensive study in English, though it does not cover the Portuguese theater [of] Brazil"—(*LJ*).

Kernan, Alvin, Ed. MODERN AMERICAN THEATRE: A Collection of Critical Essays. 1967. Twentieth Century Views *Prentice-Hall* 1967 $5.95 Spectrum pap. $1.95

Kerr, Walter. GOD ON THE GYMNASIUM FLOOR AND OTHER THEATRICAL ADVENTURES. *Dell* Delta 1973 pap. $2.65. Essays concerning recent trends in theatre and drama.

THE THEATRE IN SPITE OF ITSELF. *Simon & Schuster* 1963 $5.00. The former drama critic of the *N.Y. Herald Tribune* who is now Sunday drama critic for the *N.Y. Times* won the 1964 George Jean Nathan Award for this book.

TRAGEDY AND COMEDY. *Simon & Schuster* 1967 $5.95 Touchstone-Clarion 1968 pap. $2.45

"He has attempted no less a task than to write a modern poetics—an examination of the assumptions on which tragedy and comedy are based. Against all odds he remains sensible and persuasive"—(*N.Y. Times*).

Krutch, Joseph Wood. MODERNISM IN MODERN DRAMA. 1953. *Russell & Russell* 1962 $6.00; *Cornell Univ. Press* 1966 pap. $1.45

Lahr, John. UP AGAINST THE FOURTH WALL: Essays on Modern Theater. *Grove* 1970 pap. $2.95. Fifteen essays by an important American critic, winner of the George Jean Nathan Award for Drama Criticism.

Laver, James. COSTUME IN THE THEATRE. *Farrar, Straus* (Hill & Wang) 1965 $6.50 pap. $2.25

"Not only a vivid, factual account, but a creative, original interpretation by an able historian, former keeper of the Victoria and Albert Museum"—(*LJ*).

Lessing, Gotthold. HAMBURG DRAMATURGY. 1769. Trans. by H. Zimmern *Dover* pap. $2.75. Eighteenth-century essays combining practical criticism with an important reconsideration of the idea of tragedy.

Lewis, Allan. THE CONTEMPORARY THEATRE: The Significant Playwrights of Our Time. *Crown* 1962 rev. ed. 1970 $5.95 text ed. $4.50. An absorbing survey; 18 playwrights from Ibsen to Williams are discussed in detail.

Ley-Piscator, Maria. THE PISCATOR EXPERIMENT: The Political Theatre. *James H. Heineman* 1967 $8.50. With Bertolt Brecht (*q.v.*), Erwin Piscator, a German producer and director, was the leading force in the innovations of the German "epic" theater.

Little, Stuart W. OFF-BROADWAY: The Prophetic Theater. *Dell* Delta pap. $2.95. A survey and documentary record of the past twenty years of noncommercial theatre.

Lucas, Frank Laurence. TRAGEDY: Serious Drama in Relation to Aristotle's Poetics. 1927. *Macmillan* Collier Bks. 1966 pap. $1.25

Lumley, Frederick. NEW TRENDS IN 20TH CENTURY DRAMA: A Survey Since Ibsen and Shaw. *Oxford* 1960 1967 4th ed. 1972 $8.50

McCarthy, Mary. THEATRE CHRONICLES: Nineteen Thirty Seven to Nineteen Sixty Two. 1963. *Farrar, Straus* $4.50

Macgowan, Kenneth, and Robert Edmond Jones. CONTINENTAL STAGECRAFT. 1922 *Blom* 1964 $12.50

(With William Melnitz) GOLDEN AGES OF THE THEATER. *Prentice-Hall* Spectrum Bks. 1959 pap. $1.95. How the stage has reflected the life of the times through 2,500 years.

THE LIVING STAGE: A History of the World Theatre. *Prentice-Hall* 1955 $12.50. This well-written volume is highly recommended for playgoer and student.

Macqueen-Pope, W. A. THE CURTAIN RISES: The Story of the Theater. 1961 *Greenwood* 1974 $19.75. A popular history by the late British dramatic critic and publicity man.

Moussinac, Léon. THE NEW MOVEMENT IN THE THEATRE: A Survey of Recent Developments in Europe and America. 1930. Introd. by R. H. Packman; fwd. by Gordon Craig *Blum* 1967 $35.00

Historically "of special value for the many plates"—(*LJ*).

Muller, Herbert J. THE SPIRIT OF TRAGEDY. *Knopf* 1956 $5.95. A provocative presentation of the literature of tragedy.

Nagler, A. M. A SOURCE BOOK IN THEATRICAL HISTORY. 1952 *Dover* pap. $4.00; *Peter Smith* $6.00

"An indispensable complement to the study of the drama"—(*Educational Theater Journal*).

Nathan, George Jean. THE CRITIC AND THE DRAMA. 1922. *Fairleigh Dickinson Univ. Press* $6.75

Nathan founded *The American Mercury* with H. L. Mencken and served as its drama critic for a number of years. He wrote many books about the theater, and articles for American and foreign periodicals including the *American Spectator*, which he founded in 1943, and the daily N.Y. *Journal American*. He died in 1958.

MATERIA CRITICA. 1924. *Fairleigh Dickinson Univ. Press* 1971 $8.00

PASSING JUDGMENTS. 1935. *Fairleigh Dickinson Univ. Press* 1970 $8.00

THEATRE OF THE MOMENT. 1936. *Fairleigh Dickinson Univ. Press* 1971 $8.00

Nicoll, Allardyce. BRITISH DRAMA: An Historical Survey from the Beginnings to the Present Time. *Harper* (Barnes & Noble) 5th ed. rev. 1963 $7.50

THE DEVELOPMENT OF THE THEATRE: A Study of Theatrical Art from the Beginnings to the Present Day. *Harcourt* 1927 1937 1948 1958 5th ed. rev. 1967 $15.00

An invaluable and indispensable survey from the time of the Dionysian theater. In the new edition, "the additional sections on the Oriental stage and the theater of the 20th Century are invaluable, as are the author's selective bibliographical essays and the seldom published *Dialogues* of Leone di Somi"—(*LJ*).

A HISTORY OF ENGLISH DRAMA 1660–1900 *Cambridge* 6 vols. Vol. 1 Restoration Drama, 1660–1700 (1923 4th ed. 1952) Vol. 2 Early Eighteenth Century Drama, 1700–1750 (1925 rev. and enl. 1952) Vol. 3 Late Eighteenth Century Drama, 1750–1800 (1927 rev. and enl. 1952) Vol. 4 Early Nineteenth Century Drama, 1800–1850. Originally pub. in 2 vols. (1930 2nd ed. rev. and enl. 1955) Vol. 5 Late Nineteenth Century

Drama, 1850–1900. Originally pub. in 2 vols. (1946 rev. and enl. ed. 1959) Vol. 6 Alphabetical Catalogue of the Plays (1959) Vols. 1, 2, 3 each $19.50, Vol. 4 $23.50 Vol. 5 $35.00 Vol. 6 $23.00 set $105.00

Allardyce Nicoll is one of the world's leading theater historians. He spent a number of years in this country as Chairman of the Drama Department of Yale University.

MASKS, MIMES AND MIRACLES. *Cooper* 1964 $18.50

THE THEORY OF DRAMA. 1931. Rev. and enl. ed. of "An Introduction to Dramatic Theory. *Blom* 1966 $10.75

"A survey which enables us to appreciate the drama from Aristotle's time to the present day as the variation of a single theme and the communication of a kindred ecstasy"—(*TLS*, London).

WORLD DRAMA: From Aeschylus to Anouilh. *Harcourt* 1949 $9.75

The author "set himself a difficult task: to survey the whole of drama from its miscellaneous beginnings to its present global diversity, and in so doing to consider it as theatrical experience, literature and a way of interpreting life. The accomplishment is impressive . . . planned skillfully and written with clarity and grace"—(*N.Y. Times*).

THE WORLD OF HARLEQUIN: A Critical Study of the Commedia dell' Arte. *Cambridge* 1963 $24.50. Highly recommended to all theatrical collections and large libraries.

Olson, Elder. TRAGEDY AND THE THEORY OF DRAMA. 1961. *Wayne State Univ. Press* pap. $3.95

Palmer, Helen H., and Jane Anne Dyson. EUROPEAN DRAMA CRITICISM. *Shoe String Press* 1967 $10.00; Supplement One, to January 1970 1970 $6.50; Supplement Two 1974 $8.50

Peacock, Ronald. THE ART OF THE DRAMA. 1957 *Greenwood* $11.50

Potts, L. J. COMEDY. 1960 *Putnam* 1966 pap. $1.45

Raphael, D. D. THE PARADOX OF TRAGEDY. *Indiana Univ. Press* 1960 pap. $1.45; *Peter Smith* $3.50. Citing examples from the Greek masters to Arthur Miller, Dr. Raphael, Senior Lecturer in Moral Philosophy at the University of Glasgow, examines the essential elements of tragedy.

Ridgeway, William. THE DRAMAS AND DRAMATIC DANCES OF THE NON-EUROPEAN RACES. 1915. *Blom* 1963 $17.50

THE ORIGIN OF TRAGEDY. 1910. *Blom* 1963 $12.50

Schechner, Richard. PUBLIC DOMAIN. *Bobbs* $6.95; *Avon* 1970 pap. $1.65. Essays on criticism, classical and modern plays, and contemporary radical experiments in theatre.

Shaw, George Bernard. SHAW'S DRAMATIC CRITICISM, 1895–1898. Sel. by John F. Mathews. 1959 *Peter Smith* $3.75

Smith, Michael. THEATRE JOURNAL: Winter, 1967. 1968. *Univ. of Missouri Press* pap. $2.50. At one time chief drama critic of *The Village Voice*, Smith is closely associated with New York's "Off-Off-Broadway" drama movement.

Smith, Winifred. COMMEDIA DELL' ARTE. *Blom* rev. ed. 1964 $13.95

"The basic book on the subject published in English"—(*LJ*).

Steiner, George. THE DEATH OF TRAGEDY. 1961 *Farrar, Straus* (Hill & Wang) Dramabks. 1963 pap. $3.25. An attempt to explain why tragedy died in Western literature.

Styan, J. L. THE DARK COMEDY: The Development of Modern Comic Tragedy. *Cambridge* 1961 2nd ed. 1968 $14.75 pap. $4.95. Centers its discussion of modern drama on the audience's response to the play.

THE ELEMENTS OF DRAMA. *Cambridge* 1960 $10.95 pap. $4.95. Close analysis of excerpts from plays by Shakespeare, Ibsen, Chekhov, Shaw, and others. An introduction to theatre for the general reader.

Tynan, Kenneth. CURTAINS. *Atheneum* 1961 $10.00. A collection of the best critical writing on the theater by the English critic-at-large who has also reviewed American theater for the *New Yorker*. He is now Literary Manager of Britain's National Theater.

TYNAN RIGHT AND LEFT: Plays, Films, Places, People and Events. *Atheneum* 1967 $8.95. Selections from his writing over 10 years.

Valency, Maurice. THE FLOWER AND THE CASTLE: An Introduction to Modern Drama. 1963 *Grosset* pap. $2.95

Wagenknecht, Edward. SEVEN DAUGHTERS OF THE THEATRE. *Univ. of Oklahoma Press* 1964 $7.95. The seven daughters are Jenny Lind, Sarah Bernhardt, Ellen Terry, Julia Marlowe, Isadora Duncan, Mary Garden, Marilyn Monroe.

Wellwarth, George E. THEATRE OF PROTEST AND PARADOX: Developments in the Avant-Garde Drama. *New York Univ. Press* 1964 1970 $10.00 pap. $3.95

Whiting, Frank M. AN INTRODUCTION TO THE THEATRE. *Harper* 1961 3rd ed. 1969 $12.95

Williams, Raymond. DRAMA FROM IBSEN TO BRECHT. *Oxford* 1969 $6.50. A sharp and valuable volume.

DRAMA IN PERFORMANCE. 1973. *Penguin* pap. $1.95. Discusses relations between dramatic form and performance practice in the history of European drama.

MODERN TRAGEDY. *Stanford Univ. Press* 1966 $7.00

Professor Williams of Cambridge University concludes "that 'modern tragedy' is similar to classical tragedy in that it shows the personal and social necessity for what is rather loosely termed 'revolution' [in a study that] brings together in neat and perceptive perspective a long tradition of literary accomplishment"—(*LJ*).

Winter, Marian Hannah. THE THEATRE OF MARVELS. Trans. from the French; pref. by Marcel Marceau *Blom* 1965 $17.50

* Concerned with the "unsophisticated theater of sight and loud sound" to about 1860, this is "a useful reference tool, as well as a delight for reading"—(*LJ*).

Wright, Edward A. A PRIMER FOR PLAYGOERS. *Prentice-Hall* 1958 2nd ed. 1969 $10.60 text ed. $7.95. Fine analysis of the theater and drama in general.

Young, Stark. THE FLOWER IN DRAMA AND GLAMOUR: Theatre Essays and Criticism. 1923 and 1925 rev. ed. 1955. *Octagon* 1972 $11.50

"Stark Young, in several small books, . . . made one of the best contributions to the understanding of theater arts"—(Eric Bentley).

IMMORTAL SHADOWS. 1948 *Octagon* 1972 $12.50

See also Chapter 4, Modern British Drama, and Chapter 5, American Drama, this volume.

ORIENTAL DRAMA

Arlington, L. C. THE CHINESE DRAMA. 1937. *Blom* 1965 $32.50. Criticism.

Bowers, Faubion. THEATRE IN THE EAST: A Survey of Asian Dance and Drama. *Grove* 1960 pap. $3.95

Brandon, James R. BRANDON'S GUIDE TO THEATER IN ASIA. *Univ. Press of Hawaii* 1976 (in prep.)

KABUKI: Five Classic Plays. *Harvard Univ. Press* 1975 $20.00. Well illustrated.

THEATRE IN SOUTHEAST ASIA. *Harvard Univ. Press* 1967 $12.50

"Linguistic skill, and a talent for dedicated research have produced this authoritative, fact-filled compendium. . . . The book's magnificent bibliography, copious notes, glossary, and index make it an invaluable source of information"—(*LJ*).

Horrwitz, Ernest Philip. INDIAN THEATRE: A Brief Survey of Sanskrit Drama. 1912 *Blom* 1967 $8.50

Irwin, Vera R., Ed. FOUR CLASSICAL ASIAN PLAYS. *Penguin* 1972 pap. $3.75. Four plays representing different forms of classical Eastern drama: The Vision of Vasavadatta (India); The West Chamber (China); Ikkaku Sennin (Noh); Narukami (Kabuki).

Kincaid, Zoë. KUBUKI: The Popular Stage of Japan. 1925 *Blom* 1965 $18.50. Criticism.

Liu Jung-en, Trans. SIX YUAN PLAYS. *Penguin* 1972 pap. $2.25

Scott, A. C. TRADITIONAL CHINESE PLAYS. *Univ. of Wisconsin Press* 1967 3 vols. Vols. 1 and 2 pap. $2.50 Vol. 3 $10.00

Waley, Arthur, Trans. THE NO PLAYS OF JAPAN. 1920. *Grove* 1957 pap. $3.95. Translations of twenty plays, summaries of others. Still the definitive anthology in English.

Wells, Henry W. THE CLASSICAL DRAMA OF THE ORIENT: China and Japan. *Asia Pub. House* (dist. by Taplinger) 1965 $8.50. Criticism.

SIX SANSKRIT PLAYS IN ENGLISH TRANSLATION. *Asia Pub. House* 1964 $10.95

Zung, Cecilia. SECRETS OF THE CHINESE DRAMA: A Guide to Its Theatre Techniques. 1937. *Blom* 1963 $15.00. Includes synopses of 50 classic plays.

For further information on Oriental drama, see Chapter 19, Asian Literature, this volume.

DRAMATIC TECHNIQUE

Archer, William. PLAYMAKING: A Manual of Craftsmanship. 1912. 1959 *Peter Smith* $4.50

Baker, G. P. DRAMATIC TECHNIQUE. 1919. Theatre, Film, and the Performing Arts Ser. *Da Capo* 1971 $17.50; *Greenwood* $19.25. A classic of American dramaturgy.

Barton, Lucy. HISTORICAL COSTUMES FOR THE STAGE. Ill. with pen-and-ink drawings. *Baker* rev. ed. 1961 $10.95

Boleslavski, Richard. ACTING: The First Six Lessons. *Theatre Arts* 1933 $3.95. Pub. for the National Theater Conference.

Brooke, Iris. COSTUME IN GREEK CLASSIC DRAMA. 1962 *Greenwood* 1973 $9.25

Cartmell, Van H. AMATEUR THEATER: A Guide for Actor and Director. 1936. 1961 *T. Y. Crowell* (Funk and Wagnalls) 1968 pap. $1.50. Covers basic problems in play selection, casting, direction, and production.

Coger, Leslie Irene, and Melvin R. White. READER'S THEATRE HANDBOOK: A Dramatic Approach to Literature. *Scott, Foresman* 1967 rev. ed. 1973 pap. $5.50

Cole, Toby, Ed. PLAYWRIGHTS ON PLAYWRITING: The Meaning and Making of Modern Drama from Ibsen to Ionesco. *Farrar, Straus* (Hill & Wang) Dramabks. 1960 pap. $2.95

(With Helen Krich Chinoy, Eds.) ACTORS ON ACTING. *Crown* 1949 rev. ed. 1970 $8.95 text. ed. $6.75. Theories, techniques and practices in their own words; with introductions and biographical sketches.

DIRECTORS ON DIRECTING. *Bobbs* 1963 $5.00 pap. $3.50. Includes a historical study of the emergence of the director, essays by fifteen directors from Antoine to Logan, and valuable excerpts from rehearsal notes for famous productions.

Craig, Edward Gordon. SCENE. 1923. *Blom* 1965 $15.75. His discussion of stage design and lighting is illustrated with 19 full-page plates.

THE THEATRE ADVANCING. 1919. *Blom* 1963 $12.50. Edward Gordon Craig (1872–1966), son of the actress Ellen Terry, was an outstanding designer for the stage. See the excellent biography by Denis Bablet, "Edward Gordon Craig" (trans. by P. Woodward, *Theatre Arts* 1966 $7.75) and entry under Arnold Rood, below.

Dean, Alexander, and L. Carra. FUNDAMENTALS OF PLAY DIRECTING. *Holt* (Rinehart) 1941 1965 3rd ed. 1974 $9.95. Contains stage technique for actor and producer; a section on pantomine; diagrams and photographs and a glossary of terms.

Dolman, John. THE ART OF PLAY PRODUCTION. 1929. *Harper* 1946 3rd ed. 1973 $10.95. A very helpful manual for theater students.

Egri, Lajos. THE ART OF DRAMATIC WRITING. *Simon & Schuster* 1946 rev. ed. 1960 pap. $2.25

Freytag, Gustav. FREYTAG'S TECHNIQUE OF DRAMA. 1895. Trans. by J. Elias *Johnson Reprint* $16.75; *Scholarly Press* $19.50; 1905 *Blom* $10.75. Of historical interest.

Fuchs, Theodore. STAGE LIGHTING. 1929. *Blom* 1963 $15.00

Fuerst, René, and Samuel J. Hume. TWENTIETH CENTURY STAGE DECORATION. *Blom* 2 vols. 1965 set $18.50

Gassner, John. PRODUCING THE PLAY. *Holt* (Dryden) 2 vols. in one 1941 new rev. ed. 1953 $11.95. With the "New Scene Technician's Handbook" by Philip Barber.

Goodman, Randolph. DRAMA ON STAGE. *Holt* 1961 pap. $9.00. Production studies of six plays representing various periods and dramatic styles.

   FROM SCRIPT TO STAGE: Eight Modern Plays. *Holt* 1971 $12.50. Eight contemporary plays with elaborate commentary of theatre professionals who have been involved in their production.

Gorelik, Mordecai. NEW THEATRES FOR OLD. *French* 1940 $2.45; *Dutton* Everyman's 1962 pap. $2.45. This widely acknowledged classic presents a vivid record of the rise and fall of stage and screen techniques.

Hainaux, René, and Yves Bonnat. STAGE DESIGN THROUGHOUT THE WORLD SINCE 1935. 1950. *Theatre Arts* $29.50. Pictorial survey of experiments in opera, ballet, drama, 1935–1950. 176 photographs.

   (With the collaboration of the International Theatre Institute.) STAGE DESIGN THROUGHOUT THE WORLD SINCE 1950. *Theatre Arts* 1963 $32.50. Stage design in 33 countries with 192 pages of black-and-white illustrations and 16 pages of color; includes a "Stage Designers' Who's Who."

STAGE DESIGN THROUGHOUT THE WORLD SINCE 1960. *Theatre Arts* $39.95

Hatlen, Theodore W. ORIENTATION TO THE THEATER. 1962. *Prentice-Hall* Appleton-Century-Crofts 2nd ed. 1972 pap. $7.50. "An analysis of dramatic composition and theatrical production from age to age in Western Civilization."

Heffner, Hubert C., and others. MODERN THEATRE PRACTICE: A Handbook of Play Production. 1935. *Prentice-Hall* Appleton-Century-Crofts 5th ed. 1973 $13.50. A very helpful book on the subject.

Herman, Lewis and Marguerite Shalett Herman. AMERICAN DIALECTS: A Manual for Actors, Directors and Writers. *Theatre Arts* 1947 reprint 1960 $9.50. An excellent guide to reproducing the sounds, rhythms, lilts and stresses of representative U.S. dialects.

   FOREIGN DIALECTS: A Manual for Actors, Directors and Writers. *Theatre Arts* $9.50

Hopkins, Albert. MAGIC: Stage Illusions and Scientific Diversions. *Blom* 1966 $12.75

Hopkins, Arthur M. REFERENCE POINT: Reflections on Creative Ways in General with Special Reference to Creative Ways in the Theatre. *French* 1948 $2.50. About writing, direction, acting.

Kerr, Walter. HOW NOT TO WRITE A PLAY. *The Writer* 1955 $6.95. The author has directed plays both amateur and professional, taught playwriting and written plays himself.

Komisarjevsky, Theodore, and Lee Simonson. SETTINGS AND COSTUMES OF THE MODERN STAGE. 1933. *Blom* 1965 $15.00

Lawson, John H. THEORY AND TECHNIQUE OF PLAYWRITING. *Farrar, Straus* (Hill & Wang) Dramabks. 1960 pap. $2.45

   "Beyond doubt the most incisive and illuminating treatment of playwrighting as a dynamic art"—(John Gassner).

Le Gallienne, Eva. THE MYSTIC IN THE THEATRE: Eleonora Duse. 1966. *Southern Ill. Univ. Press* 1973 pap. $2.45

McCandless, Stanley. A METHOD OF LIGHTING THE STAGE. *Theatre Arts* rev. ed. 1954 $4.45

Macgowan, Kenneth. A PRIMER OF PLAYWRITING. *Random* 1941 $5.95; *Doubleday Bks.* pap. $.95. A sound guide to the basic rules.

Machlin, Evangeline. SPEECH FOR THE STAGE. *Theatre Arts* $6.75

Matthews, Brander, Ed. PAPERS ON ACTING. *Farrar, Straus* (Hill & Wang) 1958 $3.75 Dramabks. pap. $1.65. Contains essays by such actors as Talma, Coquelin, Booth, Irving, Kemble and others.

(Ed.) PAPERS ON PLAYMAKING. *Farrar, Straus* (Hill & Wang) Dramabks. 1957 pap. $1.35; Essay Index Reprint Ser. *Bks. for Libraries* 1957 $11.25; *Folcroft* 1973 $9.50

The first professor of dramatic literature in an American university, Brander Matthews of Columbia was an eminent theater critic and essayist. Until his death in 1929 he was prominent in numerous dramatic organizations.

Mielziner, Jo. DESIGNING FOR THE THEATRE: A Memoir and a Portfolio. 1965 *Potter* (dist. by Crown) $29.95

"One of America's top theater designers has given us in the 'Memoir' snatches of memory and a fascinating explanation of his methods"—*(LJ)*.

Newquist, Roy. SHOWCASE. Introd. by Brooks Atkinson; ill. by Irma Selz *Morrow* 1966 $5.95. Interviews with notable theater personalities.

Oxenford, Lyn. DESIGN FOR MOVEMENT. *Theatre Arts* 1954 $3.85

Parker, W. Oren, and Harvey K. Smith. SCENE DESIGN AND STAGE LIGHTING. *Holt* 1963 2nd ed 1968 $12.95. Step-by-step instruction including over 275 diagrams, sketches and photographs.

Plummer, Gail. THE BUSINESS OF SHOW BUSINESS. 1961 *Greenwood* 1973 $12.00. An authoritative book on the extremely important role of a business manager in the theater, whether commercial, educational or presumably nonprofit.

Redfield, William. LETTERS FROM AN ACTOR. 1964. *Viking* Compass Bks. 1969 pap. $1.75

Written by an actor who took part in the 1964 Gielgud-Burton production of "Hamlet," this is "a book of bright and flavorsome observations [that] abounds in inside stage talk"—(Harold Clurman).

Redgrave, Michael. MASK OR FACE: Reflections in an Actor's Mirror. Introd. by Harold Clurman *Theatre Arts* 1958 $4.15. One of the great books on acting.

Roberts, Vera Mowry. ON STAGE: A History of Theatre. *Harper* 1962 2nd ed. 1974 $12.95. Professor Roberts "minimizes the literary side to give more space to the actual evolvement of theater buildings and the stages themselves" from their beginnings in Egypt and Greece.

Rood, Arnold. EDWARD GORDON CRAIG, ARTIST OF THE THEATRE, 1872–1966: A Memorial Exhibit in the Amsterdam Gallery. 1967 N.Y. Pub. Library Publications in Reprint Ser. *Arno* 1971 $9.00

Rowe, Kenneth Thorpe. A THEATRE IN YOUR HEAD. *T. Y. Crowell* (Funk & Wagnalls) 1960 1967 $2.95

A practical handbook on how to experience a play by visualizing its production, with emphasis on the plays as dramatic literature and the playwright's collaboration with the producer, director and others; valuable previously unpublished selections from the notebooks of Elia Kazan and John Gielgud.

WRITE THAT PLAY. *T. Y. Crowell* (Funk & Wagnalls) 1969 $6.95 pap. $2.95

Rubin, Joel E., and Leland H. Watson. THEATRICAL LIGHTING PRACTICE. *Theatre Arts* 1954 $7.45

Saint-Denis, Michel. THEATRE: The Rediscovery of Style. *Theatre Arts* 1969 pap. $2.95

Seyler, Athene, and Stephen Haggard. THE CRAFT OF COMEDY. *Theatre Arts* 1944 2nd enl. ed. 1957 $4.25. One of the most useful books for any student of acting technique.

Sharp, William. LANGUAGE IN DRAMA: Meanings for the Director and the Actor. *T. Y. Crowell* (Chandler Pub.) 1970 $7.00 pap. $3.50

Simonson, Lee. THE STAGE IS SET. *Theatre Arts* 1962 $3.95. A picture of the scene designer at work in the modern theater.

Southern, Richard. THE SEVEN AGES OF THE THEATRE. *Farrar, Straus* (Hill & Wang) Dramabks. 1961 pap. $2.95. A history of theatre buildings and playing spaces, "of the first importance in its field"—(Eric Bentley).

STAGE SETTING FOR AMATEURS AND PROFESSIONALS. *Theatre Arts* $7.25

Spolin, Viola. IMPROVISATION FOR THE THEATER: A Handbook of Teaching and Directing Techniques. *Northwestern Univ. Press* 1963 $10.00 text ed. $7.50

Stanislavski, Constantin (pseud. of Konstantin Sergieevich Alekseev). AN ACTOR PREPARES. Trans. by Elizabeth Reynolds Hapgood; introd. by John Gielgud. 1930. *Theatre Arts* anniversary ed. 1948 $4.95

> By the codirector of the Moscow Art Theater in its halcyon days, the originator of "Method" acting. For further information on Stanislavski and his impact, see "The Stanislavsky Heritage: Its Contribution to the Russian and American Theatre" by Christine Edwards (*New York Univ. Press* 1965 $10.00 pap. $3.50); "Stanislavski and America: An Anthology from the *Tulane Drama Review*" edited by Erika Munck (*Hill & Wang* 1966 $5.95); and "The Stanislavski System: The Professional Training of an Actor" by Sonia Moore (*Viking* 1965 $3.50), a revised and enlarged version of "The Stanislavski Method" (1960).

> AN ACTOR'S HANDBOOK. Trans. by Elizabeth Reynolds Hapgood. *Theatre Arts* 1963 pap. $2.25

> > An alphabetical arrangement of pithy statements about the theater, published Jan. 17, 1963, to commemorate the 100th anniversary of Stanislavski's birth. Through the efforts of Moscow archivists who collated all of his papers, some extremely interesting statements, previously untranslated, have been found and are included here.

> BUILDING A CHARACTER. Trans. by Elizabeth Reynolds Hapgood; introd. by Joshua Logan. *Theatre Arts* 1949 $5.45

> MY LIFE IN ART. Trans. by J. J. Robbins. 1924. *Theatre Arts* 1948 pap. $4.25

> STANISLAVSKI'S LEGACY: A Collection of Comments on a Variety of Aspects of an Actor's Art and Life. Sel. and trans. by Elizabeth Reynolds Hapgood *Theatre Arts* 1958 rev. ed. 1968 $5.50 pap. $2.45. Hitherto unpublished material.

> STANISLAVSKY ON THE ART OF THE STAGE. Trans. with introd. by David Magarshack *Farrar, Straus* (Hill & Wang) 1960 Dramabks. 1962 $2.95. Includes "The System and Method of Creative Art," a posthumous collection of lectures given at the Bolshoi Theatre.

Sterne, Richard L. JOHN GIELGUD DIRECTS RICHARD BURTON IN HAMLET: A Journal of Rehearsals. *Random* 1967 $8.95

> Sterne, who acted Guildenstern in the 1964 production, "edited this volume from notes and tapes, adding the playing version with detailed description of stage business and retrospective interviews with the principals."—(*LJ*).

Thomas, Charles. MAKE-UP: The Dramatic Student's Approach. *Theatre Arts* $2.25

Wagenknecht, Edward. MERELY PLAYERS: A Great Actor Becomes the Second Author of His Parts by His Accents and His Physiognomy. *Univ. of Oklahoma Press* 1966 $7.95. "Psychographs" of eight great actors (Garrick, Kean, Macready, Forrest, Booth, Irving, Jefferson, and Mansfield).

Whiting, Fran M. INTRODUCTION TO THE THEATRE. *Harper* 1954 1961 3rd ed. 1969 $12.95. A recommended, copiously illustrated guide.

—D. M. B.

Chapter 2

British Drama: Early to 18th Century

"From jigging veins of rhyming mother wits,
And such conceits as clownage keeps in pay,
We'll lead you to the stately tent of war,
Where you shall hear the Scythian Tamburlaine
Threat'ning the world with high astounding terms,
And scourging kingdoms with his conquering sword.
View but his picture in this tragic glass,
And then applaud his fortunes as you please."

—MARLOWE, Prologue to "Tamburlaine"

Drama was the supreme form of literary expression in the Age of Elizabeth. So popular was it with the public that many of the authors of that day who had small faculty for the writing of drama were compelled to be poor dramatists when they might have been greater artists in some other field. Yet the dramatists and actors themselves were often treated with the disrespect accorded their nomadic, disreputable forebears. They were inveighed against by the Puritans, who were to close all theaters in 1642 because they were centers of immorality. During the reigns of Elizabeth, James, and Charles, however, they were supported by aristocratic patrons, whose funds and interest helped them create the greatest age of drama in English literature. Sir Edmund Kerchever Chambers' great four-volume work "The Elizabethan Stage" is the best background book for this period (*see Elizabethan Drama: History and Criticism, this Chapter*).

PRE-SHAKESPEAREAN DRAMA: HISTORY AND CRITICISM

Brooke, C. F. Tucker. TUDOR DRAMA: A History of English National Drama to the Retirement of Shakespeare. 1911. *Haskell* 1967 $24.25. Still a most useful survey.

Chambers, Sir Edmund K. THE MEDIEVAL STAGE. *Oxford* 2 vols. 1903 set $21.00

Craig, Hardin. ENGLISH RELIGIOUS DRAMA OF THE MIDDLE AGES. *Oxford* 1955 $13.75

Craik, T. W. THE TUDOR INTERLUDE. 1958. *Humanities Press* $6.00

Farnham, Willard. THE MEDIEVAL HERITAGE OF ELIZABETHAN TRAGEDY. *Harper* (Barnes & Noble) 1957 $10.00

Gardiner, Harold C. MYSTERIES' END. 1946. *Shoe String Press* 1967 $4.50

Knight, G. Wilson. THE GOLDEN LABYRINTH: A Study of British Drama. *Norton* 1962 $6.00 pap. $1.85. A single-volume history of the essential nature of British drama by an outstanding Shakespearean critic.

Nelson, Alan H. THE MEDIEVAL ENGLISH STAGE: Corpus Christi Pageants and Plays. *Univ. of Chicago Press* 1974 $12.50

Prosser, Eleanor A. DRAMA AND RELIGION IN THE ENGLISH MYSTERY PLAYS: A Re-evaluation. *Stanford Univ. Press* 1961 $8.50. The revised interest in medieval drama has largely been brought about by the York Festival and others held in England. Professor Prosser of San Jose State College, California, presents a new and clearer approach.

Rossiter, Arthur P. ENGLISH DRAMA FROM EARLY TIMES TO THE ELIZABETHANS. *Harper* (Barnes & Noble) 1962 $6.00 pap. $1.95

Stratman, Carl J. BIBLIOGRAPHY OF ENGLISH PRINTED TRAGEDY, 1565–1900. *Southern Illinois Univ. Press* 1966 $15.00

BIBLIOGRAPHY OF MEDIEVAL DRAMA. Fwd. by John Webster Spargo. 1954. *Ungar* 1972 $35.00

DRAMATIC PLAY LISTS, 1591–1963. *N.Y. Public Lib.* 1966 pap. $2.50

Taylor, Jerome, and Alan H. Nelson, Eds. MEDIEVAL ENGLISH DRAMA: Essays Critical and Contextual. *Univ. of Chicago Press* text ed. 1972 $14.00 pap. 1974 $3.95

Wickham, Glynne. EARLY ENGLISH STAGES 1300–1660. *Columbia* 1959 2 vols. Vol. 1 1300–1576 $17.50 Vol. 2 1577–1660 part 1 $17.50, part 2 $17.50

Williams, Arnold. DRAMA OF MEDIEVAL ENGLAND. *Michigan State Univ. Press* 1969 $6.00

Young, Karl. THE DRAMA OF THE MEDIEVAL CHURCH. *Oxford* 2 vols. 1933 set $41.00

ANTHOLOGIES OF PRE-SHAKESPEAREAN DRAMA

The beginnings of the English drama are to be found in the Miracle and Morality plays given in churches and village squares, which preceded Elizabethan drama. These early plays are best read in anthologies, listed below.

Adams, Joseph Quincy. CHIEF PRE-SHAKESPEAREAN DRAMAS. *Houghton* 1924 $11.95

Boas, Frederick S. FIVE PRE-SHAKESPEAREAN COMEDIES [Early Tudor Period]. *Oxford* 1934 1952 pap. 1970 $1.75

Creeth, Edmund, Ed. with introd. TUDOR PLAYS: An Anthology of Early English Drama. 1966. *Norton* 1972 pap. $4.95; *Peter Smith* $7.50

Gassner, John. MEDIEVAL AND TUDOR DRAMA. *Bantam* 1963 pap. $1.25. Plays from the 10th century through Elizabethan times, including early pagan drama and passion plays.

Heilman, Robert Bechtold, Ed. AN ANTHOLOGY OF ENGLISH DRAMA BEFORE SHAKESPEARE. *Holt* (Rinehart) 1952 pap. $3.95; *Peter Smith* $4.25

Hooper, Vincent F. and Gerald B. Lahey, Eds. MEDIEVAL MYSTERIES, MORALITIES AND INTERLUDES. *Barron's* 1962 $4.75 pap. $1.50. The best of early British dramas: Abraham and Isaac, Noah's Flood, The Second Shepherd's Play, Everyman, and others.

Hussey, Maurice. THE CHESTER MYSTERY PLAYS. *Theatre Arts* 1957 $2.90. Contains 16 of the 24 existing plays.

Manly, J. M., Ed. SPECIMENS OF THE PRE-SHAKESPEAREAN DRAMA. 1897. 2 vols. set *Biblo & Tannen* $17.50; *Peter Smith* $10.00

Pollard, Alfred W. ENGLISH MIRACLE PLAYS, MORALITIES AND INTERLUDES. *Oxford* 8th ed. rev. 1927 $11.25

ELIZABETHAN DRAMA: HISTORY AND CRITICISM

More criticism has been written of the literature of the Age of Elizabeth than of the literature of any other age in the world's history. The term Elizabethan Drama is often applied, as it is here, to the plays written in the reigns of Elizabeth I and her two successors, James I (1603–25) and Charles I (1625–49), up to the closing of the theaters in 1642. Sometimes the later part of the period is subdivided into Jacobean and Caroline. Criticism of Shakespeare alone is the largest tributary body of literature in existence. (*See Chapter 3, Shakespeare.*)

An excellent small background book of fine scholarship is E. M. W. Tillyard's "The Elizabethan World Picture" (1944. *Random* Vintage Bks. pap. $1.65). Some little-known views made available by modern research and other familiar beliefs, astronomical, medical and ethical, make exciting reading. " 'The Horizon Book of the Elizabethan World' by Lacey Baldwin Smith [o.p.] is a lavishly illustrated (more than 400 illustrations, over 100 in color) anthology of Elizabethan writings, plus 12 chapters of text by [the] professor of English history at Northwestern University"—(*PW*). It is a 9 ½ × 12 ¼-inch book of which the *Observer* (London) has said: "A brilliant synthesis of English and European history. . . . Certainly it stands head and shoulders above any other book on Elizabethan England published in the last 10 years. . . . By the exercise of a great literary skill all these disparate elements are woven into a fabric of great strength and beauty; the result, a real work of art." A welcome reprint of Morrison C. Boyd's "Elizabethan Music and Musical Criticism" (*Univ. of Pennsylvania Press* rev. ed 1962 $7.50), a collection of transcribed contemporary documents, is, in fact, a history of those years from the standpoint of music, writings about it, and those who made it.

For the latter part of the period Professor G. P. V. Akrigg's "Jacobean Pageant: or, The Court of James I" (*Harvard Univ. Press* 1962 pap. $3.95; *Greenwood* 1973 $15.25) is one of the best documented studies. It sets forth the manifold maneuvering, the courtside intriguing, the Catholic conflict, which beset England as it moved from the great age of the strong-minded Tudors into the troubled age of the second-rank Stuarts.

Barroll, J. Leeds, Alexander Leggatt, Richard Hosley and Alvin Kernan. THE REVELS HISTORY OF DRAMA IN ENGLISH, VOLUME III 1576–1613. *Harper* (Barnes & Noble) $37.50 pap. $15.50

Bentley, Gerald Eades. THE JACOBEAN AND CAROLINE STAGE. *Oxford* 6 vols. Vols. 1–2 Dramatic Companies and Players (1941) set $25.50 Vols. 3–5 Plays and Playwrights (1956) set $41.00 Vols. 6–7 Theatres, Appendixes to Vol. 7, and General Index (1968) set $24.00. A scholarly and invaluable supplement to Sir Edmund K. Chambers' authoritative history (*see below*). Bentley continues from the death of Shakespeare to 1642, when the theaters were closed at the outbreak of the Civil War. It is the standard authority. The skillful use of entertaining quotation and comment leavens the learning.

THE PROFESSION OF DRAMATIST IN SHAKESPEARE'S TIME, 1590–1642. *Princeton Univ. Press* 1972 $11.00

Bevington, David M. TUDOR DRAMA AND POLITICS. *Harvard Univ. Press* 1968 $10.00

Bluestone, Max, and Norman Rabkin, Eds. SHAKESPEARE'S CONTEMPORARIES: Modern Studies in English Renaissance Drama. *Prentice-Hall* 2nd ed. 1970 pap. $5.35

Boas, Frederick S. AN INTRODUCTION TO STUART DRAMA. *Oxford* 1946 $8.50 pap. $2.95. Critical analysis of the plots and characterizations of the chief playwrights.

Bowers, Fredson. ELIZABETHAN REVENGE TRAGEDY, 1587–1642. 1940. *Princeton Univ. Press* 1966 pap. $2.95; *Peter Smith* 1958 $5.00

Bradbrook, Muriel C. THE GROWTH AND STRUCTURE OF ELIZABETHAN COMEDY. *Hillary House* 1955 $8.25

THE RISE OF THE COMMON PLAYER: A Study of Actor and Society in Shakespeare's England. *Harvard Univ. Press* 1962 $5.25

THEMES AND CONVENTIONS OF ELIZABETHAN TRAGEDY. 1938. *Cambridge* 1952 $11.95 1960 pap. $3.95

Chambers, Sir Edmund Kerchever. THE ELIZABETHAN STAGE. *Oxford* 4 vols. 1923 set $51.25

ENGLISH LITERATURE AT THE CLOSE OF THE MIDDLE AGES. (Vol. 2 Part 2 of Oxford History of English Literature) *Oxford* 1945 $7.95

Creizenach, William. THE ENGLISH DRAMA IN THE AGE OF SHAKESPEARE. Trans. by Cécile Hugon. 1916. *Russell & Russell* 1967 $15.00

Doran, Madeleine. ENDEAVORS OF ART: A Study of Form in Elizabethan Drama. *Univ. of Wisconsin Press* 1954 pap. $4.95

Eliot, T. S. ESSAYS ON ELIZABETHAN DRAMA. *Harcourt* Harvest Bks. 1956 pap. $1.95

Ford, Boris, Ed. PELICAN GUIDE TO ENGLISH LITERATURE. Vol. 2 The Age of Shakespeare. 1955. *Penguin* pap. $1.65; (with title "A Guide," etc.) *Dufour* 1961 $7.50

Greenfield, Thelma N. INDUCTION IN ELIZABETHAN DRAMA. *Univ. of Oregon Bks.* 1970 $6.00

Griffin, Alice V. PAGEANTRY ON THE SHAKESPEAREAN STAGE. 1951. *College & Univ. Press* pap. $2.95

Harbage, Alfred. ANNALS OF ENGLISH DRAMA: 975–1700. *Univ. of Pennsylvania Press* rev. by S. Schoenbaum 1964 $18.00

  CAVALIER DRAMA: An Historical and Critical Supplement to the Study of the Elizabethan and Restoration Stage. 1936. *Russell & Russell* 1964 $10.00

Harrison, George Bagshawe. ELIZABETHAN PLAYS AND PLAYERS. *Univ. of Michigan Press* 1956 $4.94 Ann Arbor Bks. pap. $2.25

Jones, Inigo. DESIGNS BY INIGO JONES FOR MASQUES AND PLAYS AT COURT. Ed. by P. Simpson and C. F. Bell. 1924. *Russell & Russell* $35.00

Kaufmann, Ralph James, Ed. ELIZABETHAN DRAMA: Modern Essays in Criticism. *Oxford* 1961 Galaxy pap. $3.50

Lucas, F. L. SENECA AND ELIZABETHAN TRAGEDY. 1922. *Haskell* lib. bdg. $10.95; *Gordon Press* lib. bdg. $25.95

Nicoll, Allardyce. STUART MASQUES AND THE RENAISSANCE STAGE. *Blom* $17.50

Ornstein, Robert. THE MORAL VISION OF JACOBEAN TRAGEDY. 1960. *Greenwood* $15.50

Parrott, Thomas Marc, and Robert Hamilton Ball. A SHORT VIEW OF ELIZABETHAN DRAMA. *Scribner* 1934 1958 pap. 1960 $2.95. A standard reference work.

Prior, Moody E. THE LANGUAGE OF TRAGEDY. 1947. *Indiana Univ. Press* 1966 $2.95; *Peter Smith* $6.00

Rabkin, Norman, Ed. REINTERPRETATIONS OF ELIZABETHAN DRAMA. *Columbia* 1969 $7.00

Reed, A. W. EARLY TUDOR DRAMA. 1926. *Octagon* 1969 lib. bdg. $11.00

Ribner, Irving, Comp. TUDOR AND STUART DRAMA: Bibliography. 1966. *AHM Pub. Corp.* $2.95

Rossiter, A. P. ENGLISH DRAMA FROM EARLY TIMES TO THE ELIZABETHANS: Its Background, Origins and Developments. 1950. *Harper* (Barnes & Noble) 1959 $6.00 pap. $1.95

Simpson, Percy. STUDIES IN ELIZABETHAN DRAMA. 1955. *Folcroft* $20.00

STRATFORD-UPON-AVON STUDIES. General Eds. Bernard Harris and John R. Brown. *Crane-Russak Co.* (Shakespeare Institute, Stratford-upon-Avon) Vol. 1 Jacobean Theater (1961) Vol. 9 Elizabethan Theater (1967) pap. each $4.50

Waith, Eugene M. THE HERCULEAN HERO IN MARLOWE, CHAPMAN, SHAKESPEARE AND DRYDEN. *Columbia* 1962 $10.00. This excellent study of 7 plays, inquiring into the nature of the hero, demonstrates the relationship between the heroic and the tragic.

Welsford, Enid. THE COURT MASQUE: A Study in the Relationship Between Poetry and the Revels. 1927. *Russell & Russell* 1962 $16.00

Wilson, Frank Percy. ELIZABETHAN AND JACOBEAN. *Oxford* 1945 1953 $5.00. Excellent short, readable reference.

ANTHOLOGIES OF ELIZABETHAN DRAMA

Bald, Robert C., Ed. SIX ELIZABETHAN PLAYS. *Houghton* Riv. Eds. 1965 pap. $2.65

Brooke, C. F. Tucker, and N. B. Paradise. ENGLISH DRAMA, 1580–1642. *Heath* 1933 $12.95. One of the best of the older anthologies.

Gomme, A. H., Ed. JACOBEAN TRAGEDIES. *Oxford* 1969 pap. $2.75

Harrier, Richard C., Ed. AN ANTHOLOGY OF JACOBEAN DRAMA. *New York Univ. Press* 2 vols. 1963 each $12.50; (with title "Jacobean Drama: An Anthology") *Norton* 2 vols. 1968 Vol. 1 pap. $4.95 Vol. 2 pap. $2.95

Knowland, A. S., Ed. SIX CAROLINE PLAYS. *Oxford* $3.00

Lamb, Charles. SPECIMENS OF ENGLISH DRAMATIC POETS WHO LIVED ABOUT THE TIME OF SHAKESPEARE. 1893. *Johnson Reprint* 2 vols. set 1970 lib. bdg. $49.00

Lawrence, Robert G., Ed. EARLY SEVENTEENTH CENTURY DRAMA. *Dutton* Everymans $3.50

McIlwraith, Archibald K. FIVE ELIZABETHAN COMEDIES. *Oxford* World's Classics 1934 $3.75

FIVE ELIZABETHAN TRAGEDIES. *Oxford* World's Class. 1938 $2.75

FIVE STUART TRAGEDIES. With introd. *Oxford* World's Class. 1953 $2.95. Chapman's Bussy D'Ambois; Beaumont and Fletcher's The Maid's Tragedy; Webster's The Duchess of Malfi; Massinger's The Roman Actor; Ford's 'Tis Pity She's a Whore.

Ornstein, Robert, and Hazelton Spencer, Eds. ELIZABETHAN AND JACOBEAN COMEDY: An Anthology. *Heath* 1964 pap. $4.95

ELIZABETHAN AND JACOBEAN TRAGEDY: An Anthology. *Heath* 1964 pap. $4.95

Salgado, Gamini, Ed. THREE JACOBEAN TRAGEDIES. *Penguin* pap. $1.45

Spencer, Hazleton. ELIZABETHAN PLAYS. *Heath* 1945 $13.95

Spencer, T. J. B. A BOOK OF MASQUES. *Cambridge* 1967 $18.50

Thayer, William R., Ed. BEST ELIZABETHAN PLAYS. 1890. Play Anthology Reprint Ser. *Bks. for Libraries* $22.00

Wheeler, Charles Bickersteth. SIX PLAYS BY CONTEMPORARIES OF SHAKESPEARE. 1915. *Oxford* 1955 pap. 1971 $8.50. Beaumont and Fletcher, Dekker, Webster, Massinger.

Wine, Martin, Ed. DRAMA OF THE ENGLISH RENAISSANCE. *Random* (Modern Library) 1968 pap. $2.95

Wright, Louis B., and Virginia A. LaMar, Eds. FOUR FAMOUS TUDOR AND STUART PLAYS. *Simon & Schuster* (Washington Square Press) $ .75

SERIES OF EDITIONS

CHANDLER EDITIONS IN DRAMA. *T. Y. Crowell* (Chandler Pub.) pap. $ .60–$2.25

FOUNTAINWELL DRAMA TEXTS. *Univ. of California Press* each $6.00 pap. $1.60–$1.80. The texts of the plays are "normalised, but not modernised." Each play in the series has an introduction, textual notes, commentary, and glossary. General Editors T. A. Dunn, Andrew Gurr, John Horden, A. Norman Jeffares.

MERMAID DRAMABOOKS. *Farrar, Straus* (Hill & Wang) Dramabks. $3.95–$4.95 pap. $1.50–$2.95. Originally published from the 1880's to the early 1900's, the famous Mermaid Series of English Dramatists has been reissued here since 1956. Although not annotated, the introductions are of the best.

REGENTS RENAISSANCE DRAMA SERIES. *Univ. of Nebraska Press* 38 vols. various prices. New editions of plays of the Elizabethan, Jacobean and Caroline theatres. General Editor Cyrus Hoy, Advisory Editor G. E. Bentley.

THEATRE CLASSICS FOR THE MODERN READER. *Barron's* Library of Literary Masterpieces 1958 $4.25 pap. $1.25–$1.50. Designed to be read as living theater, each volume includes interpretations of the play and author, with staging and acting directions: All For Love, The Beaux Stratagem, The Beggar's Opera, The Way of the World, among others.

ELIZABETHAN DRAMATISTS EXCLUDING SHAKESPEARE

LYLY, JOHN. 1554–1606.

Lyly wrote eight comedies, the first prose comedies in our literature. His plays were all written to be acted at Court, where he was Assistant to the Master of the Revels. They are addressed to the most cultivated hearers, and are very witty and scrupulously refined. "Lyly raised the drama of the Court to an art and the writing of plays to the dignity of a profession"—(Schelling).

COMPLETE WORKS. 1902. Ed. by R. W. Bond. *Oxford* 3 vols. $48.00

GALLATHEA AND MIDAS. Ed. by Anne B. Lancashire. Regents Ser. *Univ. of Nebraska Press* 1969 $4.75 Bison Bks. pap. $1.85

Books about Lyly

John Lyly. By John D. Wilson. 1905. *Haskell* 1969 lib. bdg. $10.95
The Court Comedies of John Lyly, A Study in Allegorical Dramaturgy. By Peter Saccio. *Princeton Univ. Press* 1969 $8.50
Lyly. By G. K. Hunter. *British Bk. Centre* $2.95 pap. $1.20

GREENE, ROBERT. 1558–1592.

Greene was one of the first authors to write for the "entertainment of a broad reading public, and most of his output belongs to the early history of the best-sellers. . . . The best of his plays, "Friar Bacon and Friar Bungay" and "James IV" [1598], are romantic medleys. [His] method of construction with a latent or symbolic parallel between two separate plots (which may also contrast with each other) became the common method of the Elizabethans"—(Boris Ford). The standard edition of his works is that edited by J. Churton Collins.

THE LIFE AND COMPLETE WORKS IN PROSE AND VERSE. Ed. by A. B. Grosart. 1881–86. *Russell & Russell* 15 vols. limited ed. 1964 set $175.00

PLAYS AND POEMS OF ROBERT GREENE. Ed. by J. Churton Collins. 1905. *AMS Press* 2 vols. each $10.00; *Bks. for Libraries* set $24.50

FRIAR BACON AND FRIAR BUNGAY. c. 1594. 1914. *AMS Press* $17.50; ed. by Daniel Seltzer Regents Ser. *Univ. of Nebraska Press* 1963 $4.75 Bison Bks. pap. $1.85; ed. by G. B. Harrison 1927 *Richard West* $17.50

THE SCOTTISH HISTORY OF JAMES THE FOURTH. 1598. Ed. by Norman Sanders *Harper* 1970 $8.50 1973 pap. $4.00

THE TRAGICAL REIGN OF SELIMUS. Ed. by Alexander Grosart. 1898. *Richard West* $35.00

Books about Greene

Robert Greene. By John C. Jordan. *Octagon* 1965 $10.00
Robert Greene Criticism: A Comprehensive Bibliography. By Tetsumaro Hayashi. *Scarecrow Press* 1971 $5.00

KYD, THOMAS. 1558–1594.

Kyd is the tragedian of blood. His "Spanish Tragedy" is a lurid, blood-curdling tale of horror that surpassed in popularity every other play of its day. Rupert Brooke (*q.v.*) says, "Kyd filled Seneca's veins with English blood. He gave his audience living people, strong emotions, vendetta, murder, pain, real lines of verse, and, stiffly enough, the stateliness of art."

WORKS. Ed. by F. S. Boas. *Oxford* 1901 1955 $12.00

THE SPANISH COMEDY, or The First Part of Hieronimo (1605), and THE SPANISH TRAGEDY, or Hieronimo Is Mad Again (1589). Regents Ser. *Univ. of Nebraska Press* 1967 $4.75 Bison Bks. pap. $1.65. The first work was published anonymously, but is attributed to Kyd. Ed. by Andrew S. Cairncross.

THE SPANISH TRAGEDY. Ed. by Charles T. Prouty *AHM Pub. Corp.* Crofts Class. 1951 pap. $.85; ed. by Thomas W. Ross *Univ. of California Press* 1968 $6.00 pap. $1.65; ed. by J. R. Mulryne *Farrar, Straus* (Hill & Wang) Dramabks. 1970 $4.50; ed. by Philip Edwards *Harper* 1969 $5.25 pap. $3.25

Books about Kyd

Induction to Tragedy: A Study in a Development of Form in *Gorboduc, The Spanish Tragedy* and *Titus Andronicus*. By Howard Baker. 1939 *Russell & Russell* 1965 $7.50

Thomas Kyd and Early Elizabethan Tragedy. By Philip Edwards. *British Bk. Centre* 1966 $2.95
pap. $1.20

Thomas Kyd: Facts and Problems. By Arthur Freeman. *Oxford* 1967 $8.50

Thomas Kyd. By Peter B. Murray. English Authors Series *Twayne* $6.50

PEELE, GEORGE. 1558–1596?

That he was born in London, educated at Oxford and "that his latter days were spent in poverty and sickness" are the chief facts known about this dramatist and poet. His poems suggest that he moved in court circles. Virtually none of his life history is available other than his lingering reputation for wit, gaiety, quotable quips and pranks. His contribution to the drama was minor, perhaps, although his influence on Milton (*q.v.*), because of his masques and pageants, has not been fully gauged. His lyric gift, however, was genuine and won for his plays a permanent honorable mention. His play, "The Old Wives' Tale" (c. 1593), a prose and poetry medley of old folktales, is a title repeatedly borrowed.

DRAMATIC AND LITERARY WORKS. 1888. Ed. by A. H. Bullen. *Kennikat* 2 vols. set $27.50

DRAMATIC WORKS: The Araygnement of Paris (ed. by Mark R. Benbow); David & Bethsabe (ed. by Elmer M. Blistein); The Old Wives Tale (ed. by Frank S. Hook). *Yale Univ. Press* 1970 $20.00

Books about Peele

George Peele. By L. R. Ashley. English Authors Ser. *Twayne* $7.50

CHAPMAN, GEORGE. 1559–1634.

Chapman's plays are seldom if ever performed, but are known for their solid, intellectual quality. He was a poet of merit. His "Poems," edited by P. B. Bartlett is again available (1941. *Russell & Russell* 1962 $18.00). His translation of Homer, the first in English, is the work for which he is still famous today. (*See Chapter 7, Classical Greek Literature–Homer, this volume.*)

THE TRAGEDIES. Ed. by T. M. Parrott. 1910. *Russell & Russell* 2 vols. 1961 set $22.50

THE COMEDIES. Ed. by T. M. Parrott. 1914. *Russell & Russell* 2 vols. 1961 set $27.50

THE PLAYS OF GEORGE CHAPMAN: The Comedies. Ed. by Allan Holaday and Michael Kiernan *Univ. of Illinois Press* 1970 $20.00

THE WIDOW'S TEARS. 1605. Ed. by Ethel M. Smeak *Univ. of Nebraska Press* 1966 $4.75 Bison Bks. pap. $1.65; ed. by Akihoro Yamada *Harper* 1973 $15.00

ALL FOOLS. 1605. Ed. by Frank Manley Regents Ser. *Univ. of Nebraska Press* 1968 $4.75 Bison Bks. pap. $1.00

THE GENTLEMAN USHER. 1606. Ed. by John H. Smith Regents Ser. *Univ. of Nebraska Press* 1970 $4.75 Bison Bks. pap. $1.00

BUSSY D'AMBOIS. 1607. Ed. by Maurice Evans *Harper* 1964 $8.50; *Farrar, Straus* (Hill & Wang) Dramabks. 1966 pap. $1.95; ed. by Robert J. Lordi Regents Ser. *Univ. of Nebraska Press* $4.75 Bison Bks. pap. $1.00

Books about Chapman

The Tragedies of George Chapman: Renaissance Ethics in Action. By Ennis S. Rees. *Harvard Univ. Press* 1955 $4.50. Significant contribution to Elizabethan poetry and dramatic criticism.

George Chapman: A Critical Study. By Millar MacLure. *Univ. of Toronto Press* 1966 $10.00

George Chapman. By Charlotte Spivak. English Authors Series *Twayne* 1967 $6.50

George Chapman: The Effect of Stoicism upon His Tragedies. By John W. Wieler. *Octagon* 1968 lib. bdg. $10.00

MARLOWE, CHRISTOPHER. 1564–1593.

Marlowe is the greatest of all Shakespeare's predecessors and a superb poet. His use of blank verse as a medium for drama made Shakespeare's dramas possible. Marlowe's art was a great advance over that of all earlier dramatists. He abandoned rhyme, used by his brother playwrights, and adopted blank verse. He found blank verse very monotonous and set in its form; he left it plastic and varied, adapting the form to the sense in a way that had never been done before. Marlowe's plays are all tragedies and his language is the language of literature rather than of life. "The three most distinguished plays of Marlowe might well be termed a trilogy of Lust's dominion. 'Tamburlaine' illustrates the lust of boundless conquest; 'Faustus,' the lust of boundless knowledge; 'The Jew of Malta,' the lust of boundless wealth"—(Seccombe). "The Jew of Malta" led to

Shakespeare's "Shylock." "Edward II," the first great historical drama in English literature, led to "Richard II." The best known of all Marlowe's plays is "Dr. Faustus," and his rendering of the old world fable was performed by itinerant companies of English players in Germany, where it had great influence in establishing the popularity of the Faust legend in Germany and its later use by Goethe (*q.v.*). Leslie Hotson's best book was "Death of Christopher Marlowe," (1925. *Russell & Russell* 1967 $7.50).

THE WORKS AND LIFE OF CHRISTOPHER MARLOW. Ed. by R. H. Case. 1930–1933. *Gordian* 6 vols. 1966 each $10.00 set $60.00

COMPLETE WORKS. Ed. by Fredson Bowers *Cambridge* 2 vols. 1973 Vol. 1 $32.50 Vol. 2 $35.00 set $60.00

Works. Ed. by C. F. Tucker Brooke *Oxford* 1910 $6.00; 1931 *Gordian* 1966 Vol. 4 $10.00

THE COMPLETE PLAYS. Ed. by I. Ribner *Odyssey* 1963 $5.50 pap. $3.50; *Penguin* 1969 pap. $2.45

FIVE PLAYS. Ed. by Havelock Ellis; introd. by John Addington Symonds *Farrar, Straus* (Hill & Wang) Mermaid Dramabks. 1956 pap. $2.25; *Peter Smith* $4.50

PLAYS AND POEMS. Introd. by Edward Thomas *Dutton* Everyman's Am. ed. 1950 $3.95

PLAYS OF CHRISTOPHER MARLOWE. Ed. by Roma Gill *Oxford* 1971 $4.00

TAMBURLAINE THE GREAT. 1590. Ed. by Irving Ribner *Bobbs* (Odyssey) 1974 $7.95; ed. by J. W. Harper *Farrar, Straus* (Hill & Wang) Dramabks. 1973 $6.95 pap. $2.25

DIDO QUEEN OF CARTHAGE AND THE MASSACRE AT PARIS. 1594. Ed. by H. J. Oliver *Harper* 1968 $3.00

EDWARD THE SECOND. 1594. Ed. by Jacques Chwat *Avon* 1974 pap. $.75; ed. by Irving Ribner *Bobbs* Odyssey 1970 pap. $1.75; ed. by Moelwyn *Farrar, Straus* (Hill & Wang) Dramabks. 1968 $3.75

DOCTOR FAUSTUS. 1604. Ed. by Paul H. Kocher *AHM Pub. Corp.* Crofts Class. 1950 pap. $.85; ed. by John Taylor *Aurora Pub.* 1970 pap. $2.50; ed. by Russell H. Robbins *Barron's* 1948 pap. $.85; ed. by Sleight *Cambridge* $2.45; ed. by Roma Gill *Farrar, Straus* (Hill & Wang) New Mermaid 1966 pap. $1.95; ed. by John D. Jump 1962 *Harper* 1968 $8.50 pap. $2.50; ed. by Sylvan Barnet *New Am. Lib.* 1969 $.95; ed. by W. W. Greg *Oxford* 1950 $14.50; ed. by Louis B. Wright and Virginia A. LaMar *Simon & Schuster* (Washington Square) pap. $.60

THE JEW OF MALTA. 1633. Ed. by Irving Ribner *Bobbs* (Odyssey) $1.85; ed. by T. W. Craik *Farrar, Strauss* (Hill & Wang) Dramabks. 1967 $3.75 pap. $1.95; ed. by Richard W. Van Fassen Regents Ser. *Univ. of Nebraska Press* 1963 $4.75 Bison Bks. $1.85

Books about Marlowe

Christopher Marlowe. By U. M. Ellis-Fermor. 1927. *Shoe String Press* 1967 $5.00

The Assassination of Christopher Marlowe: A New View. By Samuel Tannenbaum. 1928. 1962 *Somerset Pubs.* $6.00

Christopher Marlowe: A Biographical and Critical Study. By Frederick S. Boas. *Oxford* 1940 $8.50

Marlowe's "Tamburlaine": A Study in Renaissance Moral Philosophy. By Roy Battenhouse. *Vanderbilt Univ. Press* 1942 1964 $6.50

"When first published in 1942 this study was scoffed at by many scholars . . . . Now understanding of Marlowe's life and thinking confirms Professor Battenhouse's contention that this drama represented the thinking of Protestant writers in the England of his time"—(*LJ*).

The Tragical History of Christopher Marlow. By John Bakeless. 1942. *Greenwood* 2 vols. set $34.50

Christopher Marlowe: A Study of His Thought, Learning and Character. By Paul H. Kocher. 1946. *Russell & Russell* 1961 $11.00

The Muses' Darling. By Charles Norman. 1946. *Bobbs* (Odyssey) 1960 $7.50

The Overreacher: A Study of Christopher Marlowe. By Harry Levin. 1952. *Beacon* 1964 pap. $1.75; *Peter Smith* $4.50

Marlowe and the Early Shakespeare. By Frank Percy Wilson. *Oxford* 1953 $9.00. Wit, grace and learning make these lectures enjoyable both to layman and scholar.

Marlowe: Dr. Faustus. By J. P. Brockbank. Ed. by David Daiches. *Barron's* 1962 $1.95 pap.
   $1.00. Critical study.
Suffering and Evil in the Plays of Christopher Marlowe. By D. Cole. *Gordian* $9.00
Marlowe: A Critical Study. By J. B. Steane. *Cambridge* 1964 $14.50 pap. $4.45
Marlowe: A Collection of Critical Essays. Ed. by Clifford Leech. *Prentice-Hall* 1964 $5.95
Tulane Drama Review. Summer, 1964. *Tulane University,* New Orleans, La. 70118. $2.00. This
   issue was devoted to Marlowe.
Marlowe: A Collection of Critical Essays. Ed. with introd. by Clifford Leech. 20th Century Views
   Prentice-Hall 1965 $5.95
   These "14 excellent articles, . . . beginning with T. S. Eliot's groundbreaking essay in 1918,
   focus on Marlowe's intellectual quality, complexity in writing . . . and relation to the stage"—
   (LJ).
In Search of Christopher Marlowe: A Pictorial Biography. By A. D. Wraight and Virginia F.
   Stern. *Vanguard* 1965 $12.50
   "At once a definitive work and a book many readers will enjoy browsing through"—*(LJ)*.
The Dramatist and the Received Idea. By Wilbur Sanders. *Cambridge* 1968 $14.50
Twentieth Century Interpretations of *Doctor Faustus.* Ed. by W. Farnham. *Prentice-Hall* 1969
   $4.95
Critics on Marlowe. Ed. by Judith O'Neill. *Univ. of Miami Press* 1970 $3.95
The Left Hand of God: A Critical Interpretation of the Plays of Christopher Marlowe. By John
   P. Cutts. *Haddonfield House* (Div. of Griffin Press Inc. 300 King's Hwy. E., Haddenfield, N.J.
   08033) 1974 $10.00

DEKKER, THOMAS.   1570–1641.

Dekker wrote very few plays of his own; he was usually a collaborator and something of a literary hack. The domestic drama of contemporary London life was his chosen field and all his plays
except "Old Fortunatus" are about the London of his day. Two musical versions of "The Shoemaker's Holiday," a rollicking comedy containing his best lyrics, were presented in 1967 in New
York and Minneapolis. "The Gull's Hornbooke" (1609), a prose work, is said to have suggested to
Sir Walter Scott *(q.v.)* "The Fortunes of Nigel." Dekker's masterpiece and his only unaided work,
"Old Fortunatus," is a pastoral comedy, taken from folklore, with passages that are very lyrical and
humorous and full of pleasant allegory. The character of Fortunatus is reminiscent of Faustus.
"The Merry Devil of Edmonton" (1608, ed. by W. A. Abrams 1942, o.p.), of anonymous author-
ship and one of the most popular plays of its time, is now attributed to Dekker. "The Wonderful
Year" (1603), in G. R. Hibbard's "Three Elizabethan Pamphlets" (1951 *Richard West* $9.00; *Bks. for
Libs.* $11.00) is a vivid description of the plague.

THE DRAMATIC WORKS. Ed. by Fredson Bowers *Cambridge* 4 vols. 1953–1961 Vols. 1 & 4
   $19.50 Vol. 2 $21.00 Vol. 3 $22.50. In the old spelling and with criticism.

   Vol. 1 Sir Thomas More (Dekker ed.); The Shoemaker's Holiday; Old Fortunatus; Patient Gris-
sil; Satironastix; Sir Thomas Wyatt; Vol. 2 The Honest Whore pts. I & 2; The Magnificent Entertainment; Westward Ho; Northward Ho; The Whore of Babylon; Vol. 3 The Roaring Girl; If This
Be Not a Good Play, the Devil Is in It; Troia-Nova Triumphans; Match Me in London; The Witch
of Edmonton; The Virgin Martyr; The Wonder of a Kingdom; Vol. 4 The Welsh Ambassador;
The Noble Spanish Soldier; Lust's Dominion; The Sun's Darling; London's Tempe; Britannia's
Honour.

THE NON-DRAMATIC WORKS. Ed. by A. B. Grosart *Russell & Russell* 5 vols. 1963 set
   $60.00

THE SHOEMAKER'S HOLIDAY. 1600. Ed. by Merritt Lawlis *Barron's* 1974 $1.65; ed. by
   J. B. Steane *Cambridge* 1965 $3.75; ed. by Paul C. Davies *Univ. of California Press* 1968
   $6.00 pap. $1.65

(With John Webster). SIR THOMAS WYATT. 1602. 1914 *AMS Press* $17.50

(With John Webster). WESTWARD HO. 1604. 1914 *AMS Press* $17.50

(With John Webster). NORTHWARD HO. 1605. 1914 *AMS Press* $17.50

THE NOBLE SOLDIER. 1913 *AMS Press* $17.50

Books about Dekker

Thomas Dekker. By Mary L. Hunt. 1911. *Folcroft* $25.00
Thomas Dekker: An Analysis of Dramatic Structure. By James H. Conover. *Humanities Press*
   text ed. 1969 $15.50
Thomas Dekker. By George R. Price. English Authors Series *Twayne* 1969 $6.50

JONSON, BEN.   1573–1637.

Jonson is the greatest of Shakespeare's contemporaries. He was the Poet Laureate of England and an avowed censor and reformer of the stage. He railed against public taste and sought seriously to educate his audience to better art, observing the dramatic unities of classic drama in his plays: his action takes place in a short space of time and with little change of place. "Every Man in His Humour" is his most popular work, and its title might well be the title of all his plays, since he liked to dramatize peculiarities, eccentricities or exaggerated human traits. His characters were usually personifications of human vices and follies, though he was a moralist at a loss to his art. His satirical masterpieces are "Volpone, or The Fox," and "The Alchemist." "The Alchemist," which satirized the prevailing passion for the occult, has been revived with great success on the modern English and American stage. "The Poems of Ben Jonson" is edited by George Burke Johnston (*Harvard Univ. Press* Muses Lib. 1955 pap. $2.95). It contains three collections of poems from the Folios, the great mass of ungathered poems and a selection of lyrics from his masques and plays with a biographical and critical introduction and notes. Other collections are "The Complete Poetry of Ben Jonson" edited by William B. Hunter (*Doubleday* Anchor Bks. 1963 pap. $1.95; *New York Univ. Press* 1963 $2.50) and "Ben Jonson's Literary Criticism" edited by James D. Redwine, Jr. (*Univ. of Nebraska Press* 1970 $5.95).

WORKS. Complete Critical Edition. Ed. by C. H. Herford, Percy Simpson and Evelyn Simpson. *Oxford* 11 vols. 1925–1952 each $12.00

Contents: Vol. 1–2: The Man and His Work (1925); Vol. 3: Tale of a Tub, The Case is Altered, Every Man in His Humour, Every Man Out of His Humour (1927); Vol. 4; Cynthia's Revels, Poetaster, Sejanus, Eastward Ho (1932); Vol. 5: Volpone, Epicene, The Alchemist, Cataline (1937); Vol. 6: Bartholomew Fair, The Devil is an Ass, The Staple of News, The New Inn, The Magnetic Lady (1938); Vol. 7: The Sad Shepherd, The Fall of Mortimer, Masques and Entertainments; Vol. 8: The Poems, the Prose Works (1947); Vol. 9: An Historical Survey of the Text, The Stage History of the Plays, Commentary on the Plays (1951); Vol. 10: Play Commentary, Masque Commentary (1951); Vol. 11: Commentary on the Poems and the Prose Works, Jonson's Literary Record, Supplementary Notes on Jonson's Life, and an Index (1952).

COMPLETE PLAYS. *Dutton* Everyman's 1954 2 vols. each $3.95

DRAMAS. Ed. by W. Bang. *Kraus* Pt. 1 1905 Pt.2 1908 $35.00

THE COMPLETE MASQUES. Ed. by Stephen Orgel. *Yale Univ. Press* 1969 $22.50

SELECTED MASQUES. Ed. by Stephen Orgel. *Yale Univ. Press* 1970 $17.50 pap. $4.95

THREE PLAYS. Ed. by Brinslay Nicholson and C. H. Herford. *Farrar, Straus* (Hill & Wang) Mermaid Dramabks. 2 vols. 1949 Vol. 1 pap. $2.25 Vol. 2 $2.45 1957 pap. $1.95. Vol. I: Volpone, Epicene, The Alchemist; Vol. 2: Every Man in His Humour, Sejanus, Bartholomew Fair.

FIVE PLAYS. *Oxford* World's Class. 1953 $3.95

THREE COMEDIES. Ed. by M. Jamieson. *Penguin* pap. $1.95. Volpone, The Alchemist, Bartholomew Fair.

EVERY MAN IN HIS HUMOUR. 1599. Ed. by Seymour-Smith *Farrar, Straus* (Hill & Wang) New Mermaid Dramabks. 1968 $3.75; ed. by J. W. Lever Regents Ser. *Univ. of Nebraska Press* 1971 $10.00; *Somerset Pub.* $7.50; ed. by Gabriele B. Jackson *Yale Univ. Press* 1969 pap. $2.75

SEJANUS HIS FALL. 1603. Ed. by W. F. Bolton *Farrar, Straus* (Hill & Wang) New Mermaid Dramabks. 1965 $3.75; ed. by Jonas A. Barish *Yale Univ. Press* 1965 $10.00 pap. $2.75

VOLPONE. 1605. Ed. by Jonas A. Barish *AHM Pub. Corp.* 1958 pap. $.85; ed. by Vincent F. Hopper and Gerald B. Lahey *Barron's* 1959 $4.25 pap. $1.95; ed. by Jay L. Halio *Univ. of California Press* 1968 $6.00 pap. $1.80; ed. by Philip Brockbank *Farrar, Straus* (Hill & Wang) New Mermaid Dramabks. 1969 $4.50; ed. by David Cook *Harper* (Barnes & Noble) Revels Plays Ser. 1967 $1.75; ed. by Louis B. Wright and Virginia A. LaMar *Simon & Schuster* 1970 $4.50; ed. by Alvin B. Kernan *Yale Univ. Press* 1962 $10.00 pap. $3.45

EPICŒNE, or The Silent Woman. 1609. Ed. by L. Beurline *Univ. of Nebraska Press* 1965 $4.75 Bison Bks. pap. $1.85; ed. by Edward Partridge *Yale Univ. Press* 1972 $10.00

THE ALCHEMIST. 1610. Ed. by G. E. Bentley *AHM Pub. Corp.* Crofts Class. 1947 pap. $.85; ed. by John I. McCollum, Jr. *Barron's* 1965 $5.75; ed. by Sidney Musgrove *Univ. of California Press* 1968 $6.00; ed. by Kingsford *Cambridge* $2.95; ed. by Douglas Brown *Farrar, Straus* (Hill & Wang) New Mermaid Dramabks. 1966 pap. $1.95; ed. by F. H. Mares *Harper* (Barnes & Noble) Revels Plays Ser. 1974 pap. $4.25; ed. by Alvin B. Kernan *Yale Univ. Press* 1974 pap. $2.95

CATILINE. 1611. Ed. by W. F. Bolton and Jane Gardner Regents Ser. *Univ. of Nebraska* 1973 $8.95

BARTHOLOMEW FAIR. 1614. Ed. by E. A. Horsman *Harper* (Barnes & Noble) Revels Plays Ser. 1968 $3.00 pap. $2.00; ed. by Eugene M. Waith *Yale Univ. Press* 1963 pap. $2.95

A SCORE FOR LOVERS MADE MEN: A Masque. 1617. Ed. by Andrew J. Sabol *Brown Univ. Press* 1963 pap. $4.00

THE GYPSIES METAMORPHOSED. 1621. Ed. by G. W. Cole *Kraus* 1931 pap. $14.00

JONSON'S MASQUE OF GYPSIES. 1640. In the Burley, Belvoir, and Windsor Versions. Ed. by W. W. Greg *Oxford* 1952 $5.00

An illuminating social document of the tastes and manners of James I's court. First presented in 1621, it was performed in three versions and is preserved in five independent texts. Dr. Greg has attempted for the first time a detailed reconstruction of the several versions.

Books about Jonson

Ben Jonson: The Man and His Work. By C. H. Herford and Percy Simpson. *Oxford* 2 vols. 1928 each $12.00. Vols. 1 & 2 of "Works" (*see above*).

Ben Jonson on the English Stage 1660–1776. By Robert Gale Noyes. 1935. *Blom* 1966 $12.50

Drama and Society in the Age of Jonson. By L. C. Knights. 1937. 1957 Norton 1968 pap. $2.25. An important study.

Ben Jonson of Westminster. By Marchette G. Chute. *Dutton* 1953 $6.95. She "combines with painstaking scholarship a gift for bringing facts to life."

Jonson and the Comic Truth. By John J. Enck. *Univ. of Wisconsin Press* 1957 pap. $3.95; *Brown Bk. Co.* pap. $1.95

The Broken Compass: A Study of the Major Comedies of Ben Jonson. By Edward B. Partridge. 1958 *Fernhill* $4.50

Ben Jonson's Poems: A Study of the Plain Style. By Wesley Trimpi. *Stanford Univ. Press* 1962 $8.50

Ben Jonson. Ed. by Jonas A. Barish. *Prentice-Hall* Spectrum Bks. 1963 $6.50. A collection of critical essays.

Ben Jonson: Studies in the Plays. By Calvin G. Thayer. 1963. *Univ. of Oklahoma Press* 1966 $5.95

The Jonsonian Masque. By Stephen Orgel. *Harvard Univ. Press* 1965 $6.50

Vision and Judgment in Ben Jonson's Drama. By Gabriele B. Jackson. *Yale Univ. Press* 1968 $9.50

Ben Jonson and the Language of Prose Comedy. By Jonas A. Barish. *Norton* 1970 pap. $2.45

The Compassionate Satirist: Ben Jonson and His Imperfect World. By J. A. Bryant, Jr. *Univ. of Georgia Press* 1973 $8.50

HEYWOOD, THOMAS. 1574?–1641.

Most of Heywood's work has been lost. A "writer of great industry and no small talent," he wrote or collaborated in 220 plays, of which only about 25 have come down to us. He is, like Dekker (*q.v.*), a dramatist of English domestic life, writing realistically and at the same time poetically. He is the supposed author of "Oenone and Paris by T. H. 1594," which was reprinted from the unique copy in the Folger Shakespeare Library (1943, o.p.). His best play, "A Woman Killed with Kindness," is a tale of an unfaithful wife who is tenderly punished by her husband. It closes in a death scene which gives great opportunity to the starring actress. This quiet tragedy, with its strong situations and its deep human pathos, is still popular on the modern stage. "An Apology for Actors," (1612) is his temperate answer to Puritan criticism of the stage. He succeeded Dekker in 1631 as writer of mayoral pageants for the City of London, and composed a masque with Inigo Jones in 1634 to celebrate the king's birthday.

DRAMATIC WORKS. Ed. by R. H. Shepherd 1874. *Adler's* 6 vols. 1968 set $158.00; *Russell & Russell* 6 vols. ltd. ed. 1964 set $85.00

A WOMAN KILLED WITH KINDNESS. 1603. *British Bk. Centre* 1975 $7.50 pap. $4.95; ed. by

R. W. Van Fossen *Harper* (Barnes & Noble) Revels Plays Ser. 1961 $8.50 1970 pap. $3.50

THE FAIR MAID OF THE WEST. c. 1610. Pts. 1 & 2. Ed. by Robert K. Turner Regents Ser. *Univ. of Nebraska Press* rev. ed. 1967 $4.75 Bison Bks. pap. $1.00

AN APOLOGY FOR ACTORS. 1612. *Garland Pub.* The English Stage Ser. Vol. 12 $22.00; (and "A Refutation of the Apology for Actors.") *Johnson Reprint* 1972 $16.50

Books about Heywood

Thomas Heywood, Playwright and Miscellanist. By Arthur M. Clark. 1931. *Russell & Russell* $9.00

TOURNEUR, CYRIL. 1575?–1626.

Details of Tourneur's life are known only through references in his writings. His reputation rests solely on "The Atheist's Tragedy" and "The Revenger's Tragedy"—which latter, attributed to Tourneur in the 17th century, is now thought by many critics to be by Thomas Middleton (*q.v.*). For a discussion of the entire issue see the study by Murray (*below*) and the introduction to "The Revenger's Tragedy" by R. A. Foakes in the Revels Plays series. The play has fascinated many 20th-century readers, largely because of its remarkable poetry.

WORKS. Ed. by Allardyce Nicoll 1929. *Russell & Russell* 1963 $15.00

THE ATHEIST'S TRAGEDY AND THE REVENGER'S TRAGEDY. In "Webster and Tourneur." Introd. by J. A. Symonds *Farrar, Straus* (Hill & Wang) New Mermaid Dramabks. 1956 pap. $2.65

THE REVENGER'S TRAGEDY. Ed. by B. Gibbons *Farrar, Straus* (Hill & Wang) New Mermaid Dramabks. 1967 pap. $1.95; ed. by R. A. Foakes *Harper* (Barnes & Noble) Revels Plays Ser. 1975 pap. $4.95; ed. by L. J. Ross Regents Ser. *Univ. of Nebraska Press* 1966 $4.75 Bison Bks. pap. $1.85

Books about Tourneur

A Study of Cyril Tourneur. By Peter B. Murray. *Univ. of Pennsylvania Press* 1964 $9.00

MARSTON, JOHN. 1576–1634.

Marston began as a satirist, but turned to drama in 1599. His prose, at its best, "attains a striking swiftness and pungency. [His plays are] certainly the work of a man superior to the savage caricature of him in [Jonson's] "Poetaster" [*q.v.*] by which he is unfortunately best known. . . . After a short and brilliant career broken by quarrels, disappointments, and imprisonment, he turned away from the world and retired into religion"—(Parrott and Ball, "A Short View of Elizabethan Drama"). He married a clergyman's daughter, and he became rector of a country parish in 1607. A good study is "John Marston, Satirist" by Anthony Caputi (1961, o.p.).

WORKS. Ed. by A. H. Bullen 1887. *Adler's* 3 vols. 1970 set $85.20

THE PLAYS OF JOHN MARSTON. Ed. by H. Harvey Wood 1934–1938. *Somerset Pubs.* 3 vols. set $49.50

THE SCOURGE OF VILLANIE. 1598. *Haskell* 1974 $10.95

ANTONIO AND MELLIDA. 1599. Ed. by G. K. Hunter Regents Ser. *Univ. of Nebraska Press* $4.75 Bison Bks. pap. $1.00

ANTONIO'S REVENGE. 1599. Ed. by G. K. Hunter Regents Ser. *Univ. of Nebraska Press* 1965 $4.75 Bison Bks. pap. $1.85

HISTRIOMASTIX. 1599. 1912. *AMS Press* $17.50

JACK DRUM'S ENTERTAINMENT. c. 1601. 1912. *AMS Press* $17.50

THE DUTCH COURTESAN. 1604. Ed. by Peter Davison *Univ. of California Press* 1968 $6.00; ed. by M. L. Wine Regents Ser. *Univ. of Nebraska Press* 1965 $4.75 Bison Bks. pap. $1.85

THE MALCONTENT. 1604. *British Bk. Centre* 1975 $7.50 pap. $4.95; ed. by Bernard Harris *Farrar, Straus* (Hill & Wang) New Mermaid Dramabks. 1969 $3.75; ed. by George Hunter *Harper* (Barnes & Noble) Revels Plays Ser. 1975 $17.50 pap. $10.00; ed. by M. L. Wine Regents Ser. *Univ. of Nebraska Press* 1965 $4.75 Bison Bks. pap. $1.85

THE FAWN. c. 1605. Ed. by Gerald A. Smith Regents Ser. *Univ. of Nebraska Press* 1965 $4.75 Bison Bks. pap. $1.00

Books about Marston

John Marston of the Middle Temple: An Elizabethan Dramatist in His Social Setting. By Philip J. Findelpearl. *Harvard Univ. Press* 1969 $6.00

FLETCHER, JOHN. 1579–1625. *See* BEAUMONT, FRANCIS, 1584–1616, *this Chapter.*

MIDDLETON, THOMAS. 1580–1627.

Middleton wrote the comedy of manners, dealing always with contemporary London life. "A Game at Chess," his most famous play, is a daring political satire which needs a key to be understood; its characters are all counterparts of living men and women of that day. The best plays are the tragedies, "The Changeling" and "Women Beware Women." His plots are always improbable and often impossible. A lawyer and a gentleman born, he was not above the coarse wit that made his plays popular.

WORKS OF THOMAS MIDDLETON. Ed. by A. H. Bullen. 1885–1886. *AMS Press* 8 vols. each $13.50 set $104.00

THOMAS MIDDLETON: With an Introduction by A. C. Swinburne. 1904. *Somerset Pubs.* 2 vols. $29.50

BEST PLAYS OF THE OLD DRAMATISTS. 1887. *Scholarly Press* 2 vols. each $14.50 set $26.50

THE GHOST OF LUCRECE. 1600. Facsimile of the Folger Library copy of 1600 edition; ed. with introd. by Joseph Quincy Adams 1937 *Somerset Pubs.* $6.00

MICHAELMAS TERM. 1607. Ed. by Richard Levin Regents Ser. *Univ. of Nebraska Press* 1967 $4.75 Bison Bks. pap. $1.00

A MAD WORLD, MY MASTERS. 1608. Ed. by S. Henning Regents Ser. *Univ. of Nebraska Press* 1965 $4.75 Bison Bks. pap. $1.85

A TRICK TO CATCH THE OLD ONE. 1608. Ed. by Charles Barber *Univ. of California Press* 1968 $6.00 pap. $1.65

(With Thomas Dekker). THE ROARING GIRL. 1611. *AMS Press* $17.50

THE CHANGELING. 1622. *Barron's* 1967 $.95; ed. by N. W. Bawcutt 1958 *Harper* (Barnes & Noble) Revels Play Ser. 1970 $8.00; ed by G. W. Williams *Univ. of Nebraska Press* 1965 $4.75 pap. $1.85; ed. by Matthew W. Black *Univ. of Pennsylvania Press* 1966 $5.00 pap. $2.45

A GAME AT CHESS. 1625. Ed. by J. W. Harper *Farrar, Straus* (Hill & Wang) Dramabks. 1967 $3.75 pap. $1.25; *Somerset Pubs.* repr. of 1929 ed. $7.50

A CHASTE MAID IN CHEAPSIDE. 1630. *British Bk. Centre* $7.50 pap. $4.95; ed. by Charles Barber *Univ. of California Press* 1969 $6.00 pap. $1.65; ed. by B. R. Parker *Harper* (Barnes & Noble) Revels Plays Ser. 1973 pap. $4.00

HENGIST, KING OF KENT; or The Mayor of Queenborough. 1651. 1938 *Somerset Pubs.* $7.50

WOMEN BEWARE WOMEN. 1657. Ed. by Charles Barber *Univ. of California Press* 1969 $6.00 pap. $1.80; *Farrar, Straus* (Hill & Wang) New Mermaid Dramabks. 1969 $3.75 pap. $1.25; ed. by J. R. Mulryne *Harper* (Barnes & Noble) Revels Plays Ser. 1975 $17.50 pap. $10.00

Books about Middleton

Middleton's Tragedies. By Samuel Schoenbaum. 1955. *Gordian* 1970 $8.00
Thomas Middleton. By Richard Hindry Barker. 1958. *Greenwood* 1975 $12.75. A critical study which analyzes his comedies, tragicomedies and tragedies.
The Art of Thomas Middleton. By David M. Holmes. *Oxford* 1970 $9.75
Thomas Middleton and the Drama of Realism. By Dorothy M. Farr. *Harper* (Barnes & Noble) 1973 $8.00

WEBSTER, JOHN. 1580–1625.

Webster is often a favorite Elizabethan dramatist with modern readers. Rupert Brooke (*q.v.*) devotes the greater part of his work on the Elizabethan dramatists to Webster—"John Webster and the Elizabethan Drama." He wrote mostly in collaboration. His best unaided plays are "The Duchess of Malfi" and "The White Devil," which was revived in New York and Princeton in 1962. Both of these tragedies are founded on actual historic personages and events in Italy during the Renaissance. They are known as "revenge plays"—tales of savage cruelty, the horror being intensified by making the central figure a sinful women. Kenneth Rexroth in the *Saturday Review* called "The Duchess of Malfi" probably the greatest [melodrama] ever written, . . . very great entertainment and its own excuse for being." Webster is one of the most quotable of Elizabethans because of his sententious and epigrammatic style. He is known to have kept a notebook with the aid of which he "compiled rather than composed his plays."

COMPLETE WORKS. Ed. by F. L. Lucas. *Gordian* 4 vols. 1966 set $42.50

PLAYS BY WEBSTER AND FORD. *Dutton* Everyman's pap. $3.95 & $1.75

WEBSTER AND TOURNEUR. Gen. ed. Eric Bentley; introd. and notes by John Addington Symonds *Farrar, Straus* (Hill & Wang) New Mermaid Dramabks. 1948 1956 pap. $2.65; *Peter Smith* 1960 $3.50. The White Devil, and The Duchess of Malfi by Webster; The Atheist's Tragedy, and The Revenger's Tragedy by Tourneur.

(With Thomas Dekker). NORTHWARD HO. 1605. 1914. *AMS Press* $17.50

THE WHITE DEVIL. c. 1612. *British Bk. Centre* 1975 $8.50 pap. $5.95; ed. by Clive Hart *Univ. of California Press* 1970 $6.00 pap. $1.80; introd. by Travis Bogard *Chandler Pub.* 1961 pap. $.95; ed. by Elizabeth M. Brennan *Farrar, Straus* (Hill & Wang) New Mermaid Dramabks. 1968 pap. $2.23; ed. by F. L. Lucas *Fernhill* 1959 $5.00; ed. by J. R. Brown *Harper* (Barnes & Noble) Revels Plays Ser. 1969 pap. $4.50; ed. by J. R. Mulryne Regents Ser. *Univ. of Nebraska Press* 1970 $4.75 Bison Bks. pap. $1.75

THE DUCHESS OF MALFI. 1623. Ed. by Fred B. Millet *AHM Pub. Corp.* Crofts Classics Ser. 1953 pap. $.85; ed. by Vincent F. Hopper and Gerald B. Lahey *Barron's* 1959 $4.25 pap. $1.75; ed. by Elizabeth Brennan *Farrar, Straus* (Hill & Wang) New Mermaid Dramabks. 1966 $3.75 pap. $1.25; ed. by F. L. Lucas *Fernhill* 1959 $5.50; ed. by J. R. Brown *Harper* (Barnes & Noble) Revels Plays Ser. 1969 pap. $4.50

THE DEVIL'S LAW-CASE. 1623. Ed. by Frances A. Shirley Regents Ser. *Univ of Nebraska Press* 1972 $6.95

Books about Webster

John Webster. By Clifford Leech. 1951. *Haskell* $9.95
The Tragic Satire of John Webster. By Travis Bogard. 1955. *Russell & Russell* $8.00
Webster: The Duchess of Malfi. By Clifford Leech. *Barron's* 1963 pap. $1.00
Twentieth Century Interpretations of The Duchess of Malfi. Ed. by Norman Rabkin. *Prentice-Hall* 1968 $4.95
John Webster. Ed. by Brian Morris. *Rowman* New Mermaid Critical Commentaries Ser. 1970 $6.00
The Art of John Webster. By Ralph Berry. *Oxford* 1972 $12.75

MASSINGER, PHILIP. 1583–1640.

"A New Way to Pay Old Debts" was revived by David Garrick and has held the stage ever since. It has probably been performed more often in modern times than any other Elizabethan play except Shakespeare's. "Massinger's greatest claim to distinction probably rests upon his stagecraft and his skill in dramatic construction. Likewise, Massinger's ability to write moral and rhetorical declamation is superior to that of most of his contemporaries"—(*Cyclopedia of World Authors*). A fascinating stage history is R. H. Ball's "The Amazing Career of Sir Giles Overreach" (1939, *Octagon* 1967 $12.00).

PLAYS AND POEMS OF PHILIP MASSINGER. Ed. by Philip Edwards and Colin Gibson *Oxford* 1974 4 vols. set $96.00

PLAYS. Ed. by William Gifford. 1813. *AMS Press* 4 vols. set $75.00

THE BONDMAN: An Ancient Storie. 1624. 1932 *Scholarly Press* $14.50

THE ROMAN ACTOR. 1629. 1912 *Somerset Pubs.* $19.50

THE CITY MADAM. 1632. Ed. by Cyrus Hoy Regents Series *Univ. of Nebraska Press* $4.75 Bison Bks. pap. $1.00

(With Nathan Field). THE FATAL DOWRY. 1632. Ed. by T. A. Dunn *Univ. of California Press* 1969 $6.00 pap. $1.65

A NEW WAY TO PAY OLD DEBTS: A Comedie. 1633. *British Bk. Centre* 1975 $7.50 pap. $4.95

BELIEVE AS YOU LIST. 1849. 1907 *AMS Press* $17.50

BEAUMONT, FRANCIS, 1584–1616, and JOHN FLETCHER, 1579–1625.

The most famous Elizabethan collaborators were Beaumont and Fletcher, considered in their day the equals if not the superiors of Shakespeare and Jonson. Each wrote some plays alone and Fletcher collaborated not only with Beaumont but also with Massinger and several others. The 50-odd plays of this group of playwrights are known as the "Beaumont and Fletcher" plays, though in spite of much valuable modern scholarship the exact share of each is not known. By their extensive use of romance material they laid the groundwork for heroic drama while also contributing to the vogue of tragicomedy. Fletcher's witty comedies look forward to the Restoration comedy of manners. "The Pattern of Tragicomedy in Beaumont and Fletcher" by Eugene M. Waith (1952, *Shoe String Press* 1969 $6.00) is a helpful study.

THE DRAMATIC WORKS IN THE BEAUMONT AND FLETCHER CANON. Ed. by Fredson Bowers, A. Glover and A. R. Waller. *Cambridge* 5 vols. 1966 each $23.50–$27.50

"The first new edition of the plays ascribed to the Beaumont and Fletcher canon undertaken since the gaslight era, [this is] an unhampered, unpuzzling text that should become the standard point of reference for all who read and study these authors, a model for all who edit others"— (*N.Y. Times*).

THE WORKS OF BEAUMONT AND FLETCHER. Ed. by A. Dyce. 1843–1846. *Bks. for Libraries* 11 vols. set $195.00

WORKS. Ed. by A. R. Waller and A. Glover. 1912. *Octagon* 10 vols set $175.00

SELECTED PLAYS. Introd. by G. P. Baker *Dutton* Everyman's $3.95. By Beaumont and Fletcher: The Knight of the Burning Pestle (1613); The Maid's Tragedy (1619); A King and No King (1619). Ascribed to Fletcher alone: The Faithful Shepherdess (1609); The Wild-Goose Chase (1652); Bonduca (1647).

THE KNIGHT OF THE BURNING PESTLE. 1613. Ed. by Benjamin W. Griffith, Jr. *Barron* 1963 pap. $1.25; *British Bk. Centre* 1975 $9.50 pap. $5.95; ed. by Andrew Gurr *Univ. of California Press* 1968 $6.00 pap. $1.65; ed. by John Doebler Regents Ser. *Univ. of Nebraska Press* rev. ed. 1967 $4.75 Bison Bks. pap. $1.85

A KING AND NO KING. 1619. Ed. by Robert K. Turner. Regents Series *Univ. of Nebraska Press* 1963 $4.75 Bison Bks. pap. $1.85

THE MAID'S TRAGEDY. 1619. Ed. by Andrew Gurr *Univ. of California Press* 1969 $6.00 pap. $1.65; ed. by Howard B. Norland Regents Ser. *Univ. of Nebraska Press* 1969 $4.75 Bison Bks. pap. $1.85

PHILASTER, or Love Lies a-Bleeding, 1620. *British Bk. Centre* 1975 $8.50 pap. $5.95; ed. by Andrew Gurr *Harper* (Barnes & Noble) Revels Plays Ser. 1973 pap. $4.00; ed. by Dora J. Ashe Regents Ser. *Univ. of Nebraska Press* 1974 $8.95 Bison Bks. pap. $1.85

Books about Beaumont and Fletcher

The Influence of Beaumont and Fletcher on the Restoration Stage. By J. H. Wilson. 1928. *Blom* $8.50

Poets on Fortune's Hill: Studies in Sidney, Shakespeare, Beaumont and Fletcher. By John F. Danby. 1952. *Kennikat* $7.25

Beaumont and Fletcher on the Restoration Stage. By Arthur C. Sprague. *Blom* $12.50

Beaumont and Fletcher. By Ian Fletcher. Writers & Their Work Ser. *British Bk. Centre* $2.38 pap. $1.20

FORD, JOHN. 1586–1640.

Ford, born in Devonshire and a student of law in his youth, collaborated on early plays, particularly with Dekker (*q.v.*). He is one of the most important and interesting of Shakespeare's successors. The great restraint of his style, as compared to that of Shakespeare or Webster, effectively understates the profound anxieties and doubts of his characters.

WORKS. Ed. by W. Gifford and A. Dyce; rev. by A. H. Bullen. 1895. *Russell & Russell* 3 vols. 1965 set $35.00

PLAYS BY WEBSTER AND FORD. *Dutton* Everyman's pap. $3.95 & $1.75

FIVE PLAYS. Ed. by Havelock Ellis *Farrar, Straus* (Hill & Wang) Dramabks. 1957 pap. $2.95. The Lover's Melancholy; 'Tis Pity She's a Whore; The Broken Heart; Love's Sacrifice; Perkin Warbeck.

THREE PLAYS. Ed. by Keith Sturgess *Penguin* 1974 pap. $1.95; *Peter Smith* $4.95. 'Tis Pity She's a Whore; The Broken Heart; Perkin Warbeck.

THE BROKEN HEART. 1633. Ed. by Brian Morris *Farrar, Straus* (Hill & Wang) New Mermaid Dramabks. 1966 $3.75 pap. $1.25; ed. by Donald K. Anderson Regents Ser. *Univ. of Nebraska Press* 1968 $4.75 Bison Bks. pap. $1.00

'TIS PITY SHE'S A WHORE. 1633. Ed. by Mark Stavig *AHM Pub.* Crofts Class. 1966 pap. $.85; *British Bk. Center* 1974 $8.50 pap. $5.95; ed. by Brian Morris *Farrar, Straus* (Hill & Wang) New Mermaid Dramabks. 1969 $3.75 pap. $1.95; ed. by N. W. Bawcutt Regents Ser. *Univ. of Nebraska Press* 1965 $4.75 Bison Bks. pap. $1.85

PERKIN WARBECK. 1634. Ed. by Peter Ure *Harper* (Barnes & Noble) Revels Plays Ser. 1973 $4.00; ed. by D. K. Anderson Regents Ser. *Univ. of Nebraska Press* 1965 $4.75 Bison Bks. pap. $1.00

CRITICAL EDITION OF FORD'S PERKIN WARBECK. Ed. by Mildred C. Struble *Univ. of Washington Press* 1926 pap. $3.50

Books about Ford

The Tragic Muse of John Ford. By George F. Sensabaugh. 1944. *Blom* $10.00

The Problem of John Ford. By H. J. Oliver. *Richard West* 1955 $6.50. The learned authority gives a good critical assessment

John Ford. By Clifford Leech. Writers & Their Work Ser. *British Bk. Centre* 1964 $2.95 pap. $1.20

John Ford and the Traditional Moral Order. By Mark Stavig. *Univ. of Wisconsin Press* 1968 $12.50

John Ford. By D. K. Anderson, Jr. English Authors Ser. *Twayne* $6.50

BROME, RICHARD. c. 1590–1652.

Brome, a minor dramatist and actor, was Jonson's (*q.v.*) servant in his early years. He imitated his master's "humour" comedy and wrote realistic comic plays. His concern with manners anticipates one aspect of Restoration comedy and his influential play "The Jovial Crew," presenting the beggar's world, forms a link between "Beggars' Bush" by Fletcher and Massinger, and Gay's "The Beggar's Opera" (*q.v.*). His most original play, "The Antipodes," deals with the theme of illusion and reality.

DRAMATIC WORKS. Ed. by R. H. Shepherd. 1873. *AMS Press* 3 vols. set $55.00

THE ANTIPODES. 1640. Ed. by A. Haaker. Regents Ser. *Univ. of Nebraska Press* 1966 $4.75 Bison Bks. pap. $1.00

THE JOVIAL CREW. 1641. Ed. by A. Haaker. Regents Ser. *Univ. of Nebraska Press* 1968 $4.75 Bison Bks. pap. $1.00

Books about Brome

Richard Brome, Caroline Playwright. By R. J. Kaufmann. *Columbia* 1961 o.p. The author has done "a remarkable job in resurrecting the ascertainable facts."

SHIRLEY, JAMES. 1596–1666.

One of the most successful and prolific of Caroline dramatists, Shirley wrote in the tradition of Beaumont and Fletcher. His comedies, "The Lady of Pleasure" (1635) and "Hyde Park" (1632), somewhat influenced by Fletcher's "The Wild Goose-Chase" and "Wit Without Money," clearly anticipate Restoration comedy. Shirley is the connecting link between the Elizabethan and the Restoration drama. He saw the closing of the theaters under Cromwell in 1642 and their reopening in 1660. During that interval of 18 years no dramatic performances were permitted in England.

DRAMATIC WORKS AND POEMS. Ed. by W. Gifford and A. Dyce. 1833. *Russell & Russell* 6 vols. 1965 set $75.00

THE TRAITOR. 1631. Ed. by J. S. Carter. Regents Ser. *Univ. of Nebraska Press* 1965 $4.75
Bison Bks. pap. $1.00
THE LADY OF PLEASURE. 1637. *British Bk. Centre* $9.50 pap. $5.95

RESTORATION DRAMA: HISTORY AND CRITICISM

The dominant dramatic forms of the theater when it was revived at the restoration of
Charles II were the witty and often libertine comedies of manners which are often performed today, and heroic drama, which is almost never performed. Most tragedy was
drawn into the heroic mode, but by the end of the century the emphasis fell increasingly
on pathos rather than heroism. The chief comic writers were Sir George Etherege, William Wycherley, John Dryden and William Congreve (whose "The Way of the World" is
one of the best of all English comedies). Dryden was the greatest of the writers of heroic
drama; Thomas Otway and Nathaniel Lee were chiefly responsible for the trend toward a
drama of heightened emotion.

Birdsall, Virginia O. WILD CIVILITY: The English Comic Spirit on the Restoration Stage.
Indiana Univ. Press 1970 $11.95

Brown, J. R., and B. Harris, Eds. RESTORATION THEATRE. 1965 *Putnam* 1967 $1.65

Dobrée, Bonamy. RESTORATION COMEDY, 1660–1720. *Oxford* 1924 $4.25

RESTORATION TRAGEDY, 1660–1720. *Oxford* 1929 $7.00

Holland, Norman N. THE FIRST MODERN COMEDIES: The Significance of Etherege, Wycherley, and Congreve. *Harvard Univ. Press.* 1959 $9.00; *Indiana Univ. Press* 1967 pap.
$2.95

Hotson, Leslie. THE COMMONWEALTH AND RESTORATION STAGE. 1928. *Russell & Russell*
1962 $12.50. A standard work.

THE LONDON STAGE, 1660–1800: A Calendar of Plays, Entertainments & Afterpieces together with Casts, Box-Receipts and Contemporary Comment; comp. from the Play-
bills, Newspapers and Theatrical Diaries of the Period. *Southern Illinois Univ. Press*
1960 5 pts. with critical introds. published separately. PART I 1660–1700. Ed. by Will-
am Van Lennep 1963 o.p. (critical introd. by E. L. Avery pap. $2.25); PART 2 1700–
1729. Ed. by Emmett L. Avery 2 vols. 1960 o.p. (critical introd. pap. $2.25); PART 3
1729–1747. Ed. by Arthur H. Scouten 2 vols. 1961 $50.00 (critical introd. pap.
$2.25); PART 4 1747–1776. Ed. by George Winchester Stone, Jr. 3 vols. 1963 $75.00
(critical introd. pap. $2.25); PART 5 1776–1800. Ed. by Charles Beecher Hogan 3 vols.
1968 $75.00 (critical introd. pap. $2.25). This mine of theatrical information provides
facts of performance and critical introductions which explain or interpret all aspects
of management and the production of plays in the period.

Lynch, Kathleen M. THE SOCIAL MODE OF RESTORATION COMEDY. 1926. *Octagon* 1965
$8.00

McCollum, John I., Ed. THE RESTORATION STAGE. *Greenwood* (orig.) 1961 $15.00

McMillin, Scott, Ed. RESTORATION AND EIGHTEENTH CENTURY COMEDY. Critical Editions
Ser. *Norton* 1973 $12.50 pap. $2.95

Miner, Earl R., Ed. RESTORATION DRAMATISTS. 20th Century Views *Prentice-Hall* 1966
Spectrum Bks. pap. $1.95

Nicoll, Allardyce A. A HISTORY OF ENGLISH DRAMA, 1660–1900. Now completed in 6 vols.
Cambridge 3 vols. 1952–1959 each $12.00

The three volumes covering the periods in this chapter: Vol. 1 The Restoration Drama, 1660–
1700. 1923 rev. and enl. 1952; Vol. 2 Early 18th Century Drama, 1700–1750. 1925 rev. and enl.
1952; Vol. 3 Late 18th Century Drama, 1750–1800. 1927 rev. and enl. 1952. These earlier volumes have been thoroughly revised and expanded to form a new series. This is an authoritative
reference work of great importance. *For other volumes see Chapter 1, The Drama—Dramatic Criticism
and History, this volume, under Nicoll.*

Perry, Henry Ten Eyck. THE COMIC SPIRIT IN RESTORATION DRAMA: Studies in the Comedy of Etherege, Wycherley, Congreve, Vanbrugh, and Farquhar. 1925. *Russell & Russell* 1962 $7.00

Smith, John H. THE GAY COUPLE IN RESTORATION COMEDY. 1948. *Octagon* $10.50

Summers, Montague. THE PLAYHOUSE OF PEPYS. *Humanities Press* 1964 $15.00

ANTHOLOGIES OF RESTORATION DRAMA

Harris, B., Ed. RESTORATION PLAYS. *Random* Modern Lib. $1.95. The Country Wife by Wycherley; All for Love by Dryden; The Relapse by Vanbrugh; The Way of the World by Congreve; The Beaux Stratagem by Farquhar; and others.

Loftis, John, Ed. REGENTS RESTORATION DRAMA SERIES. *Univ. of Nebraska Press* 28 vols. each $4.75 Bison Bks. pap. each $1.85

MacMillan, Dougald, and H. M. Jones, Eds. PLAYS OF THE RESTORATION AND EIGHTEENTH CENTURY. *Holt* 1931 2nd ed. 1938 $14.75

Morrell, J. M. Ed. FOUR ENGLISH COMEDIES OF THE 17TH AND 18TH CENTURIES. *Penguin* 2nd ed. 1959 pap. $1.95. Complete texts of Volpone by Jonson; The Way of the World by Congreve; She Stoops to Conquer by Goldsmith; The School for Scandal by Sheridan.

Salgado, Gamini, Ed. THREE RESTORATION COMEDIES. *Penguin* English Library Ser. 1968 pap. $1.95. Man of the Mode by George Etherege; Country Wife by William Wycherley; Love for Love by William Congreve.

TWELVE FAMOUS PLAYS OF THE RESTORATION AND THE EIGHTEENTH CENTURY. 1933 *Somerset Pubs*. 2 vols. $39.50. Congreve, Wycherley, Goldsmith, Sheridan.

Wilson, John, Ed. SIX RESTORATION PLAYS. *Houghton* 1959 pap. $2.95. Includes Country Wife by William Wycherley; Man of Mode by George Etherege; All for Love by John Dryden; Venice Preserve by Thomas Otway; Way of the World by William Congreve; Beaux Stratagem by George Farquhar.

RESTORATION DRAMATISTS

DRYDEN, JOHN. 1631–1700.

WORKS. To be completed in 21 vols. *Univ. of California Press* 2 vols. 1962 Vol. 8 $20.00 Vol. 9 $22.50. Vol. 8 Plays: The Wild Gallant (1663), The Rival Ladies (1664), The Indian Queen (1692), ed. by John Harrington Smith and Dougald MacMillan; Vol. 9 Plays: The Indian Emperour (1667), Secret Love (1668), Sir Martin Mar-all (1668), ed. by John Loftis and Vinton A. Dearing.

DRAMATIC WORKS. *Gordian* 6 vols. 1967 set $110.00

THREE PLAYS. *Farrar, Straus* (Hill & Wang) Mermaid Dramabks. 1949–50 $3.95. The Conquest of Granada (1672), Marriage à la Mode (1673), Aureng-Zebe (1676). Ed. with introd. and notes by George Saintsbury.

SELECTED WORKS. Ed. by William Frost *Holt* (Rinehart) 1953 pap. $2.25; 1971 pap. $1.95

POETRY, PROSE AND PLAYS. Sel. by Douglas Grant *Harvard Univ. Press* Reynard Lib. 1952 o.p.

FOUR COMEDIES. Ed. by L. A. Beaurline and Fredson Bowers *Univ. of Chicago Press* 1968 $12.00

FOUR TRAGEDIES. Ed. by L. A. Beaurline and Fredson Bowers *Univ. of Chicago Press* 1968 $12.00

AURENG-ZEBE. 1676. Ed. by Fredrick M. Link *Univ. of Nebraska Press* 1974 $4.75 pap. $1.85

ALL FOR LOVE, or The World Well Lost. 1678. Ed. by J. J. Enck *AHM Pub. Corp.* 1966 pap. $.85; ed. by Benjamin W. Griffith, Jr. *Barron's* 1960 $4.25 pap. $1.25; *British Bk. Centre* 1974 $15.95; ed. by David Vieth Regents Ser. *Univ. of Nebraska Press* 1972 $6.95 Bison Bks. pap. $1.95

Books about Dryden

The Intellectual Milieu of John Dryden. By Louis I. Bredvold. *Univ. of Michigan Press* 1956 Ann Arbor Bks. pap. $1.75

Dryden's Heroic Drama. By Arthur C. Kirsch. 1964 *Gordian* $7.50

Twentieth Century Interpretations of *All for Love*. Ed. by Bruce King. *Prentice-Hall* 1968 pap. $1.25

Dryden's Mind and Art. Ed. by Bruce King. *Harper* (Barnes & Noble) 1970 $4.00

See also Chapter 5, British Poetry: Early to Romantic, Readers' Adviser *Vol. 1.*

ETHEREGE, SIR GEORGE.   1634?–1691.

Almost nothing is known of Etherege's early life or the circumstances of his death, but he held various diplomatic posts abroad from time to time in his maturity. He wrote three plays, "The Comical Revenge" (1664), "She Would If She Could" (1668) and "The Man of Mode," all comedies of manners; the last is the best. "His correspondence, which included letters to and from Dryden, is full of life and gossip about wits of his time, all of it expressed with the gaiety, candour and foppish wit of which Etherege, in his plays, is the acknowledged master"—("Cambridge History of English Literature"). An excellent study is "Etherege and Seventeenth-Century Comedy of Manners" by Dale Underwood (1957, *Shoe String Press* 1969 $5.50). "The Letterbook" (ed. by Sybil Rosenfeld 1928, o.p.) "supersedes all previous biographies"—(Macmillan and Jones, "Plays of the Restoration and Eighteenth Century"). The standard edition of his works is edited by H. F. B. Brett-Smith.

THE DRAMATIC WORKS OF SIR GEORGE ETHEREGE. Ed. by H. F. Brett-Smith. 1927. *Scholary Press* 2 vols. 1971 $29.50. This is the standard edition of Etherege's plays.

THE WORKS OF SIR GEORGE ETHEREDGE. Ed. by A. Wilson Verity *Folcroft* 1973 lib. bdg. $45.00

SHE WOULD IF SHE COULD. 1668. Ed. by Charlene Taylor Regents Ser. *Univ. of Nebraska Press* 1971 $6.95

WYCHERLEY, WILLIAM.   1640–1715.

Wycherley lived the life of a man about town and court favorite from 1671—when the success of his first comedy, "Love in a Wood," brought him into the favor of the Duchess of Cleveland (the king's mistress)—until 1680, when he married the widow of the Earl of Drogheda—disastrously as it turned out. Its secrecy lost him favor at Court, and after his wife's death two years later he was imprisoned for debt. In 1685 the new king, James II, released him and provided him with a pension. In his last years he published poems, many of which his friend Alexander Pope (nearly 50 years his junior) revised.

Known as an "immoral" comic writer, Wycherley "mercilessly exposed the vice, social chicanery and hypocrisy of his age." "The Country Wife" (1674), one of the most amusing comedies of the period, and "The Plain Dealer" (1676) are his masterpieces. "In the tonic of *The Plain Dealer,* English comedy recovered momentarily a sense of the actual relations of contemporary social conditions to better standards." (Quotations are from "The Cambridge History of English Literature.")

COMPLETE WORKS. Ed. by Montague Summers. 1924. *Russell & Russell* 4 vols. 1965 set $50.00

THE COMPLETE PLAYS. Ed. with introd. by Gerald Weales *New York Univ. Press* 1967 $12.50; *Norton* 1971 pap. $3.45

THE COUNTRY WIFE. 1674? Ed. by Steven H. Rubin *British Bk. Centre* 1974 $8.50 pap. $5.95; ed. by T. H. Fujimura Regents Ser. *Univ. of Nebraska Press* 1965 $4.75 Bison Bks. pap. $1.85

THE PLAIN DEALER. 1676. Ed. by T. Ehrsam *British Bk. Centre* 1974 $12.95 pap. $7.50; *Univ. of Nebraska Press* 1967 $4.75 pap. $1.00

Books about Wycherley

Wycherley's Drama. By Rose A. Zimbardo. *Yale Univ. Press* 1965 $5.00

William Wycherley. By K. M. Rogers. English Authors Ser. *Twayne* $6.50

William Wycherley. By P. Vernon. Writers & Their Work Ser. *British Bk. Centre* 1965 $2.95 pap.
$1.20

OTWAY, THOMAS. 1652–1685.

Otway was a frustrated actor turned playwright. In 1625 he fell in love with Mrs. Elizabeth Barry, an actress; his unrequited passion caused him to enlist briefly in the army and is thought to have led to his untimely death "perhaps of starvation, but almost certainly in an ale-house"—(Macmillan and Jones, "Plays of the Restoration and Eighteenth Century"). His blank verse tragedies, "The Orphan" (1680) and "Venice Preserved," were said by a contemporary to be two of the three most successful plays of the period, and "Venice Preserved" remains, next to Dryden's "All for Love," the most admired Restoration tragedy.

THE COMPLETE WORKS. Ed. by Montague Summers. 1926. *AMS Press* 3 vols. 1967 set
$85.00

THE WORKS OF THOMAS OTWAY. Ed. by J. C. Ghosh. 1932. *Oxford* 2 vols. 1968 $17.00

VENICE PRESERVED. 1683. Ed. by Malcolm Kelsall Regents Ser. *Univ. of Nebraska Press*
1969 $4.75 Bison Bks. pap. $1.00

Books about Otway

Next to Shakespeare. By Aline Mackenzie Taylor. 1932. *AMS Press* 1950 $17.50

LEE, NATHANIEL. 1653–1692.

Unsuccessful as an actor, Lee turned to writing tragedies. His early plays were well received, but the production of "Lucius Junius Brutus," considered politically offensive, was forbidden by the Lord Chamberlain. "Indeed, the shadow of political controversy rests on all his later dramas"— (Macmillan and Jones, "Plays of the Restoration and Eighteenth Century"). Madness is a frequent theme in Lee's (usually extravagant) plays. His own tendency toward insanity confined him to a hospital from 1684 to 1689.

THE WORKS OF NATHANIEL LEE. Ed. by Thomas Stroup & Arthur L. Cooke *Scarecrow Press*
2 vols. $17.50. This is the standard edition of Lee's plays.

RIVAL QUEENS. 1677. Ed. by P. F. Vernon Regents Ser. *Univ. of Nebraska Press* 1970 $4.75
Bison Bks. pap. $1.00

LUCIUS JUNIUS BRUTUS. 1680. Regents Ser. *Univ. of Nebraska Press* rev. ed. 1967 $4.75
pap. $1.00

VANBRUGH, SIR JOHN. 1664–1726.

Vanbrugh's plays were exceedingly popular in his day and his facility with stage settings may have turned his mind to the designing of pretentious country mansions, his own theatre and other buildings. His first play to be produced was "The Relapse" (1696). He drafted a play, "The Provok'd Wife" (produced 1697) while confined for two years in a French prison after being arrested on a charge of espionage. He was serving in the English army at the time.

THE COMPLETE WORKS. Ed. by Bonamy Dobrée and Geoffrey Webb. 1927–28. *AMS
Press* 4 vols. 1967 set $100.00

THE RELAPSE. 1697. Ed. by Curt A. Zimansky Regents Ser. *Univ. of Nebraska Press* 1970
$4.75 Bison Bks. pap. $1.85

THE PROVOKED WIFE. 1697. Ed. by Curt A. Zimansky Regents Ser. *Univ. of Nebraska
Press* 1970 $4.75 Bison Bks. pap. $1.00

(With Colley Cibber). THE PROVOKED HUSBAND. Ed. by Peter Dixon Regents Ser. *Univ.
of Nebraska Press* 1973 $7.95

Books about Vanbrugh

Sir John Vanbrugh, Architect and Dramatist. By Lawrence Whistler. 1938. *Kraus* $16.00
Sir John Vanbrugh. By Bernard Harris. Writers and Their Work Ser. *British Bk. Centre* $2.95
pap. $1.20

CONGREVE, WILLIAM. 1670–1729.

Congreve wrote a novel "Incognita, or Love and Duty Reconciled," published in 1692 (*British Bk. Centre* 1974 $8.50 pap. $4.95). His first comedy, "The Old Bachelor" (1693), was tremendously popular in his day as were his later plays, including his tragedy "The Mourning Bride" (1697). Seldom read or played today, it is the source of "Music hath charms to soothe the savage breast" and "Hell hath no fury like a woman scorned." After Jeremy Collier's attack on dramatists and Congreve's reply in 1698, his next comedy, "The Way of the World" (1700), failed. It has since been recognized, however, as the masterpiece of the period—witty, cynical and epigrammatic. After its failure the dramatist wrote no more. In later life he held minor political positions. He was buried in Westminster Abbey.

COMPLETE WORKS. Ed. by M. Summers. 1923. *Russell & Russell* 4 vols. 1964 set $40.00

COMPLETE PLAYS. Gen. ed. Eric Bentley; ed. by Alexander Charles Ewald; introd. by Macaulay *Farrar, Straus* (Hill & Wang) Mermaid Dramabks. 1956 pap. $2.95; ed. by H. Davis *Univ. of Chicago Press* 1967 $15.00

COMEDIES. Ed. by Bonamy Dobrée *Oxford* World's Class. $2.75. The Old Bachelor (1693), The Double-Dealer (1693), Love for Love (1695), The Way of the World (1700).

LOVE FOR LOVE. 1695. *British Bk. Centre* 1974 $4.95; ed. by M. M. Kelsall *Farrar, Straus* (Hill & Wang) New Mermaid Dramabks. 1970 $3.95 pap. $1.50; ed. by Emmett L. Avery Regents Ser. *Univ. of Nebraska Press* $4.75 Bison Bks. pap. $1.85

THE MOURNING BRIDE. 1697. 1928 *Somerset Pubs.* $23.50

THE WAY OF THE WORLD. 1700. Ed. by Henry T. E. Perry *AHM Pub. Corp.* 1951 pap. $1.25; ed. by Vincent Hopper and Gerald Lahey *Barron's* 1958 $4.25 pap. $1.50; *British Bk. Centre* 1974 $8.50 pap. $5.95; ed. by K. M. Lynch Regents Ser. *Univ. of Nebraska Press* 1965 $4.75 Bison Bks. pap. $1.85

Books about Congreve

William Congreve. By D. Crane Taylor. 1931. *Folcroft* $20.00
William Congreve. By J. C. Hodges. 1941. *Kraus* pap. $8.00
A New View of Congreve's *Way of the World*. By Paul Mueschke. 1958. *Folcroft* $8.50
Congreve. By Bonamy Dobrée. Writers and Their Work Ser. *British Bk. Centre* 1964 $2.95 pap. $1.20
A Congreve Gallery. By Kathleen M. Lynch. *Octagon* 1966 $10.00
The Cultivated Stance: The Designs of Congreve's Plays. By W. H. Van Voris. *Dufour* 1966 $8.95
William Congreve. By M. E. Novak. English Authors Ser. *Twayne* $6.50

FARQUHAR, GEORGE. 1677?–1707.

"The Beaux' Stratagem" (1707), his justly famous masterpiece, enjoyed an immediate and lasting success. Born in Ireland, Farquhar acted on the Dublin stage before coming to London. "His comedies, though full of the easy morality of his time are sincere, artless, virile, and full of robust humor." Willard Connely's "Young George Farquhar" (1949, o.p.) is the standard biography.

COMPLETE WORKS. Ed. by C. Stonehill *Gordian* 2 vols. 1967 set $35.00

THE RECRUITING OFFICER. 1706. Ed. by M. Shugrue Regents Ser. *Univ. of Nebraska Press* 1965 $4.75 Bison Bks. pap. $1.85

THE BEAUX' STRATAGEM. 1707. Ed. by Eric Rothstein *AHM Pub. Corp.* Crofts Class. 1967 pap. $ .85; ed. by Vincent Hopper and Gerald Lahey *Barron's* 1962 pap. $1.25; *British Bk. Centre* 1975 $11.95 pap. $7.50

Books about Farquhar

George Farquhar. By David Schmid. 1904. *Johnson Reprint* pap. $19.00
George Farquhar. By A. J. Farmer. Writers and Their Work Ser. *British Bk. Centre* $2.95 pap. $1.20
George Farquhar. By Eric Rothstein. English Authors Ser. *Twayne* 1968 $6.50
The Development of George Farquhar As a Comic Dramatist. By E. Nelson James. *Mouton* (dist. by Humanities) 1973 $18.50

18TH-CENTURY DRAMA: ANTHOLOGIES AND CRITICISM

At the beginning of the 18th century the shift of sensibility which began to be felt in the last decade of the 17th became much more pronounced. In comedy there was a reaction against libertine behavior and licentious dialogue, and even George Farquhar, who continued to write "Restoration" comedy, made his rakes somewhat less reprehensible. By the time of Sir Richard Steele's (*q.v.*) "The Conscious Lovers" (1722), comedy had become self-consciously moral. Sentimentality invaded the theater, as can be seen in Steele's comedy and in the tragedies of Nicholas Rowe and Joseph Addison (*q.v.*), all of which contain scenes that aim for a tearful response. A strain of satire also carried over from the previous century, and in John Gay's "The Beggar's Opera" as well as in Joseph Fielding's (*q.v.*) plays, it was not only literary but political. Satire of the government became so outspoken that in 1737 the Licensing Act was passed, imposing a censorship which took most of the vitality out of the drama for many decades. In the late 18th century there was a revival of comedy, thanks largely to Oliver Goldsmith and Richard Brinsley Sheridan. Colley Cibber (1671–1757), actor, playwright and manager of Drury Lane, wrote thirty plays ("Dramatic Works, With a Life by D. E. Baker," 1777, *AMS Press* 5 vols. set $90.00). He is remembered for his "Apology for the Life of Colley Cibber" (1889, ed. with supplement and notes by R. W. Lowe *AMS Press* 2 vols. set $14.50; ed. by B. R. Fone *Univ. of Michigan Press* 1968 $9.75). David Garrick (1717–1779) was the greatest actor on the English stage at this time. His acquaintance was so varied that his epigrams, many of which remain unprinted, serve as a series of footnotes to the biographies of famous authors, actors, critics and statesmen, among them Addison, Chesterfield, Congreve, Fielding, George III, Goldsmith, Hogarth, Reynolds, Sheridan, Vanbrugh, John Wilkes and Peg Woffington. "A Checklist of Verse by David Garrick," by Mary E. Knapp (*Bibliographical Soc. of the Univ. of Virginia* 1955 $5.00), contains 500 bibliographical entries with indexes to persons and first lines. "As actor, manager, impresario, playwright, play-doctor and versifier of witty epilogues, he flashed with Gallic energy and spark. He amassed a fortune, solidified a reputation for middle-class virtue, and bore that hallmark of prosperity, the gout."

Bernbaum, Ernest. THE DRAMA OF SENSIBILITY: A Sketch of the History of English Comedy and Domestic Tragedy, 1696–1780. 1915. *Peter Smith* 1958 $5.00

Bettenbender, John, Ed. THREE ENGLISH COMEDIES. *Dell* pap. $.75. She Stoops to Conquer; The Rivals; The School for Scandal.

Boas, Frederick Samuel. AN INTRODUCTION TO EIGHTEENTH-CENTURY DRAMA, 1700–1780. *Oxford* 1953 $8.50. An unpretentious, imformative survey of 26 dramatists from Nicholas Rowe to Sheridan. Analysis and criticism; biographies.

Booth, Michael R., Ed. EIGHTEENTH CENTURY TRAGEDY. *Oxford Univ. Press* 1965 $3.00

Hampden, John, Ed. EIGHTEENTH CENTURY PLAYS. *Dutton* Everyman's $3.95

Krutch, Joseph Wood. COMEDY AND CONSCIENCE AFTER THE RESTORATION. 1924. *Columbia* 2nd rev. ed. 1949 pap. $2.75. One of the most important books on English eighteenth-century comedy by an authority on the period and a distinguished dramatic critic.

Loftis, John. COMEDY AND SOCIETY FROM CONGREVE TO FIELDING. *Stanford Univ. Press* 1959 $6.50

THE POLITICS OF DRAMA IN AUGUSTAN ENGLAND. *Oxford* 1963 $4.80

THE LONDON STAGE, 1660–1800. *Southern Illinois Univ. Press.* For a detailed description of this work, *see the above entry under the heading "Restoration Drama: History and Criticism," this Chapter*.

Nicoll, Allardyce. LATE EIGHTEENTH CENTURY DRAMA, 1750–1800. Vol. 3 of A History of English Drama 1660–1900. *Cambridge* rev. & enl. 1952 $19.50

Sherbo, Arthur. ENGLISH SENTIMENTAL DRAMA. *Michigan State Univ. Press* 1957 $5.75

Taylor, W. D., Ed. EIGHTEENTH CENTURY COMEDIES. *Oxford* World's Class. 1950 $2.75. The Beaux' Stratagem; The Conscious Lovers; The Beggar's Opera; The Tragedy of Tragedies; She Stoops to Conquer.

18TH-CENTURY DRAMATISTS

GAY, JOHN.   1685–1732.

Gay was a friend of Steele (q.v.) and of Pope (q.v.). He was a famous wit and one much feared by his contemporaries, many of whom he ridiculed. His reputation today rests on the often-revived "Beggar's Opera" and its sequel "Polly" (1729). "The Beggar's Opera" was revived off-Broadway early in 1963 by the Provincetown Repertory Company. Gay is buried in Westminster Abbey in a tomb for which he composed the epitaph:
"Life is a jest, and all things show it;
I thought so once, and now I know it."

THE POETICAL, DRAMATIC, AND MISCELLANEOUS WORKS OF JOHN GAY. 1795. Adler's 6 vols. set $140.00; AMS Press 6 vols. each $17.25 set $90.00

THE PLAYS OF JOHN GAY. 1922. Richard West 2 vols. set $25.00

THE POETICAL WORKS OF JOHN GAY. Ed. by G. C. Faber. 1926. Russell & Russell 1969 $15.00

THE BEGGAR'S OPERA AND COMPANION PIECES. Ed. by C. F. Burgess. AHM Pub. Corp. Crofts Class. 1966 pap. $ .85

THE BEGGAR'S OPERA. 1728. Dover 1973 pap. $3.00; Peter Smith $5.50; ed. by Edgar V. Roberts Regents Ser. Univ. of Nebraska Press 1969 Bison Bks. pap. $3.65

POLLY—AN OPERA; BEING THE SECOND PART OF THE BEGGAR'S OPERA. 1728. 1922 Richard West $20.00

Books about Gay

Gay's Beggar's Opera. By William E. Schultz. 1923. Russell & Russell $10.00
John Gay, Social Critic. By Sven M. Armens. 1954. Octagon 1966 $11.00
John Gay. By Warner Oliver. Writers and Their Work Ser. British Bk. Centre 1964 $2.95 pap. $1.20
John Gay. By Patricia Meyer Spacks. English Authors Ser. Twayne 1965 $6.50
John Gay: An Annotated Checklist of Criticism. By Julie T. Klein. Whitston Pub. 1973 $7.50

GOLDSMITH, OLIVER.   1728–1774.

Goldsmith's first play, "The Good-Natured Man," had considerable stage success, and the second, "She Stoops to Conquer" (finished only a year before he died), met with great applause and is often revived. Restoration comedy until Goldsmith had been largely the comedy of society and fashion. The first act in "She Stoops to Conquer" was a landmark in English drama, since its action centered around members of the "lower classes."

THE COLLECTED WORKS OF OLIVER GOLDSMITH. Ed. by Arthur Friedman. Oxford 5 vols. 1966 set $68.00

POEMS AND PLAYS. Ed. by Austin Dobson. Dutton Everyman's $2.25

GOLDSMITH: Four Plays. Ed. by George Pierce Baker; introd. by Austin Dobson Farrar, Straus (Hill & Wang) Dramabks. 1957 pap. $1.25. The Good Natur'd Man, She Stoops to Conquer, An Essay on the Theater, A Register of Scotch Marriages.

SELECTED WORKS. Ed. by Richard Garnett. Harvard Univ. Press Reynard Lib. 1951 $15.00 pap. $5.95

THE GOOD-NATURED MAN. 1768. 1921 Somerset Pubs. $6.00

SHE STOOPS TO CONQUER. 1773. Ed. by Katharine C. Balderston AHM Pub. Corp. 1957 pap. $5.95; Baker Bk. House $1.00; (and Sheridan's "School for Scandal") introd. by Brooks Atkinson Bantam pap. $ .45; British Bk. Centre 1975 $8.50 pap. $5.95; (and "The Vicar of Wakefield," "The Deserted Village") Collins-World $3.95; French $1.50; (and "The Vicar of Wakefield") introd. by R. H. W. Dillard Harper Perenn. Lib. pap. $ .50; Heritage Conn. $10.00; ed. by Arthur Friedman Oxford 1968 pap. $1.50; Simon & Schuster (Washington Square) 1968 $.75

Books about Goldsmith

Goldsmith: The Critical Heritage. Ed. by G. S. Rousseau. Routledge & Kegan Paul 1974 $25.00

See also Chapter 10, British Fiction: Early Period, Reader's Adviser, Vol. 1.

SHERIDAN, RICHARD BRINSLEY.   1751–1816.

Sheridan, statesman and dramatist, lived in a period when satirical comedy could easily find something to make merry over. When "The Rivals" was first presented in 1775 it was a failure. Not until it was given in revised form did it gain the popularity that it still maintains today. Sheridan's plays are skillfully constructed, his situations well conceived, his dialogue and humor clever. "The Rivals" and "The School for Scandal" are two of the most brilliant comedies in English drama; they are frequently revived. "The School for Scandal," that "scintillating look at backbiting and intrigue among the London gentry," was given remarkable production on Broadway early in 1963 by an English cast under the direction of Sir John Gielgud (who was also the star), and in 1966 the A.P.A.–Phoenix Repertory Company of New York "established itself on Broadway" (Walter Kerr) with a production of this "London game of murdering reputations to kill time"—(*Cue*).

THE DRAMATIC WORKS OF RICHARD BRINSLEY SHERIDAN. Ed. by Cecil Price. 1902. *Oxford* 2 vols. 1974 set $54.50; *Richard West* 2 vols. set $30.00

COMPLETE PLAYS. *Collins* $1.95

COLLECTED PLAYS. *Dutton* Everyman's $2.25

PLAYS AND POEMS. Ed. with introd. by R. Crompton Rhodes. 1928. *Russell & Russell* 3 vols. 1962 set $35.00

PLAYS. Ed. by Joseph Knight. *Oxford* World's Class. 1951 $2.75

SIX PLAYS. Ed. by L. K. Kronenberger. *Farrar, Straus* (Hill & Wang) Dramabks. 1957 pap. $2.25. The Rivals, St. Patrick's Day, The Duenna, A Trip to Scarborough, The School for Scandal, The Critic.

THE RIVALS. 1775. Ed. by Alan S. Downer *AHM Pub. Corp.* Crofts Class. 1932 $.95; ed. by Vincent Hopper and Gerald Lahey *Barron's* pap. $1.25; *British Bk. Centre* 1974 $11.95 pap. $6.95; *T. Y. Crowell* Chandler Pub. 1968 pap. $1.25; ed. by C. J. L. Price *Oxford* 1968 $1.60

THE SCHOOL FOR SCANDAL. 1777. Ed. by J. Loftis *AHM Pub. Corp.* Crofts Class. 1966 $.85; *Barron's* $4.25 pap. $1.25; *French* $1.50; ed. by E. M. Jebb *Oxford* 1928 $2.00; Eng. Lit. Ser. *St. Martin's* $1.20

THE CRITIC. 1779. (And Buckingham's "The Rehearsal") introd. by Cedric Gale *Barron's* pap. 1960 $1.25

Books about Sheridan

Sheridan. By W. A. Darlington. 1933. *Richard West* $10.00
Sheridan. By Lewis Gibbs. 1947. *Richard West* $9.95
Betsy Sheridan's Journal: Letters from Sheridan's Sister 1784–1786 and 1788–1790. Ed. by William Le Fanu. *Rutgers Univ. Press* 1960 $6.00

—E.J.A.

Chapter 3

Shakespeare

*"Thou in our wonder and astonishment
Hast built thy self a live-long Monument."*
—JOHN MILTON

For audiences, readers, and students today, Shakespeare remains thoroughly alive as the mirror of great drama. Indeed, we are faced with an embarrassment of riches when we turn to our century's constant flow of new productions, editions, and criticism of his plays and poems. Clearly Shakespeare still has the power to rouse our "wonder and astonishment." During the two decades of his career (ca. 1590–1611), he was the consummate man of the theater; he was not only a prolific and successful playwright, but also an actor and part-owner of his theater. We have only snatches of commentary on his works from his contemporaries, but we know that his plays were paid the high compliment of imitation and that his ease of composition was legendary. After four centuries, his reputation has flown far beyond the praises of his own times. We recognize him as the genius of our language, perhaps the greatest writer of any time in any language. All our human activities are reflected in the mirror of his art, from our private world of love and friendship to our public world of politics, economics, and philosophy. As we watch these private and public worlds separate, collide, harmonize, we discover fresh commentary on our own lives. In Shakespeare's mirror, we see ourselves as we are, as we might have been, as we should be.

That Shakespeare has had more editors than any other writer merely bears witness to his hold on our imagination. Over 100 editions of his works were published between 1623 and 1821, the years of the First Folio and of the Third Variorum, respectively. More than 100 editions have appeared since 1821, many still in print, many revised and reissued. Some important revisions of older editions include The New Temple, The New Cambridge, and The New Variorum, each of which adds the products of modern research to the original text. Of these, The New Variorum, still under revision, offers the most fully detailed notes on background, stage history, and criticism of the plays. The Arden Shakespeare is another mine of rich annotations to Shakespeare's text. The most noteworthy recent edition is The Riverside Shakespeare, which reflects G. Blakemore Evans' study of the earlier texts and editions of Shakespeare's works, and to which the "Harvard Concordance" is keyed (*see Sections on Modern Editions and Productions; Concordances and Books of Quotations*).

The fertile production of critical works on Shakespeare also testifies to his vitality. Four periodicals devote themselves entirely to studies of his works: *Shakespeare Quarterly; Shakespeare Survey; Shakespeare Studies;* and *Shakespeare Newsletter.* These magazines are sources of articles, reviews, and data on Shakespeare studies and organizations. In addition, book length criticism appears regularly from both university and commercial presses. Work is still advancing on our understanding of Shakespeare's own historical era, so that we may attempt to read the plays in their original context. Studies in Shakespeare's language, his use of rhetoric and imagery, influence our view of his style's genesis and development. Shakespeare's stage has also been the focus of critical research, since an understanding of his dramaturgy adds to our visual appreciation of the plays' form and meaning. So, too, does a thorough understanding of Shakespeare's sources and his use of them enhance our reading of the works. The future of scholarship, despite the quantity of books already available, looks very healthy. More interdisciplinary works, which relate Shakespeare's literary art to other arts and disciplines like psychology, mythology, sociology, history, and philosophy, promise a broader understanding of Shakespeare's unique genius. Modern technology will also have a strong impact on Shakespeare studies. Our sophisticated copying machines have made it possible for Samuel Schoenbaum to preserve and disseminate original and often decaying biographical records in his work "William Shakespeare: A Documentary Life" (*see Section on Biographies of Shakespeare*). Computers, too, will enrich our critical methods since we will be able to store and cross-index vast amounts of data in them. Marvin Spevack used computers to compile the new Harvard Concordance.

With interest in Shakespeare already high and increasing, with movies and television as well as theaters using their media to perform his works, and with publishing companies responding to this interest with new books and articles, it seems that Shakespeare continues to build in us his "live-long Monument."

BIBLIOGRAPHIES

Ebisch, Walther, and L. L. Schücking. A SHAKESPEARE BIBLIOGRAPHY. 1931. *Blom* 1968 $17.50; supplement for the years 1930–1935, 1937 $10.00. The standard bibliography for the period it covers. Gordon R. Smith's bibliography (*see below*) is a continuation of this work.

Jaggard, William. SHAKESPEARE BIBLIOGRAPHY. 1911. *Fernhill* 1971 $71.50

"To the bookman, Shakespeare and Jaggard are practically synonymous! Not only because the original Wm. Jaggard was Shakespeare's printer, but also because a lineal descendant of Jaggard was Shakespeare's greatest bibliographer.... There have been many WS bibs since the first appearance of this work ... but all others are selective. Jaggard included everything he could find: some 36,000 entries, annotated and indexed from the 12 largest WS libraries. This welcome reprint is long overdue and is still the cornerstone of any Shakespeare reference library"—(*Antiquarian Bookman*).

McManaway, James G., and Jeanne Addison Roberts. A SELECTIVE BIBLIOGRAPHY OF SHAKESPEARE. *The Univ. Press of Virginia* for the Folger Shakespeare Library 1974 $8.75 pap. $3.95. This valuable bibliography, covering the years 1930–1970, lists 4500 editions, books, and articles.

Smith, Gordon R., Ed. A CLASSIFIED SHAKESPEARE BIBLIOGRAPHY. 1936–1958. *Pennsylvania State Univ. Press* 1965 $49.50. This comprehensive bibliography lists some 25,000 books, articles and reviews in all major languages.

Wells, Stanley. SHAKESPEARE: Select Bibliographical Guides. *Oxford* 1973 $10.50 pap. $3.95. This book contains seventeen essays that supply reading lists and outline major critical views on the texts, plays, and poems.

Valuable annual bibliographies are to be found in Shakespeare Survey, Shakespeare Quarterly *and the Modern Language Association's periodical* PMLA.

CONCORDANCES AND BOOKS OF QUOTATIONS

Bartlett, John. A COMPLETE CONCORDANCE OF SHAKESPEARE. 1894 reissue 1937. *St. Martin's Press* 1953 $37.50. References are to Act, Scene and Line of the Globe edition.

Browning, David C., Comp. EVERYMAN'S DICTIONARY OF SHAKESPEARE QUOTATIONS. 1954 *Int. Pubns. Service* 5th ed. 1970 $7.50. From little-known "jewels five words long" to complete speeches and sonnets; detailed index.

Howard-Hill, T. H. OXFORD SHAKESPEARE CONCORDANCES. *Oxford* 37 vols. 1969–73 $8.00–$17.00. These individual volume concordances are keyed to an Oxford Old Spelling edition of Shakespeare, which is now in preparation.

Lewis, William Dodge, Ed. SHAKESPEARE SAID IT: Topical Quotations from the Works of Shakespeare. *Syracuse Univ. Press* 1961 $6.50

A "fitting supplement" to the standards, Bartlett and Stevenson, this contains hundreds of topic headings ranging from "Absence" to "Youth." Entries are identified by act, scene, and line or lines.

An extensive index provides cross-references to alternate headings. A number of the quotations are extensive, amounting to complete or condensed scenes. Footnotes by the editor are placed conveniently after each entry.

Spevack, Marvin, Ed. A COMPLETE AND SYSTEMATIC CONCORDANCE TO THE WORKS OF SHAKESPEARE. *Olms* (dist. by Adler's) 6 vols. 1968–70 set $444.00; *Hafner Service* each $49.50 set $275.30. Spevack's invaluable work is keyed to The Riverside Shakespeare (*see Section on Modern Editions and Productions, this Chapter*).

(Ed.). THE HARVARD CONCORDANCE TO SHAKESPEARE. *Harvard Univ. Press* 1973 $45.00. This single-volume concordance is an abridgement of the six-volume edition.

Stevenson, Burton Egbert, Comp. THE HOME BOOK OF SHAKESPEARE QUOTATIONS. *Scribner* $22.50. (This vol. is available only directly from the Publisher.)

"One of Burton Stevenson's great compilations . . . back in print"—(David Glixon, in *SR*).

THE STANDARD BOOK OF SHAKESPEARE QUOTATIONS. *T. Y. Crowell* (Funk & Wagnalls) 1953 $7.50. The "conclusive reference tool in this field."

GENERAL REFERENCE WORKS

Baker, Arthur E. A SHAKESPEARE COMMENTARY. (Orig. "Shakespeare Dictionary") *Ungar* 2 vols. 1957 $18.50. "Scholarly, brief, and pointed notes, regarding characters, place names, words, and allusions in each play."

Bullough, Geoffrey, Ed. NARRATIVE AND DRAMATIC SOURCES OF SHAKESPEARE. *Columbia* 8 vols. 1951–66. Vol. I Early Comedies, Poems, Romeo and Juliet (1957) Vol. 2 Comedies, 1597–1603 (1958) Vol. 3 Earlier English History Plays Henry VI Parts I, 2, 3, Richard III and Richard II (1953) Vol. 4 Later English History Plays (1962) Vol. 5 Roman Plays (1964) Vol. 6 Other Classical Plays (1966) Vol. 7 Major Tragedies: Hamlet, Othello, King Lear, Macbeth Vol. 8 Romances (1974) 8 vols. each $15.00. A collection of Shakespeare's presumed sources, the first to be published in English since 1875.

Campbell, Oscar James, and Edward G. Quinn, Eds. THE READER'S ENCYCLOPEDIA OF SHAKESPEARE. *T. Y. Crowell* 1966 $15.00. This work is a very rich source of information on Shakespeare's life, plays, and critics.

Chambers, Sir Edmund Kercheyer. THE ELIZABETHAN STAGE. *Oxford* 4 vols. 1923 set $51.25. The authoritative work.

Charney, Maurice. How to READ SHAKESPEARE. *McGraw-Hill* 1971 $6.96 pap. $1.95. The book's brevity and liveliness make it a good introduction for students.

Granville-Barker, Harley, and G. B. Harrison. A COMPANION TO SHAKESPEARE STUDIES. *Cambridge* 1934 $12.50

This is an indispensable handbook. Granville-Barker was equally famous as a producer of plays and as a dramatist, although most of his plays are now o.p. Associated in turn with the Stage Society and with the Court Theatre in London, he was prominent in the movement of the new drama and was always a great innovator and experimenter in the theater. He also wrote "On Dramatic Method" (1931 *Peter Smith* 1960 $4.00).

Halliday, F. E. A SHAKESPEARE COMPANION: 1564–1964. *Schocken* 1964 $12.00. A useful compendium of information about Shakespeare, his contemporaries and his times, arranged as an encyclopedia.

SHAKESPEARE IN HIS AGE. 1956. *A. S. Barnes* (Yoseloff) 1964 $7.50

Harbage, Alfred. WILLIAM SHAKESPEARE: A Reader's Guide. *Farrar, Straus* 1963 $6.95 Noonday pap. $3.45; *Octagon* 1972 $13.00

Dr. Harbage examines 15 of the most popular plays, first in scene-by-scene synopsis and then in evocative analysis. Always keenly observant and sharply suggestive, his brief notes on all the plays are most helpful; useful bibliographic references.

Kökeritz, Helge. SHAKESPEARE'S NAMES: A Pronouncing Dictionary. *Yale Univ. Press* 1959 $6.50

Marder, Louis. His Exits and His Entrances: The Story of Shakespeare's Reputation. (1963, o.p.)

> In this sound and comprehensive work the author "discusses Shakespeare through the centuries that followed the issuing of his plays, giving due attention to the general knowledge Shakespeare appears to have possessed, his personal and public life, the great collections, the editions produced, and the emendations which occurred. He considers the question of authorship and portraiture and describes the forgeries with humor. . . . Throughout there is an air of currency about the work; theses and comments are up to date"—(LJ).

Martin, Michael R., and Richard C. Harrier. The Concise Encyclopedia to Shakespeare. *Horizon Press* 1971 $14.95. This encyclopedia offers a listing of modern critics, theater people, productions, and recordings.

Muir, Kenneth, and Samuel Schoenbaum. A New Companion to Shakespeare Studies. *Cambridge* 1971 $13.95 pap. $4.95. This collection of critical essays updates the earlier Granville-Barker and Harrison "Companion."

Odell, George C. D. Shakespeare from Betterton to Irving. *Dover* 2 vols. 1966 pap. each $3.00; *Blom* 2 vols. $13.75. A history of the staging of Shakespearean drama from 1660 to 1902.

Onions, Charles T. The Shakespeare Glossary. 1911. *Oxford* 2nd ed. rev. 1919 $5.00. By one of the editors of the *Oxford English Dictionary*; material that resulted from his lexicographical research.

Raleigh, Sir Walter A., Ed. Shakespeare's England. *Oxford* 2 vols. 1917 set $22.00. The life and manners of the age, by various authorities.

Sternfeld, Frederick W. Music in Shakespearian Tragedy. *Routledge & Kegan Paul* 1963 $10.00

> "Secondary sources are here described and appraised [and he goes] on to make further discoveries of his own. . . . [An] important book"—(LJ).

Wilson, John Dover. Life in Shakespeare's England. 1911 1920. *Folcroft* $5.95

SHAKESPEARE'S THEATER

Adams, John C. The Globe Playhouse: Its Design and Equipment. 1943. *Harper* (Barnes & Noble) 2nd rev. ed. 1961 $12.50

Beckerman, Bernard. Shakespeare at the Globe, 1599–1609. *Macmillan* 1962 $5.95 pap. $1.95

> The author reconstructs the repertory system of the Globe, spells out the pattern of its dramaturgy, discusses the stage and staging, and evaluates the acting as an expression of the Elizabethan spirit; a "thorough, substantial work."

Gurr, Andrew. The Shakespearean Stage. *Cambridge* 1970 $12.50. A full background study of the theater from 1574 to 1642.

Harbage, Alfred Bennett. Shakespeare's Audience. *Columbia* 1941 1961 pap. $1.95; *Peter Smith* $4.25

King, T. J. Shakespearean Staging. *Harvard Univ. Press* 1971 $6.75. A discussion of the contemporary staging of Shakespeare and his contemporaries from 1599 to 1642.

Nagler, Alois M. Shakespeare's Stage. Trans. by Ralph Manheim. *Yale Univ. Press* 1958 $7.50. An excellent brief account by a distinguished theater historian.

Smith, Irwin. Shakespeare's Blackfriars Playhouse: Its History and Design. *New York Univ. Press* 1964 $15.00 pap. $4.95

Shakespeare's Globe Playhouse: A Modern Reconstruction in Text and Scale Drawings. *Scribner* 1957 $12.50. Informative introd. by James C. McManaway of the Folger Shakespeare Library; detailed scale drawings, photographs and reproductions of old prints and maps. A valuable reference work.

Styan, J. L. SHAKESPEARE'S STAGECRAFT. *Cambridge* 1967 $10.50 pap. $3.75. An exploration of the effects of acting technique, character groupings, and space utilization on our understanding of the plays.

Thorndike, Ashley H. SHAKESPEARE'S THEATRE. *Macmillan* 1916 reissue 1948 $6.95. A popular history of the Elizabethan stage to put beside the monumental work of Sir Edmund Chambers (*see General Reference Works Section, this Chapter*).

TEXTUAL STUDIES

Many of Shakespeare's plays were printed separately in quarto editions in his lifetime. In 1623, seven years after his death, two members of his company, John Heminge and Henry Condell, put together the first collected edition, published in folio. This First Folio was followed by three others in the 17th century, in one of which, the Third Folio (1663–64), seven more plays were added. Only one of these, "Pericles, Prince of Tyre," is now considered to be at least partly by Shakespeare. He probably collaborated on two other plays: "The Two Noble Kinsmen," printed in 1634 as by Shakespeare and Fletcher, and "Sir Thomas More," never printed until the 19th century. The canon of Shakespearean plays generally accepted today is therefore the contents of the First Folio and three additional plays. There has been a good deal of debate about whether some of the plays included in the First Folio contain sections written by collaborators or revisers, or sections originally written by others and rewritten by Shakespeare. Some account of these problems will be found in G. E. Bentley, "Shakespeare: A Biographical Handbook" (*see Section of this Chapter on Biographies*) and in Arthur Brown, "The Great Variety of Readers," *Shakespeare Survey*, XVIII (1965), 11–22.

Bartlett, Henrietta Collins, and A. W. Pollard, Eds. CENSUS OF SHAKESPEARE'S PLAYS IN QUARTO 1594–1709. 1916. Rev. 1939 *AMS Press* $15.00; *Richard West* 1975 $14.95
Professor Pollard's was the first census to list any separate editions after 1640. It appeared first in 1916. Miss Bartlett brought the work up to date. The bibliographical information is of incalculable value to students and scholars, collectors and reference librarians.

Bowers, Fredson Thayer. ON EDITING SHAKESPEARE. *Univ. Press of Virginia* 1966 $5.00 pap. $2.45

Craig, Hardin. A NEW LOOK AT SHAKESPEARE'S QUARTOS. *AMS Press* $12.50

Greg, Sir Walter Wilson. THE EDITORIAL PROBLEM IN SHAKESPEARE. *Oxford* 1942 1952 3rd ed. 1954 $7.00. A Survey of the Foundations of the Text. A summary of our present knowledge.

THE SHAKESPEARE FIRST FOLIO: Its Bibliographical and Textual History. *Oxford* 1955 $12.00

Hinman, Charlton. THE PRINTING AND PROOF-READING OF THE FIRST FOLIO OF SHAKESPEARE. *Oxford* 2 vols. 1963 set $44.00. The definitive work on this subject for the specialist.

Walker, Alice. TEXTUAL PROBLEMS OF THE FIRST FOLIO. 1953. *Richard West* 1973 $5.95. A sound examination of "what lies behind the Folio texts of Richard III, King Lear, Troilus and Cressida, Henry IV Pt. II, Hamlet and Othello."

MODERN EDITIONS AND PRODUCTIONS

A list of all the editions of Shakespeare's works, which we have not attempted, would show that there are almost as many editions as there are publishers. The best of the one-volume editions and of the many-volume editions (including new paperbacks) intended for the general reader will be found below.

The great rise of interest in Shakespeare festivals here, in Canada and in England has stimulated the reading of these editions. "The American Shakespeare Festival: The Birth of a Theatre" by John Houseman and Jack Landau (1959, o.p.) traces, through text and more than 200 pictures, the development of the major repertory theater at Stratford, Conn. This Stratford group now gives winter performances for students in addition to its regular summer season. The festival in Stratford, Ontario, with its complete Canadian staff, owes much to its original director, Tyrone Guthrie, who "gave it the imagination, scope and confidence that pushed it in the right direction." Begun in a tent in 1953, the permanent theater was opened in 1957.

The New York Shakespeare Festival Public Theater, under the auspices of Joseph Papp, is a welcome contribution to American theater. The Delacorte Theater in Central Park, a $400,000 2,300-seat amphitheater with an Elizabethan stage, produces free Shakespeare to enthusiastic audiences every summer. In 1975, the actors played to a total of 73,000 theatergoers. The Mitzi E. Newhouse Theater of Lincoln Center, now a branch of the New York Shakespeare Festival, ran two seasons of Shakespeare in 1973 and 1974. Joseph Papp's work, known for its flexibility and innovation, has produced exciting theatrical events from the rich mine of Shakespeare's plays. He transformed "Two Gentlemen of Verona" so successfully into a musical that it became a Broadway hit.

Other festivals and permanent companies abound throughout the English-speaking world, and new (or old) experiments with Shakespeare add exciting dimensions—or at their worst, fail to ruin him. Experiments with all-male performers, in imitation of Elizabethan practice, have been attempted; minority group casts of the plays are now familiar. Shakespeare's plays also appear frequently on film and television, thus widening even further his circle of modern devotees. Joseph Papp writes an interesting article on "Shakespeare Festivals" in "The Best Plays of 1965–66" (*Dodd* 1966 $12.50), in which he says: "Shakespeare apparently has more immediate understandability to the mass than Beckett, Pinter, Genet or John Arden, so he will continue to draw, and in fact probably outdraw modern playwrights." With competent, imaginative—even daring—productions, Shakespeare proves susceptible to endless variation and is capable of enchanting modern audiences of every kind.

One-Volume Editions

AMS Press—THE COMPLETE WORKS: Globe Edition. Ed. by William George Clark and William Aldis Wright 1864 lib. bdg. $65.00. Constantly reprinted since 1864, with a new glossary in 1891, revised in 1911.

THE SHAKESPEARE QUARTOS: The Comedies. Ed. by James G. McManaway 1970 $37.50

T. Y. Crowell—THE COMPLETE WORKS OF WILLIAM SHAKESPEARE. Ed. by George Lyman Kittredge 1966 $15.00. Ill. with photos of recent Old Vic and Royal Shakespeare productions.

Doubleday—THE COMPLETE WORKS OF WILLIAM SHAKESPEARE. Pref. by Christopher Morley; ill. by Rockwell Kent 1946 $8.95

Harcourt—THE COMPLETE SIGNET CLASSIC SHAKESPEARE. Ed. by Sylvan Barnet 1972 $12.95. A compilation of the individual-volume Signet editions into one volume with a separate editor for each play. The arrangement is chronological.

SHAKESPEARE: The Complete Works. Ed. by G. B. Harrison 1952 $11.95. Incorporates the general introduction, illustrations, text, commentaries and appendixes from the 1948 edition below.

SHAKESPEARE: The Major Plays and the Sonnets. Ed. by G. B. Harrison 1948 text ed. $10.25

Houghton—COMPLETE PLAYS AND POEMS. A new text ed. with introd. and notes by William Allan Neilson and Charles Jarvis Hill New Cambridge Edition 1942 text ed. $14.95

THE RIVERSIDE SHAKESPEARE. Ed. by G. Blakemore Evans 1974 $15.95. This authoritative edition is the product of years of work examining original texts and major editions of Shakespeare. The general introduction is written by Harry Levin, the individual introductions to the comedies, histories, tragedies, romances and poems by Anne Barton, Herschel Baker, Frank Kermode, and Hallet Smith. The arrangement is generic.

Six Plays. Ed. by Charles Jarvis Hill 1964 pap. $3.25

Irvington—Shakespeare's Principal Plays. Ed. by C. F. Tucker Brooke *Ariston Bks.* 3rd ed. 1935 text ed. $17.95

Macmillan—The Essential Shakespeare: Nine Major Plays and the Sonnets. Ed. by Russell Fraser 1972 $5.50

The Living Shakespeare: 22 Plays and the Sonnets. Ed. by Oscar J. Campbell 1949 $9.95

Oxford—The Complete Works. Oxford Standard Authors. Ed. by W. J. Craig 1943 $6.50

Random—The Complete Works. 1952 $7.95 text ed. $4.15. A new edition ed. with introd. and glossary by Peter Alexander

This completely new edition includes a biographical introduction, an appendix, containing the special transcript by Sir Walter Greg of Shakespeare's contribution to Sir Thomas More, the preliminary notes to the first folio, a glossary of 2,500 entries.

Scott, Foresman—Complete Works. Ed. by Hardin Craig 1961; rev. by David Berington 1973 $11.25

Introduction to Shakespeare: Eight Plays, Selected Sonnets. Ed. by Hardin Craig Key Eds. 1952 pap. $4.25

Shakespeare. Ed. by Hardin Craig rev. ed. 1958 $10.95. A historical and critical study with annotated texts of 21 plays.

Scribner—Shakespeare: Twenty-three plays and the sonnets. Ed. by Thomas Marc Parrott and others 1938 rev. ed. 1953 $9.75. All the plays likely to be read in schools and colleges.

Six Plays and the Sonnets. Introds. and notes by Thomas Marc Parrott and Edward Hubler 1956 pap. $2.95

Viking—The Portable Shakespeare. 1944 lib. bdg. $6.50 pap. $3.75. Seven plays complete (Hamlet, Macbeth, Romeo and Juliet, Julius Caesar, A Midsummer Night's Dream, As You Like It, The Tempest); memorable lines and passages from the other plays; all the sonnets; the songs from all the plays; and a key-word index to 1,000 quotations.

Xerox University Microfilms—Complete Works. Ed. by George Lyman Kittredge 1936 1957; rev. by Irving Ribner 1970 $14.50. Irving Ribner has revised and added to Kittredge's original notes.

Editions in Two or More Volumes

AHM Pub. Corp.—Crofts Classics Shakespeare. 15 vols. pap. each $.85. Various editors.

AMS Press—Plays. Ed. by Samuel Johnson. 1765. 8 vols. set $235.00

The Plays and Poems of William Shakespeare. Ed. by James Boswell. The Third Variorum. 1821. 21 vols. set $500.00

Works. Ed. by Alexander Pope. 1723–1725. 6 vols. set $315.00

Works. Ed. by Lewis Theobald. 1733. 7 vols. set $205.00

The Works of Mr. William Shakespeare. Ed. by Nicholas Rowe. 1709–1710. 7 vols. set $175.00

Bobbs Odyssey—Shakespeare Series. Ed. by Northrup Frye. 2 vols. pap. $1.65–$1.75

Borden-Audio Books Records—Shakespeare's Plays. 24 records with individual plays in book form each $7.50. The book alone is $1.00.

Brown, William C.—THE BLACKFRIARS SHAKESPEARE. 19 vols. 1969–1971 pap. $.95–$1.25. Various editors.

Caedmon—SHAKESPEARE RECORDING SOCIETY ALBUMS. Records boxed with complete text in book form and background notes by G. B. Harrison. 34 albums each $5.95–$23.80

Cambridge—THE NEW SHAKESPEARE. Ed. by Sir Arthur Quiller-Couch, John Dover Wilson and J. C. Maxwell 39 vols. 1921–66 each $6.50 pap. 24 vols. 1968–   each $1.65
This edition was begun in 1921. The comedies in 14 volumes were completed in 1934. With the first of the tragedies (Hamlet), Dr. Wilson became sole editor. After 16 volumes of the tragedies were published, Dr. Wilson was joined by J. C. Maxwell.

SHAKESPEARE. Ed. by E. F. C. Ludowyk 6 vols. $1.45–$1.95

Collins-World—Ed. by Peter Alexander 4 vols. COMPLETE COMEDIES with general introd., introd. to each play and glossary (1954) COMPLETE HISTORICAL PLAYS (1955) TRAGEDIES, PT. 1 (1956) TRAGEDIES, PT. 2 and POEMS (1956) New Class. each $4.95 lea. each $9.95 set $35.00

Dell—INVITATION TO SHAKESPEARE. Ed. by Edmund Fuller 8 vols. each $.50

LAUREL SHAKESPEARE SERIES. General ed. Francis Fergusson; modern commentaries by various authorities 30 vols. 1958–   pap. each $.35–$1.45

Dover—NEW VARIORUM SHAKESPEARE. Ed. by Horace Howard Furness. 1871–1901. 10 vols. pap. each $2.75–$4.00
Each play is a standard text with all textual variations from the available manuscripts and editions. Included as well are scholarly annotations and explanations of elusive references and passages, and a critical appendix of background information: dating, sources, past performances, past editions and line changes.

Dutton—COMPLETE WORKS. Ed. by Oliphant Smeaton Everyman's 3 vols. 1953 each $3.95. Comedies; Tragedies; Histories; Poems and Sonnets.

French—GLOBE THEATER STREAMLINED VERSIONS. 10 vols. each $1.00. These acting and abridged or streamlined versions have been used by many famous actors.

SHAKESPEARE'S PLAYS: Acting Edition. 20 vols. each $2.50

Funk & Wagnalls—THE ALDUS SHAKESPEARE. Ed. by Henry Norman Hudson, Israel Gollancz and C. H. Herford 19 vols. $2.95 pap. 20 vols. $.95 Consult *T. Y. Crowell* catalog.

Harcourt—THE HARBINGER SHAKESPEARES. Edited by G. B. Harrison Harbinger Bks. 1963–   Hamlet $1.85 Macbeth $1.45
These single editions have been entirely reset from Professor Harrison's great single volume "Shakespeare: The Complete Works" (*see under Section on One-Volume Editions*). Each volume contains not only the same general study of Shakespeare and the era in which he wrote, but an introduction to the particular play under discussion, with the authoritative Globe text and Professor Harrison's detailed notes.

Harper (Barnes & Noble)—THE ARDEN SHAKESPEARE. Ed. by Harold F. Brooks and Harold Jenkins 28 vols. 1951– $8.75 pap. $2.25. There are individual editors for each title of these revised editions of the original Arden Series, which was begun in 1899. It has been under the editorship of W. J. Craig, Robert H. Case and Una Ellis-Fermor.

New Am. Lib.—THE SIGNET CLASSIC SHAKESPEARE. Gen. Ed. Dr. Sylvan Barnet, Chairman of the English Department at Tufts University 38 vols. 1963–68 pap. each $.75. All plays and sonnets.

Oxford—COMPLETE WORKS: Comedies, Histories, Tragedies. Introd. by A. C. Swinburne; introd. to each play by Edward Dowden Standard Authors 3 vols. 1911–12, 1933 each $9.00

THE NEW CLARENDON SHAKESPEARE. General ed. R. E. C. Houghton, with various editors 21 vols. 1938–   each $1.50 except Measure for Measure $1.75. The text is based on the Oxford Shakespeare and is considerably less expurgated than in most existing school editions.

SHAKESPEARE QUARTO FACSIMILES. Ed. by Walter W. Greg and Charlton Hinman 11 vols. 1939–1972 $6.50–$7.00

Penguin—THE PELICAN SHAKESPEARE. Professor Alfred Harbage of Harvard, Gen. Ed. Various editors 35 vols. 1956–67 each $.45–$1.65

Random—COMPLETE WORKS. Players deluxe ed. 3 vols. 1957 boxed $30.00

Peter Smith—A NEW VARIORUM EDITION. Ed. by Horace Howard Furness. 1871. 14 vols. (Hamlet 2 vols.) each $5.50

Washington Square—FOUR GREAT COMEDIES. 1961 pap. $.75; FOUR GREAT TRAGEDIES. 1961 pap. $.75; also 39 single plays ed. by Virginia A. La Mar and Louis B. Wright Folger Library Series pap. each $.45–$.65

Xerox University Microfilms—THE KITTREDGE-RIBNER SHAKESPEARE. Ed. by George Lyman Kittredge and Irving Ribner 35 vols. 1966–1969 pap. $1.00. The text is from the Kittredge edition of Shakespeare as revised by Irving Ribner. Each volume contains notes, never before published, as well as an introduction, textual notes, and a glossarial index.

Yale Univ. Press—THE YALE SHAKESPEARE. Ed. by the members of the Department of English 40 vols. 1918–1928, 28 vols. in print: most are cloth-bound each $4.00, some are in cloth and paper, some are in paper only $.95–$1.25

SONGS, SONNETS AND POEMS

Shakespeare's sonnets, which have aroused strong critical controversy over the centuries, were first published in 1609 without his supervision. Their textual accuracy, their ordering, and their dates of composition are therefore in question. Critical interest, however, has focused primarily on the tempting autobiographical possibilities the poems appear to open up for us. Surrounding the poet are a cast of characters: The Fair Friend, The Dark Lady, The Rival Poet. Scholars have searched for biographical and historical evidence to identify these characters, with most of the interest focussed on the young man for whom Shakespeare expresses such strong attachment. He is generally assumed to be the "Mr. W. H." to whom the book was dedicated. Henry Wriothesley, the 3rd earl of Southampton and Shakespeare's patron, is a long-standing favorite among the candidates, but other names have been offered by prominent Shakespeareans. Leslie Hotson favors William Hatcliffe; John Dover Wilson suggests William Herbert, the 3rd earl of Pembroke. With Shakespeare's prodigious stature, with centuries separating us from him, and with the poverty of personal autobiographical data on his life, we are left with an overwhelming desire to satsify our curiosity about him through his sonnets. Yet, as interesting as these speculations are, they are merely guesses based on circumstantial evidence.

The search for autobiography has distracted many critics from assessing the poems as poetry. Indeed, we do not even know whether the sonnets were personal statements. Shakespeare's was one of the many sonnet sequences brought into vogue by the publication of Sidney's "Astrophel and Stella" in 1591. Although Shakespeare's is uniquely excellent poetically, it follows many of the Petrarchan conventions and contains standard, sometimes derivative single sonnets. Even the anti-Petrarchanisms, expressed so arrestingly in Sonnet 130: "My mistress' eyes are nothing like the sun . . .," had become conventional. Shakespeare's uniqueness in the sonnet sequence, therefore, is much like his uniqueness in the drama; the use he made of the conventions separates him from the pack of contemporary writers. Thematic and poetic analysis of the sonnets is consequently a valuable approach for critics. Two recent works have put aside the unanswerable questions to suggest new ways of the viewing the poems. Philip Martin's "Shakespeare's Sonnets: Self, Love and Art" examines Shakespeare's works in this genre separately and in comparison to other sonnet writers, notably Donne. He proposes that Shakespeare's sonnets are thematically concerned with the exploration of selfhood. Stephen Booth, in "An Essay on Shakespeare's Sonnets," discusses the poetic structure of individual sonnets and patterns of structure in the sequence in close detail (*see Section on Criticism*).

Less critical attention has been paid to Shakespeare's other poems, although his Ovidian narrative "Venus and Adonis" and his complaint poem "The Rape of Lucrece" were extremely popular during his lifetime. They, too, reflect Shakespeare's ability to fashion highly individual poems from conventional material. "The Phoenix and the Turtle," a mysterious and beautiful work, has also drawn commentary from those who wish to see it as an allegory of contemporary figures, but this key, if it exists, remains lost. All Shakespeare's poems inform our understanding of his drama's structure, themes, and poetry, and lend their testimony to the wide range of his art.

THE COMPLETE SONNETS, SONGS AND POEMS OF SHAKESPEARE. Ed. by Oscar J. Campbell *Schocken* 1965 $6.50 pap. $1.95; ed. by H. W. Simon *Simon & Schuster* (Washington Square) 1951 pap. $.45

SONNETS. Ed. by Hyder E. Rollins *AHM Pub. Corp.* Crofts Classics pap. $.50; ed. by Hyder E. Rollins *American Scholars Pubns.* New Variorum 2 vols. each $17.50; ed. by Martin Seymour-Smith 1966 $1.75; ed. by John Dover Wilson *Cambridge* New Shakespeare Ed. 1966 $5.50; ed. by Francis Fergusson introd. by C. L. Barber *Dell* pap. $.35; *Doubleday* Dolphin Bks. 1960 pap. $.95; ed. by A. L. Rowse *Harper* 1973 $8.95; ed. by W. G. Ingram and Theodore Redpath *Harper* (Barnes & Noble) 1965 $7.50; ed. by William Burto *New Am. Lib.* pap. $.75; ed. by Barbara H. Smith *New York Univ. Press* 1969 $8.95; ed. by Douglas Bush *Penguin* 1961 pap. $1.75; ed. by Louis B. Wright and Virginia LaMar *Simon & Schuster* (Washington Square) Folger Lib. Ser. 1969 pap. $.95; ed. by George Lyman Kittredge and Irving Ribner *Xerox College Publishing* 1968 pap. $1.00; ed. by E. B. Reed *Yale Univ. Press* Yale Shakespeare ed. 1923 $4.00

LOVE POEMS AND SONNETS. Ill. by Vera Bock *Doubleday* 1957 $3.95

THE POEMS AND SONNETS. *Assoc. Booksellers* Airmont Bks. pap. $.60; ed. by Gwyn Jones *A. S. Barnes* Golden Cockerel Press special ed. $40.00 standard ed. $20.00

POEMS. Ed. by Hyder E. Rollins *American Scholar Pubns.* $17.50 supplementary bibliography pap. $2.00; *Cambridge* New Shakespeare Ed. $6.50 pap. $1.65; comp. by Lloyd Frankenberg *T. Y. Crowell* 1966 $3.50 lib. bdg. $4.25; ed. by William Empson and William Burto *New Am. Lib.* 1968 $.95; ed. by A. Harbage and R. Wilbur *Penguin* pap. $.95; ed. by F. T. Prince *Harper* (Barnes & Noble) 1960 1969 $8.75 pap. $2.25; ed. by Louis B. Wright and Virginia LaMar *Simon & Schuster* (Washington Square) Folger Library Series 1969 $.50

TALES FROM SHAKESPEARE

The "Tales from Shakespeare" by Charles and Mary Lamb was written for William Godwin and published first in his Juvenile Library in 1807. The tragedies were told by Charles Lamb and the comedies by his sister. As the historical plays of Shakespeare were not included among the Tales, several modern editions have added them.

Chute, Marchette G. STORIES FROM SHAKESPEARE. *Collins-World* 1956 $5.95; *New Am. Lib.* Mentor Bks. 1959 pap. $1.25

A complete retelling of all the plays in 20th century language for both adults and young people. This is the very best of the modern versions. "Sensibly, she has given briefer accounts to those of least value. With the truly great plays she is admirable, blending an unobtrusive eloquence of her own and a sensitivity of interpretation with her generous use of quotations from the plays"—(*N.Y. Times*).

Deutsch, Babette. THE READER'S SHAKESPEARE. Decorations by Warren Chappell *Simon & Schuster* (Messner) 1946 $6.95. 15 of the plays are related in straight narrative prose form, using the poet's words whenever possible; intended for grown-ups, not children.

Lamb, Charles, and Mary Lamb. TALES FROM SHAKESPEARE. Ill. by Elinore Blaisdell *T. Y. Crowell* 1942 $4.50; *Dutton* Childrens Ill. Class. $4.50 Everyman's pap. $1.50; ill. by John C. Wonsetter *Macmillan* New Chil. Class. 1963 $4.95; (with title "Ten Tales from Shakespeare") *Franklin Watts* 1969 $5.95

BIOGRAPHIES

Although most readers own a well-edited Shakespeare, "it is far less certain that they possess a first-rate biography of the world's greatest poet and dramatist," writes Clifton Fadiman in the *Book-of-the-Month Club News*. "The omission is understandable, for it is commonly thought that we know so little about Shakespeare's career that a good encyclopedia summary should suffice for most purposes. The fact is, however, that we know a great deal, and that in the past twenty years or so scholars have been patiently adding to an already considerable store of reliable information. Will Shakespeare has ceased to be a shadowy figure; we can at least draw his profile and fill in here and there with rich details."

Barring some fortuitous accidents, we are unlikely to add more substance to our knowledge of Shakespeare's life. The question of Shakespeare's education being incommensurate with the learning demonstrated in his plays, which led to the controversy over his authorship, has been effectively answered by a wider understanding of the educational system in England and particularly in Stratford. No reputable Shakespeare scholar today considers the question of his authorship debatable. Recently, the Samuel Schoenbaum biography, "William Shakespeare: A Documentary Life," has enriched the materials available to us by providing facsimiles of the records relating to Shakespeare. It is a welcome addition to scholarship. Among the other biographies, E. K. Chambers' comprehensive work is notable.

Adams, Joseph Quincy. A LIFE OF WILLIAM SHAKESPEARE. 1923. *Houghton* 1927 $10.95. By the late Librarian of the Folger Library.

Bentley, Gerald Eades. SHAKESPEARE: A Biographical Handbook. *Yale Univ. Press* 1961 pap. $2.95

Chambers, Sir Edmund K. A SHORT LIFE OF SHAKESPEARE WITH SOURCES. *Oxford* 1933 $3.50. Abr. by Charles Williams from the following work. *Oxford* 1933 $3.50

WILLIAM SHAKESPEARE: A Study of Facts and Problems. *Oxford* 2 vols. 1930 set $17.00. These volumes provide a valuable, extensive collection of materials not only on Shakespeare's life but also on the customs, laws, and theaters of his day.

Chute, Marchette Gaylord. SHAKESPEARE OF LONDON. *Dutton* 1949 $8.95 pap. $2.25. An excellent and readable biography for the general reader with emphasis on the re-created background; based on source material dated up to 1635.

Eccles, Mark. SHAKESPEARE IN WARWICKSHIRE. *Univ. of Wisconsin Press* 1962 $10.00; *Somerset Pubs.* $7.50. Brings together what is known about the years in Stratford.

Neilson, William Allan and Ashley Horace Thorndike. FACTS ABOUT SHAKESPEARE. 1913 rev. ed. 1931. *Somerset Pubs.* $11.50; *Richard West* $11.25. Known facts of his life; chronology of the plays; history of the texts; Elizabethan theater; index to the characters of the plays; index to the songs; Shakespeare's will; inscription on his monument; introduction to the first folio.

Rowse, Alfred L. SHAKESPEARE THE MAN. *Harper* 1973 $10.00. The major addition to Shakespeare's biography in this work is the proposed identification of the Dark Lady of the sonnets as Emilia Lanier.

Schoenbaum, Samuel. SHAKESPEARE'S LIVES. *Oxford* 1970 $15.00. A scholarly and inter-esting evaluation of the previous biographies with a review of the available evidence.

WILLIAM SHAKESPEARE: A Documentary Life. *Oxford* 1975 $50.00. This work includes over 200 facsimiles of Shakespeare records. Its contribution to the availability and preservation of the evidence is immeasurable.

Wilson, John Dover. THE ESSENTIAL SHAKESPEARE: A Biographical Adventure. By the editor of "The New Shakespeare." *Cambridge* 1932 1960 pap. $2.65

CRITICISM

Battles continue to be fought and reappraisals made in the great field of Shakespeare criticism as evidenced by the number of new and newly reprinted titles here. (With a very few exceptions, critical books on a single play only have not been included.) The following works give a good general introduction to the plays and poems. It is a selective list, be-cause the "field of Shakespeare studies is a fertile one, and has been so for a long time, until, in our time, books and articles about Shakespeare come out at the rate of a thou-sand a year. Of course there is little agreement among them: that is why they come out in such numbers"—(Edward Hubler, in the *N.Y. Times*). (*See also* Reader's Adviser *Chapter 1, Drama, Section on Dramatic Criticism and History, and Chapter 2, British Drama: Early to 18th Century, Section on Elizabethan Drama: General History and Criticism*).

Anthologies of Criticism (by date of publication)

SHAKESPEARE CRITICISM: A Selection. Ed. by D. Nichol Smith *Oxford* 1916 $3.50

SHAKESPEAREAN CRITICISM. Ed. by Anne Bradby Ridler *Oxford* World's Class. Vol. I 1919–1935 $1.75 Vol. 2 1935–1960 (1963) $2.75. Modern criticism from the years in-dicated.

SHAKESPEARE: Modern Essays in Criticism. Ed. by Leonard Fellows Dean *Oxford* 1957 rev. ed. 1967 Galaxy Bks. pap. $3.95. A good sampler of all the "new criticism," for the general reader as well as the scholar.

THE EARLY SHAKESPEARE. Vol. 3 Stratford-upon-Avon Studies, Shakespeare Institute, Stratford-upon-Avon. Gen. Eds., Bernard Harris and John R. Brown 1961 *Schocken* 1966 pap. $1.95

HIS INFINITE VARIETY: Major Shakespeare Criticism since Johnson. Ed. by Paul N. Siegel. 1964. *Bks. for Libraries* $15.00

SHAKESPEARE'S CRITICS: From Jonson to Auden. Ed. by A. M. Eastman and G. B. Harri-son *Univ. of Michigan Press* 1964 $9.00 pap. $4.50

SHAKESPEARE: The Tragedies. Ed. by Clifford Leech *Univ. of Chicago Press* 1965 pap. $2.45

SHAKESPEARE: A Collection of Critical Essays. The Histories, ed. by Eugene M. Waith; The Comedies, ed. by K. Muir; The Tragedies, ed. by Alfred Harbage *Prentice-Hall* 3 vols. each $7.95 pap. each $1.95–$2.45

ESSAYS IN SHAKESPEAREAN CRITICISM. Ed. by James L. Calderwood and Harold E. Toliver *Prentice-Hall* 1970 pap. $4.95

TWENTIETH CENTURY INTERPRETATIONS. Ed. by Maynard Mack *Prentice-Hall* 13 vols. 1968–1970 each $6.95 pap. $1.25. These volumes are collections of critical essays, each with its own editor, for the following plays: As You Like It; Coriolanus; Hamlet; Henry IV, Part I; Henry IV, Part II; Henry V; Julius Caesar; Measure for Measure;

The Merchant of Venice; Much Ado about Nothing; Richard II; Romeo and Juliet; The Tempest; Twelfth Night.

Individual Works

Alexander, Peter. SHAKESPEARE'S LIFE AND ART. *New York Univ. Press* 1961 $7.94 pap. $2.45. A concise compendium of relevant information about each play.

Armstrong, Edward A. SHAKESPEARE'S IMAGINATION: A Study of the Psychology of Association and Inspiration. *Univ. of Nebraska Press* Bison Bks. reissue 1963 pap. $2.45; *Peter Smith* $4.50

Barber, Cesar L. SHAKESPEARE'S FESTIVE COMEDY. 1959. *Princeton Univ. Press* 1972 $11.50 pap. $3.45

Battenhouse, Roy W. SHAKESPEAREAN TRAGEDY: Its Art and Its Christian Premises. *Indiana Univ. Press* 1969 $17.50

Berry, Ralph. SHAKESPEARE'S COMEDIES: Explorations in Form. *Princeton Univ. Press* 1972 $10.00

Bethel, S. L. SHAKESPEARE AND THE POPULAR DRAMATIC TRADITION. 1945. *Octagon* $9.50

Booth, Stephen. AN ESSAY ON SHAKESPEARE'S SONNETS. *Yale Univ. Press* 1969 $10.00 pap. $2.95

Bradley, Andrew Cecil. SHAKESPEAREAN TRAGEDY: Lectures on Hamlet, Othello, King Lear, Macbeth. 1904 1905. *Fawcett* World pap. $1.50; *St. Martin's* repr. of 1905 ed. $12.95 pap. 1956 $2.75. One of the best critical commentaries.

Brown, John Russell. SHAKESPEARE AND HIS COMEDIES. 1957. 2nd ed. *Harper* (Barnes & Noble-Methuen) pap. $2.50

  SHAKESPEARE'S PLAYS IN PERFORMANCE. *St. Martin's* 1967 $8.50

  (With Bernard Harris, Eds.) HAMLET. Stratford-upon-Avon Studies No. 5. *St. Martin's* 1964 $8.95

  (With Bernard Harris, Eds.) LATER SHAKESPEARE. Stratford-upon-Avon Studies No. 8. *St. Martin's* 1967 $5.75

Burckhardt, Sigurd. SHAKESPEAREAN MEANINGS. *Princeton Univ. Press* 1968 $12.50

Campbell, Lily Bess. SHAKESPEARE'S "HISTORIES": Mirrors of Elizabethan Policy. *Huntington Library* 1947 $10.00

  SHAKESPEARE'S TRAGIC HEROES. 1930 1952. *Harper* (Barnes & Noble) 1960 $6.50 pap. $1.95

Chambers, Sir Edmund K. SHAKESPEARE: A Survey. 1926 5th impression 1951. *Farrar, Straus* (Hill & Wang) Dramabks. 1958 pap. $1.95. An invaluable book of his play prefaces.

Champion, Larry S. THE EVOLUTION OF SHAKESPEARE'S COMEDY: A Study in Dramatic Perspective. *Harvard Univ. Press* 1970 $8.50 pap. $2.95

Charney, Maurice. SHAKESPEARE'S ROMAN PLAYS. *Harvard Univ. Press* 1961 $7.00

Chute, Marchette Gaylord. INTRODUCTION TO SHAKESPEARE. *Dutton* 1951 $3.95. Excellent brief study of his world and theater written for high school age.

Clemen, Wolfgang H. THE DEVELOPMENT OF SHAKESPEARE'S IMAGERY. *Harvard Univ. Press* 1951 $6.00; *Farrar, Straus* (Hill & Wang) Dramabks. 1962 pap. $2.25. An essential and stimulating study first published in German in 1936.

Coghill, Nevill. SHAKESPEARE'S PROFESSIONAL SKILLS. *Cambridge* 1964 $11.50

Coleridge, Samuel Taylor. SHAKESPEAREAN CRITICISM. Ed. by T. M. Raysor. *Dutton* Everyman's 2 vols. each $3.95

Colie, Rosalie L. SHAKESPEARE'S LIVING ART. *Princeton Univ. Press* 1974 $18.50 pap. $9.75

Crane, Milton. SHAKESPEARE'S PROSE. *Univ. of Chicago Press* 1941 $7.50. The author "shows that Shakespeare has a dramatic reason for using prose, or for shifting from blank verse to prose and back again."

Cruttwell, Patrick. THE SHAKESPEAREAN MOMENT AND ITS PLACE IN THE POETRY OF THE SEVENTEENTH CENTURY. *Columbia* 1955 $10.00

Danby, John F. SHAKESPEARE'S DOCTRINE OF NATURE. Study of "King Lear." 1961. *Hillary House* $7.75 pap. $3.25

Dowden, Edward. SHAKESPEARE: A Critical Study of His Mind and Art. 1872. *Folcroft* repr. of 1962 ed. 1973 $8.00; *Gordon Press* $27.00. There have been many editions of this famous classic by the erudite and sensitive critic, Professor of English in the University of Dublin for many years.

Eastman, Arthur M. A SHORT HISTORY OF SHAKESPEARIAN CRITICISM. 1968. *Norton* Norton Lib. 1974 pap. $3.95

"The commentary in these pages is wide, learned, ingenious and full of penetrating and striking insights. . . . The notes . . . add up to a good-sized bibliography. . . . An example of what a scholarly work should be"—(Eliot Fremont-Smith).

Ellis-Fermor, Una. SHAKESPEARE THE DRAMATIST. Ed. by Kenneth Muir. 1948. *Harper* (Barnes & Noble) 1961 $11.50; *Folcroft* $4.50

Evans, Bertrand. SHAKESPEARE'S COMEDIES. *Oxford* 1960 $12.25 pap. $2.50

Evans, G. Blakemore, Ed. SHAKESPEAREAN PROMPT-BOOKS OF THE SEVENTEENTH CENTURY. *Univ. Press of Virginia.* The following volumes are available: Vol. 3, Pt. 1 The Comedy of Errors, Pt. 2 A Midsummer Night's Dream boxed set pap. $15.00 Vol. 4 Hamlet pap. boxed $17.00 Vol. 5 Smock Alley Macbeth pap. boxed $25.00

Farnham, Willard. SHAKESPEARE'S TRAGIC FRONTIER: The World of His Final Tragedies. 1950. *Harper* (Barnes & Noble) 1973 $9.50. An important critical study.

Frye, Northrup. FOOLS OF TIME: Studies in Shakespearean Tragedy. *Univ. of Toronto Press* 1967 $4.95 pap. $2.95

A NATURAL PERSPECTIVE: The Development of Shakespearean Comedy and Romance. *Columbia* 1965 $9.00; *Harcourt* Harbinger Bks. 1969 pap. $2.25

Goddard, Harold C. THE MEANING OF SHAKESPEARE. *Univ. of Chicago Press* 1951 $12.50 Phoenix Bks. 2 vols. 1960 pap. Vol. I $3.95 Vol. 2 $3.25

Goldsmith, Robert H. WISE FOOLS IN SHAKESPEARE. *Michigan State Univ. Press* 1963 $5.50. "Shakespeare's wise fool alters the tone and meaning of the play of which he is a part."

Granville-Barker, Harley. PREFACES TO SHAKESPEARE. *Princeton Univ. Press* 4 vols. 1965 each $7.50 pap. each $2.95. Vol. 1 Hamlet (o.p.) Vol. 2 King Lear, Cymbeline and Julius Caesar Vol. 3 Coriolanus, Antony and Cleopatra Vol. 4 Love's Labour's Lost, Romeo and Juliet, The Merchant of Venice and Othello

Granville-Barker, scholar, playwright and director wrote these prefaces over a period of nearly 20 years, the "Hamlet" preface appearing in 1937, and the others seven years earlier. This American edition is invaluable in its illumination of Shakespeare's theater intention and working practice.

Harbage, Alfred Bennett. As THEY LIKED IT: A Study of Shakespeare's Moral Artistry. *Peter Smith* 1961 $5.00; *Univ. of Pennsylvania* 1972 pap. $2.95

SHAKESPEARE AND THE RIVAL TRADITIONS. *Indiana Univ. Press* 1970 pap. $3.45

Harrison, George B. INTRODUCING SHAKESPEARE. 1939. *Penguin* 1966 pap. $1.75; *Somerset Pubs.* $6.00

SHAKESPEARE AT WORK, 1592–1603. With a new preface by the author. (First published under the title "Shakespeare under Elizabeth.") 1933. *Univ. of Michigan Press* Ann Arbor Bks. 1958 pap. $1.95

SHAKESPEARE'S TRAGEDIES. 1952. *Routledge & Kegan Paul* 1951 $9.25 pap. $3.00. Stimulating reading based on sound scholarship.

Hubler, Edward. THE SENSE OF SHAKESPEARE'S SONNETS. 1952 rev. 1954. (o.p.)

"In an appendix to a penetrating and lively discussion of the sonnets, Professor Hubler not only states the evidence and explains the reasoning that certify to Shakespeare's authorship of the plays. He also attacks the anti-Stratfordians head-on, indiscriminately lumping as 'Baconians' those who assign the authorship to Bacon, Oxford, Derby or Dyer, and he would probably add Marlowe and Queen Elizabeth today, to say nothing of the social circle of nabobs who scribbled off the dramas when they were not blowing sweet airs through recorders. . . . All the other theories (which really ought to cancel each other out) are 'monstrous nonsense,' he says"—(Brooks Atkinson, in the *N.Y. Times*).

Hunter, Robert G. SHAKESPEARE AND THE COMEDY OF FORGIVENESS. *Columbia* 1965 $10.00

Johnson, Dr. Samuel. JOHNSON ON SHAKESPEARE. Ed. by Walter A. Raleigh. Collected prefaces written for his edition of the Plays in 8 volumes in 1765. *Oxford* 1968 $3.25; ed. by Arthur Sherbo, introd. by Bertrand Bronson *Yale Univ. Press* 2 vols. 1965 set $45.00

Knight, G(eorge) Wilson. THE CROWN OF LIFE: Essays in Interpretation of Shakespeare's Final Plays. 1952 2nd ed. 1953. *Harper* (Barnes & Noble) 1961 $7.50 pap. $3.50

THE IMPERIAL THEME: Further Interpretations of Shakespeare's Tragedies Including the Roman Plays. 1931. *Harper* (Barnes & Noble) 3rd ed. 1961 $10.00 1966 pap. $2.95

THE MUTUAL FLAME: Definitive and scholarly study of the "Sonnets" and "The Phoenix and the Turtle." 1955. *Harper* (Barnes & Noble) 1962 1973 $12.50

SHAKESPEARE AND RELIGION: Essays of Forty Years. *Routledge & Kegan Paul* 1967 $14.25; *Simon & Schuster* Clarion Bks. 1968 pap. $2.95

THE SHAKESPEARIAN TEMPEST: With a Chart of Shakespeare's Dramatic Universe. 1932 3rd rev. ed. 1953. *Harper* (Barnes & Noble) $7.25 pap. $4.00

THE WHEEL OF FIRE: Interpretation of Shakespeare's Tragedies. With three new essays. 1930. *Harper* (Barnes & Noble) 4th rev. ed. 1962 $9.50 pap. $4.50

Knights, Lionel C. SOME SHAKESPEAREAN THEMES. *Stanford Univ. Press* 1960 pap. $2.95

Kott, Jan. SHAKESPEARE OUR CONTEMPORARY. Trans. from the Polish by Boleslaw Taborski; introd. by Martin Esslin. 1964. *Norton* Norton Lib. 1974 $3.95. A controversial but most interesting interpretation from the perspective of the theater of the absurd.

Leishman, J. B. THEMES AND VARIATIONS IN SHAKESPEARE'S SONNETS. 1961. *Hillary House* Hutchinson Univ. Lib. $6.50

LeWinter, Oscar, Ed. SHAKESPEARE IN EUROPE. *Peter Smith* $5.50. A careful sampling of hitherto scattered or inaccessible Continental comment; includes Voltaire, Lessing, Goethe, Schiller, Hugo, Turgenev, Tolstoy, Ortega y Gasset among others.

Ludowyck, E. F. C. UNDERSTANDING SHAKESPEARE. *Cambridge* 1962 $9.50 pap. $3.45

This is an introductory book for the general reader, the teacher and the student. It includes a general introduction to Shakespeare: his life and times, Elizabethan dramatic tradition, as well as detailed studies of Richard II, The Merchant of Venice, Henry V, Julius Caesar, Twelfth Night and Macbeth.

McElroy, Bernard. SHAKESPEARE'S MATURE TRAGEDIES. *Princeton Univ. Press* 1973 $10.00

McFarland, Thomas. SHAKESPEARE'S PASTORAL COMEDY. *Univ. of North Carolina Press* 1972 $8.95

Mack, Maynard. KING LEAR IN OUR TIME. *Univ. of California Press* 1965 $8.75 pap. $2.35

Martin, Philip. SHAKESPEARE'S SONNETS: Self, Love and Art. *Cambridge* 1972 $11.50

Nevo, Ruth. TRAGIC FORM IN SHAKESPEARE. *Princeton Univ. Press* 1972 $15.00

Ornstein, Robert. A KINGDOM FOR A STAGE: The Achievement of Shakespeare's History Plays. *Harvard Univ. Press* 1972 $11.00

Palmer, John. POLITICAL AND COMIC CHARACTERS OF SHAKESPEARE. *St. Martin's* 1945–46 1962 pap. $6.95. Studies of Berowne. Touchstone, Shylock, Bottom, Beatrice and Benedick, by an author who believes that "sympathy, . . . and not satire, is the inspiration of Shakespeare's comedy."

Parrott, Thomas M. SHAKESPEAREAN COMEDY. 1949 *Russell & Russell* 1962 $12.50. An historical and systematic study.

Partridge, Eric. SHAKESPEARE'S BAWDY: A Literary and Psychological Essay and a Comprehensive Glossary. *Dutton* 1947 rev. ed. 1955 pap. $1.95

Pierce, Robert B. SHAKESPEARE'S HISTORY PLAYS: The Family and the State. *Ohio State Univ. Press* 1971 $8.75

Proser, Matthew N. THE HEROIC IMAGE IN FIVE SHAKESPEAREAN TRAGEDIES. *Princeton Univ. Press* 1965 $10.50

Ralli, Augustus John. A HISTORY OF SHAKESPEAREAN CRITICISM. 1930. *Humanities Press* 2 vols. set $27.50. An invaluable source book.

Reese, Max Meredith. THE CEASE OF MAJESTY: A Study of Shakespeare's History Plays. *St. Martin's* 1961 $10.95. An authoritative finely written study.

   SHAKESPEARE: His World and His Work. *St. Martin's* 1953 $12.95. An excellent critical introduction, "well researched, interestingly written and scholarly"; well indexed.

Ribner, Irving. PATTERNS IN SHAKESPEAREAN TRAGEDY. *Harper* (Barnes & Noble) 1960 1969 $7.50 pap. $3.00

Rose, Mark. SHAKESPEAREAN DESIGN. *Harvard Univ. Press* 1972 $7.95 pap. $2.95

Rossiter, Arthur P. ANGEL WITH HORNS AND OTHER LECTURES ON SHAKESPEARE. *Theatre Arts* 1961 pap. $4.45. A compilation of lectures by a great English scholar and persuasive lecturer.

Schanzer, Ernest. THE PROBLEM PLAYS OF SHAKESPEARE: A Study of "Julius Caesar," "Measure for Measure," "Anthony and Cleopatra." *Schocken* 1963 pap. $1.95
   Professor Schanzer of the University of Liverpool takes over from F. S. Boas (1896), W. H. Lawrence (1931) and E. M. W. Tillyard (1951) in his well-documented study. His arguments are persuasive and his critiques are highly recommended.

Sen Gupta, S. C. SHAKESPEARE'S HISTORICAL PLAYS. *Oxford* 1964 $6.00

Seng, Peter J. THE VOCAL SONGS IN THE PLAYS OF SHAKESPEARE: A Critical History. *Harvard Univ. Press* 1967 $9.75

Sewell, Arthur. CHARACTER AND SOCIETY IN SHAKESPEARE. *Oxford* 1951 $5.00

Shaw, George Bernard. SHAW ON SHAKESPEARE: An Anthology of Bernard Shaw's Writings on the Plays and Production of Shakespeare. Ed. by Edwin Wilson. 1961. *Bks. for Libraries* $11.50

Siegel, Paul. SHAKESPEAREAN TRAGEDY AND THE ELIZABETHAN COMPROMISE. 1957. *Bks. for Libraries* $11.00

Simmons, J. L. SHAKESPEARE'S PAGAN WORLD: A Study of the Roman Tragedies. *Univ. Press of Virginia* 1973 $8.75

Simpson, Percy. STUDIES IN ELIZABETHAN DRAMA. 1955. *Folcroft* $20.00

Spencer, Theodore. SHAKESPEARE AND THE NATURE OF MAN. *Macmillan* 1942 2nd ed. 1949 reissue 1951 $6.00 pap. $1.95
   A book of "genuine scholarship with a rich cultural background, written in a style of admirable precision and at times of eloquence. I believe that it will prove a lasting contribution to the interpretation and enjoyment of Shakespeare"—(W. A. Neilson).

Spivack, Bernard. SHAKESPEARE AND THE ALLEGORY OF EVIL. *Columbia* 1958 $15.00. A massive and admirable contribution.

Sprague, Arthur C. SHAKESPEARE AND THE ACTORS: The Stage Business in His Plays (1660–1905). 1914. *Russell & Russell* 1963 $15.00

SHAKESPEARE AND THE AUDIENCE: A Study of the Technique of Exposition. 1935. *Russell & Russell* 1966 $8.50

Spurgeon, Caroline F. E. SHAKESPEARE'S IMAGERY AND WHAT IT TELLS US. 1935. *Cambridge* 1952 $13.95 pap. $3.95. A splendid book that helps to fathom the depth of the poet's character.

Stirling, Brents. UNITY IN SHAKESPEARIAN TRAGEDY: The Interplay of Theme and Character. 1956. *Gordian* 1966 $7.00. This "genuine contribution to Shakespearean scholarship" studies seven tragedies.

Stoll, Elmer Edgar. SHAKESPEARE AND OTHER MASTERS. 1940. *Russell & Russell* 1962 $9.50

Tillyard, E. M. W. ESSAYS LITERARY AND EDUCATIONAL. *Harper* (Barnes & Noble) 1962 $6.00. The first five of the Literary Essays are devoted to Shakespeare.

SHAKESPEARE'S HISTORY PLAYS. 1946. *Harper* (Barnes & Noble) 2nd ed. 1964 $8.00; *Macmillan* Collier Bks. $1.50

Shakespeare's philosophy of history in relation to Elizabethan beliefs concerning the universe. Dr. Tillyard discusses the Elizabethan view of the philosophical, spiritual and physical world in his small volume "The Elizabethan World Picture" (*Macmillan* 1944 1961 $2.50; *Random* Vintage Bks. pap. $1.25).

SHAKESPEARE'S LAST PLAYS. 1938. *Harper* (Barnes & Noble) 6th ed. 1964 $2.25. A study of Cymbeline, The Winter's Tale, and The Tempest.

SHAKESPEARE'S PROBLEM PLAYS. *Univ. of Toronto Press* 1949 pap. $2.25

Traversi, Derek Antona. AN APPROACH TO SHAKESPEARE. *Doubleday* 1938 1956 3rd ed. enl. and expanded 1969 $4.50 Anchor Bks. 2 vols. Vol. I From Henry VI to Twelfth Night Vol. 2 From Troilus and Cressida to the Tempest pap. each $1.95

SHAKESPEARE: From Richard II to Henry V. *Stanford Univ. Press* 1967 $6.00. Brilliant analysis of the second cycle of historical plays by this penetrating and readable critic.

SHAKESPEARE: The Last Phase. *Stanford Univ. Press* 1955 $7.50. Valuable criticism of Pericles, The Winter's Tale, Cymbeline and The Tempest.

SHAKESPEARE: The Roman Plays. *Stanford Univ. Press* 1963 $7.50

Van Doren, Mark. SHAKESPEARE. 1939. *Doubleday* Anchor Bks. 1953 pap. $1.95. Essays on each of Shakespeare's plays and a chapter on his poems.

Vyvyan, John. SHAKESPEARE AND THE ROSE OF LOVE. 1960. *Rowman* 1968 $4.00

Wilson, J. Dover. THE FORTUNES OF FALSTAFF. *Cambridge* 1943 $5.00

AN INTRODUCTION TO THE SONNETS OF SHAKESPEARE: For the Use of Historians. 1964, o.p. (*See comment under Section on Songs, Sonnets and Poems.*)

WHAT HAPPENS IN HAMLET. 1935. *Cambridge* 3rd ed. $13.00 pap. $3.75

Winny, James. THE PLAYER KING: A Theme of Shakespeare's Histories. *Harper* (Barnes & Noble) 1968 $6.00

—E.J.A.

Chapter 4

Modern British Drama

"ROSENCRANTZ [*practising what he'll say to Hamlet*]. *To sum up: Your father, whom you love, dies, you are his heir, you come back to find that hardly was the corpse cold before his young brother popped onto his throne and into his sheets, thereby offending both legal and natural practice. Now, why exactly are you behaving in this extraordinary manner?*"

—TOM STOPPARD

In England, playgoing has so long been a popular national habit that the outside "foreign" observer may find even a slump period in the theater relatively vigorous. To "insiders" during the early fifties however, there was a feeling that the English stage had gone stagnant. "Playgoing had become dull; it was a safety first theatre." Revivals were the order of the day along with foreign imports and long runs featuring famous actresses. "Then, on May 8, 1956, came the revolution." "The event which marks 'then' off decisively from 'now' is the first performance of 'Look Back In Anger,' " wrote John Russell Taylor in 1962. Osborne's play established "a new intellectual climate . . . a return to a direct language without polite euphemisms"—(Lumley in *Trends in 20th Century Drama*). Since that time, wrote Martin Esslin, "we have seen the emergence of a real 'new wave' of British dramatists."

Who were these new dramatists of the sixties? Their names included Osborne, Harold Pinter, Arnold Wesker, Robert Bolt, N. R. Simpson, Shelagh Delaney, Brendan Behan, Alun Owen, John Arden, John Mortimer, John Whiting, Ann Jellicoe ("The Knack"), Peter Shaffer, and Henry Livings ("Eh?"). Most of them were under forty; many were under thirty. Their youth was one of the "new" facts worth noting. Another fact that Taylor found "even stranger in the context of British drama" was that many of them came from working-class backgrounds and wrote about working-class life. Most were doing something else, unconnected with or only partially related to writing for the theater, when the commercial and critical success of Osborne's play opened the door for them.

A point of real importance to the emergence of the new drama was that the young playwright in England could manage to support himself decently by writing for stage or radio or television. BBC broadcasts over 400 plays a year, so television has been a force of inestimable benefit to the new dramatists both in commissioning work and in familiarizing a vast audience with their style. For several of the younger writers success in radio and television preceded success in theater. Frequently the work of the new dramatists was directly subsidized by Arts Council grants or play competitions.

What differentiated the "new wave" of dramatists from what was already there? Esslin has commented that "the 'new wave' . . . is above all distinguished by its determined effort to achieve a liberation from the cramping conventions of the old well-made play." And there was an attempt to discover a "new level of authenticity" in realistic drama by using the spoken vernacular of middle and lower class English.

By the seventies, the New Wave had definitely passed. The English Stage Company, which had produced "Look Back in Anger," was still doing a valuable job in promoting Edward Bond and Joe Orton at the Royal Court Theatre. But the focus for serious audiences in Britain had shifted to the vigorous productions of modern and classic drama by the Royal Shakespeare Company and, especially, the National Theatre, which had been firmly established in the previous decade under the direction of Sir Laurence Olivier and his literary manager, Kenneth Tynan. It is from the National Theatre's Old Vic stage that the major works of Stoppard, Shaffer, and Pinter today begin their transatlantic voyages.

Looking back calmly, it is hard for even the most enthusiastic publicists of the New Dra-

ma to see exactly what had struck them as "new" in the socially conscious realism of De-
lany and Wesker, the conservative plotting of Shaffer and Bolt, or even the warmed-over
Beckett and Brecht of the early Stoppard and Arden. There had been new playwrights a
decade ago; there are new playwrights today. But perhaps, a contrite John Russell Taylor
has recently confessed, there never was any such thing as a "New Drama."

What may come to seem more important than momentary drama movements is the
continuity which joins the "New Dramatist" to his forebears and successors in modern
English theatre. The traditional culture of the music hall for instance runs from O'Casey's
"Juno" through Osborne's "Entertainer" and Behan's "Hostage" (and other Joan Little-
wood entertainments) to the vaudevilles of Stoppard. English parodies of melodrama are
as old as Gilbert and Shaw, as new as Orton and Nichols. Most of all, the tradition of
modern English drama is formed around a concern with language, with a "voice" which
defines and defies the social system. From "Pygmalion" to "Roots," from Jimmy Porter's
rant to the delicate philosophic musings of the professor in "Jumpers," language has been
the subject as well as the medium of the English playwright.

RECENT COLLECTIONS

Ashley, Leonard R. N. NINETEENTH-CENTURY BRITISH DRAMA: An Anthology of Representative Plays. *Scott, Foresman* 1967 pap. (orig.) $7.50. Each of these 12 full-length
   and 3 short plays illuminates a different aspect of British drama of the period.

Bailey, James O. BRITISH PLAYS OF THE NINETEENTH CENTURY. *Bobbs* Odyssey 1966 $9.25

Clurman, Harold. SEVEN PLAYS OF THE MODERN THEATRE. *Grove* 1962 pap. $4.95. Includes
   Pinter: The Birthday Party; Behan: The Quare Fellow; Delaney: A Taste of Honey.

Corrigan, Robert W. MASTERPIECES OF THE MODERN ENGLISH THEATER. *Macmillan* Collier
   Bks. 1965 1967 pap. $1.50. Wilde, Barre, Shaw, Galsworthy, Kops.

   (Ed.) THE TWENTIETH CENTURY BRITISH DRAMA. *Dell* Laurel 1965 pap. $.95
      Shaw: Heartbreak House; Galsworthy: Loyalties; Coward: Private Lives; Bagnold: The Chalk
   Garden; Bolt: A Man for All Seasons; Jellicoe: The Knack. Each play is accompanied by an essay
   by the playwright or a critic.

Fitzjohn, Donald. ENGLISH ONE-ACT PLAYS OF TODAY. *Oxford* 1962 pap. $2.25. Eight plays
   by British and American dramatists.

Popkin, Henry, Ed. MODERN BRITISH DRAMA. *Grove* 1964 pap. $5.95
      Delany: A Taste of Honey; Behan: The Hostage; Wesker: Roots; Arden: Serjeant Musgrave's
   Dance; Simpson: One Way Pendulum; Pinter: The Caretaker. Notes on the theatre by directors
   and playwrights.

Rowley, George. NINETEENTH CENTURY PLAYS. *Oxford* The World's Classics 1972 pap.
   $2.95
      Jerrold: Black-Ey'd Susan; Bulwer-Lytton: Money; Reade and Taylor: Masks and Faces;
   Boucicault: The Colleen Bawn; Bradon and Hazlewood: Lady Audley's Secret; Taylor: The Tick-
   et of Leave Man; Robertson: Caste; Albery: Two Roses; Lewis: The Bells; Grundy: A Pair of Spec-
   tacles.

Salerno, Henry F. ENGLISH DRAMA IN TRANSITION, 1880–1920. *Pegasus* 1968 $11.95 pap.
   $3.95
      Henry Arthur Jones: The Liars; Pinero: The Second Mrs. Tanqueray; Wilde: The Importance
   of Being Earnest; Shaw: Major Barbara; Barrie: The Admirable Crichton; Galsworthy: The Silver
   Box; Yeats: Dierdre; Synge: The Playboy of the Western World; Maugham: Our Betters. Critical
   introduction and notes.

Trewin, John Courtenay, Ed. PLAYS OF THE YEAR: Selections from the London Theater
   Season. *Ungar* 2 vols. a year; available from Vol. 6 (1951) onwards each vol. $7.50

Warnock, Robert. REPRESENTATIVE MODERN PLAYS: British. *Scott, Foresman* Key Eds. 1953
   pap. $5.50

Weales, Gerald. EDWARDIAN PLAYS: Maugham's Loaves and Fishes; Hankin's The Return of the Prodigal; Shaw's Getting Married; Pinero's Mid-Channel; Granville-Barker's The Madras House. *Farrar, Straus* (Hill & Wang) Mermaid Dramabks. 1962 pap. $2.45

HISTORY AND CRITICISM

Arundell, Dennis. THE STORY OF SADLER'S WELLS 1683–1964. *Theatre Arts Bks.* 1967 $6.95

Booth, M. R., and others. THE REVELS HISTORY OF DRAMA IN ENGLISH, VOLUME SIX: 1750–1880. *Harper* (Barnes & Noble) 1974 $22.50 University Paperbacks pap. $9.75. Includes a survey of social and cultural backgrounds, theatre architecture and acting styles, as well as plays and playwrights.

Brown, John Russell, Ed. MODERN BRITISH DRAMATISTS: A Collection of Critical Essays. Introd. by the editor. Twentieth Century Views Ser. *Prentice-Hall* 1968 $5.95. Esslin Taylor, Gilman, Marowitz, Brustein and others; includes chronology of important dates and sel. bibliography.

(With Bernard Harris, Eds.) CONTEMPORARY THEATRE: Stratford-upon-Avon Studies, Vol. 4. *St. Martin's* 1962 $9.95. Chapters on Arnold Wesker and Harold Pinter, verse and prose, television theater and other topics.

Craig, Edward Gordon. *See Chapter 1, Drama, Section on Dramatic Technique.*

Donoghue, Denis. THE THIRD VOICE: Modern British and American Verse Drama. *Princeton Univ. Press* 1959 $8.50 pap. $2.95

Yeats and Eliot are treated as crucial figures with shorter studies of such dramatists as Christopher Fry, E. E. Cummings, Auden, MacLeish, Pound, Wallace Stevens and Richard Eberhart.

Guthrie, Tyrone. MY LIFE IN THE THEATRE. *McGraw-Hill* 1959 $6.95

"Hilarious, engrossing, shrewd, ironic, informative, disputatious and inspiring"—(*N.Y. Times*).

Kennedy, Andrew. SIX DRAMATISTS IN SEARCH OF A LANGUAGE: Shaw, Eliot, Beckett, Pinter, Osborne, Arden. *Cambridge* 1975 $15.95 pap. $5.95

Lumley, Frederick. NEW TRENDS IN 20TH-CENTURY DRAMA: A Survey Since Ibsen and Shaw. *Oxford* Essential Bks. 1956 1960 1967 4th ed. 1972 $8.50. This contains a revised chapter on the new British playwrights.

Lytton, Edward, Earl of [who wrote novels as Bulwer-Lytton], and William Charles Macready. BULWER AND MACREADY: A Chronicle of the Early Victorian Theatre. Ed. by Charles H. Shattuck. *Univ. of Illinois Press* 1958 $6.95

McCarthy, Desmond. THE COURT THEATRE, 1904–1907: A Commentary and Criticism. Ed. by Stanley Weintraub Bks. of the Theatre Ser. *Univ. of Miami Press* 1967 $6.50

Mander, Raymond, and Joe Mitchenson. BRITISH MUSIC HALL. *British Bk. Centre* $9.95

Marowitz, Charles, and others, Eds. THE ENCORE READER: A Chronicle of the New Drama. *Harper* (Barnes & Noble) pap. $1.50. Selections from the important English theatre magazine of the fifties and sixties.

Nicoll, Allardyce. BRITISH DRAMA: An Historical Survey from the Beginnings to the Present Time. 1925. *Harper* (Barnes & Noble) 1947 1957 1963 $7.50

A HISTORY OF ENGLISH DRAMA, 1660–1900. *Cambridge* 6 vols. $105.00. Vol. 4 Early Nineteenth Century Drama, 1800–1850, originally published in 2 vols. in 1930 as "A History of Early Nineteenth Century Drama, 1800–1850," 2nd ed. 1955 $19.50. Vol. 5 Late Nineteenth Century Drama, 1850–1900, originally published in 2 vols. in 1946, rev. and enl. ed. 1959 $23.50. Vol. 6 Alphabetical Catalogue of the Plays 1959 $35.00

Reynolds, Ernest. EARLY VICTORIAN DRAMA (1830–1870). 1936. *Blom* 1965 $7.50

Spanos, William V. THE CHRISTIAN TRADITION IN MODERN BRITISH VERSE DRAMA: The Poetics of Sacramental Time. *Rutgers Univ. Press* 1967 $12.50. This study of the development of modern religious drama in Britain offers deft analyses of important plays by Eliot, Bottomley, Williams, Sayers, Masefield, Hassall, Ridler, Nicholson, Duncan and Fry.

Sterne, Richard L. John Gielgud Directs Richard Burton in "Hamlet": A Journal of Rehearsals. *Random* 1968 $8.95

"An edited version of the comprehensive notes and recorded conversations taken during the rehearsals [with] a version of the play as it was performed complete with Gielgud's directions [and] interviews with director and star" compiled by a member of the cast. "The results ought to captivate students of the theater and of the Bard"—(*N.Y. Times*).

Stokes, John. Resistible Theatres: Enterprise and Experiment in the Late Nineteenth Century. *Harper* (Barnes & Noble) 1972 $15.75

Taylor, John Russell. The Rise and Fall of the Well-Made Play. *Farrar, Straus* (Hill & Wang) Mermaid Dramabks. $5.75 pap. $1.95. From Tom Robertson in 1870 to Terence Rattigan.

The Second Wave: British Drama for the Seventies. *Farrar, Straus* (Hill & Wang) 1971 $6.95. Successor to "Anger and After," Taylor's review of the New Drama of the sixties, now out of print.

Tindall, William York. Forces in Modern British Literature 1885–1946. 1947. *Random* Vintage Bks. rev. ed. 1956 $15.50. Many modern playwrights are included in this wise and witty book.

Literary Symbol. 1955. *Indiana Univ. Press* 1958 pap. $1.95; *Peter Smith* $4.00

Tynan, Kenneth. Curtains. *Atheneum* 1961 $10.00

The former drama critic of the *Observer* (London) and (briefly) of the *New Yorker*, now Literary Manager of Britain's National Theater, gives here a "valuable . . . picture of a decade of theater, largely in England, but also in America, France, Germany and Russia." Composed mainly of articles on plays and players published during the 50s, his "view is idiosyncratic and occasionally biased, but it is sincere, animated and often illuminating."

Tynan Right and Left: Plays, Films, People, Places and Events. *Atheneum* 1967 $8.95

Watson, Ernest Bradlee. Sheridan to Robertson: A Study of the Nineteenth Century London Stage. 1926. *Blom* 1963 $12.50

See also Chapter 1, The Drama, and Chapter 2, British Drama: Early to 18th Century, this volume.

GILBERT, SIR WILLIAM SCHWENCK. 1836–1911.

Born in London, William Schwenck Gilbert served a term as a government clerk and was called to the Bar as a barrister before being decoyed into the bohemian world of Victorian comic journalism. He first achieved popularity as the author of several volumes of "Bab Ballads" (Beerbohm praised them as "silly"). He moved on to the theatre, contributing to the current rage for travesties of operas and for one-act musical "entertainments" until a blank-verse burlesque of Tennyson's "Princess" led to commissions and full-length comedies, both mythological and "modern." Still highly regarded by critics, some of these—notably "Sweethearts" (1874) and "Engaged" (1877), recently revived at the Old Vic—should be made available to readers once again. As it is, their best memorial is the early work of Bernard Shaw, who, although he polemically rejected their cynicism, was clearly influenced by Gilbert's comedies.

By the time of "Engaged," however, Gilbert's second (and more famous) dramatic career was already well under way. The collaboration with Sir Arthur Sullivan, which had begun in 1871 with the performance of "Thespis," had been firmly established by the success of "Trial by Jury" (1875). The partnership, joined by producer Richard D'Oyly Carte, lasted stormily through 25 years and 13 "Savoy" operas (so called because many were staged in D'Oyly Carte's Savoy Theatre).

Gilbert, whose merely theatrical connections (as opposed to Sullivan's serious musical credentials) held him back from formal honors, was knighted in 1907, a few years before his death.

Gilbert before Sullivan: Six Comic Plays. Ed. by Jane W. Stedman *Univ. of Chicago Press* 1967 $10.00

One-act musical "entertainments" written for Mr. and Mrs. German Reed (*see biographical note above*). No Cards (1869); Ages Ago: A Musical Legend (1869); Our Island Home (1870); A Sensation Novel in Three Volumes (1871); Eyes and No Eyes, or The Art of Seeing (1875); and Happy Arcadia (1872)—with a selected bibliography and excellent introductory essay by the editor. "A very, very, very pleasant book"—(*N.Y. Times*).

NEW AND ORIGINAL EXTRAVAGANCES. Ed. by Sir Isaac Goldberg 1931 *Branden* 13.00

MARTYN GREEN'S TREASURY OF GILBERT AND SULLIVAN. Ed. and annot. by Martyn Green;
ill. by Lucille Corcos; arrangements by Albert Sirmay *Simon & Schuster* 1961 $19.95
This music-size volume contains the librettos of 11 works, "over 100 songs arranged quite simply for voice and piano, lively illustrations (many colored) that are much in the vein, and comments (historical, descriptive, explanatory, and reminiscent) by the knowing editor, a star of the
D'Oyly Carte Opera Company for over two decades."

THE SAVOY OPERAS. *Oxford* World's Class. 2 vols. 1962–63 Vol. 1 introd. by David Cecil,
notes by Derek Hudson. Trial by Jury; The Sorcerer; H.M.S. Pinafore; The Pirates
of Penzance; Patience; Iolanthe; Princess Ida. Vol. 2 introd. by Bridget D'Oyly Carte.
The Mikado; Ruddigore; The Yeomen of the Guard; The Gondoliers; Utopia Limited; The Grand Duke. each $2.50

POEMS OF W. S. GILBERT. Ed. by William Cole *T. Y. Crowell* Poets Ser. 1967 $3.95

THE BAB BALLADS. 1869. Ed. by James Ellis *Harvard Univ. Press* 1970 $15.00; *St. Mar-
tin's* 1953 $6.75

SONGS OF TWO SAVOYARDS. 1890. *Routledge & Kegan Paul* 1954 $5.00

Books about Gilbert

W. S. Gilbert: His Life and Letters. By Sidney Dark and Rowland Grey. 1923. *Blom* $12.75; *Gale
Research Co.* $14.00; *Richard West* $13.95
Gilbert and Sullivan: A Critical Appreciation of the Savoy Operas. By A. H. Godwin. 1926. *Ken-
nikat* 1969 $9.00; *Richard West* $20.00
A Bibliography of Sir William Schwenck Gilbert. By Townley Searle. 1931. *Burt Franklin* 1967
$15.00
The Story of Gilbert and Sullivan. By Sir Isaac Goldberg. 1935. rev. ed. *Gordon Press* $29.95;
Richard West 1973 $19.50. Biography and history.
Gilbert and Sullivan: A Biography. By Hesketh Pearson. 1935. *Scholarly Press* 1951 $19.50
A Gilbert and Sullivan Dictionary. By George A. Dunn. 1936. *Folcroft* 1972 $7.50
The World of Gilbert and Sullivan. By W. A. Darlington. 1950. *Bks. for Libraries* Select Bibliog-
raphies Reprint Ser. $8.75. A critical study.
Picture History of Gilbert and Sullivan. By Raymond Mander and Joe Mitchenson. *Dufour* 1963
$9.75
W. S. Gilbert: An Anniversary Survey and Exhibition Checklist. By Reginald Allen. *Univ. Press
of Virginia* 1964 $5.50
"Prepared with the fullest scholarship and knowledge, handsomely illustrated with facsimile
title pages, manuscripts, and so forth and readably printed, this reference tool has obvious
value for libraries"—(*LJ*). Mr. Allen, an official of the Metropolitan Opera, is a well-known
authority.
W. S. Gilbert: A Century of Scholarship and Commentary. *New York Univ. Press* 1970 $10.00. A
collection of articles.

WILDE, OSCAR. 1854–1900.

Oscar Wilde had a number of careers. The longest was the ritual tragedy played out before the
public eye. The young wit from Dublin who was recognized from the late seventies as the leader of
"aesthetic" fashion, the epigrammatist and philosopher of the artificial, the public speaker and
publicist, aged into the reckless sensualist who brought upon himself the disastrous 1895 trial for
homosexuality, which led to hard labor, illness, self-imposed exile, and sordid death. Shorter than
this langorous spectacle was Wilde's active career as a professional writer, in effect lasting little
more than the seven years from 1888 to 1895. And still shorter was the period in which he wrote
all five of his major plays—incredibly, no more than the four years from 1891 until his fall.

Three of these plays are social "problem" dramas built on the lines of a Pinero (*q.v.*) work and
propelled by the same wheezing Scribean clockwork. (It was not for nothing that Wilde had studied the French dramatists in preparation for his foray into London theatre.) "Salomé," written
originally in French, is a stiffly self-conscious piece of Biblical decadence, notable mainly as the
basis for the Strauss opera.

And then there is one incomparable comedy, "The Importance of Being Earnest," the best reason we have for remembering Oscar Fingal O'Flaherty Wilde.

COMPLETE WORKS OF OSCAR WILDE. Ed. by R. Ross 1908–1922 *Harper* (Barnes & Noble)
15 vols. 1969 set $200.00; 1927 *Richard West* 12 vols. set $200.00

THE PORTABLE OSCAR WILDE. Ed. by Richard Aldington *Viking* 1946 lib. bdg. $6.50 pap. $3.25

PLAYS, PROSE WORKS, AND POEMS. *Dutton* Everyman's $3.95 pap. $1.95

THE WORKS OF OSCAR WILDE. *Collins-World* $6.95

SELECTED WRITINGS OF OSCAR WILDE. Ed. by Richard Ellmann *Oxford* World's Class. 1961 $2.75; ed. by Russell Fraser *Houghton* Riverside Eds. 1969 $1.75. Includes five plays, essays, and poems.

THE WIT AND HUMOR OF OSCAR WILDE. Ed. by Alvin Redman *Dover* 1959 pap. $2.50; *Peter Smith* 1959 $4.00

OSCAR WILDE'S EPIGRAMS. *Peter Pauper Press* vest-pocket ed. $1.95

EPIGRAMS AND APHORISMS. *Gordon Press* $25.95

Plays:

FIVE MAJOR PLAYS. 1899. *Assoc. Booksellers* Airmont Books. Classics Series pap. $.95. Includes Lady Windermere's Fan, Importance of Being Earnest, Salomé, A Woman of No Importance, and An Ideal Husband.

PLAYS. *Penguin* pap. $1.50

LADY WINDERMERE'S FAN. 1893. *Barron's* 1960 $4.25 pap. $1.25

SALOMÉ. 1894. From Wilde's original French. The very rare text of the 1894 limited edition, trans. by Lord Alfred Douglas; ill. by Aubrey Beardsley *Dover* (orig.) pap. $2.00

SALOMÉ. Trans. from the French by Lord Alfred Douglas (bilingual); ill. by Aubrey Beardsley *Branden* pap. $1.35

THE IMPORTANCE OF BEING EARNEST. 1899. *Avon Bks.* 1965 pap. $.60; *Baker* (abr.) $1.00; ed. by Vincent F. Hopper and Gerald B. Lahey *Barron's* 1959 pap. $1.25; *Branden* pap. $.95; *French* $1.25; *Plays, Inc.* 1968 $1.65; *Franklin Watts* 1972 $3.45

THE IMPORTANCE OF BEING EARNEST: A Trivial Comedy for Serious People. *N.Y. Public Lib.* 2 vols. 1956 $20.00. In four acts as originally written.

Other Prose Works:

THE HAPPY PRINCE AND OTHER STORIES. 1888. *Dutton* Chil. Ill. Class. 1968 $4.50; (and Other Fairy Tales) *Penguin* 1962 pap. $.95

ESSAYS. Ed. and introd. by Hesketh Pearson 1950. *Bks. for Libraries* $11.75

LITERARY CRITICISM OF OSCAR WILDE. Ed. by Stanley Weintraub Regents Critics Ser. *Univ. of Nebraska Press* Bison Bks. 1968 $5.95 pap. $2.25

HISTORICAL CRITICISM. *Bern Porter* 1971 $7.70

THE PICTURE OF DORIAN GRAY. 1891. *AMSCO* School Pubns. 1970 pap. $1.40; *Assoc. Booksellers* Airmont Bks. pap. $.60; (and Thirteen Other Stories) *Collins-World* Standard Class. $3.95; *Dell* 1956 $.75; ed. by Isobel Murray *Oxford* 1974 $9.75; (and Selected Stories) *New Am. Lib.* Signet 1962 pap. $.75; *Penguin* pap. $1.10

LORD ARTHUR SAVILE'S CRIME (1891) AND OTHER STORIES. *Penguin* 1973 $1.35

THE CANTERVILLE GHOST. *Branden* 1962 pap. $.95

DE PROFUNDIS. 1905. *Random* Vintage Bks. pap. $1.85; (and Other Writings) Ed. by Hesketh Pearson *Penguin* Eng. Lib. Ser. 1973 pap. $1.25. Includes "The Soul of Man under Socialism" and "The Decay of Lying," with a selection of poems. Written in prison, "De Profundis" describes Wilde's agonies of spirit which led him in time to a kind of religion. Critics have disagreed as to its sincerity.

THE LETTERS OF OSCAR WILDE. Ed. by Rupert Hart-Davis. 1962 o.p. The first systematic, major, unexpurgated collection, including the first unexpurgated edition of "De Profundis."

The publication of 1,098 unexpurgated "Letters," written to some 300 friends, was a publishing event of the greatest importance. Printed exactly as Wilde wrote them, they contain everything from "samples of his prodigious wit to his excellent ideas on prison reform." Here can be traced the growth of his homosexual affection for Lord Alfred Douglas, which was to be the cause of his ruin and imprisonment.

Books about Wilde

A Bibliography of Oscar Wilde. By Stuart Mason. 1914. *Milford House* $30.00; *Haskell* Reference Ser. $29.95; reprint of 1919 ed. *Richard West* 1973 $30.00

Oscar Wilde: His Life and Confessions. By Frank Harris. 2 vols. 1916 rev. ed. 1930. *Horizon Press* 1974 $12.95. For many years considered the standard biography.

A Study of Oscar Wilde. By Arthur Symons. 1930. *Folcroft* $10.00

Oscar Wilde: A Summing-Up. By Lord Alfred Douglas. 1940. *Richard West* $20.00

Oscar Wilde. By Edouard Roditi. *New Directions* 1947 $4.50

Oscar Wilde. By James Laver. Pamphlet. *British Bk. Centre* $2.95 pap. $1.20

Son of Oscar Wilde. By Vyvyan Holland. 1954. *Greenwood* 1973 $11.50

Wilde and the Nineties. Ed. by Charles Ryskamp. *Princeton Univ. Lib.* 1966 $3.50

The Art of Oscar Wilde. By Epifanio San Juan, Jr. *Princeton Univ. Press* 1967 $10.00. A critical study.

Oscar Wilde: A Collection of Critical Essays. Ed. by Richard Ellmann. Twentieth Century Views Ser. *Prentice-Hall* 1969 $5.95 Spectrum Bks. pap. $1.95

Oscar Wilde. By Kevin Sullivan. Essays on Modern Writers Ser. *Columbia* 1972 pap. $1.00

Oscar Wilde. By Edward Partridge. Irish Writers Ser. *Bucknell Univ. Press* $4.50 pap. $1.95

PINERO, SIR ARTHUR WING.   1855–1934.

Pinero was an expert craftsman and measured the taste of his generation shrewdly. "The Second Mrs. Tanqueray" (1893, o.p. in a separate volume), which his public regarded as daring and thought-provoking, shows the influence of Ibsen's (*q.v.*) modern ideas. For two decades each new play was regarded as a likely source of controversy. Then in the last 20 years of his life, his popularity waned. Since his death, however, he has continued to be played by amateur groups. Recently "Trelawney of the Wells" (1898) has been revived professionally here.

SOCIAL PLAYS. Ed. with general introd. and critical pref. to each play by Clayton Hamilton. 1917–22. *AMS Press* 4 vols. each $17.50 set $70.00

THE ENCHANTED COTTAGE. 1922. *Baker* $1.00

PLAYGOERS. *French* $1.60. A one-act comedy.

THE COLLECTED LETTERS OF SIR ARTHUR PINERO. Ed. by J. P. Wearing *Univ. of Minnesota Press* 1974 $15.00

Books about Pinero

Sir Arthur Pinero: A Critical Biography with Letters. By W. D. Dunkel. 1941. *Kennikat* $6.00

Arthur Wing Pinero. By Walter Lazenby. English Authors Ser. *Twayne* $6.50

SHAW, GEORGE BERNARD.   1856–1950.   (Nobel Prize 1925)

Shaw, the expatriate Irishman, is the anomalous instance of a playwright who was a success in book form before he was a success on the stage; to be more exact, he was a failure on the stage until after he was a success in book form. His seven "Plays, Pleasant and Unpleasant" and his three "Plays for Puritans" were all written before 1900, and all but one presented on the stage. Not one met with noticeable success and most were downright failures. In 1898 appeared Shaw's first printed volume, "Plays, Pleasant and Unpleasant." The instant popularity of these led to their re-trial in the theater, where they triumphed. These early plays are unmistakably the work of a drama reviewer (*The Saturday Review,* 1895–98) who made his attacks on theatrical convention inseparable from his criticism of society. Less overtly given to parodying melodrama, the major works of the next decade and a half remain Shaw's most popular plays: "Man and Superman" (1903), "Major Barbara" (1905), "The Doctor's Dilemma" (1906), "Pygmalion" (1912). The experience of the First World War, as Stanley Weintraub has recently shown ("Journey to Heartbreak." *McKay* Weybright and Talley 1971 $8.95), had a profound effect on Shaw's work. His bitter memorial of the war, "Heartbreak House" (1919), which he apparently considered his favorite play, is in some ways his most difficult. It foreshadows the open-form fantasies and political extravaganzas which largely occupied Shaw for the next three decades. Except for "Saint Joan" (1923), the rich work of this period is unjustly neglected by anthologists and producers today.

During his 60 years of literary activity, Shaw produced a tremendous body of work. Contrary to received opinion, his prefaces, polemics, and press releases are almost as uniformly thoughtful as they are uniformly, magnificently, readable.

Plays:

COMPLETE PLAYS WITH PREFACES. *Dodd* 6 vols. 1962 each $7.50 set $45.00

THE THEATRE OF BERNARD SHAW. Ed. by Alan S. Downer *Dodd* 2 vols. 1961 pap. each
$3.25. A collection of 10 plays designed to illustrate the range and development of
Shaw's dramatic theory.

SEVEN PLAYS: With Prefaces and Notes. *Dodd* 1951 $10.00. Latest revision of text of
Ayôt St. Lawrence Ed. Caesar and Cleopatra; Mrs. Warren's Profession; Arms and
the Man; Candida; Saint Joan; Man and Superman; The Devil's Disciple.

FOUR PLAYS: Candida; Caesar and Cleopatra; Pygmalion; Heartbreak House. *Random*
Modern Lib. 1953 $2.95

FOUR PLAYS. Introd. by Paul Kozelka *Simon & Schuster* (Washington Square) pap. $.75.
Caesar and Cleopatra; Candida; The Devil's Disciple; Man and Superman.

SAINT JOAN, MAJOR BARBARA, ANDROCLES AND THE LION. *Random* Modern Lib. 1956
$2.95. Plays dealing with religion or religious thought; prefaces included.

FOUR PLAYS: Candida, The Devil's Disciple, Caesar and Cleopatra, Captain
Brassbound's Conversion. *Dell* Laurel 1957 pap. $.95

PLAYS. Introd. by Eric Bentley *New Am. Lib.* Signet pap. $1.50. Includes Arms and the
Man, Candida, Man and Superman, Mrs. Warren's Profession.

PLAYS: Major Barbara, Heartbreak House, Saint Joan, Too True to Be Good. Ed. by
Warren S. Smith *Norton* Critical Eds. 1970 $8.00 pap. $2.65

SELECTED PLAYS AND OTHER WRITINGS. Introd. by William Irvine *Holt* (Rinehart) 1956
pap. $2.00. Arms and the Man; Candida; Man and Superman; Selections from the
Quintessence of Ibsenism; Mainly about Myself.

PLAYS UNPLEASANT. 1898. *Penguin* 1961 pap. $.95. Includes Widower's Houses, The
Philanderer, Mrs. Warren's Profession.

PYGMALION AND OTHER PLAYS. *Dodd* Great Ill. Class. 1967 $5.50

SELECTED ONE-ACT PLAYS. *Penguin* pap. $1.65
The Shewing-Up of Blanco Posnet; How He Lied to Her Husband; O'Flaherty V.C.; The Inca
of Perusalem; Annajanska; The Bolshevik Empress; A Village Wooing; The Six of Calais; Overruled; Dark Lady of the Sonnets; Great Catherine; Augustus Does His Bit.

SEVEN ONE-ACT PLAYS. Fwd. by E. Martin Browne *Penguin* 1958 pap. $.65. How He
Lied to Her Husband; The Admirable Bashville; The Man of Destiny; The Dark
Lady of the Sonnets; A Village Wooing; Overruled; Passion; Poison and Petrifaction.

ARMS AND THE MAN. 1894. With sel. criticism and intro. by Henry Popkin *Avon Bks.* new
ed. 1967 $.60; *Baker* $1.25; with intro. by Louis Kronenberger *Bantam* pap. $.60; ed.
by Louis Crompton *Bobbs* pap. $.95; *Penguin* $1.65

CANDIDA. 1897. *Baker* $.75; ed. by R. S. Nelson *Bobbs* pap. $.95; *French* $.75; *Penguin*
pap. $1.95

YOU NEVER CAN TELL. 1898. *Univ. of Nebraska Press* 1961 pap. $.90

CAESAR AND CLEOPATRA. 1899. Ed. by E. T. Forter *AHM Pub. Corp.* Crofts Class. 1965
pap. $.85; *Assoc. Booksellers* Airmont Bks. pap. $.50; *Baker* $.50; ed. by Gale K. Larson
Bobbs pap. $.95

CAPTAIN BRASSBOUND'S CONVERSION. 1901. *French* $.95

THE DEVIL'S DISCIPLE. 1901. *Baker* $.50; *French* $.85; *Penguin* $.80

MAN AND SUPERMAN. 1903. *Assoc. Booksellers* Airmont Bks. pap. $.60; *Baker* $.85; *French*
$1.25; *Penguin* pap. $1.25

MAJOR BARBARA. 1905. Ed. by Elizabeth T. Forter *AHM Pub. Corp.* Crofts Class. pap.
$.85; *Baker* $.65; *French* $.75; *Penguin* pap. $1.35

JOHN BULL'S OTHER ISLAND. 1907. *French* $7.50

THE ADMIRABLE BASHVILLE. 1909. *French* $.65

THE DOCTOR'S DILEMMA. 1911. *Baker* $.65; *Penguin* pap. $.65

PYGMALION. 1913. *Baker* $.50; *French* $.65; *Penguin* pap. $.65; *Simon & Schuster* (Washington Square) pap. $.75

THE DARK LADY OF THE SONNETS. 1914. *French* $1.65

FANNY'S FIRST PLAY. 1914. *French* $7.50

MISALLIANCE. 1914. *French* $7.50

ANDROCLES AND THE LION. 1916. *Baker* $.65; *French* $.95; *Penguin* pap. $1.95.

ANDROCLES AND THE LION. *Penguin* (orig.) The Shaw Alphabet Edition. 1962 pap. $1.95
In his will Shaw directed that a new and more efficient alphabet be designed and published, to enable English "to be written without indicating single sounds by groups of letters or by diacritical marks." He further directed that this play be translated into the new alphabet and published in a special edition with the normal English spellings on facing pages. Kingsley Read, advised by experts, designed this 48-character alphabet, which was chosen following an international competition.

OVERRULED. 1916. *French* $1.65

ANNAJANSKA. 1919. *French* $1.65

AUGUSTUS DOES HIS BIT. 1919. *French* $1.65

THE GREAT CATHERINE. 1919. *French* $1.65

HEARTBREAK HOUSE. 1919. *French* $.95; *Penguin* 1965 pap. $.95

THE INCA OF PERUSALEM. 1919. *French* $1.65

O'FLAHERTY, V. C. 1919. *French* $1.65

BACK TO METHUSELAH: A Metabiological Pentateuch. 1921. *French* $1.50

SAINT JOAN. 1924. *Baker* $.65; ed. by Stanley Weintraub *Bobbs* pap. $.95; *French* $.85; *Penguin* pap. $.95; ed. as a screenplay by Bernard F. Dukore *Univ. of Washington Press* 1970 $6.95 pap. $2.45

THE APPLE CART. 1929. *French* $.50; *Penguin* pap. $.50

THE VILLAGE WOOING. 1934. *French* $1.65

THE MILLIONAIRESS. 1936. *French* $.50; *Penguin* 1961 pap. $.50

THE SIMPLETON OF THE UNEXPECTED ISLES. 1936. *French* $2.75

THE SIX OF CALAIS. 1936. *French* $1.65

Other Prose Works:

PROSE ANTHOLOGY. Ed. by H. M. Burton *Fawcett* Premier Bks. pap. $.75

SELECTED NON-DRAMATIC WRITINGS. Ed. by Dan H. Laurence; introd. by Gordon Ray *Houghton* Riv. Eds. pap. $2.95. An Unsocial Socialist, The Quintessence of Ibsenism, Essays and Reviews.

PREFACES. 1934. *Scholarly Press* 1971 $42.00

MAJOR CRITICAL ESSAYS. 1932. *Scholarly Press* 1971 $17.00

Dramatic Criticism:

PLAYS AND PLAYERS: Essays on the Theatre. Sel. with introd. by A. C. Ward *Oxford* World's Class. 1954 $2.25. Forty complete essays providing a representative cross-section of English theater history in the 1890's.

SHAW ON THEATRE. Ed. by E. J. West. *Farrar, Straus* (Hill & Wang) Dramabks. 1959 $3.95 pap. $1.75. Fifty years of essays, letters and articles, most of which are collected for the first time in book form.

SHAW'S DRAMATIC CRITICISM (1895–1898): A Selection by John F. Matthews. 1959. *Greenwood* 1961 $14.50; *Peter Smith* $4.00. Reviews from the London *Saturday Review*.

THE QUINTESSENCE OF IBSENISM. 1891. 1913. *Farrar, Straus* (Hill and Wang) Dramabks. 1957 pap. $2.75

SHAW ON SHAKESPEARE. Ed. by Edwin Wilson. 1961. *Bks. for Libraries* $11.50

Musical Criticism:

THE COLLECTED MUSIC CRITICISM. *Vienna House* 4 vols. 1973 set $50.00

LONDON MUSIC IN 1888–1889. 1937. *Vienna House* 1973 $15.00

MUSIC IN LONDON, 1890–1894. 1931. *Scholarly Press* repr. of 1956 ed. 3 vols. $49.50; *Vienna House* repr. of 1931 ed. 3 vols. each $12.50

THE PERFECT WAGNERITE. 1898. *Dover* 1966 pap. $1.75; *Peter Smith* $4.00

HOW TO BECOME A MUSICAL CRITIC. Ed. with intro. by Dan H. Laurence *Farrar, Straus* (Hill & Wang) 1961 $5.00

On Religion:

RELIGIOUS SPEECHES. *Pennsylvania Univ. Press* 1963 $5.00

While attacking "the thing miscalled religion" (in lectures given 1906–37), Shaw "presents piecemeal a kind of Bergsionian creative evolution, confessing to a mysticism that requires a 'design and purpose in the universe' and the belief that 'a religious person . . . conceives himself to be the instrument' of that purpose"—(*LJ*).

Political and Miscellaneous Essays:

THE INTELLIGENT WOMAN'S GUIDE TO SOCIALISM, CAPITALISM, SOVIETISM, AND FASCISM. 1928. *Random* Vintage 1972 pap. $2.95

FABIAN ESSAYS IN SOCIALISM. 1932. *Peter Smith* repr. of 1967 edition $4.25

THE MATTER WITH IRELAND. Ed. by Dan H. Laurence and David A. Grene *Farrar, Straus* (Hill & Wang) 1962 $5.00

THE RATIONALIZATION OF RUSSIA. Ed. by Harry M. Geduld *Indiana Univ. Press* 1964 $3.95

THE CRIME OF PUNISHMENT. 1946. *Greenwood* $7.50

ON LANGUAGE. Ed. by A. Tauber *Citadel Press* pap. $1.85

PEN PORTRAITS AND REVISIONS. 1932. *Scholarly Press* $16.00

Novels and Tales:

CASHEL BYRON'S PROFESSION. 1886. Ed. by Stanley Weintraub *Southern Illinois Univ. Press* 1968 $6.95

AN UNSOCIAL SOCIALIST. 1887. *Norton* pap. $2.95; *Scholarly Press* $14.50

TALES. *Putnam* Capricorn Bks. 1964 pap. $1.45

THE ADVENTURES OF THE BLACK GIRL IN HER SEARCH FOR GOD. 1932. *Putnam* Capricorn Bks. 1959 pap. $1.65. With the original ills. by John Farleigh. An account of a modern Candide.

Letters:

MY DEAR DOROTHEA: A Practical System of Moral Education for Females. Embodied in a Letter to a Young Person of That Sex. Ill. by Clare Winsten; with a note by Stephen Winsten *Vanguard* 1957 $3.00

LETTERS TO GRANVILLE-BARKER. Ed. by C. B. Purdom with commentary and notes *Theatre Arts* 1957 1960 $1.55

ADVICE TO A YOUNG CRITIC: Letters 1894–1928. Ed. by E. J. West *Hillary House* 1956 $3.00; *Putnam* Capricorn Bks. pap. $1.45. Shaw's views on drama culled from his 35-year correspondence with the critic Reginald Golding Bright.

COLLECTED LETTERS. Ed. with introd. by Dan Laurence *Dodd* 2 vols. of 4 projected vols.
Vol. 1 1874–1897 (1964) $12.50 Vol 2 1898–1910 (1972) $25.00

The letters Shaw wrote are estimated at 250,000. This collection brings him to his 41st year.
"Shaw's incredible energy for writing about [love and politics], as displayed in these letters, is simply a marvel, and this volume is a record of a phenomenon"—(*LJ*).

Books about Shaw

George Bernard Shaw. By G. K. Chesterton. 1909 enl. ed. 1950 *Farrar, Straus* (Hill & Wang)
Dramabks. 1957 pap. $1.25

Dictionary to the Plays and Novels of Bernard Shaw. By C. L. and V. M. Broad. 1929. Studies in
Irish Lit. Ser. *Haskell* 1969 $12.95; *Scholarly Press* 1972 $9.50. Including a bibliography of
Shaw's works and of the literature concerning him, along with a record of the principle Sha-
vian play productions (to 1929).

George Bernard Shaw: His Life and Personality. By Hesketh Pearson. 1941. *Atheneum* 1963
pap. $1.95; *Norwood Eds.* $10.00

Bernard Shaw. By Eric Bentley. *New Directions* 1947 new ed. rev. and augmented 1957 pap.
$1.95. An illuminating analysis which Shaw called "the best critical description of my public
activities I have yet come across." In the Makers of Modern Literature Series.

The Universe of G. B. S. By William Irvine. 1949. *Russell & Russell* 1968 $13.00. Useful study of
Shaw's intellectual backgrounds.

The Quintessence of G. B. S. By Stephen Winsten. 1949. *Richard West* $17.50

A Good Man Fallen among Fabians: G. B. Shaw. By Alick West. 1950. *Bks. for Libraries* Select
Bibliographies Reprint Ser. $10.00; *Folcroft* $9.95. A Marxist critique of Shaw.

Shaw and Society: An Anthology and a Symposium. Ed. by C. E. Joad. 1953. *Folcroft* $17.50.
Contributions by Leonard Woolf and Kingsley Martin, among others.

**Theatrical Companion to Shaw: A Pictorial Record of the First Performance of the Plays of
Bernard Shaw.** By R. Mander and J. Mitchenson. 1954. *Folcroft* $25.00

Men and Supermen: The Shavian Portrait Gallery. By Arthur H. Nethercot. 1954 *Blom* 1966
$12.50

Bernard Shaw: His Life, Work, and Friends. By St. John Ervine. 1956. *Morrow* 1972 pap. $3.95

George Bernard Shaw: Man of the Century. By Archibald Henderson. 1957. *Richard West*
$5.00. An encyclopedic biography.

A Glossary to the Plays of Bernard Shaw. By Paul Kozelka. 1959 *Norwood Editions* $7.50. A glos-
sary of words and phrases used in Shaw's plays.

Shaw: The Style and the Man. By Richard Ohmann. *Wesleyan Univ. Press* 1962 $9.00. This is a
meticulous analysis of "the famous, clearly idiosyncratic Shaw style according to the criteria
and methodology of structural linguistics," to discover the relation between his personality,
thought and language.

Shaw and the Nineteenth-Century Theatre. By Martin Meisel. *Princeton Univ. Press* 1963 $12.50

A Guide to the Plays of Bernard Shaw. By C. B. Purdom. *Apollo* pap. $1.75. Play descriptions,
lists of characters, critical and biographical information.

A Shavian Guide to the Intelligent Woman. By Barbara Bellow Watson. *Norton* 1964 pap. $2.45

The Unrepentant Pilgrim: A Study of the Development of Bernard Shaw. By J. Percy Smith.
Norwood Eds. 1974 $15.00; *Richard West* $20.00. Professor Smith expounds his persuasive and
provocative theory of Shaw's "conversion."

The Serpent's Eye: Shaw and the Cinema. By Donald P. Costello. *Univ. of Notre Dame Press* 1965
$7.95. Included are Shaw's opening scenes for the film version of "The Devil's Disciple," his
entire screen play for a projected filming of "Arms and the Man" and the casts and credits of
all film versions of Shaw.

G. B. Shaw: A Collection of Critical Essays. Ed. with introd. by R. J. Kaufmann. Twentieth Century Views Ser. *Prentice-Hall* Spectrum Bks. 1965 $5.95 pap. $1.95
"A well-gathered, balanced collection"—(*LJ*).

The Wit and Satire of Bernard Shaw. By Fred Mayne. *St. Martin's* 1967 $7.95
In this "admirably articulated book, . . . a combination of the inevitable and the surprising is
confirmed as the touchstone of Shaw's art"—(*LJ*).

Bernard Shaw and the Theatre in the Nineties: A Study of Shaw's Dramatic Criticism. By Harold Fromm. *Univ. Press of Kansas* 1967 $5.00. A well-researched introductory work—the first
entirely devoted to this subject.

What Shaw Really Said. By Ruth Adam. *Schocken* 1967 $6.00. An admirable slim volume guid-
ing the general reader to Shaw's major themes; includes short synopses of his best-known
works.

Shaw the Dramatist. By Louis Crompton. *Univ. of Nebraska Press* 1969 $7.95

The Shavian Playground: An Exploration of the Art of George Bernard Shaw. By Margery M.
Morgan. *Harper* (Barnes and Noble) 1972 $17.50

The Cart and The Trumpet: The Plays of George Bernard Shaw. By Maurice Valency. *Oxford* 1973 $12.50

BARRIE, SIR JAMES MATTHEW, BART. 1860–1937.

Barrie was successful first as a novelist, but after 1902 his writing was almost entirely dramatic. At first he refused to have his plays published, feeling that much of the charm and atmosphere might be lost. The early plays are typographically unique with some of the dialogue printed as in a novel. The stage directions are written in his whimsical narrative style. Though he is often criticized for sentimentality, "there were many good reasons why Barrie should have become England's best-loved modern playwright before 1920, quite apart from his exceptional understanding of the business of making a play move on stage. . . . According to many playgoers, England after 1890 was acquiring too many realists for comfort, but the deft magician from Thrums made the romantic spirit bloom again. And his romanticism was unlike that which had seethed with illicit passions and unfurled the banner of revolt in the days before respectability had mounted the throne of England with Victoria. In Barrie's enchanted gardens there were no flowers of evil"— (John Gassner). For Americans his plays are linked forever with Maude Adams, who made many of them famous here. His autobiography, "The Greenwood Hat" (1938) is now o.p.

PLAYS. *Scribner* 1928 $12.50. Omnibus vol. of 20 plays.

QUALITY STREET. 1903. *Baker* $1.25; *French* acting ed. 1946 $1.75

THE ADMIRABLE CRICHTON. 1903. *French* acting ed. 1950 $1.75

ALICE SIT-BY-THE-FIRE. 1905. *Baker* $1.25; *French* acting ed. $1.75

WHAT EVERY WOMAN KNOWS. 1908. *Baker* $1.25; *French* $1.75

HALF HOURS. 1914. Pantaloon; The Twelve-Pound Look *Baker* $.60; *French* $.85; Rosalind; The Will *French* $.85

A KISS FOR CINDERELLA. 1916. *Baker* $1.25; *French* 1948 $1.75

ECHOES OF THE WAR: The Old Lady Shows Her Medals; Barbara's Wedding; A Well-Remembered Voice. 1918. *Baker* each $.60; *French* each $.85

DEAR BRUTUS. 1922. *Baker* $1.25; *French* 1950 $1.75

SHALL WE JOIN THE LADIES? 1922. *Baker* $.60; *French* .85

MARY ROSE. 1924. *Baker* $1.25

PETER PAN. 1928. *Baker* $1.25; *French* $1.75; with an essay by the author *Scribner* $3.50

LETTERS. Ed. by Viola Meynell 1947. *AMS Press* $18.50

See also Chapter 11, British Fiction—Middle Period, Reader's Adviser, Vol. 1, where works about Barrie are listed.

GALSWORTHY, JOHN. 1867–1933. (Nobel Prize 1932)

The initial performance in 1906 of "The Silver Box" heralded Galsworthy's arrival as a dramatist of stature. That year also saw the publication of "The Man of Property," which was to become the first part of his memorable fiction trilogy, "The Forsythe Saga." In his plays Galsworthy dramatized social and ethical problems. "The Silver Box" deals with the subject of "one law for the rich and one law for the poor"; "The Pigeon" (1912) treats fully of the futility of charity toward the "submerged tenth." "Strife" deals with the war between capital and labor; "Justice" with the horrors of the prison system; "The Mob" with the jingoism of the South African war. The attention accorded to "Justice" brought about certain British penal reforms. Galsworthy's controversial themes were characteristically left unresolved—and he leveled his attack not on individuals but on the institution at fault. For all their passionate subject-matter, his plays seem relatively calm. He felt that "the aim of the dramatist employing [naturalism] is evidently to create such an illusion of actual life passing on the stage as to compel the spectator to pass through an experience of his own, to think and talk and move with the people he sees thinking, talking, and moving."

PLAYS. *Scribner* 1928 $12.50. Selected dramatic works in 1 vol.

JUSTICE. 1910. *French* $6.50

THE SKIN GAME. 1920. *French* $6.00

LOYALTIES. 1922. *French* $1.75

See also Chapter 12, Modern British Fiction, Reader's Adviser, Vol. 1, where works about Galsworthy are listed.

BENNETT, ARNOLD.   1867–1931.   *See Chapter 12, Modern British Fiction,* Reader's Adviser, *Vol. 1.*

MAUGHAM, (WILLIAM) SOMERSET.   1874–1965.

Maugham wrote that the first test of a work of art is that it shall entertain. His 30 plays—some in a serious vein, but the more successful, like "Lady Frederick," high comedies of manners—are unfailingly good entertainment. The collected edition (1934, o.p.) contained 18 plays, all that he cared to reprint. In time he gracefully retired; he said he had come to regard the writing of plays as "one of the lesser arts, like wood-carving and dancing." After 1933 he referred to himself as an ex-dramatist.

Several of his short stories have been successfully dramatized for stage and screen. The play "Rain" (*French* $1.75) was dramatized by John Colton and Clemence Randolph from "Miss Thompson" and also adapted by H. Dietz and R. Mamoulian for a spectacular musical version, "Sadie Thompson" (1944). S. N. Behrman (*q.v.*) based his comedy "Jane" (*French* $1.25) on a story (*see* "The Complete Short Stories" 1952 4 vols. *Simon & Schuster* (Washington Square) each $.75). Maugham himself, thinly disguised, is the subject of one of Noel Coward's last plays, "A Song at Twilight."

THREE COMEDIES: The Constant Wife, The Circle, Our Betters. *Simon & Schuster* (Washington Square) pap. $.90

THE LETTER. 1925. *Baker* $1.25

THE SACRED FLAME. 1928. *Baker* $1.25

THE BREADWINNER. 1930. *Baker* $1.25

Books about Maugham

The World of Somerset Maugham: An Anthology. By Klaus W. Jonas. 1959. *Greenwood* 1972 $11.50. Includes an essay on Maugham's drama by St. John Ervine.
Somerset Maugham: Writer for All Seasons. By Richard A. Cordell. *Indiana Univ. Press* 1961 $16.50. A biographical and critical study which includes a chapter on Maugham's theater.
The Dramatic Comedy of Somerset Maugham. By Ronald Barnes. *Humanities Press* 1968 $10.50
W. Somerset Maugham: An Annotated Bibliography of Writings About Him. Ed. by C. Sanders and H. E. Gerber. *Northern Illinois Univ. Press* 1970 $15.00

See also Chapter 12, Modern British Fiction, Reader's Adviser, *Vol. 1 where works about Maugham are listed.*

ELIOT, T(HOMAS) S(TEARNS).   1888–1965.   (Nobel Prize 1948)

From his pageant play "The Rock" (1934) Eliot learned some of the techniques of the stage and became interested in the possibilities of the dramatic form. "The ideal medium for poetry," he wrote, "and the most direct means of social 'usefulness' for poetry is the theatre." His tragedy of Thomas à Becket was commissioned for the Canterbury Festival and "Murder in the Cathedral" was played in 1935 within a few yards of the spot where Becket had been murdered seven and a half centuries earlier. It was then successfully produced in London. It became a film—and even a successful Italian opera, *"Assassinio Nella Cattedrale"* by Ildebrando Pizzetti. "The Family Reunion," a masterpiece of tragedy modeled on the ancient Greek, was not a successful play. But ten years later, "The Cocktail Party" won the Drama Critics' Circle Award and the London *Times* Literary Award. It has been called a modern morality play and introduced a "genuinely new note into writing for the contemporary theatre." It is written in verse "so easy most of the time that it is only barely above the level of prose"—(J. W. Krutch). Its popular success astonished even its author—it netted the "lyrical sum of $1,000,000." "The Confidential Clerk" was, wrote Paul Engle, "a wise, witty, elegant play, whose characters speak finely and shrewdly." It seemed to mark something of a climacteric in Eliot's poetic drama. "Nobody has experimented more patiently with dramatic verse than Mr. Eliot and his this . . . play he completes the elaboration of what might be called a form of serious farce, a form which is peculiarly his own invention"—(*Spectator*).

But Eliot, in "The Elder Statesman," went on to surprise practically everyone; the play was called "entertaining," "touching" and "his most human" by the critics. More than any of his previous plays or most of the poems, this play extols love. Eliot himself made a remarkable confession: "I'm just beginning to grow up, to get maturity. In the last few years, everything I'd done up to 60 or so has seemed very childish."

In "Poetry and Drama" (1951, o.p.), he "examined his own aims, techniques, and partial successes in relation to the poetic ideal in such a thoughtful spirit that this essay becomes a useful blueprint for future dramatic poets"—(*San Francisco Chronicle*). In 1948 he received the Nobel prize in literature and in the same year he was awarded the Order of Merit by King George VI.

COMPLETE PLAYS. *Harcourt* 1963 $8.50. The five major plays.

THE COMPLETE POEMS AND PLAYS. 1909–1950. *Harcourt* 1952 $9.75

The plays: Murder in the Cathedral; The Family Reunion; The Cocktail Party; Sweeney Agonistes: Fragments of an Aristophanic Melodrama is included among the Unfinished Poems in the section on collected poems 1909–1935.

MURDER IN THE CATHEDRAL. 1935. *Harcourt* 1935 $4.75 pap. $1.65; *French* $1.75. Play.

THE FAMILY REUNION: A Verse Play. 1939. *Harcourt* 1939 $4.95 Harvest Bks. pap. $1.85; *French* $1.75

THE COCKTAIL PARTY: A Verse Comedy. 1949. *Harcourt* 1950 $6.95 Harvest Bks. pap. $2.45; *French* 1950 pap. $1.75

THE CONFIDENTIAL CLERK. 1953. *Harcourt* 1954 $4.95 Harvest Bks. pap. $1.85; *French* $1.75. A play.

THE ELDER STATESMAN. 1959. *Farrar, Straus* 1959 $4.95; *French* $1.75. Play.

Books about Eliot

T. S. Eliot's Poetry and Plays: A Study in Sources and Meaning. By Grover Cleveland Smith. *Univ. of Chicago Press* 1956 2nd ed. 1975 $15.00 Phoenix Bks. pap. $4.95

The Plays of T. S. Eliot. By David E. Jones. *Univ. of Toronto Press* 1960 pap. $2.75

T. S. Eliot's Dramatic Theory and Practice: From "Sweeney Agonistes" to "The Elder Statesman." By Carol H. Smith. *Princeton Univ. Press* 1963 $6.50

T. S. Eliot. By Philip T. Headings. U.S. Authors Ser. *Twayne* 1964 $6.50

T. S. Eliot: A Collection of Critical Essays. Ed. by Hugh Kenner. Twentieth Century Views Ser. *Prentice-Hall* 1966 $5.95 Spectrum Bks. pap. $1.95

The Making of T. S. Eliot's Plays. By E. Martin Browne. *Cambridge* 1969 $15.50

Twentieth Century Interpretations of Murder in the Cathedral. Ed. by D. Clark. *Prentice-Hall* 1971 $4.95

A Half-Century of Eliot Criticism: Annotated Bibliography of Books and Articles in English, 1916–1965. Ed. by Mildred Martin. *Bucknell Univ. Press* 1972 $20.00

T. S. Eliot: Poet and Dramatist. By Joseph Chiari. *Harper* (Barnes and Noble) 1973 $8.50

See also Chapters 7, Modern British Poetry, and 15, Essays and Criticism, Reader's Adviser, *Vol. 1.*

PRIESTLEY, J(OHN) B(OYNTON). 1894–

J. B. Priestley is another English novelist turned dramatist. He is a successful playwright, theater director and producer. He was briefly (1966–67) a board member of Britain's National Theater but resigned when he found it was mainly concerned with financing. He has had more than 25 plays produced; "Dangerous Corner," the most successful, has been performed in most countries of the Western world. It concerns the tragedy that results when a group of people who have long known each other fail to turn a dangerous conversational corner and start raking over the past to discover bitter truths that should have been left buried. At the end the first scene is replayed as it might have been, with the "dangerous corner" successfully negotiated. His other plays range from light comedy of character to detective drama. His introduction to the "Collected Plays" (1951, o.p.) includes witty and candid comment on each. "The Art of the Dramatist," a lecture, has been published with appendixes and discursive notes (1957, o.p.).

DANGEROUS CORNER. 1934. *French* $1.75

LABURNUM GROVE. 1936. *French* $1.75

I HAVE BEEN HERE BEFORE. 1937. *French* $1.75

TIME AND THE CONWAYS. 1937. *French* $1.75

MYSTERY AT GREEN FINGERS. 1938. *French* $1.75

WHEN WE ARE MARRIED. 1940. *French* $1.75

AN INSPECTOR CALLS. 1946. *Dramatists* $1.25

THE LINDEN TREE. 1947. *French* $1.75

MOTHER'S DAY. (In "English One-Act Plays of Today.") Ed. by Donald Fitzjohn *Oxford* 1962 pap. $2.25

(With Iris Murdoch) A SEVERED HEAD. *French* $1.75. A comedy.

Book about Priestley

J. B. Priestley. By Ivor Brown. Pamphlet. *British Bk. Centre* $2.95 pap. $1.20

See also Chapter 12, Modern British Fiction, Reader's Adviser, *Vol. 1.*

COWARD, NOEL. 1899–1973.

"Before he was forty at least one full-length play for each year of his age had been produced and published, to say nothing of two books of one-act plays, an 'impudent' autobiography, a volume of poetry and a book of short stories"—(Harrison Smith, in *SR*). Noel Coward grew up on the stage. He was a juvenile prodigy who became "a front-rank playwright, actor director, composer, conductor, wit, raconteur and writer, who [could] also sing and dance acceptably." His light, sophisticated comedy is always good theater. His autobiography "Present Indicative" (1937, o.p.) reveals the terrific pace of his career, reflected in the tempo of his plays. "Cavalcade" (1931), one of his most spectacular productions, attended by the Royal Family in London, was a sentimental recreation of Britain's recent history as it affected an English family. He was accused of writing "nationalist propaganda," but it was tremendously popular on stage and screen. "Tonight at 8:30" was written for the purpose of restoring the short play to favor and in these nine plays the author himself played nine different parts. It was revived in New York in 1967. He considered "Hay Fever" (1925), which he wrote in three days, his best comedy, "The Vortex" (1923) his best drama. "Private Lives" was successfully revived on Broadway in 1974.

"Pretty Polly and Other Stories" (1965, o.p.) offers "fleeting prose entertainment about people and events in a variety of intriguing situations"—(*LJ*). In her delightful autobiography, "A Star Danced" (1945, o.p.), the late Gertrude Lawrence gives many glimpses of Noel Coward after their first meeting at Miss Conti's dancing school in London. "Future Indefinite," "an agreeable autobiographical diversion" (1954, o.p.), is "provocative, amusing, temperamental, lively, sly, acid and altogether engaging."

PLAYS. 13 vols. *French* each $1.75. I'll Leave It to You (1920); The Young Idea (1924); Hay Fever (1925); Private Lives (1930, acting ed. 1948); Blithe Spirit (1941, also *Baker* $1.25); Present Laughter (1947, also *Baker* $1.25); This Happy Breed (1947); Peace in Our Time (1948 acting ed. 1949); Fallen Angels; Relative Values; Nude with Violin (also *Baker* $1.25); Quadrille (also *Baker* $1.25); Waiting in the Wings.

TONIGHT AT 8:30. *French* each $.85. Nine short plays for presentation in groups of three: Hands across the Sea; The Astonished Heart; Red Peppers. We Were Dancing; Fumed Oak; Shadow Play. Ways and Means; Still Life; Family Album.

SUITE IN THREE KEYS: A Song at Twilight; Shadows of the Evening; Come into the Garden Maud. *Doubleday* 1967 $4.95 pap. $1.95; *French* $1.95

"*A Song At Twilight* . . . is one of Coward's best"—(*LJ*). It concerns homosexuality, and marks a departure for Coward in the direction of realism.

LYRICS. 1965. *Overlook Press* 1973 $12.95

NOEL COWARD READING HIS DUOLOGUES. *Caedmon* TC 1069 $6.98. Brief Encounter (complete); Blithe Spirit (Act II, Scene I); Present Laughter (Act II, Scene I). A recording with Margaret Leighton.

NOEL COWARD READING HIS POEMS. *Caedmon* TC 1094 $6.98. On one side of this record, Coward and Margaret Leighton share the reading of his verses; on the other, he and she perform a scene from G. B. Shaw's "The Apple Cart."

Books about Coward

Satire in the Comedies of Congreve, Sheridan, Wilde, and Coward. By Rose Snider. 1937. *Folcroft* $7.50
The Art of Noel Coward. By Robert Greacen. 1953. *Folcroft* $7.50
Noel Coward. By Milton Levin. English Authors Ser. *Twayne* 1969 $5.50
Noel. By Charles Castle. *Doubleday* 1973 $12.95

VAN DRUTEN, JOHN. 1901–1957.

John Van Druten was a lawyer-dramatist-director who taught law in Wales and lectured on drama throughout the United States. He became a naturalized American citizen in 1944 and lived in California. His plays show wide variety of theme and treatment. "Young Woodley," on the love affair between an older woman and a young boy in a boys' school, was refused a license in England for a time. "The Voice of the Turtle," adapted in 1967 for television by Truman Capote, is Van Druten's best comedy and his greatest success on Broadway. "I Remember Mama" was successful on the stage, in the movies and as a television feature. "Bell, Book and Candle" was a hit on stage and screen, and "I Am a Camera," based on sections of Christopher Isherwood's (*q.v.*) "Berlin Diary," received the Drama Critics Circle award in 1952. Its lively musical adaptation "Cabaret"

(*Random* 1967 $4.50) won the 1967 Drama Critics Circle award and eight "Tonys." The *N.Y. Times* said of his autobiography, "The Widening Circle" (1957, o.p.): "Casual, informal, gently sprinkled with a bit of yesterday's snows . . . the book ranges over a variety of subjects. Books are discussed . . . and [his] own gropings for a religious faith. The effect is like listening to an extremely pleasant soliloquy by a man who knows what he feels, but would not dream of imposing his feeling on anyone else." He summed up his 27 years in the theater in "The Playwright at Work" (1953, o.p.) which, he says, contains "everything I have learned, picked up and thought of as regards play-wrighting."

PLAYS. 5 vols. *French* each $1.75. Young Woodley (1925); There's Always Juliet (1932); The Distaff Side (1934); Old Acquaintance (1941); (with L. R. Morris) The Damask Cheek (1943 acting ed.).

PLAYS. 5 vols. *Dramatists* each $1.25. Make Way for Lucia (based on novels of E. F. Benson, 1949); The Druid Circle (acting ed. 1948) ms. only; The Voice of the Turtle (1944); Bell, Book and Candle (acting ed. 1951); I Am a Camera (1952).

PLAYS. 2 vols. *Dramatists* each $2.25. The Mermaids Singing (1946); I've Got Sixpence (1953).

I REMEMBER MAMA. *Harcourt* 1945 $6.50; *Dramatists* acting ed. 1945 $1.25. A play in two acts adapted from Kathryn Forbes' book, "Mama's Bank Account."

I AM A CAMERA: A Play in Three Acts. 1952. *Greenwood* 1971 $11.50

GREENE, (HENRY) GRAHAM. 1904– *See Chapter 12, Modern British Fiction*, Reader's Adviser, *Vol. 1.*

WILLIAMS, EMLYN. 1905–

Playwright, actor and producer, Emlyn Williams knew in his boyhood the Welsh background of his success, "The Corn Is Green." Son of a Welsh iron worker and miner, he was born in a tiny Welsh hamlet. He was eight before he could speak a word of English, nineteen before he saw a play. Of his "vibrant down-to-earth story of his childhood," "George: An Early Biography," (1961, o.p.) Edward Weeks said in the *Atlantic:* "The delight in this book is the emergence of young George—he was christened George Emlyn—from a shy inhibited Welsh youngster to the prize-winning scholar of Christ Church." His first theatrical success in 1930 was "A Murder Has Been Arranged." In 1935 "Night Must Fall," with the author in the leading role, was a hit in London, where it ran for over a year; it eventually became a film success and a classic of the U.S. summer theater. His great triumph here on stage and screen was "The Corn Is Green," in 1940, when the late Ethel Barrymore played the role of an understanding teacher who turns a surly-mannered, smutty-faced Welsh miner into an educated man. It won the New York Drama Critics Circle award for the best foreign play of 1941.

He has appeared in his own and others' plays in England and America and in the movies since 1932. After Williams' 1952 re-creation of Charles Dickens giving readings of his novels before American audiences and his one-man interpretation "A Boy Growing Up," based on the stories of Dylan Thomas, in 1957–58, Williams assumed the role of Sir Thomas More in "A Man for All Seasons" by Robert Bolt (*q.v.*). This play won the New York Drama Critics Circle Award for best foreign play, 1962. Like Pamela Hansford Johnson (*q.v.*), Williams has analyzed the notorious Moors murder case at book length. In "Beyond Belief: A Chronicle of Murder and its Detection" (*Random* 1968 $7.95; *Avon* pap. $.95) he presents a factual and interpretive account, deploring the emphasis on violence and crime in modern reading matter and entertainment, which he holds as partly responsible. In 1975, Williams again performed his Dickens impersonation at London's Haymarket Theatre.

PLAYS. A Murder Has Been Arranged (1931); Night Must Fall (1936). *French* 2 vols. each $1.75

PEPPER AND SAND. *Baker* $.85

THE CORN IS GREEN. 1941. *Dramatists* 1945 $1.25

SOMEONE WAITING. *Dramatists* $1.25

BECKETT, SAMUEL. 1906– *See Chapter 9, French Literature, this volume.*

FRY, CHRISTOPHER (born Christopher Harris). 1907–

Success came to Christopher Fry after 38 years of living close to poverty. He was born in Bristol, where his father, a poor architect, turned to lay missionary work in the slums. In 1940, after alter-

nating between teaching and acting, Fry became director of the excellent Oxford Playhouse. As a
Quaker conscientious objector, he refused to bear arms in World War II.

He was first "discovered" by critics and connoisseurs when "A Phoenix Too Frequent" was performed in a small London theater in 1946. Three years later, John Gielgud's production of "The
Lady's Not for Burning" brought him popular success in London and the provinces. It was produced in New York, 1950–51, received the Drama Critics Circle award, 1950, and was listed
among the Notable Books of 1950. Sir Laurence Olivier commissioned him to write "Venus Observed," which is Fry's own favorite. During one week four of his plays were running in London.
The main themes of "The Dark Is Light Enough," set in the time of the Hungarian Revolution
against the Austro-Hungarian empire in 1848–49, are "the value of a human life, and the error of
using violence even to redress deep wrongs. But, as always in Fry, the language is the thing, and to
my taste a fine thing"—(*Atlantic*). He has adapted Anouilh's (*q.v.*) "*L'Invitation au Château*," "Ring
Round the Moon" (*Dramatists* $1.25) and Giraudoux's (*q.v.*) "Tiger at the Gates" (*Oxford* 1955
$3.75; *French* $1.25). "Tiger at the Gates" received the New York Drama Critics Circle award of
1956 for the best foreign play. Fry has translated Giraudoux's "*Pour Lucrèce*" as "Duel of Angels"
(*Oxford* 1959 $3.50). He wrote the screenplay for John Huston's production "The Bible," based on
the Book of Genesis (*Pocket Bks.* 1966 pap. $.75).

As a result, perhaps, of the change in British theatrical taste, Fry suffered eclipse in the sixties.
His antiwar play "A Sleep of Prisoners" was, however, performed in churches (it takes place in a
church, where soldiers have found refuge) and on television in this country.

THREE PLAYS: The Firstborn; Thor, with Angels; A Sleep of Prisoners. *Oxford* Galaxy
   Bks. pap. $2.25

THE BOY WITH A CART: Cuthman, Saint of Sussex. 1939. *Oxford* 1950 1952 $3.00; *Baker*
   $1.25. An early play.

A PHOENIX TOO FREQUENT. *Oxford* 1946 reissue 1949 $4.00; *Dramatists* acting ed. pap.
   $1.25; (in "English One-Act Plays of Today") ed. by Donald Fitzjohn *Oxford* 1960
   pap. $2.25

THE FIRSTBORN. *Oxford* 1947 1952 3rd ed. 1958 $4.00; *Dramatists* acting ed. pap. $1.25

THE LADY'S NOT FOR BURNING. 1948. *Oxford* 1949 2nd rev. ed. 1950 $4.00; *Dramatists*
   acting ed. pap. $1.25

THOR, WITH ANGELS. *Oxford* 1949 $3.00; *Dramatists* ms. only

VENUS OBSERVED. *Oxford* 1950 $4.00; *Dramatists* acting ed. pap. $1.25

A SLEEP OF PRISONERS. *Oxford* 1951 $3.50; *Dramatists* acting ed. pap. $1.25

THE DARK IS LIGHT ENOUGH: A Winter Comedy [in 3 acts]. *Oxford* 1954 $4.00; *Drama-
   tists* 1958 acting ed. pap. $1.25

CURTMANTLE. (1961, o.p.)

A YARD OF SUN. *Oxford* 1970 $4.95

Books about Fry

   Christopher Fry. By Derek Stanford. Pamphlet. *British Bk. Centre* $2.95 pap. $1.20
   Christopher Fry. By Emil Roy. *Southern Illinois Univ. Press* 1968 $4.95
   Christopher Fry. By Stanley Wiersma. *Eerdmans* Contemporary Writers in Christian Perspective
      Ser. 1970 pap. $.95

RATTIGAN, TERENCE (MERVYN).   1911–

   Rattigan, like Fry, more or less faded from the British theatrical scene in the 1960's and never
enjoyed the great popularity here that he knew in England in the 1940's and early 1950's. His
conventional comedies, dealing sometimes with serious questions of middle-class justice and injustice, seem a far cry from revolutionary British theater.

   The success of "The Deep Blue Sea" in New York was laid to the powerful performance of the
late Margaret Sullivan. Vivian Leigh appeared in the movie version. "The Winslow Boy" won the
Ellen Terry Award in London in 1946 and the Drama Critics Circle Award in 1948, but the Maurice Evans production of "The Browning Version" failed here in 1949. Both these were made into
successful English movies. Brooks Atkinson wrote some years ago that, to London audiences, Rattigan's professional aloofness and knack of underwriting seem evidence of skill and maturity but
that "Americans expect an artist to participate more actively in a theme—to have strong opinions
about his characters, their experience and the world in which they live"—and not to rely too completely on craftsmanship—(*N.Y. Times*).

THE COLLECTED PLAYS. 3 vols. 1953–1964. *Int. Pub. Service* each $8.00

FRENCH WITHOUT TEARS. 1938. *French* $1.75

WHILE THE SUN SHINES. 1945. *French* $1.75

THE WINSLOW BOY. 1946. *Dramatists* $1.25

THE BROWNING VERSION. 1948. *French* $.85; (in "English One-Act Plays of Today") ed. by Donald Fitzjohn *Oxford* 1960 pap. $2.25

A HARLEQUINADE. 1948. *French* $.85; *Baker* $.75

O MISTRESS MINE. 1949. *French* $1.75

THE DEEP BLUE SEA. 1952. *French* $1.75

THE SLEEPING PRINCE. 1953. *Dramatists* 1957 ms. only; price on request

SEPARATE TABLES. 1954. *French* $1.75; *Baker* $1.25

MAN AND BOY. 1963. *French* $1.75

WHITING, JOHN. 1917–1963.

John Whiting had had only one play produced ("A Penny for a Song") and one other written and shelved (his first, "Conditions of Agreement," rewritten much later for television) when his "Saint's Day" was awarded first place in an Arts Council play competition in 1951. The award raised a storm of controversy. It is now difficult to guess what then seemed so exotic or obscure, but at the time the play was "decidedly new." His third play, "Marching Song," which shares with "Saint's Day" the theme of self-destruction, caused no such furor when produced in 1954; neither, however, did it do well. When it closed, Whiting withdrew from the London stage for a period of seven years and concentrated on writing screenplays; nine were produced. In 1961 "The Devils" appeared as the first play commissioned by the new London branch of the Stratford Memorial Theater. It enjoyed "considerable" success, and has been hailed as "a masterpiece, or nearly one," by the critics.

Whiting's "lifelong preoccupations with the nature of violence and of personal responsibility foreshadowed the concern of a younger generation of dramatists. . . . His achievement was unique in combining intelligence and contemporaneity while remaining relevant for the predicaments of the sixties, and in exerting, at least for a minority, a distinctively theatrical pull. The range of his relatively small output, from delicately textured comedy to physically painful near-melodrama, was enormous. Each play was at once derivative and germinal, owing some debt to the mode of the theatrical moment, but contributing its significant share to recent developments"—(*Tulane Drama Review*).

COLLECTED PLAYS. Ed. by Ronald Hayman *Theatre Arts* 2 vols. each $7.95

SAINT'S DAY. 1951. *Theatre Arts* $1.95

MARCHING SONG. 1954. *French* $1.75; *Theatre Arts* $1.95

ON THEATRE. *Dufour* 1966 $1.95

SIMPSON, N(ORMAN) F(REDERICK). 1919–

N. F. Simpson was born in London and is a schoolmaster by profession. John Russell Taylor in "The Angry Theatre" has noted "his complete abandonment of any form of continuity. Not only is there no plot, in any normal sense of the term, but there is no attempt at character differentiation. . . . In every play the pattern of constant *non sequitur* is rigidly adhered to, so that the participants, as well as being nonexistent as individual characters, cannot even communicate."

Another critic, however, finds in Simpson's work "extravagant fantasy in the vein of Lewis Carroll." Martin Esslin, in "The Theatre of the Absurd" aligns Simpson with the main stream of new European theater: "Nonsense and satire mingle with parody but the serious philosophical intent is again and again brought into the open. . . . 'One Way Pendulum' owed its considerable success with the public to the sustained inventiveness of its nonsense." However, Esslin argues, "what seems little more than . . . harmless . . . upside-down logic is essentially a ferocious comment on contemporary British life." In the same vein of "purposeful nonsense," "The Cresta Run" (1966, o.p.) satirizes the concept of organized espionage.

A RESOUNDING TINKLE. 1956. *French* 1958 $.85

THE HOLE. 1957. *French* 1958 $.85

ONE WAY PENDULUM: A Farce in a New Dimension. 1959. *French* $1.75; (in "Modern British Drama") ed. by Henry Popkin *Grove* 1964 pap. $5.95

THE FORM. *French* 1961 $.85

USTINOV, PETER. 1921–

In "Photo Finish," written, directed, and acted (on Broadway in 1963) by Ustinov, he portrayed an 80-year-old author who meets and chats with himself in his twenties, forties, and sixties. The *tour de force* is typical of this "triple-threat" man of the theatre. And some of his difficulties may derive from the fact that the playwright of more than 17 plays keeps bumping into his other selves—the film actor (who in 1961 won an Oscar for "Spartacus"), the wit and clown, the novelist and short story writer (author most recently of "The Frontiers of the Sea" *Little–Atlantic* 1966 $5.95 and "Krumnagel" *Little–Atlantic* 1971 $7.95; *New Am. Lib.* 1972 Signet pap. $1.25). Ustinov has never really duplicated the success of his early pieces, such as "The Love of Four Colonels," "No Sign of the Dove" (1965, o.p.) or "The Banbury Noses" (1944, o.p.). He is, notes Clive Barnes, "a tantalizingly good writer who has yet to write a completely satisfying play. . . . We are still waiting for him to honor the full promise he has been showing for more than 20 years." "Who's Who in Hell," a political satire which closed after a few Broadway performances in 1975, brought Ustinov no closer to that goal.

THE LOVE OF FOUR COLONELS: A Play in two acts. 1951. *Dramatists* 1953 $1.25

ROMANOFF AND JULIET. 1958. *Dramatists* $1.25

PHOTO FINISH. 1962. *Dramatists* $1.25

Books about Ustinov

Peter Ustinov. By Geoffrey Willans. *Hillary House* 1952 $4.00

MORTIMER, JOHN. 1923–

Two of the three plays published together in Mortimer's first American collection were written for television, as was "Lunch Hour." "The Dock Brief" has been shown on American TV. His affinity for the medium ("for a writer, television now seems to me the best medium after the theatre") reflects his familiarity with film techniques, gained in war work on documentary films. John Mortimer was educated at Harrow and Oxford. He became a barrister in 1948 and practised law for eight years, meanwhile writing six novels. "The Dock Brief," his first play, was written originally for radio and broadcast by BBC's Third Programme in 1957.

Mortimer's plays appear at the onset to have more in common with the "old" drama ("typical Shaftesburiana" growled one critic) than the new, partly because "he applies his exploratory techniques to the middle classes"—(John Russell Taylor). His plays take place in a "seedy middle-class world of run-down private schools, draughty seaside hotels, nine-to-five offices and the shabbier corners of the courts." He mixes the shabbiness with comedy, which is, to him, "the only thing worth writing in this despairing age, providing the comedy is truly on the side of the lonely, the neglected, the unsuccessful." Mortimer's frequent subject is the "failure of communication, confinement to and sometimes liberation from private dream-worlds."

THE DOCK BRIEF. 1957. *French* $.85; (in "English One-Act Plays of Today") ed. by Donald Fitzjohn *Oxford* 1962 pap. $2.25

WHAT SHALL WE TELL CAROLINE? 1958. *French* $.85

I SPY. 1957. *French* $.85. An unstaged play, originally for radio.

LUNCH HOUR. 1960. *French* $.85. A one-act play.

BOLT, ROBERT. 1924–

Born in Manchester, where he attended school and university, Robert Bolt had spent three years in the army and air force, and was teaching school when his play "Flowering Cherry" was presented in London with Sir Ralph Richardson as Cherry. Its success persuaded him to devote himself to the stage. His second success, "The Tiger and the Horse," proved him "a good, traditional playwright whose approach to his craft . . . is not so different from that of, say, Terence Rattigan," according to John Russell Taylor. "These two plays are 'uneasily straddled,' as Bolt himself puts it, "between naturalism and nonnaturalism . . . realistic in technique, but in their climaxes they both try something beyond realism."

In 1958 Bolt wrote a short play for BBC radio about Sir Thomas More (*q.v.*). It is this play, "A Man for All Seasons," expanded and restyled for the stage, that has won for Bolt recognition on both sides of the Atlantic. In sharp opposition to the experimentalism of contemporaries for whom the ambiguities of character and situation rob action of meaning, Bolt reaffirmed a drama in which real conflicts between meaningful alternatives can reveal "a nobility of character rarely found in the modern theatre." This play won the N.Y. Drama Critics Circle award in 1962 as the best foreign play. Since then Bolt has written three award-winning screenplays: "Lawrence of Arabia" (1962), "Doctor Zhivago" and the adapatation of "A Man for All Seasons" for the film which won the 1966 Oscars for best picture, best adapted screenplay and several other categories.

In the last, Paul Scofield recreated his brilliant portrayal of Sir Thomas against marvelous photography of the English landscape.

"Gentle Jack" (1963, o.p.), which Bolt himself does not regard as entirely successful, was written for Dame Edith Evans. It concerns a boy and an elderly woman—the boy embodying "the central human situation" in which spontaneity means tenderness but also violence. Both central characters meet violent ends. The boy is passion, the woman intellect, and Bolt is concerned about the polarity of these two elements in the modern world, "which has got to be ended pretty damned quick, because I think it has implications far beyond the world of art." "Vivat Vivat Regina," a play about Mary, Queen of Scots, was performed in 1970 at the Chichester Festival and in London.

FLOWERING CHERRY. 1958. *French* $1.75

A MAN FOR ALL SEASONS. 1961. *Random* 1962 $5.50 Vintage pap. $1.65; *Baker* $1.25; *French* $1.75; (in "New Theatre of Europe") Vol. 1 ed. by R. W. Corrigan *Dell* Delta pap. $2.25; (in "The Twentieth Century British Drama") ed. by R. W. Corrigan *Dell* Laurel 1965 $.95

THE TIGER AND THE HORSE. 1960. *French* $1.75

VIVAT VIVAT REGINA. 1971. *Random* 1972 $4.95; *French* $1.75

KOPS, BERNARD. 1926– *See Chapter 12, Modern British Fiction*, Reader's Adviser, *Vol. 1.*

SHAFFER, PETER. 1926–

Peter Shaffer differs from others of the new playwrights in his reluctance as a dramatist to reveal his private world. "The most interesting quality of his work is its impersonality," writes John Russell Taylor. Cast-iron construction, coherent plot, realistic characterization provide a conventional surface that conceals great originality of observation.

Born in Liverpool, he spent three years working in coal mines before entering Cambridge. After graduating in 1950, he came to New York and began writing plays. Two of his television plays had been produced when "Five Finger Exercise" won for him the London *Evening Standard* Drama Award as the most promising British playwright of 1958. Its New York production in 1959 won the Drama Critics Circle Award as the best foreign play of the year.

In 1962, his two one-acters "The Private Ear" (filmed in 1966 as "The Pad") and "The Public Eye" won critical praise for "technical efficiency and that ability to engage an audience which is the hall-mark of a true dramatist." "The Royal Hunt of the Sun," a dramatization in verse of the physical and philosophical confrontation between the Spanish Conquistador Pizarro and the Inca Atahuallpa, was the first contemporary play to be performed by the British National Theater under the direction of Sir Laurence Olivier. It enjoyed a successful run in New York. In a very different vein is "Black Comedy"—"a bout of the wildest slapstick that has been around here in a long, long time"—(*New Yorker*). First performed in London in 1965, it came to New York in 1967 with the curtain-raiser "White Lies," a less effective piece about a boy who invents his working-class origins, youthful poverty and whining accent "because it's *de rigueur* in Britain these days"—(*N.Y. Times*). A tautly constructed psychiatric thriller, "Equus," was given a theatrically strong production by John Dexter and London's National Theatre Company in 1973, and brought to New York in the following year. Mr. Shaffer has lived for some time in New York and has written three detective novels.

FIVE FINGER EXERCISE: A Play in Two Acts and Four Scenes. Pref. by Frederick Brisson *Harcourt* 1958 $3.00; *French* $1.75

THE PRIVATE EAR and THE PUBLIC EYE. 1962. *Stein & Day* 1964 $3.95; *French* 2 vols. each $.85. Two one-act plays.

THE ROYAL HUNT OF THE SUN. 1965. *French* $1.75

BLACK COMEDY (1965) and WHITE LIES (1967). *Stein & Day* 1967 pap. $1.95; *French* $1.75

EQUUS and SHRIVINGS. *Atheneum* 1974 $7.95. Two plays in one vol.

NICHOLS, PETER. 1928–

A Bristol-born former actor and schoolteacher, Peter Nichols got his start writing some fourteen plays for television and has continued to write for that medium even after his success in the West End. "A Day in the Death of Joe Egg," his first stage play, was produced in England in 1967 and on Broadway a year later. "Joe Egg" (as a squeamish New York management insisted it be retitled) is a "restlessly original and recklessly touching . . . comedy" (Walter Kerr) concerning a couple whose marriage is slowly being destroyed by their attempt to raise a hopelessly spastic daughter (Josephine, alias "Joe Egg," their "living parsnip"). They survive in their situation as long as they do only by ceaselessly joking about it. But this is not "black humor," Nichols insists. The black humorist "sets himself at a distance from his characters and [laughs] at them. The characters [in my play] set themselves at a distance from their own situation. . . ."

Nichols' second play, "The National Health," is about a situation no less desperate (a hospital ward filled with the suffering and dying), treated in a manner no less fantastic (scenes in the ward alternate with episodes of an outrageous medical soap-opera, "Nurse Norton's Affair," shown on a simulated TV screen). Performed in England by the National Theatre and chosen by the *Evening Standard* as the Best Play of 1969, "The National Health" was a major hit of the 1974 New York season. A third Nichols play, "Forget-Me-Not Lane," also a great success in London, has yet to be published or produced in the United States.

JOE EGG. *Grove* Evergreen Bks. 1968 (orig.) pap. $1.95; *French* $1.75

THE NATIONAL HEALTH. 1970. *Grove* 1975 pap. $3.95

OSBORNE, JOHN.   1929–

"The entry of Jimmy Porter on to the stage of the Royal Court Theatre . . . marks a turning point in recent theatrical history," writes Frederick Lumley. Jimmy Porter, villain-hero, his creator and prototype, John Osborne, and "Look Back in Anger" inaugurated in England a revitalization of British drama, the era of young writers, catagorized at the onset as "The Angry Young Men." Their appearance coincided almost simultaneously with the eruption in America of "Beat Writing." Osborne made hopes and despairs of the youth of the "lower classes"—the dispossessed in rebellion against the Establishment—a burning issue not only in the theater but in British life, and helped to make fashionable the long-despised non-Oxford accents of the Beatles and "Twiggy."

He had had two plays performed out of town when he sent the script of "Look Back in Anger" to the newly formed English Stage Company, a hopeful repertory group with the declared aim of being a "writer's theater." The play was selected for production that first season. Kenneth Tynan greeted it with wholehearted enthusiasm—"It's the best young play of the decade"—and its commercial success opened the way for Osborne and many others to find in writing drama a viable mode of expression. (*See also the introduction to this Chapter.*)

John Osborne was born and raised in a London tenement district. At 16 he left school to work at various jobs in trade magazines and intermittently as an actor until, at the age of 26, his "Look Back in Anger" was produced. The keynote of Osborne's comment on the modern world was anger, and Jimmy Porter was his voice, loud, selfish, profane, but direct. "Though Jimmy Porter and his *milieu* seem, even at this short distance of time, inescapably 'period' . . . quintessentially 'mid-fifties,' " writes Taylor, "it was precisely the quality of immediacy and topicality which makes them so now that had the electrifying effect in 1956: Jimmy was taken to be speaking for a whole generation. . . ." and Jimmy's most familiar pronouncement, "There aren't any good, brave causes left," seemed a revelation of heroic honesty.

"The Entertainer" and "Epitaph for George Dillon," Osborne's next plays, extended his popularity. Both are realistic, both are "angry" plays; in Osborne's sense "to be angry is to care." In "The Entertainer," however, Osborne attempts certain techniques borrowed from Brechtian "epic" theater. He encases the realistic scenes in an "endistancing" framework of music-hall numbers. The great success of the play may have been partially due to Sir Laurence Olivier's role as Archie Rice, the fading comedian of a holiday show. Osborne's next play, however, in which he attempted more extensive use of song, dance and satire, proved unsuccessful. "The World of Paul Slickey" and the television play, "a Matter for Scandal and Concern," both failed to reconcile the different techniques of epic and realistic theater. In "Luther" the playwright eschews Brechtian mannerisms and presents the historical material in straightforward fashion, creating a portrait of a "man who had built his strength on his own frailties"—(*N.Y. Times*). Much of the dialogue is taken verbatim from Luther's own writings. With Albert Finney in the title role, it opened in 1963 in New York, where it received the Drama Critics Circle award. Osborne also won a 1963 Tony award for his screenplay "Tom Jones."

The changes on the British dramatic scene which Osborne initiated proceeded so rapidly as almost to outdate him. Gordon Rogoff wrote in the British Theatre issue of the *Tulane Drama Review* (Winter 1966), "Osborne seen away from his first, deceptive impact—regardless of how useful that deception was to the extraordinary theatrical renaissance that followed in Britain—is, ironically, more a figure from the past than from the present. . . . As it is, the anti-hero of this past season's Broadway success, 'Inadmissible Evidence,' is still another expert monologist, Jimmy Porter not so much grown-up as grown older; and it is of some moment that his most eloquent diatribe is directed against a ruthlessly separated, uncommunicative, silent member of the new generation. The Osborne line is almost classically British in its ascent: yesterday's rebel is tomorrow's Establishment."

If Osborne's rebellion has been neutralized, his voice still insists on being heard: his is a remarkably productive playwright. There has been nothing in the seventies to match the success of "Inadmissible Evidence" and the scandal of "A Patriot for Me." But there have been television plays ("The Right Prospectus," 1970; "Very Like a Whale," 1971), adaptations ("Hedda Gabler," 1972; "Picture of Dorian Gray," 1973, performed in London in 1975), and full-length pieces ("West of Suez," 1971, and "A Sense of Detachment," 1972, both performed at the Royal Court Theatre). And, indeed, revivals of Osborne's earliest plays, provoking reassessments of his place in the history of English drama. The important British critic, Ronald Bryden, recently wondered in print whether that neglected work, "The Entertainer," in its heavy dependence on music-hall culture, might not be said to have shown the way to recent, pop-oriented English plays.

LOOK BACK IN ANGER. 1956. Ed. by John R. Taylor *Aurora* 1970 pap. $2.50; *Bantam* pap. $.95; *Dramatic* $1.25; *Phillips* $4.95

THE ENTERTAINER. 1957. *Phillips* $4.95; *Dramatic* $1.25

(With Anthony Creighton) EPITAPH FOR GEORGE DILLON. 1958. *Phillips* $3.95; *Bantam* 1964 pap. $.95; *Dramatic* $1.25

LUTHER. 1961. *Dramatic* $1.25; *New Am. Lib.* Signet 1964 pap. $.95

PLAYS FOR ENGLAND: The Blood of the Bambergs and Under Plain Cover. 1962. *Criterion* 1964 $3.50; (and The World of Paul Slickey, 1959) *Grove* 1966 pap. $1.45

INADMISSIBLE EVIDENCE. 1964. *Grove* 1965 pap. $2.45; *Dramatic* $1.50; (in "New Theatre of Europe," vol. 3) ed. by R. W. Corrigan *Dell* Delta 1968 pap. $2.25

FOUR PLAYS: West of Suez, A Patriot for Me, Time Present, The Hotel in Amsterdam. *Dodd* 1973 $7.50

Books about Osborne

John Osborne. By Martin Banham. Writers and Critics Ser. *Int. Pub. Service* 1969 $2.50
The Plays of John Osborne: An Assessment. By Simon Trussler. *Humanities Press* 1969 $7.50 pap. $3.75
John Osborne: Look Back in Anger. Ed. by J. R. Taylor Casebook Ser. *Aurora* 1970 pap. $2.50
John Osborne. By Alan Carter. *Harper* (Barnes and Noble) 1973 $11.50
John Osborne. By H. Ferrar. Essays on Modern Writers *Columbia* pap. $1.00
John Osborne. By Ronald Hayman. World Dramatists Ser. *Ungar* $7.50

ARDEN, JOHN. 1930–

Unlike many of the British "new wave" dramatists who turned unexpectedly from workaday life to drama, John Arden, born in Barnsley and educated for architecture at Cambridge and Edinburgh, has been writing dramas since his school days. And unlike most of his contemporaries writing drama, he had not, by the early sixties, achieved popular success. But in spite of almost "complete public apathy," the English Stage Company espoused his cause, producing "The Waters of Babylon," "Live like Pigs," "Happy Haven" and "Serjeant Musgrave's Dance." BBC radio and television purchased plays, and a rapidly growing audience found familiarity with his approach "breeds nothing but respect and admiration."

Sean O'Casey (*q.v.*) wrote in "Blasts and Benedictions," "Indeed, it seems to me that Arden's *Serjeant Musgrave's Dance* is far and away the finest play of the present day, full of power, protest, and frantic compassion, notwithstanding that, on its first presentation, it was scowled and scooted from the theatre by most of our intelligent and unintelligent drama critics. I wonder why!" "Live Like Pigs," produced at the Royal Court Theater in London in 1961, concerns a wild group of gypsies evicted from their home in an abandoned streetcar by "the leveling, hygienic processes of the welfare state, which cannot tolerate their dirt, their immorality, and above all, their lack of ambition"—(Quotations from the *Tulane Drama Review*).

"In America, where *Musgrave* was a flop *d'estime* and *Live like Pigs* a flop plain," wrote Robert Pasolli in the *Nation* (1967), "Arden is yet to emerge from the relative chill of admiration by university and theatre workshop coteries into the warm sun of popular and critical reception. Apparently a major American production of *Armstrong's Last Goodnight* is needed to bring that off." The latter concerns the clash between the local laird, Johnny Armstrong of Gilnockie, and the King of Scotland—the individual versus established authority. Arden's first play, "The Waters of Babylon," was produced in 1967 at the Washington (D.C.) Theatre Club—the Brechtian story of a man called Krank, a rent-gouging pimp. Pasolli finds it full of defects as a play, but "what is astounding about *Babylon* and marks it as great playwriting is the variety, imagination and poeticism of the story of Krank and his company." "Left-Handed Liberty," written on commission for the 750th anniversary of Magna Carta, is "highly dramatic, almost entirely historically accurate and beau tifully characterized"—(*LJ*). A play about Nelson, "The Hero Rises Up," which Arden wrote with his wife Margaretta D'Arcy, was briefly performed in London in 1969.

THREE PLAYS: Live like Pigs (1958), The Waters of Babylon (1957) and The Happy Haven (1960). Introd. by John Russell Taylor. *Grove* Black Cat Bks. 1966 pap. $2.45

SERJEANT MUSGRAVE'S DANCE. 1959. *Grove* $2.45; (in "Modern British Drama") ed. by H. Popkin *Grove* 1964 $5.95

(With Margaretta D'Arcy) THE BUSINESS OF GOOD GOVERNMENT. 1960. *Grove* Evergreen Bks. 1967 pap. $1.45

THE WORKHOUSE DONKEY. 1963. *Grove* Evergreen Bks. pap. $1.45

LEFT-HANDED LIBERTY: A Play about Magna Carta. 1965. *Grove* Evergreen Bks. 1966 pap. $2.45

ARMSTRONG'S LAST GOODNIGHT. 1964. *Grove* Evergreen Playscript 1968 pap. $1.50

PINTER, HAROLD.   1930–

In 1958 a television play called "A Night Out" drew the largest audience theretofore recorded in England, "with a minimum of fifteen million." It was by Harold Pinter, the London-born, East End-reared son of immigrant parents—actor, poet, novelist and playwright for radio, stage, film and television, who today stands stage-center in the British dramatic renaissance. What was important about the audience estimate that night was not just the clue it lends to the vastly creative role of television in British drama but the evidence that a mass audience, seeking entertainment, found Pinter neither esoteric nor highbrow. If he has been linked with the European tradition of Absurd theatre, so also has he "learnt a lot from the master of controlled horror, Hitchcock." Pinter wrote or collaborated in the screenplays for "The Caretaker," "The Servant" and "The Accident."

Since his first play, "The Room," his work has exhibited an obsessive, dreamlike quality that provoked the critical term "comedy of menace." "The Birthday Party," "The Dumbwaiter" and "A Slight Ache" all represent situations of mystery, of horror, in which some nameless menace intrudes upon the refuge of the safe, the known. His technique of "casting doubt upon everything by matching each clear and unequivocal statement with an equally clear and unequivocal statement to the contrary" creates mystery and uncertainty. And, "by extension, the whole question of everyday reality comes into question." With "The Caretaker" and subsequent plays, Pinter has shown a deeper mastery of psychological realism. Characters behave with comprehensible motivation: What was formerly menace from the outside is contained by a clash of personality within the play. Clifford Leech praised "The Caretaker" as "the most impressive dramatic writing in English since the War." Produced in New York in 1961, it achieved the same citical and commerical success it won in London the previous year. In 1962–63 "The Collection" and "The Dumbwaiter" played to full houses off-Broadway despite a prolonged newspaper strike.

"The Homecoming," shocking in theme and execution, hit New York like a thunderbolt early in 1967. In this production by the Royal Shakespeare Company, Vivien Merchant, Pinter's wife, played the role of a young woman who crosses the Atlantic with her husband to meet his (entirely male) family and ends by staying on, by mutual agreement, as their private whore who will do public whoring to support herself, while the apparently unaffected husband amiably returns to their children in America. With this play, Pinter's drama of mysterious intrusion achieved a rich mythic resonance. "The Homecoming" was immediately accepted as a classic. It has already been revived in New York (1971), and filmed for the American Film Theatre's repertory, in a version written by Pinter himself.

In 1969, the Royal Shakespeare Company's double bill of "Landscape" and "Silence" marked what critics have agreed is a turn in a new direction for Pinter—toward plays obsessed with memory, built of monologues and separated conversations. The first full-length experiment in the new mode, "Old Times," was produced in both London and New York in 1971. A second, "No Man's Land," was performed at London's Old Vic in 1975.

THE CARETAKER (1960) and THE DUMBWAITER (1957). *Grove* Evergreen Bks. 1961 pap. $1.75·

THE BIRTHDAY PARTY (1958) and THE ROOM (1957). *Grove* Evergreen Bks. 1961 pap. $1.75

THREE PLAYS: The Collection, A Slight Ache (1961) and The Dwarfs. *Grove* Evergreen Bks. 1961 pap. $1.95

EARLY PLAYS: A Night Out (1961), Night School, Revue Sketches (1961). *Grove* 1968 Evergreen Bks. pap. $1.95

THE LOVER AND OTHER PLAYS. *Grove* 1967 Evergreen Bks. pap. $1.95. Also includes The Tea Party (1964) and The Basement.

THE DUMBWAITER. 1957 *Dramatists* $1.75

THE COLLECTION. 1962. *Dramatists* $1.95

THE DWARFS. *Dramatists* $1.25. A one-act play and 8 revue sketches.

THE LOVER. 1963. *Dramatists* $.75

THE HOMECOMING. 1964. *Grove* $3.95 Evergreen Bks. pap. $1.95; *French* $1.95

MAC: A Memoir. *Grove* 1969 $4.50. A memoir of Anew MacMaster, an Irish actor. Pinter was his friend and, at one time, a member of his company.

LANDSCAPE AND SILENCE. *Grove* 1970 $3.95 Evergreen Bks. pap. $1.95. Includes a short piece, Night.

POEMS. *Enitharmon* (dist. by Serendipity Bk. Dist.) 1971 $4.50 pap. $2.20 signed limited ed. $25.00

OLD TIMES. *Grove* 1972 Evergreen Bks. pap. $1.95

FIVE SCREENPLAYS: The Servant, The Pumpkin Eater, The Quiller Memorandum, Accident, The Go-Between. *Grove* 1973 $10.00 Evergreen Bks. pap. $3.95

NO MAN'S LAND. *Grove* 1975 $6.95 pap. $1.95

Books about Pinter

Harold Pinter. By Arnold Hinchcliffe. English Authors Ser. *Twayne* 1967 $6.50. The author has taught British drama at Yale and is now at the University of Manchester, England.

Harold Pinter. By Walter Kerr. Essays on Modern Writers *Columbia* 1967 pap. $1.00

The Peopled Wound: The Work of Harold Pinter. By Martin Esslin. *Doubleday* Anchor Bks. 1970 pap. $1.45

The Dramatic World of Harold Pinter: Its Basis in Ritual. By Katherine H. Burkman. *Ohio State Univ. Press* 1971 $8.00

Casebook on Harold Pinter's The Homecoming. Ed. by John Lahr. *Grove* 1971 pap. $2.95

Pinter: A Collection of Critical Essays. Ed. by A. Ganz. Twentieth Century Views Ser. *Prentice–Hall* Spectrum $6.50 pap. $1.95

Harold Pinter. By Ronald Hayman. World Dramatists Ser. *Ungar* 1973 $7.50

The Plays of Harold Pinter: An Assessment. By Simon Trussler. *Humanities Press* 1974 $7.50

Harold Pinter. By John R. Taylor. Writers and Their Work Ser. *British Bk. Centre* $2.95 pap. $1.20

The Pinter Problem. By Austin E. Quigley. *Princeton Univ. Press* 1975 $13.50

WESKER, ARNOLD. 1932–

To Arnold Wesker belongs the unique distinction of having had his three related plays, now indelibly dubbed "The Wesker Trilogy," performed in repertory at the Royal Court Theater with the acclaim of critics and audience alike. The execution of this theatrical event is no less remarkable than the ambitious attempt of the plays themselves to "sum up the situation of the working class today." At the time (1960) Wesker had written only one other play. If he aspired to give voice to the complex situation of Britain's labor class, Wesker had authentic credentials. Like most of the other new-wave dramatists, he came from a working-class family. He grew up in London's East End, and was himself a working man until "Chicken Soup with Barley" was first performed on an Arts Council Grant in 1958. His years spent as a pastry cook provided background for the play and film of "The Kitchen" (1962, o.p.), which dramatizes the chaotic rush hour in the kitchen of a large restaurant. Although his style in the trilogy is unmistakably naturalist, in "The Kitchen" Wesker attempted allegorical drama. The kitchen is a world-in-miniature and "these are the conditions of capitalist life and labor, he implies. ('When the world is filled with kitchens,' says one man, 'you get pigs.')"—(Stanley Kauffmann, in the *N.Y. Times*).

"Chips with Everything", (1962, o.p.), a resounding success in its 1962 London production, grew out of Wesker's experiences in the RAF as well as his preoccupation, as he has said, "with this idea of the way in which the rebel is absorbed in English society"—(quoted in "Theatre at Work"). It represented a move still further away from naturalism. "Chips with Everything" opened on Broadway late in 1963 with unanimous critical approval.

In 1966 "Their Very Own and Golden City" was first produced (in its final version) at London's Royal Court Theater. It is his interpretation of the rise and fall of the Labor Movement—from 1926 to 1990. "The Four Seasons" (1965), a two-character love story, is unique among his plays for its heightened dialogue and for the absence of a theme of social protest. "The real interest of 'The Four Seasons' is the manner in which it indicates Wesker's dissatisfaction with working-class realistic drama," wrote Clive Barnes in 1968. "The move toward the theater of imagery is probably wise and necessary."

THE WESKER TRILOGY: Chicken Soup with Barley (1958); Roots (1959); I'm Talking about Jerusalem (1960). *Penguin* 1964 pap. $1.25

ROOTS. 1959. (in "Modern British Drama") ed. by H. Popkin *Grove* 1964 pap. $5.95

Books about Wesker

Arnold Wesker. By Harold Ribalow. English Authors Ser. *Twayne* $6.50
Arnold Wesker. By Ronald Hayman. World Dramatists Ser. *Ungar* 1973 $7.50
Arnold Wesker. By Glenda Leeming. Writers and Their Work Ser. *British Bk. Centre* 1973 $2.95 pap. $1.20

ORTON, JOE.   1933–1967.

Orton wrote his first play (for the BBC) in 1964; in 1967 he was murdered. In the short time between, he saw four radically disturbing comedies staged in London: "Entertaining Mr. Sloane" (1964), "Loot" (1965), "The Ruffian on the Stair" and "The Erpingham Camp" (1966, a double bill). "What the Butler Saw" was produced posthumously, from a perhaps unrevised draft. The first two Orton productions had great commercial success, "Entertaining Mr. Sloane" being chosen the Best New British play of 1964. It is in that play that Orton's entirely original style, combining the intricacy of melodramatic or farcial plot, dialogue of extreme—even Victorian—formality, and outrageously grotesque and violent circumstances, is best displayed.

In 1975, the English Stage Company produced a retrospective Orton Festival at London's Royal Court Theatre.

ENTERTAINING MR. SLOANE. 1965. *Grove* $2.95; *French* $1.45

LOOT. 1967. *Grove* $1.95; *French* $1.75

WHAT THE BUTLER SAW. 1969. *Grove* $2.40; *French* $1.75

BOND, EDWARD.   1935–

Because of its pivotal scene, which involves the stoning to death of a baby by a gang of young toughs in a London park, Edward Bond's first major production, "Saved" (1965), was banned in its entirety by the Lord Chamberlain. This last heroic effort of English stage censorship, whose tradition was to come to an end only three years later, necessarily drew attention away from the remarkable power of Bond's naturalistic examination of Oedipal forces in society. In the last decade Bond has put his special vision of inhumanity before the public several times in new dramatic forms: the surrealism of "Early Morning" (1968), in which Disraeli, Victoria, and Florence Nightingale share the stage with a royal pair of Siamese twins; the spare allegory of the "Japanese" fable, "Narrow Road to the Deep North" (1968); the "Shakespearean" adaptation, "Lear" (1970). In 1974, Bond's "Bingo" showed Shakespeare himself, selfish and embittered, enduring his retirement in Stratford and dying at last, a suicide.

SAVED. 1966. *Farrar, Straus* (Hill and Wang) $1.75; (in "The New Theatre of Europe" vol. 4 ed. by M. Esslin) *Dell* Delta pap. $2.25.

NARROW ROAD TO THE DEEP NORTH. 1968. *Farrar, Straus* (Hill and Wang) pap. $1.50.

LEAR. 1971. *Farrar, Straus* (Hill and Wang) 1972 pap. $2.65

BINGO AND THE SEA. 1974. *Farrar, Straus* (Hill and Wang) 1975 $3.95

STOPPARD, TOM.   1937–

When Britain's National Theater needed a last-minute substitute for its canceled production of "As You Like It," Kenneth Tynan decided to produce a script by an unknown author called "Rosencrantz and Guildenstern Are Dead," which had received discouraging notices from provincial critics at its Edinburgh Festival debut. In such an unlikely way Tom Stoppard came to light, and, when the play opened in London in April, 1967, he was "acclaimed by the critics almost to a man as the brilliant dramatic find of the sixties and the most stimulating new British dramatist—but how different!—since Harold Pinter"—(*New Yorker*). In New York, "Rosencrantz and Guildenstern" won the Drama Critics' Circle Award as Best Play of 1968.

In time, the echoes of "Godot" in this study of two offstage characters-in-waiting became more audible to the critical ear. (The play's insights, wrote Robert Brustein, "all seem to come . . . prefabricated from other plays.") Stoppard's reputation suffered through the production of a number of minor works, whose intellectual preoccupations were shrugged off by reviewers:

"Enter a Free Man" (1968: "an adolescent twinge of a play"—Marowitz in the *N.Y. Times*), "The Real Inspector Hound" (1968: "lightweight"—*N.Y. Times*), and "After Magritte" (1970).

But the initial enthusiasm aroused by "Rosencrantz and Guildenstern" has, in the seventies, been more than vindicated by the production of two full-length Stoppard plays. "Jumpers" (1972) is concerned, improbably, with politics, metaphysics, and acrobatics. "Travesties" (1974) is about the equally unlikely coincidence (if not meeting) of James Joyce, Tristan Tzara, and Lenin in Zurich during World War I, as seen through the uncomprehending eyes of a British consul (a "minor character," like Rosencrantz and Guildenstern). Immensely inventive verbally and theatrically, the plays have been successes on both sides of the Atlantic.

Brought up in England and now living in London (though born in Czechoslovakia), Stoppard began his literary career working for a Bristol newspaper. He has written a novel, "Lord Malquist and Mr. Moon" (1968 *Grove* 1975 pap. $2.45).

ROSENCRANTZ AND GUILDENSTERN ARE DEAD. 1966. *Grove* 1967 Black Cat Bks. pap. $1.95

ENTER A FREE MAN. 1968. *Grove* 1972 Evergreen Bks. pap. $1.65

THE REAL INSPECTOR HOUND. 1968. *Grove* 1969 Evergreen Bks. pap. $2.45

JUMPERS. *Grove* 1974 $5.95 Evergreen Bks. pap. $1.95

TRAVESTIES. *Grove* 1975 $6.95 pap. $1.95

DELANEY, SHELAGH.   1939–

Shelagh Delaney's career as a playwright reads like a romance novel. She is an extraordinary graduate of that untold host of would-be writers who see a play or read a novel and feel at the end they could write at least that well themselves. Shelagh Delaney saw a Terence Rattigan (*q.v.*) production on tour and dedided to better it. "A Taste of Honey" was the result—the play that enjoyed long and successful runs in the West End and on Broadway, that was promptly made into a film by Tony Richardson, and that catapulted its creator into fame. Shelagh Delaney was born and brought up in Slaford, Lancashire. She did poorly in school and left at the age of 16 to try her hand at various jobs, including work in a factory. She began to write "A Taste of Honey" when she was 17.

Her second play, "The Lion in Love" (1960, o.p.) was produced in 1960, first at the new Belgrade Theatre in Coventry, which had given Arnold Wesker (*q.v.*) his first production, and later that year in London. Though scarcely a commercial or critical success, some reviewers felt it did mark an advance in dramatic skill. Miss Delaney's pessimism and wry humor color her autobiographical "Sweetly Sings the Donkey" (1963, o.p.).

A TASTE OF HONEY. 1958. *Grove* Evergreen Bks. 1959 pap. $1.95; (in "Seven Plays of the Modern Theater") ed. by H. Clurman *Grove* 1962 $4.95; (in "Modern British Drama") ed. by H. Popkin *Grove* 1964 $5.95

IRISH DRAMA

It is the custom to group under Irish Drama not the writers who were born in Ireland, which would include Shaw (*q.v.*) and Wilde (*q.v.*), but the writers whose dramas are Irish in subject and setting. The great Renaissance of the Irish theater came with Yeats' decision to use the lives of gods and heroes of ancient Irish legends as material for the national drama. He rejected Ibsen's social themes. In the realistic period of the 20's, following the Easter Rebellion (1916), Irish folklore was discarded and the workaday world with its political and social problems took its place. O'Casey was the most dynamic force in the Post-Revolution drama. And Brendan Behan, who lived in Dublin when he was not in London, San Francisco, Toronto, Paris or New York was the youngest Irish playwright to become known here.

Three histories of Ireland's National Theater, the Abbey, are invaluable records of the tumults and triumphs from its founding in 1899 by Lady Gregory, Edward Martyn and Yeats to its burning in 1951. Peter Kavanagh's "The Story of the Abbey Theatre: From Its Origins in 1899 to the Present" (1950, o.p.) is spirited, if not impartial. "The Abbey Theatre: Cradle of Genius" (1958, o.p.) by Gerard Fay is a history, based on research into the original documents, by an author whose father and uncle were closely associated with the Theater. The official history commissioned by the Abbey Theater authorities was compiled by Lennox Robinson: "Ireland's Abbey Theatre: A History, 1899–1951" (1952. *Folcroft* $5.50; *Kennikat* $8.00). Equally absorbing is "Joseph Holloway's Abbey Theatre: A Selection from His Unpublished Journal 'Impressions of a Dublin Playgoer' " (ed. with introd. by Robert Hogan and Michael J. O'Neill, pref. by Harry T. Moore, *Southern Illinois Univ. Press* 1967 $6.95). A well-to-do architect, Holloway became greatly interested in the Abbey and candidly reported his observations in his copious journals, which ran to more than 100,000 pages. " 'He had,' as Padraic Colum remarked to us, 'the shrewdness of a first-nighter, but had, I should say, no real literary judgment' "—(Editors' introduction). His very lack of literary sophistication, however, lends the 296-page core of these diaries an air of immediacy—a sense, for the reader, of "being there" with the great personalities of the Abbey's heyday. At the turn of the century, the Abbey was "probably with the sole exception of the Moscow Art Theater, the most important and influential stage in the world" according to Tyrone Guthrie. But with the victory of Irish nationalism, it "lost a main incentive for its existence; also its policy passed out of the control of the aristocratic, but liberal members of the Protestant Ascendancy, who had created it."

Clark, William Smith. THE EARLY IRISH STAGE: The Beginnings to 1720. 1955. *Greenwood* 1973 $11.00. Well organized, comprehensive and scholarly.

Corrigan, Robert, Ed. MASTERPIECES OF THE MODERN IRISH THEATER. 1965. *Macmillan* Collier Bks. pap. $1.50. Includes Yeats: The Countess Cathleen; Synge: The Playboy of the Western World, Riders to the Sea; O'Casey: The Silver Tassie, Cock-A-Doodle-Dandy.

Coxhead, Elizabeth. J. M. SYNGE AND LADY GREGORY. *British Bk. Centre* 1962 $2.95 pap. $1.20. Pamphlet.

Ellis-Fermor, Una. THE IRISH DRAMATIC MOVEMENT. *Harper* (Barnes & Noble) 2nd ed. 1954 repr. 1967 Univ. Paperbacks pap. $6.00. An important study of Yeats, Lady Gregory, Synge and their contemporaries.

Hogan, Robert. AFTER THE IRISH RENAISSANCE: A Critical History of the Irish Drama Since "The Plough and the Stars." *Univ. of Minnesota Press* 1967 $8.50

An excellent history with an "exceptionally full" bibliography—*(PW)*

(Ed.) SEVEN IRISH PLAYS, 1946–1964. Introd. by the editor. *Univ. of Minnesota Press* 1967 $10.00

The Visiting House by Michael Molloy; Design for a Headstone by Seamus Byrne; Song of the Anvil by Bryan MacMahon; Copperfaced Jack by John O'Donovan; Sharon's Grave and Many Young Men of Twenty by John B. Keane; The Ice Goddess by James Douglas.

Kain, Richard M. DUBLIN IN THE AGE OF WILLIAM BUTLER YEATS AND JAMES JOYCE. *Univ. of Oklahoma Press* 1962 $3.95. Personalities and politics.

Malone, Andrew E. IRISH DRAMA. 1929. *Blom* 1965 $10.75

Mercier, Vivian. THE IRISH COMIC TRADITION. *Oxford* 1962 Galaxy Bks. 1969 pap. $2.50. A survey of the comic in Gaelic literature from the 9th century on, which suggests that it probably preceded tragedy.

THREE IRISH PLAYS: Iron Harp by Joseph O'Conor; Step in the Hollow by Donagh McDonagh; Moon in the Yellow River by Denis Johnston. *Branden* pap. $.95

(With D. H. Greene, Eds.) 1000 YEARS OF IRISH PROSE: Pt. 1 The Literary Revival. 1952. *Grosset* Univ. Lib. pap. $2.45

Part I includes Yeats' "Cathleen Ni Houlihan," first performed in 1902, marking the real beginning of the Irish National Theatre, and "The Resurrection" (1934). A preface and a play by Synge and one by O'Casey are the other drama entries.

GREGORY, LADY ISABELLA AUGUSTA. 1852–1932.

The manager for many years of the Abbey Theatre in Dublin, Lady Gregory was one of the founders of the Irish National Theater Society, the author of several books on Irish folklore and a playwright herself. The story of the revival of native drama for the Irish stage is told in "Our Irish Theatre." "Lady Gregory's Journals 1916–1930," ed. by Lennox Robinson (1947, o.p.) reveals her as courageous and honest, with the gift of bringing out the best in the many people she befriended. A close friend of Yeats (*q.v.*) to the end, she died on the estate in Galway immortalized in Yeats' lovely poem "The Wild Swans at Coole." With Yeats she wrote the play "Cathleen ni Houlihan" (1902). Her own—usually brief—plays were fantasies based on Irish legend, patriotic historical dramas and the comedies of Irish peasant life for which she is best known.

COLLECTED PLAYS. Ed. by Ann Saddlemyer *Oxford* 4 vols. 1971 Vol. 1 The Comedies $12.00 Vol. 2 The Tragedies and Tragi-comedies $13.75 Vol. 3 The Wonder and Supernatural Plays $15.25 Vol. 4 Translations and Adaptations and Her Collaborations with Douglas Hyde and W. B. Yeats $13.75

SEVEN SHORT PLAYS. 1910. *Scholarly Press* 1970 $14.50

IRISH FOLK HISTORY PLAYS. 1912. *Scholarly Press* 2 vols. 1971 $24.50

THREE LAST PLAYS. 1928. *Scholarly Press* 1971 $14.50

SPREADING THE NEWS. 1904. *French* $.60

THE RISING OF THE MOON. 1907. *French* $.60

THE WORKHOUSE WARD. 1908. *French* $.60; *Baker* $.60

THE TRAVELLING MAN. 1910. *French* $.60; *Baker* $.60

Nondramatic Works

KILTARTAN BOOKS. 1909–1919. Ill. by Robert and Margaret Gregory; fwd. by Padriac Colum. *Oxford* Coole Ed. 1971 $12.00. Includes Kiltartan Poetry, History and Wonder Books.

CUCHULAIN OF MUIRTHEMNE: The Story of the Men of the Red Branch of Ulster. 1902. *Oxford* Coole Ed. 5th ed. 1970 $9.50 pap. $3.95

GODS AND FIGHTING MEN. 1904. *Scholarly Press* 1971 $16.00; *Oxford* 2nd ed. 1970 $10.50

A BOOK OF SAINTS AND WONDERS. 1906. *Irish Academic Press* (Cuala Press) 1971 $10.80; *Oxford* Coole Ed. 1971 $8.50

THE KILTARTAN POETRY BOOK. 1918. *Irish Academic Press* (Cuala Press) 1971 $10.80

VISIONS AND BELIEFS IN THE WEST OF IRELAND. 1920. *Oxford* Coole Ed. 1970 $11.25

SIR HUGH LANE, HIS LIFE AND LEGACY. 1921. *Oxford* Coole Ed. 1973 $19.25

COOLE. 1931. Ed. by Colin Smythe *Humanities* (Dolmen Press) text ed. $14.75; *Irish Academic Press* (Cuala Press) rept. of 1931 ed. 1971 $10.80

Books about Lady Gregory

In Defence of Lady Gregory, Playwright. By Ann Saddlemyer. 1965. *Dufour* 1967 $5.25 "This small volume . . . whets the reader's appetite for a full-scale, modern study of the dramatist. The sections on comedy, use of dialect, and fable are of particular interest to students of drama, but the discussion of Lady Gregory's relationship with Yeats and Synge is regrettably brief"—(*LJ*).

J. M. Synge and Lady Gregory. By Elizabeth Coxhead. *British Bk. Centre* 1962 $2.95 pap. $1.20 The author is an authority on Lady Gregory and has also written her biography, "Lady Gregory: A Literary Portrait" (1961, o.p.).

Lady Gregory. By Hazard Adams Irish Writers Ser. *Bucknell Univ. Press* $4.50 pap. $1.95

YEATS, WILLIAM BUTLER. 1865–1939. (Nobel Prize 1923)

"Before [Yeats] began his work, poetry was virtually unknown in the contemporary theatre; nineteenth-century poets had either avoided drama or written plays primarily for reading. Yeats lived to see poetic drama acclimatized in Ireland, England, and America almost as it had been in Elizabethan England. This was the more remarkable in that Yeats's genius does not appear to have been primarily dramatic"—(*Oxford Companion to the Theater*).

In 1899 the new Irish Literary Theatre opened in Dublin with Yeats's "The Countess Cathleen" (1892), a five-act verse drama about a woman who sells her own soul for the sake of starving Irish peasants. The failure of his first stage organization brought Yeats into partnership with the actors William and Frank Fay. Together, they helped found the Irish National Theatre Society, which subsequently established itself in the Abbey Theatre. While encouraging Lady Gregory and J. M. Synge to write for the new stage, Yeats himself contributed "The Land of Heart's Desire" (1894),

"Cathleen ni Houlihan" (1902), and "Dierdre" (1907). He left off writing for Abbey audiences in disgust after the infamous rioting which greeted Synge's "Playboy of the Western World" (1907).

In his later plays Yeats continued to develop Irish legendary themes ("At the Hawk's Well," 1917; "The Death of Cuchulain," 1939), but also interested himself in Christian ("Calvary," 1920; "Purgatory," 1939) and classical ("Sophocles' King Oedipus," 1928) material. He turned also to the Japanese Noh for the pattern of a drama whose evolution is marked by song and dance as much as by verse and action.

COLLECTED PLAYS. *Macmillan* 1935 new ed. with additional plays 1953 $8.95. Contains all the plays published in the 1934 edition, plus five written after 1934 and printed in the "Last Poems and Plays" (1940, o.p.).

THE VARIORUM EDITION OF THE PLAYS OF W. B. YEATS. Ed. by R. K. Alspach *Macmillan* 1966 $35.00

ELEVEN PLAYS. *Macmillan* 1966 pap. $1.95

THE LAND OF HEART'S DESIRE. 1894. *Baker* $.60; French $.85

CATHLEEN NI HOULIHAN. 1902. *Gordon Press* $25.00

TWO PLAYS FOR DANCERS. 1919. *Irish Academic Press* (Cuala Press) 1971 $13.20

KING OEDIPUS. 1928. *Macmillan* 1970 pap. $1.25

THE KING OF THE GREAT CLOCK TOWER. 1934. *Irish Academic Press* (Cuala Press) 1971 $13.20

EXPLORATIONS. Ed. by Mrs. W. B. Yeats *Macmillan* 1963 $5.95

A valuable collection of essays and introductions by Yeats. "The longest section is devoted to 'The Irish Dramatic Movement,' essays written between 1901 and 1919 stating (and restating) his philosophy of theater in general and the Irish theater in particular. . . . As might be expected, all reflect in varying measure Yeats's promotion of romantic tendencies and opposition to rationalism in literature and philosophy, his anti-democratic leanings, and his concern with the great Anglo-Irish tradition and his own place in that tradition"—(*LJ*).

Books about Yeats

Yeats: The Man and the Masks. By Richard Ellmann. 1948. *Dutton* pap. $2.45
The Irish Dramatic Movement. By Una Ellis-Fermor. 1954. *Harper* (Barnes and Noble) Univ. Paperback 1967 $6.00
Prolegomena to the Study of Yeats' Plays. By George B. Saul. 1958. *Octagon Bks.* 1970 $8.00
Yeats' Vision and the Later Plays. By Helen Hennessey Vendler. *Harvard Univ. Press* 1963 $8.00
Yeats the Playwright: A Commentary on Character and Design in the Major Plays. By Peter Ure. *Routledge & Kegan Paul* 1963 $6.25 pap. $2.50
The Tragic Drama of William Butler Yeats: Figures in a Dance. By L. Nathan. *Columbia* 1965 $12.00
Masks of Love and Death: Yeats as Dramatist. By John R. Moore. *Cornell Univ. Press* 1971 $12.50
W. B. Yeats: The Writing of The Player Queen. *Northern Illinois Univ. Press* 1974 $25.00

See also Chapter 7, Modern British Poetry, Reader's Adviser, *Vol. 1*

SYNGE, JOHN MILLINGTON. 1871–1909.

If Yeats (*q.v.*) had not discovered this young man in Paris, persuading him to return to Ireland and absorb its native tradition, the Irish Renaissance might have lost one of its best playwrights. More successfully, perhaps, than any of his contemporaries, Synge blended the poetic spirit of Celtic romanticism with the realism of peasant life. As he wrote in his preface to "The Playboy": "In countries where the imagination of the people, and the language they use, is rich and living, it is possible for a writer to be rich and copious in his words, and at the same time to give the reality, which is the root of all poetry, in a comprehensive and natural form."

"The Aran Islands" (1911, o.p.) is Synge's journal of the sojourn in which he first came to know and love the Irish peasants and to catch the flavor and rhythm of their speech. Before his short life was ended by cancer, he had written poetry, six major plays and two prose works (the other being "In Wicklow and West Kerry," o.p.). "Riders to the Sea" (1904), about a mother whose last son is drowned, is a one-act tragedy "whose brevity and economy of form and intensity and simplicity of passion make it one of the finest, if not the finest, of all modern short plays"—(*Oxford Companion to the Theatre*). Three years later his comedy "The Playboy of the Western World" caused riots at the Abbey Theater—as it did later in America among Irish patriots who saw it as a slander on their countrymen. The story, of a boy who becomes a hero among the simple villagers after boasting of killing his father, makes an ironic about-face when the irate father, very much alive, suddenly appears. The never completed "Deirdre of the Sorrows" (1910), now considered a "masterpiece of Irish Romanticism," is based on Lady Gregory's (*q.v.*) English version of an old Celtic legend of ill-fated love.

THE COMPLETE WORKS. *Random* $7.95

THE COMPLETE PLAYS. *Random* Vintage Bks. 1960 pap. $1.95

PLAYS, POEMS, AND PROSE. *Dutton* Everyman's 1968 $3.95 pap. $2.25

RIDERS TO THE SEA. 1904. *Baker* $.60; *French* $.85; *Irish Academic Press* (Cuala Press) 1970 $21.00

THE PLAYBOY OF THE WESTERN WORLD. 1907. *French* $2.45; (and "Riders to the Sea") ed. by William E. Hart *AHM Pub. Co.* Crofts Class. pap. $.50; ed. by Henry Popkin *Avon* 1967 $.60; *Harper* (Barnes & Noble) 1962 pap. $.95

THE TINKER'S WEDDING. 1909. *Branden* $2.00

DIERDRE OF THE SORROWS. 1910. *Irish Academic Press* (Cuala Press) $10.80

THE ARAN ISLANDS. *Branden* 1911 $3.75. A journal which provides a good background to the plays.

SOME SONNETS FROM LAURA IN DEATH. 1909. Ed. by Robin Skelton *Humanities Press* (Dolmen Press) 1971 $9.50. Prose translations from Petrarch.

LETTERS TO MOLLY: John Millington Synge to Maire O'Neill. Ed. by Ann Saddlemyer *Harvard Univ. Press* Belknap Press 1971 $11.00

MY WALLET OF PHOTOGRAPHS: The Collected Photographs of J. M. Synge arranged and introduced by Lilo Stephens *Humanities Press* (Dolmen Press) 1971 $16.50

Books about Synge

J. M. Synge: A Critical Study. By Percival P. Howe. 1912. *Folcroft* $8.75; *Greenwood* $9.25; Studies in Irish Lit. *Haskell* 1969 $12.95

John Millington Synge and the Irish Theatre. By Maurice Bourgeois. 1913. *Blom* $10.00; *Haskell* $18.95. One of the earliest studies, this scholarly work investigates Synge's complex personality, his relation to the Abbey Theatre and its productions, and includes a study of the Irish dialect in his plays.

The Death of Synge. By W. B. Yeats. 1923. *Irish Academic Press* (Cuala Press) 1971 $13.20

Synge and Anglo-Irish Literature. By Daniel Corkery. 1931. *Russell & Russell* 1965 $8.00

J. M. Synge. By David H. Greene and Edward M. Stephens. (1959, o.p.)
"A compelling answer to Daniel Corkery's work on Synge"—(*SR*), this official biography is valuable to the student "both for its lavish quotations and summaries of his unpublished writings and for its brief but more helpful notes, bibliography and index"—(*N.Y. Times*).

Synge and Anglo-Irish Drama. By Alan F. Price. 1961. *Russell & Russell* 1972 $16.00

J. M. Synge and Lady Gregory. By Elizabeth Coxhead. Writers and Their Work Ser. *British Bk. Centre* 1962 pap. $.75

John Millington Synge. By Donna Gerstenberger. English Authors Ser. *Twayne* 1964 $6.50

John Millington Synge. By D. Johnston. Essays on Mod. Writers Ser. *Columbia* 1965 $1.00

The Writings of J. M. Synge. By Robin Skelton. *Bobbs* $8.00

Synge: A Bibliography of Criticism. Ed. by Paul Levitt. *Harper* (Barnes and Noble) 1974 $15.00

O'CASEY, SEAN. 1884–1964.

After his plays were produced at the Abbey Theatre in Dublin, Sean O'Casey's success was noised abroad. The Irish Players themselves gave "Juno and the Paycock" and "The Plough and the Stars" in New York, on a visit to this country. Since that time his plays have been produced on Broadway as well as off-Broadway and by many amateur groups. A Protestant, slum-born, slum-reared and self-educated, he was active in the rebellions for Irish independence. A haunter of the Abbey Theater, he learned playwriting by watching the productions there. The Abbey produced his two "realistic" masterpieces, "Juno and the Paycock" and "The Plough and the Stars." But a riot in the theatre greeted the second of these, a bitterly ironic attack on the romantic "patriotism" of the Easter rebellion, and alienated O'Casey from the Abbey. A dispute over the production of his pacifist play, "The Silver Tassie," led to an actual break and self-exile in England, where he was warmly received by Shaw and others. In England, away from the discipline of a working theatre, he turned to modes of expressionistic satire and "morality" drama which have not received critical praise (or attention) of the sort reserved for the lyrical realism of the earlier Irish pieces. In 1958, after a dispute with the Archbishop of Dublin over the production of "The Drums of Father Ned" at the Dublin Theatre Festival, he vowed that none of his plays would ever again appear in Ireland. When he relented—"but just this once"—in 1963, it was to allow the Abbey to perform "Juno" and "The Plough and the Stars."

O'Casey's plays and his six great autobiographical volumes (1939–1954, o.p.), written in the third person, are distinguished for a prose "beautiful, angry, touching." His style mirrors "the music of the Irish . . . savage and caustic, but . . . also rich in song and loveliness." "Green Crow" (1956, o.p.) is a collection of his delightful and provocative articles on the theater which also contains four short stories. "Under a Colored Cap" (1963, o.p.) is a collection of 12 essays. "Blasts and Benedictions" (1967, o.p.) consists of stories and articles; about half are concerned with the theater. "An excellent anthology," said Sean Cronin (in the *New Republic*); "it is typical O'Casey: provocative ideas skip lightly across the pages clad sometimes in breathlessly lyrical language; at other times the style is as plain and direct as a Swiftian tract."

COLLECTED PLAYS. *St. Martin's* 4 vols. 1950–51 each $10.00. Vol. 1 Juno and the Paycock; The Shadow of a Gunman; The Plow and the Stars; The End of the Beginning (1937); A Pound on Demand (1949) Vol. 2 The Silver Tassie (1928); Within the Gates (1933); The Star Turns Red (1940) Vol. 3 Purple Dust; Red Roses for Me; Hall of Healing (1951) Vol. 4 Oak Leaves and Lavender (1946); Cock-A-Doodle Dandy (1949); Bedtime Story (1951); Time to Go (1951).

SELECTED PLAYS. Introd. by John Gassner *Braziller* 1956 $7.50. The Shadow of a Gunman; Juno and the Paycock; The Plough and the Stars; The Silver Tassie; Within the Gates; Purple Dust; Red Roses for Me; Bedtime Story; Time to Go; a foreword on playwriting by the dramatist and an excellent comprehensive introduction by John Gassner.

FIVE ONE-ACT PLAYS. *St. Martin's* 1960 $2.25. Includes The End of the Beginning (1937); A Pound on Demand (1949); The Hall of Healing (1951); Bedtime Story (1951); Time to Go (1951).

THREE PLAYS. 1957. *St. Martin's* 1960 pap. $1.95. Juno and the Paycock; The Shadow of a Gunman; The Plough and the Stars.

THREE MORE PLAYS. *St. Martin's* 1965 pap. $2.95. The Silver Tassie; Purple Dust; Red Roses for Me.

FEATHERS FROM THE GREEN CROW: Sean O'Casey, 1905–1925. Ed. by Robert Hogan *Univ. of Missouri Press* 1962 $6.50. Early works including newspaper articles, stories, songs and two previously unpublished plays, "Kathleen Listens In" and "Nannie's Night Out."

JUNO AND THE PAYCOCK and THE PLOUGH AND THE STARS. Introd. and notes by Guy Boas *St. Martin's* 1954 $2.25

THE SHADOW OF A GUNMAN. 1923. *French* $1.75

JUNO AND THE PAYCOCK. 1925. *French* $1.75

THE PLOUGH AND THE STARS. 1926. *French* $1.75

PURPLE DUST. 1940. *Dramatists* 1957 $1.25; (in "Contemporary Drama" ed. by E. B. Watson and B. Pressey) *Scribner* 1959 pap. $3.95

RED ROSES FOR ME. 1942. *Dramatists* $1.25; (in "Six Great Modern Plays") *Dell* Laurel pap. $1.25

COCK-A-DOODLE DANDY. 1949. (In "Masterpieces of the Modern Irish Theater" ed. by R. W. Corrigan) *Macmillan* Collier pap. $1.50

BEDTIME STORY. 1951. (In "One Act: Eleven Short Plays of the Modern Theatre" ed. by S. Moon) *Grove* 1961 Black Cat Bks. pap. $2.45

THE DRUMS OF FATHER NED. 1959. *St. Martin's* 1960 $2.95

I KNOCK AT THE DOOR. Adapted by Paul Shyre *Dramatists* 1958 $1.50; *Macmillan* pap. $2.50. A dramatization in two acts of the autobiography intended for concert reading.

PICTURES IN THE HALLWAY. Adapted by Paul Shyre *French* $1.75; *Macmillan* Collier Bks. pap. $1.65. A dramatization of the autobiography.

THE FLYING WASP. 1937. *Blom* $19.75. Comments on drama criticism.

LETTERS. Vol. 1. Ed. by D. Krause *Macmillan* 1975 $35.00

Books about O'Casey

Sean O'Casey: The Man and His Work. By David Krause. *Macmillan* rev. ed. 1975 $8.95 "A serious, soberly documented study"—(*N.Y. Times*).

Sean O'Casey: The Man I Knew. By Gabriel Fallon. *Little* 1965 $5.00. The author, an Irish actor turned drama critic, was for many years a friend of O'Casey's.

Sean O'Casey: The Man and His Plays. By Jules Kaslow. *Citadel Press* 1966 pap. $1.75

Sean O'Casey: A Bibliography of Criticism. Ed. by E. H. Mikhail. *Univ. of Washington Press* 1972 $12.00

Sean O'Casey. By William A. Armstrong. Writers and their Work Ser. *British Bk. Centre* $2.95 pap. $1.20

Sean O'Casey. By Bernard Benstock. Irish Writers Ser. *Bucknell Univ. Press* $4.50 pap. $1.95

CARROLL, PAUL VINCENT.   1900–

In writing of his life in "Twentieth Century Authors," this Irish dramatist said: "I learned at the Abbey Theatre the rudiments of play-making and that unquenchable love of the drama that is the chief impetus of my life. . . . Swift so shocked and fascinated me that to this day his influence is one of the most potent factors in my writing." His play, "Shadow and Substance" portrayed Dean Swift (*q.v.*). It was only when the American critics endorsed the Abbey Theatre's opinion of this drama by giving it the N.Y. Drama Critics Circle Award in 1938, that Carroll began to take his place as a professional dramatist. George Jean Nathan said that his work "was stippled alternately with tenderness and dynamite."

In 1943 Carroll helped the late James Bridie, the Scottish playwright, to found the Glasgow Citizens' Theater and became director and production advisor. He now lives in England and writes successfully for television and the movies. "The Devil Came from Dublin," his satire on the devil's efforts to trap a gentle Irish priest, was produced on Broadway as "The Wayward Saint" early in 1955. The critics found it "warm and charming" but it had only a brief run. A number of his plays had American productions in the 1950's.

IRISH STORIES AND PLAYS. *Devin-Adair* 1958 $5.95. Eight short stories and three one-act plays, The Conspirators, Beauty Is Fled, Interlude, and the full-length drama, The Devil Came from Dublin.

SHADOW AND SUBSTANCE. 1936. *Dramatists* $1.25

Books about Carroll

Paul Vincent Carroll. By Paul A. Doyle Irish Writers Ser. *Bucknell Univ. Press* 1971 $4.50 pap. $1.95

BEHAN, BRENDAN.   1923–1964.

Writing of his early prison life in "Borstal Boy," which takes its title from England's Borstal Institutions (reform schools), this colorful Irishman from the Dublin slums told of his arrest at the age of 16 as a terrorist for the IRA (Irish Republican Army). "Confessions" begins with his deportation to Ireland after his Borstal release at 19, carries him through subsequent terms in English jails which he used as opportunities for reading and writing, and brings his later life up to his marriage in 1955. "Betwixt prisons and pubs Brendan acquired the material he adapted into two of the best Irish plays since O'Casey"—(*SR*).

"Quare Fellow" is Irish prison jargon for a man sentenced to death, and Behan's first play re-creates the prison atmosphere just before a hanging. Behan wrote "The Hostage" in Gaelic while he was living on the Spanish Balearic Islands. It was successfully produced first in Dublin, then in London and New York. It is the "ribald and hilarious" story of a British soldier held hostage in a Dublin brothel to prevent the execution of an Irish rebel; Behan aimed its satirical barbs against English snobbery, the Irish government and various "hypocritical" institutions.

Though he died too early from drink and diabetes, Behan did manage to escape what he had so dreaded—old age "with bent old legs and twisted buniony toes" (as he once wrote in prison). Posthumously published were "The Scarperer," a novel about the Dublin underworld (1964, o.p.), "Brendan Behan's New York," a series of rambling, humorous anecdotes (1964, o.p.), and "Confessions of an Irish Rebel." "Hold Your Hour and Have Another" (1964, o.p.), from his column in *The Irish Press*, is "certainly the best collection of Dublin pub conversations, real or imaginary, outside the pages of 'Ulysses' or Sean O'Casey"—(*PW*). "Richard's Cork Leg" is a version of Behan's last play manuscript, with additions by Alan Simpson.

THE QUARE FELLOW (1956) and THE HOSTAGE (1958). *Grove* Black Cat Bks. 1965 pap. $1.95

RICHARD'S CORK LEG. Ed. by Alan Simpson *Grove* Evergreen Bks. 1974 pap. $2.95

BRENDAN BEHAN'S ISLAND: An Irish Sketchbook. Ill. by Paul Hogarth. *Bernard Geis* (dist. by McKay) 1962 $5.95. A collection of anecdotes, two short stories, a one-act play and several poems.

BORSTAL BOY. Autobiography. *Knopf* 1959 $6.95

BRENDAN BEHAN SINGS IRISH FOLKSONGS AND BALLADS. *Spoken Arts* 760 (59 Locust Ave., New Rochelle, N.Y. 10801) $5.95. Includes Behan's lively commentary and several of his own songs from his two plays.

Books about Behan

Beckett and Behan and a Theatre in Dublin. By Alan Simpson. *Hillary House* 1962 $3.50

My Brother Brendan. By Dominic Behan. *Simon & Schuster* 1966 $4.50
This curious memoir is filled with quotations and witty anecdotes, yet "it becomes reasonable to wonder how well, for all his ear for bawdy Irish talk, Dominic knew his notorious [older] brother"—(*SR*). "Tell Dublin I Miss Her" (1962) by the same author is now o.p.

The World of Brendan Behan. Ed. by Sean McCann. *Twayne* 1966 $4.00. Firsthand accounts by people who knew him.

Brendan Behan. By R. Porter Essays on Mod. Writers *Columbia* 1973 pap. $1.00

Brendan Behan. By Ulick O'Connor. 1973. *Grove* pap. $1.95. Yet another biography, more comprehensive than most of the others.

Brendan Behan. By Ted E. Boyle. English Authors Ser. *Twayne* $6.50

FRIEL, BRIAN. 1929–

This "talented young Irish playwright" (*N.Y. Times*) made his American debut with his fourth play, "Philadelphia, Here I Come!," produced on Broadway in 1966. The story of the Irish youth who was about to leave for Philadelphia—and whose "public" and "private" faces were played by two actors—charmed many, and the play was chosen as one of the year's ten best. Said Walter Kerr in the N.Y. *Herald Tribune*: "*Philadelphia, Here I Come!* is a funny play, a prickly play, finally a most affecting play. . . . Author Brian Friel has set all of his cranky, fond, and obstinately shy people to searching for the one word that is everlastingly on the tip of everyman's tongue, and everlastingly not spoken. He has written a play about an ache, and he has written it so simply and honestly that the ache itself becomes a warming fire." "The Loves of Cass McGuire," in which a disillusioned, toping old woman returns to Ireland after a half-century's stay in America, was not a success in New York, where it opened, but once on native ground became a solid hit with the Irish. Walter Kerr wrote of this one that "the mood is unevenly distributed, the bits and pieces are not assimilated into one single simple truth," but he found the characterization expert and touching. "Indeed, line by line, Mr. Friel writes nearly everything well." Friel's 1967–68 triumph in Dublin was "Lovers," which had an almost unheard-of run of three months until it had to be taken off to make room for the Dublin Drama Festival. Consisting of two one-acters, "Winners" (a tragedy) and "Losers" (called "hilarious"), it opened successfully at Lincoln Center in the spring of 1968. Also in 1968, "Crystal and Fox," concerning the private life of a travelling show company, was produced in Dublin and Los Angeles. The Abbey Theatre maintained a deplorable example by turning down Friel's next play, "The Munday Scheme." But the political satire (in which it is proposed that the West of Ireland be converted for profit into an international cemetery) eventually took the stage in 1969, both in Dublin and in New York. Two other Friel plays have been produced since: "The Gentle Island" (1971) and "The Freedom of the City" (1973, at the Abbey and London's Royal Court).

Friel, who taught school in Ireland until 1960, has also published short story collections.

PHILADELPHIA, HERE I COME! 1964. *Farrar, Straus* 1966 $4.50; *French* $1.75

THE LOVES OF CASS MCGUIRE. 1966. *French* $1.75

LOVERS. *Farrar, Straus* Noonday $1.95. Two one-act companion pieces, "Winners" and "Losers."

TWO PLAYS: Crystal and Fox and The Munday Scheme. *Farrar, Straus* 1970 $6.50 Noonday pap. $2.45

Books about Friel

Brian Friel. By D. E. Maxwell Irish Writers Ser. *Bucknell Univ. Press* $4.50 pap. $1.95

—D.M.B.

Chapter 5

American Drama

"The Theatre in this country was primarily a place not in which to be serious but in which to be likeable."
—PLAYWRIGHT WILLIAM GIBSON, commenting on the production of his play "Two for the Seesaw" (1958)

American drama got off to a slow start. At first the Puritan spirit denied drama altogether. America's "first" professionally done play was Thomas Godfrey's "The Prince of Parthia" (1767), which was but a copy of English drama of the time; and although the Revolutionary War gave American dramatists the theme of liberty, the form this took in drama remained derivative. Apart from the creation of new comic types such as the Yankee in Royall Tyler's "The Contrast" (1787) our dramas had little national originality and drew heavily upon the romanticized histories and melodramas popular in England, France and Germany in the 18th and early 19th centuries. (The International Copyright Law did not materialize until 1891.)

After the Civil War, American dramatists gradually came under the influence of the realism movement which was furthered by such prose writers as Hamlin Garland and William Dean Howells. Yet dramatic dialogue remained stilted and characters were stereotypes set in the simplicities of melodrama or folk drama. Theatre historian Ralph G. Allen has argued that the only fresh theatre of this period was honky-tonk, minstrel shows, and Burlesque. *(For information on this period, see Bernard Hewitt, Daniel Havens, Hugh Rankin, and William Dunlap below.)*

At the end of the 19th century some of the leading playwrights were James Herne, whose "Margaret Fleming" (1890) is a landmark, dealing in a faintly Ibsenite manner with the double standard in marriage; Steele MacKaye, whose "Hazel Kirke" (1880) treated infidelities; and Bronson Howard, who wrote "Shenandoah" (1888), a Civil War drama. An American drama, if not literature, was developing here which Alan Downer has perceived as containing "the love of experiment in form and technique, generally swift tempo and bruising action, unexpected changes from laughter to sentiment, and the general rejection of tragedy." In the beginning of the 20th century, American plays began to reflect for the first time, if not quite treat fully, specific social issues of middle-class life: corruption in Clyde Fitch's "The City" (1909), interracial tensions in Edward Sheldon's "The Nigger" (1909), politics in the same playwright's "The Boss" (1911). *(For information on this period, see David Grimsted, Montrose Moses, Frank Rahill, and Vardac below.)*

It was only after World War I that American drama attained full maturity, acquiring a seriousness that came from a better hold on psychological and social truths. For the first time playwrights were more important to a play than the actors. Influences on the new drama were the European playwrights, especially the German expressionists Toller and Kaiser (*qq.v.*), whose productions were reported back in the United States by theatre travellers (*see McGowan and Jones below*). The "little theatre" movement brought a resurgence of life that flowered in the Provincetown Players in New York City (1916–1917), formerly at Cape Cod, and the Washington Square Players (1915), who became the Theatre Guild (1918) (*see Deutsch and Eaton below*).

Another creative force was George Pierce Baker (1866–1935) (*see Kinne below*). His 47 Workshop at Harvard was to have such illustrious students as Barry, Behrman, Howard, Sheldon, and O'Neill. Emancipation of American drama in the 1920s came with the work of Sidney Howard with his dramatic representation of an unconventional love triangle in "They Knew What They Wanted" and his Freudian play "Silver Cord." Philip Barry's comedies also questioned conventional morality; Maxwell Anderson's and Lawrence Stalling's "What Price Glory?" introduced an earthy spirit and fresh language to the stage.

Perhaps the most important new development was the expressionism introduced by Elmer Rice's "The Adding Machine" and Eugene O'Neill's "The Emperor Jones" and "The Hairy Ape." *(For information on this period, see Atkinson, "The Lively Years"; Downer, "Fifty Years . . . "; and Flexner, Krutch, Sievers, and Young below.)*

The 1930s began in a depression and ended with the rise of Fascism and the beginning of World War II. Harold Clurman has written that the most important difference between the drama of the 1920s and that of the 1930s "is the emphasis in the later period on the social, economic, and political background of the individual psychological case." Even the comic dramatists, such as S. N. Behrman and Philip Barry, wrote in a darker vein. Maxwell Anderson treated the conniving of Congress in "Both Your Houses," Odets urged strikes in "Waiting for Lefty," and Paul Green with "Johnny Johnston" and Robert E. Sherwood with "Idiot's Delight" spoke for pacificism; at the end of the decade Lillian Hellman and Sherwood turned to anti-Nazi dramas. Hellman, like Odets, raised questions about the very existence of the times. But these flashing, probing dramas did not seek easy answers for the problems. *(For information on this period, see Atkinson and Clurman, "The Fervent Years"; Flexner, Flanagan, Goldstein, and Green, "Ring Bells! Sing Songs!"; and Krutch, Matthews, Rabkin, and Young below.)*

The late 1930s and early 1940s brought the unconventional dramas of two very individual men, William Saroyan and Thornton Wilder. The end of World War II introduced Arthur Miller and Tennessee Williams, who seemed at first to continue the themes of the 1930s. However, Williams's "The Glass Menagerie" and Miller's "Death of a Salesman" revealed these playwrights to be more pessimistic about American life than the serious but essentially optimistic Odets, Sherwood and Wilder. Oversimplifying their differences, Kenneth Tynan has written, "Williams's genius has no social commitments, but many aesthetic ones . . . Miller's mind traps him wherein history is shaped . . . with action and incident. . . . Complementary, yet irreconcilable, Miller and Williams have produced the most powerful body of dramatic prose in modern English." The 1950s introduced Robert Anderson, Paddy Chayefsky and William Inge. *(For information on this period, see Bentley and Clurman, "The Divine Pastime"; Gassner, "Theater at the Crossroads"; Kerr, "Pieces at Eight" and "The Theater in Spite of Itself"; and Lewis, Tynan, and Weales, "American Drama since World War II" below.)*

The 1960s marked the period of influence of French Existentialist dramatists Ionesco and Samuel Beckett as well as the German Bertholt Brecht. Edward Albee's "Zoo Story," and "Who's Afraid of Virginia Woolf?," van Itallie's "America Hurrah," Schisgal's "Luv," and Kopit's "Indians" are openly critical of the American way of life, attempting self-definition in new modes of drama to the American stage. Black drama also reached importance in the 1960s. The Black Arts Repertory Company was founded in 1964 by Imamu Amiri Baraka (LeRoi Jones), the Negro Ensemble Company by Douglas Turner Ward and Robert Hooks in 1966, and the New Lafayette Theatre by Ed Bullins in 1967. Prominent Black dramatists who began writing plays in this decade were Lorraine Hansberry, "A Raisin in the Sun"; Baraka, "Dutchman"; James Baldwin, "Blues for Mister Charlie"; and Ed Bullins, "The Electronic Nigger." Yet another creative force that arose in the 1960s was Off-Off Broadway. Michael Smith has written, "Off-Off Broadway theatre was invented by new playwrights because they were unwanted elsewhere." Schroeder in his introduction to "The New Underground Theater" (1968, o.p.) explained the precise contribution of these playwrights. "American drama on Broadway evolves from the well-made play principles of Scribe and Hebbel, the social realism of Ibsen, Shaw and Chekhov, and the psychological probing of Strindberg and O'Neill. The underground theatre of New York and San Francisco takes the opposite tack. Its plays are spun out of fantasy and intuition. Their probing is more psychic than psychological. It intentionally sacrifices story-line, suspense, naturalistic representation, characterization, romance, vicarious identification with a star."

Some of the main groups in this alternative theatre have been La Mama Experimental Theatre Club founded by Ellen Steward and Paul Foster in 1961 in New York City, the Living Theatre founded by Judith Malina and Julian Beck, and the Open Theatre founded by Joseph Chaikin in 1963. Such groups have operated out of lofts, church basements and cafés where young writers can experiment with their craft and ignore conventional definitions of success. *(For information on this period see Brustein and Clurman, "The Divine Pastime"; Kerr, "Thirty Plays Hath November"; and Mitchell, Simon, and Weales "The Jumping Off Place" below.)*

It is too early to assess the 1970s, but one is perhaps safe in stating that more of the serious drama being written goes counter to the judgment expressed by William Gibson in 1958 and placed at the head of this chapter: American drama may not always be so "likeable" but it is "serious."

HISTORY AND CRITICISM

Abramson, Doris E. NEGRO PLAYWRIGHTS IN THE AMERICAN THEATRE, 1925–1959. *Columbia* 1969 $12.50

> The drama editor of *The Massachusetts Review* analyzes twenty plays from Garland Anderson's "Appearances" through Lorraine Hansberry's "A Raisin in the Sun." "The most comprehensive survey of 20th century Negro literature to date"—(*Choice*).

THE AMERICAN THEATRE: A Sum of Its Parts. Introd. by Henry B. Williams *French* 1971 $10.00. Excellent collection of essays by theatre scholars on the development of our drama.

Atkinson, Brooks. BROADWAY. *Macmillan* rev. ed. 1974 $12.95. A popular history, well illustrated with photographs of outstanding productions, from the turn of the century through the sixties.

(With Al Hirschfeld) THE LIVELY YEARS: 1920–1973. *Association Press* 1973 $12.50. The former drama critic of the *N.Y. Times* comments on 82 dramas, including many American ones, which he covered on opening nights. Accompanied by sketches of sheer linear magic by the great caricaturist Hirschfeld.

Belknap, Sara Yancey, Comp. GUIDE TO THE PERFORMING ARTS. *Scarecrow Press* 1965 $12.00; 1966 $10.00; 1967 $15.00; 1968 $12.50. An excellent library tool; an annual guide to periodicals in the theater, music and dance fields.

Bentley, Eric. WHAT IS THEATRE? (Incorporating "The Dramatic Event and Other Reviews, 1944–1967"). *Atheneum* 1968 $12.50 pap. $4.95. Reviews mostly written for the *New Republic* by the author of "The Life of the Theatre."

Blum, Daniel C. PICTORIAL HISTORY OF THE AMERICAN THEATRE: 1860–1970. Ed. by John Willis *Crown* 3rd enl. ed. 1969 $12.50. Many photographs with hundreds of actors identified in Broadway productions.

Bonin, Jane R. PRIZE-WINNING AMERICAN DRAMA: A Bibliographical and Descriptive Guide. *Scarecrow Press* 1973 $7.50. Describes plays which have won one or more of the five major American drama awards.

Brockett, Oscar G., and Robert R. Findlay. CENTURY OF INNOVATION: A History of European and American Theatre and Drama since 1870. *Prentice-Hall* 1973 $14.95

Broussard, Louis. AMERICAN DRAMA: Contemporary Allegory from Eugene O'Neill to Tennessee Williams. *Univ. of Oklahoma Press* 1962 $4.95. How American dramatists have used expressionism.

Brown, John Mason. DRAMATIS PERSONAE: A Retrospective Show. 1963 *Viking* Compass Bks. 1965 pap. $2.25. Selected criticism from the late critic's career on *Theatre Arts, Saturday Review* and New York newspapers. Includes "The Modern Theatre in Revolt" (1929), a chronicle of some of the major theatre tendencies as seen at that time.

Brown, John Russell, and Bernard Harris, Eds. AMERICAN THEATRE. 1967. Stratford-
upon-Avon-Studies *Crane-Russak* $9.00. Covers writers, influences, ideological and
social conditions, theatrical idioms. Contributors are English and American.

Brustein, Robert. SEASONS OF DISCONTENT: Dramatic Opinions 1959–1965. *Simon &
Schuster* 1965 $5.95 Touchstone 1967 $1.95. A sharp look at American, and other,
playwrights. Most of these articles first appeared as drama reviews in the *New
Republic*. The collection lacks the temperance of the author's "The Theatre of
Revolt." Includes Brustein's famous attack on the reputation of William Inge.

Clurman, Harold. THE DIVINE PASTIME: Theatre Essays. *Macmillan* 1974 $7.95

Reviews and essays selected from his earlier collections "Lies Like Truth" (1958) and "The
Naked Image" (1966). Clurman has been drama critic of *The Nation* since 1953. "Clurman tells us
what each production is about—its central idea or expression—out distances most reviewers"—
(Ruby Cohn, *N.Y. Times Bk. Review*).

THE FERVENT YEARS: The Story of the Group Theatre and the Thirties with a New
Chapter On the Postwar Theatre. 1945, 1957. *Harcourt* 1975 pap. $4.95. The author
is one of the founders of the Group Theatre and offers an articulate record of the
Group's members which included playwrights Clifford Odets, Irwin Shaw and
William Saroyan.

Cole, Toby, Ed. PLAYWRIGHTS ON PLAYWRITING: The Meaning and Making of Modern
Drama from Ibsen to Ionesco. Introd. by John Gassner *Farrar, Straus* (Hill & Wang)
1961 pap. $3.50. The American playwrights include O'Neill, Wilder and Williams.

Deutsch, Helen, and Stella B. Hanau. PROVINCETOWN: A Story of the Theatre. 1931
Russell & Russell $18.00

Donoghue, Denis. THE THIRD VOICE: Modern British and American Verse Drama.
Princeton Univ. Press 1959 pap. $2.95. The American playwrights discussed are Eliot,
Cummings, MacLeish, Pound, Wallace Stevens and Richard Eberhart.

Downer, Alan S. FIFTY YEARS OF AMERICAN DRAMA, 1900–1950. *Regnery* 1966 pap. $1.25
"Written in terms of plays rather than playwrights"—(Preface).

(Ed.) THE AMERICAN THEATER TODAY. *Basic Bks.* 1967 $6.95. Essays and interviews by
Eric Bentley, John Gassner, Edward Albee, Murray Schisgal, Gerald Weales and
others.

Dunlap, William. HISTORY OF THE AMERICAN THEATRE AND ANECODOTES OF THE PRINCI-
PAL ACTORS. 2nd ed. 1832 *Burt Franklin* 3 vols. in one $32.50. The first history of the
American theatre and its playwrights by the notable 19th century playwright and
stage manager.

Eaton, Walter P. THE THEATRE GUILD: The First Ten Years, with Articles by the
Directors. 1929. *Bks. for Libraries* $17.25; *Scholarly Press* $13.00

Engel, Lehman. THE AMERICAN MUSICAL THEATRE: A Consideration. *Macmillan* 1967 rev.
ed. 1975 $6.95 pap. $2.95. Both a history and an analysis of the makings of a musical.
Includes a discography and list of published librettos and vocal scores.

Ewen, David. THE NEW COMPLETE BOOK OF THE AMERICAN MUSICAL THEATER. (Orig. title
"Complete Book of The American Musical Theater") *Holt* 1958 1970 $15.00. The
most comprehensive and best-organized book on musical plays. Highly recommended.

Flanagan, Hallie. ARENA: The History of the Federal Theatre. 1940. *Arno* $20.00

A first-hand account by the woman who headed the government-established theater. "As
exciting as a novel and twice as provocative"—(John Gassner in the *N.Y. Times*).

Flexner, Eleanor. AMERICAN PLAYWRIGHTS: 1918–1938. 1938. *Bks. for Libraries* $21.00

Frenz, Horst, Ed. AMERICAN PLAYWRIGHTS ON DRAMA. *Farrar, Straus* (Hill & Wang) 1965
pap. $1.95. Articles both formal and informal by 14 American playwrights including
Albee, Behrman, Hansberry, Inge, Miller, O'Neill and Williams.

Gassner, John. DRAMATIC SOUNDINGS. (1968, o.p.)
> Posthumous collection of over 60 essays. "Learned but not pedantic . . . indispensable"—(*Choice*).

THEATRE AT THE CROSSROADS: Plays and Playwrights on the Mid-Century American Stage. *Harper* 1960 $5.95

Gottfried, Martin. A THEATER DIVIDED: The Postwar American Stage. (1968, o.p.). The author is chief drama critic for *The New York Post*.

Gould, Jean. MODERN AMERICAN PLAYWRIGHTS. 1966. *Apollo* pap. $1.95. Popularly written biographical accounts of Albee, Barry, Maxwell Anderson, Hellman, Inge, Miller, Odets, Elmer Rice, Robert Sherwood, Wilder and Williams.

Green, Stanley. RING BELLS! SING SONGS!: Broadway Musicals of the 1930's. Introd. by Brooks Atkinson *Arlington* 1972 $14.95. Discusses 175 musicals produced on Broadway during the 1930s. Presented chronologically.

THE WORLD OF MUSICAL COMEDY. *A. S. Barnes* rev. 2nd ed. 1974 $17.50

Grimsted, David. MELODRAMA UNVEILED: American Theatre and Culture, 1800–1850. *Univ. of Chicago Press* 1968 $11.50. Discusses needs of society that give melodrama its historical validity.

Guernsey, Otis L., Jr. PLAYWRIGHTS, LYRICISTS, COMPOSERS ON THEATRE. *Dodd* 1974 $15.00. Practically a text of information on practical dramatic composition and related subjects. *(See also under Mantle, Burns.)*

Havens, Daniel F. THE COLUMBIAN MUSE OF COMEDY: The Development of a Native Tradition in Early American Social Comedy, 1787–1845. *Southern Illinois Univ. Press* 1973 $6.95. For serious students of American playwriting in its early stages.

Hewitt, Bernard. THEATRE U.S.A., 1665–1957. *McGraw-Hill* 1959 text ed. $11.50
> The story of American theatre told primarily through contemporary accounts. "A miniature library of theatrical records . . . revealing reading for scholars, students and theatre buffs"— (Lewis Funke in the *N.Y. Times*).

Hughes, Glenn. HISTORY OF THE AMERICAN THEATRE, 1700–1950. *French* 1951 $6.00. A chronological review of American theatre.

Kernan, Alvin, Ed. THE MODERN AMERICAN THEATER. Twentieth Century Views Ser. *Prentice-Hall* 1967 $5.95 pap. $1.95. Includes Tynan on Miller, Guthrie on Wilder, Kaprow on "Happenings," several essays by and about Albee.

Kernoodle, George R. INVITATION TO THE THEATRE. *Harcourt* 1967 text ed. $10.95. Includes many perceptive passages on American dramatists. A superb book. Indispensable for any drama (as well as theatre) collection.

Kerr, Walter. THE GOD ON THE GYMNASIUM FLOOR. *Simon & Schuster* 1973 $7.95; *Dell* pap. $2.65. Play reviews covered for the 1969–1971 seasons. Discerning criticism by the former critic of the *New York Herald Tribune* and the present Sunday Drama Critic of the *New York Times*.

PIECES AT EIGHT. *Simon & Schuster* 1957 pap. $3.95. Reviews for 1950–1957.

THE THEATRE IN SPITE OF ITSELF. *Simon & Schuster* 1963 $5.00. Reviews 1957–1962.

THIRTY PLAYS HATH NOVEMBER: Pain and Pleasure in the Contemporary Theater. *Simon & Schuster* 1969 $6.50. Reviews for 1963–1968.

Kinne, Wisner P. GEORGE PIERCE BAKER AND THE AMERICAN THEATRE. 1954. *Greenwood* 1968 $18.00
> "A real contribution to theatrical history"—(*Nation*).

Krutch, Joseph Wood. AMERICAN DRAMA SINCE 1918: An Informal History. *Braziller* 1939 rev. ed. 1957 $5.00. Leading figures and movements up to 1939 with a brief chapter on post–World War Two that touches on Miller and Williams. The author was formerly Brander Matthews Professor of Dramatic Literature at Columbia University.

Lewis, Allan. AMERICAN PLAYS AND PLAYWRIGHTS OF THE CONTEMPORARY THEATRE. *Crown* 1965 $6.00. Popularly written account of the works of major dramatists from O'Neill to Albee.

Little, Stewart. OFF-BROADWAY. 1974. *Dell* pap. $2.95

Lovell, John Jr., Ed. GREAT AMERICAN PLAYS IN DIGEST FORM. *Apollo* pap. $2.25. Summaries of more than 100 selected plays from 1766 to 1959.

Ludlow, Noah. DRAMATIC LIFE AS I FOUND IT. Introd. by Francis Hodge *Arno* 1964 $25.00. The frontier theatre of the early 19th century.

Lumley, Frederick. NEW TRENDS IN TWENTIETH CENTURY DRAMA: A Survey since Ibsen and Shaw. 4th ed. *Oxford* 1972 $8.50. Includes American dramatists. Good survey.

McCarthy, Mary. THEATER CHRONICLES 1937–1962. (1963 o.p.). Uncompromising criticism with a social and intellectual awareness found in few other drama critics. Keen analyses of Saroyan, Odets, George Kelly, O'Neill.

MacGowan, Kenneth, & Robert Edmond Jones. CONTINENTAL STAGECRAFT. 1922. *Arno* $15.00. This book while obviously not *about* American drama was *influential* on American theatre, and is based on the author's observations of some 60 productions by Appia, Reinhardt, Craig, Stanislavsky, Copeau, etc.

Mantle, Burns, and others, Eds. THE BEST PLAYS. Annual volumes. *Dodd* annuals for 1919–1964 each $12.50 1964–1973 $15.00. Each volume includes summary and excerpts of the ten best plays of the Broadway season, plus an invaluable mine of statistics: complete listing of New York productions with dates, theaters and casts; important premières of plays in the United States and Europe; lists of drama awards; necrology. The current editor is Otis Guernsey.

Mathews, Jane DeHart. THE FEDERAL THEATER, 1935–1939: Plays, Relief, and Politics. *Princeton Univ. Press* 1967 $12.50 pap. $2.95
"A consistently engrossing account of the W.P.A. Theatre Project"—(*PW*).

Meserve, Walter J. AN OUTLINE HISTORY OF AMERICAN DRAMA. *Rowman* 1965 lib. bdg. $7.95 pap. $2.25. From colonial theater to Albee.

(Ed.) DISCUSSIONS OF AMERICAN DRAMA. *Heath* 1965 pap. $2.95. Essays by playwrights and critics on individual plays as well as periods.

Mitchell, Loften. BLACK DRAMA: The Story of the American Negro in the Theatre. *Hawthorn* 1967 $7.95 pap. $2.45. A partisan but interesting account of the rich contribution of the Negro, from the African Grove Theatre in 1820 to LeRoi Jones' (*q.v.*) Black Arts project of 1965.

VOICES OF THE BLACK THEATRE: Ruby Dee, Abram Hill, Eddie Hunter, Paul Robeson, Dick Campbell, Vinnette Carroll, Frederick O'Neill and Regina M. Andrews. *James T. White & Co.* 1975 $12.50. Interviews with major figures of the black theatre.

Mordden, Than. BETTER FOOT FORWARD: A New History of American Musical Theatre. *Viking* 1976 $12.95

Moses, Montrose. THE AMERICAN DRAMATIST. 1925. *Arno* 1964 $20.00. Discussion of all major American dramatists from the 18th century to the 1920s.

(With John Mason Brown) AMERICAN THEATRE AS SEEN BY ITS CRITICS, 1752–1934. 1934. *Cooper* $11.00. An anthology.

Nathan, George Jean. *See Chapter 1, The Drama, Section on Dramatic Criticism and History, this volume.*

THE NEW YORK TIMES DIRECTORY OF THE THEATRE. Introd. by Clive Barnes *Quadrangle* 1973 $25.00. Does not print actual reviews but cites reviews and articles on actors, actresses, playwrights, producers, directors, etc. that appeared from 1920 to 1970. A library with the *Times* for these years should have this handy index.

NOTABLE NAMES IN THE AMERICAN THEATRE. 1966. Ed. by Walter Rigdon. *James T. White & Co.* 1976 $62.50.

This is the revised edition of a work formerly known as "Encyclopaedia and Who's Who of the American Theatre." The new edition is divided into nine sections. 1) New York Productions, lists all productions in New York City since 1900, with the name of the theater, date of opening, and number of performances. 2) Premières of American Plays, lists premières throughout the country giving title, author, date and name of producing group and theater, starting with the 1968 season. 3) Premières of American Plays Abroad. 4) Theater Group Biographies, with a history of the organization, names of the present officers and the repertory. 5) Theater Building Biographies, including new information about the Lincoln Center complex, as well as facts about older theaters. 6) Awards, with the names of the recipients and description of the awards. 7) Biographical Bibliography, listing 3000 titles about 980 theatrical personalities. 8) Necrology. 9) Who's Who, containing 3,500 brief biographies.

Odell, George C. D. ANNALS OF THE NEW YORK STAGE TO 1849. 1927–1949. *AMS Press* 15 vols. 1970 each $46.50 set $695.00. This valuable history covers opera, concerts, burlesque and circus as well as theater.

Palmer, Helen H., and Jane Anne Dyson. AMERICAN DRAMA CRITICISM: Interpretations, 1890–1965 Inclusive, of American Drama Since the First Play Produced in America. *Shoe String Press* 1967 $8.50. An extremely useful bibliography of critical essays and reviews appearing in books, periodicals and scholarly journals.

Paris Review. WRITERS AT WORK. Third Series. *Viking* 1967 $7.95 pap. $1.65. Lively and fascinating interviews with contemporary authors. The American playwrights included are Lillian Hellman, Arthur Miller and Edward Albee.

See Chapter 4, Broad Studies and General Anthologies, Reader's Adviser, Vol. 1, for other volumes in this series. Wilder is in the first, Robert Lowell in the second.

Quinn, Arthur Hobson. A HISTORY OF THE AMERICAN DRAMA. 1923 1927. *Irvington Pubns.* 2 vols. 2nd eds. 1943 and 1946 Vol. 1 From the Beginning to the Civil War (2nd ed. 1943) $7.50 Vol. 2 From the Civil War to the Present Day (2nd ed. 1946) $8.00. A standard history, the bibliography and play list have been completely revised.

Rabkin, Gerald. DRAMA AND COMMITMENT: Politics in the American Theatre of the Thirties. 1964 *Haskell* 1972 $15.95

The author examines the theatrical developments of the Depression (the Theater Union, Group Theater and Federal Theater) as well as the effect of political commitment on five playwrights of the period: Lawson, Odets, Behrman, Rice and Anderson.

Rahill, Frank. WORLD OF MELODRAMA. *Pennsylvania State Univ. Press* 1967 $10.50. Follows the development of melodrama in France, England and the U.S., documenting stock characters and situations. Scholarly.

Rankin, Hugh F. THE THEATRE IN COLONIAL AMERICA. *Univ. of North Carolina Press* 1965 $7.50

"Using numerous primary sources, such as playbills, newspaper advertisements, and court records, Professor Rankin, who teaches history at Tulane University, has concentrated on the historical and sociological aspects of the American theater"—(*LJ*).

Sievers, David. FREUD ON BROADWAY. 1955. *Cooper* 1971 $12.50. The influence of Freud on dramatists from Susan Gaspell to the early plays of Arthur Miller and Tennessee Williams.

Simon, John. UNEASY STAGES: A Chronicle of the New York Theatre, 1963–1973. *Random* 1976 $15.00 pap. $5.95. Collected reviews, mostly for *New York Magazine*, by an acid-tongued writer with a Ph.D. in Comparative Literature from Harvard University. Mostly negative, these reviews are never unintelligent—only wrongheaded. A good supplement to Brustein's anthology listed above.

Sper, Felix. FROM NATIVE ROOTS. 1948 *Brown Books Co.* $4.00. A region-by-region survey follows the growth of the drama from pageant to local legend play to folk play. Important study of this genre.

Taubman, Howard. THE MAKING OF THE AMERICAN THEATRE. Fwd. by Richard Rodgers *Coward* 1965 rev. ed. 1967 $10.00. Infused with the enthusiasm of this *N.Y. Times* roving arts critic who has been a theater buff since childhood.

Tynan, Kenneth. CURTAINS. *Atheneum* 1961 $10.00. Reviews, many on American plays, by the noted British critic who was literary manager of Britain's National Theater.

Vardac, A. Nicholas. STAGE TO SCREEN: Theatrical Method from Garrick to Griffith. 1949 *Arno* 1968 $15.00. Shows how American (and British) theatre evolved cinematic methods and productional techniques which were borrowed by early film makers.

Vinson, James, Ed. CONTEMPORARY DRAMATISTS. Pref. by Ruby Cohn *St. Martin's* 1973 $30.00. Many living American playwrights have entries which include biography, a signed critical comment on the writer's work, comment by the playwright if he has chosen to make one, and a bibliography.

Weales, Gerald. AMERICAN DRAMA SINCE WORLD WAR II. (1962, o.p.)

THE JUMPING-OFF PLACE: American Drama in the Sixties. *Macmillan* 1969 $6.95. Examines Albee, Miller, LeRoi Jones, Ellen Stewart, Happenings among others. Weales is Professor of English at the University of Pennsylvania and a well-informed writer.

Wharton, John F. LIFE AMONG THE PLAYWRIGHTS: Being Mostly the Story of the Playwrights Producing Company, Inc. *Quadrangle* 1974 $15.00. A personal account from the late thirties to 1960 of the accomplishments and failures of the group that included Robert E. Sherwood, Maxwell Anderson, S. N. Behrman, Sidney Howard and Elmer Rice.

Willis, John, Ed. THEATRE WORLD. *Crown* 10 vols. currently available. Vol. 21 1964–65 Vol. 22 1965–66 Vol. 23 1966–67 Vol. 24 1967–68 Vol. 25 1968–69 Vol. 26 1969–70 Vol. 27 1970–71 Vol. 28 1971–72 Vol. 29 1972–73 Vol. 30 1973–74 each $8.95. A theater annual.

Young, Stark. IMMORTAL SHADOWS: A Book of Dramatic Criticism. 1948. *Octagon* 1973 $12.50. A selection from twenty-five years of criticism by America's finest drama critic to date.

COLLECTIONS

Almost every successful play (and many an unsuccessful one) is now published soon after opening. General trade publishers issue plays in book form without handling the performance rights, but these printed versions are sooner out-of-print than those published by the specialized publishers who handle the amateur performance rights. Of these, the best known is *Samuel French, Inc.*, 25 W. 45 St., New York, N.Y. 10036 (for eastern states), and 7623 Sunset Blvd., Hollywood, Calif. 90046 (for western states), founded in 1830. *Dramatists Play Service, Inc.*, 440 Park Ave. South, New York, N.Y. 10016, was established by the Dramatists Guild of the Author's League of America, for the handling of the nonprofessional acting rights of members' plays and the encouragement of the nonprofessional theater. "Baker's Plays" are published by *W. H. Baker Co.*, 100 Summer St., Boston, Mass. 02110. The Drama Book Shop has its own publishing house *Drama Book Specialists Pubs.*, 150 W. 52 St., New York, N.Y. 10019. To date this new concern has mostly released recordings of old plays and musicals, rather than new texts. These publishers will send catalogs free on request, and libraries are urged to obtain the catalogs from *French* and *Dramatists* for their reference shelves.

For a list of play publishers, *see under Book Publishers—Classified in the current "Literary Market Place: The Directory of American Book Publishing"* (*Bowker* $21.50).

The reader will soon discover that many American playwrights are missing from the biographical section below—dramatists from the 1920 to 1970 period, such as Ben Hecht, Charles MacArthur, Garson Kanin, John Van Druten, John Patrick, Gore Vidal, Howard

Lindway, Russel Crouse, and Jean Kerr; and even more names are lacking from the pre-1920 period. As the intent is to select those playwrights who are not only most likely to be read today with pleasure but who *also* made a significant contribution to American dramatic literature, it is assumed that readers interested in the history of American drama will use the fine anthologies of pre-1920 drama that are available (*see Barrett Clark, Richard Moody, and Arthur Quinn below*).

At the same time there will be many readers who will want to know more of what has been produced Off-Broadway in recent years. Prominent one-time or long-established Off-Broadway playwrights are given in the biographical section: Arthur Kopit, Jack Gelber, William Hanley, Jack Richardson, Edward Albee, Murray Schisgal, Israel Horovitz and Mart Crowley, but there are still other playwrights represented in recent anthologies.

Ballet, Arthur H., Ed. PLAYWRIGHTS FOR TOMORROW: A Collection of Plays. *Univ. of Minnesota Press* 13 vols.

Vol. 1 The Space Fan and the Master by James Schevill, Ex-Miss Copper Queen on a Set of Pills by Megan Terry, A Bad Play for an Old Lady by Elizabeth Johnson, And Things That Go Bump in the Night by Terrence McNally (1966) pap. $1.95; Vol. 2 (o.p.); Vol. 3 Five Easy Payments by John Lewin, With Malice Aforethought by John Stranack, The Great Git-Away by Romeo Muller, I, Elizabeth Otis, Being of Sound Mind by Philip Barber, Where Is de Queen? by Jean-Claude van Itallie (1967) $7.95; Vol. 4 Visions of Sugar Plums by Barry Pritchard, The Strangler by Arnold Powell, The Long War by Kevin O'Morrison, The World Tipped Over and Laying on Its Side by Mary Feldhaus-Weber (1967) $7.95; Vol. 5 Fair Beckoning One by Sarah Monson Koebnick, The New Chautauqua by Frederick Gaines (1969) $5.50 pap. $1.95; Vol. 6 The Thing Itself by Arthur Sainer, The Marriage Test by Jonathan Gillman, The End of the World, or Fragments from a Work in Progress by Keith Neilson (1969) $5.50 pap. $1.95; Vol. 7 Grace and George and God by Alexander Hierholzer, Assassin! by David Ball, Freddie the Pigeon by Seymour Leichman, Rags by Nancy Walter, The Orientals by Stephen Grecco, Drive-In by David Kranes (1971) $6.95 pap. $1.95; Vol. 8 A Gun Play by Yale Udoff, Anniversary on Weedy Hill by Allen Joseph, The Nihilist by William N. Monson (1972) $8.95 pap. $2.95; Vol. 9 Encore by David Korr, Madam Popov by Gladden Schrock, Children of the Kingdom by The Company Theatre Ensemble with script by Don Keith Opper, Psalms of Two Davids by Joel Schwartz (1972) $8.95 pap. $2.95; Vol. 10 The Unknown Chinaman by Kenneth Bernard, Fox, Hound and Huntress by Lance Lee, Escape by Balloon by W. E. R. La Farge, Stops by Robert Auletta, 3 Miles to Poley by Hal Lynch (1973) $8.95 pap. $3.45; Vol. 11 Boxes by Susan Yankowitz, Canvas by David Roskowski, Bierce Takes on the Railroad! by Philip A. Bosakowski, Chamber Piece by John O'Keefe (1973) $8.95 pap. $3.45; Vol. 12 The Root by McCarthy Coyle, Wilson by George Greanias, A Lean and Hungry Priest by Warren Kliewer, A Bunch of the Gods Were Sitting around One Day by James Spencer (1975) $12.95 pap. $4.95; Vol. 13 The Tunes of Chicken Little by Robert Gordon, The Inheritance by Ernest A. Joselovitz, Blessing by Joseph Landon, The Kramer by Mark Medoff (1975) $12.95 pap. $4.95

Benedikt, Michael. THEATRE EXPERIMENT. *Doubleday* 1967 pap. $2.50

A unique collection of 17 pieces: The Long Christmas Dinner by Thornton Wilder; The Ping-Pong Players by William Saroyan; The Tridget of Greva and Abend di Anni Nouveau by Ring Lardner; Three Travelers Watch a Sunrise by W. Stevens; Santa Claus by E. E. Cummings; The Birthday by Kenneth Sawyer Goodman; Benito Cereno by Robert Lowell; George Washington Crossing the Delaware by K. Koch; Hot Buttered Roll by Rosalyn Drexler; Gallows Humor by J. Richardson; The Falling Sickness by R. Edson; Poem-Plays by R. Krauss; What Happened by Gertrude Stein; Flower by Robert Whitman; Meat Joy by Schneemann; Gas by A. Kaprow and C. Frazier.

Clark, Barrett H., Gen. Ed. AMERICA'S LOST PLAYS. 1940. *Indiana Univ. Press* 20 vols. bound as 10 plus vol. 21 1963–1969 each $12.50 Vol. 21 $9.95 set $100.00. Reissue of the famous collection of popular American plays from three centuries.

(With William H. Davenport) NINE MODERN AMERICAN PLAYS. *Prentice-Hall* (Appleton) 1951 $8.50. Includes The Hairy Ape; Street Scene; Green Grow the Lilacs; High Tor; Stage Door; You Can't Take It with You; Abe Lincoln in Illinois; The Glass Menagerie; Command Decision.

Clurman, Harold, Ed. FAMOUS PLAYS OF THE SIXTIES. *Dell* pap. $.95. Contains Benito Cereno by Robert Lowell; Hogan's Goat by William Alfred; We Bombed in New

Haven by Joseph Heller; The Indian Wants the Bronx by Israel Horvitz; The Boys in the Band by Mart Crowley.

Corbin, Richard and Miriam Balf, Eds. TWELVE AMERICAN PLAYS 1920–1960. *Scribner* 1969 pap. $5.80

Contains The Sandbox by Richard Albee; Harvey by Mary Chase; The Little Foxes by Lillian Hellman; Arsenic and Old Lace by Joseph Kesselring; The Rainmaker by Ogden Nash; Beyond the Horizon by Eugene O'Neill; The Teahouse of the August Moon by John Patrick; The King and I by Richard Rodgers and Oscar Hammerstein, II; Requiem for a Heavyweight by Rod Serling; There Shall Be No Night by Robert Sherwood; Our Town by Thornton Wilder; The Glass Menagerie by Tennessee Williams.

Couch, William, Ed. NEW BLACK PLAYWRIGHTS: Six Plays. *Avon Bks.* Bard Bks. 1970 $1.65

Happy Ending and Day of Absence by Douglas Turner Ward; A Rat's Mass by Adrienne Kennedy; Tabernacle by Paul Carter Harrison; Goin'a Buffalo by Ed Bullins; Family Meeting by William Wellington Mackey. The original hardcover edition (o.p.) has Lonne Elder's Ceremonies in Dark Old Men (separately available *Farrar, Straus* 1969 $5.95 Noonday pap. $1.95).

Gassner, John, Ed. BEST PLAYS OF THE EARLY AMERICAN THEATRE: From the Beginning to 1916. *Crown* 1967 $10.95 text ed. $7.50

Uncle Tom's Cabin by G. Aiken; Superstition by J. Barker; The Octoroon by D. Boucicault; The Count of Monte Cristo by C. Fechter; The Truth by C. Fitch; Secret Service by W. Gillette; The Mouse-Trap by W. Howells; The Scarecrow by P. Mackaye; The New York Idea by L. Mitchell; The Great Divide by W. Moody; Fashion by A. Mowatt; Charles the Second by J. and Irving W. Payne; Salvation Nell by E. Sheldon; The Witching Hour by A. Thomas; The Contrast by R. Tyler; The Easiest Way by E. Walter.

BEST PLAYS OF THE MODERN AMERICAN THEATRE: 2nd Series 1939–1946. *Crown* 1947 $10.95 text ed. $7.50

The Philadelphia Story by P. Barry; Tomorrow the World by J. Gow and A. d'Usseau; Watch on the Rhine by L. Hellman; Born Yesterday by G. Kanin; The Man Who Came to Dinner by G. Kaufman and M. Hart; Arsenic and Old Lace by J. Kesselring; The Patriots by S. Kingsley; Home of the Brave by A. Laurents; Life with Father by H. Lindsay and R. Crouse; The Hasty Heart by J. Patrick; Dream Girl by E. Rice; The Time of Your Life by W. Saroyan; Abe Lincoln in Illinois by R. Sherwood; The Male Animal by J. Thurber and E. Nugent; I Remember Mama and The Voice of the Turtle by J. Van Druten; The Glass Menagerie by T. Williams.

BEST AMERICAN PLAYS: 3rd Series 1945–1951. *Crown* 1952 $10.95 text ed. $7.50

Anne of the Thousand Days by M. Anderson; Billy Budd by L. Coxe and R. Chapman; Medea by Euripides (adapted R. Jeffers); Mister Roberts by T. Heggen and J. Logan; The Autumn Garden by L. Hellman; The Moon Is Blue by F. Herbert: Come Back, Little Sheba by W. Inge; Darkness at Noon and Detective Story by S. Kingsley; State of the Union by H. Lindsay and R. Crouse; The Member of the Wedding by C. McCullers; All My Sons and Death of a Salesman by A. Miller; The Iceman Cometh by E. O'Neill; Bell, Book and Candle by J. Van Druten; A Streetcar Named Desire by T. Williams.

BEST AMERICAN PLAYS: 4th Series 1952–1957. *Crown* 1958 $10.95 text ed. $7.50

Tea and Sympathy by R. Anderson; The Seven Year Itch by G. Axelrod; A Hatful of Rain by M. Gazzo; The Fourposter by J. Hartog; Bus Stop and Picnic by W. Inge; The Solid Gold Cadillac by G. Kaufman and H. Teichman; Inherit the Wind by J. Lawrence and R. Lee; No Time for Sergeants by L. Levin; The Crucible and A View from the Bridge by A. Miller; A Moon for the Misbegotten by E. O'Neill; I Am a Camera by J. Van Druten; The Matchmaker by T. Wilder; Cat on a Hot Tin Roof and The Rose Tattoo by T. Williams; The Caine Mutiny by H. Wouk.

BEST AMERICAN PLAYS: 5th Series 1957–1963. *Crown* 1963 $10.95 text ed. $7.50

Who's Afraid of Virginia Woolf? by E. Albee; Silent Night, Lonely Night by R. Anderson; Gideon by P. Chayefsky; Look Homeward, Angel by K. Frings; A Thousand Clowns by H. Gardner; Two for the See-Saw by W. Gibson; The Dark at the Top of the Stairs by W. Inge; Mary, Mary by J. Kerr; Oh Dad, Poor Dad, Mamma's Hung You in the Closet and I'm Feelin' So Sad by A. Kopit; J. B. by A. MacLeish; All the Way Home by T. Mosel; A Touch of the Poet by E. O'Neill; The Cave Dwellers by W. Saroyan; The Best Man by G. Vidal; The Night of the Iguana and Orpheus Descending by T. Williams; The Rope Dancers by M. Wishengrad.

BEST AMERICAN PLAYS: 6th Series 1963–1967. *Crown* 1971 $10.95 text. ed. $8.25

Tiny Alice by E. Albee; Hogan's Goat by W. Alfred; You Know I Can't Hear You When the Water's Running by R. Anderson; Blues for Mister Charlie by J. Baldwin; The Last Analysis by

S. B. Bellow; In White America by M. B. Duberman; The Subject Was Roses by F. D. Gilroy; The Lion in Winter by J. Goldman; Slow Dance on the Killing Ground by W. Hanley; The Sign in Sidney Brustein's Window by L. Hansberry; The Toilet by L. Jones; The Fantasticks by T. Jones; Benito Cereno by R. Lowell; The Owl and the Pussycat by B. Manhoff; Hughie by E. O'Neill; The Odd Couple by N. Simon; Fiddler on the Roof by J. Stein.

(With Clive Barnes) BEST AMERICAN PLAYS: 7th Series 1967–1973. *Crown* 1975 $10.95

All Over by E. Albee; Play It Again, Sam by W. Allen; The Boys in the Band by M. Crowley; Ceremonies in Dark Old Men by L. Elder, III; Little Murders by J. Feiffer; Tom Paine by P. Foster; Scuba Duba by B. Friedman; The House of Blue Leaves by J. Guare; Morning by I. Horowitz; Indians by A. Kopit; Night by T. McNally; The Price by A. Miller; Subject of Fits by R. Montgomery; Sticksand Bones by D. Rabe; The Great White Hope by H. Sackler; The Prisoner of Second Avenue by N. Simon; 1776 by P. Stone and S. Edwards; Lemon Sky by L. Wilson.

BEST AMERICAN PLAYS: Supplementary Vol., 1918–1958. *Crown* 1961 $10.95 text. ed. $7.50

Here Come the Clowns by P. Barry; Biography by S. Behrman; Harvey by M. Chase; Rain by J. Colton; Ethan Frome by O. Davis and D. Davis; The Diary of Anne Frank by F. Goodrich and A. Hackett; The House of Connelly by P. Green; Yellow Jack by S. Howard and P. DeKruif; Men in White by S. Kingsley; Children of Darkness by E. Mayer; Awake and Sing by C. Odets; Morning's at Seven and On Borrowed Time by P. Osborn; The Teahouse of the August Moon by J. Patrick; The Adding Machine by E. Rice; Green Grow the Lilacs by L. Riggs; Clarence by B. Tarkington.

TWENTY BEST PLAYS OF THE MODERN AMERICAN THEATRE. *Crown* 1939 $10.95 text. ed. $8.25

Three Men on a Horse by G. Abbott and J. Holm; High Tor and Winterset by M. Anderson; The Animal Kingdom by P. Barry; End of Summer by S. Behrman; The Women by C. Booth; Green Pastures by M. Connelly; Stage Door by E. Ferber and G. Kaufman; Johnny Johnson by P. Green; You Can't Take It with You by M. Hart and G. Kaufman; The Children's Hour by L. Hellman; Dead End by S. Kingsley; Tobacco Road by J. Kirkland and E. Caldwell; The Fall of the City by A. MacLeish; The Golden Boy by C. Odets; Yes, My Darling Daughter by M. Reed; Bury the Dead by L. Shaw; Idiot's Delight by R. Sherwood; Boy Meets Girl by B. and S. Spewack; Of Mice and Men by J. Steinbeck.

TWENTY-FIVE BEST PLAYS OF THE MODERN AMERICAN THEATRE: Early Series. *Crown* 1949 $10.95 text ed. $8.25

Gods of the Lightning by M. Anderson and H. Hickerson; Saturday's Children by M. Anderson; Berkeley Square by J. Bladerston; Paris Bound by P. Barry; The Clod by L. Beach; The Second Man by S. Behrman; Minnie Field by E. Conkle; Broadway by P. Dunning and G. Abbott; Trifles by S. Glaspell; White Dresses by P. Green; The Front Page by B. Hecht and C. MacArthur; Porgy by D. Heyward and D. Heyward; They Knew What They Wanted by S. Howard; Beggar on Horseback by G. Kaufman and M. Connelly; Craig's Wife and Poor Aubrey by G. Kelly; Aria da Capo by E. Millay; Desire under the Elms, The Hairy Ape and Ile by E. O'Neill; Street Scene by E. Rice; The Road to Rome by R. Sherwood; What Price Glory? by L. Stallings and M. Anderson; Strictly Dishonorable by P. Sturges; Machinal by S. Treadwell.

(With Clive Barnes) FIFTY BEST PLAYS OF THE AMERICAN THEATER. *Crown* 1969 boxed set $45.00

Uncle Tom's Cabin by G. Aiken; Who's Afraid of Virginia Woolf? by E. Albee; High Tor M. Anderson; Tea and Sympathy by R. Anderson; The Seven Year Itch by G. Axelrod; The Philadelphia Story by P. Barry; Harvey by M. Chase; Rain by J. Colton and C. Randolph; Green Pastures by M. Connelly; Ethan Frome by O. and D. Davis; Look Homeward Angel by K. Frings; Two for the See-Saw by W. Gibson; The Diary of Anne Frank by F. Goodrich and A. Hackett; The Fourposter by J. Hartog; The Front Page by B. Hecht and C. MacArthur; Mister Roberts by T. Heggen and J. Logan; The Children's Hour by L. Hellman; Porgy by D. Heyward and D. Heyward; Come Back, Little Sheba by W. Inge; Medea by Euripides adapted by R. Jeffers; Born Yesterday by G. Kanin; The Man Who Came to Dinner and You Can't Take It with You by G. Kaufman and M. Hart; Arsenic and Old Lace by J. Kesselring; Men in White by S. Kingsley; Tobacco Road by J. Kirkland; Oh Dad, Poor Dad, Mamma's Hung You in the Closet and I'm Feelin' So Sad by A. Kopit; Life with Father and The State of the Union by H. Lindsay and R. Crouse; The Member of the Wedding by C. McCullers; The Crucible and Death of a Salesman by A. Miller; Awake and Sing and Golden Boy by C. Odets; Desire under the Elms and The Hairy Ape by E. O'Neill; On Borrowed Time by P. Osborn; The Teahouse of the August Moon by J. Patrick; Dream Girl and Street Scene by E. Rice; The Time of Your Life by W. Saroyan; Bury the Dead by I. Shaw; Salvation Nell by E. Sheldon; Abe Lincoln in Illinois by R. Sherwood; The Odd Couple by N.

Simon; Fiddler on the Roof by J. Stein; The Contrast by R. Tyler; The Matchmaker by T. Wilder; The Glass Menagerie and A Streetcar Named Desire by T. Williams.

Hatch, James V., Ed. and Ted Shine, Consulting ed. BLACK THEATER, U.S.A.: Forty-Five Plays by Black Americans 1847–1974. *Macmillan* (Free Press) 1974 $19.95

The most balanced collection. The Black Doctor (1847) by Ira Aldridge; The Brown Overcoat (1858) by Victor Séjour; The Escape; or, A Leap for Freedom (1858) by William Wells Brown; Caleb the Degenerate (1901) by Joseph S. Cotter, Sr.; Rachel (1916) by Angeline Grimke; Mine Eyes Have Seen (1918) by Alice Dunbar Nelson; They That Sit in Darkness (1919) by Mary Burrill; Balo (1924) by Jean Toomer; Appearances (1925) by Garland Anderson; The Church Fight (1925) by Ruth Gaines-Shelton; A Sunday Morning (1925) by Georgia Douglas Johnson; 'Cruiter (1926) by John Matheus; For Unborn Children (1926) by Myrtle Smith Livingston; Flight of the Natives (1927) by Willis Richardson; The Purple Flower (1928) by Marita Bonner; Graven Images (1929) by May Miller; The Idle Head (1929) by Willis Richardson; Undertow (1929) by Eulalie Spence; Job Hunters (1931) by H. F. V. Edward; Bad Man (1934) by Randolph Edmonds; Little Ham (1935) by Langston Hughes; Don't You Want to Be Free? (1937) by Langston Hughes; Natural Man (1937) by Theodore Browne; Big White Fog (1938) by Theodore Ward; Divine Comedy (1938) by Owen Dodson; Limitations of Life (1938) by Langston Hughes; Native Son (1941) by Richard Wright and Paul Green; Walk Hard (1944) by Abram Hill; District of Columbia (1945) by Stanley Richards; Dry August (1949) by Charles Sebree; Take a Giant Step (1953) by Louis Peterson; The Amen Corner (1954) by James Baldwin; In Splendid Error (1954) by William Branch; The Drinking Gourd (1960) by Lorraine Hansberry; Fly Blackbird (1960) by C. Bernard Jackson and James V. Hatch; The Slave (1964) by Imamu Amiri Baraka (LeRoi Jones); Star of the Morning (1964) by Loften Mitchell; Day of Absence (1965) by Douglas Turner Ward; The Owl Answers (1965) by Adrienne Kennedy; Goin' a Buffalo (1966) by Ed Bullins; Black Love Song #1 (1969) by Val Ferdinand; Wine in the Wilderness (1969) by Alice Childress; The Tumult and the Shouting (1969) by Thomas Pawley; Job Security (1970) by Martie Charles; Herbert III (1974) by Ted Shine; Bibliographies.

Hewes, Henry. FAMOUS AMERICAN PLAYS OF THE 1940's. *Dell* 1960 pap. $.95. Contains The Skin of Our Teeth; Home of the Brave; All My Sons; Lost in the Stars; The Member of the Wedding.

King, Woodie and Ron Milner, Eds. BLACK DRAMA ANTHOLOGY. *Columbia* 1972 $15.00

Contains Junkies are Full of (SHHH. . . .) and Bloodrites by Imamu Amiri Baraka (LeRoi Jones); Junebug Graduates Tonight by Archie Shepp; The Corner by Ed Bullins; Who's Got His Own by Ron Milner; Charades on East Fourth Street by Lonnie Elder; Gabriel by Clifford Mason; Brotherhood by Douglas Turner Ward; The One by Oliver Pitcher; The Marriage by Donald Greaves; The Owl Killer by Philip Hayes Dean; Requiem for Brother X by William Wellington Mackey; Ododo by Joseph A. Walker; All White Caste by Ben Caldwell; Mother and Child by Langston Hughes; The Breakout by Charles (Oyamo) Gordon; Three X Love by Ron Zuber; A Medal for Willie by William Branch; Ladies in Waiting by Peter DeAnda; Black Cycle by Marite Charles; Strictly Matrimony by Errol Hill; Star of the Morning by Loften Mitchell; Toe Jam by Elain Jackson.

Kozelka, Paul, Ed. FIFTEEN AMERICAN ONE-ACT PLAYS. The ANTA Ser. of Distinguished Plays. *Simon & Schuster* (Washington Square) 1961 pap. $.75

Contains Thursday Evening by Christopher Morley; Dust of the Road by Kenneth Sawyer Goodman; The Undercurrent by Fay Ehlert; The Man Who Died at Twelve O'clock by Paul Green; Aria Da Capo by Edna St. Vincent Millay; The Lottery by Brainerd Duffield from a story by Shirley Jackson; Red Carnations by Glenn Hughes; Feathertop by Maurice Valency from a story by Nathaniel Hawthorne; Sorry, Wrong Number by Lucille Fletcher; The Still Alarm by George S. Kaufman; Trifles by Susan Glaspell; The Trysting Place by Booth Tarkington; The Neighbors by Zona Gale; Impromptu by Tad Mosel; The Devil and Daniel Webster by Stephen Vincent Benet.

Lion, Eugene, and David Ball, Eds. GUTHRIE NEW THEATER, Vol. 1. *Grove* 1975 Evergreen Bks. pap. $4.95

This the first in a series of anthologies of contemporary American playwrights who are receiving productions by the Guthrie Theater 2 in Minneapolis, perhaps the foremost regional theater in the country. It includes seven plays scheduled for production by the Guthrie Theater 2 late in 1975 and early in 1976. They are: Swellfoot's Tears by Leon Katz; the Future Pit by Menzies McKillop; Cold by Michael Casale; Glutt and Taps by Gladden Schrock; Afternoon Tea by Harvey Perr; and Waterman by Frank B. Ford. Eugene Lion is the artistic director of Guthrie Theater 2, and David Ball its literary director.

MacGowan, Kenneth. FAMOUS AMERICAN PLAYS OF THE 1920's: The Moon of the Caribbees; What Price Glory; They Knew What They Wanted; Porgy; Holiday; Street
Scene. *Dell* 1959 pap. $.95

Mailman, Bruce, and Albert Poland. THE OFF-OFF BROADWAY BOOK. *Bobbs* 1972 $20.00
pap. $6.95. Some 37 plays from Off-Off Broadway productions including Sam
Shepard, van Itallie, John Guare, Rochelle Owens, David Rabe, Tom Eyen and Israel
Horovitz.

Mantle, Burns. THE BEST PLAYS OF 1894–1974. *See Chapter 1, The Drama, this volume.*

Moody, Richard, Ed. DRAMAS FROM THE AMERICAN THEATRE 1762–1909. *Houghton* 1969
$12.50

Contains A Dialogue and Ode by Francis Hopkinson; A Dialogue between an Englishman and
an Indian and A Little Tea Table Chitchat by John Smith; The Candidates, or The Humours of a
Virginia Election by Col. Robert Munford; The Contrast by Royall Tyler; Bunker-Hill, or The
Death of General Warren by John D. Burk; The Glory of Columbia: Her Yeomanry! by William
Dunlap; She Would Be a Soldier, or The Plains of Chippewa by M. M. Noah; The Forest Rose, or
American Farmers by Samuel Woodworth; A Trip to Niagara, or Travelers in America by William
Dunlap; Metamora, or The Last of the Wampandags by John A. Stone; The Gladiator by Robert
M. Bird; The Drunkard, or The Fallen Saved by W. H. Smith; Fashion by Anna C. Mowatt; Uncle
Tom's Cabin by George L. Aiken; Po-ca-hon-tas, or The Gentle Savage by John Brougham; Fran-
cesca da Rimini by George H. Boker; Minstrel Show Across the Continent, or Scenes from New
York Life and the Pacific Railroad by James J. McCloskey; The Mulligan Guard Ball by Edward
Harrigan; Shenandoah by Bronson Howard; A Letter of Introduction by William D. Howells; A
Temperance Town by Charles H. Hoyt; Shore Acres by James A. Herne; The Great Divide by
William V. Moody; The New York Idea by Langdon Mitchell; The City by Clyde Fitch.

Nelson, Stanley, Ed. THE SCENE ONE: Plays from Off-Off Broadway. *The Smith* New Egypt
$2.50. Plays by David Newgurge, Roma Greth, Guy Gauthier, Frederick Bailey,
Stanley Nelson, Ben Bradford, Fran Lohman, Robert Reinhold, Eduardo Garcia.

THE SCENE TWO: Annual Anthology of Off-Off Broadway Plays. *The Smith* New Egypt
1974 $3.50. Plays by Michael McGrinder, William Kushner, Sally Ordway, Sharon
Thie, Arthur Sainer, Oscar Mandel, Robert Patrick.

THE SCENE THREE: Annual Anthology of Off-Off Broadway Plays. *The Smith* New Egypt
1975 $4.00

Plays by Robert Houston, Robert Reinhold, Robert Herron, Jay Roth, Frederick Bailey, Ilsa Gilbert, Edna S. Chappart, Eduardo Garcia, Robert Somerfeld, Pamela Lengyel, Guy Gauthier,
Charles Wilbert, Jennine O'Reilly, Gloria Gonzalez, Joseph Lazarus. All plays in these anthologies
have been in recent production Off-Off Broadway. The texts include original casts, performance
time, and information on performing rights.

NEW AMERICAN PLAYS. Ed. by Robert Corrigan and William Hoffman *Farrar, Straus* (Hill
& Wang) Mermaid Dramabks. Vol. 1 1965 $4.95 pap. $1.95 Vol. 2 1968 $5.95 pap.
$1.95 Vol. 3 1969 $5.95 pap. $2.45 Vol. 4 1971 $6.50 pap. $2.45

Vol. 1 The Death and Life of Sneaky Fitch by James L. Rosenberg; Socrates Wounded by Al-
fred Levinson; Constantinople Smith by Charles L. Mee, Jr.; The Hundred and First by Kenneth
Cameron; Ginger Anne by Deric Washburn; Pigeons by Lawrence Osgood; The Good Bull of
Boredom by Lorees Yerby; Blood Money by Dennis Jasudowicz; Mr. Biggs by Anna Marie Bar-
low; A Summer Ghost by Claude Fredericks. Vol. 2 Futz by Rochell Owens; Until the Monkey
Comes by Venable Herdon; A Message from Cougar by Jean R. Maljean; French Gray by Josef
Bush; The Abstract Wife by Ursule Molinaro; Passacaglia by James P. Dey; The White Whore and
the Bit Player by Tom Eyen; The Owl Answers by Adrienne Kennedy. Vol. 3 The Electronic Nig-
ger by Ed Bullins; The Poet's Papers by David Starkweather; Always with Love by Tom Harris;
Thank You, Miss Victoria by William M. Hoffman; The Golden Circle by Robert Patrick; An
American Playground Sampler by Marc Estrin; The King of Spain by Byrd Hoffman. Vol. 4
Slaughterhouse Play by Susan Yankowitz; At War with the Mongols by Robert Heide; Captain
Jack's Revenge by Michael Smith; African Medea by Jim Magnuson; Icarus by Ken Rubenstein;
Moby Tick by Emanuel Peluso.

Orzel, Nick, and Michael Smith, Eds. EIGHT PLAYS FROM OFF-OFF BROADWAY. *Bobbs* 1967 pap. $2.25

Contains The General Returns From One Place to Another by Frank O'Hara; The Madness of Lady Bright by L. Wilson; Chicago by Sam Shepard; The Great American Desert by J. Oppenheimer; Balls by P. Foster; American Hurrah by J. C. van Itallie; The Successful Life of 3 by M. I. Fornes; Calm Down Mother by Megan Terry.

Parone, Edward. NEW THEATRE IN AMERICA. *Dell* 1964 pap. $2.25. Seven plays including Dutchman by LeRoi Jones and Mrs. Dally Has a Lover by William Hanley.

Patterson, Lindsay, Comp. BLACK THEATER: A 20th Century Collection of the Work of Its Best Playwrights. *Dodd* 1971 $12.95

Contains St. Louis Woman by Arna Bontemps and Countee Cullen; Take a Giant Step by Louis Peterson; In Splendid Error by William Branch; Trouble in Mind by Alice Childress; Simply Heavenly by Langston Hughes; A Raisin in the Sun by Lorraine Hansberry; Purlie Victorious by Ossie Davis; Dutchman by LeRoi Jones; The Amen Corner by James Baldwin; In the Wine Time by Ed Bullins; No Place to Be Somebody by Charles Gordone; Ceremonies in Dark Old Men by Lonne Elder III.

Quinn, Arthur Hobson, Ed. REPRESENTATIVE AMERICAN PLAYS, From 1767 to the Present Day. *Prentice-Hall* (Appleton) 1938 7th ed. rev. and enl. 1953 $12.95

Contains The Prince of Parthia by Thomas Godfrey; The Contrast by Royall Tyler; Andre by William Dunlap; Superstition by J. N. Barker; Charles the Second by J. H. Payne and Washington Irving; Pocahontas or The Settlers of Virginia by G. W. P. Custis; The Broker of Bogota by Robert M. Bird; Tortesa, the Usurer by N. P. Willis; Fashion by A. C. M. Ritchie; Francesca da Rimini by G. H. Boker; The Octoroon or Life in Louisiana by Dion Boucicault; Rip Van Winkle, as played by Joseph Jefferson; Hazel Kirke by Steele MacKaye; Shenandoah by Bronson Howard; Margaret Fleming by J. A. Herne; Secret Service by William Gillette; Madame Butterfly by David Belasco and J. L. Long; The Girl with the Green Eyes by Clyde Fitch; The New York Idea by Langdon Mitchell; The Witching Hour by Augustus Thomas; The Faith Healer by W. V. Moody.

Strasberg, Lee. FAMOUS AMERICAN PLAYS OF THE 1950's: Camino Real; The Autumn Garden; Tea and Sympathy; The Zoo Story; A Hatful of Rain. *Dell* 1963 pap. $.95

See also Chapter 1, The Drama, this volume.

KELLY, GEORGE EDWARD. 1887–1974.

A member of Philadelphia's famous Kelly clan and uncle of Princess Grace, Kelly's reputation was made by three of his plays from the 1920s. "The Torch-Bearers" pokes fun at amateur theatre groups; "The Show-Off," an expanded version of "Poor Aubrey," is a classic presentation of the bragger; "Craig's Wife" is a study of a woman who loves her home and position more than her husband.

Morris Freedman has written that "Kelly was able . . . to apply that same sort of phenomenological insight marking the work of fictionists like Lewis and Dreiser and essayists like Mencken." And beneath his domestic detail and small talk Kelly's puritanical judgment punishes the egotistical figures (often middle-aged women) in his plays.

"Kelly's portrait gallery consisted of coldly calculated . . . figures, observed with detachment. . . . Kelly points out the follies and ludicrous behaviour of his times with a crabbed cynicism that would do credit to Ben Jonson if it did not lack Jonson's raucous gusto"—(*Sievers*).

Kelly won a Pulitzer Prize for Drama for "Craig's Wife."

THE TORCH-BEARERS. *French* 1922 $2.00

THE SHOW-OFF. *French* 1924 $1.75

CRAIG'S WIFE. *French* 1925 rev. ed. 1949 $1.75

THE FLATTERING WORD. *French* 1925 $.85

POOR AUBREY. *French* 1925 $.85

THE WEAK SPOT. *French* 1925 $.85

BEHOLD THE BRIDEGROOM. *French* 1927 $1.75

REFLECTED GLORY. *French* 1937 mss.

THE FATAL WEAKNESS. *French* 1947 $1.75

Books about Kelly

George Kelly. By Foster Hirsch. *Twayne* 1976 $7.50

ANDERSON, MAXWELL. 1888–1959.

During his long successful career as a dramatist, which he turned to in 1924 after being a journalist on the West Coast and in New York, Anderson wrote about a wide range of figures: American statesmen, British royalty, Socrates, Joan of Arc, and the average man. His plays include historical dramas, musicals, patriotic plays, fantasies, and a thriller. Perhaps his best piece is "Winterset," inspired by the Sacco-Vanzetti case. It tells the search of Mio, son of a man executed ostensibly for murder but actually for his radical ideas, to clear his father's name. Mio's father is the equivalent of Vanzetti. Beginning with "Elizabeth the Queen," Anderson's most famous historical drama, the playwright employed for many years an irregular blank verse, with which he intended to heighten the emotions of his characters. However, Edmund Wilson observed that this style "has no relation to the language and tempo of our lives." Yet these verse plays collected in one volume (*see below*) constitute his best work. Harold Rosenberg writes of their common theme: "Each turns upon a . . . perfect romance . . . frustrated by another need—political ("Elizabeth the Queen" and "Mary of Scotland"), social ("The Wingless Victory" and "Winterset") or private ("High Tor" and "Key Largo"). The issue [is] an omnipresent dying within."

Anderson won the Pulitzer Prize for Drama for "Both Your Houses" and the New York Drama Critics Circle Award for "Winterset" and "High Tor."

ELEVEN VERSE PLAYS, 1929–1939: Elizabeth the Queen (1930); Night over Taos (1932); Mary of Scotland (1934); Valley Forge (1934); Winterset (1935); The Wingless Victory (1936); High Tor (1937); The Masque of Kings (1936); The Feast of Ortolans; Second Overture (1940); Key Largo (1939) *Harcourt* 1940 $15.00

FOUR VERSE PLAYS: Elizabeth the Queen; Mary of Scotland; Winterset; High Tor. *Harcourt* Harvest Bks. 1959 pap. $3.95

THREE PLAYS BY MAXWELL ANDERSON: Valley Forge; Joan of Lorraine; Journey to Jerusalem. Ed. by George Freedley *Simon & Schuster* (Washington Square) 1963 pap. $.60

ELIZABETH THE QUEEN (1930); BOTH YOUR HOUSES (1933); MARY OF SCOTLAND (1934) *French* 3 vols. each $1.75

WINTERSET (1935); JOAN OF LORRAINE (1946); ANNE OF THE THOUSAND DAYS (1948); BAREFOOT IN ATHENS (1951); THE BAD SEED (1955); THE GOLDEN SIX (1958). *The following are available in mss. only:* THE WINGLESS VICTORY (1936); THE MASQUE OF KINGS (1936); THE STAR WAGON (1937); KEY LARGO (1939); JOURNEY TO JERUSALEM (1940); SECOND OVERTURE (1940); CANDLE IN THE WIND (1941); STORM OPERATION (1944); TRUCKLINE CAFÉ (1946). *Dramatists* each $1.25

ESSENCE OF TRAGEDY AND OTHER FOOTNOTES AND PAPERS. 1939 *Russell & Russell* $6.50

Books about Anderson

Maxwell Anderson, the Playwright as Prophet. By Mabel D. Bailey. *Bks. for Libraries* 1957 $10.25

Maxwell Anderson: A Bibliography. By Martha Cox. *Folcroft* 1958 $7.50

O'NEILL, EUGENE. 1888–1953. (Nobel Prize 1936)

O'Neill remains America's finest dramatist, to date. He was born in New York City, the son of the famous actor James O'Neill. After being suspended from Princeton University, he spent five years as a drifter, including time as a seaman, before beginning to write.

In the twenties O'Neill tried various techniques, using expressionism in "The Hairy Ape" and "The Emperor Jones," symbolism in "The Fountain," interior monologues in "Strange Interlude" and masks in "The Great God Brown." In the thirties came "Mourning Becomes Electra" (a Freudian interpretation of the Greek legend of the House of Atreus) and "Ah, Wilderness!" (his only comedy). O'Neill continued in his naturalistic vein with "The Iceman Cometh," "More Stately Mansions" and "Long Day's Journey into Night."

Harold Clurman has written that "O'Neill's plays stand on well grounded pillars of strong action—melodrama in fact—and far more effectively, they are embodiments of his spiritual obsessions. . . . His dramatized preoccupations were at once profoundly personal and objectively significant. . . . Wracked by disbelief he groped toward positive affirmation."

O'Neill won the Pulitzer Prize for Drama for "Anna Christie," "Beyond the Horizon," "Strange Interlude," and "Long Day's Journey into Night," and the New York Drama Critics Circle Award for "Long Day's Journey into Night."

THE COMPLETE PLAYS OF EUGENE O'NEILL. *Random* 1941 Lifetime Lib. 3 vols. 1951 boxed set $30.00

This edition contains the author's extensive revisions. The 29 plays, published originally in a uniform edition 12 vols. (o.p.) as follows: Vol. I Strange Interlude (1928); Desire under the Elms (1924); Lazarus Laughed (1927); The Fountain (1925); The Moon of the Caribbees, Bound East for Cardiff, The Long Voyage Home, In the Zone, Ile, Where the Cross Is Made, The Rope (all these one-act plays first pub. 1919); The Dreamy Kid (1919); Before Breakfast (1916); Vol. 2 Mourning Becomes Electra (1931); Ah, Wilderness! (1933); All God's Chillun Got Wings (1923); Marco Millions (1927); Welded (1923); Diff'rent (1920); The First Man (1922); Gold (1920); Vol. 3 Anna Christie (1921); Beyond the Horizon (1920); The Emperor Jones (1921); The Hairy Ape (1922); The Great God Brown (1925); The Straw (1920); Dynamo (1929); Days without End (1934); The Iceman Cometh (1946).

NINE PLAYS. 1936. *Random* Modern Lib. Giants Nobel Prize ed. 1941 $5.95

Mourning Becomes Electra; Strange Interlude; The Emperor Jones; Marco Millions; The Great God Brown; All God's Chillun Got Wings; Lazarus Laughed; The Hairy Ape; Desire under the Elms.

THE LONG VOYAGE HOME: Seven Plays of the Sea. *Random* Modern Lib. 1919 $1.95. The Moon of the Caribbees; Bound East for Cardiff; The Long Voyage Home; In the Zone; Ile; Where the Cross Is Made; The Rope.

THE EMPEROR JONES, ANNA CHRISTIE, THE HAIRY APE. *Random* Modern Lib. 1937 $1.95

THREE PLAYS: Desire under the Elms; Strange Interlude; Mourning Becomes Electra. *Random* Vintage Bks. $1.95

TEN "LOST" PLAYS. Fwd. by Bennett Cerf *Random* 1964 $7.95

Includes five plays not in print elsewhere; "apprentice works" which O'Neill did not wish to preserve, but which are of value as a record. There is no indication of the date of each, nor of the order in which they were written.

SIX SHORT PLAYS: The Dream Kid; Before Breakfast; Diff'rent; Welded; The Straw; Gold. *Random* Vintage Bks. pap. $1.95

THE EMPEROR JONES. 1921. Ed. by Max J. Herzberg *Prentice-Hall* (Appleton) 1960 $2.25; (and "Macbeth") *Harper* (Barnes & Nobles) $3.60

THE ICEMAN COMETH. 1946. *Random* Vintage Bks. $1.95

A MOON FOR THE MISBEGOTTEN. *Random* 1952 $1.95; *French* 1958 $1.75

LONG DAY'S JOURNEY INTO NIGHT. *Yale Univ. Press* 1956 $10.00 pap. $2.95. Autobiographical play in four acts.

A TOUCH OF THE POET. *Yale Univ. Press* 1957 $10.00 pap. 1960 $2.95

HUGHIE. A one-act play. *Yale Univ. Press* 1959 $4.50

"Hughie" is a previously unpublished work in which O'Neill returned to a form with which he had experimented earlier. It is the only surviving manuscript from a series of eight one-act monologue plays that he planned in 1940 and which was completed in 1941. Its world premiere was at the Royal Dramatic Theater in Stockholm on Sept. 18, 1958.

MORE STATELY MANSIONS. *Yale Univ. Press* 1965 $10.00 pap. $3.45. Shortened from the author's partly revised manuscript by Karl Ragner Gierow and ed. by Donald Gallup. This full-length tragedy was to have been the fourth play in the saga of an American family and was first produced in Stockholm in 1962.

Books about O'Neill

Eugene O'Neill: A Critical Study. By S. K. Winter. 1934. *Russell & Russell* 2nd enl. ed. 1961 $8.50. O'Neill's main ideas behind his plays in the context of the times.

The Haunted Heroes of Eugene O'Neill. By Edwin A. Engel. (1953, o.p.). A clear and intensive critical study including analyses of most of the plays.

Eugene O'Neill and the Tragic Tension: An Interpretive Study of the Play. By Doris V. Falk. *Rutgers Univ. Press* 1958 pap. $2.95. A neo-Freudian interpretation.

O'Neill and His Plays. Ed. by Oscar Cargill, N. Bryllion Fagin and William J. Fisher. *New York Univ. Press* 1961 1963 pap. $3.95. This anthology of reviews, articles and discussions of the playwright, with O'Neill's own letters, is a valuable contribution.

O'Neill. By Arthur and Barbara Gelb. 1961. *Harper* rev. ed. 1974 $17.50 pap. $7.95. One of the best biographies.

O'Neill. By Clifford Leech. 1963. Writers and Critics Ser. Vol. 24 *Int. Pubns. Service* $2.50. A brief but well written study.

O'Neill: A Collection of Critical Essays. Ed. by John Gassner. Twentieth Century Views Ser. *Prentice-Hall* 1964 $5.95

Eugene O'Neill. By Frederic I. Carpenter. U.S. Authors Ser. *Twayne* $6.50; *College Univ. Press* $2.45. Superb short treatment of O'Neill as a writer. Highly recommended.

The Plays of Eugene O'Neill. By John Henry Raleigh. Crosscurrents/Modern Critiques Ser. *Southern Illinois Univ. Press* 1965 $4.50 pap. $2.85. Analyzes three periods in O'Neill's career, relating them to specific American cultural strains; a detailed and major study.

O'Neill, Son and Playwright. By Louis Sheaffer. *Little* 1968 $15.00 pap. $5.25. The most important biography. Supersedes the biography by Arthur and Barbara Gelb.

Drama of Souls: Studies in O'Neill's Super-Naturalistic Technique. By Egil Tornqvist. *Yale Univ. Press* 1970 $12.50. O'Neill's dramatic techniques. "Super-naturalism" was O'Neill's term for Strindberg's expressionism.

Contour in Time: The Plays of Eugene O'Neill. By Travis Bogard. *Oxford* 1972 $15.00. An important literary study.

O'Neill, Son and Artist. By Louis Sheaffer. *Little* 1973 $15.00 pap. $5.25. The second half of the monumental Shaeffer opus.

Eugene O'Neill and the American Critic: A Bibliographic Checklist. By Jordan Y. Miller. *Shoe String Press* rev. ed. 1974 $20.00. Essential for the serious student.

KAUFMAN, GEORGE S. 1889–1961.

Kaufman, who was born in Pittsburgh, attended law school for two years, was a journalist on the *Washington Times* by 1912 and drama editor for the *New York Times* in the 1920s. Kaufman was sole author of one long play and two one-act plays; he collaborated on over 25 plays. His talent was essentially complementary. Other people supplied the idea; he gave it its dramatic quality. His partnerships were usually made with other writers rather than dramatists, and the plays exhibit a composite character that always reflects Kaufman's personal signature. John Gassner wrote on Kaufman and his collaborators, they "have been marvelous recorders of American surfaces" but in their occasional critical outlook they "were either disinclined or unable to carry it to conclusions . . . their flippancy [was] amusing and at worst just a trifle too empty." Commenting once on why he did not write true satire, the playwright said, "Satire is what closes Saturday night."

Kaufman's early plays have enjoyed frequent revivals in both professional and amateur theaters.

Kaufman, Ryskind, and Ira Gershwin won the Pulitzer Prize for Drama for "Of Thee I Sing," and Kaufman and Hart for "You Can't Take It with You."

(With Moss Hart) SIX PLAYS. *Dramatists* each $1.25 except as noted

Once in a Lifetime (*French* 1930 $1.75); Merrily We Roll Along (*French* 1934 $2.95); You Can't Take It with You (1937); The American Way (1939 *Dramatists* mss. only); The Man Who Came to Dinner (1940); George Washington Slept Here (1940).

(With Marc Connelly) PLAYS: Dulcy (1921) *French* $1.75; The Beggar on Horseback (1924) *Scholarly Press* $9.00; *French* $.75

(With Edna Ferber) PLAYS: Minick (1924); The Royal Family (English title: "Theatre Royal" 1928); Dinner at Eight (1932). 3 vols. *French* each $1.25

(With Edna Ferber) PLAYS: Stage Door (1936); The Land Is Bright (1941 1946); Bravo! (1949). 3 vols. *Dramatists* each $1.25

(With various collaborators) PLAYS: First Lady (with Katherine Dayton 1935); The Late George Apley (with J. P. Marquand 1946); Small Hours (with Leueen Macgrath 1951). 3 vols. *Dramatists* each $1.25

THE BUTTER AND EGG MAN. 1926. *French* $1.75

IF MEN PLAYED CARDS AS WOMEN DO (one act). *French* 1926 $.85

THE STILL ALARM (one act). *French* 1930 $.85

(With M. Ryskind and I. Gershwin) OF THEE I SING. 1932. *French* Libretto $2.00. Vocal Score $15.00

(With Howard Teichmann) THE SOLID GOLD CADILLAC. 1954. *Dramatists* $1.25

Books about Kaufman

George S. Kaufman: An Intimate Portrait. By Howard Teichmann. *Atheneum* 1972 $10.00; *Dell* pap. $1.95

George S. Kaufman and His Friends. By Scott Meredith. *Doubleday* 1974 $12.94. There is no serious attempt to analyse Kaufman's plays but "this biography can be unenthusiastically described as the available"—(Walter Clemons in *Newsweek*).

HOWARD, SIDNEY (COE). 1891–1939.

Howard graduated from the University of California, and studied playwrighting with George Pierce Baker's 47 Workshop at Harvard. His most notable play is "They Knew What They Wanted." In this story a middle-aged Italian-American grape grower gets a young "mail-order" bride. Subsequently, she has an illegitimate child by a younger man; but the older man accepts her and the baby. Lloyd Morris has written, "the qualities which made 'They Knew What They Wanted' so remarkable continued to dominate all of Howard's work. Unlike many of his contemporaries he was neither a moralist, a sentimentalist, or a propagandist. . . . He saw [life] from a point of view . . . of common sense, unprejudiced by commitment to any doctrine."
Howard died tragically, on his farm, crushed by his own tractor.
The playwright won the Pulitzer Prize for Drama for "They Knew What They Wanted."

PLAYS. *French* each $1.75 except as noted. They Knew What They Wanted (1925 $2.00); Ned McCobb's Daughter (1926); The Silver Cord (1927); The Late Christopher Bean (founded on "Prenez Garde à la Peinture" by René Fauchois 1933).

(With Paul De Kruif) YELLOW JACK. 1934. *Dramatists* 1946 mss. only

DODSWORTH. *Dramatists* 1948 mss. only. Dramatized from the Sinclair Lewis novel with comments by Howard and Lewis on the art of dramatization.

MADAM WILL YOU WALK? *Dramatists* 1955 mss. only

RICE, ELMER. 1892–1967.

A native of New York City, Rice attended law school at night and passed his bar exams. However, he immediately began writing; and "On Trial," which employed a flashback technique, made Rice an important playwright at the age of twenty-two. He proceeded to study under Hatcher Hughes at Columbia University where he also directed. He helped found the Playwrights' Company in 1938, the Dramatists' Guild and other groups. In 1951 he came to the defense of actors whose allegedly left-wing associations were causing them to lose their jobs. During his 45 years in the theatre, Rice wrote 50 full-length plays, 4 novels, film and television scripts, as well as his autobiography, and "The Living Theatre," appraising the theatre in terms of the social and economic forces affecting its development.
His two masterpieces are "The Adding Machine," an expressionistic comedy wherein the hero remains a cipher in mechanized society, and "Street Scene," which was originally entitled "Landscape with Figures" because Rice considered "the [tenement] house as the real protagonist of the drama." Mary McCarthy has written of this naturalistic play that "the plot, like the old plots of Hamlet, Oedipus, and Orestes, is not a conflict of persons but a contest between a man and a fearful action which everything wills him to commit . . . ." The plot's *crime passionnel* is but one aspect of the crowded panorama of tenement life. Robert Hogan writes in assessing Rice's career, "Rice has produced a remarkable body of work—large, varied, experimental and honest. . . . As a consistently experimental playwright he is rivalled in our theatre only by O'Neill."
Rice won the Pulitzer Prize for Drama for "Street Scene."

THREE PLAYS: The Adding Machine; Street Scene; Dream Girl. *Farrar, Straus* (Hill & Wang) 1965 $4.95 Dramabks. pap. $3.45

PLAYS. *French* each $2.00 except as noted. The Adding Machine (1923); Street Scene (1929); Not for Children (1935 rev. ed. 1951 $1.75)

TWO ON AN ISLAND. 1940. *Dramatists* mss. only

DREAM GIRL. *Dramatists* acting ed. 1946 $1.85

THE GRAND TOUR. 1952. *Dramatists* 1952 $2.25

THE WINNER. 1954. *Dramatists* 1954 $2.50

THE LIVING THEATRE. 1959. *Greenwood* 1972 $14.75

MINORITY REPORT: An Autobiography. *Simon & Schuster* 1963 $6.50

Books about Rice

The Independence of Elmer Rice. By Robert G. Hogan. Crosscurrents/Modern Critiques Ser. *Southern Illinois Univ. Press* 1965 $6.95
Elmer Rice. By Frank Durham. U.S. Authors Ser. *Twayne* $6.50

MacLEISH, ARCHIBALD. 1892– *See Chapter 9, Modern American Poetry,* Reader's Adviser, *Vol. 1.*

BEHRMAN, S. N. 1893–1973.

Behrman once wrote, "Any good comedy has its basis in tragedy. It is a hair's breadth removed— not the tragedy of death, but the abiding one of life."

A grocer's son from Worcester, Mass., Behrman studied at Clark University and then Harvard University, where he worked in Baker's 47 Workshop. Behrman was skilled at producing polished comedies depicting fashionable persons in a comedy of manners. Often his plots involved a hero who turns against society while the heroine, usually middle-aged and charming, maintains her independence. It is in his heroines that Behrman gives life to the humanitarian spirit. His plays exhibit both an abhorrence and attraction toward the egoist. Behrman was earnest about the social and political issues in his plays, causing Rabkin to comment that "the very seriousness of the ideas involved continually threatens to destroy the trivial base upon which the wit is perched." "Biography," one of the author's best plays, has as its heroine a portrait painter who abandons both an opportunist and an idealist and keeps her detachment. Perhaps his second finest play is "End of Summer" in which the wealthy hostess is asked by various groups to provide financial aid.

FOUR PLAYS: The Second Man; Biography; Rain from Heaven; End of Summer. (1955, o.p.)

THE SECOND MAN (1927); METEOR (1930); BIOGRAPHY (1933); RAIN FROM HEAVEN (1934); NO TIME FOR COMEDY (1939); I KNOW MY LOVE (adapted from Marcel Archard's play); JANE (1952). *French* 8 vols. each $1.75

LORD PENGO. Adapted from the author's "Duveen." 1963. *French* $1.75

Books about Behrman

S. N. Behrman. By Kenneth T. Reed. *Twayne* 1976 $6.95

GREEN, PAUL. 1894–

Paul Green, born on a North Carolina farm, studied philosophy at the University of North Carolina. He began writing plays as a freshman under the guidance of Frederick Koch, whose Carolina Playmakers staged Green's first works. He is the best of our regional dramatists, portraying the plight of oppressed Southerners both of the old South and the new. His dramas used interpolations of folk songs along with authentic North Carolina dialect. Among Green's finest achievements are, "The House of Connelly" (1931, o.p.) and "Johnny Johnson." Gassner writes, " 'The House of Connelly' . . . remains the most poignant drama of the postbellum South, and 'Johnny Johnson' is the most imaginative and affecting antiwar full-length play in the American Theatre." Johnny Johnson is a young Middle West American who believes in peace, but takes war propaganda at its face value until he is disillusioned. "In Abraham's Bosom" (1926, o.p.) shows the failure of a mulatto to achieve status. This later work, performed by the Provincetown Players in New York City, won the Pulitzer Drama Prize for 1926.

Green is also largely responsible for the development of pageants or symphonic dramas, as he terms them. "The Lost Colony" (o.p.) was his first outdoor drama and was written to commemorate the 350th anniversary of Raleigh's colony at Roanoke, Virginia. Using a cast of 150, it has been performed every summer since. Other popular Green pageants, derived from the life and history of the people or single individuals from a particular locale, are "The Common Glory" and "The Stephen Foster Story." Green has written, [America's] "Richness of tradition, our imaginative folk life . . . are too outpouring for the narrow confines of the usual . . . Broadway play and stage. But they can be put to use in the symphonic drama . . . . It is wide enough, free enough, and among the people cheap enough for their joy and use."

WIDE FIELDS (1928) *AMS Press* 1970 $8.50; *Scholarly Press* 1971 $14.50

HYMN TO THE RISING SUN (1936) *French* $1.95

JOHNNY JOHNSON (1937) *French* $3.00

THE COMMON GLORY (1938) *Greenwood* $12.00

HAWTHORN TREE: Some Papers and Letters on Life and the Theatre. (1943) *Bks. for Libraries* $12.00

(With Charles G. Vardell) SONG IN THE WILDERNESS. *Univ. of North Carolina Press* 1947 $2.00

THE WILDERNESS ROAD (1956) *French* $3.00

CONFEDERACY (based on the life of Robert E. Lee) (1959) *French* $1.75

(With Abbe Abbott) I AM ESKIMO: Aknick My Name. *Alaska Northwest Pub.* 1959 pap. $3.95

THE STEPHEN FOSTER STORY. *French* $2.00

Books about Green

Paul Green. By Barrett H. Clark. *Haskell* 1974 lib. bdg. $7.95
Paul Green. By Vincent Kenny. *Twayne* $6.50

THURBER, JAMES. 1894–1961. *See Chapter 15, Essays and Criticism,* Reader's Adviser, *Vol. I.*

HAMMERSTEIN, OSCAR. 1895–1960. *See* RICHARD RODGERS, 1902– , *this Chapter.*

BARRY, PHILIP. 1896–1949.

Barry is best remembered as a writer of comedies about the well-to-do. His most noted play is "The Philadelphia Story" which revolves about a wealthy young woman who on her wedding day switches from a dull social climber to marry a man of her own background. Other drawing room successes include "Paris Bound" and "Holiday." Barry also created plays of greater seriousness— with less success, however. "Hotel Universe," where a group of strangers relive personal crises in their lives, and "Here Come the Clowns" are experimental dramas with a mystical side, reflecting Freudian interpretation of character and existential doubt. "Tomorrow and Tomorrow" presents a situation where a man discovers that his mistress, in behavior and love, is more his wife than the woman he is legally married to.

Gill has written, "No matter how ambitious the intentions of his plays, he kept the plays themselves modest in scale. He wrote often in the now unfashionable genre of high comedy but his comedies strove to be deeper than they were high."

STAGES OF GRACE: Eight Plays by Philip Barry. Ed. by Brendan Gill and Ellen Barry *Harcourt* 1974 $19.95. Contains You and I; White Wings; Hotel Universe; The Animal Kingdon; Here Come the Clowns; Philadelphia Story; Second Threshold; Holiday.

YOU AND I (1923); IN A GARDEN (1926); HOLIDAY (1929); PARIS BOUND (1929 $2.00); TOMORROW AND TOMORROW (1931 mss.); THE ANIMAL KINGDOM (1932); THE PHILADELPHIA STORY (1939); HERE COME THE CLOWNS (1939 $6.50). *French* each $1.75 (except as noted)

SECOND THRESHOLD. *Dramatists* acting ed. 1951 $1.25. His last play. With revisions and a preface by Robert E. Sherwood.

Books about Barry

Philip Barry. By Joseph P. Roppolo. U.S. Authors Series *College & Univ. Press* 1965 pap $2.45

SHERWOOD, ROBERT E(MMET). 1896–1955.

A graduate of Harvard, Sherwood wrote for *Vanity Fair* as a film critic and for the old humor magazine *Life,* of which he was editor from 1920 to 1928. Sherwood wrote in a variety of tones and of different historical periods, always with a serious purpose. Matlow writes, "His plays, however melodramatic or comic, are ideological and hortatory: early ones preach pacifism, later ones warfare against evils that have menaced democracy—slavery in Lincoln's time, and Fascist world domination in the 1930s and 1940s." "Abe Lincoln in Illinois" is a drama of Lincoln's life from the time of his early twenties until he left Springfield at the age of fifty-one. In "The Petrified Forest" a group of gangsters take over a lunchroom in the Arizona desert where a disillusioned intellectual has given his insurance policy to the young waitress so that she might have a better life. "There Shall Be No Night" has as its background the Russian invasion of Finland and the necessity for personal courage in the face of the Communist destruction.

Sherwood became overseas director for the Office of War Information and a speech writer for President Franklin D. Roosevelt during World War II.

The humane dramatist once said, "The duty of dramatists is to express their times and guide the public through the complexities of those times."

Sherwood won the Pulitzer Prize for Drama for "Idiot's Delight," "Abe Lincoln in Illinois" and "There Shall Be No Night."

Studies of Sherwood by John Mason Brown are currently o.p.: "The Worlds of Robert E. Sherwood: Mirror to His Times" (1965); "The Ordeal of a Playwright: Robert E. Sherwood and the Challenge of War" (1970); "There Shall Be No Light" (1970).

THE ROAD TO ROME (1927); TOVARICH (adapted from Jacques Déval 1937). *French* each $1.75

REUNION IN VIENNA (1932); THE PETRIFIED FOREST (1935); IDIOT'S DELIGHT (1936 mss. only); ABE LINCOLN IN ILLINOIS (1939); THERE SHALL BE NO NIGHT (1940); SMALL WAR ON MURRAY HILL (1957 $2.50). *Dramatists* each $1.85 (except as noted)

ABE LINCOLN IN ILLINOIS. *Scribner* 1939 $4.95

Books about Sherwood

Robert E. Sherwood. By R. Baird Shuman. U.S. Authors Ser. *Twayne* 1964 $6.50; *College & Univ. Press* 1964 pap. $2.45

WILDER, THORNTON. 1897–1975.

Wilder, the son of a man who was to become American consul general in Hong Kong and Shanghai, was born in Wisconsin; he attended Oberlin College, Yale University and Princeton University where he received the degree of M.A. Wilder's plays are basically about the wonder of human existence. He made use of anti-naturalistic Eastern and classical dramatic traditions and European mystery plays, and introduced a fresh dramaturgy to American literature. He experimented with stage space and time to present a generalized view of man under the aspect of eternity looking at a moment from two points in time.

"Our Town" is a tender portrait of small-town people, oblivious, except for the heroine (who dies at the end of the play), to what it is to be alive. "The Skin of Our Teeth" is an expressionist fantasy depicting a suburban family and its free-wheeling maid, surviving through war, the Great Flood and the Ice Age. Much of the material from this play is derived from Joyce's "Finnegan's Wake" (dialogue in "The Matchmaker" is from Molière). But Wilder quite reasonably argued that "Literature has always more resembled a torch race than a furious dispute among heirs."

Wilder won the Pulitzer Prize for Drama for "Our Town."

THE LONG CHRISTMAS DINNER AND OTHER PLAYS IN ONE ACT. 1931. Introd. by John Gassner *Harper* 1963 pap. $.95

THREE PLAYS: Our Town (1938); The Skin of Our Teeth (1942); The Matchmaker (1954). *Harper* 1957 $8.95; *Bantam* pap. $.95. The author's preface is a contribution of the utmost importance to dramatic technique and theatre history.

THE LONG CHRISTMAS DINNER (1931 rev. ed. 1934); LOVE AND HOW TO CURE IT (1932); THE HAPPY JOURNEY (rev. ed. 1934). *French* each $.85

OUR TOWN. 1938. *Harper* 1960 $6.95; *French* $1.75

THE SKIN OF OUR TEETH. 1942. *French* 1944 $2.00

THE MATCHMAKER. Originally produced in 1938 as "The Merchant of Yonkers." *French* 1958 $1.75

THREE PLAYS FOR BLEECKER STREET: Infancy; Childhood; Someone from Assisi. *French* $.85

Books about Wilder

Thornton Wilder. By Rex Burbank. U.S. Authors Series. *Twayne* 1961; *College & Univ. Press* 1962 pap. $2.45

Thornton Wilder. By Bernard Grebanier. Pamphlets on American Writers *Univ. of Minnesota Press* 1964 $1.25

The Art of Thornton Wilder. By Malcolm Goldstein. *Univ. of Nebraska Press* 1965 $7.95 pap. $2.95

"An excellent book on the highlights of Wilder's thought, but [there is] not enough about his art"—*(N.Y. Times)*.

The Plays of Thornton Wilder: A Critical Study. By Donald Haberman. *Wesleyan Univ. Press* 1967 $8.00. Scholarly in approach, this examines the influence of Dreiser, Stein, Joyce and Kierkegaard on Wilder. It considers Wilder's use of expressionist theater techniques and of symbol, myth and allegory.

Thornton Wilder. By Helmut Papajewski. Trans by John Conway *Ungar* 1969 $6.50

Examines his three major plays and "A Life in the Sun" which has not yet been published in the United States. "Serious, rather academic, but enlightened comment"—*(LJ)*.

Thornton Wilder. By Hermann Stresau. Trans. by Frieda Schutze *Ungar* 1971 $7.00 pap. $1.75

Thornton Wilder: An Intimate Portrait. By Richard H. Goldstone. *Saturday Review Press* (dist. by Dutton) 1975 $12.95

Analyzes the leading themes of Wilder's plays and their productions. "An artful and substantial literary biography . . . Goldstone's psychological analysis strike me as both sensible and probable"—(Carlos Baker).

See also Chapter 14, Modern American Fiction, Reader's Adviser, *Vol. 1*.

RODGERS, RICHARD, 1902– and OSCAR HAMMERSTEIN II, 1895–1960.

Hammerstein was born into a theatrical family. His grandfather was owner of the Manhattan Opera Company, his father a theatrical manager and his uncle a producer. Nevertheless the young Hammerstein studied law before turning to the theater, where his uncle gave him his start, for experience, as a stagehand. In the course of a successful career he wrote lyrics for the music of Rodgers and Jerome Kern, and at his death left an estate of over $7,000,000. There are two books of songs by the Rodgers and Hammerstein team: "The Songs We Sing from Rodgers and Hammerstein" (ed. by Mary Rodgers 1957, o.p.) and "Song Book" (*Simon & Schuster* 1958 $17.50).

Rodgers' collaboration with the lyricist Oscar Hammerstein II began with "Oklahoma!" (1943). They continued from success to success, including "Carousel" and the vastly popular "South Pacific" which won a Pulitzer award.

Six Plays: South Pacific (1949); The King and I (1951); Me and Juliet (1953); Carousel (1945); Oklahoma! (1943); Allegro (1947). Text and lyrics but no music. 1955. *Random* Modern Lib. 1959 $3.95

The Sound of Music. *Random* 1960 $5.95

The Songs of Richard Rodgers: A Definitive Collection. *Random* 1974 pap. $8.95

Musical Stages: An Autobiography. *Random* 1975 $12.50

Books about Rodgers and Hammerstein

Some Enchanted Evenings. By Deems Taylor. 1953. *Greenwood* 1972 $15.25

The Rodgers and Hammerstein Story. By Stanley Green. (1963, o.p.). The "highly recommended" account of the partnership that changed the American musical stage.

HART, MOSS. 1904–1961.

Moss Hart was born in New York. He was very successful, as he said, in his own "bailiwick of satire and light comedy." "Once in a Lifetime," the beginning of his collaboration with George S. Kaufman in 1930, was the first of a series of plays that pleased a large public. After 1940 came several successes of his own: the psychoanalytic musical comedy, "Lady in the Dark"; "Winged Victory" (1943, o.p.), written to order for the Air Force; "Light up the Sky," a comedy about the pre-Broadway tryout of a new play and others. With "The Climate of Eden," he changed pace and wrote a serious play about British Guiana.

(With George S. Kaufman). Once in a Lifetime. *French* 1930 $1.75

Merrily We Roll Along. *French* 1934 $2.95

You Can't Take It with You (1936); The American Way (1939); The Man Who Came to Dinner (1939); George Washington Slept Here (1940); Lady in the Dark (1941); Light up the Sky. *Dramatists* each $1.25

The Climate of Eden. 1953. *Dramatists* mss. A play from Edgar Mittelholzer's novel, "Shadows Move among Them."

Act One: An Autobiography. *Random* 1959 $7.95

HELLMAN, LILLIAN. 1905–

The foremost American woman playwright was born in New Orleans but educated at New York University and Columbia. She now spends her time between New York and Martha's Vineyard. Her first dramatic success, written when she was 26, was "The Children's Hour." The story came from a famous 19th-century Scottish trial. Two teachers at a girls' boarding school are implicated in a scandal; the theme is not simply sexual perversion but the destructiveness caused by well-intentioned witch-hunting. "The Watch on the Rhine" (1941, o.p.) was an early anti-Nazi play. Best known is "The Little Foxes" which depicts an avaricious family in the South of 1900. Walter Kerr said of this play, "it is not a great play, perhaps, but virtually perfect of its kind, lean and candid, muscular and mettlesome in the bold black-and-white strikes it makes against a money-guilded world." "Autumn Garden" is a Chekhovian drama about people with unfilled lives.

Robert Corrigan has observed of Hellman, "In a realistic style, characteristic of Ibsen, she writes of the conflicts of personal morality and their public consequences. . . . In each of her plays she raspingly attacks both the doers of evil and those who stand by and watch them do it."

Hellman won the New York Drama Critics Circle Award for "The Watch on the Rhine" and "Toys in the Attic."

COLLECTED PLAYS. *Little* 1972 $17.50

Contains "Another Part of the Forest," concerns the Hubbard family of "The Little Foxes" (1939) twenty years earlier; "The Autumn Garden" (1951); "The Children's Hour" (1934); "Days to Come" (1934), a labor dispute exposes anger against an indebted factory owner; "The Lark," Joan of Arc's life, portrayed in flashbacks at her trial; "Montserrat," portrays the execution of six persons, and of the hero when he refuses to testify; "My Mother My Father and Me" (1963), a comedy based on the novel "How Much!" by Burt Blechman. An aged mother is put into a nursing home after the family argues it out in their Manhattan setting; "The Searching Wind" depicts the life of an American ambassador stationed in Europe before World War II; "Toys in the Attic," sisters with too protective a hold on their brother; "Watch on the Rhine," a German anti-Nazi is tracked down by a blackmailing Nazi agent in Washington, D.C. social setting.

THE LITTLE FOXES and ANOTHER PART OF THE FOREST. *Viking* 1973 pap. $2.95

PORTRAIT OF AN UNFINISHED WOMAN. *Little* 1969 $7.50; *Bantam* 1974 pap. $1.50. Autobiography.

Books about Hellman

Lillian Hellman: Playwright. By Richard Moody. *Bobbs* Pegasus 1972 $6.95
  Phoebe Adams wrote in *Atlantic* that Moody's work is not nearly as interesting as Hellman's autobiography, but his book contains more information about the plays themselves.
Dramatic Works of Lillian Hellman. By L. Ross Holman. *Humanities Press* 1973 pap. text ed. $5.75. A close structural and thematic analysis.

KINGSLEY, SIDNEY.   1906–

Born in New York City, Kingsley graduated from Cornell University in 1928. He was a play reader and then wrote films for Columbia Pictures. "Men in White," the play about doctors which first established Kingsley, was written in three months, then rewritten for three years while he verified his medical data. The realistic production rather than the story itself was responsible for the play's success. "Dead End" combines a story of tough street kids with that of a gangster making his last efforts to see his mother; it also presents a contrast between the wealthy and slum classes. Morrison has observed, "In most of his work Kingsley relies on a sense of atmosphere generated by realistic re-creation of a particular world—hospitals, slums, police stations, prisons—a vivid milieu that supplies much of the dramatic impact of the play and also constitutes its limitations . . . timely issues have made them at first appear more substantial than they later are seen to be." And Morgan Himelstein has observed that the advent of television has lessened the effectiveness of Kingsley's type of documentary dramas.

Kingsley won the Pulitzer Prize for Drama for "Men in White" and the New York Drama Critics Circle Award for "The Patriots" and "Darkness at Noon."

MEN IN WHITE. 1933. *French* mss.

DEAD END. *Dramatists* mss. only

THE PATRIOTS. *Dramatists* $8.25

DETECTIVE STORY. 1949. *Dramatists* 1951 $1.85. A play in 3 acts.

DARKNESS AT NOON. 1951. *French* $1.75. A play based on the novel by Arthur Koestler.

NIGHT LIFE. 1963. *Dramatists* $1.85

THE WORLD WE MAKE. *Dramatists* mss. only

ODETS, CLIFFORD.   1906–1963.

Odets was born in Philadelphia, became an actor about 1923, and thereafter was associated with the theatre. In 1930 he joined the Group Theatre (*see Clurman, Harold, "The Fervent Years" in this Chapter, Section on History and Criticism*). Odets appeared in his own "Waiting for Lefty" (1935, o.p.) which established his name. This early piece uses a flashback technique whereby vignettes demonstrate the causes of a strike. Odets's finest play, and one of the major plays of American dramatic literature, is "Awake and Sing" (1935, o.p.). This drama depicts a poor Bronx family, its dominating mother, and their economic and psychological plights. In its compassion, humor, and use of poetic dialogue Odets demands comparison with O'Casey. His dialogue makes most effective use of a heightened middle-class Jewish speech. A proletarian playwright, in his early and major period of writing, Odets portrays characters tormented by economic uncertainties. "Go out and fight so life shouldn't be printed on dollar bills"—"Awake and Sing." Clurman has observed that Odets's "central theme was the difficulty of attaining maturity in a world where money as a token of success . . . plays so dominant a role."

WAITING FOR LEFTY. 1935. *Richard West* 1975 $10.00

GOLDEN BOY. 1937. *Dramatists* 1948 $1.25

THE COUNTRY GIRL. 1951. *Dramatists* $1.25

THE FLOWERING PEACH. 1955. *Dramatists* mss. only

Books about Odets

Clifford Odets. By R. Baird Shuman. U.S. Authors Series. *Twayne* 1962 $6.50; *College & Univ. Press* 1963 pap. $2.45

Clifford Odets: The Thirties and After. By Edward Murray. *Ungar* 1968 $7.50. Three of the early and five of the later plays are examined for structure; probing, original evaluations.

Clifford Odets: Humane Dramatist. By Michael Mendelsohn. *Everett Edwards* 1969 $10.00. The interviews with Odets are particularly valuable.

Clifford Odets: Playwright. *Bobbs* Pegasus 1971 $6.95. Not a complete literary estimate.

SAROYAN, WILLIAM.   1908–

An Armenian-American with little formal education, Saroyan is America's reckless dramatist of the late 1930s and early forties. He wrote, "Plot, atmosphere, style, and all the rest of it may be regarded as so much nonsense"—("Three Times Three"). And, indeed, Saroyan's plays have been criticized as formless, and his writing as undisciplined. Yet they are imbued with affection for the human race and contain an infectious enthusiasm for society's misfits and innocents. Linking Saroyan with two earlier giants of American literature, Frederic Carpenter once wrote that Saroyan "reaffirms the old American faith of Emerson and Whitman, who, . . . proclaimed that the world could be reformed only by reforming the individual, and that this could not be accomplished by social compulsion and physical violence but only by personal freedom and loving tolerance."

Saroyan's dramatic career was launched with "My Heart's in the Highlands," a fantasy. The following year "The Time of Your Life" was awarded the Pulitzer Prize (which Saroyan publicly refused on the grounds that commerce had no right to patronize art). This play, undoubtedly Saroyan's one enduring piece, takes place in a waterfront saloon where vivid characters can quite appropriately wander in and out and come into contact with the philosophical Joe, a man of unending generosity.

For the past two decades Saroyan has spent much time abroad, particularly in Paris and London.

MY HEART'S IN THE HIGHLANDS. *French* 1939 $.75

TIME OF YOUR LIFE. *French* 1939 $2.00

THE BEAUTIFUL PEOPLE. *French* 1941 $.75

LOVE'S OLD SWEET SONG. *French* 1941 $.75

HELLO OUT THERE. *French* 1942 $.75

GET AWAY OLD MAN. *French* 1944 $.75

THE CAVE DWELLERS: A Play [in 2 Acts]. *French* $.75

THE SLAUGHTER OF THE INNOCENTS. *French* $.75

Books about Saroyan

William Saroyan. By Howard R. Floan. U.S. Authors Ser. *Twayne* 1966 $6.50; *College & Univ. Press* 1966 pap. $2.45

See also Chapter 14, Modern American Fiction, Reader's Adviser, *Vol. 1.*

WILLIAMS, TENNESSEE.   1911–

Born in his grandfather's rectory in Columbus, Miss., Williams, the son of a shoe salesman, had odd jobs and transient attendances at the Universities of Washington and Iowa, graduating from the latter in 1940. Today the playwright remains peripatetic, maintaining residences in New York City, Rome, New Orleans, and Key West. Williams won his first recognition with "The Glass Menagerie" which contains characters and themes he has used frequently since. The female protagonists here are both pained by solitude, the daughter sustained by the dream of a suitor, the mother a prisoner of the past. When a young caller comes, their dream life is completely altered by reality. In each play there is some struggle to be free. The redemptive force is usually a man who is a composite figure of Christ and Dionysus. As Henry Popkin observes, "the bold nonconformism of the poet and the bohemian must actively oppose the destructive forces that threaten them: the dead hand of the past . . . convention, repression, and illusion."

In his plays Williams has used a theatrical language employing poetry of the theatre that is unexcelled by any American dramatist to date. The playwright has written, "The printed script of a play is hardly more than an architect's blueprint of a house not yet built or built and destroyed. The color, grace and levitation, the structural pattern in motion, the quick interplay of live beings . . . these things are the play not words on paper, nor thought and ideas. . . ." Yet enough of this tension in form pervades the scripts themselves to make them of enduring value.

Williams won the Pulitzer Prize for Drama for "A Streetcar Named Desire" and "Cat on a Hot Tin Roof." He won the New York Drama Critics Circle Award for these two and "The Glass Menagerie" and "The Night of the Iguana."

THE THEATRE OF TENNESSEE WILLIAMS. *New Directions* 5 Vols. Vol. 1 Battle of Angels, A Streetcar Named Desire, The Glass Menagerie $12.50 Vol. 2 The Eccentricities of a Nightingale, Summer and Smoke, The Rose Tattoo, Camino Real $10.00 Vol. 3 Cat on a Hot Tin Roof, Orpheus Descending, Suddenly Last Summer $10.00 Vol. 4 Sweet Bird of Youth, Period of Adjustment, Night of the Iguana $12.50 Vol 5. The Milk Train Doesn't Stop Here Anymore, Kingdom of Earth, Small Craft Warnings, Out Cry $12.50

DRAGON COUNTRY: Eight Plays. *New Directions* $7.50 pap. $2.95. Short Plays. Including "In the Bar of a Tokyo Hotel" and two Slapstick Tragedies.

TWENTY-SEVEN WAGONS FULL OF COTTON AND OTHER ONE-ACT PLAYS. *New Directions* 1946 1949 3rd ed. 1953 $6.50 pap. $2.25; *Dramatists* $1.95

THE GLASS MENAGERIE. 1945. *New Directions* New Class. 1949 pap. $1.75; *Dramatists* 1948 $1.25

A STREETCAR NAMED DESIRE. 1947. *New Directions* 1947 $5.25; *Dramatists* 1952 $1.25; *New Am. Lib.* Signet pap. $1.25

AMERICAN BLUES. 1948. *Dramatists* $1.25. Five one-act plays.

I RISE IN FLAME, CRIED THE PHOENIX. 1951. *Dramatists* $.50. A play about D. H. Lawrence.

BABY DOLL. *New Directions* 1956 $4.50. A screenplay and two one-act plays on which the script is based: The Unsatisfactory Supper and 27 Wagons Full of Cotton.

SWEET BIRD OF YOUTH. 1959. *New Am. Lib.* Signet 1962 $.60; *New Directions* $2.75. In three acts.

PERIOD OF ADJUSTMENT. 1960. *New Directions* 1960 $6.50; *New Am. Lib.* Signet 1962 pap. $.50

THE ECCENTRICITIES OF A NIGHTINGALE and SUMMER AND SMOKE. *New Directions* 1964 $6.50. Two different versions of the same play.

THE MUTILATED and THE GNÄDIGES FRÄULEIN. 1966. *Dramatists* 1967 each $.75. Two one-act plays produced on Broadway under the title "Slapstick Tragedy."

OUT CRY. *New Directions* 1973 $6.50 pap. $2.25

TENNESSEE WILLIAMS: Memoirs. *Doubleday* 1975 $8.95 limited ed. $50.00

Books about Williams

Tennessee Williams. By Signi Falk. U.S. Authors Ser. *Twayne* 1961 $6.50; *College & Univ. Press* pap. $2.45

Tennessee Williams: The Man and His Work. By Benjamin Nelson. *Astor-Honor* Obolensky (dist. by Grosset) 1961 $6.50 pap. $1.00
Not a definitive study, but "his family relationships are revealing and some of the remarks about the plays hit them off with sure accuracy"—(*Guardian*).

Tennessee Williams: Rebellious Puritan. By Nancy M. Tischler. 1961 *Citadel Press* 1965 pap. $1.95

"Long on plot summary and cozy biographical detail and short on criticism. . . . The account of this complex man's early life and personality is undoubtedly an important contribution"— (*LJ*).

Tennessee Williams. By Gerald Weales. Pamphlets on American Writers *Univ. of Minnesota Press* 1965 pap. $1.25

INGE, WILLIAM (MOTTER). 1913–1973.

Inge was born in Independence, Kansas. He went to Peabody College in Nashville, Tenn. and also studied theatre with Maude Adams at Stephens College in Columbia, Missouri. "Come Back Little Sheba" was his first success on Broadway. It is about an aging couple, the wife clinging to the past, the husband an alcoholic. His next play was "Picnic" (later revised as "Summer Brave") about a virile young drifter and his effect on women in a small town. "Bus Stop" involves people stranded. Each reveals his loneliness, and in the end an aspiring singer accepts the attention of a naive but rough cowboy. "Dark at the Top of the Stairs" concerns itself with a frustrated family wherein a new understanding between the mother and father, and more confidence on the part of the son and daughter eventuates.

Inge was immensely popular in the 1950s. In most of his plays the characters live a humdrum existence, usually in the Midwest Kansas-Oklahoma region of fifty years ago. Behind the naturalistic dialogue is an inner softness; and the main figures are prone to confession. His works have been called "psychodramas involving the solution of personal and social problems by introspection and togetherness"—(Eric Mottram). Inge once said, "I have never written a play that had any intended theme or that tried to propound any particular idea . . . I want my plays only to provide the audience with an experience which they can enjoy . . . and which shocks them with the unexpected in human nature."

Inge won both the Pulitzer Prize for Drama and the New York Drama Critics Circle Award for "Picnic." The latter part of Inge's career as a dramatist was not successful. He took his life in 1973.

FOUR PLAYS BY WILLIAM INGE. *Random* 1958 $7.50. Come Back, Little Sheba (1950 also *French* acting ed. 1951 $1.25); Picnic (1953 also *Dramatists* $1.25); Bus Stop (also *Dramatists* 1955 $1.25); The Dark at the Top of the Stairs (1958 also *Dramatists* $1.25)

ELEVEN ONE-ACT PLAYS. *Dramatists* $1.75

"The Boy in the Basement," an undertaker, dominated by his mother, must embalm a youth he admired; "Bus Riley's Back in Town," in a bar, a girl meets her lover who had been jailed for her pregnancy; "An Incident at the Standish Arms," a divorcee fears detection after sexual relations with a cab driver; "The Mall"; "Memory of Summer," a troubled woman continues swimming after the resort season until a guard stops her; "The Rainy Afternoon"; "A Social Event," a satire concerning an uninvited couple at a star's funeral; "Splendor in the Grass"; "The Tiny Closet"; "To Bobolink for Her Spirit"; "People in the Wind."

SPLENDOR IN THE GRASS. *Dramatists* 1966 $1.25. Adapted for the stage from Inge's screenplay by F. Andrew Leslie.

GIBSON, WILLIAM. 1914–

Gibson, a New Yorker, was educated in the New York City public schools, at Townsend Harris Hall and at City College. "The Miracle Worker" comes from a discursive TV script about the first crucial weeks in which the indomitable teacher, Annie Sullivan, is trying to communicate with the mind of a blind, deaf, mute, Helen Keller (*q.v.*). His "A Cry of Players," concerns Shakespeare's youth.

Gibson's talent appears to be for biographical dramas.

TWO PLAYS: Dinny and the Witches and The Miracle Worker. *Atheneum* 1960 $4.50

THE MIRACLE WORKER: A Play for Television. *Knopf* 1957 $4.50; *Bantam Bks.* 1962 pap. $.50

THE SEESAW LOG: A Chronicle of Stage Production, with the text of "Two for the Seesaw." *Knopf* 1959 $4.50

CRY OF PLAYERS. *Atheneum* 1969 $4.95

AMERICAN PRIMITIVE. *Atheneum* 1972

A SEASON IN HEAVEN. *Atheneum* 1974 $6.95

A MASS FOR THE DEAD. *Atheneum* 1968 $7.95. His autobiography.

MILLER, ARTHUR. 1915–

A crusader with intensity of feeling and great powers of observation, Arthur Miller has an "independent mind, professional skill and personal courage." His plays have been called "political," but he considers the areas of literature and politics to be quite separate and has said, "The only sure and valid aim—speaking of art as a weapon—is the humanizing of man." The recurring theme of all his plays is the relationship between a man's identity and the image that society demands of him. The son of a well-to-do New York Jewish family, Miller graduated from high school with poor grades and then went to work in a warehouse. "On the subway to and from work I began reading. . . . A book that changed my life was 'The Brothers Karamazov,' which I picked up, I don't know how or why, and all at once believed I was born to be a writer"—(quoted in "Twentieth Century Authors," 1955). He entered the University of Michigan, where he soon started writing plays. He graduated in 1938.

"All My Sons," a Broadway success that won the Drama Critics Circle Award in 1947, tells the story of a son, home from the war, who learns that his brother's death was due to defective airplane parts turned out by their profiteering father. "Death of a Salesman," his experimental yet classical American tragedy, "emotionally moving as it is socially terrifying," received both the Pulitzer Prize and the Drama Critics Circle Award in 1949. It is a poignant statement of man facing himself and his failure. In "The Crucible," a play about bigotry in the Salem witchcraft trials of 1692, he brought into focus "the tragedy of a whole society, not just the tragedy of an individual." It was generally considered to be a comment on the McCarthyism of its time. (Miller himself appeared before the Congressional Un-American Activities Committee and steadfastly refused to involve his friends and associates when questioned about them.)

His cinema-novel, "The Misfits," from a Miller short story, was written for his second wife, actress Marilyn Monroe. "After the Fall" has clear autobiographical overtones and involves the story of Miller's ill-fated marriage to Marilyn Monroe. In it a disillusioned lawyer named Quentin (the character representing Miller himself) converses with an (invisible) old friend, calling up scenes and people from his past. "Incident at Vichy" is a one-acter about a group of men picked off the streets one morning during the Nazi occupation of France. Miller has said of it, "I think most people seeing this play are quite aware it is not . . . a wartime horror tale; they do understand that the underlying issue concerns us now, and that it has to do with our individual relationships with injustice and violence." "The Price," is a "psychological problem drama"; it concerns two brothers, one a policeman, one a wealthy surgeon, whose long-standing conflict is explored over the disposal of their father's furniture. "The Creation of the World and Other Business" is a retelling of the story of Genesis, attempted as a comedy.

Robert Corrigan has observed the common theme in Miller's early work as well as in his later plays. "The main struggle in Miller's play through ["The Collected Plays"] shows," he writes, "each of the protagonists confronted with a situation which . . . eventually puts his 'name' in jeopardy. In the ensuing struggle his inability to answer the question 'Who am I?' produces his downfall . . . the verdict of guilty is based upon Miller's belief that if a man faced up to the truth about himself he could be fulfilled as an individual and still live within the restrictions of society." In the later plays, Miller treats "the effect his protagonist has had on the lives of others and his capacity to accept full responsibility."

Miller won the Pulitzer Prize for Drama for "Death of a Salesman" and the New York Drama Critics Circle Award for "All My Sons" and "Death of a Salesman."

COLLECTED PLAYS. *Viking* 1957 $6.95. All My Sons; Death of a Salesman; The Crucible; A Memory of Two Mondays; A View from the Bridge, in a hitherto unpublished two-act form.

THE PORTABLE ARTHUR MILLER. Ed. with introd. by Harold Clurman. *Viking* 1970 $10.00 pap. $3.95. Death of a Salesman, The Crucible, selection from The Misfits, essays and poetry; critical introduction, chronology, bibliography and notes.

ALL MY SONS. 1947. *Dramatists* $1.25

DEATH OF A SALESMAN: Certain Private Conversations in Two Acts and a Requiem. *Viking* 1949 $5.00 Compass Bks. 1958 pap. $1.45; *Dramatists* acting ed. 1952 $1.25

A VIEW FROM THE BRIDGE: Two One-Act Plays. 1949 rev. 1955. Includes also "A Memory of Two Mondays." *Viking* 1949 $4.75 Compass Bks. 1960 pap. $1.25; with a new introd. by the author *Bantam* 1962 pap. $1.25; *Dramatists* 1955 $1.25

THE CRUCIBLE. 1953. *Viking* 1964 $3.95 Compass Bks. pap. $1.35 (Text and Criticism) ed. by Gerald Weales *Viking* 1971 $6.95 pap. $2.45

AFTER THE FALL, or The Survivor. *Viking* 1964 $3.95; Compass pap. $1.45; *Bantam* pap. $1.25

INCIDENT AT VICHY. *Viking* 1965 $3.50

THE PRICE. *Viking* 1968 pap. $1.25

CREATION OF THE WORLD AND OTHER BUSINESS. *Viking* 1973 $5.95

THEATER ESSAYS OF ARTHUR MILLER. Ed. by Robert Martin *Viking* 1976 $8.95. Miller's commentary on his own work, the nature of tragedy, on theater as an institution etc.

Books about Miller

Arthur Miller. By Robert Hogan. Pamphlets on American Writers *Univ. of Minnesota Press* 1964 pap. $1.25
Arthur Miller. By Dennis Welland. Writers and Critics Ser. *Int. Pubns. Service* 1966 $2.50. Serviceable brief survey.
Arthur Miller. By Leonard Moss. U.S. Authors Ser. *Twayne* 1967 $6.50 pap. $2.45. Moss sees Miller as more than a purely "social dramatist," concluding that his "effort to unify social and psychological perspectives has been the source of his accomplishments and his failures as a dramatist."
Arthur Miller, Dramatist. By Edward Murray. *Ungar* 1967 $6.50 pap. $2.45. A critical examination of seven plays from "All My Sons" through "Incident at Vichy."
Psychology and Arthur Miller. By Richard I. Evans. *Dutton* 1969 $4.50. A discussion between a psychologist and the playwright.
Arthur Miller: A Collection of Critical Essays. Ed. by Robert W. Corrigan. *Prentice-Hall* 1969 $6.50
Arthur Miller: Portrait of a Playwright. By Benjamin Nelson. *McKay* 1970 $5.95
Arthur Miller. By Ronald Hayman. World Dramatists Ser. *Ungar* $8.50

ANDERSON, ROBERT (WOODRUFF).   1917–

The dramatist was born in New York City and graduated from Harvard where he did graduate work and assisted Harry Levin in his theatre course. He began writing plays while on a battleship in World War II. His best known work is "Tea and Sympathy," the plot of which concerns a boy falsely accused of homosexuality in a New England preparatory school. The school master's wife restores his self-respect in a final scene. The playwright has cautioned, however, not to regard the play simply in sexual terms. The play "has to do with responsibility . . . with loneliness . . . with questioning some popular definitions of manliness . . . with judgment by prejudice." "I Never Sang for My Father" focuses on a middle-aged son who has never been able to love his irascible father, but tries to come to terms with him.

TEA AND SYMPATHY. 1953. *French* $1.75

ALL SUMMER LONG: A drama in two acts adapted from the novel "A Wreath and a Curse" by Donald Wetzel. *Baker* pap. $1.25; *French* 1955 pap. $1.75

THE DAYS BETWEEN. *Random* 1965 pap. $1.95

I NEVER SANG FOR MY FATHER. *Random* 1968 $5.50

SOLITAIRE, DOUBLE SOLITAIRE. *Random* 1972 $4.95 pap. $1.95

LOWELL, ROBERT.   1917–   *See Chapter 9, Modern American Poetry,* Reader's Adviser, *Volume 1.*

LAURENTS, ARTHUR.   1918–

A native New Yorker, Laurents was educated at Cornell and wrote radio scripts before a four-year stint in the Army. "Home of the Brave" won him a Sidney Howard Award. " 'The Time of the Cuckoo' contrasts the romanticism and social naiveté of Americans with the worldliness of Europeans. . . . In view of the effortlessness of his style, the amount of insight he conveys is remarkable. Every character is a full length portrait"—(Brooks Atkinson, in the *N.Y. Times*). His Broadway hit musical, "West Side Story," is a retelling of the Romeo and Juliet theme in terms of Manhattan's juvenile delinquency. With music by Bernstein, choreography by Robbins, it had a long run in New York and became a very successful movie.

Laurents' last Broadway show, "Hallelujah, Baby!" opened in 1967, about a Negro girl who makes it in show business and eventually becomes civil-rights-conscious.

HOME OF THE BRAVE. 1946. *Dramatists* acting ed. 1946 $1.25

THE BIRD CAGE. *Dramatists* 1950 $1.25. Play in two acts.

The Time of the Cuckoo. 1953. *French* $1.75

A Clearing in the Woods. 1957. *Dramatists* $1.25

(With Stephen Sondheim) West Side Story. *Random* 1958 $5.50

Hallelujah, Baby! (1967, o.p.)

CHAYEFSKY, PADDY (born Sidney Chayefsky). 1923–

Born in the Bronx, New York, Chayefsky went to City College, receiving a bachelor's degree in social science. He first received public recognition for his television drama "Marty," a naturalistic love story of an Italian-American bachelor and the plain schoolteacher, of a different heritage, whom he marries. His first stage play was "Middle of the Night" about a middle-aged widower who loves a woman thirty years his junior. In these two pieces Chayefsky is concerned with the loneliness of his characters, lightened at the end by love. "The Tenth Man" and "Gideon" differ from the earlier works with a departure from strict realism and the use of fantasy along with a religious element. "The Passion of Joseph D." is about the leading figures of the Russian Revolution.

In recent years Chayefsky has written film scenarios.

Television Plays: Holiday Song; Printer's Measure; The Big Deal; Marty; The Mother; The Bachelor Party. *Simon & Schuster* 1955 1956 pap. $2.45

Middle of the Night. 1957. *French* $1.75

The Goddess. (1958, o.p.) His film script.

The Tenth Man. *Random* 1960 $4.50; *French* $1.75

Gideon. (1962, o.p.)

The Passion of Josef D. *Random* 1964 $5.50

The Latent Heterosexual. *Random* 1968 $5.00. A play.

FEIFFER, JULES. 1924–

Educated at the Art Students League and Pratt Institute, Feiffer is best known for his mordant cartoons for the *Village Voice*. He has also turned his satire to dramatic literature. "Little Murders" shows the meaningless violence behind American life. "The White House Murder Case" is aimed at the war posture of the United States in some future time. "Knock, Knock," which Walter Kerr termed "a good new funny American play, literate, lively, loquacious" opened Off-Broadway in 1976.

The White House Murder Case. *Grove* 1970 pap. $1.25

SIMON, NEIL. 1927–

Born in the Bronx, Simon had childhood ambitions to be a doctor, but after attending New York University and the University of Denver, he turned instead to television. His first play, "Come Blow Your Horn" (1958, o.p.) about a young rebel who moves into the luxurious apartment of his older playboy brother, is partly autobiographical. Since then, Simon has written many successful comedies; the titles and plays themselves or film versions will no doubt be familiar to the reader. Most are about the middle class with the comedy basically deriving from situations of personal frustration. His detractors have accused Simon of superficiality and being essentially a "gag writer." But Walter Kerr defends Simon's artistry in writing that Simon's work "has a much more serious, perceptive, human base to it than ordinary mechanical farce . . . he does have an eye and an ear for the crazy, cruel world about him."

Comedy of Neil Simon. *Random* 1972 $12.95; *Avon Bks.* 1973 $4.95

Contains "Barefoot in the Park," newlyweds in New York City and their attempt to provide romance for mother; "Come Blow Your Horn"; "The Gingerbread Lady," a singer fights alcoholism; "Last of the Red Hot Lovers," unsuccessful attempts of a middle-aged married man to have a love affair; "The Odd Couple," two friends whose wives have left them try to live together; "Plaza Suite"; "The Prisoner of Second Avenue," middle-aged couple living in New York apartment suffer unemployment; "The Star-Spangled Girl."

Barefoot in the Park. *Random* 1964 $6.95

The Odd Couple. *Random* 1966 $5.50

The Sunshine Boys. *Random* 1973 $5.95

God's Favorite. *Random* 1975 $6.95

ALBEE, EDWARD.   1928–

Edward Albee was raised as a "sole hope"—the pampered adopted son of millionaire parents. An indifferent, rebellious student, he attended various private schools, ending at Choate, where his gift for writing was first encouraged. He attended Trinity College briefly, then quit home and schooling at the age of 21 to live in New York City.

For nearly a decade he worked at odd jobs, writing poetry, attempting novels, publishing nothing. Just before his 30th birthday, he sat down and wrote "The Zoo Story" in two weeks. "The Sandbox" (1960), "Fam and Yam" (1960), "The American Dream" (1961) and "The Death of Bessie Smith" (1961) followed rapidly and the fame of the young dramatist was established.

These one act plays linked Albee to the Theater of the Absurd. The full-length "Who's Afraid of Virginia Woolf?" in 1962, Albee's Broadway debut, was by contrast "naturalistic." The evening-long argument between a married couple is a strong denunciation of modern marital relation-ships, "amusingly bitchy on the surface but murderously vicious underneath." "The heart of his technique is an archetypal family unity, in which the defeats, hopes, dilemmas, and values of our society (as Albee sees it) are tangibly compressed"—(Lee Baxandall in "The Theater of Edward Albee").

"The Ballad of the Sad Café," Albee's adaptation of the novella by Carson McCullers, was less successful in 1963. "Tiny Alice" had elements of the Theater of the Absurd and appeared to many who saw it to be an allegory about spiritual versus secular elements. Albee called it "something of a metaphysical dream play which must be entered into and experienced without preconception," a play that should be felt rather than analyzed. "A Delicate Balance," a more conventional comedy of serious intent, he says is "about how as you get older the freedom of choices becomes less and less, and you are left only with the illusion of freedom of action and you become a slave of compromise." In "Box" the stage is void except for the lines of a box; from the stage issues a woman's voice reciting thoughts suggested by the word box. "All Over" presents a famous person's imminent death—we never see him—attended by his nurse, doctor, wife, mistress, best friend and son. "Seascape," intended as a comedy and balance to the view of life expressed in "All Over," has a middle-aged married couple at the shore meeting a reptile. Their conversation reveals common problems in life. Of Albee plays Harold Clurman wrote (in the *Nation*): "What Albee is saying throughout his work, from 'The Zoo Story' to 'A Delicate Balance' is that we are uneasy, without comfort, unhinged. . . . We find no solace because we seek in vain for genuine substance in our professed faiths, shibboleths, institutions. We have opinions, but hardly any convictions. . . . Through the frustration of our desire for contact we take to wounding one another."

A perceptive critic of Albee, C. W. Bigsby writes, "Albee's value to the American theatre lies precisely in his determination to transcend the exhausted naturalism of the Broadway theatre, while establishing an existential drama committed to examining the metaphysical rather than the social or psychological problems of man."

Albee won the Pulitzer Prize for Drama for "A Delicate Balance" and "Seascape" and the New York Drama Critics Circle Award for "Who's Afraid of Virginia Woolf?"

THE ZOO STORY, THE DEATH OF BESSIE SMITH and THE SANDBOX: 3 Plays. Introd. by the author *Coward* 1960 pap. $2.95

THE AMERICAN DREAM, THE DEATH OF BESSIE SMITH, and FAM AND YAM. *Dramatists* 1962 $1.50

THE AMERICAN DREAM. 1961. *Coward* pap. $2.45; (and "The Zoo Story") *New Am. Lib.* 1963 Signet pap. $.75

WHO'S AFRAID OF VIRGINIA WOOLF? 1962. *Atheneum* pap. $3.95; *Simon & Schuster* (Pocket Bks.) pap. $1.50

(With Carson McCullers) THE BALLAD OF THE SAD CAFÉ. *Atheneum* pub. jointly with *Houghton* 1963 $4.95 pap. $3.45

THE SANDBOX and THE DEATH OF BESSIE SMITH. *New Am. Lib.* 1964 Signet pap. $.95

TINY ALICE. *Atheneum* 1965 $4.50; *Simon & Schuster* (Pocket Bks.) pap. $1.25; *Dramatists* $1.50

MALCOLM. *Atheneum* 1966 $4.95. Play based on the novel by James Purdy.

A DELICATE BALANCE. *Atheneum* 1966 $5.00; *Simon & Schuster* (Pocket Bks.) pap. $1.95

EVERYTHING IN THE GARDEN. *Atheneum* 1968 $5.95; *Simon & Schuster* 1969 $.95. From the play by Giles Cooper.

BOX and QUOTATIONS FROM CHAIRMAN MAO. *Atheneum* 1969 $4.50

ALL OVER. *Atheneum* 1971 $5.95; *Simon & Schuster* (Pocket Bks.) 1974 $1.25

SEASCAPE. *Atheneum* 1975 $7.95

Books about Albee

Edward Albee. By Richard E. Amacher. *Twayne* 1968 $6.50. Comments on ten plays. Believes the one-act plays and the full-length tragedies the best.

Edward Albee at Home and Abroad: A Bibliography 1938–June 1968. Ed. by Richard E. Amacher and Margaret Rule. *AMS Press* 1973 $12.50

Edward Albee: Playwright in Protest. By Michael Rutenberg. *Avon Bks.* Bard 1969 $6.95 pap. $1.65

Albee. By C. W. Bigsby. Writers & Critics Ser. *Int. Pubns. Service* Vol. 60 1969 $2.50. One of the most astute critics on Albee.

Edward Albee. By Ruby Cohn. Pamphlets on America Writers Ser. *Univ. of Minnesota Press* 1969 pap. $1.25. A study of Albee's plays up to "A Delicate Balance."

Edward Albee. By Ronald Hayman. *Ungar* $8.50

SCHISGAL, MURRAY. 1929–

The son of an immigrant from Lithuania, Schisgal was born in Brooklyn; he earned a L.L.B. degree from Brooklyn Law School but taught in New York City's public school system, and was a jazz musician and worker for the garment trades before becoming a playwright. In "The Tiger," a one-act play, a man kidnaps the first woman he can, finding this suburban housewife is also in revolt against the status quo, and he ends up taking French lessons from an all-too-willing mistress. The full length "Luv" uses the triangle situation. Walter Kerr found it "one step ahead of the avant-garde. . . . If the avant-garde, up to now, has successfully exploded the bright balloons of cheap optimism, Mr. Schisgal is ready to put a pin to the soap bubbles of cheap pessimism." "Jimmy Shine" is about a would-be artist who never quite makes it as an artist but who succeeds in becoming a human being. The one-act "The Chinese" is a satire on psychiatry.

Schisgal's plays usually have few characters and are about alienation. His stories are often fantasies, sometimes conveyed within a complex structure.

Schisgal has written about his technique, "What the painter has done with color and line, the avant-garde playwright seeks to do with language. What the painter has done with perceived subject matter, either obliterating it completely or distorting it to its bare essence, the playwright attempts to do with plot and theme."

THE TYPISTS and THE TIGER. *Coward* 1963 pap. $1.95

LUV. Introd. by Walter Kerr; interview with Schisgal by Ira Peck 1965. *Dramatists* $1.85

ALL OVER TOWN. *Dramatists* $1.85

AN AMERICAN MILLIONAIRE. *Dramatists* $1.85

DUCKS AND LOVERS. *Dramatists* $1.85

JIMMY SHINE. *Dramatists* $1.85

FRIEDMAN, BRUCE JAY. 1930–

Born in the Bronx to a garment company manager, Friedman received a bachelor's degree from the University of Missouri, where he majored in journalism. He wrote three novels before producing "Scuba Duba," a comic play of a neurotic white American liberal vacationing on the Riviera, who fears that his wife has run off with a black scuba diver. In "Steambath," the Puerto Rican attendant turns out to be a God figure, who gives out rewards and punishments in an apparently irrational manner.

SCUBA DUBA. *Dramatists* $1.85

STEAMBATH. *French* $1.75

HANSBERRY, LORRAINE. 1930–1965.

Though Lorraine Hansberry was a Negro, she refused to be typed as a Negro writer. She was the daughter of a well-to-do Chicago real estate man and studied painting before venturing to New York (in 1950), where she worked as a salesgirl, cashier and assistant to an Off-Broadway producer. She took courses in playwriting at the New School for Social Research and began working at it seriously after her marriage to the producer Robert Nemiroff. "A Raisin in the Sun," which brought her sudden success, was the warmly human story of a Negro family moving into a white neighborhood (as her father had done when she was eight). The title refers to Langston Hughes' "Harlem": "What happens to a dream deferred? Does it dry up like a raisin in the sun?" "The Sign in Sidney Brustein's Window," about the morals problems of a Jewish intellectual in Greenwich Village, was written during her final illness. She died of cancer in 1965, and in 1967 the radio station WBAI ran two moving three-hour programs on the course of her short life as described by herself and some 60 of the American theater's finest and most prominent actors and actresses, who enacted excerpts from her plays.

Hansberry won the New York Drama Critics Circle Award for "A Raisin in the Sun."

LES BLANCS AND THE LAST PLAYS OF LORRAINE HANSBERRY. *Random* 1972 $8.95 pap. $2.45

A RAISIN IN THE SUN. *Random* 1959 $5.50; *New Am. Lib.* $.95 (and "The Sign in Sidney Brustein's Window") *New Am. Lib.* pap. $.95

THE SIGN IN SIDNEY BRUSTEIN'S WINDOW. *Random* 1965 $5.50

TO BE YOUNG GIFTED AND BLACK: Lorraine Hansberry in Her Own Words. Ed. by Robert Nemiroff *Prentice-Hall* 1969 $8.95

HANLEY, WILLIAM. 1931–

Born in Ohio and educated at Cornell University and the American Academy of Dramatic Arts, Hanley has been called both "traditional" and "avant-garde." Hanley made his name in 1964 with "Slow Dance on the Killing Ground." "The 'Killing Ground' of the title is the big wide violent world, and there is temporary sanctuary from it for three people in a small Brooklyn paper-and-soda store: the store's owner, . . . a German refugee; a brilliant but eccentric Negro youth who . . . is running from the police; and a homely lass looking for an abortionist. They are three actual or potential killers"—("Best Plays of 1964–1965"). "Mrs. Dally Has a Lover," a play of humor and pathos, concerns a married woman and her conversations with a teenager. Their affair is unsordid but depicts the woman's failure both in relation to her husband and to the young man. "Today Is Independence Day" continues the story of "Mrs. Dally."

MRS. DALLY HAS A LOVER AND OTHER PLAYS. (1963, o.p.) Includes "Whisper into My Good Ear" and "Today Is Independence Day."

WHISPER INTO MY GOOD EAR and MRS. DALLY HAS A LOVER. *Dramatists* 1963 $1.25

SLOW DANCE ON THE KILLING GROUND. (1965, o.p.)

GELBER, JACK. 1932–

Gelber, a Chicagoan by birth, has a degree in journalism from the University of Illinois. He teaches at Columbia University. "The Connection," produced by the Living Theater in 1959, was hailed by Kenneth Tynan as the most exciting new American play staged Off-Broadway since World War II. Using techniques reminiscent of Pirandello, the "playwright" appears on stage to tell his public that the actors are really addicts playing actors, and that their pay will be heroin. Gelber intends the situation to carry the implication that we are all involved in some kind of "connection." Robert Brustein wrote, " 'The Connection' even avoids that over-intellectualization of human behavior which informs the work of Beckett, Ionesco and Genet. Gelber has managed to assimilate, and sometimes to parody, his borrowed techniques without a trace of literary self-consciousness." Gelber's subsequent plays to date have not had the same critical or popular success. "The Cuban Thing" shows a Cuban family's reaction to the Castro revolution. "Sleep" has psychologists testing a man who finally demands his integrity.

APPLE PIE (1961) and SQUARE IN THE EYE (1966). Introd. by Richard Gilman *Viking* Compass Bks. 1974 pap. $2.95

THE CONNECTION. *Grove* Evergreen Bks. (orig.) 1961 pap. $2.45

SLEEP. *Farrar, Straus* (Hill & Wang) 1972 $6.95 pap. $2.95

BARAKA, IMAMU AMIRI (LeRoi Jones). 1934–

Born LeRoi Jones in Newark, New Jersey, Baraka graduated from Howard University and has taught at Columbia, the New School for Social Research and at San Francisco State College. Baraka was founder of the Harlem (New York) Black Arts Repertory Theater School, using funds given by the U.S. Office of Economic Opportunity. The purpose of this school was to develop black theatrical talent and to give classes in remedial reading and mathematics. When this project closed, Baraka moved his cultural operation to Newark, forming the Spirit House Movers, a group of nonprofessional actors. In 1968 he created the Black Community Development and Defense Organization "dedicated to the creation of a new value system for the Afro-American community."

"Dutchman" marked Baraka as an important Black dramatic voice. In this one-act play a provocative white girl alternately entices, belittles and finally kills a young Negro in the subway. In "The Slave" a black revolutionary confronts his former wife, a white woman, and kills their two children. In "The Toilet" a black youth beats a white youth who has offered homosexual advances, but in the absence of others, returns to comfort the white youth. "Slave. Ship" is a indictment of white imperialism. Baraka's plays are bold in concept, strong in language and committed to revolutionary racial and social change.

DUTCHMAN and THE SLAVE. *Morrow* 1964 $4.95 pap. $2.25

THE BAPTISM and THE TOILET. *Grove* 1967 pap. $2.45

FOUR BLACK REVOLUTIONARY PLAYS: All Praises to the Black Man. *Bobbs* 1969 $5.00 pap. $2.25. Contains Experimental Death Unit#1; A Black Mass; Great Goodness of Life; Madheart.

Books about Baraka

From LeRoi Jones to Amiri Baraka: The Literary Works. By Theodore R. Hudson. *Duke Univ. Press* 1973 $7.95 pap. $4.75

See also Chapter 9, Modern American Poetry, Reader's Adviser *Vol. 1, under Jones, LeRoi.*

BULLINS, ED. 1935–

Bullins was born in Philadelphia, and educated at William Penn Business Institute, Philadelphia, Los Angeles City College and San Francisco State College. He has since become director of the New Lafayette Theatre in Harlem and an editor of *Black Theatre*. He has an individual feeling for the Black situation which he reveals as humorous, fierce and without a structured future.

FIVE PLAYS. *Bobbs* 1969 $7.50 pap. $4.95. Contains Clara's Old Man; Goin' a Buffalo; In the Wine Time; A Son Come Home; The Electronic Nigger.

FOUR DYNAMITE PLAYS. *Morrow* 1971 $5.95 pap. $2.95

THE DUPLEX: A Black Love Fable in Four Movements. *Morrow* 1971 $5.95

van ITALLIE, JEAN-CLAUDE. 1935–

After his parents fled his native city, Brussels, during the Nazi invasion, van Itallie grew up in Great Neck, N.Y., which, he says, "left me with a horror of the American suburbs." After graduating from Harvard, he supported himself mainly by writing scripts for National Educational Television; he also began working with Chaikin and the Open Theater group from which "America Hurrah" and later "The Serpent" evolved. The former play is really a trilogy, comprised of "Interview," "TV" and "Motel." "Interview" shows persons appearing in various interview situations, job, priest and parishioner, psychiatrist and patient, etc. An interwoven vocal and physical fugue of questions and responses conveys in nonrealistic fashion the impersonal, corporate approach to humans manifested by the authorities of our institutions. In "TV" researchers are merged with the banalities of the programs they are viewing. "Motel," with a cast of three huge papier-mâché dolls (there are actors inside), involves a couple at a motel. The lady motel keeper's voice drones on and on about the glories of motel civilization while her customers make love, destroy the room and finally its owner. Robert Brustein wrote of this remarkable piece, "Vladimir Nabokov effectively used motel culture, in 'Lolita,' as an image of the sordidness and tastelessness in the depths of our land; Mr. van Itallie uses it as an image of our violence, our insanity, our need to defile."

"The Serpent" is a work devised by van Itallie in conjunction with the Open Theatre. It places together moments from modern times, such as Kennedy's assassination, and episodes from *Genesis.* John Lahr writes of this important, avant-garde work, " 'The Serpent' is intended to call up dreams, not answer immediate moral questions. The action and sounds spin around an audience, reweaving the rites of birth and death as well as the Original Sin and celebration."

AMERICA HURRAH: Comprising Interview, TV, and Motel. 1967. *Dramatists.* $1.85

WAR; WHERE IS DE QUEEN?; ALMOST LIKE BEING; THE HUNTER AND THE BIRD; I'M REALLY HERE. *Dramatists* 1967 each $1.25

THE SERPENT. *Dramatists* $1.85

RICHARDSON, JACK. 1936–

Born in New York, Richardson is a graduate of Columbia University. "A truly remarkable first play" was Walter Kerr's comment on "The Prodigal," produced off-Broadway in 1960. With his reworking of the Orestes legend of idealism, political opportunism and bloody vengeance, Richardson achieved immediate success. In 1961, his double-bill one-acters "Gallows Humor" explored the problem of order and disorder in modern life, first within the prison cell of a murderer about to be hanged and then in the kitchen of the hangman. Richardson made his

Broadway debut in 1963 with "Lorenzo," in which a group of actors devoted to the "real" life of illusion are confronted by the exigencies of war. The setting is Renaissance Italy, but Richardson is clearly writing about the role of the artist in the society of his own time. Though admired in the weeklies, the play fell victim to the newspaper strike. "Xmas in Las Vegas," about a gambler, disappointed critics who had come to consider Richardson a major dramatist.

THE PRODIGAL. *Dutton* Everyman's (orig.) 1960 pap. $1.35

GALLOWS HUMOR. *Dutton* Everyman's (orig.) 1961 pap. $1.15

LORENZO. *Dramatists* mss. only

XMAS IN LAS VEGAS. *Dramatists* 1966 $1.25

ZINDEL, PAUL. 1936–

Born in Staten Island, New York, and educated at Wagner College, Zindel was a chemistry teacher for a number of years.

Zindel won the Pulitzer Prize for Drama and New York Drama Critics Circle Award for "The Effect of Gamma Rays on Man-in-the-Moon Marigolds."

THE EFFECT OF GAMMA RAYS ON MAN-IN-THE-MOON MARIGOLDS. *Dramatists* $1.85. This is a domestic play, similar in theme and characters to Williams' "The Glass Menagerie."

AND MISS REARDON DRINKS A LITTLE. *Dramatists* $1.85. The relation of three sisters whose lives have reached a point of crisis.

KOPIT, ARTHUR. 1937–

Kopit, a New Yorker, won a scholarship to Harvard to study electrical engineering. At Harvard he found his main interest was in playwrighting, however, and wrote many one-act plays there. Shortly after graduating *cum laude* Kopit wrote "Oh Dad, Poor Dad, Mamma's Hung You in the Closet and I'm Feeling So Sad." This absurdist play is about an overprotective mother who travels not only with her son, but with two Venus Flytraps and the remains of her husband, an obvious parody of Tennessee Williams' "Suddenly Last Summer." "The Day the Whores Came out to Play Tennis" is another comedy, about the grossly materialistic world of a country club. "Indians," a more ambitious play, depicts in epic style Buffalo Bill who, as a man caught in an ambivalent position between government and Indians, comes to represent the nemesis of the American Indian and the untroubled American conscience.

OH DAD, POOR DAD, MAMMA'S HUNG YOU IN THE CLOSET AND I'M FEELING SO SAD: A Pseudoclassical Tragifarce in a Bastard French Tradition. *Farrar, Straus* (Hill & Wang) 1960 pap $2.25

THE DAY THE WHORES CAME OUT TO PLAY TENNIS, AND OTHER PLAYS. *Farrar, Straus* (Hill & Wang) 1965 Dramabks. pap. $2.45

INDIANS. *Farrar, Straus* (Hill & Wang) 1969 $4.50 New Mermaid pap. $1.95; *Bantam* 1971 pap. $1.65

GUARE, JOHN. 1938–

Guare, who was born in New York, graduated from Georgetown and then received his M.F.A. from the Yale Drama School, where he started to write plays. "The House of Blue Leaves" is a wild and sad farce with such characters as the middle-aged husband with a yearning to become a songwriter, his son who is AWOL from the army, his insane wife, a wacky mistress, and a flock of nuns bent on seeing the visiting Pope on television. This is an inventive, intelligent playwright aware of society's foibles and predicaments, writing in a not entirely realistic manner.

"Rich and Famous" opened Off-Broadway in 1976. Guare has written, "I think the only playwrighting rule is that you have to learn your craft so that you can put on stage plays you would like to see."

Guare won the New York Drama Critics Circle Award for "The House of Blue Leaves."

THE HOUSE OF BLUE LEAVES. *French* 1972 $1.75

HOROVITZ, ISRAEL. 1939–

Horovitz was born in Wakefield, Mass. and went to Harvard University where he earned the degree of M.A. He received the degree of Ph.D. from the City University of New York. Horovitz caused considerable reaction with his one-act play "The Indian Wants the Bronx" wherein two teenage toughs cruelly torment an East Indian man who cannot speak English. The drama demonstrates the primitive impulse to hurt others who are helpless. His comedy "The Primary English Class" opened Off-Broadway in 1976.

THE INDIAN WANTS THE BRONX. *Dramatists* 1968 $.95

IT'S CALLED THE SUGAR PLUM. *Dramatists* $.95

SHEPARD, SAM.   1943–

Shepard, born in Illinois, created his first work "Cowboys" in 1964 and has had 26 more produced as of 1975. Shepard has said about the form of theatre, "Theatre contains all the other arts. You can put anything in that space—painting, film, dance, music, it can all be contained . . . a special art like the theatre is unlimited; there is every possibility." Most of Shepard's plays have been produced in the off-off Broadway theatre. His first full-length play "La Turista" is an allegory set in hotel rooms in the U.S. and Mexico. The hero's *"turista"* and his predicament are both irrational and uncurable. "Operation Sidewinder" is a thrilling allegory that contrasts the dehumanizing American white man with his technology and the Indian with his fundamental beliefs. The play resolves around a sophisticated Air Force computer in the form of a snake which escapes into the desert. Michael Smith has written, "All Shepard's plays use the stage to project images; they do not relate to the spectator by reflecting outside reality (they are not psychological or political); rather they relate to reality by operating directly on the spectator's mind and nerves. The imagery is surreal, the method nonrational."

FIVE PLAYS: Chicago; Icarus's Mother; Red Cross; Fourteen Hundred Thousand; Melodrama Play. *Bobbs* 1967 $5.00

UNSEEN HAND AND OTHER PLAYS. *Bobbs* 1970 $6.00

MAD DOG BLUES AND OTHER PLAYS. *Drama Bk. Specialists* 1973 $7.95 pap. $2.95

TOOTH OF THE CRIME AND GEOGRAPHY OF A HORSE. *Grove* Evergreen Bks. 1974 $3.95

OPERATION SIDEWINDER: A Play in Two Acts. *Bobbs* 1970 $5.00

—M.P.

Chapter 6

World Literature: General Works

"In the highest sense, when the aim of a translator is the re-creation of a poem (or a novel), the search he performs is not totally unlike the original search of the poet (or the novelist). It is the search for words capable of sustaining the experience."
—WALLACE FOWLIE

"Nor ought a genius less than his that writ attempt translation."
—SIR JOHN DENHAM

GENERAL REFERENCE AND BIBLIOGRAPHY

This chapter contains brief lists of books dealing with world literature in general, or, as the field is sometimes called, comparative literature. Works dealing with the literature of a specific country will be found listed under the appropriate specialized heading: French Literature, Asian Literature, and so forth.

Baldensperger, Fernand, and Werner P. Friederich. BIBLIOGRAPHY OF COMPARATIVE LITERATURE. 1950. *Russell & Russell* 1960 $20.00. An essential reference work, listing both articles and books.

CASSELL'S ENCYCLOPEDIA OF WORLD LITERATURE. Ed. by John Buchanan-Brown. 1954. *Morrow* 1973 $47.95

Curley, Dorothy Nyren, and Arthur Curley, Comps. and Eds. MODERN ROMANCE LITERATURES. *Ungar* 1967 $20.00

"Commentary of more than 400 critics about 148 mostly 20th century writers who have been selected because of their impact upon the English-speaking world."—(*LJ*)

THE FICTION CATALOG: The Standard Catalog Series. *Wilson* 9th ed. 1975 and supplement service through 1979. (U.S. and Canada) $45.00; (foreign) $50.00

Selected by experienced and outstanding librarians, this lists 4,734 works of fiction which have been found most useful in libraries throughout the United States and Canada.
Translations: Afrikans, Bengali, Bohemian, Catalan, Chinese, Czech, Danish, Dutch, Finnish, French, German, Greek, Hebrew, Hungarian, Italian, Japanese, Norwegian, Persian, Polish, Portuguese, Russian, Spanish, Swedish, Turkish, Yiddish. Also valuable are the 1951, 1956 and the 1961 volumes of the "Book Review Digest" (*Wilson* service basis) where, in the 1947–1951, 1952–1956, 1957–1961, 1962–1966 and the 1967–1971 cumulated indexes under "Fiction—Translated Stories," reviewed titles are listed under the original language. The annual volumes of the *Book Review Digest* also list "Fiction—Translated Stories" (consult *Wilson* catalog for separate volumes available).

Fleischman, Wolfgang Bernard. ENCYCLOPEDIA OF WORLD LITERATURE IN THE 20TH CENTURY. Enlarged and updated edition, translated into English, of the Herder Lexikon der Weltliteratur im 20. Jahrhundert. *Ungar* 4 vols. 1967 Vol. 1 A–F $34.50 Vol. 2 G–N $36.50 Vol. 3 O–Z $46.00 Vol. 4 Supp. and Index, ed. by Frederick Ungar and Lina Mainiero $48.00 set $155.00

This volume is impressive in its scope and detail, in its thoroughness, and in the list of contributors. The general editor, Wolfgang Fleischmann, is professor of comparative literature at the University of Massachusetts and former editor of *Books Abroad*. Until the publication of this encyclopedia there has been no comparable work in English. In addition to biobibliographical entries on most major literary figures of the 20th Century, the encyclopedia contains excellent discussions by scholars of note on literary movements, criticism, and genres. Only a few minor errors were noted in the entries, which are generally accurate and complete—(*LJ*)

Hardison, O. B., Ed. MODERN CONTINENTAL LITERARY CRITICISM. *Prentice-Hall* (Appleton) 1962 pap. $5.50

Heiney, Donald, and Lenthiel H. Downs. CONTEMPORARY LITERATURE. *Barron's* 4 vols. 1974 pap. Vols. 1, 2, & 3 each $2.95 Vol. 4 $3.95. Vol. 1 Contemporary European Literature; Vol. 2 Contemporary British Literature; Vol. 3 Recent American Literature from 1880 to 1930; Vol. 4 Recent American Literature after 1930.

Holman, Clarence H. A HANDBOOK TO LITERATURE. 1936 1960 *Bobbs* (Odyssey) 1972 $7.00 pap. $3.90. Based on the original by William Flint Thrall and Addison Hibbard.

Hopper, Vincent F., and Bernard D. N. Grebanier. WORLD LITERATURE. *Barron's* 2 vols. 1952 each $6.00 pap. each $1.95

Hornstein, Lillian Herlands, Ed., G. P. Percy, Co-Ed., Calvin S. Brown, Gen. Ed. and others. THE READER'S COMPANION TO WORLD LITERATURE: A Guide to the Enjoyment and Knowledge of the Immortal Masterpieces of Writing from the Dawn of Civilization to the Present. 1956. *New Am. Lib.* Mentor Bks. 1957 rev. ed. 1973 pap. $1.95. A most useful and authoritative, alphabetically arranged guide to titles, authors, literary periods, movements and terms from earliest times to the present.

INDEX TRANSLATIONUM. A UNESCO publication, covering material for 1964–1971. *UNESCO* 5 vols. Vol. 19 1966 $36.00 Vol. 21 1968 $40.00 Vol. 22 1971 $42.00 Vol. 23 1972 $46.00 Vol. 24 1973 $74.00. Vol. 24 contains an international bibliography of translations covering 42,970 translated books published in 1971 in 71 countries.

THE LITERATURES OF THE WORLD IN ENGLISH TRANSLATION: A Bibliography. *Ungar* Vol. 1 The Greek and Latin Literatures, ed. by George B. Parks and Ruth Z. Temple $18.50; Vol. 2 The Slavic Literatures, comp. by Richard C. Lewanski assisted by Lucia G. Lewanski and Maya Deriugin $25.00; Vol. 3 The Romance Literatures, ed. by George B. Parks and Ruth Z. Temple $45.00

Magill, Frank N., Ed. CYCLOPEDIA OF LITERARY CHARACTERS. *Harper* 1964 $15.00 lib. bdg. $12.69

(With Dayton Kohler, Eds.) CYCLOPEDIA OF WORLD AUTHORS. (Orig. "Masterplots Cyclopedia of World Authors"). *Harper* 1958 $15.00 lib. bdg. $12.69. Biographies of 753 world-famous authors, from Homer to James Gould Cozzens.

PENGUIN COMPANION TO WORLD LITERATURE. *McGraw-Hill* 4 vols. 1971. Vol. 1 British and Commonwealth Literature, ed. by David Daiches $10.95 Vol. 2 European Literature, ed. by Anthony Thorlby $11.95 Vol. 3 U.S.A. and Latin American Literature, ed. by Malcolm Bradbury, Eric Mottram and Jean Franco $9.95 Vol. 4 Classical, Oriental and African Literature, ed. by D. M. Lang and D. R. Dudley $9.95
"Each of these volumes is a solid reference work having a definite place in libraries of all sizes and types."—(*LJ*)

Richardson, Kenneth, and R. Clive Willis, Eds. TWENTIETH CENTURY WRITING; A Reader's Guide to Contemporary Literature. *Transatlantic* 1970 $15.00

Shipley, Joseph T., Ed. DICTIONARY OF WORLD LITERATURE: Criticism, Forms, Technique. With the collaboration of 250 scholars and other authorities. New rev. ed. 1953. *Littlefield* 1959 1968 pap. $2.50

Smith, Horatio, General Ed. COLUMBIA DICTIONARY OF MODERN EUROPEAN LITERATURE. *Columbia* 1947 $20.00
Nearly 1,200 articles with general surveys of the literary activities of 31 continental European countries from about 1870 to the present, written by 239 scholars and experts; articles on approximately 200 French authors, 150 German, 100 Russian, 100 Italian, 100 Spanish, 50 Polish and 40 Czechoslovakian; less familiar literatures such as Catalan, Icelandic, Flemish, Turkish are given special treatment. An excellent reference now being revised.

Wakeman, John, Ed. WORLD AUTHORS. 1950–1970: A Companion Volume to Twentieth Century Authors. *Wilson* 1975 $60.00
"A conspectus of nearly 1,000 Authors most of whom came into prominence during the years 1950 to 1970. In addition to the biographical material on each author, evaluative comments indicate the critical concensus on his writing. . . . The bibliographies for most authors list all published books (with dates of publication)"—(Publisher's catalog).

Ward, A. C. LONGMAN COMPANION TO TWENTIETH CENTURY LITERATURE. 1970 *Longman* 1975 $16.50

YEARBOOK OF COMPARATIVE AND GENERAL LITERATURE. W. P. Friedrich and Others, Eds. Pub. in collab. with the Comparative Literature Committee of the National Council of Teachers of English and the Comparative Literature Section of the Modern Language Assn. of America. 1952–1962. *Russell & Russell* 11 vols. 1965–1968 each $8.50

PERIODICALS

BOOKS ABROAD: An International Literary Quarterly. 1927– . *Univ. of Oklahoma Press* quarterly $10.00 (individual) $18.00 (institutional) per year

ERASMUS, SPECULUM SCIENTIARUM, INTERNATIONAL BULLETIN OF CONTEMPORARY SCHOLARSHIP. 1947– . *Ernst-Ludwig-Hans* (Alexandraweg 26, D-61 Darmstadt, German Federal Republic) semi-monthly $40.00 per year

"An international and interdisciplinary book review journal . . . highly recommended for academic libraries. Its coverage of many fields, the concise readability of its reviews, and the generally interesting criticism are a valuable international contribution"—(*Magazines for Libraries*, 2nd ed., Supplement).

INTERNATIONAL P.E.N. BULLETIN OF SELECTED BOOKS. 1950– . International P.E.N. quarterly $2.00 per year. Contains brief reviews of books notable for their literary value and their contribution to general knowledge of their countries.

THE TIMES LITERARY SUPPLEMENT. 1902– . *Times Newspapers of Great Britain* weekly $18.00 (surface mail) $40.00 (air mail, index included) per year

COLLECTIONS AND RELATED WORKS

The collections in this section are in English and in some cases give the original text as well as the translation. The "Oxford Book of Verse" Series contains verse anthologies in the original text: among others, German, Italian, Portuguese, Scandinavian and Spanish. The *Penguin* series of books of verse has both original texts and translations.

Anderson, George L., Ed. MASTERPIECES OF THE ORIENT. *Norton* 1961 $4.50. Both classic and modern works from the Near East, India, China and Japan; valuable introductory prefaces and excellent bibliographies.

Angus, Douglas, and Sylvia Angus, Eds. GREAT MODERN EUROPEAN SHORT STORIES *Fawcett* Premier Bks. (orig.) 1967 1973 pap. $1.50

"A really choice collection that is at the same time comprehensive. . . . Each story is preceded by a brief biographical-critical note"—(*PW*).

Barnstone, Willis, Ed. MODERN EUROPEAN POETRY. *Bantam* 1970 pap. $1.95

Burnshaw, Stanley, Ed. THE POEM ITSELF: 45 Modern Foreign Poets in a New Presentation. *Schocken* 1967 pap. $2.95

More than 150 French, Spanish, German, Italian and Portuguese poems (including those of Baudelaire, Brecht, Garcia Lorca and Quasimodo) are presented in the original language, followed by a literal rendering and analysis in prose by a distinguished critic. "The best way anyone has yet found to get an English-speaking reader to the poetry of other languages"—(John Ciardi).

Clark, Barrett H., Ed. WORLD DRAMA: An Anthology. 1933. *Dover* 1955 2 vols. each $4.00; *Peter Smith* 2 vols. $12.00. Vol. 1 Ancient Greece, Rome, India, China, Japan, Medieval Europe, and England; Vol. 2 Italy, Spain, France, Germany, Denmark, Russia and Norway.

Clifford, William, and Daniel L. Milton, Eds. A TREASURY OF MODERN ASIAN STORIES. *New Am. Lib.* Plume pap. $2.95

Cody, Sherwin, Ed. SELECTIONS FROM THE WORLD'S GREATEST SHORT STORIES. 1902. *Bks. for Libraries* 1974 $15.00

Crane, Milton, Ed. FIFTY GREAT SHORT STORIES. 1952 *Bantam* 1959 pap. $1.50

Creekmore, Hubert, Ed. LITTLE TREASURY OF WORLD POETRY. *Scribner* 1952 $10.00

"An anthology of poetry in translation taken from the literatures of ancient Egypt, Babylonia and China, down thru the ages to the modern poets of Europe, Asia and South America"—*(Book Review Digest)*.

de Bary, William Theodore, and Ainslie T. Embree. A GUIDE TO THE ORIENTAL CLASSICS. *Columbia* 1964 2nd ed. 1975 pap. $9.50

Decker, Clarence R., and Charles Angoff, Eds. MODERN STORIES FROM MANY LANDS. *Manyland Books* 1963 1972 $7.95. Never before published in English in book form, there are 24 stories from 13 countries including Austria, Chile, Greece, India, Indonesia, Ireland, Israel, Italy, Japan, Netherlands, Philippines, Turkey and the U.S.

Eberhart, Richard, and Selden Rodman. WAR AND THE POET. 1945. *Greenwood* 1974 $12.50. Some of the sources are unusual and the translations excellent of these "poets of all times and literatures."

GREAT SHORT STORIES OF THE WORLD. *Reader's Digest* (dist. by Norton) 1972 $11.95

Gullason, Thomas A., and Leonard Casper. THE WORLD OF SHORT FICTION: An International Collection. *Harper* 1962 2nd ed. 1971 pap. $4.25

Hamalian, Leo, and Edmond Volpe, Eds. INTERNATIONAL SHORT NOVELS: A Contemporary Anthology. *Wiley* 1974 $7.75

Haydn, Hiram Collins, and John Cournos, Eds. A WORLD OF GREAT STORIES. *Crown* new ed. 1956 pap. $2.45. Digests of permanent writings from ancient classics to current literature.

(With Edmund Fuller, Eds.). THESAURUS OF BOOK DIGESTS: Digests of the world's permanent writings from the ancient classics to current literature. *Crown* 1949 new ed. 1956 $5.00 pap. $1.95

Jose, F. Sionil, Ed. ASIAN P.E.N. ANTHOLOGY. Various translators; introd. by Norman Cousins *Taplinger* 1967 $7.50

"Every anthology has its duds. This one, fortunately, has its gems, and it is worthwhile combing the hills to find them"—*(SR)*. "The volume, perhaps pardonably, is marred by scores of typographical errors"—*(LJ)*.

Locke, Louis G., J. P. Kirby and M. E. Porter. LITERATURE OF WESTERN CIVILIZATION. *Ronald* 2 vols. 1952 each $9.50

Mack, Maynard, and others, Eds. WORLD MASTERPIECES. *Norton* 2 vols. 1956 3rd ed. 1973 Vol. 1 Literature of Western Culture through the Renaissance Vol. 2 Literature of Western Culture since the Renaissance each $11.95 pap. each $9.95 Continental ed. 3rd ed. 1974 2 vols. pap. each $9.95 2 vols. in one pap. $12.50

Magill, Frank Northern, Ed. MASTERPIECES OF WORLD LITERATURE IN DIGEST FORM. With the assistance of Dayton Kohler and staff; introd. by Clifton Fadiman *Harper* 1st ser. 1952 2nd ser. 1956 3rd ser. 1960 4th ser. 1959 each $15.00

Parker, Elinor, Comp. THE SINGING AND THE GOLD: Poems Translated from World Literature *T. Y. Crowell* 1962 $5.95

Patrick, Walton R., and Eugene Current-Garcia. SHORT STORIES OF THE WESTERN WORLD. *Scott Foresman* 1969 pap. $5.95

Priest, Harold M., Ed. RENAISSANCE AND BAROQUE LYRICS: An Anthology of Translations. *Northwestern Univ. Press* 1962 $11.50

Rodman, Selden. 100 MODERN POEMS. *New Am. Lib.* Mentor Bks. 1951 pap. $1.25. The first section, Beyond Frontiers, includes very readable translations from the Russian, French, Spanish, German, etc.

Ross, James Bruce, and Mary Martin McLaughlin, Eds. THE PORTABLE RENAISSANCE READER. *Viking* 1953 1958 $5.50 pap. $3.45

"This highly useful anthology is equipped with an informative introduction, a well chosen list of suggestions for wider reading, a biographical list of authors and a chronological table"—(*N.Y. Herald Tribune*).

(Eds.) THE PORTABLE MEDIEVAL READER. *Viking* 1946 lib. bdg. $6.50 pap. $3.75. Biography, history, science, theology, poetry, letters, journals, by writers of the 11th to the 15th century.

Runes, Dagobert David, Ed. TREASURY OF WORLD LITERATURE. 1956. 1961 *Greenwood* $41.00

Spender, Stephen, Irving Kristol and Melvin J. Lasky, Eds. ENCOUNTERS: An Anthology From the First Ten Years of *Encounter* Magazine. Sel. by Melvin J. Lasky 1963 *Simon & Schuster* 1965 pap. $2.45. An indispensable representative selection from the transatlantic periodical of intellectual recreation during its first ten years of life.

Trawick, Buckner B. WORLD LITERATURE. College Outline Ser. *Harper* (Barnes & Noble) 2 vols. Vol. 1 Greek, Roman, Oriental and Medieval Classics 1953 reprint 1960 pap. $1.75 Vol. 2 Italian, French, Spanish, German and Russian since 1300 1955 pap. $2.25

Van Doren, Mark. AN ANTHOLOGY OF WORLD POETRY. 1928. *Harcourt* rev. and enl. ed. 1936 $16.50. Translations by Chaucer, Swinburne, Dowson, Symons, Rossetti, Waley, Herrick, Pope, Thompson, E. A. Robinson and others.

Weber, Eugen, Ed. PATHS TO THE PRESENT: Aspects of European Thought from Romanticism to Existentialism *Dodd* 1960 pap. $6.75. Essays, letters, prefaces, pamphlets and other documents.

Yohannan, John D. A TREASURY OF ASIAN LITERATURE. 1956. *New Am. Lib.* Mentor Bks. pap. $1.50. Prose, poetry, drama and scripture selections from the leading and representative writings of the East.

See also Chapter 4, Broad Studies and General Anthologies, Reader's Adviser, *Vol. I.*

HISTORY AND CRITICISM

Auerbach, Erich. MIMESIS: The Representation of Reality in Western Literature. 1946. Trans. by Willard Trask *Princeton Univ. Press* 1953 $13.50 pap. $3.45. Twenty brilliant essays on outstanding landmarks of Western literature. A seminal study by a widely learned scholar.

Block, Haskell, and Herman Salinger, Eds. THE CREATIVE VISION: Modern European Writers on Their Art. 1960. *Peter Smith* $5.00. Twenty-two essays by Valéry, Rilke, Gide, Proust, Mann, Pirandello, Lorca, Giraudoux, Anouilh, Brecht, Malraux and Sartre. Each writer discusses and interprets his own writings or those of a contemporary or the problems of the literary artist.

Brooks, Cleanth, and R. P. Warren, Eds. UNDERSTANDING FICTION. *Prentice-Hall* (Appleton) 2nd ed. 1959 $8.50. Several foreign authors included.

Curtius, Ernst Robert. EUROPEAN LITERATURE AND THE LATIN MIDDLE AGES. 1948. Trans. by Willard Trask Bollingen Ser. *Princeton Univ. Press* 1953 $20.00 pap. $3.95

Friederich, Werner P., and D. H. Malone. OUTLINE OF COMPARATIVE LITERATURE FROM DANTE ALIGHIERI TO EUGENE O'NEILL. *Univ. of North Carolina Press* 1956 pap. $7.50

Highet, Gilbert. THE CLASSICAL TRADITION. *Oxford* 1949 $15.00 Galaxy Bks. 1957 pap. $4.95. A masterful assessment of the influence of Greek and Latin literature down through the ages. Excitingly written and admirably documented.

Jackson, W. T. H. THE LITERATURE OF THE MIDDLE AGES. *Columbia* 1960 $12.50. A smoothly written, informative survey of European literature in several genres; with summaries and commentaries on important works, and a valuable bibliography.

Krutch, Joseph Wood. FIVE MASTERS: A Study in the Mutations of the Novel. 1930. *Peter Smith* $5.00. Includes Boccaccio, Cervantes, Richardson, Stendhal, Proust.

Praz, Mario. THE ROMANTIC AGONY. Trans. by Angus Davidson. 1933. *Oxford* 1951 1970 $7.25 Galaxy Bks. pap. $4.50. One of the most literate and eloquent studies of sexuality, in the idiosyncratic forms that shaped and directed the work of romantic and decadent writers throughout European literature.

Priestley, J. B. LITERATURE AND WESTERN MAN. *Harper* 1960 $12.50
A highly personal and exuberant estimate from "Johann Gutenberg, the founding father of movable type, to Thomas Wolfe, whose books required a lot of it."

Saintsbury, George. A HISTORY OF CRITICISM AND LITERARY TASTE IN EUROPE: From Earliest Texts to the Present Day. 1949. *Humanities Press* 3 vols. 1961 each $7.50. Vol. 1 Classical and Medieval Criticism Vol. 2 From the Renaissance to the Decline of 18th Century Orthodoxy Vol. 3 Nineteenth Century.

T. L. S.: Essays and Reviews from the *Times* Literary Supplement, 1973. *Oxford* 1974 $17.75 (issued annually)

Weig, Hermann J. SURVEYS AND SOUNDINGS IN EUROPEAN LITERATURE. *Princeton Univ. Press* 1966 $15.00. Ranges from the Middle Ages and Shakespeare to Schiller, Goethe and Thomas Mann.

BOOKS ON TRANSLATION
General

Arrowsmith, William, and Roger Shattuck, Eds. THE CRAFT AND CONTEXT OF TRANSLATION. *Univ. of Texas Press* 1961 1971 $7.50
Includes articles by the editors, D. S. Carne-Ross, Kenneth Rexroth, Denver Lindley, Richard Howard, Sidney Monas and Werner Winter. The first section deals with the "craft" of translation; the second with editorial and publishing problems in the matter of translation. The third and final section presents a fascinating list of books in foreign languages which cry out for first or fresh translation.

Cary, E., and R. W. Jumpelt. QUALITY IN TRANSLATION. *Pergamon* 1964 $34.00

Citroen, I. J., Ed. TEN YEARS OF TRANSLATION: Proceedings of the Fourth Congress of the International Federation of Translators Held at Dubrovnik, 1963. *Pergamon* 1967 $15.00. As presented—in English, French or German.

Conley, C. H. FIRST ENGLISH TRANSLATORS OF THE CLASSICS. 1927. *Kennikat* $6.50. A scholarly review of great translations.

Finlay, Ian F. LANGUAGE SERVICES IN INDUSTRY. *Beekman* 1973 $12.50

Matthiessen, Francis Otto. TRANSLATION: An Elizabethan Art. 1931. *Octagon* 1965 $10.50. The late Harvard professor and literary critic discusses Hoby, North, Florio and Holland.

Proetz, Victor. ASTONISHMENT OF WORDS: An Experiment in the Comparison of Languages. *Univ. of Texas Press* 1972 $7.75

Savory, Theodore. ART OF TRANSLATION. rev. ed. *The Writer* 1968 $5.00

Steiner, George. AFTER BABEL: Aspects of Language and Translation. *Oxford* 1975 $17.50

Machine Translation

Akhmanova, Olga S., and others. EXACT METHODS IN LINGUISTIC RESEARCH. *Univ. of California Press* 1963 $10.50

Booth, A. D., Ed. MACHINE TRANSLATION. 1967. *American Elsevier* $38.50
"12 representative papers from some of the leading specialists" in many countries. A "highly technical" collection strongly recommended by *Library Journal* for libraries serving this field.

Ceccato, Silvio, Ed. LINGUISTIC ANALYSIS AND PROGRAMMING FOR MECHANICAL TRANSLATION. *Gordon & Breach* 1961 $24.50

Garvin, Paul. ON MACHINE TRANSLATION. *Humanities Press* 1972 pap. $8.50

—J.R.P.

Chapter 7

Classical Greek Literature

"A possession for all time (κτῆμα ἐς αἰεί)."
—THUCYDIDES

Every literary genre—except satire—originated with the Greeks and achieved perfect expression. The tradition begins with Homer (*q.v.*), whose "Iliad" and "Odyssey" are its bible, its storehouse of character, plot, and poetic language. Hesiod (*q.v.*) is credited as well with giving the Greeks their gods.

Homer may have come from Chios, an Ionian island not far from the coast of Asia Minor. The interaction between the Greeks and Asians on the Ionian islands in the seventh and sixth centuries B.C. produced a radiant period in intellectual history. It was then that Thales accurately predicted the "first eclipse," Anaximander inquired into the origin of the universe, Pythagoras logically analyzed the nature and destiny of the soul, Xenophanes posited the existence of one god only. His disciple Parmenides taught of the unique, eternal being; Heraclitus built on this philosophy and harmonized change and decay in an all-embracing unity, the logos or word which governs the world. Indebted to these last two, Empedocles constructed the theory of the four elements which are mixed and separated by love and strife.

At this same time literary artists flourished in Ionia. Archilochus developed elegiac and iambic verse to convey his intense loves and hates; and his elegies were probably familiar to the Spartan poet Tyrtaeus. Terpander is said to have invented solo singing to the lyre—lyric poetry—on the island of Lesbos; Alcaeus wrote his simple, short drinking and fighting songs and Sappho (*q.v.*) her exquisite love lyrics there. Half a century later, around 550 B.C., Anacreon was renowned for his witty, erotic verse appropriate to the symposium or drinking party and Simonides for choral lyric and epigram.

On the mainland in the sixth century, Theognis elaborated the elegy in celebration of aristocratic virtue; and at Syracuse and elsewhere Pindar (*q.v.*) perfected his glorious choral lyrics, occasionally in competition with Bacchylides. In Athens Solon, the lawgiver and poet, cancelled unfair debts, rescued the peasants from serfdom, introduced Attic coinage, imported craftsmen, reformed the constitution, and had a more humane law code published. His poetry, drawing on the moral code of Hesiod (*q.v.*) which glorifies the triumph of Law and Justice over *hybris* or vain lawlessness, looks forward to the great speeches in Attic tragedy and to Plato's (*q.v.*) "Republic."

In Solon's era, the beast fable was imported from the East and artfully worked into a collection of stories which have attached themselves to Aesop's (*q.v.*) name. Fables had been used earlier by both Archilochus and Hesiod for social criticism and were again retold by Babrius (*q.v.*) in the second century A.D.

Solon's poetry points to Attic tragedy. This genre probably grew out of religious festivals where the priest and the celebrants exchanged words. By introducing a second actor, Aeschylus (*q.v.*) created the possibility for real theatre, as the two actors could play many roles. The splendor of human will and divine providence shine forth in his magnificent poetry and Homeric language. His tragedies are quintessentially Athenian— or Attic—and were written in a proud epoch when Athens had thwarted the Persians in their advance from Asia to Europe. Sophocles (*q.v.*), who was Aeschylus's younger contemporary, added a third actor for more dramatic flexibility and in his noble tragedies immortalizes human greatness in defeat and in victory. He wrote in the mid- and late fifth century, the golden age of Athens. Euripides (*q.v.*) is the third preeminent Athenian tragedian. More of a skeptic and iconoclast than his predecessors, he was active late in the century when the city had overextended itself and was meeting strong resistance from its enemy Sparta.

Concurrently with the blossoming of tragedy, comedy ripened in the hands of Aristophanes (q.v.) whose exuberant social, cultural and political spoofs were popular with his fellow citizens in the democracy and tolerated by politicians as well. In the next century, Menander's (q.v.) romantic comedies of manners have Athenian settings and characters, but are concerned with personal and domestic problems. His was an era unsafe for pointed criticism.

Athens' golden age can perhaps be best characterized by two famous and extraordinary figures of whom nothing survives except their enormous influence on others and the numerous legends about them. They are Socrates and Pericles. The latter was the wise leader of Athens in the fifth century, an age since named for him. He ruled the democracy—first among equals—and by his powerful character and oratory attempted to unify all of Greece; and he extended the reach of Athenian empire to the Black Sea. He was an intimate friend of Sophocles and Phidias, the sculptor of the Parthenon—which Pericles commissioned. By personal magnetism and skillful direction, he guided and inspired his city in its most shining era—an era which in its intellectual and artistic achievements still illuminates Western history.

Socrates dominated intellectual life in Periclean Athens. He devoted himself to inquiry by cross-examination in order to discover right conduct. Indifferent to physical comfort, dispassionate, kindly, ironic, he attracted a circle of young Athenians around him, the greatest of them being Plato (q.v.) whose profoundly educational dialogues cast Socrates in conversations where he applies his critical intelligence to fundamental assumptions of morality and systematically defines the general terms used in the discussion. He is Plato's inspiration in the full-blown development of his moral philosophy and logic. Xenophon, the fourth-century historian and philosopher, made Socrates the subject of three of his works. Plato, in turn, taught Aristotle (q.v.), who took up an independent philosophical position. He believed that all speculation must be grounded in experience of reality and scientific research and thereby extended philosophy to universal science. His pupil Theophrastus (q.v.) was a scientific researcher and scholar whose writings were also authoritative. Socrates was, in short, the seminal influence on Plato, and through him, on Aristotle and his successors; and these two are the stay and support of all Western philosophy.

Growing distrust of Athenian power, especially among the Spartans, led to the outbreak of the Peloponnesian Wars in the late fifth century. Pericles died from the plague which swept Athens during the war; thereafter the city was without a leader of his intelligence. These wars are the subject of the "History" of Thucydides (q.v.). They are analyzed logically and impartially by the scientific method of cause and effect to explain political events. Written in a terse and compelling style, the "History" is, true to Thucydides' prediction, "a possession for all time." About thirty years earlier, Herodotus (q.v.) was the first to make past occurrences the subject of research and verification and is therefore called the father of history. His aim in his "History" is to record the illustrious deeds of Greeks and Barbarians of earlier times and the struggle between Asia and Greece which culminated in the Persian defeat. He extols his country in simple and charming narrative filled with lively and varied anecdotes.

Oratory took root in Attic soil because of the necessity for self-defense in a court of law, and it became essential training for a politician. Plato, Aristotle, and Theophrastus theorized about it. Around 390 B.C., Isocrates established an influential school of rhetoric which taught the "right" moral and political attitudes and attracted students from all over the Greek world. At the end of the fifth century Lysias was famous for his speeches in a pure, simple style which skillfully manipulate the listener's emotions. Other eminent orators of this age are Isaeus, Aeschines, and his famous rival Demosthenes (q.v.), who is the most distinguished of these because he combined noble thought and expression in flawlessly organized, strikingly eloquent speech. He moves easily from anger to irony to pathos, always with the intent to persuade.

In the "Philippics" and "On the Crown" Demosthenes tried to warn Athens of Philip of Macedon's dangerous encroachments. But the resistance to Philip failed; his son Alexander the Great ascended the throne, and became the new power in the Greek world. In the Alexandrian or Hellenistic Age and after, the supreme Attic self-confidence, seen so clearly in Aeschylus, Sophocles, and Demosthenes, fades and gives way to the remote and refined creations of cosmopolitan writers: to the pastoral idylls of Theocritus of Sicily, of Moschus of Syracuse, and Bion of Smyrna; to the slender elegies and hymns of Callimachus of Alexandria; to the learned epic of Apollonius of Rhodes (qq.v.). Alexandria became the cultural center and its literary artists revere the old Athenian literature, comment on it, interpret it, emend it. But they write poems divorced from contemporary politics and devoid of current caricature for an international audience. Oratory dies and is replaced by the art of rhetoric, tragedies lose their vigor, the Olympian gods are discredited. But backward-looking historical narrative is well-represented in Polybius's (q.v.) "Histories" of Rome and in Plutarch's (q.v.) "Lives of the Noble Greeks and Romans." Philosophy gets new impetus from Epicureanism and Stoicism, two moral codes for individual conduct; Greek philosophers and their doctrines are carefully described in Diogenes Laertius's compendium. Science, too, is enriched by discoveries in the fields of astronomy, mathematics, and geography.

Rome dominated the Mediterranean basin from the second century B.C., and Latin gradually replaced Greek as the common tongue. But Greek writers are still a hardy stock in the early centuries of the Christian era. "On the Sublime," a literary treatise by "Longinus" (q.v.), discourses on the sublime glory of Homer, Plato, and Demosthenes— among others. In his dialogues, Lucian (q.v.) questions and criticizes the old Greek myths and philosophies. Longus and Heliodorus (qq.v.) shape the novel as a new literary genre.

The Romans shared "Longinus's" reverence for their Greek heritage and transmitted it in Latin letters to Christian and secular writers of the Middle Ages. With the rediscovery of Greek texts in the fourteenth century and onwards, an intellectual and artistic renaissance was realized. At any time in history, however, Greek culture holds out to the individual the promise of rebirth: for anyone freshly experiencing it, a renewal of mind and spirit is possible.

CLASSICAL LITERATURE

Both Greek and Latin literature are treated in the works listed in the following two sections.

History and Criticism

Arnott, Peter Douglas. An Introduction to the Greek Theatre. Fwd. by H. D. F. Kitto. 1959. *Indiana Univ. Press* Midland Bks. 1963 pap. $2.45

Bieber, Margarete. The History of the Greek and Roman Theater. *Princeton Univ. Press* 1939 rev. ed. 1961 $25.00. Indispensable for understanding the appearance of ancient theatres.

Bolgar, R. R. Classical Influence on European Culture, a.d. 500–1500. *Cambridge* 1971 $15.00. An excellent guide to the classical tradition in European culture after the fall of Rome.

Cambridge Ancient History. *Cambridge* 12 vols. Vol. 1 Pt. 1 Prolegomena and Pre-history $32.50 Pt. 2 Early History of the Middle East $35.00 Vol. 2 Pt. 1 History of the Middle East and Aegean Region c. 1800–1380 b.c. $32.50 Pt. 2 $32.50 Vol. 3 Assyrian Empire $32.50 Vol. 4 Persian Empire and the West $32.50 Vol. 5 Athens, 478–401 b.c. $32.50 Vol. 6 Macedon, 401–301 b.c. $32.50 Vol. 7 Hellenistic Monarchies and the Rise of Rome $42.50 Vol. 8 Rome and the Mediterranean, 218–133 b.c. $32.50 Vol. 9 Roman Republic, 133–44 b.c. $37.50 Vol. 10 Augustan Empire, 44

B.C.–A.D. 70 $42.50 Vol. 11 Imperial Peace A.D. 70–192 $35.00 Vol. 12 Imperial Crisis and Recovery, A.D. 193–324 $37.50. This is the standard history of antiquity and is highly recommended for its careful, detailed presentation.

Cary, Max, and T. J. Haarhoff. LIFE AND THOUGHT IN THE GREEK AND ROMAN WORLD. 1940. *Harper* (Barnes & Noble) 5th ed. 1959 $10.00 pap. $4.25

Ceram, C. W. GODS, GRAVES, AND SCHOLARS: The Story of Archaeology. Ill. *Knopf* rev. ed. 1967 $10.00; *Bantam* 2nd rev. ed. 1972 pap. $1.95. Tells the story of archaeological discoveries in a lively and suspenseful style, which makes wonderful reading.

Donaldson, James. WOMAN: Her Position and Influence in Ancient Greece and Rome and among the Early Christians. 1907. *Burt Franklin* $15.00

Ehrenberg, Victor L. SOCIETY AND CIVILIZATION IN GREECE AND ROME. Ill. Martin Classical Lectures *Harvard Univ. Press* 1964 $4.00

Grube, G. M. A. GREEK AND ROMAN CRITICS. *Univ. of Toronto Press* 1965 $3.50

Hadas, Moses. ANCILLA TO CLASSICAL READING. *Columbia* 1954 $6.00 1961 pap. $1.95. A useful companion for the reader of Greek and Latin literature.

Highet, Gilbert. THE CLASSICAL TRADITION: Greek and Roman Influences on Western Literature. *Oxford* 1949 $14.50 Galaxy Bks. pap. $3.95. An admirably rich volume which takes into account the many ways the classical tradition has shaped European and American literature. Scholarly, humanistic, yet never pedantic.

Kerényi, C. THE RELIGION OF THE GREEKS AND ROMANS. Trans. by Christopher Holme. 1962. *Greenwood* 1973 $19.50. Combining Greek and Roman mythology, philology, literature, and Jungian psychology, this is a stimulating view of how the ancients faced the absolute.

Larsen, J. A. O. REPRESENTATIVE GOVERNMENT IN GREEK AND ROMAN HISTORY. Sather Classical Lectures *Univ. of California Press* 1955 pap. $1.75

Lattimore, Richmond. THEMES IN GREEK AND LATIN EPITAPHS. 1942. *Univ. of Illinois Press* 1962 pap. $1.95

Lemprière, John. A CLASSICAL DICTIONARY 1809. *Gale* 1973 $18.00; *Gordon Press* $34.95. Still very useful because of its wealth of anecdotes and literary references.

Marrou, Henri. HISTORY OF EDUCATION IN ANTIQUITY. 1948, 1964 o.p. An indispensable, masterful work.

OXFORD CLASSICAL DICTIONARY. Ed. by N. G. Hammond and H. H. Scullard *Oxford* 2nd ed. 1970 $30.00. The experts in all phases of classical scholarship have written articles and supplied short bibliographies on their fields of interest for this volume, which is an invaluable source of learning.

OXFORD COMPANION TO CLASSICAL LITERATURE. Comp. and ed. by Sir Paul Harvey *Oxford* 2nd ed. 1937 $10.50. A valuable reference work, which is comprehensive, concise, and well-written.

Pevsner, Nikolaus. AN OUTLINE OF EUROPEAN ARCHITECTURE. Ill. *Penguin* 1960 pap. $6.75; *Allen Lane* (dist. by Penguin) 7th ed. 1974 $9.95. This is an excellent guide to Greek and Roman architecture and its influence on later European designs.

Ramage, Edwin S. URBANITAS: Ancient Sophistication and Refinement. *Univ. of Oklahoma Press* 1973 $8.95. An original study of urbane literature.

Richter, Gisela M. FURNITURE OF THE GREEKS, ETRUSCANS, AND ROMANS. Ill. *Phaidon* (dist. by Praeger) 1966 $35.00

Rose, Herbert J. RELIGION IN GREECE AND ROME. *Harper* Torchbks. pap. $1.95. A sophisticated, terse analysis.

Rostovtzeff, Mikhail. SOCIAL AND ECONOMIC HISTORY OF THE HELLENISTIC WORLD. Ill. *Oxford* 3 vols. 1941 $100.00. A definitive study by an eminent historian.

Smith, William. Dictionary of Greek and Roman Antiquities. 1870. *Milford House* 1973 lib. bdg. $55.00

Dictionary of Greek and Roman Biography and Mythology. 1890. *Milford House* 1973 lib. bdg. $55.00

Dictionary of Greek and Roman Geography. 1873. *AMS Press* 2 vols. $90.00. All the Smith dictionaries are still valuable reference tools.

Snell, Bruno. Discovery of Mind: The Greek Origins of European Thought. *Harper* Torchbks. pap. $2.45. A stimulating overview of intellectual history.

Collections

Casson, Lionel, Trans. and ed. Masters of Ancient Comedy: Selections from Aristophanes, Menander, Plautus, and Terence. *T. Y. Crowell* (Funk and Wagnalls) 1967 pap. $2.95

MacKendrick, Paul, and Herbert M. Howe, Eds. Classics in Translation. Vol. 1 Greek Literature Vol. 2 Latin Literature *Univ. of Wisconsin Press* 2 vols. 1952 pap. each $5.00

New translations most of which were made for these volumes. Greek plays, complete translations: Aeschylus, Agamemnon, trans. by L. MacNeice; Sophocles, Antigone, trans. by M. F. Neufeld; Euripides, Medea, trans. by W. R. Agard; Aristophanes, Frogs, trans. by J. G. Hawthorne. Latin plays, complete translations: Plautus, The Haunted House, trans. by H. J. Leon; Terence, Woman from Andros, trans. by R. I. W. Westgate and R. V. Scudder; Seneca, Medea, trans. by E. C. Evans.

Murphy, Charles T., Kevin Guinagh and Whitney J. Oates, Eds. Greek and Roman Classics in Translation. *McKay* 1947 $8.75

Five complete plays: Prometheus Bound; Oedipus the King; Hippolytus; The Clouds; The Adelphi; and selections from Homer, Greek poetry, Herodotus, Thucydides, Plato, Aristotle, Epictetus, Demosthenes, Lucretius, Catullus, Cicero, Virgil, Horace, Livy, Tacitus and Juvenal.

Plutarch. Lives of the Noble Greeks and Romans. Trans. by John Dryden *Random* Modern Lib. Giants $5.95; *Dutton* Everyman's 3 vols. each $3.95. *See Chapter 9, History, Government and Politics*, Reader's Adviser, *Vol. 3*.

CLASSICAL GREEK LITERATURE

History and Criticism

Alsop, Joseph W. From the Silent Earth: A Report on the Greek Bronze Age. Ill. *Harper* 1964 $10.00

Arnott, Peter D. The Ancient Greek and Roman Theatre. *Peter Smith* $5.50

Introduction to the Greek Theatre. Ill. *Indiana Univ. Press* 1963 pap. $2.45

Introduction to the Greek World. Ill. *St. Martin's* 1967 $8.95

Beazley, John D., and B. Ashmole. Greek Sculpture and Painting. *Cambridge*. 1932, 1965 $13.50

Bonner, Robert J. Aspects of Athenian Democracy. 1933. *Russell & Russell* $7.00

Lawyers and Litigants in Ancient Athens: The Genesis of the Legal Profession. 1927. *Blom* $9.75

(With Gertrude E. Smith) The Administration of Justice from Homer to Aristotle. Ill. 1938. *Greenwood* 2 vols. set $27.50. This is *the* sourcebook on Greek law.

Bowra, C. M. Ancient Greek Literature. *Oxford* Univ. Paperbacks 1933 pap. $2.50

Early Greek Elegists. 1938. Martin Classical Lectures *Cooper* 1969 $6.00

The Greek Experience. *New Am. Lib.* Mentor Bks. pap. $1.25

Greek Lyric Poetry from Alcman to Simonides. *Oxford* 2nd ed. 1961 $10.25

Cary, Max. A History of the Greek World, 323 to 146 b.c. Methuen's History of the Greek and Roman World Ser. *Harper* Barnes & Noble (Methuen) 2nd rev. ed. 1951 1972 $13.50 University Paperbacks pap. $9.25

Cooper, Lane. Greek Genius and Its Influence: Selected Essays and Extracts. 1952. *Cornell Univ. Press* $12.50

Cottrell, Leonard. The Bull of Minos. Introd. by Prof. Alan Wace. 1953. *Holt* (Rinehart); *Grosset* Univ. Lib. pap. $2.75

Lost Cities. 1957 *Grosset* Univ. Lib. 1963 pap. $2.25

Dickinson, G. Lowes. The Greek View of Life. Pref. by E. M. Forster. 1896. *Univ. of Michigan Press* 1958 $4.40 Ann Arbor Bks. pap. $1.85; *Macmillan* Collier Bks. pap. $.95; *Peter Smith* $4.00

Else, Gerlad F. The Origin and Early Form of Greek Tragedy. Martin Classical Lectures *Harvard Univ. Press* 1965 $3.75; *Norton* Norton Lib. 1972 pap. $1.95

Finley, Moses I. The Ancient Greeks: An Introduction to Their Life and Thought. *Viking* 1963 $5.00 Compass Bks. pap. $1.45. A brief history of Greek culture from its beginnings to Roman times.

Flacelière, Robert. Love in Ancient Greece. Trans. from the French by James Cleugh. 1962. *Greenwood* 1973 $10.50

This professor at the Sorbonne and a leading French authority corrects some popular misconceptions regarding Greek attitudes toward love, sex and marriage. He "wears his erudition lightly. . . . His time-span covers Greek literature from Homer to Menander."

Graves, Robert. The Greek Myths. *Braziller* 1959 $7.50; *Penguin* Pelican Bks. 2 vols. 1955 pap. Vol I $1.75 Vol. 2 $1.45. An idiosyncratic and amusing presentation of the myths.

Guthrie, W. K. Greek Philosophers: From Thales to Aristotle. *Harper* Torchbks. pap. $1.95

The Greeks and Their Gods. *Beacon Press* 1968 pap. $4.95

History of Greek Philosophy. *Cambridge* 3 vols. Vol. I Earlier Presocratics and the Pythagoreans (1962) Vol. 2 Presocratic Tradition from Parmenides to Democritus (1965) Vol. 3 The Fifth-Century Enlightenment (1969) each $29.50. Excellent summaries.

Socrates. *Cambridge* 1971 pap. $3.95

Hadas, Moses. A History of Greek Literature. *Columbia* 1950 $10.00 pap. $1.95

Haight, Elizabeth H. Essays on Ancient Fiction. 1936. *Bks. for Libraries* $8.50

Hamilton, Edith. The Echo of Greece. *Norton* 1957 $6.95 pap. $1.75. This notable interpretation includes studies of Aristotle, Demosthenes, Alexander the Great, and Menander.

The Greek Way. *Norton* 1930 1943 new ed. 1948 $6.95; *Avon* 1973 pap. $1.50; *Franklin Watts* lg.-type ed. Keith Jennison Bks. $9.95

Mythology. *Grosset* Univ. Lib. pap. $2.50; *New Am. Lib.* Mentor Bks. pap. $1.25; *Franklin Watts* 1966 lg.-type ed. Keith Jennison Bks. $12.50. A standard retelling of the stories.

See also her main entry in Chapter 9, History, Government and Politics, Reader's Adviser, Vol. 3.

Harrison, Jane Ellen. Epilegomena to the Study of Greek Religion and Themis: A Study of the Social Origins of Greek Religion. 1921. *University Bks.* 1962 $10.00

"It is largely under her influence that Olympian gods have come to be recognized as relatively late and predominantly literary figures, whereas she maintained the idea that it was the Mysteries, Dionysian and Orphic, that were the core of the Greek religion." While she had numerous critics

among her academic peers, she also won the support and admiration of such great scholars as
Gilbert Murray, who contributed the "Jane Harrison Memorial Lecture" to this volume.

PROLEGOMENA TO THE STUDY OF GREEK RELIGION. 1957. *Arno* o.p.

Huxley, George Leonard. EARLY SPARTA. 1962. *Harper* (Barnes & Noble) 1971 $8.00
  The surviving contemporary accounts concerning their victorious enemy, Sparta, are almost all
  Athenian. In this careful study, "ancient and modern evidence is analyzed to deduce what can be
  known of Sparta from 1200 to 490 B.C., when the evidence becomes more plentiful."

Jaeger, Werner. PAIDEIA: The Ideals of Greek Culture. Trans. by Gilbert Highet *Oxford* 3
  vols. Vol. 1 Archaic Greece and The Mind of Athens Vol. 2 In Search of the Divine
  Center Vol. 3 Conflict of Cultural Ideals in the Age of Plato each $10.00 Vol. 1
  Galaxy Bks. pap. $3.95. Brilliant analysis of Greek culture by an eminent authority
  on intellectual history.

Jones, John. ON ARISTOTLE AND GREEK TRAGEDY. *Oxford* 1962 Galaxy Bks. 1968 pap.
  $2.95

Kennedy, George. THE ART OF PERSUASION IN GREECE. *Princeton Univ. Press* 1963 $13.50.
  An excellent history of Greek oratory.

Kerényi, C. THE RELIGION OF THE GREEKS AND ROMANS. Trans. by Christopher Holme,
  1962. *Greenwood* 1973 $19.50. Combining Greek and Roman mythology, philology,
  classic literature and Jungian Psychology, this is a stimulating view of how the Greeks
  and Romans faced the absolute.

Kitto, H. D. F. FORM AND MEANING IN DRAMA. *Harper* Barnes & Noble (Methuen) 1959
  pap. $5.00

  GREEK TRAGEDY: A Literary Study. *Harper* Barnes & Noble (Methuen) 3rd. rev. ed.
  1961 1966 $11.50 Univ. Paperback $5.50

  THE GREEKS. 1951. *Aldine* $7.50; *Peter Smith* $4.75
  "Written in [Kitto's] normally graceful, witty, and also opinionated way, it gives a truly
  wonderful insight into most aspects of ancient Greek civilization"—(*LJ*).

Lattimore, Richmond. THE POETRY OF GREEK TRAGEDY. *Johns Hopkins Press* 1958 $7.50.
  Penetrating critical study.

  STORY PATTERNS IN GREEK TRAGEDY. *Univ. of Michigan Press* Ann Arbor Bks. 1969 pap.
  $1.95

Lesky, Albin. GREEK TRAGEDY. Trans. by H. A. Frankfort *Barnes & Noble* 1965 o.p.

  A HISTORY OF GREEK LITERATURE. Trans. from the German by James Willis and
  Cornelis de Heer. *T. Y. Crowell* 1966 $15.00. A superb comprehensive history
  which discusses in detail all literary genres, from very early periods through the
  Hellenistic, Roman and early Christian eras. Summaries of major works are very full
  and the extensive bibliographies are up to date.

Lloyd-Jones, Hugh. THE JUSTICE OF ZEUS. Sather Class. Lectures *Univ. of California Press*
  1971 $8.50 pap. $2.85

Lullies, Reinhard. GREEK SCULPTURE. Ill. *Harry N. Abrams* rev. ed. 1957 $25.00 pap.
  $13.95. Authoritative and handsomely illustrated.

MacKendrick, Paul. THE GREEK STONES SPEAK: The Story of Archaeology in Greek
  Lands. *St. Martin's* rev. ed. 1962 $8.50 text ed. $7.50; *New Am. Lib.* Mentor Bks. pap.
  $1.50 A polished study with a wealth of detail; covers over 2,000 years from the era
  of Homeric legend to Roman occupation.

Murray, Gilbert. A HISTORY OF ANCIENT GREEK LITERATURE. 1897. *Ungar* 1966 $8.50;
  Richard West $6.25
  "Murray combined erudition, imagination, sensitivity, and enthusiasm with an urbane narrative
  style to make the reading of his book an exciting intellectual adventure"—(*LJ*).

THE RISE OF THE GREEK EPIC. *Oxford* 1911 4th ed. 1934 pap. $2.75

Norwood, Gilbert. GREEK COMEDY. 1963. *Peter Smith* $4.25

   GREEK TRAGEDY. 1920. *Farrar, Straus* (Hill & Wang) Dramabks. 1960 pap. $1.95; *Peter Smith* $4.50

Pausanias. DESCRIPTION OF GREECE. Trans. by W. H. S. Jones (Vols. 1 & 3–5), and by W. H. S. Jones and H. A. Ormerod (Vol. 2) *Harvard Univ. Press* Loeb 5 vols. 1918–1935 each $7.00. A guidebook for tourists, written in the second century A.D.

Pearson, Lionel. POPULAR ETHICS IN ANCIENT GREECE. *Stanford Univ. Press* 1962 $7.50. Covers ethical attitudes of the market place, and concepts found in Homer, Hesiod, Theognis, Solon, and 5th-century dramatists.

Pendlebury, John D. ARCHAEOLOGY OF CRETE. Ill. *Biblo and Tannen* $10.00; *Norton* 1965 pap. $3.95. First-hand account of the excavations in Crete.

Pickard-Cambridge, A. W. DITHYRAMB, TRAGEDY AND COMEDY. *Oxford* 1927 2nd ed. rev. 1962 $10.25. A learned work on the beginnings of Greek drama.

   DRAMATIC FESTIVALS OF ATHENS. *Oxford* 1953 2nd ed. by D. M. Lewis and J. P. Gould 1968 $23.50. Comprehensive account of the festivals; by a foremost scholar.

   THE THEATRE OF DIONYSUS IN ATHENS. *Oxford* 1946 $22.50. A history from the earliest days to the time of the Roman Empire.

Polybius. HISTORIES. Trans. by W. R. Paton *Harvard Univ. Press* Loeb 6 vols. 1922 each $5.50. Records the rapid rise of Rome, as seen by a Greek historian of the 2nd century A.D.

Renault. Mary. THE KING MUST DIE. *Pantheon* 1958 $7.95; *Bantam* 1974 pap. $1.75. An exciting version of the story of Theseus and Ariadne in Crete.

Richter, Gisela M. SCULPTURE AND SCULPTORS OF THE GREEKS. Ill. *Yale Univ. Press* 4th ed. rev. and enl. 1970 $37.50. The standard reference book on Greek sculpture.

Robinson, Charles Alexander, Jr. ATHENS IN THE AGE OF PERICLES. *Univ. of Oklahoma Press* 1959 $3.50 pap. $2.50. "Incisive, illuminating and relevant" comments.

Rose, H. J. A HANDBOOK OF GREEK LITERATURE. *Dutton* 1934 rev. ed. 1950 pap. $2.45. A brief work excellent for quick reference.

Scully, Vincent J. THE EARTH, THE TEMPLE, AND THE GODS: Greek Sacred Architecture. 1962. *Praeger* 1969 $16.00 pap. $5.95. Critical restudy of ancient sites with attention given to lesser-known sanctuaries; erudite, informative footnotes and rich illustrations.

Snell, Bruno. POETRY AND SOCIETY: The Role of Poetry in Ancient Greece. 1961 *Bks. for Libraries* $7.50

Ventris, Michael, and John Chadwick. DOCUMENTS IN MYCENAEAN GREEK. *Cambridge* 1956 2nd ed. 1973 $37.50. By deciphering the clay tablets found in the ruins of King Minos' palace at Knossos, Crete, Ventris, a British architect found the key to one of the last remaining lost languages—that of Homer's heroes.

Vermeule, Emily. GREECE IN THE BRONZE AGE. *Univ. of Chicago Press* 1964 $10.00 Phoenix Bks. 1972 $3.95

   "Professor Vermeule . . . presents a superb, unhackneyed, up-to-date, overall and detailed view of prehistoric Greek mainland civilization, ca. 6500–1100 B.C. . . . Generously documented and illustrated"—(*LJ*).

Warner, Rex. ETERNAL GREECE. Photography by Martin Hürlimann. 1953. *Transatlantic* 1972 $18.00. This combination of commentary, translations from classic Greek, and fine gravure plates captures the essence of the Hellenic world.

   THE STORIES OF THE GREEKS. *Farrar, Straus* 1967 $10.00 Noonday 1968 pap. $2.65. A one-volume edition of the author's three books on the gods, heroes and wars of ancient Greece: "Men and Gods," "Greeks and Trojans" and "The Vengeance of the Gods."

Webster, T. B. L. The Greek Chorus. 1970. *Harper* Barnes & Noble $11.00

  Greek Theatre Production. 1956 2nd ed. 1970 *Harper* Barnes & Noble $9.25. A chronological and geographic survey of the scenery, staging and costumes of Greek theater.

  Studies in Later Greek Comedy. *Harper* Barnes & Noble 1970 $10.00

Collections

General

The Attic Orators from Antiphon to Isaeos. Trans. and ed. by R. C. Jebb. 1875. *Russell & Russell* 2 vols. 1962 $20.00

Auden, W. H., Ed. The Portable Greek Reader. *Viking* Portable Lib. 1948 1955 $6.95 pap. $3.50. Selections from Homer to Galen; includes very useful chronological outline of classical Greek civilization.

The Greek Anthology. (And "The Garland of Philip and Other Contemporary Epigrams") trans. and ed. with notes and commentary by A. S. F. Gow and D. L. Page *Cambridge* 2 vols. 1968 set $55.00; (with title "Anthologia Graeca: The Greek Anthology") trans. and ed. by W. R. Paton *Harvard Univ. Press* Loeb 5 vols. 1916–1918 each $7.00; (with title "Poems from the Greek Anthology") trans. by Kenneth Rexroth; ill. *Univ. of Michigan Press* 1962 pap. $1.75

  An admirable anthology done with sympathy and skill. The original collection was made by Constantius Cephales about 925 A.D. The original manuscript was found in the Palatine Library at Heidelberg in the 17th century, so that it is frequently referred to as the "Palatine Anthology." It contains more than 6,000 poems classified according to type and subject and written by 320 authors beginning in the 7th century B.C.

Greek Bucolic Poets: Theocritus, Bion, and Moschus. Trans. by J. M. Edmonds *Harvard Univ. Press* Loeb $7.00

Greek Elegy, Iambus, and Anacreontea. Trans. by J. M. Edmonds *Harvard Univ. Press* Loeb 2 vols. each $7.00

Greek Lyrics. (With title "Lyra Graeca") trans. and ed. by J. M. Edmonds *Harvard Univ. Press* Loeb 3 vols. each $7.00; (with title "Greek Lyric Poetry") trans. and ed. by Willis Barnstone, introd. by William E. McCulloh, ill. by Helle Tzalos *Schocken* 1972 $9.00 pap. $2.95; (with title "Greek Lyrics") trans. by Richmond Lattimore *Univ. of Chicago Press* 1955 rev. ed. 1960 $5.00 Phoenix Bks. pap. $1.35

Greek Romances. (With title "Three Greek Romances") trans. by Moses Hadas *Bobbs* 1964 $6.00 pap. $1.45. Includes Daphnis and Chloe by Longus, The Ephesian Tale by Xenophon, and Hunters of Euboia by Dio Chrysostom.

Minor Attic Orators. Trans. K. J. Maidment and J. O. Burtt *Harvard Univ. Press* Loeb 2 vols. 1941–1954 each $7.00. Includes Antiphon and Andocides; Lycurgus, Dinarchus, Demades, Hyperides.

Oxford Book of Greek Verse in Translation. Ed. by Thomas F. Higham and C. M. Bowra. Currently o.p. Comprehensive and skillfully translated.

Greek Drama

An Anthology of Greek Drama. Ed. by Charles Alexander Robinson *Holt* (Rinehart) 2 vols. 1949 1954 pap. each $2.95. Vol. 1 Agamemnon; Oedipus Rex; Antigone; Medea; Hippolytus; Lysistrata Vol. 2 Prometheus Bound; Choephoroe; Eumenides; Philoctetes; Oedipus at Colonus; The Trojan Women; The Bacchae; The Clouds; The Frogs.

The Complete Greek Drama. Ed. by Whitney J. Oates and Eugene O'Neill, Jr. *Random* 2 vols. 1938 each $11.00 boxed $20.00. All the extant tragedies of Aeschylus, Sophocles and Euripides, and the comedies of Aristophanes and Menander, in a variety of translations.

THE COMPLETE GREEK TRAGEDIES. Ed. by David Grene and Richmond Lattimore. *See author entries for Aeschylus, Sophocles, and Euripides.*

FIFTEEN GREEK PLAYS. Trans. by Gilbert Murray and others; ed. by Lane Cooper, with an introd. and a supplement from the "Poetics" of Aristotle. *Oxford* 1943 $9.95. A revision and expansion of "Ten Greek Plays" (1929)

    Collection of plays translated as follows. Aeschylus: Prometheus, by Whitelaw; Agamemnon, Choephoroe, Eumenides, by Gilbert Murray. Sophocles: Oedipus the King, by Gilbert Murray; Antigone, by Whitelaw; Oedipus at Colonus, Electra, by Lewis Campbell, Euripides: Electra, Iphigenia in Tauris, Medea, Hippolytus, by Gilbert Murray. Aristophanes: Clouds, Birds, Frogs, by Rogers.

FOUR GREEK PLAYS. *Harcourt* Harvest Bks. 1960 1962 pap. $2.25

    Contents: Agamemnon by Aeschylus, trans. by Louis MacNeice; Oedipus Rex by Sophocles and Alcestis by Euripides, trans. by Dudley Fitts and Robert Fitzgerald; The Birds by Aristophanes, trans. by Dudley Fitts.

GREEK COMEDY. Ed. by R. W. Corrigan *Dell* Laurel Leaf Lib. pap. $1.25. Selections from Aristophanes and Menander.

GREEK DRAMA. Ed. by Moses Hadas *Bantam* 1968 pap. $1.25. Includes Agamemnon by Aeschylus, Antigone of Sophocles, Eumenides of Aeschylus, Frogs of Aristophanes, Hippolytus of Euripides, Medea of Euripides, Oedipus the King of Sophocles, Philoctetes of Sophocles, Trojan Women of Euripides.

GREEK PLAYS IN MODERN TRANSLATIONS. Ed. by Dudley Fitts *Dial* Permanent Lib. Bks. 1947 $7.50; *Holt* (Dryden) text ed. 1947 $8.25. The Trojan Women; Agamemnon; Electra; Medea; Hippolytus; Alcestis; King Oedipus; Oedipus at Colonus; Antigone; Prometheus Vinctus; Oresteia.

GREEK TRAGEDY AND COMEDY. Trans. with introd. by Frank L. Lucas *Viking* 1968 pap. $2.95. Includes Prometheus Bound of Aeschylus, Agamemnon of Aeschylus, Antigone of Sophocles, Oedipus the King of Sophocles, Hippolytus of Euripides, Bacchae of Euripides, Clouds of Aristophanes.

SEVEN FAMOUS GREEK PLAYS. With introds. by various hands. *Random* Modern Lib. 1950 pap. $1.95 Vintage Bks. 1955 pap. $1.95. Aeschylus: Agamemnon, Prometheus Bound; Sophocles: Oedipus the King, Antigone; Euripides: Medea, Alcestis; Aristophanes: The Frogs.

THREE GREEK PLAYS. Trans. and ed. by Edith Hamilton *Norton* 1937 Norton Lib. 1958 pap. $2.25. Verse translations of Prometheus, Agamemnon, and The Trojan Women.

THREE GREEK PLAYS FOR THE THEATRE. Trans. and ed. by Peter D. Arnott *Indiana Univ. Press* 1961 pap. $1.95; *Peter Smith* $4.50. The Cyclops, Medea, and The Frogs, prepared especially for the actor.

HOMER. c. 700 B.C.

    Homer is the father of European literature. The Greeks believed that both the "Iliad" and the "Odyssey" were composed by the blind bard Homer but were uncertain of his dates or of his birthplace. Seven cities claimed him—Athens, Argos, Chios, Colophon, Rhodes, Salamis, and Smyrna. Now it is conjectured that he was an Ionian, probably from Chios, and that he lived around 700 B.C. Scholars have long disputed his authorship of both poems. But, for the present, the urgency of the "Homeric Question" has given way to general agreement that he was the presiding genius behind both epics. Modern experts have shown that these epics could have been recited without a written score or text to prompt the singer's memory because he would have relied instead on his stock of formulaic phrases or epithets to keep the narrative flowing. And yet, it must be said that oral or written, real or imaginary, late or early, Homer remains a mysterious figure wrapped in the mists of the ancient past.

    The "Iliad," regarded as the earlier of the two poems, tells the story of the Trojan War and of its two heroes Achilles and Hector. The narrative, which begins in the midst of the siege and moves very rapidly towards its tragic conclusion, is often interrupted at a moment of crisis by beautiful similes drawn from nature, farming, and handcrafts. Its language is magnificent and rich and its poetry at the peak of Western literary tradition.

The "Odyssey," which may have been written in Homer's old age, recounts the wanderings of Odysseus after the Trojan War had ended and his final homecoming to Ithaca where he found his wife Penelope still faithful to him. It is a fantastical adventure story with a comic tone and a happy ending. Like the "Iliad," it is noteworthy for its beautiful poetry, simplicity of statement, dramatic plot and postponement, and nobility of character.

Also attributed to Homer are the "Homeric Hymns," invocations to such gods as Apollo, Aphrodite, Hermes. They vary in tone from tender to amusing to erotic, but all are expressed in exquisite Homeric language. Lang's translation of 1899 (*Bks. for Libraries* 1972 $13.75; *Folcroft* 1973 $25.00) and that of Evelyn-White (*Harvard* Loeb 1914 $7.00) are recommended.

Homer was a bible, an oracle, the repository of all wisdom for the Greeks. His poetry shaped the Greek character and Greek literature from its beginnings. It was the seminal influence on Latin literature and has continued to dominate European vernacular literature even down to the present: Hesiod, Pindar, Aeschylus, Sophocles, Euripides, Plato; Virgil, Horace, Ovid; Dante; Chaucer, Shakespeare, Milton; and in our time, Joyce and Kazantzakis. The idea of the hero, of tragedy and comedy, of beginning a story in the middle, dramatic postponement, divine intervention, flashback, and the rich assembly of individual plots and characters—all these fundamentals come from Homer. Many great poets have aspired to equal Homer; but in all of Western literature he has never been surpassed.

The Iliad: Older Versions

Chapman, George (1559?–1634). 1616. Translation in rhyming couplets Vol. 1 (Vol. 2 The Odyssey and the Lesser Homerica.) Ed. by Allardyce Nicoll Bollingen Ser. *Princeton Univ. Press* 2 vols. 1967 boxed $20.00; 2 vols. 1897 *Richard West* $75.00

Chapman's was the first English translation of Homer, the translation that inspired Keats (*q.v.*) to write his famous sonnet: "Much have I travelled in the realms of gold." Chapman issued his translation in 1616, the year of Shakespeare's death. For readers of the present day, Chapman's translation is rather archaic, steeped in humors, fantasticalities and conceits. "Homeric Renaissance: The Odyssey of George Chapman" by George de Forest Lord (1956, o.p.) is an "absorbingly interesting book . . . concerned to clarify and largely to vindicate Chapman's reading."

Hobbes, Thomas (1588–1679). ILIADS AND ODYSSES. 2nd ed. 1677. *AMS Press* $27.50. The famous philosopher tried his hand at Homer towards the end of his career—more, he claimed, for recreation than for any other reason. His version retains some of the vigor of the author's style as seen in his original prose works.

Pope, Alexander (1688–1744). 1720. In rhyming couplets of 18 syllables. Ed. by Robert A. Brower and W. H. Bond *Macmillan* $7.95 Collier Bks. pap. $2.95; *Heritage Press*, Conn. deluxe ed. $11.95; ed. by Maynard Mack and others *Yale Univ. Press* Twickenham ed. 2 vols. 1967 set $50.00. Pope's translation, a literary *tour de force*, remained for many years the standard English version, and as such had a great influence on English poetry as well as on the reputation of Homer.

Bryant, William Cullen (1794–1878). 1870. In rhymeless iambic pentameter. o.p.

Derby, Edward, Earl of (1799–1869). 1864. In heroic blank verse. Everyman's Dictionary Catalog characterized Lord Derby's translation (o.p.) as one "marked by simplicity, dignity, and sincerity; . . . its ease of style makes it eminently readable."

Butler, Samuel (1835–1902). 1898. Prose translation. o.p.

The author of "Erewhon" and "The Way of All Flesh" (*q.v.*) translated both the "Iliad" and the "Odyssey" into prose in an effort "to rescue them from the clutches of a blighting academism; for he knew that the terriblest thing Homer, a vital and living artist, has to fight against is the fact that his work has been a school book for over two thousand five hundred years."

Lang, Andrew (1844–1912), Walter Leaf (1852–1927) and Ernest Van Ness Myers (1844–1921). *Assoc. Booksellers* Airmont Bks. pap. $.60; introd. by Louise Pound *Macmillan* 1924 rev. ed. 1947 $3.95; *Random* Modern Lib. 1929 $3.95; (in "Complete Works") Giants 1935 $4.95; *St. Martin's* Globe Lib. 1914 $4.50. In prose. "Of the prose translations, that of Andrew Lang and his friends is as perfect as prose translation of verse can be." Written in biblical diction.

Hewlett, Maurice (1861–1923). 1928. The Iliad (first 12 books) in blank verse. This posthumous book (o.p.), because of its beauty and simplicity, was greeted with acclaim.

The Iliad: Modern Versions

Murray, Augustus Taber. In prose; bilingual. *Harvard Univ. Press* Loeb 2 vols. 1924–25 each $5.50. The rendering is smooth, fluent and exact.

Andrew, S. O., and M. J. Oakley. Introd. by John Warrington; pref. by M. J. Oakley. In verse. *Dutton* Everyman's 1935 1955 $3.95

Rouse, William Henry Denham. Prose translation. 1938. *New Am. Lib.* Mentor Bks. 1950, 1954 pap. $.75. This is a readable and vigorous rendering.

Rieu, E. V. In prose. *Penguin* Classics (orig.) 1953 pap. $1.65. This followed his translation of "The Odyssey" in 1945.

Richards, Ivor Armstrong. THE WRATH OF ACHILLES: The Iliad Shortened and in a New Translation. *Norton* 1950 Norton Lib. 1959 pap. $1.45. A very readable modern version of strong continuing action has been made by cutting many passages and omitting entirely Books 2, 10, 13 and 17.

Graves, Robert. THE ANGER OF ACHILLES: Homer's Iliad. Ill. by Ronald Searle. In prose with occasional ballad-like verse. o.p.

"He is magnificently and unfailingly readable"—(Dudley Fitts, in the *N.Y. Times*).

Lattimore, Richmond Alexander. A new verse translation in a free six-beat line. *Univ. of Chicago Press* 1951 2nd ed. with drawings by Leonard Baskin 1962 $6.95 Phoenix Bks. pap. $2.45. Considered the most faithful to Homer of all the modern translations, Lattimore's version is highly respected. It can, however, be difficult and obscure like the original.

Logue, Christopher. THE PATROCLEIA OF HOMER. A new version in verse of the 16th book of The Iliad. Fwd. and postscript by D. S. Carne-Ross *Univ. of Michigan* 1963 $4.00

Fitzgerald, Robert. *Doubleday* 1974 Anchor Bks. pap. $2.95. Fluent and graceful and eminently readable.

The Odyssey: Older Versions

Chapman, George (1559?–1634). 1616. Translation in rhyming couplets. Vol. 2 (and "The Lesser Homerica"). (Vol. 1 The Iliad) Ed. by Allardyce Nicoll *Princeton Univ. Press* 2 vols. 1967 boxed $17.50

Chapman's "Odyssey" is in all features like his "Iliad." The only change was the use of a line of five accented syllables instead of seven accented syllables as in the "Iliad." The ballad style remains the same. Roloff Beny becomes "a photographer in the wake of Odysseus," in his book of 148 handsome photographs, "A Time of Gods" (*Viking* Studio Bks. 1962 $20.00). He successfully evokes the mood and place of the "Odyssey" as he follows the story through free, not literal, quotations from Chapman's translation.

Pope, Alexander (1688–1744). In rhyming couplets. Ed. by Maynard Mack and others *Yale Univ. Press* Twickenham ed. 2 vols. 1967 set $50.00. *(See comment on his translation of the "Iliad.")*

Cowper, William (1731–1800). 1791. In blank verse. o.p.

Although Cowper (*q.v.*) translated the "Iliad" also, he was not nearly so successful with it as with the "Odyssey." His version of the "Iliad" is found only in his collected poetical works (*Macmillan* Globe Eds. o.p.). His attempt to render Homer in Miltonic blank verse is slow and elaborate. *(See Cowper's main entry in Chapter 5, British Poetry: Early to Romantic, Reader's Adviser Vol. 1.)*

Bryant, William Cullen (1794–1878). 1871–1872. In blank verse. Rhymeless iambic pentameter similar in excellence to his "Iliad." o.p.

Morris, William (1834–1890). 1887. In verse. o.p.

Butler, Samuel (1835–1902). 1900. In prose. Ed. by Malcolm M. Willock *Simon & Schuster* (Washington Square) pap. $.60 Reader's Enrich. Ser. pap. $.75. *(See comment on his translation of the "Iliad.")*

Palmer, George Herbert (1842–1933). *Houghton* 1884 ill. by N. C. Wyeth, Holiday Ed. $5.00 Riv. Lib. $3.20; *Bantam* 1962 pap. $.95. Written in simple American prose.

Butcher, Samuel H. (1850–1910), and Andrew Lang (1844–1912). 1879. *Random* Modern
Lib. 1929 college ed. pap. $.85 (in "Complete Works") Giants 1935 $4.95; *Franklin
Watts* lg.-type ed. Keith Jennison Bks. $7.95 Watts Class. $4.50. In prose. Translated,
like the "Iliad," into the language of the King James Bible. One of the very best of
earlier translations.

Mackail, J. W. (1859–1945). 1903–1910. Translated into quatrains modeled on E. Fitz-
Gerald's "Rubaiyat of Omar Khayyam." o.p.

The Odyssey: Modern Versions

Rouse, William Henry Denham. *New Am. Lib.* Mentor Bks. 1949 pap. $.75. A prose
translation; recommended.

Murray, Augustus Taber. *Harvard Univ. Press* Loeb 2 vols. 1919 each $5.50. In prose.

Andrew, S. O. Introd. by John Warrington *Dutton* Everyman's 1953 $3.95. In verse; a
literal translation.

Rieu, E. V. In prose. *Penguin* Class. (orig.) 1945 pap. $1.45. After several experiments
and many years, Rieu evoked an easy, unaffected and rapid style. It is a genuine
translation, as is his "Iliad," which followed (*q.v.*).

Lawrence, T. E. (T. E. Shaw). *Oxford* 1932 pap. $1.95. This rendering of the "Odyssey" by
Lawrence of Arabia is written in straightforward, compelling prose and is faithful to
the intent of the original. It reads better than the other modern translations and
comes with a brilliant, eccentric introduction.

FitzGerald, Robert. *Doubleday* 1961 $5.50; *Anchor Pr.* $12.50 1963 pap. $1.95

This new blank verse translation by an American poet, who worked on it for seven years, has
been called a "masterpiece." "One of the great merits of FitzGerald's book is its rendering of
Homer's heroic dignity, his moral force, his religious spirit—and this without loss of narrative,
clarity and action. . . . One never forgets that Homer was a poet, a poet of serious purpose and
austere imagery"—(*N.Y. Times*).

Lattimore, Richmond. *Harper* 1967 $8.95 Torchbks. pap. $1.95

"Lattimore's [verse] translation . . . is the most eloquent, persuasive and imaginative I have seen.
It reads as few translations ever do—as if the poem had been written originally in English, and in
language idiomatic, lively, and urgent"—(Paul Engle). "On the basis of purity and exactitude I
recommend this translation strongly. . . . The best *Odyssey* in modern English"—(Gilbert Highet).

Cook, Albert. *Norton* 1967 $6.00 pap. $1.95

The author has made a "literal translation following the original line for line. These lines scan
easily and move rapidly, thus reproducing one of the special delights of Homeric style. It is always
a real pleasure to read a translation which [reflects] faithfully what the poet says"—(Francis D.
Lazenby, Classics Department, Notre Dame).

Books about Homer

The Authoress of the Odyssey. By Samuel Butler. 1897. *Univ. of Chicago Press* 1967 $8.75 pap.
$2.45 This heterodox study of the epic argues that it was written more than two centuries
after the "Iliad" and that its author was a young Sicilian woman of Trapani; it is worth
reading.

On Translating Homer. By Matthew Arnold. 1905. *AMS Press.* 1972 $7.00. Arnold believed that
Homer is eminently rapid, eminently plain and direct in expression, eminently simple and
direct in ideas and eminently noble.

The Unity of Homer. By John A. Scott. 1921 *Biblo & Tannen* $8.50

A Lexicon of the Homeric Dialect. By Richard John Cunliffe. 1924. *Univ. of Oklahoma Press* reprint
1963 $9.95

For English-speaking readers of Homer in the original, this reprint based on the Oxford
Classical Text editions includes all words except, unfortunately, names. "The author's
scholarship is matched by his (and the printer's) accuracy."

Tradition and Design in the Iliad. By C. Maurice Bowra. *Oxford* 1930 $8.25. Argues that the
poem was constructed by one poet using traditional sources and adding new material of his
own.

Homer and Mycenae. By Martin P. Nilsson. 1933. *Cooper Sq.* $10.00; Ill. *Pennsylvania Univ. Press* 1972 pap. $3.95. A compelling theological and anthropological study.

The Odyssey: A Modern Sequel. By Nikos Kazantzakis. 1938. *Simon & Schuster* 1958 $14.95 1962 pap. $2.95 Touchstone Bks. pap. $4.95. This modern epic was first published in Athens in 1938. The author takes up the story where Homer left off.

Folk Tale, Fiction, and Saga in the Homeric Epics. By Rhys Carpenter. *Univ. of California Press* 1946 1962 pap. o.p.

On the Iliad. By Rachel Bespaloff. Trans. from the French by Mary McCarthy; introd. by Hermann Broch. *Princeton Univ. Press* 1947 $4.50 pap. $1.45. Engaging analysis showing the relationship of Homer's characters and ethical ideas to the present day.

The World of Odysseus. By Moses I. Finley. Pref. by Mark Van Doren. *Viking* 1954 Compass Bks. 1965 pap. $1.95. A background book on the ways of the Homeric world for the delight and enlightenment of all readers.

Iliad, or The Poem of Force. By Simone Weil. *Pendle Hill* 1956 pap. $.70.
This was written by a victim of the Nazi concentration camps who brings her original mind to bear on the meaning of force in the "Iliad."

Homer and the Heroic Tradition. By Cedric H. Whitman. *Harvard Univ. Press* 1958 $10.00; *Norton* Norton Lib. 1965 pap. $2.75
Chiefly devoted to the "Iliad" (the "Odyssey" is considered in the final chapter), the book presents arguments, both historical and contemporary, with clarity and objectivity; valuable for Whitman's judgments resulting from recent discoveries.

Daily Life in the Time of Homer. By Emile Mireaux. Trans. by Iris Sells *Macmillan* 1959 $5.95. Good background reading.

History and the Homeric Iliad. By Denys Lionel Page. *Univ. of California Press* 1959 pap. $3.85. A heavily annotated and exhaustive study of the preclassical world, based on recent archaeological finds.

Singer of Tales. By Albert B. Lord. *Harvard Univ. Press* 1960 $10.00; *Atheneum* 1965 pap. $3.95. Using the parallel case of Yugoslavian oral epic, this work explains why Homer may have been an oral poet. A landmark in Homeric studies.

The Songs of Homer. By Geoffrey S. Kirk. *Cambridge* 1962 $15.50

A Companion to Homer. Ed. by Alan J. B. Wace and Frank H. Stubbings. *Macmillan* 1963 $17.50
"Started before 1939, having lost by death editor Wace and three others but having gained from new excavations and the decipherment of Linear B, the publication of this giant in every sense is an important event. The list of 17 contributors resembles a Homeric Who's Who, the contents a Homeric What's What. Though intended chiefly for those reading Homer in Greek, this *Companion* has much also for those reading him in English"—*(LJ)*.

Essays on the Odyssey. Ed. by Charles H. Taylor, Jr. *Indiana Univ. Press* 1963 Midland Bks. pap. $1.95. Seven essays published since 1950.

The Ulysses Theme: A Study in the Adaptability of a Traditional Hero. By W. B. Stanford. *Univ. of Michigan* Ann Arbor Bks. 1968 pap. $2.65

Ulysses Found. By Ernle Bradford. *Harcourt* 1964 Harvest Bks. pap. $1.65
Since the age of 19, Bradford has sailed the Mediterranean in search of the route of Ulysses and has found Homeric geography to bear out in fact—"it is the very authenticity of the winds and weathers, ports and harbors, which acts as a solid backbone to the poem." " 'Ulysses Found' is highly literate, full of wit and wry humor, a delight from start to finish"— (Francis D. Lazenby, in *LJ*).

Homer and the Epic. By Geoffrey S. Kirk. *Cambridge* 1965 pap. $2.95. A shortened version of "The Songs of Homer."

Homer and the Bible: The Origin and Character of East European Literature. By Cyrus H. Gordon. *Ventnor Pubs.* 1967 pap. $2.50. Explores the connections and interactions of the Mediterranean cultures.

The Iliad, the Odyssey and the Epic Tradition. By Charles Rowan Beye. *Gordian Press* $10.00; *Peter Smith* $5.00

The Art of the Odyssey. By Howard Clarke. *Prentice-Hall* 1967 Spectrum Bks. pap. $1.45
Five essays intended for readers of Homer in translation. There is an interesting chapter on the history and problems of English translations on the "Odyssey." "A welcome addition to the ever-increasing Homeric literature"—*(LJ)*.

Archery at the Dark of the Moon: Poetic Problems in Homer's Odyssey. By Norman Austin. *Univ. of California Press* 1975 $14.75

Nature and Culture in the Iliad: The Tragedy of Hector. By James M. Redfield. *Univ. of Chicago Press* 1975 $13.50

Spontaneity and Tradition: A Study in the Oral Art of Homer. By Michael Nagler. *Univ. of California Press* 1975 $12.50

HESIOD. c. 700 B.C.

Hesiod tells us that his father gave up sea-trading and moved from Ascra to Boeotia, that he himself as he tended sheep on Mount Helicon was commanded by the Muses to sing of the gods, and that he won a tripod for a funeral song at Chalcis. His date falls around 700 B.C. The poems credited to him with certainty are the "Theogony," concerning the origins and genealogies of the gods, and the "Works and Days," a wise sermon addressed to his brother Perses with maxims for farmers and lucky days for their activities. Uncertain attributions are the "Shield of Heracles" and the "Catalogue of Women." Hesiod is a didactic and individualistic poet who is often compared and contrasted with Homer, as both are representative of early epic style.

WORKS. Trans. by Thomas Cooke. 1728. *AMS Press* 2 vols. each $12.50

HESIOD. Homeric Hymns, Fragments of the Epic Cycle, Homerica. Trans. by Hugh G. Evelyn-White *Harvard Univ. Press* Loeb 1914 $7.00. A careful, highly respected scholarly translation of Hesiod.

THE WORKS AND DAYS; THEOGONY; THE SHIELD OF HERAKLES. Trans. by Richmond Lattimore *Univ. of Michigan Press* 1959 $4.95

This translation in verse is always readable and never strained, and the excellent introductory essay gives much valuable information about a neglected epic tradition. "Hesiod is earth-bound and dun colored; indeed part of his purpose is to discredit the brilliance and the ideals of heroism glorified in the Homeric tradition. But Hesiod too is poetry, though of a different order, and Lattimore's is the only version that makes the English reader aware that it is"—(Moses Hadas, in the *N.Y. Times*).

THEOGONY. Trans. with introd. by Norman O. Brown. 1953. *Bobbs* Liberal Arts $1.25. The translator gives a fascinating introduction to the poet.

Books about Hesiod.

The World of Hesiod: A Study of the Greek Middle Ages c. 900–700 B.C. By Andrew Robert Burn. 1936. *Blom* $12.50
Hesiod and Aeschylus. By Friedrich Solmsen. 1949. *Johnson Reprint* $21.00. The author is a leading classicist and scholar of Hesiod.
Hesiod and the Near East. By P. Walcott. *Verry* 1966 $5.50. An illuminating study of the interaction between Greece and the Near East in the late 8th and early 7th centuries B.C.
The Winged Word: A Study in the Technique of Ancient Greek Oral Composition as Seen Principally through Hesiod's Works and Days. By Berkley Peabody. *State Univ. of New York Press* 1975 $40.00. Convincing analysis of verse patterns and oral recitation in Hesiod, Homer, and Eastern literatures.

SAPPHO. c. 612 B.C.

Sappho, whom Plato called "the tenth Muse," was the greatest of the early Greek lyric poets. She was born at Mytilene on Lesbos and was a member, perhaps the head, of a group of women who honored the Muses and Aphrodite. Her brilliant love lyrics, marriage songs, and hymns to the gods are written in Aeolic dialect in many meters, one of which is named for her—the Sapphic. Only fragments survive. Her verse is simple and direct, exquisitely passionate and vivid. Catullus (*q.v.*), Ovid (*q.v.*), and Swinburne (*q.v.*) were among the many later poets influenced by her.

THE POEMS OF SAPPHO. A prose translation by J. M. Edmonds. 1922. (In "Lyra Graeca") *Harvard Univ. Press* Loeb 3 vols. each $7.00. A sometimes obscure, but generally faithful translation.

POEMS. Trans. by Suzy Q. Groden *Bobbs* Liberal Arts 1966 $6.00 pap. $1.75

POEMS AND FRAGMENTS. Trans. with introd. by Guy Davenport *Univ. of Michigan Press* 1965 $3.95

SAPPHO: A New Translation. By Mary Barnard; fwd. by Dudley Fitts *Univ. of California Press* 1958 pap. $1.65

LYRICS IN THE ORIGINAL GREEK. Trans. and ed. by Willis Barnstone *New York Univ. Press* 1965 $6.95. A vivid, impressionistic version.

Books about Sappho

Sappho and Her Influence. By David M. Robinson. 1930. *Cooper* $3.50
Sappho and Alcaeus: An Introduction to the Study of Ancient Lesbian Poetry. By Denys Lionel Page. *Oxford* 1955 $8.50. Text, translation, and commentary with an introductory essay to the two poets from Lesbos. This distinguished book is required reading for the serious student.

Greek Lyric Poetry from Alcman to Simonides. By C. M. Bowra. *Oxford* 2nd ed. 1962 $10.25. A sensitive critique of Sappho's lyrics and of problems associated with the text.

AESOP.   fl.   570 B.C.

The Greek slave of Samos was said to have composed the animal "Fables" although the sources of many of them have been traced to earlier literature. "He is illustrated listening to a fox on an Attic cup of about 450 B.C., and is mentioned by Aristophanes (*q.v.*) and by Socrates (*q.v.*) in Plato's 'Phaedo' "—(Cassell). Babrius (fl. 2nd cent. A.D.), a Greek fabulist, and Phaedrus (c. 15 B.C.-c. 50 A.D.), a Latin writer from Macedonia, versified Aesop's fables; their versions were rendered into prose during the Middle Ages. "Babrius and Phaedrus" (trans. and ed. by Ben Edwin Perry *Harvard Univ. Press* Loeb 1965 $7.00) includes a comprehensive survey of Greek and Latin fables in the Aesopic tradition. William Caxton's "Here begynneth the book of the sybtyl Historie and Fables of Esope" was translated "out of the French into Englysshe" in 1484. Sir Roger L'Estrange "did his work of translation with the utmost thoroughness" in 1669. "His chiefest qualification for the task was his mastery of his own language. . . . The work by which he is best remembered, is his version of Aesop's Fables. . . . His Aesop, stripped of its 'reflexions,' still remains the best we have"—(Charles Whibley, in "Cambridge History of English Literature"). "Aesop: Five Centuries of Illustrated Fables" by John J. McKendry (*N.Y. Graphic Society* 1964 $5.95) is an interesting and "beautifully designed" (*LJ*) history of the illustrations by Oudry, Bewick, Doré, Walter Crane and Calder, among others.

FABLES. [Fables from Caxton's "Aesop" (1484), from Thomas James's "Aesop" (1848) and "Fables from Aesop, Phaedrus," etc., by Sir Roger L'Estrange.] Ill. by Alexander Calder *Dover* 1967 pap. $1.50; trans. by S. A. Handford *Penguin* 1964 pap. $1.50

FABLES. Trans. by John Warrington *Dutton* 1961 1966 $3.95. Specially translated from the Greek and Latin texts of Babrius, Phaedrus and other ancient or medieval writers.

FABLES. (With title "Twelve Fables") ed. by Glenway Wescott, ill. by A. Fransconi *Museum of Modern Art* (dist. by N.Y. Graphic Society) 1964 pap. $.95; told by Valerius Babrius, ed. and trans. by Denison B. Hull *Univ. of Chicago Press* 1960 $8.50

Books about Aesop

Aesopica: A Series of Texts Relating to Aesop or Ascribed to Him or Closely Connected with the Literary Tradition that Bears His Name. By Ben Edwin Perry. *Univ. of Illinois Press* 1952 $15.00. This valuable source book has ancient testimonies about Aesop.

The Ancient Romances: A Literary-Historical Account of Their Origin. By Ben Edwin Perry. Sather Classical Lectures *Univ. of California Press* 1967 $12.50. This work places Aesop in the romance tradition.

The Fables of Aesop, Vol. 1: History of the Aesopic Fable. Ed. by Joseph Jacobs. 1889. *Burt Franklin* 1970 $20.50. A careful account of the transmission of the fables in antiquity, the middle ages, and down to modern times.

A Manual of Aesopic Fable Literature: A First Book of Reference for the Period Ending A.D. 1500. (And "The History of French Fable Manuscripts") 1896. *Burt Franklin* 1927 $15.00. A useful handbook showing the extent of Aesop's influence throughout history.

AESCHYLUS.   524–456 B.C.

Aeschylus was born at Eleusis of a noble family. He fought at the Battle of Marathon (490 B.C.) where a small Greek band heroically defeated the invading Persians. At the time of his death, Athens was in its golden age. In all of his extant works, his intense love of Greece and Athens finds expression.

Of the nearly ninety plays attributed to him, only seven survive. These are the "Persians" (produced in 472 B.C.), the "Seven against Thebes" (467 B.C.), the "Oresteia" (458 B.C.)—which includes the "Agamemnon," the "Libation Bearers," and the "Eumenides" (or "Furies")—the "Suppliants" (463 B.C.), and the "Prometheus Bound" (c. 460 B.C.). Aeschylus called his prodigious output "dry scraps from Homer's banquet" because his plots and solemn language are derived from the epic poet. But a more accurate summation of Aeschylus would emphasize his grandeur of mind and spirit and the tragic dignity of his language. Because of his patriotism and belief in divine providence, there is a profound moral order to his plays. Characters such as Clytemnestra, Orestes, and Prometheus personify a great passion or principle. As individuals they conflict with divine will but ultimate justice prevails.

Aeschylus' introduction of the second actor made real theatre possible because the two could address each other and act several roles. His successors imitated his costumes, dances, spectacular effects, long descriptions, choral refrains, invocations, and dialogue.

Swinburne's enthusiasm for the "Oresteia" sums up all praises of Aeschylus; he called it simply "the greatest achievement of the human mind."

COMPLETE PLAYS. Trans. into English rhyming verse by Gilbert Murray *Oxford* 1920–1939 $7.50. Available also in separate vols.: Agamemnon 1920 pap. $1.95; Choephoroe (Libation Bearers) 1923 pap. $1.75; The Eumenides 1925 pap. $1.95; The Persians 1939 pap. $1.95; Prometheus Bound 1931 pap. $1.95; The Suppliant Women 1930 $1.50. Murray's English strikes the modern reader as somewhat archaic.

TRAGEDIES. Trans. by Herbert Weir Smyth *Harvard Univ. Press* Loeb 2 vols. 1922 1926 each $7.00. Vol. 1 The Suppliant Maidens (c. 463 B.C.); The Persians (472 B.C.); Prometheus (c. 460 B.C.); Seven against Thebes (467 B.C.). Vol. 2 Agamemnon; The Libation Bearers; Eumenides (all 458 B.C.); Fragments.

AESCHYLUS I. (A volume of "The Complete Greek Tragedies," ed. by David Grene and Richmond Lattimore.) *Univ. of Chicago Press* 1953 Phoenix Bks. pap. $1.95. This volume contains The Oresteia. This and the following volume are excellent and authoritative modern translations which convey the complexity and the metrics of the originals.

AESCHYLUS II. (A volume of "The Complete Greek Tragedies," ed. by David Grene and Richard Lattimore.) *Univ. of Chicago Press* 1956 Phoenix Bks. pap. $1.95. Prometheus Bound and Seven against Thebes, trans. by David Grene; The Persians and The Suppliant Maidens, trans. by Seth G. Benardete.

SEVEN AGAINST THEBES. Trans. by Anthony Hecht and Helen Bacon Greek Tragedy in New Translations Ser. *Oxford* 1973 $7.95. A readable version.

THE SUPPLIANTS. Trans. by Janet Lembke and William Arrowsmith The Greek Tragedy in New Translations Ser. *Oxford* 1975 $6.95

PROMETHEUS BOUND. Trans. by Warren Anderson *Bobbs* Liberal Arts 1963 pap. $1.00; trans. by James Scully and C. J. Herington, ed. by William Arrowsmith The Greek Tragedy in New Translations Ser. *Oxford* 1975 $6.95; trans. and ed. by Edith Hamilton *Norton* 1937 pap. $1.25; (and "Other Plays: Suppliants, Seven, and Persians") trans. by Philip Vellacott *Penguin* 1961 pap. $2.25

ORESTEIA. Trans. and ed. by Peter Arnott *AHM Pub. Corp.* Crofts Classics 2 vols. 1964 Vol. 1 Agamemnon Vol. 2 Libation Bearers and Eumenides pap. each $.85; (and "Prometheus Bound") trans. by M. W. B. Townsend, introd. by Lionel Casson *T. Y. Crowell* (Chandler Pub.) 1965 pap. $2.25; (with title "The Orestes Plays of Aeschylus") trans. by Paul Roche *New Am. Lib.* Mentor Bks. 1963 pap. $.95; (with title "The Oresteian Trilogy") trans. by Philip Vellacott *Penguin* 1956 $1.45; trans. by Robert Fagles *Viking* 1975 $15.00

THE HOUSE OF ATREUS. Adapted from the Oresteia by John Lewin; ed. by Tyrone Guthrie Minnesota Drama Eds. *Univ. of Minnesota Press* 1966 $5.00. This adaptation of the trilogy "Agamemnon," "The Libation Bearers" and "The Furies" is for contemporary stage presentation and is the version used by the Minnesota Theater Company for its production at the Tyrone Guthrie Theater in Minneapolis.

AGAMEMNON. Trans. by Walter Headlam, ed. by Alfred C. Pearson *Cambridge* 1910 $12.50; (in "Three Greek Plays") trans. and ed. by Edith Hamilton *Norton* Norton Lib. 1937 pap. $1.25; ed. by Eduard Fraenkel Vol. 1 Prolegomena, Text and Translation Vols. 2 and 3 Commentary *Oxford* 3 vols. 1950 set $48.00. Fraenkel's introduction, critical edition of the Greek text, English translation, and commentary represent the best of modern scholarship on this most difficult and profound of plays.

Books about Aeschylus

Tragic Drama in Aeschylus, Sophocles and Shakespeare. By Lewis Campbell. 1904. *Russell & Russell* 1965 $8.50

Aeschylean Tragedy. By Herbert W. Smyth. 1924. *AMS Press* $7.50; *Biblo & Tannen* 1969 $6.50. Written by an American authority on Aeschylus.

Aeschylus and Sophocles: Their Work and Influence. By J. T. Sheppard. 1927. Our Debt to Greece and Rome Ser. *Cooper* $3.75

Aeschylus and Athens. By G. Thomson. 1940. *Beekman Pubs.* 1974 $15.00; *Haskell* 1969 $19.95

Aeschylus: The Creator of Tragedy. By Gilbert Murray. *Oxford* 1940 $8.50

The Style of Aeschylus. By Frank R. Earp. 1948. *Russell & Russell* 1970 $9.00

Hesiod and Aeschylus. By Friedrich Solmsen. 1949. *Johnson Reprint* $21.00. A sophisticated study of the relationship between the two poets; by a leading Hellenist.

Pindar and Aeschylus. By John H. Finley, Jr. Martin Classical Lectures Ser. *Harvard Univ. Press* 1955 $10.00

The Political Background of Aeschylean Tragedy. By Anthony J. Podlecki. *Univ. of Michigan Press* 1966 $7.50. A carefully presented argument.

Author of the Prometheus Bound. By C. J. Herington. New Delphin Ser. *Univ. of Texas Press* 1970 $5.50. An intelligent discussion of problems in the "Prometheus."

Aeschylus: A Collection of Critical Essays. By March McCall, Jr. *Prentice-Hall* 1972 $6.95 pap. $1.95

PINDAR. 518–c. 438 B.C.

Pindar, a Boeotian aristocrat who wrote for aristocrats, lived at Thebes, studied at Athens and stayed in Sicily at the court of Hieron at Syracuse. His epinicians, or choral odes in honor of victors at athletic games, survive almost complete and are divided into four groups dependent on whether they celebrate victory at the Olympian, Pythian, Nemean, or Isthmian games. It is surmised that these are representative of his other poetry—such as the hymns, processional songs, dirges—which are extant in fragments.

The odes joyfully heap up praises for beautiful, brilliant athletes who are like the gods in their moment of triumph. Bold mythological metaphor, dazzling intricacy of language, and metrical complexity together create sublimity of thought and of style. Pindar was famous in his lifetime and later throughout the Hellenistic world, as is attested by the story that Alexander the Great in 335 B.C. ordered the poet's house spared when his army sacked Thebes.

The "Pindaric ode" form used in England in the 17th and early 18th centuries was based on an incorrect understanding of Pindar's metrical schemes and was characterized by grandiose diction. Abraham Cowley (1618–1667) published his "Pindarique Odes" in 1656, and the form was used by Dryden (*q.v.*), Pope (*q.v.*), Swift (*q.v.*) and others. Cowley's odes were paraphrases rather than translations, according to his preface; he said that "if a man should undertake to translate Pindar word for word, it would be thought that one madman had translated another." Sir John E. Sandys' prose translation is "scholarly and dignified." The more recent free verse renderings used by Professor Lattimore in an effort to suggest Pindar's own meters give us a version which is "clear and lucid, except when Pindar himself is otherwise, and then Mr. Lattimore, like a true translator, reproduces the obscurity of the original by an obscurity transferred to the English"—(David Grene, in *Poetry*).

ODES AND FRAGMENTS. Trans. by Sir John Sandys *Harvard Univ. Press* Loeb 1915, 1919 $7.00

THE ODES OF PINDAR. Trans. by Richmond Lattimore *Univ. of Chicago Press* 1947 Phoenix Bks. pap. $2.25

ODES OF PINDAR. Trans. by C. Maurice Bowra *Penguin* Class. 1969 pap. $1.75. An excellent version.

SELECTED ODES. Trans. by Carl A. Ruck and William H. Matheson *Michigan Univ. Press* 1968 $10.00

Books about Pindar

Pindar and Aeschylus. By John Huston Finley. *Harvard Univ. Press* 1955 $10.00. An important study of the relationship between the two poets who met at Hieron's court in Syracuse.

Pindar's Pythian Odes: Essays in Interpretation. By Reginald W. B. Burton. *Oxford* 1962 o.p. A classic study.

Pindar. By C. Maurice Bowra. *Oxford* 1964 $13.00. Indispensable for understanding the difficult poetry of Pindar.

Pindar. By Gilbert Norwood. Sather Classical Lectures *Univ. of California Press* 1974 $12.00

SOPHOCLES. c. 496–406 B.C.

Sophocles was born to a wealthy family at Colonus, near Athens, was admired as a boy for his personal beauty and musical skill. He served faithfully as treasurer and general for Athens when it was expanding its empire and influence. In the dramatic contests, he defeated Aeschylus (*q.v.*) in

468 B.C. for first prize in tragedy, wrote a poem to Herodotus (*q.v.*), and led his chorus and actors in mourning for Euripides (*q.v.*) just a few months before his own death. He wrote approximately 123 plays, of which seven tragedies are extant, as well as a fragment of his satiric play, *"Ichneutae"* ("Hunters"). His plays were produced in the following order: "Ajax" c. 450 B.C., "Antigone" 441 B.C., "Oedipus Tyrannus" c. 430 B.C., "Trachiniae" c. 430 B.C., "Electra" between 418 and 410 B.C., "Philoctetus" 409 B.C., and "Oedipus at Colonus," posthumously, in 401 B.C. With Sophocles Greek tragedy reached its most characteristic development. He added a third actor, made each play independent, that is not dependent on others in a trilogy, increased the numbers of the chorus, introduced the use of scenery and brought language and characters, though still majestic, nearer to everyday life. His finely delineated characters are responsible for the tragedy which befalls them and accept it heroically. Aristotle (*q.v.*) states that Sophocles said he portrayed people as they ought to be, Euripides (*q.v.*) as they are. His utter command of tragic speech shown in the simple grandeur of his choral odes, dialogues and monologues, encourages the English reader to compare him to Shakespeare.

THE TRAGEDIES OF SOPHOCLES. Trans. by Richard C. Jebb. 1904. *Bks. for Libraries* $14.50

THE COMPLETE PLAYS. Trans. by Richard C. Jebb; ed. with introd. by Moses Hadas *Bantam* World Drama Orig. 1967 pap. $1.50. A newly revised edition of the famous Jebb translations.

DRAMAS. Trans. by Sir George Young *Dutton* Everyman's 1906 $3.95

TRAGEDIES. Trans. by Francis Storr *Harvard Univ. Press* Loeb 2 vols. 1912 each $7.00. Vol. 1 Oedipus the King: Oedipus at Colonus; Antigone. Vol. 2 Ajax; Electra; Trachinae; Philoctetes; contains bibliography of editions and translations.

SOPHOCLES I. (A volume of "The Complete Greek Tragedies," ed. by David Grene and Richmond Lattimore.) *Univ. of Chicago Press* 1954 Phoenix Bks. pap. $1.25. Oedipus the King, trans. by David Grene; Oedipus at Colonus, trans. by Robert Fitzgerald; Antigone, trans. by Elizabeth Wyckoff.

SOPHOCLES II. (A volume of "The Complete Greek Tragedies," ed. by David Grene and Richmond Lattimore.) *Univ. of Chicago Press* 1957 Phoenix Bks. pap. $2.95. Ajax, trans. by John Moore; The Women of Trachis, trans. by Michael Jameson; Electra, Philoctetes, trans. by David Grene.

FOUR PLAYS: Ajax; Philoctetes; Electra; The Women of Trachis. Trans. by Theodore Howard Banks *Oxford* 1966 $4.00 pap. $2.50

THREE THEBAN PLAYS: Antigone; Oedipus the King; Oedipus at Colonus. Trans. by Theodore Howard Banks *Oxford* 1956 pap. $1.95

THE OEDIPUS CYCLE: An English Version. *Harcourt* Harvest Bks. 1955 pap. $1.35. Oedipus Rex, trans. by Dudley Fitts and Robert Fitzgerald; Oedipus at Colonus, trans. by Robert Fitzgerald; Antigone, trans. by Dudley Fitts and Robert Fitzgerald.

THREE TRAGEDIES: Antigone; Oedipus the King; Electra. Trans. into verse by H. D. F. Kitto *Oxford* 1962 pap. $1.95

THE ANTIGONE OF SOPHOCLES. Trans. by Michael Townsend *T. Y. Crowell* (Chandler Pub.) 1962 pap. $1.25; (and "Electra, Oedipus the King, Philoctetes") ed. by Robert Corrigan Classical Drama Ser. *Dell* Laurel pap. $.95; trans. by Gilbert Murray *Oxford* 1941 $2.75; trans. by Richard Braun Greek Tragedy in New Translations Ser. *Oxford* 1973 $7.95

OEDIPUS, KING OF THEBES. Trans. into rhyming verse with notes by Gilbert Murray *Oxford* 1911 $2.95

OEDIPUS, THE KING. (And "Antigone") trans. and ed. by Peter D. Arnott *AHM Pub. Corp.* Crofts Class. 1960 pap. $.85; trans. by Bernard M. Knox *Simon & Schuster* (Washington Square) 1959 pap. $.75. Two excellent versions.

OEDIPUS REX. Trans. by Stephen Berg and Clay Diskin. Greek Tragedy in New Translations Ser. *Oxford* 1975 $7.95

WIFE OF HERACLES: Being Sophocles' play, The Trachinian Women. Trans. by Gilbert Murray into English verse with notes *Oxford* 1948 $1.95

WOMEN OF TRACHIS. *New Directions* 1957 $5.75. A poetic version by Ezra Pound.

ELECTRA. Trans. by R. C. Jebb; introd. by J. F. Charles *Bobbs* Lib. Arts $.75; (and "Women of Trachis, Philoctetes") trans. by E. F. Watling *Penguin* (orig.) 1953 pap. $2.50; trans. by F. Fergusson *Theater Arts* pap. $1.90

PHILOCTETES. Trans. by K. Cavander. *Chandler Pub.* 1965 pap. $.95

THE SEARCHERS (Ichneutae, in "Literary Papyri: Poetry"). Trans. by Denys L. Page *Harvard Univ. Press* Loeb 1941 rev. ed. 1942 $7.00

OEDIPUS AT COLONUS. (And "Electra") trans. by Peter Douglas Arnott *AHM Pub. Corp.* Crofts Class. 1974 pap. $1.25; trans. by Gilbert Murray *Oxford* 1948 pap. $2.25; trans. by Anthony Hecht and George Dimock Greek Tragedy in New Translations Ser. *Oxford* 1975 $7.95

Books about Sophocles

Tragic Drama in Aeschylus, Sophocles and Shakespeare: An Essay. By Lewis Campbell. 1904. *Russell & Russell* 1965 $8.50

Aeschylus and Sophocles: Their Work and Influence. By J. T. Sheppard. 1927. Our Debt to Greece and Rome Ser. *Cooper* $3.95

An Introduction to Sophocles. By T. B. L. Webster. 1936. *Richard West* $4.00. An excellent, basic study.

Sophocles. By William N. Bates. 1940. *A. S. Barnes* Perpetua Bks. 1961 pap. $1.95; *Russell & Russell* 1969 $16.00

Sophoclean Tragedy. By C. M. Bowra. *Oxford* 1944 pap. $3.95. A sensitive and comprehensive study.

The Style of Sophocles. By Frank R. Earp. 1944. *Russell & Russell* 1972 $12.00

Sophocles: A Study of Heroic Humanism. By Cedric H. Whitman. *Harvard Univ. Press* 1951 $10.00. This author analyzes the plays as "literary monuments, social documents ... philosophical treatises."

Sophocles and Pericles. By Victor Ehrenberg. *Humanities Press* 1954 $7.25. The author describes the friendship between these two great Athenians.

A Study of Sophoclean Drama. By G. M. Kirkwood. 1957. *Johnson Reprint* $21.00. An illuminating and important analysis.

The Heroic Temper: Studies in Sophoclean Tragedy. By Bernard M. Knox. Sather Classical Lectures Ser. *Univ. of California Press* 1965 $9.00. A perceptive study by a foremost scholar of Sophocles.

Sophocles the Dramatist. By A. J. A. Waldock. *Cambridge* 1966 $11.50 pap. $4.45

Sophocles: A Collection of Critical Essays. Ed. with introd. by Thomas M. Woodward Twentieth Century Views Ser. *Prentice-Hall* 1966 $5.95

Reality and the Heroic Pattern: Last Plays of Ibsen, Shakespeare and Sophocles. By David Grene. *Univ. of Chicago Press* 1967 $7.00 Phoenix Bks. pap. $1.95. A "basic and lucid study" *(LJ)* by the noted editor of "The Complete Greek Tragedies"; three of the ten essays included treat Sophocles' "Ajax," "Philoctetes" and "Oedipus at Colonus."

HERODOTUS. c. 490–c. 425 B.C. *See Chapter 9, History, Government and Politics: Ancient Greek Historians,* Reader's Adviser, *Vol. 3.*

EURIPIDES. c. 485–c. 406 B.C.

The third of the three great Greek tragedians was born in Attica and lived most of his life in Athens. Out of some 80 plays by him only 19 are extant; the dates of the following plays are known: "Alcestis" 438 B.C., "Medea" and "Philoctetes" 431 B.C., "Hippolytus" 428 B.C., "Hecuba" c. 424 B.C., "Electra" 417 B.C., "Troades" 415 B.C., "Iphigenia in Tauris" c. 413 B.C., "Helen" 412 B.C., "Phoenissae" after 412 B.C. and before 408 B.C., "Ion" c. 411 B.C., "Orestes" 408 B.C., "Bacchus" and "Iphigenia in Aulis" c. 405 B.C. The "Rhesus"—if indeed it is genuine—is the earliest.

When Gilbert Murray's translations made the dramatist popular in the early 1900s, readers were impressed by the author's modernity of thought and spirit, the feeling for human life and problems of pain. Euripides' attitude toward the gods was iconoclastic and rationalistic, toward humans—notably his passionate female characters—deeply sympathetic.

Euripides separated the chorus from the action, the first step toward its complete elimination. He used the prologue as an introduction and explanation and was charged with intemperate use of the "deus ex machina," by which artifice a god is dragged in abruptly at the end to resolve a confusion beyond human powers. He developed the literary devices of reversal, recognition by means of rings and necklaces, substitution of children, violations of maidens on all of which New Comedy (*see Menander*) depends. His language is simple and direct, well tuned to the expression of passion.

Despite criticism and satire against him, Euripides did win several prizes for tragedy in his lifetime and shortly after his death his reputation rose and has never diminished.

EURIPIDES. Trans. by Arthur S. Way *Harvard Univ. Press* Loeb 4 vols. 1912 each $7.00. Vol. 1: Iphigeneia at Aulis, Rhesus, Hecuba, The Daughters of Troy, Helen; Vol. 2: Electra, Orestes, Iphigeneia in Taurica, Andromache, Cyclops; Vol. 3: Bacchanals, Madness of Hecules, Children of Hercules, Phoenician Maidens, Suppliants; Vol. 4: Ion, Hippolytus, Medea, Alcestis.

EURIPIDES I. (A volume of "The Complete Greek Tragedies," ed. by David Grene and Richmond Lattimore.) *Univ. of Chicago Press* 1955 Phoenix Bks. pap. $2.95. Four Tragedies: Alcestis (438 B.C.), trans. by Richmond Lattimore; The Medea (431 B.C.), trans. by Rex Warner; The Heracleidae (c. 427 B.C.), trans. by Ralph Gladstone; Hippolytus (428 B.C.), trans. by David Grene; with an introd. by Richmond Lattimore.

EURIPIDES II. (A volume of "The Complete Greek Tragedies," ed. by David Grene and Richmond Lattimore.) *Univ. of Chicago Press* 1956 Phoenix Bks. pap. $2.95. Four Tragedies: The Cyclops (c. 423 B.C.), Heracles (c. 422 B.C.), trans. by William Arrowsmith; Iphigenia in Tauris (c. 413 B.C.), trans. by Witter Bynner; Helen (412 B.C.), trans. by Richmond Lattimore.

EURIPIDES III. (A volume of "The Complete Greek Tragedies," ed. by David Grene and Richmond Lattimore.) *Univ. of Chicago Press* Phoenix Bks. 1958 pap. $2.95; *Simon & Schuster* (Washington Square) pap. $.95. Four Tragedies: Hecuba (c. 424 B.C.), trans. by William Arrowsmith; Andromache (c. 426 B.C.), trans. by John Frederick Nims; The Trojan Women (415 B.C.), trans. by Richmond Lattimore; Ion (c. 411 B.C.), trans. by Ronald Frederick Willetts.

EURIPIDES IV. (A volume of "The Complete Greek Tragedies," ed. by David Grene and Richmond Lattimore.) *Univ. of Chicago Press* Phoenix Bks. 1958 pap. $3.45. Four Tragedies: Rhesus, trans. by Richmond Lattimore; The Suppliant Women (c. 421 B.C.), trans. by Frank William Jones; Orestes (408 B.C.), trans. by William Arrowsmith; Iphigenia in Aulis (c. 405 B.C.), trans. by Charles R. Walker.

EURIPIDES V. (A volume of "The Complete Greek Tragedies," ed. by David Grene and Richmond Lattimore.) *Univ. of Chicago Press* 1959 Phoenix Bks. pap. $2.45; *Simon & Schuster* (Washington Square) pap. $.95. Three Tragedies: Electra (417 B.C.), trans. by Emily Townsend Vermeule; The Phoenician Women (c. 409 B.C.), trans. by Elizabeth Wyckoff; The Bacchae (c. 405 B.C.), trans. by William Arrowsmith.

TEN PLAYS. Trans. by Moses Hadas and J. H. McLean; introd. by Moses Hadas *Bantam* (orig.) pap. $1.25. Alcestis; Medea; Hippolytus; Andromache; Ion; The Trojan Women; Electra; Iphigenia Among the Taurians; Bacchants; Iphigenia at Aulis.

THREE PLAYS. Trans. and introd. by Paul Roche *Norton* 1974 $6.95 pap. $1.95. Alcestis, Medea, and the Bacchae.

RHESOS. Trans. by Gilbert Murray *Oxford* 1916 pap. $1.95; trans. by Richard Braun Greek Tragedy in New Translations Ser. *Oxford* 1975 $7.95

ALCESTIS. Trans. by Gilbert Murray *Oxford* 1915 pap. $2.95; trans. by William Arrowsmith Greek Tragedy in New Translations Ser. *Oxford* 1973 $6.95; (and "Other Plays") trans. by Philip Vellacott *Penguin* rev. ed. 1975 pap. $1.95

MEDEA. (And "Hippolytus") trans. by Sydney Waterlow 1906 *AMS Press* $9.00; trans. by Michael Townsend, introd. by William Arrowsmith *T. Y. Crowell* (Chandler Pub.) 1966 pap. $1.25 (a "colloquial rendition" which misses the poetry of the Greek original—*Choice*); (and "Hippolytus, Alcestis, Bacchae") trans. by Robert W. Corrigan Masterpieces of Classical Drama Ser. *Dell* Laurel Eds. pap. $.95; trans. by Gilbert Murray *Oxford* 1906 pap. $2.50; (and "Hecabe, Electra, Hercules") trans. by Philip Vellacott *Penguin* 1963 pap. $1.75; *Peter Smith* $4.00

HIPPOLYTUS. Trans. by Gilbert Murray *Oxford* 1902 pap. $2.75; trans. by Robert Bagg Greek Tragedy in New Translations Ser. *Oxford* 1973 $7.95

ELECTRA. Trans. by Moses Hadas *Bobbs* Liberal Arts pap. $1.00; trans. by Gilbert Murray *Oxford* 1905 pap. $2.25; trans. into prose with introd. and notes by D. W. Lucas *Verry* 1951 $1.75

THE TROJAN WOMEN. Trans. into rhyming verse with introd. and notes by Gilbert Murray *Oxford* 1915 pap. $2.75; adapted by Jean-Paul Sartre and trans. by Ronald Duncan into verse *Random* Vintage Bks. 1967 pap. $1.65

IPHIGENIA IN TAURIS. Trans. by Gilbert Murray *Oxford* 1910 pap. $1.95; trans. by Richmond Lattimore Greek Tragedy in New Translations Ser. *Oxford* 1973 $7.95

ION. Trans. into rhyming verse with notes by Gilbert Murray *Oxford* 1954 pap. $2.25; trans. by D. W. Lucas *Verry* 1949 $1.75

THE BACCHAE. Trans. into rhyming verse with notes by Gilbert Murray *Oxford* 1904 pap. $2.95; trans. by Robert Bagg Greek Tragedy in New Translations Ser. *Oxford* 1975 $7.95; (and "Women of Troy, Helen, Ion") trans. by Philip Vellacott rev. ed. *Penguin* pap. $2.50; trans. with critical essay by Donald Sutherland *Univ. of Nebraska Press* 1968 pap. $2.45

Books about Euripides

Euripides the Rationalist. By Arthur W. Verrall. 1895. *Russell & Russell* 1967 $8.00

Euripides and the Spirit of His Dramas. By Paul De Charme. Trans. by J. Loeb. 1906. *Kennikat* 1968 $12.50

Euripides and His Age. By Gilbert Murray. 1913. A stimulating study, now o.p.

New Chapters on the History of Greek Literature. Ed. by J. U. Powell and E. A. Barber. 1921. *Biblo & Tannen* $10.00; (Second Ser.) 1929 $12.50. *(See the Pickard-Cambridge article on Euripides.)*

Drama of Euripides. By G. M. Grube. 1941 *Harper* Barnes & Noble 1973 $23.75

Euripides and His Influence. By F. L. Lucas. 1930. Our Debt to Greece and Rome Ser. *Cooper* $3.95; *Gordon Press* $35.00

The Greeks and the Irrational. By E. R. Dodds. 1951. o.p. A brilliant analysis of the Dionysian tendencies in Greek letters and thought—particularly relevant to the "Bacchae."

The Greek Tragic Poets. By D. W. Lucas. 1958. *Folcroft* 1973 $20.00. Valuable for understanding Euripides.

Euripides: A Collection of Critical Essays. Ed. by Erich Segal. *Prentice-Hall* 1968 $6.95

Euripides and the Full Circle of Myth. By Cedric Whitman. *Harvard Univ. Press* 1974 $8.00

Ironic Drama. By Philip Vellacott. *Cambridge* 1975 $17.95 pap. $6.95

THUCYDIDES. c. 460–c. 400 B.C. *See Chapter 9, History, Government and Politics: Ancient Greek Historians,* Reader's Adviser, *Vol. 3.*

ARISTOPHANES. c. 450–c. 385 B.C.

Aristophanes is the great master of Athenian "Old Comedy." In addition to the eleven of his plays which are extant, we have 32 titles and many fragments. We know very little of his life. Greek drama had reached its peak and was declining when he began to write. His comedies are full of a peculiar mixture of broad political, social and literary satire, discussions of large ideas and boisterous vulgarities. His characters are like normal human beings in absurd and preposterous situations. His Greek is exceptionally beautiful and his idyllic lyrics delightful.

Edith Hamilton says: "To read Aristophanes is in some sort like reading an Athenian comic paper. All the life of Athens is there: the politics of the day and the politicians; the war party and the anti-war party; pacifism, votes for women, free trade, fiscal reform, complaining taxpayers, educational theories, the current religious and literary talk—everything, in short, that interested the average citizen. All was food for his mockery. He was the speaking picture of the follies and foibles of his day." His sharp barbs were aimed at such targets as Socrates, Euripides, and Aeschylus. He spared no class, no profession, and no age group.

ARISTOPHANES. Trans. by Benjamin Bickley Rogers *Harvard Univ. Press* Loeb 3 vols. 1924 and later rev. each $7.00

Vol. 1 The Acharnians (425 B.C.); The Clouds (423 B.C.); The Knights (424 B.C.); The Wasps (422 B.C.) Vol. 2 The Peace (421 B.C.); The Birds (414 B.C.); The Frogs (405 B.C.) Vol. 3 Lysistrata (411 B.C.); Thesmophoriazusae (411 B.C.); Ecclesiazusae (392 or 391 B.C.); Plutus (388 B.C.). Excellent notes for this inspired verse translation, with the "indecencies" toned down.

COMPLETE PLAYS. Ed. by Moses Hadas *Bantam* (orig.) 1962 pap. $1.95

THE ELEVEN COMEDIES. Athenian Society trans. *Liveright* Black and Gold Lib. 1930 $7.95

PLAYS. Trans. by Patric Dickinson *Oxford* 2 vols. 1970 Vol. 1 The Acharnians, The Knights, The Clouds, The Wasps, and Peace Vol. 2 The Birds, Lysistrata, Thesmophoriazusai, The Frogs, Ecclesiazusai, and Ploutos pap. each $4.95

FIVE COMEDIES: The Wasps; The Birds; The Clouds; The Frogs; Lysistrata. Trans. by Benjamin Bickley Rogers; complete and unabridged with Rogers' introds. and notes; ed. by Andrew Chiappe *Doubleday* Anchor Bks. 1955 pap. $1.95

THE ACHARNIANS. Trans. by William Arrowsmith *New Am. Lib.* Mentor Bks. 1973 pap. $.75; trans. by Douglass Parker (in "The Complete Greek Comedy" ed. by William Arrowsmith) *Univ. of Michigan Press* 1961 $4.95

THE KNIGHTS. Trans. into rhyming verse with introd. and notes by Gilbert Murray *Oxford* 1967 pap. $1.95

THE CLOUDS. (With Plautus' "Pot of Gold") trans. and ed. by Peter D. Arnott *AHM Pub. Corp.* Crofts Class. 1967 pap. $.85; trans. by William Arrowsmith *New Am. Lib.* 1970 pap. $.95

PEACE. Trans. by R. H. Webb *Univ. Press of Virginia* 1964 pap. $2.75

THE BIRDS. (With Plautus' "Brothers Menaechmus") trans. and ed. by Peter D. Arnott *AHM Pub. Corp.* Crofts Class. 1958 pap. $.85; trans. by Dudley Fitts *Harcourt* 1957 $4.95 (in "Four Greek Plays") Harvest Bks. (orig.) 1960–62 pap. $2.25; trans. by William Arrowsmith *New Am. Lib.* 1970 pap. $.95; trans. into verse with introd. and notes by Gilbert Murray *Oxford* 1950 pap. $2.50

LYSISTRATA. Trans. by Donald Sutherland *T. Y. Crowell* (Chandler Pub.) 1961 pap. $1.25; trans. by A. H. Sommerstein *Penguin* 1974 pap. $2.65; trans. by Douglass Parker into "American" English verse ill. by Ellen Raskin (in "The Complete Greek Comedy" ed. by William Arrowsmith) *Univ. of Michigan Press* 1964 $4.95; *New Am. Lib.* 1970 pap. $.95; trans. by Robert H. Webb *Univ. Press of Virginia* 1963 $4.75

LADIES' DAY (*Thesmophoriazusae*). Trans. by Dudley Fitts *Harcourt* 1959 $4.50

"An excellent new adaptation . . . which should receive wide production because of its lively nature."

THE FROGS. Trans. by Richmond Lattimore *New Am. Lib.* Mentor Bks. 1973 pap. $.75; trans. by Gilbert Murray 1908 *Oxford* pap. $2.50; (and "Other Plays") trans. by David Barrett *Penguin* pap. $1.75; trans. by Richmond Lattimore (in "The Complete Greek Comedy" ed. by William Arrowsmith) *Univ. of Michigan Press* 1962 $4.95

THE CONGRESSWOMEN (*Ecclesiazusae*). Trans. by Richmond Lattimore *New Am. Lib.* Mentor Bks. 1970 pap. $.95; trans. with introd. by Douglass Parker, ill. by Leo and Diane Dillon (in "The Complete Greek Comedy" ed. by William Arrowsmith) *Univ. of Michigan Press* 1967 $4.95

Books about Aristophanes

Aristophanes: His Plays and His Influence. By Louis E. Lord. 1925. Our Debt to Greece and Rome Ser. *Cooper* 1930 $3.95

Aristophanes: A Study. By Gilbert Murray. *Oxford* 1933 $3.95; *Russell & Russell* 1964 $8.00

The People of Aristophanes: A Sociology of Old Attic Comedy. By Victor Ehrenberg. 1943. *Harper* Barnes & Noble repr. of 1951 ed. $21.00. A careful study.

Aristophanes and the Comic Hero. By Cedric H. Whitman. Martin Classical Lectures *Harvard Univ. Press* 1964 $11.50. "This full-fledged, thoroughly documented, sympathetic and sensitive study of the Aristophanic hero and of the nature of Aristophanic comedy is excellent"—*(LJ)*.
Aristophanic Comedy. By K. J. Dover. *Univ. of California Press* 1972 $11.50 pap. $3.85
The Living Aristophanes. By Alexis Solomos. Trans. by Marvin Felheim *Univ. of Michigan Press* 1974 $10.00
The Stage of Aristophanes. By C. W. Dearden. *Humanities Press* (Athlone Press) 1975 $18.00

PLATO. c. 429–347 B.C. *See Chapter 5, Philosophy: Ancient Philosophers,* Reader's Adviser, *Vol. 3.*

XENOPHON. c. 428/7–c. 354 B.C. *See Chapter 9, History, Government and Politics: Ancient Greek Historians,* Reader's Adviser, *Vol. 3.*

ARISTOTLE. 384–322 B.C. *See Chapter 5, Philosophy: Ancient Philosophers,* Reader's Adviser, *Vol. 3.*

DEMOSTHENES. 384–322 B.C.

Demosthenes, the magnificent orator, is said to have had to conquer an originally ineffective vocal delivery. After years of private law practice, he delivered the first of his three "Philippics" against Philip of Macedon in 351 B.C. He saw danger to Athens in the tyrannical expansion of the Macedonian state, but his passionate and compelling exhortations did not save the Greeks from defeat at Chaeronea in 338 B.C. Exiled in 324 B.C., he was recalled after the death of Alexander the Great in 323 B.C. Again he tried to organize the Greek resistance, but failed and was forced to flee when Athens was taken. He took poison to avoid capture. His great speeches are characterized by deep sincerity, prodigious power of verbal suggestion, and intricate structure. His influence on Cicero and the Roman rhetoricians was enormous.

ALL THE ORATIONS OF DEMOSTHENES. Trans. by Thomas Leland. 1757. *AMS Press* 2nd ed. $17.50

PHILIPPICS (351–41), OLYNTHIACS (349–48), AND MINOR PUBLIC ORATIONS. Trans. by J. H. Vince and ed. by E. H. Warmington *Harvard Univ. Press* Loeb 1930 $7.00

DEMOSTHENES' PUBLIC ORATIONS. Trans. with introd. by A. W. Pickard-Cambridge. 1912. *Dutton* Everyman's 1963 $3.95. The translator has rendered "the speeches into such English as a political orator of the present day might use."

PRIVATE ORATIONS. Trans. by A. T. Murray *Harvard Univ. Press* Loeb 3 vols. 1936–39 each $7.00

DEMOSTHENES: Six Private Speeches. By Lionel Pearson. *Univ. of Oklahoma Press* 1972 $4.95

MEIDIAS, ANDROTION (355), ARISTOCRATES (352), TIMOCRATES (352), ARISTOGEITON. Trans. by J. H. Vince *Harvard Univ. Press* Loeb 1935 $7.00

FUNERAL SPEECH, EROTIC ESSAY, EXORDIA AND LETTERS. Trans. by Norman W. DeWitt and Norman J. DeWitt *Harvard Univ. Press* Loeb 1949 $7.00

ON THE CROWN. (with title *"De Corona"* and *"De Falsa Legatione"*) trans. by C. A. Vince and J. H. Vince *Harvard Univ. Press* Loeb 1926 $7.00

DEMOSTHENES' ON THE CROWN: A Critical Case Study of a Masterpiece of Ancient Oratory. Ed. by James Jerome Murphy, with a new translation by John J. Keaney *Random* 1967 pap. $2.95

LETTERS OF DEMOSTHENES. By Jonathan A. Goldstein. *Columbia* 1968 $12.00. A revision of the author's thesis, Columbia, 1959, with a translation of four letters.

Books about Demosthenes

Demosthenes and the Last Days of Greek Freedom. By A. W. Pickard-Cambridge. 1914. *AMS Press* $24.50. Convincingly and carefully describes fourth-century issues and problems.
Demosthenes and His Influence. By Charles D. Adams. 1930. Our Debt to Greece and Rome Ser. *Cooper* $3.95
Demosthenes. By Werner W. Jaeger. *Octagon* 1963 $11.50. A brilliant study of Demosthenes' thought.

THEOPHRASTUS. c. 370–288/5 B.C.

The pupil and successor of Aristotle (q.v.) as head of the Peripatetic school of philosophy wrote on a variety of subjects—botany, metaphysics, physics, and law—but is best known for his "Characters," 30 satiric sketches of different character types. These were imitated by English writers of the seventeenth century and by La Bruyère in his famous "Caractères."

CHARACTERS. (And "Herodes, Cercidas, and the Greek Choliambic Poets") trans. by J. M. Edmonds *Harvard* Loeb 1929 $7.00

MORAL CHARACTERS OF THEOPHRASTUS. Trans. by Benjamin Boyce. 1642. *Humanities Press* 1967 $13.75; trans. by Eustace Budgell. 1714. *AMS Press* $7.50

ENQUIRY INTO PLANTS, AND MINOR WORKS ON ODOURS AND WEATHER SIGNS. Trans. by Sir Arthur Hort *Harvard* Loeb 1916 $7.00

MENANDER. 342/1–293/89 B.C.

The late fourth century gave rise to New Comedy, a comedy of manners, more refined and lacking the robustness of the Old Comedy. Until the latter part of the 19th century Menander's plays were known only through adaptations and translations made by the Roman dramatists, Plautus (q.v.) and Terence (q.v.), and by the comments of Ovid (q.v.) and Pliny (q.v.). Menander wrote about 100 plays and the few we have in the Greek text were found on papyrus rolls in the rubbish heaps of Roman Egypt; however "The Dyskolos" (o.p. in separate ed.), the first complete Menander "New Comedy" ever to be discovered intact turned up on papyrus in a private Swiss collection. His comedies are skillfully constructed, his characters well-delineated types, his diction excellent, his themes mostly the trials and tribulations of young love with conventional solutions.

Menander was born in Athens of the upper classes, and studied under the philosopher-scientist Theophrastus, the successor of Aristotle (qq.v.).

THE COMEDIES. Trans. by Frank G. Allinson *Harvard Univ. Press* Loeb 1921 1950 $7.00

THE GIRL FROM SAMOS. Trans. by E. G. Turner *Humanities Press* (Athlone Press) 1972 $2.75

MENANDER, THE PRINCIPAL FRAGMENTS. Trans. by Frank G. Allinson 1921 *Greenwood* $22.00

Books about Menander

The Birth of Modern Comedy of Manners. By T. B. L. Webster. *Int. Scholarly Bk. Services* (Sydney Univ. Press) pap. $1.25; *Folcroft* $4.00

Menander: A Commentary. By A. W. Gomme and F. H. Sandbach. *Oxford* 1973 $38.50 lib. bdg. $30.42. Based on the Oxford Classical Texts of Dysckolos, and Reliquiae Selectae also ed. by Sandbach.

CALLIMACHUS. c. 305–c. 240 B.C.

At Alexandria Callimachus was bibliographer for the great library, teacher of Apollonius Rhodius (q.v.), and a famous, prolific poet. His beautiful, elegant and refined epigrams, hymns, elegiacs (the "Aetia" or "Causes"), iambics and little epic survive in varying degrees of completeness. In his day he was widely admired and later served as a model for Catullus (q.v.) and the Roman elegiac poets, especially Ovid (q.v.).

AETIA, IAMBI, HECALE AND OTHER FRAGMENTS. Trans. by C. A. Trypannis *Harvard* Loeb 1958 $7.00. For the elegiacs, iambics and little epic.

LYCOPHRON, ARATUS. Trans. by A. W. Mair *Harvard* Loeb 1921 $7.00. For the hymns and epigrams.

THEOCRITUS. c. 300–c. 260 B.C.

Regarded as the creator of pastoral poetry, Theocritus was a native of Syracuse and lived in Alexandria. About 30 idylls and a number of epigrams are extant. His genuine love of the country lends freshness and great beauty to the idylls; his bucolic characters are realistic and alive. He is a master of dramatic presentation, description, and lyrical refinement. He has had many imitators, among them Virgil (q.v.) and Spenser (q.v.). The surviving works of two other pastoral poets are often included with those of Theocritus: Moschus of Syracuse who lived in the second century B.C. and Bion, who was born near Smyrna, lived in Sicily probably in the second century B.C. and is best known for his "Lament for Adonis." The Andrew Lang translation in prose of these three poets is considered an English classic (1889, 1924, o.p.).

THE GREEK BUCOLIC POETS. Trans. by J. M. Edmonds *Harvard Univ. Press* Loeb 1912 $7.00. Theocritus, Bion, Moschus and others. An accurate version which is recommended.

THEOCRITUS. Trans. by Charles S. Calverley. 1869. *Bks. for Libraries* $11.00. Appealing versions by an accomplished Victorian poet-translator.

POEMS. Trans. and ed. by A. S. F. Gow *Cambridge* 2 vols. 1952 set $42.50. Beautifully produced textual edition and translation with an excellent introduction and commentary by a foremost scholar.

IDYLLS. A verse translation by Barriss Mills *Purdue Univ. Studies* 1963 $2.95

Books about Theocritus

Theocritus in English Literature. By Robert T. Kerlin. 1910. *Folcroft* $25.00

The Green Cabinet: Theocritus and the European Pastoral Lyric. By Thomas G. Rosenmeyer. *Univ. of California Press* 1969 $10.75 pap. $3.65. A literary critique of Theocritus and his later influence.

APOLLONIUS RHODIUS.   3rd century B.C.

This Greek epic poet was a scholar of some note, which is reflected in his main work, based on the legend of the Argonauts—Jason's voyage in search of the Golden Fleece. Somewhat pedantic, the "Argonautica" is enlivened by the character of Medea. Virgil (*q.v.*) used Apollonius as a source for his portrayal of Dido in the "Aeneid." Apollonius may have been librarian of the great library of Alexandria built by Ptolemy II and certainly studied in Alexandria with Callimachus (*q.v.*). His name is derived from his supposed retirement in Rhodes, probably after a literary feud with Callimachus over the relative merits of long traditional epic as opposed to short, finished poems.

THE ARGONAUTICA. Trans. in prose by R. C. Seaton *Harvard Univ. Press* Loeb 1912 $7.00. Text and translation recommended.

VOYAGE OF ARGO. Trans. by E. V. Rieu *Penguin* 1959 pap. $2.95

MOSCHUS.   fl. 150 B.C. *See Theocritus.*

BION.   fl. c. 100 B.C. *See Theocritus.*

PLUTARCH.   c. 46–c. 125 A.D. *See Chapter 9, History, Government and Politics,* Reader's Adviser, *Vol. 3.*

LONGINUS.   c. 1st century A.D.

"Longinus" is the author assigned to "On the Sublime," a treatise which defines the sublime in literature, using Homer, Plato, and Demosthenes (*qq.v.*) as the chief examples. Translated by Boileau in 1674, this greatly influenced literary theory until the early nineteenth century and is of lasting importance as a brilliant critique of classical literature.

ON SUBLIMITY. Trans. by D. A. Russell *Oxford* 1965 $1.70

ON THE SUBLIME. Trans. by G. M. A. Grube *Bobbs* 1957 pap. $1.25; (with Aristotle's "Poetics" and "On Style" by Demetrius) *Harvard Univ. Press* Loeb $7.00; (with Aristotle's "Poetics" and Horace's "Ars Poetica") trans. by T. S. Dorsch *Penguin* Classics Ser. pap. $1.25

BABRIUS.   fl. 2nd cent. A.D. *See Aesop.*

LUCIAN (Lucianus Samosatensis).   c. 120–c. 185 A.D.

Lucian, the wit and satirist, was a brilliant Greek writer in the time of the Roman Empire. He was born in Samosata, Syria, traveled and lectured in Italy, Asia Minor and Gaul and in later life held a government position in Egypt. Of nearly 80 works the most important and characteristic are his essays, written in dialogue form. "Dialogues of the Gods," "Dialogues of the Dead" and "The Sale of Lives" show his knowledge of classical Greek and ancient mythology. He is a good critical source for ancient art and for information about his literary contemporaries. The "True History," a nonsense fantasy and parody of incredible adventure stories, influenced Rabelais (*q.v.*) and Swift (*q.v.*).

SELECTED WORKS. Trans. by B. P. Reardon *Bobbs* Liberal Arts 1965 $6.50 pap. $2.75

SELECTED SATIRES. Trans. and ed. by Lionel Casson *Norton* Norton Lib. 1968 pap. $3.75

DIALOGUES. Trans. by Austin Morris Harmon; vol. 8 trans. by M. D. Macleod *Harvard Univ. Press* Loeb 8 vols. 1913–1936 each $7.00

SATIRICAL SKETCHES. Trans. by Paul Turner *Peter Smith* 1962 $3.75

TRUE HISTORY AND LUCIUS OR THE ASS. Trans. by Paul Turner; ill. *Indiana Univ. Press* Midland Bks. 1974 pap. $1.95

Books about Lucian

Essays and Addresses. By R. C. Jebb. 1907. *Richard West* 1973 $30.00. Contains a chapter on Lucian.

Lucian, Satirist and Artist. By Francis G. Allinson. 1950. Our Debt to Greece and Rome Ser. *Cooper* $3.95

The Sophists in the Roman Empire. By G. W. Bowerstock. *Oxford* 1969 $7.25. See Chapter 9 for Lucian.

Studies in Lucian. By Barry Baldwin. *Hakkert* 1974 $8.00

LONGUS.   fl. 2nd or 3rd cent. A.D.?

The pastoral "Daphnis and Chloe," the best of the ancient Greek romances, is attributed to Longus. Nothing is known of his life. His passionate love story of two foundlings raised together by shepherds on Lesbos is sweetly told and has been persistently admired for its bucolic charm.

DAPHNIS AND CHLOË (and Xenophon's "An Ephesian Tale," Dio Chrysostom's "The Hunters of Euboéa"). Trans. by Moses Hadas *Bobbs* Liberal Arts $6.00 pap. $1.45; (and Parthenius, "Love Romances") trans. by Thornley, rev. by J. M. Edmonds *Harvard Univ. Press* Loeb rev. ed. 1955 $7.00

Books about Longus

The Ancient Romances: A Literary-Historical Account of Their Origins. By Ben Edwin Perry. Sather Classical Lectures *Univ. of California Press* 1967 $11.50. This work places Longus in the context of the romance tradition.

Longus. By William McCulloh. World Authors Ser. *Twayne* $6.95

HELIODORUS OF EMESA.   fl. 220–250 A.D.

One of the earliest and longest of the surviving Greek novels, the "Aethiopica" is a romance of two young lovers, Theagenes and Charicleia, set in the 5th century B.C., which shows considerable insight and narrative skill. It was much read by the Byzantines and in the 16th and 17th centuries was translated into many languages. Almost nothing is known of the author except that he was a native of Emesa in Syria and perhaps later became Bishop of Tricca in Thessaly.

THE AETHIOPIAN HISTORY OF HELIODORUS. In Ten Books, The First Five Translated by a Person of Quality, the Last Five by Nahum Tate. To Which are Prefixed the Testimonies of Writers, Both Ancient and Modern Concerning This Work. 1686. *AMS Press* $18.00

AETHIOPIAN HISTORY. Trans. by Thomas Underdowne. 1895. *AMS Press* $15.00

ETHIOPIAN STORY. Trans. by Sir Walter Lamb *Dutton* Everyman's 1961 $3.95

—E.C.K.S.

Chapter 8

Latin Literature

"Rome. It has resonance like a deep bronze bell. It clangs like a heavy shield struck by a heavy sword. It is the keynote of a noble theme in which other names are overtones: Caesar, triumph, legion, forum, senate, emperor, pope. The majestic word has rung through 27 centuries. It is one of the greatest utterances of mankind: it is heard all round the world and will not soon be silenced."

—GILBERT HIGHET

Latin literature must always be seen in light of its Greek antecedents and of contemporary Roman history. *"Arma virumque cano"* ("Of arms and the man I sing"), the opening words of Virgil's "Aeneid," tell us that the poem will comment on Homer's "Iliad" (the arms) and "Odyssey" (the man). Viewed in another way, however, these words mean the Roman Empire and the Emperor Augustus. The poem is both the noblest Roman epic and the imperially sanctioned history of Rome.

The early poets, Livius Andronicus, Naevius, and Ennius (their works survive only in fragments), adapted Homer and the Greek tragedians in lustrous Latin verse and thereby laid the foundations of the literature. Influenced by Greek New Comedy and native Italian farce, Plautus (*q.v.*) was a popular playwright when Rome was expanding in the Mediterranean and developing a taste for Hellenic culture. As Greek fashions took firm hold in the second century B.C., particularly in the brilliant circle associated with Scipio Africanus Minor, Terence (*q.v.*) was admired for his polished romantic comedies written after the style of his Greek predecessor Menander.

The first century B.C., an era of debilitating civil wars at home and conquest abroad, when Rome had replaced Athens and Alexandria as the political and intellectual center of the Mediterranean world, boasts very great literary artists. Cicero (*q.v.*) is preeminent as orator, philosopher, and statesman. He translated the eloquence of Demosthenes (*q.v.*) and the logic of Plato (*q.v.*) to Latin letters, which he dominated thereafter. The philosopher Epicurus (*q.v.*) is interpreted by Lucretius (*q.v.*) in his melancholy hexameter poem, *"De Rerum Natura"* ("On the Nature of the Universe"). His metrical skill and beautiful phrases were imitated by Virgil, Horace, and Catullus (*qq.v.*). This last celebrates his loves and his hates in a manner suggestive of the Greek Alexandrian poets, who preferred a personal statement in short, elegant verse to the "swollen" epic. Republican Rome ends with the assassination of Julius Caesar (*q.v.*), himself an intelligent propagandist of his own military acumen in the "Commentaries."

The Augustan or Golden Age of Roman literature (c. 44 B.C. to 17 A.D.) acclaims the political harmony achieved by the Emperor Augustus after almost a century of civil strife. Its brightest light is Virgil whose "Aeneid" immortalized the Roman genius for ruling the world with law, establishing the custom of peace, sparing the conquered, subduing the proud. Virgil's friend Horace sang of Roman virtues, such as moderation and patriotism, with technical virtuosity and self-mocking wit. Also at the emperor's court was Ovid whose clever elegiac treatises on love's vagaries and fantastical *"Metamorphoses"* gently mocked imperial Rome. The elegiac poets, Tibullus and Propertius (*qq.v.*), proclaimed their personal—even idiosyncratic—loves.

Livy's (*q.v.*) anecdotal histories are to prose what Virgil's epic is to poetry in the Augustan epoch. Writing nearly a century later, Tacitus (*q.v.*) never shares Livy's optimism. Rather, his "Annals" emphasize the loss of liberty and the resulting moral weakness caused by the absolutism of empire. His acute and pessimistic analysis is reminiscent of Sallust (*q.v.*), an historian of Cicero's age. And the thread of Tacitus' narrative is taken up again in the fourth century A.D. by Ammianus Marcellinus, who is the last great chronicler of Rome.

Phaedrus (*q.v.*), a Greek freedman attached to Augustus' household, composed beast fables for advice and entertainment. He, the satirist Petronius (*q.v.*), the philosopher Seneca (*q.v.*), and the epic poet Lucan (*q.v.*) all offended imperial dignity with their veiled criticism of despotism, and for that reason were harshly punished. Persius and Juvenal, and Horace before them, developed satire as an original Roman genre. Juvenal was the most incisive of these: he chafed under the tyranny of the Emperor Domitian, and he suffered for speaking the truth. Others in the first century A.D. (known as the Silver Age of Latin literature) chose not to satirize their own era. Quintilian's (*q.v.*) manual of rhetoric is a valuable, wise guide to teaching the art of oratory; Pliny's (*q.v.*) letters offer a fascinating picture of contemporary Roman life and a tactful account of current politics. Suetonius (*q.v.*) looks back in time to the private lives of the Caesars, and Statius (*q.v.*) writes of mythological heroes and wars in epic verse. Martial's (*q.v.*) epigrams can be biting, cruel, and obscene, yet they "spare the sinner but denounce the sin."

Apuleius (*q.v.*), the only Latin novelist, flourished in the second century A.D. His was a time of peace and prosperity, the height of the *pax Romana*, before the collapse of empire. Donatus and Servius, the biographer and the scholiast of Virgil, recall the glories of the Augustan Age. Priscian's grammar became a source book for the Middle Ages; Martianus Capella codified the liberal arts for centuries to come; and Macrobius wrote influential commentaries on Cicero and Virgil.

Christian doctrine rules the literary imagination from the third century onwards to the fall of Rome in the fifth century. Tertullian used his training in Roman rhetoric to champion Christianity and is really the first Latin advocate of the new religion. The most classical of all the early apologists is Lactantius, the Christian Cicero. Later, in the fourth century, Prudentius unified classical poetry with Christian thought in his allegory of the soul which is modeled on Virgil.

The fifth century, dark days for Rome, is illuminated by Christian thinkers. Trained in classical rhetoric, Christian theology, Greek, Hebrew, and with a mastery of Cicero, Virgil, and Horace, St. Jerome made a fresh translation of the scriptures from the original Hebrew and Greek into a literary Latin called the Vulgate, thereby shaping Christian thought and expression for all time. St. Augustine's knowledge of Latin writers and of Neoplatonism deepened his presentation of Christianity in the seminal "Confessions" and "City of God."

After the fall of Rome in the fifth century, Latin continued to be the official language of the West. It survived when Greek was forgotten. Vernacular European authors regarded extant Latin works, especially those of Cicero, Virgil, Horace, and Ovid, as paragons. These models of perfection from antiquity stimulated fertile literary activity just as the Greek masters had for the Romans centuries earlier. Virgil interpreted Homer and Roman history in sublime Latin verse, and, in turn, fed the genius of Dante and Milton, the consummate poets of Christianity. Cicero transmitted a Latinate Plato to the Church Fathers and medieval apologists. These two, and their Greek predecessors, are the pillars of European and American thought and letters.

HISTORY AND CRITICISM

Works treating both Latin and Greek literature are listed at the beginning of the bibliographies in Chapter 7.

Appian. ROMAN HISTORY (c. 150 A.D.). Trans. by H. E. White *Harvard Univ. Press* Loeb 4 vols. $7.00 each. A fascinating, anecdotal account written by a Greek living in Rome at the time of Antoninus Pius.

Beare, William. THE ROMAN STAGE: A Short History of Latin Drama in the Time of the Republic. Rev. by N. G. L. Hammond 3rd ed. 1965 *Harper* Barnes & Noble (Methuen) $9.00

Bury, J. B. A History of the Later Roman Empire: From the Death of Theodosius to the Death of Justinian. 1889. *Dover* 2 vols. 1957 pap. each $4.50. This is the foremost history of the empire in the fourth, fifth and sixth centuries.

Carcopino, Jerome. Daily Life in Ancient Rome: The People and the City at the Height of the Empire. Trans. by E. O. Lorimer; ed. by Henry T. Rowell *Yale Univ. Press* 1940 $15.00 pap. $3.95

Cary, M. and H. H. Scullard. A History of Rome. 2nd ed. Ill. *St. Martin's* 1975 $12.95

D'Alton, John F. Roman Literary Theory and Criticism. 1931. *Russell & Russell* 1962 $12.50. A valuable outline of the literary canons which influenced Roman writers.

Duckworth, George Eckel. Nature of Roman Comedy: A Study in Popular Entertainment. *Princeton Univ. Press* 1952 $17.50 pap. $3.95

Duff, John Wight. A Literary History of Rome: From the Origins to the Close of the Golden Age. Ed. by A. M. Duff. 1928. *Harper* Barnes & Noble 1953 3rd ed. 1960 $8.50 pap. $5.00. A reset edition of a standard work with a supplementary bibliography of writings which have appeared since 1909; includes a preliminary study of the origins, language and character of the Romans and a history of Latin literature from the earliest times to the death of Augustus.

A Literary History of Rome in the Silver Age: Tiberius to Hadrian. Ed. by A. M. Duff. 1927. *Harper* Barnes & Noble 1960 $10.00 3rd ed. 1964 pap. $4.25

Fowler, Warde. The Religious Experience of the Roman People: From the Earliest Times to the Age of Augustus. 1911. *Cooper* 1971 $13.50. Respected and authoritative.

Frank, Tenney. Life and Literature in the Roman Republic. 1930. Sather Classical Lectures *Univ. of California Press* 1957 pap. $2.65

Giannelli, Giulio, Ed. The World of Ancient Rome. *Putnam* 1967 $20.00

An "excellent" discussion (*LJ*) of Roman life by 12 noted classical scholars of Italy, France and England. "Both text and pictures make this book a welcome companion to all studies in the history, language and literature of Rome"—(*LJ*).

Gibbon, Edward. The Decline and Fall of the Roman Empire. 1776–1788. *Dutton* Everyman's 6 vols. each $3.95; *Random* Modern Lib. Giants 3 vols. each $5.95; (and "Other Selected Writings") ed. by Hugh R. Trevor-Roper *Simon and Schuster* (Washington Sq. Press) 3 vols. in 1 pap. $4.95. The classic analysis of Roman history, famous for its incisive observations and impressive prose style.

Grant, Michael. The World of Rome. 1960. *New Am. Lib.* Mentor Bks. pap. $1.25; *Praeger* 1970 $10.00

Graves, Robert. I, Claudius. *Random* Vintage Bks. pap. $1.95. This sympathetic and witty portrait of the Emperor Claudius vividly portrays life at the courts of Augustus, Tiberius, and Claudius.

Hadas, Moses. A History of Latin Literature. 1952. *Columbia* 1964 $11.00 pap. $2.95. The distinguished classical authority who died in 1966 draws upon modern scholarship and newer techniques of analysis and appreciation for his interpretations of the classics.

Hamilton, Edith. The Roman Way. *Norton* 1932 $6.95 pap. $1.25; *Avon* 1973 pap. $1.50

Highet, Gilbert. Poets in a Landscape. *Knopf* 1957 $8.95

Seven Latin poets: Catullus, Virgil, Propertius, Horace, Tibullus, Ovid, and Juvenal. The career and work of each is discussed, with generous quotation. "A delightful book by a scholar in whose mind the ancient world has evidently remained vididly alive"—(*New Yorker*).

Johnston, Mary. Roman Life. *Scott, Foresman* 1957 $13.95. Successor to the author's father's "Private Life of the Romans," long a standard reference work. Much revised and enlarged, with a wealth of illustrative material, this volume is recommended for the general reader. The bibliography is especially comprehensive.

Kennedy, George. THE ART OF RHETORIC IN THE ROMAN WORLD. *Princeton Univ. Press* 1972 $19.50 pap. $9.75. A first-rate study of a subject of central importance in Latin literature.

Löfstedt, Einar. ROMAN LITERARY PORTRAITS: Aspects of the Literature of Roman Empire. Trans. by P. M. Fraser *Oxford* 1958 $6.00

Lück, Georg. LATIN LOVE ELEGY. *Harper* Barnes & Noble 2nd ed. 1969 pap. $4.50. Illuminates the poetry of Catullus, Ovid, Propertius, and Tibullus.

Mackendrick, Paul. THE MUTE STONES SPEAK: The Story of Archaeology in Italy. *St. Martin's* text ed. 1960 $7.50; *New Am. Lib.* Mentor Bks. pap. $1.50

Nash, Ernest. PICTORIAL DICTIONARY OF ANCIENT ROME. *Praeger* 2 vols. 1967–68 each $38.50

   An essential reference work, valuable to classicists, archeologists and informed laymen, this is a systematic pictorial survey of all Roman Buildings and monuments with old etchings, plans, drawings to document the original appearance of destroyed or altered monuments; thorough bibliography.

Plutarch. LIVES. 105–115 A.D. Trans. by John Dryden *Random* Modern Lib. Giants $5.95; *Dutton* Everyman's 4 vols. each $3.95. Wonderfully entertaining biographies of the elite of antiquity written in graceful English prose.

Rose, H. J. A HANDBOOK OF LATIN LITERATURE. *Dutton* 1936 $7.95 pap. $2.45. A brief scholarly guide which is somewhat idiosyncratic.

Rostovtzeff, Mikhail. SOCIAL AND ECONOMIC HISTORY OF THE ROMAN EMPIRE. 1926. Ed. by E. J. Bickerman; trans. by J. D. Duff *Oxford* 1960 pap. $3.50. Authoritative and widely respected.

Rowell, Henry Thompson. ROME IN THE AUGUSTAN AGE. *Univ. of Oklahoma Press* 1962 $3.50 pap. $2.50. Interesting and authoritative material by the Director of the American Academy in Rome; excellent index and bibliography.

Sellar, William Young. THE ROMAN POETS OF THE AUGUSTAN AGE. With a memoir of the author by Andrew Lang. *Biblo & Tannen* 2 vols. Vol. 1 Horace and the Elegiac Poets (1892) Vol. 2 Virgil (3rd ed. 1908) each $12.50

   THE ROMAN POETS OF THE REPUBLIC. 3rd ed. 1889. *Biblo & Tannen* $12.50. Each of Sellar's studies is thorough and learned.

Syme, Ronald. THE ROMAN REVOLUTION. *Oxford* 1939 pap. $7.50. A sophisticated scholar examines the changeover from republic to monarchy after the death of Caesar in convincing and devastating detail.

Wilder, Thornton. THE IDES OF MARCH. *Harper* 1948 $7.95; *Avon* 1975 pap. $1.75; *Grosset* 1956 pap. $2.95. A brilliant fictional portrait of Julius Caesar and the intrigue and passion which involved him with Catullus and Clodia, Cicero, Mark Antony, and Cleopatra.

Wilkinson, L. P. GOLDEN LATIN ARTISTRY. *Cambridge* 1963 $15.00. Analyzes Latin literature of the Golden Age with sensitivity and understanding.

Yourcenar, Marguerite. MEMOIRS OF HADRIAN. Ill. *Farrar, Straus* 1963 $8.95 Noonday pap. $4.50. A memorable portrayal of the Emperor Hadrian, his peaceful and prosperous reign, and his love for the boy Antinous.

See also Chapter 7, Classical Greek Literature, Section on Classical Literature, this Vol.

COLLECTIONS

Copley, Frank O., and Moses Hadas, Trans. ROMAN DRAMA ANTHOLOGY: Plays by Seneca, Terence, and Plautus. *Bobbs* Liberal Arts $6.50 pap. $2.65

Davenport, Basil, Ed. THE PORTABLE ROMAN READER. *Viking* Portable Lib. 1951 $6.50 pap. $2.95

Plautus's "Amphitryon"; Seneca's "Medea"; Terence's "Phormio"; Lucretius' "De Rerum Natura" Bks. 1 and 3; Virgil's "Aeneid" Bks. 2, 3 and 4; Ovid's "Metamorphoses" Bk. 3; selections from lyric poets, historians and philosophers. A competent survey.

Duckworth, George E., Ed. THE COMPLETE ROMAN DRAMA. *Random* Lifetime Lib. 2 vols. 1942 each $10.50 boxed set $20.00. All the extant comedies of Plautus and Terence and the tragedies of Seneca in a variety of translations.

Duff, John W., and A. M. Duff, Trans. and eds. MINOR LATIN POETS. *Harvard Univ. Press* Loeb 1934 $7.00

Grant, Michael, Ed. ROMAN READINGS: Translations from Latin Prose and Poetry. 1957. *Peter Smith* $4.25. Includes selections from Plautus, Ovid, Virgil, Caesar, and Cicero.

Guinagh, Kevin, and Alfred P. Dorjahn, Eds. LATIN LITERATURE IN TRANSLATION. *McKay* 1942 2nd ed. 1952 $7.95

Selections from 28 authors, among them Plautus, Terence, Caesar, Cicero, Catullus, Virgil, Horace, Livy, Ovid, Seneca, Pliny, Tacitus, Juvenal and St. Augustine; some short bibliographies, a map and glossary. The second edition contains additional material.

Harsh, Philip W., Ed. AN ANTHOLOGY OF ROMAN DRAMA. *Holt* 1960 pap. $2.95

Mackail, John W. LATIN LITERATURE. Introd. and revision by Harry C. Schnur. 1895. *Folcroft* $12.50; *Macmillan* Collier Bks. 1962 pap. $1.50; *Ungar* 1966 $7.50. History, criticism and selections.

Rieu, Emil V., Ed. A BOOK OF LATIN POETRY. *St. Martin's* 4th ed. 1953 1961 $3.50. From Ennius to Hadrian.

Wedeck, Harry E., Ed. CLASSICS OF ROMAN LITERATURE. *Littlefield* 1964 pap. $2.95. Annotated, with many new translations.

PLAUTUS, TITUS MACCIUS.   d.c. 184 B.C.

Plautus and Terence founded comedy as we know it today. Each uses stock characters (the young lovers, the clever slave, the irate father) and devices (mistaken identity), but each handles these conventions in his own distinct manner.

Plautus was the son of a poor Umbrian farmer who may have fought in the Second Punic War. The playwright is said to have been a popular actor, a true comedian, jovial, tolerant, rough of humor. He not only modeled his plays on the Greek New Comedy, but unhesitatingly inserted long passages translated from the Greek originals. He was the master of comic irony and, as its originator, copied by Molière, Corneille, Jonson, Dryden and Fielding. Shakespeare's "Comedy of Errors" was based on Plautus's "Menaechmi." Of more than 100 plays, 21 survive.

WORKS. Trans. by Paul Nixon *Harvard Univ. Press* Loeb 5 vols. 1916–38 each $7.00

This is the best translation for most of the plays; Vol. 5 includes selected fragments and index to proper names. Vol 1 Amphitryon; The Comedy of Asses; The Pot of Gold; The Two Bacchises; The Captives. Vol. 2 Casina (c. 185 B.C.); The Casket Comedy (c. 202 B.C.); Curculio; Epidicus; The Two Menaechmuses. Vol. 3 The Merchant; The Braggart Warrior (c. 205 B.C.); The Haunted House; The Persian (after 196 B.C.). Vol. 4 The Little Carthaginian; Pseudolus (191 B.C.); The Rope. Vol. 5 Stichus (200 B.C.); Three Bob Day (194 B.C. or later); Truculentus; The Tale of a Travelling Bag (Fragments).

THREE COMEDIES. Trans. by Erich Segal *Harper* 1969 $10.00

AMPHITRYON AND TWO OTHER PLAYS. Ed. and trans. by Lionel Casson *Norton* Norton Lib. 1971 pap. $1.65

THE MENAECHMI. (And Aristophanes' "The Birds") trans. and ed. by Peter D. Arnott *AHM Pub. Corp.* Crofts Class. pap. $.85; trans. with introd. by Frank O. Copley *Bobbs* Liberal Arts pap. $1.10; (with title "Menaechmi: The Original of Shakespeare's Comedy of Errors") ed. by W. H. D. Rouse the Latin text together with the Elizabethan translation 1912. *Folcroft* 1973 $12.50; (with title "The Menaechmus Twins and Two Other Plays") ed. and trans. by Lionel Casson *Norton* Norton Lib. 1971 pap. $1.95; *Richard West* 1973 $15.00

THE POT OF GOLD. (And Artistophanes' "The Clouds") trans. and ed. by Peter D. Arnott *AHM Pub. Corp.* Crofts Class. pap. $.85; (and "Other Plays") trans. by E. F. Watling *Penguin* pap. $1.45

THE ROPE. Trans. with introd. by Frank O. Copley *Bobbs* Liberal Arts pap. $.65; (and "Other Plays") trans. by E. F. Watling *Penguin* 1964 pap. $1.65

Books about Plautus

Plautus and Terence. By Gilbert Norwood. 1930. Our Debt to Greece and Rome Ser. *Cooper* $3.75

Roman Laughter: The Comedy of Plautus. By Erich Segal. *Harvard Univ. Press* 1968 $6.95; *Harper* Torchbks. 1971 pap. $3.00. A knowledgeable and entertaining presentation of Plautus by a famous classicist and novelist.

TERENCE (Publius Terentius Afer).   c. 190–159 B.C.

Terence was born in Carthage. As a boy, he was the slave of Terentius Lucanus, a Roman senator, who educated him and set him free. He was an intimate friend of the younger Scipio and of the elegant poet, Laelius. They were the gilded youth of Rome and Terence's plays were undoubtedly written for this inner circle, not for the vulgar crowd. They were adapted from Menander (*q.v.*) and other Greek writers of the New Comedy and, in the main, are written seriously on a high literary plane with careful handling of plot and character. The six comedies are all extant. The Liberal Arts translations are in the spirit of the originals—elegant, witty, and lucid.

COMEDIES. Trans. by John Sargeaunt *Harvard Univ. Press* Loeb 2 vols. 1912 each $7.00. Vol. 1 The Lady of Andros (166 B.C.); The Self-Tormentor (163 B.C.); The Eunuch (161 B.C.) Vol. 2 Phormio (161 B.C.); The Mother-in-Law (160 B.C.); The Brothers (160 B.C.).

THE COMEDIES OF TERENCE. Trans. by Frank O. Copley *Bobbs* Liberal Arts 1967 $7.50 pap. $2.50; trans. by Laurence Echard (1670–1730); ed. with fwd. by Robert Graves 1962 *Ungar* 1969 $6.50

THE WOMAN OF ANDROS. Trans. by Frank O. Copley *Bobbs* Liberal Arts 1949 pap. $.65

THE SELF-TORMENTOR. Trans. by Frank O. Copley *Bobbs* Liberal Arts 1963 pap. $1.25

THE EUNUCH. Trans. by Frank O. Copley *Bobbs* Liberal Arts 1963 pap. $.85

PHORMIO. Trans. by Frank O. Copley *Bobbs* Liberal Arts 1958 pap. $.65

THE MOTHER-IN-LAW. Trans. by Frank O. Copley *Bobbs* Liberal Arts 1962 pap. $1.00

THE BROTHERS. Trans. by Frank O. Copley *Bobbs* Liberal Arts 1962 pap. $.65

Books about Terence

The Art of Terence. By Gilbert Norwood. 1923. *Russell & Russell* 1965 $7.50
Plautus and Terence. By Gilbert Norwood. 1930. Our Debt to Greece and Rome Ser. *Cooper* $3.75

CICERO or TULLY (Marcus Tullius Cicero).   106 B.C.–43 B.C.

Cicero is Rome's great prose stylist. Of his speeches, 58 are extant, as well as about 900 of his letters, many political and philosophical writings, and rhetorical treatises. As a youth he studied law, oratory, Greek literature and philosophy. He became consul in 63 B.C., uncovered the conspiracy of Catiline and aroused the people by his famous "Orations Against Catiline." His political career was a long, stormy and often inconsistent one. When out of favor or banished he devoted himself to literary composition, wrote his many revealing letters and such well-known essays as those "On Friendship," "On Duties," "On Old Age," which together with the "Tusculans" and the "Dream of Scipio" have deeply influenced European thought and literature.

During the civil war he sided with Pompey, but after Pompey's decisive defeat at the battle of Pharsalus in 48 B.C., Cicero became reconciled with Caesar. After Caesar's assassination, Cicero attacked Antony in his "Philippics." When the Second Triumvirate was established, Antony demanded the head of his enemy. Cicero escaped but was overtaken by soldiers. He died courageously; at Antony's command, his head and hands were displayed over the orators' rostra in Rome.

The Loeb edition of the "Complete Works" is excellent. The Everyman's volume containing the early (1699) translation of "The Offices" by T. C. Cockman and W. Melmoth's translation of the "Essays" and "Select Letters" (1753–1777) is still considered "a good piece of work." Cicero is one of the subjects of Plutarch's "Lives" (*Dutton* Everyman's 3 vols. each $3.95).

WORKS. Various translators *Harvard Univ. Press* Loeb 28 vols. 1912–1958 each $7.00

SELECTED WORKS. Trans. with introd. by Michael Grant *Penguin* 1960 pap. $1.45. Includes: Against Verres, 23 Letters, 2nd Philippic Against Anthony, On Duties, On Old Age.

SELECTIONS. Trans. by Joseph Pearl *Barron's* 1967 $5.50 pap. $1.25. Orations, philosophical writings and letters.

MURDER TRIALS. Trans. by Michael Grant *Penguin* pap. $1.95

THE OFFICES (*De Officiis, c.* 43 B.C.); LAELIUS, AN ESSAY ON FRIENDSHIP (*De Amicitia, c.* 44
B.C.); CATO, AN ESSAY ON OLD AGE (*De Senectute, c.* 44 B.C.) and SELECT LETTERS.
Offices trans. by Thomas Cockman; Essays and Letters by W. Melmoth *Dutton.*
Everyman's 1909 reprinted 1937–1953 introd. by John Warrington 1955 $3.95

ON OLD AGE and ON FRIENDSHIP. *Bobbs* Liberal Arts pap. $1.25; trans. with introd. by
Frank O. Copley *Univ. of Michigan Press* 1967 $4.95 Ann Arbor Bks. pap. $1.95

CICERO ON ORATORY AND ORATORS. (55 B.C.) Trans. by J. S. Watson *Southern Illinois
Univ. Press* 1970 $8.50

ON THE COMMONWEALTH (C. 51 B.C.) Trans. by G. H. Sabine and S. B. Smith 1929.
Bobbs 1959 $5.00 Liberal Arts pap. $1.75

ON THE NATURE OF THE GODS. (46 B.C.) Trans. by Horace C. P. McGregor *Penguin* 1972
pap. $2.25

CICERO'S BRUTUS, or History of Famous Orators. (46 B.C.) Trans. by Ernest Jones.
1776. Augustan Translators Ser. *AMS Press* $22.50

THE BEST OF LIFE. (44 B.C.) A translation of "*De Senectute*" by Georgia W. Dingus. *Naylor*
1968 $4.95

DE OFFICIIS. (43 B.C.) Trans. by Harry G. Edinger *Bobbs* 1970 $7.50 pap. $2.95

LETTERS OF CICERO: A Selection in Translation. Trans. and ed. by L. P. Wilkinson *Norton* Norton Lib. 1968 pap. $1.95; *Hillary House* (Hutchinson Univ. Lib.) 1966 $5.50

Books about Cicero

Cicero and the Fall of the Roman Republic. By J. L. Strachan-Davidson. 1894. Select Bibliogra-
phies Reprint Ser. *Bks. for Libraries* 1972 $19.75
CICERO AND HIS FRIENDS: A Study of Roman Society in the Time of Caesar. By Gaston Boissier.
1897. Trans. by A. D. Jones *Cooper* 1970 $10.00. Well-known and respected.
Cicero of Arpinum: A Political and Literary Biography. By E. G. Sihler. 1914. *Cooper* 1969
$15.00
Cicero: A Biography. By Torsten Petersson. 1920. *Biblo & Tannen* $12.50
Cicero and His Influence. By John C. Rolfe. 1923. *Cooper* $3.75
Cicero: The Secrets of His Correspondence. By J. Carcopino. Trans. by E. O. Lorimer *Greenwood*
2 vols. 1951 set $18.00. An influential study which is recommended.
Cicero and the Roman Republic. By F. F. Cowell. *Penguin* Pelican Bks. 1956 rev. ed. 1973 pap.
$1.95; *Peter Smith* $4.25
Cicero. Ed. by T. A. Dorey. *Basic Bks.* 1965 $5.95. Seven scholars evaluate Cicero "in the light of
modern literary and historical criticism."
Cicero the Statesman. By R. E. Smith. *Cambridge* 1966 $13.50
Cicero: A Political Biography. By David Stockton. *Oxford* 1971 $12.00
Cicero. By D. R. Shackleton Bailey. *Scribner* 1973 $10.00 pap. $3.50

CAESAR, GAIUS JULIUS.   100 B.C.–44 B.C. *See Chapter 9, History, Government and Politics, Section on Ancient Roman Historians*, Reader's Adviser, *Vol. 3.*

LUCRETIUS (Titus Lucretius Carus).   c. 94 or 99 B.C.–c. 55 B.C.

Almost nothing is known of Lucretius' life but legends have attached themselves to him. Donatus says that Virgil (*q.v.*) assumed the toga of manhood the very day Lucretius died (that is,
October 15, 55 B.C.); and Jerome states that the poet was poisoned by a love potion, wrote his "*De
Rerum Natura*" at lucid intervals, and then committed suicide. He may have been one of the Lucre-
tii, an aristocratic Roman family, or a native of Campania who studied Epicureanism at Naples. It
is certain, however, that he was a friend or dependent of C. Memmius (who was also the patron of
Catullus) to whom the poem is dedicated.

The "*De Rerum Natura*" ("On the Nature of the Universe"), Lucretius' only work, is written in six
books and expounds the philosophy of Epicurus (*q.v.*). Because the universe and all things in it are
made up of atoms swirling about in different combinations, the human soul perishes with the
body. Lucretius is intent on proving this so that he might persuade his audience to give up their
fear of death and of punishment in the afterlife and their superstitious belief in divine inter-

vention. His logical exposition of the mechanical nature of the universe shows intensity of thought and feeling and is expressed in beautiful, vivid images. His lovely invocation to Venus in Book I and his bitter denunciation of women and the passion of love in Book IV are famous and their influence enduring.

ON THE NATURE OF THINGS. (With title "On Nature") trans. by Russel M. Geer *Bobbs* 1965 $6.50 pap. $3.00; trans. by William Ellery Leonard *Dutton* pap. $1.35; trans. by W. H. D. Rouse *Harvard Univ. Press* Loeb 1924 $7.00. The translations of Leonard (in verse) and of Rouse (in prose) are both recommended.

THE NATURE OF THE UNIVERSE. Trans. by Ronald E. Latham *Penguin* pap. $2.50; trans. by James H. Mantinband *Ungar* pap. $2.95

LUCRETIUS: The Way Things Are. *Indiana Univ. Press* 1969 $8.95 pap. $1.95. A translation of "On Nature" in English blank verse by Rolfe Humphries.

Books about Lucretius

Lucretius. By W. H. Mallock. 1878. *Richard West* $15.00
Three Philosophical Poets. By George Santayana. 1910. *Cooper* 1971 $6.75
Lucretius and His Influence. By George D. Hadzsits. 1930. Our Debt to Greece and Rome Ser. *Cooper* 1963 $3.95. Valuable for its careful presentation of Lucretius' later influence.
Lucretius, Poet and Philosopher. By Edward E. Sikes. 1936. *Russell & Russell* 1971 $12.00. An important critical study of the poet.
Lucretius. *De Rerum Natura.* Ed. by Cyril Bailey. *Oxford* 3 vols. 1947 $41.00. Vol. 1 is a superb introduction to the poet—his life, philosophy, and poetic technique; vols. 2 and 3 are the Latin text with commentary. The complete set is a model of scholarship.
Epicurus and His Philosophy. Norman W. De Witt. 1954. *Greenwood* 1973 $17.25. Clarifies Lucretius' relationship to Epicurus.
Epicurus and His Gods. André M. Festugière. Trans. by C. W. Chilton. 1955. *Russell and Russell* 1969 $7.50. A basic analysis of the Greek philosopher and Lucretius' indebtedness to him.
Imagery and Poetry of Lucretius. By David West. *Aldine* 1969 $7.95
The Lyre of Science: Form and Meaning in Lucretius' *De Rerum Natura.* By Richard Minadeo. *Wayne State Univ. Press* 1969 $9.95

CATULLUS (Gaius Valerius Catullus).   84? B.C.–54? B.C.

Catullus was born in Verona of a wealthy family, but spent much of his short life in Rome. He moved in fashionable society there and was captivated by a woman he calls Lesbia, who has been identified as Clodia, a notorious aristocrat. His 25 poems to her tell the story of his tormented love. These together with his other verse—occasional, satiric, epic-like, and epigrammatic—have been widely imitated. The Latin poets, Horace, Virgil, Propertius, and Martial, were all indebted to him and he has been translated into English by such eminent poets as Campion, Jonson, Byron, and Tennyson (*see Duckett below*). By his successors he was called *doctus* (learned) because of his ideal of technical perfection, development of new literary forms (miniature epic, elegy, and epigram), and erudition.

To date the best commentary on the poems is that of R. Ellis (1889, 2nd ed., now o.p.); Horace Gregory's translation of Catullus (*see entry below*) conveys the direct appeal of the originals.

THE POEMS OF GAIUS VALERIUS CATULLUS IN ENGLISH VERSE. Trans. by John Knott. 1795. Augustan Translators Ser. *AMS Press* 2 vols. each $15.00 set $29.50. With the Latin text revised, and classical notes; prefixed are engravings of Catullus and his friend Cornelius Nepos.

WORKS OF CATULLUS AND TIBULLUS with Pervigilium Veneris. Catullus trans. by F. W. Cornish *Harvard Univ. Press* Loeb 1913, 1935 rev. reprinted 1939 $7.00

THE COLLECTED POEMS. Trans. by Jack Lindsay. 1956. *Norton* Norton Lib. 1972

POEMS. Trans. by Horace Gregory. 1956. *Norton* Norton Lib. 1972 pap. $1.95; trans. with introd. by Peter Whigham *Penguin* bilingual ed. pap. $1.95; (with title "Poetry") ed. by James Michie *Random* $7.95 Vintage Bks. pap. $1.95; trans. with introd. by P. Whigham *Univ. of California Press* 1969 $8.95

CATULLUS: The Complete Poetry. A new trans. with introd. and notes by Frank O. Copley *Univ. of Michigan Press* 1957 Ann Arbor Bks. 1964 pap. $1.95
Without the Latin. A "superior" translation—(*LJ*).

ODI ET AMO: The Complete Poetry of Catullus. Trans. with introd. by Roy Arthur Swanson *Bobbs* Liberal Arts 1959 $5.00 pap. $2.00

CARMINA. A verse trans. by Barriss Mills; ill. by Iola J. Mills *Purdue Univ. Studies* 1965 $4.95

"A rendition that is as attractive as it is basically unambitious—which is meant as a compliment"—(*LJ*).

POETRY. Trans. by the English poet, C. H. Sisson, with the complete Latin text *Grossman* Orion Press 1967 $6.00; *Viking* Compass Bks. 1969 pap. $1.85

Includes the Poems to Lesbia, the Hymn to Attis, his epigrams and elegies. "Every generation should read Catullus in a translation suitable to the period, so I hope Sisson's will spread far and wide"—(Cyril Connolly).

Books about Catullus

Catullus in English Poetry. Ed. by Eleanor S. Duckett. 1925. *Russell & Russell* 1972 $13.00; *Richard West* $12.95. A careful compilation of English poems which imitate Catullus, this includes some of the most beautiful of English lyrics.

Catullus and Horace: Two Poets in Their Environment. By Tenney Frank. 1928. *Russell & Russell* 1965 $9.50. A learned and sympathetic portrait of Catullus.

Catullus and His Influence. By Karl P. Harrington. 1930. Out Debt to Greece and Rome Ser. *Cooper* $3.50

The Lyric Genius of Catullus. By Eric Alfred Havelock. 1939. *Russell & Russell* 1967 $12.00. A penetrating critical analysis which includes the Latin text of the poems with free translations by the author; bibliography.

Catullus in Strange and Distant Britain. By James A. McPeek. 1939. *Russell & Russell* 1972 $20.00

Catullus, Poems: A Commentary. By Kenneth Quinn. *St. Martin's* 1970 $8.95. Quinn examines the literary, political and social aspects of the poems with passionate interest. All of his studies are good reading.

Catullan Questions. By T. P. Wiseman. *Humanities Press* 1970 pap. $3.50

Approaches to Catullus. Ed. by Kenneth Quinn. Views & Controversies About Classical Antiquity Ser. *Harper* Barnes & Noble 1972 $10.95

Catullus: An Interpretation. By Kenneth Quinn. *Harper* Barnes & Noble 1973 $12.75

VIRGIL or VERGIL (Publius Vergilius Maro). 70 B.C.–19 B.C.

The reign of Augustus, grandnephew of Julius Caesar, who became the first Roman emperor (27 B.C.–14 A.D.), marked the Golden Age of Latin literature. "The writers of the time were moved to celebrate the greatness of Rome, past, present, and to come. The great monument is, of course, Virgil's 'Aeneid,' which links the foundation of Rome to the fall of Troy, traces the ancestry of Julius Caesar to the gods, and makes the greatness of Rome the subject of divine intervention and prophecy"—(Basil Davenport).

Virgil was given a good education by his father, a prosperous farmer living near Mantua. After his studies at Rome and Naples, Virgil completed in 37 B.C. his "Eclogues" or "Bucolics" which idealize rural life and are modeled on his Greek predecessor Theocritus (*q.v.*). At that time Maecenas, a trusted counselor of Augustus, became the poet's patron and was introduced by him to Horace (*q.v.*). The "Georgics," a didactic, realistic treatise on farming in the manner of the Greek poet Hesiod (*q.v.*) and honoring Maecenas, followed the "Bucolics"; and then Virgil devoted the rest of his life to the "Aeneid." This epic poem, derived from Homer's "Iliad" and "Odyssey" and drawing on much of Greek and earlier Latin literature, reveals the greatness of the Roman empire and is written with perfection of technique and tenderness and melancholy of mood. Virgil considered it still in need of polishing and revision at the time of his death and asked his executor to destroy the manuscript, but this order was rescinded by Augustus. Virgil died at Brindisi, and was buried at Naples where his tomb was revered thereafter—St. Paul is said to have wept over it. Master Virgil came to be regarded as a magician and as a prophet of Christianity. And his poetry, particularly the "Aeneid," is a dominant influence on later European literature. He is Dante's (*q.v.*) guide through Hell in the "Divine Comedy"; and in English letters, Chaucer, Surrey, Spenser, Milton, Dryden, Pope, and Tennyson (*qq.v.*) venerate him.

WORKS. Trans. by Henry Rushton Fairclough Vol. 1 Eclogues, Georgics, Aeneid 1–6 Vol. 2 Aeneid 7–12, Minor Poems. *Harvard Univ. Press* Loeb 1916–18 new rev. ed. 2 vols. 1935 each $7.00

THE AENEID (c. 29–19 B.C.); ECLOGUES (c. 40–37 B.C.); GEORGICS (c. 37–29 B.C.). Trans. by John William Mackail *Random* Modern Lib. 1934 pap. $1.95

THE ECLOGUES (or BUCOLICS, 42–37 B.C.) and GEORGICS. Trans. by C. Day Lewis *Doubleday* Anchor Bks. 1964 pap. $1.25; trans. by Thomas Fletcher Royds *Dutton* Everyman's 1924 $3.95

THE PASTORAL POEMS. Trans. by E. V. Rieu *Penguin* 1968 pap. $1.25. Contains the Latin text and the translation. Faithful to the literal sense of the original.

THE GEORGICS (30 B.C.). *Doubleday* Anchor Bks. and *Dutton* Everyman's (*see "The Ecologues" above*); trans. by Smith Palmer Bovie *Univ. of Chicago Press* 1956 $5.00 Phoenix Bks. pap. $1.75. Bovie's translation reads well.

THE AENEID. Trans. into Scottish verse by Gavin Douglas (1512–1513, printed 1553), ed. by George Dundas. 1839. *AMS Press* 2 vols. set $45.00; *Johnson Reprint* $45.00; trans. by Edward Fairfax Taylor, ed. by Edward Morgan Forster. 1906. *AMS Press* $18.50; trans. by John Dryden *Assoc. Booksellers* Airmont Bks. pap. $.75; trans. by Allen Mandelbaum *Bantam* pap. $1.25; trans. by Frank O. Copley *Bobbs* Liberal Arts 1965 $6.50 pap. $2.25; trans. by C. Day Lewis *Doubleday* Anchor Bks. 1953 pap. $2.50; trans. into English verse by Michael Oakley *Dutton* Everyman's 1957 $3.95; trans. by John Dryden, ed. by R. Fitzgerald *Macmillan* 1965 $7.95 Collier Bks. pap. $2.45; trans. by Patric Dickinson *New Am. Lib.* Mentor Bks. 1961 pap. $.95; trans. by W. F. Jackson Knight *Penguin* 1956 pap. $1.45; trans. into verse and ed. by Rolfe Humphries *Scribner* 1950 $7.95 pap. $2.95; trans. with introd. by James H. Mantinband *Ungar* 1964 $6.50 pap. $3.25; trans. by Allen Mandelbaum *Univ. of California Press* 1971 $10.00; trans. into prose by John Conington (1872) *Simon & Schuster* (Washington Square) pap. $.95. The translations by Gavin Douglas and John Dryden are classic renderings by influential British poets. Mackail's version is written in graceful English prose. Jackson Knight is faithful to the literal sense of the original. That of Humphries is a modern poetic interpretation.

Books about Virgil

Vergil; A Biography. By Tenney Frank. 1922. *Russell & Russell* 1965 $7.50
Harvard Lectures on the Vergilian Age. By Robert S. Conway. 1928. *Biblo & Tannen* $7.50
Virgil and Spenser. By Merritt Y. Hughes. 1929. *AMS Press* $7.00; *Folcroft* $6.95; *Kennikat* 1969 $8.25
Virgil and His Meaning to the World of Today. By J. W. Mackail. 1930. Our Debt to Greece and Rome Ser. *Cooper* $3.75
Comparative Study of the Beowulf and the Aeneid. By Tom B. Haber. 1931. *Phaeton Press* (dist. by Gordian) 1968 $6.50; *Richard West* 1973 $6.45
Virgil in English Poetry. By George Gordon. 1931. *Folcroft* $5.50
Virgil, Father of the West. By Theodor Haecker. 1934. *Folcroft* $10.00
An Introduction to Virgil's Aeneid. By J. W. Mackail. 1946. *Richard West* $10.00. Highly recommended.
Virgil's Mind at Work. By Robert W. Cruttwell. 1947. *Cooper* $6.00; *Greenwood* 1971 $8.75
The Art of Virgil: Image and Symbol in the Aeneid. By Viktor Poeschl. Trans. from German by Gerda Seligson *Univ. of Michigan Press* 1962 $5.95 Ann Arbor Bks. 1970 pap. $2.25. A profound analysis of the unity of the "Aeneid."
Virgil: A Study in Civilized Poetry. By Brooks Otis. *Oxford* 1964 $11.00. Readable and comprehensive.
Poetry of the Aeneid: Four Studies in Imaginative Unity and Design. By Michael C. Putnam. *Harvard Univ. Press* 1965 $7.00
Virgil: A Collection of Critical Essays. Ed. by Steele Commager. *Prentice-Hall* 1966 $5.95 Spectrum Bks. pap. $1.95. Various approaches to Virgil which are provocative and well written.
Virgil: Epic and Anthropology. By W. F. Knight; ed. by J. D. Christie. *Fernhill* $9.50
Virgil's Aeneid: A Critical Description. By Kenneth Quinn. *Univ. of Michigan Press* 1968 $9.75
Introduction to Virgil's Aeneid. By W. A. Camps. *Oxford* 1969 $4.25
Virgil's Pastoral Art: Studies in the Eclogues. By Michael C. Putnam. *Princeton Univ. Press* 1970 $14.50
The Speeches in Vergil's Aeneid. By Gilbert Highet. *Princeton Univ. Press* 1972 $14.50. A thorough, illuminating, always interesting study of a subject of central importance for the poem and for Latin literature in general.

HORACE (Quintus Horatius Flaccus). 65 B.C.–8 B.C.

Horace's father was an ambitious "freedman of modest circumstances," who gave his son the best available education. While a student in Athens, Horace met Brutus and fought in the battle of Philippi. After that defeat he returned to Italy to find his farm confiscated, became a clerk in the civil service, and started writing. Through Virgil (q.v.) he met Maecenas, the great patron of literature, who gave him the Sabine farm which Horace celebrated in his poetry. His circumstances improved as his friendship with Maecenas and the Emperor Augustus grew, and the sarcasm and occasional obscenity of the "Epodes" and "Satires" gave way to the more genial and mellow mood of the "Odes" and "Epistles." He is acknowledged as one of Rome's greatest poets because of his perfection of verse technique, his candid self-portraiture, urbane wit, sincere patriotism, and sensible commendation of the golden mean. He makes the Rome of his day come alive in street scenes, private banquets, love affairs, country weekends, and in personalities great and small, rich and poor. The literary canons set forth in his *"Ars Poetica"* dominated literary criticism throughout the Middle Ages and into the eighteenth century. His impeccable and very quotable use of language has been widely admired, and his influence on English letters extensive. Poetic translations of Horace into English include those by Jonson, Dryden, Milton, Congreve, and Pope (qq.v.). The prose translation in the Loeb is recommended; Fraenkel's and Wilkinson's commentaries (*see below*) are basic; Commager's study is enthusiastic. Of Helen Rowe Henze's English version in Horace's original meters, *Library Journal* said: "The translation is both authentic and, considering the difficulty and strictures of her method, unforced." Of the James Michie "Odes" the same journal commented: "Michie, a published British poet with Oxford degrees in Classics and English, attempts much and, surprisingly, is nearly always successful."

WORKS. Trans. into English prose by David Watson. New ed. rev. and corrected by W. Crakelt. 1792. Augustan Translators Ser. *AMS Press* 2 vols. each $21.50 set $40.00; (with title "Poems of Horace") paraphrased by several hands, ed. and largely trans. by Alexander Brome. 1666. Augustan Translators Ser. *AMS Press* $21.50

COLLECTED WORKS. Trans. by Lord Dunsany and Michael Oakley *Dutton* Everyman's 1961 $3.95; (with title "Horace for English Readers") trans. by E. C. Wickham. 1903. *Richard West* $20.00

SATIRES, EPISTLES, and ARS POETICA. Trans. by H. Rushton Fairclough *Harvard Univ. Press* Loeb 1926 rev. ed. 1929 $7.00. A standard translation; faithful to the original.

SATIRES (35–30 B.C.) and EPISTLES (20–13 B.C.). Trans. with introd. and notes by Smith Palmer Bovie *Univ. of Chicago Press* 1959 $8.50 Phoenix Bks. pap. $2.95

"Documented and based on a sound text, thorough scholarship, and poetic sensitivity"—(*LJ*).

HORACE TALKS: The Satires. Trans. by Henry H. Chamberlain. 1940. *Bks. for Libraries* $9.00

"All the elements of Horace's art, both in its spirit and in its form, come to life again in Chamberlain's translation"—(E. K. Rand, in the Preface).

THE SATIRES OF HORACE AND PERSIUS. Trans. by Niall Rudd Classics Ser. *Penguin* 1974 pap. $2.45

ODES (23–13 B.C.) and EPODES (30 B.C.). Trans. by John Marshall. 1907. *AMS Press* $15.00; trans. by C. E. Bennett *Harvard Univ. Press* Loeb 1914 rev. ed. 1927 $7.00; trans. by Joseph P. Clancy *Univ. of Chicago Press* Phoenix Bks. 1960 pap. $2.95; (with title "Selected Odes") trans. by Skuli Johnson *Univ. of Toronto Press* 1952 $3.50

THE ODES OF HORACE: 103 Horatian Odes Newly Translated from the Latin and Rendered into the Original Metres. Trans. by Helen Rowe Henze *Univ. of Oklahoma Press* 1961 $5.95

THE ODES OF HORACE. Trans. by James Michie; introd. by Rex Warner *Grossman* Orion Press 1963 (bilingual) $6.00; *Simon & Schuster* (Washington Square) pap. $.90

ODES AND THE CENTENNIAL HYMN (17 B.C.). Trans. by James Michie *Bobbs* Liberal Arts 1965 pap. $2.25

AD PYRRHAM. Assembled with introd. by Ronald Storrs *Oxford* 1959 $4.00. A polyglot collection of translations of Horace's ode to Pyrrha (Bk. 1, Ode 5). Some 144 translations; among the translators are Milton, Gladstone, Lord Norwich Simon, Hood, and others.

ARS POETICA (13–8 B.C.). Trans. by Burton Raffel and James Hynde *State Univ. of New York Press* (bilingual ed.) 1974 $6.00 pap. $1.95. A fast-moving and colloquial translation; (with title "Epistola ad Pisones, De Arte Poetica, The Art of Poetry, An Epistle to the Pisos") trans. with notes by George Colman. 1783. Augustan Translators Ser. *AMS Press* $20.00; (with title "Horace His Arte of Poetrie, Pistles and Satyrs") trans. by Thomas Drant 1567; with an introd. by Peter E. Medine *Scholars' Facsimiles* 1972 $15.00

"An important example of Renaissance efforts to adapt a pagan form to Christian goals"— (Publisher's catalog).

Books about Horace

Studies Literary and Historical in the Odes of Horace. By A. W. Verrall. 1884. *Kennikat* 1969 $8.00

The Influence of Horace on the Chief English Poets of the Nineteenth Century. By Mary R. Thayer. 1916. *Russell & Russell* 1967 $5.75

Catullus and Horace: Two Poets in Their Environment. By Tenney Frank. 1928. *Russell & Russell* 1965 $9.50. A vivid and sensitive portrait of the two poets.

Horace and His Influence. By Grant Showerman. 1930. Our Debt to Greece and Rome Ser. *Cooper* $3.75. A careful and detailed study.

Horace: A Biography. By Henry D. Sedgwick. 1947. *Russell & Russell* $7.50

Horace. By Eduard Fraenkel. *Oxford* 1957 $14.50 pap. $4.50. This is a basic and comprehensive work by a first-rate scholar; any serious student of Horace must consult it.

The Odes of Horace: A Critical Study. By Steele Commager. *Yale Univ. Press* 1962 $17.50; *Indiana Univ. Press* 1967 pap. $2.95.

"This is good modern criticism, finely calibrated to a classical writer and sustained by firm and conscientious, if somewhat showy, scholarship. . . . The great, compelling virtue of Commager's study is that it restores to Horace the features of a man; that in place of the silly, moralizing, Sabine Micawber of philology, it gives us at last a credibly complex picture of a great poet"—*(N.Y. Times)*.

Horace. By Kenneth J. Reckford. World Authors Ser. *Twayne* $6.95

Horace. By Jacques Perret; trans. from the French by Bertha Humez; fwd. by Jotham Johnson *New York Univ. Press* 1964 $7.50 Gotham Lib. pap. $1.95

Mr. Perret is a professor of Latin at the Sorbonne. His "analysis is fresh, wise, perceptive, with excellent insights. . . . The lover of Horace will like this eye-opener; the newcomer will find it a handsome introduction to the poet"—*(LJ)*.

Satires of Horace. By W. J. Rudd. *Cambridge* 1966 $14.50

Horace and His Lyric Poetry. By L. P. Wilkinson. *Cambridge* 1968 $8.50 pap. $2.95. This sensitive and scholarly study is highly recommended.

Sound and Image in the Odes of Horace. By M. Owen Lee. *Univ. of Michigan Press* 1969 $4.95

Horace. By C. D. Costa. Greek & Latin Studies *Routledge & Kegan Paul* 1973 $10.00

LIVY (Titus Livius). 59 B.C.–17 A.D. *See Chapter 9, History, Government and Politics, Reader's Adviser, Vol. 3.*

PROPERTIUS (SEXTUS). c. 50 B.C.–c. 16 B.C.

Propertius was deprived of his Umbrian estate in the confiscations of the Civil War. He applied his rhetorical education not to the courts, but to poetry. His first book of elegies to "Cynthia" won him the patronage of Maecenas and established his reputation as a passionate, witty, self-absorbed, and learned poet. The three books which followed invoke Cynthia, but carry as well tributes to Maecenas, to Roman greatness, addresses to friends, and antiquarian fragments.

Butler's translation in the Loeb is faithful and Carrier's imaginative. Gilbert Highet's essay on Propertius in "Poets in a Landscape" (*see general Latin list*) is sympathetic and original.

PROPERTIUS. Trans. by H. E. Butler *Harvard Univ. Press* Loeb 1912 $7.00. A careful, scholarly translation.

POEMS. Trans. by Constance Carrier; introd., notes and glossary by Smith Palmer Bovie *Univ. of Indiana* Midland Bks. 1963 pap. $1.95; *Peter Smith* $4.50; trans. by J. P. McCulloch *Univ. of California Press* (bilingual ed.) 1972 $15.00 pap. $3.45

POEMS. Trans. by A. E. Watts *Branden* 1967 $7.50; *Saifer* $7.50

TIBULLUS (ALBIUS). 48 B.C.?–19 B.C.

Tibullus became the poet laureate of the republican literary circle which had as its leader Messalla Corvinus. The chief inspirations of his elegies were his sentimental longing for rustic simplicity and his amorous longing for two women (whom he called Delia and Nemesis) and a boy (Marathus). Tibullus contributed refinement of form and simplicity of language to Roman elegy. (*See Gilbert Highet's illuminating comments on Tibullus in "Poets in a Landscape" listed in the general Latin list.*)

WORKS OF CATULLUS AND TIBULLUS WITH PERVIGILIUM VENERIS. Tibullus trans. by J. P. Postgate *Harvard Univ. Press* Loeb 1913 rev. ed. 1939 $7.00

POEMS. Trans. by Constance Carrier; introd., notes and glossary by Edward M. Michael *Indiana Univ. Press* 1968 $6.50 Midland Bks. pap. $1.95

Books about Tibullus

A Critical Concordance of the Tibullan Corpus. By Edward N. O'Neil. *Am. Philological Assn.* (dist. by Press of Case Western) 1963 $10.00

Tibullus: A Commentary. By Michael C. Putnam. *Univ. of Oklahoma Press* 1973 $4.95. Includes the latest scholarship on the poet; the work of a versatile scholar.

OVID (Publius Ovidius Naso).   43 B.C.–17 A.D.

Born of an equestrian family in Sulmo, Ovid was educated in rhetoric at Rome but gave it up for poetry. He counted Horace and Propertius (*qq.v.*) among his friends and wrote an elegy on the death of Tibullus (*q.v.*). He became the leading poet of Rome but was banished in 8 A.D. by an edict of Augustus to the remote Tomis on the Black Sea because of a poem and an indiscretion. Miserable in provincial exile, he died there ten years later.

His brilliant, witty, fertile elegiac poems include the *"Amores"* ("Loves"), *"Heroides"* ("Heroines"), *"Ars Amatoria"* ("Art of Loving"), but he is perhaps best known for the "Metamorphoses," a marvelously imaginative compendium of Greek mythology where every story alludes to a change in shape. Ovid was admired and imitated throughout the Middle Ages and Renaissance; Chaucer, Spenser, Shakespeare, and Jonson knew him well. His mastery of form, gift for narration, and amusing urbanity are irresistible.

Good translations of the "Metamorphoses" include Golding's (which Shakespeare used), and those by the modern poets, Rolfe Humphries, and Horace Gregory (*see below*).

SELECTED WORKS. Ed. with introd. by J. C. and M. J. Thornton; trans. by Christopher Marlowe and others *Dutton* Everyman's 1939 $2.25

AMORES (c. 3 B.C.). Trans. by Guy Lee *Viking* 1968 $5.75 Compass Bks. pap. $1.65

HEROIDES (c. 5 B.C.–8 A.D.) AND AMORES. Trans. by Grant Showerman *Harvard Univ. Press* Loeb 1914 1921 1931 1947 $5.50

THE ART OF LOVE (c. 1 B.C.). Trans. by J. Dryden and others. 1712. Tudor Trans. Ser. *AMS Press* $24.50; trans. by Jack Shapiro *Borden* pap. $2.00; trans. by J. H. Mozley *Harvard Univ. Press* Loeb 1929 rev. 1939 $7.00; trans. by Rolfe Humphries *Indiana Univ. Press* Midland Bks. 1958 pap. $1.95; trans. by Jack Shapiro *Laurida* 1967 $4.95 pap. $2.00; trans. by Charles D. Young (with "Elegies" trans. by Christopher Marlowe) *Liveright* 1931 $6.95; trans. by Henry T. Riley *Stravon* 1949 $2.00

METAMORPHOSES, or Stories of Changing Forms (c. 2 A.D.). Trans. by John Dryden and others. 1717. Tudor Translators Ser. *AMS Press* $49.50; trans. by F. J. Miller *Harvard Univ. Press* Loeb 1916 2nd ed. 1921 2 vols. each $7.00; trans. into modern verse by Rolfe Humphries *Indiana Univ. Press* 1955 $7.50 Midland Bks. 1957 pap. $2.95; trans. by Arthur Golding, ed. by J. F. Nims *Macmillan* 1965 Collier Bks. 1968 pap. $2.95; trans. by Horace Gregory *New Am. Lib.* Mentor Bks. (orig.) 1960 pap. $1.50; trans. by Mary Innes *Penguin* (orig.) 1955 pap. $1.75; trans. by Arthur Golding, ed. by W. H. Rouse *Southern Illinois Univ. Press* 1962 $19.50; trans. by Horace Gregory with decorations by Zhenya Gay *Viking* 1958 $7.50

METAMORPHOSES. Trans. in blank verse by Brookes More (sold only with corresponding vol. of Wilmon Brewer's "Ovid's Metamorphoses in European Culture.") 3 units of 2 vols. *Marshall Jones* Vol. 1 Bks. I–V 1933 Vol. 2 Bks. VI–X 1941 Vol. 3 XI–XV 1956 each unit $1.50

THE FASTI (c. 8 A.D.). Trans. by Sir James George Frazer *Harvard Univ. Press* Loeb 1931 $7.00

TRISTIA (c. 9–12 A.D.) and EX PONTO (c. 13–17 A.D.). Trans. by Arthur Leslie Wheeler *Harvard Univ. Press* Loeb 1914 1921 1931 1947 $7.00

Books about Ovid

Ovid. By E. K. Rand. 1930. Our Debt to Greece and Rome Ser. *Cooper* $3.75. This is indispensable for understanding Ovid's poetry and his influence on later European literature.

Ovid's Metamorphoses in European Culture. By Wilmon Brewer. Sold only with Brookes More's translation of the "Metamorphoses."

Ovid: A Poet between Two Worlds. By Hermann Frankel. 1945 Sather Classical Lectures & California Library Reprint Ser. *Univ. of California Press* 1969 $9.50. An excellent study by a mature scholar.

Ovid Surveyed. By L. P. Wilkinson. *Cambridge* 1962 pap. $3.95. A penetrating critique of Ovid's poetry.

The Mystery of Ovid's Exile. By John C. Thibault. *Univ. of California Press* 1964 $7.75

Ovid and the Canterbury Tales. By Richard L. Hoffman. *Univ. of Pennsylvania Press* $7.50

Ovid and the Elizabethans. By Frederick S. Boas. Studies in Shakespeare *Haskell* 1970 pap. $2.95

Ovid's Heroides. By Howard Jacobson. *Princeton Univ. Press* 1974 $19.50

PHAEDRUS. c. 15 B.C.–c. 50 A.D. *See Aesop in Chapter 7, Classical Greek Literature, this Vol.*

PETRONIUS (Gaius Petronius Arbiter). d. 65 A.D.

Tacitus (*q.v.*) called this Roman dandy—the director of entertainments at the Emperor Nero's court—"Arbiter Elegantiae" (arbiter of refined taste), and says further that Petronius was in high favor, having been governor of Bithynia and consul, but he was finally denounced by Nero's favorite, Tigellinus, and forced to commit suicide. He is generally considered to have written the "Satyricon," a satirical picaresque romance, in prose interspersed with verse, which is extant only in fragments. Its subject is Italian low life and it is characterized by "brilliant wit and riotous obscenity." The chief episode describes the vulgarian upstart Trimalchio and his rich banquet for the hero. William Arrowsmith has made a vigorous, appropriately colloquial American English translation. "We savor the satire and the parodies of practically every Greek or Roman literary type, and we see the universal applications behind the catalogue of the vices and excesses of Nero's Rome"—(*LJ*).

WORKS OF PETRONIUS ARBITER IN PROSE AND VERSE. Trans. by Joseph Addison. 1736. Tudor Translators Ser. *AMS Press* $17.50. Prefixed by the Life of Petronius, done from the Latin, and a character of his writings by Monsieur St. Evremont.

THE SATYRICON (c. 60 A.D.). (And Seneca's "Apocolocyntosis") Petronius trans. by M. Heseltine, Seneca by W. H. D. Rouse *Harvard Univ. Press* Loeb $7.00; trans. by William Burnaby *Heritage Press, Conn.* deluxe ed. $11.95; trans. by W. C. Firebaugh *Liveright* $6.95; trans. by William Arrowsmith *New Am. Lib.* Mentor Bks. 1960 pap. $1.25; (and "Fragments") trans. by John P. Sullivan *Penguin* pap. $1.45; trans. by William Arrowsmith *Univ. of Michigan Press* 1959 $4.95; trans. by W. C. Firebaugh *Simon & Schuster* (Washington Square) pap. $.75. The translations by Sullivan and by Arrowsmith are particularly recommended.

Books about Petronius

Arbiter of Elegance: A Study of the Life and Works of C. Petronius. By Gilbert Bagnani. *Univ. of Toronto Press* 1954 pap. $4.50. A sound and scholarly work.

Petronius. By Philip B. Corbett. World Authors Ser. *Twayne* $6.95

Satire: Critical Essays on Roman Literature. Ed. by John P. Sullivan. *Humanities Press* $7.75; *Indiana Univ. Press* Midland Bks. 1968 pap. $1.95. The chapter on Petronius is very useful.

Roman Novel. By P. G. Walsh. *Cambridge* 1970 $13.50

SENECA, LUCIUS ANNAEUS. c. 3 B.C.–65 A.D.

Seneca was born in Spain of a wealthy Italian family. His father, Lucius Annaeus Seneca, wrote the well-known "*Controversaie*" ("Controversies") and "*Suasoriae*" ("Persuasions"), which are collections of arguments used in rhetorical training; and his nephew, Lucan, is the epic poet of the Civil War. Educated in rhetoric and philosophy at Rome, he found the Stoic doctrine especially compatible. The younger Seneca became famous as an orator but was exiled by the emperor Claudius. He was recalled by the empress Agrippina to become the tutor of her son, the young Nero. After the first five years of Nero's reign, Agrippina was murdered and three years later Octavia, Nero's wife, was exiled. Seneca retired as much as possible from public life and devoted himself to philosophy, writing many treatises at this time. But in 65 A.D. he was accused of conspiracy and, by imperial order, committed suicide by opening his veins. He was a Stoic philosopher and met his death with Stoic calm. "The Stoic Philosophy of Seneca: Essays and

Letters" is available (trans. with introd. by Moses Hadas *Peter Smith* 1959 $4.25; *Norton* Norton Lib. 1968 pap. $2.45).

His writings show his nobility. It is thought that his tragedies might never have been presented on the stage. They are stilted and rhetorical, mostly imitative of Euripides (*q.v.*). But he tried to unify the plots, added psychological motivation to action and attempted to show the human problems of life on a human plane. His ten tragedies are all believed to be genuine, with the exception of "Octavia," which is now considered to be by a later writer. Translations of the tragedies influenced English dramatists such as Jonson, Marlowe, and Shakespeare, who all imitated Seneca's scenes of horror and his characters—the ghost, nurse, and villain. Seneca's "Moral Essays" and "*Epistulae Morales*" ("Letters") are in print in the Loeb Classical Library (*Harvard Univ. Press* 6 vols. each $5.50).

SENECA's TRAGEDIES. Trans. in prose by Frank Justus Miller *Harvard Univ. Press* Loeb 2 vols. 1917 each $7.00. Vol. 1 Hercules Furens; Troades; Medea; Hippolytus; Oedipus Vol. 2 Agamemnon; Thyestes; Hercules Oetaeus; Phoenissae; Octavia. Comparative analysis, bibliographies, index with identification of mythological and historical characters included.

SENECA: His Tenne Tragedies. Trans. into English and ed. by Thomas Newton. 1581. Fwd. by T. S. Eliot *AMS Press* 2 vols. each $15.00 set $30.00; fwd. by T. S. Eliot *Indiana Univ. Press* 1966 $9.50; *Burt Franklin* repr. of 1887 ed. 2 vols. in 1 1966 $37.00

FOUR TRAGEDIES AND OCTAVIA. Trans. by E. F. Watling *Penguin* pap. $1.75; *Gannon* $5.00

OEDIPUS. Trans. by Moses Hadas *Bobbs* Liberal Arts 1955 pap. $.65

MEDEA. Trans. by Moses Hadas *Bobbs* Liberal Arts 1956 pap. $.80

THYESTES. Trans. by Moses Hadas *Bobbs* Liberal Arts 1957 pap. $.65

Books about Seneca

The Influence of Seneca on Elizabethan Tragedy. By John W. Cunliffe. 1893. *Shoe String Press* 1965 $5.00

Seneca, the Philosopher, and His Modern Message. By R. M. Gummere. 1900. Our Debt to Greece and Rome Ser. *Cooper* $2.95

PERSIUS (Aulus Persius Flaccus). 34 A.D.–62 A.D.

Persius was a native of Etruria and was educated at Rome where he became Lucan's (*q.v.*) friend. He wrote six satires in a somewhat contorted style which inculcate Stoic morality. His sanity and wit have direct appeal.

THE SATIRES OF PERSIUS. Trans. by W. S. Merwin. 1961. *Kennikat* 1973 $7.25. The notes and introd. of W. S. Anderson are recommended.

THE SATIRES OF HORACE AND PERSIUS. Trans. by Niall Rudd Classics Ser. *Penguin* 1974 pap. $2.45

Books about Persius

R. G. M. Nisbet in Critical Essays on Roman Satire. Ed. by John P. Sullivan. *Humanities* 1963 $7.75; *Indiana Univ. Press* Midland Bks. 1968 pap. $1.95

QUINTILIAN (Marcus Fabius Quintilianus). c. 35 A.D.–c. 95 A.D.

The "*Institutio Oratoria*" in 12 books was written by the most famous of the Roman rhetoricians during his later years. It contains the principles of rhetoric, especially in public speaking, and is a practical treatise on the complete education of a Roman and the best methods used in the Roman schools. It offers, in the tenth book, a famous critique of Greek and Latin authors. His ideal orator is a good man skilled in speaking. Quintilian was born in northern Spain but educated in Rome, where he began to teach oratory in 68 A.D. He was the first rhetorician to establish a public school and to receive a salary from the state.

INSTITUTIONIS ORATORIAE (On the Training of an Orator). Trans. by H. E. Butler *Harvard Univ. Press* Loeb 4 vols. 1953 each $7.00. An excellent translation.

ON EDUCATION: Being a Translation of Selected Passages from the "*Institutio Oratoria.*" Ed. by W. M. Smail. *Teachers College* $5.95 pap. $2.50

ON THE EARLY EDUCATION OF THE CITIZEN-ORATOR. *Bobbs* Liberal Arts 1965 $6.00 pap. $1.45. A revision of the John Selby Watson translation.

Books about Quintilian

Roman Education from Cicero to Quintilian. By Aubrey Gwynn. *Teachers College* 1926 $6.95
   pap. $3.50; *Russell & Russell* 1964 $8.50

Quintilian. By George Kennedy. World Authors Ser. *Twayne* 1969 $6.95. By a leading authority
   on Roman rhetoric.

Quintilian as Educator. By Frederick M. Wheelock. *Twayne* 1974 $7.95

LUCAN (Marcus Annaeus Lucanus).   39 A.D.–65 A.D.

Grandson and nephew of Seneca the Rhetorician and Seneca the Philosopher, Lucan was born
in Spain and educated in rhetoric at Rome. He was a favorite at Nero's court until the emperor
took offense at his precocious literary talent and prevented him from displaying it in public. Lucan
then joined a conspiracy against the monarch and was forced to commit suicide. His epic poem,
the *"Bellum Civile"* ("The Civil War"), also called the "Pharsalia," sides with Pompey in his fatal
struggle with Julius Caesar. His complex rhetorical style was acclaimed in the Middle Ages; Dante
and Chaucer ranked him high as a poet.

CIVIL WAR. Trans. by J. D. Duff *Harvard Univ. Press* Loeb 1928 $7.00

MARTIAL (Marcus Valerius Martialis).   40? A.D.–104? A.D.

Martial's 12 books of "Epigrams" are written for the most part in elegiac couplets modeled on
Ovid (*q.v.*) and Catullus (*q.v.*). They show his acute observation of Roman life in the last third of
the first century and were written with wit and brevity, often postponing the point or sting until
the end. They are frequently insulting and obscene. Not much is known of his life except that he
left his home in Bilbilis, Spain, in 64 A.D. to live by his writing and his wits in Rome. He courted the
favor of the rich and powerful, was a friend of Seneca, Lucan, Juvenal, and Quintilian (*qq.v.*), and
Pliny the Younger (*q.v.*) lamented his death after his return to Spain. The "Epigrams" have been
read and imitated throughout the centuries; one of them was translated as the memorable "I do
not love thee, Dr. Fell." The version by Francis and Tatum (*Cambridge* 1924, o.p.) is "the work of
sound scholars, has the advantage of brief notes, and is sometimes, perhaps generally, the more
literal." (A. Y. Campbell). Of the Fitts translation, Horace Gregory said (in the *N.Y. Times*): "It is a
book of singular charm and gay indiscretion. One might almost say that a transmigration of souls
from Martial to Fitts had taken place, and, if anything, the wit on the right-hand page is more
brightly polished than the Latin on the left." Fitts has not hesitated to make his (Martial's) barbs
American and contemporary. *Library Journal*, on the other hand, feels that Fitts *misses* Martial's
elegance: "For the urbanity and elegance that were part and parcel of Martial's poetic soul, we
must still return to the charming renderings of Paul Nixon" (*see his book below*). The Ker translation
is literal but misses, says Charles Simmons (*N.Y. Times*), the "fun."

THE EPIGRAMS. 80–84. Trans. by Walter C. A. Ker *Harvard Univ. Press* Loeb 2 vols.
   1919–20, 1947–50 each $7.00; trans. by James A. Michie *Random* 1973 $6.95 Vintage
   Bks. pap. $1.95

SELECTED EPIGRAMS. Trans. by Ralph Marcellino *Bobbs* Liberal Arts 1967 $7.00 pap.
   $2.25; trans. by Rolfe Humphries *Indiana Univ. Press* 1963 Midland Bks. pap. $2.45

SIXTY POEMS. Trans. by Dudley Fitts (bilingual) *Harcourt* 1967 $4.75. "Free paraphrases
   of the original [Latin] by a contemporary poet and critic."

Books about Martial

Martial and English Epigram from Sir Thomas Wyatt to Ben Jonson. By Thomas K. Whipple.
   1925. *Phaeton* 1970 $6.00

Martial and the Modern Epigram. 1927. By Paul Nixon. *Cooper* $3.75

Poems after Martial. By Philip Murray. *Weslyan Univ. Press* 1967 $6.00
   Free adaptations of some 70 epigrams in all. "A few of the renderings are brilliant," many are
   "witty and urbane"—(*LJ*).

STATIUS, PUBLIUS PAPINIUS.   c. 45 A.D.–c. 96 A.D.

Born in Naples the son of a schoolmaster, Statius became prominent in Rome for his verse. He
was a favorite in the court of Emperor Domitian, and his lyric verse includes elegies, odes and
poems in praise of the emperor. The *"Thebaid"* is an epic in 12 books about the struggle of the two
sons of Oedipus to rule Thebes. Only fragments are extant of the unfinished *"Achilleid"* (Story of
Achilles). His *"Silvae"* are pleasant occasional verses to his friends, his wife, and the emperor. His
influence continued through the Middle Ages. Dante (*q.v.*) regarded him as a Christian; Chaucer
(*q.v.*) imitated his *"Thebaid"* in *"Troilus and Criseyde"* and considered him one of the world's great
poets.

Silvae, Thebaid, or Thebais, Achilleid, or Achilleis. Trans. by J. H. Mozley *Harvard Univ. Press* Loeb 2 vols. 1955 each $7.00. A readable and accurate translation.

Books about Statius
The Influence of Statius upon Chaucer. By Boyd A. Wise. 1911. *Phaeton* 1967 $6.00

TACITUS, CORNELIUS. c. 56 A.D.–115 A.D. *See Chapter 9, History, Government and Politics, Reader's Adviser, Vol. 3.*

JUVENAL (Decimus Junius Juvenalis). 60? A.D.–140? A.D.

The 16 "Satires" of Juvenal, which contain a vivid picture of contemporary Rome under the Empire, have seldom been equaled as biting diatribes. The satire was the only literary form that the Romans did not copy from the Greeks. Horace (*q.v.*) merely used it for humorous comment on human folly. Juvenal's invectives in powerful hexameters, exact and epigrammatic, were aimed at lax and luxurious society, tyranny (Domitian's), criminal excesses, and the immorality of women. He is so sparing of autobiographical detail that we know very little of his life. He was desperately poor at one time and may have been an important magistrate at another.

His influence was great in the Middle Ages; in the 17th century he was well translated by Dryden (1693) and in the 18th century he was paraphrased by Dr. Johnson in his "London" and "Vanity of Human Wishes." He inspired in Swift the same savage bitterness. The prose translation of the "Satires" by G. G. Ramsay in the Loeb edition, Dryden's version and the verse translation by William Gifford (1802) are recommended. The poet Rolfe Humphries has made the first verse translation since William Gifford's—one "as real as an angry Irishman reading the daily newspaper"—(*SR*).

Satires (c. 110–127). With Persius' "Satires." Trans. by John Dryden. 1697. Tudor Translators Ser. *AMS Press* $32.50. Some of the Juvenal "Satires" were translated by hands other than Dryden. Persius' "Satires" are the work of Dryden, and carry explanatory notes at the end of each satire.

Satires. Trans. by Thomas Sheridan. 1739. Tudor Translators Ser. *AMS Press* $21.50
"With explanatory and classical notes relating to the laws and customs of the Greeks and Romans"—(AMS catalog).

Satires. Trans. by William Gifford. Explanatory notes and introd. by Arthur Frederic Andrew Cole. 1906. *AMS Press* $15.00

Satires. With Persius' "Satires." Trans. by William Gifford *Dutton* Everyman's 1954 $3.95; trans. by G. G. Ramsay *Harvard Univ. Press* Loeb 1918, 1924 rev. 1950 $7.00

Satires. Trans. by Rolfe Humphries *Indiana Univ. Press* 1958 Midland Bks. pap. $1.95; trans. by Hubert Creekmore *New Am. Lib.* Mentor Bks. 1963 pap. $.95; trans. by Jerome Mazzaro, notes and introd. by Richard E. Braun *Univ. of Michigan Press* 1965 $5.00

Sixteen Satires. Trans. with introd. and notes by Peter Green *Penguin* 1967 pap. $2.50

Books about Juvenal
Juvenal the Satirist: A Study. By Gilbert Highet. *Oxford* 1954 $7.20 Galaxy Bks. pap. $1.85
"An admirable book, informative well-written," for the general reader and the more advanced student.

PLINY THE YOUNGER (Gaius Plinius Caecilius Secundus.) c. 61–112. A.D.

Raised by his uncle, Pliny the Elder, who was a scholar and industrious compiler of the "Natural History," Pliny the Younger intended his "Letters" for posterity and polished them with extreme care. He was an orator, statesman, and well-educated man of the world. He wrote with discretion on a variety of subjects, and without the bitterness of his friends, Tacitus (*q.v.*) and Suetonius (*q.v.*), or the disgust for the social conditions of those troubled times found in the writings of his contemporaries, Juvenal (*q.v.*) and Martial (*q.v.*). In the introduction to the Loeb edition, Hutchinson writes: "Melmoth's translation of Pliny's letters, published in 1746, not only delighted contemporary critics . . . but deservedly ranks as a minor English classic. Apart from its literary excellence, it has the supreme merit of reflecting the spirit of the original. . . . No modern rendering can capture the ease and felicity of Melmoth's; for they came of his living in a world like Pliny's own."

LETTERS. Trans. by William Melmoth (1746), revised by W. M. L. Hutchinson *Harvard Univ. Press* Loeb 2 vols. 1915, 1931–32, 1952 each $7.00

THE LETTERS OF THE YOUNGER PLINY. An original translation by Betty Radice *Penguin* 1963 pap. $1.65; *Peter Smith* $4.25

Books about Pliny

Scribe and Critic at Work in Pliny's Letters. By Selatie E. Stout. 1954. *Haskell* 1972 $13.95
Letters of Pliny: A Historical and Social Commentary. By A. N. Sherwin-White. *Oxford* 1966 $22.50

For Pliny the Elder, see Chapter 7, Science, Reader's Adviser, *Vol. 3.*

SUETONIUS (Gaius Suetonius Tranquillus).   c. 69 A.D.–160? A.D.

Suetonius is noted for "The Lives of the Twelve Caesars," which survives almost intact. Only fragments remain of his much larger collection, "Illustrious Men." He recorded the most minute details of his subjects' lives in a lively informative style which became a model for many later biographers. The brief period as secretary to the Emperor Hadrian probably gave him access to official archives, so that his background data are authentic, spiced with the gossip of the times.

The 1606 version by Philemon Holland was influential. Rolfe's version "does not lack the qualities of vigor and lightness: on the contrary it is decidedly readable," J. Wright Duff reported in the *Classical Review,* but the 1914 edition suffered from "defective proof-reading, inaccuracies in translation, and neglect of sound English." Of the Robert Graves translation the *Christian Science Monitor* said: "Astonishing truly, that the stiffly framed Latin language that we learn about in our school texts and grammars is capable of such elasticity and color as we find in this reproduction by Mr. Graves."

THE LIVES OF THE TWELVE CAESARS. c. 121. An unexpurgated English version edited with notes and an introd. by Joseph Gavorse *Modern Library* 1931 $1.95; trans. by Philemon Holland. 1606. 1899. *AMS Press* 2 vols. each $15.00

THE LIVES OF THE CAESARS. Trans. by J. C. Rolfe *Harvard Univ. Press* Loeb 2 vols. 1914, 1920 each $7.00

THE TWELVE CAESARS. Trans. by Robert Graves *Penguin Bks.* 1957 (orig.) pap. $1.50

LIVES OF THE FIRST TWELVE CAESARS. Trans. with annotations, and a review of the government and literature of the different periods, by Alexander Thomson. 1796. Tudor Translators Ser. *AMS Press* $30.00

APULEIUS, LUCIUS.   fl. 2nd cent. 114? A.D.–? A.D.

Apuleius, of African birth, was educated at Carthage and Athens. His most famous work, "The Golden Ass," is often considered the first novel. It is the tale of a young philosopher who transformed himself not into a bird as he had expected, but into an ass. After many adventures he was rescued by the goddess Isis. The episode of "Cupid and Psyche," told with consummate grace, is the most celebrated section. A fine version is given in Walter Pater's "Marius the Epicurean." This romance of the declining Empire influenced the novels of Boccaccio (*q.v.*), Cervantes (*q.v.*), Fielding (*q.v.*) and Smollett (*q.v.*); Heywood (*q.v.*) used the theme for a drama and William Morris (*q.v.*) used some of the material in "The Earthly Paradise." The early translation (1566) by William Adlington is graceful. Robert Graves' version (*see below*) has the advantage of recent studies and revision in the original text. "Graves' translation abandons the aureate Latinity of Apuleius for a dry, sharp, plain style—which is itself a small masterpiece of twentieth-century prose"—(Kenneth Rexroth, in *SR*).

THE GOLDEN ASS, or Metamorphoses. c. 150. Trans. by William Adlington (1566) introd. by Charles Whibley. 1893. *AMS Press* $15.00; trans. by Robert Graves *Farrar, Straus* 1967 Noonday pap. $2.25; trans. by William Adlington *Harvard Univ. Press* 1919 Loeb $7.00; trans. by Jack Lindsay *Indiana Univ. Press* Midland Bks. 1962 pap. $2.25; trans. by William Adlington, introd. by Charles Whibley *Liveright* rev. ed. 1927 $6.95; trans. by William Adlington, ed. by Harry C. Schnur *Macmillan* Collier Bks. 1962 pap. $.95; trans. by Jack Lindsay *Peter Smith* $4.25

APOLOGIA and FLORIDA. Trans. by H. E. Butler. 1909. Greenwood $11.50

Books about Apuleius

Apuleius and His Influence. By Elizabeth H. Haight. 1930. Our Debt to Greece and Rome Ser. *Cooper* $3.75

Amor and Psyche: The Psychic Development of the Feminine. By Erich Neumann. Trans. from the German by Ralph Manheim Bollingen Ser. *Princeton Univ. Press.* 1956 $8.50 pap. $2.95. A commentary on the tale by Apuleius.

Roman Novel. By P. G. Walsh. *Cambridge* 1970 $13.50

—E.C.K.S.

Chapter 9

French Literature

"French literature, taken as a whole, overtops in richness, artistic quality, and historical influence, all literatures since those of Greece and Rome."
—C. H. CONRAD WRIGHT

From the Middle Ages arguably, from the Renaissance certainly, French literature has continued to hold a high place in Western civilization and, from the nineteenth century onward, has been a principal representative of occidental culture in the Orient. No other literature has held so consistently high the ideal of thought and expression as inseparable couple; no other civilization has attached so much importance to the purity and good usage of its language. From the sixteenth-century *"Défense et illustration de la langue française"* by Du Bellay to very recent concerns about the intrusion of other modern languages into French (e.g. *franglais*), the French language has adapted, but slowly and carefully, to contemporary pressures.

Ideas come through, for better or for worse, in translation; the style of their expression much less easily. That is why translation into English produces at best only an approximation of the original, why poetry can be perhaps adapted but surely not brought over from French into English. The English-reading public has been well served in recent years by the admirable achievements in this field of translators like Richard Howard, Willard Trask and Louise Varese. It must be remembered that this chapter covers only translations of French literature—prose, poetry and theater—now in print. The date directly· after a title is that of the first publication in French.

Genêt (Janet Flanner) wrote from Paris in the *New Yorker* of June 10, 1967: "It seems odd that the most popular among the new books recently published here have assumed less significance than the phenomenon of the old books that are being republished. The Cercle du Bibliophile has just brought out a new edition of the complete works of Stendhal, but its biggest success is with the republishing of Victor Hugo, in forty volumes, and the next in popularity is the Club du Livre Français' reissue of Balzac. The most widespread revival has been that of Zola. The French young read them with passion, like reading terrible true stories of their great-grandfathers' lives and times. [Zola furnishes] raw meat to satisfy youth's appetite today for violence." That both young and old French readers have gone back, at least temporarily, to the nineteenth-century novels of French literary genius certainly indicates a kind of reader rebellion against current French fiction.

The *nouveau roman*, new in the 1950s, continues to be discussed and its principal authors (Butor, Duras, Robbe-Grillet, Sarraute and Claude Simon) continue to add titles. More recently, the literary scene—particularly in criticism—has been occupied by the structuralists and the semiologists (Barthes, Dérida, Kristeva) as voices in the creative field—novel and theater—seem relatively silent. The novels and theater of Samuel Beckett, a member of no school, continue to enjoy international reputation although there is little new even from him.

French Canadian literature, about which the first general work by Ian Forbes Fraser ("Spirit of French Canada") dates from 1939, has continued to grow in interest and importance for the Canadian reader. Marie-Claire Blais, Anne Hébert and Réjean Ducharme continue to find a growing public for their novels. The theater written in *joual* (Quebec idiom) has enjoyed growing success although the text often remains less important than the production.

The "Oxford Companion to French Literature" (*see under Harvey below*) is the most comprehensive work available on French literature in one volume. Still of great value and now in the process of revision by Jean-Albert Bédé is the "Columbia Dictionary of

Modern European Literature" originally edited by Horatio Smith (*Columbia* 1947 $20.00). French novelists are included under "Translations" in "The Fiction Catalog: The Standard Catalog Series" (*Wilson* 9th ed. 1975 and supplement service through 1980 U.S. and Canada $25.00). Henri Peyre's (Professor and Executive Officer of the Graduate Center of the City University of New York) "French Novelists of Today" (1967 *Oxford Univ. Press* pap. $3.50) presents a valuable panorama of modern literature from a traditional point of view. Leon S. Roudiez' "French Fiction Today: A New Direction" (*Rutgers* 1972 $15.00) gives a sympathetic hearing to the new writers. Professor Cazamian's history in English (*see below*) covers his native literature from the "Cantilène de Sainte Eulalie" to Jean Anouilh. Another work in English, with quotations in French, is the five-volume *Barnes and Noble* "A Literary History of France" (*see below*).

For general background on the changes in France since the 1930s, "In Search of France" (1963, o.p.) is a thoughtful and well-coordinated symposium with very well-written articles. Worked out as part of the research program of the Harvard Center for International Affairs, it has benefited by the give and take among specialists in three years of discussions at Harvard and in France.

The theater has always been a strong force in French literature with some of its writers ranking amongst the most celebrated and respected; e.g., Corneille, Molière, Racine. It was in the mid-seventeenth century—with influences from antiquity by way of the Renaissance and from Spain which was finishing its *siglo de oro*—that notions of French comedy and tragedy were formulated after initial experiment during the sixteenth century and the early years of the seventeenth century. The kind of rigid formality which made the careers of Molière and Racine at the end of the seventeenth century falls under questioning in the eighteenth century with Voltaire writing theater on the established model and Marivaux adding a new dimension. It is above all Diderot, and particularly in his theoretical essays on theater, who introduces into France and Europe in general (cf. Lessing in Germany) the new theater that shuns the excess of classical formality and moves toward contemporary realism called drama. Beaumarchais, at the end of the century, will be the most gifted translator of these theories to the stage ("Barber of Seville," "Marriage of Figaro").

The nineteenth century is characterized by the Romantic Theater (already adumbrated by Diderot) from roughly 1815–1840 (Hugo, Musset, Vigny and others) and thereafter by the socially conscious realists, purveyors of the well-made play (Dumas fils, Sardou, Scribe) until the end of the century when neoromantic tendencies (Rostand), symbolist redirection (Maeterlinck, Claudel) and uncharted experiments put an end to the "problem theater" of ideas (Curel, Hervieux, Brieux, Porto-Riche, and others).

A particularly rich moment in French theater comes between the two world wars of the twentieth century when Freudian ideas, surrealist disenchantment and a renaissance of the ideal of classical expression (e.g., Gide) all work together as ingredients to produce playwrights like Lenormand, Cocteau, Giraudoux, Montherlant, Anouilh, Aymé, etc., some of whom have continued to write after 1950.

French theater in its contemporary form may be said to have its sources (aside from the long tradition beginning at the end of the Renaissance) in reformers like Antoine, Copeau and the *cartel des quatre* (Baty, Dullin, Jouvet and Pitoeff), in dramatists like Alfred Jarry, Apollinaire and the surrealists. Of particular relevance in the last years are the writings of Antonin Artaud (1895–1948), in particular "The Theater and its Double" (1938, trans. by Mary Caroline Richards, *Grove* Evergreen Books 1958 pap. $2.95).

The group loosely identifiable as absurdists continues to be marked by the contributions of Adamov, Beckett, Ionesco, Pinget and particularly Genet.

The most useful sources of information on the genesis and development of the New Theater are Martin Esslin's book, "The Theater of the Absurd" (*Doubleday* Anchor Bks. 1961 pap. $2.50; *Overlook Press* $12.50), Jacques Guicharnaud's "Modern French Theater" (1967) and David Grossvogel's "The Self-Conscious Stage in Modern French

Drama" (1958) [*see below*]. An anthology of Artaud's writing in translation is published by *City Lights* ("Anthology" 2nd ed. rev. pap. $3.00).

BIBLIOGRAPHY

Cabeen, David Clark, Ed. A CRITICAL BIBLIOGRAPHY OF FRENCH LITERATURE. *Syracuse Univ. Press* to be 7 vols. 1947– Vol. 1 The Mediaeval Period ed. by U. T. Holmes, Jr. 1947 rev. ed. 1952 $10.00 Vol. 2 The Sixteenth Century ed. by Alexander H. Schutz 1956 $12.00 Vol. 3 The Seventeenth Century ed. by Jules Brody 1961 $16.00 Vol. 4 The Eighteenth Century ed. by George Havens and Donald Bond 1951 $12.50, and Vol. 4a The Eighteenth Century–Supplement ed. by Richard A. Brooks 1968 $12.00 Vol. 5 The Nineteenth Century ed. by J-A. Bédé (in prep.) Vol. 6 and Vol. 7 The Twentieth Century ed. by D. Alden and R. Brooks (in prep.)

Harvey, Sir Paul, and Janet Ewing Heseltine, Eds. THE OXFORD COMPANION TO FRENCH LITERATURE. *Oxford* 1959 $15.00. Covering the period from about 400 A.D. to the years immediately preceding World War II, there are approximately 6,000 articles on every aspect of French literature, with a selection of some postwar entries.

Wicks, C. Beaumont, Ed. THE PARISIAN STAGE: Alphabetical Indexes of Plays and Authors. *Univ. of Alabama Press* Vol. 1 1800–1815 (1950) pap. $4.00 Vol. 2 1816–1830 (1953) pap. $4.00 Vol. 3 ed. by C. Beaumont Wicks and Jerome W. Schweitzer 1830–1850 (1960) $4.00 Vol. 4 1851–1875 $6.95

HISTORY AND CRITICISM

Babbitt, Irving. THE MASTERS OF MODERN FRENCH CRITICISM. Introd. by Milton Hindus. 1912. *Richard West* $25.00

By a noted Harvard professor, this discussion of the most significant of the 19th-century critics, in which Babbitt describes his own critical position, is still of importance. His insistence that what writers write can be studied independently of their lives helped inspire the "New Criticism."

Balakian, Anna Elizabeth. LITERARY ORIGINS OF SURREALISM: A New Mysticism in French Poetry. 1947. *New York Univ. Press* 1966 $6.95 pap. $1.95

This book "has the rare virtue of giving a clear, precise synthesis of a long literary tradition without ponderous parentheses and footnoting"—(*Choice*).

Barnes, Hazel E. HUMANISTIC EXISTENTIALISM: The Literature of Possibility. *Univ. of Nebraska Press* 1959 Bison Bks. 1962 pap: $2.45. An exposition of the works of Sartre, Camus and de Beauvoir.

Barthes, Roland. WRITING DEGREE ZERO AND ELEMENTS OF SEMIOLOGY. *Beacon Press* 1970 pap. $2.95. A landmark for a recent school of criticis.

Bersani, Leo. BALZAC TO BECKETT: Center and Circumference in French Fiction. *Oxford* 1970 $8.95

Brandes, Georg. REVOLUTION AND REACTION IN NINETEENTH CENTURY FRENCH LITERATURE. 1905. *Russell & Russell* 1960 $8.00

Braun, Sidney D., Ed. DICTIONARY OF FRENCH LITERATURE. 1958. *Greenwood* 1971 $18.00

Brée, Germaine, and Margaret Guiton. AN AGE OF FICTION: The French Novel from Gide to Camus. *Rutgers Univ. Press* 1957 $7.50. Excellent critical work.

Brereton, Geoffrey. AN INTRODUCTION TO THE FRENCH POETS: Villon to the Present Day. *Harper* (Barnes & Noble) 1961 rev. ed. 1973 $13.50 pap. $6.75

A SHORT HISTORY OF FRENCH LITERATURE. 1962 currently o.p. A valuable study.

Brombert, Victor. INTELLECTUAL HERO: Studies in the French Novel 1880–1955. *Univ. of Chicago Press* 1961 pap. $1.95

Butler, K. T. A HISTORY OF FRENCH LITERATURE. 1923. *Russell & Russell* 2 vols. 1967 set

$20.00. A penetrating and lucid survey of the literature of France from its beginnings to the 1920's. The textbook-style subheadings are most helpful for student or researcher. Chronology, bibliography, index.

Campos, Christopher. VIEW OF FRANCE: From Arnold to Bloomsbury. *Oxford* 1965 $6.00. France as seen through English eyes, 1840–1918.

Cazamian, Louis F. A HISTORY OF FRENCH LITERATURE. *Oxford* 1955 $13.00 pap. $4.95

"Charming and informative, this handsome volume is the work of a distinguished scholar who was for many years Professor of English Literature at the Sorbonne and whose teaching has left its brilliant mark upon generations of French students of English. It is a comprehensive and thorough account . . . from the earliest times to the present day"—*(Manchester Guardian)*.

Cobban, Alfred. A HISTORY OF MODERN FRANCE. *Braziller* 1965 $10.00; *Penguin* 3 vols. 1966 Vol. 1 1715–1799 pap. $1.95 Vol. 2 1799–1871 pap. $1.45 Vol. 3 1871–1962 pap. $1.45

"The history of France covered here is so interesting and so well told that the book should be purchased by all libraries, large and small"—*(LJ)*.

Crocker, Lester. AN AGE OF CRISIS: Man and World in Eighteenth-Century French Thought. *Johns Hopkins Univ. Press* 1959 $19.50

NATURE AND CULTURE: Ethical Thought in the French Enlightenment. *Johns Hopkins Univ. Press* 1963 $19.50

Cruickshank, John, Ed. FRENCH LITERATURE AND ITS BACKGROUND. *Oxford* 6 vols. Vol. 1 The Sixteenth Century 1968 Vol. 2 The Seventeenth Century 1969 Vol. 3 The Eighteenth Century 1968 Vol. 4 The Early Nineteenth Century 1969 Vol. 5 The Late Nineteenth Century 1969 Vol. 6 The Twentieth Century pap. each $3.25

THE NOVELIST AS PHILOSOPHER: Studies in French Fiction 1935–1960. *Oxford* 1962 $7.00

Curley, Dorothy Nyren, and Arthur Curley, Comps. and Eds. MODERN ROMANCE LITERATURES. *Ungar* 1967 $15.00. Extracts from book reviews on major writers.

Demorest, Jean-Jacques, Ed. STUDIES IN SEVENTEENTH-CENTURY FRENCH LITERATURE. *Cornell Univ. Press* 1962 $10.00

Doubrovsky, Serge. THE NEW CRITICISM IN FRANCE. Trans. by Derek Coltman *Univ. of Chicago Press* 1973 $10.50

Flanner, Janet. PARIS JOURNAL, 1944–1965. *Atheneum* 1965 $8.95

PARIS JOURNAL, 1965–1971. *Atheneum* 1971 $10.00. This, and the preceding collection of letters by the Paris correspondent of the *New Yorker*, known as Genêt, give admirably written accounts of events of all sorts on the French scene.

Fowlie, Wallace. THE AGE OF SURREALISM. 1950. *Indiana Univ. Press* Midland Bks. 1960 pap. $2.25; *Peter Smith* 1960 $4.25. Essays on Lautréamont, Rimbaud, Mallarmé, Breton, Apollinaire, Cocteau, Eluard, etc.

THE CLIMATE OF VIOLENCE: The French Literary Tradition from Baudelaire to the Present. *Macmillan* 1967 $6.95
A "distinguished book"—*(LJ)*.

FRENCH LITERATURE: Its History and Meaning. *Prentice-Hall* 1973 $8.95 pap. $4.95

A GUIDE TO CONTEMPORARY FRENCH LITERATURE: From Valéry to Sartre. *Peter Smith* $6.00

Fraser, Ian Forbes. SPIRIT OF FRENCH CANADA: A Study of the Literature. 1939. *AMS Press* $10.00

Frohock, Wilbur Merrill. STYLE AND TEMPER: Studies in French Fiction 1925–1960. *Harvard Univ. Press* 1967 $5.00

Gaulle, Charles de. COMPLETE WAR MEMOIRS. *Simon & Schuster* 1964 Touchstone-Clarion Bks. pap. $4.95

Gay, Peter. THE PARTY OF HUMANITY: Essays on the French Enlightenment. 1963. *Norton* 1971 pap. $2.65

"A provocative volume"—(Henri Peyre). By the winner of the 1967 National Book Award for "The Enlightenment."

Gibson, Robert D. D. MODERN FRENCH POETS ON POETRY. *Cambridge* 1961 $14.00

Gide, André. PRETEXTS: Reflections on Literature and Morality. Ed. by Justin O'Brien. 1959. *Bks. for Libraries* $12.75

Ginestier, Paul. THE POET AND THE MACHINE. Trans. by Martin B. Friedman. 1961. *College & Univ. Press* 1965 pap. $1.95. An appraisal of French, American and English poetry in the machine age.

Gleason, Judith. THIS AFRICA: Novels by West Africans in English and French. *Northwestern Univ. Press* 1965 $6.50

Hatzfield, Helmut A. LITERATURE THROUGH ART: A New Approach to French Literature. 1952 *International Scholarly Bk. Services* 1969 pap. $8.45

TRENDS AND STYLES IN TWENTIETH CENTURY FRENCH LITERATURE. *Catholic Univ. of America Press* 1966 $11.95

Havens, George R. THE AGE OF IDEAS: From Reaction to Revolution in Eighteenth-Century France. 1955. *Macmillan* (Free Press) pap. $3.50. Readable and memorable introduction to the lives, personalities and ideas of such French philosophers as Voltaire, Rousseau and Diderot.

Jahn, Janheinz. NEO-AFRICAN LITERATURE. Trans. by Oliver Coburn and Ursula Lehrburger 1969 *Grove* Evergreen Bks. pap. $1.95

James, Henry. FRENCH POETS AND NOVELISTS. 1878. *Bks. for Libraries* $15.00; *Folcroft* 1973 $12.75; *Gordon Press* $29.95; *Richard West* repr. of 1893 ed. $13.50

King, Bruce. INTRODUCTION TO NIGERIAN LITERATURE. *Holmes and Meier* (Africana Pub. Corp.) 1972 $8.00

"The broadest treatment thus far of Nigerian writing"—(Herdeck).

Kohn, Hans. MAKING OF THE MODERN FRENCH MIND. *Van Nostrand-Reinhold* 1955 Anvil Bks. pap. $2.95

Lancaster, H. Carrington. A HISTORY OF FRENCH DRAMATIC LITERATURE IN THE SEVENTEENTH CENTURY. *Gordian* 1966 Pt. 1, 2 vols. each $14.00 Pt. 2, 2 vols. Vol. 1 $14.00 Vol. 2 $15.00 Pt. 3, 2 vols. Vol. 1 $14.00 Vol. 2 $15.00 Pt 4, 2 vols. each $15.00 Pt. 5 $10.00 set of 9 vols. $125.00. The classic work on the period.

LeSage, Laurent. THE FRENCH NEW CRITICISM: An Introduction and a Sampler. *Pennsylvania State Univ. Press* 1967 $6.50. In his "provocative and controversial book" (*SR*), Professor LeSage discusses the new trend on the part of French critics to evaluate a book with reference to the society from which it emerges.

THE FRENCH NEW NOVEL: An Introduction and a Sampler. *Pennsylvania State Univ. Press* 1962 $6.00. An important introduction to the French "antinovels" of Beckett, Bessette, Blanchot, Butor, Cayrol, Duras, Lagrolet, Ollier, Pinget, Robbe-Grillet, Sarraute, Simon and Yacine.

Levin, Harry. THE GATES OF HORN. A Study of Five French Realists. *Oxford* 1963 $10.50 Galaxy Bks. pap. $3.95. A major work by an important critic (*q.v.*) on the relation between literature and life in the realistic novels of Stendhal, Balzac, Flaubert, Zola and Proust.

A LITERARY HISTORY OF FRANCE. *Harper* Barnes & Noble 5 vols. Vol. 1 2 pts. Pt. 1 The Middle Ages by John Fox 1974 $16.50 Pt. 2 Renaissance France, 1470–1589 by I. D. McFarlane 1974 $18.00 Vol. 2 The Seventeenth Century, 1600–1715 by P. J. Yarrow 1967 $11.50 Vol. 3 The Eighteenth Century, 1715–1789 by Robert Niklaus 1970 $6.00 Vol. 4 The Nineteenth Century, 1789–1870 by P. E. Charvet 1967 $11.50 Vol.

5 The Nineteenth and Twentieth Centuries, 1870–1940 by P. E. Charvet 1967 $10.00. A concentrated view of the whole of French literary history. Each volume is written by an English authority on the period.

Lockert, Lacy. STUDIES IN FRENCH CLASSICAL TRAGEDY. *Vanderbilt Univ. Press* 1958 $7.50

Lough, John. PARIS THEATER AUDIENCES IN THE SEVENTEENTH AND EIGHTEENTH CENTURIES. *Oxford* 1957 $11.25

Mallinson, Vernon. MODERN BELGIAN LITERATURE, 1830–1960. This work, the only recent study of its kind in English, is currently o.p.

Matthews, Brander. FRENCH DRAMATISTS OF THE NINETEENTH CENTURY. 1901. *Blom* 1968 $12.50

Mauriac, Claude. THE NEW LITERATURE. Trans. by Samuel I. Stone. An excellent analysis of 17 contemporary essayists, poets and novelists who are experimenting with new forms. The volume (1959) is currently o.p.

Nadeau, Maurice. A HISTORY OF SURREALISM. Trans. by Richard Howard; introd. by Roger Shattuck *Macmillan* Collier Bks. 1965 pap. $2.45. The origin and history of the surrealist school in literature, by the editor of *Les Lettres Nouvelles*.

O'Brien, Justin. CONTEMPORARY FRENCH LITERATURE: Essays edited by Leon S. Roudiez. *Rutgers Univ. Press* 1971 $12.50

   THE FRENCH LITERARY HORIZON. *Rutgers Univ. Press* 1967 $9.00. Essays on noted French writers of the 20th century by an important critic. Most were previously published as articles, introductions, etc.

Patterson, Warner F. THREE CENTURIES OF FRENCH POETIC THEORY: A Critical History of the Chief Arts of France, 1328–1640. 1935. *Russell & Russell* 1955 Pts. 1 & 2 in 3 vols. $32.50

Pei, Mario. FRENCH PRECURSORS OF THE CHANSON DE ROLAND. 1948. *AMS Press* $8.50. A study showing the influences of French poetry of the 9th to 11th centuries on the 13th-century *chanson de geste*.

Peyre, Henri. FRENCH NOVELISTS OF TODAY. *Oxford* 1967 $11.75 pap. $3.50
   This revision of Peyre's "The Contemporary French Novel" (1955) "is so extensive and contains such an abundance of important, new and useful material, . . . that it not only supersedes the earlier version, but also amounts to a new and original work itself. . . . A supremely lucid and vigorous survey of the novel in France from 1920 to the present, [the book] is at once an authoritative history, a highly personal critique in the traditionalist mold, and a detailed and efficient work of reference; one does not hesitate to call it the essential guide"—(*N.Y. Times*).

   MODERN LITERATURE: The Literature of France. A study of American scholarship in the field of French literature. 1966 o.p.

Pierce, Roy. CONTEMPORARY FRENCH POLITICAL THOUGHT. *Oxford* 1966 pap. $3.50. The ideas of Mounier, Weil, Camus, Sartre, de Jouvenel and Aron are stressed in this overview of French political philosophy since World War II.

Poulet, Georges. STUDIES IN HUMAN TIME. Trans. by Elliott Coleman *Johns Hopkins Univ. Press* 1956 $11.00

Robbe-Grillet, Alain. FOR A NEW NOVEL: Essays on Fiction. Trans. by Richard Howard *Bks. for Libraries* $10.25; *Grove* 1966 Black Cat Bks. pap. $2.25

Roudiez, Leon S. FRENCH FICTION TODAY: A New Direction. *Rutgers Univ. Press* 1972 $15.00

Saintsbury, George. A HISTORY OF THE FRENCH NOVEL: To the Close of the 19th Century. 1917–1919. *Russell & Russell* 1964 2 vols. set $25.00; *Richard West* $24.95

Sarraute, Nathalie. THE AGE OF SUSPICION: Essays on the Novel. Trans. by Maria Jolas *Braziller* 1963 $5.00. In these four essays Mme Sarraute considers a wide range of past masters and seeks to relate their theory and practice to those of the makers of the New French Novel (*see her main entry, this Chapter*).

Strachey, G. Lytton. Landmarks in English Literature. 1912. *Oxford* 1969 pap. $1.95; *Richard West* $10.00

Tilley, Arthur Augustus. Literature of the French Renaissance: An Introductory Essay. 1885. *Folcroft* repr. of 1885 ed. lib. bdg. $20.00; *Macmillan* (Hafner) repr. of 1904 ed. 2 vols. 1959 set $25.00; *Richard West* repr. of 1885 ed. 1973 $20.00

Turnell, Martin. The Art of French Fiction. *New Directions* 1968 $8.50 pap. $2.95. A perceptive critical analysis of the Abbe Prevost, Stendhal, Zola, Maupassant, Proust, Gide and Mauriac.

The Novel in France. 1951 *Bks. for Libraries* $16.50

Ullmann, Stephen. Style in the French Novel. *Harper* Barnes & Noble 1064 $8.50

Wilson, Edmund. Axel's Castle: A Study in the Imaginative Literature of 1870–1930. *Scribner* 1931 $6.95 pap. $2.95. Symbolism: Valéry, Proust and Rimbaud, and others.

O Canada: An American's Notes on Canadian Culture. *Farrar, Straus* 1965 $4.95. Wilson's comprehensive report on Canadian literature in French and on the political mood of French Canadians.

COLLECTIONS

Aspel, Alexander, and Donald Justice, Eds. Contemporary French Poetry: Fourteen Witnesses of Man's Fate. *Univ. of Michigan Press* bilingual ed. 1965 lib. bdg. $4.40 Ann Arbor Bks. pap. $1.95

Various translators, mostly connected with the Univ. of Iowa Translation Workshop; "the book lacks unity of tone and is quite uneven" but "useful"—(*LJ*).

Brians, Paul, Ed. Bawdy Tales from the Courts of Medieval France. *Harper* 1972 pap. $2.95

Carey, Henry F. Early French Poets. 1923 *Kennikat* 1970 $7.50

Comfort, Andrew, Ed. Seven French Short Novel Masterpieces. Introd. by Henri Peyre *Popular Lib.* (orig.) pap. $.95

Dupee, F. W., Ed. Great French Short Novels. (1952, o.p.)

Flores, Angel, Ed. An Anthology of French Poetry from Nerval to Valéry in English Translation. *Doubleday* Anchor Bks. 1958 pap. $1.95; *Peter Smith* $4.25. This collection includes the texts of the original French poems.

Fowlie, Wallace, Trans. and ed. Mid-Century French Poets. *Twayne* 1955 $7.00. Renderings by various translators of poems by Jacob, Fargue, Supervielle, Perse, Cocteau, Breton, Eluard, Desnos, Michaux, Emmanuel; with notes and bibliographies.

Green, F. C., Ed. French Short Stories of the 19th and 20th Centuries. *Dutton* Everyman's 1962 pap. $1.55

Legge, J. F. Chanticleer: A Study of the French Muse. 1935. *Kennikat* 1969 $12.50

Lyon, Pamela, Ed. French Short Stories. *Penguin* Parallel Text pap. $1.45. French texts with English translations of eight stories by contemporary writers such as Robbe-Grillet, Gascar, and Queneau.

MacIntyre, Carlyle F., Trans. French Symbolist Poetry. *Univ. of California Press* 1958 pap. $1.95. Both French and English texts.

Marks, Elaine, Ed. French Poetry from Baudelaire to the Present. *Dell* Laurel Eds. pap. $.75. Both French and English texts.

O'Brien, Justin, Ed. From the N.R.F.: An Image of the Twentieth Century from the Pages of the *Nouvelle Revue Francaise*. 1958 o.p. This important collection contains 45 essays which appeared between 1919 and 1940. The magazine from which they are taken was founded by a small group centering around André Gide. Its writing helped to set the literary tone of the period throughout the field of European letters.

PENGUIN BOOK OF FRENCH VERSE. *Penguin* one-volume ed. $4.25. Pt. 1 To the 15th Century, ed. by B. Woledge Pt. 2 16th–18th Centuries, ed. by Geoffrey Brereton Pt. 3 19th Century, ed. by Anthony Hartley Pt. 4 20th Century

Shapiro, Norman R., Trans. THE COMEDY OF EROS: Medieval French Guides to the Art of Love. *Univ. of Illinois Press* 1971 $4.95

Watson-Taylor, Simon, and Edward Lucie-Smith, Eds. FRENCH POETRY OF TODAY. *Schocken* 1972 $10.00

THEATER

Benedikt, Michael, and George E. Wellwarth, Trans. and eds. MODERN FRENCH THEATRE: The Avant-Garde, Dada, and Surrealism. *Dutton* 1964 pap. $2.95. A collection of 17 representative pieces.

Bishop, Thomas. PIRANDELLO AND THE FRENCH THEATER. *New York Univ. Press* 1970 $6.95 pap. $2.25

Corrigan, Robert, Ed. MASTERPIECES OF THE MODERN FRENCH THEATRE. *Macmillan* Collier Bks. 1967 pap. $1.50. Plays by Becque, Giraudoux, Montherlant, Anouilh, Ionesco, Ghelderode. This volume is one of a series called "Masterpieces of the Modern Theatre."

Esslin, Martin. THE THEATRE OF THE ABSURD. *Doubleday* Anchor Bks. 1961 pap. $2.50; *Overlook Press* $12.50. Analysis of the works of Beckett, Ionesco, and others.

Fowlie, Wallace. DIONYSUS IN PARIS: A Guide to Contemporary French Theatre. *Peter Smith* $5.50

Grossvogel, David. I. TWENTIETH CENTURY FRENCH DRAMA. (Orig. "The Self-Conscious Stage in Modern French Drama") *Columbia* 1958 pap. 1961 $2.25; *Gordian* 1961 $7.50. A remarkably comprehensive account, with analyses of the best plays of the 20th century, including most of those by Adamov, Anouilh, Apollinaire, Beckett, Claudel, Cocteau, Giraudoux, Ionesco, Jarry, and Sartre.

Guicharnaud, Jacques, and June Guicharnaud. MODERN FRENCH THEATRE: From Giraudoux to Genet. *Yale Univ. Press* 1967 $17.50

A revision and expansion of the author's excellent 1961 volume covering French theater since World War II. The revised edition includes new chapters on Vauthier, Arrabal, Duras, Dubillard, Pichette, Vian, Adamov, Gatti and Billetdoux. Three appendixes provide annotated lists of directors, producers and performances. Excellent bibliography of critical works.

Hobson, Harold. THE FRENCH THEATRE TODAY. 1953. *Blom* 1966 $8.75. The English critic reviews the work of French playwrights working in the 1940s and 1950s: Sartre, Montherlant, Salacrou, and Anouilh.

Pronko, Leonard Cabell. AVANT-GARDE: The Experimental Theater in France. *Univ. of California Press* 1962 $6.50. An analytical study largely concerned with Beckett and Ionesco. The volume contains lists of English translations, of French producers, and a bibliography of material about the dramatists.

Waxman, Samuel M. ANTOINE, AND THE THEATRE LIBRE. 1926. *Blom* $10.75

THE SONG OF ROLAND (*Chanson de Roland*). 11th century.

The Song of Roland, a grandly heroic poem, and one of the greatest monuments of medieval literature, recounts in artfully crafted poetic stanzas the deeds of the Count Roland, the strongest of the band of Charlemagne. The events appear to have originated in an actual historical event in which Charlemagne's troops were attacked by Saracens, and suffered a grave defeat. But in losing the battle, the defeated warriors, as the poet tells the story, appear even more bold than the victors, because they are armed with the courage that Christianity gives them. The poem contains vivid battle scenes, with both sides showing brave strength. Roland's last act is to send forth a mighty blast on his horn; he calls for help, and dies from the immense effort, last on the field.

The name of the author of the poem is not known for sure. But his hero appears in Italian literature as the central character of *"Orlando Furioso"* by Ariosto (*q.v.*), whose poem was a model for "The Faerie Queene" by Edmund Spenser (*q.v.*).

The best inexpensive edition of "The Song of Roland" is translated by Dorothy L. Sayers (*Penguin* 1957 pap. $1.25). The author, at first famous for her mystery novels, turned to translation, and produced a marvelously close poetic rendering of "The Song of Roland." Her English stanza forms closely reflect the construction and tempo of the French original, and her work is enriched by a very valuable introduction. Other translations are available as follows: trans. by Patricia Terry *Bobbs* 1965 $5.00 Lib. Arts pap. $1.75; trans. by Jessie Crosland 1926 Medieval Library *Cooper* $5.00; trans. by Frederick Bliss Luquiens *Macmillan* 1952 pap. $1.25; trans. by Robert Harrison *New Am. Lib.* Mentor Bks. 1970 pap. $.95; trans. by William S. Merwin *Random* Vintage Bks. pap. $1.65; trans. by Howard S. Robertson *Rowman* 1973 $5.75 pap. $2.75; trans. by C. K. Scott-Moncrieff *Univ. of Michigan Press* Ann Arbor Bks. 1959 pap. $1.65; trans. by Isabel Butler *Richard West* $10.00; trans. by Jessie Crosland. 1924. *Richard West* $15.00; trans. by Leonard Bacon. 1919. *Richard West* $20.00; trans. by C. K. Scott-Moncrieff. 1919. *Richard West* $15.00; trans. by John O'Hagan. 1883. *Richard West* $20.00; trans. by Arthur S. Way. 1913. *Richard West* $20.00.

AUCASSIN AND NICOLETTE.   c. 1130.

The romance of Aucassin and Nicolette, by an unknown author who lived about 1130, belongs to the beginnings of French literature. A *"chante-fable"*—narrative in alternate prose and verse—it tells of Aucassin's love for a captive maiden, Nicolette. After her escape from prison, the two are captured by the Saracens, placed on different ships and separated for years. Nicolette returns to Provence in the disguise of a harper, sings a song to Aucassin about the love of Aucassin and Nicolette, and the lovers are reunited. There are translations now o.p. by Edward Everett Hale (1875); Rodney MacDonough (1880); F. J. Gibbs (1887); F. W. Bourdillon (1887); Andrew Lang (1887); and Laurence Housman (1930).

AUCASSIN AND NICOLETTE AND OTHER MEDIEVAL ROMANCES AND LEGENDS. Trans. by Eugene Mason *AMS Press* repr. of 1931 ed. $10.00; *Dutton* Everyman's 1910 pap. $1.35; *Richard West* repr. of 1919 ed. $9.50

ABÉLARD, PIERRE, 1079–1143, and HÉLOÏSE, 1101–1164.

Abélard was a brilliant and respected philosopher who, as tutor of Héloïse, fell in love with and secretly married his pupil. Her suspicious uncle had him seized and emasculated. He became a monk and she a nun, and the letters were written after their renunciation of each other. The lovers are buried in one grave in the Pére-Lachaise cemetery in Paris.

THE LETTERS OF ABÉLARD AND HÉLOÏSE. Trans. by C. K. Scott-Moncrieff. 1926. *Cooper* repr. of 1946 ed. 1974 lib. bdg. $7.50. The "Letters" of Héloïse and Abélard, written in Latin, were translated in most cases from the French. C. K. Scott-Moncrieff made a beautiful translation for the first time from the Latin.

ETHICS. Trans. and ed. by D. E. Luscombe *Oxford* 1971 $13.75

THE STORY OF MY MISFORTUNES (Historia Calamatatum). Trans. by Henry Bellows *Macmillan* 1972 pap. $1.50

Books about Abélard and Héloïse

Héloïse and Abélard. By George Moore. *Liveright* Black & Gold Lib. 2 vols. in 1 1921 $7.50. A novel.

Peter Abélard. By Helen Waddell. 1933. *Harper* Barnes & Noble 1971 $6.00; *Peter Smith* 1959 $4.00; *Viking* Compass Bks. 1959 pap. $1.95. A fictional retelling of the tragic love story by a wll known medievalist.

Héloïse and Abélard. By Etienne Gilson. *Univ. of Michigan Press* 1960 $4.95 Ann Arbor Bks. pap. $2.25. The medieval love story retold by an eminent French scholar, widely respected for his work on medieval philosophy and literature.

Abélard. By Cedric Whitman. *Harvard Univ. Press* 1965 $5.50
This retelling of the love story, a narrative poem by a professor of Latin and Greek at Harvard, is "an exploration of the philosophical and psychological dimensions of an archetypal tragic situation . . . [a] charming volume"—(*LJ*).

CHRÉTIEN DE TROYES (also Chrestien de Troyes).   fl. c. 1170.

Almost nothing is known of the life of this poet—one of the first to compose after models established by the troubadours of southern France. His romances, two of which were written for patrons, were intended to entertain an elegant and sophisticated court society. The unfinished "Perceval, or the Grail" is generally regarded as the earliest work on the theme of the Holy Grail.

Chrétien is a gifted storyteller, and a true poet. It was he who first took the odd bits and pieces of the Arthurian material, and moulded them into coherent and individually brilliant works of literary art.

ARTHURIAN ROMANCES. Trans. with introd. by W. W. Comfort *Dutton* Everyman's 1956 $3.95

CLIGES. Trans. by L. J. Gardiner. 1926. *Cooper* $4.50

YVAIN, or The Knight with the Lion. Trans. by Ruth H. Cline *Univ. of Georgia Press* 1975 $11.50; trans. into prose by Robert W. Ackerman and Frederick W. Locke *Ungar* 1957 $4.50 pap. $1.45

Books about Chrétien

> Iwain: A Study of the Origin of the Arthurian Romance. By Arthur C. Brown. 1903. Studies in Arthurian Legend and Literature Ser. *Haskell* $10.95
> Chrétien de Troyes: Inventor of the Modern Novel. By Foster Guyer. *AMS Press* $10.00
> The Grail Castle and Its Mysteries. By Leonardo Olschki. Trans. from the Italian by J. A. Scott; ed. with fwd. by Eugène Vinaver *Univ. of California Press* 1966 $3.75
> Myth and Celebration in Old French Narrative Poetry. By Karl D. Utti. *Princeton Univ. Press* 1973 $11.00
> The Allegory of Adventure: Reading Chrétien's Erec and Yvain. By Tom Artin. *Bucknell Univ. Press* 1974 $12.00

TRISTAN AND ISEULT.   c. 1185

The story of Tristan and Iseult has held the romantic imagination more strongly perhaps than any other of the medieval legends. The hero takes Iseult to Cornwall to become the bride of his kinsman, King Mark. But on the ship they unwittingly drink a love potion intended for the bride's wedding night. Doomed to love each other, and doomed to betray each other and all around them, they play out their fate to a beautiful and tragic death.

The tale was clearly a favorite from early times, for there are numerous medieval versions of it. The earliest poems of consequence are by Thomas of Britain, and by Béroul, a French author. Their poems are known to us only in fragments. Chrétien de Troyes wrote a version called "Marc et Iseut," now lost; and versions abound in other European languages. Gottfried von Strassburg (*q.v.*) composed a magnificent version in German; a less accomplished, but undeservedly neglected version was composed in Middle English by a poet named Thomas ("Sir Tristrem," ed. by G. P. McNeill. 1886. *Johnson Reprint* $18.25). In modern times, many poets have turned their hands to the theme, notably Matthew Arnold, A. C. Swinburne, Alfred Tennyson (*see their main entries in Reader's Adviser, Vol. 1*), and others. The most widely known of modern versions is by Richard Wagner, "Tristan and Isolde," for which he first wrote the poetic text (1859. Trans. by Stewart Robb *Dutton* pap. $2.00), and then the music (1861). His oceanic musicdrama represents the culmination of the view of romantic love as the highest source of human inspiration and redemption.

THE ROMANCE OF TRISTAN AND ISEULT. As retold by Joseph Bédier; trans. by Hilaire Belloc and Paul Rosenfeld; introd. by Padraic Colum; ill. by Serge Ivanoff *Random* Vintage Bks. pap. $1.65. Bédier was a brilliant, learned scholar of medieval French literature, and a brilliant prose stylist in his own right. He took the various fragmentary remains of the Tristan legend and recast them into a version which is part translation into modern French, and part a literary masterpiece by itself. It has been for several generations the principal avenue of introduction to the story for French and English speaking readers alike.

THE ROMANCE OF TRISTAN AND ISOLT. Trans. by Norman B. Spector Medieval French Texts *Northwestern Univ. Press* 1973 $5.50

THE ROMANCE OF TRISTAN AND THE TALE OF TRISTAN'S MADNESS. Trans. by Alan S. Frederick *Penguin* 1970 pap. $1.45; *Peter Smith* $4.00

Books about Tristan and Iseult

> Tristan and Isolt: A Study of the Sources of the Romance. By Gertrude Loomis. Research & Source Work *Burt Franklin* 2nd ed. 2 vols. in 1 1970 $25.00
> The Tristan Legend: A Study in Sources. By Sigmund Eisner. *Northwestern Univ. Press* 1969 $7.00
> The Tristan of Béroul: A Textual Commentary. By T. B. Reid. *Harper* Barnes & Noble 1972 $9.50

The Conflict of Love and Honor: The Medieval Tristan Legend in France, Germany and Italy. By Joan M. Ferrante. *Humanities Press* 1974 pap. $13.75

LORRIS, GUILLAUME DE, fl. c. 1236, and JEAN (CLOPINEL) DE MEUNG (or Meun), c. 1240–1305.

The *"Roman de la Rose"* enjoyed an immense popularity during the Middle Ages and Renaissance. Guillaume de Lorris began the work and wrote a considerable portion of it around 1236. His portion is an elaborate allegory of courtly love, in which the lover, upon entering a garden, must learn to be worthy before he can enjoy the perfect rose that he has fallen in love with. The lines that concern his education form a mirror of medieval ideals and a storehouse of chivalric conventions. The unfinished work was taken up by Jean de Meung about 40 years later; he completed it in a satirical, philosophic manner rather at variance with the tone of the composition he built upon. The poem was widely influential, particularly upon Chaucer (*q.v.*), and it enjoyed a revival among the Pre-Raphaelite poets and painters of late nineteenth-century England. Robbins, in his translation, "has rendered the work into flowing English iambic pentameter which is readable and contemporary yet preserves the elegant air of the original"—(*LJ*).

THE ROMANCE OF THE ROSE. Trans. by Frederick S. Ellis. 1900. *AMS Press* 3 vols. set $37.50; trans. into English verse by Harry W. Robbins; ed. by Charles Dunn *Dutton* 1962 pap. $3.25; trans. by C. R. Dahlberg *Princeton Univ. Press* 1971 $16.50

VILLON, FRANÇOIS (François de Moncorbier). 1431–1465?

Villon is one of the first great French lyric poets, and one of the greatest French poets of any age. His "Testaments" are mock-wills, written in a racy blend of French and underworld slang. Scattered here and there among the ironic items of bequest are exquisite ballads and lyrics, some crystallizing classic themes of medieval literature, such as the *"Ballade des dames du temps jadis"*—the ballad of dead ladies; the poet rhetorically asks "Where are they?" and answers his question with the elegiac refrain, "But where are the snows of yesteryear?" His ballad to Our Lady is a delicate hymn of contrite prayer to the Virgin; and his "Ballad of Fat Margot," a rollicking bawdy-house song. One of his masterpieces, the ballad of the hanged men, was written with the thought that he might soon go to join the spare skeletons that swung upon the public gibbet at Montfaucon. After a chequered career at the Sorbonne, Villon embarked upon a mad career of drinking, whoring, and thieving in the Paris underworld, writing poems when he had a bellyful, some paper, and some fuel (so that the ink in the well was not frozen solid). He was at various times arrested, imprisoned, tortured, and nearly put to death; his final sentence was commuted to exile by King Louis XI on his accession to the throne, when he declared amnesties of all sorts, according to the usual practice of the time. After Villon's release from prison, he disappears from our view, and it is not known how he spent his last years.

Villon's poetry was vigorously revived and promoted during the nineteenth century. English readers became acquainted with it through the translations of John Payne, D. G. Rossetti (*q.v.*) and A. C. Swinburne (*q.v.*).

COMPLETE POEMS. Trans. by Berman Saklatvala (bilingual); introd. by John Fox *Dutton* Everyman's 1967 pap. $3.95; trans. by John Heron Lepper, including the text of John Payne and others *Liveright* 1927 $6.95

THE COMPLETE WORKS OF FRANÇOIS VILLON. Trans. from the medieval French by Anthony Bonner (bilingual); introd. by William Carlos Williams *McKay* 1960 $3.95

BOOK OF FRANÇOIS VILLON. Trans. by Algernon Charles Swinburne, Dante Gabriel Rossetti and John Payne *Branden* $1.95. Some of Swinburne's most lively and impressive translations of Villon are available only in "New Writings by Swinburne" (ed. by Cecil Y. Lang *Syracuse Univ. Press* 1964 $8.50).

Books about Villon

François Villon. By D. B. Wyndham Lewis. 1928. *Richard West* $15.00. A fascinating biographical reconstruction, using Villon's own poems, and numerous documents of the period. An excellent introduction to the poet and his work.
The Poetry of Villon. By J. H. Fox. 1962. *Hillary House* $6.50
François Villon. By Robert H. Anacker. World Authors Ser. *Twayne* 1969 $6.95

RABELAIS, FRANÇOIS. c. 1490–1553

The works of Rabelais are filled with life to the overflowing. His chief actors, Gargantua and his son Pantagruel, are appropriately giants—not only in size, but also in spirit and action. The five books of their adventures are separate works, containing, in different measure, adventures, discussions, farcical scenes, jokes, games, satires, philosophical commentaries, and (one might say) everything else that a worldly, learned man of genius such as Rabelais was could pour into his work. His style is innovative and idiosyncratic, marked by humorous words made up from the learned languages, Greek and Latin, side by side with the most earthy, humble, and rough words of the street and barnyard—all of which he uses with equal skill and relish. One of the most memorable moments in the story is the foundation of the Abbey of Thélème, a castle where beautiful and good young men and women could go and live together under only one rule: *"Fais ce que voudras"*—"Do as you like."

Rabelais' work is one of the great masterpieces of world literature. It is a monument of humanism, with its enthusiastic celebration of the worth of soul and body, and it is a testimony to the richness of the author's all-encompassing humanity.

THE COMPLETE WORKS OF RABELAIS (the five books of Gargantua and Pantagruel). In the modern trans. of Jacques Le Clercq *Random* Modern Lib. Giants 1944 $3.95; *Tudor* 1963 $3.95

THE PORTABLE RABELAIS. Trans. and ed. by Samuel Putnam *Viking* 1946 lib. bdg. $4.95 pap. $2.95. Contains all except a few of the archaic, obscure and the less "Rabelaisian" portions of the Gargantua and Pantagruel.

GARGANTUA AND PANTAGRUEL. 1532–35. Trans. by Sir Thomas Urquhart and Peter Le Motteux (1653–94) *AMS Press* 3 vols. each $15.00; (with title "The Heroic Deeds of Gargantua and Pantagruel") trans. by Thomas Urquhart and Peter Le Motteux (1653–94) *Dutton* Everyman's 2 vols. 1954 each $3.95

The Urquhart-Motteux translation is a classic in its own right, for the authors did not so much translate, as recreate Rabelais in English. And their old-fashioned language has much of the flavor of the French original. For literal accuracy a modern translation, such as that of J. M. Cohen (*Penguin* 1963 pap. $2.65) is preferable; but the spirit of the original is perhaps more vividly represented in the older version. There is a modern volume of selections translated and edited by F. Gray (*AHM Pub. Corp.* Crofts Class. pap. $.85).

Books about Rabelais

François Rabelais. By Arthur Tilley. 1907. *Richard West* 1973 $12.00

Rabelais. By Anatole France. 1928. *Richard West* 1973 $25.00

François Rabelais: Man of the Renaissance. By Samuel Putnam. 1929. *Bks. for Libraries* 1973 $22.00

The Life of François Rabelais. By Jean Plattard. 1930. *Fernhill* 1968 $11.00. The author is one of the most respected authorities on French literature.

Dr. Rabelais. By D. B. Wyndham Lewis. 1957. *Greenwood* 1969 $15.00

Rabelais and the Franciscans. By A. J. Krailsheimer. *Oxford* 1963 $8.60

Rabelais. By Michael Tetel. *Twayne* 1967 $6.95. An introductory study of Rabelais' work seen as satire, stressing the writer's verbal imagery; with a bibliography, a chronology, and an index.

Rabelais. By D. G. Coleman. *Cambridge* 1971 $11.50

Rabelais: A Dramatic Game in Two Parts. Trans. by Robert Baldick; ed. by Jean-Louis Barrault *Farrar, Straus* (Hill & Wang) Dramabks. 1971 $4.95 pap. $1.95

CALVIN, JOHN. 1509–1564. *See Chapter 4, World Religions, Reader's Adviser, Vol. 3*

RONSARD, PIERRE DE. 1524–1585.

Ronsard is one of the principal originators of European poetic tradition as it has existed since the Renaissance. Dissatisfied with native French poetic models, and taken with the example of Greek, Latin, and Italian poetry, he set about to make French poems according to their models. He was the first to imitate systematically forms such as the ode, the sonnet, the epic, the eclogue, the elegy. He attracted a circle of sympathetic poets; since the group amounted to seven, they called themselves the *Pléiade*, after the seven-starred constellation. Their professed aim (like that of all revolutionaries) was to go back to the original foundations, and they found these in the poetry of early Italy, and ancient Greece and Rome. Their manifesto was an essay by Joachim du Bellay (1525–1560) called *"Défense et Illustration de la Langue Française"* (1549), the first significant work of French literary criticism.

Of Ronsard's large and varied literary works, the best known are his sonnets, rich in images and delicate of construction. They have been often translated into English sonnets, notably by Humbert Wolfe.

SELECTED POEMS. Ed. by Christine M. Scollen *Humanities Press* (Athlone Press) 1975 $9.50 pap. $4.50

SONNETS POUR HÉLÈNE. Trans. by Humbert Wolfe. 1934. *Richard West* $20.00

Books about Ronsard

Ronsard, Prince of Poets. By Morris Bishop. 1940. *Univ. of Michigan Press* Ann Arbor Bks. 1959 pap. $1.85

Ronsard: His Life and Times. By D. B. Wyndham Lewis. 1946. *Norwood Editions* $22.50

Spenser, Ronsard and Du Bellay: A Renaissance Comparison. By A. W. Satterthwaite. 1960. *Kennikat* 1971 $10.00

Critical Theory and Practice of the Pléiade. By Robert J. Clements. *Octagon* 1969 $11.50

Pierre de Ronsard. By K. R. Jones. World Author Series *Twayne* $6.95

MONTAIGNE, MICHEL EYQUEM DE. 1533–1592.

Montaigne's essays are a vast compendium of his own thoughts, sentiments, reflections, and opinions, as they were put down and gathered together by him in the course of a long, peaceful life at his chateau near Bordeaux. Aside from a journey to Italy (of which he kept a delightfully detailed diary), and two terms as mayor of Bordeaux, the principal occupation of his mature years was the nurture of his book, which first appeared in 1580, and of which revised editions appeared in 1588 and 1595. We know more perhaps about Montaigne than about any other person of his time; not so much in his outward circumstances, as in his private traits. But his essays are far from being exercises in egotism. One of the author's dominant qualities is his humility, expressed, for example, in the motto in his library, which can still be seen by visitors there today: *"Que scay-je?"*— "What do I know?" In turning to the nearest subject at hand—himself—and letting his well-furnished, supple mind play upon this familiar subject, Montaigne created for us a mirror of ourselves. He is at once a most particular and a most universal author.

The tone and the form of his writings, which he called "essays"—that is, "trial efforts"—was imitated by English writers such as Francis Bacon (*q.v.*) and Thomas Fuller, in the 17th century, and in the 19th century by Lamb and Hazlitt (*qq.v.*), and by their successors in our own time.

COMPLETE WORKS: Essays, Travel Journal, Letters. Newly trans. by Donald M. Frame *Stanford Univ. Press* 1957 $18.50. This translation, the first complete one since 1887, was written by a life-long student of Montaigne. His version is highly readable, and done according to the highest standards of scholarly accuracy, by one who has both knowledge of and sympathy for his subject.

MONTAIGNE'S ESSAYS AND SELECTED WRITINGS. Trans. and ed. by Donald M. Frame (bilingual) *St. Martin's* 1963 pap. $4.50. A beautiful large-print, fully annotated edition.

COMPLETE ESSAYS. Trans. by George B. Ives. *Heritage Press Conn.* 3 vols. each $8.95; trans. by J. M. Cohen *Penguin* pap. $2.25; trans. by Donald M. Frame *Stanford Univ. Press* 1958 $10.00 pap. $4.95

ESSAYS. 1580–1588. Trans. by John Florio (1603); ed. with introd. by George Saintsbury. 1892–1893. *AMS Press* 3 vols. each $15.00; introd. by L. C. Harmer *Dutton* Everyman's 3 vols. each $3.95. Florio's translation, the first into English, is famous for its richness of style. What he loses in strict literal accuracy he gains through infusing the work with his own personality.

SELECTIONS FROM THE ESSAYS. Trans. by Donald M. Frame *AHM Pub. Corp.* Crofts Class. 1973 pap. $.85

IN DEFENSE OF RAYMOND SEBOND. Trans. by Arthur H. Beattie *Ungar* $4.75 pap. $1.95. Raymond Sebond was a 15th-century Spanish theologian, whose work on natural theology Montaigne translated from Latin into French. This lengthy essay in reality has less to do with Sebond and his book than with larger questions of religion and revelation.

AUTOBIOGRAPHY. Trans. by Marvin Lowenthal *Random* Vintage Bks. 1956 pap. $1.45

Books about Montaigne

Montaigne. By Fortunat Strowski. 1931. Philosophy Monograph Ser. *Burt Franklin* 1972 $17.50

Montaigne. By André Gide. 1939. A classic study, currently o.p.

Montaigne's Discovery of Man: The Humanization of a Humanist. By Donald M. Frame. *Columbia* 1955 $10.00. The evolution of Montaigne's "meditative journey" through life as revealed in the several editions of the Essays.

Montaigne: A Biography. By Donald M. Frame. *Harcourt* 1965 $10.00
"Mr. Frame in his preface states that it has been his intention that 'the nonspecialist may read this book with interest, the scholar with confidence'; he has succeeded admirably. . . .Written in a style which is both exact and pleasant . . . the biography is soundly based on the best documentary and critical sources"—*(LJ)*.

Montaigne's Essays: A Study. By Donald M. Frame. Landmark in Literature Ser. *Prentice-Hall* 1969 $5.95 pap. $1.95

Essays of Montaigne: A Critical Exploration. By R. A. Sayce. *Northwestern Univ. Press* 1972 $15.00

DESCARTES, RENÉ. 1596–1650. *See Chapter 5, Philosophy,* Reader's Adviser, *Vol. 3.*

CORNEILLE, PIERRE. 1606–1684.

Corneille is the first French dramatist; that is to say, the first to write plays according to modern (as opposed to medieval) notions of French drama. He achieved the establishment of a pattern that was to be followed by successive generations of dramatists, such as Racine. His plays deal with noble characters, in closely defined situations of high moral intensity, developed within the limits of the "three unities"—a term derived from the writings of the Greek philosopher Aristotle, and interpreted to mean that the dramatic action must happen in the same locality (unity of place), within the span of time covered by the stage presentation (unity of time), and in a coherent sequence of events (unity of action). The original model for the "unities" was the practice of Greek dramatists. Corneille's most admired play is "The Cid," a tale of vengeance and divided allegiance. It vividly represents the dominant theme of his tragedies—the inner struggle between duty and passion—a theme which Racine was later to treat after his own different fashion. Corneille, in his shaping of language and form to his dramatic purposes, had a great effect upon the development of French literature; more specifically, it can be said that he gave form and aim to French neo-classicism. Far from being cold masterpieces of the past, Corneille's plays live today in the French theater, where they are regularly performed and enthusiastically received.

CHIEF PLAYS. Trans. into English blank verse; introd. on Corneille by Lacy Lockert *Princeton Univ. Press* 1952 rev. ed. 1957 $9.50

"Well translated by Lacy Lockert, who provided an excellent critical introduction, this is a valuable selection. . . . Included are *Horace, Cid, Cinna, Polyeucte, Rodogune, Nicomède*"—*(LJ)*.

MOOT PLAYS OF CORNEILLE. Ed. and trans. into blank verse by Lacy Lockert *Vanderbilt Univ. Press* 1959 $7.50. Includes *La Mort de Pompée, Héraclius, Don Sanche d'Aragon, Sertorius, Othon, Attila, Pulchérie* and *Suréna*.

SEVEN PLAYS. Trans. by Samuel Solomon *Random* 1969 $15.00

LE CID. 1636. *AHM Pub. Corp.* Crofts Class. pap. $.85; trans. by Rosalie Feltenstein *Barron's* 1953 $2.95 pap. $.95; ed. by A. Donald Sellstrom *Prentice-Hall* 1967 pap. $1.95

POLYEUCTE. 1643. Trans. by Eric Steel *Barron's* 1974 pap. $1.50. The hero, an Armenian convert to Christianity, defends his faith with his life, and wins the conversion of others with his death.

RODOGUNE. 1645. Trans. by William G. Chubb, with facing French and English texts *Univ. of Nebraska Press* 1974 $12.00

Books about Corneille

Ariosto, Shakespeare, and Corneille. By Benedetto Croce. Trans. by D. Ainslie. 1920. *Russell & Russell* $8.50. The author is one of the most profound and influential of modern critics and philosophers.

The Classical Moment: Studies in Corneille, Molière, and Racine. By Martin Turnell. 1948. *Greenwood* 1971 $13.50

Corneille: His Heroes and Their Worlds. By Robert J. Nelson. *Univ. of Pennsylvania Press* 1964 $8.50. The author studies the morality upon which Corneille based his dramatic practice.

Pierre Corneille. By Claude Abraham. World Authors Ser. *Twayne* $6.95

SCARRON, PAUL. 1610–1660.

Poet, playwright, novelist, Paul Scarron was a purveyor of realism in the novel before realism existed. Paralyzed and misshapen after 1638, he married Mlle D'Aubigné who would after his death become Mme de Maintenon, mistress and eventually wife of Louis XIV. His role in French 17th-century literature continues to grow in importance as craftsman and student of human psychology.

Whole Comical Works. Foundations of the Novel Ser. *Garland Pub.* Pt. I (vol. 2) $25.00 Pts. 2 & 3 (vol. 3) $25.00

Innocent Adultery and Other Short Novels. Trans. by Tom Brown *Blom* 1968 $10.00

The Comical Romance. 1651. Trans. by Tom Brown *Blom* 1968 $12.50

Books about Scarron

Paul Scarron. By Frederick A. De Armas. World Authors Ser. *Twayne* $6.95

LA ROCHEFOUCAULD, FRANÇOIS, DUC de. 1613–1680.

La Rochefoucauld, in his "Maxims," pares down the limits of literary expression to the finely balanced measure of a sentence, or a brief paragraph. In his careful words, he points out the hypocrisies of mankind. All human behavior, good, evil, or merely ordinary, is, in his eyes, tainted by self-interest: "Virtue runs to selfishness like rivers to the sea. Vice is compounded into virtue like poison into medicines." The views expressed in the "Maxims" were the bitter fruit of the author's years as a courtier. When his expectations of favor were at last disappointed, he retired from the royal circle, and enjoyed the company and conversation of talented and sympathetic writers, such as Mme de Sévigné and Mme de Lafayette.

The Maxims of François, Duc de la Rochefoucauld. 1665. Trans. by John Heayd *Branden* pap. $.95

Books about La Rochefoucauld

La Rochefoucauld: His Mind and Art. By Will G. Moore. *Oxford* 1969 $5.25 pap. $3.25

LA FONTAINE, JEAN de. 1621–1695.

La Fontaine's "Fables" are children's classics and sophisticated works of art. He adapted the stories of Aesop and other ancient authors of moral tales and turned them into concise, highly polished verse. His version of the story about the ant and the grasshopper is one of the most widely known of French poems.

Fables. Trans. into English verse by Sir Edward Marsh *Dutton* Everyman's 1952 $3.95; trans. by Marianne Moore *Viking* 1954 $5.00 Compass Bks. pap. $1.65

The Best Fables. Trans. by Frances Duke *Univ. Press of Virginia* 1965 $7.50

Selected Fables. Trans. by Eunice Clark; ill. by Alexander Calder. 1948. *Dover* pap. $1.50

Books about La Fontaine

Young La Fontaine: A Study of His Artistic Growth in His Early Poetry and First Fables. By Philip A. Wadsworth. 1952. *AMS Press* 1970 $15.00

La Fontaine: Poet and Counterpoet. By Margaret Guiton. *Rutgers Univ. Press* 1961 $5.00

Esthetics of Negligence: La Fontaine's Contes. By John C. Lapp. *Cambridge* 1971 $12.50

La Fontaine and His Friends. By Agnes MacKay *Braziller* 1973 $8.95

MOLIÈRE (Jean-Baptiste Poquelin). 1622–1673.

Molière is the creator of French comedy. A master of all comic forms, he knew how to combine lofty satire with broad slapstick, and he left a collection of comedies unique in Western literature. He also directed, acted, and was for many years manager of his own company. He died on the night he performed the title role in his play, "The Imaginary Invalid." He held no orthodoxy except that of reason and common sense. He was at once a free thinker and a satirist of the nonconformist of his day.

His plays lead a vigorous life. Their scenes are located in the seventeenth century, but the characters and situations are as alive now as ever. The plays are regularly performed in France and in the United States, and they have been made into successful screen versions.

The Works of Molière. Trans. by John Ozell. First English edition of Molière's collected works (1714) *Blom* 6 vols. in 3, set $57.50. It was not highly regarded by 18th-century critics, says the modern publisher, because of its "colloquial, lively" (and today attractive) translations.

Comedies. Trans. by H. Baker and J. Miller *Dutton* Everyman's 2 vols. 1955 each $3.95

The Misanthrope and Other Plays: The Misanthrope, Tartuffe, The Imaginary Invalid, A Doctor in Spite of Himself, The Sicilian. Trans. by John Wood *Penguin* 1959 pap. $1.75

THE MISER AND OTHER PLAYS. Trans. by John Wood *Penguin* pap. $1.55. The Would-Be Gentleman, That Scoundrel Scapin, The Miser, Love's the Best Doctor, Don Juan.

TARTUFFE AND OTHER PLAYS. Newly trans. by Donald M. Frame *New Am. Lib.* 1967 Signet pap. $1.50. The Precious Ladies, The School for Husbands, The School for Wives, Critique of the School for Wives, The Impromptu of Versailles, Don Juan.

SIX PROSE COMEDIES: The Pretentious Young Ladies, Don Juan, The Unwilling Doctor, The Miser, The Middle-Class Gentleman, Scapin. Trans. by George Graveley *Oxford* World's Class. 1968 $3.00

THE KILTARTAN MOLIÈRE. Trans. by Lady Gregory. 1910. *Blom* $10.50. The Miser, The Doctor in Spite of Himself, Scapin.

THE PRETENTIOUS YOUNG LADIES (*Les Précieuses Ridicules*). 1659. Trans. by Herma Briffault *Barron's* pap. $.95

THE SCHOOL FOR HUSBANDS (*L'École des Maris*). 1661. Trans. and adapted by Arthur Guiterman and Lawrence Langner in rhyme *French* 1933 1935 $1.25

THE SCHOOL FOR WIVES (*L'École des Femmes*). 1662. An adaptation in Rhymed Verse by Eric M. Steel *Barron's* 1971 pap. $1.50; adapted by Miles Malleson *French* $1.25; trans. by Richard Wilbur *Harcourt* 1971 $5.75 Harvest Bks. 1972 pap. $1.25

DON JUAN (*Dom Juan*). 1665. Trans. by Wallace Fowlie *Barron's* 1964 pap. $1.25

THE MISANTHROPE. 1666. Trans. by B. D. N. Grebanier *Barron's* 1959 $2.95 pap. $1.25; (and "Tartuffe") trans. and ed. by Richard Wilbur *Harcourt* 1965 Harvest Bks. pap. $2.25

THE UNWILLING DOCTOR (*Le Médecin Malgré Lui*). 1666. Trans. by Lisl Beer *Branden* 1961 $1.00; (with title "The Reluctant Doctor") trans. by W. Hannan *Theater Arts Books* $1.25

THE MISER. 1668. Trans. by Wallace Fowlie *Barron's* 1964 pap. $.95; a new acting version based upon the 1739 English trans. by H. Baker and J. Miller, arr. by Walter F. Kerr *Dramatic* 1942 $.85

TARTUFFE: A Comedy in Five Acts. 1669. Trans. and ed. by Haskell M. Block *AHM Pub. Corp.* Crofts Class. pap. $.85; trans. by Renée Walsinger *Barron's* 1959 $2.95 pap. $.95; trans. by R. Hartle *Bobbs* Liberal Arts 1965 pap. $1.10; trans. by Rosenberg *T. Y. Crowell* (Chandler Pub.) pap. $1.50; trans. by Richard Wilbur *Harcourt* 1963 $3.95 Harvest Bks. pap. $1.45

THE MIDDLE-CLASS GENTLEMAN (*Le Bourgeois Gentilhomme*). 1670. Trans. by Herma Briffault *Barron's* 1957 pap. $1.25

SCAPIN (*Les Fourberies de Scapin*). 1671. Trans. by Donald Sutherland. *T. Y. Crowell* (Chandler Pub.) pap. $.85

THE LEARNED LADIES (*Les Femmes Savantes*). 1672. Trans. by Renée Waldinger *Barron's* 1957 pap. $1.25

THE IMAGINARY INVALID (*Le Malade Imaginaire*). 1673. (With title "The Would-Be Invalid") trans. and ed. by Morris Bishop *AHM Pub. Corp.* Crofts Class. pap. $.85; arr. and adapted by K. W. Turner *Dramatic* 1939 $.85; trans. and adapted by Merritt Stone *French* 1939 $.75; *French & European* bilingual ed. pap. $1.50

Books about Molière

Molière. By John Palmer. 1930. *Blom* 2nd ed. 1965 $12.50; *Richard West* $12.45
Molière: A New Criticism. By Will Grayburn Moore. *Oxford* 1949 $3.75 pap. $1.60
Molière and the Comedy of the Intellect. By J. D. Hubert. *Univ. of California Press* 1962 $12.75
Men and Masks: A Study of Molière. By Lionel Gossman. *Johns Hopkins Press* 1963 $10.00 pap. 1969 $2.95
   Library Journal highly recommends this work on Molière as "a reflection of French historical events" and "the most complete study of its kind."
Molière: A Collection of Critical Essays. Ed. with introd. by Jacques Guicharnaud. *Prentice-Hall* 1964 $5.95

"Seventeen excellent essays on Molière by important French, British and American critics. . . . A Molière chronology, notes on critics, commentary on notable performances and
judiciously selected bibliography are included"—(*LJ*).
Molière: Stage and Study. Ed. by W. D. Howarth and J. Merlin Thomas. *Oxford* 1973 $17.75

PASCAL, BLAISE.   1623–1662. *See Chapter 5, Philosophy*, Reader's Adviser, *Vol. 3*.

SÉVIGNÉ, MME DE (Marie de Rabutin-Chantal, Marquise de Sévigné).   1626–1696.

Mme de Sévigné's letters (written mostly to her daughter from 1648 to 1696) "reflect so
accurately the spirit of the time in which they were written and the character and spirit of the
woman who wrote them that the reader lives for a while in 17th century France." "They provide
vivid pictures of French society in the age of Louis XIV, of the life of the aristocracy in Paris, at
court, and in the provinces; and in them figure many of the great personages of the time." Mme
de Sévigné is noted for "the unaffected elegance of her style" and "the acuteness of her
observations."

LETTERS TO HER DAUGHTER AND HER FRIENDS. Sel. with introd. by Richard Aldington
from the nine-vol. London ed. of 1811; biographical and historical app. 1927. *Folcroft*
2 vols. $85.00

The 1500 "Letters" form "one of the great masterpieces of French Literature"—(*LJ*).

SELECTED LETTERS OF MADAME DE SÉVIGNÉ. Sel. and trans. with introd. by H. T.
Barnwell *Dutton* Everyman's 1960 $3.95

Books about Mme de Sévigné

Mme de Sévigné: Her Letters and her World. By Arthur Stanley. 1946. *Richard West* 1973
$20.00
Madame de Sévigné: A Portrait in Letters. By Harriet Ray Allentuch. *Johns Hopkins Press* 1963
$12.00

A study of Mme de Sévigné as seen in her letters. It is written as "scientific characterology," a
discipline, says *Library Journal*, "much cultivated in France." "One is bound to admire the
manner in which Mrs. Allentuch has laid bare the complex and even contradictory elements
of an extraordinary personality."

LA FAYETTE, MARIE MADELEINE, Comtesse DE (Pioche de la Vergne).   1634–1693.

Well-educated and with high connections at court, Mme de La Fayette sought refuge from an
unhappy marriage in the company of such literary figures as Mme de Sévigné (*q.v.*), La Rochefoucauld (*q.v.*) and Jean Regnault de Segrais, a 17th-century poet and novelist. "The Princess of
Cleves" is considered the first great French novel. Supposed to have been written with the
assistance of Segrais and La Rochefoucauld, it is notable for quiet wit, simplicity and psychological
realism.

THE PRINCESS OF CLÈVES. (In "Seven French Short Novel Masterpieces" ed. by Andrew
Comfort) *Popular Lib.* $.95

Books about Mme de La Fayette

Madame de La Fayette. By Sterling Haig. World Author Ser. *Twayne* $6.95

RACINE, JEAN BAPTISTE   1639–1699.

Racine is the great tragic dramatist of French literature. He takes his themes from classical,
biblical, and Oriental story, and treats them in the neoclassic manner: keeping to few characters,
observing the "three unities" (*see above, under Corneille*), and writing in regular verses called
"alexandrines." He wrote only twelve plays, but each is original and highly polished. His
masterpiece is "Phèdre," a tale of powerful passions and contradictions, based upon an ancient
Greek story. Racine is in many ways the most "French" of authors; he is the national dramatist, as
Shakespeare is for the English-speaking world. Their differences are less in rank than in kind, that
is, in outlook and inspiration. To understand Racine is to understand some of the distinctive traits
of the literature of France. As with the other French "classics," the plays of Racine are regularly
performed by French acting companies.

COMPLETE PLAYS. Trans. by Samuel Solomon *Random* 2 vols. 1968 boxed set $20.00

THE BEST PLAYS. Trans. by Lacy Lockert into rhyming verse *Princeton Univ. Press* 1936
pap. $3.95. Contains Andromache, Britannicus, Phaedra, Athalia.

RACINE'S MID-CAREER TRAGEDIES. Trans. by Lacy Lockert *Princeton Univ. Press* 1958 $7.50. English rhyming verse translations of Berenice, Bajazét, Mithridate, Iphigenie.

JEAN RACINE: Five Plays. Trans. by Kenneth Muir *Farrar, Straus* (Hill & Wang) 1960 $4.50 Dramabks. pap. $2.25. Contains Andromache, Britannicus, Berenice, Phaedra, Athalia.

THREE PLAYS: Phaedra, Andromache, Britannicus. Trans. by George Dillon *Univ. of Chicago Press* 1961 Phoenix Bks. pap. $2.45

PHAEDRA AND OTHER PLAYS. Trans. by John Cairncross *Penguin* 1964 $1.95. Includes Iphigenia and Athaliah.

PHAEDRA and FIGARO. *Farrar, Straus* 1961 Noonday pap. $2.25; *Octagon* 1972 $8.00

ANDROMACHE. 1667. Trans. by Herma Briffault *Barron's* $4.25 pap. $1.25

PHAEDRA (*Phèdre*). 1677. Trans. and ed. by Oreste F. Pucciani *AHM Pub. Corp.* Crofts Class. pap. $.85; trans. by Bernard Grebanier *Barron's* pap. $.75; trans. by W. Goddard *T. Y. Crowell* (Chandler Pub.) 1961 pap. $1.50; trans. by Margaret Rawlings (bilingual) *Dutton* Everyman's 1962 pap. $1.25; trans. in rhymed alexandrine couplets by William Packard *French* 1966 pap. $1.25; trans. and ed. by R. C. Knight Edinburgh Bilingual Lib. *Univ. of Texas Press* 1972 $5.75 pap. $2.25

Books about Racine

Racine. By Jean Giraudoux. Trans. by P. Mansell Jones *Folcroft* 1938 $5.00
Aspects of Racinian Tragedy. By John Lapp. *Univ. of Toronto Press* 1955 $10.00
The Hidden God. By Lucien Goldman. Trans. by Philip Thody *Humanities Press* 1964 $15.50
On Racine. By Roland Barthes. Trans. by Richard Howard (1964, *o.p.*)
    Three essays by a Sorbonne professor on the meaning of Racine's 11 tragedies, on a famous French production of Phèdre and on the origins of Racine's present reputation. Critic Lionel Abel called the studies "simply first rate: one of the best pieces of criticism in recent years and probably the best book on Racine ever written."
Racine's Rhetoric. By Peter France. *Oxford* 1966 $8.50
    A scholarly, "full-scale study of Racine's rhetoric against the background of contemporary theory and practice. . . . The investigation is wide and deep, but its value lies in the clarity of exposition, the modest, unpedantic approach and the sensitivity of the analysis"—(*TLS*, London).
The Art of Jean Racine. By Bernard Weinberg. *Univ. of Chicago Press* 1969 pap. $3.45

MARIVAUX, PIERRE CARLET CHAMBLAIN DE. 1688–1763.

Marivaux, whose style gave birth to the term *marivaudage*, is a major writer—European as well as French—in the novel and theater. The refinement of thought and expression (bordering for some on preciosity) which is his trademark, is particularly clear in his plays, of which perhaps the most widely known are "*Les Fausses Confidences*" and "*Le Jeu de l'amour et du hasard.*" In his "*La Vie de Marianne*" and "*Le Paysan parvenu*" (both unfinished at his death), he did much to bring the novel into its own as an important genre. He was not a *philosophe* and no love was lost between him and them.

SEVEN COMEDIES. Trans. by Oscar and Adrienne Mandel; ed. by Oscar Mandel *Cornell Univ. Press* 1968 $14.50

PHARSAMOND, or The New Knight-Errand. 1715. Trans. 1750. Ed. by Michael F. Shugrue The Flowering of the Novel 1740–1755 Ser. *Garland Pub.* 1974 $25.00

Books about Marivaux

Marivaux: A Study in Sensibility. By Ruth K. Jamieson. 1941. *Octagon* 1969 $9.50
    "A fresh approach which adds much to our understanding of the subject"—(Brenner). This well-established study concerns particularly the novels.
Theater of Marivaux. By Kenneth N. McKee. *New York Univ. Press* 1958 $8.95
Marivaux. By Oscar Haac. World Authors Ser. *Twayne* 1974 $6.95
Marivaux's Novels: Theme and Function in Early 18th-Century Narrative. By Ronald C. Rosbottom. *Fairleigh-Dickinson Univ. Press* 1975 $10.00
    "Rosbottom's study is a serious contribution to the continuing enlightenment of the sources, circumstances and achievements of Marivaux's role in critical and creative literature at the

post-classic moment of turn to enlightenment and modernity. Admirably read in both primary and secondary sources"—(J. R. Loy).

MONTESQUIEU, CHARLES LOUIS DE SECONDAT, Baron DE LA BREDE ET DE. 1689–1755.

Montesquieu, of Bordeaux nobility of the robe and member of that city's *parlement* and *président à mortier* for a time, is the first of the great French philosophers. His youthful "Persian Letters" (1741) was an epistolary novel that set a style for the rest of the century; his "Considerations on the Grandeur and Decadence of the Romans" (1734) is an important example of the sociological "case study" before its time; and his masterly "Spirit of the Laws" (1748), his life work, became a source book, not on laws, but on where laws come from, for future generations of political scientists and sociologists in Europe and America.

PERSIAN LETTERS. 1721. Trans. and ed. by J. Robert Loy 1962 *New Am. Lib.* pap. $2.95; trans. by C. J. Betts *Penguin* 1973 pap. $2.65

CONSIDERATION ON THE CAUSES OF THE GREATNESS OF THE ROMANS AND THEIR DECLINE. 1734. Trans. by David Lowenthal *Cornell Univ. Press* 1968 pap. $1.95

THE SPIRIT OF THE LAWS. 1748. Trans. by Thomas Nugent (1750); introd. by Franz Neumann *Macmillan* (Hafner) 1949 pap. $4.95

Books about Montesquieu

Montesquieu in America, 1760–1801. By Paul M. Spurlin. 1940. *Octagon* 1969 $11.00
Montesquieu: A Critical Biography. By Robert Shackleton. *Oxford* 1961 $9.50
Montesquieu. By J. Robert Loy. World Authors Ser. *Twayne* 1968 $6.95

VOLTAIRE (François-Marie Arouet de Voltaire).   1694–1778.

Voltaire was born François-Marie Arouet into a prospering middle-class family. His satires on the king and ruling class twice caused him imprisonment; and in 1727 he was exiled for a time to England. There he came to admire English rationalism, freedom and progress—ideas which, as he expressed them, were seminal for the French Revolution.

His writings, noted for their incisive wit, included epic, lyric and dramatic poetry, novels, philosophical essays, criticism and historical narrative. Highly regarded in his lifetime as a dramatist, he is better known today for his novel "Candide" and for his historical and philosophical works. The "Philosophical Dictionary" and other philosophical works like the "Philosophic Letters" and the "Treatise on Tolerance" set forth his credo of "natural religion"—a belief in God and the practice of virtue but a disbelief in dogma and revelation. In the Age of Enlightenment, Voltaire was the foe of religious hypocrisy, corruption and priestcraft. He was long regarded as an infidel, but the modern verdict is that "a foe to religion, he made religion and the world more honest." His many thousands of letters contain much of his thought and personality.

The novel, "Candide, or Optimism," is an entertaining attack on the optimistic philosphy of Leibnitz, which Voltaire turned against after the terrible Lisbon earthquake of 1755, in which many lives were lost. Each of the hero's catastrophic adventures leaves his Leibnitz-oriented friend, Dr. Pangloss, declaring: "Whatever is, is right," and "Everything is for the best in this best of all possible worlds."

THE PORTABLE VOLTAIRE. Ed. with introd. by Ben Ray Redman *Viking* 1949 $6.50 pap. $2.95. Contains Candide, Zadig, Micromegas, The Story of a Good Brahmin, Letters to Frederick the Great and others, The Lisbon Earthquake, Selections from the Philosophical Dictionary and other works.

VOLTAIRE ON RELIGION: Selected Writings. Trans. and ed. by Kenneth W. Appelgate *Ungar* 1974 $7.50

SHORTER WRITINGS. *A. S. Barnes* Perpetua Bks. pap. $1.45

VOLTAIRE: Alphabet of Wit. *Peter Pauper Press* $1.95

CANDIDE AND OTHER WRITINGS. (With title "Candide and Zadig) introd. by Raymond R. Canon *Assoc. Booksellers* Airmont Bks. pap. $.60; (with title "Voltaire's Candide, Zadig, and Selected Stories") trans. by Donald M. Frame *New Am. Lib.* Signet pap. $.60; (with title "Candide and Other Stories") trans. by Joan Spencer; introd. by Theodore Besterman *Oxford* World's Class. pap. $3.00; ed. with introd. by Haskell M. Block *Random* (Modern Lib.) 1956 pap. $1.95; ed. with introd. by Lester Crocker *Simon & Schuster* (Washington Square) 1962 pap. $.60

ELEMENTS OF ISAAC NEWTON'S PHILOSOPHY. 1738. Trans. by John Hanna *International Scholarly Bks. Services* (Frank Cass Ltd.) 1967 $14.00

MAHOMET THE PROPHET, or Fanaticism. 1741. Trans. by Robert L. Myers *Ungar* $4.50 pap. $1.25

ZADIG (1748). With Crébillon's "Zeokinizal, King of the Kofranis." Ed. by Michael Shugrue *Garland Pub.* 1974 lib. bdg. $25.00

THE AGE OF LOUIS XIV. 1751. *Dutton* Everyman's $3.95 pap. $1.95

THE VIRGIN OF ORLEANS (*La Pucelle*). 1755. Trans. by Howard Nelson *Swallow* 1965 $5.00

CANDIDE. 1759. Ed. by N. L. Torrey *AHM Pub. Corp.* Crofts Class. pap. $.85; trans. by Lowell Blair 1932 *Bantam* 1959 pap. $.60; ill. by Rockwell Kent *Barron's* 1963 pap. $1.75; introd. by André Morize *Branden* 1936 $.95; (and "Other Tales") trans. by Tobias Smollett, rev. by James Thornton *Dutton* Everyman's 1955 $3.95 pap. $1.95; trans. and ed. by Robert M. Adams *Norton* Critical Eds. 1966 pap. $1.95; trans. by John Butt *Penguin* $.95; ill. by Fritz Kredel *Peter Pauper Press* de luxe artist's ed. 1948 $4.95; trans. and ed. by Peter Gay (bilingual) *St. Martin's* 1963 pap. $3.95; trans. by Tobias Smollett *Simon & Schuster* (Washington Square) Collateral Class. 1962 pap. $.50

VOLTAIRE'S PHILOSOPHICAL DICTIONARY. 1764. Trans. and ed. by Peter Gay; pref. by André Maurois *Basic Bks.* 2 vols. 1962 $12.50; trans. by Peter Gay *Harcourt* Harvest Bks. 1967 pap. $2.95; trans. by Theodore Besterman *Penguin* 1972 pap. $2.45; trans. by Theodore Besterman *Peter Smith* $4.50

THE PHILOSOPHY OF HISTORY. 1765. Pref. by Thomas Kiernan *Citadel Press* pap. $2.25

SELECTED LETTERS. Trans. by Richard A. Brooks *New York Univ. Press* 1973 $12.95

LETTERS CONCERNING THE ENGLISH NATION. 1733. Trans. by Lockman (1733) with introd. by Charles Whibley. 1926. *Burt Franklin* 1974 lib. bdg. $12.50

PHILOSOPHICAL LETTERS. 1773. Trans. with introd. by Ernest Dilworth *Bobbs* Liberal Arts 1961 pap. $1.45

Books about Voltaire

Voltaire. By Gustave Lanson. 1906. Trans. by Robert A. Wagoner *Wiley* 1966 $9.25 pap. $5.50 "After more than a half century, this classic study is still probably the best single work on Voltaire"—(Topazio). The author is famous for his "History of French Literature."
Spirit of Voltaire. By Norman L. Torrey. 1938 *Russell & Russell* 1968 $11.00
Voltaire and Madame du Châtelet. By Ira O. Wade. 1941. *Octagon* 1966 $10.00. Voltaire was involved in a long intellectual friendship and love affair with this scientist.
The Search for a New Voltaire. By Ira O. Wade. *American Philosophical Soc.* 1958 pap. $5.00. Based on materials at the American Philosophical Society.
Voltaire and Candide. By Ira O. Wade. 1959. *Kennikat* $13.50
Voltaire and the Calas Case. By Edna Nixon. *Vanguard* 1962 $5.95. A *cause célèbre* to which Voltaire brought all his brilliance and courage.
Voltaire Essays and Another. Ed. by Theodore Besterman. *Oxford* 1962 $6.00
A collection of papers and addresses covering a wide field of Voltaire scholarship. "It is safe to say that no one in the world today has a more thorough knowledge of Voltaire than Mr. Besterman, who has literally lived and breathed Voltaire . . . these many years"—(Topazio).
Voltaire. By H. N. Brailsford. *Oxford* 1963 pap. $1.50. A study of his style.
Voltaire: A Critical Study of His Major Works. By Virgil W. Topazio. 1966 *Peter Smith* 1967 $5.00
The Intellectual Development of Voltaire. By Ira O. Wade. *Princeton Univ. Press* 1969 $20.00
Voltaire and the Century of Light. By A. Owen Aldridge. *Princeton Univ. Press* 1975 $20.00

CRÉBILLON (fils), CLAUDE PROSPER JOLYOT DE. 1707–1777.

Son of the playwright rival of Voltaire (Crébillon *père*), Crébillon the younger was a writer of boudoir novels which are contemporary with the *comédie larmoyante* in France, and with Richardson, Fielding, and Cleland in England. His role in the development of the French novel has come to be appreciated by recent perceptive critics. Perhaps his best known novel is "The Sofa" (1745).

LETTERS FROM THE MARCHIONESS DE M. TO THE COMTE DE R. Foundations of the Novel
Ser. *Garland Pub.* $25.00

Books about Crébillon

Essay on Crébillon Fils. By Clifton Cherpack. *Duke Univ. Press* 1962 $7.25

ROUSSEAU, JEAN JACQUES. 1712–1778.

Rousseau's writings mark the beginning of Romanticism in French literature. "Julie, or the New Héloïse" (1760), an epistolary novel, marks a milestone in the development of the French novel. "Émile," published in 1762, is a philosophical novel, or pedagogical romance, divided into five books. The first four deal with the education of the boy, Émile; the last one with the education of the girl, Sophie, destined to be Émile's wife. This work is the foundation of much modern pedagogy, having influenced both Pestalozzi and Froebel in their educational methods. Rousseau advocated education by observation rather than by textbook, and manual training along with mental training. "The Social Contract," a treatise on political rights, was a strong influence in the development of the French Revolution. Many of his political ideas were carried out, and many of his socialistic theories put into effect in its early days. In rebellion against the rationalism of Voltaire and others, he called for a return to human feeling as a guide and maintained that man, basically good, has been corrupted by his society. Rousseau has had his passionate partisans and opponents ever since, but we are now, says Peter Gay in the *N.Y. Times*, beginning to see him in perspective, as a serious, complex, "even a consistent," thinker.

He was the son of a watchmaker and had an erratic career at many occupations until his writings won him prominence. His life as a literary rebel continued stormy and included a period of exile, but he returned to finish his "Confessions" and died in Paris in 1778.

POLITICAL WRITINGS: Containing The Social Contract, Considerations on the Government of Poland and Pt. 1 of The Consitutional Project for Corsica. Trans. and ed. by Frederick Watkins (1953, o.p.). An important collection.

MINOR EDUCATIONAL WRITINGS. Sel. and trans. by William H. Boyd *Teachers College* 1962 $4.95 pap. $2.25

MISCELLANEOUS WORKS. 1767. *Burt Franklin* 5 vols. 1973 set $75.00

FIRST AND SECOND DISCOURSES. 1750 and 1754. Trans. by Roger D. and Judith R. Masters; ed. with introd. by Roger D. Masters *St. Martin's* 1964 pap. $3.95. The first, which won him early fame, was on "the arts and sciences," the second on "inequality"; both expressed the central thesis of his life (*see below*).

LA NOUVELLE HÉLOÏSE. 1761. Trans. by Judith H. McDowell *Pennsylvania State Univ. Press* 1968 $10.00

ÉMILE, or Treatise of Education. 1762. Trans. by Barbara Foxley *Dutton* Everyman's 1955 $3.95; trans. and ed. by William H. Boyd *Teachers College* 1962 $2.95 pap. $1.50

THE SOCIAL CONTRACT. 1762. (With title "Social Contract: Essays by Locke, Hume, and Rousseau") ed. by Sir Ernest Barker *Oxford* World's Class. 1951 pap. $2.95. This edition contains works on the same subject by three great political thinkers.

THE SOCIAL CONTRACT (1762) AND OTHER DISCOURSES. Trans. with introd. by G. D. H. Cole *Dutton* Everyman's Am. ed. 1950 $3.95

THE SOCIAL CONTRACT. 1762. An 18th-century trans. rev. and ed. by Charles Frankel *Macmillan* (Hafner) 1953 1954 pap. $2.50; trans. by Maurice Cranston *Penguin* 1968 pap. $1.25; trans. with introd. by Willmoore Kendall *Regnery* Gateway Eds. 1954 pap. $1.15

THE CREED OF A PRIEST OF SAVOY. 1762. Trans. with introd. by Arthur H. Beattie *Ungar* 2nd ed. 1956 $3.75 pap. $.95

THE GOVERNMENT OF POLAND. 1772. Trans. by Willmoore Kendall *Bobbs* Liberal Arts 1972 $6.00 pap. $1.95

ON THE ORIGIN OF LANGUAGE. 1781. With J. G. Herder's essay on the same subject. Trans. by John H. Moran and Alexander Gode *Ungar* $4.75 pap. $1.75

THE REVERIES OF A SOLITARY. 1781. Trans with introd. by John Gould Fletcher. 1927. *Burt Franklin* 1972 lib. bdg. $14.50

CONFESSIONS. 1782. *Dutton* Everyman's 2 vols. each $3.95; trans. by J. M. Cohen *Penguin* pap. $2.25

POLITICS AND THE ARTS: Letter to d'Alembert. 1758. Trans. by Allan Bloom *Cornell Univ. Press* 1968 pap. $2.45. This famous letter, opposing the opening of a Geneva theater (he considered all theater a depraving influence), set off a feud with Voltaire, a theater enthusiast.

Books about Rousseau

Montesquieu and Rousseau: Forerunners of Sociology. 1880. By Emile Durkheim. Trans. by Ralph Manheim; fwd. by Henri Peyre and notes by Georges Davy and A. Cuvillier *Univ. of Michigan Press* Ann Arbor Bks. pap. $1.95

Rousseau and Romanticism. By Irving Babbitt. 1919 o.p. An attack on Rousseau's ideas by the famous Harvard humanist.

Jean-Jacques Rousseau. By Matthew Josephson. 1931. *Russell & Russell* 1970 $21.00

Rousseau and the Modern State. By Alfred Cobban. 1934 *Shoe String Press* 1961 $5.50

Rousseau, Kant, Goethe: Two Essays. By Ernst Cassirer. Trans. by James Gutman, Paul O. Kristeller and John H. Randall, Jr.; introd. by Peter Gay. 1945. *Princeton Univ. Press* 1970 $8.50 pap. $1.95

Jean-Jacques Rousseau: A Critical Study of His Life and Writings. By Frederick C. Green. 1955 o.p.

Jean-Jacques Rousseau: A Study in Self-Awareness. By Ronald Grimsley. 1961. *Verry* 1970 $8.50

The Question of Jean-Jacques Rousseau. By Ernst Cassirer. Trans. and ed. by Peter Gay *Indiana Univ. Press* Midland Bks. 1963 pap. $1.65; *Peter Smith* $4.60

Rousseau and the French Revolution: 1762–1791. By Joan McDonald. 1965. *Humanities Press* (Athlone Press) $9.00

Jean-Jacques Rousseau. By Jean Guéhenno. Trans. by John and Doreen Weightman *Columbia* 2 vols. 1966 set $20.00

A "splendid book by Jean Guéhenno, critic, author and member of the Académie Française. . . . In gratifying detail and with complete lucidity [the author shows us Rousseau] as neither angel nor devil, but as a man"—(Peter Gay, in the *N.Y. Times*).

Jean-Jacques Rousseau: Vol. 1, The Great Quest (1712–1758). By Lester G. Crocker. *Macmillan* 1968 $9.95

"Highly readable, well researched"—(*LJ*).

Rousseau in America. By Paul M. Spurlin. *Univ. of Alabama Press* 1969 $6.00

The Art and Influence of J.-J. Rousseau. By Mark J. Temmer. *Univ. of North Carolina Press* 1973 $5.50

Jean-Jacques Rousseau on the Individual and Society. By Merle L. Perkins. *Univ. of Kentucky Press* 1974 $10.50

DIDEROT, DENIS. 1713–1784.

Diderot, coeditor with D'Alembert of the "*Encyclopédie*," has finally come into his own in the last forty years to rank with Montesquieu, Voltaire, and Rousseau as one of the great movers of the French enlightenment. Philosopher, playwright, novelist, essayist, and theorist of literature, he left behind him works of genius that were appreciated properly only long after his death. His "D'Alembert's Dream" (1769) is a statement of his philosophic thought in an experimental form—for he was as interested in literature as in ideas. His theories on theater and the new genre, drama, were taken up by later generations in France (starting with Beaumarchais) and influenced the formation of ideas about theater in Germany beginning with Lessing. In the novel, he produced three experimental works—all masterpieces: "The Nun" (in the style of the English novelist, Samuel Richardson (*q.v.*), "Rameau's Nephew" (a philosophic dialogue) and "Jacques the Fatalist" (a work almost in the manner of Lawrence Sterne [*q.v.*], but finally in a class by itself). His correspondence (particularly to Sophie Volland) gives a valuable picture of society, with its portrait of a proto-romantic in the age of reason. His "Salons" (1757–1781), reviews of painting exhibitions in Paris, are fascinating early examples of a later established genre: art criticism.

Materialist and humanitarian, in the end it was the charitable deed bringing happiness that won over a frigidly objective atheism and materialism.

SALONS. Ed. by Jean Seznec and Jean Adhémar. Ill. *Oxford* Vol. 1 1757, 1761, 1763 (1975) $45.00 Vol. 2 1765 o.p. Vol. 3 1767 (1963) $32.00 Vol. 4 1769 1171 1775 1781 (1967) $51.25

THE NUN. 1760. Trans. by Leonard Tancock *Penguin* 1974 pap. $1.25

RAMEAU'S NEPHEW AND OTHER WORKS. 1762. Trans by Jacques Barzun and Ralph Bowen *Bobbs* 1964 pap. $1.65

ENCYCLOPEDIA: Selections. 1765. Trans. by Nelly S. Hoyt and Thomas Cassier *Bobbs* 1965 $7.50 pap. $4.25

ENCYCLOPÉDIE: Two vols. of Plates. 1765. Ed. by Charles C. Gillespie *Dover* 1959 each $15.00

THEATRE ARCHITECTURE AND STAGE MACHINES. *Blom* 1968 $37.50. Engravings from the "*Encyclopédie*."

JACQUES THE FATALIST AND HIS MASTER. 1773. Trans. by J. Robert Loy *Macmillan* Collier Bks. 1962 pap. $1.50

LETTERS TO SOPHIE VOLLAND. Trans by Peter France *Oxford* 1972 $11.75

Books about Diderot

The Embattled Philosopher. By Lester G. Crocker. 1954. *Macmillan* Free Press 1966 $7.55
Diderot. By Arthur M. Wilson. *Oxford* 1972 $25.00
Diderot: The Virtue of a Philosopher. By Carol Blum. *Viking* 1974 $8.95

RESTIF DE LA BRETONNE, NICHOLAS EDMÉ. 1734–1806.

Restif de la Bretonne, the poor man's Rousseau, with Laclos and Sade, is an important figure—uneven polygraph as he is—in understanding what happens to French literature in the hands of the disciples of Jean-Jacques at the time of the French Revolution and before Romanticism.

LES NUITS DE PARIS, or The Nocturnal Specters: A Selection. 1788–1794. Trans. by Linda Asher and Ellen Fertig *Random* 1964 o.p.

Books about Restif de la Bretonne

Utopian Thought of Restif de la Bretonne. By Mark Poster. *New York Univ. Press* 1971 $9.50

SADE (DONATIEN ALPHONSE FRANÇOIS), Comte DE (called Marquis de Sade). 1740–1814.

Of "The Complete Justine" volume *Library Journal* said: "Relentlessly shocking, these explorations—fictional and otherwise—of eroticism, perversity, evil and ugliness, show the Marquis de Sade at his best"—or, one might say, without fear that the author would have disapproved, at his worst. Sade spent much of his chaotic career in prison. Legend has it that he was one of the handful of prisoners released from the Bastille when it was destroyed in the French Revolution. The charges against him stemmed from his habit of luring young girls to his chateau and molesting them in elaborately perverse fashion. The tendency to derive pleasure from inflicting pain upon others is called sadism after his name.

Sade wrote many novels, plays, tracts, and letters. A number of the literary works were published in his own time, if not always with approval, at least in some cases with grudging toleration. In the course of the 19th century his work was publicly condemned; but it acquired a wide fame through clandestine circulation. Writers such as Baudelaire and Swinburne (*qq.v.*) were admirers of his work. The relaxation of the laws of censorship has now made his books accessible to a wide public. Simone de Beauvoir, in "The Marquis de Sade: A Study with Selections" (U.S. 1953, o.p.), wrote that he "must be given a place in the great family who wish to cut through the banality of everyday life." He is, in effect, a revolutionary, and to this extent a representative of his age.

COMPLETE WORKS. Trans. by Paul J. Gillette *Holloway* (orig.) 2 vols. 1966 pap. set $3.00

THE COMPLETE JUSTINE (1791), PHILOSOPHY IN THE BEDROOM (1795), EUGENIE DE FRANVAL (1797), AND OTHER WRITINGS. Trans. and compiled by Richard Seaver and Austryn Wainhouse; introds. by Jean Paulhan and Maurice Blanchot *Grove* 1966 Black Cat Bks. pap. $3.95; *Putnam* Capricorn Bks. pap. $.95

THE 120 DAYS OF SODOM (1785) AND OTHER WRITINGS. Trans. and compiled by Richard Seaver and Austryn Wainhouse; introds. by Simone de Beauvoir and Pierre Klossowski *Grove* 1966 Black Cat Bks. pap. $1.75. "The 120 Days of Sodom," written in 1785, was not published until 1904, when the manuscript was discovered in Germany.

JULIETTE. 1797. Trans. by Austryn Wainhouse *Grove* 1968 $17.50 Black Cat Bks. pap. $3.95

SELECTED LETTERS. Trans. by W. J. Strachan; ed. by Margaret Crosland; pref. by Gilbert Lély *October House* 1966 $8.50

"The Sade revival continues apace with publication of this translated selection of 33 out of some nearly 200 of the ill-fated Marquis' missives known to be still extant. A judicious assortment, it runs from 1777 to 1794, thus covering the period of Sade's imprisonment at Vincennes and several years following his liberation from the Bastille"—(*Choice*). Some of these letters, written mainly to his wife, were discovered as late as 1948. They are all "fascinating examples of epistolary prose, explications of a most complicated and brilliant mind, and documents of prison life before and during the French Revolution"—(*LJ*).

Books about Sade

The Marquis de Sade. By Gilbert Lély. Trans. by Alec Brown *Dufour* 1961 $10.00; *Grove* 1962 Black Cat Bks. pap. $1.95. A scholarly study by an authority on the subject.

Portrait of De Sade: An Illustrated Biography. Ed. by Walter Lennig. *McGraw-Hill* 1971 $6.95

CHODERLOS DE LACLOS, PIERRE AMBROISE FRANÇOIS. 1741–1803.

"*Les Liasons Dangereuses*," by Laclos, is the last of the important epistolary novels, and, by common agreement, one of the key French novels of the 18th century. Disciple of Rousseau, precursor of Sade, this sober military man, presumably sincere in his moral intent, wrote precisely one work of literary importance. It is a story of adultery and seduction, told in a series of letters by the principal actors in the drama. In the 19th century the book had a reputation as an unsavory specimen of libertine literature, but discerning readers recognized it as a brilliant work of art. In England, A. C. Swinburne (*q.v.*) admired it and imitated it in his own epistolary novel, "A Year's Letters" (*New York Univ. Press* 1974 $10.00). André Gide included it among his "ten titles." Laclos is now securely recognized as an exact stylist and a refined analyst of human psychology.

LES LIAISONS DANGEREUSES. 1784. Trans. by Richard Aldington *New Am. Lib.* 1962 Signet pap. $.95; trans. by P. W. Stone *Penguin* 1973 pap. $1.95

CHATEAUBRIAND, FRANÇOIS RENÉ, Vicomte DE. 1768–1848.

The work of Chateaubriand, writer and statesman, illustrates Romanticism before-the-movement in France. In his "*Essai Historique Politique et Moral sur les Révolutions*" (1797), he took a stand as a mediator between the royalist and revolutionary ideas and as Rousseauistic freethinker in religion. "*Atala, ou les amours de deux sauvages dans le désert*" is known for its lush descriptions of nature. The poetic "*Génie du Christianisme, ou les beautés de la religion chrétienne*" (1802), appealing to the emotions rather than to reason, tried to show that all progress and goodness stemmed from the Christian religion. "René," a short novel, largely autobiographical, is taken from this work. Its extremely sensitive hero, who feels ill at ease in the conditions of his time, is overwhelmed by life and becomes depressed and incapable of functioning. His "*mal du siècle*" afflicted many of Chateaubriand's contemporaries and successors. His "*Memoires d'Outre-tombe*," published in 1849, has been praised as his masterpiece; a selection under the title, "Memoirs of Chateaubriand," trans. and ed. by Robert Baldick, 1961 is currently o.p.

ATALA (1801) and RENÉ (1802). Trans. by Irving Putter *Univ. of California Press* 1957 pap. $2.25

TRAVELS IN AMERICA. 1810. Trans. and ed. by Richard Switzer *Univ. Press of Kentucky* 1969 $7.95

Books about Chateaubriand

Chateaubriand at the Crossways: A Character Study. By Henry P. Spring. 1924. *AMS Press* $15.00

Chateaubriand. By Richard Switzer. World Authors Ser. *Twayne* $6.95

STENDHAL (pseud. of Marie Henri Beyle). 1783–1842.

Stendhal's great popularity in America, writes Henri Peyre in the *Saturday Review*, dates from "the eve of World War II, [when] a new generation of readers arrived on the college campuses, eager to analyze their feelings and to affect a cynical attitude which, as in Stendhal, only half disguised a repressed sentimentality." "*Le Rouge et le Noir*" is a superb chronicle of the period in French history following the downfall of Napoleon. Of "The Charterhouse of Parma," Peyre says, "One of the claims to uniqueness of the *Chartreuse* lies . . . in the dreamlike atmosphere in which Stendhal steeped the impossible adventures of his characters, and in the creation of a woman who may well be the truest and most appealing of all French fictional heroines." The "Charterhouse" was based on an Italian novel of the 17th century which Stendhal discovered in manuscript in 1834; he wrote it in seven weeks in a dry, spare style ("Every morning I read two or three pages of the *code civil* [civil law] so as to be always natural"). At the book's end is his dedication in English,

"TO THE HAPPY FEW." These two novels are his masterpieces. Stendhal shows keen psychological insight into character and his writing is very clear and direct. His "Racine and Shakespeare" (1823) (U.S. 1962, o.p.) is his famous pamphlet on the Classic *vs.* Romantic controversy, in which he took the side of the Romantics. Stendhal also wrote some 30 volumes of biography, travel, and art and music criticism, as well as the "Diaries" and "Memoirs of an Egotist" (1892, U.S. 1949, o.p.); his "To the Happy Few: Selected Letters" (U.S. 1952 1955) is o.p. The *Nation* called the "Diaries," begun at 18 in 1801 and continued until 1823, "a brilliant record of society in the Napoleonic epoch and a very peculiar kind of sensibility."

THE SHORTER NOVELS. Trans. by C. K. Scott-Moncrieff *Liveright* Black & Gold Lib. $7.95

HAYDEN, MOZART AND METASTASIO. 1814. Trans. by Richard N. Coe *Grossman* 1972 $15.00

ON LOVE. 1822. Trans. by Vyvyan B. Holland under the direction of C. K. Scott-Moncrieff *Grosset* Univ. Lib. 1967 pap. $2.95; *Liveright* 1927 Black & Gold Lib. 1947 $7.95
This "remains one of the very few readable treatises on that subject so often mishandled by Psychologists"—(Henri Peyre, in *SR*).

LIFE OF ROSSINI. 1824. Trans. and ed. by Richard N. Coe *Univ. of Washington Press* 1972 pap. $3.95

ARMANCE, or Scenes from a Parisian Salon in 1827. 1827. *Dufour* 1961 $3.95. First published in English in 1928. Newly trans. by Gilbert and Suzanne Sale. This, his first novel, though lacking their power, foreshadows his later works.

THE RED AND THE BLACK (*Le Rouge et le Noir*). 1830. Trans. by Lowell Bair *Bantam* pap. $.95; trans. by C. K. Scott-Moncrieff *Liveright* 1927 Black and Gold Lib. 1947 $8.95; trans. by Charles Tergie *Macmillan* Collier Bks. 1961 pap. $.95; trans. by Lloyd C. Parks *New Am. Lib.* Signet 1970 pap. $.95; trans by M. R. B. Shaw *Penguin* pap. $1.95; trans. by Charles Tergie *Simon & Schuster* (Washington Square) 1963 pap. $.95

MEMOIRS OF AN EGOTIST. 1832. Trans. by David Ellis *Horizon Press* 1974 $7.59

MEMOIRS OF A TOURIST. 1838. Trans. by Allan Seager *Northwestern Univ. Press* 1962 $10.50
This is the only edition in English of "*Mémoires d'un Touriste,*" which pretends to be the journal of a merchant, curious about life, art and history, traveling in almost every part of France. "The quality of Mr. Seager's translation of the excerpts from Stendhal's considerable work . . . is exceedingly poor"—(*LJ*).

THE CHARTERHOUSE OF PARMA (*La Chartreuse de Parme*). 1839. Trans. by Lowell Bair *Bantam* 1960 pap. $.75; trans. by C. K. Scott-Moncrieff *Liveright* Black & Gold Lib. 1925 $8.95; trans. by C. K. Scott-Moncrieff *New Am. Lib.* Signet pap. $.75; trans. by M. R. B. Shaw *Penguin* 1968 pap. $2.65

THE LIFE OF HENRI BRULARD. 1890. Trans. by Jean Stewart and B. C. J. Knight. 1958. *T. Y. Crowell* (Funk & Wagnalls) Minerva Bks. 1968 pap. $2.50

LUCIEN LEUWEN. 1901. Trans. by Louise Varèse *New Directions* 2 vols. 1950 Vol. 1 The Green Huntsman o.p. Vol. 2 The Telegraph $3.50 pap. $1.75

FEDER, or The Moneyed Husband. Trans. by Dr. H. R. L. Edwards *Dufour* 1962 $2.95. Pub. for the first time in English.

A ROMAN JOURNAL. Trans. and ed. by Haakon Chevalier o.p. Though Stendhal was traveled and had been in Rome, this book is a *tour de force*. It was pillaged and rewritten from standard texts in the Bibliothèque Nationale.

TRAVELS IN THE SOUTH OF FRANCE. Trans. by Elisabeth Abbott *Grossman* 1970 $12.50

PRIVATE DIARIES. Trans. and ed. by Robert Sage. 1954. *Norton* 1962 pap. $1.95

Books about Stendhal

Stendhal. By Armand Caraccio. 1951. Trans. by Dolores Bagley *New York Univ. Press* 1965 $7.50 pap. $2.25

A professor at the University of Grenoble shows the close relationship between Stendhal's life and works. "Concise, lucid, Stendhalian in its swift and vivid tempo, with only very little of the ironical condescension with which his biographers have often patronized Stendhal's naiveté and his famous fiascoes in love"—(Henri Peyre, in *SR*).

The Man of Sensibility. By Jean Dutourd. *Simon & Schuster* 1961 $3.95

Stendhal: A Collection of Critical Essays. Ed. by V. H. Brombert. *Prentice-Hall* 1962 $5.95 Spectrum Bks. pap. $1.95

Stendhal: A Study of His Novels. By F. W. Hemmings. *Oxford* 1964 $7.75

Stendhal: Fiction and the Themes of Freedom. By Victor Brombert. *Random* 1968 $5.95

Stendhal. By Marcel Gutwirth. World Authors Ser. *Twayne* $6.95

Stendhal: Notes on a Novelist. By Robert M. Adams *T. Y. Crowell* Funk & Wagnalls 1968 pap. $2.50

Stendhal. By Joanne Richardson. *Coward* 1974 $10.00

BALZAC, HONORÉ DE. 1799–1850.

Balzac is often said to be the greatest of French novelists. His greatness is not only in the richness of his work, which is comparable to that of Dickens, but also in its extent. Even though he died at the age of 51, he left, among other writings, 92 novels (out of over 100 which he had projected) which taken together form what he called "The Human Comedy." His purpose in this gigantic undertaking was to make an inventory of all the vices and virtues of French society in the first half of the 19th century, and to write a history of the manners and customs of the period. "The Human Comedy" is divided into three parts: Studies of Manners, Philosophic Studies, and Analytical Studies. Studies of Manners is subdivided into Scenes of Private Life, of Provincial Life, of Parisian Life, of Country Life, of Political Life, and of Military Life. It is one of the most ambitious literary plans ever conceived or accomplished; the work contains 2,000 distinctly drawn characters. Among the best known of the novels are "Père Goriot," "Cousin Bette," and "Eugenie Grandet." Three stories in the Philosophic Series form an exceptional psychological trilogy: "The Wild Ass's Skin," "Louis Lambert," and "Séraphita." The last is a Swedenborgian romance and the most mystical of Balzac's works. "Droll Stories," written earlier in the vein of Rabelais (*q.v.*), are 30 in number and do not belong to "The Human Comedy." "Balzac," says André Maurois, "was by turns a saint, a criminal, an honest judge, a corrupt judge, a minister, a fop, a harlot, a duchess and always a genius."

WORKS. Introds. by George Saintsbury. 1901. *Bks. for Libraries* 18 vols. set $434.50

THE SHORT NOVELS. Ed. by Jules Romains *Dial* 1948 $7.50

THE MYSTERIES OF HONORÉ DE BALZAC: The Gonderville Mystery, trans. by Katharine Prescott Wormeley; La Grande Bretêche, trans. by Clara Bell *Juniper Press* 1961 $5.50 pap. $2.45

THE CHOUANS. 1827. Trans. by Marion A. Crawford Class. Ser. *Penguin* 1972 pap. $2.95

THE PHYSIOLOGY OF MARRIAGE. 1830. *Grove* Black Cat Bks. pap. $.75; *Liveright* Black and Gold Lib. $6.95

THE WILD ASS'S SKIN (*La Peau de Chagrin*). 1831. Trans. by Ellen Marriage *Dutton* Everyman's 1961 pap. $2.25

DROLL STORIES (*Contes Drolatiques*). 1832. Trans. by Alec Brown *Dufour* $12.50; ed. by Ernest Boyd *Liveright* Black & Gold Lib. $7.95

THE COUNTRY DOCTOR. 1833. Trans. by Ellen Marriage *Dutton* Everyman's 1961 $3.95

EUGÉNIE GRANDET. 1833. Trans. by Ellen Marriage *Dutton* Everyman's $3.95 pap. $1.50; trans. by Merloyd Lawrence *Houghton* 1964 Riv. Eds. pap. $2.95; trans. by Marion A. Crawford Class. Ser. *Penguin* 1969 pap. $1.50

PÈRE GORIOT. 1834. Trans. by Geoffrey Tickell *Assoc. Booksellers* Airmont Bks. pap. $.60; (with title "Old Goriot") trans. by Ellen Marriage *Dutton* Everyman's $3.95 pap. $1.35; trans. by Jane Minot Sedgwick, with introd. and notes by Wallace Fowlie *Holt* 1950 pap. $3.95; trans. by Henry Reed *New Am. Lib.* Signet 1962 pap. $.60; (with title "Old Goriot") trans. by Marion Crawford *Penguin* pap. $1.75; (and "Eugénie Grandet") trans. by E. K. Brown and others *Random* Mod. Lib. 1946 $1.95 pap. $.60.

HISTORY OF THE THIRTEEN (*Histoire des Treize*). 1834. Trans. by Herbert Hunt Class. Ser. *Penguin* 1974 pap. $2.25

SÉRAPHITA. 1835. Trans. by Katherine Prescott Wormeley with introd. by George Frederick Parsons. 1889. *Bks. for Libraries* 1971 $9.75

A MURKY BUSINESS (*La Rabouilleuse*). 1841. Trans. by Herbert J. Hunt *Penguin* 1972 pap. $1.95

CONJUGAL LIFE: Pinpricks of Married Life. 1845. Trans. by Geoffrey Tickell. (And "The Physiology of Marriage" sel. and ed. by Derek Stanford *Assoc. Booksellers* 1958 2 pts. in 1 $3.75

COUSIN BETTE. 1846. Trans. by Anthony Bonner *Bantam* 1961 pap. $.75; trans. by M. A. Crawford *Penguin* pap. $1.95; trans. by Kathleen Raine *Random* (Modern Lib.) 1958 $1.95

HARLOT HIGH AND LOW (*Splendeur et Misère des Courtisanes*). 1846. Trans. by Rayner Heppenstall Class. Ser. *Penguin* 1970 pap. $2.95

EPIGRAMS ON MEN AND WOMEN. Sel. and trans. by Jacques Le Clercq *Peter Pauper Press* $1.95

Other famous novels now o.p. in separate volumes: A Passion in the Desert, 1830; Louis Lambert, 1832; César Birotteau, 1837; Lost Illusions, 1837–1843; Bachelor's House, 1841; Catherine de Médici, 1843; Cousin Pons, 1845.

Books about Balzac

The Evolution of Balzac's Comédie Humaine. By E. Preston Dargan. 1942 *Cooper* 1973 $12.50

Honoré de Balzac: A Biography. By Herbert Hunt. 1957. *Greenwood* $11.00

Balzac's Comédie Humaine. By Herbert Hunt. 1959. *Humanities Press* (Athlone Press) pap. $3.25. A companion volume to Hunt's excellent biography.

Honoré de Balzac. By E. J. Oliver. Masters of World Literature Ser. *Macmillan* 1964 $3.95
Concentrating on Balzac's major works rather than his life, this "will serve a useful purpose to students and general readers alike"—(*N.Y. Times*).

Balzac and the Human Comedy. By Philippe Bertault. Trans. by Richard Monges *New York Univ. Press* 1963 $8.00 pap. $2.95
"A critical potpourri . . . both an introductory study and one which will delight even the most zealous Balzacians"—(*LJ*). Bibliography, index.

Prometheus: The Life of Balzac. By André Maurois. Trans. by Norman Denny *Harper* 1966 $10.00
The definitive life—the last Maurois says he will ever write. "A superb biography . . . enriched by much enlightening criticism of all Balzac's books separately and with a brilliant exposition of *La Comédie Humaine*"—(*N.Y. Times*). "André Maurois possesses a genius for depicting the life of a genius. . . . Beyond a shadow of a doubt, this is a book for all to read, whether or not they are familiar with *The Human Comedy* in any language"—(Justin O'Brien, in *SR*).

Balzac. By V. S. Pritchett. *Knopf* 1973 $15.00

DUMAS, ALEXANDRE (*père*). 1802–1870.

Dumas, perhaps the most broadly popular of French romantic novelists, published during his lifetime some 1,200 volumes, but these works were not all written by him. He employed a body of collaborators with whom he would develop the outline of a story to be elaborated and finished. His methods were a literary scandal, and led to many lawsuits and accusations of plagiarism. Even his best works were based on borrowed material. "The Three Musketeers," his great tale of derring-do, was taken from the "Memoirs of Artagnan" by an 18th-century writer, and "The Count of Monte Cristo" from Penchet's "A Diamond and a Vengeance." "The Chronicles of France," as he called his romances, were the work of "Dumas & Co." The historical novel was his chosen field, as it supplied him with a ready-made outline. He called himself a "vulgarizer of fiction." His stories are melodramatic and improbable, but they are well told and swiftly moving, with an irrepressible gaiety.

It is to be regretted that there is no adequate English translation of the "Memoirs," one of Dumas' most entertaining works. Of its more than 6,000 pages, only some 250 have appeared in an abridged version, "My Memoirs" (U.S. 1961, o.p.), of which the *Library Journal* reported that "little of the charm and warmth of the original remain in the undistinguished translation." The various travel journals of Dumas—describing his adventures in Algeria, Spain, Switzerland and Russia—are now o.p. in this country.

SHORT STORIES. 1927. *Bks. for Libraries* 10 vols. in 1 $36.75

THE THREE MUSKETEERS. 1844. Introd. by Raymond R. Cannon *Assoc. Booksellers* Airmont Bks. pap. $.95; trans. by William Barrow with introd. by Sidney Dark *Collins-World* Standard Class. $4.95; ill. by M. Lelior *Dodd* Gt. Ill. Class. 1940 $5.50; *Dutton* Everyman's $3.95 pap. $2.25; ill. by N. Price and E. C. Van Swearingen *Grosset* Ill. Jr. Lib. 1953 $2.95 special ed. $3.95 deluxe ed. $4.95; *Macmillan* $4.95 lib. bdg. $4.94; *New Am. Lib.* Signet 1974 pap. $1.25; *Pyramid Bks.* pap. $1.25; *Simon & Schuster* (Washington Square) pap. $.95

THE COUNT OF MONTE CRISTO. 1844–45. *Bantam* abr. ed. pap. $.95; *Collins-World* Standard Class. $3.95; *Dodd* abr. ed. $5.00; *Dutton* Everyman's $3.95; *Grosset* 1953 $5.95; *Hart* pap. $1.50

MARGUERITE DE VALOIS. 1845. *Dutton* Everyman's $3.95

CHEVALIER DE MAISON-ROUGE. 1846. *Dutton* Everyman's $3.95

CHICOT THE JESTER (*La Dame de Monsereau*). 1846. *Dutton* Everyman's $3.95

THE FORTY-FIVE (*Les Quarante-cinq*). 1848. *Dutton* Everyman's $3.95

THE MAN IN THE IRON MASK (*Vicomte de Bragelonne*). 1848. *Assoc. Booksellers* Airmont Bks. pap. $.75; *Collins-World* Standard Class. $3.95; *Dodd* Gt. Ill. Class. $5.50

THE BLACK TULIP. 1850. *Dutton* Everyman's 1931 $3.95 pap. $1.95

ROBIN HOOD, PRINCE OF OUTLAWS. Trans. by Lowell Bair *Dell* $.45

THE JOURNAL OF MADAME GIOVANNI. Trans. for the first time from the 1856 ed. by M. E. Wilbur *Liveright* Black & Gold Lib. 1944 $6.95

Books about Dumas

Alexandre Dumas: A Great Life in Brief. By André Maurois. Trans. by Jack Palmer White Great Lives in Brief *Knopf* 1955 $3.95

The Titans: A Three Generation Biography of the Dumas. By André Maurois. Trans. by Gerard Hopkins 1957 *Greenwood* 1971 $23.95. A biography of Thomas Alexandre, Alexandre *père*, and Alexandre *fils*.

HUGO, VICTOR MARIE, Vicomte. 1802–1885.

The figure of Victor Hugo dominates the landscape of French literary history. Like a vast colossus he bestrides the century, from the time that it was two years old until the sunset years of the eighties. In the realms of poetry, criticism, drama, and fiction, he left an indelible mark.

The revolutionary song of his *"Odes et Ballades"* (1826) and *"Les Orientales"* (1829) is alive with music and rich in words and images. *"Les Châtiments"* (1853) is a collection of invectives directed against Louis Napoleon from Hugo's exile in the island of Guernsey. *"La Légende des Siecles"* (1859, 1877, and 1883) is a vast poetic vision of world history from the creation to the present and beyond. Hugo's poems are perhaps the greatest of his works, and among the greatest productions of modern literature. It is unfortunate that of all of his work, this part has proved least amenable to translation into English.

In the realm of drama, his "Cromwell" (1827) and "Hernani" (1830) won him notoriety for breaking away from the French neoclassic traditions of the drama. His defense, the "Preface to Cromwell" is one of the essential documents in the history of criticism.

To English-speaking readers, Hugo is probably best known as the author of *"Notre Dame de Paris"* (1831) ("The Hunchback of Notre Dame"), and of *"Les Miserables"* (1862), an immense tale of human courage and social oppression set in the era of the first Napoleon. Both novels were made into classic motion pictures.

When Hugo returned from exile in 1870, at the collapse of the empire of Napoleon III, he was welcomed and propelled into the arena of politics, where he remained a controversial voice to the last. When he died in 1885, the entire nation went into mourning, as if not an author, but a national hero had passed from the scene.

CROMWELL. 1827. *Greenwood* repr. of 1935 ed. $18.75

THREE PLAYS: Hernani (1830), The King Amuses Himself (1832) and Ruy Blas (1838). Ed. by Helen A. Gaubert *Simon & Schuster* (Washington Square) 1964 pap. $.60

THE HUNCHBACK OF NOTRE DAME (*Notre Dame de Paris*). 1831. *Assoc. Booksellers* Airmont Bks. pap. $.75; trans. by Lowell Bair *Bantam* pap. $1.25; trans. by Beckwith *Collins-World* Standard Class. 1955 $3.95; *Dodd* Gt. Ill. Class. $5.50; (with title *"Notre Dame de*

Paris") trans. by Herbert Fallin with introd. by Denis Saurat *Dutton* Everyman's 1931 $3.95; *New Am. Lib.* Signet pap. $.95

LES MISÉRABLES. 1862. *Collins-World* Standard Class. $3.95; *Dodd* 1925 $5.50; trans. by Charles E. Wilbour with introd. by Denis Saurat *Dutton* Everyman's 2 vols. each $3.95; abr. by James Robinson *Fawcett* Premier Bks. Pap. $.95; trans. by Charles E. Wilbour *Simon & Schuster* (Washington Square) Collateral Class. abr. ed. pap. $.95

WILLIAM SHAKESPEARE. 1864. Trans. by Melville B. Anderson. 1906. *AMS Press* $17.50; *Bks. for Libraries* repr. of 1886 ed. $14.50

TOILERS OF THE SEA. 1866. Trans. by W. M. Thomas *Dutton* Everyman's $3.95

JOURNAL, 1830–1848. 1954. *Greenwood* $14.75

Books about Hugo

The Career of Victor Hugo. By Elliott M. Grant. 1945. *Kraus* pap. $16.00; *Norwood Editions* $17.50
Victor Hugo: A Tumultuous Life. By Samuel Edwards. *McKay* 1971 $8.95
Stage for Poets: Studies in the Theater of Hugo and Musset. By Charles Afron. *Princeton Univ. Press* 1972 $9.50

MÉRIMÉE, PROSPER.   1803–1870.

Mérimée is the master of the *nouvelle*, the long short story, written with restraint and psychological characterization rare in the Romanticists of his time. He was a Parisian man of fashion and culture with a phlegmatic strain of English blood, whose earlier historical novels are filled with his archeological preoccupations and lack strong emotion. "Colomba" (1840) is his most finished novel. "Carmen" (1845) is loosely constructed, but furnished the famous plot for Georges Bizet's opera (1875).

TALES OF LOVE AND DEATH. Sel. by J. I. Rodale. 1948. *A. S. Barnes* Perpetua Bks. 1961 pap. $1.65

CARMEN. 1845. Trans. with introd. by Walter Ade *Barron's* 1975 pap. $1.50

A SLIGHT MISUNDERSTANDING. (In "Three Great Classics") ed. by Fred Honig *Arco* pap. $1.45

Books about Mérimée

Prosper Mérimée. By Maxwell A. Smith. World Authors Ser. *Twayne* $6.95

SAINTE-BEUVE, CHARLES-AUGUSTIN.   1804–1869.

Sainte-Beuve, the great French critic, liked to examine an author's work in the light of his personal life and particular psychology, through a scrupulous investigation of memoirs, correspondence and journals. "I would go to the end of the world for a minute detail, like a mad geologist after a pebble," he once said. Though he is often criticized for having misjudged highly gifted writers like Baudelaire (*q.v.*), "the touch of his feelers, so to speak, probing the features and quality of a literary object, is infinitely delicate, supple, and insinuating; his valuations are almost always just, and take full account of the finer shades that make a work of art unique"—(L. Cazamian). Sainte-Beuve found his outlet in the newspapers and reviews which became increasingly popular in his lifetime. His collected critical essays, from periodicals such as the *Revue des Deux Mondes*, were published in more than 35 volumes. Five of these made up *"Critiques et Portraits Littéraires"* ("Criticism and Literary Portraits"), from which the translated "Portraits" are taken. Sainte-Beuve became a member of the French Academy in 1845 and a senator in 1865.

SELECTED ESSAYS. Trans. and ed. by Francis Steegmuller and Norbert Guterman. 1963. *Bks. for Libraries* $12.25

LITERARY CRITICISM OF SAINTE-BEUVE. Ed. by Emerson R. Marks Regents Critics Ser. *Univ. of Nebraska Press* 1971 $10.00

ESSAYS ON MEN AND WOMEN. Ed. by William Sharp 1890 *Richard West* $10.00

PORTRAITS OF THE SEVENTEENTH CENTURY: Literary and Historic. Sel. from *"Critiques et Portraits Littéraires,"* 1836–39. Trans. by Katherine P. Wormeley; introd. by Ruth Mulhauser *Gordon Press* $30.00; *Ungar* 2 vols. set $18.00

PORTRAITS OF THE EIGHTEENTH CENTURY: Literary and Historic. Sel. from *"Critiques et Portraits Littéraires."* Trans. by Katherine P. Wormeley; introd. by Ruth Mulhauser *Ungar* 2 vols. set $18.00

MONDAY-CHATS. 1851–62. Trans. by William Matthews. 1891. *Richard West* $25.00

ENGLISH PORTRAITS. 1875 *Folcroft* 1975 lib. bdg. $25.00

PORTRAITS OF WOMEN. 1884. Trans. by Helen Stott. 1891. *Folcroft* 1974 $15.00

PORTRAITS OF MEN. Trans. by Forsyth Edereain. 1891. *Bks. for Libraries* $11.00

Books about Sainte-Beuve

Sainte-Beuve: A Literary Portrait. By William F. Giese. 1931. *Greenwood* 1974 $15.50

Sainte-Beuve to Baudelaire: A Poetic Legacy. By Norman Barlow. *Duke Univ. Press* 1964 $7.25 Though primarily known as a critic, Sainte-Beuve was also a novelist and wrote poetry. This book is "a slim but delicate study of his influence as a poet on Baudelaire"—(Henri Peyre).

TOCQUEVILLE, ALEXIS (CHARLES HENRI MAURICE CLÉREL) DE. 1805–1859 *See Chapter 9, History, Government and Politics,* Reader's Adviser, *Vol. 3.*

MUSSET, (LOUIS CHARLES) ALFRED DE. 1810–1857.

Alfred de Musset, poet and dramatist, born a Parisian nobleman, began writing verse at an early age. His book of poems, "Romances of Spain and Italy" (1829), was an immediate success but provoked bitter opposition for its cynicism, particularly in respect to some of the older Romantic poets. Musset became known as the *enfant terrible* of Romanticism. In 1833 he wrote "The Caprices of Marianne," still a classic in the Théâtre Français. His catastrophic love affair with George Sand began in 1833 in Paris and ended in Italy in 1835. Musset went on to write "Lorenzaccio," a tragedy (1834), "Confessions of a Child of the Century," a semiautobiographical novel (1836), and poetry—inspired by his unhappy liaison—expressing the theme that poetic greatness is achieved through suffering.

Two of his well-known comedies are "No Trifling with Love" (1834) and "One Can Never Tell" (1836), which reveal his sense of humor. In this and in his indifference to Nature or to social reform he was unlike the older generation of Romantics. He eventually became a member of the French Academy. Kathleen Butler tells the story of one Academician saying to another, *"Musset s'absente trop."* The reply was *"Il s'absinthe trop,"* and from this kind of life he died at 47, still much loved by his friends. His plays are performed today by the Comédie Française only slightly less often than those of Racine and Molière.

ALFRED DE MUSSET: Seven Plays. Trans. with introd. by Peter Meyer *Farrar, Straus* (Hill & Wang) Dramabks. 1962 pap. $1.95. Fantasio, A Diversion, The Candlestick, Journey to Gotha, A Door Must Be Kept Open or Shut, Camille and Perdican, Marianne.

CAMILLE AND PERDICAN. Trans. by Peter Meyer *T. Y. Crowell* (Chandler Pub.) 1961 pap. $1.25

FANTASIO. 1834. (In "From the Modern Repertoire," Series 7. Ed. by Eric Bentley) *Indiana Univ. Press* 1949 $10.00

GAMIANI, or Two Nights of Excess. *Universal Pub.* Award Bks. 1968 pap. $.95

Books about Musset

Three French Dramatists: Racine, Marivaux, Musset. By Arthur A. Tilley. 1933. *Russell & Russell* 1967 $8.50

Alfred de Musset. By Margaret A. Rees. World Authors Ser. *Twayne* $6.95

Stage for Poets: Studies in the Theater of Hugo and Musset. By Charles Afron. *Princeton Univ. Press* 1972 $9.50

Theater of Solitude: The Drama of Alfred de Musset. By David Sices. *Univ. Press of New England* 1974 $11.00

BAUDELAIRE, CHARLES (PIERRE). 1821–1867.

Baudelaire was the poet of decadence of his period. His collected poems, "Flowers of Evil," celebrate "the pursuit of lust, the faculty of self-torment in love, and moral anarchy." Their literary form is so polished as to be almost faultless. In 1857 he was tried on charges of obscenity for this volume, and six of the more controversial poems had to be deleted before it could be sold. "It is Baudelaire's painting of the pleasures and resulting horrors of vice which so scandalised the critics. Yet he was a moralist in the Christian tradition, who expresses revolt against the lure of the flesh, and the horror of the pleasures which leave a bitter taste of ashes in the mouth"—(Enid Starkie). Throughout the years, in numerous Baudelaire revivals, different aspects of his work have been hailed: the symbolic, the decadent, the erotic, the cynical and the spiritual. Now he is "probably the poet most widely read all over the world. . . . At the distance of a century [it is] as if he had written for the present generation with a knowledge of its problems and interests"—(Starkie). He was also a perceptive literary and art critic, extolling artists like Courbet, Corot and Manet at a time when they were objects of general derision. He translated Poe's tales into French. The American's love of horror and mystery had a strong influence on Baudelaire's prose writings.

Born to a bourgeois family, Baudelaire for a while lived the modish life of a literary dandy on an inheritance from his father, reluctantly joining the "Paris *bohème*" when his fortune ran dry. "His character," says Morris Bishop, "is perverse and fascinating. Critics see in him a conflict of many dualisms; he was both Catholic and satanist, debauchee and mystic, cynical sensualist and yearner for purity. . . . Unable to excel in virtue, he made himself a legend of vice." The "Intimate Journals" are now o.p.

SELECTED VERSE. Trans. in prose.and ed. by Francis Scarfe *Penguin* (orig.) 1961 pap. $1.65

LES FLEURS DU MAL: Flowers of Evil and Other Poems. Trans. by Francis Duke *Univ. Press of Virginia* bilingual ed. 1961 $6.50

LES FLEURS DU MAL (Flowers of Evil). 1857. Trans. by Florence Friedman *Dufour* 1966 $5.50; trans. by James Laver *Heritage Press, Conn.* deluxe ed. $12.50; (with title "Selected Flowers of Evil") ed. by Marthiel and Jackson Mathews *New Directions* bilingual ed. 1958 pap. $1.50; trans. by Jacques Leclercq *Peter Pauper Press* $1.95

FLOWERS OF EVIL: An Anthology of Translations. Ed. by Marthiel and Jackson Mathews (bilingual). *New Directions* 1955 rev. ed. 1962 $10.00. The result of a six-year search for the best available translation for each of the 163 poems, including new translations; a centenary edition.

PARIS SPLEEN. 1869. Trans. by Louise Varèse. *New Directions* 1970 pap. $1.75

ART IN PARIS, 1845–1862. Trans. and ed. by J. Mayne. *Phaidon* (dist. by Praeger) $7.95

ON POE: Critical Papers. Trans. and ed. by Lois and Francis E. Hyslop, Jr. *Bald Eagle Press* 1952 $4.00

BAUDELAIRE AS A LITERARY CRITIC. Trans. and ed. by Lois B. and Francis E. Hyslop, Jr. *Pennsylvania State Univ. Press* 1964 $9.50. Criticism by Baudelaire.

ARTIFICIAL PARADISE: Hashish and Wine as Means of Expanding Individuality. 1860. *McGraw-Hill* 1971 pap. $2.95

MY HEART LAID BARE AND OTHER ESSAYS. Ed. by Peter Quennell. *Haskell* 1974 lib. bdg. $11.95

LETTERS OF CHARLES BAUDELAIRE TO HIS MOTHER, 1833–1866. Trans. by Arthur Symons. 1927. *Blom* $13.50; *Haskell* 1971 repr. of 1928 ed. $14.95

Books about Baudelaire

Baudelaire the Critic. By Margaret Gilman. 1943 *Octagon* 1971 $11.00
Baudelaire. By Jean-Paul Sartre. Trans. by Martin Turnell *New Directions* 1950 $1.75
Baudelaire: A Study of His Poetry. By Martin Turnell. *New Directions* 1954 pap. $2.20. A "carefully documented, knowledgeable and suggestive study."
Baudelaire. By Enid Starkie. 1933. *New Directions* rev. ed. 1957 $12.50
   The *N.Y. Times* called this "one of those rare biographies of which the reader feels: What else is there left to record?" Miss Starkie rewrote her biography from new material and out of a desire to demolish the falsities which legend has ascribed to Baudelaire. "The figure which emerges . . . is hypersensitive, tortured, helplessly self-destructive, physically ill, and bears little resemblance to the foppish, philandering, wild, and wastrel poet which popular legend describes."
Baudelaire: A Collection of Critical Essays. Ed. by Henri Peyre. *Prentice-Hall* 1962 $5.95
A Concordance to Baudelaire's *Les Fleurs du Mal*. By Robert T. Cargo. *Univ. of Alabama Press* 1965 $7.00
Baudelaire. By Marcel A. Ruff. Trans. by Agnes Kertesz *New York Univ. Press* 1965 $6.95 pap. $1.95
   "The best work on the poet"—(Starkie).

FLAUBERT, GUSTAVE. 1821–1880.

Flaubert's masterpiece, "Madame Bovary," is a study of a woman of romantic temperament and upbringing who ruins herself in her thirst for romantic experience. (With the subtitle "Provincial Morals" it caused a scandal, though Flaubert was declared innocent of offense against public and religious morality in a court case.) "The Sentimental Education" has a similar theme—with a male protagonist. A novel in quite another vein, intended to shock, was "Salammbô," a story of sex and violence in ancient Carthage. It leaves "an overwhelming impression" of "nightmarish brutality," even "sadism"—(Victor Brombert). A year after Flaubert's death appeared his colossal work, "Bouvard and Pécuchet," "a precious wilderness of wonderful reading," as H. G. Wells (q.v.) called it. Flaubert was possibly the most painstaking writer in all literature. He wrote slowly and laboriously, and his books followed one another at long intervals. "Madame Bovary" took him 6 years; "Bouvard and Pécuchet" remained unfinished after 13 years of work. His tireless search for the right word, and his habit of reading aloud every sentence until its cadence was perfect to the ear, have earned for him a reputation as perhaps the greatest stylist of all time. He prided himself on being a scrupulously objective literary realist who described life as he saw it (in minute detail), but as a serious artist he became involved with his characters: "I am myself Madame Bovary."

A depiser of the bourgeoisie and bourgeois thinking, he compiled a witty book of clichés, "The Dictionary of Accepted Ideas" (trans. with introd. and notes by Jacques Barzun *New Directions* 1954 rev. ed. 1968 pap. $1.45), also published with the title "A Dictionary of Platitudes: Being a Compendium of Conversational Clichés, Blind Beliefs, Fashionable Misconceptions and Fixed Ideas" (trans. and ed. by Edward J. Fluck *A. S. Barnes* Perpetua Bks. 1961 pap. $1.45). The *Nation* said of his "Selected Letters": "They are among the finest literary letters in the whole of epistolary literature, and Francis Steegmuller . . . has edited them with discretion after translating them with authority."

MADAME BOVARY. 1857. Introd. by Raymond R. Canon *Assoc. Booksellers* Airmont Bks. pap. $.60; trans. by Lowell Bair with introd. by Malcolm Cowley *Bantam* pap. $1.25; trans. by Eleanor Marx-Aveling *Dutton* Everyman's $3.95; *Heritage Press, Conn.* deluxe ed. $11.95; trans. by Merloyd Lawrence with introd. by Germaine Brée *Houghton* Riv. Eds. 1969 $2.95; trans. by Mildred Marmur with fwd. by Mary McCarthy *New Am. Lib.* Signet 1964 pap. $.75; (text with critical essays) rev. trans. and ed. by Paul de Man *Norton* Critical Eds. 1966 lib. bdg. $6.00 pap. $1.95; trans. by Alan Russell *Penguin* pap. $1.95; trans. by Francis Steegmuller *Random* Modern Lib. $2.95 pap. $1.95; trans. by Eleanor Marx-Aveling *Simon & Schuster* (Washington Square) pap. $.95

SALAMMBÔ. 1862. Trans. by J. C. Chartres with introd. by F. C. Green *Dutton* Everyman's 1956 $3.95 pap. $1.75

THE SENTIMENTAL EDUCATION (*L'Education Sentimentale*). 1869. Trans. with introd. and notes by Anthony Goldsmith *Dutton* Everyman's 1941 $3.95 pap. $1.35; *New Am. Lib.* Signet pap. $1.50; trans. by Robert Baldick Class. Ser. *Penguin* 1964 pap. $1.95

THE FIRST SENTIMENTAL EDUCATION. Trans. by Douglas Garman; introd. by Gerhard Gerhardi *Univ. of California Press* 1972 $10.00

THREE TALES: A Simple Heart, St. Julian, Herodias. 1877. Trans. by Robert Baldick *Penguin* 1961 $1.25

BOUVARD AND PÉCUCHET. 1881. Trans. by Earp and Stonier; introd. by Lionel Trilling *New Directions* $6.50 pap. $2.50

THE SELECTED LETTERS OF GUSTAVE FLAUBERT. Trans. and ed. by Francis Steegmuller. 1953. *Bks. for Libraries* $13.75

Books about Flaubert

Flaubert and Madam Bovary: A Double Portrait. By Francis Steegmuller. 1939. *Farrar, Straus* 1968 $6.95 Noonday pap. $2.45
The Novels of Flaubert: A Study of Themes and Techniques. By Victor Brombert. *Princeton Univ. Press* 1966 $11.50 pap. $2.95
Includes bibliography and index. "This brilliant, detailed examination of Flaubert's fictional canon nearly destroys a mass of critical platitude"—(*LJ*). "Although marred by tiresome affectations of style, Professor Brombert's book is a full and very suggestive scrutiny of Flaubert's love-hate of realism, as it is woven into the texture of his narratives"—(V. S. Pritchett, in *N.Y. Review of Books*).

Madame Bovary and the Critics: A Collection of Essays. Ed. by B. F. Bart. *New York Univ. Press*
1966 $6.95 pap. $2.25
This "valuable little volume [comprises] a well chosen group of 12 essays which range in date
from the 19th century to the 1960s. They provide excellent examples of many of the
approaches and points of view that are possible when one deals with Flaubert's masterpiece"—(*Choice*).
Gustave Flaubert. By Stratton Buck. World Authors Ser. *Twayne* 1966 $6.95
Flaubert: The Making of the Master. By Enid Starkie. *Atheneum* 1967 $8.50
Flaubert: The Master. By Enid Starkie. *Atheneum* 1971 $10.00. This volume, together with its
predecessor, gives a brilliant, thoughtful view of its subject. The author is known for her
landmark biographical-critical studies of Rimbaud and Baudelaire.

GONCOURT, EDMOND DE, 1822–1896, and JULES DE GONCOURT, 1833–1870.

Artists, critics and novelists, the brothers Goncourt bequeathed the money for the Goncourt
Prize of 10,000 francs awarded annually since 1903 to the author of an imaginative prose work of
high merit. They were among the earliest of the impressionist writers, and their work paved the
way for naturalism as well. The "Journals" were not to be published until a generation after their
deaths. However, the surviving brother, Edmond, allowed an expurgated version to be printed in
France in 1887. Litigation over the allegedly scandlous nature of the diary followed. The
"Journals," covering the years 1851–1896, contain intimate descriptions of the great writers of the
day. The 1937 one-volume English translation by Lewis Galantière ends with Jules' death. It is not
superseded, but to a considerable extent supplemented by "Pages from the Goncourt Journal,"
which was selected from the full manuscript (not published in its entirety, even in France, until
1959). The Goncourts wrote their novels jointly, drawing on the "Journals" for material. They
focused on the abnormal, even pathological, their style giving "no impression of unity, because it is
made up of an infinite number of details, all of equal prominence"—(Kathleen Butler).

GERMINIE. 1865. Trans. by Ernest Boyd. 1922. *Greenwood* 1955 $11.75

SISTER PHILOMÈNE. 1861. Trans. by L. Ensor. 1890. *Howard Fertig* 1974 $11.50

WOMAN OF THE EIGHTEENTH CENTURY. 1862. Trans. by Jacques LeClercq and Ralph
Roeder. 1928. *Bks. for Libraries* 1972 $16.00

ELISA. 1878. Trans. by M. Crosland. 1959. *Howard Fertig* 1974 $9.50

THE GONCOURT JOURNALS, 1851–1870. Trans. by Lewis Galantière. 1958. *Greenwood*
1969 $19.75

PAGES FROM THE GONCOURT JOURNAL. Trans. and ed. with introd. by Robert Baldick
Oxford 1962 $6.10

(Eds.) FRENCH EIGHTEENTH CENTURY PAINTERS. 1859–1875. Trans. and ed. by Robin
Ironsides *Phaidon* (Praeger) pocket ed. $2.95

Books about the Goncourts

The Goncourts. By Robert Baldick. *Hillary House* 1960 $2.75
The Goncourt Brothers. By R. B. Grant. World Authors Ser. *Twayne* $6.95

RENAN, ERNEST. 1823–1892.

"The Life of Jesus" was the first of an eight-volume "History of the Origins of Christianity"
(1863–83), by which Renan popularized the use of scientific and historical methods in the study of
the Bible. It created a sensation at the time. His historical work is now outdated, but the brilliance
and originality of his style, "sentimental yet ironic and skeptical," has influenced many later
writers, particularly Anatole France (*q.v.*). Renan was intended originally for the priesthood, but
the scientific bent of his mind turned him from orthodox Christianity to a faith in science and in
social regeneration under the guidance of the intellectually elite.

THE POETRY OF THE CELTIC RACES. 1860. Trans. by William G. Hutchinson. 1896.
Kennikat $9.50; *Richard West* $9.25

THE LIFE OF JESUS (*Vie de Jésus*). 1863. *Belmont-Tower Bks.* 1972 pap. $1.25

Books about Renan

Ernest Renan as an Essayist. By Richard M. Chadbourne. *Cornell Univ. Press* 1957 $4.50
Professor Chadbourne provides a perceptive analysis of Renan's thoughts and style and "has
rendered a service in talking so well about [his minor writings]"—(*TLS*, London).

Ernest Renan: A Critical Biography. By H. W. Wardman. *Humanities Press* (Athlone) 1964 $10.00. Traces Renan's religious crisis through his major works, correspondence and autobiographical recollections.

Ernest Renan. By Richard M. Chadbourne. World Authors Ser. *Twayne* 1968 $6.95

DUMAS, ALEXANDRE *(fils)*.   1824–1895.

Dumas, the playwright, is known as Dumas *(fils)* to distinguish him from his father, the author of the "Count of Monte Cristo" and other popular historical romances. Dumas *(fils)* is the author of the most important and representative theater of mid-nineteenth century France: plays dealing with social and domestic problems and written close to the tradition of the soon-to-be-decried "well-made play." The best known of these is his *"La Dame aux Camélias"* (1852), based on his own novel, and made famous through the opera version by Verdi, *"La Traviata,"* and a motion picture version starring Greta Garbo, "Camille."

CAMILLE. 1856. Trans. by Mathilde Heron *Bks. for Libraries* $8.25

Books about Dumas (Fils)

Alexandre Dumas, Fils, Dramatist. By Stanley H. Schwartz. 1927 *Richard West* $25.00

The Titans: A Three-Generation Biography of the Dumas. By André Maurois. Trans. by Gerard Hopkins. 1957. *Greenwood* 1971 $23.95. A biography of Thomas Alexandre, Alexandre *(père)*, and Alexandre *(fils)*.

VERNE, JULES.   1828–1905.

Verne's novels of scientific adventure, or "extraordinary voyages," as he named them, anticipated many modern inventions and appeal to the boyish imagination. They are not great literature, but show an uncanny prescience. "Twenty Thousand Leagues Under the Sea" prophesied the submarine, and the voyages to the planets predicted the airplane and space capsule. "Five Weeks in a Balloon" was the first of Verne's *voyages imaginaires;* it describes an adventurous voyage across Africa by an English scientist and his two devoted companions. This novel combines rapid travel (steamer and train) with many adventures; the two chief characters are the "strange Englishman" Phineas Fogg and his French manservant Passepartout. The father of "science fiction" is today enjoying a tremendous revival in France and elsewhere.

FITZROY EDITIONS OF JULES VERNE NOVELS. Newly trans. and ed. by J. O. Evans *Assoc. Booksellers* 51 vols. each $3.95 set $215.00

THE JULES VERNE OMNIBUS: Twenty Thousand Leagues under the Sea (1869–1870); Around the World in Eighty Days (1873); The Blockade Runners; From the Earth to the Moon (1865). *Lippincott* 1951 4 vols. in 1 $5.95

FIVE WEEKS IN A BALLOON (1865) and AROUND THE WORLD IN EIGHTY DAYS (1873). *Dutton* Everyman's 1962 $3.95

TO THE SUN? and OFF ON A COMET! Trans. by Edward Roth *Peter Smith* $4.75

JOURNEY TO THE CENTER OF THE EARTH. 1864. *Dodd* Gt. Ill. Class. 1959 $5.50; *Penguin* 1965 pap. $1.25

FROM THE EARTH TO THE MOON (1865) and ALL AROUND THE MOON (1870). Trans. by Edward Roth *Dover* pap. $3.50; *Heritage Press, Conn.* deluxe ed. $12.50; (with title "From the Earth to the Moon and a Trip around It") *Lippincott* 1958 $3.95; *Peter Smith* $4.00

TWENTY THOUSAND LEAGUES UNDER THE SEA. 1869–70. *Collins-World* Standard Class. $3.95 Rainbow Class. $2.95; *Dodd* Gt. Ill. Class. $5.50; *Dutton* Everyman's $3.95; *Macmillan* 1962 $4.95; trans. by Mendor T. Brunetti *New Am. Lib.* Signet 1969 pap. $.95; (and "Around the Moon") Gt. Writers Collection Ser. *Platt & Munk* 1965 $3.95; *Scribner* Ill. Class. 1925 $6.00

AROUND THE MOON. 1870. *Dutton* Chil. Ill. Class. 1970 $4.50

AROUND THE WORLD IN EIGHTY DAYS. 1873. *Collins-World* Standard Class. $4.95; *Dodd* Gt. Ill. Class. 1956 $5.50

DR. OX'S EXPERIMENT. 1874. *Macmillan* 1962 $4.95

THE MYSTERIOUS ISLAND. 1874. *Dodd* Gt. Ill. Class. 1958 $5.50; *Scribner* Ill. Class. 1920 $7.50

MICHAEL STROGOFF. 1876. *Assoc. Booksellers* Airmont Bks. pap. $.60; *Scribner* Ill. Class. 1927 $5.00

MASTER OF THE WORLD. 1904. *Assoc. Booksellers* Airmont Bks. pap. $.50

Books about Verne

Jules Verne. By Kenneth Allott. 1954. *Kennikat* 1970 $11.00

Jules Verne and His Work. By I. O. Evans. 1966 o.p. A lively, illustrated study by the translator of the Fitzroy Edition. Bibliography and Index.

The Political and Social Ideas of Jules Verne. By Jean Chesneaux. Trans. by Thomas Wikely. *Transatlantic* 1973 $10.00

DAUDET, ALPHONSE. 1840–1897.

Daudet is a delightful storyteller as well as the gentlest of satirists and the most genial of humorists. His first successful books were collections of short stories—"Monday Tales" and "Letters from My Windmill." The former contained his famous "The Last Lesson" (which takes place during one of the recurring changes in national ownership of Alsace, a border province). "Little What's His Name" (*"Le Petit Chose"*) is a child autobiography that made him famous. Daudet is the creator of two immortal characters, "Tartarin" and "Sapho." "Sapho" (1884, o.p.) is the typical French courtesan-heroine, like "Mlle de Maupin" and "Manon Lescaut." "Tartarin" has been called "The French Pickwick." Daudet came from Provence and in his three very popular "Tartarin" novels he satirized his fellow southerners with their riotous imagination, boastfulness, habit of hyperbole, and sunny temperament.

SELECTED STORIES. *A. S. Barnes* 1951 Perpetua Bks. pap. $1.45

LETTERS FROM MY MILL. 1869. Trans. by J. MacGregor *Taplinger* 1966 $4.50; (and "Letters to an Absent One" 1875) trans. by Frank Hunter Potter. 1900. *Bks. for Libraries* $11.75

MONDAY TALES. 1873. *Bks. for Libraries* repr. of 1900 ed. $13.25

TARTARIN OF TARASCON (1882) and TARTARIN ON THE ALPS (1885). *Dutton* Everyman's $3.95

LA BELLE NIVERNAISE AND OTHER STORIES. 1895. Trans. by R. Routledge *Bks. for Libraries* $8.75

THE MULE OF AVIGNON. Trans. by John Lawrence *T. Y. Crowell* 1973 $4.50. A children's edition.

Books about Daudet

The Career of Alphonse Daudet: A Critical Study. By Murray Sachs. *Harvard Univ. Press* 1965 $5.95

ZOLA, ÉMILE. 1840–1902.

Zola was the spokesman for the naturalistic novel in France and the leader of a school which championed a scientific approach to literature. He was the author of the 20-novel Rougon-Macquart series, in which he attempted to trace scientifically the effects of heredity through five generations of the Rougon and Macquart families. The three outstanding volumes are *"L'Assommoir,"* a story of alcoholism and the working class; *"Nana,"* about a prostitute who is a *femme fatale;* and *"Germinal,"* about a strike at a coal mine. All gave scope to Zola's gift for portraying crowds in turmoil. Later series were "The Three Cities" and "The Four Gospels," (U.S. o.p.). His newspaper article *"J'Accuse,"* written in defense of Alfred Dreyfus, was one of the most dramatic episodes in what was known as the "Affair." "Thérèse Raquin" has been dramatized by Thomas Job as "Thérèse" (*French* 1947 $2.00 pap. $1.25).

THREE FACES OF LOVE. Trans. by Roland Gant *Vanguard* 1967 $4.95. For One Night of Love, Round Trip, Winkles for Mister Chabre. Early Zola short stories now appearing for the first time in English.

THÉRÈSE RAQUIN. 1867. Trans. by L. W. Tancock *Penguin* (orig.) 1962 pap. $1.75; *Peter Smith* $3.75

MADELINE FERAT. 1868. Trans. by Alec Brown *Dufour* 1957 $7.95

THE KILL. 1872. Trans. by A. Texeira de Mattos *Dufour* $7.95

SAVAGE PARIS (*Le Ventre de Paris*). 1873. Trans. by David Hughes and Marie J. Mason *Dufour* 1955 $7.95

ABBE MOURET'S SIN. 1875. Trans. by Alec Brown *Dufour* $7.95

HIS EXCELLENCY (*Son Excellence Eugène Rougon*). 1876. Trans. by A. Brown *Dufour* 1958
$7.95

THE LOVE AFFAIR (*Une Page d'amour*). 1878. Trans. by Jean Stewart *Dufour* 1955 $7.95

L'ASSOMMOIR. *Penguin* 1970 pap. $2.65; *Peter Smith* $4.75

NANA. 1880. *Assoc. Booksellers* Airmont Bks. 1969 pap. $.95; trans. by Victor Plarr
Dufour 1957 $8.95; *Macmillan* Collier Bks. 1962 pap. $.65; trans. by George Holden
Penguin 1972 $2.95; trans. by Charles Duff 1956 *Rowman* 1974 $10.00

THE EXPERIMENTAL NOVEL AND OTHER ESSAYS. 1880. Trans. by Belle M. Sherman.
1893. *Haskell* $18.95

GERMINAL. 1885. *Dutton* Everyman's $3.95; *New Am. Lib.* Signet 1970 pap. $1.75; trans.
by L. W. Tancock *Penguin* pap. $2.25; trans. by Havelock Ellis 1962 *Peter Smith* $4.50

THE MASTERPIECE (*L'Oeuvre*). 1886. Trans. by Thomas Walton *Dufour* 1960 $8.50;
Univ. of Michigan Press Ann Arbor Bks. 1968 pap. $2.95

EARTH. 1887. Introd. by Angus Wilson *Dufour* 1954 $8.95

THE BEAST IN MAN (*La Bête humaine*). 1890. Trans. by Alec Brown *Dufour* $8.95

THE DEBACLE. 1892. Trans. by John Hands *Dufour* 1970 $9.50

DOCTOR PASCAL. 1893. Trans. by V. Kean *Dufour* 1958 $7.95. The final volume of the
Rougon-Macquart series.

THE RESTLESS HOUSE (*Pot Bouille*). 1895. Trans. by Percy Pinkerton 1953 *Dufour* $7.95

Books about Zola

Émile Zola. By Angus Wilson. *Apollo* 1961 pap. $1.50
Émile Zola: An Introductory Study of His Novels. By Angus Wilson. *Peter Smith* 1962 $4.00
Émile Zola. By. F. W. J. Hemmings. 1953 *Oxford* Clarendon Press rev. ed. 1966 $11.25 pap.
$3.50
 The revised edition of his "masterly study"—(*TLS* London), incorporating the vast amount of
 new material on Zola since 1953.
Zola before the Rougon-Macquart. By John C. Lapp. *Univ. of Toronto Press* 1964 $7.50
Émile Zola. By Elliot M. Grant. World Authors Ser. *Twayne* 1966 $6.95

MALLARMÉ, STEPHANE.   1842–1898.

Mallarmé, the leader of the symbolist group of poets, has had great influence on French,
English and American poetry. He learned English in order to read Poe (*q.v.*) in the original, then
taught English in various provincial lycées and finally in Paris. His poem "*L'Après-midi d'un Faune*"
(1876) is known primarily because it inspired the musical prelude of Debussy, which the Russian
dancer Nijinsky later used for one of his famous roles. Mallarmé believed that the "music" of
words "is more significant than their conventional meanings" and that "suggestion and implication
are superior to statement." He is not an easy poet to understand, and the critical works below may
be helpful to readers new to his work.

SELECTED POEMS. Trans. by C. F. MacIntyre *Univ. of California Press* bilingual ed. 1959
$4.50 pap. $2.45

DICE THROWN NEVER WILL ANNUL CHANCE. 1897. Trans. by B. Coffey *Dufour* 1965
$4.95; *Humanities Press* (Dolmen Press) 1965 $2.00. An early example of odd
typographical arrangement for poetry—as specified by Mallarmé for this single
poem.

Books about Mallarmé

Mallarmé. By Wallace Fowlie. With 10 line drawings by Henri Matisse *Univ. of Chicago Press*
1953 $9.00 Phoenix Bks. pap. $2.45
 "Probably the best" introduction to Mallarmé in English. "Charming and intuitive"—(*LJ*). "It
 comprises a biographical introduction, a detailed study of individual poems, which are
 quoted in full with a prose translation, and a final chapter on Mallarmé's influence upon
 Valery, Gide, Claudel and others"—(*New Statesman*).
Mallarmé and the Symbolist Drama. By Haskell Block. *Wayne State Univ. Press* 1963 $6.50

Toward the Poems of Mallarmé. By Robert Greer Cohn. *Univ. of California Press* 1965 $11.50
"Detailed interpretations" of 28 important poems provide a useful "companion to Mallarmé
studies." Professor Cohn "tries to relate Mallarmé to the development of French lyricism"
and "fills a gap in Mallarmé criticism"—*(TLS, London)*.

Mallarmé and the Language of Mysticism. By Thomas Williams. *Univ. of Georgia Press* 1970
$6.00

FRANCE, ANATOLE (pseud. of Jacques-Anatole Thibault). 1844–1924. (Nobel Prize 1921)

Anatole France was the son of a bookseller. His literary criticism records "the adventures of his
soul among masterpieces" and often appears, together with autobiographical elements, under a
thin disguise of fiction. Some of the best of this genre are "On Life and Letters" (1910–24, U.S.
o.p.), "My Friend's Book," "The Opinions of Jerome Coignard" and "Little Peter." "The Crime of
Sylvester Bonnard" (1881, o.p.), France's first success has enjoyed great popularity. His fiction
covers a wide range of subjects and historical periods. His autobiographies of his own childhood
give evidence of his understanding of child nature. Widely respected as a distinguished "prince of
letters," and "the leading exemplar of French intelligence, wisdom and wit," he was elected to the
French Academy. France received the Nobel Prize (1921) for "the most remarkable literary work
of idealistic stamp." But his own ironic, yet compassionate, point of view made him keenly aware
of living at the end of an era.

WORKS. 1924. *Folcroft* autograph ed. 1924 30 vols. $600.00

BEE: The Princess of the Dwarfs. 1883. Trans. by Peter Wright *Folcroft* lib. bdg. $6.50

MY FRIEND'S BOOK. 1885. Trans. by R. Feltenstein *Barron's* pap. $1.25

BALTHASAR. 1889. Trans. by Mrs. John Lane *Folcroft* lib. bdg. $8.50

TALES FROM A MOTHER-OF-PEARL CASKET (*L'Etui de Nacre*). 1892. Trans. by Henri Pene
du Bois. 1896. *Bks. for Libraries* $11.00; (with title "Mother of Pearl") trans. by
Frederic Chapman 1908. *Bks. for Libraries* $11.25; *Folcroft* $8.50

AT THE SIGN OF THE REINE PÉDAUQUE. 1893. Trans. by Mrs. Wilfrid Jackson. (And "The
Revolt of the Angels") *Dutton* Everyman's $3.95; *Folcroft* repr. of 1924 ed. lib. bdg.
$8.50

THE OPINIONS OF MR. JEROME COIGNARD. 1893. Trans. by Mrs. Wilfrid Jackson *Folcroft*
lib. bdg. $8.50

THE WELL OF SAINT CLARE. 1895. Trans. by Alfred Allinson 1909. *Bks. for Libraries*
$12.25

THE AMETHYST RING. 1899. Trans. by B. Drillien. 1919. *Folcroft* lib. bdg. $8.50

CLIO. 1899. Trans. by Winifred Stephens. 1922. *Bks. for Libraries* $10.25

CRAINQUEBILLE. 1901. Trans. by Winifred Stephens. 1922. *Bks. for Libraries* $9.25

THE MERRIE TALES OF JACQUES TOURNEBROCHE. 1908. Trans. by Alfred Allinson. 1909.
Bks. for Libraries $10.75; *Folcroft* lib. bdg. $8.50

PENGUIN ISLAND. 1908. *New Am. Lib.* Signet pap. $1.50

THE SEVEN WIVES OF BLUEBEARD. 1909. Trans. by D. B. Stewart. *Bks. for Libraries* repr.
of 1923 ed. $10.00; 1920 *Folcroft* lib. bdg. $8.50

THE MAN WHO MARRIED A DUMB WIFE. 1913. Trans. by Curtis H. Page. 1915. *Folcroft*
lib. bdg. $7.50

LATIN GENIUS. 1924. Trans. by F. Chapman and J. L. May. *Bks. for Libraries* $14.50

PREFACES, INTRODUCTIONS AND OTHER UNCOLLECTED PAPERS. 1927. *Kennikat* 1970
$9.25

RABELAIS. 1928. Trans. with introd. by Ernest Boyd. 1928. *Folcroft* lib. bdg. $30.00;
Haskell 1974 $18.75; *Richard West* 1973 $25.00

ON LIFE AND LETTERS. 1910–1924. Four series. Trans. by A. W. Evans *Folcroft* 1st ser.
lib. bdg. $8.50; trans. by Frederic Chapman *Bks. for Libraries* Ser. 1 $12.50 Ser. 2
$13.00 Ser. 3 $13.50 Ser. 4 $13.50

Books about France

Anatole France: The Politics of Skepticism. By Carter Jefferson. *Rutgers Univ. Press* 1965 $8.00

Anatole France. By David Tylden-Wright. 1967. *Int. Pubns. Service* $10.50

"Tylden-Wright has written a splendid biography. . . . He writes with complete ease and with perception and verve. If this man doesn't send you back to France's novels, probably no one can"—*(PW)*.

Anatole France. By Reino Virtanen. World Authors Ser. *Twayne* 1969 $6.95

VERLAINE, PAUL. 1844–1896.

The dissolute, erratic leader of the "Decadents" and one of the early symbolists, Verlaine wrote 18 volumes of verse in alternating moods of sensuality and mysticism. He wandered over Europe with Arthur Rimbaud (*q.v.*) and was imprisoned for two years after shooting his companion. "*Sagesse*," his collection of religious poems of great melodic and emotional beauty, is generally considered his finest volume. Verlaine's poem "*Art Poétique*" asks that poetry be musical and suggestive rather than descriptive. Mallarmé called the collection in which it appears—"*Jadis et Naguère*" (1884)—"almost continuously a masterpiece . . . disturbing as a demon's work," and described Verlaine's skill as that of a guitarist.

SELECTED POEMS. Ed. with introd. and notes by R. C. D. Perman *Oxford* 1965 $1.95; trans. by C. F. MacIntyre *Univ. of California Press* bilingual ed. 1948 pap. $2.25

SAGESSE. 1881. *Humanities Press* (Athlone Press) 1942 $7.50 pap. $2.75

Books about Verlaine

Poet under Saturn: The Tragedy of Verlaine. By Marcel Coulon. Trans. by Edgell Rickword. 1932. *Kennikat* 1970 $7.50

The Art of Paul Verlaine. By Antoine Adam. Trans. by Carl Morse *New York Univ. Press* 1963 $6.95 pap. $1.95

Almost half of this handbook is a biography, a simple statement of the more obvious facts of Verlaine's life; most of the rest of the study is a book-by-book account of his literary development. A brief chapter of conclusions and a bibliography are included.

Paul Verlaine. By A. E. Carter. World Authors Ser. *Twayne* $6.95

Verlaine. By Joanna Richardson. *Viking* 1971 $10.00

Verlaine. By C. Chadwick. *Humanities Press* (Athlone Press) 1973 $9.00 pap. $3.50

LAUTRÉAMONT, LE COMTE DE (pseud. of Isidore Lucien Ducasse). 1846–1870.

"*Les Chants de Maldoror*" has won wide acceptance as a minor classic of French literature, but there is very little authentic information about its author except that he was born in Uruguay and settled in Paris about 1860. Lautréamont received no recognition during his lifetime for this remarkable book which has been called "a poetic nightmare epic." He came to fame only when his book was taken up by the surrealists a good half century after his death. It is considered today a landmark of early surrealism.

MALDOROR. 1868–70. Trans. by Guy Wernham *New Directions* 1943 pap. $3.45. Also includes a translation of his *Poésies*.

Books about Lautréamont

Lautréamont. By Wallace Fowlie. World Authors Ser. *Twayne* 1974 $6.95

Nightmare Culture. By Alex De Jonge. *St. Martin's* 1974 $10.95

HUYSMANS, J(ORIS)-K(ARL) (Charles Marie Georges Huysmans). 1848–1907.

Huysmans, a Frenchman with a Dutch father, began as a follower of Zola's (*q.v.*) school of naturalism and wrote his early novels in that vein. "*À Rebours*," the story of a nobleman who seeks escape from contemporary monotony through decadence and artificiality, marked a new phase in Huysmans' development; it profoundly influenced the English Decadents of the 1890's. He moved through a period of interest in diabolism and the Black Arts to a return to the religion of his fathers—the Catholic faith. "The Cathedral" ("*La Cathédrale*," 1898), a major novel, was his expression of the Christian mysticism, ritual and symbolism that Chartres Cathedral evoked for him.

AGAINST THE GRAIN (*À Rebours*). 1884. Introd. by Havelock Ellis. 1931. *Dover* 1969 pap. $2.50; trans. by Robert Bladick *Penguin* 1959 pap. $2.50; *Peter Smith* $4.00

DOWN THERE (*Là Bas*). 1891. Trans. by Keene Wallace. 1928. *Dover* 1972 pap. $2.50

Books about Huysmans

Huysmans. By Henry R. T. Brandreth. *Hillary House* 1963 $2.75
Joris-Karl Huysmans. By George R. Ridge. World Authors Ser. *Twayne* 1968 $6.95

LOTI, PIERRE (pseud. of [Louis Marie] Julien Viaud). 1850–1923.

Loti was a French naval officer whose fiction and books of travel reflect his voyages, especially those to the Orient. "The Iceland Fisherman," the novel for which he is best known today, deals with Breton fisherfolk, and is a tragic tale of the sea. There is a subtle melancholy in all Loti's novels, heightened by an exotic, impressionistic style.

THE ICELAND FISHERMAN (*Pêcheur d'Islande*). 1886. Translated by W. P. Baines *Dutton* Everyman's $3.95; *Folcroft* repr. of 1896 ed. lib. bdg. $10.00

MADAME CHRYSANTHEME. 1887. Trans. by Laura Ensor *Tuttle* 1973 pap. $2.50; *Folcroft* $12.50

RAMUNTCHO. 1897. Trans. by W. P. Baines *Folcroft* 1917 $12.50

THE DISENCHANTED. 1906. Trans. by Clara Bell *Folcroft* $10.00

ON LIFE'S BYWAYS (*Reflets sur la sombre route*). 1914. Trans. by Fred Rothwell *Folcroft* 1914 $12.50

Books about Loti

Pierre Loti. By Edmund B. D'Auvergne. 1926. *Kennikat* 1970 $10.00

MAUPASSANT, (HENRI RENÉ ALBERT) GUY DE. 1850–1893.

Maupassant was the godson and disciple of Gustave Flaubert (*q.v.*), who trained him in writing for seven years before allowing him to publish. Maupassant may be considered the creator of the short story in its modern form; he himself wrote more than 200, of which "Mademoiselle Fifi" and "The Necklace" are two of the most famous. Tolstoy (*q.v.*) pronounced "A Woman's Life" (1883, o.p.) to be the best novel in French literature since *"Les Misérables."* It is the story of a woman who is deceived by those for whom she sacrifices herself. "Peter and John" (*"Pierre et Jean,"* 1888), a maturer, more sympathetic novel about two sons, is especially notable for Maupassant's preface, an essay on his theories of fiction.

COLLECTED NOVELS AND STORIES. *Bks. for Libraries* 7 vols. available 1922–1925 each $11.25

Vol. 1 Boule de Suif (1880) and Other Stories trans. by Ernest Boyd 1922 Vol. 2 Mademoiselle Fifi (1882) and Other Stories trans. by Ernest Boyd 1922 Vol. 5 The Sisters Rondoli and Other Stories trans. by Ernest Boyd 1923 Vol. 6 Miss Harriett and Other Stories trans. by Ernest Boyd 1923 Vol. 9 Day and Night Stories trans. by Ernest Boyd 1924 Vol. 10 Little Rogue and Other Stories trans. by Storm Jameson, ed. by Ernest Boyd 1924 Vol. 14 The Olive Orchard and Other Stories trans. by Storm Jameson, ed. by Ernest Boyd 1925.

COMPLETE SHORT STORIES. Trans. with introd. by Artine Artinian 1955 o.p. Professor Artinian, an eminent Maupassant scholar, presents this carefully researched volume of 273 stories with several newly translated. He includes every story known to have been written by Maupassant and excludes many erroneously attributed to him.

THE ODD NUMBER. Short Stories. Trans. by Jonathan Sturges *Harper* 1889 $6.95

SHORT STORIES. Trans. by Marjorie Laurie; introd. by Gerald Gould *Dutton* Everyman's $3.95 pap. $1.35

BEST SHORT STORIES *Assoc. Booksellers* Airmont Bks. pap $.60

SELECTED SHORT STORIES. Trans. by Roger Colet *Penguin* 1971 pap. $1.95

YVETTE, A NOVELLETTE AND TEN OTHER STORIES. Trans. by Ada Galsworthy. 1916. *Bks. for Libraries* $9.25

SAINT ANTHONY AND OTHER STORIES. Trans. by Lafcadio Hearn. 1924. *Bks. for Libraries* $10.50

THE DIAMOND NECKLACE AND FOUR OTHER STORIES. *Franklin Watts* 1967 lib. bdg. $3.45

THE COCOTTE AND THREE OTHER STORIES. *Franklin Watts* 1972 $3.95

MADEMOISELLE FIFI (1882) AND OTHER STORIES. Trans. by Ada Galsworthy; pref. by Joseph Conrad *Branden* pap. $.95

THE COLONEL'S NIECES. 1885. *Branden* pap. $1.95

BEL AMI. 1885. *Heritage Press, Conn.* deluxe ed. $12.50; *Popular Lib.* 1963 pap. $.50

Books about Maupassant

Guy de Maupassant. By Leo Tolstoy. *Haskell* 1974 $7.95
Maupassant: A Lion in the Path. By Francis Steegmuller. 1949. *Bks. for Libraries* $14.00
Maupassant the Novelist. By Edward D. Sullivan. 1954. *Kennikat* 1971 $8.50. An "excellent critique, scholarly, thoughtful, and spare" which reappraises the novels.
Guy de Maupassant. By Albert H. Wallace. World Authors Ser. *Twayne* 1973 $6.95

RIMBAUD, (JEAN NICOLAS) ARTHUR. 1854–1891.

Rimbaud, a symbolist poet and visionary, abandoned literature at 19. He was shot and wounded in a quarrel with the poet Verlaine (*q.v.*), left France, wandered in many countries and finally became a trader in Abyssinia. He returned to France to die in 1891.

Roger Shattuck, in a most illuminating article in the *N.Y. Review of Books* for June 1, 1967, finds that Rimbaud's work divides itself "naturally into three parts. There are the poems, highly personal and written in more or less regular verse . . . from 1870 to 1872. Then there is the autobiographical prose work, 'A Season in Hell,' thirty intense and loosely connected pages composed in four months beginning in April, 1873. Passing harsh judgment on his past, Rimbaud appears to bid farewell to the long turbulent relationship with Verlaine and to the 'madness' that Rimbaud had cultivated in order to achieve a new level of living and writing. Thirdly, there is the miscellaneous collection of prose poems called 'Illuminations' " (probably written 1872–74). In " 'Illuminations,' he appears finally to make peace with the world and to seek, by name, the order and reason he had scorned earlier." Shattuck believes that the secret of Rimbaud's brilliantly concentrated brief life in literature was the result of precociously swift emotional and mental development which allowed intelligence to separate itself from emotion—a mark of maturity—at a very early age. This produced a poetic harvest "incredibly rich and convincing." Rimbaud has fascinated English-speaking poets from Hart Crane and Pound to the present generation. The preoccupations "fused" in his poetry were, says Shattuck, adventure, magic, alchemy, drugs, the "abominations" fostered by the Decadents, and a form of "messianic evolutionism that proclaimed a world made new through the mechanics of history."

COMPLETE WORKS WITH SELECTED LETTERS. Trans. with introd. and notes by Wallace Fowlie *Univ. of Chicago Press* bilingual ed. 1966 $12.50 Phoenix Bks. pap. $3.95
Prose translations that are "models of scholarly integrity and poetic sensibility"—(*LJ*).

ILLUMINATIONS (1886) AND OTHER PROSE POEMS. Trans. by Louise Varèse *New Directions* bilingual ed. rev. and enl. ed. 1957 pap. $1.75

SELECTED VERSE. Trans. and ed. with introd. by Oliver Bernard 1962. *Peter Smith* bilingual ed. $4.50

A SEASON IN HELL (*Une Saison en Enfer,* 1873) and THE DRUNKEN BOAT (*Le Bateau Ivre,* 1920). Trans. by Louise Varèse *New Directions* bilingual ed. 1961 pap. $1.50

A SEASON IN HELL (1873) and ILLUMINATIONS (1886). Trans. by Enid R. Peschel *Oxford* 1973 $8.95 Galaxy Bks. pap. $2.95

Books about Rimbaud

Arthur Rimbaud. By Enid Starkie. *New Directions* rev. ed. 1968 $4.75. The definitive biography, first published in 1947, now completely rewritten, with much new material.
Rimbaud's Illuminations: A Study in Angelism. Ed. by Wallace Fowlie. 1953. *Greenwood* $12.25
The Time of the Assassins: A Study of Rimbaud. By Henry Miller. *New Directions* 1956 pap. $2.75
 A "poignant and concentrated analysis of the artist's dilemma"—more of an autobiography of Henry Miller than a criticism of Rimbaud.
Rimbaud: A Critical Study. By Wallace Fowlie. *Univ. of Chicago Press* 1966 $8.00 Phoenix Bks. pap. $2.45
 "For whatever understanding we now have of the French Symbolists . . . we are heavily indebted to Professor Wallace Fowlie . . . scrupulous scholar, impeccable translator, and thorough critic." Intended as a companion volume to the "Complete Works" (*see above*), this new study, a revision of two earlier books, "presents a compact life of Rimbaud and detailed explication of the poetry. Essential for students of modern poetry and of interest to informed laymen"—(*LJ*).
Rimbaud. By Yves Bonnefoy. Trans. by Paul Schmidt *Harper* 1973 $11.50

COURTELINE, GEORGES (pseud. of Georges Moineaux). 1860–1929.

Son of a Parisian journalist, Courteline began in 1883 to write humorous articles for various newspapers and by 1890 had formed a close association with the *Écho de Paris*—which became the major outlet for his short stories, prose pieces and reminiscences. But he is best known today for his one-act plays—character sketches ranging from satire to farce, which derive their "classic French" humor from his ironic caricatures of bureaucrats (whom he had known in the French civil service) and of military men (he had served in the army). Only in *"Boubourouche,"* a domestic drama about a cuckold, with large implications about human society in general, does bitterness creep in. As in all serious comedy, tragedy lies just below the surface of his plays. They have been compared to those of Molière and (by Geoffrey Brereton) to medieval farce.

PLAYS: Volume 1. Trans. and ed. by Albert Bermel and Jacques Barzun *Theatre Arts* 1961 pap. $1.90. Badin the Bold; Hold On, Hortense; Afraid to Fight; Boubouroche (1893).

MAETERLINCK, MAURICE, Comte. 1862–1949. (Nobel Prize 1911)

Maeterlinck was a Belgian, trained for the legal profession, who decided to become a writer on a visit to Paris in 1887. Here he married his first wife, a handsome opera singer, and together they maintained a brilliant salon. He received the Nobel Prize for Literature in 1911, but he declined membership in the Académie Française because he was unwilling to give up his Belgian nationality for French. The Belgian king raised him to the rank of Count on his 70th birthday.

Maeterlinck's early plays—like "The Intruder," a one-act mood piece—were in the symbolist tradition. Later he turned to dramas of action, of which "Monna Vanna" (1902) is the strongest. Medieval and fantastic themes provided the means of expression for his developing philosophy—from skepticism to faith and hope ("The Life of the Bee," "The Bluebird") to, in the end, a kind of sad agnosticism. His philosophical bent is exemplified in "On Emerson and Other Essays: Three Great Transcendentalists" (1912, *Kennikat* 1967 $6.75). "The Blue Bird" mingles symbolism and allegory and has been performed throughout the world. "Pelléas and Mélisande" (1893) was made into an opera by Debussy and Fauré. In "The Life of the Bee" (1901, *Dodd* $3.00), not a scientific tract but a sensitive observation of the beauty and meaning to be found in bee society, he illuminated human life from an unusual perspective.

THE INTRUDER. 1890. (In "Five Modern Plays" ed. by Edmund R. Brown) *Branden* $.95

THE BLUE BIRD. 1908. *Dodd* $4.00; *French* $3.50

Books about Maeterlinck

Maurice Maeterlinck: A Critical Study. By Una Taylor. 1915. *Kennikat* $7.50

RENARD, JULES. 1864–1910.

Renard became a well-known author of novels, short stories and plays, a member of the Goncourt Academy and mayor of his home town. Though he was associated with the *Mercure de France*, a major symbolist review, his work had little in common with that of the symbolists or of any other group. Jean-Paul Sartre said of him: "Directly or indirectly, Renard is at the origin of contemporary literature." In the "Journal" he set forth "unorthodox and not always impartial views of literary personalities; . . . impressions of the countryside he loved; aphorisms, ironical, witty, deflationary and yet not bitter; . . . a real underlying compassion [giving the 'Journal'] a multidimensional quality. . . . Of all diarists Jules Renard is surely the one who comes closest to absolute sincerity"—(Brée).

JOURNAL, 1887–1910. Trans. and ed. by Louise Bogan and Elizabeth Roget; pref. by Louise Bogan; biographical note by Elizabeth Roget *Braziller* 1964 $6.00

Selected from Renard's unedited journal, which formed part of his "Complete Works" pub-. lished in France, 1925–27. "Perceptive and straightforward, Louise Bogan's introduction and Elizabeth Roget's short biographical page give just the insight that can make the journal come alive for the reader"—(Germaine Brée, in *SR*).

POIL DE CAROTTE. 1893. Trans. by Ralph Manheim; ill. by Felix Valloton 1967 o.p. An account of the author's childhood years in Burgundy.

"Poil de Carotte" ("Carrot Top"), Renard's account of his lonely, profoundly unhappy boyhood, is "his most successful work"—(Germaine Brée, in *SR*). It was made into an excellent French movie.

ROLLAND, ROMAIN. 1866–1944. (Nobel Prize 1915)

Rolland was a novelist, playwright, biographer and critic. Professor of the History of Music at the Sorbonne, he wrote a number of books about music and musicians, as well as one on the great ambition of his life, the establishment of a People's Theater. "Essays on Music" (*Dover* 1948 pap $3.50; *Peter Smith* 1960 $4.75) has been translated by David Ewen. His "Prophets of New India" has been published in two volumes as "The Life of Ramakrishna" and "The Life of Vivekananda" (*Vedanta Press* 1952 2 vols. each $2.95). "Jean-Christophe" (1904–1912) is a fine example of the "biographical" novel, a form of fiction in which the narrative follows exactly the sequence of events in the hero's life. It was the first great novel about a musical genius and contains interesting reflections on music, art and letters. On completion of "Jean-Christophe," Rolland was awarded the Grand Prize in Literature by the Académie Française (1913) and the Nobel Prize (1915).

JEAN-CHRISTOPHE. 1904–1912. Trans. by Gilbert Cannan *Avon Bks.* 3 vols. 1969 Bard Bks. pap. each $.95

TOLSTOY. 1911. Trans. by Bernard Miall. 1911. *Garland Pub.* lib. bdg. $19.00; *Kennikat* 1971 $10.00; *Richard West* 1973 $9.95

MUSICIANS OF TO-DAY. 1914. Trans. by Mary Blaiklock. 1915. *Bks. for Libraries* $11.00

HANDEL. 1916. Trans. by A. Eaglefield Hull. 1916. *AMS Press* 1971 $8.00; *Johnson Reprint* 1969 lib. bdg. $12.50

I WILL NOT REST. (*15 Ans de Combat*). 1919–1934. Trans. by K. S. Shelvankar. 1937. *Bks. for Libraries* 1973 $13.75

MUSICAL TOUR THROUGH THE LAND OF THE PAST. 1922. Trans. by B. Miall. 1922. *Bks. for Libraries* 1967 $9.00

Books about Rolland

A Critical Bibliography of the Published Writings of Romain Rolland. By William Thomas Starr. *Northwestern Univ. Press* 1950 $3.50
Romain Rolland and a World at War. By William T. Starr. 1956 *AMS Press* $17.50
Romain Rolland. By Harold March. World Authors Ser. *Twayne* $6.95

CLAUDEL, PAUL. 1868–1955.

Claudel was a poet, dramatist, essayist, and religious thinker of great power and originality whose works are suffused with his ardent Catholicism. "The Tidings Brought to Mary" (1912, 1916) is a modern miracle play. His dramas mark a high point of symbolism in French theater. His poetry abounds in metaphor and is often elliptical. Claudel served as minister to Denmark and ambassador to Japan, to the United States and to Belgium. After his retirement he lived in the country, devoting himself to writing prose of a religious nature. He was elected to the French Academy in 1946. When he died the *N.Y. Times* wrote, "Whatever he touched he enriched, and those who came in contact, however briefly, with the man or with his works count it a privilege to have lived in the same age with him."

"The publication in 1949, of the correspondence of Gide and Claudel was an event of capital importance. The translation . . . is a faithful performance which conveys much of the original tone and vigor. . . . The Catholicism of Paul Claudel is impressive and majestic. He is a poet speaking with the force of lyricism. He communicated his exultation. The answers of Gide have their own formal beauty, their own careful refinement and reticence"—(*SR*).

TWO DRAMAS: The Break of Noon and Tidings Brought to Mary. Trans. by Wallace Fowlie *Regnery* 1960 $4.75

CLAUDEL ON THE THEATRE. Trans. by Christine Trollope, ed. by Jacques Petit and Jean-Pierre Kempf *Univ. of Miami Press* 1972 $10.00

POETIC ART. 1907. Trans. by Renée Spodheim. 1948. *Kennikat* $6.50

FIVE GREAT ODES. 1910. Trans. by Edward Lucie-Smith *Dufour* 1970 $7.50

CRUSTS. 1918. Trans. by John Heard *Branden* $3.00. Play.

HUMILIATION OF THE FATHER. 1920. Trans. by John Heard *Branden* $3.00. Play.

WAYS AND CROSSWAYS (*Positions et Propositions*). 1928. Trans. by Fr. J. O'Connor in collaboration with the author. 1933. *Bks. for Libraries* $9.50; *Kennikat* $8.50

A POET BEFORE THE CROSS. Trans. and introd. by Wallace Fowlie. 1932 *Regnery* 1958 $7.50. A series of meditations and commentaries on the Passion of Christ.

THE EYE LISTENS (*L'oeil écoute*). 1946. Trans. by Elsie Pell. 1950. *Kennikat* 1969 $11.00

CORRESPONDENCE 1899–1926: Paul Claudel and André Gide. Trans. with pref. by John Russell; introd. and notes by Robert Mallet 1964 o.p.

LETTERS FROM PAUL CLAUDEL, MY GODFATHER. Ed. by Sister Agnes du Sarment *Christian Class.* 1964 $4.95

Books about Claudel

Paul Claudel. By Wallace Fowlie. *Hillary House* 1957 $2.75. "His book is a skillful and lucid exposition both of Claudel's poems and his poetic dramas"—(*N.Y. Times*).

The Inner Stage: An Essay on the Conflict of Vocations in the Early Works of Paul Claudel. By Richard Berchan. *Michigan State Univ. Press* 1966 $3.50
"A carefully researched and penetrating study of the conflict between Claudel's powerful poetic vocation and his desire to devote himself to the service of God [which] adds appreciably to our understanding of the works of Claudel and of the man himself"—(*Choice*).

Paul Claudel. By Harold A. Waters. World Authors Ser. *Twayne* $6.95

ROSTAND, EDMOND. 1868–1918.

Rostand, important at the turn of the century as a neoromantic dramatist, wrote only poetic plays. At a time of realism and naturalism on the stage, he revived the old romantic themes of chivalry in dramas that "reveal sadness and frustration beneath their superficial bravura."

Sarah Bernhardt created three title roles. Her first was that of *"La Princesse Lointaine"* ("The Far-Away Princess," 1895)—the beautiful Melisande, Countess of Tripoli, beloved by the troubadour Rudel. The great actress also starred as *"La Samaritaine"* ("The Woman of Samaria," 1897) and *"L'Aiglon"* ("The Eaglet," 1900), which has often been performed in the United States.

"Cyrano de Bergerac," Rostand's masterpiece, in which the great actor Coquelin starred is based on the life of an early French novelist, dramatist, and *libertin* (1619–55). He was the author of "Voyages to the Empires of the Moon and the Sun," a work which supplied Rostand with some of the lines of his play.

THE ROMANCERS. 1894. Trans. by Barrett H. Clark *French* $.60; *Baker* $.75

CYRANO DE BERGERAC. 1897. Trans. by Brian Hooker *Bantam* 1962 pap. $.75; trans. by Erna Krukenmeyer, adapted from the Kingsbury-Mansfield version *French* $1.75; trans. by Brian Hooker *Holt* 1923 $4.50; trans. by Anthony Burgess *Knopf* 1971 $5.95; trans. by Lowell Bair *New Am. Lib.* 1972 pap. $.75; trans. by Christopher Fry *Oxford* 1975 $7.50; Readers Enrich. Ser. *Simon & Schuster* (Washington Square) pap. $.60; trans. by Helen B. Dole *Richard West* repr. of 1925 ed. $10.00

CHANTECLER: A Play in Four Acts. 1899. *Richard West* 1925 $6.50

GIDE, ANDRÉ. 1869–1951. (Nobel Prize 1947)

Gide, the reflective rebel against bourgeois morality and one of the most important and controversial figures in modern European literature, published his first book anonymously at the age of 18. As a young man he was an ardent member of the symbolist group; but the style of his later work is more in the tradition of classicism. His sympathies with communism prompted him to travel to Russia, where he found the realities of Soviet life less attractive than he had imagined. His accounts of his disillusionment were published as "Return from the U.S.S.R." (1937) and "Afterthoughts from the U.S.S.R." (1938). His novels and theater mark him as an imaginative innovator, and his "Journals" are valuable documents of an age.

He was the founder of the influential *Nouvelle Revue Française* in which appeared the works of many prominent modern European authors, and was a director until 1941. He resigned when it passed into the hands of the Collaborationists. Always preoccupied with freedom, a champion of the oppressed, a skeptic, he remained an incredibly youthful spirit. "More even than for the intrinsic . . . value of his work, [Gide,] literary artist, critic, satirist, moralist, compelling personality, . . . will be remembered for the direction he gave to a whole generation"—(Milton H. Stansbury). He was, says André Maurois, "the author most beloved by adolescents of my generation. . . . Young people read him less today." Henri Peyre describes Gide as "the novelist of sincerity." He adds, however, that "Claudel . . . may not have been far wrong when he stigmatized his great contemporary and rival as a man fascinated by mirrors. . . . Narcissus is one of the underlying myths of literature." Gide received the Nobel Prize in 1947 and was made an Honorary Corresponding Member of the American Academy of Arts and Letters in 1950.

"The first English publication of the correspondence of André Gide and Paul Valéry cannot but be a literary event. The letters were written over a period of 50 years and the friendship they record evolved through many stages: youthful enthusiasm, literary rivalry, comfortable intimacy, mutual sympathy"—(*LJ*). "Valéry was to realize that Gide could sacrifice everything and everybody to his work, whereas Valéry was never really convinced of the value of anything. [The letters] remind us that we have not yet the whole story even of Gide, and that we should look for new meanings in the books of both"—(*SR*).

THE IMMORALIST. 1902. Trans. by Dorothy Bussy *Knopf* 1930 new ed. 1948 $5.00; *Random* Vintage Bks. 1956 pap. $1.95; *Bantam* pap. $1.25. Novel.

STRAIT IS THE GATE (*La Porte Étroite*). 1909. Trans. by Dorothy Bussy *Knopf*. 1943 $4.95; *Random* Vintage Bks. 1956 pap. $1.95. Novel.

TWO SYMPHONIES: Isabel (1911) and La Symphonie Pastorale (1919). Trans. by Dorothy Bussy *Knopf* 1949 $6.95

LAFCADIO'S ADVENTURES (*Les Caves du Vatican*). 1914. Trans. by Dorothy Bussy 1925 *Random* Vintage Bks. 1943 pap. $1.95

DOSTOEVSKY. 1923. Introd. by Albert J. Guerard. 1949. *New Directions* 1961 pap. $2.25

THE COUNTERFEITERS. 1926. Trans. by Dorothy Bussy *Random* (Modern Lib.) 1962 $3.95 Vintage Bks. pap. $2.45

TWO LEGENDS: Oedipus and Theseus (1946). Trans. by John Russell *Random* 1950 Vintage Bks. 1958 pap. $1.65

(With Jean-Louis Barrault). THE TRIAL. 1947. *Schocken* 1963 $3.50 pap. $2.25. Play: an adaptation from Kafka.

PRETEXTS: Reflections on Literature and Morality. Sel. and ed. by Justin O'Brien. 1959. *Bks. for Libraries* $12.75. Some 40 lectures, essays and prefaces which show his perceptiveness, sense of values, brilliance and honesty.

TRAVELS IN THE CONGO. 1927. Trans. by Dorothy Bussy *Univ. of California Press* 1957 pap. $1.95. Diaries.

THE WHITE NOTEBOOK. Trans. by Wade Baskin *Citadel Press* 1965 pap. $1.25

JOURNALS, 1889–1949. Trans. with introd. and notes by Justin O'Brien. 1947–51. *Howard Fertig* 4 vols. Vol. 1 1889–1913 $15.00 Vol. 2 1914–1927 $16.00 Vol. 3 1928–1939 $16.00 Vol. 4 1939– 1949 $15.00

THE CORRESPONDENCE OF ANDRÉ GIDE AND EDMUND GOSSE, 1904–1928. Trans. and ed. with introd. and notes by Linette F. Brugmans *New York Univ. Press* 1959 $7.50. Over 100 letters covering a 20-year period of exchange reproduced in full. Gide's appear in both French and English; annotations by the editor.

SELF PORTRAITS: The Gide-Valéry Letters, 1890–1942. 1955. Trans. and abr. by June Guicharnaud; ed. with introd. by Robert Mallet *Univ. of Chicago Press* 1966 $15.00

"Judicious" choice of 263 of the 462 letters originally selected by Mallet. A sensitively translated, "handsomely presented, well-edited volume [with] a thoughtful, penetrating and valuable preface"—(Germaine Brée, in the *N.Y. Times*).

Books about Gide

André Gide. By Aibert Joseph Guerard. 1951. *Harvard Univ. Press* rev. ed. 1969 $6.95. A brilliant study of Gide.

Gide and the Hound of Heaven. By Harold March. *A. S. Barnes* 1961 Perpetua Bks. pap. $2.25; *Univ. of Pennsylvania Press* 1952 $5.00. A fine introduction.

Gide. By Germaine Brée. *Rutgers Univ. Press* 1963 $6.00
Professor Brée, "a stout defender of Gide, as an artist and person, has here written a careful and thorough account of his abundant and varied works: autobiographical tales, novels, theatrical pieces"—(*LJ*).

The Youth of André Gide. By Jean DeLay. Trans. by June Guicharnaud *Univ. of Chicago Press* 1963 $12.00. A biography by a distinguished psychiatrist.

Three Philosophical Novelists: Gide, Joyce, and Mann. By Joseph G. Brennan. *Macmillan* 1963 $6.50. The author, a philosopher, questions whether Gide was really a novelist.

André Gide: His Life and Art. By Wallace Fowlie. *Macmillan* 1965 Collier Bks. pap. $1.95
"An excellent first book for the reader interested in the life and work of André Gide. [It shows that] the work was often a form of confession or compensation for the life"—(*LJ*).

André Gide: The Evolution of an Aesthetic. By Vinio Rossi. *Rutgers Univ. Press* 1967 $7.50
A careful, appreciative and very readable study of the development of Gide through the

whole body of his work. "Of all the French writers of the first half of the twentieth century, Gide offers by far the greatest resistance to the . . . one-word or one-phrase description." Professor Rossi considers later works masterpieces which prepared the way for Anouilh, Sartre, Montherlant and, especially, Camus.

André Gide. By Jean Hytier. Trans. by Richard Howard *Ungar* 1967 pap. $1.95

VALÉRY, PAUL. 1871–1945.

In 1966 Harry T. Moore wrote (*see his helpful summary in "Twentieth Century French Literature to World War II"*), "Paul Valéry, who published his most important verse between 1917 and 1922, is the greatest French poet the twentieth century has so far produced. . . . Few modern poets . . . have presented richer experience through their verses. Valéry . . . could handle abstractions with a living and always poetic concreteness, and put them into incomparable verse-music." He was also a critic and esthetic theorist, interested in art, architecture and mathematics. His skepticism, malice and learning brought him both admiration and hostility.

Valéry had been a member of the Mallarmé (*q.v.*) circle in the 1890's and wrote much symbolist poetry at that time, but an unhappy love affair caused him to fall poetically silent (he earned his living as a journalist) until Gide (*q.v.*) and others persuaded him, 20 years later, to publish some of his youthful work. He had thought to add a short new poem and instead wrote *"La Jeune Parque"* ("The Young Fate," 1917), several hundred lines in length. It is technically "superb" and "deals movingly with the problems all mankind must face" (Moore), and it won him instant recognition in poetic circles. Several collections of his earlier poems were published in the 20's, as well as the great "Cemetery by the Sea" (1920). From then until his death in 1945 he wrote chiefly esthetic theory, criticism and an unfinished play ("My Faust," 1946). He helped to revive lively interest in the symbolists and had a pervading influence on French culture generally, though his poetry is not easy for the casual reader.

He was elected to the French Academy in 1925. His "Collected Works" are being published in expert translations by the Bollingen Foundation. Of "Aesthetics," Volume 13 of the series, *Library Journal* said: "One realizes he is in the power of an amazing artist who cannot only create, but who has the rare ability to search deeply within himself to . . . examine his own creative process. . . . His language and reason are inspiring."

COLLECTED WORKS. Ed. by Jackson Matthews Bollingen Ser. *Princeton Univ. Press* 1957–

Vol. 1 Poems. Trans. by James Lawler and David Paul (1971) $15.00 Vol. 2 Poems in the Rough. Trans. by Hilary Corke (1970) $9.50 Vol. 3 Plays. Trans. by David Paul and Robert Fitzgerald (1960) $9.50 Vol. 4 Dialogues. Trans. by William M. Stewart with two prefaces by Wallace Stevens (1957) $7.00 Vol. 5 L'Idée Fixe. Trans. by David Paul (1965) $6.00 Vol. 6 Monsieur Teste. Trans. by Jackson Matthews (1973) $7.50 Vol. 7 The Art of Poetry. Trans. by Denise Folliot (1958) $10.50 Vol. 8 Leonardo, Poe, Mallarmé. Trans. by James Lawler and Malcolm Cowley (1956, 1972) $12.50 Vol. 9 Masters and Friends. Trans. by Martin Turnell (1968) $10.00 Vol. 10 History and Politics. Trans. by Denise Folliot (1962) $12.50 Vol. 11 Occasions. Trans. by Jackson Matthews (1970) $8.50 Vol. 12 Degas, Manet, Morisot. Trans. by David Paul (1960) $6.50 Vol. 13 Aesthetics. Trans. by Ralph Manheim (1964) $8.50 Vol. 14 Analects. Trans. by Stuart Gilbert (1970) $12.50 Vol. 15 Moi. Trans. by James Lawler and Malcolm Cowley (1956, 1975 in prep.)

SELECTED WRITINGS. Various translators *New Directions* bilingual ed. 1950 pap. $3.25. Poetry, essays, dialogues, critiques.

SELF-PORTRAITS: The Gide-Valéry Letters, 1890–1942. 1955. Trans. and abr. by June Guicharnaud; ed. with introd. by Robert Mallet *Univ. of Chicago Press* 1966 $15.00 (*see comment under André Gide*).

Books about Valéry

The Poetics of Paul Valéry. By Jean Hytier. 1953. Trans. by Richard Howard *Peter Smith* $4.25
"Not a study of Valéry's verse, but a survey of his critical thinking, his efforts to penetrate the secrets of poetic creation"—(*PW*).

Paul Valéry and the Civilized Mind. By Norman Suckling. *Oxford* 1954 $9.75
"A lecturer in French at the University of Durham writes with admirable force and clarity if also with something like well-bred fanaticism"—(*Nation*).

The Poetic Theory of Paul Valéry: Inspiration and Technique. By W. N. Ince. *Humanities Press* 2nd ed. 1970 pap. $6.00

Rilke, Valéry and Yeats: The Domain of the Self. By Priscilla Shaw. *Rutgers Univ. Press* 1964 $6.00

Paul Valéry. By Henry A. Grubbs. World Authors Ser. *Twayne* 1968 $6.95

PROUST, MARCEL. 1871–1922.

Proust, a cultured dilettante, conditioned by chronic asthma, wrote—mostly at night—in the seclusion of a cork-walled room. His vast novel recounts the life of the narrator as he surveys French society at the turn of the century. Involuntary memory plays a large part in the construction of the work. But in spite of the unorthodox features of Proust's method, he achieves a portrait of the social fabric that is in some ways comparable to Balzac's "Human Comedy." The comments of a (publisher's) reader of the manuscript in 1912 were recently discovered—and printed in the *N.Y. Times* of Jan. 22, 1967. Ironically, the first third of "Remembrance of Things Past," "so very rich in aesthetic, scientific, and philosophic learning" (André Maurois), and today considered perhaps "the most remarkable literary work produced in the first half of the twentieth century" (Germaine Brée), was rejected—on the grounds, among others, that "one has no idea what it's all about . . . nothing happens in these 700 pages. . . ." It was eventually published only with heavy financing from Proust himself. Henri Peyre says: "His deep penetration both into reality and into man's emotions and thoughts is hardly equaled anywhere."

REMEMBRANCE OF THINGS PAST (*À la Recherche du Temps Perdu*). 1913–1927. Definitive edition. Trans. by C. K. Scott-Moncrieff and Frederick A. Blossom; introd. by Joseph Wood Krutch *Random* 2 vols. 1934 ea. $15.00 boxed set $30.00 Vintage 1970 7 vols. pap. ea. $1.95 (except as noted).

Vol. 1 Swann's Way (*Du Côté de Chez Swann*). 1913; Vol. 2 Within a Budding Grove (*À l'Ombre des Jeunes Filles en Fleurs*). 1919. 1934 pap. $2.45 (Proust was awarded the Goncourt prize for this novel in 1919); Vol. 3 The Guermantes Way (*Le Côté de Guermantes*). 1920. 1933 pap. $2.95; Vol. 4 The Cities of the Plain (*Sodome et Gomorrhe*). 1921. 1941; Vol. 5 The Captive (*La Prisonnière*). 1923. 1941; Vol. 6 The Sweet Cheat Gone (*Albertine Disparue*). 1925 1948; Vol. 7 The Past Recaptured (*Le Temps Retrouvé*). 1927. Trans. by Andreas Mayor 1951 $7.95.

APHORISMS AND EPIGRAMS FROM REMEMBRANCE OF THINGS PAST. Ed. by Justin O'Brien *McGraw-Hill* 1948 pap. $2.75

JEAN SANTEUIL. 1951. Trans. by Gerard Hopkins; pref. by André Maurois *Simon & Schuster* 1956 $5.95

When Proust died, he left behind some 70 notebooks and several boxes of detached manuscript pages. Shortly after World War II a young Proust scholar, Bernard de Fallois, was given access to this material by the novelist's niece. Among these papers M. de Fallois discovered—and prepared for publication—this novel, the existence of which had not been suspected. "Undeniably the germ of Proust's later, famous work is here, although he has not yet learned to orchestrate his themes"—(Justin O'Brien, in the *N.Y. Times*). "It was unfortunately badly edited, put together very arbitrarily and prepared . . . by a very inadequate introduction. . . . Valuable as some of its chapters are, [it] fails to come to life"—(Henri Peyre).

A READING OF PROUST: Melusine in Paris, an Informal Guide. Ed. by Wallace Fowlie *Peter Smith* $5.00

ON READING. 1906. Trans. and ed. by Jean Autret and William Burford *Macmillan* 1968 $7.95

LETTERS TO HIS MOTHER (1887–1905). 1953. Trans. by George D. Painter. 1956. *Greenwood* 1973 $10.75

Books about Proust

Proust and His French Critics. By Douglas W. Alden. 1940. *Russell & Russell* 1973 $16.00
The Mind of Proust: A Detailed Interpretation of "*À la Recherche du Temps Perdu*." By Frederick C. Green. 1949. This classic study is currently o.p.
Proust. By Samuel Beckett. *Grove* $4.00 Evergreen Bks. 1957 pap. $2.45
A remarkable critical essay which has been called "a masterpiece of irascible insight worthy to rank with Johnson on Savage"—(*Nation*).
Proust and Literature: The Novelist as Critic. By Walter A. Strauss. *Harvard Univ. Press* 1957 $4.75. On Proust's search for the secret of other authors in an attempt to find his own form, style and aesthetic.
Marcel Proust and His Literary Friends. By Laurent LeSage. *Univ. of Illinois Press* 1958 $3.50 pap. $2.50
Proust: The Early Years. By George Painter. *Little-Atlantic* 1959 $8.50
"All things considered, this is the most accurate and complete life of Proust yet written"—(André Maurois, in the *N.Y. Times*). It covers the years between the author's birth and the death of his father in 1903. Mr. Painter is a librarian at the British Museum.

Proust: The Later Years. By George Painter. *Little-Atlantic* 1965 $8.50
The final volume of Painter's definitive work; it "renders obsolete or superfluous all the Proust biography that has preceded it, and prohibits, for a long time to come, anything but minor amplification or correction." This second part especially, however, will probably not "appeal or even mean very much to readers not thoroughly familiar with Proust's writings"— (Laurent LeSage, in *SR*).

The Magic Lantern of Marcel Proust. By Howard Moss. 1962. *Grosset* Univ. Lib. pap. $1.95
"This vivid, lively discussion centers around selected themes and images which appear in '*A la recherche du temps perdu*'—gardens, windows, parties, church spires—and one is impressed not so much by what is said as by the manner in which it is presented"—(*LJ*).

Proust: A Collection of Critical Essays. Ed. by René Girard. *Prentice-Hall* 1962 $5.95

Proust's Nocturnal Muse. By William Stewart Bell. *Columbia* 1963 $10.00
"Proust himself referred to the dream as an integral part of his thought and methods, and Bell here has undertaken to trace the use of dreams throughout Proust's work. It is an intensive, detailed study"—(*LJ*).

The World of Marcel Proust. By Germaine Brée. *Houghton* Riv. Lib. 1966 pap. $4.95. A study of his life and works.

Marcel Proust. By Henri Peyre. Essays on Modern Writers Ser. *Columbia* 1970 pap. $1.00

Marcel Proust and the Creative Encounter. By George Stambolian. *Univ. of Chicago Press* 1972 $12.00

A Foretaste of Proust. By Margaret Mein. *Saxon* 1974 $10.00

Marcel Proust. By Roger Shattuck. *Viking* 1974 $5.95 pap. $2.25

COLETTE (SIDONIE GABRIELLE) (Colette Willy, pseud.). 1873–1954.

"La grande Colette," *"romancière,* short-story writer, playwright, journalist, editor, actress, dramatic critic, fashion columnist, book reviewer, feature writer, wife and nurse" received the "greatest honor possible for a woman writer in France: the presiding chair in the Goncourt Academy." Her first "Claudine" novels were published in collaboration with her first husband, the notorious "Willy," whom she had married at 20 and divorced when she was 33. Under M. Willy's "editorship" she became a master craftsman. During her varied, active life, reflected in her novels, she became known for her subtle psychological insight and masterly style. The "Claudine" series is taken from her youth, "The Vagabond" (1910) from her days as a music-hall dancer, and *"Chéri"* from an affair with a "dissolute" young man. "She was her own most interesting character, and beneath her attempts at fictional delineation of a Claudine, a Lea, a Gigi was Colette's palpitating heart, faintly veiled, disarming in its candid subjectivity"—(Anna Balakian, in *SR*). Gide (*q.v.*) praised her, and Proust (*q.v.*) wept on reading *"Mitsou."* A Grand Officer of the Legion of Honor, she was accorded a formal state funeral, and in 1967 Paris named a street in her honor.

SIX NOVELS. *Random* Modern Lib. 1960 $2.45

PLACES. Trans. by David Le Vay. 1970. *Bobbs* 1971 $6.95. A collection selected from *"Trois-six-neuf," "En pays connu," "Prisons et paradis," "Paysages et portraits,"* and *"Journal intermittent."*

THE RETREAT FROM LOVE. 1907. Trans. by Margaret Crosland *Bobbs* $7.95

THE VAGABOND. 1911. Trans. by Enid McLeod. 1955. *Farrar, Straus* 1974 $8.95 pap. $2.95

MITSOU (1918) and MUSIC-HALL SIDELIGHTS (1913). *Farrar, Straus* 1958 $3.75. Two novels: Mitsou, trans. by Raymond Postgate; Music-Hall Sidelights, trans. by Anne-Marie Callimachi.

CHÉRI (1920) and THE LAST OF CHÉRI (1926). Trans. by Roger Senhouse *Penguin* 1974 pap. $1.50

JOURNEY FOR MYSELF. 1922. Trans. by David Le Vay *Bobbs* 1972 $6.95

MY MOTHER'S HOUSE (1922) and SIDO (1929). Trans. by Una V. Troubridge and Enid McLeod *Farrar, Straus* 1974 $7.95

BREAK OF DAY (1928) and THE BLUE LANTERN (1949). Break of Day trans. by Enid McCleod; The Blue Lantern trans. by Roger Senhouse; introd. by Glenway Wescott *Farrar, Straus* 1966 $5.95

THE OTHER ONE. 1929. Trans. by Elizabeth Tait and Roger Senhouse. 1960. *Greenwood* 1972 $10.00

The Cat. 1933. Trans. by Antonia White *Popular Lib.* 1974 pap. $.95

Duo 1934. Trans. by Frederick A. Blossom. 1935 *Bobbs* 1975 $6.95

Look Backwards. 1941. Trans. by David Le Vay *Indiana Univ. Press* 1975 $10.00

The Pure and the Impure. 1941. Trans. by Herma Briffault; introd. by Janet Flanner *Farrar, Straus* 1967 $4.75. Colette said of this book about love and eroticism, "It will perhaps be one day recognized as my best work."

Gigi (1944) and Selected Writings. *New Am. Lib.* Signet 1954 pap. $1.25

The Evening Star. 1946. Trans. by David Le Vay *Bobbs* 1974 $5.95

The Blue Lantern: Memoir by Colette. 1949. Trans. by Roger Senhouse *Farrar, Straus* 1963; *Greenwood* 1972 $8.50

This was her last major work, "but her senses were alert, and she missed nothing as she looked over the gardens of the Palais Royal from her window or had an occasional motor trip to not-too-far places, or attended a meeting of the Académie Goncourt. . . . Genius is the word for Colette, and her last word is no exception"—(*LJ*).

Gigi. 1954. *French* $1.75. A play adapted from Collette's novel by the author with Anita Loos (author of "Gentlemen Prefer Blondes").

The Thousand and One Mornings. 1970. Trans. by Margaret Crosland and David Le Vay *Bobbs* 1973 $6.95

Earthly Paradise: An Autobiography of Colette (as Drawn from Her Writings). Trans. by Herma Briffault, Derek Coltman and others; ed. by Robert Phelps. *Farrar, Straus* 1966 Sunburst Bks. pap. $5.95

Books about Colette

Close to Colette. By Maurice Goudeket. 1957 *Greenwood* 1972 $11.25
Colette. By Elaine Marks. *Rutgers Univ. Press* 1960 $5.00. A critical biography by a scholar who had access to Colette's papers and manuscripts.
Colette. By Robert D. Cottrell. *Ungar* 1974 $6.00
Colette: The Difficulty of Loving. By Margaret Crosland. Introd. by Janet Flanner. *Bobbs* 1974 $8.95. The best general study of Colette.

JARRY, ALFRED. 1873–1907.

Gabriel Brunet said: "Jarry's life seems to have been directed by a philosophical concept. He offered himself as a victim to the derision and to the absurdity of the world. His life is a sort of humorous and ironic epic, which he carried to the point of the voluntary, farcical and thorough destruction of the self."

A playwright who anticipated the Theater of the Absurd, Jarry at the time of his death "was regarded as little more than one of those bizarre specimens of the Paris Bohème . . . that disappear when they perish, as Jarry did, from overindulgence in absinthe and dissipation. Yet Jarry left an oeuvre that has been exerting a growing influence ever since he died and that still continues to increase." (Quotations are from "The Theater of the Absurd" by Martin Esslin.) "*Ubu Roi*" was originally conceived when Jarry was 15—to mock one of his teachers. His Ubu, a vulgar tyrant who thrashed about and behaved with heartless, humorously Rabelaisian eccentricity, appeared ludicrously exaggerated in 1896; but he was rehabilitated by the Surrealists, by the practitioners of the Theater of Cruelty and by the Absurdists. He became central to the adherents of Pataphysics, a literary "philosophy" drawn from his works. The play appears, in light of subsequent developments, as "a landmark and a forerunner." Jarry wrote a sequel, "*Ubu Chained*" (1900), and a number of novels.

Selected Works. Ed. by Roger Shattuck and Samuel Watson Taylor *Grove* 1965 $7.95 Evergreen Bks. pap. $2.95

Ubu Roi (King Ubu). 1896. Trans. by Barbara Wright *New Directions* (orig.) 1961 pap. $1.65; (in "Four French Comedies") *Putnam* 1960 pap. $1.35

A drama in five acts together with "The Song of the Disembraining," and two essays on the theater explaining his theories. "With 2 portraits of the author by L. Lantier and F. A. Cazels and several drawings by Jarry and Pierre Bonnard and 204 drawings by Fracizka Themerson doodled on lithographic plates"—(Title page).

Books about Jarry

The Banquet Years. By Roger Shattuck. 1958. *Peter Smith* rev. ed. 1968 $5.50
The Theater of the Absurd. By Martin Esslin. *Doubleday* 1961 $1.45

PÉGUY, CHARLES. 1873–1914.
   During World War II, the mystic-religious writings of Péguy, who was killed in action in World War I, were rediscovered and reapplied. His life and work were filled with baffling contradictions and idiosyncrasies. Born of humble parents, he was educated by numerous scholarships and opened a socialist bookstore and press. When these failed and the socialists refused to back him in founding a review, he started alone the *Cahiers de la Quinzaine* (1900), in which most of his work appeared. He published his most memorable religious poetry, much of it on the theme of Joan of Arc, in the last four years of his life. All his writing was imbued with idealism, which expressed itself in Péguy's ardent Christianity and in his patriotism. His work is repetitious and slow-moving, but displays nobility and mystic vision. He has been called the father of the French Catholic contemporary renaissance.

BASIC VERITIES: Prose and Poetry. Trans. by Anne and Julian Green. 1943. *Bks. for Libraries* $11.00

GOD SPEAKS: Religious Poetry. Trans. with introd. by Julian Green. 1945. *Pantheon* 1957 $5.95

Books about Péguy
   Charles Péguy: The Decline of an Idealist. By Hans A. Schmitt. *Louisiana State Univ. Press* 1967 $6.00

APOLLINAIRE, GUILLAUME (pseud. of Guillaume de Kostrowitski). 1880–1918.
   This French poet was widely read and his influence has been great. His most important works are two volumes of poems, *"Alcools"* (1913) and *"Calligrammes"* (1918). Symbolism was still alive when he went to Paris in 1898 and he was to "inherit some of its tenets, enrich its tradition, and by embracing its spirit of liberty, develop from it the new movements, modernism, cubism, dada, surrealism. . . . He studied his times like an anthropologist eager to detect in customs and costumes what, for lack of a better word, he called *l'esprit nouveau*"—(René Taupin). His great "technical skill, his varied versification, now free, now classical, his use of traditional phrases in a new composition, his grouping of images, the absence of punctuation, create an original unity of tone that involves not sentimentality but intimacy, the intimacy resulting from the somewhat casual alternating between the contemporary and the classical."
   His real name was that of his mother, of Polish origin, and he was born either in Rome, where he was baptized, or in Monaco, where he was educated at the Lycée Saint-Charles. In Paris he wrote novels, short stories and plays as well as poetry and "developed his erudition in different ways, including the editorship of rare books and responsibilities as censor during the First World War. He edited for the Bibliothèque des Curieux erotic books of repute and helped to catalogue the Enfer de la Bibliothèque Nationale." He became the friend of the great cubists including Picasso and Braque and wrote *"Les Peintres Cubistes"* (1913, *see below*), which first defined the nature of cubism. An Apollinaire revival, steadily on the rise in France since 1945, has crossed the Atlantic, marked by the appearance here of new translations, new biographies and numerous articles.

SELECTED WRITINGS. Trans. by Roger Shattuck *New Directions* bilingual ed. 1950 $6.50 rev. ed. 1971 pap. $2.95

APOLLINAIRE ON ART: Essays and Reviews. Trans. by Susan Suleiman; ed. by Leroy C. Breunig *Viking* 1972 $17.50 pap. $5.95

ALCOOLS: Poems, 1898–1913. 1913. Trans. by William Meredith; introd. and notes for all poems by Francis Steegmuller *Doubleday* Anchor Bks. bilingual ed. pap. $1.25; trans. by Anne Hyde Greet *Univ. of California Press* bilingual ed. 1965 $9.50 pap. $3.45
   Library Journal found William Meredith's translations "compromises between exactness and elegant sound, with the bias toward sound over sense." Those by Anne Hyde Greet, though "considerably more literal," are perhaps of greater value "in informing the beginning reader of just what Apollinaire, that difficult and strange poet, is saying."

DEBAUCHED HOSPODAR (*Les onze mille verges*) and MEMOIRS OF A YOUNG RAKEHELL (*Exploits d'un jeune Don Juan*). 1907. *Holloway* pap. $1.25

THE CUBIST PAINTERS. 1913. Trans. by Lionel Abel Documents of Modern Art *Wittenborn* 1949 1962 pap. $3.00

THE BREASTS OF TIRESIAS. 1917. (In "Modern French Theatre: The Avant-Garde, Dada, and Surrealism."). Trans. and ed. by Michael Benedikt and George E. Wellworth *Dutton* $6.95 pap. $2.75. A symbolic play called by Apollinaire a *"drame surréaliste"*—the first known use of the term *surréaliste*.

CALIGRAMS. 1918. Trans. by Anne Hyde Greet *Unicorn Press* bilingual ed. 1973 $4.95 pap. $1.95

Books about Apollinaire.

Apollinaire: Poet among the Painters. By Francis Steegmuller. 1963. *Bks. for Libraries* $19.50. A biography stressing the poet's relationship with the painters of his period.

Apollinaire. By Scott Bates. World Authors Ser. *Twayne* 1967 $6.95. The first critical study to make use of several works by Apollinaire not previously known to scholars. Bibliography, chronology, and index.

Guillaume Apollinaire. By Leroy C. Breunig. Essays on Modern Writers Ser. *Columbia* 1969 $1.00

MARTIN DU GARD, ROGER.   1881–1958.   (Nobel Prize 1937)

The Nobel Prize winner of 1937, novelist and playwright, was the chronicler of another famous family in French literature, the Thibaults, whose pre-1914 "World" he described in a lengthy novel. It follows the fortunes of two brothers who question the strict bourgeois values by which they have been raised—one reacts conservatively, the other in open revolt. The style is, said Martin du Gard, "as objective as humanly possible." The author was interested in the general ideas and attitudes which molded family and personal life in the early 20th century rather than in political or social reform, though his "Jean Barois," a novel on the Dreyfus affiar (1913), first won him recognition. He was associated with the *Nouvelle Revue Française* from its earliest years.

JEAN BAROIS. 1913. Trans. by Stuart Gilbert; ed. by Eugen Weber *Bobbs* Lib. Arts 1969 $7.50 pap. $3.25

THE WORLD OF THE THIBAULTS. 1922–1940. Trans. by Stuart Gilbert 1941 o.p.

NOTES ON ANDRÉ GIDE. Trans. by John Russell. 1953. *Richard West* $15.00

Books about Martin du Gard

Roger Martin du Gard. By R. Gibson. *Hillary House* 1962 $2.50

Roger Martin du Gard. By Denis Boak. *Oxford* 1963 $8.50. A study of his work and its place in modern French literature.

Roger Martin du Gard: The Novelist and History. By David L. Schalk. *Cornell Univ. Press* 1967 $6.75. Schalk examines his literary development during the 1930's in the context of historical events.

Roger Martin du Gard. By Catherine Savage. World Authors Ser. *Twayne* 1968 $6.95

GIRAUDOUX, JEAN.   1882–1944.

"The Madwoman of Chaillot" won the N.Y. Drama Critics Circle Award in 1949 as the best foreign play. Paris copies of the exotic costumes that Berard had designed for the 1945 production gave the play unusual style, but Giraudoux's commercial success seemed to break all the old dramatic rules. "What Giraudoux does is to create, upon a stage permeated with realism, a theatre of the unreal. . . . Paradox is the essence of his form. . . . There is nothing of Ibsen in his work, nothing of Shaw or Scribe; there is a great deal of 'A Midsummer Night's Dream' "— (Maurice Valency, in *Theatre Arts*). Giraudoux spent most of his life in government service and rose from the rank of consular attaché to that of cabinet minister. He traveled widely (he was always fascinated by Germany) and had published about 30 titles, most of them novels, before he became a dramatist at 46. He wrote plays at top speed entirely for his own pleasure. He was "more interested in ideas than in dramatic action, more interested in conversation than in ideas." His was a "baroquely opulent dialogue. [He] could skate across a polished verbal mirror with emotional and intellectual freight, as in his *Electra* and *Judith*, no less gracefully and provocatively than when he brought his audiences the light comic fantastication of *Amphitryon 38*"—(Gassner).

"Tiger at the Gates" was produced successfully on Broadway in 1955. Its French title, "The Trojan War Will Not Take Place" explains the dramatist's wry but grand theme—Hector's "fierce and fruitless effort" to prevent the Trojan War. *Time* said of it: "Just how good an orthodox play is this sunburst of dialectics and wit may be open to question; beyond question the play exhibits the elegance, the light-fingered thoughtfulness, the ironic lyricism of the most civilized playwright of the era between the wars. And Christopher Fry's (*q.v.*) translation not only does brilliantly by the play but may even be Fry's solidest writing for the theater." Two plays won the N.Y. Drama Critics Circle Award: "Ondine" in 1954 and "Tiger at the Gates" in 1956. The *Tulane Drama Review* (May 1959) was an all-Giraudoux issue with articles by Anouilh, Gassner, Germaine Breé and others.

FOUR PLAYS. Adapted by Maurice Valency *Farrar, Straus* (Hill & Wang) Mermaid Dramabks. 1958 $2.25. Ondine; The Enchanted; The Madwoman of Chaillot; The Apollo of Bellac.

THREE PLAYS. Trans. by Phyllis LaFarge and Peter Judd. *Farrar, Straus* (Hill & Wang) Mermaid Dramabks. 1964 pap. $2.25. Siegfried (1928); Amphitryon 38; Electra (1937).

THREE PLAYS: Judith (1938); Tiger at the Gates (1935); Duel of Angels (1953). Trans. by Christopher Fry with introd. by Harold Clurman *Oxford* 1963 $7.50

Books about Giraudoux

Jean Giraudoux: His Life and Works. By Laurent LeSage. *Pennsylvania State Univ. Press* 1959 $8.50. Scholarly well-documented analysis.

Jean Giraudoux: The Theatre of Victory and Defeat. By Agnes G. Raymond. *Univ. of Massachusetts Press* 1966 pap. $5.00

Giraudoux: Three Faces of Destiny. By Robert Cohen. *Univ. of Chicago Press* 1968 $8.70 1970 pap. $2.45

MARITAIN, JACQUES.   1882–   *See Chapter 5, Philosophy*, Reader's Adviser, *Vol. 3.*

RÉAGE, PAULINE.   1884?–

The pseudonym of this writer with few but sensational titles to her credit, probably masks the personality of a well-known writer-critic. The "Story of O" has lately been made into a startling, X-rated motion picture.

THE STORY OF O. Trans. by Sabine D'Estrée. 1966. *Grove* $6.00 pap. $1.95; *Ballantine* 1973 pap. $1.95

RETURN TO THE CHATEAU. Trans. by Sabine D'Estrée *Grove* 1973 pap. $2.95

SUPERVIELLE, JULES.   1884–1960.

Supervielle, born like Lautréamont in South America, proposed himself as a "reconciler of ancient and modern poetry." He possessed, says Boisdeffre, "the sense of mysterious correspondences which unite man to the Cosmos." His world and his imagination are essentially and delightfully childlike and his excellent short stories are inspired with that elusive quality.

SELECTED WRITINGS. *New Directions* 1967 $7.50 pap. $2.75

DUHAMEL, GEORGES.   1885–1966.

One of the stalwarts of the cycle or *roman-fleuve* novel of the beginning of this century, Duhamel (a physician by profession) is best known for his Salavin and Pasquier cycles (e.g. *"Confession de Minuit"* 1920, *"Le Notaire du Havre"* 1933). They present, in traditional post-naturalism style, the interrelationships between typical French bourgeois families, showing also the independence of the individual.

AMERICA THE MENACE (*Scènes de la vie future*). 1931. Trans. by Charles M. Thompson *Arno* 1974 $12.00

IN DEFENCE OF LETTERS. 1939. *Folcroft* 1973 $8.00; *Kennikat* 1968 $8.25; *Richard West* 1973 $8.00

MAURIAC, FRANÇOIS.   1885–1970.   (Nobel Prize 1952)

On the publication of "The Lamb" in 1956, Charles Poore wrote in the *N.Y. Times*: "François Mauriac, who won the Nobel Prize in 1952, has passed the three-score-and-ten mark and is still writing novels with a vitality and drive that should give courage to all sad young men of letters. His new book . . . brilliantly combines mystical symbolism with tense, dramatic action. It is often said of Mauriac that he is the leading novelist of the Catholic Renascence. Perhaps the idea of renascence helps to keep him young in spirit." And the *Saturday Review* said: "Surely, among French writers, he is the greatest artist in fiction. 'The Lamb' may represent the summit of Mauriac's attainment . . . a point of unsurpassable mastery."

Most of Mauriac's novels are laid in his birthplace, Bordeaux. They reflect his classical culture and his meditation on the Gospels and the Catholic contemplative writers. He is a moralist, presenting always the eternal conflict: the world and the flesh against Christian faith and charity. "Every one of his novels is a fresh attempt and an adventure into the unknown, though every one of them ends monotonously with the gift of grace that the novelist insists upon imparting to his sinners"—(Henri Peyre). Mauriac resisted the Nazi invaders and the Vichy regime consistently and courageously during World War II. He was involved in a number of political and literary controversies. He was elected to the French Academy in 1933 and received the Nobel Prize in 1952. His son Claude Mauriac (*q.v.*) (b. 1914) is a novelist and critic.

A MAURIAC READER. Trans. by Gerard Hopkins *Farrar, Straus* 1968 $10.00

YOUNG MAN IN CHAINS. 1913. Trans. by Gerard Hopkins *Farrar, Straus* 1963 $3.75. His first novel.

THÉRÈSE: A Portrait in Four Parts (*Thérèse Desqueyroux*). 1927. Trans. by Gerard Hopkins *Farrar, Straus* 1947 1951 Noonday pap. $3.45

ANGUISH AND JOY OF THE CHRISTIAN LIFE. 1931. *Christian Class.* 1964 $3.95; *Univ. of Notre Dame Press* 1967 pap. $1.25

VIPERS' TANGLE (*Le Noeud de Vipères*). 1932. Trans. by Warre B. Wells 1933 *Doubleday* Image Bks. 1957 pap. $.95. A novel of vicious family entanglements which Henri Peyre calls "an artistic masterpiece."

ASMODÉE. 1938. Trans. by Beverly Thurman. *French* $1.75
   A play "with beautiful scenes and touching moments. . . . Mauriac is a writer of conscience who has insight into human motivations and faith in divine mysteries"—(Brooks Atkinson, in the *N.Y. Times*).

THE LOVED AND THE UNLOVED. 1945. Trans. by Gerard Hopkins 1952 *Farrar, Straus* 1967 Noonday pap. $1.95

MEN I HOLD GREAT (*Les Grands Hommes*). 1949. Trans. by Elsie Pell 1951 *Kennikat* 1971 $7.00; (with title "Great Men") *Richard West* 1949 $17.50

THE HOLY TERROR (*Le Drôle*). 1951. Trans. by Anne Carter *T. Y. Crowell* (Funk & Wagnalls) 1967 $3.95

THE SON OF MAN. 1958. Trans. by Bernard Murchland *Macmillan* Collier Bks. pap. $.95. Reflections on the inner meaning of Christ's life.

SECOND THOUGHTS: Reflections on Literature and on Life. 1961. Trans. by Adrienne Foulke. 1961. *Bks. for Libraries* $9.25

DE GAULLE. 1966. Trans. by Richard Howard. o.p.
   "With his almost religious devotion to de Gaulle, [Mauriac's book is] one continuous hymn of praise." "Rather than the biography of an individualistic statesman, [he] has given us the apologia for his own Gaullism"—(*SR*). Indeed, his staunch admiration for the French President has stirred up so much controversy that a book on the subject called "*Mauriac sous de Gaulle*" has recently been published in France.

MALTAVERNE (*Un adolescent d'autrefois*). 1970. Trans. by Jean Stewart *Farrar, Straus* 1970 $5.95

MÉMOIRES INTÉRIEURS. 1959. Trans. by Gerard Hopkins *Farrar, Straus* 1961 $4.95

LETTERS ON ART AND LITERATURE. Trans. by Mario Pei. 1953. *Kennikat* 1970 $6.00

Books about Mauriac

François Mauriac: A Critical Study. By Michael F. Moloney. *Swallow* $3.75
Faith and Fiction: The Creative Process in Greene and Mauriac. By Philip Stratford. *Univ. of Notre Dame Press* 1964 pap. $2.95. A thorough critical examination of the works of Graham Greene and François Mauriac.
Mauriac. By Cecil Jenkins. *Int. Pubns. Service* 1965 $2.50
   "Compact and articulate introduction to a writer who is one of the most widely translated authors in the Anglo-Saxon world and, yet, one who has received very little book-length criticism in English. . . . A valuable starting point for undergraduates"—(*Choice*).
François Mauriac. By Maxwell A. Smith. World Authors Ser. *Twayne* $6.95
Intention and Achievement: An Essay on the Novels of François Mauriac. By J. E. Flower. *Oxford* 1969 $5.00

MAUROIS, ANDRÉ (pseud. of Émile Herzog). 1885–1967.

Maurois first came into prominence with his war story about his British comrades, "The Silence of Colonel Bramble" (1918), which was read with delight in the trenches. His "Ariel: The Life of Shelley" (1924 *Ungar* 1958 $7.50 pap. $2.75), intended for Frenchmen unacquainted with the life of Shelley, won, to his great surprise, an even greater success among English-speaking people, and he became a professional and most gifted biographer. (His books in this vein are treated in Chapter 16, Literary Biography and Autobiography, Vol. 1.) He possessed "a brilliant mind steeped in French history, literature, and art, capable of independent thought, and open to the best of the foreign"—(Justin O'Brien, in *SR*). An ardent Anglophile, he combined this passion with another—that for Marcel Proust (*q.v.*)—in "The Chelsea Way," which recounts in Proustian style an imaginary trip to England by the narrator of "Remembrance of Things Past."

COLLECTED STORIES. Trans. by Adrienne Foulke *Washington Square* 1967 $5.95

THE ART OF WRITING. Trans. by Gerard M. Hopkins. 1960 *Bks. for Libraries* $11.75. Collection of literary essays.

THE ART OF LIVING. Trans. by James Whitall; introd. by the author *Harper* rev. ed. 1967 $6.95

FROM PROUST TO CAMUS: Essays on Modern French Writers. 1963. Trans. by Carl Morse and Renaud Bruce *Doubleday* 1966 $5.95 Anchor Bks. pap. $1.45

Originally prepared for students. Although it contains interesting personal reminiscences, the book is not Maurois at his best. David Pryce-Jones, in the *Observer*, found that "all these French writers have become one and the same, the National Genius in 15 reproductions." "This sort of treatment is mildly boring [and sometimes] downright silly"—(*LJ*).

WEIGHER OF SOULS (1931) and THE EARTH DWELLERS. *Macmillan* 1963 $3.95

THE CHELSEA WAY: A Proustian Parody. 1929. Trans. with introd. and notes by George Painter; ill. by Philippe Jullian *James H. Heineman, Inc.* 1967 $3.95

ATMOSPHERE OF LOVE. 1929. Trans. by Joseph Collins *Ungar* $4.50 pap. $1.75

FATTYPUFFS AND THINIFERS. 1930. *Knopf* 1969 $3.95 lib. bdg. $4.79

PRIVATE UNIVERSE. Trans. by Miles Hamish. 1932. *Bks. for Libraries* $12.75

PROPHETS AND POETS. 1935. *Kennikat* 1968 $11.00

RICOCHETS: Miniature Tales of Human Life. Trans. by Miles Hamish. 1935. *Bks. for Libraries* $8.25

THE ART OF HAPPINESS. 1939. Ed. by Karen Middaugh *Hallmark* 1972 $3.00

LIFE OF SIR ALEXANDER FLEMING: Discoverer of Penicillin. 1959. Trans. by Gerard Hopkins *Dutton* 1959 $7.95

FROM THE NEW FREEDOM TO THE NEW FRONTIER. 1962. Trans. by Patrick O'Brian *McKay* 1963 $5.00

Maurois' history of the United States from 1912 to the present. It stresses the interaction of political, economic and cultural movements in molding the mind and heart of America. The parallel volume (planned as such—the two were published in many countries) is Louis Aragon's (*q.v.*) "History of the USSR from Lenin to Krushchev" (*McKay* 1964 $12.00).

AN ILLUSTRATED HISTORY OF ENGLAND. Trans. by Miles Hamish; fwd. by Sir Arthur Bryant *Viking* 1964 $20.00

A revision of his popular 1937 "History of England" brought up to 1962; the editors have now added more than 200 illustrations of "commendable taste"—(*LJ*).

AN ILLUSTRATED HISTORY OF GERMANY. Trans. by Stephen Hardman *Viking* Studio Bks. 1966 $22.50

Although criticized for its brief treatment of Nazi Germany, this is otherwise "an excellent overview of German history"—(*LJ*).

A HISTORY OF FRANCE. From early times to 1956. *T. Y. Crowell* (Funk & Wagnalls) 1968 $2.50

"One of the most absorbing histories you can read"—(*PW*).

OPEN LETTER TO A YOUNG MAN. 1966. *James H. Heineman, Inc.* 1968 $2.25

A "letter of apprenticeship" to an imaginary 20-year-old, this is "a short book of wit, wisdom and optimism in which Maurois encourages youth to enjoy and make full use of the opportunities the modern world gives him"—(*PW*).

MEMOIRS, 1885–1967. Trans. by Denver Lindley *Harper* 1970 $12.50

Books about Maurois

Maurois: The Writer and His Work. By Georges Lemaitre. *Ungar* rev. ed. 1968 $7.50

See also Chapter 16, Literary Biography and Autobiography, Reader's Adviser, *Vol. 1.*

ROMAINS, JULES (pseud. of Jules Louis Farigoule).   1885–

M. Romains first appeared in English as a medical researcher, with his scientific work, "Eyeless Sight: A Study of Extra-Retinal Vision and the Paroptic Sense" (1920, 1924, o.p.). He then became known as a dramatist. His first novel, "The Death of a Nobody," is still considered by many his masterpiece. In it, Romains "boldly did away with the existing props of the novel," an innovation at that time. The serial novel "Men of Good Will" begins in 1933, with its political unrest recalling the sixth of October 1908, six years before the First World War, the day with which the first volume opens. The narrative combines imaginary events with historical, and fictitious characters with actual. Lenin, Poincaré, the Kaiser, Jean Jaurès, Briand and others meet and converse with the people of the story. Not until Volume 7 does the war begin, and "Verdun," the high point of the work, was published just as world events of 1939 paralleled those of 1914. This epic novel, with its vast canvas and mass of characters, is an expression of the author's "unanimist" conception of life, a theory which defines society through the individual's relation to masses or groups, and contends that a group of people with a unanimous emotion (such as goodwill) can develop a mass power superior to any other force. Romains was international president of the P.E.N. Club from 1938 to 1941 and was elected to the French Academy in 1946.

DR. KNOCK. 1925. Trans. by James B. Gidney *French* $.95. A play.
"Bold and spinning scenes of delightful satire"—(*N.Y. Times*).

BODY'S RAPTURE. 1933. *Liveright* Black and Gold Lib. $7.95

MEN OF GOOD WILL. 1932–46. 14 vols. Vols. 1, 2, 3 trans. by Warre B. Wells, the rest by Gerard Hopkins. o.p.

The original U.S. edition was divided as follows: 1. Men of Good Will, 1933; 2. Passion's Pilgrims, 1934; 3. The Proud and the Meek, 1934; 4. The World from Below, 1935; 5. The Earth Trembles, 1936; 6. The Depths and the Heights, 1937; 7. Death of a World, 1938; 8. Verdun, 1939; 9. Aftermath, 1941; 10. The New Day, 1942; 11. Work and Play, 1944; 12. The Wind Is Rising, 1945; 13. Escape in Passion, 1946; 14. The Seventh of October, 1946.

Books about Romains

Drama of the Group. By P. J. Norrish. *Cambridge* 1958 $10.00
Jules Romains. By Denis Boak. World Authors Ser. *Twayne* 1974 $6.95

ALAIN-FOURNIER, HENRI.   1886–1914.

Alain-Fournier was a symbolist greatly influenced by Rimbaud (*q.v.*) and Baudelaire (*q.v.*). "The Wanderer," which has been called a "minor masterpiece," was partly based upon his own life and partly on that of John Keats (*q.v.*). His only finished work, it is a story of adolescent longing, of the discrepancy between a young man's dream and actuality. He died at 28, in action during World War I.

THE WANDERER (*Le Grand Meaulnes*). 1913. Trans. by François Delisle 1928. *Doubleday* Anchor Bks. 1958 pap. $1.95; trans. by François Delisle. 1928. *Kelley* $13.50; trans. by Lowell Bair *New Am. Lib.* Signet 1971 pap. $1.25

CENDRARS, BLAISE (pseud. of Frédéric-Louis Sauser).   1887–1961.

Born in Switzerland, but brought up in England, France and Germany as well, Cendrars, an important avant-garde poet, "prose-poet" and novelist, "went far beyond the surrealistic paths of Apollinaire. . . . From the early poetry of 'Easter in New York' to the late prose of 'The Detonated Man,' throughout, Cendrars astonishes"—(*LJ*). A bohemian afflicted with wanderlust, he traveled to Russia, Canada, the United States, South America and England—always returning to Paris, where he wrote and dabbled in film-making. Among his adventures were a music-hall stint as a juggler and a period in the French Foreign Legion (from 1914), which ended when he lost his right arm. Henry Miller (*q.v.*) called his literary attitude one of "instinctive, ordained defiance; . . . the word 'rebel' sounds ridiculous when applied to him. Cendrars was an absolute traitor to the race, and as such I salute him." His "novel *To the End of the World*, (1956, o.p.) is certainly picaresque, both in the subject matter and in the frenetic surge of its intention. The result is overwhelmingly and vastly funny"—(*New Statesman*).

SELECTED WRITINGS. Ed. with introd. by Walter Albert; pref. by Henry Miller *New Directions* bilingual ed. 1966 $7.50 pap. $2.45. Contains most of his poetry and some of his major prose writings.

AFRICAN SAGA (in *Anthologie Nègre*). 1921–1927. Trans. by Margery Dickinson Bianco. 1927. *Greenwood* (Negro Univs. Press) $14.25

THE ASTONISHED MAN (*Homme foudroyé*). 1945. Trans. by Nina Rootes 1970 o.p.

PLANUS (*Bourlinguer*). 1948. Trans. by Nina Rootes *Int. Pubns. Service* 1972 $13.00

Books about Cendrars

> The Inner Theatre of Recent French Poetry: Cendrars, Tzara, Peret, Artaud, Bonnefoy. By Mary Ann Caws. Princeton Essays in Lit. *Princeton Univ. Press* 1972 $9.50

MARAN, RENÉ. 1887–1961.

Born in Guyane, French Guinea, and educated in France, Maran was a government bureaucrat in the now Central African Republic from 1915 to 1921. As government representative, he was first-hand witness of colonial injustice. Of an older generation, he, despite his colonial disillusionment, claimed never to have understood the real meaning of negritude. Winner of several literary prizes during the forties, he finally was awarded the poetry prize of the French Academy.

BATOUALA. 1921. Trans. by Barbara Beck and Alexandre Mboukou *Fawcett* 1974 pap. $1.25; *Inscape Corp.* 1972 $9.50 1973 pap. $2.95

PERSE, ST.-JOHN (pseud. of Aléxis Saint-Léger Léger). 1887– (Nobel Prize 1960)

"Anabasis," the work which established St.-John Perse as the symbolist successor to Arthur Rimbaud (*q.v.*), was generally considered his masterpiece until the publication of the long poem "Seamarks." The *New Republic* said that this, "a moving celebration set in the ambience of the sea, establishes him once again as the major poet of our time in any language." "Birds," a meditation on flight illustrated by his close friend Braque, "contains some of the poet's finest lines"—(*LJ*).

Perse managed to combine poetry with diplomacy most of his life. He was born on a small family-owned island off Guadaloupe. He became a member of the French diplomatic corps and was Permanent Secretary of Foreign Affairs after Briand's death and until the Germans invaded France. He refused to become a collaborationist, fled to England, then Canada, and, at the request of Archibald MacLeish (*q.v.*), came to the United States to act as Consultant on French Poetry to the Library of Congress. Manuscripts left behind when he left France were destroyed by the Nazis. He received the Nobel Prize in 1960.

COLLECTED POEMS and ANABASIS. Collected Poems trans. by W. H. Auden and others; Anabasis trans. by T. S. Eliot Bollingen Ser. *Princeton Univ. Press* bilingual ed. 1972 $18.50

ANABASIS. 1924. First trans. 1930. Rev. trans. by T. S. Eliot. *Harcourt* new bilingual ed. 1949 pap. $1.85

All the Perse books in the list below are in the Bollingen Series, distributed by Princeton University Press.

ÉLOGES (1910) AND OTHER POEMS. Rev. trans. by Louise Varèse bilingual ed. 1944. 1956 $8.50

EXILE (1942) AND OTHER POEMS. Trans. by Denis Devlin bilingual ed. 1953. $8.50

WINDS. 1946. Trans. by Hugh Chisholm bilingual ed. 1953 2nd ed. 1961 $8.50

CHRONIQUE. Trans. by Robert Fitzgerald bilingual ed. 1961 $8.50

BIRDS. 1962. Trans. by Robert Fitzgerald bilingual ed. With reproductions of four original color etchings by Georges Braque 1966 $20.00
"Beautifully printed"—(*LJ*).

TWO ADDRESSES. Trans. by W. H. Auden and Robert Fitzgerald bilingual ed. His Nobel Prize speech "On Poetry" (1960) and Inauguration Address at the 7th Centenary of the birth of Dante (1965). 1966 $6.00

Books about Perse

> Saint-John Perse: A Study of his Poetry. By Arthur Knodel. *Edinburgh Univ. Press* (dist. by Aldine) 1966 $5.75
> This "helpful volume," the first full-length work on Perse in English, treats "the genesis, development, and maturation of the poet's art"—(*LJ*).

BERNANOS, (PAUL LOUIS) GEORGES. 1888–1948.

"The Diary of a Country Priest," awarded the Grand Prix by the Académie Française in 1936, records events matter-of-factly, almost monotonously. Its unpretentious hero, a young priest of peasant origin, sickly and somewhat ineffectual but in search of God, is "a defenseless child who is nevertheless capable of hurting both himself and other people"—(Robert Coles, in the *New Republic*). "Mouchette," a short novel, concerns a wretchedly poor, ungainly adolescent girl who, raped and betrayed by the epileptic town poacher, is ultimately drawn to suicide—feeling that death "is something to be achieved in the absence of love." Both novels are set in bleak villages untouched by the 20th century. "In different ways [these books] treat of pride and innocence, those two states of mind and soul that struggle within us for command of whatever destiny we may have in this universe. [They] are suffused with spiritual concerns, but the mystery of Christianity, of salvation and damnation, remains almost austerely beyond analysis or even speculation"— (Coles). Both have been made into films. The *New Yorker* called Robert Bresson's "Mouchette," shown at the 1967 Cannes Film Festival, the "season's one artistically great French film."

For over a year Bernanos lived at Palma in the Balearic Islands. His "A Diary of My Times" (1938, o.p.) was written as a result of what he saw happening there during the Spanish Civil War. After the "treason of Munich" he left France, settled in Brazil and wrote from there the powerful exhortations, "Plea for Liberty" (1944, o.p.). He was a brilliant polemicist, an ardent Catholic and fervent Frenchman.

THE DIARY OF A COUNTRY PRIEST. 1926. Trans. by Pamela Morris. 1962. *Doubleday* Image Bks. 1974 pap. $1.75

MOUCHETTE. 1937. Trans. by J. C. Whitehouse *Holt* 1966 $3.95
"Whitehouse has done a lovely job"—*(New Republic)*.

LAST ESSAYS. 1955. Trans. by Joan and Barry Ulanov. 1955. *Greenwood* 1968 $12.00

Books about Bernanos
Bernanos: An Introduction. By Peter Hebblethwaite. *Hillary House* 1965 $2.75
Study of the religious aspects of Bernanos' works by a member of the Society of Jesus. "A good introduction . . . especially for the lay reader"—*(Choice)*. Bibliography.
The Poetic Imagination of Georges Bernanos: An Essay in Interpretation. By Gerda Blumenthal. *Johns Hopkins Press* 1965 $8.00
Georges Bernanos. By William Bush. World Authors Ser. *Twayne* $6.95
Georges Bernanos: A Biography. By Robert Speaight. *Liveright* 1974 $8.95

MARCEL, GABRIEL.   1889–   *See Chapter 5, Philosophy*, Reader's Adviser, *Vol. 3*.

COCTEAU, JEAN.   1891–1963.
This versatile, sophisticated, eccentric, exuberant poet-dramatist-novelist experimented with almost every literary and artistic form: novels, plays, poems, film scenarios, ballet, criticism, drawing, painting. "Prodigal son of a wealthy notary," he became the spokesman for literary modernism and surrealism. His artist friends and collaborators included Picasso, Diaghilev and Rilke (*q.v.*). His career is said to have been sparked by Diaghilev's request that he do something "astonishing": Cocteau became adept at it. Generous and alert for fresh talent, he "launched a number of gifted adolescents like Raymond Radiguet or outlaws like Genet on their paths to fame"—(Henri Peyre). Though he is even now under attack as a "juggler" or "poseur," the American critics who take Cocteau seriously, admitting his failures, appear to be in the majority. Among the nonliterary achievements of this extraordinary man are the decoration of the City Hall of Menton and the fisherman's chapel at Villefranche, both on the French Riviera.

Francis Fergusson considers Cocteau one of the most dexterous and resourceful "poets of the theatre" in our time. "He is a master of the make-believe; of the glamour and the trickery of the stage. But, as he himself explains, he composes his theatrical effects with the rigor of a *symboliste* poet, putting together the words of a small subtle lyric. Sometimes he will play with ancient legends, as in *Antigone* and *Orphée*; sometimes with themes from contemporary fiction or the contemporary theatre, as in *The Eagle with Two Heads, Intimate Relations* and *The Holy Terrors*. But he always catches the familiar figures in unexpected light, that of his own unique, poetic intelligence."

Somewhat surprisingly, Cocteau was elected to the Académie Française in 1955. As he "took his place at last in the charmed circle of immortality," he said, "Entrance to the Académie is the last scandal I will create."

THE INFERNAL MACHINE AND OTHER PLAYS. Trans. by W. H. Auden, Albert Bermel, E. E. Cummings, Dudley Fitts, Mary Hoeck and John Savacool *New Directions* 1967 $8.75 pap. $2.75
Six of the most famous plays: "virtually all of this great poet's contribution to the stage. . . . Highly recommended"—*(LJ)*.

FIVE PLAYS. *Farrar, Straus* (Hill & Wang) 1961 $4.50 Mermaid Dramabks. pap. $3.95.
Includes The Eagle with Two Heads (1946), Antigone (1926), Orphée (1926),

Intimate Relations (*Les Parents Terribles* 1938), The Holy Terrors (*Les Monstres Sacrés* 1939).

COCTEAU'S WORLD: An Anthology of Major Writings by Jean Cocteau. Trans. and ed. by Margaret Crosland *Dodd* 1973 $8.95

SCREENPLAYS AND OTHER WRITINGS ON THE CINEMA. Trans. by Carol Martin-Sperry *Grossman* (Orion Press) 1968 $5.95. Includes The Blood of a Poet and The Testament of Orpheus. Illustrated with photographs from the films.

THREE SCREENPLAYS. *Grossman* 1972 $8.95 pap. $4.95. Includes Beauty and the Beast, Orpheus, The Eternal Return. Over 100 photographs from the films.

TWO SCREENPLAYS. Trans. by Carol Martin-Sperry *Penguin* Pelican Bks. 1969 pap. $1.25

CALL TO ORDER. 1918–26. Trans. by Rollo H. Myers. 1927. *Haskell* 1974 $12.95

THE HOLY TERRORS (*Les Enfants Terribles*). 1929. Trans. by Rosamond Lehmann; 20 drawings by Cocteau. *New Directions* 1957 pap. $2.25

MAALESH: A Theatrical Tour in the Middle East. 1949. Trans. by Mary C. Hoeck *Hillary House* 1956 $5.50

BEAUTY AND THE BEAST: Diary of a Film. (Orig. "Diary of a Film") 1950. *Dover* 1972 pap. $2.75; *Peter Smith* $5.00

THE HAND OF A STRANGER (*Journal d'un inconnu*). 1953. Trans. by Alec Brown. 1956. *Bks. for Libraries* 1959 $11.50

OPIUM: A Diary of a Cure. 1930. Trans. by Margaret Crosland *Hillary House* 1957 $7.25. Relates how Cocteau overcame his addiction to opium, which he had begun using after the death of his great friend Raymond Radiguet.

JOURNALS. Trans. and ed. with introd. by Wallace Fowlie; ill. with drawings by the author 1964 *Peter Smith* $4.50. The imprint of the forceful personality behind the public figure is here, with revealing portraits of Proust, Maritain, Picasso and others.

PROFESSIONAL SECRETS: An Autobiography of Jean Cocteau. Trans. by Richard Howard, ed. by Robert Phelps *Farrar, Straus* 1970 $8.50; *Harper* Colophon Bks. pap. $3.25

COCTEAU ON THE FILM. Trans. by Vera Traill. 1954. With new introd. by George Amberg *Dover* 1972 pap. $2.00. Conversations with Cocteau recorded by André Fraigneau.

DRAWINGS: 129 Drawings from Dessins. Trans. by Stanley Applebaum. 1924. New fwd. by Edouard Dermit *Dover* 1972 pap. $3.00; *Peter Smith* $6.00

Books about Cocteau

Jean Cocteau: A Biography. By Margaret Crosland. 1956 o.p. The standard biography, with a critical estimate of his creative work and various public activities.

Scandal and Parade: The Theatre of Jean Cocteau. By Neal Oxenhandler. *Rutgers Univ. Press* 1957 $9.00
"The best study we have of Cocteau the dramatist"—(*N.Y. Times*).

Jean Cocteau: The History of a Poet's Age. By Wallace Fowlie. *Indiana Univ. Press* 1966 $6.95
"A book of criticism ... mostly free from portentous considerations, by the foremost American interpreter of contemporary French literature. ... This intelligent volume would have pleased [Cocteau]"—(Henri Peyre, in the *N.Y. Times*). "Warm portrait of a brilliant, generous soul"—(*SR*).

Jean Cocteau: The Man and the Mirror. By Elizabeth Sprigge and Jean-Jacques Kihm. *Coward* 1968 $5.95
A "gossipy and entertaining biography"—(*The Kirkus Service*).

Jean Cocteau. By Bettina L. Knapp. World Authors Ser. *Twayne* $6.95

Cocteau. By Francis Steegmuller. *Little* 1970 $12.50

DRIEU LA ROCHELLE, PIERRE. 1893–1945.

One of the most controversial of writers between the wars, Drieu came out of the First World War to join the generation of Malraux and Aragon. His *"La Comédie de Charleroi"* (1934) is a reflection of his military service. His adhesion to fascist ideology, from the thirties to the end of

World War II, made him an unpopular figure in a France he would not abandon. He was editor of the prestigious *NRF* (*Nouvelle Revue Française*) during the war. After the liberation, he succeeded after several attempts in committing suicide. *"Gilles"* (1939) and *"Les Chiens de Paille"* (1964) are the best known of his representative work.

SECRET JOURNAL AND OTHER WRITINGS. 1951 1961. Trans. by Alastair Hamilton *Howard Fertig* 1974 $9.50

Books about Drieu la Rochelle

Drieu la Rochelle and the Fiction of Testimony. By Frederic Grover. *Univ. of California Press* 1958 o.p.

CÉLINE, LOUIS-FERDINAND (pseud. of Louis-Ferdinand Destouches).   1894–1961.

Céline, an imaginative, "shocking" writer, horrified his readers in "Journey to the End of the Night" and "Death on the Installment Plan," which are to a great extent autobiographical; nevertheless, these novels were translated into all European languages. Céline's world as portrayed in these books is brutal and violent—a place of filth, perversion, obscenity, perfidy and crime, but there is "fierce sincerity" in his writing. "The great snarling cascade of whores and pimps and cretins, . . . the souped-up colors, the hallucinatory slides from the real to the dream, the mad polar swings from blackness to cascades of life, the taking of truth to the tenth power, the 'improvement' on reality, the prose that flies along at treetop level—all are Céline's trademarks, an innovative earthquake in French letters"—(Bruce Jay Friedman, in the *N.Y. Times*). He wrote in the slang of the French underworld, which he called "the language of hatred."

A violent anti-Semite, he was a known collaborationist during the German occupation of France. Fleeing to Denmark after the German collapse, he was imprisoned and later permitted to return to France, mentally unstable and partly paralyzed. Céline's work is now enjoying a great revival: seen in perspective, his influence on contemporary literature eclipses his warped personality. To Bruce Jay Friedman he is "a black 20th-century genius without peer." "To Henry Miller, Jack Kerouac, Allen Ginsberg, and many other writers he is Saint Céline, the man who showed them what could be done, how to howl"—(*N.Y. Review of Books*).

JOURNEY TO THE END OF THE NIGHT. 1932. Trans. by John H. P. Marks *New Directions* 1949 1959 pap. $2.95

DEATH ON THE INSTALLMENT PLAN (*Mort à Crédit*). 1936. Trans. by Ralph Manheim *New Directions* new ed. 1966 pap. $4.75

A "new rendering, . . . more in keeping with today's usage, [of the work] considered by many critics to be his best"—(*LJ*).

CASTLE TO CASTLE. 1959. Trans. by Ralph Manheim *Delacorte* Seymour Lawrence 1968 $7.50; *Dell* 1970 pap. $.95. This volume won the National Book Award for translation in 1969.

NORTH. 1969. Trans. by Ralph Manheim *Delacorte* Seymour Lawrence 1972 $10.00

RIGADOON. 1969. Trans. by Ralph Manheim *Delacorte* Seymour Lawrence 1974 $8.95

Books about Céline

Louis-Ferdinand Céline. By David Hayman. Essays on Modern Writers *Columbia* 1965 pap. $1.00. An excellent critical essay with a selected bibliography.
Céline and his Vision. By Erika Ostrovsky. *New York Univ. Press* 1967 $7.95 pap. $2.25 "Brilliantly written, exquisitely researched critical analysis"—(*N.Y. Times*).
Céline: The Novel as Delirium. By Allen Thiher. *Rutgers Univ. Press* 1972 $12.50
Céline: Man of Hate. By Bettina Knapp. *Univ. of Alabama Press* 1974 $10.00

ELUARD, PAUL (pseud. of Eugène Grindel).   1895–1952.

At first associated with the dadaists and surrealists, Eluard "since 1918 has been one of France's most original and imaginative poets." Love is the theme he consistently celebrated. Private love inspired his best poetry and expanded into love for humanity at large. This led him in 1938 to join the Communist Party and to be active in the French Resistance during World War II, but his greatest "private" poem, "Poetry Uninterrupted" (*"Poésie Ininterrompue"*), was written in 1946. "Eluard will remain, not as a political poet, but as a writer who restored, after Symbolism, simplicity to poetry and reintroduced reality without becoming prosaic"—(Geoffrey Brereton). *"Le Dur Désir de Durer"* (U.S. 1950, ltd. ed., o.p.) is a book of poems translated into verse by Stephen Spender (*q.v.*) and Frances Cornford, with illustrations by Marc Chagall.

SELECTED WRITINGS. Trans. by Lloyd Alexander; introd. notes by Aragon and others *New Directions* bilingual ed. 1951 $7.50

UNINTERRUPTED POETRY: Selected Writings. Trans. by Alexandre Lloyd *New Directions* 1973 pap. $3.95

CAPITAL OF PAIN. 1926. Trans. by Richard Weisman *Grossman* 1973 $12.50 pap. $4.95

GIONO, JEAN. 1895–1970.

"When Giono's first novel, *'Colline'* (Hill of Destiny) appeared in 1929, it struck a fresh, new note. . . . After Proust and Gide, Duhamel and Romains, Cocteau and Giraudoux, what could be more restful than a world of wind and sun and simple men who apparently had never heard of psychological analysis, never confronted any social problems, never read any books. . . . For Giono the world of his imagination was undoubtedly a refuge. . . . Brought up by his father, a shoemaker, in the small town of Manosque, Giono, except for one brief interval, had never left home before 1914." When, as a boy of 19, he was sent to the front with the infantry, he was totally unprepared. "Four years later, when release came, his revolt was complete; he fled from the modern world and banished it from his novels." After the shock of World War II his novels seemed to gain in stature. One of his best is the "strange, terrible and beautiful" "Horseman on the Roof," his chronicle of the great cholera epidemic of 1838. "Giono's vast frescoes reflect his fundamental optimism and love of life, his deliberate refusal to deal with the complications of human psychology." (*See the chapter on private worlds in "An Age of Fiction" by G. Brée and M. Guiton, from which these quotations have been taken.*)

TO THE SLAUGHTERHOUSE (*Le Grand Troupeau*). 1931 *Dufour* $7.95

THE MAN WHO PLANTED HOPE AND GREW HAPPINESS. 1954. Fwd. by Gaylord Nelson *Friends of Nature* 1967 pap. $.75. A pamphlet telling the (true) story of Elzéard Bouffier, who in 1910, for his own pleasure, began planting acorns and seedlings on a barren wasteland in Provence, creating by 1945 a vast, beautiful forest.

THE BATTLE OF PAVIA, 24 FEBRUARY 1525. 1963. Trans. and ed. by A. E. Murch. *Dufour* $7.95. Novel.

TWO RIDERS OF THE STORM (*Deux Cavaliers de l'orage*). 1965. Trans. by Alan Brown *Dufour* 1967 $7.50

ENNEMONDE. 1968. *Dufour* $7.95

Books about Giono

Jean Giono. By Maxwell A. Smith. *Twayne* 1966 $6.95
     The first study of Giono in English. Alternating biographical and critical chapters; chronology; bibliography; index. "More complete biographies are needed. But this is an honest, worthwhile study of Giono the Provençal regionalist and universal writer"—(*Choice*).
Giono. By W. D. Redfern. *Duke Univ. Press* 1967 $6.75. Critical study of his development and thought as reflected in his fiction.
Giono: Master of Fictional Modes. By Norma L. Goodrich. *Princeton Univ. Press* 1973 $12.00

BRETON, ANDRÉ. 1896–1966.

At the time of his death, André Breton's novel "Nadja," about a young dreamer in love with a "hallucinated and ethereal heroine, . . . his brightest literary jewel . . . was finally reaching beyond the limited circle of friends and coterie disciples . . . to a new generation of youth"—(Anna Balakian in *SR*). Breton, dynamic personage, poet, novelist, philosophical essayist and art critic, was the father—he was often called the "pope"—of surrealism. From World War I to the 1940s he was at the forefront of the numerous avant-garde activities that centered in Paris. A prolific producer of pamphlets and manifestoes, he also edited two surrealist periodicals. "Automatic writing," defined by Breton in his "Manifesto of Surrealism" (1924) as a process "by which one strives to express . . . the genuine functioning of the mind in the absence of all control exercised by reason" was his method of creation. The Manifesto implied "that surrealism was not simply a reform in prosody or in the techniques of the artist but a reformation of the mental process of the writer and the artist, and by the same token of the reader and the viewer"—(Balakian). Breton, says the *N.Y. Times*, "exercised a worldwide influence on the art and literature of this century." Picasso, Derain, Magritte, Giacometti, Cocteau, Eluard and Gracq are among the many whose work was affected by his thinking. From 1927 to 1933 he was a member of the Communist Party, but thereafter he opposed communism. He said in *"L'Amour Fou"* (1937), "I had . . . willed never to become unworthy of the power which, in the direction of eternal love, had made me *see* and granted me the privilege, even more rare, of making others see. I had never been undeserving of it, I have never ceased to make into one the flesh of the being I love and the snow of the summits in the rising sun."

SELECTED POEMS. Trans. by Kenneth White *Grossman* Cape Eds. 1969 $3.50 pap. $1.95

MANIFESTOES OF SURREALISM. 1924 1930. Trans. by Richard Seaver and Helen R. Lane *Univ. of Michigan Press* 1969 $8.50 Ann Arbor Bks. 1972 pap. $3.25

NADJA. 1928. Trans. by Richard Howard *Grove* 1960 Evergreen Bks. pap. $2.95; *Peter Smith* pap. $5.00

SURREALISM AND PAINTING. 1928. Trans. by Simon W. Taylor *Harper* 1973 $25.00 pap. $7.95

WHAT IS SURREALISM? 1934. 1936. *Haskell* lib. bdg. $7.95

YOUNG CHERRY TREES SECURED AGAINST HARES (*Jeunes Cerisiers Garantis contre les Lièvres*). Trans. by Edouard Roditi; ill. by Arshile Gorky *Univ. of Michigan Press* bilingual ed. 1969 $5.00 Ann Arbor Bks. pap. $1.95

ODE TO CHARLES FOURIER. Trans. by Kenneth White *Grossman* Cape Eds. 1970 $4.50

Books about Breton

Surrealism and the Literary Imagination: A Study of Breton and Bachelard. By Mary Ann Caws. *Humanities Press* 1966 $5.50

André Breton. By J. H. Matthews. Essays on Modern Writers *Columbia* 1967 pap. $1.00

André Breton: Magus of Surrealism. By Anna Balakian. *Oxford* 1971 $10.95. A serious and comprehensive study.

André Breton and Surrealism. By Michel Carrouges. Trans. by Maura Prendergast *Univ. of Alabama Press* 1974 $10.75

MONTHERLANT, HENRY (MILLON) DE. 1896–1973.

Born in Paris of a very old French family, Henry de Montherlant was a disciple of "tradition, authority, classicism, and nationalism," and many of his writings are cynical and misogynous in tone. He has often been compared with Ernest Hemingway (*q.v.*), with whom he had much in common temperamentally. Montherlant was primarily a novelist, though he also wrote poetry, plays and essays. His first success as a dramatist came with "*La Reine Morte*" in 1942. After that time he wrote 12 plays—tragedies probing psychological conflicts. "Port-Royal," about Jansenist nuns considered heretics by the Catholic church, is the last and most dramatic part of what he called a "Catholic trilogy." He won the highest literary award granted by the French Academy, the Grand Prix de Littérature, for "*Les Célibataires*" ("Perish in Their Pride," or "The Bachelors"), a novel about the decadence and ruin of two old bachelors of the French nobility. "Chaos and Night," his first novel in many years, describes the approach to death of a Spanish Civil War veteran who is also a bullfighter. Its general pessimism and disgust with mankind again reveals the somewhat petulant idealist *manqué*. Henri Peyre finds that Montherlant did not fulfill his early promise, hampered by "prolonged boyishness and woeful inadequacy of theme to a masterful style." He was elected to the French Academy in 1960.

THE BACHELORS (*Les Célibataires*). 1934. Trans. with introd. by Terence Kilmartin. o.p. His best and most successful novel.

GIRLS (*Les Jeunes Filles*). 1935–40. Trans. by Terence Kilmartin *Harper* 1969 $8.95

CHAOS AND NIGHT. 1963. Trans. by Terence Kilmartin 1964 *Grosset* pap. $2.45

His first major novel in more than 20 years, it presents "his final commentary on the state of man [and] seems, in spirit, to be largely autobiographical"—(*SR*).

Books about Montherlant

Existence and Imagination: The Theatre of Henry de Montherlant. By John Batchelor. *Humanities Press* 1967 $11.00

Henry de Montherlant. By Robert B. Johnson. World Authors Ser. *Twayne* 1968 $6.95

Henry de Montherlant: A Critical Biography. By Lucille F. Becker. *Southern Illinois Univ. Press* 1970 $4.95

ARAGON, LOUIS. 1897–

Aragon began his literary career as a surrealist poet. In 1931 he visited the Soviet Union (his wife is Elsa Triolet, sister-in-law of the Russian poet Mayakovsky) and became strongly Marxist-oriented—a writer "most likely to go down to posterity as a virtuoso master of prose and as a novelist"—(Henri Peyre). He has written nine novels, somewhat sentimental in tone, and is noted for his clandestine political poetry composed during the French Resistance in World War II. In 1965 the *Saturday Review* reported that "Aragon, having completed with André Maurois their *Parallel History* (in which Maurois traces the history of the USA while Aragon presents a chronicle of the USSR), now launches another collective project—this time with his wife. . . . This marital team has begun to publish its complete works in alternating volumes, the first being her juvenilia and the second his earliest works. It is a pleasant idea, and appropriate, since Mme Triolet inspired some of Aragon's finest poetry."

HENRI MATISSE. 1971. Trans. by Jean Stewart *Harcourt* 1972 $7.50

Books about Aragon

Malraux, Sartre, and Aragon as Political Novelists. By Catherine Savage. *Univ. Presses of Florida* 1965 pap. $2.00

Louis Aragon. By Lucille F. Becker. World Authors Ser. *Twayne* $6.95

BATAILLE, GEORGES.   1897–

Bataille, known chiefly as an essayist, has written novels (e.g. *"Le Bleu de Ciel,"* 1957) in which, says Boisdeffre, "he has not succeeded in giving a concrete approximation of the modern hero." He has also written erotic tales (*"Histoire de l'oeil," "Mme Edwarda," "L'Abbé"*). In *"L'Expérience intérieure"* (1943), *"Le Coupable"* (1943), and *"Haine de la Poésie"* (1946), he has invented a genre that, says Nadeau, "marries stark confession with philosophic reflection and mystical research." In search of the absolute, any road seems good to him; no rule, no social or moral compunction stands in his way. Literature is a manner of expression and language is a tool.

LITERATURE AND EVIL. 1957. Trans. by Alastair Hamilton *Humanities Press* 1973 $7.50

GHELDERODE, MICHEL DE.   1898–1962.

Born in Brussels, Ghelderode was a hermit and an invalid, a scholar and a gentleman. His dark bachelor apartment was filled with objects that might have been collected by a European Andy Warhol. The reputation of "one of the world's best-known, little-known playwrights of this century" (Clive Barnes) started to grow in the 1940's in France and has been spreading since then through radio and television broadcasts and performances in theaters all over the world.

"The uniqueness of Ghelderode's plays is largely due to the intensity of their romantic characteristics. The plays are not so much set in the past as wrought out of the past. The sensuous elements are vivid and persistent, often brutal. The works do not deal with mystery, they are permeated with mystery. And everywhere sin and death are the constant accompaniments of human existence. The plays are shot with laughter; but with that Flemish laughter that rings with the gnashing of teeth. . . . His artistic life was as intense and as consistent as his plays. He was a man of deep feeling, great sensitivity, and enormous industry, and he was utterly undeterred by the fact that he was, as he himself put it, 'a no-making-money author.' At a time when so much homage was paid to logic, he kept his eyes fixed on what seemed to him to be truth. If the truth turned out to be illogical, his reaction was 'so much the worse for logic.' "—(Introduction to "Seven Plays: Volume 2"). Martin Esslin classifies Ghelderode as an exponent of the "poetic avant-garde" theater—drama "more lyrical" than that of the Theater of the Absurd. "It aspires to plays that are in effect poems, images composed of a rich web of verbal associations."

Ghelderode's work has long been known to the avant-garde, but with the playing of "Escurial" on U.S. NET Television in the spring of 1967 a wider American public became aware of him. "Escurial" is a harsh duologue between an unfeeling king (whose queen is dying) and his victim, the sentient human being who is his court jester. "Pantagleize" received ecstatic reviews as performed by the APA on Broadway in December 1967. Clive Barnes, who expected bombast and intellectualism, wrote in the *NY. Times:* " 'Pantagleize' is a marvelous play, the production is excellent, and the whole thing is funny, thoughtful, stimulating and entertaining." The antihero Pantagleize, a "Chaplinesque everyman," through farcical misadventures "discovers a destiny"— before a firing squad. He is "whirled along to his destruction," says Harold Clurman (in the *Nation*), "by the absurd tides of a movement of which he is wholly unaware and to which he is entirely indifferent." Ghelderode himself called "Pantagleize" "a farce to make you sad."

Important articles on various aspects of the theater and thought of Ghelderode appeared in the *Tulane Drama Review*, vol. 8, 1963.

SEVEN PLAYS. Trans. with introd. by George Hauger *Farrar, Straus* (Hill & Wang) 2 vols.
   Vol. 1 1960 $4.95 Mermaid Dramabks. pap. $2.25 Vol. 2 1964 pap. $2.75

   Vol. 1 The Women at the Tomb; Barabbas (1928); The Blind Men (1933); Chronicles of Hell (1929); Lord Halewyn; Three Actors and Their Drama; Pantagleize Vol 2. Red Magic (1931); Hop Signor! (1935); The Death of Doctor Faust (1925); Christopher Columbus (1927); A Night of Pity (1921); Piet Bouteille (1918); Miss Jairus (1934)

CHRONICLES OF HELL. 1929. (In "Modern Drama" ed. by Otto Reinert) *Little* 1966 pap.
   $5.50

CHRISTOPHER COLUMBUS. 1932. (In "Masterpieces of Modern French Theater" ed. by
   Robert W. Corrigan) *Macmillan* Collier Bks. 1967 pap. $1.50

SCHOOL FOR BUFFOONS. 1937. *T. Y. Crowell* (Chandler Pub.) 1968 pap. $.95

ESCURIAL. (In "The Modern Theatre" Vol. 5 ed. by Eric Bentley) *Peter Smith* 1957 $6.00

KESSEL, JOSEPH. 1898–

"A few, a very few novels have the quality of folk tales passed on from generation to generation, the simplicity dusted with wonder, the essential truth, the unstated but inherent message, the rightness of man's relationship to nature and to his fellow man—the qualities of stories told and retold because truth is in them. Such a rare novel is 'The Lion' "—(*Chicago Sunday Tribune*). A novelist of "action and adventure" (Henri Peyre), Kessel spent part of his childhood in Russia, and went to France before World War I, when he served in the French Air Force. He worked with the French Underground in World War II and did some "superb [wartime] reporting from London"—(Peyre). In June 1967, Genêt of the *New Yorker* reported that "No. 1 [on the French best-seller list was] the tremendous, gusty Joseph Kessel adventure novel 'Les Cavaliers.' . . . It is written with that natural exhilarating verbal gift, somewhat Oriental in flavor, that has promoted Kessel to a seat in the Académie Française and has made him one of the most popular of France's writers since his first book, in 1923, to which he has added twenty-eight more."

THE LION. 1958. Trans. by Peter Green *Knopf* 1959 2nd ed. 1962 $3.95 lib. bdg. $5.99; *Avon* 1970 pap. $.75

THE MAN WITH THE MIRACULOUS HANDS. 1960. Trans. by Helen Weaver and Leo Raditsa. 1961. *Bks. for Libraries* $12.50. The story of Dr. Felix Kersten, physician to Heinrich Himmler during World War II.

THE HORSEMEN (*Les Cavaliers*). 1967. *Farrar, Straus* 1968 $6.95; *New Am. Lib.* Signet pap. $1.50

KISLING. 1971. Ed. by Jean Kisling; trans. by B. D. Conlan *Harry N. Abrams* 1973 $35.00; *Newbury Bks.* bilingual ed. 1972 $55.00

PONGE, FRANCIS. 1899–

A poet, long unread, who has come into his own since the 1950s with admirers from Sartre to Sollers. The publication in 1961 of his "*Grand Receuil*" was somewhat disappointing, says Boisdeffre, for these "essential texts cruelly exposed the absence of a global architecture." The poet, says Ponge, should never propose a thought but rather an object. He has become a particular favorite of the group of young semiologists around the literary review *Tel Quel*.

THINGS. 1942 *Grossman* 1971 $12.95 pap. $4.95; (with title "The Voice of Things") trans. by Beth Archer *McGraw-Hill* 1974 pap. $2.95

SOAP. 1967. Trans. by Lane Dunlop *Grossman* 1969 $3.50 pap. $1.50

GREEN, JULIEN. 1900–

Julien Green, who writes in French, was born in Paris of American parents. He spent his childhood in France, returning to the United States only to study at the University of Virginia and to serve in both World Wars. American life is the background for his two novels, "*Mont-Cinère*" (1926, U.S. 1927, o.p.) and "Moira" (1950, U.S. 1951, o.p.). French provincial life is the setting for "*Adrienne Mesurat*" ("The Closed Garden" 1927, U.S. 1928, o.p.), which won the Prix Femina and was honored by the Académie Française, and also for "Léviathan" ("The Dark Journey"), which won the Harper Prize Novel Contest for 1929–30. "The Transgressor," set in a French provincial town, was described by the London *Sunday Times* as "rare and memorable." "Each in His Darkness" (U.S. 1961, o.p.) is a novel about a Frenchman and his dying uncle in America. In his diary, Julien Green, a "fascinating personality," reveals his "sensitive, poetic nature" and provides insights into the obsessive, nightmarish atmosphere of his works as well as into the major conflicts of his life—Catholicism vs. Protestantism, and "the struggle between spiritual energy and sensual emotion"—(Justin O'Brien in *SR*). In 1966 he was awarded France's Grand Prix National des Lettres for his lifetime achievements.

THE DARK JOURNEY (*Léviathan*). 1929. Trans. by Vyvyan Holland. 1929. *Greenwood* $16.75

MEMORIES OF HAPPY DAYS. 1942. *Greenwood* $13.75. Composed in English.

THE OTHER ONE (*L'Autre*). 1971. Trans. by Bernard Wall *Harcourt* 1973 $6.95

DIARY. 1928–1957. Trans. by Anne Green; sel. by Kurt Wolff *Harcourt* 1964 $6.50

"Kurt Wolff has used a delicate scalpel to cut out for us the most characteristic and revealing passages [from the 8-volume diary], which the author's sister, the distinguished American novelist Anne Green, has beautifully translated from her brother's French"—(Justin O'Brien, in *SR*).

Books about Green

Julien Green and the Thorn of Puritanism. By S. E. Stokes, Jr. *Greenwood* 1972 $8.75. The most sympathetic and measured study of the man and his works.

Julien Green. By G. Burne. World Authors Ser. *Twayne* $6.95

SAINT-EXUPÉRY, ANTOINE DE. 1900–1944.

After escaping death in several accidents while flying as a pilot over the most dangerous sections of the French airmail service in South America, Africa and the South Atlantic, Saint-Exupéry was reported missing over southern France in 1944. He was mourned as a hero who had caught the imagination of men and women throughout the world. His books are written in beautifully simple poetic prose, exalting man's courage and heroic hope. He has a rare gift for coining unusual images. "Night Flight" was introduced by André Gide (*q.v.*) and was at once proclaimed a masterpiece. "Wind, Sand and Stars" is a series of tales, interspersed with philosophical reflections on the earth as a planet and on the nobility of the common man. "Flight to Arras" is the author's own account of a hopeless reconnaissance sortie during the tragic days of May 1940. He probes the meaning of death and war with a courageous belief in the final victory of love and good.

AIRMAN'S ODYSSEY: Wind, Sand and Stars (1939) trans. by Lewis Galantière; Night Flight (1931) trans. by Stuart Gilbert; Flight to Arras (1942) trans. by Lewis Galantière *Harcourt* 3 vols. in 1 1943 $9.50 pap. 3 vols. each $1.25

SOUTHERN MAIL. 1929. Trans. by Curtis Cate *Harcourt* 1972 pap. $1.45

NIGHT FLIGHT. 1931. Fwd. by André Gide *New Am. Lib.* Signet pap. $.95

WIND, SAND AND STARS. 1939. Trans. by Lewis Galantière, appreciation by Anne Morrow Lindberg, ill. by John O'Hara Cosgrave II 1940 *Harcourt* Harbrace Mod. Class. 1949 $2.95 pap. $1.15

THE LITTLE PRINCE. Trans. by K. Woods; ill. by the author *Harcourt* 1943 $5.95 pap. $.95 anniversary ed. 1973 $7.50. A poetic allegory for adults, a charming fantasy for children.

THE WISDOM OF THE SANDS. 1948. Trans. by Stuart Gilbert *Harcourt* 1950 $8.50. Saint-Exupéry's philosophy of life, published posthumously.

A SENSE OF LIFE. Trans. by Adrienne Foulke; introd. by Claude Reynal *T. Y. Crowell* (Funk & Wagnalls) 1965 $5.00

Posthumously collected "reports, news items, prefaces, and political essays. . . . Short thoughts of a great man, marvelous for reading aloud"—(*LJ*).

Books about St. Exupéry

Saint-Exupéry. By Marcel Migeo. *McGraw-Hill* $5.95. A biography.

Antoine de Saint-Exupéry. By Curtis Cate. *Putnam* 1970 $10.00

MALRAUX, ANDRÉ. 1901–

"Man's Fate," dealing with the Shanghai revolution, won the Goncourt Prize. It is the first of three war novels of great emotional intensity. "Man's Hope" (1938, o.p.), about the civil war in Spain, was made into a stirring film. "Days of Wrath" tells of the horrors of a concentration camp in Germany. These novels have little plot; they are crowded with characters and read like firsthand historical testimonies of the events they narrate. Malraux's heroes are men of action passionately devoted to their cause. And though it was Sartre (*q.v.*) who was to preach *l'engagement* (involving oneself in the moral struggles of mankind), Malraux "practised commitment in a much more impressive way. . . . He also expressed the concepts of the 'Absurd' and 'Existentialist Man' well in advance of the time when these terms became part of common parlance"—(*N.Y. Review of Books*). In committing himself, Malraux lived many lives. An airplane pilot, explorer and guerilla revolutionary in China and Spain, he later served under General de Gaulle in the French Resistance. A radical novelist—read by radicals—in his youth, he has become art critic, art historian and was de Gaulle's Minister for Cultural Affairs.

"The Voices of Silence" has been hailed as his masterpiece. It is a survey of the whole history of art in relation to man's religious beliefs and aspirations. André Maurois (*q.v.*) has said: "It would be easier to write another book rather than an article on this teeming, brilliant work. The reader will [here] discover the story of man."

THE TEMPTATION OF THE WEST. 1926. Trans. with introd. by Robert Hollander. 1961. *Jubilee Bks.* lib. bdg. $12.50

MAN'S FATE (*La Condition Humaine*). 1934. Trans. by Haakon Chevalier *Random* (Modern Lib.) 1936 pap. $1.95 Vintage Bks. pap. $1.65

THE VOICES OF SILENCE. 1951. Trans. by Stuart Gilbert *Doubleday* 1953 ltd. ed. $100.00. Printed in France; with 465 ills.

MUSEUM WITHOUT WALLS: The Voices of Silence. Trans. by Stuart Gilbert and Frances Price *Doubleday* 1968 pap. $2.49. A reworking of the first volume of "The Voices of Silence."

FELLED OAKS: Conversations with De Gaulle (*Les Chênes qu'on abat*). 1971. Trans. by Irene Clephane *Holt* 1972 $6.95

Books about Malraux

André Malraux and the Tragic Imagination. By Wilbur M. Frohock. *Stanford Univ. Press* 1952 $7.00 pap. $1.95
Still "the best full-length study of Malraux that has so far appeared"—(*N.Y. Review of Books*, Oct. 6, 1966).

André Malraux: The Conquest of Dread. By Gerda Blumenthal. *Johns Hopkins Press* 1960 $6.50. An analysis of his novels in terms of his esthetic theories.

Malraux: A Collection of Critical Essays. Ed. by R. W. B. Lewis. *Prentice-Hall* 1964 Spectrum Bks. $1.95
"Twelve essays by eminent American, French, and other critics [including Trotsky]. A very useful collection"—(*N.Y. Review of Books*).

Malraux, Sartre, and Aragon as Political Novelists. By Catherine Savage. *Univ. Presses of Florida* 1965 pap. $2.00

André Malraux: The Indochina Adventure. By Walter G. Langlois. *Praeger* 1966 $5.95
"Unquestionably of value to students of literature" (*LJ*), the book resolves existing rumors about Malraux's 1923–25 jaunt in Indochina, while showing how it influenced his later writings. (He had removed some Khmer sculptures, neglected in the jungle, to sell—when he needed money. Malraux was briefly imprisoned for theft.)

Memoirs. By Clara Malraux. Trans. by Patrick O'Brian *Farrar, Straus* 1967 $6.95
These reminiscences of Malraux's first wife, who during their 20-year marriage shared his many adventures and worked feverishly to obtain his release from prison after the Indochina episode (*see entry just above*), are "an important contribution to information about Malraux and good reading in itself"—(*LJ*). It was a best seller in Paris, where its propriety has been much debated.

André Malraux. By Cecil Jenkins. World Authors Ser. *Twayne* $6.95

André Malraux. By Jean Lacourture. Trans. by Alan Sheridan *Pantheon* 1976 $12.95

AYMÉ, MARCEL. 1902–1967.

Aymé was one of France's leading humorous writers. He was "insurance broker, bricklayer, journalist, salesman," then—after 1938—a prolific author. "In M. Aymé's writing fantasy is curiously compounded with an earthy but cheerful cynicism, and he rarely fails to be entertaining. He inclines to beat the drum of his preoccupation too loudly and too long, but in spite of what the green mare says there appears to be plenty of room in his world and his book for other elements—such as kindliness, affection, a strong feeling for, and familiarity with the countryside—as well as sex"—(*TLS*, London). Aymé's plays have been hits on the Parisian stage since 1945. His last, "*La Convention Belzébir*" (1967), in which permits to kill are sold for large sums, satirizes the absurdities of our world. An early article on his view of the world is J. Robert Loy's "The Real World of Marcel Aymé" in *French Review*, 1951.

ACROSS PARIS AND OTHER STORIES. Trans. by Norman Denny 1957 o.p. These fantasies of a master are essential Aymé.

THE GREEN MARE. 1933. Trans. by Norman Denny. *Atheneum* 1963 pap. $1.45. Novel.

CLÉRAMBARD. 1950. English version by Alvan Sapinsley and Leo Kerz; basic trans. by Norman Denny. *French & European* 1958 $5.50
This play "makes a motley of jest of the difference between aspiration and reality, which is always the soul of wit in the theatre."

Books about Aymé

Marcel Aymé. By Dorothy Brodin. Essays on Modern Writers *Columbia* 1968 $1.00

SARRAUTE, NATHALIE.   1902–

Nathalie Sarraute is the "thinker" among the practitioners of the New Novel. In her essay on the art of fiction, "The Age of Suspicion," she condemned the techniques used in the novel of the past and took a stand beside Robbe-Grillet (*q.v.*) as a leader of the avant-garde. The novel, she feels, must express "that element of indetermination, of opacity, and mystery that one's own actions always have for the one who lives them." Her works have now become known to an international public. Her ability to render fleeting awareness, and the psychological states underlying articulate speech has won both praise and disdain. So much of this revelation is built (says Henri Peyre) on "garrulous talk around trifles" that "French wits have disparagingly [coined the word] 'sarrauteries.' " Genêt (Janet Flanner) has called Mme Sarraute "the only one among the New Novel experimenters who appears finally to have struck her own style—intense, observational, and personal."

Of her novels, "The Golden Fruits" (1964, o.p.)—about the Paris literary fortunes of an imaginary novel called "The Golden Fruits"—is "the most barren of extraneous decor, the most accomplished from the standpoint of her esthetic aims"—(*SR*). It was awarded the International Literary Prize for the best work of fiction of 1964. *Life* found it a "murderously funny parable." Henri Peyre, who is not a devotee of the New Novel, says of the same book: "She who intends to portray insignificance and tedium should probably not banish all humor, forcefulness, and even exaggeration . . . and incur the one unforgivable charge in literature: that of unshakable dullness."

"Tropisms," her earliest (very brief) book, contains "all the raw material that I have continued to develop in my later works." Her "tropisms," she says, are instinctive "sensations," or even "movements," "produced in us by the presence of others, or by objects from the outside world. [They hide] beneath the most commonplace conversations and the most everyday gestures." She regards her novels as composed of a series of tropisms of varying intensity. "Nathalie Sarraute believes the artist's task is to reveal new aspects of reality that earlier generations have ignored. If she is right in that assumption, her success is undeniable. . . . Creative spirit, while guided by the theorist and craftsman in her, has carried the day"—(*SR*).

TROPISMS. 1939 rev. 1957. Trans. by Maria Jolas *Braziller* 1967 $3.50 pap. $1.95

"24 brief descriptions of moments of inner movement or change . . . of interest to writers and to specialists in the French new novel"—(*LJ*).

PORTRAIT OF A MAN UNKNOWN. 1948. Trans. by Maria Jolas *Braziller* 1958 $4.50

MARTEREAU. 1953. Trans. by Maria Jolas *Braziller* 1959 $4.50

THE AGE OF SUSPICION: Essays on the Novel (*L'Ère du Soupçon*). 1956. Trans. by Maria Jolas *Braziller* 1963 $5.00. The title of her well-known essay was given to this collection of four written from 1947 to 1956. She considers the work of Balzac, Joyce, Kafka and other masters in relation to her own novelistic aims.

DO YOU HEAR THEM? 1970. Trans. by Maria Jolas *Braziller* 1973 $5.95 pap. $2.95

Books about Sarraute

Nathalie Sarraute. By Ruth Z. Temple. Essays on Modern Writers *Columbia* 1968 $1.00. A compact study by a qualified scholar.

VERCORS (pseud. of Jean Bruller).   1902–

Vercors, who uses his real name, Jean Bruller, as the well-known satiric artist-illustrator, was cofounder of the leading French underground publishing house, *Aux Editions de Minuit.* "Le Silence de la Mer" was its first publication during the German occupation in 1942. It was translated as "The Silence of the Sea" by Cyril Connolly (*Macmillan* 1944, o.p.) and revealed by implication the impossibility of French-German collaboration. The allegorical "You Shall Know Them," about a man who fathers—and later is put to trial for killing—a half-human, half-animal "tropi," raises several disturbing moral questions. "Sylva" (1951, U.S. 1961, o.p.) is a story about a fox who turns into a woman. "Vercors is a skillful renovator of the fable and a master at blending moral and fantastic elements in a purely written tale"—(Henri Peyre). Rita Barisse, Vercors' translator, is Mme Bruller, his wife.

YOU SHALL KNOW THEM (*Les Animaux Dénaturés*). 1952. Trans. by Rita Barisse *Popular Lib.* 1967 pap. $.60

THE BATTLE OF SILENCE. 1967. Trans. by Rita Barisse *Holt* 1969 $5.95

QUENEAU, RAYMOND.   1903–

This author of treatises on mathematics and other scholarly works, who has made his reputation writing comic novels, is "recognized as one of the five or six major writers of the generation born at the beginning of the century"—(Guicharnaud). Queneau (through one of his characters) once defined humor as "an attempt to purge lofty feelings of all the baloney." Roger Shattuck interprets his philosophy: "Life is of course absurd and it is ludicrous to take it seriously; only the comic is serious." Life is so serious to Queneau that only laughter makes it bearable. He has written a play, screenplays, poetry, numerous articles and 15 novels—the first of which, "Le Chiendent," was published in 1933. In "Exercises in Style" (1947, U.S. 1955, o.p.), he tells a simple anecdote 99 different ways.

"The Blue Flowers," says Life, "represents Queneau at his best. . . . The jokes, puns, double-entendres, deceptions, wild events, tricky correspondences—and always the bawdy language growing in fields of glorious rhetoric—make it a feast of comic riches." The influences of Charlie Chaplin as well as James Joyce are detectable in his fiction. Queneau has been a member of the Goncourt Academy since 1951.

THE BARK TREE (Le Chiendent). 1933. Trans. by Barbara Wright New Directions 1971 $9.50 pap. $3.95

THE BLUE FLOWERS. 1965. Trans. by Barbara Wright Atheneum 1967 $5.00

THE FLIGHT OF ICARUS (Vol d'Icare). 1968. Trans. by Barbara Wright New Directions 1973 $7.50 pap. $2.25

Books about Queneau

Raymond Queneau. By Jacques Guicharnaud. Essays on Modern Writers Columbia 1965 pap. $1.00

RADIGUET, RAYMOND. 1903–1923.

This genius died of typhoid fever at 20, leaving one volume of unpublished poems, "The Devil Within," and two novels, "Le Diable au Corps" and "Le Bal du Comte d'Orgel." He was a close friend of Cocteau (q.v.), who said of him: "One is rather appalled by a boy of twenty who publishes the sort of book that can't be written at his age." Radiguet's novels depict the new "mal de siècle" which had broken out during the years following the war. He combines ingeniously a formal elegance with a licentious content. Radiguet's works richly deserve republication, both for their inherent excellence and for their influence upon Cocteau and others of his generation.

DEVIL IN THE FLESH (Le Diable au Corps). 1923. Trans. by Kay Boyle 1960 o.p.

COUNT D'ORGEL. 1924. Trans. by Violet Schiff. 1955 o.p.

YOURCENAR, MARGUERITE (pseud., an anagram of Crayencour). 1903–

The fictional autobiography, written by the Roman Emperor Hadrian to his 17-year-old grandson, Marcus Aurelius, is based on Hadrian's writings and the writings of "historians, friends and enemies." The work received the Prix Femina in 1952 and the 1955 Page One Award of the Newspaper Guild of New York: "As a work of art, of psychological insight, of historical intuition, [it] is an extraordinarily expert performance. . . . It has a quality of authenticity, of verisimilitude, that delights and fascinates"—(N.Y. Herald Tribune). Miss Yourcenar, a translator of Henry James and Virginia Woolf, is French but spends much of her time in this country. She has taught in the Romance Language Department at Sarah Lawrence College in Bronxville, N.Y.

COUP DE GRACE. 1939. Trans. by the author and Grace Frick Farrar, Straus 1957 $4.95

HADRIAN'S MEMOIRS. 1954. Trans. by the author and Grace Frick Farrar, Straus 1963 deluxe ed. $8.95 Noonday pap. $4.50

CURIE, EVE. 1904– See Chapter 7, Science, Reader's Adviser, Vol. 3.

THOBY-MARCELIN, PHILIPPE, 1904– , and PIERRE MARCELIN, 1908–

These brothers have written several works in the vein of Roumain but with greater detachment. Their works include "Le Crayon de Dieu" (1951 "The Pencil of God" o.p.), "Canapé Vert" (1944, o.p.), and "La Bête de Musseau" (1946 "Beast of the Haitian Hills" o.p.). Some of their works, praised by Edmund Wilson, have appeared in English translation before publication in French.

ALL MEN ARE MAD (Tous les Hommes sont fous). Trans. by Eva Thoby-Marcelin Farrar, Straus 1970 $6.95

SINGING TURTLE AND OTHER TALES. Trans. by Eva Thoby-Marcelin Farrar, Straus 1971 $3.95

ARON, RAYMOND. 1905– See Chapter 8, The Social Sciences: Social Scientists etc., and Chapter 9, History, Government and Politics: Modern and World History, Reader's Adviser, Vol. 3.

SARTRE, JEAN-PAUL.   1905–

In the leading French existentialist's first novel, "Nausea," he emphasized "the breakdown of meaning and the nausea resulting from a sudden apprehension of the existence of things." His concern with the "recognition of existence as a starting point in man's creative life" (*Cyclopedia of World Authors*) was continued in his volume of short stories, "The Wall and Other Stories" (1939, 1948, o.p.). Henri Peyre writes in "French Novelists of Today": "Sartre's fiction is original on many counts. First of all, his mastery of the language is extraordinary. . . . The great moments when the characters, suddenly aware of their existence or of their nascent freedom, seem to be favored with a gift of second sight, are impregnated with a severe and precise beauty. [His use of words] revivifies French through integrating into the written style all the fluid and picturesque, or malodorous, wealth of the language of the common people. . . . Sartrian fiction avoids most of the dangers of philosophical literature, and it gains, in our opinion, far more than it loses, in paralleling an arresting philosophy."

It is "evident [too] not only that Sartre is one of the great literary critics of our age, but that his criticism is perhaps the finest part of his work"—(Thomas Bishop, in *SR*). His study of Genet (*q.v.*), though "exasperating, [with] nothing made easy or clear, [is] crammed with stunning and profound ideas"—(Susan Sontag). "Situations," ten critical essays "uniformly outstanding, [reveal] the constant incisiveness of Sartre's mind and his forceful, free-flowing style wherein complexity and clarity go hand in hand. 'Situations' is first-rate criticism"—(Bishop). Sartre has expressed himself on many French writers, as well as on Négritude—the philosophy of Africans writing in French (*see Chapter 17, African Literature, this Vol.*). He is the editor of the review *Les Temps Modernes* and has been a close associate of Simone de Beauvoir (*q.v.*).

Sartre's first play, "The Flies" (*"Les Mouches"*), was produced during the German Occupation despite its underlying message of defiance. Before the end of World War II, his "No Exit" (*"Huis Clos"*) had also been presented in Paris. It received the 1947 N.Y. Drama Critics Circle Award as the best foreign drama but had a very short run here. The "impressive" film version opened in New York in January, 1963. It is about three evildoers in Hell and provides an introduction to the stark philosophy of French Existentialism, first propounded by Sartre. His caustic melodrama about a lynching in the South, "The Respectful Prostitute," was successfully presented in New York in 1948. The authorized translation of "Dirty Hands" is "incomparably better" than its acting version, "Red Gloves," which was unsuccessful on Broadway in 1948. "Sartre publicly denounced the American producers for mutilating the script and producing an entirely different play, leaving nothing of his 'but trivial melodrama full of talk on politics with no political meaing' "—(*Theatre Arts*, March 1949). After three years of theatrical, if not literary silence, Sartre's long play, "The Condemned of Altona" opened in Paris in the fall of 1959, and a London production followed. It concerns the fears and guilt of a German family after World War II, and is one of Sartre's most difficult and controversial plays.

THE WRITINGS OF JEAN-PAUL SARTRE. Trans. by Richard C. McCleary; ed. by Michel Contat and Michel Rybakla *Northwestern Univ. Press* 2 vols. 1974. Vol. 1 comp. by McCleary and Rybakla. A Bibliographic Life $30.00 Vol. 2 Selected Prose $10.00 set $35.00

Nondramatic Works

INTIMACY AND OTHER STORIES. *Berkley* Medallion Bks. pap. $.95; trans. by Lloyd Alexander *New Directions* 1952 1958 1969 pap. $1.75

NAUSEA. 1938. Trans. by Lloyd Alexander *New Directions.* 1949 pap. $1.50

ROADS TO FREEDOM: Three Novels of Modern Europe. The Age of Reason and The Reprieve (1945) trans. by Eric Sutton *Knopf* 1947 each $7.95 Troubled Sleep (1949) trans. by Gerard Hopkins *Knopf* 1951 $7.95; *Random* Vintage Bks. 3 vols. 1972 pap. each $1.95

BAUDELAIRE. 1947. Trans. by Martin Turnell *New Directions* 1950 $2.25

WHAT IS LITERATURE? 1948. (With title "Literature and Existentialism") trans. by Bernard Frechtman *Citadel* 1962 pap. $1.75; *Harper* Colophon Bks. pap. $1.95; *Peter Smith* $4.00

LITERARY ESSAYS. *Philosophical Lib.* Wisdom Lib. pap. $.95

LITERARY AND PHILOSOPHICAL ESSAYS. Trans. by Annette Michelson *Macmillan* Collier Bks. 1962 pap. $1.50

SEARCH FOR A METHOD. *Knopf* 1963 $5.95; *Random* Vintage Bks. pap. $1.65

SITUATIONS (*Situations* IV). 1964. Trans by Benita Eisler *Braziller* 1965 $5.95; *Fawcett* Premier Bks. pap. $1.25

"Interpretations of Camus, Gide, Sarraute and other writers, artists and thinkers in an analysis of man and the human situation"—(Publisher's note).

SAINT GENET. 1952. Trans. by Bernard Frechtman *Braziller* 1963 $8.50; *New Am. Lib.* Plume Bks. pap. $3.95. An interpretation of the life and work of Genet (*see below*).

THE WORDS. 1964. Trans. by Bernard Frechtman *Fawcett* Premier Bks. pap. $.95

"An essay in autobiography and self-contained first volume of a projected many-volumed work [in which] Sartre examines the formation of his character during his childhood years. . . . The central event . . . was the discovery of the world of words, of language. . . . [A] brilliant work . . . excellently translated"—(*LJ*).

Plays

NO EXIT AND THREE OTHER PLAYS. Trans. by Stuart Gilbert and Lionel Abel *Random* Vintage Bks. 1955 pap. $1.45. Includes The Flies; Dirty Hands (1948); The Respectful Prostitute (1947). These earliest plays of Sartre are vital to understanding the author.

NO EXIT (1944) and THE FLIES (1943). English version by Stuart Gilbert *Knopf* 1947 $4.95. Two plays.

THE DEVIL AND THE GOOD LORD (1951) AND TWO OTHER PLAYS. Trans. by Kitty Black and Sylvia and George Leeson *Knopf* 1960 $5.95; *Random* Vintage Bks. pap. $1.95. Includes Kean (1954) and Nekrassov (1956).

THE CONDEMNED OF ALTONA (*Les Séquestrés d'Altona*). 1959. Trans. by Justin O'Brien *French* 1967 $1.25; trans. by Sylvia and George Leeson *Knopf* 1961 $4.95; *Random* Vintage Bks. pap. $1.65

THE TROJAN WOMEN. 1965. *Knopf* 1967 $4.95. Sartre's adaptation of the play by Euripides (*q.v.*) for France's Théâtre National Populaire.

Books about Sartre

Sartre: Romantic Rationist. By Iris Murdoch. *Hillary House* 1953 $2.00; *Yale Univ. Press* 1953 pap. $1.95. An estimate by the noted British novelist.

Stages on Sartre's Way, 1938–1952. By Robert Jean Champigny. *Kraus* Indiana Univ. Press Series 1959 $13.00

Sartre. By Maurice Cranston. 1962. *Int. Pubns. Service* $2.50

To Be and Not to Be: An Analysis of Jean-Paul Sartre's Ontology. By J. L. Salvan. *Wayne State Univ. Press* 1962 $3.95

Sartre: A Collection of Critical Essays. Ed. by Edith Kern. *Prentice-Hall* 1963 Spectrum Bks. pap. $1.95

Malraux, Sartre, and Aragon as Political Novelists. By Catherine Savage. *Univ. Presses of Florida* 1965 pap. $2.00

See also Chapter 5, Philosophy, Reader's Adviser, *Vol. 3.*

BECKETT, SAMUEL. 1906–

Samuel Beckett, who became known here for his play, "Waiting for Godot," was born in Dublin and educated at Trinity College. He lectured in Paris at the École Normale Supérieure and then at Dublin University. He returned to France to settle there permanently in 1937 and abandoned English for French in his writing. Several novels and plays were written in French and translated into English by the author. His brilliant, highly individual style makes his work more appreciated perhaps in France. The *Manchester Guardian* said of "Malone Dies": "Superbly written throughout, it is a disturbing and memorable work of genius." Beckett shares with Sartre (*q.v.*) and Camus (*q.v.*) an "intense sense of the pervasiveness of misery, solitude, paralysis of will, and above all, the horror of nothingness. His obscure and difficult style is peculiarly suited to the portrayal of a world where, amidst obscenity and occasional blasphemy, the characters create their personal hells in the prisons of their own dark minds." "Poems in English" show his "vivid word sense, sexual imagery, telescoped meanings, violent *non sequiturs*, eruditions, and his Irishness, which, as was said of Joyce, he carried with him into exile"—(*LJ*). "In 'Stories and Texts for Nothing,' we have Beckett at his acrid best," wrote Charles Poore (in the *N.Y. Times*), who says he feels "invigorated

after a bout with Samuel Beckett's stylish sad works. He brings a wild Irish jiggery to man's fate."
Beckett's profound examination of "Proust" (*q.v.*) (*Grove* 1957 pap. $2.45) has been called "one of the
very best pieces of modern criticism."

Nondramatic Works

MORE PRICKS THAN KICKS. 1934. *Grove* 1970 $5.00 Evergreen Bks. pap. $1.95

MURPHY. 1938. *Grove* 1957 $5.00 Evergreen Bks. pap. $1.95

MALONE DIES. 1951. Trans. by the author *Grove* 1956 $4.00

MOLLOY. 1951. Trans. by the author and Patrick Bowles *Grove* 1955 $5.00

THE UNNAMABLE. 1953. Trans. by the author *Grove* 1958 $5.00

MOLLOY, MALONE DIES and THE UNNAMABLE. *Grove* Black Cat Bks. 1959 pap. $1.95

WATT. 1953. *Grove* 1959 $5.00 Evergreen Bks. pap. $3.95

STORIES AND TEXTS FOR NOTHING. 1958. Trans. by the author *Grove* 1967 $5.00
Evergreen pap. $2.95

POEMS IN ENGLISH. *Grove* 1963 pap. $4.00 Evergreen Bks. 1964 pap. $1.45

HOW IT IS. Trans. by the author *Grove* 1964 $5.00 Evergreen Bks. pap. $1.95

Plays

KRAPP'S LAST TAPE (1959) AND OTHER DRAMATIC PIECES. *Grove* $5.00 Evergreen Bks.
1960 pap. $2.45

WAITING FOR GODOT. 1952. Trans. by the author *Grove* 1954 5.00 Evergreen Bks. 1956
pap. $1.95. A tragicomedy in two acts.

ENDGAME. 1958. Trans. by the author *Grove* 1958 $4.00 Evergreen Bks. pap. $1.95

HAPPY DAYS. 1960. *Grove* 1961 $4.00 Evergreen Bks. pap. $1.65

CASCANDO (1963) AND OTHER SHORT DRAMATIC PIECES. *Grove* 1969 $4.00 Evergreen
Bks. pap. $1.95. Includes Words and Music, Eh Joe, Play, Come and Go, Film.

FILM: A Film Script. 1966 *Grove* 1969 $4.00 Evergreen Bks. pap. $1.95

FIRST LOVE (*Premier Amour*) AND OTHER SHORTS. 1970 Trans. by the author *Grove* 1974
$6.95 Evergreen Bks. pap. $1.95

THE LOST ONES (*Le Dépeupleur*). 1970 *Grove* 1973 $4.95 Evergreen Bks. pap. $1.95

Books about Beckett

Samuel Beckett: The Comic Gamut. By Ruby Cohn. *Rutgers Univ. Press* 1962 $7.00
Samuel Beckett. By William Y. Tindall. Essays on Modern Writers *Columbia* 1964 pap. $1.00
Samuel Beckett: A Collection of Critical Essays. By Martin Esslin. *Prentice-Hall* 1965 $6.95 pap.
$1.95
Casebook on Waiting for Godot. By Ruby Cohn. *Grove* Evergreen Bks. 1967 pap. text ed. $3.95
Samuel Beckett: Poet and Critic. By Lawrence E. Harvey. *Princeton Univ. Press* 1970 $14.50
A Reader's Guide to Samuel Beckett. By Hugh Kenner. *Farrar, Straus* 1973 $7.95 Noonday pap.
$2.95
Back to Beckett. By Ruby Cohn. *Princeton Univ. Press* 1974 $12.50
Samuel Beckett: A Critical Study. By Hugh Kenner. California Library Reprint Ser. *Univ. of
California Press* 1974 $9.75 pap. $2.45
Casebook on Waiting for Godot: The Impact of Beckett's Modern Classics Reviews, Reflections
and Interpretations. *Peter Smith* $5.00

DIOP, BIRAGO ISMAIL.   1906–

A veterinarian by profession, Diop was born in Dakar and educated in Senegal and Toulouse
(National School of Veterinary Medicine). He served for many years in high administrative
positions concerning animal husbandry, and in 1960 was the ambassador from Senegal to Tunisia.
A member of the P.E.N. Club and president of the Writers' Association of Senegal, he has written
in addition, "*Leurres et Lueurs*" and "*Contes et Lavanes.*" The latter work won the *Prix d'Afrique Noire*
in 1964. Diop has been a friend of Senghor (*q.v.*) since the thirties when he collaborated with him
on "*L'Étudiant Noir.*"

TALES OF AMADOU KOUMBA. 1947. Trans. by Dorothy S. Blair *Oxford* 1966 $4.50.
Winner of the *Grand Prix Littéraire de l'Afrique Occidentale.*

ROUGEMONT, DENIS (LOUIS) DE. 1906–

"One of the more imaginative critical thinkers of our time, . . . this Swiss-born French writer confronts the world as a Christian and a European, a witness to his age, a firm believer in engaged literature. He . . . [comes] to grips with great issues and movements, with which he always deals in an intellectually probing manner. His *Love in the Western World* was an admirable study wherein he brilliantly linked love, for Western man, to the concept of death and to a search for an absolute. In *The Christian Opportunity* (1963, o.p.) he applied his insight to a vast panorama of contemporary concepts, displaying what several critics have termed a Catholic perspective or imagination and a Protestant conscience"—(Thomas Bishop, in *SR*). In his other works, notably "Love Declared" and "Dramatic Personages," he pursues other aspects of the thesis that has become his life's study: that for European man there is a radical dualism of *agape*—selfless Christian love for God or fellow man—and *eros*—acquisitive love.

Irving Singer, in the *N.Y. Review of Books,* Jan. 28, 1965, is skeptical of de Rougemont's complex theses and their application: "His major talent consists in the ability to see interesting parallels between dissimilar writers or between situations in literature and those in life. . . . We end up convinced of the man's cleverness, but uncertain about his ultimate integrity." De Rougemont's "Love in the Western World," however, continues to be widely mentioned and quoted. An editor and professor, M. de Rougemont has lectured in New York and in universities throughout Western Europe. He founded and now directs the European Culture Centre in Geneva.

LOVE IN THE WESTERN WORLD. 1939. Trans. by Montgomery Belgion *Harper* Colophon Bks. 1974 pap. $3.25. His best known work.

DRAMATIC PERSONAGES. 1944. Trans. by Richard Howard *Kennikat* 1971 $8.00. Essays on a widely differing group of writers.

TALK OF THE DEVIL. 1945. *Richard West* $15.00

MAN'S WESTERN QUEST (*L'adventure occidentale de l'homme*). 1956. Trans. by Montgomery Belgion. 1957. *Greenwood* 1973 $10.00

THE MEANING OF EUROPE. Trans. by Alan Braley *Stein & Day* 1965 $3.95

BLANCHOT, MAURICE. 1907–

Blanchot has been praised by Henri Peyre as "one of the three or four acute critics in France today." He is also a writer of fiction. Like others of his generation, he returns constantly to the theme of the solitude of the artist for whom communication by traditional language is difficult. His best-known novels are *"Thomas l'Obscur"* (1941), *"Aminadab"* (1942) and *"Le Très-Haut"* (1948).

THOMAS THE OBSCURE. 1941 trans. by Robert Lanberton *David Lewis Pubns.* 1973 $8.50

Books about Blanchot

The Novelist as Philosopher: Studies in French Fiction 1935–1960. Ed. by John Cruickshank. *Oxford* 1962 $7.00. Contains an essay on Blanchot by Geoffrey Hartman.

CHAR, RENÉ. 1907–

Albert Camus (*q.v.*) said: "I consider René Char our greatest living poet. . . . This poet of all time speaks immediately to our own. He is in the midst of the fight. He formulates for us both our suffering and our survival." Louise Bogan (*q.v.*) wrote in the *New Yorker:* "The contrast, for example, between, Char, now considered by many to be the most important poet in France, and his British and American contemporaries is marked. Char . . . writes in almost hermetic terms, with a touch of Blake's feeling for the enigmatic aphorism. He celebrates life's more joyful mysteries." "Char matured through a surrealistic period of collaboration with Breton and Éluard toward a reflective pessimism, faintly tinged with hope"—(Robert J. Clements, in *SR*).

Char speaks in the rhythms of Provence, where he was born, where he grew up and where he still often resides. He studied at the Lycée in Avignon and at the University in Aix. "But it was the war and his experience as the leader of a Maquis group in Provence that have most deeply affected his work—channeled his major themes, furnished the substance and many of the subjects of his later poems. The privation, the hunger, the moral suffering of those years were somehow turned into the passionate economy of his style, his rage to compress everything into aphorisms and short bursts of prose"—(Editor's note, in "Hypnos Waking"). He was awarded the French Prix des Critiques in 1966.

HYPNOS WAKING: Poetry and Prose. Trans. and sel. by Jackson Mathews with William Carlos Williams, Richard Wilbur, William Jay Smith, Barbara Howes, W. S. Merwin and James Wright. 1956 o.p.

LEAVES OF HYPNOS (*Feuilles d'Hypnos*). 1946. Trans. by Cid Corman *Grossman* 1973
    $20.00 pap. $5.95

PEYREFITTE, ROGER. 1907–

After serving briefly in the French Diplomatic Corps, as Secretary to the Embassy in Athens
from 1933 to 1938 and as part of the Vichy government's delegation in Paris, 1943 to 1945, Roger
Peyrefitte wrote two very successful satirical novels about the Corps, "Diplomatic Diversions"
(1951, U.S. 1953, o.p.) and "Diplomatic Conclusions" (1953, U.S. 1954, o.p.). He is, says the
Saturday Review, "a specialist in scandal," very much the best-seller *enfant terrible* of the contemporary French literary world. Henri Peyre has called him "a genteel humanist . . . and an elegant
stylist [whose] sensationalism has spoiled a talent which at one time was great." Peyre says "The
Jews" "brought only ridicule to the author"—but it sold 200,000 copies as a satire on French high
society.

KNIGHTS OF MALTA. Trans. by Edward Hyams *Phillips* 1959 $6.95

MANOUCHE. 1972. Trans. by Sam Flores *Grove* 1974 $8.95

ROUMAIN, JACQUES. 1907–1944.

Posthumous work of a Haitian intellectual, "The Masters of the Dew" is a "powerful and
realistic portrayal in creolized French of life in a peasant community." Roumain was one of those
educated young who were interested in folkways (e.g. those who founded *La Revue Indigène* in
1927), an experience which generated social protest as well as literary nationalism. Roumain has
written poems, novels, and ethnological studies. Among his novels are *"La Proie et l'Ombre," "La
Montagne Ensorcelée"* (1931), *"Les Fantoches"* (1931), and *"Bois d'Ebène"* (1945).

MASTERS OF THE DEW *(Gouverneurs de la Rosée)*. 1944. Trans. by Langston Hughes and
    Mercer Cook. 1947. *Macmillan* Collier Bks. 1971 $1.50

LÉVI-STRAUSS, CLAUDE. 1908– *See Chapter 8, The Social Sciences,* Reader's Advis-
er, *Vol. 3.*

ADAMOV, ARTHUR. 1908–

This Russian-born author, originally one of the group of avant-garde Parisian writers, has
turned his back upon them. From "Absurd" theater and a preoccupation with his own neuroses
and sense of futility he has turned to socially committed drama close to the "epic" mode of Brecht
(*q.v.*), sharing Brecht's (never total) leaning toward the Communist faith. Adamov left Russia at
the age of four, began his schooling in Geneva, later attended the French lycée in Mainz, and
completed his studies in Paris, where he has lived since 1924.

In speaking of his earlier, avant-garde period, Leonard Cabell Pronko has said: "A play of
Adamov must be seen to be appreciated, for the text is only a scenario, describing in rather great
detail the physical movement that is to take place, and will constitute the major impact and the
principal means of communicating with the audience. Dialogue has been reduced to dry and
frequently dull platitudes. . . . Adamov's works tend to be still-born because they depend too
exclusively upon the visual element, they are moving pictures but they do not move in any
particular direction (and this is, of course, part of the point)."

"Taranne" ("*Le Professeur Taranne*"), taken from one of his dreams and written in two days,
represents "the nightmare of man trying to hold on to his identity, unable to establish conclusive
proof of it," according to Martin Esslin, whose chapter on Adamov in "The Theatre of the
Absurd" is recommended. Between "Taranne" and "Paolo Paoli" the transition to a new Adamov
has taken place: "*Paolo Paoli* is an epic drama depicting the social and political causes of the
outbreak of the First World War and examining the relationship between a society based on profit
and the forces of destruction to which it gives rise. [It is] a political play . . . brilliantly constructed
and executed"—(Esslin). The two protagonists are a dealer in rare butterflies and an importer of
ostrich feathers. The economic motif is in the fortunes of these rather ridiculous wares, representing money, which becomes the focus of the two ignoble lives, though Paoli (the butterfly man)
undergoes conversion at the end and vows to help the poor.

"Ping Pong" represents an intermediate stage between the early mood and the later, and is, says
Esslin, Adamov's best play to date. "*Le Ping-Pong* belongs in the category of the Theatre of the
Absurd; it shows man engaged in purposeless exertions, in a futile frenzy of activity that is bound
to end in senility and death. [The play centers on a pinball game, and] the pinball machine has all
the fascinating ambiguity of a symbol"—(Esslin); it stands for anything to which one chooses to
devote one's life. The theme of "Ping Pong" is a large one. *Paolo Paoli* becomes narrower and
specific and, while "epic," has not lost all elements of the Absurd. The main influences on
Adamov's work, says the playwright, are Brecht, Strindberg (*q.v.*) and Kafka (*q.v.*). He is a master
of both his chosen genres.

Two Plays: Professor Taranne (1953) and Ping-Pong (1955). Trans. by A. Bermel and Richard Howard. 1962. *Humanities Press* (Fernhill) pap. $4.25

Paolo Paoli: A Play in Twelve Scenes Satirizing Middle-Class Society in the French Edwardian Era. 1956. Trans. by G. Brereton. 1959. *Humanities Press* (Fernhill) $3.75

BEAUVOIR, SIMONE DE.   1908–

Simone de Beauvoir and the existentialist Sartre (*see above*) have been leaders among French intellectuals since World War II. She grew up in Paris, received her doctorate from the Sorbonne and taught until 1943. In 1947 she made a four-month, coast-to-coast tour here under the auspices of the French Cultural Service. She has written novels, essays and plays. "The Second Sex" is a study of the role and destiny of woman in ancient and modern times. The *New Yorker* calls it "more than a work of scholarship; it is a work of art, with the salt of recklessness that makes art sting." "The Mandarins," for which she received the Goncourt Prize in 1954, is "a group portrait of the Existentialist clique, its fellow travelers and its adversaries, and a chronicle of the political role played by the leading Existentialists from the Liberation to the late nineteen-forties"— (*Atlantic*). A 1967 best seller in France was "*Les Belles Images,*" her first novel in ten years. Written under the influence of the "New Novel," it describes a woman's rejection of her own narrow world for her daughter.

"Memoirs of a Dutiful Daughter" is a frank confession about "an anguished adolescence during one of the most disturbed periods of French social and intellectual life"—World War I and the aftermath. It closes with her fateful meeting with Sartre and is "a case history of growing up; and though we may find the austerity with which it is told frenzied and feverish, we must honor the intention and applaud the accomplishment whole-heartedly"—(Elizabeth Janeway, in the *N.Y. Times*). The *N.Y. Times* wrote that "The Prime of Life" is "tiresome at times and overly charged with unnecessary detail . . . [but] is a work of considerable importance." *Library Journal* called it a "valuable source book" for students of the period (1929–1944): "Because the life she led before and during the war was one of intellectual excitement and included a long-lasting liaison with Jean-Paul Sartre as well as friendships with Picasso, Giacometti, Camus, and others of similar stature, her avid seizure on detail is justified and results in a fascinating accumulation of data." The third volume of her autobiography, "Force of Circumstance," "looks with despair on old age and its encroachments but, for all that, the book contains many subtle, magnificent responses to the genuine wealth of the world—its art, its variety of peoples, cultures, techniques, and adaptations to life"—(*SR*).

The Ethics of Ambiguity. 1947. Trans. by Bernard Frechtman *Citadel* 1962 pap. $2.25

The Second Sex. 1949. Trans. and ed. by H. M. Parshley *Knopf* 1953 $12.95; *Random* Vintage Bks. 1974 pap. $2.95

The Mandarins 1954. Trans. by Leonard M. Friedman. o.p.

Brigitte Bardot and the Lolita Syndrome. 1960. Trans. by Bernard Frechtman *Arno* 1972 $9.00

The Coming of Age (*La Vieillesse*). 1960. Trans. by Patrick O'Brian *Putnam* 1972 $10.00; *Paperback Lib.* pap. $2.25

A Very Easy Death. 1964. Trans. by Patrick O'Brian *Paperback Lib.* pap. $.95. Her reactions to the slow dying of her 77-year-old mother.

All Said and Done (*Tout Compte Fait*). 1972. Trans. by Patrick O'Brian *Putnam* 1974 $8.95

Memoirs of a Dutiful Daughter. 1958. Trans. by James Kirkup *Harper* Colophon Bks. 1974 pap. $3.95. Autobiography of her early years.

The Prime of Life. 1960. Trans. by Peter Green *Lancer* pap. $1.95. The second volume of her autobiography covers the years 1929 to 1944.

Force of Circumstance. 1963. Trans. by Richard Howard 1965 o.p. The third volume of her autobiography, covering the years 1944 to 1963.

Books about Simone de Beauvoir

Simone de Beauvoir: Encounters with Death. By Elaine Marks. *Rutgers Univ. Press* 1973 $8.00

MARCELIN, PIERRE. 1908– *See* THOBY-MARCELIN, PHILIPPE, 1904– , *this Chapter.*

GRACQ, JULIEN (pseud. of Louis Poirer). 1909–

Julien Gracq, novelist, playwright and history teacher, refused to accept the 1951 Goncourt Prize, France's most important literary award because, as he said, of the "commercialism" of literary prizes. A surrealist, Gracq feels that writing is "the expression of the inexpressible." "Balcony in the Forest" concerns men on duty in the Maginot line on the edge of a forest in the autumn of 1939, waiting for the Germans to attack. He himself served in the French Army during World War II and was taken prisoner. In this novel, the reader experiences "the terrible endurance of the soldier ... and the effects of soldiering on a man with a meditative turn of mind"—(*SR*). Gracq is an ardent admirer of André Breton (*q.v.*), and Breton professed equal admiration for him. Henri Peyre says, "We must declare that [Gracq's] novels appear to us unbearably pseudo-romantic." Nonetheless, his role as a late surrealist justifies republication of his works in English.

Balcony in the Forest. 1958. Trans. by Richard Howard 1959 o.p.

ROY, GABRIELLE. 1909–

This novelist, born in Manitoba, writes vividly and compassionately but not sentimentally about her fellow French Canadians. She has become known for her fine descriptive power, her delicacy of feeling and her humor. Her first novel, "The Tin Flute" (1947, o.p.) won the Prix Femina in France; she received the Duvernay Prize in 1956. "The Hidden Mountain" (1962, o.p.) is the moving story of a sensitive self-made artist in two utterly different worlds—the great cold North and Paris. "The nostalgic love that gilds both characters and scene makes 'The Street of Riches' (1957, o.p.) a charming memoir"—(*N.Y. Herald Tribune*). "The Road Past Altamont" (1966, o.p.), four episodes in the life of a young French-Canadian girl, was called by *Library Journal* a "charming book ... a refreshing change from the fiction of the contemporary neo-realists." In "O Canada," Edmund Wilson (*q.v.*) writes, "I have found one French Canadian idyl that is distinguished and quite delightful: *La Petite Poule d'Eau*, by Gabrielle Roy." This book, not yet translated, deals with isolated sheep farmers. Her enviable position in French Canadian letters surely justifies republication of her work in English.

SIMENON, GEORGES. 1909–

The prolific Belgian-born writer, Georges Simenon, has produced to date more than 350 fictional works under his own name and 17 pseudonyms in addition to some 70 books about Inspector Maigret, long "the favorite sleuth of highbrow detective-story readers"—(*SR*). Over 50 "Simenons" have been made into films. In addition to his mystery stories, since 1936 he has been writing what he calls "hard" books, the serious psychological novels now numbering about 100. Brief, tense, somber, written "in a lean and supple style" (*N.Y. Times*), they are compelling studies of human motivation—attempts to understand the forces that push men to their limits. "The Snow Was Black," a novel of violence, "is excellently written and full of suspense"—(*N.Y. Times*). "The Blue Room" and "The Accomplices" reveal a special quality "that makes 'a Simenon' unique. There is a real sense of tragedy, of human waste, of the beauty that could have been." "What the brilliant and fecund [author] has done [in "The Premier" and "The Train"] is to produce two ... Greek tragedies"—(*SR*). In "The Bells of Bicêtre" a dying man is forced to reexamine the worth of his life. "The Little Saint," about a child of poverty endowed with saintly qualities, "may be the most joyous novel Simenon has written [and] is at once lively, realistic, genial, and magnetic"—(*SR*). Simenon's "flawless camera lens captures every nuance of psychological metamorphosis" in "The Old Man Dies"—(*LJ*). Of the same book, the *New Yorker* wrote: "Simenon is today's great proof that a real writer ... can never write himself out. ... He is writing better than ever." The autobiographical "Pedigree," set in his native town of Liège, is perhaps his finest work. Simenon himself once said that he would never write a "great novel": some, like Henri Peyre, who writes "that none of his works are likely to survive," would be quick to agree. Yet Gide called him "a great novelist, perhaps the greatest and truest novelist we have in French literature today" and Thornton Wilder found that Simenon's narrative gift extends "to the tips of his fingers." Legions of his detective-story fans were delighted to learn that in 1966 Inspector Maigret was "eternalized in bronze at Delfzijl, where the point of the Lowlands loses itself in the North Sea"—(*SR*).

The following are some of Simenon's novels exclusive of the Maigret detective stories.

The Bells of Bicêtre. 1963. Trans. by Jean Stewart *Harcourt* 1964 $6.95

The Confessional. Trans. by Jean Stewart *Harcourt* 1968 $7.50

November. 1969. Trans. by Jean Stewart *Harcourt* 1970 $5.75

The Rich Man (*Le Riche Homme*). Trans. by Jean Stewart *Harcourt* 1971 $5.95

When I Was Old (*Quand j'étais vieux*). Trans. by Helen Eustis *Harcourt* 1971 $8.50

THE DISAPPEARANCE OF ODILE (*La Disparition d'Odile*). Trans. by Lyn Moir *Harcourt* 1972 $5.95

TEDDY BEAR (*L'Ours en peluche*). Trans. by John Clay *Harcourt* 1972 $5.95

THE GLASS CAGE (*La Cage de Verre*). 1973. Trans. by Antonia White *Harcourt* 1973 $5.50

THE INNOCENTS. 1973. Trans. by Eileen Ellenbogen *Harcourt* 1974 $6.50

THE VENICE TRAIN (*Le Train*). 1973. Trans. by Alastair Hamilton *Harcourt* 1974 $6.50

THE MAN ON THE BENCH IN THE BARN. Trans. by Moura Budberg *Harcourt* 1974 $5.95

PEDIGREE. 1948. Trans. by Robert Baldick *British Bk. Centre* 1963 $4.95. An autobiographical novel.

Other titles are available from Harcourt, Curtis Bks., and Penguin.

WEIL, SIMONE.   1909–1943.

Twentieth-century Pascal, this ardently spiritual woman in search of certitude was also a social thinker aware of the human lot. Jewish by birth and Greek by aesthetic choice, she has influenced religious thinking profoundly in the twenty years since her death. "Humility is the root of love," she said (in *"La Connaissance Surnaturelle"*) as she questioned traditional theologians and held that the Apostles had badly interpreted Christ's teaching. Christianity was, she felt, to blame for the heresy of progress.

NEED FOR ROOTS. 1949. Trans. by Arthur Wills. 1952. *Harper* 1971 pap. $4.25

ILIAD, or Poem of Force. 1953 *Pendle Hill* 1956 $.70

OPPRESSION AND LIBERTY. 1955. Trans. by Arthur Wills and Joan Petrie *Univ. of Massachusetts Press* 1973 $8.50

ON SCIENCE, NECESSITY AND THE LOVE OF GOD. 1966. Trans. by Richard Rees *Oxford* 1968 $10.50

SEVENTY LETTERS. 1957. Trans. by Richard Rees *Oxford* 1965 $7.00

Books about Simone Weil

Simone Weil. By Eric W. F. Tomlin. 1954 *Humanities Press* $2.75
Simone Weil: A Sketch for a Portrait. By Richard Rees. *Southern Illinois Univ. Press* 1966 $6.95
Simone Weil. By David Anderson. 1971 *Allenson* pap. $1.95

ANOUILH, JEAN.   1910–

While Paris and most of France were under German occupation, the character of Antigone, from Greek legend, was used symbolically in three new French plays. The most striking, played in modern dress, was Anouilh's. It provided a "rallying point for the aspirations of insurgent youth." His is a distinct and highly original talent. He combines the serious with the fantastic and is "less concerned with making innovations than with returning to a tradition." Anouilh himself groups his works as either *"pièces roses,"* where the good triumph, or *"pièces noires,"* where the evil are victorious, in the clash between the symbolic characters prevalent in his drama. His usual themes (said *Library Journal* in its warm review of "Poor Bitos") "are the impossibility of attaining what one once had thought was goodness, the corruptibility of human endeavors and the pitifulness of the pretenses of those who believe themselves to be distinguished." His style is "deceptively easy."

Anouilh was born in Bordeaux, came to Paris when he was very young, began to study law, then worked for a time in an advertising agency. Always interested in the theater, he became secretary to Louis Jouvet, the famous actor-manager, in 1931, and his first play was produced during the following year.

His moving dramatization of the trial of Joan of Arc, "The Lark," was first presented in New York in 1955 as adapted by Lillian Hellman (*q.v.*). The language was described as having a "simple, clear, timeless ring to it, and its directness is exhilarating." "The Waltz of the Toreadors" (1951, o.p.) received the N.Y. Drama Critics Circle Award as the "Best Foreign Play," 1957. Brooks Atkinson called it "a riotous farce written by a somberminded dramatist." "Although the manner is antic the substance is melancholy. M. Anouilh and Mr. Richardson (who plays the lead) know how to make a vastly entertaining rumpus out of blistering ideas." "Time Remembered," a romantic love story with satiric overtones and undertones, was Anouilh's first Broadway hit. "Becket," in which Laurence Olivier and Anthony Quinn exchanged the leading roles, was another in 1960. "Beckett" also became a successful film with Richard Burton and Peter O'Toole. "Thieves' Carnival," "the nicest play about an identity crisis ever written" (Walter Kerr), received an excellent performance in 1967 at the Tyrone Guthrie Theater in Minneapolis, as did "Antigone" at the American Shakespeare Festival Theater in Stratford, Conn.

SEVEN PLAYS. Trans. by Lucienne Hill, Luce and Arthur Klein and Miriam John *Farrar, Straus* (Hill & Wang) Dramabks. pap. $2.45. Thieves' Carnival (1938), Medea (1946), Cécile (1951), Traveler without Luggage (1936), The Orchestra, Episode in the Life of an Author, Catch as Catch Can.

FIVE PLAYS. *Farrar, Straus* (Hill & Wang) $3.95 Mermaid Dramabks. 2 vols. pap. $2.45 and $2.25

Vol. 1 1958 Romeo and Jeanette (1945), The Rehearsal (1950), Ermine (1932), Antigone (1942)
Vol. 2 1959 Ardèle (1948), Time Remembered (Léocadia, 1942), Mademoiselle Colombe (1951), Restless Heart, The Lark (1953)

THE LARK. 1953. Trans. by Christopher Fry *Oxford* 1956 $3.75

ORNIFLE. 1955. Trans. by Lucienne Hill *Farrar, Straus* (Hill & Wang) Mermaid Dramabks. $4.95 pap. $1.95

BECKET. 1959. Trans. by Lucienne Hill *Coward* (orig.) 1960 pap. $2.45; *New Am. Lib.* Signet 1964 pap. $.75

DEAR ANTOINE. 1966. Trans. by Lucienne Hill *Farrar, Straus* (Hill & Wang) Dramabks. $4.95 pap. $1.95

Books about Anouilh

The World by Jean Anouilh. By Leonard Cabell Pronko. *Univ. of California Press* 1961 $5.75 pap. $2.25

Anouilh: A Study in Theatrics. By John Harvey. 1964 *French & European* $10.50
Professor Harvey has done an "interesting and informative study. . . . Not merely another scholarly work, this is an absorbing and penetrating analysis of a modern playwright and an important phase of contemporary theater"—(*LJ*).

Jean Anouilh. By Alba Della Fazia. World Authors Ser. *Twayne* $6.95

Jean Anouilh. By Marguerite Archer. Essays on Modern Writers *Columbia* 1971 $1.00

GENET, JEAN. 1910–

Many of his contemporaries consider Genet one of France's greatest writers, as does Sartre (*q.v.*), who wrote an appreciation of his work—poetry, novels, drama, in that sequence (*see below*). While serving one of his many prison sentences for theft, Genet produced his first novel, "Our Lady of the Flowers" (1944, o.p.) Tom F. Driver (in *SR*) called another autobiographical novel, "Miracle of the Rose" (1946, *Grove* 1965 $7.50), "a major achievement of modern literature. . . . Genet transforms experiences of degradation into spiritual exercises and hoodlums into the bearers of the majesty of love." The last of his five major prose works, "The Thief's Journal" (1949, *Grove* 1964 Black Cat Bks. pap. $1.95), an account of "Genet's adolescence and young manhood as a beggar, homosexual, convict, and petty thief, is perverse in every sense of the word [but] a literary creation of great importance and midnight beauty"—(*LJ*). According to Sartre, Genet then "turned dramatist because the falsehood of the stage is the most manifest and fascinating of all."

Genet was born in Paris in 1910, an illegitimate child who never knew his parents. Abandoned to the "Assistance Publique," he was adopted by a peasant family in the Morvan. At ten he was sent to a reformatory for stealing. After many years of institutions he escaped and joined the Foreign Legion, but soon deserted. In traveling through Europe he begged, thieved, smuggled and was imprisoned in almost every country he visited. He escaped life imprisonment in France in 1948 when the President of the Republic, petitioned by a group of eminent writers and artists, granted him a pardon.

Genet's plays in lacking plot and other conventions of the prewar theater have many elements of the Theater of the Absurd. But his "theatre is, profoundly, a theatre of social protest. Yet . . . it resolutely rejects political commitment, political argument, didacticism, or propaganda. In dealing with the dream world of the outcast of society, it explores the human condition, the alienation of man, his solitude, his futile search for meaning and reality"—(Martin Esslin).

THE MAIDS (1948) and DEATHWATCH (1949). Trans. by Bernard Frechtman *Grove* Evergreen Bks. 1954 pap. $2.45

FUNERAL RITES. 1948. Trans. by Bernard Frechtman *Grove* 1969 $7.50 Black Cat Bks. pap. $1.50

MIRACLE OF THE ROSE. 1950. Trans. by Bernard Frechtman *Grove* 1966 $7.50 Black Cat Bks. pap. $1.50

THE BALCONY. 1956. Trans. by Bernard Frechtman *Grove* Evergreen Bks. 1958 pap. $2.25

THE BLACKS: A Clown Show. 1958. Trans. by Bernard Frechtman *Grove* Evergreen Bks. 1960 pap. $2.25

THE SCREENS: A Play in Seventeen Scenes. 1961. Trans. by Bernard Frechtman *Grove* 1962 pap. $1.95

MAY DAY SPEECH. *City Lights* 1970 pap. $1.00

THE THIEF'S JOURNAL. 1949. Trans. by Bernard Frechtman *Grove* 1964 Black Cat Bks. 1973 pap. $1.95

LETTERS TO ROGER BLIN. 1966. Trans. by Richard Seaver *Grove* 1969 Evergreen Bks. pap. $1.95

Books about Genet

Four Playwrights and a Postscript: Brecht, Ionesco, Beckett, Genet. By David I. Grossvogel. *Cornell Univ. Press* 1962 $5.00

Saint Genet: Actor and Martyr. By Jean-Paul Sartre. Trans. by Bernard Frechtman *Braziller* 1963 $8.50; *New Am. Lib.* Plume Bks. pap. $1.25

The Imagination of Jean Genet. By Joseph H. McMahon. *Yale Univ. Press* 1963 $6.50; pap. $1.75

"A detailed study of all the works of Jean Genet . . . useful as an introduction to [his] prose and dramatic work"—(*LJ*).

Jean Genet. By Tom F. Driver. Essays on Modern Writers *Columbia* 1966 pap. $1.00

Jean Genet. By Bettina Knapp. World Authors Ser. *Twayne* 1968 $6.95

Jean Genet: A Critical Appraisal. By Philip Thody. *Stein & Day* 1970 pap. $2.45

LEDUC, VIOLETTE. 1910–

Violette Leduc had been publishing works of an autobiographical nature in France since 1945 but, aside from the enthusiastic support of Simone de Beauvoir, Sartre and certain other intellectuals, she had gone unnoticed until the publication of *"La Bâtarde"* propelled her to fame—in part, no doubt, for "the candor in the totally uninhibited descriptions of [her] Lesbian loves. . . . But it was not Mme Leduc's design . . . to titillate the pruriency of readers or to indulge any lewdness. This, the story of [her] first forty years, is a courageous confession and a work of art, . . . a weird mixture of burning, naïve, lucid, and unadorned sincerity . . . and of poetic inner monologue"—(Henri Peyre, in *SR*). Elizabeth Janeway, reviewing "The Woman with the Little Fox," (1958, o.p.), wrote in the *N.Y. Times*: "There are no adjectives for Mlle Leduc's work beyond the obvious one, astonishing. To read her is to be astonished by the experience of an enlarged world." Of the title story the *New Yorker* said, "Only a writer as particularly gifted as Miss Leduc could have enclosed, as in thin glass, the silent storm of feeling, sensation, and understanding that is at the heart of this work." More conventional in form than the writers of the *nouveau roman*, Miss Leduc shares with them an interest in the significance of small events. She involves the reader by vivid characterization and by her sensuous evocation of French rural life. The Lesbian love story of "Thérèse and Isabelle" (1967, o.p.) was originally intended as part of *"La Bâtarde."* Henri Peyre (in *SR*) called it "a thin tale . . . unworthy of Mme Leduc's talent, which, at other moments, has been great."

LA BÂTARDE. 1965. Trans. by Derek Coltman; fwd. by Simone de Beauvoir *Farrar, Straus* 1965 $7.95

MAD IN PURSUIT (*La chasse à l'amour*). 1970. Trans. by Derek Coltman *Farrar, Straus* 1971 $8.95

THE TAXI. 1971. Trans. by Helen Weaver *Farrar, Straus* 1972 $5.95

TROYAT, HENRI (born Lev Tarassov). 1911–

The vast novel, "My Father's House" (1947, U.S. 1951, o.p.), tells of the Russia Troyat knew in his youth. He and his family fled during the Revolution, and he later became a naturalized French citizen. He received the Prix Goncourt in 1938 for the novel *"L'Araignée"* and the Louis Barthou Prize—awarded by the Académie Française, to which he has been elected a member—for the excellence of his writing. Many of Troyat's novels are parts of cycles, "a genre," says the *Saturday Review*, "in which the French have always excelled." Such series as "My Father's House," "The Seed and the Fruit" (of which "Tender and Violent Elizabeth" and "The Encounter" form the last two parts) and "The Light of the Just," set in the Napoleonic era, are all extremely popular. The third volume of a new cycle, *"Les Eygletière,"* the saga of a 20th-century family, was published in France in 1967. The *N.Y. Times* said of the original "Elizabeth," "The whole art of Henri Troyat is to turn Paris streets, a country school, a village house and all the characters of various ages who people them, into that extraordinary thing which is life itself."

AMELIE IN LOVE (*Sémailles et les moissons*). 1954. *Simon & Schuster* 1956 Pocket Bks. 1974 pap. $1.25

AMELIE AND PIERRE (*Amélie et Pierre*). 1957. *Simon & Schuster* Pocket Bks. 1974 pap. $1.25

ELIZABETH. 1957. *Simon & Schuster* 1959 Pocket Bks. pap. $1.25

TENDER AND VIOLENT ELIZABETH. 1957. Trans. by Mildred Marmur *Simon & Schuster* Pocket Bks. pap. $1.25

THE ENCOUNTER. 1958. Trans. by Gerard Hopkins *Simon & Schuster* 1962 Pocket Bks. pap. $1.25

DAILY LIFE IN RUSSIA UNDER THE LAST TSAR. 1959. Trans. by Malcolm Barnes *Macmillan* 1962 $4.00

THE BARONESS. 1960. *Simon & Schuster* 1961 $4.50

TOLSTOY. 1965. Trans. by Nancy Amphoux *Dell* Laurel Eds. pap. $1.65
"The final, complete portrait of the man as he surely was . . . endlessly informative and absorbing"—Genêt (Janet Flanner).

DIVIDED SOUL: The Life of Gogol. 1971. Trans. by Nancy Amphoux *Doubleday* 1973 $12.95

BOULLE, PIERRE.   1912–

"The Bridge over the River Kwai," based on Boulle's own war experiences in Asia, was called by the *Atlantic* "an exciting story of action which centers on a situation that is simultaneously droll, pathetic, and appalling." It was made into an excellent film starring Alec Guinness—which was awarded seven Oscars. The *N.Y. Herald Tribune* called "Not the Glory," "a penetrating, ironic, but deeply sympathetic study of the British national character." In "s.o.p.h.i.a.," Boulle tells the story of an "organization man" in the Malayan jungle. The *New Yorker* said of it: "M. Boulle has astonishing command when he sets out to convey a certain atmosphere or a certain mood or change of mood, but there are times when his writing is so clinical that he seems to be making a study of the reaction of human beings to prearranged conditions of climate and discipline, rather than writing a novel." His near-religious fable, "The Executioner," is an unusual and gripping story about Chong, official executioner of the Chinese province of Li-Kang. Maurice Evans and Charlton Heston appeared together in 1968 as co-stars of a film version of "Planet of the Apes." *Library Journal* described that novel as "a Swiftian fable in which Boulle gives full play to his not inconsiderable gift for irony and satire." "Garden on the Moon" has as its theme the race between nations to get to the moon first—and the implications of the race for humanity.

NOT THE GLORY. 1950 (with title "William Conrad"). Trans. by Xan Fielding *Vanguard* 1955 $6.95; Manor Bks. pap. $1.25

THE BRIDGE OVER THE RIVER KWAI. 1952. Trans. by Xan Fielding *Vanguard* 1954 $6.95; *Bantam* pap $.75; *Franklin Watts* lg. type ed. Keith Jennison Bks. $7.95

FACE OF A HERO (*La Face*). 1953. Trans. by Xan Fielding *Vanguard* 1956 $6.95

TEST (*L'Epreuve des hommes blancs*). 1955. Trans. by Xan Fielding *Vanguard* 1957 $6.95

THE OTHER SIDE OF THE COIN. Trans. by Richard Howard *Vanguard* 1958 $6.95

S.O.P.H.I.A. Trans. by Xan Fielding *Vanguard* 1959 $6.95

A NOBLE PROFESSION (*Un métier de seigneur*). Trans. by Xan Fielding *Vanguard* 1960 $6.95

THE EXECUTIONER. Trans. by Xan Fielding *Vanguard* 1961 $6.95

PLANET OF THE APES. 1963. Trans. by Xan Fielding *Vanguard* $6.95; *New Am. Lib.* Signet pap. $.95

GARDEN ON THE MOON. Trans. by Xan Fielding *Vanguard* 1965 $6.95; *New Am. Lib.* Signet $.95

TIME OUT OF MIND AND OTHER STORIES. Trans. by Xan Fielding *Vanguard* 1966 $6.95; *New Am. Lib.* Signet pap. $1.25

MY OWN RIVER KWAI. *Vanguard* 1967 $6.95. The true story of Boulle's adventures as a secret agent in Indo-China.

THE PHOTOGRAPHER. Trans. by Xan Fielding *Vanguard* 1968 $6.95

BECAUSE IT IS ABSURD (*Quia Absurdum*). 1970. *Vanguard* $6.95

DESPERATE GAMES (*Les Jeux de L'esprit*). 1971. Trans. by Patricia Wolf *Vanguard* 1973 $6.95

BARS OF THE JUNGLE (*Les Oreilles de jungle*). 1972. Trans. by Xan Fielding *Vanguard* 1972 $6.95

THE VIRTUES OF HELL. 1974. Trans. by Patricia Wolf *Vanguard* 1974 $6.95

ELLUL, JACQUES. 1912–   *See Chapter 9, History, Government and Politics,* Reader's Adviser, *Vol. 3.*

IONESCO, EUGÈNE. 1912–

The Rumanian-born French dramatist first attracted critical notice when "The Chairs" was produced in New York. Wildly improbable, hilarious and wholly original, all his plays combine and contrast the comic and the tragic, the possible and the unlikely. The dramatist has said, "the comic is tragic and man's tragedy a matter of derision." He ranks with Beckett (*q.v.*) and Adamov (*q.v.*) among the contemporary leading exponents of the experimental European theater.

His plays have been performed in Germany, Italy, Switzerland, Poland, Yugoslavia and Israel. Several have been produced off-Broadway and "The Lesson" appeared on television in 1966. In January, 1960, for the first time, an avant-garde author was performed in a French national theater. It was Ionesco's 13th play, "Rhinoceros." The crowded theater was the Théâtre de France, the director Jean-Louis Barrault. (Ten years before, Ionesco's first play, "The Bald Soprano," had been performed at the Théâtre des Noctambules with three persons in the audience on opening night.) The plot of "Rhinoceros" deals with a young man, a nonconformist, who refuses to heed the admonition of his friends that "you must be in step with the time" and "turn into a rhinoceros." The main criticism was not of the theme but that the dramatist had deserted the avant-garde and fallen into the very type of theater that he previously execrated. Ionesco replied: "They attack me with my own weapons. They used to accuse me of giving no message in my plays, now they accuse me of the exact contrary. They accused me of being incomprehensible, now they accuse me of being too clear." This satiric play was successful on Broadway in the 1960–1961 season. "Exit the King," an allegory about a king who has reigned for several centuries over a now decaying nation and must prepare to die, provides "a tiny, capricious universe with a dream logic of its own—small in conception, perfect in execution"—(*LJ*). It was produced by the APA Phoenix Repertory Company, opening January 11, 1968, with Richard Easton, Eva Le Gallienne and Patricia Conolly in the leading roles. "It is the most personal and moving of all Ionesco's plays," wrote Clive Barnes in the *N.Y. Times*, "and . . . incomparably his greatest work. . . . It is Ionesco's concern that 'in this life we must never forget our final destiny,' and his play reeks with the smell of mortality." Another "conventional" play, *"Soif et Faim"* ("Thirst and Hunger"), received mixed reviews (but drew 24 curtain calls) when performed at the Comédie Française in the summer of 1966. "Victims of Duty," a one-acter, appeared off-Broadway in 1968. Ionesco has adapted several plays from his short stories, published here by Grove as "The Colonel's Photograph and Other Stories."

PLAYS. Trans. by Donald Watson *Int. Pubns. Service* 9 vols. Vols. 1-7 each $7.50 Vol. 8 $9.00 Vol. 9 $11.50

FOUR PLAYS: The Bald Soprano (1950); The Lesson (1951); Jack, or The Submission (1955); The Chairs (1952). Trans. by Donald M. Allen *Grove* 1958 Evergreen Bks. pap. $1.95

THREE PLAYS: Amédée (1954); The New Tenant (1957); Victims of Duty (1953). Trans. by Donald Watson *Grove* Evergreen Bks. pap. $2.95

RHINOCEROS AND OTHER PLAYS. Includes The Leader (1958); The Future Is in Eggs (1958). Trans. by Derek Prouse *Grove* Evergreen Bks. 1960 pap. $1.95; *Peter Smith* $4.00

THE KILLER (1950) and OTHER PLAYS: Improvisation, or The Shepherd's Chameleon; Maid to Marry; The Killer. *Grove* Evergreen Bks. 1959 pap. $2.45

KILLING GAME. 1957. Trans. by Helen Gary Bishop *Grove* 1974 $5.95 Evergreen Bks. pap. $2.95

A STROLL IN THE AIR (*Piéton de l'air,* 1962) and FRENZY FOR TWO (*Délire à deux,* 1962). Trans. by Donald Watson *Grove* 1968 Evergreen Bks. pap. $2.45

EXIT THE KING. 1963. Trans. by Donald Watson *Grove* Evergreen Bks. 1967 pap. $1.95

HUNGER AND THIRST (1966) AND OTHER PLAYS: The Picture, Anger, Salutations. Trans. by Donald Watson *Grove* 1969 $3.95 Evergreen Bks. pap. $1.95

THE COLONEL'S PHOTOGRAPH (*La Photo du Colonel*) AND OTHER STORIES. Trans. by Jean Stewart and John Russell *Grove* 1969 $4.95 Evergreen Bks. pap. $1.95

PRESENT-PAST, PAST-PRESENT (*Présent-passé, passé-présent*). 1970. Trans. by Helen R. Lane *Grove* 1971 $5.95 Evergreen Bks. pap. $1.95

MACBETT. 1972. Trans. by Charles Marowitz *Grove* 1974 $6.95 Evergreen Bks. pap. $1.95

STORY NUMBER 4 (*Conte #4*). Trans. by Ciba Vaughan *Dial* (Harlin Quist) 1973 $4.95

THE HERMIT (*Le Solitaire*). 1973. Trans. by Richard Seaver *Viking* 1974 $6.95

NOTES AND COUNTER-NOTES: Writings on the Theatre. 1962. Trans. by Donald Watson *Grove* 1964 pap. $2.45

A "valuable collection of 'essays, interviews, exchanges and polemics with fellow dramatists and critics,' as well as Ionesco's discussions of his own plays and the modern theater in general"—(*LJ*).

FRAGMENTS OF A JOURNAL (*Journal en miettes*). 1967. Trans. by Jean Pace *Grove* 1968 Evergreen Bks. pap. $1.95

Books about Ionesco

Four Playwrights and a Postscript: Brecht, Ionesco, Beckett, Genet. By David I. Grossvogel. *Cornell Univ. Press* 1962 $5.00

Eugène Ionesco. By Leonard Cabell Pronko. Essays on Modern Writers *Columbia* 1965 pap. $1.00

Eugène Ionesco: A Study of His Work. By Richard N. Coe. *Grove* 1968 pap. $1.50

Eugène Ionesco. By Allan Lewis. World Authors Ser. *Twayne* $6.95

Ionesco: A Collection of Critical Essays. Ed. by Rosette Lamont. *Prentice-Hall* 1973 $5.95 pap. $1.95

CAMUS, ALBERT.   1913–1960.   (Nobel Prize 1957)

Albert Camus, the novelist and playwright, who won the Nobel Prize in Literature in 1957, died in 1960 in an auto accident near Sens, France. For his friends and admirers all over the world "it was and would always remain an unbearable, an irreparable catastrophe." He was the second youngest man in history to receive the Nobel honor. (Kipling was younger when he was cited in 1907.) Camus was a member of the Académie Française.

As one of the leading authors in the French Resistance, he wrote daily outspoken articles in the underground *Combat*, now an important Paris daily. He was a native of Algiers and lived there until 1940. He was never really committed to the existentialists' view but formulated a modern kind of stoicism: when confronted with the inevitable absurdities of life, man can do nothing but courageously face up to them in full awareness of his situation. As Camus himself once put it, "The aim is to live lucidly in a world where dispersion is the rule."

"*The Stranger* is a minor masterpiece of restraint and of effectiveness"—(Henri Peyre). "The Plague," symbolizing Europe under Hitler, was the most admired French novel after World War II. Of "The Fall," the *N.Y. Herald Tribune* wrote: "If power and sincerity and sheer beauty such as is rare in any age are criteria of literary greatness, this is a book that will live."

"Camus was a versatile writer, with a mastery of style almost unique among his contemporaries. 'The last of the heirs of Chateaubriand,' Sartre called him. His language is rich in imagery and highly controlled. He was a 'Latin.' . . . 'Every artist, no doubt [he wrote], is in quest of his truth. If he is great, each work brings him closer to it, or, at least, gravitates more closely to that central, hidden sun, where all, one day, will be consumed' "—(Germaine Brée, *N.Y. Times*, Jan 24, 1960). The publication of the first volume of his "Notebooks" was a literary event of 1963. The translator has included in this volume a biographical record, bibliographies and notes, showing how some of the entries made their way into Camus' early essays and his first two novels. The second "volume of *Notebooks* reflects the quieter Camus and contains less of the personal tumult of the young man"—(*SR*). "Each of the many disconnected entries [reveals] his love and compassion for mankind tempered by his clarity of thought"—(*LJ*).

Nondramatic Works

THE STRANGER. 1942. Trans. by Stuart Gilbert *Knopf* 1946 $4.95; *Heritage Press, Conn.* deluxe ed. $11.95; *Random* Vintage Bks. pap. $1.65. Novel.

THE MYTH OF SISYPHUS (1942) AND OTHER ESSAYS. Trans. by Justin O'Brien *Knopf* 1955 $4.00; *Random* 1955 Vintage Bks. pap. $1.25

THE PLAGUE. 1947. Trans. by Stuart Gilbert *Knopf* 1948 $5.95; *Random* (Modern Library) $2.95 Vintage Bks. pap. $1.95. Novel.

THE REBEL: An Essay on Man in Revolt. 1951. Trans. by Anthony Bower *Knopf* 1954 $5.95; *Random* 1954 Vintage Bks. pap. $1.95

THE FALL. 1956. *Knopf* 1957 $4.95; (and "Exile and the Kingdom") trans. by Justin O'Brien. *Random* (Modern Lib.) $2.95 Vintage Bks. 1963 pap. $1.95. Novel.

EXILE AND THE KINGDOM. 1957. Trans. by Justin O'Brien *Knopf* 1958 $5.50; *Random* Vintage Bks. pap. $1.95

"Of the six stories, three have the imprint of the solid craftsmanship that made 'The Stranger' one of the most significant works of fiction of recent years"—(*N.Y. Herald Tribune*).

LYRICAL AND CRITICAL ESSAYS. *Knopf* 1968 $6.95; *Random* Vintage Bks. pap. $1.95

A HAPPY DEATH (*La Mort heureuse*). 1971. Trans. by Philip Thody *Knopf* 1972 $5.95; *Random* Vintage Bks. pap. $1.95

Plays

CALIGULA AND THREE OTHER PLAYS. 1944–49. Trans. by Stuart Gilbert *Knopf* 1958 $5.95; *Random* 1962 Vintage Bks. pap. $1.95. Includes: The Misunderstanding, State of Seige, and The Just Assassins.

THE POSSESSED: A Play in Three Parts. 1959. Trans. by Justin O'Brien *Knopf* 1960 $5.95; *Random* Vintage Bks. pap. $1.65. A modern dramatization of Dostoyevsky's novel.

RESISTANCE, REBELLION AND DEATH (*Actuelles I, II, III*). 1950–58. Trans. by Justin O'Brien *Knopf* 1960 $5.95; *Random* (Modern Lib.) 1963 $2.95 Vintage Bks. pap. $1.95

THE GROWING STONE. (In "Seven French Short Novel Masterpieces") ed. by Andrew Comfort; introd. by Henri Peyre *Popular Lib.* (orig.) pap. $.95

NOTEBOOKS. Vol. 1 1935–42 1962 trans. by Philip Thody *Knopf* 1963 $5.95; *Random* (Modern Lib.) $2.95 Vol. 2 1942–51 1965 trans. by Justin O'Brien *Knopf* 1965 $5.95. The first 2 of 3 projected vols.

Books about Camus

Camus. By Germaine Brée. *Rutgers Univ. Press* 1959 rev. ed. 1961 $7.50; *Harcourt* 1964 Harbinger Bks. pap. $3.75
"An admirably independent and objective study."
Albert Camus and the Literature of Revolt. By John Cruickshank. *Oxford* 1959 Galaxy Bks. pap. $2.25
"As a searching commentary on the significance, the literary devices and the style of Camus' novels and plays, John Cruickshank's essay is unsurpassed and is likely to remain so for many years"—(Henri Peyre, in the *N.Y. Times*).
Camus: A Collection of Critical Essays. Ed. by Germaine Brée. *Prentice-Hall* 1962 $6.50 Spectrum Bks. pap. $1.95
Albert Camus. By Germaine Brée. Essays on Modern Writers *Columbia* 1964 $1.00
Camus: The Artist in the Arena. By Emmett Parker. *Univ. of Wisconsin Press* 1965 pap. $3.50
"A thorough study [that] explores the novelist through his articles as a journalist and has a valuable bibliography"—(Henri Peyre).
Albert Camus. By Adele King. 1965 *Putnam* 1971 $1.25
Albert Camus. By Philip H. Rhein. World Authors Ser. *Twayne* 1969 $6.95
Sea and the Prisons: Reflections on the Life and Thought of Albert Camus. By Roger Quilliot. Trans. by Emmett Parker *Univ. of Alabama Press* 1970 $10.00

CÉSAIRE, AYMÉ.   1913–

Césaire, with Senghor (*q.v.*), at the heart of the *négritude* movement and manner in French literature since the 1930s, was born on the island of Martinique. Like so many other French writers, he is an alumnus of the *École normale supérieure*, having arrived in Paris in 1929. Strangely of a mind with the surrealists with which group he was not connected, he has reacted strongly against the rational and Cartesian in French civilization. "Poetry," he holds, "begins with excess, extravagance, research into the forbidden, in the grand blind tam-tam, to the incomprehensible rain of stars." "For we hate you," he continues, "you and your reason, we demand dementia precox, flaming folly, tenacious cannibalism."

DISCOURSE ON COLONIALISM. 1955. Trans. by Joan Pinkham *Monthly Review* 1972 $4.94 pap. $2.50

RETURN TO MY NATIVE LAND. 1956. Trans. by Emile Snyders *Panther House* 1971 $2.50; *Penguin* 1970 pap. $2.95

CADASTRE. 1961. New ed. trans. by Gregson Davis *Third Press* 1972 $4.95 pap. $1.95; trans. by Emile Snyder *Third Press* 1973 $5.95 pap. $2.95

SEASON IN THE CONGO. Trans. by Ralph Manheim *Grove* Evergreen Bks. 1969 pap. $2.45

TRAGEDY OF KING CHRISTOPHE. Trans. by Ralph Manheim *Grove* Evergreen Bks. 1970 pap. $2.45

THE TEMPEST. *Third Press* 1974 $5.95 pap. $2.95

DANINOS, PIERRE.   1913–

Early in 1954 a mysterious British major appeared in the pages of *Figaro*—Marmaduke Thompson, who had abandoned tiger-hunting to track down the idiosyncrasies of the French. *Un vrai succès fou*, the most talked-about book on both sides of the Channel, sold over 400,000 copies during its first year in France. The second book reports on a visit to England and the U.S. The *Saturday Review* reported that in 1964 Daninos's "*snobissimo*" (sic), a "history and anatomy of snobbism," and in 1966 his "*Le 36° Dessous*," a "seriocomic book" about his nervous breakdown, were high on French best-seller lists. Major Thompson's creator was born in Paris, worked as a foreign correspondent in the United States, joined the French Army in 1939 and took part in the retreat from Dunkirk as a liaison agent with a British unit. He wrote numerous books of humor between 1942 and 1952.

THE NOTEBOOKS OF MAJOR THOMPSON: An Englishman Discovers France and the French. 1954. Trans. by Robin Farn *Knopf* 1955 $4.95

SIMON, CLAUDE.   1913–

Claude Simon, whose novels were influenced by both Faulkner and Camus, creates a universe dominated by fatality and pervaded with doom. His heroes are outsiders like Meursault, and testify to Simon's leaning toward the philosophy of the absurd. Simon makes great use of the interior monologue and consciously maintains a single point of view in his novels. In "The Flanders Road," three French POW's in a German camp pass the time by recalling incidents, trivial and otherwise—"all in precise detail, dissecting each component, then synthesizing it into one vast jumble of incidents and impressions—a sort of stream-of-consciousness technique with its interminable sentences and indeterminable scenes." Of "The Palace," Henri Peyre says, "Nothing happens in this novel, made up of shadowy dialogues and Proustian reminiscences. . . . The chief concern of the novelist, who no longer relates a story or presents images of real people, is to devise a language which may be true to his purely subjective vision." Though Simon has limited appeal as a writer for the vast majority, "he may well be the novelist of the nineteen-sixties most likely to endure"—(Peyre). In 1967 he received the Médicis Prize for "*Histoire*."

THE GRASS. 1959. Trans. by Richard Howard *Braziller* 1958 $4.50

THE FLANDERS ROAD. 1960. Trans. by Richard Howard *Braziller* 1961 $4.00

THE PALACE. 1962. Trans. by Richard Howard *Braziller* 1964 $4.50

HISTOIRE. 1967. Trans. by Richard Howard *Braziller* 1968 $5.95

THE BATTLE OF PHARSALUS. 1969. Trans. by Richard Howard *Braziller* 1971 $5.95

CONDUCTING BODIES (*Corps conducteurs*). 1971. Trans. by Helen R. Lane *Viking* 1974 $7.95

Books about Simon

The French New Novel: Claude Simon, Michel Butor, Alain Robbe-Grillet. By John Sturrock. *Oxford* 1969 $6.95

DURAS, MARGUERITE.   1914–

Born in Indochina, Marguerite Duras went to Paris at the age of 17 and studied mathematics at the Sorbonne. Her fame in literature dates from "The Sea Wall" (1953, o.p.)—about white settlers in Vietnam—called by Germaine Brée "a resilient, robust novel in which all the characters, even the most incidental, live with a kind of elemental gusto and genuineness." Mme Duras now has ten novels to her credit—all "setting powerful subconscious mechanisms in motion behind a screen of trivia"—(SR). In a review of "The Ravishing of Lol Stein" the *N.Y. Times* praised her "remarkable objective style, full of strange contrasts, sudden insights and haunting images." The characters in her novels, developed chiefly by means of dialogue, play out the entire human drama. Seeking meaning and fulfillment, they are sacrificed to the ever-flowing tide of existence, and life is perhaps over before they are fully aware of what has been happening. Although some of her material may seem repellent and disconcerting, her technique is faultless. She is usually grouped with the (in fact, widely disparate) "New Novelists."

Mme Duras has taken a great interest in the cinema, composing the scenario and dialogue for the prize-winning "Hiroshima Mon Amour." Films have been made of her novels "The Sea Wall," "Moderato Cantabile," "Ten-thirty on a Summer Night" and "The Sailor from Gibraltar."

FOUR NOVELS: The Square (1955); Moderato Cantabile (1958); Ten-thirty on a Summer Night (1960); The Afternoon of Mr. Andesmas (1962). Trans. by Sonia Pitt-Rivers, Irina Morduch, Richard Seaver and Anne Borchardt; introd. by Germaine Brée *Grove* 1965 Black Cat Bks. pap. $1.95

HIROSHIMA MON AMOUR. Trans. by Richard Seaver *Grove* Evergreen Bks. 1961 pap. $2.95; *Peter Smith* $4.25. Script for film.

THE RAVISHING OF LOL STEIN. 1966. Trans. by Richard Seaver *Grove* 1967 Black Cat Bks. pap. $.95

GARY, ROMAIN (pseud. of Romain Kacew).   1914–

A diplomat who has served in French embassies in England, Bulgaria and Switzerland, Gary was French Consul in Los Angeles in 1956. A pilot in World War II, he flew his plane to Britain after the fall of France, joined the R.A.F., and flew in attacks all over Europe. He has many decorations and was made a Chevalier of the Legion of Honor. He is a "social critic who knows how to write."

"The Roots of Heaven," which won the Prix Goncourt in 1956, was a best seller here. An allegory about the moral crisis of modern man, it is, on the surface, an exciting tale of elephants and high adventure in the African wilds. The *Atlantic* said that the "novel throughout is as densely packed with ideas as with action. It is a rich and exciting work, compellingly readable." A film was made of "Lady L" (1963, o.p.), another clever and successful novel. "A European Education," fiction about the Polish underground, "is one of the few unforgettable books on World War II"— (Henri Pyre). It was awarded the Prix des Critiques and translated into 14 languages.

Gary's "autobiography . . . is written with Gallic flair, frankness and humor. It is as much the biography of his amazingly strong-willed and worshipping mother, once an actress in Moscow, who scrimped and sacrificed for him and who influenced him throughout her life and directly even after her death. The book tells the story of Gary's boyhood in Moscow, Vilno, and Nice, . . ." of the war years and the fall of France. It skips from the end of World War II to his later life at Big Sur, California, "but by then it has chronicled enough adventures to fill nine lives"—(LJ).

A EUROPEAN EDUCATION. 1945 rev. 1959. Trans. by Viola Garvin *Simon & Schuster* 1960 $3.75 Pocket Bks. 1961 pap. $.50

THE ROOTS OF HEAVEN. 1956. Trans. by Jonathan Griffin. 1958. *Popular Lib.* $1.25

HISSING TALES. Trans. by Richard Howard *Harper* 1964 $4.95

Fifteen short stories revealing his "irony, invention, humor, sensitivity, and verbal artistry"—(LJ).

THE SKI BUM. *Harper* 1965 $4.95; *Bantam* pap. $.75

PROMISE AT DAWN. 1960. Trans. by John Markham Beach *Harper* 1961 $5.00; *Simon & Schuster* Pocket Bks. 1963 pap. $.50. His autobiography.

WHITE DOG. *New Am. Lib.* (dist. by Norton) 1970 $6.95

THE GASP. *Putnam* 1973 $6.95; *Simon & Schuster* Pocket Bks. pap. $1.25

MAURIAC, CLAUDE.   1914–

Claude Mauriac, son of novelist François Mauriac, has occupied an important place in modern French letters as essayist, literary critic and novelist. Depth and know-how characterize him, says

Boisdeffre. He has consistently shown himself aware of new directions from the recent past and in the present. His books, "The New Literature" (1958), "Dinner Party" (1959), and "The Marquise Went Out at 5" (1961), are currently o.p.

ANDRÉ BRETON. 1949. Trans. by Richard Howard *Grossman* (in prep.)

CONVERSATIONS WITH ANDRÉ GIDE. 1951. Trans. by Richard Howard *Braziller* 1965 $5.00

THE OTHER DE GAULLE. *T. Y. Crowell* (John Day) 1973 $12.95

DADIE, BERNARD. 1916–

Born in the Ivory Coast, Dadie is novelist, poet, and playwright. On the death of his guardian-uncle in 1929, he had a chance to have an education in Martinique but his father refused. He finally got to the École Normale in Dakar where he prepared a degree in administration. He is at present Director of Cultural Affairs in the Ivory Coast. He has written three volumes of poetry, three plays and several novels. "Present-day African poems," he has said, "must cry out encouragement to overcome our difficulties."

CLIMBIÉ. 1956. Trans. by Karen C. Chapman *Holmes & Meier* 1971 $7.95 pap. $2.75

GASCAR, PIERRE (pseud. of Pierre Fournier). 1916–

Gascar, "one of France's most exciting younger writers" (*SR*), first became known in 1953 when he received both the Prix Goncourt and the Prix des Critiques. He "ranks among the most original talents of contemporary France and easily . . . among the best authors of *récits* and short stories since Maupassant"—(Henri Peyre, in *SR*). His most famous story is "The Horses" (in "Beasts and Men"); here he displays an unusual awareness of the psychology of animals in a finely drawn tale of starving horses in the early days of World War II. It is based on his own observations as a prisoner in an East German POW camp. "Lambs of Fire," "entertaining as a novel [and] at the same time an illuminating inquiry into the rationale and workings of extremist movements everywhere" (*LJ*), describes a fictional conspiracy to overthrow de Gaulle for his stand on Algeria. Of "Women" (1955, o.p.) and "The Sun" (1960, o.p.) Henri Peyre wrote: "The concreteness of the imagery, the parsimony of language, the unremitting tension, and the avoidance of all rhetoric or sentimentality should fascinate and delight." In "The Fugitive" (1961, o.p.), a novel about an escaped prisoner in Germany (Gascar himself escaped twice during his captivity), he reveals "the intense lyricism of his prose and his *vision sans recul,* his relentless pursuit of an inner truth"—(*SR*). Set in the remote Aquitaine region of southern France, "The Best Years" provides vivid descriptions of rural life. "There is no spiritual quest in this solid, taut book. And yet its social examination of the natural world is a near-documentary on religious feeling in contemporary France"—(*N.Y. Times*). Peyre describes Gascar as "in France today . . . the closest approximation to Hemingway, with no trace of any American influence on him." Gascar has said, "Literature is to me . . . a moral life. . . . To write is a . . . self-punishment, a drive for redemption."

BEASTS AND MEN (1953) and THE SEED (1955). Trans. by Merloyd Lawrence 1960 o.p.

LAMBS OF FIRE. 1953. Trans. by Merloyd Lawrence *Braziller* 1965 $5.00

THE BEST YEARS. 1964. Trans. by Merloyd Lawrence *Braziller* 1967 $5.00

"It is remarkable for a translation to convey so much of the character of what must surely be the high literary quality of the original"—(*LJ*).

OLDENBOURG, ZOÉ. 1916–

Mme Oldenbourg is one of the most outstanding (and scholarly) historical novelists writing anywhere. "The World Is Not Enough" (1948, o.p.), the story of the medieval House of Linnières, "is a huge French tapestry of a book, a piece of work in which each leaf and plume and battlement has been picked out lovingly and with knowledge. This novel has a wonderful breadth of feeling, is kept sharply contemporary with its period"—(*New Statesman*). "The Cornerstone" (1953, o.p.) won the Prix Femina, was a Book Society Choice in England and a Book-of-the-Month Club selection here. "The Awakened" (o.p.) is a story of starcrossed lovers. *Library Journal* said of "Destiny of Fire" (1961, o.p.): "Obviously possessed of a deep and loving knowledge of the Middle Ages, Mme Oldenbourg achieves a remarkable compassionate historical novel dealing with the Albigensian heresy and the unusually cruel 'Fourth Crusade.' The characters are intensely alive. . . . A brilliant and unspoiled work of literature." Henri Peyre defines all the works described above as "novels." The *Saturday Review* called the biography "Catherine the Great" (chiefly about Catherine's early years) "well written and at times fascinating" but presented "from the standpoint of the historical novelist rather than the scholarly biographer." The *Christian Science Monitor* said of "The Crusaders" (1963, o.p.): "If any book can make us see through the eyes of the Crusaders and feel what they went through, it is this volume."

Zoé Oldenbourg was born in Leningrad. Her parents were both scholars, her father a historian, her mother a mathematician, refugees from Bolshevist Russia. When she was nine they took her to Paris, where she studied for a time to be a painter but found herself more interested in writing. As the family was desperately poor, she took a job in a textile firm, did research on her free days and wrote at night.

MASSACRE AT MONTSÉGUR: A History of the Albigensian Crusade. 1960. Trans. by Peter Green 1962 *Funk & Wagnalls* Minerva Bks. 1968 pap. $2.95

CATHERINE THE GREAT. 1965. Trans. by Anne Carter *Pantheon* 1965 $8.95

THE HEIRS OF THE KINGDOM (*La joie des pauvres*). 1970. Trans. by Anne Carter *Pantheon* 1971 $8.95

PINGET, ROBERT. 1919–

Before deciding to write professionally, Pinget practiced law in his native city of Geneva and studied painting at the École des Beaux Arts in Paris. Of all the "New Novelists" he is one of the more abstruse, and has seemed little interested in attracting a following. Nevertheless, "The Inquisitory" (1962, o.p.), awarded the 1962 Prix des Critiques, became a best seller in France. It is essentially a monologue—a deaf old servant's meandering, half-truthful responses to the terse questions of an interrogator seeking information on a man who has vanished. As the old man speaks, he brings to light all the vice and corruption of what appears to be a placid provincial town. "The *Inquisitory* is, in fact, a disturbing, bewildering book. But its very confusion dazzles rather than dazes"—(Thomas Bishop, in *SR*). In 1965 Pinget's "*Quelqu'un,*" about a man's search for a scrap of paper, won the Prix Femina. Author of 11 novels, Pinget is also a dramatist. *Library Journal* describes his "Three Plays," admired by Samuel Beckett, as "dialogues really." Though not without humor, their mood is sad and disillusioned, their themes old age, loneliness, defeats. "On their own terms they are exceedingly well written"—(*LJ*).

THREE PLAYS. The Old Tune (1960), adapted by Samuel Beckett; Clope (1961) and Dead Letter (1959) trans. by Barbara Bray *Farrar, Straus* (Hill & Wang) Dramabks. 1966 $5.00

ARCHITRUC. 1961. (In "Modern French Theatre: The Avant-Garde, Dada, and Surrealism") trans. and ed. by Michael Benedikt and George E. Wellwarth *Dutton* pap. $2.95. Play.

DIB, MOHAMMED. 1920–

One of the best-known and representative Moslem writers in French, Dib belongs to what might be called the North-African School. His "Grande Maison" (1952) is his best-known novel.

EROS FAIR. *Red Hill* 1975 pap. $2.50

DUTOURD, JEAN. 1920–

"M. Dutourd is a fine craftsman, whose work has the classic virtues of brevity, lucidity and concentration"—(*N.Y. Times*). "Five A.M." (o.p.) is a witty novel written in the "stream-of-consciousness" style. In "Taxis of the Marne" (1955, o.p.) Dutourd combines autobiographical material with a study of the decline and fall of France in World War II. "It is a serious and thought-provoking confession of patriotism. It is also a loud and lonely warning [about] the stupidity, complacency and individual selfishness that brought about France's defeat"—(*Chicago Sunday Tribune*). André Maurois found "The Horrors of Love" (1963, o.p.) "a great book and one which will last." It concerns, says Henri Peyre in *SR*, "the banality and the dreariness of adultery. [It is a] strange, unwieldy, hybrid . . . an original mixture of some fictional elements with autobiographical ones, of sundry reflections on literature, art, and delectable eating interspersed with vituperations against the modern world."

Jean Dutourd, born in Paris, was drafted in 1940. He was taken prisoner and escaped to join the Resistance movement. In 1943 he was caught by the Gestapo and sentenced to death but again escaped to resume his underground activities. He worked for some time in London, and is a painter as well as a writer. In 1961 he was awarded the Monaco Prize; he is a member of the Académie Française.

THE BEST BUTTER (*Le Bon Beurre*). 1952. Trans. by Robin Chancellor. 1955. *Greenwood* $11.50

THE SPRINGTIME OF LIFE. 1972. Trans. by Denver and Helen Lindley *Doubleday* 1974 $6.95

VIAN, BORIS. 1920–1959.

Vian, the favorite writer of contemporary French youth and the subject today of much French critical attention, was known in his lifetime as "the prince of Saint-Germain des Prés," where he was a charming, dynamic figure of the literary cafés. "He was educated as an engineer . . . but his life was a catalogue of other occupations: actor, auto mechanic, carpenter and cabinet maker," to name only four of some 25 described in "Plays for a New Theater," which include also "essayist," "science-fiction writer," "journalist," "novelist," "film technician," "translator." When he died at 39, the note on him in that anthology continues, "Vian left behind him 9 novels, 4 plays, 3 opera librettos, 9 ballet scenarios, 93 cabaret skits, many short stories, 3 volumes of poetry, 400 songs, a patent for an elastic wheel, 20 major works of translation, 8,911 articles printed in 40 different publications, many pencil sketches, and some paintings. Singing his own songs in Paris nightclubs, he was a social force as a popular poet."

"The General's Tea Party" and "Knackery for All" (also translated "The Knacker's ABC"; a knacker is one who slaughters old horses for meat and hides) are biting antiwar satires. The 1950 Paris production of "Knackery for All," coming with its sharp, irreverent humor so soon after World War II, caused an uproar. Vian retorted: "There is nothing scandalous in trying to evoke hilarity over war. . . . For me, it inspires only a desperate and total anger against the absurdity of battles made of words which kill men made of flesh. Unfortunately, this anger is ineffectual. One means of expression, however, is mockery." "The Empire Builders"—which has to do with the daily activity of all of us and seems almost certainly intended as a satire on the Algerian War—has been produced in many countries. A family, trying to escape a frightening noise, moves higher and higher in its apartment house until it is reduced to the father in the attic room—who dies. Always silently present is the *"schmürz"*—a hideous, living, ragged and bleeding blob. He is ignored by the others and may represent *Schmerz*, the German word for pain. Life, as we go on, becomes mercilessly narrower, says Vian, in anticipation perhaps of his own early death at 39. "Jean-Sol Partre," a main character in the play, is one of several thinly disguised celebrities portrayed.

Vian came to prominence as a novelist with the sensational "American" thriller "I'll Spit on Your Grave" (filmed in 1959), which he wrote under the pseudonym of Vernon Sullivan. "The Froth on the Daydream," another novel, was well received by the critics. Though he often shocked the bourgeois world, Vian was not personally given to license; he lived intensely, but he worked intensely as well. Marc Slonim of the N.Y. Times has written that, for many Frenchmen, "Vian understood the evil of this world but was not contaminated by it, and preserved the innocence of childhood. Perhaps this partly explains his magic hold over French youth."

FROTH ON THE DAYDREAM (*L'Écume des jours*). 1947. Trans. by Stanley Chapman. 1967. *Int. Pubns. Service* $7.50; (with title "Mood Indigo") trans. by John Sturrock *Grove* 1968 Evergreen Bks. pap. $1.95

KNACKERY FOR ALL (*L'Equarrissage pour Tous*). 1950. Trans. by Simon Watson Taylor *Grove* Evergreen Bks. 1968 pap. $1.95; (in "Plays for a New Theater") trans. by Marc Estrin *New Directions* Playbook 2 1966 $7.50 pap. $.95

THE EMPIRE BUILDERS. 1959. Trans. by Simon Watson Taylor *Grove* Evergreen Bks. (orig.) 1967 $2.95

THE HEARTSNATCHER (*L'Arrache-coeur*). 1962. Trans. by Stanley Chapman. 1968. *Int. Pubns. Service* $7.50

THE GENERAL'S TEA PARTY. Trans. by Simon Watson Taylor *Grove* Evergreen Bks. (orig.) 1967 pap. $1.95

ROBBE-GRILLET, ALAIN. 1922–

It is around the person of this brilliant young writer that most of the controversy over the "new novel" has turned. Robbe-Grillet focused his acute attention on the most minute photographic detail. His method has been heatedly discussed by his critics. In explanation, Robbe-Grillet's "For a New Novel" (*Grove* 1965 Black Cat Bks. pap. $1.65; *Bks. for Libraries* $9.25) outlines his aims "quite clearly and unpretentiously" (*LJ*); here one cannot doubt his intelligence and sincerity. More recently, he has turned his creative talents to cinema and is currently interested in painting.

The publication of "The Erasers" in France in 1953 appeared to mark the debut of the *nouveau roman*, but as Leon S. Roudiez points out in the *Saturday Review* of October 10, 1964, various authors now considered part of the movement had been writing since the early 1940s. All are talented, and none is exactly like another. Robbe-Grillet's *"La Maison de Rendez-Vous,"* a kind of involuted detective story, is "a treat for the mind," said Thomas Bishop (in *SR*). Frederic Morton (in the *N.Y. Times Book Review*) wrote of the same book: "It's playing with the optics of experience. . . . It's not enough. . . . The novelist, no matter how *nouveau*, will [still] need an ancient quality called 'emotion.' " Eliot Fremont-Smith (daily *N.Y. Times*), discussing the same novel, said of the new form: "It is . . . probably the least understood experiment in modern literature. What Robbe-Grillet is after . . . is not simply the 'objectification of things' but the forced inclusion of the reader in the process of inventing art, inventing stories, inventing experience." This critic found *"La Maison"* "neither difficult nor dull. It is a funny book, a provocation, a do-it-yourself mystery or fairy tale." Surely what is involved here is the always painful process of change, and to one reader Robbe-Grillet seems a good deal more substantial than certain of the avant-garde at home. "The Voyeur" won the Prix des Critiques in 1955. "Last Year at Marienbad" was a successful film.

TWO NOVELS: Jealousy (1957) and In the Labyrinth (1959). Trans. by Richard Howard *Grove* Black Cat Bks. pap. $2.45

THE ERASERS. 1953. Trans. by Richard Howard *Grove* 1966 Black Cat Bks. pap. $1.95

THE VOYEUR. 1955. Trans. by Richard Howard *Grove* 1958. Black Cat Bks. 1967 pap. $1.95

LAST YEAR AT MARIENBAD. 1961. Trans. by Richard Howard *Grove* Evergreen Bks. (orig.) 1962 pap. $1.95

LA MAISON DE RENDEZ-VOUS. 1965. Trans. by Richard Howard *Grove* 1966 Black Cat Bks. pap. $1.95

PROJECT FOR A REVOLUTION IN NEW YORK. 1972. Trans. by Richard Howard *Grove* 1972 $5.95 Black Cat Bks. pap. $1.65

SNAPSHOTS. 1972. Trans. by Richard Howard *Grove* Evergreen Bks. 1973 pap. $2.45
Books about Robbe-Grillet

Alain Robbe-Grillet. By Bruce Morrissette. Essays on Modern Writers *Columbia* 1965 pap. $1.00
French New Novel: Claude Simon, Michel Butor, Alain Robbe-Grillet. By John Sturrock. *Oxford* 1969 $6.95

OUSMANE, SEMBENE (also Sembene, Ousmane). 1923–

Born in Senegal, Sembene (the family name) is an autodidact having become after elementary school a fisherman like his father. Drafted into the French army, he saw service in Germany and Italy. Before settling in Dakar in 1957, he lived in Marseille, becoming a trade-union leader there at the time he started writing. Aside from novels, he has written and directed films after studying in Moscow.

His best-known novels are *"O pays, mon beau peuple"* (1957), *"Les bouts de bois de Dieu"* (1960), *"L'Harmattan"* (1964). Of "God's Bits of Wood," Jame Fernandez said: "Ousmane captures expertly the contrast between bush and bidonville Africa and the European colonials."

GOD'S BITS OF WOOD (*Les Bouts de bois de Dieu*). 1960. Trans. by Francis Price *Doubleday* 1970 $1.95

SEMPRUN, JORGE. 1923–

Born in Madrid to a father who was a professor of law and a diplomat, Semprun was educated in Paris (Faculty of Letters) and served for some years as a translator for UNESCO. In 1964, he adapted Rolf Hochhuth's *"Vicaire"* for the film. He wrote the scenario and dialogue for *"La Guerre est finie"* (1966) and for "Stavisky" (1974). He has most recently written scripts for Costa-Gavras and Yves Boisset—notably for the film "Z" (1968). In 1963, he wrote the short novel *"Le Grand Voyage,"* *"L'Evanouissement"* in 1967 and *"La Deuxième Mort de Ramon Mercader"* in 1969 for which he won the Prix Femina.

LA GUERRE EST FINIE. 1966. Trans. by Richard Seaver *Grove* 1967 pap. $2.95; *Peter Smith* $4.75

STAVISKY. 1974. Trans. by Sabine Destrée *Viking* 1975 $3.95

BUTOR, MICHEL (or Michael). 1926–

Although closely associated with the "New Novelists," Butor has enjoyed considerable general popularity. "A Change of Heart" was awarded one of the major French literary prizes of 1957 and put Butor before the general public. The subject of his novels is consciousness, frequently presented in the form of the interior monologue and described in painstaking detail. "Degrees" is "a complex novel about a secondary school teacher of history and geography at the Lycée Taine in Paris who attempts to reveal with infinite veracity and detail the actions and thoughts of an entire 11th-grade class and its various teachers—in and out of the classroom. . . . Though the story line is usually buried within snatches and bits of dialogue and detail, and though the numerous flashbacks from three points of view occasionally puzzle the reader, the interwoven strands of the book provide a brilliant picture of the perennial schoolboy—and the perennial teacher."

In "Mobile," a sort of pastiche or verbal photomontage of catchwords recalling many areas of the United States, unique typographical arrangements substitute for conventional syntax in connecting words and phrases, and also signify various themes. "It is not, most people would agree, a novel. Some people in France wondered if it was even a book"—(Roudiez). Of Butor's French publication, "6,810,000 *Litres d'eau par Seconde*" (trans. "Niagara: A Stereophonic Novel," 1965), inspired by Niagara Falls, Robert J. Clements wrote (in *SR*): "Butor continues to exhibit a fascination with typography on the loose: boldface, roman, and italic fonts jostling one another, uneven margins, incomplete lines, etc." To his visual gimmicks in this work he has added aural ones: suggestions for making this a "stereophonic" novel—indeed several *different* novels—by varying the tone of voice in different ways while reading it aloud. No wonder a French critic discusses him (1965) in terms of *le livre futur*. Recently he is said to have returned to more conventional literary forms.

PASSING TIME (*L'Emploi du Temps*) (1956) and A CHANGE OF HEART (*La Modification*) (1957). Trans. by Richard Howard *Simon & Schuster* Touchstone-Clarion Bks. 1969 pap. $3.45

INVENTORY. 1960 1964. Trans. by Richard Howard *Simon & Schuster* 1969 $7.95

MOBILE: Study for a Representation of the United States. 1962. Trans. by Richard Howard *Simon & Schuster* 1963 $6.00

NIAGARA: A Stereophonic Novel. 1965. Trans. by Elinor S. Miller *Regnery* 1969 $7.95

Books about Butor

Michel Butor. By Michael Spencer. World Authors Ser. *Twayne* 1974 $6.95
French New Novel: Claude Simon, Michel Butor, Alain Robbe-Grillet. By John Sturrock. *Oxford* 1974 $6.95

FOUCAULT, MICHEL. 1926–

Foucault comes to literature through philosophy. His *"Les Mots et les Choses"* (1966) has established itself as an important text for understanding recent literature. An article in *Critique*, "Distance, Aspect, Origine," is a structuralist commentary on the new novel.

MADNESS AND CIVILIZATION: A History of Insanity in the Age of Reason. 1961. Trans. by Richard Howard. 1965. *Random* 1973 pap. $2.45

ARCHAEOLOGY OF KNOWLEDGE (*Archéologie du Savoir*). 1969. Trans. by A. M. Sheridan-Smith *Pantheon* 1972 $10.00; *Irvington Pubns.* 1972 $19.95

I, PIERRE RIVIÈRE, HAVING SLAUGHTERED MY MOTHER, MY SISTER, AND MY BROTHER. 1973. *Pantheon* 1975 $10.00

SCHWARTZ-BART, ANDRÉ. 1928–

"Powerful memorialist of the Passion of Israel" (Boisdeffre), Schwartz-Bart won the Goncourt Prize in 1959 with his *"Le Dernier des Justes."* A Polish Jew who suffered horrible loss of family under the Nazis, he is motivated by deep spiritualism to bring serious questions to his reader with "warmth and generosity"—(Peyre).

THE LAST OF THE JUST. 1959. Trans. by Stephen Becker 1960 *Atheneum* 1973 pap. $3.95; *Bantam* 1973 pap. $1.50

A WOMAN NAMED SOLITUDE (*La Mulâtresse Solitude*). 1972. Trans. by Ralph Manheim *Atheneum* 1973 $5.95; *Bantam* 1974 pap. $1.75

WIESEL, ELIE. 1928–

Hungarian-born Elie Wiesel (who is generally regarded as a French author) went to Paris and began writing after a period in Auschwitz. Now living in New York, he is literary critic and UN correspondent for a major Israeli newspaper. His novels "are driven by an ardor that gives form to the terrible passions that play beneath the surface of civilization. . . . Masterfully, passionately, desperately, he has dredged from the horror of the holocaust a vision of man as moving as his suffering and as powerful as his survival"—(*Nation*). Wiesel's first book, "Night," a recounting in starkly simple prose of the author's own experience as a child during the Nazi holocaust in Europe, received wide acclaim. "Dawn" is an illuminating document about terrorists in Palestine. "The Accident," set in New York, describes a man who has lost the will to live because he has seen too much of death. "The Gates of the Forest," a novel on the Nazi period, is "an excellent . . . four-part parable about God's and man's inhumanity to man"—(*LJ*). "The Jews of Silence," says the *New Yorker*, "is not journalistic but subjective and poetic. He found the Jews of the Soviet Union living in 'an enclosed and silent fear,' discriminated against at every level of life and cut off by government censorship from any contact with the Jews of other countries." Therefore they cling with especial tenacity to their religion. Isaac Bashevis Singer (in the *N.Y. Times*) described the book as "one passionate outcry, both in content and in style."

THREE TALES: Night (*La Nuit*, 1958), trans. by Stella Rodway; Dawn (*L'Aube*, 1960), trans. by Frances Frenaye; The Accident (*Le Jour*, 1962), trans. by Ann Borchardt *Farrar, Straus* (Hill & Wang) 1972 $7.95

NIGHT. 1958. Trans. by Stella Rodway *Avon* Bard Bks. pap. $1.25. A fictional account based upon his family's experience in the Nazi concentration camps.

DAWN. 1960. Trans. by Frances Frenaye *Avon* Bard Bks. pap. $1.25

THE ACCIDENT. 1961 Trans. by Ann Borchardt *Avon* Bard Bks. pap. $1.25

THE TOWN BEYOND THE WALL. Trans. by Stephen Becker *Holt* 1967 $4.95; *Avon* Bard Bks. pap. $1.25

THE GATES OF THE FOREST. 1964. Trans. by Frances Frenaye *Holt* 1966 $4.95; *Avon* 1967 pap. $1.25

THE JEWS OF SILENCE: A Personal Report on Soviet Jewry. 1966. Trans. from the Hebrew with a historical afterword by Neal Kozodoy. *Holt* 1966 $4.95; *New Am. Lib.* Plume Bks. pap. $1.95. Based on Wiesel's series of articles for an Israeli newspaper about his 1965 visit to the Soviet Union.

LEGENDS OF OUR TIME (*Le Chant des Morts*). 1966. Trans. by Stephen Donadio *Holt* 1968 $5.95; *Avon* Bard Bks. 1970 pap. $1.25

ZALMAN, or The Madness of God (*Zalman ou la folie de Dieu*). 1968. Trans. by Nathan Edelman. *Random* 1975 $6.95

ONE GENERATION AFTER (*Entre deux soleils*). 1970. Trans. by Lily Edelman *Random* 1970 $5.95; *Avon* Bard Bks. 1971 pap. $1.75

SOULS ON FIRE: Portraits and Legends of Hasidic Masters (*Célébration hassidique*). 1972. Trans. by Marion Wiesel *Random* 1972 $7.95 Vintage Bks. 1973 pap. $1.65

THE OATH (*Le Serment du Kolvillaq*). 1973. *Random* 1973 $7.95; *Avon* 1974 pap. $1.75

ANI MAAMIN: A Song Lost and Found. 1974 *Random* 1974 $7.50. Text for a cantata by Darius Milhaud.

THE DAY THE PIGS REFUSED TO BE TAKEN TO MARKET. *Random* 1974 $7.95

OYONO, FERDINAND.   1929–

Born in the Cameroon, Oyono was educated in Africa and France: Provins and Paris (Law School and National School of Administration). In 1956 he wrote *"Une Vie de boy"* and *"Le Vieux Nègre et la Medaille"* which gave him a European reputation. Diplomat in various capacities since 1960, he now serves as Ambassador of the United Republic of Cameroon in France. Oyono, humorous in his refined satire, shows constantly the impoverishment (material and spiritual) that is the result of colonialism for both Europeans and Africans.

BOY. 1956. Trans. by John Reed *Macmillan* Collier Bks. 1970 pap. $1.25

OLD MAN AND THE MEDAL. 1956. *Macmillan* Collier Bks. 1971 pap. $1.50

MALLET-JORIS, FRANÇOISE.   1930–

"Neither an autobiography nor confession, ["A Letter to Myself"] is a searching and contemplative examination of her experiences, her friends, her way of life and her own truths. . . . To read this book is to follow a fascinating and cultivated mind"—(*N.Y. Herald Tribune*). "From the very first words, it moves with the swiftness and strength of a masterpiece"—(Germaine Brée, in *SR*).

The work of this Belgian writer, daughter of a Belgian playwright, Suzanne Lilar, has been highly praised both here and abroad. "The Illusionists," her first book (1951, U.S. 1952, o.p.), was published when she was only 20. "Mme Françoise Mallet-Joris proves in 'The Red Room' (1956, o.p.) that she constructs her stories with solid understanding of human nature"—(*N.Y. Times*). Frances Keen, who reviewed "The House of Lies" (1956, o.p.) in the *N.Y. Times* wrote: "Françoise

Mallet-Joris is, I believe, the only woman writing in French today who deserves the title of novelist." "Café Celeste" (1958, U.S. 1959, o.p.), which won the Prix Femina, has been called "a feast uncommonly and memorably rich"—(*TLS*, London). The stories in "Cordelia" concern the psychology and reactions of women in various situations. Her latest novel, "Signs and Wonders," ostensibly about two writers covering the story of Algerian repatriates, delves deeply into questions of morality, philosophy and love. The *N.Y. Times*, daily and Sunday, was lukewarm. "The very success of [her character] sketches," says Eliot Fremont-Smith, "detracts from the success of the book as a whole. They fragment . . . emotional response." And Elizabeth Janeway writes: "Mme Mallet-Joris's talent is (in my opinion) for big, old-fashioned three-decker novels, emotional and unsubstantial." Germaine Brée said of her in 1964, however: "If the mantle of Colette is to fall on another woman writer in France, Françoise Mallet-Joris, different though she be, is certainly at the moment the most likely heir."

SIGNS AND WONDERS. 1966. Trans. by Herma Briffault *Farrar, Straus* 1967 $6.95

A LETTER TO MYSELF. 1963. Trans. by Patrick O'Brian *Farrar, Straus* 1964 $4.95

THE UNDERGROUND GAME. 1973. *Dutton* 1975 $6.95

BETI, MONGO (pseud. of Alexandre Biyidi).   1932–

A young Cameroonian professor, Beti is "undoubtedly" (Paulin Joachim) the most gifted of the French-speaking African writers. He wrote his first novel, *"Ville Cruelle"* under the pseudonym of Eza Boto. Despite the good intentions of the two main characters, they eventually both acquire the self-centeredness of Europeans and the materialism of Africans exploiting their newly won authority. Born near Yaoundé, Beti was educated in local schools until expelled at age 14. He continued his education in Yaoundé and France (Aix-en-Provence) and the Sorbonne. A favorite theme of Beti is the failure of colonial missionary efforts in Africa; he speaks not so much against Christianity as against the futile Europeanization of Africans in the name of religion.

POOR CHRIST OF BOMBA. 1956. Trans. by Gerald Moore *Humanities* 1972 $2.50

MISSION TO KALA (*Mission terminée*). 1957. *Humanities* 1966 pap. $1.75. Winner of the Ste-Beuve Prize, 1948.

KING LAZARUS (*Le Roi miraculé*). 1958. *Macmillan* Collier Bks. 1970 $1.50

NIANE, DJIBRIL TAMSIR.   1932–

Born of *Griot* ancestors, Niane has collected oral literature, the province of the story-telling *Griot*. Born in Conakry, Guinea, he was educated in Dakar and Bordeaux. Returned home in 1959, he taught history in lycées, rose steadily in educational administration and since 1968 has been Dean of the Faculty of Social Sciences at Conakry's Polytechnic Institute. His specialization in history has been medieval African empires; he has written *"Recherches sur l'empire du Mali"* (1959), and (in collaboration with Jean Suret-Canale) *"Histoire de l'Afrique occidentale"* (1961).

SUNDIATA: An Epic of Old Mali. 1960. *Humanities* 1965 pap. $2.00

SAGAN, FRANÇOISE (pseud. of Françoise Quoirez).   1935–

"Bonjour Tristesse," winner of the Prix des Critques, is a "remarkable combination of precocity, immaturity, majesty, and amorality," says *Booklist*, a novel which "will shock or repel some readers, while those who can tolerate other moral standards than their own will find in the clear-cut writing and stark thinking a noteworthy achievement for the eighteen-year-old author." With *"Aimez-Vous Brahms,"* Miss Sagan's talent began to mature. Marya Mannes wrote (in the *N.Y. Times*) that this short novel "is the work of a serious writer, firmly disciplined and touched with compassion. . . . Miss Sagan handles a simple triangle involving complicated people with the sobriety and depth of the mature artist." "Miss Sagan is a technician of a high order, working with exceptional economy and elegance in the tradition of Colette and Benjamin Constant"—(*Atlantic*). *"La Chamade,"* again about a love triangle, reveals her "deepened sense of life and an artistic expansion that carries her strides ahead as a writer"—(*N.Y. Times*). Her novels express the philosophical, political and religious disillusionment of many intellectuals, the vapid life of the rich and the cynicism of French youth.

After failing in her examination at the Sorbonne in the summer of 1953 she wrote *"Bonjour Tristesse"* during the month of August, submitted it to a publisher and overnight became an international literary figure. She was born in France and lives in Paris. Fond of sports, jazz, dancing and fast cars, she was severely injured early in 1957 when driving her Italian racing car, allegedly at 175 miles per hour. *"Bonjour Tristesse"* has been translated into some 20 languages, and both it and *"Aimez-Vous Brahms"* have been made into motion pictures. She has also written five plays. The first of these, *"Château en Suède"* (Paris, 1960), was called by Genêt of the *New Yorker*, "a modern French classic in lunatic fantasy, rich characterizations, amorality." *"Le Cheval Évanoui,"* her latest play, was much praised by French critics—"the major social and theatrical Paris event" (says Genêt) of the 1966 season.

BONJOUR TRISTESSE. 1954. Trans. by Irene Ash. 1955. *Popular Lib.* pap. $.95

A CERTAIN SMILE. 1956. Trans. by Anne Green. 1956. *Popular Lib.* pap. $.95

THE WONDERFUL CLOUDS. 1956. Trans. by Anne Green. 1962. *Popular Lib.* pap. $.95

THOSE WITHOUT SHADOWS (*Dans un Mois, Dans un An*). 1957. Trans. by Frances Frenaye. 1957. *Popular Lib.* pap. $.95

AIMEZ-VOUS BRAHMS. 1959. Trans. by Peter Wiles. 1960. *Popular Lib.* pap. $.95

LA CHAMADE. 1965. Trans. by Robert Westhoff *Popular Lib.* pap. $.95. The title means a roll of drums signifying defeat.

A FEW HOURS OF SUNLIGHT (*Un peu de soleil dans l'eau froide*). 1969. *Harper* pap. $1.25

SCARS ON THE SOUL (*Des Bleus a l'âme*). 1973. Trans. by Joanna Kilmartin *McGraw-Hill* 1974 $6.95

THE HEART KEEPER (*La Garde du coeur*). 1968. Trans. by Robert Westhoff *Popular Lib.* pap. $.95

SOLLERS, PHILIPPE. 1936–

Sollers, since 1960 the editor of the provocative French literary review *Tel Quel*, was born in Talence in the suburbs of Bordeaux and finished his secondary studies there. At the age of 17, he came to Versailles to study with the Jesuits. He finished his degree at the École Supérieure de Sciences Economiques et Commerciales and has lived in Paris ever since. He has published several experimental novels: *"Une Curieuse Solitude," "Le Parc," "Nombres," "Lois," "Drame,"* and *"H."*

He has guided *Tel Quel* since its founding. His wife is Julia Kristeva, intellectual writer of the *Tel Quel* group of semiologists.

THE PARK. 1961. Trans. by A. Sheridan Smith 1968 *Red Dust* 1969 $4.25

LE CLEZIO, JEAN-MARIE. 1940–

Le Clezio, the most promising young writer of the post-war generation, made his debut with *"Le Procès-Verbal,"* a great literary success. A book of short stories entitled *"La Fievre"* is "remarkable for its psychological accuracy and its warm emotion" (Peyre). He has continued to add titles that find popular success quite apart from the semiologic specialists of the past years.

FOOD. 1966. Trans. by Peter Green *Atheneum* 1968 $5.95

TERRA AMATA. 1967. Trans. by Peter Green *Atheneum* 1969 $5.95

BOOK OF FLIGHTS. 1969. Trans. by Peter Green *Atheneum* 1972 $6.95

WAR. 1970. Trans. by Peter Green *Atheneum* 1973 $6.95

THE GIANTS. 1973. Trans. by Peter Green *Atheneum* 1975 $10.00

OUOLOGUEM, YAMBO (also pseud. Utto Rodolph). 1940–

Ouologuem, only son of a school inspector, was educated in local schools, the lycée in Bamako (Mali) and in Paris (English Literature, Sociology). His novel "Bound to Violence" precipitated a literary battle because, it was said, he lifted whole passages from Schwartz-Bart's "Last of the Just" and from Graham Greene's "It's a Battlefield." The authors concerned have brought no such charges. In 1969, under the pseudonym of Utto Rodolph, he published *"Les mille et une Bibles du sexe."* He has also written significant and original poetry. He disapproves of bleeding-heart liberals who approve of everything black; this, he says, is worse than racism.

BOUND TO VIOLENCE. 1968. Trans. by Ralph Manheim 1971 o.p.

BLAIS, MARIE-CLAIRE. 1941–

This gifted young French-Canadian writer was first brought to the attention of the American public by Edmund Wilson (*q.v.*)—who says of her in "O Canada": "Mlle Blais is a true 'phenomenon'; she may possibly be a genius. [Her work is] of a passionate and poetic force that, as far as my reading goes, is not otherwise to be found in French-Canadian fiction."

Mlle Blais, in appearance "a schoolgirl, with fine little features" (Wilson), was educated at a convent in Quebec and later at Quebec's Laval University. Though her themes, like those of many of her French-Canadian contemporaries, usually involve tragic love affairs or the situation of outcasts from society, they go "beyond the regional or polemical to involve the human condition"—(*SR*). "The idea that man is born to sorrow, the agony of expiation, is at the basis of her tragic consciousness." And her novels express "the desperate cry that arises from the poverty, intellectual and material, the passionate self-punishing pity and the fierce defeated pride of Quebec"—(Wilson). In "The Day Is Dark" and "Three Travelers" (1967, o.p.) she displays "an intense virtuosity that commands our admiration [in describing] creatures of romantic dream, in love with easeful death"—(*N.Y. Times*). "A Season in the Life of Emmanuel," for which she won the 1966 French Prix Médicis, concerns the lot of a poor family with 16 offspring. "Intense flashes of humor, affection, and poetry illuminate this account of general misery, which otherwise might become so dreadful as to topple into the ludicrous"—(*SR*). Mlle Blais has also written poetry.

A SEASON IN THE LIFE OF EMMANUEL. 1966. Trans. by Derek Coltman. 1966. *Grosset* Univ. Lib. pap. $1.95

THE MANUSCRIPTS OF PAULINE ARCHANGE. 1968. Trans. by Derek Coltman *Farrar, Straus* 1970 $5.95

SAINT LAWRENCE BLUES (*Un joualonais, sa joualonie*). 1974. Trans. by Ralph Manheim *Farrar, Straus* 1974 $7.95

DAVID STERNE. *Bks. Canada* (McClelland & Stewart) 1973 $5.95

Chapter 10

Italian Literature

*"For the ancient valor
in Italian hearts is not yet dead."*

—FRANCESCO PETRARCA

In the world of letters the years 1974–1975, which mark the three-quarter point in the twentieth century, will be long remembered. In 1975 Eugenio Montale (*q.v.*) won the Nobel Prize for literature, the fifth Italian to be so honored (along with Carducci, Deledda, Pirandello, and Quasimodo). Montale is described in the *Times Literary Supplement* (Oct. 31, 1975) as "a writer preeminent in his own country whose values are simple and universal. What Montale has stood for throughout his long life is above all intelligence and what he calls 'decenza quotidiana.' He may be classified as a lyric poet—and as the finest of lyric poets since Leopardi—but he is also a poet for whom intelligence matters more than sentiment, and common decency more than any high flown political or metaphysical allegiance. Montale is in this respect a contradiction: a wonderfully varied and resourceful poet who holds essentially prosaic values." It was in the years 1974 and 1975 that three long-awaited works appeared: *"Corporale"* (*Einaudi*, 1974) by Paolo Volponi, which probes the contemporary human condition and reveals the stark nature of man's alienated state; *"La Storia"* (*Einaudi*, 1974) by Elsa Morante, which has aroused much critical attention and public furor for its provocative account of the war years (1941–1947) in Italy; and *"Horcynus Orca"* (*Mondadori*, 1975) by Stefano D'Arrigo, which invites comparison both with the Homeric epics and the epic novels of Melville and Joyce and has caused mixed responses from critics regarding its literary merits. We eagerly await their eventual translation into English. These years are those in which the voices of several outstanding authors, critics, and historians were silenced forever: Carlo Levi, Giacomo Devoto, Guido Piovene, Luigi Salvatorelli, Pier Paolo Pasolini, and Aldo Palazzeschi. Finally, both years have occasioned celebrations: 1974 marked the 600th anniversary of the death of Francesco Petrarca (1304–1374) and 1975 was the 600th anniversary of the death of Giovanni Boccaccio (1313–1375). Each author was commemorated by an international symposium: the World Petrarch Congress at the Folger Library in Washington D.C. and the International Boccaccio Symposium at the University of California at Los Angeles. Moreover, in the course of each year numerous monographs, translations, and articles were published, and special numbers of periodicals appeared in honor of Italy's outstanding luminaries of the Trecento. Among the more important of these publications, we might call attention to Aldo Bernardo's "Petrarch, Laura and the Triumphs" (*State Univ. of New York Press* 1974 $17.00), Vittore Branca's "Boccaccio: The Man and His Works" (*New York Univ. Press* 1975 $19.50), Stravros Deligiorgis' "Narrative Intellection in the *Decameron*" (*Univ. of Iowa Press* 1974 $12.95), Thomas G. Bergin's translation of Petrarch's "Bucolicum Carmen" (*Yale Univ. Press* 1974 $15.00), Aldo Bernardo's version of Petrarch's *"Rerum Familiarium Libri* I–VIII" (*State Univ. of New York Press* 1975 $30.00), and Anthony Cassell's translation of Boccaccio's "The Corbaccio" (*Univ. of Illinois Press* 1975 $7.95).

The following lists contain works of a general cultural, literary, or historical character, including some monographs on individual authors for whom there are no translations in print, and anthologies of essentially literary texts.

HISTORY AND CRITICISM

Allen, Don Cameron. MYSTERIOUSLY MEANT: The Rediscovery of Pagan Symbolism and Allegorical Interpretation in the Renaissance. *Johns Hopkins Press* 1971 $16.00
  "A major scholarly contribution to Renaissance studies, without rival"—(*Choice*).

Baron, Hans. CRISIS OF THE EARLY ITALIAN RENAISSANCE: Civic Humanism and Republican Liberty in an Age of Classicism and Tyranny. *Princeton Univ. Press* rev. ed. 1966 $18.50 pap. $4.95

FROM PETRARCH TO LEONARDO BRUNI: Studies in Humanistic and Political Literature. *Univ. of Chicago Press* 1968 $12.00 pap. $3.25

HUMANISTIC AND POLITICAL LITERATURE IN FLORENCE AND VENICE AT THE BEGINNING OF THE QUATTROCENTO: Studies in Criticism and Chronology. 1955. *Russell & Russell* 1968 $9.50

Barzini, Luigi. FROM CAESAR TO THE MAFIA. *Open Court* 1971 $8.95

THE ITALIANS. *Atheneum* 1964 $6.95; *Bantam* 1965 1972 pap. $1.25

"Barzini is a craftsman with words and an Italian; . . . a beautiful book about *cose all'italiana*, why they are the way they are. Highly recommended"—*(LJ)*.

Biasin, Gian-Paolo. LITERARY DISEASES: Theme and Metaphor in the Italian Novel. *Univ. of Texas Press* 1975 $10.95

Brown, Peter M. LIONARDO SALVIATI: A Critical Biography. *Oxford* 1974 $32.00

"Brown has provided the first biography of one of Renaissance Europe's major intellectual figures in the field of vernacular philology, and admirably measured and described the cultural climate in Florence during the last half of the 16th century, using Salviati as a barometer of tastes and tendencies"—*(Choice)*.

Bruckner, Gene. RENAISSANCE FLORENCE. *Wiley* 1969 pap. $5.95

THE SOCIETY OF RENAISSANCE FLORENCE: A Documentary Study. *Harper* 1972 Torchbks. pap. $3.95

Burckhardt, Jacob. THE CIVILIZATION OF THE RENAISSANCE IN ITALY. 1860. *Harper* Torchbks. 2 vols. Vol. 1 pap. $2.45 Vol. 2 pap. $1.95; *Peter Smith* 2 vols. set $11.00. Extremely important study which represents the first attempt to synthesize the period.

Burke, Peter. CULTURE AND SOCIETY IN RENAISSANCE ITALY, 1420–1540. *Scribner* 1972 $14.95. A fine contribution to the sociology of art and literature.

Cassirer, Ernst. THE INDIVIDUAL AND THE COSMOS IN RENAISSANCE SOCIETY. 1963. Trans. by Mario Domandi *Univ. of Pennsylvania Press* 1972 pap. $2.95

Cochrane, Eric, Ed. FLORENCE IN THE FORGOTTEN CENTURIES, 1527–1800: A History of Florence and the Florentines in the Age of the Grand Dukes. *Univ. of Chicago Press* 1973 $12.50

THE LATE ITALIAN RENAISSANCE, 1525–1630. *Harper* Torchbks. 1970 pap. $3.45; *Peter Smith* $6.00

Collison-Morley, Lacy. ITALY AFTER THE RENAISSANCE: Decadence and Display in the Seventeenth Century. 1930. *Russell & Russell* 1972 $19.00

Corrigan, Beatrice, Ed. ITALIAN POETS AND ENGLISH CRITICS, 1755–1859: A Collection of Critical Essays. *Univ. of Chicago Press* 1968 $10.50 pap. $3.45

Crane, Thomas Frederick. ITALIAN SOCIAL CUSTOMS OF THE SIXTEENTH CENTURY AND THEIR INFLUENCE ON THE LITERATURES OF EUROPE. 1920. *Russell & Russell* 1971 $20.00

Dolci, Danilo. REPORT FROM PALERMO. Trans. by P. D. Cummins *Viking* 1970 pap. $2.45. Dolci, the great Italian reformer and battler against the Mafia exploitation of the poor in Sicily, won the Lenin Peace Prize in 1958 and was nominated in 1967 for the Nobel Prize.

Dole, Nathan H. A TEACHER OF DANTE AND OTHER STUDIES IN ITALIAN LITERATURE. 1908. *Bks. for Libraries* $10.00

Donadoni, Eugenio. HISTORY OF ITALIAN LITERATURE. Trans. by Richard Monges *New York Univ. Press* 2 vols. 1969 set $17.50 pap. set $6.95

Duchartre, Pierre Louis. THE ITALIAN COMEDY: The Improvisation, Scenarios, Lives, Attributes, Portraits and Masks of the Illustrious Characters of the Commedia dell'Arte. *Dover* rev. ed. 1967 pap. $5.00; *Peter Smith* $8.75

Emerton, E. HUMANISM AND TYRANNY: Studies in the Italian Trecento. *Peter Smith* $5.50

Foligno, Cesare. EPOCHS OF ITALIAN LITERATURE. 1920. *Kennikat* 1970 $5.00

Gage, John. LIFE IN ITALY AT THE TIME OF THE MEDICI. Ed. by Peter Quennell *Putnam* 1968 $5.60 Capricorn 1970 pap. $2.45

Gardner, Edmund G. THE ARTHURIAN LEGEND IN ITALIAN LITERATURE. 1930. *Octagon* 1970 $14.00

DUKES AND POETS IN FERRARA: A Study in the Poetry, Religion and Poetics of the 15th and Early 16th Centuries. 1904. *Haskell* 1969 $24.95; *Scholarly Press* 1972 $29.50

ITALIAN LITERATURE. 1928. *Richard West* $10.00

Garin, Eugenio. PORTRAITS FROM THE QUATTROCENTO. Trans. by V. A. and E. Velen *Harper* 1972 $3.95. Includes portraits of Ficino, Poliziano, Pico della Mirandola, Savonarola, and others.

SCIENCE AND CIVIC LIFE IN THE ITALIAN RENAISSANCE. Trans. by Peter Munz *Peter Smith* $4.75

Garnett, Richard. A HISTORY OF ITALIAN LITERATURE. 1898. *Kennikat* 1970 $13.50; *Richard West* 1973 $20.00

Gilmore, Myron P. WORLD OF HUMANISM, 1453–1517. 1952. *Harper* Torchbks. pap. $2.25

Grendler, Paul F. CRITICS OF THE ITALIAN WORLD, 1530–1560: Anton Francesco Doni, Nicolo Franco and Ortensio Lando. *Univ. of Wisconsin Press* 1969 $12.50

"A welcome addition to the very sparse materials in English relating to the decay, or decline, or crisis of the Italian Renaissance in the mid-16th century"—(*Choice*).

Grillo, Ernest. STUDIES IN MODERN ITALIAN LITERATURE. 1930. *Richard West* 1973 $25.00

Hall, Robert A., Jr. A SHORT HISTORY OF ITALIAN LITERATURE. 1951. *Richard West* $40.00

Hare, Christopher. LIFE AND LETTERS OF THE ITALIAN RENAISSANCE. *Haskell* 1974 $17.95

Hathaway, Baxter. THE AGE OF CRITICISM: The Late Renaissance in Italy. 1962. *Greenwood* 1972 $22.25. A scholarly consideration of literary theory from 1540 to 1613.

MARVELS AND COMMONPLACES: Renaissance Literary Criticism. *Philadelphia Bk. Co.* 1968 pap. $3.95

Herrick, Marvin T. ITALIAN COMEDY IN THE RENAISSANCE. *Univ. of Illinois Press* 1966 pap. $1.75; Essay Index Reprint Ser. *Bks. for Libraries* 1970 $12.25

(Comp. and ed.) ITALIAN PLAYS 1500–1700 IN THE UNIVERSITY OF ILLINOIS LIBRARY. *Univ. of Illinois Press* 1966 $5.75

Hyde, John K. SOCIETY AND POLITICS IN MEDIEVAL ITALY: The Evolution of the Civil Life 1000–1350. *St. Martin's* 1973 $13.95 pap. $4.95

"In a remarkable synthesis of scholarship, both old and recent, Hyde focuses on the development of civic life in Medieval Italy from its beginning to the establishment of the despotisms of the 14th century"—(*Choice*).

Larner, John. LORDS OF ROMAGNA: Romagnol Society and the Origin of the Signorie. *Cornell Univ. Press* 1966 $12.50

Lipari, Angelo. THE DOLCE STIL NUOVO ACCORDING TO LORENZO DE'MEDICI. 1936. *AMS Press* 1973 $17.50

Logan, Oliver. CULTURE AND SOCIETY IN VENICE, 1470–1790. Culture and Society *Scribner* 1972 $12.50. Well-documented study of Venice from the Renaissance to the second "Golden Age" of the 18th century.

McLeod, Addison. PLAYS AND PLAYERS IN MODERN ITALY. 1912. *Kennikat* 1970 $13.00. Commentary on playwrights such as Butti, Rovetta, Rasi, Bracco, Benelli, and players such as Duse, Borelli, Galli, Salvini, Ruggieri, Falconi, Novelli, and Zacconi.

Miller, Frank J. STUDIES IN THE POETRY OF ITALY. 1913. *Richard West* 1973 $15.00

Mitchell, Bonner. ROME IN THE HIGH RENAISSANCE: The Age of Leo X. Centers of Civilization *Univ. of Oklahoma Press* 1973 $3.95. Covers the period 1503–1527 with emphasis on the papacy of Leo X.

Nichols, Peter. ITALIA, ITALIA. *Little* 1974 $8.95. Cultural account of post-war Italy and Italian life, especially in the sixties and early seventies. A good companion piece to Barzini's "The Italians" (*q.v.*).

Nolthenius, Helene. DUECENTO: The Late Middle Ages in Italy. *McGraw-Hill* 1969 $8.95

Owen, John. THE SKEPTICS OF THE ITALIAN RENAISSANCE. 1908. *Kennikat* 1970 $17.50; *Gordon Press* $35.00; *Richard West* $17.00

Pacifici, Sergio. A GUIDE TO CONTEMPORARY ITALIAN LITERATURE: From Futurism to Neorealism. *Southern Illinois Univ. Press* 1972 $7.00 pap. $2.95

THE MODERN ITALIAN NOVEL: From Capuana to Tozzi. Crosscurrents-Modern Critiques Ser. *Southern Illinois Univ. Press* 1973 $6.95

THE MODERN ITALIAN NOVEL: FROM MANZONI TO SVEVO. Pref. by Harry T. Moore. *Southern Illinois Univ. Press* 1967 $6.95

(Ed.) FROM VERISMO TO EXPERIMENTALISM: Essays on the Modern Italian Novel. *Indiana Univ. Press* 1970 $8.95 pap. $2.95

Praz, Mario. THE FLAMING HEART: Essays on Crashaw, Machiavelli, and Other Studies in the Relations between Italian and English Literature from Chaucer to T. S. Eliot. *Peter Smith* 1958 $5.50; *Norton* 1973 pap. $3.95

Procacci, Giuliano. HISTORY OF THE ITALIAN PEOPLE. Trans. by Anthony Paul *Harper* 1971 $10.95

Quinones, Riccardo. THE RENAISSANCE DISCOVERY OF TIME. *Harvard Univ. Press* Studies in Comparative Literature 1972 $16.00

"Superbly suggestive and intricate work in the Renaissance attitude towards its discovery of the 'doubleness' of time: caught in the promise of the present moment, man tends to forget its ephemeral nature. Fearing the 'all consuming' power of time, the Renaissance man seeks to conquer it by changing the present with meaningful activity"—(*Choice*). Sections on Dante and Petrarch.

Radcliffe-Umstead, Douglas. THE BIRTH OF MODERN COMEDY IN RENAISSANCE ITALY. *Univ. of Chicago Press* 1969 $12.50

Riccio, Peter. ITALIAN AUTHORS OF TODAY. 1938. *Bks. for Libraries* $10.25

Rice, Eugene F. THE RENAISSANCE IDEA OF WISDOM. 1958. *Greenwood* 1973 $12.50

Robb, Nesca A. NEOPLATONISM OF THE ITALIAN RENAISSANCE. *Octagon* 1968 $11.00

Ruggiers, Paul G. FLORENCE IN THE AGE OF DANTE. *Univ. of Oklahoma Press* 1964 1968 $3.95

"Small but elegantly written . . . a remarkably concise account"—(*LJ*).

Snell, F. J. PRIMER OF ITALIAN LITERATURE. 1893. *Richard West* 1973 $12.50

Sturm, Sara. LORENZO DE' MEDICI. World Authors Ser. *Twayne* 1974 $7.95

"The first book in English to attempt an overall view of Lorenzo de' Medici as man of letters . . . a clear presentation of Renaissance Florence's most enigmatic figure. . . ."—(*Choice*).

Symonds, John A. ITALIAN LITERATURE. *Putnam* Capricorn Bks. 2 vols. Vol. 1 From the Beginnings to Ariosto Vol. 2 From Ariosto to the Late Renaissance, pap. each $1.85; *Peter Smith* 2 vols. each $4.50

THE RENAISSANCE IN ITALY. *Peter Smith* 3 vols. Vol. 1 The Fine Arts Vol. 2 The Revival of Learning Vol. 3 The Age of Despots, each $6.50, set $19.50

Tedeschi, John. THE LITERATURE OF THE ITALIAN REFORMATION. *Newberry Lib.* 1971 pap. $1.25

Thayer, William R. ITALICA: Studies in Italian Life and Letters. 1908. *Richard West* 1973 $25.00

Trail, Florence. A HISTORY OF ITALIAN LITERATURE. 1903. *Haskell* 1972 $17.95; *Richard West* 1972 repr. of 1914 ed. $14.75

Trinkaus, Charles. ADVERSITY'S NOBLEMEN. Rev. ed. 1965. *Octagon* $9.00

IN OUR IMAGE AND LIKENESS. *Univ. of Chicago Press* 1970 2 vols. set $27.50

Venturi, Franco. ITALY AND THE ENLIGHTENMENT. *New York Univ. Press* 1973 $10.00

Vittorini, Domenico. THE MODERN ITALIAN NOVEL. 1930. *Russell & Russell* 1967 $8.50

Weinberg, Bernard. HISTORY OF LITERARY CRITICISM IN THE ITALIAN RENAISSANCE. *Univ. of Chicago Press* 1961 2 vols. pap. set $33.50

Weiss, Roberto. DAWN OF HUMANISM IN ITALY. 1947. *Haskell* 1970 $7.95

SPREAD OF ITALIAN HUMANISM. *Hillary House* 1964 $3.00

Whitfield, John H. A SHORT HISTORY OF ITALIAN LITERATURE. *Harper* (Barnes & Noble) 1962 $3.75. A Survey from Dante to Pirandello.

Wilkins, Ernest Hatch. A HISTORY OF ITALIAN LITERATURE. *Harvard Univ. Press* 1954 $13.50 rev. ed. by Thomas G. Bergin 1974 $15.00

COLLECTIONS

Bentley, Eric, Ed. THE CLASSIC THEATRE. Vol. 1 Six Italian Plays: The Mandrake (Machiavelli), Ruzzante Returns from the Wards (Beolco), The Three Cuckolds (Anon.), The King Stag (Gozzi), The Servant of Two Masters, and Mirandolina (Goldoni). *Doubleday* Anchor Bks. pap. $2.95; *Peter Smith* $5.50

Bond, Richard Warwick, Ed. EARLY PLAYS FROM THE ITALIAN. *Blom* 1967 $12.50. Includes Supposes (Ariosto), The Buggbears (Grazzini), Misogonus.

BOTTEGHE OSCURE. *Wesleyan Univ. Press* 1948–60 25 vols. Vols. 7, 8, 11–25 in print each $5.00. This international review, which ceased publication in the early 1960's, was very important to numerous young writers of various nationalities (English, Italian, French, etc.) in that it helped them launch their careers. Selections in the language of the original. (*See also below under Caetani and Garrett.*)

Caetani, Marguerite, Ed. ANTHOLOGY OF NEW ITALIAN WRITERS. 1950. *Greenwood* 1972 $18.75. Selections from the review *Botteghe Oscure* (*q.v.*).

Capocelli, Ginevra, Trans. and ed. THE OUTLOOK ON LIFE OF VARIOUS ITALIAN WRITERS. *William-Frederick Press* 1963 $4.00. Contains selections from Dante, Petrarch, Leonardo da Vinci, Leopardi, Croce, et al.

Cassirer, Ernst, Paul Oskar Kristeller and John Herman Randall, Jr., Eds. THE RENAISSANCE PHILOSOPHY OF MAN. *Univ. of Chicago Press* 1948 $12.50 Phoenix Bks. 1967 $3.45. Includes On His Own Ignorance (Petrarch), Dialogue on Free Will (Valla), Five Questions concerning the Mind (Ficino), Oration on the Dignity of Man (Pico della Mirandola), On the Immortality of the Soul (Pomponazzi), and others.

Corrigan, Robert, Ed. MASTERPIECES OF THE MODERN ITALIAN THEATER. *Macmillan* Collier Bks. 1967 pap. $1.50. Includes The Pleasure of Honesty and Six Characters in Search of an Author (Pirandello), Crime on Goat Island (Betti), Filumena Marturana (De Filippo), The Academy and The Return (Fratti).

Crane, Thomas Frederick, Trans. with commentary. ITALIAN POPULAR TALES. 1885. *Gale Research Co.* (Singing Tree Press) 1968 $12.50; *Gordon Press* $35.00

De Luca, A. Michael, and William Giuliano, Trans. and eds. SELECTIONS FROM ITALIAN POETRY. *Harvey House* 1966 $6.00. A good brief introduction to Italian verse with some 57 poems by poets from St. Francis to Quasimodo.

De' Lucchi, Lorna, Trans. and ed. ANTHOLOGY OF ITALIAN POEMS, 13TH–19TH CENTURY. 1922. *Biblo & Tannen* $12.50

Fulton, Robin, Trans. ITALIAN QUARTET: Versions after Saba, Ungaretti, Montale, Quasimodo. *Dufour* 1966 pap. $2.25

Garrett, George, Ed. with the assistance of Katherine Garrison Biddle. THE BOTTEGHE OSCURE READER. *Wesleyan Univ. Press* 1974 $12.50 pap. $2.95

Guercio, Francis M., Trans. and ed. ANTHOLOGY OF CONTEMPORARY ITALIAN PROSE. 1931. *Kennikat* 1970 $7.50

Howells, W. D. MODERN ITALIAN POETS: Essays and Versions. 1887. *Bks. for Libraries* 1972 $18.50; *Russell & Russell* 1973 $20.00. Includes translations from Alfieri, Parini, Monti, Foscolo, Manzoni, Leopardi, Giusti, and others.

Kennard, Joseph S. ITALIAN ROMANCE WRITERS. 1906. *Folcroft* 1973 $12.45; *Kennikat* $12.50

Lind, Levi Robert, Trans. and ed. TWENTIETH-CENTURY ITALIAN POETRY: A Bilingual Anthology. *Bobbs* Liberal Arts 1974 $8.95 pap. $5.95. Excellent introduction to modern Italian poetry.

Marchione, Margherita, Trans. and ed. TWENTIETH-CENTURY ITALIAN POETRY: A Bilingual Anthology. *Fairleigh Dickinson Univ. Press* 1974 $10.00 A collection of contemporary religious poetry.

PALACE OF PLEASURE. Trans. by William Painter. Ed. by Hamish Miles. 1929. *AMS Press* 4 vols. each $31.50 set $125.00; ed. by Joseph Jacobs *Dover* 1966 3 vols. pap. each $4.00. Includes *novelle* by Boccaccio, Bandello, et al.

Pasinetti, Pier M., Ed. GREAT ITALIAN SHORT STORIES. *Dell* 1959 pap. $.60

Rebay, Luciano, Trans. and ed. ITALIAN POETRY: A Selection from St. Francis of Assisi to Salvatore Quasimodo. *Dover* 1970 pap. $2.00; *Peter Smith* $4.50

Ross, James Bruce, and Mary Martin McLaughlin, Eds. THE PORTABLE RENAISSANCE READER. *Viking* 1953 $4.95 pap. $3.45. Includes the Italian and Northern Renaissance (c. 1350–1600).

Schevill, Ferdinand, Ed. THE FIRST CENTURY OF ITALIAN HUMANISM. 1928. *Gordon Press* $35.00; *Haskell* 1970 $6.95; *Russell & Russell* 1967 $5.00. Selections from Petrarch (Secretum and Letters), Boccaccio (Decameron), Salutati (Letters), Valla, Piccolomini, and others.

Smith, William Jay. POEMS FROM ITALY. *T. Y. Crowell* 1972 $4.50; *Apollo* 1974 pap. $2.45. This illustrated, bilingual anthology contains selections from all centuries of Italian literature.

Speroni, Charles, Trans. WIT AND WISDOM OF THE ITALIAN RENAISSANCE. *Univ. of California Press* 1964 $11.50. Selections from Bracciolini, Poliziano, Leonardo da Vinci, Castiglione, and others.

Thompson, David, and Alan F. Nagel, Trans. THE THREE CROWNS OF ITALY: Humanist Assessments of Dante, Petrarca and Boccaccio. *Harper* Torchbks. 1972 pap. $2.95. Selections from Salutati, Bruni, Landino, Bembo, and others.

THREE RENAISSANCE CLASSICS. Introd. and notes by Burton A. Milligan *Scribner* Lyceum Ed. 1971 pap. $3.95. Includes Machiavelli's The Prince and Castiglione's The Courtier.

Trevelyan, Raleigh, Ed. ITALIAN SHORT STORIES. *Penguin* 1965 pap. $1.25. Includes Pratolini, Pavese, Moravia, Soldati, Ginzburg, Gadda, Cassola, and Calvino.

Tusiani, Joseph, Trans. THE AGE OF DANTE: An Anthology of Early Italian Poetry. *Baroque Press* 1973 $12.50

FROM MARINO TO MARINETTI: An Anthology of Forty Poets. *Baroque Press* 1973 $17.50

ITALIAN POETS OF THE RENAISSANCE. *Baroque Press* 1971 $12.50

LITERATURE BEFORE DANTE 1200–1300

Beginning with the Sicilian poets at the court of Frederick II (*q.v.*) at Palermo, Italian literature (especially lyric poetry) gradually developed in the course of the 13th century, passing through the so-called Guittonian phase (after the poet Guittone d'Arezzo) and through the *Dolce Stil Nuovo* ("Sweet New Style"), as exemplified in the verses of the two Guidos: Guinizzelli and Cavalcanti (*q.v.*), finally concluding with the sublime poetry of Dante (*q.v.*). In addition to the courtly lyric which celebrates the love of a noble lady (based in part on the Provençal notion of *fin'amors* and gradually becoming more spiritualized), there are several areas of literary production in Italy during this century, among which are religious, popular and bourgeois lyrics and longer narrative poems, original prose romances and *novelle,* and a large number of translations into Italian from other literatures, especially Latin and Old French. The relatively few works available in English translation reflect, nevertheless, a good many aspects of this richly varied period: from religious treatises to love poetry to the epic tales of Troy and the adventures in the Far East of Marco Polo to the homely, often crude verses of Cecco Angiolieri. Useful general collections are: "German and Italian Lyrics of the Middle Ages: An Anthology and a History," trans. by Frederick Goldin (*Doubleday* Anchor Bks. 1973 pap. $4.95), which presents lyrics with translations of some 15 poets with interesting introductory essays for the major figures (Guittone, Guinizzelli, Cavalcanti, and Dante); and "The Age of Dante: An Anthology of Early Italian Poetry," trans. by Joseph Tusiani (*Baroque Press* 1973 $12.50).

INNOCENT III, POPE (Lothario dei Segni). 1160/61–1216.

As Pope from 1198 to 1216, he had complex dealings with Frederick II and other European monarchs and gave the Franciscan Order permission to teach and preach.

On the Misery of the Human Condition. Trans. by Margaret Mary Dietz *Bobbs Liberal Arts* 1969 $6.50 pap. $2.25

Two Views of Man: On the Misery of Man; On the Dignity of Man. With Giannozzo Manetti's treatise on the "Dignity of Man." Trans. by Bernard Murchland Milestones of Thought Ser. *Ungar* 1966 $4.75 pap. $1.45

ST. FRANCIS OF ASSISI. 1181/82–1226.

The founder of the Franciscan Order embraced poverty by renouncing all material possessions and loved the beauty of nature. We know of his many deeds through the popular 14th-century stories, the *Fioretti* ("Little Flowers"), which grew up to enhance his legend.

The Little Flowers of Saint Francis d'Assisi. Trans. by Thomas Okey *Dutton* Everyman's 1951 $3.95; trans. by Raphael Brown *Doubleday* 1971 pap. $1.95. Includes The Mirror of Perfection and The Life of St. Francis.

Books about St. Francis

Franciscan Poets of the Thirteenth Century. By Frederick Ozanam. Trans. and annotated by A. E. Nellen and N. C. Craig. 1914. *Kennikat* 1969 $11.00

Saint Francis of Assisi. By G. K. Chesterton. 1936. *Doubleday* 1957 pap. $1.45

Saint Francis, Nature Mystic: The Derivation and Significance of the Nature Stories in the Franciscan Legend. By Edward A. Armstrong. *Univ. of California Press* 1963 $13.50 pap. $3.95

Saint Francis of Assisi. By Thomas Celano. *Franciscan Herald Press* 1963 $11.95 pap. $3.25

Francis of Assisi. By John Holland Smith. *Scribner* 1972 $8.95

Saint Francis of Assisi. By Morris Bishop. *Little* 1974 $6.95

Saint Francis of Assisi. By Johann Jorgensen. *Doubleday* pap. $1.95

FREDERICK II (Friedrich von Hohenstaufen). 1194–1250.

Holy Roman Emperor, at whose cosmopolitan court in Sicily gathered intellectuals from Provence, Islam, Italy, and virtually all other parts of Europe. Referred to as the "Stupor mundi," he had many and diverse interests, one of which may be seen in his work on falconry, *"De arte venandi cum avibus."*

THE ART OF FALCONRY. Trans. and ed. by Casey A. Wood and Marjorie F. Fyfe *Stanford Univ. Press* 1943 $25.00

GUIDO DELLE COLONNE.   1210?–1287?

One of the poets in the Sicilian School at the court of Frederick II, Guido is the author of the Latin version of Benoît de Sainte-Maure's *"Roman de Troie."*

THE "GEST HYSTORIALE" OF THE DESTRUCTION OF TROY. 1874. *Kraus* $26.00

HISTORIA DESTRUCTIONIS TROIAE. Trans. by Mary Elizabeth Meek Humanities Ser. *Indiana Univ. Press* 1974 $12.50

CAVALCANTI, GUIDO.   1254–1300.

A member of the poetic school of the *Dolce Stil Nuovo* ("Sweet New Style"), Cavalcanti was a fellow Florentine and a close friend of Dante, who dedicated his *"Vita Nuova"* ("New Life") (*q.v.*) to him. Cavalcanti's lyrics may be divided into two main groups: those highly exuberant poems exalting his sensual love for a lady and those brooding, tragic compositions in which he laments the intellectual and physical torment induced by love.

TRANSLATIONS. Trans. by Ezra Pound. 1926. *New Directions* 1953 rev. ed. pap. $5.25. Cavalcanti's poems (sonnets, *canzoni*, and ballads) are found on pp. 17–141 in both the English and Italian texts. Especially interesting to see how Pound renders Cavalcanti, a poet with very similar tastes and sensibilities.

POLO, MARCO.   1254–1324.

One of the first and greatest of the early travelers, the Venetian-born Marco Polo began his fabled journey to China in 1270, met Kublai Khan in 1275, remained at his court for 17 years, and finally returned to Italy in 1294. In 1299–1300 he made public the account of his travels and adventures, complete with geographical and cultural observations of extreme interest then as now.

THE TRAVELS OF MARCO POLO. 1818. Trans. by William Marsden; ed. by T. Wright *AMS Press* 1968 $17.50; *Assoc. Booksellers* Airmont Bks. 1968 pap. $.60; (with title "The Most Noble and Famous Travels,") 1579. Trans. by John Frampton, ed. by N. M. Penzer *Da Capo* $31.50; *Dutton* Everyman's 1926 1954 $3.95; ed. by Manuel Komroff *Liveright* 1939 $6.95

CECCO ANGIOLIERI.   1260?–1312?

Born in Siena, Cecco is the author of some 150 sonnets, most of which are in the so-called comic-realistic vein.

THE SONNETS OF A HANDSOME AND WELL-MANNERED ROGUE. Trans. by Thomas Caldecot Chubb *Shoe String Press* 1970 $5.00. Well-translated sonnets of one of the more important minor, popular poets of the thirteenth century. Valuable for the light they shed on the age of Dante.

LITERATURE FROM DANTE TO MODERN TIMES

DANTE (originally Durante, Alighieri).   1265–1321.

The 700th anniversary of Dante's birth was celebrated in the spring of 1965 at Ravenna, following a pilgrimage from Florence—where St.-John Perse gave the opening address—of 18 international Dante scholars. The tribute lasted eight days and the American Robert J. Clements made the concluding talk, on Dante's contemporary significance. This he described as "a personal, rather than a social one. Ask just as easily, what is the value of a medieval cathedral, with its stone demons threatening hell and its rose windows promising heaven?"—(*SR*). Thomas Bergin has written (in "Perspectives on the Divine Comedy," *see below*): "Dante lives on—and will live— . . . because his poem discloses to us a fellow man, greater in intellectual range, deeper in strength of passion perhaps than most of us, and certainly more articulate, but for all that our kinsman—and with the aforesaid gifts, fit, as no other in our span of memory, to be our spokesman."

Santayana (*q.v.*) said that Dante's long epic poem "besides being a description of the other world is a dramatic view of human passions in this life; a history of Italy and of the world; a theory of Church and State; the autobiography of an exile; and the confessions of a Christian and of a lover." T. S. Eliot (*q.v.*) calls Dante "the great master of the simple style." "Linguistically Florentine, with borrowings from other dialects, it has been a major factor in the making of literary Italian." Dante called it a *"Commedia"* because of this homely diction and because it ended happily.

Its later 16th-century readers added the epithet *"Divina."* It is an account of the poet's journey through Hell and Purgatory accompanied by Virgil (*q.v.*) and through Paradise with his Beatrice, for whom the poem was written as a memorial.

Dante first met Beatrice Portinari, a Florentine noblewoman, about 1274, and his first book, *"La Vita Nuova"*("The New Life"), written in 1292, tells the story of his love. This collection of 31 poems, chiefly sonnets, with prose commentary has been translated by poets (such as Dante Gabriel Rossetti, Ralph Waldo Emerson) and scholars alike.

Dante married Gemma Donati in 1293 and became occupied with public affairs. After the uprising of the Black Guelphs (papists) the poet, as a White Guelph (supporter of the emperor and the merchant class) was fined and banished in 1302. He spent the rest of his life wandering through Italy and never returned to Florence. The "Divine Comedy" was composed during his exile (1302–1321).

THE DIVINE COMEDY (Hell, Purgatory and Paradise). 1302–1321.

Few authors enjoy the enduring fame of the Florentine poet, and indeed the volume of textual and interpretative criticism, in the form of editions and translations of his works and books, articles and commentaries on his literary production, has increased every year since 1965, the 700th anniversary of his birth (1265). The *"Divina Commedia,"* of course, attracts the greatest share of these scholarly contributions. Recently completed is Charles S. Singleton's monumental six-volume set of translation and commentary on Dante's *magnum opus (see below)*. Of these volumes Morton Bloomfield writes (in *Speculum* XLVIII, January 1973, p. 127): "With the publication of Singleton's edition of the *Divine Comedy*, we have in English the solid beginning of a truly scholarly edition which can at last vie with comparable ones in Italian and German. [This] monumental work . . . will be indispensable for all lovers of this masterpiece who wish to root it in its linguistic, historic, and social reality. Although we have had many translations of the *Comedy* since the eighteenth century, some of them notable re-creations, we have not really had a scholarly edition which aims at relative completeness of information about the language, ideas and background of the poem. This Professor Singleton has provided." Other recent translations include that of Mark Musa (*see below*), whose poetic ear has enabled him to render one of the more interesting and valid versions in the English language and that of Allan Gilbert (*see below*). Of the standard prose translations those of John Sinclair and Carlyle-Okey-Wicksteed are, after that of Singleton, the most faithful and, for the budget-minded student, the most economical. Among the numerous translations in verse it would be remiss not to mention those of Ciardi, Sayers and Tiller, the last of which represents the result of a very interesting experiment: each canto or group of cantos has been translated by a different modern poet and placed together in this composite volume.

Dante's meter is known as *terza rima*, triple rhyme. It consists of stanzas of three lines each, line 2 of each stanza rhyming with line 1 and 3 of the next stanza. Each line has 11 syllables—hendecasyllabic measure. As this measure was foreign to English prosody, early translators used various equivalents for it: blank verse, heroic couplets, quatrains and Spenserian stanzas. Modern translators, however, have rendered the original meter in English with increasing fidelity and the measure is now an accepted English form. Certain recent English versions attempt even Dante's feminine endings, many lines finishing with a participle.

Translations of "The Divine Comedy"

Carlyle, J. A., T. Okey, and P. H. Wicksteed. *Dutton* 3 vols. bilingual 1933 each $2.95; ed. by H. Oelsner *Random* Modern Lib. 1932 reissue 1950 $2.45 pap. $.95;introd. by C. H. Grandgent *Random* Vintage Bks. pap. $1.25

The *Dutton* is a new edition of the famous Temple Classics edition of 1899–1901 in three volumes. Carlyle translated the "Inferno," Okey the "Purgatorio," Wicksteed the "Paradiso." The prose of all three translators is of even rhythmic excellence.

Fletcher, Jefferson Butler. 1931. *Columbia* 4th ptg. 1951 $10.00

In rhymed tercets, unlinked, with the second verse blank, a translation that conveys the ruggedness, force and vigor of the original. It has the drawings which Botticelli made for the "Divine Comedy" between 1492 and 1495, lost until the 19th century and found in Scotland. The preface compares all the important translations of Dante.

Lockert, L. *Princeton Univ. Press* 1931 $8.50 (Inferno only)

Sinclair, John D. 1939–47. *Oxford* 3 vols. 1948 1961 pap. each $2.95

Prose translation with comment. The Italian text from the Società Dantesca Italiana text has been revised by G. Vandelli with Sinclair's very readable English prose on the opposite page. His translation adheres closely to the text and at the end of each canto he gives a few pages of notes and helpful interpretative comment.

Ciardi, John. *New Am. Lib.* Mentor Bks. 1954 1971 pap. $1.50 (Inferno); *New Am. Lib.* Mentor Bks. 1971 pap. $1.50 (Purgatorio)

Huse, H. R. *Holt* (Rinehart) 1954 1962 pap. $1.25. A new prose translation with introd. and notes. While omitting rhyme and meter, this version keeps Dante's short lines and tercets.

Sayers, Dorothy L. *Penguin* 3 vols. Vol. 1 Inferno 1955 pap. $1.65 Vol. 2 Purgatory 1956 pap. $1.65 Vol. 3 Paradise, trans. by Dorothy Sayers and Barbara Reynolds pap. $1.95

Bergin, Thomas G. 1955. *AHM Pub. Corp.* Crofts Class. pap. $1.95 individual vols. each $.95. A modern translation in verse; cut considerably.

Bickersteth, Geoffrey. 1965. *Rowman* bilingual ed. 1973 $17.50. Translation in the meter of the original.

Tiller, Terrance, Ed. *Schocken* 1967 $5.95 (Inferno only)

Gilbert, Allan H. *Duke Univ. Press* 1969 $13.50 (Inferno only)

Musa, Mark. (With title "Dante's Inferno") *Indiana Univ. Press* 1971 $8.50 pap $2.50

Singleton, Charles S. Bollingen Ser. *Princeton Univ. Press* 1970–1975 6 vols. set $90.00 (two volumes for each canticle, set $30.00 each)

Other Works

THE PORTABLE DANTE. Ed. by Paolo Milano *Viking* 1947 rev. ed. 1969 $5.50 pap. $3.50

"The Divine Comedy" in its entirety, translated by Laurence Binyon; the complete *"Vita Nuova"* ("The New Life") in Rossetti's version; and a selection from Dante's treatises on politics and language *"De Monarchia"* and *"De Vulgare Eloquentia,"* as well as from his "Rhymes" and his "Letters."

LA VITA NUOVA (The New Life). c. 1292. Trans. by Theodore Martin 1861 *Bks. for Libraries* Select Bibliographies Ser. $9.50; trans. by Mark Musa *Indiana Univ. Press* 1962 new ed. 1973 $8.50 pap. $2.50; trans. by Ralph Waldo Emerson *Johnson Reprint* 1960 $8.00; trans. by Barbara Reynolds *Penguin* 1964 pap. $1.25

DE MONARCHIA (Monarchy). 1310–1312. (With Title "On World Government") trans. by Herbert W. Schneider *Bobbs* Lib. Arts pap. $1.25; Library of War and Peace *Garland Pub.* $14.00; (no translator given) *Gordon Press* $9.75

THE LITERARY CRITICISM OF DANTE ALIGHIERI. Trans. and ed. by Robert S. Haller Regents Critics Ser. *Univ. of Nebraska Press* 1974 $11.00

"Dante's ideas on poetic art have been culled from his various Italian and Latin works (*De vulgari eloquentia, Convivio, Vita nuova, Commedia*, etc.) and are brought together for the first time in this little book which does a giant's job in helping modern students . . . to understand the immense task Dante set before him: the recognition and establishment of respect for a humanistic tradition in the vernacular culture of Europe"—(*Choice*).

ODES OF DANTE. Trans. by H. S. Vere-Hodge *Oxford* 1963 $7.00

DANTE'S LYRIC POETRY. Trans. and ed. by Kenelm Foster and Patrick Boyde *Oxford* 2 vols. bilingual ed. 1967 Vol. 1 The Poems Vol. 2 Commentary set $34.00

Books about Dante

Dante's Ten Heavens. By Edmund G. Gardner. 1898. *Bks for Libraries* Select Bibliographies Ser. $13.50 (repr. of 1900 ed.); *Haskell* 1970 $14.95; *Richard West* 1973 $12.75

Earliest Lives of Dante. By Giovanni Boccaccio and Lionardo B. Aretino. Trans. by James R. Smith. 1901. *Folcroft* $5.00; *Haskell* 1974 $9.95; *Russell & Russell* 1968 $5.00; *Ungar* $4.50 pap. $1.25

Dante and the Animal Kingdom. By Richard T. Holbrook. 1902. *AMS Press* $15.00

Dante and His Time. By Karl Federn. 1902. *Haskell* 1970 $16.95; *Kennikat* $10.50; *Richard West* 1973 $9.75

Dante Alighieri: His Life and Works. By Paget Toynbee. 1910. Ed. by Charles S. Singleton *Peter Smith* $5.50; *Richard West* $17.50

Dante and the Mystics: A Study of the Mystical Aspects of the Divine Comedy. By Edmund G. Gardner. 1913. *Haskell* 1969 $12.95; *Octagon* 1968 $9.00

Concise Dictionary of Proper Names and Notable Matters in the Works of Dante. By Paget Toynbee. 1914. *Phaeton Press* (dist. by Gordian) 1968 $9.00; 2nd ed. rev. by Charles S. Singleton *Oxford* 1968 $25.50. Invaluable reference tool.

Dante. By Jefferson B. Fletcher. 1916. *Richard West* $10.00; *Univ. of Notre Dame Press* 1965 $5.95 pap. $2.25

The Ladies of Dante's Lyrics. By C. H. Grandgent. 1917. *Gordon Press* $11.95

Dante. By C. H. Grandgent. 1921. *Folcroft* $30.00

Symbolism in the Divine Comedy. By Jefferson B. Fletcher. 1921. *AMS Press* $10.00

Dante: Essays in Commemoration, 1321–1921. Ed. by A. Cippico and others. 1921. *Bks. for Libraries* $9.75; *Haskell* 1970 $14.95; *Richard West* 1973 $8.75

The Poetry of Dante. By Benedetto Croce. 1922. *Gordian* $8.50

Dante. By Edmund G. Gardner. 1923. *Richard West* 1973 $25.00

Discourses on Dante. By C. H. Grandgent. 1924. *Russell & Russell* 1970 $9.00

Power of Dante. By C. H. Grandgent. 1924. *Folcroft* $17.50

Essays on the Vita Nuova. By James E. Shaw. 1929. *Kraus* pap. $13.00

Dante. By T. S. Eliot. 1929. *Haskell* 1974 $8.95

The Life of Dante. By Michele Barbi. Trans. and ed. by Paul G. Ruggiers. 1933. *Univ. of California Press* 1954 pap. $1.25; *Peter Smith* $3.50. This English translation appeared long after the first publication of the work, in Florence, in 1933. The volume is concise and authoritative, with a critical appraisal of the works.

Dante and Philosophy. By Étienne Gilson. Trans. by David Moore. 1949. *Peter Smith* $5.00

The Myth of Felt. By Leonardo Olschki. *Univ. of California Press* 1949 $4.75. An attempt to explain the allusion to the Veltro.

Handbook to Dante Studies. By Umberto Cosmo. 1950. *Folcroft* $17.50

Dante as a Political Thinker. By Alexander P. D'Entrèves. *Oxford* 1952 $3.00

Dante and the Legend of Rome. By Nancy Lenkeith. 1952. *Richard West* 1973 $30.00

Introductory Papers on Dante. By Dorothy Sayers. 1954. *Harper* (Barnes & Noble) 1969 $10.00

Dante Studies I—Commedia: Elements of Structure. By Charles S. Singleton. *Harvard Univ. Press* 1954 pap. $3.00

Dante and the Early Astronomers. By Mary E. Orr. 1956. *Kennikat* 1969 $11.00

De Sanctis on Dante. Trans. by Joseph Rossi and Alfred Galpin *Univ. of Wisconsin Press* 1957 $15.00

Further Papers on Dante. By Dorothy Sayers. 1957. *Harper* (Barnes & Noble) 1973 $11.50

Dante's Other World: The Purgatorio as Guide to the Divine Comedy. By Bernard Stambler. *New York Univ. Press* 1957 $8.95

Mediaeval Culture: An Introduction to Dante and His Times. By Karl Vossler. *Ungar* 2 vols. 1958 $17.50

Structure and Thought in the Paradiso. By Joseph A. Mazzeo. 1958. *Greenwood* 1968 $13.00

Medieval Cultural Tradition in Dante's Comedy. By Joseph A. Mazzeo. 1960. *Greenwood* 1968 $14.00

The Ladder of Vision: A Study of Dante's Comedy. By Irma Brandeis. 1960. *Univ. Place Book Shop* pap. $2.00

Dante, Poet of the Secular World. By Erich Auerbach. Trans. from the German by Ralph Manheim *Univ. of Chicago Press* 1961 $7.00 Phoenix Bks. 1974 pap. $2.95
A "classic study, first published in Germany in 1929 and newly translated into English, this provocative treatment contains notes and bibliographical references, which have been changed in form but not amended. No account is given of any recent Dante scholarship, which is far from static."

The Divine Comedy. Ed. by Irma Brandeis. *Heath* Discussions of Literature 1961 pap. $2.25

The Figure of Beatrice: A Study in Dante. By Charles Williams. 1961. *Octagon* 1973 $10.50

Dante and His Comedy. By Allan Gilbert. *New York Univ. Press* 1963 $7.50 pap. $1.95
An "extensive and penetrating study"—(*LJ*).

Dante into English: A Study of the Translation of the Divine Comedy in Britain and America. By William J. DeSua. 1964. *Johnson Reprint* $13.25

Essays on Dante. Ed. by Mark Musa. 1964. *Peter Smith* $4.50
Nine essays by distinguished American and European scholars. "Very significant Dante criticism"—(*LJ*).

Dante: A Collection of Critical Essays. Ed. by John Freccero. *Prentice-Hall* 1965 $6.50. Essays by the best-known Dante scholars, including Spitzer, T. S. Eliot, Singleton and Auerbach. With a chronology of Dante's life and a selected bibliography.
"Very useful"—(*Choice*).

Dante Alighieri: Three Lectures. By J. Chesley Mathews. *Richard West* 1965 $10.00

Centenary Essays on Dante. By the Oxford Dante Society. *Oxford* 1965 $7.00

Dante's Conception of Justice. By Allan H. Gilbert. 1965 *Gordon Press* $11.95

World of Dante: Six Studies in Language and Thought. Ed. by S. Bernard Chandler and Julius A. Molinaro. *Univ. of Toronto Press* 1966 $7.50

Dante. By Francis Fergusson. *Macmillan* 1966 $4.95

Dante's Fame Abroad, 1350–1850. By Werner P. Friederich. Studies in Comparative Literature *Univ. of North Carolina Press* 1966 pap. $12.00

The Mind of Dante. Ed. by Uberto Limentani. *Cambridge* 1966 $11.50

Castelvetro's Annotations to the Inferno: A New Perspective in 16th Century Criticism. By Robert C. Melzi. *Humanities Press* 1966 pap. $11.00

Events and Their Afterlife: The Dialectics of Christian Typology in the Bible and Dante. By A. C. Charity. *Cambridge* 1966 $14.50

Perspectives on the Divine Comedy. By Thomas G. Bergin. *Rutgers Univ. Press* 1967 $4.00; *Indiana Univ. Press* 1970 pap. $1.65

An "absorbing piece of criticism" (*LJ*), for the general reader as well as the student by the eminent translator of Dante and Sterling Professor of Romance Languages at Yale.

American Critical Essays on the Divine Comedy. Ed. with introd. by Robert J. Clements. *New York Univ. Press* 1967 $8.00 pap. $2.25. Sixteen essays for the serious student by such scholars as Erich Auerbach, Thomas Bergin, Charles Singleton, and the editor.

From Time to Eternity: Essays on Dante's Divine Comedy. Ed. by Thomas G. Bergin. *Yale Univ. Press* 1967 $8.75. Lectures given at Yale by various critics.

The Divine Comedy in English: A Critical Bibliography, Vol. 2, 1900–1966. By Gilbert F. Cunningham. *Harper* (Barnes & Noble) 1968 $7.50

Dante's Drama of the Mind: A Modern Reading of the Purgatorio. By Francis Fergusson. *Princeton Univ. Press* 1968 $9.00 pap. $2.95. An excellent interpretative study by an extremely intelligent and attentive reader of Dante.

A Diversity of Dante. By Thomas G. Bergin. *Rutgers Univ. Press* 1969 $6.00

Illuminated Manuscripts of the Divine Comedy. By Peter Brieger, Millard Meiss, and Charles S. Singleton. Bollingen Ser. *Princeton Univ. Press* 2 vols. 1969 set $50.00

Dante's Craft: Studies in Language and Style. By Glauco Cambon. *Univ. of Minnesota Press* 1969 $7.50

Allegory in Dante's Commedia. By Robert Hollander. *Princeton Univ. Press* 1969 $12.50

"The six closely reasoned essays and four appendices that comprise this study ally Hollander with the important critical approaches of C. S. Singleton and Erich Auerbach. He insists on the continuous validity for understanding the Commedia of Dante's own fourfold interpretation of allegory in the letter to Can Grande"—(*Choice*).

Dante's Style in His Lyric Poetry. By Patrick Boyde. *Cambridge* 1971 $18.50

This excellent work provides "scholars with finer tools for better calculating the immense contribution made by Dante to contemporary rhetorical custom and aesthetic practice. While accomplishing this, it renders many informative and invaluable insights on (medieval) poetry in expression"—(*Choice*).

Dante's Journey to the Center: Some Patterns in His Allegory. By Sheila Ralphs. *Harper* (Barnes & Noble) 1973 $3.75

Dante's Epic Journeys. By David Thompson. *Johns Hopkins Press* 1974 $4.95. Interesting study of the figure of Ulysses.

The Invention of Dante's Commedia. By John Demarey. *Yale Univ. Press* 1974 $12.50

The five essays in this volume "urge a more consciously literal reading of the Commedia than is congenial to some recent critics . . . who stress a basically fictional structure for Dante's journey. Demarey examines early accounts of pilgrimages that circled from Italy to Egypt, where the pilgrims reenacted the Exodus to Mr. Sinai, to Jerusalem, to Rome; he traces routes on pilgrimage maps and explores typological readings of scripture and of the world of nature"—(*Choice*).

Advent at the Gates: Dante's Comedy. By Mark Musa. *Indiana Univ. Press* 1974 $6.95

PETRARCH, FRANCESCO. 1304–1374.

Petrarch, in Italian literature surpassed only by Dante (*q.v.*), has been called the "first modern man of letters." One of the greatest humanists, he made Italian letters supreme in European literature. "*Le Rime*," written after 1327, and "The Triumphs" (c. 1352–1374) contain the lyrics for which he is most famous. These are mostly love poems inspired by Laura, a lovely lady whose identity he never revealed. To her he wrote one of the most beautiful collections of amorous verse in literature—366 odes, sonnets and lyrics. "Because of their concern with love and the ancient world [the] six 'Triumphs' became one of the most popular poems of the early Renaissance, for some time outshining both the 'Divine Comedy' and their author's own sonnets and canzoni."

In "Letters from Petrarch," as revealed by Morris Bishop, "[he] is the perfect 14th-century charmer. The style of his letters is exemplary of elegant informality"—(*N.Y. Times*).

Petrarch's influence as a lyric poet has been worldwide. The delicacy and technical excellence of his sonnets set the form for the English Elizabethan sonnet through the translations of Henry Howard, Earl of Surrey and Sir Thomas Wyatt.

SELECTED SONNETS, ODES AND LETTERS. Ed. by Thomas Goddard Bergin *AHM Pub. Corp.* Crofts Class. 1966 pap. $1.25

PETRARCH: A Reader. Ed. by David Thompson *Harper* Torchbks. 1971 pap. $2.95

PETRARCH'S BUCOLICUM CARMEN. 1346–1348. Trans. by Thomas G. Bergin *Yale Univ. Press* 1974 $15.00

"This authoritative first English translation of the eclogues represents a distinguished addition to recent treatments of the Latin works, as demonstrated by D. D. Carnicelli's edition of Lord Morley's Tryumphes of Fraunces Petrarcke.... An indispensable source book for Petrarch scholarship"—(*Choice*).

RERUM FAMILIARIUM LIBRI I–VIII. 1325–1356. Trans. by Aldo S. Bernardo *State Univ. of New York Press* 1975 $30.00. Masterful translation of the crucial first books of the *Familiari*. Indispensable for anyone intending to do serious scholarly work on Petrarch.

THE SONNETS OF PETRARCH. 1336–1374. Trans. by Thomas G. Bergin *Heritage Conn.* $11.95

LORD MORLEY'S TRYUMPHES OF FRAUNCES PETRARCKE: The First English Translation of the Trionfi. 1356–1374. Ed. by D. D. Carnicelli *Harvard Univ. Press* 1971 $12.00

"This first critical edition of Petrarch's *Trionfi* in Lord Morley's 16th-century translation will be welcomed by students of the history of translation and literary theory, as well as of Renaissance literature and iconography. Morley rendered Petrarch's *terza rima* by heroic couplets. He expanded the poem to almost half again its original length, and his translation abounds in errors, omissions, and additions, all painstakingly catalogued in Carnicelli's copious notes"—(*Choice*).

TESTAMENT. 1374. Trans. by Theodor E. Mommsen. 1957. *Burt Franklin* $14.50

PETRARCH'S SECRET, or the Soul's Conflict with Passion. 1341–1345. Trans. by William H. Draper. 1911. *Richard West* 1973 $25.00. Fundamental work for an understanding of Petrarch's inner conflict between his love for Laura and his desire for God.

LETTERS FROM PETRARCH. Trans. by Morris Bishop *Indiana Univ. Press* 1966 $6.95

Books about Petrarch

Petrarch the First Modern Scholar and Man of Letters. By James H. Robinson and Henry Winchester Rolfe. 1898. *Greenwood* repr. of 1914 ed. $19.75; *Haskell* 1970 $18.95; *Richard West* $14.95

Petrarch and the Ancient World. By Pierre de Nolhac. 1907. *Folcroft* $15.00

Petrarch: His Life and Times. By H. C. Hollway-Calthrop. 1907. *Cooper* 1972 $10.00; *Richard West* $9.75

Francesco Petrarca: Poet and Humanist. By Maud F. Jerrold. 1909. *Kennikat* 1970 $12.50; *Richard West* $12.25

Francesco Petrarch, the First Modern Man of Letters: Early Years and Lyric Poems. By Edward H. Tatham. 1925. *Richard West* 1973 $45.00

Petrarch and the Renascence. By John H. Whitfield. 1943. *Haskell* 1969 $11.95; *Russell & Russell* 1965 $7.50

Studies in the Life and Works of Petrarch. By Ernest Hatch Wilkins. *Mediaeval* 1955 $8.00

Petrarch's Eight Years in Milan. By Ernest Hatch Wilkins. *Mediaeval* 1958 $8.00

Petrarch's Later Years. By Ernest Hatch Wilkins. *Mediaeval* 1959 $8.00

Life of Petrarch. By Ernest Hatch Wilkins. *Univ. of Chicago Press* 1961 Phoenix Bks. 1963 pap. $1.95

"This historical biography ... may well be regarded by its eminent author as a fitting culmination of a long and fruitful period of scholarly work. Dr. Wilkins is internationally recognized as the great Petrarch scholar of [this century].... The chronologically fashioned account is capped by a portrait ... in which the author aptly describes him as one whose 'mind was amazingly inclusive.' ... highly readable and enjoyable"—(*LJ*).

Petrarch, Scipio, and the Africa: The Birth of Humanism's Dream. By Aldo S. Bernardo. *Johns Hopkins Press* 1962 $10.00

Petrarch and His World. By Morris Bishop. 1963. *Kennikat* 1973 $15.00
  Petrarch in his roles of poet, humanist, political commentator and advisor to popes and
  emperors. A "witty, unobtrusively scholarly biography"—(*LJ*).
The Icy Fire: Four Studies in European Petrarchism. By Leonard W. Forster. *Cambridge* 1969
  $8.00
Petrarch. By Thomas G. Bergin. World Authors Ser. *Twayne* $6.95. Excellent introduction to
  the life and works by the eminent Italianist.
Petrarch in America. By Michael Jasenas. *Pierpont Morgan Lib.* 1974 $10.00
Petrarch, Laura and the "Triumphs." By Aldo S. Bernardo. *State Univ. of New York Press* 1974
  $17.00. Brilliant, penetrating study by the eminent Petrarchist on the essentially humanistic
  inspiration that Laura provided to Petrarch.
Francis Petrarch, Six Centuries Later: A Symposium. Ed. by Aldo Scaglione. *Univ. of North
  Carolina* Studies in Romance Languages and Literatures and the *Newberry Lib.* 1975 price not
  available. Outstanding collection of some 24 essays by well-known scholars in the United
  States.

BOCCACCIO, GIOVANNI.   1313–1375.

Boccaccio as author of the "Decameron" is known as the father of classic Italian prose. He was
born in Certaldo, near Florence, but went to Naples when he was ten. His chief source of
inspiration, whom he called "Fiammetta" in his writings, was the illegitimate daughter of Robert
d'Anjou, King of Naples, whose court Boccaccio frequented. After he went to Florence, about
1340, he met and formed a close friendship with Petrarch, was sent on several diplomatic missions
and became a lecturer on Dante two years before his death.

THE DECAMERON. 1348–1353.

"The Decameron," meaning "Ten Days," is a collection of one hundred prose tales, supposed to
have been told in ten days by a party of ten young persons, seven ladies and three men, who had
fled from Florence to escape the plague of 1348. "Realistic, witty, popular and licentious, these
tales, often freely adapted from traditional material, represent a reaction against medieval
asceticism and vividly portray the society of 14th-century Italy"—(*Cassell's Encyclopedia of World
Literature*). Boccaccio's is the "Human Comedy" of Italian literature as Dante's (*q.v.*) is the "Divine
Comedy." "The Decameron," which introduced the novella as a literary form, has been a source of
plots for many great writers. Chaucer, Shakespeare, Dryden and Molière were among those who
borrowed from it freely. Its design as a whole suggested to Chaucer (*q.v.*) the plan of the
"Canterbury Tales." The first complete translation into English was made by John Payne for the
Villon Society in 1886.

TALES FROM THE DECAMERON. *Nelson-Hall* $2.95. Selections.

EARLY ENGLISH VERSIONS OF THE TALES . . . FROM THE DECAMERON. 1937 *Kraus* $12.00

Translations

Hutton, Edward. 1620. 1909. *AMS Press* 4 vols. each $15.00 set $60.00

Payne, John. 1842–1916. Introd. by Sir Walter Raleigh *Stravon* 2nd ed. 1952 $4.00

Aldington, Richard. Ill. by Rockwell Kent *Doubleday* 1949 $6.95; *Dell* pap. $.95

Rigg, J. M. *Dutton* Everyman's 2 vols. 1953 each $3.95 pap. $1.50

Winwar, Frances. *Random* Modern Lib. 1955 $2.95

McWilliam, G. H. Class. Ser. *Penguin* 1972 pap. $4.95

Other Works

THE FILOSTRATO. 1335. Trans. by N. E. Griffin and A. B. Myrick (bilingual); introd. by
  N. E. Griffin 1929 *Biblio & Tannen* 1967 $12.50; *Octagon* 1973 $16.00. Boccaccio's
  Filostrato served as the model for Chaucer's "Troilus and Criseyde."

THIRTEEN MOST PLEASANT AND DELECTABLE QUESTIONS OF LOVE ENTITLED A DISPORT
  OF DIVERSE AND NOBLE PERSONAGES (*Filocolo*). 1336. *Clarkson N. Potter* (dist. by Crown)
  1974 $7.95

"A modernized version of the English translation, first published in 1587 and then reprinted by
Peter Davies in London in 1927, of the most readable section of the *Filocolo*, Boccaccio's earliest
prose work in Italian"—(*Choice*).

THE BOOK OF THESEUS (*Teseida*). 1340–41. Trans. by Bernadette Marie McCoy *Medieval
  Text Assn.* 1974 $15.00 pap. $6.95

NYMPHS OF FIESOLE (*Ninfale Fiesolano*). 1340–45. Trans. by Joseph Tusiani *Fairleigh Dickinson Univ. Press* 1971 $9.50; (with title "The Nymph of Fiesole") trans. by Daniel J. Donno into prose with commentary 1969 *Greenwood* 1974 $9.25

AMOROUS FIAMMETTA. 1343–1344. Trans. by Bartholomew Young. 1926. *Greenwood* $15.25

BOCCACCIO ON POETRY. 1350–1375. *Bobbs* Liberal Arts 1956 $5.00 pap. $2.50. Being the preface and 14th and 15th books of Boccaccio's *Genealogia Deorum Gentilium* in an English version with introd. essay and commentary by Charles G. Osgood.

FATES OF ILLUSTRIOUS MEN. 1355–1374. Trans. and ed. by Louis B. Hall *Ungar* $7.00 pap. $1.95

THE CORBACCIO. 1355. Trans. and ed. by Anthony K. Cassell *Univ. of Illinois Press* 1975 $8.95. Excellent first English translation of this controversial work.

CONCERNING FAMOUS WOMEN (*De claris Mulieribus*). 1361–75. (With title "Forty-Six Lives") ed. by Herbert G. Wright *Oxford* 1943 $10.50; trans. by Guido Guarino *Rutgers Univ. Press* 1962 $7.50

Books about Boccaccio

Giovanni Boccaccio as Man and Author. By John A. Symonds. 1895. *AMS Press* $10.00; *Folcroft* 1973 $9.95

Origin and Development of Troilus and Criseyde. By Karl O. Young. 1908. *Gordian* 1968 $6.50 (*see above under Filostrato*)

The Decameron: Its Sources and Analogues. By A. Collingwood Lee. 1909. *Haskell* $16.95; *Richard West* 1973 $14.75

Giovanni Boccaccio. By Edward Hutton. 1910. *Richard West* $40.00

Indebtedness of Chaucer's Works to the Italian Works of Boccaccio. By Hubertis M. Cummings. 1916. *Folcroft* 1973 $5.75; *Haskell* 1969 $11.95; *Phaeton Press* (Dist. by Gordian) 1967 $6.50

Some Aspects of the Genius of Giovanni Boccaccio. By Edward Hutton. 1922. *Richard West* $4.00

Life of Giovanni Boccaccio. By Thomas C. Chubb. 1930. *Kennikat* 1969 $9.00

The Tranquil Heart: Portrait of Giovanni Boccaccio. By Catherine Carswell. 1937. *Richard West* 1973 $17.50

Chaucer's Troilus: A Study in Courtly Love. By Thomas A. Kirby. 1958 *Peter Smith* $5.00

Design in Chaucer's Troilus. By Sanford B. Meech. 1959 *Greenwood* $20.50

Narrative Intellection in the *Decameron*. By Stavros Deligiorgis. *Univ. of Iowa Press* 1975 $12.95

Boccaccio: The Man and His Works. By Vittore Branca. Trans. by Richard Monges; ed. by Dennis McAuliffe *New York Univ. Press* 1975 $19.50

ALBERTI, LEON BATTISTA.   1404–1472.

Born illegitimate in Genova, Alberti received his education first in Venice then in Padua (1415–1418) and finally at Bologna, where he obtained the degree in canonical law. He became what is today known as the "universal man of the Renaissance," demonstrating his vast culture and knowledge in various disciplines.

ON PAINTING. 1435–36. Trans. by John R. Spencer *Yale Univ. Press* 1966 pap. $1.95

LEON BATTISTA ALBERTI ON PAINTING AND ON SCULPTURE. Trans. by Cecil Grayson *Phaidon Press* (dist. by Gordian) 1972 $12.50

DELLA FAMIGLIA. 1437–41. Trans. by Guido Guarino *Bucknell Univ. Press* 1971 $12.00

THE FAMILY IN RENAISSANCE FLORENCE. Trans. by Renee Neu Watkins *Univ. of South Carolina Press* 1969 $14.95

Books about Alberti

Leon Battista Alberti: Universal Man of the Early Renaissance. By Joan Gadol. *Univ. of Chicago Press* 1969 $14.50 Phoenix 1973 $5.95

"Important to anyone interested in the cultural history of the Renaissance"—(*Choice*).

PICCOLOMINI, AENEAS SILVIUS (Pope Pius II).   1405–1464.

A member of the illustrious Sienese family, Piccolomini received an excellent humanistic education under Francesco Filelfo in Florence and became the private secretary of Emperor

Frederick III, who made him poet laureate. He was later bishop of Trieste and of Siena, becoming cardinal priest of St. Sabina in 1456 and Pope Pius II in 1458.

SELECTED LETTERS. Trans. by Albert R. Baca. Renaissance Editions Ser. *California State Univ.* 1969 $7.00 pap $5.00

LEONARDO DA VINCI. 1452–1519. *See Chapter 2, General Biography and Autobiography, Reader's Adviser, Vol. 3.*

SANNAZZARO, JACOPO. 1456–1530.

Neapolitan by birth, Sannazzaro wrote many poems in the Petrarchan mode, but his most famous and influential work is the *Arcadia*, a pastoral romance, in part autobiographical and in part allegorical, written in eclogues linked by prose narrative.

ARCADIA, and PISCATORIAL ECLOGUES. Trans. by Ralph Nash *Wayne State Univ. Press* 1966 $8.95

PICO DELLA MIRANDOLA, GIOVANNI. 1463–1494.

Important Renaissance philosopher and scholar, who was associated with the famous Platonic Academy in Florence.

OF BEING AND UNITY. 1491. Trans. by Victor M. Hamm *Marquette Univ. Press* 1943 pap. $2.00

ON THE IMAGINATION. Trans. by Harry Caplan. 1930. *Greenwood* $8.75

ORATION ON THE DIGNITY OF MAN. Trans. by Robert A. Caponigri *Regnery* 1956 pap. $.95

ON THE DIGNITY OF MAN. 1495–6. Trans. by Charles G. Wallis and others *Bobbs* Liberal Arts 1965 $6.00 pap. $2.25. Includes "On Being and the One" and "Heptaplus."

MACHIAVELLI, NICCOLO. 1469–1527.

It is ironic that Machiavelli the Florentine, born into a noble family of modest means, who thought of himself as a lover of liberty, justice and truth, should have given his name to all that is diabolical, unscrupulous and wily in politics. The legend grew up because he acknowledged in "The Prince" that, while a strong central state under one ruler was desirable, the man who would achieve such power must resort to disreputable means. Machiavelli wrote "The Prince" while banished, in an attempt to ingratiate the Medici. Because of the democratic views stated in his "Discourses on Livy" (1513–1521), it is now thought that he intended the established monarchy merely as a first step toward a sound republic. He has been called the "first realist in politics."

Celebrated in his own day for his patriotism, military skill, historical and political studies, the statesman also wrote popular plays. "Mandragola" is one of the most distinguished comedies of the Italian Renaissance.

"Machiavelli reveals many facets of the Renaissance humanist: as a government official he was primarily interested in the worldly prosperity of Italian cities; as a Florentine gentleman and playwright he viewed life as a source of pleasure and took no interest in asceticism; as a historian he paid no attention to the teachings of the Church Fathers nor to the webs of the scholastics, but sought the solution for political problems not in moral laws but in a study of historical experience and current events"—*(The Reader's Companion to World Literature).*

THE CHIEF WORKS OF MACHIAVELLI AND OTHERS. Trans. and ed. by Allan H. Gilbert *Duke Univ. Press* 3 vols. 1964 set $50.00

THE PRINCE (*Il Principe*). Written 1513, first pub. 1532. Trans and ed. by Thomas G. Bergin *AHM Pub. Corp.* Crofts Class. 1947 pap. $.85; *Assoc. Booksellers* Airmont pap. $.60; (and "Selected Discourses") trans. by Daniel Donno *Bantam* pap. $.95; ed. by James Atkinson *Bobbs* (in prep.); (and "The Life of Castruccio Castracani of Lucca; The Means Duke Valentine Us'd to Put to Death Vitellozzo Vitelli, Oliverotto of Fermo, Paul, and the Duke of Gravina") trans. by Edward Dacres *British Bk. Centre* 1974 $16.95 pap. $6.95; *Dutton* Everyman's $3.95; (and "Other Works") trans. by Alan H. Gilbert *Hendricks House* 1964 $3.50 pap. $1.95; *New Am. Lib.* Mentor 1952 $.75; trans. by Luigi Ricci *Oxford* World's Class. 1906 $2.00; trans. by George Bull Classics Ser. *Penguin* 1961 pap. $1.25; (and the "Discourses") trans. by Luigi Ricci *Random* (Modern Lib.) pap. $2.95; ed. by Mark Musa *St. Martin's* 1964 pap. $3.95; *Simon & Schuster* (Washington Square) pap. $.75

THE HISTORY, POLITICAL AND DIPLOMATIC WRITINGS OF NICCOLO MACHIAVELLI. *Gordon Press* 4 vols. set $140.00

THE DISCOURSES. 1513. Trans. by Leslie J. Walker Rare Masterpieces of Philosophy and Science Ser. *Routledge & Kegan Paul* 2 vols. 1950 set $45.00; ed. by Bernard Crick *Peter Smith* $5.50

MANDRAGOLA (The Mandrake). 1518? Trans. by Anne and Henry Paolucci *Bobbs* Liberal Arts 1957 pap. $1.50. A five-act comedy.

THE ART OF WAR. 1519–20. Trans. by Peter Whitehorne (1560) *AMS Press* $15.00 (includes "The Prince" trans. by Edward Dacres 1640); trans. by Ellis Farnseworth *Bobbs* Liberal Arts rev. ed. 1965 $6.50 pap. $3.50

CLIZIA. 1525. Trans. by Oliver Evans *Barron's* 1962 $4.25 pap. $1.50

THE HISTORY OF FLORENCE (1532) AND OF THE AFFAIRS OF ITALY. Trans. by T. Bedingfeld (1595) 1905. (With title "The Florentine History") *AMS Press* $15.00; *Peter Smith* $7.50

THE LETTERS OF MACHIAVELLI. Ed. by Allan H. Gilbert *Putnam* Capricorn Bks. 1961 pap. $1.65

Books about Machiavelli

Machiavelli and the Elizabethans. By Mario Praz. 1928. *Folcroft* $5.00

The Life and Times of Niccolo Machiavelli. By Pasquale Villari. 1892. 1929. Trans. by Linda Villari *Greenwood* 2 vols. 1968 repr. of 1892 ed. set $34.75; *Haskell* 1969 repr. of 1892 ed. $43.95; *Scholarly Press* 2 vols. 1972 repr. of 1929 ed. set $25.00; *Richard West* 2 vols. 1973 repr. of 1929 ed. set $33.75

Statecraft of Machiavelli. By Herbert Butterfield. 1940 *Macmillan* Collier Bks. 1962 pap. $.95

Machiavelli. By John H. Whitfield. 1947. *Russell & Russell* 1965 $7.50

Machiavelli: Cynic, Patriot, or Political Scientist. By DeLamar Jensen. *Heath* 1960 pap. $2.50

Machiavelli and Renaissance Italy. By John R. Hale. *Verry* 1961 $5.50; *Macmillan* Collier Bks. 1963 pap. $.95

English Face of Machiavelli. By Felix Raab. *Univ. of Toronto Press* 1964 $12.50

Machiavelli and Guicciardini: Politics and History in Sixteenth-Century Florence. By Felix Gilbert. *Princeton Univ. Press* $11.50

Machiavelli. By Giuseppe Prezzolini. Trans. by Gioconda Savini *Farrar, Straus* 1967 $8.50 "Fictional Machiavellis are not yet dead, for Guiseppe Prezzolini presents one in the book under review. Ignoring most post-war scholarship, Prezzolini sees Machiavelli as anti-christian and atheistical, believing in nothing save amoral political force"—(*N.Y. Review of Books*). "The author, who is a professor emeritus of Italian literature at Columbia University, has compiled much information about the subject and his writings [but] one must search elsewhere for a sensitive examination of Machiavelli's life or influence. However, in spite of criticism, many holdings would profit by purchasing this book"—(*LJ*).

Machiavelli and the Renaissance. By Federico Chabod. Trans. by David Moore *Harper* Torchbks. pap. $2.75

Machiavelli and the United States. By Anthony J. Pansini. *Greenvale Press* 6 vols. in one 1969 $20.00

Discourses on Machiavelli. By John H. Whitfield. *Saifer* 1969 $10.00

Thoughts on Machiavelli. By Leo Strauss. *Univ. of Washington Press* 1969 $7.95 pap. $2.95

Machiavelli: A Dissection. By Sidney Anglo. *Harcourt* 1970 $7.95 pap. $2.85

Political Calculus: Essays on Machiavelli's Philosophy. Ed. by Anthony Parel. *Univ. of Toronto Press* 1972 $10.00. Essays presented during the International Machiavelli Symposium held in honor of the 500th anniversary of his birth (1469–1969).

Machiavelli and the Nature of Political Thought. Ed. by Martin Fleisher. *Atheneum* 1972 $10.00 pap. $4.95

Vision of Politics on the Eve of the Reformation: More, Machiavelli, Syssel. By J. H. Hexter. *Basic Bks.* 1972 $9.50

Machiavelli. By John Plamanatz. *Harper* Torchbks. 1973 pap. $3.95

Corruption, Conflict, and Power in the Works and Times of Niccolo Machiavelli. By Alfredo Bonadeo. Pub. in Modern Philology *Univ. of California Press* 1973 pap. $4.25

The Prince: An Analysis of Machiavelli's Treatise on Power Politics. By Jean-Pierre Barricelli. *Barron's* 1974 pap. $1.95

Machiavelli and the Art of Renaissance History. By Peter E. Bondanella. *Wayne State Univ. Press* 1974 $10.95

The Machiavellian Moment: Florentine Political Thought and the Atlantic Republican Tradition. By J. G. Pocock. *Princeton Univ. Press* 1975 $22.50

BEMBO, PIETRO.   1470–1547.

A cardinal and scholar, Bembo was very influential in the *cinquecento*, especially for his views on language, as expressed in the *"Prose della volgar lingua"* (1525). In the *"Asolani,"* which was dedicated to Lucrezia Borgia, he discusses platonic love, using the same argument that he presents in his role as a character in Castiglione's "Courtier" (*q.v.*).

GLI ASOLANI. 1505. Trans. by Rudolf B. Gottfried 1954 *Bks. for Libraries* 1971 $11.25

ARIOSTO, LUDOVICO.   1474–1533.

"Orlando Furioso," the masterpiece of a courtier, statesman and country gentleman, is perhaps the major literary achievement of the Italian Renaissance—the greatest of the poetic romances. Based on a romance of chivalry, it is written in *ottava rima*. Within a half century of his death Ariosto's poem was translated into a dozen languages. Its popularity and significance are indicated also by the fact that Cervantes (*q.v.*) mentions its Spanish translation in "Don Quixote" (1605), and that it was one of the influences on Edmund Spenser's (*q.v.*) "Faerie Queene" (1590–1595).

"Although *Orlando furioso* is perhaps the most important literary achievement of the Italian Renaissance, it has not, in any of the several translations, enjoyed the success or popularity among English readers that it so richly deserves. To be sure, there are innumerable and formidable difficulties involved in rendering an accurate yet not banal, a modern yet not colloquial, version of this monumental poem"—(*Choice*).

ORLANDO FURIOSO. 1516–32. Trans. by Sir John Harrington. 1591. Ed. by Rudolf Gottfried *Indiana Univ. Press* 1963 Midland pap. $2.95; ed. by Robert McNulty *Oxford* 1972 $41.00; *Peter Smith* $5.25; ed. by Graham Hough *Southern Illinois Univ. Press* 1963 $30.00

With McNulty's version "We finally have a scholarly edition of Sir John Harrington's free translation-paraphrase in strict 'heroical' octaves of the *Orlando furioso*.... The editor sensibly bases his on the first (1591) edition and consigns variants from two extant manuscripts and two later editions to the footnote apparatus, which does not detract from the high readability of the text. The allegories are sometimes informative, often amusing, always illustrative of Elizabethan culture in its native treatment of the foreign. This is also true of Harrington's sprightly prefatory 'Defense of poesie,' heavily dependent on Sidney, and his personal defense of his own undertaking"—(*Choice*).

Trans. by William Stewart Rose; ed. by Stewart A. Baker and A. Bartlett Giamatti Library of Literature Ser. *Bobbs* 1968 $15.00 pap. $7.50. Early 19th-century version in rhyming octaves with a good, informative introduction.

Trans. by Guido Waldman *Oxford* 1974 $19.25 pap. $5.95

"Waldman's complete and very readable prose translation, which faithfully captures all of the narrative line and much of the magic and majesty of the *Furioso*, renders an invaluable service to students and scholars, and especially to the general readership"—(*Choice*).

Trans. by Barbara Reynolds *Penguin* 1975 vol. 1 $5.95

"This long-awaited version of Reynold's in rhymed-verse octaves is most welcome: it is lucid, lively and eminently readable and, one hopes, will assure greater appreciation for a masterwork long neglected in the English-speaking world"—(*Choice*).

THE COMEDIES OF ARIOSTO. Trans. and ed. by Edmond M. Beame and Leonard G. Sbrocchi *Univ. of Chicago Press* 1974 $19.50

"Ariosto's comedies are among the earliest examples of secular theater in the vernacular, and for their historical significance alone deserve a wider audience; thus the translators and editors of the present volume have done an admirable service for students of theater history"—(*Choice*).

ARIOSTO'S SATIRES. Trans. by Peter DeSa Wiggins *Ohio Univ. Press* 1974 $9.00

Books about Ariosto

King of the Court Poets: A Study of the Work, Life and Times of Lodovico Ariosto. By Edmund G. Gardner. 1906. *Greenwood* $13.75; *Haskell* 1969 $18.95

Ariosto, Shakespeare and Corneille. By Benedetto Croce. Trans. by Douglas Ainslie. 1920. *Russell & Russell* 1966 $10.00

Spenser's Use of Ariosto for Allegory. By Susannah J. McMurphy. 1924. *Folcroft* $6.50

The Influence of Ariosto's Epic and Lyric Poetry on Ronsard and His Group. By Alice Cameron. 1930. *Johnson Reprint* 1973 $14.00

Ludovico Ariosto. By Robert Griffin. World Authors Ser. *Twayne* 1974 $6.95

MICHELANGELO (BUONARROTI). 1475–1564.

Michelangelo is, of course, far better known for his paintings (e.g. the ceiling of the Sistine Chapel in Rome) and his sculptures (e.g. "David," "Moses," "Pietà") than for his literary works. But they offer still further proof, it proof were needed, of the range and profundity of his genius.

THE COMPLETE POEMS AND SELECTED LETTERS OF MICHELANGELO. Trans. with fwd. and notes by Creighton Gilbert; ed. and with biographical introd. by Robert N. Linscott *Random* 1963 $5.95

The poems, "which can be construed as a spiritual autobiography of the artist, are the principal part of this work. The letters and the biography included in the same volume have the merit of adding substance to their spirit. In his translations, Gilbert has sacrificed rime in order to be faithful to the meaning of the poems, which he has translated phrase by phrase in their original beat . . . What is lost in rime, however, is compensated for by the preservation of Michelangelo's imagery . . . Recommended for academic and public libraries"—(*LJ*).

THE SONNETS OF MICHELANGELO. Trans. by Elizabeth Jennings *Doubleday* 1970 $3.95

"Students of the master painter-poet will do better to search out "Complete Poems of Michelangelo" (1970) (*q.v.*) edited by Joseph Tusiani for a truer interpretation and recreation of the genius' thoughts"—(*Choice*).

THE COMPLETE POEMS OF MICHELANGELO. Trans. with introd. by Joseph Tusiani. 1960. *Humanities Press* 1969 $6.50. A new translation including, for the first time, not only all the sonnets and madrigals, but all the lyric poems.

THE LETTERS OF MICHELANGELO. Trans., ed. and annot. by E. H. Ramsden *Stanford Univ. Press* 2 vols. 1963 boxed $45.00

The poet, painter, sculptor, architect, in his own day called "divine," embodied the Italian Renaissance. "As a poet he reflects the petrarchism and neo-platonism of his age but the vigour and originality of his expression give his poems an authentic Michelangelesque quality. His letters are of a comparable spontaneity and vividness"—(Barbara Reynolds). A beautiful edition, carefully annotated.

I, MICHELANGELO, SCULPTOR: An Autobiography through Letters. Trans. by Charles Speroni; ed. by Irving and Jean Stone *New Am. Lib.* Signet pap. $.95. Michelangelo's letters newly arranged and annotated, interspersed with relevant sonnets.

Books about Michelangelo

Michelangelo: His Life, His Times, His Era. By Georg Brandes. Trans. by Heinz Norden. 1921. *Ungar* 1967 $12.00

Michelangelo. By C. I. DeTolnay. *Princeton Univ. Press* 6 vols. Vol. I Youth of Michelangelo 1943 rev. 1947 1969; Vol. 2 Sistine Ceiling 1945 1969; Vol. 3 Medici Chapel 1948 1970; Vol. 4 The Tomb of Julius II 1954 1970; Vol. 5 The Last Judgment 1960 1970; Vol. 6 Michelangelo as Poet and Architect 1960 in prep. each $40.00.

This is a "monumental work of scholarship," a most unusual type of biography that "includes and examines every fact of an artist's life; that relates his life to his art and his art to his time, to our times, and to timelessness . . ."—(*N.Y. Times*). "One of the major critical biographies in the literature of art"—(*LJ*).

Michelangelo's Theory of Art. By Robert J. Clements. *New York Univ. Press* 1961 $12.50

"From the poetry and letters . . . from his recorded conversations, from contemporary biographies, and from his art, Professor Clements . . . has reconstructed the artist's theory of art, and perhaps of greater significance, has placed that theory in context with the thinking of the Renaissance . . . The result is a major contribution to literature on the Renaissance and on Michelangelo"—(*LJ*).

The Poetry of Michelangelo. By Robert J. Clements. *New York Univ. Press* 1965 $10.00 pap. $3.95

This study, which includes many translated quotations from his poems, does much to explain the man and his work. "Highly recommended"— (*LJ*).

Michelangelo. By Creighton Gilbert. Color Slide Program of the Great Masters Ser. *McGraw-Hill* 1967 $8.95

Michelangelo: A Self-Portrait: Texts and Sources. Ed. by Robert J. Clements. *New York Univ. Press* 1968 $8.50

Michelangelo. By Rolf Schott. *Scribner* 1973 pap. $3.95

Michelangelo. By Howard Hibbard. *Harper* 1975 $10.00

CASTIGLIONE, BALDASSARE, Conte.   1478–1529.

"The Book of the Courtier," a manual of gracious living written in dialogue, defines the ideal of aristocratic Renaissance society. The speakers—actual, well-known humanists—discuss with urbanity and dignity, every aspect of the life of an ideal aristocratic gentleman, not disdaining anecdote and witty repartee. Attached to the courts of Milan and Urbino, Castiglione exemplified in his own handsome, intelligent person this ideal courtier. His treatise was immensely popular: there were 50 Italian editions in the 16th century alone and it was translated into the principal languages of Europe. Sir Thomas Hoby made the first English translation (1561)—one which influenced Sir Philip Sidney, Spenser, Shakespeare and Milton, and which Samuel Johnson called "the best book that was ever written upon good breeding."

THE BOOK OF THE COURTIER. 1528. 1900. Trans. by Sir Thomas Hoby *AMS Press* $15.00; trans. by Charles S. Singleton *Doubleday* Anchor Bks. 1959 pap. $2.45; trans. by Sir Thomas Hoby *Dutton* 1975 $4.95; trans. by L. E. Opdyke and John Warrington 1928. University Library Ser. *Rowman* 1974 $10.00; trans. by Friench Simpson *Ungar* 1959 $4.50 pap. $1.75

Books about Castiglione

Baldassare Castiglione: The Perfect Courtier, His Life and Letters, 1478–1529. By Julia M. Ady. 1908. *AMS Press* 2 vols. set $42.50

GUICCIARDINI, FRANCESCO.   1483–1540.

Guicciardini was an important Florentine historian and statesman, whose works provide a well-documented and, in many cases, critical eye-witness account of contemporary events.

THE HISTORY OF FLORENCE. 1509. Trans. by Mario Domandi *Harper* 1970 $9.00 Torchbks. pap. $3.75

THE HISTORY OF ITALY. 1561. Trans. by Sidney Alexander *Macmillan* Collier Bks. pap. $3.95

MAXIMS AND REFLECTIONS OF A RENAISSANCE STATESMAN. 1576. Trans. by Mario Domandi *Univ. of Pennsylvania Press* 1972 pap. $2.25; *Peter Smith* $5.50

BANDELLO, MATTEO.   1485–1561.

Bandello had great influence on the literary production in Spain, France and England. His *"Novelle"* (1554–73), reminiscent of Boccaccio's *"Decameron"* (q.v.), was translated into French by François de Belleforest and into English by Geoffrey Fenton.

CERTAIN TRAGICAL DISCOURSES OF BANDELLO. Trans. by Geoffrey Fenton. 1567. *AMS Press* 2 vols. each $15.00. Translations from Belleforest's *"Histoires Tragiques"* (1559).

TRAGICAL TALES. Trans. by Geoffrey Fenton; ed. by Hugh Harris. 1923. *Greenwood* $20.00

ARETINO, PIETRO.   1492–1556.

This colorful Renaissance writer and dramatist, described as the first journalist of his century, was probably the son of a cobbler, although he preferred to claim that he was illegitimate, of noble origin. He first achieved notoriety for satirical verses extolling his patron Giulio de' Medici as a papal candidate, and for a series of indecent sonnets. Later he was known and admired for his *ragionamenti*—dialogues, often scandalous, on contemporary Roman life. He also wrote comedies and one tragedy, *"Orazia"* (1546), as well as poetry and religious works.

LETTERS OF PIETRO ARETINO. 1537–57. Trans. by Thomas Caldecot Chubb *Shoe String Press* 1967 $10.00

Books about Aretino

Renascence Portraits. By Paul Van Dyke. 1905. Essay Index Reprint Ser. *Bks. for Libraries* $11.25

CELLINI, BENVENUTO.   1500–1571.

The well-known goldsmith and sculptor (e.g. of "Perseus with the Head of Medusa") gives an account of his own life which is immediate, forceful and spell-binding. In it we see an intimate self-portrait of one of the greatest artists of Renaissance Florence.

THE TREATISES ON GOLDSMITHING AND SCULPTURE. 1545. Trans. by C. R. Ashbee *Dover* 1966 $3.00; *Peter Smith* $5.50

THE LIFE OF BENVENUTO CELLINI. 1558–66. (With title "The Autobiography of Benvenuto Cellini") trans. by John A. Symonds *Doubleday* Anchor Bks. 1960 pap. $2.95; trans. by Anne MacDonnell 1909. *Dutton* Everyman's $3.95 pap. $1.95; trans. by John A. Symonds *Liveright* 1942 $6.95

TASSO, TORQUATO. 1544–1595.

Son of the poet Bernardo Tasso of Naples, the young Tasso abandoned law for literature and soon found a patron at Ferrara, then a stimulating cultural center—in the person of Cardinal Luigi d'Este. Later he was court poet to the Cardinal's brother, Alfonso II, Duke of Ferrara, whose family he celebrated in his masterpiece, *"Gerusalemma Liberata."* Even before its writing he had suffered periods of insanity and restless travel. "Madness waxed as genius waned," and he died in the monastery of Sant'Onofrio near Rome.

"Jerusalem Delivered," "the greatest poem of the Counter-Reformation," was modeled on Virgil (*q.v.*) in its classical form, but was actually more like a medieval romance, peopled with battling heroes and fair ladies in love. Its theme is the recapture of Jerusalem in the First Crusade. "His poetry is finest when his fantasy is least fettered by historical, literary, or orthodox preoccupations. At such moments Tasso is capable of great feeling, conveyed more by the atmosphere of words than by their meaning, and of a religious sentiment which is not found in his heavy handling of the supernatural, but in his attitude to powers and passions greater than himself"—(Quotations are from *Cassell's Encyclopedia of World Literature*).

JERUSALEM DELIVERED. Trans. by Joseph Tusiani *Fairleigh Dickinson Univ. Press* 1970 $22.00; *Putnam* Capricorn Bks. 1963 pap. $3.95; *Peter Smith* $5.25; trans. by Edward Fairfax *Southern Illinois Univ. Press* 1962 $17.50. Finished in 1575, it was published in an incomplete version in 1580 and in its entirety in 1581.

"Tusiani's aim is a translation of Tasso's octaves into acceptable contemporary English, while remaining close to the original in form and content . . . the result is a half-slave, half-free version of middling success. This is not to say that this first American translation of Tasso is not a very commendable effort. It is readable and useful"—(*Choice*). Fairfax's translation of 1600 was a major poetic feat with lasting influence; John Dryden praised the work in the following way: "For Spenser and Fairfax both . . . saw much farther into the Beauties of our Numbers, than those who immediately followed them."

DISCOURSES ON THE HEROIC POEM. 1594. Trans. by Mariella Cavalchini and Irene Samuel *Oxford* 1973 $24.00. An excellent translation of an important work of literary history, in which Tasso presents the theory of his own epic, the *Gerusalemma Liberata*, and discusses other contemporary critical theories.

Books about Tasso

Tasso. By E. J. Hasell. 1882. *Richard West* 1973 $15.00

Tasso and His Times. By William Boulting. 1907. *Haskell* 1969 $19.95; *Richard West* $13.75

Torquato Tasso: A Study of the Poet and His Contribution to English Literature. By C. P. Brand. *Cambridge* 1965 $17.50

"This scholarly, well-written study of Tasso's life and work constitutes a significant contribution to both Italian and English literary criticism"—(*LJ*).

Landscape of the Mind: Pastoralism and Platonic Theory in Tasso's Aminta and Shakespeare's Early Comedies. By Richard Cody. *Oxford* 1969 $12.00

BRUNO, GIORDANO. 1548–1600. *See Chapter 5, Philosophy*, Reader's Adviser, *Vol. 3*.

GALILEI, GALILEO. 1564–1642. *See Chapter 7, Science*, Reader's Adviser, *Vol. 3*.

CAMPANELLA, TOMMASO. 1568–1639.

In his utopian philosophy Campanella attempted the reconciliation of the naturalistic theories of the late Renaissance with the orthodox positions of the Counter-Reformation. In his "City of the Sun" he presents his model of the ideal state, a republic governed by pure reason. His work invites comparison with More's "Utopia."

THE CITY OF THE SUN. 1602. (In "The Ideal Commonwealth," introd. by Henry Morley) trans. by Thomas W. Halliday *Kennikat* 1968 $12.50

THE DEFENSE OF GALILEO. 1616. *Arno* 1975 $8.00

MARINO, GIAMBATTISTA (also Giovanni or Giovan Battista). 1569–1625.

Marino enjoyed political favor and patronage as well as a period of exile for his satirical writings. "Adonis" includes an assessment of Marino's career and work as well as an outline of the complete poem. "*L'Adone*" is a 45,000-line, 20-canto poem which describes in highly ornamented language the love of Venus and Adonis. Its Neapolitan author, whose avowed aim was to astonish the reader, has given his name to this flowery, Baroque manner of writing (marinism).

ADONIS: Selections from *L'Adone*. 1623. Trans. with introd. by Harold Martin Priest *Cornell Univ. Press* 1967 $11.50

BASILE, GIOVANNI BATTISTA. 1575–c. 1632.

The Neapolitan Basile's best-known work is the *Pentameron*, or in its dialectal title, the "*Cunto de li Cunti*," which contains a number of tales and fables generally reflecting popular traditions and legends.

IL PENTAMERONE, or The Tale of Tales. Trans. by Sir Richard Burton *Liveright* 1927 $6.95

VICO, GIAMBATTISTA. 1668–1744.

The Neapolitan-born philosopher of law and cultural historian, Vico, in his so-called "new science of humanity" attempted to fuse, or to blend the various disciplines (history with the social sciences, philology with philosophy) so as to be able to understand more clearly those institutions of human culture, a knowledge of which is given expressly to man. His work has greatly influenced modern thinkers and literary authors, such as Croce and James Joyce.

ON THE STUDY METHODS OF OUR TIME. 1709. Trans. by Elio Gianturco *Bobbs* Liberal Arts 1965 $5.00 pap. $2.25

THE NEW SCIENCE. 1725. Trans. by Thomas G. Bergin and Max Howard Fisch *Cornell Univ. Press* 1968 $19.50 abr. ed. 1970 pap. $4.95

"A must for all students of the humanities and social sciences"—(*Choice*).

THE AUTOBIOGRAPHY OF GIAMBATTISTA VICO. 1725–31. Trans. by Thomas G. Bergin and Max Howard Fisch *Cornell Univ. Press* 1963 pap. $2.95

Books about Vico

The Philosophy of Giambattista Vico. By Benedetto Croce. 1911. Trans. by R. G. Collingwood. 1913. *Russell & Russell* 1964 $8.50

The Life and Writings of Giambattista Vico. By Henry P. Adams. 1935. *Russell & Russell* 1970 $10.50

Time and Idea: The Theory of History in Giambattista Vico. By Robert A. Caponigri. *Univ. of Notre Dame Press* 1968 pap. $2.95

The Theory of Knowledge of Giambattista Vico: On the Method of the New Science Concerning the Common Nature of the Nations. By Richard Manson. *Shoe String Press* 1969 $6.50

Giambattista Vico: An International Symposium. Ed. by Giorgio Tagliacozzo and Hayden V. White. *Johns Hopkins Press* 1969 $16.50

A Study of the New Science. By L. Pompa. *Cambridge* 1975 $14.95

Giambattista Vico's Science of Humanity. Ed. by Giorgio Tagliacozzo and Donald P. Verene. *Johns Hopkins Press* 1976 $16.50

GOLDONI, CARLO. 1707–1793.

Goldoni, who wrote about 150 comedies for two theaters in Venice, created the modern natural Italian comedy in the style of Molière (*q.v.*). This superseded the conventional *commedia dell' arte* in which only a plot was provided and the actors, in masks, improvised the dialogue.

THREE COMEDIES: Mine Hostess (1753), trans. by Clifford Bax; The Boors (1760), trans. by I. M. Rawson; The Fan (1763), trans. by Eleanor and Herbert Farjeon. Introd. by Gabrielle Baldini *Oxford* 1961 $2.90

SERVANT OF TWO MASTERS. 1745. Ed. by E. J. Dent *Cambridge* 1928 2nd ed. 1952 1970 $3.45; trans. by Frederick H. Davies *Theatre Arts* $1.40

THE COMIC THEATRE: A Comedy in Three Acts. 1750. Trans. by John W. Miller *Univ. of Nebraska Press* 1969 $4.75

THE LIAR. 1750. Trans. and ed. by Frederick H. Davies *Theatre Arts* pap. $1.60

IT HAPPENED IN VENICE. 1761. Trans. and ed. by Frederick H. Davies *Theatre Arts* pap. $1.60

Books about Goldoni

Goldoni and the Venice of His Time. By Joseph S. Kennard. 1920. *Blom* $12.50; *Gordon Press* $28.00. Includes a discussion of the Italian theater of the period.
Carlo Goldoni. By Heinz Riedt. Trans. by Ursule Molinaro *Ungar* 1974 $7.50
"This well-informed, stimulating study fills a long-standing void"—(*Choice*).

CASANOVA (Giovanni Jacopo Casanova de Seingalt). 1725–1798. *See Chapter 16, Literary Biography and Autobiography*, Reader's Adviser, *Vol. 1.*

ALFIERI, VITTORIO, Conte. 1749–1803.

This Italian tragic dramatist, whose plays and poems show his love of freedom and hatred of tyranny, influenced greatly subsequent Italian writers and nationalists. His 19 tragedies, all classical in form, include "Saul" (1782), usually considered the best, and the last, "Brutus the Second," posthumously published and dedicated "to the future Italian people." His autobiography tells of his schooling in Turin, his extensive travels in England and Europe, his love affairs and his literary career in the service of freedom.

TRAGEDIES OF VITTORIO ALFIERI. Trans. by Edgar Alfred Bowring. 1876. *Greenwood* 2 vols. set $34.50. A great improvement over the translation done in 1815 by Charles Lloyd.

OF TYRANNY. 1777. Trans. by James Molinaro and B. M. Corrigan *Univ. of Toronto Press* 1961 $10.00. A political treatise.

THE PRINCE and LETTERS. Trans. by Beatrice Corrigan and Julius A. Molinaro *Univ. of Toronto Press* 1972 $10.00

Books about Alfieri

Vittorio Alfieri, Forerunner of Italian Nationalism. By Gaudens Megaro. 1930. *Octagon* 1971 $10.00

FOSCOLO, UGO. 1778–1827.

Poet and novelist, Foscolo expressed the aspirations of his fellow countrymen during the French Revolutionary and Napoleonic Wars. The protagonist of the "Last Letters of Jacopo Ortis" (*Univ. of North Carolina Press* 1970, o.p.) is reminiscent of Goethe's Werther. In the *"Sepolcri"* Foscolo, starting with the notion that the tombs of great men serve as inspiration to the living, weaves a resounding patriotic poem urging Italians to be worthy of their national heritage.

ON SEPULCHRES: An Ode to Ippolito Pindemonte. 1807. Trans by Thomas G. Bergin *Bethany Press* 1971 $9.00

Bergin captures "Foscolo's varying moods of anguish and hope, and emulates his faultless classical form"—(*Choice*).

Books about Foscolo

Ugo Foscolo. By Douglas Radcliffe-Umstead. World Authors Ser. *Twayne* $6.95
Ugo Foscolo. By E. K. Vincent. 1953. *Folcroft* 1974 $27.50

MANZONI, ALESSANDRO. 1785–1873.

One of the most famous and important of Italian novels written in 1825–1826, during the early stages of the Italian nationalist movement, "The Betrothed" is an historical study of 17th-century Italy and a model of modern Italian prose. The novelist and poet was the leader of the Italian Romantic school and his novel is considered by many Italians to be their greatest work after Dante's "Divine Comedy" (*q.v.*).

THE BETROTHED: A Tale of XVII Century Milan (*I Promessi Sposi*, 1825–1827). Trans. by Archibald Colquhoun *Dutton* 1951 Everyman's 1956 $3.95 pap. $2.45

THE LINGUISTIC WRITINGS OF ALESSANDRO MANZONI. Trans. by Barbara Reynolds *Saifer* $5.00. Important for their relationship with the *questione della lingua* and for the light they shed on Manzoni's role in shaping the modern Italian language.

Books about Manzoni

Alessandro Manzoni. By Bernard Wall. 1954. *Hillary House* $2.75. An outstanding biography in English.

BELLI, GIUSEPPE GIOACCHINO. 1791–1863.

In his satirical poems, composed in dialect, Belli criticized every segment of the society of his day.

THE ROMAN SONNETS OF G. G. BELLI. 1830. Trans. by Harold Norse, with an introd. *Perivale Press* (dist. by B & H Bks.) 1974 pap. $3.00. Small, generally disappointing translation.

LEOPARDI, GIACOMO. 1798–1837.

Giacomo Leopardi, "the greatest Italian poet of recent centuries, held views of man's condition that were bleak indeed. . . . Subjected in his provincial town to well-meant but rigid parental custody, [he] . . . felt, at 'eighteen,' that his health had been ruined by the philological studies which consumed his youth. Sensitive and in need of the affection of women, he was attractive to few: a hunchback and semi-invalid to whom at times any change of light or breath of air was painful. Out of these experiences he generalized his own suffering into a philosophy of despair. But though the poet insisted that life was nothing but boredom and pain, the poetry had different and more dazzling insights—as if the pessimism were some black shadow thrown by a splendid sun"—("The Poem Itself," ed. by Stanley Burnshaw *Schocken* 1967 pap. $2.95).

Leopardi disliked the affectation and pedantry of contemporary Italian poetry. In his own verse he used a simpler, more limited vocabulary for the same reasons as Wordsworth (*q.v.*) and achieved "a fusion of Romantic sentiment and classical elegance"—(*LJ*). In many ways Leopardi's life and work epitomizes the Romantic age but his metaphysical despair—his conviction that all we cherish is illusory—and his rejection of religious formulae anticipates our own time.

POEMS AND PROSE. Various translators; ed. by Angel Flores with introd. by Sergio Pacifici *Indiana Univ. Press* bilingual ed. 1966 $9.50 pap. $2.95

"A very good introduction to the work . . . with a fine [foreword]"—(*Choice*). Chronology and bibliographical note.

SELECTED PROSE AND POETRY. Trans. and ed. by John Heath-Stubbs and Iris Origo *New Am. Lib.* bilingual ed. 1967 $7.00 Signet Class. pap. $1.25. Includes selections from his letters and notebooks.

THE POEMS OF LEOPARDI. Trans. & ed. by Geoffrey L. Bickersteth. 1923. *Russell & Russell* 1973 $25.00

Books about Leopardi

Leopardi and Wordsworth: A Lecture. By Geoffrey L. Bickersteth. *Folcroft* $4.50
Four in Exile: Critical Essays on Leopardi, Hans Christian Andersen, Christina Rossetti and
 A. E. Housman. By Nesca A. Robb. 1948. *Kennikat* 1968 $7.00
Leopardi and the Thoery of Poetry. By G. Singh.   *Univ. Press of Kentucky* 1964 $7.50

VERGA, GIOVANNI. 1840–1922.

William Dean Howells (*q.v.*) first presented "one of the most significant prose artists" and "the father of the Italian novel of our century," to Americans in 1891 with "The House by the Medlar Tree." This great novel of three generations of Sicilian fisher folk and their struggle for survival is regarded as the classic work of Italian realism. The Rosenthal translation is the first complete version in English and a good one, "conveying [well] the color of the language of the Sicilian fishermen and peasants. . . . A valuable edition"—(*Choice*). D. H. Lawrence translated several volumes of *novelle* and considered Verga "surely the greatest writer of Italian fiction after Manzoni." There has recently been extensive litigation in Italy about jurisdiction over the 15,000 pages of the Verga archive, which are soon, it is hoped, to provide a complete Italian edition of his works.

THE HOUSE BY THE MEDLAR TREE. 1881. Trans. by Eric Mosbacher. 1953. *Greenwood* 1975 $15.00; *Farrar, Straus* (in prep.)

THE SHE-WOLF AND OTHER STORIES. 1880–1883. Trans by Giovanni Cecchetti *Univ. of California Press* 1958 new ed. 1973 $10.00 pap. $3.25. Important for the new third section which contains *novelle* never before translated. Part I contains most of the stories from "*Vita dei campi,*" and II has a large selection from the "*Novelle rusticane.*" Cecchetti's translations are accurate, critically sound in every way, and a great improvement over those of Lawrence.

CAVALLERIA RUSTICANA. 1883. Trans. by D. H. Lawrence. 1928. *Greenwood* 1975 $14.75

Books about Verga

Giovanni Verga. By Thomas G. Bergin. 1931. *Greenwood* $9.00

Giovanni Verga: A Great Writer and His World. By Alfred Alexander. *Grant & Cutler* (London: order from British Bk. Centre, 996 Lexington Ave., New York, N.Y. 10021) 1972. A good biography, less valuable as a critical work.

GIOLITTI, GIOVANNI.   1842–1928.

An Italian statesman, Giolitti served five terms as prime minister between 1898 and 1921, his last term of office taking place in those turbulent post-war years.

MEMOIRS OF MY LIFE. 1923. Trans. by Edward Storer *Howard Fertig* 1973 $16.00. The text concludes in 1921 with the last of Giolitti's premierships and the advent of Fascism.

SVEVO, ITALO (pseud. of Ettore Schmitz).   1861–1928.

Svevo was born in Trieste of an Italianized Austrian-Jewish family. After working in a bank, he became a manufacturer and remained in industry in his native city until his death. "Svevo, the writer of genius, was recognized as such only tardily, fleetingly and abroad; Schmitz, the distrait and erratic man of affairs, had a very considerable business success and became almost rich"— (*N.Y. Times*). His first major work, "As a Man Grows Older," remained unnoticed for many years. It did have one intelligent admirer, the young James Joyce (*q.v.*) who at the time was an obscure language teacher at the Trieste Berlitz and who later became Svevo's tutor in English. "The Confessions of Zeno," published 20 years later, was given a push by the then famous Joyce. This novel about an aging man obsessed with illness and death, and acutely aware of his own absurdity, touches in many ways on the literary concerns and moods of the 1960s; it has been called "the first full-scale treatment of psychoanalysis in fiction"—(*New Yorker*). Glauco Cambon in his introduction to Montale's (*q.v.*) poetry describes Montale's "discovery" of Svevo in 1925, "a discovery amounting to self-recognition since Svevo's muffled prose, Svevo's urbane pessimism, Svevo's irony are germane to Montale's stern vision and style."

SHORT SENTIMENTAL JOURNEY AND OTHER STORIES. 1910–28. Trans. by Beryl de Zoete, L. Colison-Morley and Ben Johnson *Univ. of California Press* 1967 $8.95

A LIFE. 1893. Trans. by Archibald Colquhoun *Knopf* 1963 $7.95

AS A MAN GROWS OLDER. 1898. Trans. by Beryl de Zoete. 1932. *New Directions* $3.00; *Bantam Bks.* 1968 $.95

THE CONFESSIONS OF ZENO. 1923. Trans. by Beryl de Zoete. 1930. *Greenwood* 1973 $15.25; *Random* Vintage Bks. 1958 pap. $1.95

JAMES JOYCE. 1927. Trans. by Stanislaus Joyce *City Lights Bks.* 1968 pap. $1.25

FURTHER CONFESSIONS OF ZENO. Trans. by Ben Johnson and Philip Nicholas Furbank *Univ. of California Press* 1969 $8.95 pap. $2.45. Contains unfinished works all published posthumously: The Old Old Man (1929), An Old Man's Confession, Umbertino, A Contract, This Indolence of Mine (last four items 1949), and the play Regeneration (1960).

Books about Svevo

Italo Svevo: The Man and the Writer. By Philip Nicholas Furbank. *Univ. of California Press* 1966 $8.95

"A very nearly perfect critical biography"—(*N.Y. Times*).

D'ANNUNZIO, GABRIELE.   1863–1938.

Poet, novelist, dramatist and in his later years an ardent nationalist, D'Annunzio's reputation in his own country was greatly inflated by his sensational exploits. He lost an eye in aerial combat during World War I, seized Fiume (1919) for Italy in defiance of the Treaty of Versailles, and later championed Mussolini and the Fascist party. Born into a patriarchal family, his luxurious, sensual life and innumerable love affairs, especially that with the actress Elenora Duse, became famous in current annals of literature and scandal. It was said that he gave Italy a new aesthetic consciousness, and he was widely imitated. In his writing as in life he seemed always in search of a new sensation. He combined keen, cold perception and aesthetic sensibility with cruel barbarism. His novels, of extraordinary range and popularity in his own day, are now all o.p. here in translation.

TALES OF MY NATIVE TOWN. Trans. by Rafael Mantellini. 1920. *Greenwood* $16.00

THE DAUGHTER OF JORIO: A Pastoral Tragedy. 1904. Trans. by Charlotte Porter and others. 1907. *Greenwood* $14.00. A forceful peasant tragedy, set in the Abruzzi and replete with popular myths and superstitions.

Books about D'Annunzio

Gabriele D'Annunzio. By Gerald Griffin. 1935. *Kennikat* 1970 $10.00. Early, pre-revisionist account of D'Annunzio's life.

D'Annunzio. By Tom Antongini. 1938. *Bks. for Libraries* $19.00. The first unveiling of the controversial life of D'Annunzio when the poet was still alive.

D'Annunzio: The Poet as Superman. By Anthony Rhodes. *Astor-Honor* 1960 $6.95

Gabriele D'Annunzio in France: A Study in Cultural Relations. By Giovanni Gullace. *Syracuse Univ. Press* 1966 $6.25
An intelligent discussion of why "his reputation was greater in France than in Italy. Written in an easy, pleasant style that is a delight"—(*LJ*).

D'Annunzio. By Philippe Jullian. Trans. by Stephan Hardman *Viking* 1973 $12.95. Interesting, provocative biography of the multifaceted Italian poet, novelist, soldier, demagogue and lover.

CROCE, BENEDETTO. 1866–1952.

Croce was an idealist philosopher, critic, and man of letters whose influence on modern literary criticism spanned half a century in the journal, *La Critica*, and is still, in some quarters, a vital element. In commemoration of the 20th anniversary of his death (1952–1972), Pietro Citati wrote in *Il Giorno* (November 19, 1972): "Never has the relationship between Italian culture and Benedetto Croce been so poor as it is today. At the end of the war, after a brief period of faithful discipleship or perhaps Babylonian captivity, his followers began, one after another, to claim their freedom. . . . Now, however, indifference reigns. It is as if the eighty volumes of 'Saggi filosofici' and the 'Scritti di storia letteraria e politica' tucked away in an old Neapolitan palace no longer existed. At the bottom of both the former love and the contemporary indifference there is a misunderstanding: the artificial necessity of a choice between adoration of the master and the desire to destroy him, considering him all the while as the great renovator of Italian philosophy, historiography, literary criticism and linguistics. Personally, I do not know whether Croce renovated or renewed all these things, and I do not care whether his opinions were right or wrong. But one thing I do know: that he was the most complex, difficult and misunderstood prose writer of our century." Nicola Abbagnano writes (in *La Stampa*, November 21, 1972) that " 'Esthetics' is the subject in which Croce has proved to be the most lasting. It is the base of Croce's esthetics that art is the intuition and expression of feeling. True, Croce distinguished between artistic expression, which calms and transfigures feeling, and other non-artistic expressions which, in their use of words, make for, in his view, only 'articulated sounds' rather than for the authentic language of poetry. But, apart from these limitations, Croce's esthetic theory is accepted and followed in every sector of contemporary art, where there is a place for everyone who, in his own way and with his own tools, tries to express what he feels. In this respect the art of our day may not have gone so very far."

PHILOSOPHY, POETRY, HISTORY: An Anthology of Essays. Trans. by Cecil Sprigge *Oxford* 1966 $17.00

AESTHETIC AS SCIENCE OF EXPRESSION AND GENERAL LINGUISTIC. 1902. Trans. by Douglas Ainslie. 1909. *Farrar, Straus* Noonday 1965 pap. $3.95; *Peter Smith* $6.00

THE PHILOSOPHY OF GIAMBATTISTA VICO. Trans. by R. G. Collingwood. 1913. *Russell & Russell* 1964 $8.50

GUIDE TO AESTHETICS. 1913. Trans. by Patrick Romanell *Bobbs* Lib. Arts 1965 $5.00 pap. $1.75

EUROPEAN LITERATURE IN THE NINETEENTH CENTURY. 1923. Trans. by Douglas Ainslie. 1924. *Haskell* 1969 $16.95

THE DEFENCE OF POETRY. Trans. by E. F. Carritt. 1933. *Folcroft* $5.00

AN AUTOBIOGRAPHY. Trans. by R. G. Collingwood. 1927. *Bks. for Libraries* $9.00

See also Chapter 9, History, Government and Politics, Reader's Adviser, Vol. 3.

PIRANDELLO, LUIGI. 1867–1936. (Nobel Prize 1934)

Pirandello wrote several novels and many short stories before he achieved fame as a dramatist; most are still unknown in this country, though in Italy he is often thought of as a writer of fiction. Frederick May's book of Pirandello short stories "contains a fine selection of text [and] enables the reader to trace Pirandello's development . . . in this genre"—(*SR*)..Included is an appendix listing his more than 200 short stories and a table relating them to his plays. In his fiction as in his plays, Pirandello liked to ponder such matters as why a human being fails in life, or the wisdom of taking sense impressions, surface appearances, and sanity for granted.

The presentation of "Six Characters in Search of an Author" in Rome in 1921 resulted in a riot, and Pirandello's fame as a dramatist was made overnight. This, the most famous of all his plays, is adapted from "A Character in Distress," a volume of his short stories. He was 46 before his first play was produced but in his remaining 23 years he wrote over 50 more plays. His theater was called *grotesco* by the Italians but elsewhere is known as expressionist.

Martin Esslin, writing in the *N.Y. Times* on the centennial of Pirandello's birth in 1967, wrote that Pirandello "sets out to strip [the] masks off his characters, to get the naked truth, only to find that it is impossible to establish the truth about any human being because, life being change, change in the observer as well as the observed, there can never be an absolute, *fixed* truth about anyone. . . . Many of Pirandello's plays deal with [the related] problem of stage illusion vs. illusion in life, stage truth vs. truth in life." The playwright had hit upon what was to become a major concern of the contemporary New Theater—in part as a result of his great impact. Esslin defines the debt to Pirandello of Brecht, Genet, Sartre and Weiss, among others: "Pirandello's influence pervades all contemporary drama."

Fiction

SHOOT (*Si Gira*): The Notebooks of Serafino Gubbio, Cinematograph Operator. 1915. Trans. C. K. Scott Moncrieff. 1926. *Howard Fertig* 1975 $13.75

BETTER THINK TWICE ABOUT IT AND TWELVE OTHER STORIES. 1934. *Bks. for Libraries* $16.00

THE MERRY-GO-ROUND OF LOVE, and SELECTED STORIES. Trans. by Lily Duplaix and Frances Keene; fwd. by Irving Howe *New Am. Lib.* 1964 Signet pap. $.75

SHORT STORIES. Trans. and ed. by Frederick May Lib. of Italian Class. *Oxford* 1965 $5.00; *Simon & Schuster* pap. $1.95

Plays

PIRANDELLO'S ONE ACT PLAYS. Trans. by William Murray *T. Y. Crowell* (Funk & Wagnalls) 1970 $7.95 Minerva Press pap. $2.95. Contains: Vice, Sicilian Lives, The Doctor's Duty, The Jar, The Licence, Chi Chi, At the Exit, The Imbecile, The Other Son, Festival of Our Lord, The Ship, Bella Vita, I'm Dreaming but Am I.

NAKED MASKS: Five Plays. Ed. by Eric Bentley *Dutton* Everyman's 1952 pap. $2.25. Liolà (1916); It Is So (if You Think So) (1917); Henry IV (1922); Six Characters in Search of an Author (1921); Each in His Own Way (1924).

TO CLOTHE THE NAKED (1922) AND TWO OTHER PLAYS: Includes The Rules of The Game (1918); The Pleasure of Honesty (1917). Trans. by William Murray *Dutton* 1962 pap. $1.95

THE PLEASURE OF HONESTY. 1917. Trans. by William Murray *French* $1.75

CAP AND BELLS. 1918. Trans. by John and Marion Field *Manyland* 1974 $4.00

THE RULES OF THE GAME. 1918. Trans. by William Murray *French* $1.75

DIANA AND TUDA. 1927. Trans. by Marta Abba *French* $1.75

THE WIVES' FRIEND. 1927. Trans. by Marta Abba *French* $1.75

AS YOU DESIRE ME. 1930. Trans. by Marta Abba *French* $1.75

TONIGHT WE IMPROVISE. 1930. Trans. by Marta Abba *French* $1.75

TO FIND ONESELF. 1932. Trans. by Marta Abba *French* $1.75

WHEN ONE IS SOMEBODY. 1933. Trans. by Marta Abba *French* $1.75

NO ONE KNOWS HOW. 1935. Trans. by Marta Abba *French* $1.75

Pirandello plays are also to be found in the paperbound general anthologies edited by E. Bentley; A. Caputi; R. W. Corrigan; S. Johnson and others; A. B. Kernan; S. Moon; O. Reinert; G. Weales.

Essays

ON HUMOR. 1908. Trans. by Antonio Illiano and Daniel P. Testa Studies in Comparative Lit. *Univ. of North Carolina Press* 1974 $6.00

"The most complete statement of the Italian playwright's aesthetic and, as such, an important text for the study of his dramatic literature. . . . The translation is a lucid reading of a difficult text"—(*Choice*).

Books about Pirandello

Luigi Pirandello, 1867–1936. By Walter Starkie. 1926. *Univ. of California Press* 3rd ed. rev. 1965 $5.00 pap. $2.25

"The best general introduction in English to Pirandello and his work"—(*TLS*, London).

Age of Pirandello. By Lander MacClintock. 1951. *Kraus* $16.00

The Drama of Luigi Pirandello. By Domenico Vittorini. 1957. *Russell & Russell* 2nd ed. rev. & enl. 1969 $16.00

Pirandello and the French Theater. By Thomas Bishop. *New York Univ. Press* 1960 $6.95 pap. $2.25

Pirandello. By Oscar Büdel. *Hillary House* 1966 $3.25

Pirandello: A Collection of Critical Essays. Ed. with an introd. by Glauco Cambon *Prentice-Hall* 1967 pap. $1.95

There are 13 essays in "this useful collection." Those by Wylie Sypher, Robert Brustein, Stark Young and Francis Fergusson "attest to his revolutionary influence on 20th century theater and novelists"—(*LJ*).

Luigi Pirandello. By Olga Ragusa. Essays on Modern Writers *Columbia* 1968 pap. $1.00

Luigi Pirandello. By Renate Matthaei. Trans. by Simon and Erika Young *Ungar* 1973 $7.50

"This valuable little book has the virtue of brevity, is gracefully written and unpretentious, and mercifully avoids contributing to the frightfully snowballing jargon which plagues so many of the current crop of bloated books in drama and theater. It provides a neatly organized discussion of Pirandello, cautiously working in some meaningful biographical details"—(*Choice*).

Pirandello's Theater: The Recovery of the Modern Stage for Dramatic Art. By Anne Paolucci. *Southern Illinois Univ. Press* 1974 $6.95. A judicious analysis of 14 plays shows the gradual development of Pirandello's art from Sicilian naturalism to the concern with character and reality-illusion to the philosophical bent of the late works.

DELEDDA, GRAZIA. 1871–1936. (Nobel Prize 1927)

Deledda was a Sardinian-born novelist whose works reflect the wild starkness, the lonely expanses, the closed, morally rigid culture of her native island. Geno Pampaloni, writing on the 100th anniversary of her birth (in the *Corriere della Sera*, September 26, 1971), comments: "She wrote from instinct, in the closed circuit of a cultural inheritance which sufficed to provide her severe moral inspiration. Her style is not inventive because of her very self-sufficiency. And, like many other self-taught writers, she wrote too much, rising only by virtue of her intense spiritual quality above the level of what we might call 'women's-magazine' stories. . . . She remained rooted in reality, discovering the rhythm of its dark colors, its ancient fables, its secret side and its despair. I don't think we can go so far as to speak of a levitation of reality into symbol or of a decadent musical transfiguration; such a process was not within her cultural possibilities. Rather, a subtle religious sensibility was grafted upon a dramatic popular tradition. Her work was not, as Borgese called it, a 'neighborhood epic'; it was the epic of a secret world."

THE MOTHER. 1920. Trans. by Mary G. Steegman *Norman S. Berg* 1974 $7.95

GENTILE, GIOVANNI. 1875–1944.

A philosopher and politician, Gentile collaborated with Benedetto Croce (*q.v.*) on the journal, *La Critica*, but eventually broke his intellectual ties with Croce over Fascism.

THE PHILOSOPHY OF ART. 1931. Trans. by Giovanni Gullace *Cornell Univ. Press* 1972 $18.50

GENESIS AND STRUCTURE OF SOCIETY. Trans. by H. S. Harris *Univ. of Illinois Press* 1960 $4.50 pap. $1.95

MARINETTI, FILIPPO. 1876–1942.

Marinetti launched the literary Futurist movement on February 20, 1909, by publishing the original "Manifesto" in the Parisian journal *Figaro*. Although he waged an active campaign against all forms and ideas of the past, he essentially advocated in its place a new "futurist" style and rhetoric.

SELECTED WRITINGS. Trans. by Arthur A. Coppotelli and R. W. Flint. *Farrar, Straus* 1972 $12.95 Noonday pap. $4.95

PAPINI, GIOVANNI. 1881–1956.

Poet, novelist and critic, Papini, in the course of his long literary career, collaborated with Prezzolini on *"La Voce"* and with Soffici on *"Lacerba."* In the years following the First World War he gave up his atheist views and became a fervent adherent to Catholicism.

FOUR AND TWENTY MINDS. 1916. Trans. by Ernest Hatch Wilkins. 1922. *Bks. for Libraries* $12.50; *Richard West* 1973 $11.00

LABOURERS IN THE VINEYARD. Trans. by Alice Curtayne. 1930. *Kennikat* 1970 $8.75

THE FAILURE. 1911. Trans. by Virginia Pope. 1924. *Greenwood* 1973 $13.25. An account of the first twenty years of his life.

UNGARETTI, GIUSEPPE. 1888–1970.

Since the twenties Ungaretti has received more critical attention than any other recent Italian poet. Born in Alexandria, he lived most of his young manhood in Paris and later (1936–1942) taught at the University of São Paolo in Brazil. His first lyrics demonstrate his attempt to find a "new" language, which would express the anguish of modern man. Allen Mandelbaum, translator, said of the poems in "Life of a Man" (1947, U.S. 1958, o.p.), "Ungaretti purged the language of all that was but ornament, of all that was too approximate for the precise tension of his line. Through force of tone and sentiment, and a syntax stripped of its essential sinews, he compelled words to their primal power." "He dedicated himself to making his readers conscious of the beauty of the written word. He also created, with a style probably unmatched in contemporary Italy for its sheer melody, a vast landscape of dreams, of feelings, and, in spite of its pain and sorrow, peace."

Luciano Rebay wrote in the *N.Y. Times* of Nov. 20, 1966: "It was Allan Tate who remarked a few years ago that with the death of Paul Valéry in 1945 the poetic center of continental Europe shifted from France to Italy, the country of two great poets: Giuseppe Ungaretti and Eugenio Montale."

SELECTED POEMS OF GIUSEPPE UNGARETTI. Trans. and ed. by Allen Mandelbaum *Cornell Univ. Press* 1975 $15.00

Books about Ungaretti

Giuseppe Ungaretti. By Glauco Cambon. Essays on Modern Writers *Columbia* 1967 pap. $1.00
Three Modern Italian Poets: Saba, Ungaretti, and Montale. By Joseph Cary. *New York Univ. Press* 1969 $10.00

GRAMSCI, ANTONIO. 1891–1937.

Co-founder, with Palmiro Togliatti, of the Italian Communist Party, Gramsci began in 1919 the influential Torinese daily newspaper, *L'Ordine Nuovo.* Two years after his election to the Chamber of Deputies (1924), he was arrested and incarcerated until his death.

SELECTIONS FROM THE PRISON NOTEBOOKS OF ANTONIO GRAMSCI. Trans. and ed. by Quintin Hoare and Geoffrey Nowell Smith *International Pubs.* 1971 $13.50 pap. $4.25

LETTERS FROM PRISON BY ANTONIO GRAMSCI. Trans. with an introd. by Lynne Lawner *Harper* 1973 $10.00 pap. 1975 $3.95

Books about Gramsci

Antonio Gramsci and the Origins of Italian Communism. By John M. Cammett. *Stanford Univ. Press* 1967 $8.50 pap. $2.95
Antonio Gramsci, Life of a Revolutionary. By Giuseppe Fiori. *Dutton* 1971 $8.95; *Schocken* 1973 pap. $3.45

BETTI, UGO. 1892–1953.

In Italy Betti is regarded as the successor to Pirandello. Betti's three volumes of lyric poetry, his three collections of short stories and one short novel are distinguished, but it is his succession of 25 plays that convinced critics of his extraordinary genius. "Apart from a handful of comedies, his plays are tragic in cast, and often violent, frightening or bizarre. They are also ... austerely Christian in implication. His subject is wickedness; perhaps his life as a judge showed him more curious varieties of it than most of us come upon; at all events he studies its preposterous growths with an habituated candour"—(Henry Reed).

"Goat Island" and "Corruption in the Palace of Justice" are among the best of his plays. His first, *"La Padrona"* (1926), was awarded first prize in a dramatic competition in Rome. His fifth, and first dramatic masterpiece, was "Landslide at the North Station" (1932). In the late 1930s he began to write the comedies that won him popular favor. Between 1941 and 1943, he produced the great series of 13 plays—"all concerned with one aspect or another of men's fatal disregard or defiance of God"—(Reed). "While Betti excoriates the moral and social evils which infect society, he at the same time draws a compassionate portrait of modern man, who though largely responsible for his own corruption, nevertheless seeks to recapture the innocence which was lost in Eden"—(*LJ*).

THREE PLAYS ON JUSTICE. Trans. by G. H. McWilliam *T. Y. Crowell* (Chandler Pub.) pap. (orig.) $2.50. Landslide (1932); The Fugitive (1952–53); Struggle Till Dawn (1945).

THREE PLAYS. Trans. with fwd. by Henry Reed. 1955 *Grove* 1958 pap. $3.95; *Baker* $2.45. The Queen and the Rebels; The Burnt Flower-Bed; Summertime.

CORRUPTION IN THE PALACE OF JUSTICE. 1944. (In "The New Theatre of Europe") *French* 1967 $2.25

CRIME ON GOAT ISLAND. 1946. Trans. by Henry Reed; introd. by G. H. McWilliam *T. Y. Crowell* (Chandler Pub.) 1961 pap. $.95. A play.

GADDA, CARLO EMILIO. 1893–1973.

One of the most difficult of modern Italian writers, Gadda is widely known in Italy though largely unfamiliar to American readers. His involved style and fanciful use of language—he employs various Italian dialects as well as expressions from French, Spanish, Latin and Greek—has led many critics to compare "That Awful Mess on Via Merulana," his comic "anti-epic" (*SR*), to James Joyce's (*q.v.*) "Ulysses." On the surface a detective story, this novel has much to say about Italian life and the roots of Mussolini's fascism. It introduces a series of grotesque and extraordinary characters and situations which may or may not be intended as symbols of the spiritual condition of modern Italy. One critic writes that "Gadda is self-indulgent, bitter, ironic, malicious, hateful, shrill, despairing and human, so that even while boring us he and his book achieve a species of luminescence. . . . Behind the language and self-conscious posturing, the man is in agony"—(*N.Y. Times*).

THAT AWFUL MESS ON VIA MERULANA. 1957. Trans. by William Weaver *Braziller* 1965 $5.95

LAMPEDUSA, GIUSEPPE DI (or Tomasi, Giuseppe, Duke of Palma, Prince of Lampedusa). 1896–1957.

"The Leopard" was begun when its author was 60 and completed a few months before his death. He never saw his single novel in print. *Giangiacomo Feltrinelli* brought out the book, which was at first believed to have been written by a prominent Italian writer hiding under a pen-name.

The Prince of Lampedusa, widely traveled Sicilian aristocrat, probably drew his main character, Prince Salina, from his paternal great grandfather; "but it is also quite obvious that he gave him his own traits, thus accomplishing a curious fusion of imagination and self expression, of historical exposition and psychological confession." He "used devices that belong more to Flaubert or Stendhal than to modern fiction of symbolic allusions and surrealistic constructions. But [the book's] spirit of inner struggle and frustrated humanity, of social ambivalence and spiritual search is that of our times, and the genius of its author and the thrill it gives the reader are probably for all time"—(*N.Y. Times*).

Although it was at first thought that this was the Prince of Lampedusa's only literary work, some short stories and an essay were found among his papers. Some of these are included in "Two Stories and a Memory" which contains an autobiographical memoir, a short story and the beginning of an unfinished novel. The most compelling is the short story, "The Professor and the Mermaid," a romantic fantasy. The "Memory" is a nostalgic account of events and places from the author's childhood.

THE LEOPARD. 1958. Trans. by Archibald Colquhoun *Pantheon* 1960 $7.95; *New Am. Lib.* Signet pap. $.75; *Avon* 1975 pap. $1.75

TWO STORIES AND A MEMORY. 1961. Trans. by Archibald Colquhoun *Grosset* 1968 pap. $2.45

MONTALE, EUGENIO. 1896– (Nobel Prize 1975)

Although he has published only a few slim volumes of verse, Eugenio Montale has achieved an international reputation (with Ungaretti and Quasimodo) as one of the three greatest Italian poets of his time. The 60 "Selected Poems" (about half his output) include examples from his three important collections, *"Ossi di Seppia"* ("Cuttlefish Bones," 1925), *"Le Occasioni"* ("Occasions," 1939) and *"La Bufera e Altro"* ("The Storm and Other Things," 1956). Born and educated in Genoa, Montale served in World War I in the Italian infantry. He has edited his own magazine, worked as a librarian in Florence, and is now a contributing editor of the literary page of a Milanese newspaper. The events of his life have played little part in his poetry, for Montale's concern is with ultimate questions, and with the individual only as he encounters the universals of life, death and fate. Montale's poetry is difficult and pessimistic, but his harsh, brooding vision and poetic understatement (as in the poem "The Wall") can be suddenly illumined by delight and hope (as in "The Lemon Trees") when he becomes the "poet of colors and light and landscapes, the poet who has written some of the most striking love poems in modern Western literature"—(Luciano Rebay, in the *N.Y. Times*). His usual dry precision and lack of sentimentality has been compared to T. S. Eliot (*q.v.*), but unlike Eliot, Montale has no faith to provide him with answers; even in his early poems he "bears the mark of the later existentialists"—(Carlo Golino, *"Contemporary Italian Poetry"*). In 1967 he received an honorary degree from Cambridge University and was named by President Saragat of Italy a lifetime Senator of the Republic.

In 1975 Eugenio Montale won the Nobel Prize. A recent issue of the *TLS* (London) carried the following remarks: "His dislike of grandiloquence and cosmic speculation, his frequently very witty pessimism about the contemporary world, and his refusal of any vatic privileges for the poet, all make Montale a particularly congenial figure for English readers and one who, although he has been regularly translated into English (beginning in 1928, when he appeared in *The Criterion* translated by Mario Praz), ought to be more widely appreciated still. At the age of 79 he is still writing poetry (though no longer the literary and other journalism in which he was once prolific) and poetry which is continually different from what he wrote earlier. It is reassuring that the Nobel Prize should go to so thoroughly independent and literary a man" (October 31, 1975).

SELECTED POEMS. Various translators; introd. by Glauco Cambon *New Directions* bilingual ed. 1966 $7.50 pap. $2.25. The first American edition of his work in English translation.

PROVISIONAL CONCLUSIONS: A Selection of the Poetry of Eugenio Montale. Trans. by Edith Farnsworth *Regnery* 1970 $10.00

THE BUTTERFLY OF DINARD. 1956. Trans. by G. Singh *Univ. Press of Kentucky* 1971 $5.95

"Adepts of Montale will recognize in these prose divagations the predominant lyric themes and language of this greatest of living Italian poets. The same stoniness and essentiality of style is evident, now accommodated to a more colloquial and discursive register. In the vortex of these darting, whimsical memories one can distinguish various exotic Montalian interests: birds, insects, gastronomy, bel canto, dialectology. The stories, or sketches, like the butterfly that came to visit him every day in the café in the square of Dinard, are but fleeting images, the vagaries of a literary solfège. They reflect the bleak post-war days in which they were originally written"—(*Choice*).

XENIA POEMS. 1966. Trans. by G. Singh *Black Sparrow* 1970 signed limited ed. $20.00; *New Directions* signed limited ed. $20.00

Books about Montale

Montale and Dante. By Arshi Pipa. Monographs in the Humanities Ser. *Univ. of Minnesota Press* 1968 $6.00

Three Modern Italian Poets: Saba, Ungaretti, Montale. By Joseph Cary. *New York Univ. Press* 1969 $10.00

Eugenio Montale. By Glauco Cambon. Essays on Modern Writers *Columbia* 1972 pap. $1.00

Eugenio Montale, A Critical Study of His Poetry, Prose and Criticism. By G. Singh. *Yale Univ. Press* 1973 $15.00. Excellent comprehensive study by the well-known translator of Montale's works. This volume contains some 60 new translations from Montale's poetry.

MALAPARTE, CURZIO (pseud. of Kurt Erich Suckert). 1898–1957.

Undaunted Fascist and controversial writer.

THOSE CURSED TUSCANS. 1956. Trans. by Rex Benedict *Ohio Univ. Press* 1964 $7.00

SILONE, IGNAZIO (pseud. of Secondo Tranquilli). 1900–

Silone, portrayer of peasant life, was born in Abruzzi. He began his political and literary activities in the twenties and continued them unabated during a long exile in Switzerland. After the fall of fascism he returned to Rome. When "his books could be printed for the first time in Italy, he decided to modify the novels published during his exile . . . feeling that they were too topical and dated, too representative of the passions of the day. A comparison of the 1937 version of 'Bread and Wine' and this [1962] one shows that he has effected some improvement. The plot and style remain essentially unchanged. However, as Silone says in his preface, 'secondary elements and affairs of only contemporary concern have been removed.' 'Bread and Wine' is the story of . . . a Christlike socialist, disguised in priest's robes, who alone tries to fight the tyranny of fascism. In the end, sensing that Soviet communism is merely Red fascism, he also turns against it"—(*LJ*).

Silone's first novel, "Fontamara" (1933, U.S. 1960, o.p.), is "a choral presentation of the tragedy of a whole village, and a beautiful example of how local realism may become, through a writer's sensibility, a medium of universal human emotions." His later books show, in general, broader interest and more elaborate fictional techniques. The setting of "The Fox and the Camellias" (1961, o.p.) is a Swiss farm where the hero maintains a secret outpost for the Italian anti-Fascist underground. The *Saturday Review* said of it: "A great deal is suggested, and that is both the charm and the significance of the book." "The Seed Beneath the Snow" (1942, U.S. 1965, o.p.) "functions as a kind of reflective sequel to his more elemental *Bread and Wine*"—(*LJ*). The *N.Y. Herald Tribune* called it "a soul-stirring anti-Fascist experience, an orchestration of hope and fresh courage, a reservoir of wit and satire."

BREAD AND WINE. 1936. rev. version 1962. Trans. by Harvey Fergusson II; pref. by the author *Atheneum* 1962 $5.00; with afterword by Marc Slonim *New Am. Lib.* Signet Class. $1.25

THE STORY OF A HUMBLE CHRISTIAN. 1968. Trans. by William Weaver *Harper* 1971 $5.95. A morality play about Celestine V, the Franciscan friar who was elected Pope in 1294 as a compromise between the warring Orsini and Colonna families.

PICCOLO, LUCIO. 1901–1969.

Born in Palermo, Piccolo led, all of his life, a very secluded existence. Although he entered the world of letters at a relatively late date (1956), he played host to several of the foremost Italian literary figures, among whom are Montale and Bassani. In fact, it was at his house that his cousin, Giuseppe Tomasi di Lampedusa (*q.v.*), made his first literary contacts.

COLLECTED POEMS OF LUCIO PICCOLO. Trans. by Brian Swann and Ruth Feldman; fwd. by Glauco Cambon; afterword by Eugenio Montale *Princeton Univ. Press* 1973 $8.50

"If ever poetry was a challenge to a translator, it is that of Lucio Piccolo. And if ever a challenge was nobly met, it is in this translation"—(*Choice*).

QUASIMODO, SALVATORE. 1901–1968. (Nobel Prize 1959)

This Sicilian poet and critic—a former civil engineer of humble origin—was awarded the Nobel Prize for Literature in 1959, the first Italian in 25 years to receive it. The citation praised his "lyrical poetry which with classic fire expresses the tragic experience of life in our time." In 1941 he became a professor of Italian literature at the Giuseppe Verdi Conservatory in Milan. He was the founder and foremost representative of the "hermetic"—an intensely personal, cryptic—school of Italian poetry, which also included Ungaretti (*q.v.*) and Montale (*q.v.*). Quasimodo's maturer work, however, moved in the direction of greater social involvement. Most of the poems in "Selected Writings" appeared in 11 slender volumes covering the years 1930–58. "As the present selection shows, the greatness of Quasimodo is in his traditional power of nature description, classical expression, and concern with the eternal themes of death, love, solitude, campanilism, and reminiscence. The recollections of Sicily's harsh beauties are magnificent, even though his pity for the South equals his love for it"—(*SR*). Quasimodo was also a translator of Shakespeare, E. E. Cummings and others. An ardent opponent of Mussolini, he was once asked "how he would like posterity to remember him. 'As a man who never compromised,' he replied"— (*N.Y. Times*).

THE SELECTED WRITINGS. Trans. by Allen Mandelbaum. 1960. *T. Y. Crowell* (Funk & Wagnalls) Minerva 1969 pap. $2.95

THE POET AND THE POLITICIAN AND OTHER ESSAYS. Trans. by Thomas G. Bergin and Sergio Pacifici *Southern Illinois Univ. Press* 1964 $6.95. Essays which reflect the poet and critic's reaction to modern society.

TO GIVE AND TO HAVE AND OTHER POEMS. Trans. by Edith Farnsworth. 1966. *Regnery* 1969 $7.95 pap. $4.95

"The title of the collection is a little misleading, for the 'other poems' considerably outnumber the selections from the poet's last published work, *Dare e avere*. A 1972 translation by Jack Bevan, published by Anvil Press Poetry in England, seems much superior to Farnsworth's. He gets the title right, for one thing (*Debit and credit*), preserving the accounting metaphor. There is a surer, finer touch in the rendering, free of the verbosity and frequent awkwardness of Farnsworth's version"—(*Choice*).

LEVI, CARLO.   1902–1975.

Levi, born and brought up in Turin, was doctor, artist and author. Early in his career he abandoned medicine for painting. An active anti-Fascist, he was arrested twice in 1934–1935 and again in 1943. "Christ Stopped at Eboli" is the story of his subsequent political exile in the poverty-stricken region of Lucania (Italy). He is perceptive, reflective and a polished stylist. It has been observed that his writing is of two kinds: the vivid journalistic impressionism of his travel books and the sensitive poetic style shown in other books, which he uses "to add depth and dimension to his great skill as a reporter." "Words are Stones" (1955, U.S. 1958, o.p.) is a personal narrative written as the result of various journeys to Sicily. The beauty of the land, poetically described, is in tragic contrast to the miserable condition of the people. Modern Germany, as experienced on a brief journey, is dissected and described in "The Linden Trees" (U.S. 1962, o.p.).

CHRIST STOPPED AT EBOLI. 1945. Trans. by Frances Frenaye; reissued with new introd. by the author *Farrar, Straus* Noonday pap. $2.95

SOLDATI, MARIO.   1906–

"The Capri Letters" (1954, U.S. 1956, o.p.), which won one of Italy's two major prizes, the Premio Strega, in 1954, concerns Americans in Italy—"a mordant and perceptive study of the perversities of the puritan conscience confronted by pagan sensuality"—(*N.Y. Times*). "The Confession" (1955, U.S. 1958, o.p.) is a character study of a young Jesuit student who is trying to evade the temptation of Woman. "Mario Soldati tells his tale with great restraint, but with full control of its many ironies"—(*N.Y. Herald Tribune*). "[He] has unquestionably aimed a savage thrust at the teachings of the Roman Catholic Church, and Catholic readers are hereby warned that they may find the point of his story highly offensive"—(*N.Y. Times*). *Library Journal* calls "The Real Silvestri" (1960, o.p.) "a subtle and penetrating view of human frailty and character . . . beautifully written." Soldati is well known in Italy, not only for his varied fiction, but also for his art criticism, his radio lectures, and his work in the cinema, in which he has been a leading director since 1939.

THE MALLACCA CANE. 1964. Trans. by Gwyn Morris. *St. Martin's* 1973 $8.95

MORAVIA, ALBERTO (pseud. of Alberto Pincherle).   1907–

Born in Rome, the son of a successful architect, Moravia is "the contemporary Italian writer best known outside Italy, and at the same time he is the least provincial of Italy's well-known novelists. In the years since the war, nearly all of his books have been published in English." Reviews of the fifties and early sixties gave Moravia high praise: "His method is akin to that of the American realist but more economical in description and innocent of stylistic mannerisms. His success in projecting the reader into the life of a troubled adolescent, a Roman courtesan, or even a frustrated writer and jealous husband, makes him a novelist of the broadest appeal"—(Charles Rolo). "The bizarre, shocking, or macabre quality of such stories [as those in 'The Wayward Wife'] may blind the reader to the quiet perfection of Moravia's artistry, or to the less quiet quality of his morality. In their judicious union of incident, character, setting, mood and idea, these stories are frequently masterly. . . . Story by story, novel by novel, Moravia has emerged as one of the major fiction writers of his generation"—(*N.Y. Times*).

In 1952 he was elected an officer of the French Legion of Honor. "Several years ago, the Vatican placed Moravia's work on the [now abolished] Index of Forbidden Books. The Italian intellectual world responded promptly by awarding him the Strega Prize—an award given by a vote (in this case, unanimous) of several hundred of the country's leading writers and critics."

THE TIME OF INDIFFERENCE. 1928. Trans. by Angus Davidson *Manor Bks.* 1974 pap. $1.50. Moravia's first novel.

THE FANCY DRESS PARTY. 1941. Trans. by Angus Davidson *Manor Bks.* 1973 pap. $1.50

THE WOMAN OF ROME. 1947. Trans. by Lydia Holland *Manor Bks.* 1974 pap. $1.75

CONJUGAL LOVE. 1949. Trans. by Angus Davidson *Manor Bks.* 1973 pap. $1.25

THE WAYWARD WIFE AND OTHER STORIES. 1951. Trans. by Angus Davidson. 1960. *Manor Bks.* 1973 pap. $1.25

THE BITTER HONEYMOON. 1952. Trans. by Frances Frenaye and others *Manor Bks.* 1973 pap. $1.25

ROMAN TALES. 1954. *Manor Bks.* 1974 pap. $1.50

TWO WOMEN. 1957. Trans. by Angus Davidson. 1959. *Manor Bks.* 1974 pap $1.50

BEATRICE CENCI. 1958. Trans. by Angus Davidson *Farrar, Straus* 1966 $4.50. A Play.

THE EMPTY CANVAS. 1960. Trans. by Angus Davidson *Manor Bks.* 1973 pap. $1.50

THE FETISH AND OTHER STORIES. 1963. Trans. by Angus Davidson *Manor Bks.* 1973
pap. $1.25

THE LIE. 1965. Trans. by Angus Davidson *Manor Bks.* 1973 pap. $1.25

THE RED BOOK AND THE GREAT WALL. 1967. Trans. by Ronald Strom *Farrar, Straus*
1968 pap. $1.95

COMMAND AND I WILL OBEY YOU. 1967. *Manor Bks.* 1973 pap. $.95

TWO: A Phallic Novel. 1970. Trans. by Angus Davidson *Farrar, Straus* 1972 $7.95;
Manor Bks. 1973 pap. $1.50

BOUGHT AND SOLD. Trans. by Angus Davidson *Farrar, Straus* 1970 $6.95; *Manor Bks.*
1974 pap. $1.50

WHICH TRIBE DO YOU BELONG TO? 1972. Trans. by Angus Davidson *Farrar, Straus*
1974 $7.95. Record of impressions and perceptions obtained during five journeys to
Africa in the late 1960s and early 1970s.

Books about Moravia

Alberto Moravia. By Luciano Rebay. Essays on Modern Writers *Columbia* 1970 pap. $1.00
The Existentialism of Alberto Moravia. By Joan Ross and Donald Freed. Crosscurrents/Modern
Critiques Ser. *Southern Illinois Univ. Press* 1972 $5.95
"The book should serve as a good introduction to this Italian literary report, with the
exception that the writers take their Moravia too seriously"—(*Choice*).
Alberto Moravia. By Jane E. Cottrell. *Ungar* 1974 $6.00. Generally superficial study of little
value to serious students.

PIOVENE, GUIDO. 1907–1974.

Born in Piacenza, Piovene has gained a substantial reputation as a man of letters, as an elegant
and extremely cultured essayist, and as a shrewd observer of Italian and American life. His
treatment of the United States ("*De America*") (1953) is a prime document in the history of Italo-
American cultural relations—(S. Pacifici, in "*A Guide to Contemporary Italian Literature*").

IN SEARCH OF EUROPE. 1973. *St. Martin's* 1975 $5.25

GUARESCHI, GIOVANNI. 1908–1968.

The humorous creator of the parish priest Don Camillo and his adversary the Communist
mayor Peppone has been compared to Thurber (*q.v.*). *Commonweal* has commented on his
"brilliant, satirical, wise, apt, stunning creative power." "My Home, Sweet Home" is a collection of
vignettes about his family. "If the book—which is unpretentious and often engaging—has
anything to say, it is that 'Life with Father' is no different under the Italian sun than . . . anywhere
else"—(*N.Y. Times*).
Guareschi barely survived the German concentration camps of World War II. "My Secret Diary"
(1958, o.p.) tells of his experiences in these camps (1943–45). He was editor, principal writer and
cartoonist of the monarchist magazine *Candido,* which he founded in 1945.

THE LITTLE WORLD OF DON CAMILLO. Trans. by U. V. Troubridge *Farrar, Straus* 1951
$5.95; *Simon & Schuster* (Washington Square) 1967 pap. $.75; *EMC Corp.* pap. $1.90

MY HOME, SWEET HOME. Trans. by Joseph Green *Farrar, Straus* 1966 $4.50

A HUSBAND IN BOARDING SCHOOL. Trans. by Joseph Green *Farrar, Straus* 1967 $4.50
A comic novel "heavily embroidered with cute complications"—(*LJ*).

THE FAMILY GUARESCHI: Chronicles of the Past and Present. Trans. by L. K. Conrad
Farrar, Straus 1970 $6.50

LANDOLFI, TOMASSO. 1908–

The stories in "Gogol's Wife and Other Stories" (*see below*) are representative of Landolfi's 25
years of writing. Neither simple farce nor straight symbolism, his style combines both. "Probably
because his stories at first appear forbiddingly difficult, Tomasso Landolfi, whose fiction ranks him
among the major Italian contemporary writers, has never before had a book published in
America. . . . He is a master of the symbolic tale, in which, as in Kafka, strange happenings become
stand-ins for literal facts. . . . [His] best stories place him firmly among the most important
contemporary Italians"—(*N.Y. Times*). Susan Sontag compares him to Borges (*q.v.*) and Isak
Dinesen (*q.v.*). "It is likely, however, that he is a greater writer than either"—(in *N.Y. Review of
Books*).

Gogol's Wife and Other Stories. Trans. by Raymond Rosenthal, John Longrigg and Wayland Young; introd. by Alberto Moravia *New Directions* 1963 $6.50 pap. $1.95

Cancerqueen and Other Stories. 1961–1966. Trans. by Raymond Rosenthal *Dial* 1971 $7.95

"In more than 30 years of creative activity, beginning in 1938 with *Dialogo dei massimi sistemi,* Landolfi has won the respect of Italian critics for his remarkable narrative talents . . . as well as for his excellent translations from Russian literature (Gogol, Turgenev, Tolstoy, Chekhov). Nevertheless, his success in the U.S. has been limited, an unfortunate consequence of infrequent appearances of his works [the last in 1963, *see above 'Gogol's Wife'*]. Therefore, this admirable and much awaited translation of 17 short stories . . . does the English reader a distinct and double service. First, it permits him to enjoy and marvel at the unconventional subject matter (a surrealistic blending of the real and fantastic, a variety of science fiction as it were). Second, the precise translation enables the reader to assay Landolfi's diverse narrative techniques"—*(Choice)*.

PAVESE, CESARE. 1908–1950.

This novelist, poet, critic and translator was born in a small town in Piedmont. He was one of Italy's major post-war literary figures. According to Paolo Milano "both as a translator and as essayist, Cesare Pavese probably did more than any single man to make American literature known, loved, and imitated in Italy." He translated Melville, Dos Passos, Sinclair Lewis and others into Italian. Pavese said of his own works that "the theme of all his books is 'the rhythm of what happens.' "

His diaries (o.p.), recording his pessimistic observations on life and literature, have been hailed as "the finest literary journals since Gide." In "Dialogues with Leuco," "he takes the ideas baldly sketched in his diary and, to underscore their significance and universality, makes them the topics of imaginary dialogues between figures from Greek mythology"—*(SR)*. Pavese's death by suicide took place a few days after his acceptance of Italy's highest literary award, the Strega Prize.

Selected Works. Trans. with introd. by R. W. Flint *Farrar, Straus* 1968 $10.00 pap. $4.50

Contains the novels, The Beach; The House on the Hill; Among Women Only; The Devil in the Hills. "Now there can be no excuse for not reading Pavese, one of the few essential novelists of the mid-twentieth century. The translations and the introduction are admirable"—(Susan Sontag).

Dialogues with Leuco. 1946. Trans. by William Arrowsmith and D. S. Carne-Ross *Univ. of Michigan Press* 1964 $5.00

American Literature: Essays and Opinions. 1951. Trans. by Edwin Fussell *Univ. of California Press* 1970 $7.95

Books about Pavese

The Smile of the Gods: A Thematic Study of Cesare Pavese's Works. By Gian-Paolo Biasin. Trans. by Yvonne Freccero *Cornell Univ. Press* 1969 $9.50

VITTORINI, ELIO. 1908–1966.

Ernest Hemingway (*q.v.*) called Vittorini "one of the very best of the new Italian writers." Born in Syracuse in Sicily, he became with Pavese (*q.v.*) "one of the leaders of the 'new realism.' " He was noted as well for his sensitive Italian translations of Poe, D. H. Lawrence, Faulkner and Hemingway, and for his encouragement of younger Italian writers. In his work he uses "a rhythmic expansion and contraction, which continually contrasts the aspirations and the strangling destiny of this twilight of life. . . . He concerns himself with man's passage from doubt, apathy, and despair, to his realization and acceptance of himself and his world." This contrast is shown in "The Dark and the Light" (1956, U.S. 1961, o.p.), two novellas which illuminate the will for life in two women of very different character and circumstances. Together they reflect the dominant moods—gaiety and sadness—of Vittorini's writing. Vittorini's break with the Communist Party was a central fact of his life. Donald Heiney, in his study "Three Italian Novelists: Moravia, Pavese, Vittorini" (1968, o.p.), speaks of "The Red Carnation" as "a realistic-psychological novel more or less in the tradition of the *Bildungsroman;* in such matters as its treatment of the theme of sacred and profane love it resembles typical examples of the genre like Hesse's *"Demian."* It shows no visible mark of Svevo or any of the American influences in Vittorini's formation. Technically it is a kind of distillation or lowest common denominator of the European psychological novel: Proust, Lawrence, Maupassant, Hesse, Alain Fournier, Dostoevski" (pp. 165–166).

A Vittorini Omnibus. *New Directions* 1973 $9.50 pap. $3.75. Contains In Sicily trans. by Wilfred David; La Garibaldina trans. by Frances Keene; and The Twilight of the Elephant trans. by Cinina Brescia.

THE RED CARNATION. 1948. Trans. by Anthony Bower. 1952. *Greenwood* 1972 $12.00

WOMEN OF MESSINA. 1949. Trans. by Frances Frenaye and Frances Keene. 1950. *New Directions* 1973 $9.50 pap. $3.75

The poetical story of a commune established in the Apennines by refugees after the Second World War. "Vittorini's own disillusionment in the Communist solution is mirrored in this, his last novel. It is an uneven book but an important one for anyone interested in a more complete understanding of post-war Italy and modern Italian literature"—(*Choice*).

DESSÌ, GIUSEPPE. 1909–

Born in Sardinia and educated at the University of Pisa under Luigi Russo, he has won several literary prizes, including the Bagutta Prize in 1962 for *"Il Disertore"* ("The Deserter").

THE DESERTER. 1961. Trans. by Virginia H. Moriconi *Harcourt* 1962 $3.50

THE FORESTS OF NORBIO. *Harcourt* 1975 $7.95

CESPEDES, ALBA DE. 1911–

"De Cespedes is probably one of the most successful women writers in Italy today. Her novels are sympathetic treatments of the predicament of the modern Italian woman, who is destined to give of herself all her life without necessarily being understood and often, alas, unloved by her mate"—(S. Pacifici, in *"A Guide to Contemporary Italian Literature"*).

LA BAMBOLONA. 1967. Trans. by Isabel Quigley *Simon & Schuster* 1970 $6.50

D'ALESSANDRIA, PIA (pseud. of Pia Benadusi Maltesi). 1911–

Born in Alessandria and educated in France (at Grenoble), she is an active collaborator with several literary magazines, among which are *Nuova Antologia* and *La Fiera Letteraria*.

BULL'S EYE. 1962. Trans. by J. R. Chanter *Verry* 1962 $3.50

PRATOLINI, VASCO. 1913–

Pratolini, who has won many literary prizes, was the son of a Florentine waiter and worked at various lowly jobs. Unable to go beyond primary school, he studied and wrote on his own so feverishly and under such bad conditions that he became seriously ill. Pratolini's works are now both a literary and popular success and record the effect of brutal poverty, war and Fascism upon his countrymen, particularly the poor of Florence. But as Hamilton Basso (*q.v.*) has said, his writing "has a quiet, gentle, completely unsentimental compassion that lifts it high above the rather dehumanized plane that realistic and naturalistic writing in this country so often rests on." "The Naked Streets" (1945, U.S. 1952, o.p.) depicts a group of working class youths in the Florence of the thirties. In "Two Brothers" (U.S. 1962, o.p.), the two, reared in different homes because of the death of their mother, find themselves alienated by their divergent experiences. This fragile work was made into the Award Winner of the 1962 Venice Film Festival. "Bruno Santini" (1963, U.S. 1965, o.p.) tells of the rise to maturity of a boy of Tuscany. Though the story is familiar, "the novel is graced by skillful writing, by a taut and credible plot, and by ... understanding of what mades people tick"—(*LJ*). Pratolini avoids the oddities of language and structure of some of his younger contemporaries.

In 1967 Pratolini completed a trilogy, "An Italian Story," published in Italy. "Pratolini's many novels ... all fit into a vast *tragedie humaine*. ... The trilogy is merely an integral part of this *roman fleuve* which is still to be completed"—(Robert J. Clements, in *SR*). "Metello," the story of a young Italian working man's struggle toward maturity is o.p. Readers of Italian literature in translation should hope that his works will be reissued.

Books about Pratolini

Vasco Pratolini: The Development of a Social Novelist. By Frank Rosengarten. *Southern Illinois Univ. Press* 1965 $4.50

BERTO, GIUSEPPE. 1914–

An essentially neo-realist writer, Berto received much critical acclaim for his first novel, *"Il Cielo è Rosso"* ("The Sky Is Red"), which was perhaps the first Italian novel dealing with the Second World War and was written by the author when he was a prisoner of war in Texas. His best known work, a psychological novel *"Il Male Oscuro"* ("Incubus," 1966, o.p.), received in 1964 the double honor of the Viareggio and the Campiello Prizes.

THE SKY IS RED. 1947. Trans. by Angus Davidson *Greenwood* 1971 $17.25

LUZI, MARIO. 1914–

One of the most important poets in Italy today, Luzi has, as Wallace Craft notes (*Books Abroad*, Winter, 1975, p. 34), "through four decades of his professional career ... resisted the idea of poetry as the vehicle of preconceived programs or dogmas. . . . Luzi's only serious commitment has always been to life itself: an open, spontaneous confrontation with life in all its sensible manifestations." G. Syngh has remarked (*Books Abroad*, Autumn, 1968, p. 528) that "Luzi's poetry adds a new and authentic voice to contemporary Italian poetry—the voice of spiritual interiority rendered in terms of a semimystical and semiromantic passion."

IN THE DARK BODY OF METAMORPHOSIS AND OTHER POEMS. Trans. by I. L. Salomon *Norton* 1975 $6.95 pap. $2.50

CECCHERINI, SILVANO. 1915–

Ceccherini is an intensely autobiographical writer who in *"La Traduzione"* ("The Transfer") recounts an 18-year period of his life spent in prison.

THE TRANSFER. 1963. Trans. by Isabel Quigly *Braziller* 1966 $6.00

BASSANI, GIORGIO. 1916–

Born in Bologna, Bassani spent most of his youth in Ferrara, his ancestral home. During the Second World War he took an active part in the Resistance and was imprisoned in 1943. After the war he moved to Rome, where he still resides today. He received the Strega Prize in 1953 and the Campiello Prize in 1968 for "The Heron."

FIVE STORIES OF FERRARA. 1960. Trans. by William Weaver *Harcourt* 1971 $5.95

THE GARDEN OF THE FINZI-CONTINI. 1962. Trans. by Isabel Quigly *Melvin McCosh* 1965 $9.50

BEHIND THE DOOR. 1964. Trans. by William Weaver *Harcourt* 1972 $5.95

THE HERON. 1968. Trans. by William Weaver *Harcourt* 1970 $5.95

THE SMELL OF HAY. 1972. *Harcourt* 1975 $7.95

GINZBURG, NATALIA. 1916–

"An accomplished writer gifted with a remarkable style, Natalia Ginzburg is a perceptive novelist, capable of distilling so much of our own anguish in simple and unusually poetic stories. The world her characters live in is a strange one: although the action acknowledges the existence of an external world, little or no attention is paid to it. . . . The focus of her attention is always upon the way in which the interior life of her characters is reflected externally, by way of acts, gestures, and words"—(Sergio Pacifici). Born in Palermo, she began her literary career by writing short pieces for the Florentine magazine *Solaria*. In 1938 she married Leone Ginzburg, an editor and writer on political subjects later executed by the Germans for anti-fascist activities. In her autobiographical "Family Sayings" (U.S. 1963, o.p.) Signora Ginzburg recalls not only the history of her closely knit family but also, implicitly, the recent history and development of Italy.

No WAY. Trans. by Sheila Cudahy *Harcourt* 1974 $5.95. The novel deals with the isolation, fragmentation, and loneliness of an upper-middle-class family and its friends and is written mainly in the form of letters exchanged among them.

MORANTE, ELSA (Mrs. Alberto Moravia). 1916–

"Miss Morante possesses the Italian gift of distilling universality out of the primitive. But she also has a fine feminine instinct for the singing detail. The combination enables her to create a poetic, princely savage of a hero, half freebooter, half Huckleberry Finn. She catches the echo and iridescence of a tragedy from which lucky old Huck was spared: growing up"—(*N.Y. Times*). For the past several years Morante has been living in isolation, describing herself as an anarchist. In an article "Pro and Con the Atomic Bomb" she defines her recent writing in the following manner: "What is reality? . . . Anyone who asks me this question can't be my reader. In recent years, at the risk of appearing a fanatic or worse, I have written of no other subject. I have been trying all this time to explain the nature of things." Her most recent novel, *"La Storia,"* which caused such critical furor in Italy, will be published soon by *Knopf*. Her novel, "Arturo's Island" (U.S. 1959, o.p.), which had such critical acclaim in 1957, deals with the coming of age of the title character.

SCIASCIA, LEONARDO. 1921–

Born in Sicily, Sciascia is well-respected for his literary genius and his critical sensibility. Most of his novels, written in the neo-realist vein, deal with the political problems of modern Italy, but do so in a thinly veiled allegorical manner. In an article published in *Il Messaggero* (December 15, 1971), Giacinto Spagnoletti writes that Sciascia in *"Il Contesto"* ("Equal Danger") analyzes "the interests and passions that have for several years occupied our society. [He] treats the use and abuse of power which, he says on his final pages, 'is slipping gradually into a tangled concatenation that we may loosely define as having something of a mafia about it.' "

EQUAL DANGER. 1971. Trans. by Adrienne Foulke *Harper* 1973 $5.95

"Sciascia presents an absorbing tale in the best tradition of the *roman policier* and reveals with cynical clarity the *malaise* that afflicts those engaged in public life; moreover, he poses for the reader's consideration the universal problem of the determination and administration of human justice, as well as the corruptness and the corruptive nature of a society that has abandoned its principles, becoming in the process a hollow shell eroded from within and besieged from without"—*(Choice)*.

CALVINO, ITALO. 1923–

This writer's work "recalls the Grimm Brothers and Swift, or especially to the Italian reader, Boccaccio, and, above all Ariosto. Calvino, much like Ariosto, abstracts from our historical time certain verities that he weaves into fantastic stories about knights and their adventures"—(Sergio Pacifici). Despite his relative youth, he has already written four novellas, a two-volume collection of fables ("Italian Fables," U.S. 1961, o.p.) and an imposing collection of short stories which won the Bagutta Prize in 1959. Since 1947 he has demonstrated his interest both in reality and in a fantastic world of fairies and knights. He has no doubt been influenced by his family's professional interest in botany and by his own penchant for science and folk tales. "Calvino combines ironic fantasy with symbolic and moral preoccupations; like Vittorini before him, he suffered deep emotional disturbance on leaving the Communist Party." He has aroused considerable interest recently by the publication of *"Le Cosmocomiche"* ("Cosmicomics"), whose narrator is called Qfwfq—it is something between science fiction and an antinovel, says Robert J. Clements (in *SR*).

THE PATH TO THE NEST OF SPIDERS. 1947. Trans. by Archibald Colquhoun *Old Oregon Book Store* 1957 $4.75. His first novella.

THE WATCHER AND OTHER STORIES. 1963. Trans. by William Weaver and Archibald Colquhoun; ed. by Helen and Kurt Wolff *Harcourt* 1971 $5.95 1975 pap. $2.45

COSMICOMICS. 1965. Trans. by William Weaver *Macmillan* Collier 1970 pap. $1.25

T ZERO. 1967. Trans. by William Weaver *Macmillan* Collier 1970 pap. $1.25

INVISIBLE CITIES. 1972. Trans. by William Weaver *Harcourt* 1974 $6.50

"The brilliant Italian fantasist, Italo Calvino . . ., leaves outer space for a trip through human history, the yearnings and disasters of city life everywhere, and the accumulative pressures of 20th century life. . . . Just as Mr. Calvino brought into his outer space tales the pressures of contemporary history, so he invests his 'imaginary cities' with the alternatively witty and grimy reality of what we all know"—*(PW)*.

GHIOTTO, RENATO. 1923–

A journalist by profession (editor of *Il Mondo*), Ghiotto published his first novel in 1967, *"Scacco alla Regina"* ("Check to the Queen"), an allegorical and psychological narrative in the best Kafkian tradition.

CHECK TO THE QUEEN. 1967. Trans. by Isabel Quigly *Putnam* 1969 $6.95

VOLPONI, PAOLO. 1924–

Born in Urbino, Volponi reveals his attachment to his native locale in his early works. In his important novels of the 1960s he constantly confronts the problem of the incommunicability and alienation of man caused by industrialized society and the inability of man to integrate himself into a world governed by technology. He has recently concluded his trilogy on these themes, begun with *"Memoriale"* in 1962 and continued with *"La Macchina Mondiale"* (awarded the Strega Prize in 1965) and *"Corporale,"* which we hope will appear soon in English translation.

MY TROUBLES BEGAN. 1962. Trans. by Belén Sevareid *Grossman* 1964 $5.00

THE WORLDWIDE MACHINE. 1965. Trans. by Belén Sevareid *Grossman* 1967 $6.00

VENTURI, MARCELLO. 1925–

From his early experience as a partisan in the Second World War, Venturi draws part of the inspiration for his novels, the other part deriving from his acute awareness of the ideological problems and moral dilemmas confronting the modern intellectual.

WHITE FLAG. 1963. Trans. by William Clowes *Vanguard* 1966 $5.95

ARPINO, GIOVANNI. 1927–

Born at Pola, Arpino attended the University of Torino. He began his literary career in 1952 with the novel *"Sei stato felice, Giovanni."* In 1960 he won the Borselli Prize for *"La suora giovane"* ("The Novice," 1962, o.p.) and in 1964 the Strega Prize. One of his best novels, *"Un delitto d'onore"*

("A Crime of Honor") comes to grips with the ambiguous, if not contradictory moral code in southern Italy, by relating the marital tragedy of a nobleman and a commoner.

A CRIME OF HONOR. 1961. Trans. by Raymond Rosenthal *Braziller* 1963 $4.00

MARAINI, DACIA.   1936–

Born in Florence, Maraini published her first novel in 1962, *"La vacanza"* ("The Holiday"), and won the Formentor Prize in 1963 with a novel on the same subject, *"L'età dellmalessere"* ("The Age of Malaise," 1963, o.p.).

MEMOIRS OF A FEMALE THIEF. 1972. Trans. by Nina Rootes *Transatlantic* 1974 $9.50

—C.K.

Chapter 11

Spanish Literature

"This eternal dramatic dualism of the Spanish soul will also be the unifying principle of its literature. And it is probably also this grand duality which lends to Spanish culture its bitter, strange, and virginal enchantment. It is the duality itself rather than any of the contrasting elements considered separately that is peculiarly Spanish."

—DÁMASO ALONSO

"Without the Arabs Don Quixote and Sancho Panza would forever have remained a single person."

—ANGEL GANIVET

Spain's geographical situation—a peninsula effectively divided from Europe by the Pyrenees, a few miles across the Straits of Gibraltar from Africa, and the gateway to the Mediterranean—has influenced her history as well as her literature. Spain has been inhabited since prehistoric times by a succession of peoples—Greeks, Carthaginians, Phoenicians, and Romans—all of whom sought to take advantage of her location and to extract riches from her earth. What is perhaps the first Spanish literature is usually attributed to the Romans, for Seneca the Younger, Lucan, Martial, and Quintilian (*qq.v.*) were born in Spain.

"The Poem of the Cid" was widely considered to be the first extant Spanish literature until 1948 when S. M. Stern discovered in a Cairo synagogue 20 poems in Hebrew, the final verses of which were in Spanish, dated around 1040. Since that time 50 such poems have come to light, and they constitute the oldest known lyric poetry in a Romance language. These anonymous verses, born out of the mixture of Arabic, Hebrew, and Spanish cultures, are an appropriate beginning for Spanish literature, which is characterized by its popular roots and deeply affected by eight centuries of occupation by the Arabs. Further, in their subject matter, the laments of a young girl for an absent love, and in their nostalgic tone, they introduce love as an important theme in Spanish poetry.

"The Poem of the Cid" (c. 1140), Spain's only complete epic poem, was fed by the popular ballad tradition in which contemporary events, weddings, and battles were recounted. Many other epics are considered to have been lost, and their fragments remain in ballad form. Spontaneity, brevity, and dramatic substitution of narration with dialogue characterize these ballads, which have inspired Spanish writers of all centuries. During the twelfth to the fourteenth centuries in the northwest sector of Spain, a tradition of stylized love poetry and bawdy, satirical songs in *gallego*, a combination of Spanish and Portuguese, developed which also influenced the style and substance of Spanish poetry. King Alphonse X (1221–1284), known as Alphonse the Wise, wrote a volume of poetry in *gallego*. He also ordered the compilation of "The Book of Laws" (1256–1265), a compendium of legal theory and codes, and the "General Chronicle" (1270), the first history of Spain. The concept of a unified Spain with Castile as the nucleus is already evident here.

Alongside the ballad and minstrel tradition existed a priestly school represented by Gonzalo de Berceo (1195?–1265?), the first author known by name. His poems consist of popular legends about miracles performed through the intercession of the Virgin Mary. Juan Ruiz's "The Book of Good Love" shares with the priestly school its verse form and spiritual themes, but represents a break with medieval religious attitudes and the beginning of Renaissance humanism.

The Renaissance came late to Spain, which had first to expel the Arabs before turning to intellectual pursuits. The Catholic kings, Ferdinand and Isabel, under whom the nation was finally united, sponsored intellectual inquiry and the dissemination of books and knowledge and commissioned the first grammar of a modern language. Due to the history and character of Spain, however, the Renaissance never completely manifested itself there. The undertaking of the battle to preserve Catholicism with the Counter Reformation and the Inquisition, as well as a fundamental resistance to foreign ideas, are often cited as reasons. Nevertheless, Spain enjoyed a period, termed the Golden Age, which at its outer limits ran from 1530 and the poetry of Garcilaso de la Vega to 1681 and the death of Calderón de la Barca.

The Golden Age saw important developments in poetry and the novel, and perhaps the most fecund area was the theater. The influence of Italian humanism may be discerned in Garcilaso de la Vega's "Eclogues," pastoral poetry of notable classical influence. The Spanish mystics, Santa Teresa de Jesús, Fray Luís de León, and San Juan de la Cruz, used language renovated by the Renaissance spirit to communicate their religious ecstasy. They are distinguished from other European mystics for the commingling of everyday reality with spiritual flight. Toward the end of the Golden Age the Baroque style was introduced in Spanish literature, which became highly ornamented, convoluted, and intellectually oriented. Luis de Góngora is its representative in poetry, and gongorism or culteranism came to mean an embellished poetic style characterized by extravagant metaphors, neologisms, twisted syntax, and mythological allusions. The school of culteranism was opposed by that of conceptism, a movement led by Francisco de Quevedo and Baltasar Gracián, which called for concise language and use of the conceit, a philosophical paradox postulated through elaborate and strained metaphors. Although the proponents of the two styles carried on often vituperative debate, both styles are manifestations of the Baroque spirit.

The Spanish novel also was born during the Golden Age with the anonymous "*Lazarillo de Tormes*," which spawned a succession of picaresque novels, most notably "*Guzmán de Alfarache*" and "*El Buscón*." The picaresque novels became increasingly more satirical and pessimistic while the style became more conceptist. Miguel de Cervantes' "*Don Quijote*," although it shares some elements of the picaresque tradition as well as of the pastoral novel and the novel of chivalry, transcends all of its precursors. Cervantes, who probably began the novel as a burlesque of these previous forms, produced one of the great masterpieces of world literature, a complex, subtle novel providing extraordinary insights into the nature of reality and truth.

For Spanish theater the Golden Age was a period of development and plenitude comparable to that of Elizabethan England. Lope de Vega not only produced an extraordinary number of dramas but also provided the theoretical basis for the development of a uniquely Spanish national theatre. Lope knew instinctively the concerns of the people—religious faith, the monarchy, honor, and love—and treated them in an entertaining manner, thus attaining large audiences of common people and nobility alike. One of his followers, Tirso de Molina, excelled Lope in character development and is credited with the creation of the Don Juan figure. Calderón de la Barca, the last great dramatist of the Golden Age, brought to the theatre the Baroque styles of culteranism and conceptism, as well as philosophical and metaphysical interpretations of the traditional Spanish themes Lope had treated. He also mastered the *auto sacramental*, a short allegorical religious play.

In the eighteenth century, called the neoclassical period, Spain stagnated both politically and culturally. Its status as a world power definitely at an end, Spain's throne was occupied by members of the French house of Bourbon. Perhaps as a consequence, the literature of the century demonstrates French influence, particularly in the spirit of rationalism as seen in the works of Benito Jerónimo Feijóo and Ignacio Luzán. The literary values of the age were defined by the newly founded Royal Academy of Spain. Golden Age drama was banned in favor of works like those of Leandro Fernández de Moratín, who adhered to neoclassical rules and forms. The result was a dry and lifeless formalism. By the end of the century, however, authors such as Gaspar Melchor Jovellanos began to restore vitality to the literature, and the initial signs of Romanticism were seen.

While much of Spanish literature may be designated romantic, Romanticism itself lived a relatively brief life in Spain, from 1833 to 1848. The movement in Spain was characterized by nationalism and an emphasis on Spain's history and literature. Mariano José de Larra, a journalist who argued for the modernization of Spain, and playwright José Zorrilla, who adapted Tirso de Molina's Don Juan figure in *"Don Juan Tenorio,"* were motivated by such nationalistic sentiments. José de Espronceda and Gustavo Aldolfo Bécquer are Spain's important romantic poets.

During the second half of the nineteenth century the Spanish novel entered an extraordinary period of development, beginning with a romantic novel in the *costumbrista* tradition, "The Sea Gull" by Fernán Caballero. From these roots grew the novelistic tradition which culminated in the majestic realistic and historical novels of Benito Pérez Galdós, the regional novels of Juan Valera and Jose María de Pereda, and the naturalistic novels of Leopoldo Alas and Vicente Blasco Ibáñez.

A new era began in the year 1898 with Spain's defeat in Cuba, an event which called attention to her decline over the centuries. Amid the despair and confusion caused by the loss, a group of writers emerged who had a variety of concerns in common: preoccupation with Spain's condition and formulation of solutions, resurrection of the true spirit of Spain, a *fin-de-siècle* pessimism and anguish, a desire to renew the Spanish language, and a reaction against the scientific and the mechanistic. Angel Ganivet is generally considered a precursor of the movement with his *"Idearium Español"* (1897) in which he proposed that Spain revitalize herself by looking to past glories. The so-called Generation of 1898 included Miguel de Unamuno, Azorín, Pío Baroja, Antonio Machado, Juan Ramón Jiménez, Ramón del Valle-Inclán, Ramiro de Maeztu, and Jacinto Benavente, although various critics would exclude one or more of these. Alongside the ideological movement appeared the aesthetic movement of modernism, characterized by preoccupation with formal beauty. Introduced by the Nicaraguan poet Rubén Darío with the volume "Azure" in 1888, modernism's primary sources were French symbolism and Parnassianism, the Spanish poetry of Garcilaso, Góngora, and others, and New World traditions. The members of the Generation of 1898 most influenced by modernism were Jiménez and Valle-Inclán.

The early years of the twentieth century brought an important renovation in poetry with the Generation of 1927, the core of which includes Pedro Salinas, Jorge Guillén, Dámaso Alonso, García Lorca, and Rafael Alberti. This group tended toward gongorism, surrealism, and "pure poetry," the elimination of all nonpoetic elements. A later generation, sometimes labelled the Generation of 1936, rejected their aestheticism in favor of clarity, directness, and the expression of social concerns. That group, which includes Miguel Hernández, looked to Antonio Machado rather than to Jiménez as a master. During this time Ramón Pérez de Ayala and Gabriel Miró were the novelists of significance, while Federico García Lorca dominated the theatre.

The Spanish Civil War (1936–1939) marks a break in the development of Spanish literature, for many writers were killed, imprisoned, or exiled, and those who remained in Spain were often effectively silenced by stiff censorship. The Spanish novel entered a period of renewal with the publication of Camilo José Cela's "The Family of Pascual Duarte" in 1942. That novel initiated a movement called *tremendismo*, a style of naturalism focusing on the grotesque and violent which has been continued by Miguel Delibes and Ana María Matute. A network of underground dramatists has developed, of whom Alfonso Sastre, tried in 1967 for "blasphemy and calumny" is perhaps the best known. Since the death of Franco in 1975, some writers have announced their intentions of returning to Spain, and many are hopeful that restrictions will soon be removed.

HISTORY AND CRITICISM

Adams, Nicholson B., and John E. Keller. A HISTORY OF SPANISH LITERATURE. 1962. *Littlefield* 3rd ed. 1974 pap. $2.50

Bell, Aubrey F. G. CASTILIAN LITERATURE. 1938. *Russell & Russell* 1968 $8.00. An attempt to define the literary genius of Spain for the English-language reader. Concentrates on medieval, Renaissance, and Baroque periods.

Benson, Frederick R. WRITERS IN ARMS: The Literary Impact of the Spanish Civil War. *New York Univ. Press* 1967 $9.75 pap. $2.95

Mr. Benson "skillfully interweaves literary criticism with political analysis; he includes a useful chronology and . . . an excellent selective bibliography"—(*LJ*).

Bleiberg, German, and E. I. Fox, Eds. SPANISH THOUGHT AND LETTERS IN THE TWENTIETH CENTURY. *Vanderbilt Univ. Press* 1966 $12.50. Proceedings of an international symposium held at Vanderbilt University in 1964 commemorating the centenary of the birth of Miguel de Unamuno.

Bourland, Caroline Brown. THE SHORT STORY IN SPAIN IN THE SEVENTEENTH CENTURY. With a Bibliography of the Novela from 1576–1700. 1927. *Burt Franklin* $17.00; *Folcroft* lib. bdg. $14.75

Brenan, Gerald. THE LITERATURE OF THE SPANISH PEOPLE FROM ROMAN TIMES TO THE PRESENT DAY. *Cambridge* 1951 2nd ed. 1953 $17.50

THE SPANISH LABYRINTH. *Cambridge* 2nd ed. 1950–60 $14.50 pap. $3.95. The political and social background of the Spanish Civil War.

Chandler, Richard E., and Kessel Schwartz. A NEW HISTORY OF SPANISH LITERATURE. *Louisiana State Univ. Press* 1961 $12.00. Authoritative volume covering poetry, drama, fiction, and nonfiction with a succinct discussion of Spanish culture and history; appendixes and classified bibliography.

Clarke, H. Butler. SPANISH LITERATURE. 1893. *Kennikat* $9.00

Crawford, James P. Wickersham. SPANISH DRAMA BEFORE LOPE DE VEGA. 1937. *Greenwood* 1975 $12.75. A standard critical work.

Crow, John A. SPAIN, THE ROOT AND THE FLOWER: A History of the Civilization of Spain and the Spanish People. *Harper* 1963 rev. ed. 1974 $10.95. Spanish culture, particularly during the Golden Age, is interestingly treated here.

Descola, Jean. A HISTORY OF SPAIN. Trans. from the French by Elaine P. Halperin. *Knopf* 1963 $8.95. Presentation by a French historian of the evolution of a people; not a factual reference work.

Díaz-Plaja, Guillermo. HISTORY OF SPANISH LITERATURE. Trans. by Hugh Harter. *New York Univ. Press* 1970 $12.00. A valuable introduction with substantial excerpts from each author by an eminent Spanish historian; published in Spanish in 1948–1949.

Eoff, Sherman H. THE MODERN SPANISH NOVEL: Comparative Essays Examining the Philosophical Impact of Science on Fiction. *New York Univ. Press* 1961 $8.50 pap. $1.95. A study of the modern Spanish philosophical novel through comparisons with works in other European literatures.

Green, Otis H. THE LITERARY MIND OF MEDIEVAL AND RENAISSANCE SPAIN: Essays by Otis H. Green. Ed. by John Keller. Studies of Romance Languages *Univ. Press of Kentucky* $8.50. A compilation of articles on Spanish literature from the Middle Ages through Cervantes.

SPAIN AND THE WESTERN TRADITION: The Castilian Mind in Literature from El Cid to Calderón. 4 vols. *Univ. of Wisconsin Press* Vol. 1 1963 Vol. 2 1964 Vol. 3 1965 Vol. 4 1966 each $15.00

Ilie, Paul. THE SURREALIST MODE IN SPANISH LITERATURE: An Interpretation of Basic Trends from Post Romanticism to the Spanish Vanguard. *Univ. of Michigan Press* 1968 $6.50. Concludes that antecedents for Spanish surrealism are found in the Spanish grotesque and in gongorism; delineates the differences between French and Spanish surrealism.

Kazantzakis, Nikos. SPAIN. *Simon & Schuster* 1963 $5.00. *See also Chapter 15, Other European Literature: Greek Literature, this Volume.*

Ley, Charles David. SPANISH POETRY SINCE 1939. *Catholic Univ. of America Press* (dist. by Herder) 1962 $11.95. A useful critical study with translations.

McClellan, I. L. ORIGINS OF THE ROMANTIC MOVEMENT IN SPAIN: A Study of Aesthetic Uncertainties in the Age of Reason. 1926. *Harper* (Barnes and Noble) 2nd ed. 1975 $15.00. Using a broad definition of Romanticism, the author explores romantic tendencies and theories with reference to many periods in Spanish literature.

Madariaga, Salvador de. GENIUS OF SPAIN AND OTHER ESSAYS ON SPANISH CONTEMPORARY LITERATURE. 1923. *Bks. for Libraries* facs. ed. 1968 $9.00

Monteser, Frederick. THE PICARESQUE ELEMENT IN WESTERN LITERATURE. *Univ. of Alabama Press* Studies in the Humanities 1975 $6.75

Morris, C. B. A GENERATION OF SPANISH POETS: 1920–1936. *Cambridge* 1969 $16.95. A comprehensive study of this period of transition and renovation in Spanish poetry.

SURREALISM AND SPAIN: 1920–1936. *Cambridge* 1972 $18.50. A complex study intended for the reader of Spanish and French; includes appendixes of documents of Spanish and French surrealism.

Muste, John M. SAY THAT WE SAW SPAIN DIE: The Literary Consequences of the Spanish Civil War. *Univ. of Washington Press* 1966 $5.95

Northup, George T. AN INTRODUCTION TO SPANISH LITERATURE. 1925. *Univ. of Chicago Press* 3rd ed. rev. and enl. 1960 $6.00 pap. $3.95

Parks, George B. ROMANCE LITERATURES. *Ungar* 1970 2 vols. set $45.00. Vol. 1 contains bibliographies of English translations of Spanish, Spanish American, Portuguese, and Brazilian literatures.

Peers, Edgar Allison, Ed. SPAIN: A Companion to Spanish Studies. 1938. *Pitman* 5th ed. 1957 $10.95

THE SPANISH TRAGEDY, 1930–1936: Dictatorship, Republic, Chaos. 1936. *Greenwood* 1975 $13.25

Rennert, Hugo A. SPANISH STAGE IN THE TIME OF LOPE DE VEGA. 1909. *Kraus* $24.00

Rudder, Robert S. THE LITERATURE OF SPAIN IN ENGLISH TRANSLATION: A Bibliography. *Ungar* 1975 $25.00. A comprehensive work listing all translations of each author, whether in book, magazine, or anthology form and in or out of print.

Salinas, Pedro. REALITY AND THE POET IN SPANISH POETRY. Trans. by Edith Fishtine Helman; introd. by Jorge Guillén. 1940. *Johns Hopkins Press* 1966 pap. $1.95

Shaw, Donald Leslie. THE GENERATION OF EIGHTEEN NINETY-EIGHT IN SPAIN. *Harper* (Barnes and Noble) 1975 $11.50

A LITERARY HISTORY OF SPAIN: The Nineteenth Century. Vol. 5 *Harper* (Barnes and Noble) 1972 $8.00 pap. $4.00

Shergold, N. D. A HISTORY OF THE SPANISH STAGE: From Medieval Times until the End of the Seventeenth Century. *Oxford* 1967 $20.50. A complete account of the early Spanish theater.

Sponsler, Lucy. WOMEN IN MEDIEVAL SPANISH EPIC AND LYRIC TRADITIONS. Studies in Romance Languages *Univ. Press of Kentucky* 1975 $11.25. An exploration of women's occupations, responsibilities, education, and legal rights as revealed in medieval Spanish epic and lyric poetry, concluding that Spain has a "unique respect for women."

Stansky, Peter, and William Abrahams. JOURNEY TO THE FRONTIER. *Norton* 1966 new ed. 1970 pap. $3.75. The story of two young English poets, Julian Bell and John Cornford, who died in the Spanish Civil War.

Ticknor, George. HISTORY OF SPANISH LITERATURE. 1849. *Gordian* 6th ed. 1891 3 vols. set $45.00; *Richard West* repr. of 1849 ed. 2 vols. set $65.00. A classic in the field by the American "arbiter of culture in Brahmin Boston," who founded the Boston Public Library, where he initiated an extensive Spanish literature collection.

Young, Howard T. THE VICTORIOUS EXPRESSION: A Study of Four Contemporary Spanish Poets, Unamuno, Machado, Jimenez, and Lorca. *Univ. of Wisconsin Press* 1964 $8.50 pap. $3.50

An "excellent study"—*(LJ)* including criticism and the author's translation of poems by these important poets; a well-written book valuable to both the scholar and the student.

Wellwarth, George E. SPANISH UNDERGROUND DRAMA. *Pennsylvania State Univ. Press* 1972 $8.50. A critical study of Spanish playwrights forced "underground" by censorship during the Franco regime.

Wilson, Margaret. SPANISH DRAMA OF THE GOLDEN AGE. Pergamon Oxford Spanish Ser. *Pergamon Press* 1969 $5.50

COLLECTIONS

Alpern, Hyman, Ed. THREE CLASSIC SPANISH PLAYS. *Simon & Schuster* (Washington Square Press) pap. $.60. Sheep Well by Lope de Vega, Life Is a Dream by Calderón de la Barca, and None beneath the King by Francisco de Rojas Zorrilla.

Alpert, Michael, Trans. TWO SPANISH PICARESQUE NOVELS. *Penguin* 1969 pap. $1.45. Lazarillo de Tormes (anon.) and The Swindler by Francisco Quevedo.

Barnes, Richard G., Trans. and ed. THREE SPANISH SACRAMENTAL PLAYS. *T. Y. Crowell* (Chandler Pub.) 1969 pap. $2.25. For Our Sake by Lope de Vega, The Bandit Queen by Josef de Valdivielso, and King Belshazzar's Feast by Calderón de la Barca.

Bentley, Eric, Ed. SIX SPANISH PLAYS. The Classic Theatre *Doubleday* 1959 Anchor Bks. pap. $2.95. Celestina by Fernando de Rojas, Siege of Numantia by Miguel de Cervantes, Fuente Ovejuna by Lope de Vega, Trickster of Seville by Tirso de Molina, Love after Death and Life Is a Dream by Calderón de la Barca.

Bly, Robert, Trans. and ed. LORCA AND JIMÉNEZ: Selected Poems. *Beacon* 1973 $7.95 pap. $2.95

Cannon, Calvin, Ed. MODERN SPANISH POEMS. *Macmillan* 1965 pap. $2.50

Cohen, John M. PENGUIN BOOK OF SPANISH VERSE. *Penguin* 1966 $2.50. A bilingual volume with prose translations.

Colford, William E., Trans. CLASSIC TALES FROM MODERN SPAIN. *Barron's* 1964 $5.50 pap. $1.95

Corrigan, Robert W. MASTERPIECES OF MODERN SPANISH THEATRE. *Macmillan* 1967 pap. $1.50. Witches' Sabbath by Jacinto Benaventa, Cradle Song by Gregorio Martínez Sierra, Belisa in the Garden by Federico García Lorca, Dream Weaver by Antonio Buero Vallejo, and Death Trust by Alfonso Sastre.

Farnell, Ida, Trans. SPANISH PROSE AND POETRY, OLD AND NEW. 1920. *Folcroft* 1973 $20.00 pap. $10.50. Includes short biographical sketches and translations of poems or a portion of prose for each author covered.

Flores, Angel, Ed. GREAT SPANISH SHORT STORIES. *Dell* 1962 pap. $.95. Seventeen stories spanning four centuries.

SPANISH STORIES/CUENTOS ESPAÑOLES. Dual-Language Book *Bantam* 1960 pap. $1.25. Spanish and English versions are on facing pages in this collection of stories from medieval to modern Spain.

Florit, Eugenio, Ed. SPANISH POETRY: A Selection from the *Cantar de Mío Cid* to Miguel Hernández. *Peter Smith* $4.50

(Trans.). SPANISH POETRY: A Selection. *Dover* 1970 pap. $2.00

Holt, Marion, Ed. THE MODERN SPANISH STAGE: Four Plays. *Farrar, Straus* (Hill and Wang) 1970 $6.50 Mermaid Dramabks. $2.45. The Concert at Saint Ovide by Antonio Vallejo, Condemned Squad by Alfonso Sastre, The Blindfold by José L. Rubio, and The Boat without a Fisherman by Alejandro Casona.

Lockhart, John Gibson, Trans. and ed. ANCIENT SPANISH BALLADS, HISTORICAL AND ROMANTIC. 1841. *Blom* $12.50; *Richard West* 1973 $12.75

Mandel, Oscar, Ed. THEATRE OF DON JUAN: A Collection of Plays and Views. *Univ. of Nebraska Press* 1963 $12.50

(Ed.). THREE CLASSIC DON JUAN PLAYS. *Univ. of Nebraska Press* 1971 pap. $1.95

Peers, E. Allison, Trans. MYSTICS OF SPAIN. *Humanities Press* (Fernhill) 1951 $3.25. Translations from excerpts of writings of fifteen Spanish mystics with an introduction by Peers.

Resnick, Seymour, and Jeanne Pasmantier, Eds. AN ANTHOLOGY OF SPANISH LITERATURE IN ENGLISH TRANSLATION. *Ungar* 1958 2 vols. $15.00. Includes works by many of the authors discussed below as well as selections from authors not currently available in English translation.

THE BEST OF SPANISH LITERATURE IN TRANSLATION. *Ungar* 1975 pap. $3.75. An abridgment of the above.

Rexroth, Kenneth, Trans. THIRTY SPANISH POEMS OF LOVE AND EXILE. *City Lights* (Pocket Bookshop) 1956 pap. $1.00. Includes selections from Rafael Alberti, Mariano Brull, Nicolás Guillén, Pablo Neruda, Arturo Serrano Plaja, Federico García Lorca, and Antonio Machado.

Turnbull, Eleanor I., Ed. CONTEMPORARY SPANISH POETRY: Selections from Ten Poets. 1945. *Greenwood* $17.25. Selections from José Moreno Villa, Pedro Salinas, Jorge Guillén, Gerardo Diego, Federico García Lorca, Rafael Alberti, Emilio Prados, Vicente Aleixandre, Luis Cernuda, and Manuel Altolaguirre.

TEN CENTURIES OF SPANISH POETRY: An Anthology in English Verse with Original Texts from the XIth Century to the Generation of 1898. Introds. by Pedro Salinas. 1955. *Johns Hopkins Press* 1969 $14.95 pap. $3.95

Wellwarth, George, Ed. NEW WAVE SPANISH DRAMA: An Anthology. Gotham Library *New York Univ. Press* $10.00 pap. $3.95. The Man and the Fly and The Jackass by J. Ruibal, Train to H . . . by J. M. Bellido, Bread and Rice, or Geometry in Yellow by J. M. Bellido, The Hero and The Best of All Possible Worlds, by A. M. Ballesteros, and Sad Are the Eyes of William Tell by Alfonso Sastre.

THE POEM OF THE CID. c. 1140.

The manuscript of "The Poem of the Cid" was transcribed in 1307 by Pedro Abad and lay undiscovered in the monastery of Vicar until 1779. This epic poem recounts in 3,730 lines of verse the character and adventures of a Castilian soldier and nobleman, Rodrigo Díaz de Vivar, or El Cid (d. 1099). While the inspiration of the poem has been attributed to a variety of sources—Germanic, French *chansons de geste*, and Arabic—the Castilian spirit pervades the poem. According to Menéndez Pidal's theory of the gathering of the epic, the songs originated close to the dates of the events related and were transmitted orally through many voices, giving the poem a collective, popular flavor characteristic of much Spanish literature. Around 1140, a Spaniard, thought to be a Christian living in Moslem territory, integrated the tales to create this manuscript as it now exists.

El Cid, sent into exile by Alfonso VI of León after being accused of withholding some of the tribute money due the king, eventually recaptured the city of Valencia for Castilla, thereby giving the Spaniards access to the Mediterranean. Depicted as a protective father, a loving husband, a loyal vassal, and a servant of God, he remains a human being, rather than becoming a superhuman or mythical figure. Although the reality of his deeds is somewhat idealized, the Spanish epic is considerably more grounded in reality and history than the "Song of Roland," for example.

Some of the unique qualities of the "Poem of the Cid" are realism, powerful description, spontaneity, poetic terseness, and vitality. The democratic spirit, respect for the law, political and social consciousness, and religious spirit reflect the Castilian society of the Middle Ages. In his

"History of Spanish Literature," Ticknor wrote, "During the thousand years which elapsed from the time of the decay of Greek and Roman culture, down to the appearance of the *'Divina Commedia,'* no poetry was produced so original in its tone, or so full of natural feeling, picturesqueness, and energy." The figure and story of the Cid has been developed by Corneille (*"Le Cid"*), Herder, Southey, Hugo, Heredia, Leconte de Lisle, and Manuel Machado.

THE POEM OF THE CID: Selections. Trans. by Leonard E. Arnaud *Barron's* 1953 pap. $.95; trans. by Archer M. Huntington (originally published in 1897) *Kraus* 1965 $12.50; trans. by Lesley Byrd Simpson *Univ. of California Press* 1957 pap. $1.95

Books about "The Poem of the Cid"

The Cid and His Spain. By Ramón Menéndez Pidal; trans. and new ed. by Harold Sunderland; fwd. by the Duke of Berwick and Alba. *International Scholarly Bk. Services* 1971 $22.00

Cidean Ballads: Ballads about the Great Spanish Hero, El Cid. By Merrill G. Christopherson and Adolfo León. Comparative Literature Studies *Westburg* $10.00

RUÍZ, JUAN. 1283?–1350?.

Little is known of the life of Juan Ruíz, often described as Spain's greatest writer of the Middle Ages and likened to Chaucer and Boccaccio for various aspects of his work. In his term as archpriest of Hita, a small Castilian town east of Madrid, he apparently collected his own verses and songs into book form around 1330 and then revised and expanded it during a term in prison under sentence by the Archbishop of Toledo. In the prose introduction to the "Book of Good Love," Ruiz defines two categories of love: "good love" or the love of God and "crazy love" or carnal love. While avowing that his purpose is to expose the evils of worldly love and to lead his readers to the exclusive love of God, he admits that his text may provide those who reject divine love with useful knowledge of the other sort of love. Thus the ironic tone of the book, as well as its humorous, satirical, and didactic nature, become apparent in this introduction. Juan Ruíz's self-consciousness as a writer and his awareness of the qualities of his art provide a glimpse of the Renaissance spirit. The primary literary source for the "Book of Good Love" is "Pamphilus and Galatea," an anonymous twelfth-century play in Latin by a French poet. Américo Castro and others have suggested the possible influence of Arabic models as shown by the work's composite form, ambiguousness, and sensual elements. In its anticlerical attitudes the book reflects the crisis of faith facing the Catholic Church towards the end of the Middle Ages, a crisis complicated in Spain by the necessity of maintaining the religious fervor of the Reconquest. The most vital character in the work is Trotaconventos (convent trotter), a procuress, the archetype of Celestina. She aids a young man, Don Melon de la Huerta (Sir Melon of the Orchard) in securing the love of a widow through a series of deceptions culminating in a boccaccian lover-in-disguise scene, and in obtaining for him a number of other lovers, including a nun.

THE BOOK OF GOOD LOVE. Trans. by Elisha K. Kane. 1933. *Univ. of North Carolina Press* 1968 $10.00; trans. by Rigo Mignani and Marie A. DiCesare *State Univ. of New York Press* 1970 $10.00 pap. $2.95 microfiche $5.00

ROJAS, FERNANDO DE. 1475?–1538?.

Fernando de Rojas, thought to be of Jewish parentage and a convert to Christianity during the Inquisition, is generally considered to have written all but the first act of "Celestina." This drama, or novel in dialogue, first appeared in 1499 as "The Comedy of Calisto and Melibea," then in 1502 as "Tragi-Comedy" with five additional acts, and finally in 1519 as "Celestina" in the version now read. While grounded in medieval morality and conventions of courtly love, the work has been designated by Menéndez y Pelayo as marking the birth of the Spanish Renaissance. The tragic nature of the story of the lovers Calisto and Melibea, whose passions lead to their own destruction, the use of elegant language, the individualization of the characters, the glorification of the pleasures of this life, and the emphasis on luck as the law of the universe are indeed Renaissance in nature. Celestina, a worldly-wise old schemer who is totally preoccupied with procuring sexual love, once for herself and now for others, is the grand creation of the work. The most important source for the character of Celestina is Juan Ruíz's "Book of Good Love"; the influence of Boccaccio (*q.v.*) (through the Archpriest of Talavera) as well as of Greek and Latin classics may also be detected. Some critics consider "Celestina" to be surpassed in Spanish literature only by *"Don Quijote."*

CELESTINA. 1499. (With title "Celestina, or The Tragi-Comedy of Calisto and Melibea") trans. by Phyllis Hartnell *Dutton* Everyman's 1959 pap. $3.95; (with title "Celestina, or The Spanish Bawd") trans. by John M. Cohen *New York Univ. Press* 1966 $6.95; (with title "La Celestina: A Novel in Dialogue") trans. by Lesley Byrd Simpson *Univ. of California Press* 1955 pap. $1.95; (with title "Celestina: A Play in Twenty-One Acts

Attributed to Fernando de Rojas") trans. by Mack H. Singleton *Univ. of Wisconsin Press* 1958 pap. $4.50; (with title "Celestina, or the Tragicke-Comedy of Calisto and Melibea") trans. by James Mabbe 1634 *AMS Press* $15.00

Books about Rojas

Petrarchan Sources of La Celestina. By A. D. Deyermond. *Greenwood* 1961 $8.75
Toward a Critical Edition of Celestina. By J. Homer Herriott. *Univ. of Wisconsin Press* 1964 $12.00
The Spain of Fernando de Rojas. By Stephen Gilman. *Princeton Univ. Press* 1972 $17.50
Fernando de Rojas. By Peter N. Dunn. World Authors Ser. *Twayne* 1975 $7.95

TERESA OF JESUS, ST.   1515–1582.

St. Teresa recorded her extraordinary mystical experiences through metaphor ("the soul as a castle with seven rooms enclosing it") and paradox ("I die because I do not die"). At the same time, her style is simple, clear, and marked by lower-class archaisms and expressions. Personal, rather than literary, experience was the source of her poetry. She was known for her practicality and attention to everyday realities ("the Lord requires works"). She devoted herself to reforming the Carmelite Order against strenuous opposition, founding seventeen convents. One of her contemporaries called her "a very great woman as regards the things of this world and, as regards the things of the next, greater still." She is one of the saints in Gertrude Stein's (*q.v.*) play "Four Saints in Three Acts."

THE COLLECTED WORKS OF ST. TERESA. Trans. and ed. by Edgar Allison Peers *Sheed & Ward* 1972 3 vols. set $22.50

THE INTERIOR CASTLE. Trans. and ed. by Edgar Allison Peers *Doubleday* Image Bks. 1972 pap. $1.75

THE LIFE OF TERESA OF JESÚS: The Autobiography of St. Teresa of Avila. Trans. and ed. by Edgar Allison Peers *Doubleday* Image Bks. 1973 pap. $1.95

THE WAY OF PERFECTION. Ed. by Edgar Allison Peers *Doubleday* Image Bks. 1964 $1.45

Books about St. Teresa

Santa Teresa de Ávila. By Helmut Hatzfeld. World Authors Ser. *Twayne* 1969 $6.95
Art of Ecstasy: Teresa, Bernini and Crashaw. By Robert T. Peterssen. *Atheneum* 1970 $8.95 pap. $3.95

JOHN OF THE CROSS, ST. (Juan de Yepes y Álvarez).   1542–1591.

St. John of the Cross represents the pinnacle of Spanish mysticism. In contrast to St. Teresa's works, which refer frequently to the things of this world, his poetry is on a purely spiritual, abstract plane. His poems consist of allegorical descriptions of the journey of his spirit through mortification of earthly appetites, illumination, and purification of the soul to union with God. In his prose commentaries on his own poems he laments the insufficiency of language to communicate the true nature of his mystical experiences and his interior life.

A disciple of St. Teresa, he became the spiritual director of her convent at Avila in 1572 and was responsible for carrying out many of her rigorous new programs for the Carmelite Order. Objections to his extreme reforms led to a period of imprisonment and torture in Toledo. During this time, according to tradition, he wrote "Spiritual Canticle." His concentrated symbolic poetry has been studied with enthusiasm by such modern poets as T. S. Eliot, Paul Valéry, and Jorge Guillén (*qq.v.*).

THE COMPLETE WORKS OF ST. JOHN OF THE CROSS. Trans. by Edgar Allison Peers Christian Classics *Paulist-Newman* 1953 $22.50

POEMS OF ST. JOHN OF THE CROSS. Trans. with introd. by Willis Barnstone *New Directions* bilingual ed. 1972 pap. $1.95

POEMS OF SAINT JOHN OF THE CROSS. Trans. by Roy Campbell *Grosset* 1967 pap. $1.95

ASCENT OF MT. CARMEL. Trans. and ed. by Edgar Allison Peers *Doubleday* Image Bks. 1973 pap. $1.65

THE DARK NIGHT OF THE SOUL. Trans. and ed. by Kurt F. Reinhardt Milestones of Thought Ser. *Ungar* 1957 pap. $2.25; trans. and ed. by Edgar Allison Peers *Doubleday* Image Bks. 1959 $1.45

THE LIVING FLAME OF LOVE. Trans. by Edgar Allison Peers *Doubleday* Image Bks. 1971 pap. $1.45

SPIRITUAL CANTICLE. Trans. and ed. by Edgar Allison Peers *Doubleday* Image Bks. 1975 pap. $2.75

Books about St. John of the Cross

St. John of the Cross and Other Lectures and Addresses, 1920–1945. By Edgar Allison Peers. Biography Index Reprint Ser. *Books for Libraries* 1970 $11.25

St. John of the Cross. By Gerald Brenan. With translations by Lynda Nicholson *Cambridge* 1973 $14.95 pap. 1975 $5.95

ALEMÁN, MATEO.   1546–1614.

Mateo Alemán spent much of his life in a kind of picaresque existence, going from the universities of Salamanca and Alcalá to small government jobs to debtor's prison. It was perhaps in a Seville jail that he wrote the "First Part of the Life of the Pícaro Guzmán de Alfarache," published in Madrid in 1599; the second part, written by an imitator, was published in Lisbon in 1604. Using some formal aspects of "Lazarillo de Tormes"—autobiographical form, the lower class hero, his service to several masters, and portraits of diverse classes and characters—Alemán developed the picaresque genre by taking his character through adulthood, when he becomes a gambler, thief, and beggar. Thus he contributes to the corruption of society rather than merely being its victim, as is Lazarillo. Guzmán draws a bitter moral lesson from his experiences: life is cruel, hunger is the rule, and honor cannot be preserved.

THE ROGUE. 1599. (With subtitle "or the Life of Guzmán de Alfarache") Trans. by James Mabbe. 1622. *AMS Press* 4 vols. 1924 set $60.00

Books about Alemán

Mateo Alemán. By Donald McGrady. World Authors Ser. *Twayne* 1969 $6.95

CERVANTES SAAVEDRA, MIGUEL DE.   1547–1616.

The son of a poor apothecary–surgeon, Cervantes believed that "two roads lead to wealth and glory, that of letters and that of arms." He first tried that of arms, seeing service with the Spanish–Venetian–Papal fleet in the Battle of Lepanto, in which the Turkish invasion of Europe was thwarted. After being captured by Turkish pirates and held for ransom, he returned to Spain, where he attained a post as commissary of the Spanish Armada and tax collector. He was imprisoned when a banker to whom he entrusted government funds went bankrupt.

His first attempts at the road of letters having proved unsuccessful, for he could not compete with Lope de Vega in the theatre, he began writing his satirical novel, "*Don Quijote*," in 1603 while still in prison. In the novel, Alonso Quijano, his head turned from excessive reading, can no longer distinguish between everyday reality and that depicted in the novels of romance and chivalry in fashion during his day. Dubbing himself Don Quijote, he sets out on his bony nag, Rocinante, determined to restore justice to the world. He acquires the rotund peasant Sancho Panza as his squire and a barber's basin for a helmet. One of his most famous adventures involves combat with a giant who turns out to be a windmill, thereby originating the expression "to tilt at windmills." His further efforts are equally "quixotic," but he emerges as a tragic figure striving to maintain his illusions. Under his gaze the most base reality becomes idealized: a homely servant girl becomes a princess, and all whom Don Quijote encounters must swear to her beauty. Part Two, completed in 1615, continues the narrative of adventures and introduces philosophic observations on human nature. At the end of Part Two Cervantes has a disillusioned and humbled Don Quijote die as a precaution against imitations of his work. Sancho, however, now shares Don Quijote's faith and will continue his mission.

This first modern novel, dealing with the nature of reality and truth, is said to have been translated into more languages than any other book except the Bible. It appeared in English in 1612–1620, French in 1614–1618, Italian in 1622–1625, German in 1683, and Russian in 1769. Kenneth Rexroth has written of "*Don Quijote*," "Many people, not all of them Spanish, are on record as believing that '*Don Quijote*' is the greatest prose fiction every produced in the Western World. . . . It epitomizes the spiritual world of European man at mid-career as the 'Odyssey' and 'Iliad' do at his beginnings and 'The Brothers Karamozov' does in his decline."—(*SR*).

"The Exemplary Novels" (1613) are short stories with a moral which have provided plots for the plays of Fletcher (*q.v.*) and Middleton (*q.v.*). The "Interludes" (1615), one-act theatrical sketches, represent Cervantes's most successful attempts at writing drama.

DON QUIJOTE DE LA MANCHA. Part I 1605, Part II 1615

Early Translations of "Don Quixote"

Shelton, Thomas. 1612–20. *AMS Press* (reprint of 1896 edition) 4 vols. set $60.00. The first translation in English; nearly contemporaneous with "*Don Quijote*."

Motteux, Pierre Antoine. 1690. *Dutton* 1932 1954 Everyman's 2 vols. each $3.95; Ozell's revision, introd. by Henry Grattan Doyle *Modern Library* new ed. 1950 $2.45 pap. $1.25, ill. by Doré, rev. by Ozell, Giants 1934 $4.95

Pierre Motteux was born in France but fled to England upon the revocation of the Edict of Nantes. His conquest of the English language was rapid, complete and expert. His version of "Don Quixote" is known as "the ribald rendering" because he translated it freely, often in slang, sparing no pains to make it diverting and peppering it with contemporary allusion.

Modern Translations of "Don Quijote"

Cohen, John M. 1950. Classics Ser. *Penguin* 1950 pap. $2.75. A strong translation in modern English which is faithful to the Spanish, by an eminent translator of Spanish literature.

Putnam, Samuel. The Ingenious Gentleman, Don Quixote de La Mancha. A new translation from the Spanish, with a critical text based upon the 1st editions of 1605 and 1615; includes variant readings, variorum notes, and an introd. by the translator. *Viking* 1-vol. ed. 1954 $8.95

Putnam, the Renaissance specialist who made the best translation of Rabelais (*q.v.*), produced here a translation of Cervantes "that is nothing less than magnificent. Now, for the first time, those whose knowledge of Cervantes' native tongue is too rudimentary to cope with his seventeenth-century Spanish will be able to appreciate the humor, intellectuality, and humanity that made 'Don Quixote,' like the plays of Shakespeare and the vision of Dante, one of the greatest achievements of the literary imagination"—(Hamilton Basso, in the *New Yorker*).

Starkie, Walter. A new translation. *New Am. Lib.* Signet Class. 1957 1964 pap. $1.95

"Starkie is an eminent Hispanist whose publications on Spanish literature, life and lore are well known throughout the English-speaking world. . . . It is a close translation and, to the average American reader, may seem a bit more stiff in places than that of Putnam. The translation is, however, pleasantly readable and clearly and compactly presented in a single and inexpensive volume. Helpful and excellent introduction and a selected bibliography"—(*Choice*).

Abridged Editions of "Don Quijote"

(With title "Selections from Don Quixote") trans. by Florence Fishman *Barron's* 1950 $.95; introd. by J. K. Leslie *Dodd* Great Ill. Class. 1962 $5.95; ed. by Paul T. Manchester *Fawcett* World Library 1973 pap. $1.25; ed. by Daniel M. Crabb *Littlefield* $1.00; trans. by Walter Starkie *New Am. Lib.* abr. ed. 1957 pap. $1.25; ed. by W. Crocker *Simon & Schuster* (Washington Square) 1967 1972 $.95

Other Works

THE PORTABLE CERVANTES. Trans. and ed. with an introd. and notes by Samuel Putnam. *Viking* Portable Lib. 1951 $5.95 pap. $3.50

Includes a "reading version" of "*Don Quixote*" condensed by the editor from his own translation; two complete "Exemplary Novels"; Cervantes' farewell to life called "Foot in the Stirrup"; interesting critical introduction with modern revaluation.

THE EXEMPLARY NOVELS. 1613. Trans. by Harriet de Onís (Dialogue of the Dogs, The Gypsy Maid, The Illustrious Kitchen Maid, The Jealous Hidalgo, The Master Glass, Rinconete and Cortadillo) *Barron's* 1961 pap. $2.50; trans. by C. A. Jones Classics Ser. *Penguin* pap. $2.15; trans. anonymously and ill. by Kenneth Hassrick (The Generous Lover, The Little Gypsy, The Jealous Extremaduran) *A. S. Barnes* pap. $1.25; trans. by J. Lorente (Rinconete and Cortadillo) *Branden* 1917 $.85

INTERLUDES. 1615. Trans. by Edwin Honig *New Am. Lib.* 1964 Signet Classics pap. $.75; trans. by S. Griswold Morley *Greenwood* 1948 $12.25

Books about Cervantes

Hamlet and Don Quijote. By Ivan Turgenev. 1930. *Folcroft* $5.50

Don Quijote: An Introductory Essay in Psychology. By Salvador de Madariaga. *Oxford* 1935 1961 pap. $1.50

Index to Don Quijote. By Richard L. Predmore. 1938. *Kraus* $6.00

Cervantes across the Centuries: A Quadricentennial Volume. By Angel Flores and Mair J. Benardete. 1947. *Gordian* 1969 $9.00

Cervantes's Theory of the Novel. By Edward C. Riley. *Oxford* 1962 $8.50

The World of Don Quixote. By Richard L. Predmore. *Harvard Univ. Press* 1967 $5.75; *Dodd* 1973 $15.00

> *Library Journal* called this "an indispensable study"; a useful work, "whatever the level of the reader's sophistication."

Cervantes: A Collection of Critical Essays. By Lowry J. Nelson, Jr. Twentieth Century Views *Prentice-Hall* 1969 $6.95

Magic Realism in Cervantes: Don Quijote as Seen through Tom Sawyer and The Idiot. By Arturo Serrano Plaja. Trans. by Robert S. Rudder *Univ. of California Press* 1970 $8.50

Novel to Romance: A Study of Cervantes's Novelas Ejemplares. By Ruth El Saffar. *Johns Hopkins Press* 1973 $10.50

Distance and Control in Don Quijote. By Ruth El Saffar. *International Scholarly Bk. Services* 1975 $7.80 pap. $3.95

THE LIFE OF LAZARILLO DE TORMES.   1554.

The composition of "The Life of Lazarillo de Tormes," published in Burgos, Alcalá, and Antwerp in 1554, has been placed between 1525 and 1550, but both the date and the identity of the author remain unknown. The novel gained immediate popularity and is the prototype of the picaresque novel, a genre episodic in form which features the adventures of an antihero, usually young, matching his wits against cruel masters and an indifferent, corrupt society. Among the innovations of "The Life of Lazarillo of Tormes" are the first-person narrative technique, concentration of interest on a lower class figure, and the rejection of chivalric and sentimental literature which is further developed in *"Don Quijote."* Lazarillo, "born in the river Tormes" to a thieving father and a mother of questionable reputation, serves a crafty blind man, a greedy and hypocritical priest, and a starving gentleman striving to keep his appearance of wealth, among others. In each situation the boy must struggle continually for enough food to stay alive. Lazarillo accepts his fate with resignation, drawing no moral generalizations from his experiences. Fortune, which he naively considers to be good, brings him a marriage with the mistress of the archpriest and a job as a bell ringer. The author, however, strips the church, Spain, and human nature in general of its illusions of grandeur, and the next picaresque novel to appear, *"Guzmán de Alfarache"* (1599) by Mateo Alemán, is considerably more bitter in tone and pessimistic in outlook.

THE LIFE OF LAZARILLO DE TORMES. 1554. (With subtitle "His Fortune and Adversities") trans. by J. Gerald Markley with introd. by A. G. Holaday *Bobbs* Lib. Arts 1954 pap. $.95; trans. by Harriet de Onís *Barron's* 1959 pap. $1.25; (with subtitle "His Fortune and Adversities") trans. by W. S. Merwin *Peter Smith* 1964 $4.25; (with subtitle "His Fortunes & Misfortunes as Told by Himself") trans. by Robert S. Rudder *Ungar* 1975 $8.50 pap. $2.95

GÓNGORA y ARGOTE, LUIS de.   1561–1627.

Born in Córdoba, Luis de Góngora studied for the priesthood there and then served as private chaplain to King Philip III in Madrid. As a member of the Court he became involved in the literary controversy of his day, the antagonism between the exponents of conceptism, led by Quevedo and Gracián, and culteranism, led by Góngora himself. Both schools were manifestations of the baroque spirit, culteranism being characterized by neologism, hyperbaton, and use of metaphors as a poetic substitution for reality, and conceptism relying on conceits and philosophical paradoxes. While Góngara's early poetry consists of relatively simple romances and sonnets, his second period, that of the "Solitudes," reveals the culteranism style at its extreme. The "Solitudes" are characterized by pastoral subject matter, artificial language, intricate metaphors, mythological allusions, and musical verse. The French symbolist poets of the late nineteenth century and the Spanish poets of the Generation of 1927 have praised the poetry of Góngora, finding there "delicate imagery, poetic insight and a heightened awareness of the descriptive capacities of the Spanish language"—(Stamm).

SOLITUDES OF LUIS DE GÓNGORA. Trans. by Gilbert E. Cunningham *Johns Hopkins Press* 1968 $7.50; trans. by Edward M. Wilson *Cambridge* 1965 $6.50

POEMS. Ed. by R. O. Jones *Cambridge* 1966 $8.50 pap. $3.75

LOPE DE VEGA CARPIO, FELIX.   1562–1635.

Lope de Vega is the creator of the national theater in Spain, and his achievements in drama are comparable in many respects to those of Shakespeare in England. Lope embraced all of Spanish life in his drama, combining strands of previous Spanish drama, history, and tradition to produce a drama with both popular and intellectual appeal. A prodigious writer whom Cervantes called the "monster of nature," Lope is attributed by his biographer with nearly 2,000 plays, 400 religious dramas, and hundreds of pieces of poetry and literature in every form. He was also involved throughout his life in numerous amorous and military adventures and was ordained as a priest in 1614. In his didactic poem "New Art of Writing Plays" (1609) Lope defined his primary purpose as entertainment of the audience. He recommended a three-act play in which the outcome is withheld until the middle of the third act, when the *dénouement* should be swiftly developed. Maintaining that the possibilities of classical theater had been exhausted, he advocated casting Terence and Plautus (*qq.v.*) aside, that is, abandoning the classical unities. His definition of drama was eclectic, admitting combinations of comedy and tragedy, noble and lower class characters, a variety of verse forms as demanded by different situations, and a wide panoply of themes—national, foreign, mythological, religious, heroic, pastoral, historical, and contemporary. His major strength was in the execution of plot; he created no character of the depth or complexity of Shakespeare's (*q.v.*) major figures. He captured the essence of Spanish character with his treatment of the themes of honor, Catholic faith, the monarchy, and jealousy. In one of his best dramas, "Peribáñez" (c. 1610), a lower class hero is shown to be more honorable than a nobleman. King Henry the Just, a fictional creation, pardons Peribáñez for his revenge killing of the nobleman who contrived to dishonor him by abusing his new bride. In *"Fuente Ovejuna"* (1612–1614), a play based on an event narrated in the Spanish chronicles, the people resist a cruel overlord, refusing to join the army he tries to mount against Ferdinand and Isabel. After he interrupts a village wedding, the townspeople of Fuente Ovejuna collectively murder him and finally receive pardon and gratitude from the Catholic Kings.

Towards the end of his life Lope lost popularity, but all of Madrid attended his funeral, and his death was mourned throughout Spain. In this century, Albert Camus (*q.v.*) adapted his play "The Knight of Olmedo" for French-speaking audiences.

FIVE PLAYS: Peribáñez (1610?); Fuenteovejuna (1613?); The Dog in the Manger; The Knight from Olmedo (1623?); Justice without Vengeance (1631). Trans. by Jill Booty; ed. by R. D. F. Pring-Mill *Farrar, Straus* (Hill & Wang) Mermaid Dramabks. 1961 $2.45

THE PILGRIM, or The Stranger in His Own Country. With Jorge de Montemayor's "Diana" and Gaspar Gil Polo's "Diana Enamored." Trans. anon. 1738. Foundations of the Novel Ser. *Garland Pub. Co.* lib. bdg. $22.00

Books about Lope de Vega

The Dramatic Art of Lope de Vega. By Rudolph Schevill. 1918. *Russell & Russell* 1964 $8.50
The Life of Lope de Vega. By Hugo A. Rennert. 1904 rev. ed. 1937. *Blom* $12.50
The Goldfinch and the Hawk: A Study of Lope de Vega's Tragedy, El Caballero de Olmedo. By William C. McCrary. *Univ. of North Carolina Press* 1966 $5.00
Lope de Vega. By Francis C. Hayes. World Authors Ser. *Twayne* 1968 $6.95
Lope de Vega: Monster of Nature. By Angel Flores. *Kennikat* 1969 $9.00

QUEVEDO y VILLEGAS, FRANCISCO GÓMEZ DE. 1580–1645.

Born into an aristocratic family and educated in classics at the universities of Madrid and Alcalá, Quevedo spent much of his adult life in the Court of Madrid. His experiences in the court of the declining Spanish monarchy contributed to his skepticism and bitterness. In "The Swindler," Don Pablos narrates his picaresque adventures of the most brutal sort, and unlike the naive Lazarillo or the philosophizing Guzmán, this *pícaro* is completely amoral and misanthropic. The language of the work, densely filled with complex puns, jokes, and obscure allusions, amplifies the confusion of the world portrayed. In "Visions," Quevedo satirizes and ridicules the foibles and defects of man and society. For his nihilism and pessimism he has been compared to Swift, Dostoyevsky, Kafka (*qq.v*), and the twentieth-century existentialists.

THE SWINDLER. 1626. Trans. by Michael Alpert (in "Two Picaresque Novels"—*see Collections*) Classics Ser. *Penguin* 1969 pap. $1.45

VISIONS. 1627. Trans. by Roger L'Estrange (1667); ed. by John M. Cohen *Southern Illinois Univ. Press* Centaur Class. 1963 $12.00

Books about Quevedo

Quevedo. By Donald Bleznick. World Authors Ser. *Twayne* 1972 $6.95
Francisco de Quevedo and the Neostoic Movement. By Henry Ettinghausen. Modern Languages and Literatures Monographs *Oxford* 1972 $11.25

TIRSO DE MOLINA (Fray Gabriel Téllez). 1584–1648.

Tirso de Molina, a priest active in the religious order of La Merced, was also a prolific writer, producing over 400 plays. Adopting Lope de Vega's principles of dramatic composition, he excelled Lope in character development and is credited with the creation of the Don Juan figure. Although the theme had long been a subject in Spanish folklore and the character had been treated previously by Cervantes and Lope de Vega, it is in Tirso's play "The Trickster of Seville" that the Don Juan figure comes to life, attaining a stature with figures such as Hamlet, Don Quijote, and Faust. Don Juan, who represents complete devotion to worldly pleasures, refuses to repent for his deceptions, seductions, and finally a murder, always maintaining that he still has sufficient time since, according to Roman Catholic doctrine, even a word of repentance on the deathbed suffices to save a sinner from hell. In the most famous scene of the play, the stone sepulcher of Don Gonzalo invites him to supper in his grave, where he surprises him with a death by poison. Don Juan dies unrepentant and descends into hell for his punishment. The Don Juan theme and figure have been developed by Molière, Byron, Zorrilla, Shaw, Camus, and Motherlant (*qq.v.*), among many others.

THE PLAYBOY OF SEVILLE, or Supper with a Statue. 1630. (In "Three Classic Don Juan Plays," ed. by Oscar Mandel and trans. by S. Schezzano and Oscar Mandel) *Univ. of Nebraska Press* Bison Bks. 1971 pap. $1.95

Books about Tirso

The Don Juan Legend. By Otto Rank; ed. by David G. Winter *Princeton Univ. Press* 1975 $8.50
Metamorphoses of Don Juan. By Leo Weinstein. 1959. *AMS Press* $14.00

CALDERÓN DE LA BARCA, PEDRO.   1600–1681.

Calderón de la Barca was master of the Spanish stage from Lope de Vega's death in 1635 until his own in 1681, serving as court poet to King Philip IV. While lacking Lope's spontaneity and vitality, he surpassed him in profundity of thought and in depicting interior conflicts in his characters. Much of Calderón's work is abstract and probes metaphysical questions about free will, predestination, and the brevity of life. In addition, he provided theoretical interpretations of many of the same themes—honor, religion, the monarchy—which were presented by Lope. His style differs from Lope's in being more condensed, symbolic, and decorative, sharing characteristics of both culteranism and conceptism. These differences between Lope and Calderón are products of their respective times as well as of personality differences. Lope still enjoyed the optimistic humanism of the Renaissance, while Calderon's world had already begun to disintegrate.

Calderón's piece "Life Is a Dream," deals with the kind of prophecy about an infant found in the Oedipus myth. A king, told that his son will step on his head, locks him away from all contact with the world. When the youth awakes, he struggles with his instincts for revenge, finally moderating them. "The Mayor of Zalamea" is a reworking of a play by Lope on the theme of honor. "The Phantom Lady" is a romantic intrigue, while "Devotion to the Cross" is an example of the religious play, *auto sacramental,* for which Calderón is most famous. He led a comparatively quiet life and after his ordination in 1651, he retired from the world, writing only two religious plays a year for the city of Madrid and some plays on mythological themes for the Court's entertainment.

FOUR PLAYS. Trans. and ed. by Edwin Honig. Secret Vengeance for Secret Insult (1635), The Phantom Lady (1629), The Mayor of Zalamea (c. 1642); Devotion to the Cross (1633) *Farrar, Straus* (Hill & Wang) Mermaid Dramabks. pap. $2.95

LIFE IS A DREAM. c. 1635. Trans. by William E. Colford *Barron's* 1958 pap. $1.25; (with title "Life's a Dream") trans. by Kathleen Raine and R. M. Nadal *Theatre Arts Books* 1969 $3.85; trans. by Edwin Honig *Farrar, Straus* (Hill & Wang) $4.50 Mermaid Dramabks. pap. $2.50

THE MAYOR OF ZALAMEA. c. 1642. Trans. by William E. Colford. *Barron's* 1959 pap. $1.25

Books about Calderón

Critical Essays on the Theatre of Calderón. Ed. by Bruce W. Wardropper. *New York Univ. Press* 1965 pap. $2.25
Calderón de la Barca. By Everett W. Hesse. World Authors Ser. *Twayne* 1968 $6.95
Calderón and the Seizures of Honor. By Edwin Honig. *Harvard Univ. Press* 1972 $11.50

GRACIÁN, BALTASAR.   1601–1658.

A Jesuit priest, Baltasar Gracián was the theoretician of conceptism and the great moralistic and didactic writer of his day. In "The Oracle" he presents examples of ideal men of several types—the hero, the discreet man, and the politician—examples needed because he believed man to be cruel and barbaric by nature. "The Art of Worldly Wisdom" is an explanation and defense of conceptism in which he advocates extreme brevity of expression.

THE ORACLE: A Manual of the Art of Discretion. 1647. Trans. by L. B. Walton. *Dutton Everyman's* 1953 $3.95

THE ART OF WORLDLY WISDOM. 1648. Trans. by Joseph Jacobs. 1892. *Ungar* $5.00 pap. $1.75; (with title "Gracián's Manual: A Truth-Telling Manual and the Art of Worldly Wisdom") trans. by Martin Fischer *Charles C Thomas* 1964 $4.50

Books about Gracián

Gracián. By Virginia R. Foster. World Authors Ser. *Twayne* 1975 $7.95

VALERA Y ALCALÁ GALIANO, JUAN. 1827–1905.

A realistic and regional novelist, Valera is best known for his creation of Andalusian atmosphere, sensual themes, and psychological depth. "Pepita Jiménez," an ironic novel in epistolary form, explores the inner turmoil of a young seminarian distracted from his religious study by Pepita Jiménez, who is engaged to his own widower father. A moralist concerned with correct behavior, Valera indicates through his conclusion to the novel that Luis's romantically inspired religious faith is hollow and that service to God may take the form of human, as well as spiritual, love. "Doña Luz" deals with the same themes.

PEPITA JIMÉNEZ. 1874. Trans. and introd. by Harriet de Onís. *Barron's* 1965 pap. $1.50

DOÑA LUZ. 1879. Trans. by M. J. Serrano. 1891. *Howard Fertig* $12.50

Books about Valera

Language and Psychology in Pepita Jiménez. By Robert E. Lott. *Univ. of Illinois Press* 1970 $8.95
Juan Valera. By Cyrus de Coster. World Authors Ser. *Twayne* 1974 $8.50

ALARCÓN, PEDRO ANTONIO DE. 1833–1891.

An anticlerical radical in his youth, Alarcón became religious and conservative after an opponent in a duel spared his life. He is best known for his novella, "The Three-Cornered Hat," which Emilia Pardo Bazán called "the king of Spanish tales." The plot, reminiscent of many of Boccaccio's (*q.v.*) tales, involves a jealous miller who disguises himself to revenge what he supposes to be his wife's infidelities with the Corregidor of the village. "The Three-Cornered Hat," in which Alarcón skillfully combines humor, picaresque elements, the popular tradition, and a polished style, has served as the basis for operas in French, German, and English and a ballet by Manuel de Falla.

THE THREE-CORNERED HAT. 1874. Trans. by Harriet de Onís *Barron's* 1958 pap. $1.50; trans. by H. F. Turner *Dufour* 1965 $5.95 pap. $3.50

BÉCQUER, GUSTAVO ADOLFO (pseud. of Gustavo Adolfo Domínguez Bastida). 1836–1870.

Bécquer is the archetype of the Romantic poet, devoting his life to poetry and dying at 34 of tuberculosis and the effects of his bohemian life of poverty. "The Rhymes," published during his lifetime in newspapers and collected by friends in a volume a year after his death, are characterized by subjectivity, musicality, and the traditional Romantic themes of love, death, the idealized past, and evocative landscapes. "The Rhymes," which describe the spiritual quest of the poet for ineffable beauty and inspiration, use the metaphor of yearning for an unattainable woman, first an imaginary muse and then a real woman who rejects him. His unrequited love produces the tremendous sadness revealed here. Bécquer's brother was a painter, and his poetry has been called plastic and painterly for its emphasis on color, light, and architecture. Influences on "The Rhymes" are said to be primarily foreign—Heine, Byron, Goethe, Schiller, Musset, and Lamartine (*qq.v.*). An atmosphere of magic and fantasy pervades the romantic "Legends," which are set in distant places, such as India, and remote times, primarily the Middle Ages. Dámaso Alonso has called Bécquer's work the beginning of contemporary poetry, and he was admired deeply for his lyric poetry by the Generation of 1927: Guillén, Salinas, García Lorca, and Alberti.

ROMANTIC LEGENDS OF SPAIN. 1860–1864. Trans. by Cornelia Frances Bates and Katherine Lee Bates. 1909. *Bks. for Libraries* 1971 $13.00

SYMPHONY OF LOVE: Las Rimas. 1871. Trans. by David F. Altabe. *Regina Publishing House* 1974 $5.95 pap. $3.50

PÉREZ GALDÓS, BENITO. 1843–1920.

Pérez Galdós is Spain's outstanding nineteenth-century novelist. In scope, purpose, and achievement he is comparable to Dickens and Balzac, two writers he acknowledged as models. At a time when most Spanish novelists were limited by their regional backgrounds, Galdós possessed the intellect and vision to embrace the Spanish people as a nation. In 1873 he began the "National Episodes," a 46-volume series of historical novels in which he is concerned less with the details and facts of history than with their impact on the lives of ordinary people.

His works are sometimes divided into two periods: Novels of the First Period and Contemporary Spanish Novels. His early novels, "Doña Perfecta," "Gloria," "Marianela," and "The Family of Leon Roch," may be characterized as realistic with touches of romanticism. The novels are united by common characters and themes in the manner of Balzac's (q.v.) "Human Comedy." "Doña Perfecta" is a denunciation of intolerance. "Marianela" explores the irony and tragedy of the destruction of love by scientific progress. "Fortunata and Jacinta," a four-volume masterpiece of the second period, contrasts two women—Jacinta, wife of a wealthy middle-class man, and Fortunata, wife of a lower class man. Both are admirable characters, but it is Fortunata who has the fortune of bearing a son, a demonstration of the vitality of the lower classes. The character of Maxi reveals Galdós's interest in mental illness and his naturalistic strain.

Born and educated in the Canary Islands, Pérez Galdós studied law briefly and spent most of his adult life in Madrid. His study of lower class Spanish life and his attempts to improve it led him to the advocacy of more equal distribution of wealth and outspoken opposition to the Catholic Church at the same time that he advocated Christian charity as a solution to many social problems. While always popular with the people, he fared less well in official literary circles. In 1889 he sought admission to the Royal Academy, an honor he was refused until 1897, and the Nobel Prize went to a contemporary, José Echegaray, of considerably less talent. Galdós died poor and blind. Although the government refused him a state funeral, the entire Spanish nation mourned him. English translations of his novels now out of print are "The Disinherited Lady" (1881), "Miau" (1888), "Compassion" (1897), and "Tristana."

DOÑA PERFECTA. 1876. Trans. by Harriet de Onís. *Barron's* 1960 pap. $1.50

GLORIA. 1877. Trans. by Clara Bell. 1882. *Howard Fertig* 2 vols. in 1 1974 $18.50

MARIANELA. 1878. Trans. by Clara Bell. 1883. *Howard Fertig* 1974 $10.50

THE FAMILY OF LEON ROCH. 1879. Trans. by Clara Bell. 1882. *Howard Fertig* 2 vols. in 1 $17.50

FORTUNATA AND JACINTA: Two Stories of Married Women. 1886–1887. Trans. by Lester Clark. Classics Ser. *Penguin* 1973 pap. $4.95

Books about Pérez Galdós

Pérez Galdós and the Spanish Novel of the Nineteenth Century. By Leslie B. Walton. 1927. *Gordian* 1970 $7.50

Pérez Galdós, Spanish Liberal Crusader. By H. C. Berkowitz. 1948 *Russell & Russell* 1974 $24.00

Humor in Galdós: A Study of the Novelas Contemporaneas. By Michael Nimitz. Romanic Studies, Second Ser. *Yale Univ. Press* 1968 $11.50

PARDO BAZÁN, EMILIA. 1851–1920.

The countess Emilia Pardo Bazán introduced the French naturalistic movement to Spain with "The Burning Question" (1881, o.p.). While she recognized the excesses of naturalism in its exclusive concentration on the sordid aspects of life, she saw in it possibilities for directing the Spanish novel to social and political issues. "The Son of the Bondwoman" ("*Los Pasos de Ulloa*"), which deals with the degeneration of an aristocratic family, is naturalistic in subject and in its deterministic outcome.

THE SON OF THE BONDWOMAN. 1886. Trans. by E. H. Hearn. 1908. *Howard Fertig* $13.50

UNAMUNO y JUGO, MIGUEL DE. 1864–1936.

Philosopher, essayist, poet, and novelist, Unamuno was a central figure of the Generation of 1898. His primary concerns were man's destiny, Spain, the nature of human relationships, and renewal of artistic forms. In his major philosophical work, "The Tragic Sense of Life," Unamuno struggles with his uncertainty about immortality, the ultimate problem in his estimation, since if man is to die completely, then nothing in life has meaning. The only possible solution Unamuno sees is a desperate resignation and struggle for an irrational faith which will permit him to live, a solution often compared to Kierkegaard's (q.v.) "leap of faith." Man, then, must conduct himself "passionately well" in order to deserve immortal life. Loving other human beings is the key to living well and the only possibility for salvation: the shoemaker who would mourn the death of a client does a religious work. Reevaluating the figure of Don Quijote, Unamuno sees him as a model for the new man who will save the world, for he acts by faith and love rather than by reason. In "The Agony of Christianity," Unamuno describes the struggle to believe and the agony involved in the preservation of Christian faith.

Many of Unamuno's novels exemplify his philosophical and religious ideas. "Mist," dealing with the theme of immortality, is also an important work for its contributions to the theory of the modern novel. Augusto Pérez protests to the author of the work, a *persona* of Unamuno, when he is about to be killed for plot purposes. "Abel Sánchez," a novel on the Cain and Abel theme, develops the existentialist theme of "the other," the theory that envy is self-hatred, and that the envied person is inevitably a participant in the envy. Unamuno's poetry covers the range of his contradictory ideas and emotions, but it is in the poetry, particularly the verses evoking his homeland written during his exile in France, that the aspect of the author which has been called "the contemplative Unamuno" (Blanco-Aguinaga) is found. Rejecting modernism and aestheticism, he subordinated form to ideas in his poetry.

The dictator Primo de Rivera sent Unamuno into exile in the Canary Islands in 1924, but he soon escaped to Paris where he remained until 1930, when he returned to Spain. In 1936 he was placed under house arrest when he spoke out against anti-intellectualism, and he died on the final day of that year.

SELECTED WORKS. Trans. by Anthony Kerrigan; ed. by Anthony Kerrigan and Martin Nozick. Bollingen Ser. *Princeton Univ. Press* Vol. 3 Our Lord Don Quixote (1905) 1958–1959 $12.50; Vol. 4 The Tragic Sense of Life (1912) 1968 $13.50; Vol. 5 The Agony of Christianity (1925) and Essays on Faith 1974 $11.00

PERPLEXITIES AND PARADOXES. Trans. by Stuart Gross. 1945. Philosophical Lib. *Greenwood* $8.75. A collection of early essays.

THE TRAGIC SENSE OF LIFE. 1912. Trans. by J. Crawford Fitch. 1921. *Dover* 1954 pap. $2.50

MIST: A Tragi-Comic Novel. 1914. Trans. by Warner Fite. 1928. *Howard Fertig* 1974 $12.50

ABEL SÁNCHEZ (1917) AND OTHER STORIES (The Madness of Doctor Montarco and Saint Emmanuel the Good). Trans. by Anthony Kerrigan. *Regnery* Gateway 1956 $1.95

THREE EXEMPLARY NOVELS (The Marquis of Lumbria, Two Mothers, Nothing Less Than a Man). 1920. Trans. by Angel Flores; introd. by Angel del Río. *Grove* Evergreen 1956 pap. $2.95

THE AGONY OF CHRISTIANITY. 1925. Trans. by Kurt F. Reinhardt. *Ungar* 1960 $5.00 pap. $1.75

Books about Unamuno

Unamuno: A Philosophy of Tragedy. By Jose Ferrater Mora. Trans. by Philip Silver. *Univ. of California Press* 1962 pap. $1.50

Unamuno and the Novel as Expressionistic Conceit. By David William Foster. *Inter-American Univ. Press* 1973 pap. $2.50

BENAVENTE, JACINTO. 1866–1954. (Nobel Prize 1922).

Benavente, recipient of the Nobel Prize in 1922, marks the beginning of modern Spanish drama for his break with the melodrama and affectation of the previous style, represented by another Nobel Prize winner, José Echegaray. He professed his masters to be Lope de Vega, Calderón, Shakespeare (*q.v.*), Ibsen (*q.v.*), and Galdós, but beside their works his seem bland and static. He is noted for elegant dialogues, and indeed he uses conversation to relate action which takes place offstage. He excels in the use of social satire, ironic presentations of human weaknesses, and in psychological penetration of character. "The Bonds of Interest," considered his best play, utilizes puppet figures, "the same grotesque masks of that Italian *commedia dell'arte*, but not as gay as they were, for in all this time they have thought a great deal," as Crispín explains in his introduction. Crispín contrives to secure a financially advantageous marriage for his poverty-stricken master Leonardo with Silvia, daughter of the city's richest man. His thesis that the bonds of money are stronger than those of love seems disproved by the hints of love present in the marriage he finally arranges, but is confirmed in the sequel, which reveals that Leonardo's love waned soon after the marriage.

THE BONDS OF INTEREST. 1907. Trans. by J. G. Underhill; ed. by Hyman Alpern *Ungar* bilingual ed. 1967 $4.50 pap. $1.75

Books about Benavente

Jacinto Benavente. By Marcelino C. Peñuelas. World Authors Ser. *Twayne* 1969 $6.95

BLASCO IBÁÑEZ, VICENTE.   1867–1928.

Blasco Ibáñez is considered the last of the nineteenth-century realistic and naturalistic novelists even though he actually produced most of his work in the twentieth century. Although he is more than a regional novelist, his finest works are set in his native Valencia, depicting the harsh and brutal existence of peasant farmers and fishermen—for example "Reeds and Mud" and "The Cabin." In "Blood and Sand," made into a popular film in the United States, he attacked the Spanish passion for bullfighting as primitive and blood-thirsty. He is most famous abroad for "The Four Horsemen of the Apocalypse" (1916), a naturalistic novel on the horrors of war provoked by the Battle of Marne in which he predicted the involvement of the United States in World War I.

The Last Lion and Other Stories. *Branden* 1962 pap. $.95

The Cabin. 1898. Trans. by F. H. Snow. 1919 *Fertig* $13.50

Reeds and Mud. 1902. Trans. by Lester Beberfall. *Branden* 1966 pap. $2.95

Blood and Sand. 1908. Trans. by Frances Partridge. *Ungar* 1962 pap. $3.25

The Four Horsemen of the Apocalypse. 1916. Trans. by Charlotte Brewster Jordan. *Dutton* 1918 new ed. 1941 $7.50

BAROJA y NESSI, PÍO.   1872–1956.

Pío Baroja, whose works were admired by Hemingway, is one of Spain's foremost twentieth-century novelists. A socially conscious writer whose mission was to expose injustices, Baroja chose as central characters those who live outside society—bohemian vagabonds, anarchists, degenerates, persons from the lower classes, and tormented intellectuals. In "The Restlessness of Shanti Andía," Baroja uses Basque sailors as protagonists to dramatize his view of life as a constant struggle for survival and to present a world aboard ship which functions outside society's laws. In "The Tree of Science," medical student Andres Hurtado sees his intelligence as a disease and a disgrace which incapacitates him in life. For its treatment of *abulia* (lack of will) Valbuena Prat has called this "the novel most typical of the Generation of 1898." Baroja's view that the concepts of beginning and end are human inventions to satisfy unattainable desires for meaning influences the form of his novels, often a series of episodes without cause and effect which end with unresolved problems.

Baroja studied medicine, a discipline reflected in his works by an interest in the pathological. During the twenties he was popular in the United States, where many of his novels appeared in translation. In 1936 he was elected to the Spanish Academy. Franco later banned all but one of his nearly 100 books, but Baroja continued to live and write, although less assertively, in Spain until his death.

The Restlessness of Shanti Andía and Other Writings. 1911. Trans. by Anthony Kerrigan. *Univ. of Michigan Press* 1959 $7.50

The Tree of Knowledge. 1911. Trans. by Aubrey F. G. Bell. 1928. *Howard Fertig* 1974 $12.50

Books about Baroja

Negation in Baroja: A Key to His Novelistic Creativity. By Leo L. Barrow. *Univ. of Arizona Press* 1971 $5.95

Pío Baroja. By Beatrice P. Patt. World Authors Ser. *Twayne* 1971 $6.95

MACHADO y RUIZ, ANTONIO.   1875–1939.

Machado's great love for Castile, nourished during his years as a teacher of French in Soria, is the source of much of his poetry. Rejecting modernism and gongorism, he wrote simple, natural, and spare verses. Sadness and melancholy are his dominant moods, deriving from the somber, barren atmosphere of the Castilian landscape, the death of his young wife in 1912, his own solitary nature, and the pessimism of his generation about Spain. In "Campos de Castilla," generally considered to mark his poetic height, his themes are lost youth, time, death, religion, and Spain. Machado believed that memory, capable of transforming and reliving experience, was man's only defense against time. His preoccupation with the concept of time as a stream carrying man to his end in nothingness may have developed from his study with Henri Bergson. In "Juan de Mairena," Machado the poet carried on a dialogue with a *persona* of himself, Machado the philosopher, discussing philosophy, metaphysics, and the anguish of existence, topics which characterize him as a member of the Generation of 1898.

Castilian Ilexes. 1912. Trans. by Charles Tomlinson and Henry Gifford. *Oxford* 1963 $4.75

JUAN DE MAIRENA: Epigrams, Maxims, Memoranda, and Memoirs of an Apocryphal Professor with an Appendix of Poems from "The Apocryphal Songbooks." Trans. and ed. by Ben Belitt. *Univ. of California Press* 1963 $6.95 pap. $1.50

Books about Machado

Antonio Machado: A Dialogue with Time. By Norma L. Hutman. *Univ. of New Mexico Press* 1969 $7.95

Antonio Machado. By Carl W. Cobb. World Authors Ser. *Twayne* 1971 $6.95

PÉREZ DE AYALA, RAMÓN. 1880–1962.

Pérez de Ayala experimented with a variety of novelistic forms. His controversial novels have been criticized by some as pedantic, nihilistic, and pornographic, while others have praised their intellectual orientation, realistic portrayal of human weaknesses, and frank treatment of sex. "Belarmino and Apolonio" is a novelistic treatment of the philosophy of perspectivism. At least two versions of an event are narrated, and characters are described from many angles, some even having more than one name. In "Honeymoon, Bittermoon" Pérez de Ayala constructs a grotesque, stylized world through skillful use of poetic language, symbol, and caricature, attacking hypocritical prudishness with the story of a young man's initiation into amorous adventures.

BELARMINO AND APOLONIO. 1921. Trans. by Gabriel Burns and Murray Baumgarten. *Univ. of California Press* 1971 $8.95

HONEYMOON, BITTERMOON. 1923. Trans. by Barry Eisenberg. *Univ. of California Press* 1972 $8.95

Books about Pérez de Ayala

Literary Perspectivism of Ramón Pérez de Ayala. By Frances W. Weber. Romance Languages and Literatures Studies *International Scholarly Bk. Services* 1966 $6.50

JIMÉNEZ, JUAN RAMÓN. 1881–1958. (Nobel Prize 1956)

On receiving the Nobel Prize in 1956, Juan Ramón Jiménez was praised for "his lyrical poetry, which constitutes an inspiring example in the Spanish language of spirituality and artistic purity." Jiménez's works have indeed provided inspiration for many younger Spanish poets—García Lorca, Pedro Salinas, and Jorge Guillén among them—as well as to Latin American poets. His poetic world is both aesthetic and spiritual. Through poetry Jiménez endeavored not only to express his interior reality but also to reach the highest levels of spiritual experience.

His early work is marked by a short period of modernism followed by a rejection of it in favor of simpler forms, particularly that of the traditional Spanish ballads. The turmoil and anxiety produced by his sea voyage to the United States to marry an American, Zenobia Camprubí, and their return as newlyweds begins his second period. That phase is characterized by increasing subjectivity and purification of his poetry, a process furthered by Zenobia, who protected him from intrusions of the world. His use of woman to symbolize the object of his desires to know and experience reveals the influence of Bécquer. In his final stage he embarks on a mystical search for the absolute. His revelation is that "God desired" and "God desiring" reside within his own soul.

"Platero and I," a poignant and charming story in poetic prose about a silver-gray donkey named Platero, is popular with children. Jiménez did not intend it for children exclusively, however, but rather as a celebration of the essence of the child, "a spiritual island fallen from heaven."

Jiménez left Spain at the beginning of the Civil War and was never to return to his native land. He lived in the United States for a time and then moved to Puerto Rico, where he taught at the University of Puerto Rico in San Juan.

JUAN RAMÓN JIMÉNEZ: Three Hundred Poems, 1903–1953. Sel. and trans. by Eloïse Roach; introd. by Ricardo Gullón. *Univ. of Texas Press* 1962 $10.00. This fine representative collection includes those poems which the poet and his wife considered his best. The translator selected them from the Nobel Prize collection "*Libros de Poesía*" and from books published between 1903 and 1914.

PLATERO AND I. 1914. Trans. by Eloïse Roach *Univ. of Texas Press* 1946 1957 $4.75; trans. by William H. and Mary M. Roberts *New Am. Lib.* Signet 1960 pap. $.75

Books about Jiménez

Circle of Paradox: Time and Essence in the Poetry of Juan Ramón Jiménez. By Paul R. Olson. *Johns Hopkins Univ. Press* 1967 $9.50

Juan Ramón Jiménez. By Howard T. Young. Essays on Modern Writers *Columbia* 1967 pap $1.00

ORTEGA Y GASSET, JOSÉ. 1883–1955. *See Chapter 5, Philosophy*, Reader's Adviser, *Vol. 3.*

SALINAS, PEDRO. 1891–1951.

Pedro Salinas was one of several modern Spanish poets who have taken doctorates and taught in universities. After leaving Spain in 1936, Salinas had a distinguished career as a professor at Cambridge, the University of Puerto Rico, Wellesley, and the Johns Hopkins University. While Salinas also wrote criticism, essays, drama, and fiction, he is remembered chiefly as a poet. Love is one of his principal subjects, and in *"La voz a ti debida"* ("To Live in Pronouns"), his love for a woman is transformed into the quest for spiritual love, which symbolizes his attempt to reconcile the interior and exterior worlds. Salinas regarded love as the power to create a stable inner reality as protection against the chaos of the world. In this treatment of love and his idealization of women, he resembles Bécquer and Jiménez, two of his masters. In *"El contemplado"* ("Sea of Puerto Rico") he discovers peace through a contemplation of the waters of Puerto Rico. In his final volume, "The Incredible Bomb," he asserts faith in love even in this loveless, dangerous nuclear age.

TO LIVE IN PRONOUNS: Selected Love Poems. 1933. Trans. by Edith Helman and Norma Farber. *W. W. Norton* 1974 $12.50

SEA OF SAN JUAN: A Contemplation. 1946. Trans. by Eleanor Turnbull. *Branden* 1950 $2.75

GUILLÉN, JORGE. 1893–

Guillén's poetry celebrates this life and things of this world. In *"Cántico,"* first published in 1928 and then substantially revised numerous times by the poet, he exalts the pure joy of being: "To be, nothing more. And that suffices." He finds beauty in a walnut table top. This enthusiasm for life is sustained until *"Clamor"* (three volumes published in 1957, 1960, and 1963), when the brutal realities of the modern world break into his joyous vision. Even so, Guillén remains optimistic about the future, and in his poem "Goodbye, Goodbye, Europe," he speaks of escaping the old decaying world to an "innocent new world," a reference to the United States where he has taught in universities since 1936. Guillén's style is concentrated, economical, disciplined, and polished, showing the influence of classical forms as well as of the gongorist style. His is a "pure poetry" from which he has attempted to remove all nonpoetic elements, such as narrative and anecdote. He has translated Valéry (*q.v.*) and Claudel (*q.v.*) into Spanish.

AFFIRMATION: A Bilingual Anthology. 1919–1966. Trans. by Julian Palley. *Univ. of Oklahoma Press* 1971 $6.95 pap. $2.95

Books about Guillén

The Vibrant Silence in Jorge Guillén's "Aire Nuestro." By F. L. Yudin. *International Scholarly Bk. Services* 1975 $5.40

BAREA, ARTURO. 1897–1957.

An exile who died in England, Barea achieved international acclaim for his trilogy, "The Forging of a Rebel," which was published in English prior to its publication in Spanish in 1952. The first two volumes consist of a novelistic treatment of the events which led him to become a socialist, while the third volume is a powerful narrative of actual events of the Civil War, more properly labelled a history than a novel.

THE FORGING OF A REBEL. 1940 1943 1946. Trans. by Ilsa Barea. Richard Seaver Bk. *Viking* 1974 $15.00

ALONSO, DÁMASO. 1898–

Although the major portion of Alonso's work is literary history and criticism, he established himself as a very reputable poet with "Children of Wrath." The metaphysical and religious poetry of this volume deals with the despair of modern life and man's search for salvation. The poetic form is free verse, adopted by Alsonso in the belief that aesthetic preoccupations were irrelevant considering the state of the world.

CHILDREN OF WRATH. 1944. Trans by Elias L. Rivers. *Johns Hopkins Press* 1971 $6.95

GARCÍA LORCA, FEDERICO. 1899–1936.

García Lorca is perhaps the best known of modern Spanish writers, partly because of his brutal execution outside Granada by Franco's army at the beginning of the Civil War, but primarily because of his genius for poetry and drama. In 1928 Lorca published "Gypsy Ballads," which won him immediate success and is considered one of the most important volumes of poetry of the century. Attracted to the gypsies for their exotic folklore, primitive sexual vitality, and their status as a group on the fringe of Spanish society, Lorca enlarged the gypsy people and their traditions to mythic proportions. Nature takes on human form while reality acquires a dream-like quality in this powerful transformation of the world into myth. The verse is colorful, rhythmic, dramatic, symbolic, and suggestive. Lorca's visit to New York in 1929 produced in him a deep despair from his confrontation with a mechanical and dehumanized society, and he saw in the Negro the only hope for revitalization of that world. The volume "Poet in New York" shows the influence of Negro spirituals and the American poets Walt Whitman and T. S. Eliot (qq.v.).

Although García Lorca was interested in drama throughout his life, he did not produce much of significance until the 1930s. Most important is his trilogy of Spanish rural life, "Blood Wedding," "Yerma," and "The House of Bernarda Alba," all tragedies with women as protagonists. In each play, the fall of the heroine, and that of those around her whom she pulls down, is caused by frustrations produced by society. "Blood Wedding" demonstrates the sterility of the traditional code of honor, "Yerma" reveals the emptiness of a traditional marriage in which the woman must bear her husband children to prove her fidelity, and "The House of Bernarda Alba" dramatizes the destructive nature of Bernarda's dictatorial rule over her house, a microcosm of Spain. "The Butterfly's Evil Spell" is Lorca's first play; "The Shoemaker's Prodigious Wife" and "Don Perlimplín" are farces; "The Billy-Club Puppets" is a puppet play.

SELECTED POEMS. Trans. by Jaime de Angulo and others; ed. by Francisco García Lorca and Donald M. Allen. *New Directions* bilingual ed. 1955 $1.50

THE GYPSY BALLADS OF GARCÍA LORCA. 1928. Trans by Rolfe Humphries. Poetry Ser. *Indiana Univ. Press* 1953 $1.45

POET IN NEW YORK. 1929. Trans by Ben Belitt. *Grove Press* Evergreen bilingual ed. 1955 pap. $2.95; *Peter Smith* 1955 1957 1968 $4.50

FIVE PLAYS: Comedies and Tragicomedies. Trans. by Richard L. O'Connell and James Graham-Luján. *New Directions* 1963 $2.75. The Shoemaker's Prodigious Wife (1931), Don Perlimplín (1931), Doña Rosita the Spinster (1925), Billy-Club Puppets (1931), The Butterfly's Evil Spell (1919).

THREE TRAGEDIES. Trans. by Richard L. O'Connell and James Graham-Luján. *New Directions* 1956 pap. $1.75. Blood Wedding (1933), Yerma (1934), The House of Bernarda Alba (1936).

Books about García Lorca

Lorca: The Poet and His People. By Arturo Barea. 1949. *Cooper* 1973 lib. bdg. $6.00
The Symbolic World of Federico García Lorca. By Rupert C. Allen. *Univ. of New Mexico Press* 1972 $8.95
Psyche and Symbol in the Theater of Federico García Lorca: Perlimplín, Yerma, Blood-wedding. By Rupert C. Allen. *Univ. of Texas Press* 1974 $9.50
The Comic Spirit of Federico García Lorca. By Virginia Higginbotham. *Univ. of Texas Press* 1975 $10.50

ALBERTI, RAFAEL. 1902–

Alberti began his career as a painter, exhibiting his own work in Madrid before the age of 20. Forced to rest because of poor health, he turned to reading and writing poetry and published his first volume, "*Marinero en la tierra*," a book of lyrics evoking lost childhood, in 1924. His poetry remained conventional until 1927, when he wrote "*Cal y canto*" (published in 1929), poems in the gongorist style dominated by intricate and incongruous images. Alberti has said of that volume, "Formal beauty took hold of me until it almost petrified my feelings." In 1929 he published the volume considered to be his most important, "Concerning the Angels," which deals with the good and bad angels inhabiting modern man's shattered psyche. This volume is difficult and surreal, mingling prose and poetry, logic and incoherence, reason and the irrational. At the same time he was becoming active politically, founding a Communist newspaper, *Octubre*, in 1934. His poetry during the 1930s became more political than poetic, as for example in "*El poeta en la calle*" (1931–1936). After fighting on the side of the Republic during the Civil War, he was forced to flee Spain and since then has lived in Argentina and Italy. His poetic imagination, revived by the birth of a daughter in 1941, surfaced in "To Painting" (1945), a series of odes and sonnets addressed to famous painters.

Of the "Selected Poems," *Library Journal* said, "Alberti's tumultuous spiritual pilgrimage is well defined by the selections in this volume." Interspersed are sections of his autobiography, "A Vanished Grove."

Selected Poems. Trans and ed. by Ben Belitt; introd. by Luis Munguió. *Univ. of California Press* 1966 $7.50 pap. $1.75

The Owl's Insomnia. Trans. by Mark Strand. *Atheneum* 1973 pap. $4.95. A bilingual collection.

Concerning the Angels. 1929. Trans. by Geoffrey Connell. *Swallow Press* 1967 $4.95

SENDER, RAMÓN J. 1902–

"Seven Red Sundays," involving radical labor movement activities that culminate in a strike, reflects Sender's left-wing political views. In 1935 he won Spain's national prize for literature with "Mr. Witt among the Rebels" (1937, o.p.), a novel set in 1873 during Spain's first republic. He escaped to France after the fall of the second republic in 1936, then fled to Mexico, and finally settled in the United States, becoming an American citizen in 1942. In spite of his status as an exile, he is widely read in Spain and, upon the publication there of "Three Novelettes on St. Teresa" in 1967 (o.p.), was hailed by a Spanish critic as "our foremost living novelist" (according to Robert J. Clements in *SR*).

Seven Red Sundays. 1932. Trans. by Sir Peter Chalmers Mitchell. *Macmillan* Collier Bks. 1961 pap. $.95

HERNÁNDEZ, MIGUEL. 1910–1942.

Little educated, Hernández studiously imitated the style of Góngora in his first volume of poetry, published in 1933. In his best volume, *"El rayo que no cesa"* (1936), he finds his own voice, expressing powerful emotion in classical sonnet form. After fighting for the Republic during the Civil War, Hernández was imprisoned in a concentration camp, where he died of tuberculosis at the age of 32 in spite of international protests for his freedom. "The Songbook of Absences," written during his years as a political prisoner, are a painful record of his suffering upon the separation from his wife, his sorrow at the death of his son, and yearning for the simple country life of his youth.

The Songbook of Absences. 1938–1941. Trans. by Tom Jones. *Charioteer Press* 1972 $5.00

CELA, CAMILO JOSÉ. 1916–

In Cela's first novel, "The Family of Pascual Duarte," a condemned criminal relates in letters published after his execution the degrading circumstances which led him to commit a series of brutal murders, including that of a mare, his pet dog, his sister's lover, and his mother. Ironically, he receives the death sentence not for these murders but for killing a local boss. Narrative techniques employed by Cela are epistolary form, stream of consciousness, rupture of chronological sequence, and perspectivism. Cela produced no novel of real literary value after "The Family of Pascual Duarte" until "The Hive" in 1951, a portrait of the sordid world of lower class Madrid, and "Mrs. Caldwell Speaks to Her Son" in 1953. The subject of the latter is a mother writing notes to her dead son to try to reconstruct his life as she gradually lapses into insanity and senility: "Mr. Cela narrates it in a beautiful, stylized way, with a tone of surrealistic casualness and a dash of old-fashioned, good-hearted cynicism"—*(New Yorker)*. "Journey to the Alcarria," a description of his walking tour through Spain in the 1940s, is "recommended for larger travel or literature collections"—*(LJ)*.

The Family of Pascual Duarte. 1942. Trans. by Anthony Kerrigan. *Avon* 1972 pap. $1.45

Journey to the Alcarria. 1948. Trans. by Frances M. López-Morillas. *Univ. of Wisconsin Press* 1964 $10.00

Mrs. Caldwell Speaks to Her Son. 1953. Trans. by J. S. Bernstein. *Cornell Univ. Press* 1968 $7.50 pap. $2.45

Books about Cela

Novels and Travels of Camilo José Cela. By Robert Kirsner. Romance Languages and Literatures Studies *International Scholarly Book Services* 1964 $6.50

GIRONELLA, JOSÉ MARÍA. 1917–

Gironella is best known for his trilogy "The Cypresses Believe in God" (1953), "One Million Dead" (1961), and "Peace after War" (1966), about Spanish life from the final years of the Republic to the present day. "The Cypresses Believe in God" deals with social and political activities leading up to the Civil War as they affect life in the Catalan city of Gerona. The point of view is that of its hero, Ignacio de Alvear, who in his contacts with people from various political parties and social classes views a wide spectrum of Spanish society. Gironella claims to be objective and impartial, but critics have noted, particularly in the second volume, a gentleness toward the Falange, and indeed he has been labeled a "*Franquista*." Others have suggested that perhaps he has moderated his views to prevent censorship of his work.

Born in Gerona and educated in primary school and an ecclesiastical seminary until he was 13, Gironella worked at a series of odd jobs until the Spanish Civil War, when he served at the front in Franco's army from 1936 to 1939. His first novel, "*Un Hombre*," published in 1946, won the Nadal Prize, the Spanish equivalent of the French Prix Goncourt.

THE CYPRESSES BELIEVE IN GOD. 1953. Trans. by Harriet de Onís. *Knopf* 1955 $10.00

PEACE AFTER WAR. 1966. Trans. by Joan MacLean. *Knopf* 1969 $10.00

GOYTISOLO, JUAN.   1931–

Goytisolo first became known in the United States for his novel "The Young Assassins" (1954, trans. by John Rust 1959 o.p.), the story of juvenile delinquents corrupted by social conditions during and immediately after the Spanish Civil War. His depictions of the spiritual emptiness and moral decay of Spain under the Franco regime led to the censorship of some of his works there, and he moved to Paris in 1957. "Count Julian" is an exile's view of Spain, with Spanish history, literature, and language derisively viewed across the narrow straits in Tangiers for the purpose of destroying them so that they might be reinvented. Formally, it is a "new novel" along the lines of Robbe-Grillet's formulations.

COUNT JULIAN. 1970. Trans. by Helen R. Lane *Viking* 1974 $7.95

Books about Goytisolo

Juan Goytisolo. By Kessel Schwartz. World Authors Ser. *Twayne* 1970 $6.95

—C.S.

Chapter 12

German Literature

> *"German literature is troublesome material for those who like to make trim patterns out of untidy realities. Because of its richness and diversity, it fits awkwardly into a scheme of periods and movements. . . . Writers in the German language have rarely been supported, or constrained, by well-established native traditions and have veered, since they lacked this stabilizing influence, from one extreme to another; they have either set the pace or followed in the wake of literary fashion, striving to overhaul their contemporaries elsewhere in Europe."*
>
> —C. P. Magill, "German Literature"

A major change from the last edition of *"The Reader's Adviser"* is the inclusion of authors from Germany, Austria, and German-speaking Switzerland within this chapter. Further, modern German dramatists are also considered here. The date following a title is that of original publication in Germany.

In recent years there has been a renascence of interest in Germany. Former Federal Chancellor Willi Brandt won the Nobel Peace Prize (1971), and then resigned his office because of scandal in his administration, an action not unnoticed by Americans who were sitting in the middle of the Watergate misery. Tentative contacts were also established between the Federal Republic of Germany and the German Democratic Republic. Although no startling breakthrough has occurred, this does show that the West German government is accepting postwar reality. This situation was further accentuated by the establishment of diplomatic relations between the United States Government and the German Democratic Republic as well as the seating of delegates from both Germanies in the United Nations. Further, in recent years there have been a number of attempts by West Germans to come to grips with the Nazi past. Biographies and studies of Hitler and the Nazi phenomenon are flooding the West German market; some are sensational but most are honest, sober, guilt-free evaluations of a bizarre and unfortunate period.

This revival of interest in Germany is also evident in the field of literature, if such a judgment can be made on the basis of the number of translations and studies of German literature now available to English readers. Further evidence is seen in the popularity of German Literature in Translation courses on the nation's campuses in which German authors from the medieval period to the present are read and discussed with enthusiasm. Such writers as Hermann Hesse and Franz Kafka continue to enjoy a great vogue among readers, and Thomas Mann, whose 100th anniversary was celebrated in 1975, is again the object of interest. By winning the Nobel Prize for Literature (1972) Heinrich Böll joined the select company of German Laureates, Theodor Mommsen (1902), Rudolf Eucken (1908), Paul Heyse (1910), Gerhart Hauptmann (1912), Thomas Mann (1929), Hermann Hesse (1946), and Nelly Sachs (1966), and is again attracting readers in this country.

Like the historians, modern German writers are also facing the past and, to a large extent, overcoming it, concentrating instead on the problems which beset present-day German society. This trend can only be construed as a sign of a return to health.

The lack of adequate translations poses a problem for English readers. Important writers whose works either do not exist in translation or are very poorly represented are the medieval poet Walther von der Vogelweide and the modern poet Paul Celan. As in the last edition of *"Reader's Adviser,"* the writers Canetti, Faeke, Lenz, Nossack, and the Austrian dramatist Nestroy are not included. Another writer who will be held in abeyance is Hans Herlin, whose first novel "Commemorations" (*St. Martin's* 1975 $8.95) has been well received on both sides of the Atlantic. According to *Newsweek,* "this novel marks the debut of a significant and disturbing new writer." Writers from the German Democratic Republic are still inadequately represented; it is to be hoped that the establishment of diplomatic relations will rectify that situation. Deleted from this edition because of the lack of translations are Hans Fallada, Ernst Jünger, Ingeborg Bachmann, Alexander Kluge, and Gisela Elsner.

Theatrically speaking, pre-Nazi Germany was adventurous, spurred in great part by the talented producer Max Reinhart (1873–1943). Carl Zuckmayer (b. 1896) was an important dramatist of the period of the Weimar Republic, when he enjoyed great success with "The Captain from Köpenick" (1931), a humorous satire on Prussian militarism. "The Devil's General" (1946) was written when Zuckmayer, in exile, was struggling for a living on a farm in Barnard, Vermont, during World War II. (Films were made of both.) After the war Zuckmayer went to live in Switzerland. Now in his seventies, he has been publishing his reminiscences, "A Piece, as It Were, of Myself" (in German), which now includes several volumes containing his fascinating recollections of theatrical figures such as Reinhardt, Brecht and Frisch. The Nationalist countercurrent in the drama of the thirties had its source in the patriotic plays of World War I. Especially after 1933, "blood-and-soil" dramas, plays about war and German history, and popular farces accompanied the rise of Nazism. After World War II, vitality in German drama came from Switzerland, the only German-speaking country where the continuity of cultural life had not been broken by Nazi rule, though Bertolt Brecht, returning to Germany after a long absence, was soon to bring his revivifying influence to East Berlin.

Progress in the drama has been exciting in recent years. Peter Weiss continues his experiments in "documentary theater," and "Trotsky in Exile" is his most superb expression to date. Peter Handke, not included in this edition, is emerging as the most disturbing and avant-garde voice in drama today. By rejecting the traditional illusory and entertainment aspect of drama, including Marxist drama, Handke takes an anti-theater stance, one which moves from distrust of language ("Kaspar" *Farrar, Straus* 1967 $4.95 Noonday 1970 pap. $2.95) to distrust of reason ("The Ride over Lake Constance" *Farrar, Straus* 1975 $8.95 Noonday 1976 pap. $3.95). He regards both reason and language as restraints imposed on the individual by society in order to control him and make true communication impossible. Handke has alternately enraged and fascinated his critics and it remains to be seen whether he will be able to maintain his momentum. In any event, the continuance of Weiss and the experiments of Handke auger well for the future of German drama.

For an introduction to German literature, the histories by both Robertson and Boesch are highly recommended *(see History and Criticism below)*. The following titles have been selected as background reading:

Barraclough, Geoffrey. THE ORIGINS OF MODERN GERMANY. *Macmillan* 2nd ed. 1946 $6.50; 1946. *Putnam* Capricorn Bks. 1963 pap. $2.95. A clear and detailed presentation of German history from the earliest period to the middle of the twentieth century. The chapters on the medieval centuries are especially noteworthy.

Brandt, Willy. THE ORDEAL OF COEXISTENCE. *Harvard Univ. Press* 1963 $3.00. Brandt talks soberly of the tragedies caused by the building of the Wall, but regards it as "the most convincing propaganda against Communism there has been since 1917." (Lectures given at Harvard, October 1962.)

Bruford, W. H. CULTURE AND SOCIETY IN CLASSICAL WEIMAR, 1775–1806. *Cambridge* 1962 $22.50

GERMANY IN THE EIGHTEENTH CENTURY. *Cambridge* 1935 $14.50 pap. $3.95. One of the most important and original studies in the field of German literature, it has as its task the definition of the sociological background of the period known as the Age of Goethe.

Dawidowicz, Lucy S. THE WAR AGAINST THE JEWS, 1933–1945. *Holt* 1975 $15.00

"Mrs. Dawidowicz's (work) comes to us as a major work of synthesis, providing for the first time a full account of the holocaust not merely as it completed the Nazi vision but as it affected the Jews of Eastern Europe"—(*N.Y. Times*).

Holborn, Hajo. GERMANY AND EUROPE: Historical Essays. *Doubleday* 1971 pap. $2.50

"In this book are assembled some of [Holborn's] most important essays. New (and searching) are his analyses of German idealism in the light of social history (and) his appraisal of the opposition to Hitler. Recommended"—(*LJ*).

A HISTORY OF MODERN GERMANY. *Knopf* 3 vols. Vol. 1 The Reformation Vol. 2 1648–1840 Vol. 3 1840–1945 1959 each $11.95. These volumes represent the most thorough, scholarly, and readable treatment of modern German history available in English. Highly recommended.

Jay, Martin. THE DIALECTICAL IMAGINATION: A History of the Frankfurt School and the Institute of Social Research, 1923–1950. *Little* 1973 pap. $3.95

Merkl, Peter H. GERMANY: Yesterday and Tomorrow. *Oxford* 1965 $10.00

Professor Merkl of the University of California assesses Germany's past aggressiveness, which he feels will not occur again. "A perceptive review"—(*SR*).

Mosse, George L. THE CRISIS OF GERMAN IDEOLOGY: Intellectual Origins of the Third Reich. *Grosset* Univ. Lib. 1964 pap. $2.95

THE NATIONALIZATION OF THE MASSES: Political Symbolism and Mass Movements in Germany from the Napoleonic Wars Through The Third Reich. *Howard Fertig* 1975 $14.00

Pfeiler, William K. WAR AND THE GERMAN MIND: The Testimony of Men of Fiction Who Fought at the Front. 1941. *AMS Press* $11.50

Recent reprint of this investigation into their pre-World War II psychological conditioning. "Professor Pfeiler's extremely fair study will increase our understanding of . . . modern Germany"—(Hans Kohn, in the *Nation*).

Steiner, Jean-François. TREBLINKA. Trans. by Helen Weaver; pref. by Simone de Beauvoir. *Simon & Schuster* 1967 $5.95

A "nonfiction novel" re-creating the horrors of the Polish concentration camp. Based on diaries, documents and interviews with the 40 survivors of the 600 who escaped on August 2, 1943. "A powerful, unforgettable book" (*PW*), which has also proved controversial.

Wiesenthal, Simon. THE MURDERERS AMONG US: The Wiesenthal Memoirs. Ed. with introd. by Joseph Wechsberg. *McGraw-Hill* 1967 $6.95; *Bantam* 1973 pap. $1.25

The story of the man who made hunting escaped Nazi war criminals his life's work. "Wiesenthal emerges as a man full of compassion and human understanding, driven by an insatiable urge for justice. . . . A great book"—(*LJ*).

See also Chapter 9, History, Government and Politics, Reader's Adviser, *Vol. 3.*

HISTORY AND CRITICISM

Benedikt, Michael, and George E. Wellwarth, Trans. and eds. POSTWAR GERMAN THEATRE. *Dutton* 1967 pap. $2.75

An anthology of plays by Kaiser, Borchert, Sylvanus, Dürrenmatt, Frisch, Dorst, Laszlo, Grass, Hildesheimer, Weiss. "The translations are excellent but the leitmotif of this disappointingly biased selection is the entrapped and self-pitying and intellectual in the modern world, which does not give a fair picture of the German drama today"—(E. R. von Freiburg, in the *Nation*). The *Nation's* critic (an East and a West German writing as one) notes the omission of the West Germans Hochhuth, Walser, Geissler, and all of East Germans (the latter, Wellwarth explains, because little of literary value is being produced under the present East German regime) and points out four excellent plays that *are* included. *Library Journal* also found the selection unrepresentative.

Bennett, E. K. A HISTORY OF THE GERMAN NOVELLE. Ed. by H. M. Waidson. *Cornell Univ. Press* 2nd rev. ed. 1961 $15.50 1974 pap. $4.95. Bennett's study still remains a classic of *Novelle* scholarship and is among the best in either German or English.

Bentley, Eric. THE THEATRE OF COMMITMENT AND OTHER ESSAYS ON DRAMA IN OUR SOCIETY. *Atheneum* 1967 $5.00. A study of political engagement in drama, especially as seen in the plays of Brecht, Weiss, and Hochhuth.

Bithell, Jethro. MODERN GERMAN LITERATURE, 1880–1950. *Ungar* 3rd rev. ed. 1959 $12.00

GERMANY: Companion to German Studies. *Pitman* 5th ed. 1955 $12.50

Boesch, Bruno, Ed. GERMAN LITERATURE: A Critical Survey. Trans. by Ronald Taylor. *Harper* (Barnes & Noble) 1972 $17.25 pap. 1973 $8.25. This work, long a standard literary history in Germany, contains a series of essays on the various periods of German literature by noted German scholars. Its translation is to be welcomed. Highly recommended.

Boeschenstein, Hermann. GERMAN LITERATURE OF THE 19TH CENTURY. *St. Martin's* 1969 $7.95

Closs, August. THE GENIUS OF THE GERMAN LYRIC: An Historical Survey of Its Formal and Metaphysical Values. *Dufour* rev. ed. 1962 $12.95 pap. $4.95

Daemmrich, Horst, and Diether H. Haenicke, Eds. THE CHALLENGE OF GERMAN LITERATURE. *Wayne State Univ. Press* 1971 $13.95

Emrich, Wilhelm. THE LITERARY REVOLUTION AND MODERN SOCIETY AND OTHER ESSAYS. Trans. by Alexander and Elizabeth Henderson. *Ungar* 1971 $7.50

Friederich, Werner P. AN OUTLINE HISTORY OF GERMAN LITERATURE. College Outline Ser. *Harper* (Barnes & Noble) 2nd rev. ed. 1961 pap. $2.25. Good skeletal reference; recommended.

Fuchs, Georg. REVOLUTION IN THE THEATRE: Conclusions Concerning the Munich Artist's Theatre. Condensed and adapted from the German by Constance Connor Kuhn. 1959. *Kennikat* $9.50

Fuerst, Norbert. THE VICTORIAN AGE OF GERMAN LITERATURE: Eight Essays. *Pennsylvania State Univ.* 1966 $8.50. Readably describes the biographical, historical, and philosophical factors affecting the literature of 1820–1880.

Gray, Ronald. THE GERMAN TRADITION IN LITERATURE, 1871–1945. *Cambridge* 1966 $17.50

Analyzes the tradition which flourished in Goethe's time to what the author considers its aberration in the early 20th century. "[A] wealth of stimulating observations and suggestions"— (*LJ*).

INTRODUCTION TO GERMAN POETRY. *Cambridge* 1965 $8.50 pap. $3.75

Gropius, Walter H., Ed. THE THEATRE OF THE BAUHAUS. Trans. by Arthur S. Wensinger; introd. by editor. *Wesleyan Univ. Press* 1961 pap. 1971 $4.95

The book is for the experienced man of the theater. The three contributors are Oscar Schlemmer, Laszlo Moholy-Nagy, and Farkas Molnar. The avant-garde Bauhaus, a school devoted to all the arts in the Munich of the 1920s had a vast influence on theater throughout the world and on such artists as Robert Edmond Jones and Frank Lloyd Wright.

Haile, H. G. THE HISTORY OF DOCTOR JOHANN FAUSTUS. Trans. by the author. *Univ. of Illinois Press* 1965 pap. $1.45

The anonymous "Story of Dr. Faustus" (1587) illuminates the beliefs and superstitions of its century. Professor Haile describes how "a quite simple reality turned into one of the most striking sagas of the Germanic world"—(*LJ*).

Hamburger, Michael. CONTRARIES: Studies in German Literature. *Dutton* 1970 $8.95 pap. $2.95. This is basically the revised edition of his 1957 book, "Reason and Energy" (o.p.). For this edition Hamburger has added a new essay on Hölderlin and Milton as well as the sections on Nietzsche and Thomas Mann from his 1965 work "From Prophecy to Exorcism" (o.p.).

Hatfield, Henry. CRISIS AND CONTINUITY IN MODERN GERMAN FICTION: Ten Essays. *Cornell Univ. Press* 1969 $8.50

The essays deal with representative authors such as Thomas Mann, Hesse, Kafka and Uwe Johnson. "The essays should prove valuable to all . . . interested in modern German literature, Western culture, and the novel"—(*LJ*).

MODERN GERMAN LITERATURE: The Major Figures in Context. 1967. Midland Bks. *Indiana Univ. Press* pap. $1.85. A critical survey covering the period 1890–1956.

Heitner, Robert R. GERMAN TRAGEDY IN THE AGE OF ENLIGHTENMENT: A Study in the Development of Original Tragedies, 1724–1768. *Univ. of California Press* 1963 $11.50

Heller, Erich. THE ARTIST'S JOURNEY INTO THE INTERIOR. 1965. *Random* Vintage Bks. 1968 pap. $1.65

"[Heller] reassesses the conflict between the aesthetic and the ethical approach to the foundations of human existence, with emphasis on Goethe, Schiller, Hegel, Nietzsche, Rilke and Wittgenstein. . . . Keen analysis [combined] with brilliancy of style"—(*LJ*).

THE DISINHERITED MIND. 1957. *Harper* (Barnes & Noble) 3rd ed. 1971 $7.50 pap. $2.95. Essays on modern German literature and thought as expressed in the works of Goethe, Burckhardt, Nietzsche, Rilke, Spengler, Kafka, and Karl Kraus; highly recommended.

Heller, Peter. DIALECTICS AND NIHILISM: Essays on Lessing, Nietzsche, Mann, and Kafka. *Univ. of Massachusetts Press* 1969 $15.00

Kayser, Wolfgang. THE GROTESQUE IN ART AND LITERATURE. Trans. by Ulrich Weisstein. *McGraw-Hill* 1957 pap. $2.45. A classic of modern criticism, covering artists and writers from the 16th century to the present.

Kohn, Hans. THE MIND OF GERMANY; The Education of a Nation. *Harper* Torchbks. pap. $2.75. The last 200 years of German intellectual and political history, with chapters on Goethe, Romanticism, Heine, Nietzsche, and related subjects.

Ley-Piscator, Maria. THE PISCATOR EXPERIMENT: The Political Theatre. *James H. Heineman, Inc.* 1967 $8.50

An "affectionate and impassioned memoir" (Howard Taubman), by his wife, of Erwin Piscator and this Proletarian Theater (Berlin, 1920s), his collaboration on "epic" and political theater with Brecht, his New School for Social Research (N.Y.) experience, and his *Volksbühne* (People's Theater) of Berlin in the 1960s, where he was able to put his "epic theater" theories into practice and where he produced, among other dramatists, Hochhuth and Weiss.

Morgan, Bayard Quincy. A CRITICAL BIBLIOGRAPHY OF GERMAN LITERATURE IN ENGLISH TRANSLATION, 1481–1927. 1938. *Scarecrow Press* 2nd ed. 1965 $10.00 Suppl. 1928–1955 $14.00

Natan, Alex, Ed. GERMAN MEN OF LETTERS. *Dufour* 6 vols. Vol. I 1962 $12.95 Vols. 2–3 1964 each $10.95 Vol. 4 ed. by Brian Keith-Smith 1965 $12.95 Vols. 5–6 ed. by Alex Natan and Brian Keith-Smith 1973 $12.95 and $13.95 Vols. 1–3 pap. each $6.95. Each volume presents essays by prominent scholars on various German writers. Vol. 4 also contains an essay on East German literature. The series offers a very useful and sound first introduction to the writers under discussion.

Pascal, Roy. THE GERMAN NOVEL. *Univ. of Toronto Press* 1956 pap. $2.95

GERMAN STURM UND DRANG. *Rowman* 1967 $8.50

Pascal, Roy, and Hannah A. Closs. GERMAN LITERATURE OF THE 16TH AND 17TH CENTURIES: Renaissance, Reformation and Baroque. Introductions to German Literature Vol. 2 *Harper* (Barnes & Noble) 1968 $5.75

Prawer, Siegbert Salomon. GERMAN LYRIC POETRY: A Critical Analysis of Selected Poems from Klopstock to Rilke. *Routledge & Kegan Paul* 1965 $8.50

THE ROMANTIC PERIOD IN GERMANY. *Schocken* 1970 $10.50

Raabe, Paul, Ed. THE ERA OF GERMAN EXPRESSIONISM. 1965. Trans. by J. M. Ritchie. *Overlook Press* 1974 $15.00. Contains a collection of essays, notes, letters, and other documents by the creative artists of the period. Some are contemporary to the period and others written by those who survived. No other book of its kind exists for this period and it should be among the first works consulted for orientation in the Expressionist era.

Ritchie, J. M., Ed. PERIODS IN GERMAN LITERATURE. *Dufour* 3 vols. Vol. 1 1967 $15.95 Vol. 2 1970 $10.95 Vol. 3 o.p. A symposium on movements in German literature (17th century to the present) in light of recent research.

Robertson, John G. A HISTORY OF GERMAN LITERATURE. 1962. Rev. by Dorothy Reich and others. *British Bk. Centre* 6th ed. 1971 $11.50. There is no finer general literary history of Germany available in English.

Sagarra, Eda. TRADITION AND REVOLUTION: German Literature and Society, 1830–1890. *Basic Bks.* 1971 $8.95

Salmon, Paul. LITERATURE IN MEDIEVAL GERMANY. Introductions to German Literature Vol. 1 *Harper* (Barnes & Noble) 1967 $6.00

Silz, Wlater. REALISM AND REALITY. *Univ. of North Carolina Press* 1954 $6.00. Silz's work is the classic study of the 19th-century *Novelle* of German Realism. Recommended.

Stern, J. P. IDYLLS AND REALITIES: Studies in Nineteenth Century German Literature. *Ungar* 1971 $8.00

  RE-INTERPRETATIONS: Seven Studies in Nineteenth Century German Literature. *Basic Bks.* 1964 $10.00

Taylor, Archer. THE LITERARY HISTORY OF MEISTERGESANG. 1937. *Kraus* pap. $6.00

Thalmann, Marianne. THE ROMANTIC FAIRY TALE: Seeds of Surrealism. Trans. by Mary B. Corcoran. *Univ. of Michigan Press* 1964 $3.95. A scholarly work on the German literary fairy tale, 1796–1822—in the period of German Romanticism.

Walzel, Oskar. GERMAN ROMANTICISM. *Putnam* 1966 Capricorn Bks. pap. $1.45

Weigand, Hermann J. SURVEYS AND SOUNDINGS IN EUROPEAN LITERATURE. Ed. by A. Leslie Willson. *Princeton Univ. Press* 1966 $15.00. Selected essays, all but two on German literature, by an eminent American Germanist on such subjects as Schiller, Goethe, Chamisso, Hauptmann, and Mann—in graceful, readable prose.

Ziolkowski, Theodore. DIMENSIONS OF THE MODERN NOVEL: German Texts and European Contexts. *Princeton Univ. Press* 1969 $11.50

Zipes, Jack. THE GREAT REFUSAL: Studies of the Romantic Hero in German and American Literature. *Adler's* 1970 $14.00

COLLECTIONS

Bentley, Eric, Ed. FIVE GERMAN PLAYS: Goethe's "Egmont," Schiller's "Don Carlos" and "Mary Stuart," and Kleist's "Penthesilea" and "The Prince of Homburg." In The Classic Theatre, Vol. 2. *Doubleday* Anchor Bks. 1959 pap. $2.50; *Peter Smith* $4.50

Corrigan, Robert, Ed. MASTERPIECES OF THE MODERN CENTRAL EUROPEAN THEATER. Masterpieces of the Modern Theater Ser. *Macmillan* Collier Bks. 1967 pap. (orig.) $1.50. Includes plays by Schnitzler and Hofmannsthal.

  MASTERPIECES OF THE MODERN GERMAN THEATER. Büchner, Hebbel, Hauptmann, Wekdekind, Brecht. Masterpieces of the Modern Theater Ser. *Macmillan* Collier Bks. 1966 pap. (orig.) $1.50

Engel, Eva J., Ed. GERMAN NARRATIVE PROSE. *Dufour* 3 vols. Vol. 1 1966 $13.50 Vol. 2 ed. by H. Yuill 1966 $13.50 Vol. 3 ed. by W. Rehfield 1967 $12.95

Flores, Angel, Ed. AN ANTHOLOGY OF GERMAN POETRY FROM HÖLDERLIN TO RILKE IN ENGLISH TRANSLATION. *Peter Smith* 1960 $6.00. Over 250 poems in English with German originals.

Forster, Leonard, Trans. and ed. with introd. THE PENGUIN BOOK OF GERMAN VERSE. *Penguin* (orig.) bilingual ed. 1957 rev. ed. 1959 1964 pap. $1.45. Prose translations.

Gode, Alexander, and Frederick Ungar, Eds. ANTHOLOGY OF GERMAN POETRY THROUGH THE NINETEENTH CENTURY. (German and English) *Ungar* 2nd ed. 1963 $8.50 pap. $2.95

A "labor of love" and "valuable"—(*LJ*), although translations are uneven in quality.

Hamburger, Michael, Ed. EAST GERMAN POETRY: An Anthology. *Dutton* 1973 $10.00 pap. $5.95

Lamport, F. J., Ed. THE PENGUIN BOOK OF GERMAN STORIES. *Penguin* 1974 pap. $2.50. A representative selection of 19th- and 20th-century *Novellen* by Geothe, Kleist, Büchner, Hauptmann, Mann, Kafka, and Böll, among others.

Lange, Victor, Ed. GREAT GERMAN SHORT NOVELS AND STORIES. *Random* (Modern Lib.) 1952 $2.95. A new selection.

Pick, Robert, Ed. GERMAN STORIES AND TALES. *Simon & Schuster* (Washington Square) 1966 pap. $.95. An excellent variety from the well-known and the lesser known German and Austrian writers.

Rothenberg, Jermone, Trans. and ed. NEW YOUNG GERMAN POETS. *City Lights* 1959 $1.00. Translations of ten poets, among them Enzensberger, Piontek, Bachmann, Celan, and Grass.

Rus, Vladimir, Trans. and ed. SELECTIONS FROM GERMAN POETRY. Bilingual. Fwd. by Lotte Lenya; ill. by Elizabeth Korolkoff. *Harvey House Pubs.* $6.00 lib. bdg. $4.89. A good introductory text; the selection spans the period from the first century to the present day.

Spender, Stephen, Ed. GREAT GERMAN SHORT STORIES. *Dell* 1960 pap. $.95. Includes Mann, Kafka, Rilke, and others.

Waidson, H. M., Ed. GERMAN SHORT STORIES, 1900–1945; 1945–1955. *Cambridge* 2 vols. Vol. 1 $1.75 Vol. 2 $2.75

RUODLIEB. c. 1050.

"Ruodlieb" was composed in Latin hexameters sometime in the eleventh century, probably in the Bavarian monastery of Tegernsee. Unfortunately it is preserved only in fragments. It relates the tale of a young knight, Ruodlieb, who is forced to leave home because of the actions of his enemies. He places himself in the service of a foreign monarch known as the "great king," who becomes involved in a war with the "lesser king." The war is concluded to the great king's advantage. Upon being called home by his mother Ruodlieb is given twelve pieces of advice by the great king. Presumably all twelve axioms would have been acted on in dramatic situations in the complete story; only three are extant.

The "Ruodlieb" is surprising in many ways. The rulers, both the great king and the lesser king, are men of justice and restraint. In place of the ancient warrior ethic, according to which the greatest honor in battle was to win, a milder spirit enters here, in which concluding peace to the satisfaction of both parties is more important. This new aspect points ahead to the romances of the courtly age. In addition, the poem gives us many realistic portraits of early medieval court life as it depicts feasts, entertainments, and ceremonies. It is quite probable that the direction indicated by the "Ruodlieb" would have been taken over into the vernacular fairly soon had not the great strife between Church and Empire, the Investiture Controversy (1075), intervened. This upheaval assured the dominance of religious reform literature for the next century.

RUODLIEB, The Earliest Courtly Novel. Ed. by Gordon B. Ford, Jr. *Adler's* 1965 pap. $10.00; trans. and ed. by Edwin H. Zeydel. *AMS Press* $12.50

THE NIBELUNGENLIED. c. 1200.

The *"Nibelungenlied"* is the most powerful and dramatic work of the courtly period. It was also one of the most popular works, and complete or partial versions appear in over 30 manuscripts. Although the ultimate sources of the epic are to be found in ancient Germanic heroic songs, the medieval German poet, whose identity is still not known and probably never will be, took the matter of these ancient legends and rearranged them to fit his own contemporary situation. The *"Nibelungenlied"* is a strong criticism of aspects of the political system of feudalism, especially that of taking revenge, a custom which had great currency in the poet's world. Thus, although Hagen had every legitimate right to kill Siegfried because Siegfried's wife insulted his queen, he is castigated by the poet. Likewise when Kriemhild, Siegfried's wife, takes revenge on the murderers of her husband, the poet does not spare her his vilification. In both instances the protagonists had the legal right, indeed the obligation, to act as they did, but obviously the poet does not approve.

In the nationalistic nineteenth century, this aspect of the *"Nibelungenlied"* was overlooked, and instead the warrior ethos of battle and victory at any price was glorified. This outlook persisted through the Third Reich. The reasons for this misunderstanding are complex, and the reader is advised to refer to George Mosse, "The Nationalization of the Masses," listed in the first part of this Chapter. It is only recently that the humane strivings of the *Nibelugen* poet have been recognized and emphasized in scholarship. The tragedy of the *Nibelungen* has attracted the fancy of many German writers and composers. Most noteworthy are Friedrich Hebbel, who adapted the legend well in his dramatic trilogy *"Die Nibelungen"* (1862), and Richard Wagner, who based his massive opera tetralogy *"Der Ring des Nibelungen"* on it (1848–1874).

Although both the translations below are satisfactory, the one by Hatto is preferred. A prose translation, it has many excellent appendixes, most noteworthy of which is the "Introduction to a Second Reading."

THE NIBELUNGENLIED. Trans. and ed. by D. G. Mowatt *Dutton* Everyman's 1962 $3.95; trans. by A. T. Hatto *Penguin* 1964 pap. $1.95

THE SONG OF THE NIBELUNGS: A Verse Translation from the Middle High German *Nibelungenlied*. Trans. by Frank G. Ryder. *Wayne State Univ. Press* 1962 $11.00 pap. $4.95

Books about the "Nibelungenlied"

Richard Wagner's "The Ring of the Nibelungs" has been translated with an introduction by Stewart Robb (*Dutton* 1950 $4.50 Everyman's pap. $1.95). Robert Donington has written a detailed study of the symbolism in the music and the myth in his "Wagner's 'Ring' and Its Symbols" (*St. Martin's* 1963 $10.00).

The Nibelungenlied: A Literary Analysis. By Hugo Bekker. *Univ. of Toronto Press* 1971 $10.00. Although this book contains many interesting insights, Bekker's treatment of characterization is highly uneven and detracts from the work's general usefulness.

The Nibelungenlied: An Interpretative Commentary. By David G. Mowatt and Hugh Sacker. *Univ. of Toronto Press* 1968 $7.50. This work, too, has occasional good insights, but it is written with a basic Freudian thrust which tends to distort the analyses of the characters and their actions. *Caveat lector!*

HARTMANN VON AUE. c. 1160–c. 1220.

Hartmann von Aue is generally credited with having introduced Arthurian romance into German literature. He was born in Swabia. It seems evident that he attended a monastery school and visited in France during his youth. He entered service with a lord of Aue to whom he was deeply attached. When his master died, Hartmann joined the crusade of Henry VI in 1197. He wrote epics, love songs, and crusading lyrics, as well as a *"Büchlein,"* a lover's complaint in form of a debate between the heart and the body. His "Erec" is the first known Arthurian romance in German. It closely follows its French model, the "Eric" of Chrétien de Troyes (*q.v.*). Hartmann's *"Der Arme Heinrich"* and his "Iwein" are famous and influential romances.

In the poem "Gregorius," Hartmann virtually created a new genre, the so-called "courtly legend," in which an edifying story is told with all the refinements of courtly style. "Gregorius" is a moral tale of sin and suffering in which penance is followed by reward. The hero is the child of an incestuous union of brother and sister. The boy is abandoned, discovered, raised by monks, becomes a knight-errant, saves a lady in distress, and marries her. Later he discovers that she is his mother. In despair he undertakes a prolonged and bitter expiation. His penance is at last accepted, his virtue recognized, and he is crowned Pope. Hartmann's version of the ancient Oedipus legend became the source for Wolfram's "Parzival" (*see below*), and for Thomas Mann's (*q.v.*) "The Holy Sinner."

GREGORIUS: The Good Sinner. c. 1195. Trans. by Sheema Zeben Buehne; introd. by Helen Adolf. With facing Middle High German text. *Ungar* 1966 $6.50 pap. $2.75

GREGORIUS: A Medieval Oedipus Legend. Trans. into rhyming couplets with introd. and notes by Edwin H. Zeydel and B. Q. Morgan. 1955. *AMS Press* $12.50

GOTTFRIED VON STRASSBURG. 1170?–1210?.

Little is known about the greatest stylist of the medieval German period. Only one work of his "Tristan and Isolde," has been preserved (indeed, it may well be the only one he ever wrote) and it is incomplete. Gottfried did not identify himself as the poet, and it is only through later sources that his name is linked with the "Tristan." It is also impossible to give his life dates with any certainty. Internal evidence in Tristan suggests that Gottfried left off working on it around 1210 and it is assumed that he died shortly thereafter. Further, it has been suggested that he died in his prime so that a possible date of birth might be 1170–1175.

Gottfried was probably a native of Strasbourg and was a very learned man, well versed in Latin, French, and German. Unlike his brother poets, Hartmann von Aue (q.v.) and Wolfram von Eschenbach (q.v.), Gottfried was not a knight but a member of the urban patrician class. This accounts for the title of "meister" (master) given him by later poets instead of "hêr" (sir) which would indicate a member of the nobility. He was urbane, sophisticated, learned—more cannot be said of this great poet.

TRISTAN, Trans. by Arthur T. Hatto. 1960. *Penguin* pap. $2.25

Gottfried based his "Tristan" on the "Tristan" of a Latin poet named Thomas, who tells of the ill-fated lovers Tristan and Isolde. In his prologue Gottfried makes clear that he is writing a love story only for those who truly understand love. He calls those people the "noble hearts" and emphasizes that they are not necessarily noble by birth, but rather are noble in attitude. In "Tristan" Gottfried moves far beyond the conventions of "courtly love" and examines the phenomenon of love in great detail, so that love assumes an individuality of its own and is viewed as a powerful, independent mystical force in the world, on a level with religion.

In "Tristan" Gottfried also takes time out from telling his tale to present a view of the poets of his day. In the famous "Literary Excursus" he praises Hartmann von Aue for his clarity of style and criticizes an unnamed poet whom he calls the "companion of the hare, leaping willy-nilly over the word heath." It is generally accepted that Gottfried is taking his colleague Wolfram von Eschenbach to task, for if there is any medieval German poet who lacks those qualities of clarity which Gottfried prizes, it is Wolfram.

Books about Gottfried

Gottfried von Strassburg. By Michael S. Batts. World Authors Ser. *Twayne* 1971 $6.95
Anatomy of Love: A study of the Tristan of Gottfried von Strassburg. By W. T. H. Jackson. *Columbia* 1971 $12.50

WOLFRAM VON ESCHENBACH.   1170?–1220?

"I am Wolfram von Eschenbach and I know a little about singing"; thus does perhaps the most unique personality in medieval German literature introduce himself to his readers. The second part of the statement is one of the greatest understatements in the realm of literature. He is the author of two works not available in translation, "Willehalm" and "Titurel" (incomplete), and of lyrics—the few songs which have survived all show great innovativeness and skill. He is best known to general audiences as the author of "Parzival," a Grail romance of over 24,000 lines. His main source is the incomplete "Perceval, or The Grail" of Chrétien de Troyes (q.v.). Whether Wolfram had another source which supplied him with the end of the tale or whether he provided it himself is not definitely known. Wolfram teases his audience on several occasions by reference to a mysterious Kyot who supposedly transmitted the tale and who was Wolfram's chief source. Modern scholars have given up the search for Kyot, and most now assume that the completion of the "Parzival" story is by Wolfram himself.

The basic theme of "Parzival" is like that of the other German courtly romances, examining how a person can so arrange his life that he is pleasing to both God and man. As in the other tales, the answer lies in compassion. When first confronted with the great suffering of the Grail king, Parzival keeps silent. He then spends much time and effort in learning the basic lesson of human existence, which becomes clear to him on Good Friday when the hermit Trevrizent points out the true nature of love and compassion as exemplified by Christ's death on the cross. Parzival is now ready to become Grail king himself, and upon his next meeting with the king he asks the vital question, "oheim waz wirret dir?" ("uncle, what troubles you?"). With this simple question Parzival has shown himself capable of true humanity and has thus achieved his destiny. Wolfram's "Parzival" also provided the material used in Wagner's libretto for "Parsifal."

THE PARZIVAL OF WOLFRAM VON ESCHENBACH. Trans. into English verse with introd., notes, and connecting summaries by Edwin H. Zeydel and B. Q. Morgan 1951. *AMS Press* $12.50; trans. by Helen Mustard and Charles E. Passage *Random* Vintage Bks. (orig.) 1961 pap. $1.95

Books about Wolfram

Introduction to Wolfram's Parzival. By Hugh D. Sacker. *Cambridge* 1963 $13.00
Wolfram von Eschenbach. By James F. Poag. World Authors Ser. *Twayne* 1972 $6.95

JOHANNES VON SAAZ (or VON TEPL).   c. 1350–c. 1414.

Johannes von Saaz was born in the village of Schüttwa and studied at the University of Prague. From 1383 he was town clerk, headmaster, and archiepiscopal notary in Saaz. His young wife

Margaretta died in 1400, and "The Plowman" is her literary memorial. Written as a legal debate between the Plowman as plaintiff and Death as the accused, it forms a perfect miniature play.

"This little book in dialogue form is the first really important work of prose literature in the German language," writes M. O'C. Walshe in "Medieval German Literature." It was the fruit of an early wave of humanism in Bohemia.

THE PLOWMAN FROM BOHEMIA. Trans. by Alexander and Elizabeth Henderson. *Ungar* 1966 $4.50 pap. $1.45

BRANT, SEBASTIAN (also Brandt).   1457?–1521.

Sebastian Brant was born in Strassburg and studied at Basel, where he became a lecturer. When Basel joined the Swiss Confederacy, he returned to Strassburg and became the town clerk. He was author of a number of political and religious pamphlets. Katherine Anne Porter (*q.v.*) drew on *"Das Narrenschiff"* for her novel "Ship of Fools."

His famous parody of the late medieval period depicts life as a paradise for simpletons. It is a series of rhymed sermons excoriating sin and folly with grotesque satire. The crew of a seabound vessel is made up of 112 fools, each representing a "fashionable foible" of man. In their foolishness, they perish. Although of secondary literary merit, the book became immensely popular. It was translated into Low German, Latin, French, and English. A famous early edition of the work was translated by Alexander Barclay in 1509 (ed. by T. H. Jamieson, 1874, with original woodcuts *AMS Press* 2 vols. set $27.50).

THE SHIP OF FOOLS (*Das Narrenschiff*). 1494. Trans. into rhyming couplets by E. H. Zeydel; ill. with facsimiles of the 114 original woodcuts. *Dover* (orig.) 1962 pap. $3.50; *Peter Smith* $4.50

Books about Brant

Sebastian Brant. By Edwin H. Zeydel. World Authors Ser. *Twayne* 1967 $6.95

LUTHER, MARTIN.   1483–1546.   *See Chapter 4, World Religions,* Reader's Adviser, *Vol. 3.*

GRIMMELSHAUSEN, HANS JAKOB CHRISTOFFEL VON.   1620?–1676.

A popular didactic novel of the Reformation period, Grimmelshausen's "Simplicissimus" has been called "undoubtedly the greatest novel of the seventeenth century." It is an early example of the picaresque genre. The hero of the novel, who shares some of his creator's adventures, is no conventional "fool" reflecting on the follies of mankind, but a real soldier of fortune in the Thirty Years' War. The miseries he experiences force him to search for an answer to the riddle of human existence. One of the sequels to "Simplicissimus" was *"Landstörtzerin Courasche"* (two translations of which are given below), a bawdy, picaresque tale of a woman camp follower in an ugly world, "a symbol of the age and a lively individual [who] comes out on top in any situation with unimpaired self-assurance if not virtue"—(*LJ*). Bertolt Brecht (*q.v.*) drew on this source for his play "Mother Courage and Her Children." "The False Messiah," in which a thief poses as the Prophet Elijah, "paints an equally grotesque picture of the world. . . . It is hard to comprehend how the Victorians could have made a religious author out of Grimmelshausen"—(*SR*).

THE ADVENTUROUS SIMPLICISSIMUS. 1669. Trans. by George Schulz-Behrend. *Bobbs Liberal Arts* $5.00 pap. $2.65; (with title "Adventures of a Simpleton") trans. by Walter Wallich *Ungar* $6.50; trans. by A. T. S. Goodrick; pref. by Eric Bentley *Univ. of Nebraska Press* Bison Bks. 1962 pap. $2.25

THE RUNAGATE COURAGE. 1670. Trans. with introd. by Robert L. Hiller and John C. Osborne; pref. by Eric Bentley. *Univ. of Nebraska Press* 1965 $5.00 Bison Bks. pap. $2.40. Good introductory essay linking the work to Brecht's drama "Mother Courage and Her Children."

COURAGE, THE ADVENTURESS (1670) and THE FALSE MESSIAH (1672). Trans. by Hans Speier. *Princeton Univ. Press* $6.95 pap. $3.95

Excerpts from two works admirably translated by "a specialist on baroque literature"—(*SR*). The second selection is taken from "The Enchanted Bird's Nest."

Books about Grimmelshausen

Hans Jakob Christoffel von Grimmelshausen. By Kenneth Negus. World Authors Ser. *Twayne* 1974 $6.95

LESSING, GOTTHOLD EPHRAIM. 1729–1781.

Lessing, one of the outstanding literary critics of all time, was "the first figure of European stature in modern German literature." The son of a Protestant pastor, he was educated in Meissen and at Leipzig University, then went to Berlin as a journalist in 1749. While employed as secretary to General Tauentzien (1760–65), he devoted his leisure to classical studies. This led to his critical essay "Laocoon," in which he attempts to clarify certain laws of esthetic perception by comparing poetry and the visual arts. He fought always for truth and combined a penetrating intellect with shrewd common sense.

He furthered the German theater by his weekly dramatic notes and theories, found mainly in the "Hamburg Dramaturgy," which he wrote during his connection with the Hamburg National Theater as critic and dramatist (1768–69). His plays include "Miss Sara Sampson" (1755), important as the first German prose tragedy of middle-class life; "Minna von Barnheim" (1767), his finest comedy and the best of the era; and his noble plea for religious tolerance, "Nathan the Wise."

LAOCOON AND OTHER WRITINGS. *Dutton* Everyman's $3.95

LAOCOON. 1766. Trans. by Ellen Frothingham. *Farrar, Straus* Noonday 1957 pap. $1.45; trans. by E. A. McCormick *Bobbs* Liberal Arts 1962 pap. $1.75

MINNA VON BARNHEIM. 1767. Trans. with introd. by Kenneth J. Northcott. *Univ. of Chicago Press* 1972 $6.50 Phoenix Bks. 1973 pap. $1.95

HAMBURG DRAMATURGY. 1769. 1890. Trans. by Helen Zimmern with new introd. by Victor Lange. *Dover* 1962 pap. $2.75; *Peter Smith* $4.75

EMILIA GALOTTI: A Tragedy in 5 Acts. 1772. Trans. with introd. by Anna Johanna Gode von Aesch. *Barron's* 1959 pap. $1.25; trans. by Edward Dvoretsky *Ungar* pap. $1.45

NATHAN THE WISE: A Dramatic Poem in 5 Acts. 1779. Trans. by Walter F. Ade *Barron's* 1950 pap. $1.95; trans. into English verse by Bayard Quincy Morgan *Ungar* pap. $1.45

LESSING'S THEOLOGICAL WRITINGS: Selections in Translation. Trans. by Henry Chadwick. *Stanford Univ. Press* 1957 pap. $1.45

Books about Lessing

Lessing's Relation to the English Language and Literature. By Curtis C. D. Vail. 1936. *AMS Press* $17.50. The effect of English sources on the form, style and spirit of Lessing's dramas.

Lessing: The Founder of Modern German Literature. By Henry B. Garland. 1937. 1962. *Folcroft* 1973 lib. bdg. $15.00. The classic study of his life and work.

Lessing and the Enlightenment: His Philosophy of Religion and Its Relation to Eighteenth-Century Thought. By Henry E. Allison. *Univ. of Michigan Press* 1966 $7.50
"This rich and significant work [explores] the Leibnizean origins of much in Lessing's mature theological thought"—(*LJ*).

Lessing's Dramatic Theory: Being an Introduction to and Commentary on His "Hamburgische Dramaturgie." By John George Robertson. *Blom* $15.00. Lessing's analysis of "the theory of tragedy and the nature of drama." Includes some selections from other Lessing works and from those of European contemporaries.

Gotthold Ephraim Lessing. By F. Andrew Brown. World Authors Ser. *Twayne* 1971 $5.95

Lessings' Aesthetica in Nuce: An Analysis of the May 26, 1769, Letter to Nicolai. By Victor A. Rudowski. *Univ. of North Carolina Press* 1971 $6.70

Goethe and Lessing: The Wellsprings of Creation. By Ilse Graham. *Harper* (Barnes & Noble) 1973 $15.00

HERDER, JOHANN GOTTFRIED VON. 1744–1803.

Herder, humanist philosopher, poet, and critic, was born in Mohrungen in East Prussia. He suffered a deprived childhood but managed to attend the University of Königsberg, where he soon abandoned medical studies for theology. It was then that he came under the aegis of Kant (*q.v.*), an influence which led to Herder's revolutionary approach to history. In his major work, "Ideas on a Philosophy of Human History" (4 vols.), he proclaimed "humanity to be the essence of man's character as well as the irrevocable aim of history"—(Ernst Rose).

J. G. Robertson describes his influence on German Romanticism: "The winter which Herder spent in Strassburg (1770–1771) was of the first importance, for from it may be said to date the origin of the movement of 'Sturm und Drang.' During these months . . . Goethe sat at Herder's feet and learned the new faith from his lips. Herder opened the young poet's eyes to the greatness of Shakespeare, revealed to him the treasures of national poetry in the songs of the people, and endowed the traceries of the Gothic cathedral above their heads with a new meaning and a new gospel. In this momentous period and the few years that immediately followed, Herder was a force of the first magnitude in German literature, a force which is impossible to overestimate."

Herder later broke with Goethe and with most of his other followers. His last years were spent in bitterness and intellectual isolation.

GOD: Some Conversations. Trans. with introd. by Frederick H. Burkhardt. *Bobbs* Liberal Arts 1962 pap. $1.75

(With Jean-Jacques Rousseau) ON THE ORIGIN OF LANGUAGE. Trans. by John H. Moran and Alexander Gode; introd. by Alexander Gode. *Ungar* 1966 $4.75. Two essays.

Books about Herder

Herder and the Foundations of German Nationalism. By Robert R. Ergang. 1931. *Octagon* 1967 $11.50

Herder: His Life and Thought. By Robert T. Clark, Jr. *Univ. of California Press* 1955 $13.75

Herder's Social and Political Thought: From Enlightenment to Nationalism. By F. M. Barnard. *Oxford* 1965 $7.00

The Psychological Basis of Herder's Aesthetics. By Joe K. Fugate. *Humanities Press* 1966 pap. $14.75

GOETHE, JOHANN WOLFGANG von.   1749–1832.

Johann Wolfgang von Goethe, "Europe's last universal man," belongs with the most remarkable writers of all time. Poet, dramatist, critic, novelist, artist, and scientist, he once remarked that all his works were "fragments of a great confession." In 1775, at the time of his "Werther" success, he was invited to the court of Weimar, where he became advisor to the young Duke. Here he settled, engaging in political and cultural activities and eventually becoming himself the object of cultural pilgrimage. To Weimar, in time, came Schiller (*q.v.*), and the two pursued their fruitful friend-ship. Goethe's love affairs, which he managed to combine with a stable marriage, continued throughout his long life and provided him with literary material as well as inspiration.

With his play "Götz von Berlichingen" and his novelette "The Sorrows of Young Werther" Goethe became the standard bearer of the *Sturm und Drang* movement, which represented a youthful, idealistic revolt against the constraints of European neoclassicism and particularly French rationalism. His plays "Iphigenia in Tauris" and "Torquato Tasso" are representative of the classical rigor of his second phase.

His last period, when he was the great and somewhat lonely Olympian of world literature, produced creative work of amazing vitality and diversity: novels, narrative poems, autobiographi-cal works, and the monumental poetic drama "Faust," which represents the best thought of 60 years of Goethe's life.

In Goethe's "Faust," with its breadth of vision and grandeur of poetic expression, the emphasis is upon man's constant striving toward the full range of human experience—cultural, intellectual, and spiritual—beyond the search for mere abstract knowledge or purely physical pleasures. The earliest manuscript of "Faust," the "Urfaust," was not discovered until 1887. "Faust Part I" was completed in two stages in 1775 and 1790, and it was not published until after his death in 1832.

Goethe's greatness lay in his combination of intellectual energy, modesty, and "reverence for life" (Albert Schweitzer's key phrase) and in his continual protest against the rationalization and mechanization of the cosmos, including man.

FAUST: PART I (1808) and PART II (1832).

The legend of Dr. Johann Faust is as much a part of Western literary tradition as that of King Arthur. Its most famous treatments have been the versions of the Chapbooks, and those by Christopher Marlowe and Goethe. Goethe has taken the basic tale of a scholar who strikes a bargain with the devil but changes the object of Faust's desire from power to knowledge. Nor does Goethe's drama set a time limit—Mephistopheles can claim Faust's soul at whatever time Faust can say that he is satisfied. After the death of Gretchen in Part I and of his son Euphorion (from his union with Helen of Troy) in Part II, Faust turns his energies toward improving the lot of his fellow man, and it is while he is engaged in clearing a marsh that he sees the purpose of earthly existence, namely that only the man who constantly strives deserves the privilege of life and freedom. This moment of insight provides him with the satisfaction he has been seeking and he dies. Mephistopheles, believing he has won the wager, summons his demons, but the angels of God appear and take Faust's soul into heaven. As they take his soul they sing, "He who constantly strives is worthy of salvation," thus confirming Faust's ultimate insight. Faust's salvation is also a major departure from the traditional Faust legend. Instead of providing a warning to all Christians, which the Chapbook version hoped to accomplish with its vivid description of Faust's inglorious end, Goethe instead investigates the meaning of human existence, and, more important, provides an answer.

Part I appeared for the first time in 1808; Part II in 1832. The earliest extant version, the so-called "Urfaust," had been brought to Weimar by Goethe in 1775. This fragment is available in German in this country (ed. by Harold Lenz and F. J. Nock *Harper* 1938 $2.95; ed. by R. H. Samuels *St. Martin's* 1958 $1.50; trans. by Douglas M. Scott *Barron's* pap. $1.25). There are over 50 English translations of "Faust." The first three in English are no longer in print: that of Francis Leveson Gower, 1823; Abraham Layward, 1833, a prose translation; and John Stuart Blackie, 1834. The Bohn Library edition (o.p.) of Anna Swanwick's translation has a good bibliography. This verse rendering (Part I 1850; Part II 1878) was a popular one, both very spirited and very literal. It was originally part of the "Complete Dramatic Works of Goethe" translated by Anna Swanwick and Sir Walter Scott. Albert G. Latham made a verse translation of the complete "Faust" in the original meters, published first in 1902 in the Temple Classics and later in *Dutton* Everyman's (1928, o.p.).

Older Translations of "Faust"

Anster, John (1793–1867). Part I (1835) and Part II (1864). With Marlowe's "Doctor Faustus." *Oxford* World's Class. 1946 $2.25. In verse.

Dr. John Anster, Irish educator and poet, made the earliest English translation of "Faust" now in print. His work is more of a paraphrase than a translation. It is published together with Christopher Marlowe's "Doctor Faustus," a rendering of the Faust legend which was published in England in 1604, 200 years before Goethe wrote his version.

Martin, Sir Theodore (1816–1909). Parts I and II. Introd., rev., and annotated by W. H. Bruford. *Dutton* Everyman's 1954 $3.95. In verse.

Taylor, Bayard (1825–1878). 1870–1871. *Macmillan* Collier Bks. Part I 1961 pap. $.95 1963 bilingual ed. pap. $1.95 Part II 1962 bilingual ed. pap. $.95; Part 1 ed. by B. Q. Morgan *AHM Pub. Corp.* Crofts Class. pap. $.85; *Random* (Modern Lib.) pap. $1.75; *Oxford* World's Class. $3.00; Parts I and II *Simon & Schuster* (Washington Square) pap. $.95. In verse. Taylor translated the whole of "Faust" in the meters of the original—the work of a scholar who was also a poet.

Modern Translations of "Faust"

Kaufmann, Walter. *Doubleday* 1961 $4.50 Anchor Bks. 1963 pap. $2.95. Part I and significant sections of Part II; with a synopsis of and excerpts from the omitted portions. Bilingual.

MacIntyre, Carlyle F. *New Directions* 1941 new ed. 1945, English only text ed. 1949 $1.50. A new American free-verse translation. Part I ill. by Rockwell Kent.

MacNeice, Louis. Parts I and II. *Oxford* World's Class. 1960 pap. $2.50. An abridged version in verse. The poet cut the poem by a third for BBC's Goethe celebrations. An animated version, but the original suffers somewhat.

Morgan, Bayard Quincy. *Bobbs* Part I 1954 $5.00 Liberal Arts. pap. $1.25 Part II 1965 Liberal Arts $1.65

Passage, Charles. *Bobbs* 1965 $6.00 Liberal Arts pap. $2.25. Parts I and II.

Wayne, Philip. *Penguin* Part I 1959 pap. $1.45, Part II 1959 pap. $1.25

Other Works in Translation

GREAT WRITINGS OF GOETHE. Ed. by Stephen Spender. *New Am. Lib.* Mentor Bks. (orig.) pap. $1.25

POEMS. Trans. in the original meters by E. A. Bowring and others. 1882. *Richard West* $25.00; translations facing the original, with an introd. and list of musical settings by Edwin H. Zeydel. 1957. *AMS Press* $12.50

NOVELS AND TALES. Trans. and ed. by R. D. Boyler. 1890. *Richard West* $20.00

THE PARABLE (*Märchen.*) Trans. and introd. by Alice Raphael. *Harcourt* 1963 $3.95. A smoothly reading translation of the *Märchen* (literal trans.: "Tale") plus a learned commentary that identifies the work as a "mystery drama."

URFAUST. 1771. Trans. by Douglas M. Scott. *Barron's* 1958 pap. $1.25

GÖTZ VON BERLICHINGEN. 1773. Trans. with introd. by Charles E. Passage. *Ungar* pap. $1.95. Drama.

THE SORROWS OF YOUNG WERTHER. 1774. Trans. with introd. by Victor Lange. *Holt* 3 bks. in 1 The Sorrows of Young Werther, The New Melusina, Novelle 1948 pap. $3.95; (and "Selected Writings") trans. by Catherine Hutter *New Am. Lib.* Signet 1962 pap. $1.25; (and "Novella") trans. by Elizabeth Mayer and Louise Bogen, with poems trans. by W. H. Auden *Random* Vintage Bks. pap. $1.95; (with title "The Sufferings of Young Werther") trans. by Bayard Quincy Morgan *Ungar* 1957 $5.00 pap. $1.95; (with title "The Sufferings of Young Werther") trans. by Harry Steinhauer *Norton* 1970 $6.00 pap. $2.45

EGMONT: A Tragedy in Five Acts. 1778. Trans. by Willard R. Trask, Jr.; introd. by Alexander Gode von Aesch. *Barron's* 1960 $4.25 pap. $1.25

IPHIGENIA IN TAURIS. 1779 in prose, 1787 final poetic version. Trans. by John Prudhoe. *Harper* (Barnes & Noble) 1966 $2.25; trans. by Sydney E. Kaplan *Barron's* 1953 pap. $1.25; trans. with introd. by Charles E. Passage *Ungar* $5.00. Drama.

TORQUATO TASSO. 1790. Trans. with introd. by Charles E. Passage. *Ungar* pap. $1.95. Drama.

ROMAN ELEGIES AND VENETIAN EPIGRAMS. 1795 and 1794. Trans. by L. R. Lind. *Univ. Press of Kansas* 1974 $11.00

WILHELM MEISTER'S APPRENCTICESHIP. 1795–1796. Trans. by Thomas Carlyle; introd. by Victor Lange. *Macmillan* Collier Bks. pap. $1.50. Novel.

HERMANN AND DOROTHEA. 1797. Trans. with introd. by Daniel Coogan. *Ungar* $5.00 pap. $1.95. A provincial "epic."

ELECTIVE AFFINITIES. 1809. Trans. by Elizabeth Mayer and Louise Bogan, introd. by Victor Lange. *Regnery* 1963 $5.95; trans. by J. A. Froude and R. D. Boylan *Ungar* $6.50 pap. $1.75

An "extraordinary and unforgettable novel . . . about the elemental power of love"—(*SR*).

THEORY OF COLOURS. 1810. Trans. by Charles Eastlake. *International Scholarly Bk. Services* 1967 $19.00; *Gordon Press* $34.95; *M.I.T. Press* $12.50 pap. $2.95

ITALIAN JOURNEY (1786–1788). 1816–1817. 1962. *Schocken* $10.00. Trans. with introd. by W. H. Auden and Elizabeth Mayer; includes Goethe's own paintings and drawings. Travel sketches.

CONVERSATIONS OF GOETHE WITH ECKERMANN. 1836–1848. Trans. by Gisela C. O'Brien, ed. by Hans Kohn. *Ungar* (abr.) $6.00 pap. $1.45

GOETHE'S WORLD VIEW: Presented in His Reflections and Maxims. Trans. by Heinz Norden (bilingual); ed. with introd. by Frederick Ungar. *Ungar* $5.00 pap. $1.95

GOETHE: Wisdom and Experience. Sel. by Ludwig Curtius; trans. and ed. by Herman J. Weigand. *Ungar* $6.50

CRITICISMS, REFLECTIONS AND MAXIMS. Trans. with introd. by R. D. Rönnfeldt. *Richard West* $15.00; (with title "Maxims and Reflections") trans. by Bailey Saunders. 1893. *Richard West* $17.50

AUTOBIOGRAPHY: Poetry and Truth from My Own Life. 1811–33. Trans. by John Oxenford. *Horizon Press* $15.00; *Univ. of Chicago Press* 1975 2 vols. each $15.00 Phoenix Bks. pap. each $5.25

Books about Goethe

George Ticknor's The Sorrows of Young Werther. Ed. with introd. and critical analysis by Frank G. Ryder. 1952. *Johnson Reprint* 1966 $11.00. Ticknor (1791–1871), an American scholar and literary historian, did much of his work in Germany and other parts of Europe. His translation of "The Sorrows of Young Werther" was finished in 1814, but was not published until this edition came out in 1952.

Goethe and Mendelssohn, 1821–1831. By M. E. von Glehn. 1874. *Richard West* $35.00

Life of Johann Wolfgang Goethe. By James Sime. 1888. *Kennikat* 1971 $9.50; *Richard West* 1973 $9.45

Three Philosophical Poets. By George Santayana. 1910. *Cooper* 1971 lib. bdg. $6.00. The three poets are Lucretius, Dante, and Goethe.

Emerson and Goethe. By Frederick B. Wahr. 1915. *Folcroft* lib. bdg. $17.50; *Gordon Press* $26.00

Goethe. By Calvin Thomas. 1917. *Richard West* $25.00 An old work but still worthwhile.

Laurence Sterne and Goethe. By W. R. Pinger. 1920. *Folcroft* $7.50

Goethe. By Benedetto Croce. 1923. *Kennikat* 1970 $8.00. Recommended.

Goethe and Byron. By John G. Robertson. 1925. *Folcroft* $12.50. An excellent appraisal of the communication between the two poets.

Matthew Arnold and Goethe. By John G. Robertson. 1925. *Folcroft* $12.50

Matthew Arnold and Goethe. By James B. Orrick. 1928. *Folcroft* $7.75; Studies in Comparative Lit. Ser. *Haskell* 1972 $7.95

Goethe and Beethoven. By G. A. Pfister and E. S. Kemp. 1931. *Richard West* 1973 $25.00

Goethe's Knowledge of English Literature. By James Boyd. 1932. *Haskell* 1972 $15.95; *Richard West* 1973 $12.75

Goethe's Conception of the World. By Rudolf Steiner. 1932. *Haskell* 1972 lib. bdg. $11.95

Goethe's Interest in the New World. By Walter Waldepuhl. 1934. German Lit. and Letters Ser. *Haskell* 1973 lib. bdg. $9.95

Goethe and the Greeks. By Humphry Trevelyan. 1941. *Octagon* 1972 lib. bdg. $13.00

Rousseau, Kant, Goethe. By Ernst Cassirer. Trans. by James Gutmann, Paul O. Kristeller, and John H. Randall, Jr.; introd. by Peter Gay. 1945. *Princeton Univ. Press* pap. $1.95

Goethe and World Literature. By Fritz Strich. Trans. by C. A. Sym. 1949. *Greenwood* 1971 $17.95; *Kennikat* 1971 $13.50

Goethe the Thinker. By Karl Vietor. Trans. by Moses Hadas. 1949. *Russell & Russell* 1970 $16.00

Goethe on Human Creativeness and Other Goethe Essays. Ed. by Rolf King. *Univ. of Georgia Press* 1950 $6.50. Various authors (one writes in German).

Byron and Goethe: Analysis of a Passion. By E. M. Butler. *Hillary House* 1956 $6.50. Recommended.

Goethe's Faust: A Literary Analysis. By Stuart Atkins. *Harvard Univ. Press* 1958 $8.50. A recommended study.

The Christian Renaissance: Interpretations of Dante, Shakespeare and Goethe and New Discussions of Oscar Wilde and the Gospel of Thomas. By G. Wilson Knight. *Norton* 1962. pap. $1.85

Culture and Society in Classical Weimar, 1775–1806. By W. H. Bruford. *Cambridge* 1962 $22.50. Analyses of life and times in Weimar closely relating Goethe's life and activity to his environment.

Goethe: A Psychoanalytic Study, 1775–1786. By K. R. Eissler, M.D. *Wayne State Univ. Press* 1963 2 vols. $40.00. A monumental psychoanalytic biography.

Goethe. By Henry Hatfield. *Harvard Univ. Press* 1963 $5.00; *New Directions* (orig.) 1963 pap. $2.25. Detailed treatment of the fiction, poetry and drama with bibliography.

Goethe's Life in Pictures. By Walter Hoyer. *Adler's* 1963 $2.95; *Dufour* 1969 $4.50

Goethe: A Collection of Critical Essays. Ed. by Victor Lange. Twentieth Century Views Ser. *Prentice-Hall* 1967 $5.95 pap. $1.95

Goethe: A Critical Introduction. By Ronald Gray. *Cambridge* 1967 $14.95 pap. $5.50

Goethe's Die Wahlverwandtschaften: A Literary Interpretation. By H. G. Barnes. *Oxford* 1967 $8.50

Goethe's Faust: Its Genesis and Purport. By Eudo C. Mason. *Univ. of California Press* 1967 $11.50

"This book, which contains selected bibliography, is indispensable"—(*LJ*).

The Russian Image of Goethe. By André von Gronicka. Haney Foundation Ser. *Univ. of Pennsylvania Press* 1968 $9.00

Goethe and His Age. By Georg Lukacs. *Grosset* 1969 pap. $2.45. A sociological discussion.

Goethe: New Perspectives on a Writer and His Time. By Derek van Abbé. *Bucknell Univ. Press* $8.00

Goethe's Faust, Part I: Essays in Criticism. Ed. by John B. Vickery and J'nan Sellery. *Wadsworth* 1969 pap. $3.50

Drama of Language: Essays on Goethe and Kleist. By Sigurd Burckhardt. *Johns Hopkins Univ. Press* 1970 $8.00

Goethe's Novels. By Hans Reiss. *Univ. of Miami Press* 1971 $10.00

The Poem as Plant: A Biological View of Goethe's Faust. By Peter Salm. *Press of Case Western* 1971 $5.95. An original and insightful analysis of "Faust." Recommended.

Goethe's Faust: A Critical Reading. By Liselotte Dieckmann. *Prentice-Hall* 1972 pap. $1.95

Goethe and Rousseau. Resonances of the Mind. By Carl Hammer, Jr. *Univ. Press of Kentucky* 1973 $10.50

Artist in Chrysalis: A Biographical Study of Goethe in Italy. By H. G. Haile. *Univ. of Illinois Press* 1973 $7.95. An informative and well-written study; recommended. Contains numerous illustrations.

Johann Wolfgang Goethe. By Liselotte Dieckmann. World Authors Ser. *Twayne* 1974 $7.50. Excellent; highly recommended.

SCHILLER, (JOHANN CHRISTOPH) FRIEDRICH von. 1759–1805.

Schiller was the first German dramatist to have his plays translated widely into English. More than 200 such translations were published between 1792 and 1900. Each of his nine dramas is a masterpiece of situation, characterization, subtle psychology, and exalted artistic conception of the dramatic form. "The Robbers" (1781), his first play (prose), was the last of the great works of the German *Sturm und Drang* period (*see Goethe, above*) and an immediate success, a rallying cry for the freedom and idealism of youth against tyranny and hypocrisy the young Schiller found in the times. "Mary Stuart," one of the great verse dramas of his "classical" maturity, was "a psychological tragedy in a very modern sense" (J. G. Robertson) and has been the play of Schiller's most often produced abroad. His themes, usually expressed through historical persons and situations, were freedom, justice, heroism—the noblest aspirations of man. (A poem of his, the "Ode to Joy," was set to music by Beethoven as part of the Ninth, or Choral, Symphony.)

Schiller's life was a struggle against poverty and in his last years against tuberculosis. His friendship with Goethe was a rewarding one for both writers and led to Schiller's settling in Weimar. "The German classical age attains its culmination in the friendship of Goethe and Schiller," says Robertson. Together they revitalized German poetry and the German stage. "Schiller's view of life was no calm and dispassionate one like Goethe's. [He] was always a partisan, a champion of high ideas. . . . He remains Germany's greatest dramatist and, after Goethe, the poet whose work has had the firmest hold upon the affections of his people"—(Robertson).

FRIEDRICH SCHILLER: An Anthology for Our Time. New English trans. by Jane Bannard Greene and others (bilingual). *Ungar* 1960 $7.50 pap. $3.75. With an account of his life and work by Frederick Ungar.

THE BRIDE OF MESSINA, WILLIAM TELL, and DEMETRIUS. Trans. by Charles E. Passage. *Ungar* 1962 $6.50 pap. $2.75

DON CARLOS, INFANTE OF SPAIN: A Drama in Five Acts. 1787. Trans. by Charles E. Passage. *Ungar* 1959 $6.00 pap. $2.75

WALLENSTEIN: A Historical Drama in Three Parts. 1798–1799. Trans. by Charles E. Passage. *Ungar* 1959 pap. $2.75

MARY STUART (1801) and THE MAID OF ORLEANS (1802): Two Plays. Trans. by Charles E. Passage. *Ungar* 1960 $5.00

MARY STUART. 1801. Trans. by Sophie Wilkins. *Barron's* 1959 $4.25 pap. $1.50

WILLIAM TELL. 1804. Trans. by Sidney Kaplan *Barron's* 1954 pap. $1.25; trans. by Gilbert Jordan. *Bobbs* 1964 $6.00 Liberal Arts pap. $1.65; (with title "Wilhelm Tell") trans. by John Prudhowe. *Harper* (Barnes & Noble) 1970 pap. $3.25; trans. by William F. Mainland *Univ. of Chicago Press* 1972 $7.75 Phoenix Bks. pap. 1973 $2.45

LOVE AND INTRIGUE. 1784. Trans. by Frederick Rolf. *Barron's* 1959 new trans. 1961 $4.25 pap. $1.25; (with title "Intrigue and Love") trans. by Charles E. Passage *Ungar* 1971 $6.50 pap. $1.75

ON NAIVE AND SENTIMENTAL POETRY and ON THE SUBLIME: Two Essays. Trans. with introd. and notes by Julius Elias. *Ungar* 1967 $6.50 pap. $2.45

ON THE AESTHETIC EDUCATION OF MAN (in a Series of Letters). 1793–1795. Trans. by Reginald Snell. *Ungar* $5.50 pap. $2.45

Books about Schiller

Last Essays. By Thomas Mann. Trans. by Richard and Clara Winston and Tania and James Stern. *Knopf* 1959 $5.95. Four essays, including discussion of Schiller.

Schiller, 1759–1959. Ed. by John R. Frey. *Univ. of Illinois Press* 1959 pap. $3.50

Schiller. By Bernt von Heiseler. Trans. and annot. by John Bednall. 1963. *Richard West* $20.00. With a selective bibliography and a descriptive list of the principal plays.

HÖLDERLIN, (JOHANN CHRISTIAN) FRIEDRICH. 1770–1843.

Only during the last half century has Hölderlin come to be recognized as a great lyric poet. Except for his philosophical novel "Hyperion" and translations of two of Sophocles' plays, his works were published by friends after he became hopelessly insane in his thirties. He spent his early life as a private tutor. Hellenic in feeling, his best poetry is written in the classical meters or in free verse on Greek themes. Hölderlin knew and wrote of the tragic elements in life, but his poems encompass and transcend these in a vision of ultimate harmony. "He aimed at balance even in his rhythms, matching ascending units with descending ones and uniting many voices in a symphony. . . . He has become a guidepost for moderns"—(Ernst Rose).

ALCAIC POEMS. Trans. by Elizabeth Henderson (bilingual). *Ungar* $4.50. Some 21 poems in Alcaic meter.

POEMS AND FRAGMENTS. Trans. by Michael Hamburger (bilingual). *Univ. of Michigan Press* 1967 $12.50. The largest selection of his poems available. Includes two fragments of the tragedy "The Death of Empedocles."

SELECTED POEMS OF FRIEDRICH HÖLDERLIN AND EDUARD MÖRIKE. Trans. by Christopher Middleton. *Univ. of Chicago Press* 1972 $11.50 Phoenix Bks. pap. $3.75

HYPERION. 1797–1799. Trans. by Willard R. Trask; fwd. by Alexander Gode von Aesch. *New Am. Lib.* 1965 pap. $.75; *Ungar* $5.00; trans. by Walter Silz *Univ. of Pennsylvania Press* 1970 $6.95

THE POET'S VOCATION: Selections from the Letters of Hölderlin, Rimbaud and Hart Crane. Ed. and trans. by William Burford and Christopher Middleton; ill. by Cyril Satorsky. *Univ. of Texas Press* 1967 $3.75. A charming brief selection, handsomely produced.

Books about Hölderlin

Hölderlin. By Lore Sulamith Salzberger. *Hillary House* 1952 $2.00
A scholarly work. "Particularly valuable are the pages interpreting Hölderlin's prophetic mission of the poet, the relationship between theology and poetry, and the history of this doctrine"—(SR).

NOVALIS (pseud. of Friedrich Leopold, Freiherr von Hardenberg). 1772–1801.

Novalis, one of the early poets of German Romanticism, provided the movement with its best known symbol, the "blue flower," from his fragmentary novel "Heinrich von Ofterdingen." The blue flower became the symbol for the deep-rooted romantic yearning, the search which would never end. Novalis himself was a Saxon nobleman and a government official who was fated to die young from tuberculosis. His most famous achievement, the "Hymns to the Night," might strike some readers as an exercise in morbidity. They were written in the memory of his fiancée, Sophie von Kühn, who died in 1797 at the age of fifteen. His "Hymns" eloquently express his grief at the death of Sophie and are a unique mixture of religious, mystical feeling and personal sadness. In them he comes to view the night (death) as actually the gateway to a higher and better life, and thus night becomes the true light. The "Hymns" were composed in 1800 and the death he so longed for struck him a year later.

HYMNS TO THE NIGHT AND OTHER SELECTED WRITINGS. Trans. by Charles E. Passage. *Bobbs* Liberal Arts 1960 pap. $.95

HENRY VON OFTERDINGEN. 1802. Trans. from the German by Palmer Hilty. *Ungar* pap. $2.75

An excellent translation of a work expressing "Novalis's own ideas and [those of] early German Romanticism in general"—(LJ). For the well-informed reader.

Books about Novalis

Novalis. By Frederick Hiebel. 1954. *AMS Press* 1959 $12.50
Novalis and Mathematics. By Martin Dyck. *AMS Press* 1960 $12.50
Novalis: The Veil of Imagery, A Study of the Poetic Works of Friedrich von Hardenberg. By Bruce Haywood. *Harvard Univ. Press* 1959 $4.50
Novalis' Fichte Studies: The Foundations of His Aesthetics. By Geza von Molnar. *Humanities Press* 1970 $7.25
Bifocal Vision: Novalis' Philosophy of Nature and Disease. By John Neubauer. *Univ. of North Carolina Press* 1971 $7.75

HOFFMANN, E(RNST) T(HEODOR) A(MADEUS).   1776–1822.

Hoffmann was among the foremost raconteurs of the late Romantic period in Germany. His "Gothic" influence was felt widely throughout France, England, and America—in the works of Musset, Baudelaire, Walter Scott, and Poe, among others. Offenbach used three of his stories for the opera "Tales of Hoffmann" (1881). Fascinated by the morbid and grotesque, Hoffmann breathed life into his imaginary world and made it seem quite real. "His writing is . . . plastic, a quality which is conspicuous in his power of endowing with reality the supernatural phantasms of his brain"—(J. G. Robertson).

Although he was musically productive in his early years, Hoffmann turned to literature for financial reasons and published his first work, "Weird Tales," with a preface by Jean Paul (Richter), in 1814–1815. He settled in Berlin, where his literary circle, the *Serapionsabende*, included Chamisso (*q.v.*) and provided material for "The Serapion Brethren" (1819–1821, o.p.), a collection of stories supposed to be told by a similar group of friends. The gruesome and chilling "Devil's Elixir" (1815–1816, o.p.), a novel, is interesting for its psychological insights. The tales told by Hoffmann's fictional counterpart, the musician Kreisler, in "Weird Tales," as well as the novel "Murr the Tomcat" (1820–1822, o.p.), are in part autobiographical.

THE TALES OF HOFFMANN. (With title "The Best Tales of Hoffmann") ed. by E. F. Bleiler; ill. by the author; various translators. *Dover* (orig.) 1966 pap. $3.00; *Peter Smith* $5.00; trans. by Michael Bullock *Ungar* $5.00 pap. $2.25

THREE MÄRCHEN. Trans. by Charles E. Passage. *Univ. of South Carolina Press* 1971 $14.95. The volume includes Little Zaches, Surnamed Zinnober, Princess Brambille, and Master Flea, which is among Hoffmann's masterpieces.

WEIRD TALES. 1814–1815. Trans. by J. T. Bealby. 1923. *Bks. for Libraries* 2 vols. in 1 $18.50

Books about Hoffmann

The Influence of E. T. A. Hoffmann on the Tales of Edgar Allen Poe. By Palmer Cobb. 1908. Burt Franklin $13.50. In some ways outdated, but still interesting.

Hoffmann. By Ronald J. Taylor. *Hillary House* 1963 $2.75

E. T. A. Hoffmann's Other World: The Romantic Author and His "New Mythology." By Kenneth Negus. *Univ. of Pennsylvania Press* 1965 $7.50
For readers who know German. "A competent and well written analysis"—(*Choice*).

Russian Hoffmannists. By Charles E. Passage. *Humanities Press* 1963 $16.50

E. T. A. Hoffmann's Reception in Russia. By W. Norman Ingham. *Humanities Press* 1974 pap. $24.00

KLEIST, HEINRICH VON.   1777–1811.

This German dramatist, poet, and novelist of a Prussian military family disliked the army and resigned his commission to become a journalist and pamphleteer. None of his literary work had any real success in his short lifetime; none of his eight plays was performed. Poverty-stricken and despondent, he killed himself and a newfound, seriously ill friend, a Frau Vogel, by mutual agreement. Yet "The Broken Jug" is one of the funniest comedies in German literature, a realistic picture of village life in which a slovenly local judge is exposed. "Amphitryon," also a comedy, studies the dilemma of a young matron whom Jupiter seduces in the guise of her husband. Kleist's tragedy "The Prince of Homburg" is generally considered his masterpiece. Of his novelettes, "Michael Kohlhaas" (1810) is outstanding. In Kleist was embodied the great conflict between Classicism and Romanticism, and his general theme was the conflict between individual human feelings—often erratic—and the impersonal harshness of manmade law, which he saw as nevertheless necessary for the functioning of society.

AMPHITRYON: A Comedy. 1807. Trans. by Marion Sonnenfeld. *Ungar* $3.75 pap. $1.25

THE BROKEN JUG. 1808. (With title "The Broken Pitcher") trans. by Bayard Quincy Morgan *AMS Press* 1961 $12.50; trans. by John T. Krumpelmann *Ungar* 1962 $3.75 pap. $1.45

THE PRINCE OF HOMBURG. 1810. Trans. with introd. by Charles E. Passage *Bobbs* Liberal Arts 1956 pap. $1.25; (with title "Prince Frederick of Homburg") trans. by L. Robert Scheuer *Barron's* 1962 $2.95 pap. $1.95. A play in 5 acts.

THE MARQUISE OF O AND OTHER STORIES. 1810–1811. Trans. by Martin Greenberg. *Ungar* 1973 $8.50 pap. $3.25

Books about Kleist

Kleist In France. By F. C. Richardson. *AMS Press* 1962 $12.50

Heinrich von Kleist's Drama. By Ernst L. Stahl. *Hillary House* 1961 $4.00

Heinrich von Kleist: A Study in Tragedy and Anxiety. By John Gearey. *Univ. of Pennsylvania Press* 1967 $9.00

Drama of Language: Essays on Goethe and Kleist. By Sigurd Burckhardt. *Johns Hopkins Univ. Press* 1970 $8.00

CHAMISSO, ADELBERT von (Louis Charles Adélaide de Chamisso). 1781–1838.

This German romantic writer and naturalist was born in France and forced to flee at the time of the French Revolution. He was a member of the literary circle of Mme de Staël near Geneva. Some of his verse was set to music by Schumann. He is best known for his humorous tale of "Peter Schlemihl," the man who sold his shadow to the devil.

Peter Schlemihl. 1814. (In "Three Great Classics") ed. by Fred Honig. *Arco* $4.50 Arc Bks. pap. $1.45

GRIMM, JACOB (LUDWIG KARL), 1785–1863, and WILHELM (KARL) GRIMM, 1786–1859.

A persistent element in the German Romantic movement was the nationalism that found expression in collections of folksongs and folktales. One of the first was *"Das Knaben Wunderhorn"* ("The Boy's Magic Horn"), 1805, edited by two poets of the later Romantic literary circle, Clemens Brentano and Achim von Arnim. In 1812, the brothers Grimm published their collection of *"Kinder- und Hausmärchen"* ("Household Tales"), which has become a staple of world literature.

This interest in the past, and especially the Germanic past, gave impetus to the field of Germanic philology. The Grimms and those inspired by them worked feverishly to collect and edit ancient manuscripts of Germanic heroic tales and to produce a grammar of the German language, and the Grimms themselves began work on the monumental *"Deutsches Wörterbuch"* ("German Dictionary"), which was not finished until 1961. They departed from the indiscriminate patriotic fervor of the early Romanticists and insisted that the past and its literary monuments be approached with a strict scientific method. This is their greatest legacy.

Grimm's Household Tales. 1884. Trans. by Margaret Hunt. *Gale Research Co.* (Singing Tree Press) 1968 2 vols. $27.50

Household Stories from the Collection of the Bros. Grimm. Trans. by Lucy Crane *Dover* 1963 pap. $2.00; *Peter Smith* $3.75. These editions, illustrated by Walter Crane, the pre-Raphaelite painter, have a charming, antique atmosphere about them; they are unabridged republications of the *Macmillan* edition of 1886.

German Folk Tales. Trans. by Francis P. Magoun, Jr., and Alexander H. Krappe. *Southern Illinois Univ. Press* 1960 pap. $4.95

Teutonic Mythology. 1835. By Jacob Grimm. Trans. by James Stallybrass. 1966. *Peter Smith* 4 vols. pap. set $10.00. An examination of the roots of German law and religion.

EICHENDORFF, JOSEPH, Freiherr von. 1788–1857.

Born in Silesia, von Eichendorff studied in Breslau, Halle, Heidelberg, and Vienna. A devout Roman Catholic, he expresses a serene attitude toward life in all his writings. His poems are beautifully balanced lyrics that embody the romantic and transcendental fashions of his time. Ernst Rose writes in "A History of German Literature": "Of all romantic poets who have proceeded from folk-song, he is without doubt the most intimate." Among his Novellen, *"Aus dem Leben eines Taugenichts"* ("Memoirs of a Good-for-Nothing") is especially delightful in its light-hearted spontaneity.

Memoirs of a Good-For-Nothing. 1821. Trans. by Bayard Q. Morgan. *Ungar* 1955 pap. $1.45

Books about Eichendorff

Joseph von Eichendorff. By Egon Schwarz. World Authors Ser. *Twayne* $6.95

GRILLPARZER, FRANZ. 1791–1872.

"Hebbel and Grillparzer . . . can be regarded as the last direct heirs to the classical tradition created by Goethe and Schiller. . . . Their works are poetic dramas in blank verse, treating historical and mythological subjects in the grand manner. But although in form they look back to the classical age, their spiritual and psychological content points to the future, heralding the dawn of modern drama"—(H. F. Garten in "Modern German Drama").

Grillparzer was the first Austrian writer to achieve international standing. He was born and lived in a Vienna where music was all-important and literature strictly controlled by the Church and the imperial court. His career as a playwright and as a minor government official was beset with difficulty. His plays repeatedly state his personal conviction that to be involved in love or in political power is to invite disaster. He never married his fiancée, though he never released her from their betrothal, and died her lodger. An ardent patriot, he sought to glorify Austria in his historical plays but met with censorship from Prince Metternich's government. After the failure of his play *"Weh Dem, Der Lügt"* ("Thou Shalt Not Lie") in 1838, he permitted no new play to be performed or published, though he continued to write for more than 30 years.

Medea (1818); King Ottocar: His Rise and Fall (1825); Hero and Leander: The Waves of the Sea and of Love (1831); The Jewess of Toledo (1855). Trans. by Arthur Burkhard. 1953–1962. *Burkhard* 4 vols. each $3.00

The Poor Fiddler. 1844. Trans. by Alexander and Elizabeth Henderson; introd. by Ivar Ivask. *Ungar* $5.00 pap. $1.45. A novella.

Books about Grillparzer

Franz Grillparzer in England and America. By Arthur Burkhard. *Arthur Burkhard* 1961 $2.00

HEINE, HEINRICH. 1797–1856.

Heinrich Heine is the best-known representative of the political and intellectual movement of the nineteenth century called "Young Germany." The son of a Düsseldorf merchant, Heine's young years were ones of misadventure and failure. Born a Jew, he converted to Christianity in order to receive his law degree from the University of Göttingen in 1825. But his first love did not lie with law, and with the publication of the "Travel Sketches" (1826–1831) he became a full-time writer. True to the spirit of the "Young Germans," Heine idolized things French and eventually settled in Paris in 1831. There he was active as a journalist and attempted to interpret Germany and events in Germany to his French readers. He never lost his love for Germany, however, and some of his most beautiful poetry reveals the depths of his longing and love for his native land. From 1848 until his death in 1856 he was almost totally paralyzed, but he continued to produce some of the most sensitive poetry in the German language during those years. Brilliant, mercurial in both poetry and prose, he combined romanticism and sentiment with irony and satire. Abroad, his fame equaled Goethe's (*q.v.*). Many of his poems have been set to music by Schubert, Schumann, and Brahms.

The Bibliothèque Nationale in Paris in 1966 acquired a collection of Heine's manuscripts which include "more than 2,500 unpublished pages written by Heinrich Heine and another 2,500 pages of letters to the poet and documents about him"—(*N.Y. Times*).

Selected Works. Trans. by Helen Mustard. *Random* 1973 $12.50 Vintage Bks. pap. $2.95

Lyric Poems and Ballads. Trans. by Ernst Feise. *Univ. of Pittsburgh Press* 1961 pap. $2.75

The North Sea. Trans. by Howard Mumford Jones *Open Court* bilingual ed. $6.00 pap. $1.95. Poems.

Selected Poems. Ed. by Barker Fairley. *Oxford* 1965 $7.00

The Rabbi of Bacherach. Trans. by E. B. Ashton. *Schocken* 1947 $1.50. An unfinished novel.

Heinrich Heine: Self Portrait and Other Prose Writings. Trans. by Frederic Ewen. *Citadel Press* 1974 pap. $4.95

Books about Heine

Heine, the Tragic Satirist: A Study of the Later Poetry, 1827–1856. By Siegbert Salomon Prawer. *Cambridge* 1961 $16.50
Heinrich Heine, the Elusive Poet. By Jeffrey L. Sammons. *Yale Univ. Press* 1969 $20.00. A sensitive, scholarly study by one of the foremost Heine scholars in this country.

BÜCHNER, GEORG. 1813–1837.

"Büchner's genius, though it had no time to mature fully, is unsurpassed in German Literature after Goethe's death, but his reputation is entirely a product of the years since about 1910."

The life of Georg Büchner was short, intense, and tragic—and extremely significant for the development of modern drama. He started a literary revolution which continues to the present day. His three plays "Danton's Death," "Leonce and Lena," and "Woyzeck," "drastic, incredibly modern plays" (Henry Hatfield), were greatly ahead of their time in their penetrating dramatic and psychological treatment. They served as an impetus for contemporary schools of drama as different as the Theater of the Absurd of Ionesco (*q.v.*) and the Epic Theater of Brecht (*q.v.*). Alban Berg based the libretto of his opera "Wozzeck" on "Woyzeck." "Danton's Death," a powerful drama of the French Revolution, is, like "Woyzeck," still popular.

COMPLETE PLAYS AND PROSE: Danton's Death (1835); Leonce and Lena (1836, pub. 1838); Woyzeck (1836–1837, pub. 1879); Lenz (1836, pub. 1839); The Hessian Courier (1834). Trans. with introd. by Carl R. Mueller. *Farrar, Straus* (Hill & Wang) 1963 Mermaid Dramabks. pap. $2.25

PLAYS. Trans. with introd. by Victor Price. *Oxford* 1971 pap. $2.75. Includes Danton's Death, Leonce and Lena, Woyzeck.

LEONCE AND LENA; LENZ; WOYZECK. Trans. by Michael Hamburger. German Literary Class. in Trans. *Univ. of Chicago Press* Phoenix Bks. 1973 pap. $1.95

WOYZECK and LEONCE AND LENA. Trans. by Carl R. Mueller; introd. by Lee Baxandall. *Chandler Pub.* pap. $.75

DANTON'S DEATH. Trans. by James Maxwell; introd. by Theodore Hoffman. *T. Y. Crowell* (Chandler Pub.) pap. (orig.) $.95; *Avon* Bard Bks. pap. $1.25

LENZ. Trans. by Michael Hamburger. *Frontier Press* (dist. by Book People) pap. $1.00

Books about Büchner

Georg Büchner. By Herbert Lindenberger. *Southern Illinois Univ. Press* 1964 $4.50
Georg Büchner. By Ronald Hauser. World Authors Ser. *Twayne* 1974 $6.95. Hauser presents a well-thought-out, clear introduction to the life and works of Büchner. Recommended.

HEBBEL, FRIEDRICH. 1813–1863.

Hebbel, a North German by birth, lived abroad most of his life. The son of a stonemason and a servant girl, his childhood was passed in dire poverty, and his later travels, though sponsored in part by the Danish King Christian VIII, were marked by financial difficulties. His education was scanty and largely self-achieved. His ties to his early patroness, the novelist Amalia Schoppe, and to Elsie Lensing, a woman some years his senior, caused constant stress. Only in Vienna, where he married the well-known actress Christine Enghaus, did he settle down to a reasonably peaceful existence.

Hebbel wrote plays, short stories, lyric poems, an epic poem, and a great deal of criticism and dramatic theory. His plays are linked with those of the Viennese Grillparzer as examples of late Classicism (*see note under Grillparzer*).

THREE PLAYS BY HEBBEL. Trans. by Marion W. Sonnenfeld. *Bucknell Univ. Press* 1972 $12.00

HEROD AND MARIAMNE. 1850. Trans. by Paul H. Curts. 1950. *AMS Press* $12.50. A tragedy in five acts.

STORM, THEODOR. 1817–1888.

Storm, the poet and writer of Novellen (long short stories or short novels), was a lawyer by profession who entered the Prussian government service in 1853 and held many judicial posts until his retirement in 1880. His subjects were village people and farmers in the natural setting of his own North Sea coastal region. His earlier stories, of which "Immensee" is a charming example, are lyrical in mood; later his study of character became sharper and he reached "the height of his art" in "great tales" such as "The Rider on the White Horse"—(Professor Willy Schumann, Smith College).

IMMENSEE. 1852. Trans. by Guenther Reinhardt. *Barron's* 1950 $3.50 pap. $.95

CURATOR CARSTEN (1877) and VIOLA TRICOLOR (1873). Trans. by Bayard Quincy Morgan and Frieda M. Vought. *Ungar* $5.00 pap. $1.45

THE RIDER ON THE WHITE HORSE. 1888. Trans. by Muriel Almon (in "Three Eerie Tales from 19th Century German") ed. by Edward Mornin. *Ungar* 1975 $7.50 pap. $2.95

Books about Storm

> Theodor Storm's Craft of Fiction: The Torment of a Narrator. By Clifford A. Bernd. *Univ. of North Carolina Press* 1963 2nd ed. 1966 $6.00. Includes some material on Storm's manuscripts and letters and recent criticism of him.
> Theodor Storm's Novellen. By E. Allen McCormick. 1964. *AMS Press* $12.50
> The Theme of Loneliness in Theodor Storm's Novellen. By Lloyd W. Wedburg. *Humanities Press* pap. $9.00
> Theodor Storm. By Arthur T. Alt. World Authors Ser. *Twayne* 1971 $6.95. As is to be expected from this generally excellent series the Storm volume gives a solid introduction to the life of this great writer.

FONTANE, THEODOR. 1819–1898.

Fontane's fictional studies of nineteenth-century Berlin society, written in his late maturity, secured him a firm place in literature as the first master of the German realist novel; his declared aim was to show "the undistorted reflection of the life we lead." "He introduced his people in spirited conversations at picnics and banquets, and developed a broad and yet intimate perspective of background conditions; he was less interested in plots, and often would make a point by silence" (Ernst Rose). "Effi Briest," his masterpiece, is a revealing portrait of an individual victimized by outmoded standards. Fontane, on whom Sir Walter Scott had made a deep impression, traveled to England as a journalist and wrote two books based on his experiences: "A Summer in London" (1854) and "Across the Tweed" (1860, o.p.). He also wrote historical novels, poetry, and dramatic criticism.

A MAN OF HONOR (*Schach von Wuthenow*). 1883. Trans. by E. M. Valk. *Ungar* 1975 $7.50 pap. $2.45

BEYOND RECALL (*Unwiederbringlich*). 1891. Trans. with introd. by Douglas Parmée. *Oxford* World's Class. $2.50

EFFIE BRIEST. 1895. Trans. by W. A. Cooper. *Ungar* abr. ed. 1966 $6.50 pap. $2.45

Books about Fontane

> Theodor Fontane as a Critic of the Drama. By Bertha E. Trebein. 1916. *AMS Press* $12.50
> The Influence of Walter Scott on the Novels of Theodor Fontane. By Lambert Armour Shears. 1922. *AMS Press* $5.50
> Gentle Critic: Theodor Fontane and German Politics, 1848–1898. By Joachim Remak. *Syracuse Univ. Press* 1964 $4.75

KELLER, GOTTFRIED. 1819–1890.

This Swiss German-language poet and novelist, born in Zurich, is known for his widely read realistic short stories of Swiss provincial life. The *Saturday Review* said of the autobiographical "Green Henry": "The book's instantly captivating quality is the charm with which a quietly sequential life of curiosity and perception is narrated in the pellucid recollection of the mature poet. Keller's eye for the colorful scene and his skill in endowing the concrete particular with something like archetypal significance make him an artist of rare integrity." "His masterpiece is the story . . . 'A Village Romeo and Juliet,' . . . which tells of the tragic fate of two youthful lovers who are prevented from making an honest marriage by the sins of their fathers"—(Ernst Rose).

PEOPLE OF SELDWYLA and SEVEN LEGENDS. 1856 and 1872. Trans. by M. D. Hottinger. 1929. *Bks. for Libraries* $9.50. These two collections are Keller's most famous. The first takes a nonsentimental but gentle view of the events (sometimes tragic) which take place in the lives of "typical" Swiss people in his mythical village of Seldwyla. The second pokes gentle fun at the Virgin Mary and other inhabitants of heaven.

A VILLAGE ROMEO AND JULIET. 1876. (In "Three German Classics") trans. by R. Taylor. *Transatlantic* 1967 $5.75; trans. by Paul Bernard Thomas with Bayard Quincy Morgan *Ungar* 1955 $3.75 pap. $1.45

THE BANNER OF THE UPRIGHT SEVEN AND URSULA. 1878. Trans. by Bayard Q. Morgan. *Ungar* 1974 $6.50 pap. $1.95

GREEN HENRY. 1854–55; final version 1880. Trans. by A. M. Holt. *Transatlantic* 1967 $5.75 pap. $5.25

Books about Keller

> Gottfried Keller as a Democratic Idealist. By Edward Franklin Hauch. 1916. *AMS Press* $10.00
> Gottfried Keller: Life and Works. By James M. Lindsay. *Dufour* 1969 $9.95

NIETZSCHE, FRIEDRICH (WILHELM). 1844–1900. *See Chapter 5, Philosophy,* Reader's Adviser, *Vol. 3.*

"His reputation as a poet is all but non-existent in England and the United States. In Germany, on the other hand, it is a commonplace that he is one of the most important and influential poets since Hölderlin"—(Walter Kaufmann in "20 German Poets," 1962).

HAUPTMANN, GERHART (JOHANN ROBERT). 1862–1946. (Nobel Prize 1912)

Hauptmann, Germany's outstanding playwright of the naturalist school, was by nature an experimenter. He was a strange mixture: sometimes a revolutionary, as in his greatest play, "The Weavers"; sometimes the compassionate creator, as in "Hannele," (1893) about a beggar girl dreaming of heaven. "The Sunken Bell," his most famous drama, is an allegorical verse play on the quest for an ideal, similar in theme to Ibsen's (*q.v.*) "Peer Gynt." Hauptmann won the Nobel Prize in 1912, and was given an honorary degree by Columbia University in 1932, at which occasion he delivered an oration on Goethe (*q.v.*).

Hauptmann ranks in Germany after Schiller, Goethe, and Brecht as the most widely performed German playwright. He stands as a landmark between the classic and the modern theater. "The heroes of his plays were not from either the ruling class or the bourgeoisie, but almost always from the masses. . . . By 1913, Hauptmann's naturalism was known throughout the world"—(*N.Y. Times*).

Hauptmann deserves no less fame as a writer of prose. His earlier works, such as "Thiel the Crossing Keeper," show him at his strongest in the naturalistic mode. His characters are enslaved by their enviromnent and by their own drives, especially the sex drive. In the "Heretic of Soana" Hauptmann still concentrates on the power of the sexual urge in man in the story of the priest who gave up his church for the love of a woman, but he has by this time moved away from the brooding excesses of Naturalism.

Frowned upon by the Nazis for having been a prominent figure under the Republic, which once favored nominating him for the Presidency, Hauptmann never spoke out against Nazi tyranny, but shook hands with Goebbels and accepted a medal. Yet when he died at his home in the Silesian Mountains he had been about to move to Berlin at the invitation of the Soviet Military Government. These events were forgotten or ignored during the 1962 centennial celebrations of his birth in the two Germanys. During the Memorial Week in Cologne, seven different plays of his were performed—three of them by Cologne's own repertory theater and the others by companies from Munich, Düsseldorf, Hamburg and Göttingen. In West Germany alone, more than 20 of Hauptmann's plays were presented in theaters throughout the country.

THIEL THE CROSSING KEEPER. 1888. (In "The Penguin Book of German Stories") ed. by F. J. Lamport. *Penguin* 1974 pap. (orig.) $2.50

THE WEAVERS. 1892. (In "Masterpieces of the Modern German Theater") ed. by Robert Corrigan. Masterpieces of Mod. Theater Ser. *Macmillan* 1966 pap. (orig.) $1.50

HANNELE. 1893. (In "International Modern Plays") ed. by Antony Dent. *Dutton* Everyman's $3.95 pap. $2.95

THE HERETIC OF SOANA. 1918. Trans. by Bayard Quincy Morgan; introd. by Harold von Hofe. *Hillary House* 1960 $3.00

Books about Hauptmann

Hauptmann Centenary Lectures. Ed. by K. G. Knight for London University, Institute of Germanic Studies. *Dufour* 1964 $8.50

SCHNITZLER, ARTHUR. 1862–1931.

Arthur Schnitzler, Viennese playwright, novelist, short story writer, and physician, "caught in his gentle hand the last golden glow of Vienna's setting glory and converted it to art." A sophisticated writer much in vogue in his time, he chose themes of an erotic, romantic or social nature, expressed with clarity, irony and subtle wit. *"Reigen,"* a series of ten dialogues linking people of various social classes through their physical desire for one another, has been filmed many times as *"La Ronde."* As a Jew he was sensitive to the problems of anti-Semitism, which he explored in the play "Professor Bernhardi" (1913), seen in New York in a performance by the Vienna Burgtheater in 1968. "You don't have to speak German," said Dan Sullivan (in the *N.Y. Times*), "to know that this is theater." Henry Hatfield calls Schnitzler "second only to Hofmannsthal among the Austrian writers of his generation and one of the most underrated of German authors. . . . He combined the naturalist's devotion to fact with the impressionist's interest in nuance; in other words, he told the truth"—(in "Modern German Literature").

In his most famous story "Lieutenant Gustl" (1901) Schnitzler employs the stream-of-consciousness technique in a brilliant exposition of the follies and gradual disintegration of society in *fin de siècle* Vienna. Schnitzler has also been linked with Freud and is credited with consciously introducing elements of modern psychology into his works.

THE GAME OF LOVE and LA RONDE (*Reigen*). (In "Masterpieces of the Modern Central European Theater") ed. by Robert Corrigan. *Macmillan* Collier Bks. (orig.) pap. $1.50

BEATRICE. 1900. Trans. by Agnes Jacques. 1926. *AMS Press* 1972 $9.00

LIEUTENANT GUSTL. 1901. (In "The Penguin Book of German Stories") ed. by F. J. Lamport. *Penguin* 1974 pap. (orig.) $2.50

PROFESSOR BERNHARDI. 1913. Trans. by Hetty Landstone. 1928. *AMS Press* 1972 $9.00

DANCE OF LOVE (*Reigen*). 1920. Ed. by Eric Bentley. *Doubleday* Anchor Bks. (orig.) pap. $1.45; (with title *"La Ronde,"* in "Modern Theatre," Vol. 2) *Peter Smith* $3.00. Written in 1900, this play was not performed until 1920 because of its controversial erotic theme.

FRÄULEIN ELSE. 1925. Trans. by Robert A. Simon. 1925. *AMS Press* 1972 $9.00

NONE BUT THE BRAVE. 1926. Trans. by Richard L. Simon. 1926. *AMS Press* 1972 $9.00

RHAPSODY. 1926. Trans. by Otto P. Schinnerer. 1927. *AMS Press* 1972 $9.00

THE FAREWELL SUPPER. (In "Five Modern Plays") ed. by Edmund R. Brown. *Branden* pap. $.95

CORRESPONDENCE OF ARTHUR SCHNITZLER AND RAOUL AUERNHEIMER. With Auernheimer's "Aphorisms." Ed. by Donald G. Daviau and Jorun B. Johns. Studies in Germanic Languages and Literatures *Univ. of North Carolina Press* 1972 $7.50

Books about Schnitzler

Studies in Arthur Schnitzler. Centennial Commemorative Volume. Ed. by H. W. Reichert and H. Salinger. *AMS Press* 1963 $12.50

Annotated Arthur Schnitzler Bibliography. By Richard H. Allen. *Univ. of North Carolina Press* 1966 $6.00

Arthur Schnitzler: A Critical Study. By Martin Swales. *Oxford* 1972 $14.50

Arthur Schnitzler. By Reinhard Urbach; trans. by Donald Daviau. World Dramatists Ser. *Ungar* 1973 $8.50. Illustrated.

WEDEKIND, FRANK (BENJAMIN FRANKLIN). 1864–1918.

This poet-playwright turned actor in order to produce the effect he wanted in his plays. Like most innovators, "his has always been the fate of being misunderstood, misrepresented or misinterpreted by critics." Though as a young writer he associated himself with the naturalists, "Wedekind was not a consistent naturalist," says John Gassner (in "Treasury of the Theatre"). "An original artist who was not apt to follow fashions, he helped himself to much naturalistic detail to support his personal crusade for frankness about the elemental power of the sexual instinct. . . . No prurience, but a primal amorality, characterizes his studies of Lulu, the heroine of "Earth Spirit" (1894, o.p.) and "Pandora's Box" (1903, o.p.) who destroys man after man, only to be destroyed herself by a male counterpart. . . . The weird—now and then macabre—and explosive dramaturgy and style of much of his work, make Wedekind, indeed, a precursor of 'expressionism' [and] his importance in the modern theatre cannot be underestimated." The Earth Spirit (*Erdgeist*) was his symbol for the primitive strain in human beings. "Five Tragedies of Sex"—containing "Spring's Awakening," "Earth Spirit," "Death and the Devil," "Castle Wetterstein" and "The Box of Pandora" (1952, o.p.)—was translated by Stephen Spender and Frances Fawcett with an introduction by Lion Feuchtwanger.

PRINCESS RUSSALKA. 1897. *Branden* 1924 $3.50

Books about Wedekind

Frank Wedekind. By Sol Gittleman. World Authors Ser. *Twayne* 1969 $6.95

GEORGE, STEFAN. 1868–1933.

"Something . . . of the atmosphere and coloring of the English Pre-Raphaelites and aesthetes illumines the Mallarmèan scroll of George," writes Jethro Bithell in "Modern German Literature: 1880–1950." The notion of himself as a kind of poetic "Messiah to Nietzsche's John the Baptist" (Walter Kaufmann in "20 German Poets") characterizes George's role as poet-philosopher, poet-priest, poet-king. Aristocratic, recondite, he wrote deliberately difficult poetry for those few destined to understand him. Gathered about him was a group of gifted, often physically beautiful young men, the so-called *George Kreis* (George Circle), to whom he charged the spreading of his ideas. George's poems continue to influence young writers—not so much for their themes as for their austere formal style and perfection of diction, a diction expanded by his vast knowledge of languages ancient and modern. Many young poets today would aspire to Bithell's praise: "George paints with vowels or plays on them just as a pianist plays on keys; he tangles his construction; he swathes the inner meaning of the poem in a floating veil of symbol."

WORKS. Trans. by Olga Marx and Ernst Morwitz. 1949. *Univ. of North Carolina Press* 2nd rev. and enl. ed. 1974 $12.90. The translations are faithful and readable.

Books about George

Stefan George: A Study of His Early Work. By Ulrich K. Goldsmith. *Univ. of Colorado Press* 1959 pap. $3.00

Stefan George. By Ulrich K. Goldsmith. Essays on Mod. Writers Ser. *Columbia* 1970 $1.00

Stefan George. By Michael and Erika Metzger. World Authors Ser. *Twayne* 1972 $6.95

MANN, HEINRICH. 1871–1950.

"The work of the two brothers Heinrich and Thomas Mann [*q.v.*] has from first to last been an [intensely personal] blending of confession and mental evolution, and at the same time criticism of society, gently ironic in the work of Thomas, corrosive in that of Heinrich, who has been called the German Juvenal"—(Jethro Bithell, in "Modern German Literature, 1880–1950"). Heinrich Mann wrote about artists and poets, and voluptuaries, for whom art is a "perverse debauch." His novels set in Germany are usually grotesque caricatures with political implications; those set in Italy tend to be "riotous paeans of life lived at fever heat in a world where common sense and goodness and pity do not count." His "Professor Unrat" (1905, o.p.) was made into the famous film "The Blue Angel." "The Little Town" is perhaps his most benign novel.

Heinrich (like Thomas) Mann fled Nazi Germany and came to the United States. He died in California. His literary reputation is stronger in Europe—in America his face is clouded partly by the rancor of his brilliant, hectic prose, partly by his admiration of the Soviet Union.

THE LITTLE TOWN. 1909. Trans. by Winifred Ray. *Ungar* 1962 pap. $1.75

Books about Mann

Heinrich Mann. By Rolf N. Linn. World Authors Ser. *Twayne* 1968 $6.95

Heinrich Mann and His Public: A Socioliterary Study of the Relationship between an Author and His Public. By Lorenz Winter. Trans. by John Gorman. *Univ. of Miami Press* 1970 $5.95

WASSERMANN, JAKOB. 1873–1934.

Wassermann's novels deal chiefly with psychological, philosophical, and Jewish problems. He was born in Bavaria of Jewish parents and lived in Austria for many years, experiencing many difficulties before he achieved recognition as a writer.

According to Jethro Bithell ("Modern German Literature"—*see this Chapter, Section on History and Criticism*), Wassermann, a forerunner of the expressionists, was interested as a novelist in "the investigation of strange crimes, and [tended] to interpret them as the effect of primitive urges, or . . . psychic transferences." From his discoveries in morbid psychology he drew the conclusion that "only religious heroism of character . . . can lead out of the . . . quagmire of life in general . . . while those who have not this heroic strength of will . . . sink deeper and deeper into it"—(Bithell).

CASPAR HAUSER. 1908. Trans. by Caroline Newton. *Liveright* 1928 1963 $6.95; *Multimedia* Steiner Bks. pap. $2.95

THE MAURIZIUS CASE. 1928. Trans. by C. Newton. *Liveright* 1929 1960 $6.95

DR. KERKHOVEN. 1931. Trans. by Cyrus Brooks. *Liveright* 1932 $6.95

THE WEDLOCK. Trans. by Ludwig Lewisohn. *Liveright* 1961 $6.95

HOFMANNSTHAL, HUGO VON. 1874–1929.

Hofmannsthal wrote the libretti for Richard Strauss's *"Der Rosenkavalier," "Ariadne auf Naxos"* and *"Die Frau ohne Schatten."* Both men of genius, they preferred to work miles apart and depend upon the mail. Their divergent personalities emerge through their letters: "Strauss, genial, calm and absolutely insistent upon stageworthy librettos; von Hofmannsthal, introspective, sensitive, and possessed of his own high literary standards. Each recognized in the other his opposite number and determined to make the partnership work," as it did in many instances.

Hofmannsthal's plays are all written in verse and most of them are modernized adaptations from other dramatists. His masterpiece, "Electra," a modern treatment of the Greek tragedy, was set to music by Richard Strauss. Dramas such as *"Jedermann"* ("Everyman," 1911) and "The Tower" (1925, o.p.) showed him to be a serious and responsible social critic. Their "deep symbolism is pervaded by an uncanny insight into the demonic forces and potentialities of our century"—(*LJ*). With Max Reinhardt he helped to found the Salzburg Festival of music and theater, which still occurs annually. "One of the representative minds of European humanism, and the unsurpassed embodiment of the values of Christian Western tradition in the anticipation and experience of crisis and breakdown"—(*LJ*).

In his poetry he proved himself to be the most socially sensitive of the Viennese poets of the 1890s. He "developed the resources of his Austrian heritage into a body of disciplined verse and prose so distinguished that the impressionistic idiom of his early poetry was but the promising beginning of a literary career which surpasses in variety, breadth, and wisdom that of any of his contemporaries"—(Victor Lange).

SELECTED WRITINGS. Bollingen Ser. *Princeton Univ. Press* 3 vols. Vol. 1 Selected Prose trans. by Tania and James Stern with introd. by Hermann Broch 1952 $4.50 Vol. 2 Poems and Verse Plays various trans. (bilingual) ed. with introd. by Michael Hamburger 1961 $17.50 Vol. 3 Selected Plays and Libretti various trans. ed. with introd. by Michael Hamburger 1963 $17.50

Vol. 1 includes tales, novellas, essays, notes on his travels and the unfinished novel "Andreas." Vol. 2 includes Death and the Fool; The Emperor and the Witch; The Little Theatre of the World; The Mine at Falun; The Marriage of Zobeide; Prologue to the Antigone of Sophocles. Vol. 3 includes three plays and three libretti, chosen to show the range of his theatrical writings. "The notes at the end of the volume attest to the competence of the editor"—(*LJ*).

ELECTRA. 1903. (In "Masterpieces of the Modern Central European Theater") ed. by Robert W. Corrigan. *Macmillan* Collier Bks. (orig.) pap. $1.50

A WORKING FRIENDSHIP: The Correspondence Between Richard Strauss and Hugo von Hofmannsthal. Trans. by Hanns Hammelmann and Ewald Osers. Introd. by Edward Sackville-West. 1962. *Vienna House* 1974 pap. $5.95

Books about Hofmannsthal

Hofmannsthal. By Hans Hammelman. *Hillary House* 1957 $3.00

Hofmannsthal: Studies in Commemoration. Ed. by Frederick Norman for London Univ., Institute of Germanic Studies. *Dufour* 1963 $8.50. A useful scholarly volume, but recommended for those with some knowledge of Hofmannsthal.

Hofmannsthal's Festival Dramas: Jedermann, Das Salzburger Grosse Welttheater, Der Turm. By Brian Coghlan. *Cambridge* 1964 $23.50

"A general and comprehensive work on Hofmannsthal the poet and the thinker. The striking picture of the cultural and political background makes this book valuable also to all those interested in Austrian history"—(*LJ*).

Hofmannsthal: Three Essays. By Michael Hamburger. *Princeton Univ. Press* 1970 pap. $2.95. Recommended.

MANN, THOMAS.   1875–1955.   (Nobel Prize 1929)

Although Mann suffered some diminution in popularity after his death, his hundredth anniversary and the general renewed interest in Germany and German literature (*see the introduction to this Chapter*) have succeeded in bringing Mann again to the fore of literary discussion.

His achievement remains tremendous. "Buddenbrooks," his first novel, sprang full-fledged upon the world when Mann was 26. An intricate panoramic history of the decline of a German mercantile family not unlike Mann's own, it introduced (in the persons of several family members) what was to be the dominant Mann theme-with-variations: the isolation of the artist in society, intellectualism versus the life of the emotions and senses, decay and death as sharpeners of life, and the relationship of all these to the political and social climate in which Mann found himself. In "The Magic Mountain" he studies the fringe world of a tuberculosis sanatorium. "Doctor Faustus," his culminating masterpiece, describes the life of a composer who sells his soul to the Devil as the price of his genius. The stories "Death in Venice" and "Mario the Magician," about two different varieties of artist, portray with consummate skill and dramatic tension an atmosphere of mounting evil.

Mann's tone was ironic; his concern was with the ideas that move the intellectual man. Though early in life he claimed to be "unpolitical," the harsh realities of Germany before and throughout World War II drove him eventually to devote much of his time to lecturing and writing against the Hitler government. The "Joseph" tetralogy is "implicitly related to the experiences of that time [1926–1943, when it was written] in being Mann's tribute to the national life and religious spirit of the Jews in their darkest hour"—(J. P. Stern).

An anti-Nazi from the beginning, Mann fled Germany in 1933—to live, eventually, the life of an exile in the United States during the period in which his worldwide reputation reached its zenith.

With his family, he settled here successfully but left in the McCarthy era—finally—for Switzerland, from which he was able to make lecture tours in both zones of Occupied Germany. His daughter Monika Mann has written a memoir of her father "Past and Present." Her sister Erika Mann is the author of "The Last Year of Thomas Mann" (trans. by Richard Graves 1958. *Bks. for Libraries* $7.75).

All books translated by H. T. Lowe-Porter unless otherwise specified.

STORIES OF THREE DECADES. *Knopf* 1936 $10.00. Shorter fiction, 1896–1929.

BUDDENBROOKS. 1901. *Knopf* 1924 1938 1964 $8.95; *Random* Vintage Bks. pap. $2.45

TONIO KRÖGER (1903) AND OTHER STORIES. Trans. by David Luke. *Bantam* 1970 pap. $1.25

ROYAL HIGHNESS. 1909. Trans. by A. C. Curtis; with new pref. by H. T. Lowe-Porter. 1916. *Knopf* reissue 1939 $5.95

DEATH IN VENICE. 1912. Trans. by Kenneth Burke. *Heritage Press* deluxe ed. $12.50; *Knopf* new ed. 1965 $8.95; (and "Seven Other Stories") *Random* Modern Lib. pap. $1.95 Vintage Bks. 1954 pap. $1.95

THE MAGIC MOUNTAIN. 1924. *Knopf* 1927 rev. 1938 $8.95; *Random* (Modern Lib.) pap. $2.95 Vintage Bks. pap. $2.45

PAST MASTERS AND OTHER PAPERS. 1933. *Bks. for Libraries* $10.00

JOSEPH AND HIS BROTHERS. *Knopf* 4 vols. in 1 1948 $13.95. Vol. 1 Joseph and His Brothers (1933); Vol. 2 Young Joseph (1934); Vol. 3 Joseph in Egypt (1936); Vol. 4 Joseph the Provider (1943).

THE BELOVED RETURNS: Lotte in Weimar. 1939. *Knopf* 1940 $6.95

THE TRANSPOSED HEAD: A Legend of India. 1940. *Random* 1941 Vintage Bks. pap. $1.65

THE TABLES OF THE LAW. 1944. *Knopf* 1945 $4.50. Novelette based on the life of Moses.

DR. FAUSTUS: The Life of the German Composer, Adrian Leverkühn, as Told by a Friend. 1947. *Knopf* 1948 $7.95; *Random* (Modern Lib.) $2.95 Vintage Bks. pap. $2.45. Novel.

THE HOLY SINNER. *Knopf* 1951 $7.95. A retelling of a medieval legend.

THE BLACK SWAN. Trans. by Willard R. Trask. 1953. *Knopf* 1954 $4.95

THE CONFESSIONS OF FELIX KRULL, CONFIDENCE MAN: The Early Years. 1954. Trans. by Denver Lindley. *Knopf* 1955 $8.95; *Random* Vintage Bks. 1969 pap. $1.95
   A continuation of the short story, "Felix Krull," about a handsome 19th-century swindler. "A self-sufficient masterpiece of story telling . . . clear-cut in structure and swift-moving in pace . . . one of the most intricate examples of Mann's craft"—(*New Republic*).

ESSAYS OF THREE DECADES. *Knopf* 1947 $6.75; *Random* Vintage Bks. pap. $2.45. The author's choice is creative criticism at its best.

LAST ESSAYS. Trans. by Richard and Clara Winston and Tania and James Stern. *Knopf* 1959 $5.95

THE STORY OF A NOVEL: The Genesis of Doctor Faustus. Trans. by Richard and Clara Winston. *Knopf* 1961 $4.95. A fascinating account of literary creation, 1943–1947.

LETTERS TO PAUL AMANN, 1915–1952. Trans. by Richard and Clara Winston. Ed. by Herbert Wegener. *Wesleyan Univ. Press* 1960 $4.50. In his correspondence with a Viennese scholar Mann discussed the meaning of his work and the growth of his ideas.

A SKETCH OF MY LIFE. *Knopf* 1960 $3.95. An engrossing memoir of a young solitary's rise to world fame.

LETTERS, 1889–1955. Ed. by Richard and Clara Winston. *Knopf* 1971 $17.50

MYTHOLOGY AND HUMANISM: The Correspondence of Thomas Mann and Karl Kerényi. Trans. by Alexander Gelley. *Cornell Univ. Press* 1975 $12.50

AN EXCEPTIONAL FRIENDSHIP: The Correspondence of Thomas Mann and Erich Kahler. Trans. by Richard and Clara Winston. *Cornell Univ. Press* 1975 $12.50

UNWRITTEN MEMORIES (1974). By Katia Mann. Ed. by Elisabeth Plessen and Michael Mann; trans. by Hunter and Hildegarde Hannum. *Knopf* 1975 $7.95. This book represents Katia Mann's tribute to her husband of more than fifty years on the occasion of the hundredth anniversary of his birth.

Books about Mann

Thomas Mann's World: The Novels' Revelation of Art, Life and Disease. By J. G. Brennan. 1942. *Russell & Russell* 1967 $10.00

Thomas Mann. By Henry Hatfield. *New Directions* rev. ed. 1952 pap. $1.95. Excellent critical study.

Thomas Mann: The Mediation of Art. By Richard Hinton Thomas. *Oxford* 1956 $4.50

Thomas Mann: The World as Will and Representation. By Fritz Kaufmann. 1957. *Cooper* 1973 lib. bdg. $9.00. Mann's philosophy as a formative element in his art.

The Magic Mountain: A Study of Thomas Mann's Novel "Der Zauberberg." By Hermann J. Weigand. *Univ. of North Carolina Press* 1964 $6.50
"Originally published in 1933 (Appleton), this authoritative study is again available. . . . Thomas Mann himself gave it the stamp of his approval in the Princeton essay included in both the German and the American editions of *The Magic Mountain*"—(*LJ*).

Thomas Mann: A Collection of Critical Essays. Ed. by Henry Hatfield. Not the same as *New Directions* book above. *Prentice-Hall* 1964 $5.95

In Another Language: A Record of the Thirty-Year Relationship between Thomas Mann and His English Translator, Helen Tracy Lowe-Porter. By John C. Thirlwall. *Knopf* 1966 $6.95
"A delightful volume, rich in literary meaning. . . . She was a congenial translator of the highest caliber, an author in her own right, who caught the essence and the 'atmosphere' of his novels and essays almost to perfection"—(*LJ*). The book includes two essays by Mrs. Lowe-Porter.

Thomas Mann. By J. P. Stern. Essays on Modern Writers *Columbia* 1967 pap. $1.00. A good, concise analysis of Mann's major works and present significance by a lecturer in German at Cambridge University. Bibliography.

Thomas Mann Studies, Vol. 2. Ed. by Klaus W. Jonas and Ilsedore B. Jonas. *Univ. of Pennsylvania Press* 1968 $15.00. A listing of 4,000 critical works on Mann, many of which are not found in any previous bibliography (Vol. 1 is o.p.). The majority of the sources given are in German.

Thomas Mann: A Chronicle of His Life. By Hans Burgin and Hans-Otto Mayer. Trans. by Eugene Dobson *Univ. of Alabama Press* rev. ed. 1969 $10.00. Illustrated.

Thomas Mann. By Ignace Feuerlicht. World Authors Ser. *Twayne* 1969 $6.95

Orbit of Thomas Mann. By Erich Kahler. Princeton Essays in Lit. *Princeton Univ. Press* 1969 $6.95. An informative study by a long-time friend and intimate of Thomas Mann and his family.

Thomas Mann. By Arnold Bauer. Trans. by Alexander and Elizabeth Henderson. Modern Literature Monographs *Ungar* 1971 $6.00

Thomas Mann: A Critical Study. By R. J. Hollingdale. *Bucknell Univ. Press* 1971 $8.00

Thomas Mann: Artist and Partisan in Troubled Times. By Walter Berendsohn. Trans. by George C. Buck. *Univ. of Alabama Press* 1973 $10.00

Faust as Musician: A Study of Thomas Mann's Novel "Dr. Faustus." By Patrick Carnegy. *New Directions* 1973 $9.25

Thomas Mann: The Uses of Tradition. By T. J. Reed. *Oxford* 1974 $27.25

RILKE, RAINER MARIA. 1875–1926.

Germany's greatest modern poet was born in Prague of old Bohemian and Alsatian stock. He lived for many years in Paris, where he was secretary to Auguste Rodin; then he traveled in all parts of Europe. His popularity and influence have been international. He began—at the castle of Duino in Istria (1911–1912)—but did not complete until 1922—at Castle Muzot in the Swiss Valais—the ten poems comprising the "Duino Elegies," his masterpiece. "Sonnets to Orpheus," 55 joyous and brilliant songs, followed, and completed his poetic vision of man's struggle. Not easy to summarize, Rilke's themes are love and death, expressed in symbols at once subtle and simple, concrete yet mystical and profound. An affirmer of life, he could not bear World War I, in which he was very briefly a soldier. His extraordinary letters form a part of his great literary achievement.

Poetry and Prose

SELECTED WORKS. Vol. 1 Prose. Trans. by G. Craig Houston. *New Directions* 1960 $8.75. Vol. 2 Poetry. Trans. by J. B. Leishman. *New Directions* 1960 $8.75. Vol. 1 includes his study of Rodin and such shorter pieces as "Concerning Landscape" and "Some Reflections on Dolls." Vol. 2 contains translations of all Rilke's poetry not included in "Poems 1906–1926."

POEMS FROM THE BOOK OF HOURS. 1905. Trans. by Babette Deutsch (bilingual) 1941. *New Directions* 1968 $3.00

POEMS, 1906–1926. Trans. with introd. by J. B. Leishman. *New Directions* $8.50. The introduction is excellent; contains poems discovered after Rilke's death.

NEW POEMS. 1907–1908. Trans. with introd. by J. B. Leishman (bilingual). *New Directions* 1964 $8.75

Some 189 of Rilke's poems expertly translated with "a penetrating introduction [on their] origin and nature"—(*LJ*).

TRANSLATIONS FROM THE POETRY OF RANIER MARIA RILKE. By M. D. Herter Norton (bilingual). *Norton* 1962 pap. $1.95

SELECTED POEMS. Trans. by C. F. MacIntyre (bilingual). *Univ. of California* 1958 pap. $1.95. Originally pub. as "Fifty Selected Poems."

REQUIEM AND OTHER POEMS. Trans. by J. B. Leishman. 1957. *Humanities Press* $4.25

THE LAY OF THE LOVE AND DEATH OF CORNET CHRISTOPHER RILKE. 1906. Trans. by M. D. Herter Norton (bilingual). *Norton* 1959 pap. $1.25. Short prose poem.

THE NOTEBOOKS OF MALTE LAURIDS BRIGGE (also trans. "The Journal of My Other Self"). 1910. Trans. by John Sinton. 1959. *Humanities Press* (Fernhill) $6.75; trans. by M. D. Herter Norton *Norton* 1964 pap. $1.45. Novel.

LIFE OF THE VIRGIN MARY. 1913. Trans. by C. F. MacIntyre 1947. *Greenwood* 1972 $7.75

DUINO ELEGIES. 1923. Trans. by David P. Young. *Barn Dream* (dist. by Serendipity) 1974 $10.00 ltd. ed. $30.00 pap. $5.00; trans. by Stephen Garmey and Jay Wilson *Harper* 1972 lib. bdg. $6.00 Colophon Bks. pap. $1.95; trans. by J. B. Leishman and Stephen Spender *Norton* 1939 $3.95 pap. $1.25; trans. by C. F. MacIntyre *Univ. of California Press* bilingual ed. 1961 pap. $1.50

SONNETS TO ORPHEUS. 1923. Trans. by M. D. Herter Norton *Norton* 1942 pap. $1.25; trans. by C. F. MacIntyre *Univ. of California Press* bilingual ed. 1960 pap. $1.95

VISIONS OF CHRIST: A Posthumous Cycle of Poems. Trans. by Aaron Kramer; ed. by Siegfried Mandel. *Colorado Assoc. Univ. Press* 1967 $7.50

FROM THE REMINISCENCES OF COUNT C. W. Trans. by J. B. Leishman. 1952. *Humanities Press* (Fernhill) $3.50

LETTERS TO A YOUNG POET. 1929. Trans. by M. D. Herter Norton. *Norton* 1934 rev. ed. 1954 pap. $1.25

WARTIME LETTERS OF RAINER MARIA RILKE, 1914–1921. Trans. by M. D. Herter Norton. *Norton* 1940 pap. $1.65

LETTERS TO FRAU GUDI-NÖLKE. Trans. by Violet M. Macdonald. 1955. *Humanities Press* (Fernhill) $4.25

LETTERS. Trans. by M. D. Herter Norton and Jane B. Greene. *Norton* 2 vols. Vol. 1 1892–1910 pap. $2.95 Vol. 2 1910–1926 pap. $3.95; trans. by Norton and Greene. *Peter Smith* 2 vols. set $10.00

Books about Rilke

Rainer Maria Rilke: The Years in Switzerland. By J. R. von Salis. 1936. Trans. by N. K. Cruickshank. *Univ. of California Press* 1964 pap. $1.75

"A lucidly informative account [of Rilke's last seven years. His] death from leukaemia is

related with dignity and feeling, and Professor von Salis adds modest personal reminiscences"—(*New Statesman*).

Rainer Maria Rilke. By Eliza M. Butler. 1941. *Octagon* 1973 $16.00. A sensitive, well-balanced
study.

Rilke's Duino Elegies: An Interpretation. By Romano Guardini. 1953. Trans. by K. G. Knight.
Regnery 1961 $6.50. The author, a theologian, deals primarily with the poet's concepts of love
and death.

Rilke's Craftsmanship. By H. W. Belmore. 1955. *Humanities Press* (Fernhill) $5.50

Phases of Rilke. By Norbert Fuerst. 1958. *Haskell* 1972 $10.95

Rainer Maria Rilke: Masks and the Man. By H. F. Peters. *Univ. of Washington Press* 1960
microfiche only $6.50. In addition to his own views on Rilke's poetry, the author presents
those of many Rilke scholars, critics, friends, and those of Rilke himself.

Rilke, Europe and the English Speaking World. By Eudo C. Mason. *Cambridge* 1961 $12.50

Rilke, Valéry and Yeats: The Domain of the Self. By Priscilla Shaw. *Rutgers Univ. Press* 1964
$6.00. A close reading of specific texts and a theoretical elaboration of the questions to which
they give rise.

Rainer Maria Rilke: The Poetic Instinct. By Siegfried Mandel. *Southern Illinois Univ. Press* 1965
$4.50

An excellent study of Rilke's works and personality. The author captures the nuances of
the German language in his interpretations and provides insight into the poet's style for
readers who do not know German. "The best introduction to Rilke in English"—(*SR*).
Translations are by Stephen Spender, M. D. Herter Norton, J. B. Leishman, and Mandel
himself.

Rilke in Transition: An Exploration of His Earliest Poetry. By James Rolleston. Germanic
Studies *Yale Univ. Press* 1970 $12.50

Portrait of Rilke: An Illustrated Biography. By Hans Egon Holthusen. Trans. by W. H.
Hargreaves. *McGraw-Hill* 1971 $6.95. This is a worthwhile introduction by the well-known
German critic and poet.

Rainer Maria Rilke. By Arnold Bauer. Trans. by Ursula Lamm. Modern Literature Monograph
Ser. *Ungar* 1972 $6.00

Proust and Rilke: The Literature of Expanded Consciousness. By E. F. Jephcott. *Harper*
(Barnes & Noble) 1972 $12.00

HESSE, HERMANN. 1877–1962. (Nobel Prize 1946)

When this German novelist, poet, and essayist publicly denounced the savagery and hatred of
World War I, he was considered a traitor, and he moved to Switzerland, becoming in time a
naturalized Swiss citizen. He warned of the advent of World War II, predicting too that cultureless
efficiency would destroy the modern world. Hesse is "a novelist of ideas and a moralist of a high
order"—(Joseph P. Bauke). His theme is the conflict between the elements of man's dual nature
and the problem of spiritual loneliness. His first novel, "Peter Camenzind," was published in 1904.
"Death and the Lover" (*see below*) contrasts a scholarly abbot and his beloved pupil, who leaves the
monastery for the adventurous world. This has been considered his masterpiece. "Steppenwolf," a
European best seller, was published when defeated Germany had begun to plan for another war.
It is the story of Haller, who recognizes in himself the blend of the human and wolfish traits of the
"Wolf of the Steppes." "Magister Ludi" is a fantasy about men who devote their lives to a
completely sterile scholarly project. Hesse won the Nobel Prize in 1946.

POEMS. Trans. by James Wright (bilingual). *Farrar, Straus* 1969 $4.95 Noonday pap.
$1.95; *Bantam* 1974 pap. $1.45

STORIES OF FIVE DECADES. Trans. by Ralph Manheim and Denver Lindley. *Farrar,
Straus* 1973 $8.95 Noonday 1973 pap. $2.95; *Bantam* 1974 pap. $1.95

PETER CAMEZIND. 1904. Trans. by Michael Roloff. *Farrar, Straus* 1969 $5.95 Noonday
pap. $1.95; *Bantam* 1975 pap. $1.50

BENEATH THE WHEEL. 1906. Trans. by Michael Roloff. *Farrar, Straus* 1968 $5.95
Noonday pap. $1.95; *Bantam* 1970 pap. $1.25

GERTRUDE. 1910. Trans. by Hilda Rosner. *Farrar, Straus* 1969 $6.95 Noonday pap.
$1.95; *Bantam* 1974 pap. $1.50; lg.-type ed. *G. K. Hall* 1974 $9.95

ROSSHALDE. 1914. Trans. by Ralph Manheim. *Farrar, Straus* 1970 $5.50 Noonday pap.
$1.95; *Bantam* 1972 pap. $1.50

DEMIAN: The Story of Emil Sinclair's Youth. 1919. Trans. by Michael Roloff and Michael Lebeck; introd. by Thomas Mann. *Harper* reissue 1965 $5.95; *Bantam* pap. $1.50

"Portrays a young boy's discovery of the chaos that lies beneath the surface respectability of everyday life"—(*SR*).

KLINGSOR'S LAST SUMMER. 1920. Trans. by Richard and Clara Winston. *Farrar, Straus* 1971 $6.95 Noonday pap. $1.95

WANDERING. 1921. Trans. by James Wright. *Farrar, Straus* 1972 $4.95 Noonday pap. $1.95

SIDDHARTHA. 1922. Trans. by Hilda Rosner. *New Directions* 1951 $7.50 pap. $1.75; *Bantam* pap. $1.25. A novel inspired by Hesse's travels in India.

STEPPENWOLF. 1927. Trans. by Basil Creighton. 1929 1947. Ed. by J. Mileck *Holt* (Rinehart) 1963 $5.95 pap. $1.25; *Random* (Modern Lib.) 1963 $2.95; *Bantam* pap. $1.50

NARCISSUS AND GOLDMUND (also trans. "Death and the Lover"). 1930. Trans. by Ursule Molinaro. *Farrar, Straus* 1968 $6.95 Noonday pap. $2.25; *Bantam* pap. 1971 $1.50

MAGISTER LUDI (*Das Glasperlenspiel*, also trans. "The Bead Game"). 1943. Trans. by Mervyn Savill; fwd. by Eric Peters. *Ungar* 1957 $7.50 pap. $2.25; *Bantam* 1971 pap. $1.50; (with title "The Glass Bead Game") *Holt* 1969 $7.95 pap. 1970 $3.00

THE JOURNEY TO THE EAST. 1932. Trans. by Hilda Rosner. *Farrar, Straus* 1956 $4.95 Noonday pap. $1.45; *Bantam* 1970 pap. $1.50

IF THE WAR GOES ON. Trans. by Ralph Manheim. *Farrar, Straus* 1971 $6.95 Noonday pap. $1.95

STRANGE NEWS FROM ANOTHER STAR. Trans. by Denver Lindley. *Farrar, Straus* 1972 $5.95 Noonday pap. $1.95; lg.-type ed. *G. K. Hall* 1973 $6.95

REFLECTIONS. Trans. by Ralph Manheim; ed. by Volker Michels. *Farrar, Straus* 1974 $6.95 Noonday pap. $1.95

AUTOBIOGRAPHICAL WRITINGS. Trans. by Denver Lindley; ed. by Theodore Ziolkowski. *Farrar, Straus* 1972 $8.95 Noonday 1973 pap. $2.65

MY BELIEF: Essays on Life and Art. Trans. by Denver Lindley and Ralph Manheim; ed. by Theodore Ziolkowski. *Farrar, Straus* 1974 $8.95

Books about Hesse

Hermann Hesse and His Critics. By Joseph Mileck. 1958. *AMS Press* $12.50
Still "the best introduction to Hesse's life and works"—(*Modern Language Journal*, Oct. 1966).
The Lyrical Novel: Studies in Herman Hesse, André Gide and Virginia Woolf. By Ralph Freedman. *Princeton Univ. Press* 1963 $9.25 pap. $3.45
Faith from the Abyss: Hermann Hesse's Way from Romanticism to Modernity. By Ernst Rose. *New York Univ. Press* 1965 $7.50 pap. $2.45. Essentially a noncritical work; useful as an introduction to Hesse.
The Novels of Hermann Hesse: A Study in Theme and Structure. By Theodore Ziolkowski. *Princeton Univ. Press* 1965 $9.50 pap. $2.00
"For anyone concerned with Hesse or even the modern novel in general, [this] book will remain a landmark, notable for its new insights and perspectives and stimulating even where one disagrees"—(G. W. Field in *The German Quarterly*). By a professor of German at Princeton.
Hermann Hesse. By Theodore Ziolkowski. Essays on Modern Writers *Columbia* 1966 pap. $1.00. A brief, gracefully written account by the same authority as the above work.
C. G. Jung and Hermann Hesse: A Record of Two Friendships. By Miguel Serrano. Trans. by Frank MacShane. *Schocken* 1966 pap. $1.95
Hermann Hesse: His Mind and Art. By Mark Boulby. *Cornell Univ. Press* 1967 $12.50. An analysis of all of Hesse's major works, including his early novels.
Hermann Hesse. By Franz Baumer. Trans. by John Conway. Modern Literature Monographs *Ungar* 1969 $6.00 pap. $1.75
Portrait of Hesse: An Illustrated Biography. By Bernhard Zeller. *McGraw-Hill* 1971 pap. $2.95

Herman Hesse. By G. W. Field. World Authors Ser. *Twayne* 1970 $6.95

Hesse: A Collection of Critical Essays. Ed. by Theodore Ziolkowski. 20th Century Views Ser. *Prentice-Hall* 1973 $5.95 Spectrum Bks. pap. $1.95. This excellent collection should be used by those with a more intimate knowledge of Hesse.

DÖBLIN, ALFRED.   1878–1957.

Novelist, playwright, poet, essayist, Alfred Döblin was one of the most prolific writers of his time. He was also a practising physician in the working-class district of Alexanderplatz. His novel of this name is considered his best work, and represents, in its montage technique, Döblin's experimental attitude toward prose writing. Döblin fled the Nazi regime in 1933 and lived for a while in the United States. Later he became a French citizen and a convert to the Roman Catholic Church.

ALEXANDERPLATZ, BERLIN: The Story of Franz Biberkopf. 1930. Trans. by Eugene Jolas. *Ungar* 1958 $8.50 pap. $2.95

Books about Döblin

Alfred Döblin. By Wolfgang Kort. World Authors Ser. *Twayne* 1974 $6.95. This is a worthwhile, gracefully written introduction to Döblin. It is especially valuable for readers who are familiar with Döblin's works.

KAISER, GEORG.   1878–1945.

In the "GAS trilogy" ("The Coral," "Gas I" and "Gas II") Kaiser's fundamental theme, the regeneration of man, is presented in terms of contemporary social conflicts. The cycle of plays encompasses the entire evolution of capitalism within an abstract scheme. In essence it is a morality play.

Kaiser was the leading playwright of German expressionism, exponent of its meager settings, violent contrasts and love of the grotesque and shocking—all aimed at arousing in the beholder an intense "awareness of life." His more than 50 plays include every variety of style and subject matter—social drama, comedy, farce, romance, legend, and history. His characters are types shorn of individual subtleties, embodiments of ideas pure and simple. Kaiser stands as one of the boldest and most fascinating of the older generation of modern dramatists, and his impact on the contemporary theater, inside and outside Germany, has been considerable. "A brilliant technician, he called his plays thought dramas. They deal chiefly with social themes and were not of a kind to please the Nazis, upon whose rise to power Kaiser left Germany." He died in Switzerland.

THE CORAL. 1917. Trans. by Winifred Katzin. *Ungar* $4.75 pap. $1.75

GAS I. 1918. Trans. by Herman Scheffauer; ed. with introd. by Victor Lange. *Ungar* 1957 pap. $1.75. A play in five acts.

GAS II. 1920. Trans. by Winifred Katzin; introd. by Victor Lange. *Ungar* pap. $1.75

THE RAFT OF THE MEDUSA. 1943. (In "Postwar German Theatre") ed. by M. Benedikt and G. E. Wellwarth. *Dutton* 1967 pap. $2.75. Thirteen children on a raft are "a microcosm of the world" in this anti-Nazi play.

Books about Kaiser

Georg Kaiser. By E. Schuerer. World Authors Ser. *Twayne* $6.95

MUSIL, ROBERT.   1880–1942.

"The Man without Qualities," Musil's magnum opus, is a novel about the life and history of prewar Austria. It was unfinished when he died, though he had labored over it for ten years and it fills three volumes. Encyclopedic in the manner of Proust or Dostoyevsky, "it is a wonderful and prolonged firework display, a well-peopled comedy of ideas" (V. S. Pritchett)—and a critique of contemporary life. Ulrich, the protagonist, is the "cool" modern man who avoids involvement. The book "demands an intellectual effort comparable to that required by the more abstruse of German philosophers" (*SR*), but it made Musil's largely posthumous reputation. "Musil's whole scheme prophetically describes the bureaucratic condition of our world, and what can only be called the awful, deadly serious and self-deceptive love affair of one committee for another"— (Pritchett).

"Young Törless" is a novel of troubled adolescence set in a military school, modeled on the one attended by both Musil and Rilke. It was his first book and was immediately successful. He then abandoned his studies in engineering, logic, and experimental psychology and turned to writing. He was an officer in the Austrian army in World War I, lived in Berlin until the Nazis came into power and settled finally in Geneva. He also wrote plays, essays, and short stories. A useful study is "Robert Musil: An Introduction to His Work" by Burton Pike (1961. *Kennikat* 1971 $10.00).

YOUNG TÖRLESS. 1906. Trans. by Ernst Kaiser and Eithne Wilkins; afterword by John Simon. *New Am. Lib.* Signet pap. $.75

THE MAN WITHOUT QUALITIES. Vol. 1 (1930): Pt. 1 A Sort of Introduction; Pt. 2 The Like of It Now Happens. Trans. with introd. by Eithne Wilkins and Ernst Kaiser. *Putnam* Capricorn Bks. 1965 pap. $2.75. Vols. 2 and 3 are o.p.

A "perfect translation"—*(SR)*.

ZWEIG, STEFAN. 1881–1942.

"Each period produces writers who, while falling short of real greatness, are significant representatives of their age and society. Stefan Zweig belonged to this group"—*(LJ)*. Born in Vienna, the prolific Zweig was a poet in his early years. In the 1920s he achieved fame with the many biographies he wrote of famous people including Balzac, Dostoevsky, Dickens, and Freud. Erasmus, with whom he closely identified, was the subject of a longer biography. He also wrote the novellas "Amok" (1922) and "The Royal Game" (1944). As Nazism spread, Zweig, a Jew, fled to the United States and then to Brazil. He hoped to start a new life there but the haunting memory of Nazism, still undefeated, proved too much for him, and he died with his wife in a suicide pact.

EMILE VERHAEREN. 1910. Trans. by Jethro Bithell. 1914. *Bks. for Libraries* 1975 $9.50

ROMAIN ROLLAND: The Man and His Works. 1920. *Blom.* 1973 $12.50; *Haskell* 1970 $18.95; *Richard West* $12.00

PASSION AND PAIN. 1925. Trans. by Eden and Cedar Paul. 1925. *Bks. for Libraries* $9.50

ERASMUS OF ROTTERDAM. 1934. *Richard West* $20.00

MENTAL HEALERS: Franz Anton Mesmer, Mary Baker Eddy, Sigmund Freud. *Ungar* $8.50 pap. $2.95

THE WORLD OF YESTERDAY: An Autobiography. 1943. Introd. by Harry Zohn. *Peter Smith* $4.50; *Univ. of Nebraska Press* Bison Bks. 1964 pap. $2.50. This intensely moving document eloquently expresses Zweig's bitter disappointment with the changes that Nazism brought about not only externally but also, and more importantly, in the souls of people.

Books about Zweig

Stefan Zweig: A Bibliography. By Randolph J. Klawiter. *Univ. of North Carolina Press* 1965. $9.50. Lists more than 3,400 items and includes an essay on Zweig's life and personality.

Stephan Zweig. By Elizabeth Allday. *O'Hara* 1972 $12.50

European of Yesterday: A Biography of Stephan Zweig. By D. A. Prater. *Oxford* 1972 $13.75. This is a solid, well-written, compassionate biography. It is, above all, informative and objective. Recommended.

KAFKA, FRANZ. 1883–1924.

Kafka, a Czech who wrote in German, is now known for his "surpassing originality as an innovator in creative method." Very little of his work was published during his lifetime. The first three uncompleted novels form what Max Brod, his close friend, called a "trilogy of loneliness." "Like every other work, they reflect in a profoundly religious sense the experience of human isolation and the pathos of exclusion." He was born in Prague of middle-class Jewish parents and seems early to have suffered serious personality difficulties as the son of a domineering father. He took a law degree at the German University of Prague, then obtained a position in the workmen's compensation division of the Austrian government. Always neurotic, enigmatic, obsessed with a sense of inadequacy, failure, and sinfulness, his writing was a quest for fulfillment. He spent several years in sanatoriums and died of tuberculosis in a hospital near Vienna. Before his death he asked Max Brod to burn all his manuscripts. But Brod disregarded this injunction and was responsible for the posthumous publication of Kafka's longer narratives which have brought him worldwide fame in the past 25 years. The nightmare world of "The Castle" and "The Trial," in which the little man is at the mercy of heartless forces that manipulate him without explanation, has become frighteningly relevant to the period of the modern mammoth (or authoritarian) state, whose ordinary citizen finds himself increasingly helpless.

The publication of Kafka's letters to his fiancée, Felice Bauer, will help to demystify him somewhat, something that is needed. Kafka, like the Bible, seems to have universal application, and when reading much of the literary criticism on Kafka, one is many times unable to determine whether one is reading about Kafka and his neuroses or those of the critic.

All translated by Edwin and Willa Muir unless otherwise noted:

SELECTED SHORT STORIES. Introd. by Philip Rahv. *Random* (Modern Lib.) 1952 $2.95. Fifteen of the best-known stories.

PARABLES AND PARADOXES. Ed. by Nahum Glatzer. Various translators (bilingual). *Schocken* 1962 $6.00 pap. $1.95. A selection from his works.

THE METAMORPHOSIS (*Die Verwandlung*). 1916. Trans. and ed. by Stanley Corngold. *Bantam* crit. ed. 1972 pap. $1.95; (in "Seven Short Novel Masterpieces") ed. by Leo Hamalian and Edmond L. Volpe *Popular Lib*. pap. $.95; *Schocken* (bilingual ed.) 1948 $7.50 pap. $2.45; trans. by A. L. Lloyd *Vanguard* 1946 $5.95

IN THE PENAL COLONY: Stories and Short Pieces. 1920. *Schocken* 1948 $7.50 pap. $2.45

THE TRIAL. 1925. *Knopf* 1937 rev. ed. 1957 $6.95; *Random* (Modern Lib.) $2.95 Vintage Bks. pap. $1.95; ill. by the author *Schocken* 1969 pap. $1.95

THE CASTLE. 1926. Trans. by Willa and Edwin Muir with added material trans. by Ernst Wilkins and Eithne Kaiser and essay by Thomas Mann. *Knopf* rev. ed. 1954 $6.95; *Random* (Modern Lib.) 1969 $3.95 Vintage Bks. pap. $2.45; *Schocken* 1974

AMERIKA. 1927. Trans. by Edwin Muir; introd. by Klaus Mann; ill. by Emlen Etting. *New Directions* 1940 pap. $1.75; *Schocken* 1962 $7.50 pap. $1.95

THE GREAT WALL OF CHINA: Stories and Reflections. 1931. 1946. *Schocken* 1970 $7.50 pap. $2.25

DESCRIPTION OF A STRUGGLE (1936) AND OTHER STORIES. Trans. by Tania and James Stern. *Schocken* 1958 $1.50. More than a dozen very short pieces, three stories, and a dramatic piece.

I AM A MEMORY COME ALIVE: Autobiographical Writings. Ed. by Nahum N. Glatzer. *Schocken* 1974 $10.00

DIARIES. Vol. 1 1910–13. 1948. Trans. by Joseph Kresh; ed. by Max Brod; ill. by the author. Vol. 2 1914–23. 1949. Trans. by Martin Greenberg and Hannah Arendt; ed. by Max Brod. *Schocken* 2 vols. each $7.50 pap. each $2.95

LETTERS TO FELICE. 1912–1917. Trans. by James Stern and Elizabeth Duckworth; ed. by Erich Heller and Juergen Born. *Schocken* 1973 $17.50. The publication of the translation of Kafka's letters to his fiancée, Felice Bauer, marks a milestone event in Kafka studies in this country. Felice, whose identity was not known for years, was one of the few people, male or female, who was able to evoke feelings of tenderness and intimacy in Kafka. The letters chronicle their courtship, carried on mainly in letter form. Felice died in 1960.

LETTERS TO MILENA. Trans. by T. and J. Stern; ed. by Willi Haas. *Schocken* 1952 in German $4.50, in English 1962 $7.50 pap. $2.75

LETTER TO HIS FATHER (*Brief an Den Vater*). Trans. by Ernst Kaiser and Eithne Wilkins (bilingual) *Schocken* 1966 $6.00 pap $1.95. A lengthy autobiographical letter written at the age of 36. "You made me lose all possible self-confidence and exchange a boundless sense of guilt for it," he wrote.

Books about Kafka

Franz Kafka: A Biography. By Max Brod. Trans. by G. Humphreys Roberts and Richard Winston. 1947. *Schocken* 2nd enl. ed. 1960, 1961 $7.50 pap. $2.45
Kafka's lifelong friend and literary executor, the man who knew him as well as anyone, wrote this intimate biography which Alfred Kazin (*q.v.*) described as "invaluable to anyone at all interested in the mind of the genius."
Four Prophets of Our Destiny: Kierkegaard, Dostoevsky, Nietzsche, Kafka. By William Hubben. 1952. *Macmillan* Collier Bks. reissue 1966 pap. $1.25
Franz Kafka Today. Ed. by Angel Flores and Homer Swander. *Univ. of Wisconsin Press* 1958 pap. $1.95. Eighteen essays on the short stories, novels, letters and diaries.
Kafka. By Gunther Anders. Trans. by A. Steer and A. K. Thorlby. *Hillary House* 1960 $2.75

Franz Kafka: Parable and Paradox. By Heinz Politzer. *Cornell Univ. Press* 1962 rev. ed. 1966 $15.00 pap. $2.95

Dickens and Kafka: A Mutual Interpretation. By Mark Spilka. *Peter Smith* 1963 $5.00
"Spilka has assiduously and ingeniously studied the whole spectrum of Dickens-Kafka affinities to solve three major problems; first, the full . . . direct evidence of continuity and kinship . . . second, the form of grotesque comedy which these authors share . . . third, the illumination of specific texts"—*(LJ)*.

Kafka: A Collection of Critical Essays. Ed. by Ronald D. Gray. *Prentice-Hall* 1963 $5.95 pap. $1.95

Kafka Bibliography. By Angel Flores. *Bern Porter* 3rd ed. 1969 $5.00

Franz Kafka. By Walter H. Sokel. Essays on Mod. Writers Ser. *Columbia* 1966 pap. $1.00. Good, nonsensational analysis.

Kafka. By Charles Osborne. Ed. by Norman Jeffares. *Int. Pubns. Service* 1967 $2.50

Franz Kafka. By Wilhelm Emrich. Trans. by Sheema L. Buehme. *Ungar* 1967 $15.00
"An illuminating study of Franz Kafka's writings, examining Kafka's philosophic design by the square inch. . . . A remarkable study"—*(PW)*.

Twentieth Century Interpretations of The Castle. Ed. by Peter F. Neumeyer. *Prentice-Hall* 1968 $4.95 pap. $1.25

The Commentators' Despair: The Interpretation of Kafka's Metamorphosis. By Stanley Corngold. *Kennikat* 1973 $12.50 pap. $3.95

On Kafka's Castle: A Study. By Richard Sheppard. *Harper* (Barnes & Noble) 1973 $13.75

Kafka's Other Trial: The Letters to Felice. By Elias Canetti. Trans. by Christopher Middleton. *Schocken* 1974 $6.50. This critical study of the letters shows how the correspondence and the situation from which it arose greatly inspired Kafka's writings. This book can be considered essential.

The Kafka Problem: An Anthology of Criticism about Franz Kafka. Ed. by Angel Flores. *Gordian* 1974 $15.00

Franz Kafka: A Collection of Criticism. Ed. by Leo Hamalian. Contemporary Studies in Lit. *McGraw-Hill* 1974 pap. (orig.) $2.25

Franz Kafka. By Erich Heller. *Viking* 1975 $7.95 pap. $2.95
"Heller's is one of the more enlightened Kafka studies of recent years"—*(N.Y. Times)*.

FEUCHTWANGER, LION (J. L. Wetcheek, pseud.). 1884–1958.

The novelist and dramatist was born in Munich, the son of a wealthy Jewish manufacturer. The rise of the Nazis drove him to France, and after the collapse of that country he escaped with great difficulty to Spain; he reached the United States in 1940. A major work is his trilogy on the Jewish historian: "Josephus" (1932), "The Jew of Rome" (1935, o.p.) and "Josephus and the Emperor" (1942, o.p.). He was best known in Germany as a dramatist, but his international success was due to his revival of the historical novel written with modern psychological understanding. "Wetcheek," the pseudonym he occasionally used, is a literal translation of "Feuchtwanger."

JOSEPHUS. 1932. *Atheneum* 1972 pap. $4.95

PROUD DESTINY. 1947. Trans. by Moray Firth from the German manuscript *"Waffen für Amerika"* ("Arms for America"). *Popular Lib.* Eagle Bks. pap. $1.25
"Makes the reader feel the mighty pulse of history"—*(SR)*.

THIS IS THE HOUR. 1951. Trans. by Moray Firth. *Popular lib.* pap. $1.25

THE HOUSE OF DESDEMONA, or The Laurels and Limitations of Historical Fiction. Trans. by Harold A. Basilius. *Wayne State Univ. Press* 1963 pap. $3.95. An evaluation and analysis of some 100 historical novels of world literature.

(With Bertolt Brecht). VISIONS OF SIMONE MARCHARD. 1959. Trans. with pref. by Carl R. Mueller. *Grove* Black Cat Bks. (orig.) 1965 pap. $1.25. A play.

Books about Feuchtwanger

Lion Feuchtwanger: The Man, His Ideas and His Work. Ed. by John M. Spalek Univ. of Southern California Studies in Comparative Lit. *Hennessey & Ingalls* 1972 $12.95
A collection of critical essays. "Contributions by eighteen noted authorities with fully documented analyses of the important historical novels and dramas, discussion of the recurring themes, style, and social background, as well as a biography, chronology and bibliography"—(Publisher's catalog).

Insight and Action: The Life and Works of Lion Feuchtwanger. By Lothar Kahn. *Fairleigh Dickinson Univ. Press* 1974 $15.00

BENN, GOTTFRIED. 1886–1956.

"Benn was a striking figure in his time, but he has hardly survived it in his work, although he has been a powerful influence on recent younger Germanic poets"—(Harry T. Moore). The publication of his first volume of poems, "Morgue," in 1912, established him as a member of the European avant-garde and an *enfant terrible* of expressionism. A Berlin physician, Benn brought to his early poems a medically based obsession with the phenomena of physical and mental decay and a radical disillusionment with the bourgeois world.

PRIMAL VISION, SELECTED PROSE AND POETRY. Ed. by E. B. Ashton. *New Directions* 1960 pap. 1971 $3.25

BROCH, HERMANN. 1886–1951.

Born in Vienna, this novelist, philosopher, and playwright came to America in 1938, was awarded a Guggenheim Fellowship for 1941–1942, a membership in the American Institute of Arts and Letters 1942, and a Rockefeller Fellowship for Philosophical and Psychological Research at Princeton, 1942–1944. He had been a mathematician, engineer, and director of a Viennese textile concern. His remarkable prose trilogy describing three stages in the disintegration of modern European society, "The Sleepwalkers," is "a striking example of a new type of European cultural portraiture in which scientific speculation and poetic imagination are combined to represent the incoherent variety of contemporary experience"—(Victor Lange). "The Death of Virgil," whom Broch regarded "as a prototype of the modern man . . . depicts the last eighteen hours of Virgil's life—an obvious parallel to Joyce's work. [Broch] was conscious of a mission . . . to which he devoted himself with . . . an almost messianic zeal. Yet the reader who is willing to follow Broch into the mazes of his works . . . will come away enriched by a new dimension. Broch's vision of the immanence of death will probably be regarded as his most original contribution to human experience. His evocation of the totality and simultaneity of life is his greatest achievement in literature."—(Theodore Ziolkowski).

THE SLEEPWALKERS. 1932. Trans. by Willa and Edwin Muir; introd. by Hannah Arendt. *Grosset* Univ. Lib. 1964 pap. $3.95; *Pantheon* 1964 $10.00

THE DEATH OF VIRGIL. 1945. Trans. by Jean Starr Untermeyer; introd. by Hannah Arendt. *Grosset* Univ. Lib. pap. $2.95; *Peter Smith* $5.25

THE GUILTLESS. 1950. Trans. by Ralph Manheim. *Little* 1974 $8.95

Books about Broch

Hermann Broch. By Theodore Ziolkowski. Essays on Modern Writers *Columbia* 1964 pap. $1.00. A brief, authoritative survey of his life and works.

The Sleepwalkers: Elucidations of Hermann Broch's Trilogy. By Dorit C. Cohn. 1966. *Humanities Press* $10.50

WERFEL, FRANZ. 1890–1945.

Born in Prague, Czechoslovakia, of Jewish parents, Werfel served in World War I, 1915–1917, then lived and wrote in Vienna until driven out by the Nazi occupation of Austria. "And the Bridge Was Love: Memories of a Lifetime" by his wife, the late Alma Werfel, in collaboration with E. B. Ashton (1958, o.p.), is a deeply personal autobiography of a remarkable life in Vienna by the woman who was married to the composer-conductor Mahler and the architect Gropius. Werfel escaped to the United States after the fall of France in 1940. He won international recognition for his fiction; he also wrote lyrical poetry and drama. His comedy "Jacobowsky and the Colonel" (1944, U.S. o.p.) was successfully produced in New York in 1944. In 1967 the Hamburg Opera presented Giselher Klebe's operatic version of the play at the Metropolitan Opera House in New York.

THE FORTY DAYS OF MUSA DAGH. 1934. *Pocket Bks.* 1962 pap. $.75; trans. by Geoffrey Dunlop *Viking* Compass Bks. 1962 1967 pap. $2.25. Historical novel of the Armenian resistance to the Turks in 1915.

THE SONG OF BERNADETTE. 1942. *Avon Bks.* 1975 pap. $1.95

BETWEEN HEAVEN AND EARTH. 1944. *Bks. for Libraries* $11.25

SACHS, NELLY. 1891–1970. (Nobel Prize 1966)

When Nelly Sachs became cowinner of the 1966 Nobel Prize for Literature with S. Y. Agnon (*q.v.*), she was little known outside Germany and Sweden. Born in Berlin of an upper-middle-class Jewish family, she began writing poetry and puppet plays at the age of 17. She clung to conventional forms, especially the sonnet, ignoring the expressionist movement of her day. A volume of legends and stories, dedicated to her friend Selma Lagerlöf, (*q.v.*) and published in

1921, went largely ignored by the critics. During the Hitler years she continued to write in isolation, reading widely in the works of the German and Jewish mystics—who exerted a profound influence on her later poetry.

In 1940, on Selma Lagerlöf's request, Prince Eugene of Sweden granted refuge to Nelly Sachs and her mother. She continued to write in German, expressing through poetry her torment over the fate of her people. "I represent the tragedy of the Jews," she said in her Nobel Prize speech. She studied Swedish and translated several leading Swedish poets into German. For this service to Swedish literature she was awarded the Prize of the (Swedish) Poets' Association. Her own first volume of verse, "In the Habitations of Death," was published in Germany in 1946, and a second, "Eclipse of the Stars," in Amsterdam in 1949. Not until the appearance of her third book, "Flight and Metamorphosis" (1958) did the German critics take notice of her.

"Eli: A Mystery Play of the Sufferings of Israel," broadcast on German radio stations in 1958, brought her further prominence. In the simple style of the medieval miracle plays, it tells of a young flute-player who is killed by a German soldier. Two operas, one Swedish and one German, have been based on it. In 1961 Miss Sachs was awarded the first Nelly Sachs Prize established by the city of Dortmund, Germany, and in 1965 the Peace Prize of the German Book Publishers' Association.

"In her verse, Miss Sachs has raised a monument to the Jews that is at once modern and timeless. Combining impulses from the German world of Hölderlin, Novalis and Rilke, from surrealism, Chassidism and the Old Testament, she has found a language uniquely her own. Totally free of irony, understatement and anger, her verse reaches the hymnic pathos of prophecy"—(J. P. Bauke, in the *N.Y. Times*).

THE SEEKER AND OTHER POEMS. Trans. by Matthew Mead and others (bilingual). *Farrar, Straus* 1970 $12.50

O THE CHIMNEYS: Selected Poems, Including the Verse Play, "Eli" (1951). Trans. by Michael Hamburger and others (bilingual); introd. by Hans Magnus Enzensberger. *Farrar, Straus* 1967 $10.00 Sunburst Bks. pap. $2.75. This first English volume contains about half her poetry including "Glowing Enigmas, I, II, and III" in its entirety.

TOLLER, ERNST. 1893–1939.

A German-Jewish dramatist who fought in World War I, Toller was later imprisoned for trying to stop the war by organizing a strike of the munition workers. For his part in the Bavarian revolution he was exiled by the Nazis and his books were burned. He then came to New York. His plays and lectures spoke for the millions of Germans "who have been deprived of their voices." A radical, he identified himself strongly with the proletariat. His autobiography "Learn from My Youth—I was a German" (1934, 1936) is o.p. He took his own life in despair, following the victory of Franco in Spain and the Munich Pact, perhaps unable to bear the prospect of an inevitable World War II.

THE SWALLOW BOOK. 1924. *Haskell* 1974 lib. bdg. $7.95

Books about Toller

Ernst Toller and His Critics. By John M. Spalek. 1968 *Haskell* 1972 lib. bdg. $28.95

DODERER, HEIMITO VON. 1896–1966.

"The Demons" is the magnum opus of a writer highly respected in Germany and his native Austria. Written over a period of 30 years, the novel chronicles life in Vienna during the late 1920s. An officer in World War I, Doderer was captured on the Eastern front and sent to Siberia, where he remained for several years as a POW. He served in the German Air Force in World War II. His theme, says Claude Hill (in *SR*), is the "shrinkage of 'real' reality in the contemporary world": only the artist can liberate men from the artificialities in which they are willy-nilly enmeshed. In a comment on his life and work, he once said "I am an absolute realist and work only with realistic means. It's a matter of slipping into an invented garment and sticking your arms through real sleeves." He was awarded the Grand Prize of the Austrian Republic for his novels and poetry.

THE DEMONS. 1956. Trans. by Richard and Clara Winston. *Knopf* 1961 2 vols. $15.00

BRECHT, BERTOLT. 1898–1956.

"The German *avant-garde* in drama *is* Brecht. . . . His work is fresh, vital, and pertinent enough to give a new direction to theatrical history"—(Eric Bentley). He left Germany because of Hitler in 1933, and many of his vigorous plays, radio scripts, and poems were written against Hitlerism. He was one of the editors of a short-lived anti-Nazi magazine in Moscow (1936–1939) and came to the United States in 1941. In 1949 his wife, Helen Weigel, starred successfully in his play "Mother

Courage and Her Children," "a Brecht masterpiece and a relentless Marxist indictment of the economic motives behind internal aggression"—(Robert Brustein). It was presented on Broadway in the spring of 1963. Brecht's plays are now in the programs of many American repertory companies. "The Caucasian Chalk Circle" was played at Lincoln Center in 1966. "Galileo," in 1967, was "easily the Vivian Beaumont's best production to date"—(N.Y. Times). Brecht has also found a large audience off-Broadway, especially as librettist for Kurt Weill's "Threepenny Opera"—an adaptation of John Gay's (q.v.) "Beggar's Opera"—which ran for 2,611 performances. "Drums in the Night" (1918)—one of director Theodore Mann's "latest triumphs" (N.Y. Times)— was produced at the Circle in the Square in 1967. His most ambitious venture in verse drama, "Saint Joan of the Stockyards," was written in Germany shortly before Hitler came to power.

Brecht was "a playwright with a point of view not only toward society but toward the theatre. He saw the stage as a platform for the promulgation of a message. His aim . . . was to 'develop the means of entertainment into an object of instruction and to change certain institutions from places of amusement into organs of public communication' "—(N.Y. Times). He called himself an "epic realist." Howard Taubman has defined the Berlin "epic theater" concept, developed by Brecht and the director Erwin Piscator, in its simplest terms (it involved a good deal more than this and had a tremendous impact on world drama) as a theater "which aims to make one think rather than feel." The "conflict in Brecht's plays is almost always the same: Those who, compelled by compassion, set out to change the world cannot afford to be good"—(Hannah Arendt, in the New Yorker).

Brecht's only piece of long fiction is the "Three Penny Novel" (trans. by D. I. Vesey, verses trans. by Christopher Isherwood, 1956 o.p.). Nine volumes of Brecht's collected poetry have recently appeared in West Germany, with a tenth to come. "The material now available," says Martin Esslin (in the Drama Review), "establishes Brecht as one of the greatest of German lyrical poets, with an oeuvre of surprising richness and variety." Brecht was the subject of Grass's (q.v.) play "The Plebeians Rehearse the Uprising," which portrays him as betraying his own ideals but is generally acknowledged to have distorted the facts of the true episode with which it deals.

Brecht felt able in his last years, at the height of the Cold War, to settle in East Berlin, where he died in 1956 of a heart attack. Martin Esslin has cited evidence that, although he was certainly a radical and accepted assistance in his theatrical efforts from the East German Government, his heart belonged to no government or ideology. On his 1947 American visit he was summoned to Washington by the House Un-American Activities Committee, before which he testified as to his right of Marxist dissent. "In the end the Committee thanked him for having been a cooperative witness; he firmly denied that he had ever been a member of the Communist Party"—(Harry T. Moore). How radical Brecht really was has been the subject of considerable controversy; but, for literary purposes, his politics need only be judged as they contributed to his artistry.

In his final years Brecht experimented powerfully with his own theater and company—the Berliner Ensemble—which put on his plays under his direction and which continued after his death with the assistance of Frau Brecht (Helen Weigel). Brecht's fecundity, originality and versatility were matched by his genius, which still looms immense over Europe today.

COLLECTED WORKS. Plays. Vols. 1, 5, 7, 9. Ed. by Ralph Manheim and John Willett. *Pantheon* Vol. 1 1971 Vol. 5 1972 Vol. 9 1973 each $10.00; *Random* Vol. 7 1975 $15.00 Vintage Bks. Vols. 1, 5, 7, 9 pap. each $2.95

THE SONGS OF BERT BRECHT AND HANS EISLER. Trans. and introd. by Eric Bentley (bilingual). *Oak* 1967 $10.00

SELECTED POEMS. Trans. and introd. by H. R. Hayes (bilingual). *Harcourt* Harvest Bks. pap. $1.95

SEVEN PLAYS. Ed. by Eric Bentley. *Grove* 1961 $8.50. In the Swamp; A Man's a Man; Saint Joan of the Stockyards; Mother Courage; Galileo; The Good Woman of Setzuan; The Caucasian Chalk Circle.

EARLY PLAYS. Trans. by Eric Bentley *Grove* Black Cat Bks. 1964 pap. $1.95. Baal (1922); A Man's a Man (1927); The Elephant Calf (1924–1925).

THE JEWISH WIFE AND OTHER SHORT PLAYS. Trans. by Eric Bentley. *Grove* Black Cat Bks. 1965 pap. $1.65. The Informer; In Search of Justice; The Exception and the Rule; The Measure Taken; The Elephant Calf; Salzburg Dance of Death.

PARABLES FOR THE THEATRE. 1948. Trans. by Eric and Maja Bentley. *Univ. of Minnesota Press* 1965 $4.95. Two "epic" plays: The Caucasian Chalk Circle; The Good Woman of Setzuan.

EDWARD II: A Chronicle Play. 1924. *Grove* Black Cat Bks. (orig.) pap. 1966 $1.45

MANUAL OF PIETY. 1926. Trans. by Eric Bentley. *Grove* Black Cat Bks. 1966 pap. $1.95

THE THREEPENNY OPERA. 1928. Trans. by Eric Bentley and Desmond I. Vesy. *Grove* Black Cat Bks. 1964 pap. $1.45; *Peter Smith* $3.50

THE MOTHER. 1932. Trans. with introd. by Lee Baxandall. *Grove* Black Cat Bks. 1965 pap. $1.45. Brecht's dramatic adaptation of Gorky's novel.

MOTHER COURAGE. 1941. Trans. and adapted by Eric Bentley as produced on Broadway in 1963. *Grove* Black Cat Bks. 1963 pap. $1.50; *French* 1967 $1.25

GALILEO. 1942. Trans. by Charles Laughton *French* 1968 $1.45; trans. by Charles Laughton, ed. by Eric Bentley *Grove* Black Cat Bks. (orig.) 1966 pap. $1.65

THE GOOD WOMAN OF SETZUAN. 1943. Trans. by Eric Bentley. *French* $1.25; *Grove* Black Cat Bks. 1965 pap. $1.50

THE CAUCASIAN CHALK CIRCLE. 1947. Trans. by Eric and Maja Bentley. *French* $1.25; *Grove* Black Cat Bks. 1965 pap. $1.45

(With Lion Feuchtwanger) VISIONS OF SIMONE MARCHARD. 1959. Trans. with preface by Carl Richard Mueller. *Grove* Black Cat Bks. (orig.) 1965 pap. $1.25

BRECHT ON THEATRE. Trans. by John Willett. *Baker* $6.50; *Farrar, Straus* (Hill & Wang) 1964 $6.50 Dramabks. pap. $3.45. His own ideas on the theater and esthetics.

BRECHT ON BRECHT. 1962. Trans. and arranged by George Tabori. *French* 1967 $1.75

"A selection of the German playwright's writings, carefully edited to cast a warm glow"— (Robert Brustein).

BRECHT BEFORE THE UN-AMERICAN ACTIVITIES COMMITTEE. *Folkways* (FD 5531) $5.95

"A recording of the actual encounter of Brecht with the notorious Parnell Thomas," who was later imprisoned for fraud.

Books about Brecht

The Theatre of Bertolt Brecht: A Study from Eight Aspects. By John Willett. *New Directions* 1959 rev. ed. 1968 pap. $3.50. Indispensable to any Brecht scholar and a great aid to the beginner; excellent chronologies and bibliographies of the plays.

Brecht: The Man and His Work. By Martin Esslin. 1960. *Norton* pap. 1974 $3.95. A lucid exposition of the life and works with a chronology and bibliography.

Brecht: A Collection of Critical Essays. Ed. by Peter Demetz. *Prentice Hall* 1962 Spectrum Bks. pap. $1.95

The Art of Bertolt Brecht. By Walter Weideli. *New York Univ. Press* 1963 $5.00 pap. $1.95

The Blasphemers: The Theater of Brecht, Ionesco, Beckett, Genet. By David I. Grossvogel. *Cornell Univ. Press* 1965 pap. $1.95

Brecht's Tradition. By Max Spalter. *Johns Hopkins Univ. Press* 1967 $11.00. A discussion of the works of Lenz, Grabbe, Büchner, Wedekind, and Kraus in relation to those of Brecht.

Bertolt Brecht: His Art, His Life, His Times. By Frederick Ewen. *Citadel* Press 1967 pap. $3.95. A biography emphasizing his struggle against Nazism in the late 1920s and early 1930s.

Bertolt Brecht. By Martin Esslin. Essays on Mod. Writers Ser. *Columbia* 1969 pap. $1.00. A well-written and informative brief introduction to Brecht and his work.

Bertolt Brecht. By Willy Haas. Modern Literature Monographs Ser. *Ungar* 1970 $6.00 pap. $1.75

Brecht and Ionesco: Commitment in Context. By Julian Wulbern (ill.). *Univ. of Illinois Press* 1971 $8.95

The Essential Brecht. By John Fuegi (ill.). Univ. of Southern California Studies in Comparative Literature *Hennessey & Ingalls* 1972 $12.95. Highly Recommended.

REMARQUE, ERICH MARIA. 1898–1970.

In 1947, after eight successful years in this country, Remarque became an American citizen. During World War I he was drafted into the German army at 18. After the war he tried various occupations and in his spare time or between jobs he wrote the antimilitaristic "All Quiet" that became a classic of modern warfare. "The Road Back" (1931, o.p.) is the sequel. His later novels deal with World War II; they have had greater popular than critical success.

ALL QUIET ON THE WESTERN FRONT. Trans. by A. W. Wheen. *Little* 1929 $6.95; *Fawcett* Crest Bks. pap. $.95 Premier Bks. 1969 pap. $.95

THREE COMRADES. Trans. by A. W. Wheen. *Little* 1937 reissue 1946 $6.95

A TIME TO LOVE AND A TIME TO DIE. Trans. by Denver Lindley. *Harcourt* 1954 $7.95
The horrors of bombing raids and Nazi brutality as experienced by a German soldier
in World War II.

THE BLACK OBELISK. 1956. Trans. by Denver Lindley. *Harcourt* 1957 $5.75

HEAVEN HAS NO FAVORITES. Trans. by Richard and Clara Winston. *Harcourt* 1961 $4.50

THE NIGHT IN LISBON. Trans. by Ralph Manheim. *Harcourt* 1964 $4.95
"An understanding and compassionate picture of human beings in a state of total dis-
location. . . . [A] gripping, well-wrought novel of suspense"—(*LJ*).

SHADOWS IN PARADISE (*Schatten im Paradies*). 1971. Trans. by Ralph Manheim. *Harcourt*
1972 $6.95; *Fawcett* Crest Bks. 1973 pap. $1.25

KÄSTNER, ERICH (or KAESTNER). 1899–1974.

If Erich Kästner is chiefly known as a writer of children's books (author of "Emil and the
Detectives," he was awarded the International Hans Christian Andersen Medal in 1960), it may be
related to the fact that he was among 24 authors especially singled out for "literary cremation" at
the Nazi book burning in 1933. Strictly forbidden to publish anything within the country, though
permitted to publish abroad whatever passed censorship, Kästner continued to live in Germany
during the Nazi regime, writing poetry and children's books. "The Little Man" (trans. by James
Kirkup, ill. by Rick Shreiter *Knopf* 1966 $3.95 lib. bdg. $3.59) is a delightful tale about a boy two
inches tall. His verse is satirical and humorous; at times open and childlike, at times bitterly witty.

A SALZBURG COMEDY. Trans. by Cyrus Brooks; ill. by Walter Trier. *Ungar* 1957 $4.50

WHEN I WAS A BOY. Trans. by Isabel and Florence McHugh. *Franklin Watts* 1961 $3.95.
A charming autobiography.

Books about Kästner

Social Criticism in the Early Works of Erich Kästner. By John Winkelman. *Univ. of Missouri Press*
1953 pap. $2.50

BONHOEFFER, DIETRICH. 1906–1945. *See Chapter 4, World Religions*, Reader's
Adviser, *Vol. 3*

KUBY, ERICH. 1910–

Erich Kuby was born in Baden-Baden. He studied at Munich University, worked in a publishing
house, served in the army, and after the war became editor of an important newspaper for the
younger generation, *Der Ruf*. His novel "Rosemarie" (1957, U.S. 1959, o.p.) brought him
international fame. "*Sieg! Sieg!*" (literally "Victory! Victory!") is a seriocomic comment on the
predicament of a sensitive man forced to serve a vicious and stupid cause, exemplified by the
German army.

RUSSIANS AND BERLIN: 1945. Trans. by Arnold J. Pomerans. *Farrar, Straus* 1968 $6.95

THE SITZKRIEG OF PRIVATE STEFAN (*Sieg! Sieg!*). 1960. Trans. by Theodore H. Lustig.
Farrar, Straus 1962 $5.50

FRISCH, MAX. 1911–

Max Frisch has been for some 20 years one of the outstanding literary figures in Europe. He is a
Swiss architect by profession and a dramatist and novelist by avocation. This may account for his
persistent experimentalism and his indifference to commercial considerations. His style, as
exemplified in "The Chinese Wall," is indebted to Brecht (*q.v.*) but even more to Thornton Wilder
(*q.v.*), whose "The Skin of Our Teeth" may be seen as the optimistic other side of the coin to
Frisch's deeply pessimistic dramatic mood in "The Chinese Wall." *Library Journal* called "Andorra"
"a powerful play. . . . Bearing down with fierce dramatic irony, Frisch continues his major themes:
man totally dependent, both individually and collectively; although he is subjected to bitter
experiences, he does not learn from them." In recent years he has received a number of literary
prizes. He travels frequently; after World War II he spent a year in America on a Rockefeller
grant. In 1963 "The Firebugs" was produced off-Broadway and "Andorra" not so successfully on
Broadway. "The Firebugs," about a callous hair-lotion manufacturer whose ostrich mentality
blinds him to the designs of a group of arsonists intent on destroying him and his community, has
many elements of the Theater of the Absurd, but also the political symbolism of the smug
bourgeoisie that allows a Hitler government or other evil leadership to bring it to catastrophe. It
has appeared successfully on Broadway, first in 1963 and then, in 1968, adapted to the theme of
the American black-white struggle. The *Saturday Review* reported in 1966 that Frisch was in the
process of "busily and successfully revising his plays."

Frisch is no less renowned for his novels, of which "Stiller" remains his masterpiece. He has, by his own admission, reached a dead end with his *"Mein Name sei Gantenbein,"* ("A Wilderness of Mirrors," 1966 o.p.). Whether this is true or not remains to be seen. One thing that is certain, however, is that significant things are still to be awaited from the pen of this great writer.

THREE PLAYS. Trans. by James L. Rosenberg. Don Juan, or the Love of Geometry (1953); The Great Rage of Philip Hotz; When the War Was Over (1949). *Farrar, Straus* (Hill & Wang) Mermaid Dramabks. 1967 pap. $2.50

"That the world shapes men rather than the other way around, is the shared theme of these three plays"—*(LJ)*.

THE CHINESE WALL. 1947. Trans. by James Rosenberg; introd. by Harold Clurman. *Farrar, Straus* (Hill & Wang) Mermaid Dramabks. 1961 pap. $1.75

COUNT OEDERLAND, or the Public Prosecutor Is Sick of It All. 1951. rev. version 1956. Trans. by Michael Bullock. *Third Press* 1974 $5.95 pap. $2.95

The basic motif of [this play] may be defined as the "individual's revolt against a world of law and order, and his desire to find fulfillment in an untrammelled life providing physical and emotional freedom"—(Weisstein).

I'M NOT STILLER. 1954. Trans. by Michael Bullock. *Random* 1958 Vintage Bks. pap. $1.95

This novel is an "elaborate and powerful illustration of Kierkegaard's thesis that man's road to freedom lies through self-acceptance. . . . What gives it stature as a novel is Frisch's dissection of the tormented and tormenting relationship between Stiller and his wife. The real heart of the situation—and of the book—lies in the fifty-page postscript by the public prosecutor"—*(N.Y. Herald Tribune)*.

HOMO FABER. 1957. Trans. by Michael Bullock. *Harcourt* Harvest Bks. 1971 pap. $2.95. Frisch's next novel after "I'm Not Stiller."

THE FIREBUGS *(Biedermann und die Brandstifter)*. 1958. Trans. by Mordecai Gorelik. *Farrar, Straus* (Hill & Wang) 1963 Mermaid Dramabks. pap. $1.50

ANDORRA: A Play in Twelve Scenes. 1961. Trans. by Michael Bullock. *Farrar, Straus* (Hill & Wang) $3.50 Mermaid Dramabks. 1964 pap. $1.95. The play on anti-Semitism that created a sensation in Europe.

BIOGRAPHY: A Game. Trans. by Michael Bullock. *Farrar, Straus* (Hill & Wang) 1969 $4.50 Mermaid Dramabks. pap. $1.75

SKETCHBOOK, 1966–1971. Trans. by Geoffrey Skelton. *Harcourt* 1974 $10.00

Books about Frisch

Max Frisch. By Ulrich Weisstein. World Authors Ser. *Twayne* 1968 $6.95. A well-written introduction to Frisch with many insightful analyses of his works. Recommended.

Max Frisch. By Carol Petersen. Trans. by Charlotte LaRue. Modern Literature Monographs *Ungar* 1972 $6.00

HAGELSTANGE, RUDOLF. 1912–

A poet deeply concerned with the meaning of the war experience, Hagelstange himself served in the German army during World War II. While a soldier, he wrote "The Venetian Credo," a cycle of 35 anti-Nazi sonnets which describe the "moral bankruptcy" that led to Hitler's rise. The work was secretly circulated and published only after the war had ended. "Ballad of the Buried Life" tells the fantastic story, based on a true incident, of a group of soldiers buried alive by bombing in a vast subterranean supply dump. Unlimited quantities of canned foods and wine sustain their material needs, but each must seek out faith to prolong an existence that holds no hope for truly human dimensions. Long after the war, streetworkers clear away the rubble that blocks entrance to the vaults. One soldier emerges—the only survivor.

Hagelstange employs the bizarre tale to examine the meaning of withdrawal as a path to transcendental revelation. He has also written essays, short prose pieces and a novel.

BALLAD OF THE BURIED LIFE. 1952. Trans. by Herman Salinger; introd. by Charles W. Hoffmann. 1962. *AMS Press* $12.50

KIRST, HANS HELLMUT. 1914–

Kirst drew on his experiences as a soldier and officer in World War II to become "the number one chronicler of the German military mind"—*(SR)*. He has been a farmer, playwright, and critic

and is now one of Germany's most successful novelists—translated into 24 languages. Of the
Gunner Asch trilogy 1954–1955, which brought him fame, Harry T. Moore writes: "The
character of Asch is something which can be experienced only in the reading, for he is the
humanized soldier in conflict with the machine, and the burr under the saddle of bullying
sergeants." The *Atlantic* said of "The Revolt of Gunner Asch": "A tale in which elements of drama
and suspense are skillfully fused with high comedy—a tale which the author brings to a startling
and altogether delightful conclusion. . . . Kirst has succeeded in distilling robust fun out of brutal
realities without ever suggesting that the realities were other than brutal." The trilogy was
followed by a sequel, "What Became of Gunner Asch." Barely touching on Asch (the German title
makes no mention of him), it is "exclusively concerned with life in the new *Bundeswehr*. . . . Vastly
entertaining"—(*SR*).

"The Officer Factory" (1963, o.p.) is a tale of murder set in a Nazi officer training school in 1944.
"The Night of the Generals," made into a motion picture in 1966, is also a tale of murder and is
caustic not only about the *Wehrmacht* but also about the current revival of German militarism.
Orville Prescott called it "an engrossing thriller. . . . It crackles with sardonic humor and bristles
with quantities of furious satire and much moral indignation." "Brothers in Arms" (o.p.) is about
the reunion of six men, members of the same company during the war, who share equally the guilt
of a rape and a death. "Kirst's sense of construction is masterly, as is his illumination of the morals
and mores of the German Economic Miracle. A vivid, meaningful, and wonderfully readable
book"—(Anthony Boucher, in the *N.Y. Times*). "The whole book can be considered a plea to all
mankind to eschew complacency and stupidity"—(*LJ*). Kirst's popular thrillers have a social
conscience which raises them above the level of the literature of mere suspense.

THE REVOLT OF GUNNER ASCH. 1956. Trans. by Robert Kee. *Pyramid Bks*. 1975 pap. (in
prep.)

THE NIGHT OF THE GENERALS. 1962. *Harper* 1964 $7.95; *Bantam* pap. $1.25

WHAT BECAME OF GUNNER ASCH. 1963. *Harper* 1965 $4.95; *Pyramid Bks*. pap. $.75

HERO IN THE TOWER. 1970. *Coward* 1972 $6.95; *Pinnacle Bks*. 1973 pap. $1.50

NO FATHERLAND. *Coward* 1970 $5.95

THE ADVENTURES OF PRIVATE FAUST. *Coward* 1971 $5.95

DAMNED TO SUCCESS. 1971. *Coward* 1973 $6.95; *Berkley* 1975 pap. $1.50

A TIME FOR TRUTH. *Coward* 1974 $7.95

EVERYTHING HAS ITS PRICE. *Coward* 1976 $7.95

All translated by J. Maxwell Brownjohn unless otherwise noted.

WEISS, PETER.   1916–

In December 1965 Peter Weiss's "Marat/Sade," in a brilliant presentation by Britain's Royal
Shakespeare Company, stormed the Broadway stage, captivating audience and critic alike. The
assumption that a play about the murder of Marat by Charlotte Corday might have been one of
the many dramatic pieces written by Sade (*q.v.*)—and enacted by his fellow inmates for "therapeu-
tic" reasons during the Marquis's confinement at Charenton—provided Weiss (who maintains that
"every word I put down is political") with his framework for the "confrontation of the revolutionary Marat as the apostle of social improvement and the cynical individualist, the Marquis de
Sade"—(*N.Y. Times*). Their polemic is argued against a backdrop of hideous, flailing, drooling
madmen, who, like themselves, are acting roles in the play; the physical demands on the actors are
strenuous indeed. Winner of the "Tony" Award for best play of the year and the N.Y. Drama
Critics Circle Award for best foreign play, "Marat/Sade" also captured nearly every major award for
drama in Europe. Peter Brook, whose inventive staging on Broadway won him the 1965–1966
Best Director award, made a "brilliant film version . . . so intrinsic and creative in itself that it
sweeps the viewer into a totally new involvement in this agitating play"—(Bosley Crowther, in the
N.Y. Times). In 1967 "Marat/Sade"—"total theater, with no holds barred" (*Times*, London)—was
revived on Broadway by the National Players Company.

Peter Weiss was an unknown novelist, painter, and filmmaker when, at the age of 49, "Marat/
Sade" propelled him to fame. Because his father was Jewish, Weiss and his family fled their native
Germany in 1934, when the Nazis began to assume power. In 1939 he settled in Sweden, where he
still lives with his Swedish Wife, Gunilla Palmstierna, a stage designer. He maintains some 60
filing-cabinet drawers of research materials for his "documentary" plays. All, he says, are written
in sympathy with the human condition and "the oppressed of the world." Through the theater he
would like "to create a new kind of world." "The Investigation," which Weiss considers his best
play, was first presented in 20 theaters in East and West Germany; Ingmar Bergman was its
Swedish director. It was staged in New York in 1966. Taken almost entirely from the actual

proceedings of the 1965 Frankfurt War Crime Tribunal on Auschwitz, "The Investigation" is a "harrowing but insistently commanding experience"—(Walter Kerr, in the *N.Y. Times*). The audience, in effect, reenacts the role of the original courtroom spectators in this shattering true account of man's depravity.

"The Lusitanian Bogey," a protest play about the evils of Portugal's colonialism in Africa, was the first production of the new Negro Ensemble Company at St. Mark's Playhouse, New York, late in 1967. The *N.Y. Times'* Clive Barnes found the work "passionately committed, interesting and moving." "Mr. Weiss," he says, "does not write plays as other people do. He creates a highly dramatic framework, or perhaps better a magnetic field of dramatic force . . . to pin the audience's ears back, stab it with facts, karate-chop it with the passionate blows of insensate statistics." The Portuguese are represented by a huge tin "Bogeyman" on stage. Walter Kerr felt that the impersonality of this representation of evil robbed the play of true conflict: the bad men should have faces, should show their motivation, should be white. "Mr. Weiss," he says, "did manage to bring off this sort of mixed vision in 'The Investigation,' which was precisely what made that journalistic collage so frightening." Mr. Weiss is the most brilliant star to have lately arisen in the European theater. With the publication of "Trotsky in Exile," his most disturbing play to date, Weiss again shows himself to be the master of the form and moves ever further into Marxist political theater. His autobiographical novel, "Leavetaking" (1960), published here by *Harcourt* in 1962, is now o.p. "Exile" is another strongly autobiographical novel, about a young German Jew "finding himself" during his exile in postwar Europe.

THE TOWER. 1948. (In "Postwar German Theatre") ed. by M. Benedikt and G. E. Wellwarth. *Dutton* 1967 pap. $2.75. A dream play, with elements of the Theater of the Absurd—"doubtless his least horrifying."

THE PERSECUTION AND ASSASSINATION OF JEAN-PAUL MARAT AS PERFORMED BY THE INMATES OF THE ASYLUM OF CHARENTON UNDER THE DIRECTION OF THE MARQUIS DE SADE ("Marat/Sade"). 1964. Trans. by Geoffrey Skelton; verse adaptation by Adrian Mitchell; introd. by Peter Brook. Music examples; biographical note. *Atheneum* pap. $3.95; *Simon & Schuster* (Pocket Bks.) 1967 pap. $1.25

THE INVESTIGATION: A Play. 1965. Trans. by John Swan and Ulu Grosbard. *Atheneum* 1966 pap. $3.95

PETER WEISS READING FROM HIS WORKS. *Caedmon* TC 1131 1967 $6.98 (record) $7.95 (cassette). A recording of Weiss reading in English excerpts from "Marat/Sade," "The Investigation," "Leavetaking," and "I Come Out of My Hiding Place"—a speech given at Princeton in 1966. The album cover is designed by Weiss.

TWO PLAYS: The Song of the Lusitanian Bogey (1967) and Discourse on the Prolonged War in Vietnam (1968). *Atheneum* 1970 $6.95

NOTES ON THE CULTURAL LIFE OF THE DEMOCRATIC REPUBLIC OF VIET NAM. 1968. *Dell* Delta Bks. 1970 pap. $2.25

EXILE. Trans. by E. B. Garside, H. Hamilton, and C. Levenson. *Delacorte* (dist. by Dial) 1968 $5.95

TROTSKY IN EXILE. 1970. Trans. by Geoffrey Skelton. *Atheneum* 1971 $4.95; *Simon & Schuster* Pocket Bks. 1973 pap. $1.50

"Weiss is heir to Brecht and the whole school of 20th century drama committed to contemporary social themes. . . . In its grip on social and human issues the play towers above most modern drama."—(*PW*).

Books about Weiss

Peter Weiss. By Otto F. Best. Trans. by Ursule Molinaro. *Ungar* 1975 $7.00. A critical evaluation of Weiss' work which demonstrates clearly the various stages in his life which ultimately led him to his present Marxist stance.

BÖLL (or BOELL), HEINRICH. 1917– (Nobel Prize 1972)

Although Böll had won three literary prizes in Germany and had had earlier novels in translation published here (they are now o.p.), it was not until "Billiards at Half-Past Nine" that he became established abroad as one of the most important German novelists to have emerged since World War II. "It tells the story of an aristocratic family of architects, and covers the period from World War I to the present. . . . Written in an ironic style and utilizing the interior monologue technique, the novel is practically Joycean in scope. And just as the subject of 'Ulysses' is Joyce's

Dublin, so the real subject of 'Billiards at Half-Past Nine' is Germany"—(LJ). "The Clown," his story of the antihero who cannot make a go of life but continues ruefully to try, is intensely cynical in a lighthearted way about modern Germany. Of a *Gauleiter* who had "protected" a radical in the Hitler period, and who in turn then was bound to swear to a "denazification" court that he owed his life to that "swine," Böll writes: "Needless to say he [the Gauleiter] didn't hold his protective hand over everyone, not over Marx the leather merchant and Krupe the Communist. They were murdered. And the Gauleiter is doing all right today. He has a construction business." Said the *Saturday Review:* "Böll's clown is an outsider, whose personal disappointments have deepened his insight into the hypocrisies people live by. . . . An engaging and distinguished novel."

"Absent without Leave" and "Enter and Exit" are "essential reading for all who care about the contemporary German conscience, consciousness, and literary sensibility"—(SR). "With his sensitive, tight, allusive prose, shorn of sentimentality, Mr. Böll turns the German soldier into a portrait of every soldier"—(LJ). "18 Stories," written over a period of 20 years, "satirizes the indignities and absurdities of making a living in postwar Germany. . . . A shrewd and skillful translation"—(SR).

The son of Victor Böll the sculptor, Heinrich was born in Cologne. He was drafted in 1938 shortly after finishing his schooling and served seven years in the infantry before his demobilization in 1945. "Böll reminds one of Thomas Mann at his peak as an uncompromising foe of conventionality and political faddism, as well as a writer who in many respects courts the label of 'old-fashioned' by putting narrative ahead of experimentation. Equally unusual is Böll's dedication to literary art, his conviction that it is one of the few contemporary means of free expression"—(N.Y. Times).

"Böll began as an exponent of the literature of debris, the wreckage left behind by the tide of war. The suffering of soldiers and civilians alike on the Eastern front, the plight of war-widows, orphans, and maladjusted ex-servicemen, the corruption and callousness bred by war, the senselessness of military life. . . . During the period of Germany's economic miracle, Böll turned a critical eye on the complacent materialism and rat-race ethos of the affluent society"—(C. P. Magill, "German Literature"). In his latest work, "The Lost Honor of Katharina Blum," Böll continues to focus on modern German society and the destructive possibilities latent in it. "What is strong and attractive here, as in Böll's other novels, is the sense of the faint weirdness of daily life in a conformist country. Everything so aspires to order that the very slightest deviation smacks of a disturbing anarchy"—(N.Y. Times).

AND WHERE WERE YOU, ADAM? (1951) and THE TRAIN WAS ON TIME (1949). Trans. by Leila Vennewitz. *McGraw-Hill* 1970 $6.95 pap. 1974 $2.95

BILLIARDS AT HALF-PAST NINE. 1959. Trans. by Patrick Bowles. *McGraw-Hill* 1962 $4.95 pap. $2.95

THE CLOWN (*Ansichten eines Clowns*). 1963. Trans. by Leila Vennewitz. *McGraw-Hill* 1965 $5.50 pap. $2.95

"Smoothly translated"—(SR).

ABSENT WITHOUT LEAVE and ENTER AND EXIT: Two Novellas. Trans. by Leila Vennewitz. *McGraw-Hill* 1965 $4.50

18 STORIES. Trans. by Leila Vennewitz. *McGraw-Hill* 1966 $5.95

END OF A MISSION. Trans. by Leila Vennewitz. *McGraw-Hill* 1968 $5.95 pap. $2.95. A humorous satire on contemporary German society.

CHILDREN ARE CIVILIANS TOO. Trans. by Leila Vennewitz. *McGraw-Hill* 1970 $5.95

GROUP PORTRAIT WITH LADY. 1971. Trans. by Leila Vennewitz. *McGraw-Hill* 1973 $7.95; *Avon Bks.* 1974 pap. $1.75

THE LOST HONOR OF KATHARINA BLUM. 1974. Trans. by Leila Vennewitz. *McGraw-Hill* 1975 $7.95

IRISH JOURNAL. 1957. Trans. by Leila Vennewitz. *McGraw-Hill* 1967 $4.95 pap. $1.95

Seventeen sketches of Ireland in the mid-1950s updated with an epilogue. "Böll has an affinity for Ireland and things Irish, a fresh outlook and an uncluttered style"—(PW).

Books about Böll

Heinrich Böll, Teller of Tales. By Wilhelm J. Schwarz. Trans. by Alexander and Elizabeth Henderson *Ungar* 1968 $6.50

HEINRICH, WILLI. 1920–

"Heinrich has rightfully been called Germany's angry young man. He blasted war and militarism in 'Cross of Iron' and 'Crack of Doom.' Now he is blasting the Germany born out of war and defeat [in 'Mark of Shame,' U.S. 1959 o.p.]"—(N.Y. Herald Tribune).

The *N.Y. Herald Tribune* called "The Cross of Iron" the "most important post-war novel to be published in the United States." *Time* said that the author "has written this first novel with the passionate intensity of a man plucking shell fragments out of his own memory. A corporal himself in a German infantry division, he marched across 8,000 miles of Russian soil, was severely wounded five times, saw his division lose twelve times its original manpower. In 'The Cross of Iron' Heinrich does what a good war novelist should and few can. He makes the private inferno of his war roar all over again, but as if for the very first time and for all men."

"The Crumbling Fortress" (1964, o.p.) describes a group of fleeing German soldiers in World War II, who encounter a motley group of European refugees. In the deserted fortress in which all are forced to take perilous refuge the conflicts of contemporary Europe play a dramatic role. Heinrich was in the grocery business before he turned to writing in 1955.

THE CROSS OF IRON. Trans. by Richard and Clara Winston. 1956. *Bantam* pap. $1.25

THE CRACK OF DOOM. Trans. by Oliver Coburn. 1958. *Bantam* pap. $1.25

BORCHERT, WOLFGANG. 1921–1947.

Borchert grew up under the Nazi regime. During the war he was imprisoned and even (abortively) sentenced to death for his "defeatist" attitude. He died at the age of 26, the night before the Hamburg première of his great success, "The Outsider." Surrealistic in technique, the play concerns the return of a maimed German prisoner of war who finds everything destroyed, all hope shattered, even the symbolic "God" perplexed. The only one who flourishes is the undertaker. The hero's pitiful efforts to make a place for himself end in failure. "If there is one word that could possibly sum up the spirit of *The Outsider*"—says Wellwarth, in his introduction to "Postwar German Theatre" (*see Benedikt and Wellwarth above under History and Criticism*)—"it is outrage. The play is . . . a graphic and mercilessly unrestrained excoriation of the sinister and diabolic system that had destroyed Germany so completely, both morally and physically. [It] remains important first because it is an excellent drama in itself, the only completed play by one of Germany's greatest modern poetic geniuses; second, because it is the most perfect expression of postwar German youth's disillusionment with the system which had ruined their country and their own best years; and third, because it is the only really successful re-creation of the World War I art form known as Expressionism."

THE OUTSIDER (*Draussen vor der Tür*). 1947. (In "Postwar German Theatre") ed. by M. Benedikt and G. E. Wellwarth *Dutton* 1967 pap. $2.75; trans. by A. D. Porter *New Directions* 1971 $5.75 pap. $2.75

THE SAD GERANIUMS. 1962. Trans. by Keith Hamnet. *Ecco Press* (dist. by Viking) 1974 $5.95

DÜRRENMATT (or DUERRENMATT), FRIEDRICH. 1921–

The Lunts starred in the memorable performance of that "corrosive" play, "The Visit," which Brooks Atkinson called "devastating. A bold, grisly drama of negativism and genius." Dürrenmatt's seventh play, it received the N.Y. Drama Critics Circle Award for "Best Foreign Play" in 1959. Dürrenmatt was born near Berne, Switzerland, the son of a Protestant clergyman. He studied philosophy and theology and orignially planned to become a painter. "All of a sudden," he has said, "I began to write, and I just had no time to finish my University degree." He has called his first play, "It Is Written" (1947, o.p.), "a wild story of Anabaptists during the Reformation." When it was produced in Zurich, it caused a minor theatrical scandal because of its somewhat unorthodox sentiments, but "after the scandal subsided," he commented, "they gave me a prize for it." "The Marriage of Mr. Mississippi," his first successful comedy, was produced in Munich in 1952, and, as adapted by Maximilian Slater with the title "Fools are Passing Through," had a brief off-Broadway production in 1958. With this play he became established as one of the most popular European dramatists writing in German. In 1962 Gore Vidal's adaptation of "Romulus the Great" appeared on Broadway as "Romulus" starring Cyril Ritchard. It is a "wry comedy, somewhat in the manner of George Bernard Shaw. . . . The emperor, Romulus Augustus . . . is more interested in raising chickens than in ruling Rome"—(Harry T. Moore, in "20th Century German Literature").

His style is a peculiar mixture of the comic and the macabre. He "breaks all the rules usually set down for popular success in the American theatre. He is a mordant, cynical writer, with the blackest view of human nature. . . . Yet somehow [he] is never a depressive writer, a negative writer. He is saved from this by his wild irrepressible vitality. His view of life may be black, but his way of presenting it is colorful. . . . He presents us with a world that is absurd, macabre, improbable, then fills it with people who take it completely for granted, who live in it just as naturally as if it were the real world. . . . He is essentially a writer of melodrama, what we might call 'the melodrama of ideas' "—(James Yaffe). Dürrenmatt's "The Physicists" was a Broadway success of 1964–1965. It takes place in an insane asylum, and in the course of the play a number of nurses are murdered. The investigation reveals that the physicists are pawns in a worldwide plot by a power-mad paranoid. "It is not developed in the area of serious ideas and remains more in the realm of chilling entertainment"—(Moore).

Dürrenmatt, in his nondramatic work, turns out "some of the most wry and bitter writing of this wry and bitter time." In the novel "The Pledge" (1958, o.p.) (film version: "It Happened in Broad Daylight"), a police inspector, tracking down the murderer of a child, ends in complete moral and physical disintegration. In "Traps," a mock trial staged as a game becomes all too real for the volunteer "defendant," a man with a dreadful secret of his own. "I can best be understood if one grasps grotesqueness," Dürrenmatt once wrote. "But here a clear distinction must be made. I am not grotesque as a Romantic . . . but grotesque as once Arisotphanes or Swift was grotesque: out of the necessity at the same time to produce a pamphlet and a work of art." An unabashed intellectual thriller, "The Quarry" (U.S. 1962, o.p.) is "shocking, macabre, death-driven," words which so often describe the work of this playwright-novelist. In an interview published in *Esquire*, the author was asked what reaction he most preferred his audiences to have to his work. "Fright!" he replied. "That is the modern form of empathy." "The Judge and His Hangman" is the best of his detective stories *qua* mystery, lacking the explicit moral concern which informs his other books of this genre. "Once a Greek . . ." is about a sober clerk who attains fame and fortune through marriage to a lady he finds has once been a courtesan. He flees her on making this discovery—"the moralist whose principles stand in the way of natural law. The comic situations made inevitable by this . . . juxtaposition are varied, spasmodic and unpredictable . . . exactly the reverse of the prim logic of Duerrenmatt's detective novels. They are also more entertaining"—(*SR*).

Dürrenmatt now lives with his family near the Lake of Neuchâtel.

Plays

ROMULUS THE GREAT. 1949 rev. 1957. (And Gore Vidal's "Romulus"—the Broadway adaptation) trans. by Gerhard Nellhaus; pref. by Gore Vidal. *Dramatists* $1.25

"This volume consists of two different versions of the same play [the original by Dürrenmatt and Vidal's adaptation for the American stage]. The plays, so similar in many respects, do differ in tone, texture, and in the end, meaning. But—which is better theater? The reader will make his own diagnosis. The comparison alone provides a unique, exciting insight into the American theater. Highly recommended"—(*LJ*).

THE MARRIAGE OF MR. MISSISSIPPI (1952) and PROBLEMS OF THE THEATRE. Trans. by M. Bullock *Grove* Evergreen Bks. 1966 pap. $1.95

AN ANGEL COMES TO BABYLON (1953) and ROMULUS THE GREAT. Trans. by William McElwee and Gerhard Nellhaus. *Grove* Evergreen Bks. 1966 $1.95

THE VISIT: A Play in Three Acts. 1956. Trans. by Patrick Bowles. *Grove* Evergreen Bks. 1962 pap. $1.95

INCIDENT AT TWILIGHT. 1959. (In "Postwar German Theatre") trans. and ed. by M. Benedikt and G. E. Wellwarth. *Dutton* 1967 pap. $2.75

THE PHYSICISTS. 1962. Trans. by James Kirkup. *Grove* Evergreen Bks. 1964 pap. $1.95

THE METEOR. 1966. Trans. by James Kirkup. *Grove* 1974 $5.95

PLAY STRINDBERG. 1969. Trans. by James Kirkup. *Grove* 1973 $6.95 Evergreen Bks. pap. $1.95

Fiction

Traps (*Die Panne*). 1956. Trans. by Richard and Clara Winston. 1960. *Ballantine Bks.* 1973 pap. $.95

Books about Dürrenmatt

Friedrich Dürrenmatt. By Murray B. Peppard. World Authors Ser. *Twayne* 1969 $6.95
Friedrich Dürrenmatt. By Armin Arnold. Modern Literature Monographs *Ungar* 1972 $6.00

GRASS, GÜNTER. 1927–

The outspoken Günter Grass is West Germany's outstanding contemporary writer, its *Wunderkind.* He is poet, novelist, painter and sculptor. He won an immediate and enormous audience in Europe and the United States with his first novel, "The Tin Drum," the "allegorical" story of Oskar Matzerath, who decides at the age of three to stop growing—and thereby absolves himself of the responsibility of making adult decisions. He is the rogue, the picaresque outsider, who communicates only by banging his ever-present little drum. The story of Oskar's fantastic progress is a scandalous sardonic satire of Nazi Germany. In "Cat and Mouse," Grass again journeys into the realm of the grotesque to tell the story of Joachim Mahlke, another antihero—a youth with an enormous Adam's apple, an outsider because of his peculiarity. A cat one day mistakes it for a mouse. Mahlke tries to adapt, in scenes often of Grass's characteristic and deliberate grossness, to the "cats" of conventionality. (In the German film version of 1967, Lars Brandt, son of Foreign Minister Willy Brandt, played the leading role. The Interior Ministry, which subsidized the film, threatened to withdraw its funds because of a scene in which Brandt toys with the Iron Cross, one of Germany's highest wartime decorations. "For Grass, the scene symbolizes young Germany playing on the wreck of Hitler's Reich"—[N.Y. Times].)

"The Tin Drum," "Cat and Mouse," and "Dog Years" form a kind of trilogy. "Dog Years" is "the story of an incredible odyssey through the jungle of life in Germany just before, during and after the Hitler era. . . . Monstrous, magnificent, and unforgettable"—(SR). "This is Mr. Grass's most ambitious work. It will be studied, I predict, by many generations of readers"—(Richard K. Burns, in LJ). It concerns a Jew who creates weird scarecrows—the symbols on which Grass again builds his grimly humorous picture of modern man violating all the standards of decency to which he gives lip service.

"The World of Günter Grass" (adapted by Dennis Rosa from "The Tin Drum," "Dog Years," and "Selected Poems") was produced off-Broadway in 1966, as was "The Wicked Cooks" in 1967. Of the latter, Library Journal wrote, "The world as seen through the eyes of Günter Grass is a grotesquely cruel and preposterous place. . . . All in all, his pre-Tin Drum plays reflect the zaniness of the theater of the absurd, and, as such, are welcome additions to the club." "The wicked cooks," said Walter Kerr (in the N.Y. Times), "who are everywhere in [the] play—and they represent everyone, for 'we are all cooks,' you see—lay their hands on [the antihero] regularly, clipping him flat to the floor, strangling him with checkered dish towels, whacking him with clown's slapsticks. . . ." In "The Plebeians Rehearse the Uprising" the June 1953 East Berlin rebellion interrupts the rehearsal of Berthold Brecht's (q.v.) "Coriolanus." With Brecht the barely disguised protagonist, Grass examines the committed intellectual who fails to take a decisive stand when he should. Most reviewers felt that "The Plebeians" distorted the actual circumstances and was unfair to Brecht. The N.Y. Review of Books found it difficult to make out the play's (Grass's) own point of view and called it "less than gripping."

Mr. Grass has visited the United States; in 1967 he read from his poetry at the YMHA Poetry Center in New York. Of his "Selected Poems" the N.Y. Times said, "The freewheeling German romps through the brambles of his imagination, sticks his tongue out provocatively, or bewilders his audience with an innocence that is only slyly feigned. . . . [Though tamer for the queasy than his novels], not all poems are recommended for a ladies' literary Kranzchen—they might not relish, for example, the aborted embryos in glass jars worrying about their parents' future."

In his more recent works Grass gives evidence that the former enfant terrible is approaching middle age and is becoming more moderate. Grass now faces up to a new generation of Germans unburdened by guilt and impatient, and instead of barging ahead full steam he now recommends that slow deliberate progress be considered desirable. In his recent "Aus dem Tagebuch einer Schnecke" ("From the Diary of a Snail," 1972), Grass presents the snail as a model worthy of imitation.

Grass was born in Danzig, the son of a grocer, and was once a member of the Hitler Youth; later, at 16, he was drafted for World War II. Taken prisoner, and released after the war, he became first a farm laborer and stonecutter and eventually a sculptor and stage designer until successful writing claimed all his time. Richard Kluger wrote of him in Harper's: "His command of words is so complete—he walks them, makes them do nip-ups, trots them, gallops them, galvanizes them (fission and fusion both)—that it must be called Joycean in its virtuosity."

SELECTED POEMS. Trans. by Michael Hamburger and Christopher Middleton (bilingual). Harcourt 1966 $4.50. Selections from his first two volumes of poems published in Germany in 1956 and 1960.

THE TIN DRUM. 1959. Trans. by Ralph Manheim. Pantheon 1963 $8.95; Random Vintage Bks. pap. $2.45

CAT AND MOUSE. 1961. Trans. by Ralph Manheim. Harcourt 1963 $5.95; New Am. Lib. Signet 1964 pap. $.95

DOG YEARS. 1963. Trans. by Ralph Manheim. Harcourt 1965 $6.95; Fawcett Premier Bks. pap. $1.50

FOUR PLAYS: Flood; Mister, Mister; Only Ten Minutes to Buffalo; The Wicked Cooks. Trans. by Ralph Manheim and A. Leslie Willson; introd. by Martin Esslin. Harcourt 1967 Harvest Bks. pap. $2.45

THE WICKED COOKS. (In "The New Theatre of Europe," Vol. 2) ed. by Robert W. Corrigan. Dell Delta Bks. (orig.) $2.25

ROCKING BACK AND FORTH. (In "Postwar German Theatre") trans. and ed. by Michael Benedikt and George E. Wellwarth. *Dutton* 1967 pap. $2.75

THE PLEBEIANS REHEARSE THE UPRISING: A German Tragedy. Trans. by Ralph Manheim; introd. by the author. *Harcourt* 1966 $4.50 Harvest Bks. pap. $2.35

SPEAK OUT: Speeches, Open Letters, Commentaries. 1968. Trans. by Ralph Manheim. *Harcourt* 1969 $5.75 Harvest Bks. pap. $2.45

LOCAL ANAESTHETIC. 1969. Trans. by Ralph Manheim. *Harcourt* 1970 $6.95; *Fawcett* Crest Bks. 1971 pap. $1.25 Premier Bks. pap. $1.50

MAX: A Play. 1970. Trans. by A. Leslie Willson and Ralph Manheim. *Harcourt* Harvest Bks. 1972 pap. $3.25

FROM THE DIARY OF A SNAIL. Trans. by Ralph Manheim. *Harcourt* 1973 $7.95

INMARYPRAISE. 1973. Trans. by Christopher Middleton. *Harcourt* (ill.) 1974 $15.00

Books about Grass

Gunter Grass. By Norris W. Yates. Contemporary Writers in Christian Perspective Ser. *Eerdmans* 1968 pap. $.85
Gunter Grass. By W. Gordon Cunliffe. World Authors Ser. *Twayne* 1969 $6.95
Gunter Grass. By Kurt L. Tank. Trans. by John Conway. Modern Literature Monographs *Ungar* 1969 $6.00
Gunter Grass. By Irene Leonard. Modern Writers Ser. *Harper* (Barnes & Noble) 1974 $5.75. Good introduction.
A Select Bibliography of Gunter Grass from 1956 to 1973. By George A. Everett, Jr. *Burt Franklin* 1974 $10.00

LIND, JAKOV. 1927–

Maxwell Geismar (in the *N.Y. Times*) has called Jakov Lind "the most notable short-story writer to appear in the last two decades." An Austrian Jew whose parents were exterminated during World War II, Lind has translated the bitter memories of his youth into grotesque tales illustrating the horror of the Nazi years. The title story from "Soul of Wood" (1962, o.p.), actually a short novel, concerns the fate of a paralytic Jewish boy, the son of Nazi victims. He is left on a mountaintop by his guardian, who then vies with others to reclaim the boy for exploitation; all the horrors of Nazism are encountered as events transpire. "Journey Through the Night," another story, describes with black humor the bizarre intellectual game between an admitted cannibal and his proposed victim in a railway compartment. "Lind's stories are fluid, inventive, surrealistic, and fantastic, though based in reality, bitter, and grimly savage. Expert, well-translated nightmares"— (*LJ*). "Mr. Lind's theme—or his obsession—the depravity of the man next door, is defined with a completeness that makes him one of the most important writers in Germany"—(*N.Y. Times*).

"Landscape in Concrete" (1964, o.p.) tells of the mad adventures of Sergeant Bachmann, a discharged officer in search of a regiment to join. He kills as he goes. Lind exploits the comic irony in the Sergeant's startling reversals of mood: Bachmann "is full of philosophical maxims for good behavior on which he reflects between murders . . . [Lind's] man is a meaning-seeking animal. And in his own wild way he has not stopped seeking"—(*SR*). [The author] has worked out this grotesque tale with nearly perfect cerebral irony. . . . The focal character is everybody's German soldier, a commodious receptacle for all the outrage, disgust and loathing inspired by Germany's conduct in World War II"—(*N.Y. Times*). "Ergo" is "a wild, strange, bawdy book for lovers of paradox and black comedy. The story is set in postwar Austria, and that is about all anyone can be sure of"—(*PW*). In 1968 it was successfully presented in dramatic form at Joseph Papp's Anspacher Theater in New York. Lind was born in Vienna and lived through World War II in Holland, to which he had escaped with forged papers. He tried many trades before succeeding as a writer. During 1966–1967 he was a writer-in-residence at Long Island University. He now makes his home in London.

ERGO. Trans. by Ralph Manheim. 1967. *Farrar, Straus* (Hill & Wang) Minerva Bks. pap. $1.75. A novel.

ENZENSBERGER, HANS MAGNUS. 1929–

Enzensberger is one of the "angry" satirical writers. He was born in Bavaria and raised in Nuremberg in the Nazi period. At the age of 16 he was drafted into the German army; later he traveled (often on foot as a hiker) in Europe and the United States. In the spring of 1967 he read his poems at the Poetry Center of the YMHA, sharing the platform with Günter Grass. Today he maintains a residence in Norway but is active on the German literary scene as editor-in-chief of the magazine *Kursbuch* and as translator—of five languages—for German publishers. He has contributed a regular column to the topical journal *Der Spiegel*.

His poetical works include *Verteidigung der Wölfe* ("Vindication of the Wolves," 1957), *Landessprache* ("National Tongue," 1960) and *Gedichte* ("Poems," 1960). His interesting essay on the present-day avant-garde movements of the Western world appears in Philip Rahv's anthology "Modern Occasions" (*Farrar, Straus* 1966 $6.95; *Kennikat* 1974 $9.95). Enzensberger's poetry is sharp and disillusioned, compellingly visual and almost surrealistic at times; he is for the enduring things of nature as against a civilization whose corruption and unpleasantness he describes in scathing, searing images. He has been awarded the *Kritiker Preis für Literatur* (1961–1962) and the Georg Büchner Prize (1963).

THE CONSCIOUSNESS INDUSTRY. Trans. and ed. with postscript by Michael Roloff. *Seabury Press* Continuum Bks. 1974 $6.95

POLITICS AND CRIME. Trans. and ed. by Michael Roloff. *Seabury Press* Continuum Bks. 1974 $6.95

HOCHHUTH, ROLF. 1931–

"The Deputy," an epic drama in the manner of Schiller (*q.v.*), on its simultaneous first publication and opening performance by Erwin Piscator's company in Berlin, 1963, raised a storm. "It is almost certainly the largest storm ever raised by a play in the whole history of drama," said Eric Bentley in "The Storm over the Deputy" (1967 o.p.). Reading "like a German doctoral dissertation in verse," (Robert Brustein, in the *New Republic*), it is a searing indictment of Pope Pius XII, "God's deputy" on earth, for not having intervened publicly when Hitler organized and carried out the massacre of six million Jews. A Jesuit priest, the only invented character, reasons with the Pope in the play and in despair "becomes" a Jew and goes off to his death at Aushwitz. "To me," said Hochhuth, "Pius is a symbol, not only for all leaders but for all men . . . who are passive when their brother is deported to death."

The storm raged—with bannings, picketings, and riots in various parts of the world, and countless articles pro and con. Cardinal Spellman and Pope Paul VI were only two of the Catholic churchmen who came to the defense of Pope Pius, the latter on the ground that had he spoken out he "would have been guilty of unleashing on the already tormented world still greater calamities involving innumerable innocent victims." This conclusion is also in part that of Pinchas E. Lapide, an "Orthodox Jewish scholar and former Israeli diplomat" whose book "Three Popes and the Jews" (1967, o.p.) is "scholarly, thorough and well balanced," wrote Bernhard E. Olson (in *SR*). Lapide also describes Pius's many personal efforts to save Jews—such as sheltering some 4,000 in Rome's churches. Nor, says Lapide, was Pius silent in interchurch and private communications.

Pointing the finger again at an institutional idol, Hochhuth followed his first controversial play with a second—"The Soldiers," which opened in Berlin—with boos for the playwright at its final curtain—on Oct. 9, 1967. Sir Laurence Olivier and Kenneth Tynan were sufficiently impressed with its dramatic merit to wish to produce it in their British National Theater, but the Theater's board refused permission on the ground that it "grossly maligned" the late Sir Winston Churchill. Here Hochhuth, working (he said) from "secret" documentation by a Briton who had deposited it with a Swiss bank for the next half century, makes Churchill, for reasons of war in which he is caught, personally responsible for sabotage resulting in the death of the Polish General Vladislav Sikorski. (Sikorski was killed in a plane accident near Gibraltar in 1943.) There was a Toronto production early in 1968, and in May, 1968, New York saw "The Soldiers" in an excellent performance, the "Churchill" part being played by John Colicos. Clive Barnes found it "a play more interesting for what it is about than what it is. However, dramatically and structurally, it shows a marked advance on 'The Deputy,' if only because its point of view is theatrical more than polemical." The *New Yorker* found its thesis not supported by the recorded facts.

Hochhuth worked as an editor until 1959 and as a boy was member of a Hitler youth group. He is now, with Weiss (*q.v.*), one of the two chief exponents of "documentary drama" in Europe, but he has been unable to match his earlier success and has not produced anything of significance in recent years. It appears that in Hochhuth's case the material was the master of the playwright, but he may again find his talent and put it to good use.

THE DEPUTY. 1963. Trans. by Clara and Richard Winston, pref. by Albert Schweitzer, with "Sidelights on History" by the author. *Grove* 1964 Black Cat Bks. pap. $2.95; trans. by Jerome Rothenberg *French* 1967 pap. $1.25

THE SOLDIERS. Trans. by David MacDonald. *Grove* 1968 Black Cat Bks. pap. $1.50

Books about Hochhuth

The Deputy Reader: Studies in Moral Responsibility. Ed. by Dolores B. Schmidt and E. R. Schmidt. *Scott, Foresman* pap. $4.35

JOHNSON, UWE. 1934–

"Contemporary Germany is Johnson's all-purpose modern symbol of confused human motives, social forces that drive people frantic, and frustrations in communication that finally choke men into silence"—(Webster Schott, in the *N.Y. Times*). "The Third Book About Achim," winner of the $10,000 International Publishers' Prize in 1962, is a novel about divided Germany—and treats one of the crucial philosophical problems of any age, but particularly ours: What is objective truth? Is there such a thing at all? Karsch, a West German journalist, attempts to write the third biography of the East German bicyclist and sports hero "Achim T." The first two biographies, written in East Germany, seem propagandistic to the Western mentality of Karsch and he hopes in his to arrive at the "truth." Biographer and subject too quickly reach an impasse—their differing ideologies prevent them from communicating and the book is never written. Johnson's style is difficult: "bewildering time-sequences; abrupt and arbitrary shifts in point of view; shadowy characters; huge, eccentrically punctuated sentences; tortured syntax; esoteric excursions; oceanic digressions"—(*SR*). Joachim Remak, in *Harper's*, says "It is an easy book to dislike at first [but] in the course of the novel all the annoying traits suddenly vanish or become unimportant. For this is a great book; literary award judges can be right." The novel was catharsis for Johnson's own personal conflicts: he had reluctantly left his home in East Germany in 1959 in order to have his first novel published without censorship.

This first novel, "Speculations about Jacob," was praised for a style that "defies the traditional structure of the novel and indeed of language." William L. Shirer in the *N.Y. Herald Tribune* likened Johnson's fantastic rendering of narrative "to a sort of polyphonic chorus." The conflict between East and West Germany is the basis of the "speculations" arising from the death of an East German railroad dispatcher mysteriously killed by a switch engine. "Two Views," about a nurse and her lover on two sides of the Berlin Wall, "is a political allegory told as an affair of the heart. With fascination the reader discovers that, in Johnson's view, both ventricles are empty"—(*SR*). Oscar Handlin in the *Atlantic* called "Two Views" "one of the finest novels to come out of post-war Germany." There is an autobiographical element here too: Mrs. Uwe Johnson escaped from East Germany to be married after the Wall was erected. She accompanied her husband and their small daughter to New York, where Mr. Johnson spent 1966–1967 working as an editor for *Harcourt Brace*. "America was a rumor," he said. "I came here to verify the rumor"—(*N.Y. Times*).

In his recent "Anniversaries," Johnson again treats pressing moral and political issues by having the scene of the novel switch from New York City during the Vietnam War to Mecklenburg, Germany, in the Nazi period. One of the major themes of the book is the failure of liberalism, in the United States in the sixties and in Germany in the thirties. Johnson's work is consistent, never pedestrian and sometimes brilliant.

SPECULATIONS ABOUT JACOB. 1959. Trans. by Ursule Molinaro. *Harcourt* 1962 Harvest Bks. 1972 pap. $2.45

THE THIRD BOOK ABOUT ACHIM. 1962. Trans. by Ursule Molinaro. *Harcourt* 1967 $5.75

TWO VIEWS. 1965. Trans. by Richard and Clara Winston. *Harcourt* 1966 $4.50

ABSENCE. 1970. *Grossman* Cape Eds. $3.50 pap. $1.50

ANNIVERSARIES. 1970–1973. Trans. by Leila Vennewitz. *Harcourt* 1975 $10.00

Books about Johnson

Uwe Johnson. By Mark Buolby. Modern Literature Monographs *Ungar* 1974 $6.00

—F.G.G.

Chapter 13

Scandinavian Literature

"I belong to an ancient, idle, wild and useless tribe, perhaps I am even one of the last members of it, who, for many thousands of years, in all countries and parts of the world, has, now and again, stayed for a time among the hard-working honest people in real life, and sometimes has thus been fortunate enough to create another sort of reality for them, which in some way or another, has satisfied them. I am a storyteller."

—Karen Blixen

In the United States, three organizations are most responsible for the publication of Scandinavian literature in translation. *Twayne Publishers*, in the series Scandinavian Literature in Translation and Twayne World Authors, systematically encourages American awareness of these literatures. These series, which include reprints as well as new translations and critical studies, may be acquired on a standing order basis. *The American-Scandinavian Foundation* (127 East 73 St., New York, N.Y. 10021) has published some 125 books on Scandinavian topics, often in cooperation with university presses. Several new titles are added each year. The *University of Wisconsin Press* has provided many translations of Scandinavian literary works in its Nordic Translation Series; consult the latest catalogue of the press. In order to keep abreast of current titles of literature in translation, one should note three journals: *The Scandinavian Review* of the American-Scandinavian Foundation; *Scandinavian Studies*, the journal of the Society for the Advancement of Scandinavian Studies; and *Scandinavica* (Academic Press, New York and London). All are quarterlies.

The press of the University of Oslo, Norway, initiated in 1964 a valuable English-language series called Scandia Books. The titles, some 20 to date, have recently included five volumes of modern Scandinavian drama in translation. Publications of the *Universitetsforlag* may be ordered in the United States without difficulty.

HISTORY, CRITICISM, COLLECTIONS

Bredsdorff, Elias, and others. Introduction to Scandinavian Literature. 1951. *Greenwood* $11.50

Butler, E. The Horizon Concise History of Scandinavia. *McGraw-Hill* 1974 $8.95

Gustafson, Alrik. Six Scandinavian Novelists. 1940. *Biblo & Tannen* 1968 $7.50. Discussions of Lie, Jacobsen, Heidenstam, Lagerlöf, Hamsun, and Undset.

Hallmundsson, Hallberg, Ed. An Anthology of Scandinavian Literature. *Macmillan* Collier Bks. 1966 pap. $3.45. Includes a bibliography of literature in English translation.

Hovde, B. J. The Scandinavian Countries, 1720–1865. 1948. 2 vols. *Kennikat* set $27.50

Leach, Henry G., Ed. Pageant of Old Scandinavia. 1946. *Bks. for Libraries* $11.00

SCANDINAVIAN DRAMA

The figures of Henrik Ibsen and August Strindberg loom in the background as one views the development of Scandinavian drama in the twentieth century. Of Ibsen it can be said that his realistic plays of the period 1877–1883 created a norm for many Scandinavian dramatists who followed him. For others, the Ibsen tradition became a stale convention to be avoided. The other main dramatic tradition was created by the egocentricity of Strindberg. Rather than the outer, social reality of Ibsen's problem plays, Strindberg cultivates the subjective reality of an inner consciousness where no natural laws can be observed.

For all the power of Scandinavian theater at the turn of the century, it must be said that the real strength of Scandinavian literature since Ibsen and Strindberg has been in prose and poetry. Few are the dramatists who are not better known as novelists (e.g., Lagerkvist and Moberg in Sweden, H. C. Branner and Isak Dinesen in Denmark, Tarjei Vesaas in Norway), and with few exceptions the theater has not had great masters in recent decades. Yet there are very talented dramatists in Scandinavia today, and the theater does have a large and loyal audience. Thanks to the series Scandia Books, we now have, in the five volumes of "Modern Nordic Plays," a selection from recent Scandinavian drama.

The student of film is also aware that Ingmar Bergman (q.v.) is essentially an excellent and complex dramatist whose medium happens to be photographic. Literature by and on Bergman, including published scripts of his films, is abundant.

FIRE AND ICE: Three Icelandic Plays. Trans. and ed. by Einar Haugen and G. M. Gathorne-Hardy. Nordic Translation Ser. *Univ. of Wisconsin Press* 1967 $8.00. Includes "The Wish" by Jóhann Sigurjónsson; "The Golden Gate" by David Stefánsson; and "Atoms and Madams" by Agnar Thördarson.

FIVE MODERN SCANDINAVIAN PLAYS. Introd. by Henry W. Wells. *Twayne* 1971 $8.50. Includes "Lion with Corset" by Carl Eric Soya; "Our Power and Our Glory" by Nordahl Grieg; "The Sisters" by Valentin Chorell; "The Golden Gate" by David Stefánsson; "The Man Who Lived His Life Over" by Pär Lagerkvist.

MASTERPIECES OF MODERN SCANDINAVIAN THEATER. Ed. by Robert Corrigan. *Macmillan* Collier Bks. 1967 pap. $1.50. Includes "Hedda Gabler" by Henrik Ibsen; "Miss Julie" by August Strindberg; "Difficult Hour" by Pär Lagerkvist; "Defeat" by Nordahl Grieg; "Anna Sophie Hedvig" by Kjeld Abell.

MODERN NORDIC PLAYS. *Universitetsforlag* (Twayne) 5 vols. 1974 each $8.95

Vol. 1 Finland: "The Superintendent" by Paavo Haavikko; "Eva Maria" by V. V. Järner; "Snow in May" by Eeva-Liisa Manner; "Private Jokinen's Marriage Leave" by Veijo Meri. Vol. 2 Iceland: "The Pigeon Banquet" by Halldór Laxness; "The Seaway to Baghdad" by Jökull Jakobsson; "Mink" by Erlingur E. Halldórsson; "Ten Variations" and "Yolk-life" by Oddur Björnsson. Vol. 3 Sweden: "The Madcap" by Lars Forssell; "One Man's Bread" by Folke Fridell; "The Sandwiching" by Lars Görling; "Isak Juntti Had Many Sons" by Björn-Erik Höijer Vol. 4 Norway: "The House" by Johan Borgen; "The Injustice" by Finn Havrevold; "The Bleaching Yard" by Tarjei Vesaas; "The Lord and His Servants" by Axel Kielland Vol. 5 Denmark: "Thermopylae" by H. C. Branner; "The Bookseller Cannot Sleep" by Ernst Bruun Olsen; "Developments" by Klaus Rifbjerg; "Boxing for One" by Peter Ronild.

DANISH LITERATURE

Andersen, Benny. SELECTED POEMS. Trans. by Alexander Taylor. Lockert Lib. of Poetry in Translation *Princeton Univ. Press* 1976 $9.50 pap. $2.95. A rough comparison of Andersen (born 1929) with E. E. Cummings is appropriate; his irony, humor and word-play make for extremely enjoyable reading.

Billeskov Jansen, F. J., and P. M. Mitchell. ANTHOLOGY OF DANISH LITERATURE. Arcturus Books Paperbacks Ser. *Southern Illinois Univ. Press* bilingual ed. 2 vols. 1972 each $2.95. Vol. 1 Middle Ages, Romanticism Vol. 2 Realism to the Present

Bodelsen, Anders. STRAUS. 1971. Trans.. by Nadia Christensen and Alexander Taylor. *Harper* 1974 $5.95. Realistic depiction of contemporary society characterizes the many novels in which Bodelsen (born 1937) describes social and inner conflict.

Bredsdorff, Elias. DANISH LITERATURE IN ENGLISH TRANSLATION. 1950. *Greenwood* 1974 $9.50. Covers the period 1533–1950.

Brønner, Hedin. THREE FAROESE NOVELISTS: An Appreciation of Jørgen-Frantz Jacobsen, William Heinesen and Hedin Brú. Lib. of Scandinavian Studies *Twayne* 1973

Brú, Hedin. THE OLD MAN AND HIS SONS. 1940. Trans by John F. West. *Eriksson* 1970 $5.95. Along with William Heinesen, Brú (born 1901) is one of the leading writers of the Faroe Islands. This novel shows the generation gap in Faroese terms.

Dal, Erik, Ed. DANISH BALLADS AND FOLK SONGS. Trans. by Henry Meyer; ill. by Marcel Rasmussen. *American-Scandinavian Foundation* 1967 $7.50. Dal's knowledge of medieval Danish literature is expert; this fine collection of early verse does not include music.

Grundtvig, Svend, Ed. DANISH FAIRY TALES. Trans. by J. Grant Cramer. *Peter Smith* $5.00

Hein, Piet. GROOKS. Trans. by Jens Arup. *Doubleday* pap. 5 vols. Vol. 1 1969 $3.50 Vol. 2 1969 $3.50 Vol. 3 1971 $3.50 Vol. 4 1972 $3.95 Vol. 5 1973 $3.95. The mathematician Piet Hein is famous for his modern aphorisms, which he calls "grooks."

Jones, Gwyn W. DENMARK. Nations of the Modern World Ser. *Praeger* 1970 $8.00

Mitchell, Philip M. A HISTORY OF DANISH LITERATURE. Introd. by Mogens Haugsted. *Kraus* 2nd enl. ed. 1971 $18.00

Oakley, Stewart. A SHORT HISTORY OF DENMARK. Short Histories Ser. *Praeger* 1972 $10.00

Panduro, Leif. KICK ME IN THE TRADITIONS. 1958. Trans. by Carl Malmberg. 1961 o.p.

ONE OF OUR MILLIONAIRES IS MISSING. 1966. Trans by Carl Malmberg. 1967 o.p. Panduro (born 1923) frequently deals with problems of puberty and identity in his many novels and plays; his humor and satire have earned him a prominent place in current Danish literature.

Rode, M., and B. Rying. DENMARK: An Official Handbook. 1972. Trans. by Reginald Spink. *Vanous* $17.50. A compendious and rich source of information on Danish culture, business, and education.

Starcke, Viggo. DENMARK IN WORLD HISTORY. *Univ. of Pennsylvania Press* 1963 $12.00. The subtitle of this useful book notes its main thrust: "The External History of Denmark from the Stone Age to the Middle Ages with Special Reference to the Danish Influence on the English-Speaking Nations."

HOLBERG, LUDVIG. 1684–1754.

Holberg, the outstanding genius of the Danish Enlightenment, contributed in the areas of history, philosophy, and literature; his name stands by that of Molière as a master of European comedy. His 33 comedies created a national repertoire and a theatrical tradition. Holberg's strength in creative writing lies not in extended plot but in the individual scene, the anecdote, the characterization. "Peder Paars," a mock-heroic poem, gives Holberg the framework in which to satirize the government, the Church, and the university. The novel "Niels Klim" likewise reports on human foibles. Students of eighteenth-century European literature will want to seek out older translations of Holberg's philosophical writing (e.g., "Selected Essays of Ludvig Holberg," trans. and introd. by P. M. Mitchell 1955, o.p.), and to note that other comedies have been translated ("Four Plays by Holberg," trans. by Henry Alexander 1946, o.p.; "Three Comedies," trans. by Reginald Spink 1958, o.p.).

SEVEN ONE-ACT PLAYS. Trans. by Henry Alexander; introd. by Svend Kragh-Jacobsen (1950). *Kraus* $14.00. Includes The Talkative Barber (1722), The Arabian Powder (1724), The Christmas Party (1724), Diedrich the Terrible (1724), The Peasant in Pawn (1726), Sgnarel's Journey to the Land of the Philosophers (1751), The Caged Bridegroom (1753).

PEDER PAARS. 1719. Trans. by Bergliot Stromsoe; introd. by Børge Gedsø Madsen. *American-Scandinavian Foundation* 1962 $5.00

THE JOURNEY OF NIELS KLIM TO THE WORLD UNDERGROUND. 1741. (This edition based on a translation published in London 1742) ed. with introd. by James I. McNelis, Jr. (1960). *Greenwood* 1975 $11.50

Books about Holberg

Ludvig Holberg. By F. J. Billeskov Jansen. World Authors Ser. *Twayne* 1974 $6.95. A study by one of the deans of modern Danish literary scholarship.

ANDERSEN, HANS CHRISTIAN.   1805–1875.

Fairy tales comprise only a rather small part of Andersen's life's work—his novels and travel books were more warmly received by his contemporaries. During his lifetime, his talent was more esteemed in other countries than it was in his native Denmark—Dickens called the Dane "a great writer." Andersen complained bitterly about the lack of encouragement for his first volume of "Fairy Tales, Told for Children" (May 1835). The second volume appeared in December, 1835, the third in 1837. In 1838 came the first volume of the "New Collection," in 1839 the second volume, and, 1841, the third. In 1843, the series called "New Adventures" was begun and the title no longer addressed itself exclusively to children. Other volumes followed until Andersen's death. "There is no longer any doubt that Andersen was born so that he could write these fairy tales and stories: they are his contribution to world history"—(Fredrik Böök). "My fairy tales are written as much for adults as for children," said Andersen in his old age, "children understand only the trimmings, and not until they are mature will they see and comprehend the whole." The Paul Leyssac and Reginald Spink translations are recommended, as is that by Jean Hersholt (1958, o.p.).

Interest in Andersen's life and complex personality—and in his autobiographical writings—will certainly be increased by the new biography by Elias Bredsdorff, who draws his knowledge from decades of research in Denmark and at the University of Cambridge.

IT's PERFECTLY TRUE AND OTHER STORIES. *Harcourt* 1938 $6.95. Twenty-eight stories. Trans. by Paul Leyssac.

TALES. (In "Tales of Grimm and Andersen") sel. by Frederick Jacobi, Jr.; introd. by W. H. Auden; based partially on translations by Mrs. E. V. Lucas and Mrs. H. B. Paull. 1952 o.p.

FAIRY TALES AND STORIES. Trans. with introd. by Reginald Spink. *Dutton* Children's Ill. Class. $3.95 Everyman's 1960 $3.50. Fifty-one stories in modern translations for both adult and juvenile reading.

THE COMPLETE FAIRY TALES AND STORIES. Trans. by Eric Haugaard. *Doubleday* 1974 $15.00

THE IMPROVISATORE. 1835. Trans. by Mary B. Howitt (1897). *Folcroft* $25.00. A novel of a young writer's life; delightful scenes from nineteenth-century Italy.

O. T.: A Danish Romance. 1836. Trans. by Mary B. Howitt (1871). *Folcroft* $20.00. "O.T." abbreviates "Odense Jail," where the main figure is born to experience great social and personal handicaps.

THE STORY OF MY LIFE. 1867. Trans. by Mary B. Howitt (1871). *Folcroft* $15.00; (with title "The Fairy Tale of My Life: An Autobiography") *Two Continents* (co-publ. by Paddington) 1975 $10.95

Books about Andersen

Hans Christian Andersen: A Biography. By Fredrik Böök. Trans. from Swedish by George C. Schoolfield. 1962 o.p. An authoritative biography, "persevering in hunting the true Andersen."
The Wild Swan: The Life and Times of Hans Christian Andersen. By Monica Sterling. 1965 o.p.
Hans Christian Andersen: The Man and His World. By Reginald Spink. Pictorial Biographies Ser. *Putnam* 1972 $6.95
Hans Christian Andersen: The Man and His Work. By Reginald Spink. *Vanous* 1975 pap. $3.50
Hans Christian Andersen. By Elias Bredsdorff. *Scribner* 1975 $15.00

KIERKEGAARD, SÖREN (AABYE).   1813–1855.   *See Chapter 4, World Religions, Reader's Adviser, Vol. 3.*

BRANDES, GEORG (MORRIS COHEN).   1842–1927.

Georg Brandes "for more than 30 years was the Minos of Danish literature"—and its greatest critic. A student of all the European literatures, he traveled abroad throughout his life, coming under the influence of the ideas of Ibsen, Taine, Zola, the Goncourts, John Stuart Mill, and Nietzsche, all of whose works he promoted within Denmark. In time he succeeded in bringing Denmark's then provincial culture into the mainstream of European literature. "The motto of Brandes was 'freedom of inquiry and freedom of thought' "; in 1870 he was kept from the promised chair of esthetics at the University of Copenhagen as "a Jew, a radical and an atheist. He remained all three throughout his long life, gradually winning his way to literary canonization, then deliberately sacrificing his popularity in old age for the sake of his principles"—(*Twentieth Century Authors*). In 1911 the same university held a celebration in his honor. "At that time it was remarked, 'During those 40 years it was not *Brandes* who changed his ideals.' " In World War I he maintained an attitude of strict neutrality, which lost him many friends in Denmark and in Allied Europe generally.

Brandes was a foe of Romanticism—a pleader for realism and the expression of a social ethic in literature: "he sustained that a literature is shown to be alive by its ability and willingness to discuss problems." His *magnum opus* was "Main Currents in Nineteenth Century Literature" in six volumes (1872–1890), of which the first two volumes ("Naturalism" and "Revolution") in the listing below are in print in English. "A lawyer with a case to plead," he inspired the experimental novel of the 1870s which gave the form a new lease on life in Denmark. Prodigiously productive, Brandes is still widely read and cited today. Unattributed quotations above are from Giovanni Bach and others: "The History of Scandinavian Literatures" (1938, o.p.).

NATURALISM IN NINETEENTH CENTURY ENGLISH LITERATURE. 1872–1890. *Russell & Russell* 1957 $9.50

REVOLUTION AND REACTION IN NINETEENTH CENTURY FRENCH LITERATURE. 1872–1890. *Russell & Russell* 1960 $8.00

LORD BEACONSFIELD: A Study. 1878. Introd. by Salo W. Baron. *Apollo* pap. $1.95; *Peter Smith* $4.25. A classic study of Benjamin Disraeli, stressing his political career.

FERDINAND LASSALLE. 1881. *Greenwood*. repr. of 1911 ed. $12.50

IMPRESSIONS OF RUSSIA. 1888. Introd. by Richard Pipes. *Apollo* pap. $1.95; *Peter Smith* $4.25

WILLIAM SHAKESPEARE: A Critical Study. 1895–1896. Trans. by William Archer and Diana White. *Ungar* 1963 2 vols. set $15.00

HENRIK IBSEN. 1899. *Blom* 1964 $8.75

VOLTAIRE. 1916–1917. Trans. by Heinz Norden. *Ungar* 2 vols. set $15.00

MICHELANGELO: His Life, His Times, His Era. 1921. Trans. by Heinz Norden. *Ungar* $12.00

FRENCH ROMANTICS. 1923. *Russell & Russell* $8.50

CREATIVE SPIRITS OF THE NINETEENTH CENTURY. 1923. Trans. by R. B. Anderson. *Bks. for Libraries* $16.50; *Scholarly Press* $29.50; *Richard West* $12.00

JACOBSEN, JENS PETER. 1847–1885.

Jacobsen, Denmark's foremost novelist of naturalism, expressed in his small body of work his rejection of religion and his enthusiasm for the new doctrine of evolution. In his autobiographical novel "Niels Lyhne," sometimes called "the bible of atheism" in its time, he wrote that "there is no God and man is his prophet." During his troubled life, cut short by tuberculosis, he translated into Danish nearly all of Darwin's (*q.v.*) writings. His own work—two novels, a book of short stories, and a few poems—strove to "bring into the realm of literature the eternal laws of nature" and to free the concept of nature from the distortion of Romanticism. The novella "Mogens" was Jacobsen's first publication; it became famous as an example of the new naturalistic current in literature. In it, life is seen as perceptions of the instant, and people are motivated by natural laws and drives. In "Marie Grubbe," externally a seventeenth-century historical romance, the life of Marie is determined by her erotic needs; although born into the nobility, she finally finds happiness in life as the wife of a coarse stableman. Jacobsen's concern with anxiety and inner torment brings to mind the great nineteenth-century Russian novelists, while his naturalism and interest in psychology is reminiscent of Flaubert (*q.v.*). Jacobsen's influence on major European writers who followed him, such as Rilke (*q.v.*), is well documented.

MOGENS AND OTHER STORIES. 1872–1885. Trans. by Anna Grabow. *Bks. for Libraries* $10.00

MARIE GRUBBE. 1876. Trans. by Hanna Astrup Larsen; introd. by Robert Raphael. *Twayne* 1975 $7.95

NIELS LYHNE. 1880. Trans. by Hanna Astrup Larsen; introd. by Börge Gedsö Madsen. Lib. of Scandinavian Lit. *Twayne* 1966 $4.50

NEXÖ, MARTIN ANDERSEN.   1869–1954.

Andersen Nexö, the first prominent voice in Danish literature of trade unionism and proletarian solidarity, spent an impoverished youth working at various trades in Copenhagen and on the island of Bornholm. After 1901 he supported himself by writing. A communist and enemy of injustice, he avoided arrest during the Nazi occupation in World War II by fleeing, first to Sweden and then to the Soviet Union. He died in East Germany. "Pelle the Conquerer" and "Ditte" are Nexö's classic proletarian novels. "Pelle" describes the development of Danish trade unionism in the nineteenth century; its blend of autobiographical insights with a passionate sense of justice cast in epic narrative remind one of Gorki (q.v.) in Russia. "Ditte" charts the struggle of a young woman against poverty and cold indifference, not to mention exploitation; her goodness and warmth are totally unrewarded before she dies in misery. Ditte's fate is described in basic moral terms and is not linked with political events; thus it differs rather sharply from "Pelle."

DITTE: Ditte, Daughter of Man (trans. by A. G. Chater and Richard Thirsk); Girl Alive!; and Towards the Stars (trans. by Asta and Rowland Kenney). 1920–1922. *Peter Smith* 1930 3 vols. in 1 $7.50

PELLE THE CONQUEROR. 1906–1910. Trans. by Jessie Muir and Bernard Miall. *Peter Smith* 1930 1950 4 vols. in 2 $10.00. Boyhood; Apprenticeship; The Great Struggle; Daybreak.

IN GOD'S LAND. 1929. Trans. by Thomas Seltzer. *Peter Smith* 1933 $4.00

JENSEN, JOHANNES V(ILHELM).   1873–1950.   (Nobel Prize 1944)

Jensen has had great influence on Danish literature both as a lyric poet and as a novelist. He was born in a village in northwest Jutland where his father was a veterinary and his grandfather a farmer and weaver. He studied medicine in Copenhagen, but did not become a doctor. His great interest in anthropology and biology was concentrated in the theory of evolution. Darwinian philosophy permeates the six novels which comprise the epic "The Long Journey." His deep sense of science, or all-including nature, was what aroused his imagination—his "philosophy includes both fortitude and tenderness, while as a writer he gives us treasures unsurpassed for their fusing of rare sight and rarer insight."

THE LONG JOURNEY. 1908–1922. Nobel Prize edition 1945 o.p.

DINESEN, ISAK (pseud. of Karen Blixen).   1885–1962.

Isak Dinesen is a unique figure in the literature of modern Denmark, quite distant from the trends of the 1930s and later. She lived the happiest and most eventful years of her life in Africa rather than Denmark; she wrote primarily in a faultless and yet quite personal variety of literary English; and she found her most receptive audience, not in Denmark, but in the United States. From 1914 to 1931 Karen Blixen—her married name, by which she is known in Europe—struggled to maintain a coffee plantation in the British colony of Kenya. In contrast to the poor prospects of the farm, she was surrounded by a wealth of European and native friends in a relatively unwesternized land of enormous beauty. "Out of Africa" and its late sequel "Shadows on the Grass" are not memoirs in the usual sense. Facts are insignificant as she assesses her African experience; it is the spirit of a primitive and yet noble culture which gives these books their enduring evocative power. Karen Blixen perceived an Africa where man and nature were still one. Here she came to terms with life and acquired a proud, exquisite fatalism. The two African books are definitely a key to a greater appreciation of her works of pure fiction. If her pastorals in memory of Kenya helped Karen Blixen overcome her grief at losing her home there, then her stories, with their finely wrought fantasy, contain undercurrents of the truths she discovered in Africa. Her stories are "eccentric masterpieces; ostensibly Gothic pastiche, their outward form conceals epic wisdom, profound feminine sorrow, and a clean magic almost lost today. She is undoubtedly the princess of modern aristocratic storytellers, a delight and a revelation"— (Seymour Smith). In 1957 Karen Blixen received honorary membership in the American Academy and National Institute of Arts and Letters, an honor which only 50 foreigners may share.

SEVEN GOTHIC TALES. 1934. *Random* Vintage Bks. 1972 pap. $1.95

OUT OF AFRICA. 1938. *Random* Vintage Bks. 1972 pap. $1.95

WINTER'S TALES. 1942. *Bks. for Libraries* $12.25; *Random* Vintage Bks. pap. $2.45

THE ANGELIC AVENGERS. 1944. By Pierre Andrézel (pseud.). First American ed. 1947. *Univ. of Chicago Pr.* 1975 $8.95

LAST TALES. 1957. *Random* Vintage Bks. 1975 pap. $2.45

ANECDOTES OF DESTINY. 1958. *Random* Vintage Bks. 1974 pap. $2.45. A collection of five stories.

SHADOWS ON THE GRASS. 1961. *Random* Vintage Bks. 1974 pap. $1.65. Four sketches; a sequel to "Out of Africa."

EHRENGARD. 1963. *Random* Vintage Bks. 1975 pap. $1.95

Books about Isak Dinesen

The World of Isak Dinesen. By Eric O. Johannesson. *Univ. of Washington Pr.* 1961 $5.50
Titania: The Biography of Isak Dinesen. By Parmenia Migel. *Random* 1967 o.p.
The Life and Destiny of Isak Dinesen. Comp. and ed. by Frans Lasson; text by Clara Svendsen. 1970 o.p. An excellent photographic biography.
Isak Dinesen and Karen Blixen. By Donald Hannah. 1971 o.p.
The Gayety of Vision: A Study of Isak Dinesen's Art. By Robert Langbaum. *Univ. of Chicago Pr.* Phoenix Bks. 1975 pap. $4.95
Longing for Darkness: Kamante's Tales from out of Africa. Ed. by Peter H. Beard. *Harcourt* 1975 $19.95

PALUDAN, (STIG HENNING) JACOB (PUGGAARD). 1896–

Paludan is a novelist and essayist who began as a pharmacist. He spent part of his youth in South America (Ecuador) and New York City. "Jörgen Stein," his outstanding work, showed Denmark at the outset of World War I and is a scathing indictment of the materialism and complacency of the period. Paludan is known for his acute psychological penetration and his fine style.

JÖRGEN STEIN. 1932–1933. Trans. by Carl Malmberg; introd. by P. M. Mitchell. Nordic Translation Ser. *Univ. of Wisconsin Press* 1966 $14.00

MUNK, KAJ (HARALD LEININGER). 1898–1944.

Deep religious conviction and love of the heroic, inspired individual are blended in the personality and work of Kaj Munk, perhaps Denmark's most significant dramatist in the twentieth century. As a Lutheran minister he became a magnetic preacher whose political and cultural criticism had certain philosophical aspects in common with the antirationalism of contemporary European fascism. The irony in this lies in the fact that Munk's heroic ideal is humane and Christian; in the spirit of his heroes, Munk persistently and publicly attacked Nazism during the occupation of Denmark and was murdered by the Gestapo in 1944.

In "Before Cannae," Hannibal the ruthless empire-builder is opposed by the humanitarian Fabius. In "He Sits at the Melting Pot," God endows a man with the strength of love with which to do battle against the power-hungry of this world. "The Word," Munk's greatest success on the stage, confirms that miracles through faith are possible in modern times.

FIVE PLAYS. Trans. by R. P. Keigwin. *American Scandinavian Foundation* 1964 $5.00. Includes Herod the King (1928), The Word (1932), Cant (1931), He Sits at the Melting Pot (1938), Before Cannae (1943).

Books about Munk

Portraits of Destiny. By Melville Harcourt. *Twin Circle* (Sheed and Ward) 1966 $5.00

HEINESEN, WILLIAM. 1900–

As a young man in the Faroe Islands, William Heinesen thought of a profession in art or music; his early poetry—he writes in Danish rather than Faroese—from the 1920s demonstrates keen sensitivity to the powerful sensual contrasts of nature in the Atlantic islands. In the 1930s his elegiac and yet ecstatic pantheism received a social awareness. Of novels from this period, "*Noatun*" (1938) has appeared in English translation (London, 1939). Here we meet the vital people of a Faroese settlement bravely surviving storms, sickness, and exploitation as they struggle to establish a *noatun*, or new town. The individualistic people and sharp beauty of the Faroes are Heinesen's subjects; his strong satire, humor, and imagination have made him one of Denmark's finest prose writers. "The Lost Musicians" and "The Kingdom of the Earth" share many of the same characters, created by Heinesen to depict fantastic events in Torshavn a generation or so ago. In Heinesen's rich fantasy is an expression of the antinaturalism and unrealism that also mark the writing of Isak Dinesen and Martin A. Hansen (*qq.v.*). It is not necessary to have even heard of the Faroes to enjoy the magic of William Heinesen.

THE LOST MUSICIANS. 1950. Trans. by Erik J. Friis. *Twayne* 1972 $7.95; *Hippocrene Bks.* 1972 $3.95

THE KINGDOM OF THE EARTH. 1952. Trans. by Hedin Brönner. *Twayne* 1973 $7.50

FAROESE SHORT STORIES. Ed. and trans. by Hedin Brönner. *Twayne* and *American Scandinavian Foundation* 1972 $8.50

Books about Heinesen

William Heinesen. By W. Glyn Jones. World Authors Ser. *Twayne* 1974 $7.95

Three Faroese Novelists: An Appreciation of Jörgen-Frantz Jacobsen, William Heinesen, and Hedin Brú. By Hedin Brönner. *Twayne* 1973

BRANNER, HANS CHRISTIAN. 1903–1966.

Freudian psychoanalysis, existentialism, and modern humanism are the driving forces in Branner's fine short stories and novels. While the psychological view of human personality presented by Branner seems very simplistic today, his symbolism is intriguing as he describes with great finesse the erotic awakening of youth and adult sexual relationships. "The Story of Börge" is one of Branner's best studies of child psychology. "The Riding Master" (1949, no American edition), his most famous novel, prompted a spirited public reaction by Isak Dinesen (*q.v.*), who found fundamental fault with Branner's conception of "humanism."

THE STORY OF BÖRGE. 1942. Trans. by Kristi Planck. *Twayne* 1973 $8.50

TWO MINUTES OF SILENCE: Selected Short Stories. 1944. Trans. by Vera Lindholm Vance; introd. by Richard B. Vowles. Nordic Translation Ser. *University of Wisconsin Press* 1966 $8.00. Includes a detailed bibliography.

Books about Branner

H. C. BRANNER. By Thomas L. Markey. World Authors Ser. *Twayne* 1973 $6.95

HANSEN, MARTIN A. 1909–1955.

As a critic of the form and content of civilization since the Middle Ages, Martin A. Hansen sees a deterioration of humanity and morality as rationalism and scientism have become the guiding lights of European culture. Hansen points to the coherent culture of the Danish Middle Ages as the humane condition we have lost. In his childhood Hansen personally observed the disintegration of rural folk culture as economic and agricultural requirements "modernized" country life. His participation in the Danish Underground during World War Two also greatly increased his sense of failure of modern times to provide ethical stability. A very learned and Christian romanticism imbues his many novels and stories; he is at times very obtuse and allegorical. In "Lucky Kristoffer," a historical novel set in the sixteenth century, combatants in the strife of Reformation times express both medieval and modern attitudes, both harmony and disharmony. "The Liar," written in the form of a schoolteacher's diary, presents a psychological critique of modern times as the teacher experiences a crisis of faith.

LUCKY KRISTOFFER. 1945. Trans. by John J. Egglishaw. Scandinavian Literature in Translation Ser. *Twayne* $8.50; *American Scandinavian Foundation* 1974 $7.50

THE LIAR. 1950. Trans. by John J. Egglishaw. Scandinavian Literature in Translation Ser. *Twayne* $6.95

FINNISH LITERATURE

Ahokas, Jaakko. A HISTORY OF FINNISH LITERATURE. *American-Scandinavian Foundation* 1973 $20.00; *Humanities Press* 1973 pap. $22.00; *Indiana University Research Center* 1974 pap. $22.00

Binham, Philip, and Richard Dauenhauer, Eds. SNOW IN MAY: An Anthology of Finnish Writing, 1945–1972. *Fairleigh Dickinson Univ. Press* 1975 $15.00

Bradley, David. LION AMONG ROSES: A Memoir of Finland. *Holt* 1965 $5.95

By an American who spent two years teaching in Finland, "*Lion among Roses* (the coat-of-arms of Finland) is superbly written"—(*LJ*).

Jansson, Tove. THE SUMMER BOOK. 1972. Trans. by Thomas Teal. *Pantheon* 1975 $6.95. A Swedo-Finnish writer (although of Finnish nationality, she uses the Swedish language), Tove Jansson (born 1914) is a master creator of sophisticated children's literature. "The Summer Book" is the best introduction to her world of fantasy.

Jutikkala, Eino, and Kauko Pirinen. A HISTORY OF FINLAND. Trans. by Paul Sioblom. *Praeger* 1962 $10.00. This short history is quite exceptional and, although almost entirely political, is included for its usefulness in showing religious development and the language conflict between Finnish and Swedish adherents.

Pekkanen, Toivo. MY CHILDHOOD. Trans. by Alan Blair; introd. by Thomas Warburton. Nordic Translation Ser. *Univ. of Wisconsin Press* 1966 $8.00. Pekkanen writes with warmth and emotion of his first 16 years. The son of a stonecutter, he tells of his growing awareness of his family's poverty and of the pleasures he discovered in books and nature.

Saarikoski, Pentti. HELSINKI: Selected Poems. *Swallow Press* 1967 $4.95. Saarikoski (born 1927), a rebel against the status quo in general, defies logic and optimism.

Schoolfield, George C., Trans. and ed. SWEDO-FINNISH SHORT STORIES. Scandinavian Lit. in Translation Ser. *Twayne* $13.50

"This first collection in English presents a competent and skillful translation of a little-known part of Scandinavian writing"—(*LJ*)

Wuorinen, John H. HISTORY OF FINLAND. *Columbia* 1965 $17.50

THE KALEVALA (The Land of the Heroes). 1835–1849.

The Finnish national epic of three semidivine brothers living in Kaleva, a mythical land of abundance and happiness, was known to scholars as early as 1733 but was ignored until the nineteenth century. The verses were collected by two Finnish physicians, Zakarias Topelius, who published the first fragments in 1822, and Elias Lönnrot (1802–1884), who continued to travel and sift the folk songs chanted to him by rune singers, and who gave the cycle its present form (1835–1836). His second edition (1849) has remained the definitive version. Rich in mythology and folklore, its influence in all branches of the arts has been great. Sibelius used it in a number of his compositions. Longfellow (*q.v.*) borrowed its poetic form for "The Song of Hiawatha." Kenneth Rexroth (in *SR*) finds the Kirby translation "in rather antiquated language with poor notes." The Lönnrot-Magoun version he calls "a fine, scholarly edition." Rexroth says: "Recited in the original language, the *Kalevala* has a gripping sonority and haunting cadences quite unlike any other great poem in any language."

THE KALEVALA: The Land of the Heroes. Trans. by W. F. Kirby, with introd. by J. B. C. Grundy. *Dutton* Everyman's 1956 2 vols. each $3.95

THE KALEVALA, or Poems of the Kaleva District: A Prose Translation. Comp. by Elias Lönnrot; fwd. and appendices by Francis Peabody Magoun, Jr. *Harvard Univ. Press* 1963 $14.00

SILLANPÄÄ, FRANS EEMIL. 1888–1964. (Nobel Prize 1939)

The son of a landless peasant, Sillanpää studied natural science at Helsinki University, but his interest soon shifted to writing. His first novel was published in 1916, and his second, "Meek Heritage" (1919), established him as the foremost Finnish writer—entitled to a lifetime pension from the government. His next book to achieve international fame was "The Maid Silja" (1931), a novel of the Finnish Civil War of 1918. In 1936 he was made an honorary Doctor of Philosophy by Finland's State University, and in 1939 received the Nobel Prize for Literature. "People in the Summer Night," says *Choice*, "is written to a Finnish audience largely agrarian. . . . Sillanpää is good at capturing the smells, textures and colors of Finnish country life."

MEEK HERITAGE. 1919. *Eriksson* (dist. by Independent Publishers Group, c/o David White, 60 E. 55 St., New York, N.Y. 10022) 1972 $5.95

THE MAID SILJA. 1931. Trans. by Alexander Matson. *Norman S. Berg* 1974 lib. bdg. $10.63

PEOPLE IN THE SUMMER NIGHT: An Epic Suite. 1934. Trans. by Alan Blair; introd. by Thomas Warburton. Nordic Translation Ser. *Univ. of Wisconsin Press* 1966 $9.50

OLSSON, HAGAR. 1893–

"The formidable Hagar Olsson, critical firebrand of Finnish modernism," as she has been called by Alrik Gustafson, became a foremost expressionist writer and editor in the 1920s. "The Woodcarver and Death" is based on a legend and has been praised for its poetic simplicity.

THE WOODCARVER AND DEATH. 1940. Trans. by George C. Schoolfield. Nordic Translation Ser. *Univ. of Wisconsin Press* 1965 $10.00

WALTARI, MIKA TOIMI.   1908–

"The Egyptian," a great success in Europe, where it was translated into many languages, brought Waltari into prominence here. He was born in Helsinki. After his university education he went to Paris in 1927. There he wrote his first published novel, a success. He returned to Helsinki in 1929 and continued to write—poems, plays, novels, and fairy tales. He became editor of Finland's principal illustrated weekly, *Suomen Kuvalehti*, in 1936, and his three-volume historical novel "From Father to Son" appeared the next year. It won the National Literary Prize, was filmed and translated into fourteen languages.

THE EGYPTIAN. 1949 *Berkley* Medallion 1970 pap. $1.25

THE SECRET OF THE KINGDOM. *Putnam* 1961 $4.95

THE TREE OF DREAMS AND OTHER STORIES. 1965 o.p.

THE ROMAN. 1966. *Berkley* Medallion pap. 1967 $1.25

THE ETRUSCAN. *Berkley* Medallion 1971 pap. $1.25

All translated by Naomi Walford unless otherwise noted.

MERI, VEIJO.   1928–

"A brilliant work by an important and exciting young Finnish writer"—(*LJ*), "Manila Rope" combines terse narrative with a series of symbolic folktales. Both the hero's war adventures and the tales he is told have the grim absurdity of black comedy. "The modern line [in Finnish literature] is perhaps most clearly represented by Veijo Meri, who in recent years has begun to attract international attention. . . . War loses all its meaning in Meri's works and becomes merely grotesque. Nevertheless his small characters somehow survive and extricate themselves"—(P.E.N. *International*). Mr. Meri studied in Helsinki and worked in a publishing house before devoting himself wholly to writing.

THE MANILA ROPE. Trans. by John McGahern and Annikki Laaksi. 1967 o.p.

ICELANDIC LITERATURE

In medieval times the island-nation of Iceland produced a body of literature which was unsurpassed in Europe in its quality, variety, and sheer quantity. Although the English use of "saga" suggests adventure and dramatic events, the Icelandic word "saga" is a general term for any fictional or nonfictional account. Icelandic narrative prose embraces several kinds of themes. "The Sagas of Icelanders" tell of local events and personalities from the more recent historical past, although these sagas were not meant and should not be understood to be historically accurate in detail. "Njal's Saga" exemplifies this group, which is the one best represented in English translation. "The Sagas of Antiquity" deal with mythical–heroic figures (e.g., "Völsunga Saga" and "Hrolf's Saga Kraka"), while the "Sagas of Knights" are the Scandinavian counterpart to the chivalric literature of medieval France and Germany (e.g., "The Saga of Tristram and Isönd"). The "Sagas of the Sturlungs" deal with twelfth and thirteenth-century Icelandic history. The descendants of Sturla Thordarson, including Snorri Sturluson, played a decisive role in Icelandic politics in this period. "The Sagas of Kings," accounts of the lives of West Norse rulers, are best known through the translations of Snorri Sturluson's *"Heimskringla."*

The literary activity of modern Iceland seldom gains the attention of the English-speaking world. This is due partly, one suspects, to the relative scarcity of competent translators. Works by Nobel Prize winner Halldor Laxness are most familiar. Ardent friends of Icelandic literature will wish to consult the series "Islandica" (*Cornell Univ. Press* o.p., some volumes available from *Kraus*). In this series Halldor Hermannsson prepared a wealth of bibliographical and historical commentary on both medieval and modern Icelandic literature. See also the "Bibliography of Modern Icelandic Literature in Translation" by P. M. Mitchell and Kenneth H. Ober (*below*). Valuable information on current English-language publications will be found in the journals *Scandinavian Studies* and *Scandinavica*.

Andersson, Theodore M. THE PROBLEM OF ICELANDIC SAGA ORIGINS: A Historical Survey. 1964 o.p.

"His study is detailed, objective and thorough but only quotes in Scandinavian languages have been translated and lengthy French and German quotes make this study available only to advanced students and scholars"—(*LJ*).

Beck, Richard. HISTORY OF ICELANDIC POETS. 1800–1940. *Kraus* $14.00

(Trans. and Ed.). ICELANDIC POEMS AND STORIES. 1943. *Bks. for Libraries* $10.00. A selection of modern Icelandic literature.

Einarsson, Stefán. HISTORY OF ICELANDIC LITERATURE. *Johns Hopkins Press* 1957 $18.80

HISTORY OF ICELANDIC PROSE WRITERS, 1800–1940. *Kraus* pap. $12.00

Firchow, Evelyn Scherabon, Trans. and ed. ICELANDIC SHORT STORIES. Scandinavian Lit. in Translation Ser. *Twayne* 1975 $10.95. Good translations of 25 modern stories.

Hallberg, Peter. THE ICELANDIC SAGA. Trans. by Paul Schach. *Univ. of Nebraska Press* 1962 $4.50 Bison Bks. pap. $2.35. A stimulating and readable introduction.

Haugen, Einar. FIRE AND ICE: Three Icelandic Plays. Trans. by Einar Haugen and G. M. Gathorne-Hardy. Nordic Translation Ser. *Univ. of Wisconsin Press* 1967 $8.00. The Wish by Jóhann Sigurjónsson; The Golden Gate by David Stefánsson; and Atoms and Madams, by Agnar Thórdarson.

Hermannsson, Halldor. BIBLIOGRAPHICAL NOTES ON ICELANDIC AND OLD NORSE LITERATURE. 1942. *Kraus* $6.50

BIBLIOGRAPHY OF THE EDDAS. 1920. *Kraus* pap. $6.00

BIBLIOGRAPHY OF THE ICELANDIC SAGAS AND MINOR TALES. 1908. *Kraus* pap. $6.00

ICELANDIC AUTHORS OF TODAY. 1913. *Kraus* pap. $4.50

OLD ICELANDIC LITERATURE: A Bibliographical Essay. 1933. *Kraus* pap. $4.50

Hollander, Lee M., Trans. and ed. THE SAGAS OF KORMÁK and THE SWORN BROTHERS. 1949. *Kraus* 1972 $13.00

THE SKALDS: A Selection of Their Poems with Introduction and Notes. *Univ. of Michigan Press* 1968 $4.40 pap. $1.95. Lee M. Hollander was a master interpreter of this complex Old Norse poetic genre. This book will be of interest to all students of medieval poetry.

VÍGA-GLÚMS SAGA AND THE STORY OF ÖGMUND DYTT. Scandinavian Literature in Translation Ser. *Twayne* $7.50

Ingstad, Helge. WESTWARD TO VINLAND. Trans. by Erik J. Friis. *Harper* Colophon Bks. 1969 pap. $3.45. The fascinating story of the Norwegian archaeologist's search for medieval Norse house-sites on the Atlantic coast of North America.

Johnston, George, Trans. THE SAGA OF GISLI THE OUTLAW. Notes and essay by Peter Foote. *Univ. of Toronto Press* 1963 $6.00 pap. $3.95

Jones, Gwyn. A HISTORY OF THE VIKINGS. *Oxford* 1968 pap. 1973 $3.95. A thorough study of the material and intellectual culture of medieval Scandinavia.

(Trans. and ed.) EIRIK THE RED AND OTHER ICELANDIC SAGAS. *Oxford* World's Class. 1961 $3.00

Laxness, Halldór, and Sigurdur Thorarinsson. ICELAND: Impressions of a Heroic Landscape. 1960 o.p.

MacCulloch, John A. EDDIC MYTHOLOGY. *Cooper* $12.50

Magnusson, Magnus, and Hermann Pálsson, Trans. and ed. THE VINLAND SAGAS: The Norse Discovery of America. *Penguin* Classics 1965 pap. $1.95. This edition contains the literary sources regarding Norse exploration and settlement in North America (Newfoundland).

Mitchell, P. M., and Kenneth H. Ober, Eds. BIBLIOGRAPHY OF MODERN ICELANDIC LITERATURE IN TRANSLATION. Islandica Ser. *Cornell Univ. Press* 1975 $32.50

Pálsson, Hermann, Trans. and ed. HRAFNKEL'S SAGA AND OTHER STORIES. *Penguin* Classics 1971 pap. $1.95

(With Paul Edwards, Trans. and ed.) GAUTREK'S SAGA AND OTHER MEDIEVAL TALES. *New York Univ. Press* 1968 $6.95

Simpson, Jacqueline, Trans. and ed. NORTHMEN TALK: A Choice of Tales from Iceland. *Univ. of Wisconsin Press* 1965 $7.50

Turville-Petre, Gabriel. ORIGINS OF ICELANDIC LITERATURE. *Oxford* 1953 $13.75

THE BOOK OF SETTLEMENTS. c. 1130

This early work of Scandinavian historiography, along with *"Islendingabók"* (The Book of the Icelanders), is a primary source for medieval Icelandic history.

THE BOOK OF SETTLEMENTS (*Landnámábok*). Trans. and ed. by Hermann Pálsson and Paul Edwards. Icelandic Studies Ser. *Univ. of Manitoba Press* (Fort Garry, Winnipeg, Canada) 1975 $12.00 deluxe ed. $20.00

SNORRI STURLUSON. 1179–1241.

Snorri Sturluson's fame as an historian—his main work is the 16 sagas included in *"Heimskringla,"* a monumental history of Norway from its beginning until 1177—lies both in his critical approach to sources and in his fine, realistic exposition of event and motivation. To this day *"Heimskringla"* is read with gusto all over Scandinavia, and Norwegians know it as a major sourcebook of their nation's history. ("King Harald's Saga," edited separately by Magnusson and Pálsson, is part of *"Heimskringla."*) "The Prose Edda" by Snorri Sturluson was intended to be a handbook in skaldic poetry; it includes invaluable mythological tales which were on the verge of being forgotten even in Snorri's time. Many expert Scandinavian medievalists (e.g., Sigurdur Nordal and Björn M. Olsen) have pointed to Snorri as the author of the anonymous "Egil's Saga." In spite of the lack of absolute proof in this regard, included here under Snorri's name is this fascinating account of the life in Norway, England, and Iceland of the poet-warrior whose skaldic verse is renowned for its unusually emotional, personal qualities. Snorri Sturluson's own life was as eventful as those he wrote of. Returning to Iceland from exile in 1239, he again became deeply involved in serious power struggles and was murdered in 1241.

EGIL'S SAGA. 1200–1230. Trans. and ed. by Gwyn Jones. 1960. Library of Scandinavian Lit. in Translation *Twayne* 1972 $7.00

HEIMSKRINGLA. Trans. by Samuel Laing; rev. with introd. by Jacqueline Simpson *Dutton* Everyman's 2 vols. 1964 Vol. 1 The Olaf Sagas Vol. 2 Sagas of the Norse Kings each $3.95; trans. and ed. with introd. by Lee M. Hollander ill. by famous Norwegian artists *Univ. of Texas Press* 1964 $15.00

A "major sourcebook of early Norwegian history" in a smooth translation"—(*LJ*).

KING HARALD'S SAGA. Trans. by Magnus Magnusson and Hermann Pálsson. 1967. *Gannon* lib. bdg. $4.50

THE PROSE EDDA OF SNORRI STURLUSON. Trans. by A. G. Brodeur 1916 *Am. Scandinavian Soc.* $5.00; trans. by Jean I. Young *Univ. of California Press* 1964 $5.25 pap. $2.25

THE POETIC EDDA. 12th or 13th century.

A major source of insight into pagan Germanic religious concepts and cosmology, "The Poetic Edda" (also called "The Elder Edda," in contrast to the "Prose Edda" of Snorri Sturluson) was written in the twelfth or thirteenth century. Thus it was the product of Christian times but nevertheless gives a glimpse of heathen thought. Serious students of Eddic verse will find it useful to consult all available translations of the original Old Icelandic text.

THE POETIC EDDA. Trans. and rev. by Lee M. Hollander *Univ. of Texas Press* 1961 $6.00; a revision of Hollander's 1928 translation ed. and trans. by Ursula Dronke *Oxford* Vol. 1 Heroic Poems 1969 $12.00 Vol. 2 will contain the mythical poems; trans. and ed. by Henry Adams Bellows 1923 *American Scandinavian Foundation* $6.00; *Biblo and Tannen* 1969 $8.50

TRISTAN AND ISOLT (Icelandic version). 1226.

Icelandic versions of chivalric themes have their origins in medieval French literature. To assign this medieval Scandinavian "literature in translation" to Iceland is somewhat arbitrary, for interest in French courtly culture was officially promoted by the Norwegian king Hákon Hákonarson (reigned 1217–1263), who saw political value in an emulation of French aristocratic ideals. Courtly literature, through its ideals of knighthood and kingship, reinforced the royal hierarchy of Norway. By way primarily of the West Norwegian cultural center of Bergen, English (Arthurian) and German (the Nibelungen theme) literature reached Norway–Iceland. For further information, consult "Angevin Britain and Scandinavia" by Henry Goddard Leach (1921, o.p.).

In 1226 a certain "Brother Robert" was assigned the task by King Hákon of translating the "Roman de Tristan et Iseult" by the Anglo-Norman poet Thomas of Brittany. This translation is the earliest of the Norwegian–Icelandic "Sagas of Knights." Brother Robert's version of the French original is especially valuable as a complement to the now incomplete French "Tristan and Iseult" (q.v.) and the German version of Gottfried von Strassburg (q.v.).

THE SAGA OF TRISTRAM AND ÍSÖND. Trans. and ed. by Paul Schach. *Univ. of Nebraska Press* 1973 $9.50

EYRBYGGJA SAGA.   1230–1280.

This "saga of Icelanders" tells of the people of the farmstead Eyrr and their enemies. The story is told with great interest in local tradition and ancient customs, so the saga is especially valuable for students of early Scandinavian culture.

EYRBYGGJA SAGA. Trans. by Paul Schach; introd. and verse translations by Lee M. Hollander 1959 o.p.; trans. by Hermann Pálsson and Paul Edwards New Saga Lib. Ser. *Univ. of Toronto Press* 1972 $6.00

LAXDAELA SAGA.   c. 1250

This unforgettable "family saga" is "a tale of a love triangle with all its subterfuges, vicious insinuations, retaliations, and heartaches, presented with the detachment and subtle discernment so typical of the sagas"—(Arent in her edition). The story is not tightly knit, yet the numerous subplots do point to the broad design.

LAXDAELA SAGA. Trans. and ed. by Magnus Magnusson and Hermann Pálsson *Penguin* Classics 1969 pap. $1.95; trans. and ed. by H. Margaret Arent 1964 o.p.

NJÁL'S SAGA.   c. 1280.

"Njál's Saga" may well be Iceland's most magnificent literary work of the Middle Ages. Written by an anonymous author—a situation typical of "Sagas of Icelanders"—the saga tells of events in southern Iceland in the years 960–1015, the period in which Iceland was formally converted to Christianity. The nuances of characterization achieved by the author are unique in saga literature. The ethical views observed in the story are both heathen and Christian; the two philosophies conflict in a fateful drama. Note that the translation by Dasent is very old and extremely Victorian in style. The edition by Magnusson and Pálsson is superb and equipped with a fine introduction and notes.

THE STORY OF BURNT NJÁL. Trans. by Sir George W. Dasent. 1861. *Dutton* Everyman's $3.95

NJÁL'S SAGA. Trans. by Magnus Magnusson and Hermann Pálsson. *Penguin* Classics pap. $1.95

Books about Njal's Saga

Njal's Saga: A Critical Approach. By Lars Lönnroth. *Univ. of California Press* 1975 $15.00
Njal's Saga: A Literary Masterpiece. By Einar Olafur Sveinsson. Trans. and ed. by Paul Schach. *Univ. of Nebraska Press* 1974 $9.50. A very useful edition of the important study from 1933.

THE KING'S MIRROR (SPECULUM REGALE).   13th century.

This didactic work on courtly behavior belongs, strictly speaking, to Old Norwegian literature; similar works are present in Old French and medieval English literature. Because it illuminates the social concepts illustrated by the Old Norse–Icelandic sagas in many instances, "The King's Mirror" is essential reading for the student of medieval Icelandic literature and for the student of medieval European history in general. In the form of a conversation between father and son, the relationships of various social classes to one another and to God are discussed.

THE KING'S MIRROR. Trans. and ed. by Laurence Marcellus Larson. 1917. Scandinavian Lit. in Translation *Twayne* 1973 $8.50

STURLUNGA SAGA.   c. 1300.

The thirteenth century in Iceland was one of great literary production, especially in the area of biographies of nobility and kings. Both individuals and events in the twelfth and thirteenth centuries are the stuff of the large collection of accounts entitled "Sturlunga Saga," so named because of the prominence of the Sturlung family in Icelandic affairs. The heart of this work is formed by Sturla Tordsson's account of the period 1200–1262, at which time Iceland lost its independence and came under the power of the king of Norway.

STURLUNGA SAGA. Trans. by Julia McGrew; introd. by R. George Thomas. *Twayne* 1974 2 vols. each $12.50

VÖLSUNGA SAGA.   13th century.

The Icelandic prose saga of the Volsungs tells of the ruin of their chief, Sigurd, by Gudrun, his wife. In this saga Brynhild is the chief of the Valkyries, whom Sigurd had saved and loved. The same poetic materials were used in the German *"Nibelungenlied,"* (*q.v.*) where Sigurd becomes Siegfried, Gudrun is Kriemhild and Brynhild is Brunhild or Brünnehilde. Wagner used them in his opera cycle, "The Ring of the Nibelungs," Ibsen (*q.v.*) in "The Vikings at Helgeland" and Hebbel in his dramatic trilogy, "The Nibelungs." William Morris (*q.v.*) made them known to English readers through his "Lovers of Gudrun" in "The Earthly Paradise" (3 vols. 1868–1870, o.p.) and "Sigurd the Volsung" (1876). His own poetic adaptations do not measure up to his translation. A rare edition of this was reprinted at the Chiswick Press and published by *Longmans, Green* in 1901 with the Golden type designed by Morris for his Kelmscott Press.

THE SONG OF THE VOLSUNGS AND THE NIBELUNGS. Trans. by William Morris. 1870. (With title "Volsunga Saga") ed. by Robert W. Gutman. *Macmillan* 1962 Collier Bks. pap. $1.50

SIGURJÓNSSON, JÓHANN.   1880–1919.

Sigurjónsson is one of the best of modern Icelandic dramatists. His recurrent theme was the tragedy inevitable in the lives of those whose passionate ambition drives them to exceed their limitations—the Greek sin of *hubris*. In "The Wish," Loftur, a student, seeks power through the black arts of sorcery, bringing misery to the girl who loves him and death to himself.

Sigurjónsson, scion of a wealthy family, was sent to Copenhagen University to become a veterinarian but left it to write plays (in Danish and Icelandic—"The Wish" exists in both versions) and was the first modern writer of Iceland to achieve fame beyond its borders. "Eyvind of the Hills" (1911), first produced in Copenhagen, brought him his initial success and was later performed in Reykjavik and other Scandinavian cities. An early Swedish film was made from it. Sigurjónsson's approach to his characters is lyrical and compassionate, but fate in his plays is inexorable.

LOFT'S WISH. 1915. *Branden* 1967 $3.00; (trans. as "The Wish" in "Fire and Ice: Three Icelandic Plays") ed. by Einar Haugen Nordic Translation Ser. *Univ. of Wisconsin Press* 1967 $8.00

GUNNARSSON, GUNNAR.   1889–

"In the forefront of Icelandic writers now living, who have . . . sought a wider public through the medium of a foreign tongue, stands the novelist Gunnar Gunnarsson. . . . Enormously productive, he is one of the most widely read writers in Scandinavia, and known far beyond the borders of the northern countries"—(Bach, "The History of the Scandinavian Literatures"). Novelist, poet, and dramatist, Gunnarsson has been prolific in all the creative literary fields, including the historical novel and short story. Like many other Icelandic authors, Gunarsson spent a period in Copenhagen, returning to Iceland in 1939 and writing both in Danish and Icelandic. He is known as a brilliant interpreter of Icelandic life, particularly that of its humble people, and as a writer of subtle psychological novels of romantic theme. "The Black Cliffs" is one of these, having to do with the involvement of a young couple in a sensational murder case. "The History of the Family at Borg," translated as "Guest the One-Eyed" (1912–1914), and the autobiographical "The Church on the Mountain" (1924–1928) are Gunnarsson's best-known works.

THE BLACK CLIFFS. 1929. Trans. from the Danish by Cecil Wood; introd. by Richard N. Ringler. Nordic Translation Ser. *Univ. of Wisconsin Press* 1967 $7.50

THÓRDARSON, THORBERGUR.   1889?–

"In Search of My Beloved," a novella by the Icelandic poet, essayist, and novelist is part of a longer autobiographical novel, "An Iceland Aristocracy," and "tells of a young poet travelling around Iceland in search of his [dream girl] whom he is too shy to approach. . . . Well written, with a touch of humour, and ably translated"—(*LJ*). Thórdarson too was something of a "drifter" in his youth until he was given a place in the University of Iceland in 1913, where he began to find himself and grew interested in the language and folk culture of Iceland. He devoted himself to "word collecting" for a while, which meant further wandering, but became interested in mysticism and the supernatural, as well as in social problems, all of which became elements in his work. His essays "A Letter to Laura" created a stir on publication and had an influence on Laxness (*q.v.*). In recent years he has written chiefly novels. (Thórdarson's birth date is variously given as 1899, 1891, or 1889, of which the latter—Bach's—seems the most likely.)

IN SEARCH OF MY BELOVED. 1938. Trans. by Kenneth G. Chapman; introd. by Kristján Karlsson. *American-Scandinavian Foundation* and *Twayne* 1967 $4.00

LAXNESS, HALLDÓR KILJAN.   1902–   (Nobel Prize 1955)

When making the 1955 Nobel Prize award to Laxness, the Swedish Academy of Letters cited "his vivid epic writing, which has renewed the great Icelandic narrative art." He had been awarded the Stalin Prize for literature in 1943. "Independent People" (1934–1939, U.S. 1939, 1946, o.p.) was a best seller in this country. "Paradise Reclaimed," based in part on his own experiences in the United States, is a novel about a nineteenth-century Icelandic farmer and his travels and experiences, culminating in his conversion to the Mormon Church. Although Laxness has been by turns a Catholic convert, a Communist and a target of the radical press, he has described himself as one "who loves the Russians but practices a lot of the American way of life." "Though Laxness came to believe that the novelist's best material is to be found in the proletariat, his rejection of middle-class concerns was never complete, and the ambiguity of his attitude toward the conflict of cultural values accounts for the mixture of humor and pathos that is characteristic of all his novels"—(*SR*). He owes much to the tradition of the sagas, and writes with understated restraint, concentrating almost entirely on external details—from which he extracts, by the manner of his telling, the utmost in absurdity. The *Atlantic* finds that "The Fish Can Sing," the adventures of a young man of 1900 who wants to be a singer, "simmers with an ironic, disrespectful mirth which gives unexpected dimensions to the themes of lost innocence and the nature of art."

SALKA VALKA. 1931–1932. Trans. by F. H. Lyon. 1963 o.p. A novel of socialistic vision and love set in an Icelandic fishing village.

THE FISH CAN SING. Trans. by Magnus Magnusson. 1967 o.p.

(With Sigurdur Thorarinsson) ICELAND: Impressions of a Heroic Landscape. o.p.

WORLD LIGHT. 1955. Trans. by Magnus Magnusson. Nordic Translation Ser. *Univ. of Wisconsin Press* 1969 $14.00

PARADISE RECLAIMED. 1960. Trans. by Magnus Magnusson. 1962. *Melvin McCosh Bookseller* $8.50

Books about Laxness

Halldór Laxness. 1952. By Peter Hallberg. Trans. by Rory McTurk. World Authors Ser. *Twayne* 1969 $6.95

NORWEGIAN LITERATURE

Asbjörnsen, P. C., and Jörgen E. Moe. EAST OF THE SUN AND WEST OF THE MOON. *Macmillan* 1953 $3.95. Norwegian fairy tales are best known in the form given them by the two nineteenth century collectors Asbjörnsen and Moe.

Beyer, Harald. A HISTORY OF NORWEGIAN LITERATURE. Trans. and ed. by Einar Haugen. *New York University Press* (for the American-Scandinavian Foundation) 1956 $10.00

Christiansen, Reidar T., Ed. FOLKTALES OF NORWAY. Trans. by Pat S. Iversen. Folktales of the World Ser. *Univ. of Chicago Press* 1964 $9.00 pap. $3.95

Christiansen, Sigurd W. CHAFF BEFORE THE WIND. 1925–1929. *Greenwood* 1974 $13.75

TWO LIVING AND ONE DEAD. 1931. *Greenwood* 1975 $14.25. Novel depicting religious and ethical conflict in small-town Norway.

Derry, T. K. A. A HISTORY OF MODERN NORWAY, 1814–1972. *Oxford* 1973 $16.00. A well-done overview of political, cultural (including literary), and economic development.

Popperwell, Ronald G. NORWAY. Nations of the Modern World Ser. *Praeger* 1972 $11.50. An excellent presentation of the modern nation and its development.

Sandemose, Aksel. THE WEREWOLF. 1958. Trans. by Gustaf Lannestock; introd. by Harald S. Naess. Nordic Translation Ser. *Univ. of Wisconsin Press* 1966 $6.50. The author's last novel, written in surrealist manner. Sandemose is a more important writer than this one translation would suggest; he is concerned with psychological conflict between individual and society. The "werewolf" symbolizes the spiritual repression that keeps the individual from happiness.

Snorri Sturluson. *See his main entry under Iceland, this Chapter, for "Heimskringla," a major source of early Norwegian history.*

Undset, Sigrid. SAGA OF SAINTS. 1937. Trans. by E. C. Ramsden. *Bks. for Libraries* 1968 $13.00. Medieval Norwegian church history presented by the major writer and devout Catholic Sigrid Undset.

TRUE AND UNTRUE AND OTHER NORSE TALES. *Knopf* 1945 $3.00 lib. bdg. $5.69. These renditions of folktales originally collected by Asbjörnsen and Moe show yet another aspect of Undset's writing.

IBSEN, HENRIK (JOHAN). 1828–1906.

It has now been almost a century since the appearance of Ibsen's "The Pillars of Society," the first of the "social plays" by the Norwegian who has had the most profound influence on the direction and techniques of modern stagecraft. The timelessness of the dramas from this period—including "A Doll's House," "Ghosts," and "An Enemy of the People"—is attested by the many Broadway, television, and repertory productions that pay perennial tribute to Ibsen's incisive characterizations of individuals in conflict. Conflict with self rather than social forces best describes the plays of the next period, 1884–1890: "The Wild Duck," "Rosmersholm," "The Lady from the Sea," and "Hedda Gabler." "A Doll's House" and "Hedda Gabler" present two equally acute views of the price and value of women's liberation; Ibsen clearly did not offer simplistic programs for social groups but rather wrote about unique individuals. Ibsen's last plays, in the years 1892–1899, "The Master Builder," "Little Eyolf," "John Gabriel Borkman," and "When We Dead Awaken," generally concern the self-destructive aspects of artistic ambition. The symbolism in these plays makes them more demanding and less well known today, as are Ibsen's early work (including "Brand," 1866, and "Peer Gynt," 1867) reflecting romantic and nationalistic preoccupations. Nevertheless, Ibsen's genius inspires modern producers to stage "Peer Gynt," a technical venture which Ibsen himself may never have intended for his dramatic poem (set to music by Edvard Grieg in 1876).

The reader's needs may serve as guide when the wealth of Ibsen editions is surveyed. The library and the professional student of modern drama will turn to James W. McFarland's edition, "The Oxford Ibsen," of which seven volumes are in print. The eighth and final volume will contain "Little Eyolf," "John Gabriel Borkman," and "When We Dead Awaken." The standard English-language edition of earlier generations (trans. and ed. by William Archer, 1906–1912, o.p.) will perhaps be consulted for the sake of Archer's introductions, but the modern reader will find that the English of the plays has aged considerably. Similarly, the translations by R. Farquharson Sharp are now more than 60 years old. Currency of language is very important for an appreciation of Ibsen's major plays, and in recent years the efforts of Una Ellis-Fermor, Rolf Fjelde, Eva Le Gallienne, Michael Meyer, and Peter Watts have provided good translations of the essential plays. In discussing the drama of Ibsen, Eva Le Gallienne is also able to draw from her distinguished career in the theater, both as actress and manager.

F. L. Lucas' treatment of Ibsen, "The Drama of Ibsen and Strindberg" (1962), is still o.p. On the positive side, we now have the translation by Einar Haugen and A. E. Santianello of the second, revised edition of Halvdan Koht's "The Life of Ibsen" (1956). Koht's biography is the most authoritative, but in the United States more publicity has been given Michael Meyer's "Ibsen, a Biography" (1971). The virtue of Meyer's biography is the vast amount of information brought together from other sources, including Koht; yet he does not advance new insights.

THE OXFORD IBSEN. Ed. by James Walter McFarlane. Vols. 1–7 are available. *Oxford* Vol. 1 Early Plays trans. by Graham Orton 1970 $27.25 Vol. 2 The Vikings at Helgeland; Love's Comedy; The Pretenders trans. by Jens Arup, James W. McFarlane, Evelyn Ramsden, and Glynne Wickham 1962 $12.00 Vol. 3: Brand; Peer Gynt trans. by James Kirkup and Christopher Fry 1972 $22.00 Vol. 4 The League of Youth; Emperor Galilean trans. by James W. McFarlane and Graham Orton 1963 $12.00 Vol. 5 Pillars of Society; A Doll's House; Ghosts trans. by James W. McFarlane 1961 $12.00 Vol. 6 An Enemy of the People; The Wild Duck; Rosmersholm trans. by James W. McFarlane 1960 $12.00 Vol. 7 The Lady from the Sea; Hedda Gabler; The Master Builder trans. by Jens Arup and James W. McFarlane 1966 $13.75

In the following list, collections are grouped first by translator; these are followed by editions of individual plays and other material.

SEVEN FAMOUS PLAYS. Trans. and ed. by William Archer. *Humanities Press* 1961 $8.25

MASTER BUILDER AND OTHER PLAYS. Trans. by Una Ellis-Fermor. *Penguin.* pap. $2.95. Includes Rosmersholm; Little Eyolf; John Gabriel Borkman.

HEDDA GABLER AND OTHER PLAYS. Trans. by Una Ellis-Fermor. *Penguin* pap. $2.25. Includes Pillars of the Community and The Wild Duck.

GHOSTS. (And "Enemy of the People," "Warriors of Helgeland") trans. by R. Farquharson Sharp. *Dutton* Everyman's 1935 $3.95

PRETENDERS. (And "Pillars of Society," "Rosmersholm") trans. by R. Farquharson Sharp. *Dutton* Everyman's $3.95

FOUR GREAT PLAYS. Trans. by R. Farquharson Sharp. *Bantam* pap. $1.25. Includes Doll's House; An Enemy of the People; Ghosts and The Wild Duck.

FOUR MAJOR PLAYS. Trans. by Rolf Fjelde. *New Am. Lib.* Signet 2 vols. Vol. 1 1965 Doll's House; The Wild Duck; Hedda Gabler; and The Master Builder pap. $.95 Vol. 2 1970 Ghosts; An Enemy of the People; Lady from the Sea; and John Gabriel Borkman pap. $1.25

THREE PLAYS BY IBSEN. Introd. by Seymour L. Flaxman. *Dell* Laurel Leaf Lib. pap. $1.25. Includes Hedda Gabler; A Doll's House; and The Wild Duck.

SIX PLAYS. Trans. by Eva Le Gallienne. *Random* Modern Lib. pap. $2.95. Includes Doll's House; Enemy of the People; Rosmersholm; Hedda Gabler; The Master Builder.

THE WILD DUCK AND OTHER PLAYS. Trans. by Eva Le Gallienne. *Random* Modern Lib. pap. $2.95. Includes Pillars of Society; Lady from the Sea; Little Eyolf; John Gabriel Borkman; and When We Dead Awaken.

PLAYS: An Enemy of the People; The Wild Duck; Rosmersholm. Trans. and ed. by James W. McFarlane. *Oxford* 1971 pap. $4.50

PLAYS. Trans. and ed. by James W. McFarlane. *Oxford* Paperback Ser. 1970 pap. $2.95. Includes Pillars of Society; A Doll's House; and Ghosts.

GHOSTS AND THREE OTHER PLAYS. Trans. by Michael Meyer. *Doubleday* Anchor Bks. 1966 pap. $2.95. Includes A Doll's House; An Enemy of the People; and Rosmersholm.

HEDDA GABLER AND THREE OTHER PLAYS. Trans. by Michael Meyer. *Doubleday* Anchor Bks. 1961 pap. $2.50. Includes The Pillars of Society; The Wild Duck; and Little Eyolf.

WHEN WE DEAD AWAKEN AND THREE OTHER PLAYS. Trans. by Michael Meyer. *Doubleday* Anchor Bks. 1971 pap. $2.50. Includes The Lady from the Sea; The Master Builder; and John Gabriel Borkman.

EARLY PLAYS. Trans. by Anders Orbeck. 1921. *Kraus* $16.00. Includes Cataline; The Warrior's Barrow; and Olaf Liljekrans.

LATE PLAYS OF HENRIK IBSEN. Trans. by Arvid Paulson. *Harper* 1972 pap. $3.95

A DOLL'S HOUSE AND OTHER PLAYS. Trans. by Peter Watts. *Penguin* pap. $1.95. Includes League of Youth and Lady from the Sea.

GHOSTS AND OTHER PLAYS. Trans. by Peter Watts. *Penguin* $1.95. Includes Public Enemy and When We Dead Awaken.

FOUR PLAYS. *Holt* 2nd ed. 1970 pap. $2.00

ELEVEN PLAYS OF HENRIK IBSEN. Introd. by Henry L. Mencken. *Random* (Modern Lib.) Giants $5.95

TERJE WIEGEN. 1862. Trans. by D. Svennungsen 1923. *Melvin McCosh Bookseller* $10.00. Poems by Ibsen.

BRAND. 1866. *Dutton* Everyman's 1959 $3.95; trans. by Michael Meyer. *Doubleday* Anchor Bks. pap. $1.45

PEER GYNT. 1867. *Assoc. Booksellers* Airmont pap. $.60; trans. by R. Farquharson Sharp. *Dutton* Everyman's $3.95; trans. and ed. by Kai Jurgensen and Robert Schenkan. *AHM Pub. Corp.* Crofts Class. 1966 pap. $.85; trans. by Michael Meyer. *Doubleday* Anchor Bks. 1963 pap. $1.45; trans. by Peter Watts. *Penguin* pap. $1.75

PEER GYNT: A Play in Five Acts. 1867. Ed. and trans. by James Walter McFarlane. *Oxford* 1970 pap. $1.95

A DOLLS' HOUSE. 1879. *Dutton* Everyman's pap. $1.95; (and "The Wild Duck") *Dutton* Everyman's $3.95

GHOSTS. 1881. *Dutton* Everyman's pap. $1.50; *Avon* Bard Bks. 1965 pap. $.95

THE WILD DUCK. 1884. Trans. and ed. by Kai Jurgensen and Robert Schenkan. *AHM Pub. Corp.* 1966 pap. $.85; *Avon* Bard Bks. 1965 pap. $.60; trans. and ed. by Dounia B. Christiani. *Norton* Critical Eds. $5.00 pap. $1.95; trans. by Max Faber. *Theatre Arts* pap. $2.35

ROSMERSHOLM. 1886. Trans. by Ann Jellicoe. *T. Y. Crowell* (Chandler Pub.) 1961 pap. $1.25

HEDDA GABLER. 1890. Trans. and ed. by Alan S. Downer. *AHM Pub. Corp.* Crofts Class. 1961 pap. $1.25; ed. by Henry Popkin; trans. by Kai Jurgensen and Robert Schenkkan. *Avon* Bard Bks. 1975 pap. $.95

THE MASTER BUILDER. 1892. Trans. with commentary by Eva Le Gallienne. *New York Univ. Press* 1955 $7.95; ed. by Emlyn Williams. *Theatre Arts* 1967 pap. $1.95. A thorough study of the play and its production.

CORRESPONDENCE OF HENRICK IBSEN. Ed. by Mary Morrison 1905. *Haskell* 1975 lib. bdg. $19.95

SPEECHES AND NEW LETTERS. Trans. by Arne Kildal 1910. *Haskell* 1972 $12.95

LETTERS AND SPEECHES. Trans. and ed. by Evert Sprinchorn. *Farrar, Straus* 1964 o.p.

Books about Ibsen

Henrik Ibsen: A Critical Biography. 1890. By Henrik Jaeger. *Blom* $12.75; *Richard West* repr. of 1901 ed. 1973 $11.75

Henrik Ibsen. 1899. By Georg Brandes. *Blom* $8.75; *Richard West* $8.50. A discussion of the style and themes, with emphasis on the social dramas, by the Danish scholar–critic, a contemporary of Ibsen.

Ibsen: The Intellectual Background. 1946. By Brian W. Downs. *Octagon* 1969 $10.00

The Life of Ibsen. By Halvdan Koht. 2nd rev. ed. 1956. Trans. by Einar Haugen and A. E. Santaniello. *Blom* 1971 $17.50

Ibsen Bibliography, 1928–1957. Ed. by Ingrid Tedford. Norsk Bibliografisk Bibliotek Ser. *Universitetsforlag* 1961 pap. $7.00

Ibsen: A Collection of Critical Essays. Ed. by Rolf Fjelde. *Prentice-Hall* 1965 $6.95 pap. $1.95

Contemporary Approaches to Ibsen. By Alex Bolckmans and others. *Humanities Press* 1966 $5.50

Ibsen's Dramatic Method: A Study of the Prose Dramas. Scandia Bks. *Universitetsforlag* 1971 pap. $10.00

Ibsen: The Man and the Dramatist. By Francis Bull. *Folcroft* 1973 $7.50

Henrik Ibsen: A Bibliography of Criticism and Biography, with an Index to Characters. By Ina T. Firkins. *Folcroft* 1973 lib. bdg. $10.00

Henrik Ibsen: A Critical Anthology. Ed. by James W. McFarlane. *Peter Smith* $6.00. A very informative collection of comments from Ibsen's time to the present; includes selected bibliography.

Ibsen: A Critical Study. By John Northam. Major European Authors Ser. *Cambridge* 1973 $14.95 pap. $5.95

The Ibsen Cycle. By Brian Johnston. International Studies and Translation Ser. *Twayne* 1975 $17.50

The Modern Ibsen: A Reconsideration. By Hermann J. Weigand. 1953. Select Bibliographies Reprint Ser. *Bks. for Libraries* $16.00; *Dutton* pap. $2.25

A Study of Six Plays by Ibsen. 1950. By Brian W. Downs. *Octagon* 1972 $11.00

HAMSUN, KNUT. 1859–1952. (Nobel Prize 1920)

The writing of Knut Hamsun introduced into Norwegian literature a predominant concern with the immediate emotional life of the individual without reference to social programs or abstract "truths." The very title of Hamsun's first major work, "Hunger," suggests its theme: the psychic ebb and flood of a brilliant young writer who actually starves but who is filled with spontaneity and emotional freedom which brings both joy and misery. Hamsun sharply criticized naturalist writers for the gray superficial reality they described. He made it his goal, through art and psychology together, to illuminate the mysterious realities of the individual psyche. Yet as a poetic philosopher Hamsun is clearly anti-intellectual.

Influences such as Strindberg (*q.v.*), Nietzsche (*q.v.*), and Georg Brandes (*q.v.*) are present in Hamsun's development, but his childhood in the intensely dramatic natural world of northern Norway did as much to create his basic mood. The shifting weather and rich colors of his early home are expressed anew in Hamsun's lyrical and often ecstatic treatment of a wide range of fictional and yet psychologically credible personalities. Both "Pan" and "Victoria" are rich in the prose poetry, eroticism, and pantheism which inspired Hamsun throughout his life. His almost mystical admiration for the spontaneous individual living close to nature led Hamsun to despise industrial society and to mythologize traditional rural Norwegian patriarchal families. He saw degeneracy—money-grubbers and weak conformists—where others saw progressive industrialism. "Growth of the Soil," for which Hamsun received the Nobel Prize in 1920, is his gospel of the simple life and by implication a beautiful attack on modern civilization. It is ironic that Hamsun's visionary and violent love of traditional country life coaxed him in the latter part of his life into a fateful intellectual sympathy with Nazi dogma. Although he was scorned and severely punished by his countrymen after World War II, Hamsun's contribution to world literature is great and beyond reproach.

THE CULTURAL LIFE OF MODERN AMERICA. 1889. Trans. and ed. by Barbara G. Morgridge. *Harvard Univ. Press* 1969 $10.00. Hamsun's early views—rather casually documented but firmly espoused throughout his life—on American life and society, based on his experience in the United States in the 1880s.

HUNGER. 1890. New translation by Robert Bly; introd. by Isaac Bashevis Singer. *Farrar, Straus* 1967 $7.75 Noonday pap. $3.45; *Avon* pap. $1.95

MYSTERIES. 1892. Trans. by Gerry Bothmer. *Farrar, Straus* 1971 $8.95; *Avon* 1975 pap. $1.95

PAN: From Lieutenant Thomas Glahn's Papers. 1894. Trans. by James W. McFarlane. *Farrar, Straus* $5.95 Noonday 1955 pap. $2.65; *Avon* 1975 pap. $1.75

VICTORIA. 1898. Trans. by Oliver Stallybrass. *Farrar, Straus* 1969 Noonday pap. $2.95

THE WANDERER. 1906–09. Trans. by Oliver and Gunnvor Stallybrass. *Farrar, Straus* 1975 $7.95

GROWTH OF THE SOIL. 1917. Trans. by W. W. Worster. 2 vols. 1921 o.p. *Knopf* 1-vol. ed. 1953 $8.95; *Random* Vintage Bks. pap. $2.45

ON OVERGROWN PATHS: A Memoir. 1949. Trans. with introd. by Carl L. Anderson. 1967 o.p. Hamsun's lucid account of the treatment he received after arrest for treason during the German occupation of Norway.

RÖLVAAG, OLE EDVART. 1876–1931.

Norwegian-born Rölvaag emigrated to the United States (South Dakota) at the age of twenty in 1896. Following a college education in Minnesota and Norway, he began the teaching (at St. Olaf College, Minnesota) and writing career that was to bring him fame as an interpreter of the Norwegian–American cultural experience. Rölvaag's understanding of immigrant life on the prairie is the source of the novels that have given his name a solid place in both American and Norwegian literature. His first, highly autobiographical work, "The Third Life of Per Smevik," was published under the pseudonym Paal Mörck. Rölvaag's major work, "Giants in the Earth," is a translation of the first two of four novels dealing with the family of Per Hansa; "Peder Victorious" and "Their Fathers' God" complete the epic, although these two novels are considered to be less compelling. A new Norwegian edition of the tetralogy was published in 1975 by the Norwegian Book Club. The fascinating novels of Rölvaag, Alfred Hauge (*q.v.*) and Vilhelm Moberg (*q.v.*) bear witness to the fact that emigration to America was a major phenomenon in Scandinavian history. Americans may read them as an accurate comment on American social history.

THE THIRD LIFE OF PER SMEVIK. 1912. Trans. by Ella Valborg Tweet and Solveig Zempel. *Dillon* 1971 $5.95

THE BOAT OF LONGING. 1921. Trans. by Nora O. Solum. *Greenwood* 1974 $13.00

GIANTS IN THE EARTH. 1925. Trans. by Lincoln Colcord and the author. *Harper* lib. bdg. $12.50 pap. $1.25

PEDER VICTORIOUS: A Tale of the Pioneers Twenty Years After. 1928. Trans. by Nora O. Solum. *Greenwood* 1973 $14.25

PURE GOLD. 1930. Trans. by Sivert Erdahl. *Greenwood* 1973 $13.50

THEIR FATHERS' GOD. 1931. Trans. by Trygve M. Ager. *Greenwood* 1974 $13.75

Books about Rölvaag

Rölvaag: His Life and Art. By Paul Reigstad. *Univ. of Nebraska Press* 1972 $8.50

SANDEL, CORA (pseud. of Sara Fabricius).   1880–1974.

"Alberta Alone," a Norwegian classic, is an autobiographical trilogy ("Alberte and Jacob," 1926; "Alberte and Freedom," 1931; and "Just Alberte," 1939) in the tradition of Sigrid Undset (*q.v.*). Cora Sandel describes with insight and honesty the coming to maturity of a small-town Norwegian girl in a "magnificent work of introspection"—(*LJ*). "If the book has a fault, it is in being a little too unhurried in its wanderings. Miss Sandel is a stylist, a writer of marvelous delicacy; and the standard trouble with beautiful writers is that not enough happens in their books. Alberta merely exists in Norway, only begins to live in Paris, has a child by a painter, tries sometimes to write. Nothing more. *Alberta Alone* is not one of the very great novels . . . but it is one of those that make you remember certain things you thought you had forgotten. To read it is, in part, to relive the painful experience of growing human"—(*SR*). Cora Sandel has written other novels as well as short stories. Her insight into the psyches of women and artists is especially acute and justly praised.

ALBERTA ALONE. Trilogy. Trans. by Elizabeth Rokkan. 1966 o.p.

UNDSET, SIGRID.   1882–1949.   (Nobel Prize 1928)

The daughter of archeologist Ingvald Undset, Sigrid Undset's comprehensive knowledge of medieval Scandinavian culture has its literary monuments in "Kristin Lavransdatter" and "The Master of Hestviken," historical novels that depict both the concrete and psychological dimensions of life in the Norwegian Middle Ages. In Norway, Undset's fiction is categorized according to the time of the action: medieval or modern. "Jenny," an idealistic and tragic love story, is one of the latter novels. Norwegian criticism of Sigrid Undset's writing centers on her religiosity—she became a conservative, almost reactionary Catholic in Lutheran Norway in the 1920s—an intensity of belief rather naturally expressed in the medieval novels. On the polemical side, she has written works of primarily religious moment, for example, "Saga of Saints" (trans. by E. C. Ramsden. 1937. *Bks. for Libraries* 1968 $13.00). Yet the medieval novels are not polemical. In fact, the central motifs are eroticism, marriage, and family life, in short, the full life of a medieval woman who sees herself in the light of contemporary Christian beliefs. These novels are great, realistic delineations of medieval personalities. Cultural, autobiographical, and religious topics constitute a large and interesting portion of Undset's writing. "Longest Years" and "Stages on the Road" are autobiographical, while "Men, Women and Places" is a collection of essays. "Happy Times in Norway," also autobiographical, was written in the United States during World War II, when Sigrid Undset escaped the German occupation of Norway.

JENNY. 1911. Trans. by W. Emmé. *Fertig* 1975 $12.00

KRISTIN LAVRANSDATTER: The Bridal Wreath; The Mistress of Husaby; The Cross. 1920–1922. Trans. by C. Archer and J. S. Scott. *Knopf* 1935 $10.00

THE MASTER OF HESTVIKEN: The Axe; The Snake Pit; The Son Avenger; In the Wilderness. 1925–1927. Trans. by A. G. Chater. *Knopf* 1952 $8.95

MEN, WOMEN AND PLACES. 1938. Trans. by A. G. Chater. U.S. 1939. *Bks. for Libraries* $13.25

STAGES ON THE ROAD. 1933. Trans. by A. G. Chater. U.S. 1934. *Bks. for Libraries* $12.25

LONGEST YEARS. 1934. Trans. by A. G. Chater. U.S. 1935. *Kraus* $18.00

HAPPY TIMES IN NORWAY. 1942. Trans. by Joran Birkeland. 1942 o.p.

Books about Sigrid Undset

Sigrid Undset. By Carl F. Bayerschmidt. World Authors Ser. *Twayne* 1970 $7.50
Sigrid Undset. A Study in Christian Realism. 1949. By Andreas H. Winsnes. Trans. by Peter G. Foote 1953. *Greenwood* $12.75

VESAAS, TARJEI. 1897–1970.

By 1934, when "The Great Cycle" appeared, Tarjei Vesaas had published eleven works. In this novel he clearly shows the enduring qualities of his later work: delicate human portraiture, compelling symbolism and allegory, and constant sensitivity to universal problems (hope, fear, love) of the human being both alone and in society. At the end of his life Vesaas had written some 35 works of prose and poetry and had received the Venice Triennale Prize in 1952 and the Nordic Council Prize for literature in 1964. Perhaps the foremost writer of novels and short stories of his generation in Norway, he wrote of common people in rural Norway who represented humanity at its best and its worst. His realism is psychological rather than historical, as in "The Seed," which deals with the hatred, fear, and mass psychosis spawned in a small community by the murder of a girl. It is apparent that the barbarous acts of the killer's lynchers mirror the hideous transformation of decent people in fascist Europe of the late 1930s. Children and adolescents occupy a special place in Vesaas' writing; in both "Spring Night" and "Birds" the reader participates in the inner life of youth observing the adult world. As for Vesaas' poetry, published rather late in his career, it "has contributed significantly to the liberation of Norwegian poetry from conventional patterns. His form is modern and international, free from the musical regularity of the popular ballad, and . . . his themes are mostly the things which gladden his inland heart—the mountain, the snow, and the trees"—(Naess).

THE GREAT CYCLE. 1934. Trans. by Elizabeth Rokkan; introd. by Harald Naess. Nordic Translation Ser. *Univ. of Wisconsin Press* 1967 $6.50

THE SEED and THE SPRING NIGHT. (1940 and 1954). Trans. by Kenneth Chapman. *Universitetsforlag* 1964 $10.00. Two novels.

LAND OF THE HIDDEN FIRES. 1953. Trans. by Fritz König and Jerry Crisp; introd. by Fritz König. *Wayne State Univ. Press* 1973 $9.95. Poetry.

BIRDS. 1957. Trans. by Torbjorn Stoverud and Michael Barnes. *Morrow* 1972 pap. $2.25

BRIDGES. 1966. Trans. by Elizabeth Rokkan. *Morrow* 1970 $5.00

BOAT IN THE EVENING. 1968. Trans. by Elizabeth Rokkan. *Morrow* $5.95

THIRTY POEMS. Trans. by Kenneth Chapman. *Universitetsforlag* 1971 $6.00

Books about Vesaas

Tarjei Vesaas. By Kenneth Chapman. World Authors Ser. *Twayne* 1970 $6.95

HAUGE, ALFRED. 1915–

Religious problems viewed from a distinctly Christian point of view are the themes of this important writer's recent work, yet his fame in Scandinavia rests upon the dramatic historical trilogy "Cleng Peerson" from the early 1960s. These carefully researched and exciting novels are in the form of letters written by the poor farmer's son Cleng Peerson (1782–1865) who has become known as "the father of Norwegian emigration" in the early nineteenth century. The original Norwegian version was slightly abridged by the author for this American translation. Thanks to its general factual basis and realistic depiction of conditions in Norway and the United States, "Cleng Peerson" has quasi-documentary value as a comment on the making of American society. Hauge has written some thirty other books, four in 1975 alone.

CLENG PEERSON. 1961–65. Trans. by Erik Friis. *Twayne* 1975 2 vols. $25.00

MYKLE, AGNAR. 1915–

Ben Ray Redman once wrote in the *Saturday Review:* "Mykle's talent is one of the greatest that I have encountered in forty years of reviewing. He is a passionate poet and a naked realist, and he can speak with the organ tones of a prophet." His three powerful and extraordinarily vivid novels were at once successful, but he was accused of eroticism and "The Song of the Red Ruby" was withdrawn from circulation in Norway until eventually cleared of obscenity charges by the Norwegian Supreme Court. Mykle's essential message is man's restless search for understanding of self, and his early novels express this theme with rich poetic lyricism. These autobiographical works ("Lasso" and "Ruby") have been compared to those of Thomas Wolfe (*q.v.*). "Rubicon," which *Library Journal* calls a "novel of the absurd," is the story of a cowardly, somewhat pathetic Norwegian who comes to Paris seeking adventures. Richard Rhodes writes in the *N.Y. Times* that "though it is a decent enough book, it commands no such majesty [as his fine earlier works]. In content, it fits neatly between episodes in 'The Song of the Red Ruby.' More compressed than its predecessors, more dramatic, more focused, it is nevertheless a leftover, and I find sorrow in the fact that its author spent nine years at it." Agnar Mykle lives in Norway, the land of his birth. He

has a Norwegian degree in Political and Economic Sciences and has studied drama and the
amateur theater in France, England, and the United States, where he held a Fulbright Scholarship.

THE HOTEL ROOM. Trans. by Maurice Michael. 1963 o.p. The first novel with which he
achieved prominence in his own country.

LASSO ROUND THE MOON. Trans. by Maurice Michael. 1960 o.p.

THE SONG OF THE RED RUBY. Trans. by Maurice Michael. 1961 o.p.

RUBICON. Trans. by Maurice Michael. 1967, o.p.

BJØRNEBOE, JENS. 1920–

When "The Least of These" appeared as Bjørneboe's second novel, the major critic and author
Sigurd Hoel described it as "the most important novel since the war." It has enjoyed great
popularity since then. With fine realism—typical of Bjørneboe—the novel describes the brutal
treatment received by the little boy Jonas at the hands of teachers who are too stupid and
indifferent to realize that the child has dyslexia, that he is word-blind. The boy is the helpless
victim of an unfeeling, bureaucratic welfare state administered by colorless nonpersons driven by
self-interest.

An almost humorous interlude in Bjørnboe's career as a writer of verse, novels, and plays
occurred in 1966, when a small publisher of pornography announced "Without a Stitch," "by a
well-known Norwegian author." The detailed and monotonous erotic performances of the
heroine prompted the book's confiscation by the police and its official condemnation as "indecent"
by the courts, even though evidence presented at the trials proved that the official guardians of
morality in Norway were very capricious in their treatment of erotic literature.

The horrors of recent German history are brought together in the complicated novel "Moments
of Freedom," whose narrator is a bailiff in an Alpine city. The landmarks in this man's experience
of life are the atrocities of the twentieth century, and he consequently has begun to write a 12-
volume "history of bestiality." In form, the novel is something of a collage with philosophical,
psychological, political, and mythological elements, to name a few; its black humor is that of
modern history. One of the most important novels of the 1960s in Norway, "Moments of
Freedom" was followed in 1969 by a sequel, "The Powder House." Both suggest that cruelty is a
congenital trait of humanity.

THE LEAST OF THESE. 1955. Trans. by Bernt Jebsen and Douglas K. Stafford. *Bobbs*
1960 o.p.

WITHOUT A STITCH. 1966. Trans. by Walter Barthold. *Grove* 1969, o.p.

MOMENTS OF FREEDOM: The Heiligenberg Manuscript. 1966. Trans. by Esther Green-
leaf Murer. *Norton* 1975 $6.95

STIGEN, TERJE. 1922–

Stigen, a gifted storyteller influenced by Knut Hamsun, is able to create narrative climates
where reality and fantasy intermingle. In his novels he frequently returns to northern Norway
with its powerful and mysterious beauty. In "An Interrupted Passage," three men and a woman in
a fishing boat pass the time in storytelling; their secret thoughts are revealed and their common
fate is seen. In several works Stigen has dealt realistically with historical themes.

AN INTERRUPTED PASSAGE. 1956. Trans. by Amanda Langemo. *Twayne* 1974 $8.50

SWEDISH LITERATURE

Almqvist, Carl (Jonas Love). SARA VIDEBECK AND THE CHAPEL. Trans. by Adolph B.
Benson. 1919. Scandinavian Literature in Translation Ser. *Twayne* $6.95. Classical
short novels, depicting Swedish folk life, from the older narrative tradition. Almqvist's dates are 1793–1866.

Anderson, Ingvar. A HISTORY OF SWEDEN. Trans. by Carolyn Hannay. 1968. *Greenwood*
1975 $25.00

Bly, Robert, Trans. and ed. FRIENDS, YOU DRANK SOME DARKNESS. *Beacon Press* 1975 $8.95
pap. $3.95. Bilingual edition of poetry by the major writers Gunnar Ekelöf (*q.v.*),
Harry Martinson (Nobel Prize 1974), and Tomas Tranströmer (*q.v.*)

Enquist, Per Olov. THE LEGIONNAIRES. 1968. *Delacorte Press* (Seymour Lawrence) 1973 $10.00. In this novel, the politically involved Enquist (born 1934) deals with the fate of the Baltic nations in World War II. Enquist has received the Literary Award of the Nordic Council and The Swedish State Literary Award.

Fleisher, Frederic. THE NEW SWEDEN: The Challenge of a Disciplined Democracy. *McKay* 1967 $6.95

A "good and interesting book"—*(LJ)* by an American who served in the American Embassy at Stockholm and has lived there 15 years.

Friberg, Gösta, and Göran Palm. GÖSTA FRIBERG AND GÖRAN PALM: Two Swedish Poets. Trans. by Siv C. Fox. Chapbook Ser. *New Rivers Press* pap. $1.25. Poetry by two of the freshest figures in recent Swedish writing.

Gustafson, Alrik. A HISTORY OF SWEDISH LITERATURE. *Univ. of Minnesota Press* 1961 $15.00. The most complete study available in English. Includes a detailed critical bibliographical guide and list of Swedish literature in translation.

Mattsson, Gunnar. THE PRINCESS. Trans. by Joan Bulman. *Dutton* 1967 $3.95

The factual story of a marriage shadowed by the wife's cancer, which recedes when she has a child. "A simple and moving love story. . . . A true narrative of a physical miracle"—*(Atlantic)*.

Morris, Edita. DEAR ME AND OTHER TALES FROM MY NATIVE SWEDEN. *Braziller* 1967 $5.00

"Exquisite miniatures of life and death in Sweden" by "a writer of subtlety and compassion"— *(PW)*. They "could almost be authentic folk tales. Readers who do not find [them] too quaint will undoubtedly like them very much"—*(LJ)*.

Oakley, Stewart. A SHORT HISTORY OF SWEDEN. *Praeger* 1966 $8.50

Wahlöö, Per, and Maj Sjöwall. THE ABOMINABLE MAN. *Pantheon* 1974 $4.95; *Bantam* 1974 pap. $.75

THE COP KILLER. *Pantheon* 1974 $7.95

THE LOCKED ROOM AND THE DISCOVERY OF A CRIME. *Pantheon* 1973 $5.95

MURDER AT THE SAVOY. *Pantheon* 1971 $4.95; *Bantam* 1972 pap. $.75

The mystery novel had not been counted a Scandinavian strength until Wahlöö (born 1926) and Sjöwall (born 1935) began to write together.

SWEDENBORG, EMANUEL. 1688–1772. *See Chapter 4, World Religions, Reader's Adviser, Vol. 3.*

STRINDBERG, (JOHAN) AUGUST. 1849–1912.

Strindberg is Sweden's greatest dramatist. His pessimism and his ferocious hatred of women have won for him the title of "the Swedish Schopenhauer." "He was an extremely productive writer in many fields; poet, journalist, social critic, historical and 'regional' novelist as well as dramatist (not to mention his painting); but the Strindberg with whom the world is mainly concerned is the writer of a dozen or so plays."—(Alan Harris). "The Father," "Miss Julie," "Creditors," and "Comrades" contain his severest arraignment of women. He was three times married and three times divorced, and his woman-hating plays reflect many of his own marital difficulties. In 1967 Britain's National Theater starred its director, Sir Laurence Olivier, in "The Dance of Death," another naturalistic play involving the duel of the sexes. His "stark portrayal of a schizoid, aging Swedish Army Captain fighting to sustain his ferocity and arrogance with animal disregard for other people was a superb and mysterious creation"—(Henry Hewes, in *SR*).

Not all of his work was cynical, however. "Lucky Per" (1912, o.p. in separate ed.), an allegorical play in five acts, is said to have greatly influenced Maeterlinck's "The Blue Bird" (*q.v.*). "Swan-white" is a fairy drama for children, and "The Dream Play" is a delicate fantasy. He is a master of the one-act play. "To Damascus," in which he "abandoned traditional dramatic techniques in order to dramatize his own inferno of soul in his search for religious certainty," has been called the first expressionistic drama, and his plays in this vein have influenced the drama of O'Neill and other moderns. Brooks Atkinson, writing about "The Scapegoat" (1906, o.p.) in the *N.Y Times* of Oct. 1, 1967, points out that what Strindberg contributed to modern drama were his understanding "that human motives are complex"—he created *individuals*—and the craftsmanship of virtuoso. "Strindberg," Atkinson concludes, "led a tragic life. It was squalid, quarrelsome, vindictive and irrational. But those baleful eyes . . . saw many things that other writers did not see, or evaded as being in bad taste. 'For my part,' he said, 'I find the joy of life in the hard and cruel battles of life—and to be able to add to my store of knowledge, to learn something, is enjoyable to me.' He made that valiant remark in 1888. It provides a sound prologue to the existentialism of today."

The excellent translations by Walter G. Johnson ("The Washington Strindberg") will be the standard English-language edition for years to come; the introductions provide a wealth of information, interpretation, and bibliography for further study. Elizabeth Sprigge's fine translations of the major dramas are to be had in inexpensive editions. Also especially recommended are the editions and translations by Evert Sprinchorn and Arvid Paulson, who have made accessible less well-known plays (e.g., "World Historical Plays") and letters and autobiographical writing essential for a full understanding of Strindberg's life and work (e.g., "Inferno," "The Son of a Servant," and "Letters to Harriet Bosse").

Fascination with the genius of August Strindberg has not slackened 65 years after his death. His enormous influence, along with that of Ibsen, on European and world literature can hardly be exaggerated. In general, however, English-speaking readers are perhaps least familiar with Strindberg's autobiographical writing and novels. Strindberg is here no less an entrancing master of language and alarming self-revelation than in the dozen or so expressionist plays so frequently cited and produced. In fact, the novel "The Natives of Hemsö" is one of Strindberg's most popular works in Scandinavia, where it has had numerous stage and television dramatizations.

THE WASHINGTON STRINDBERG, Trans. and ed. by Walter G. Johnson *Univ. of Washington Press* 9 vols. Vol. 1 The Last of the Knights (1908), The Regent (1908), Earl Birger of Bjalbo (1908) 1956 $5.95 Vol. 2 Gustav Adolf (1900) *Univ. of Washington* with the *Scandinavian American Foundation* 1957 $5.00 Vol. 3 The Vasa Trilogy: Master Olof (1877), Gustav Vasa (1899), Erik XIV (1899) 1966 pap. $2.95 Vol. 4 Saga of the Folkungs (1899), Engelbrekt (1901) 1959 $5.00 Vol. 5 Queen Christina (1901), Charles XII (1901), Gustav III (1902) *Univ. of Washington* with the *Scandinavian American Foundation* 1968 $6.95 pap. $2.95 Vol. 6 Pre-Inferno Plays: The Father (1887), Lady Julie (1888), Creditors (1888), The Stronger (1889), The Bond (1892) 1971 $8.95 Vol. 7 A Dream Play and Four Chamber Plays (1901, 1907) 1973 $10.00 Vol. 8 Open Letters to the Intimate Theater 1967 $6.95 pap. $2.95 Vol. 9 Dramas of Testimony: The Dance of Death I and II (1900), Advent (1898), Easter (1900) 1975 $12.50

A DREAM PLAY AND FOUR CHAMBER PLAYS. Trans. and ed. by Walter G. Johnson. *Norton Lib.* 1975 pap. $2.75

PLAYS OF STRINDBERG. Trans. by Michael Meyer. *Random* Vintage Bks. pap. $2.45

WORLD HISTORICAL PLAYS. 1903. Trans. by Arvid Paulson; introd. by Gunnar Ollén. International Studies and Translation Ser. *Twayne* 1970 $7.50. Includes The Nightingale of Wittenberg, Through Deserts to Ancestral Lands, Hellas, and The Lamb and The Beast; the main characters are Luther, Moses, Socrates, and Christ.

STRINDBERG'S ONE-ACT PLAYS. Trans. with introd. by Arvid Paulson. *Simon & Schuster* (Washington Square) pap. $.90. Includes Outlaw (1871), Miss Julie, Creditors, The Stronger, Pariah (1889), Simoon (1889), First Warning (1892), Debit and Credit (1892), In the Face of Death (1892), Mother Love (1892), Playing with Fire (1892), The Bond, and The Pelican.

FIVE PLAYS OF STRINDBERG. Trans. with introd. by Elizabeth Sprigge. *Doubleday* Anchor Bks. 1960 pap. $1.95. Includes Creditors (1888), Crime and Crime (1899), The Dance of Death, Swanwhite (1901), and The Great Highway (1909).

SIX PLAYS OF STRINDBERG. Trans. with introd. by Elizabeth Sprigge. *Doubleday* Anchor Bks. 1955 pap. $2.95. Includes The Father, Miss Julie, The Stronger, Easter, A Dream Play, and The Ghost Sonata.

CHAMBER PLAYS. Trans. and ed. by Evert Sprinchorn and Seabury Quinn, Jr. *Dutton* pap. $2.75. Includes The Ghost Sonata (1907), The Pelican (1907), The Burned House (1907), and Storm Weather (1907).

INFERNO, ALONE AND OTHER WRITINGS. Trans. and ed. by Evert Sprinchorn. *Peter Smith* $4.50

EIGHT EXPRESSIONIST PLAYS. Trans. and ed. by Arvid Paulson; introd. by John Gassner. *New York Univ. Press* 1972 $12.00 pap. $4.50. Includes Lucky Per's Journey (1882), The Keys to Heaven (1892), To Damascus I (1898), To Damascus II (1898), To Damascus III (1904), A Dream Play (1901), The Ghost Sonata (1907), and The Great Highway (1909).

THREE PLAYS. Trans. by Peter Watts. *Penguin* pap. $1.50. Includes The Father, Miss Julie, and Easter.

THE RED ROOM. 1879. Trans. and ed. by Elizabeth Sprigge. *Dutton* Everyman's $3.95

THE FATHER. 1887. (And "A Dream Play") trans. and ed. by Valborg Anderson. *AHM Pub. Corp.* Crofts Class. 1964 pap. $.95

MISS JULIE. 1888. *Avon* Bard Bks. 1965 pap. $.70

THE NATIVES OF HEMSÖ. 1889. Trans. and ed. by Arvid Paulson. *American-Scandinavian Foundation* 1965 $5.00; *Liveright* 1973 pap. $2.95; (with title "The People of Hemsö") trans. by Elspeth H. Schubert *Greenwood* 1974 $10.50

ON THE SEABOARD: A Novel of the Baltic Islands. 1890. Trans. by Elizabeth E. Westergren (1913). *Howard Fertig* 1975 $13.50; (with title "By the Open Sea") *Haskell* 1972 $14.95. Antidemocratic novel.

A MADMAN'S DEFENSE. 1895. Trans. with introd. by Evert Sprinchorn. *Peter Smith* $4.50. The following two entries are translations of the same autobiographical piece by Strindberg, written by him in French (1887–1888).

THE CONFESSION OF A FOOL. Trans. by Ellie Schleussner. 1913. *Haskell* 1972 $14.95

A MADMAN'S MANIFESTO. Trans. and ed. by Anthony Swerling. *Univ. of Albama Press* 1971 $7.50

A DREAM PLAY. 1901. Trans. by Michael Meyer; ed. by Ingmar Bergman. *Dial* 1973 $6.00; trans. and ed. by Jacque Chwat *Avon* Bard Bks. 1974 pap. $.75

FAIR HAVEN AND FOUL STRAND. 1902. 1914. *Haskell* $12.95

THE SON OF A SERVANT: The Story of the Evolution of a Human Being, 1849–1909. Trans. with introd. and notes by Evert Sprinchorn. *Peter Smith* $4.50. Autobiographical novel.

IN MIDSUMMER DAYS AND OTHER TALES, Vol. 1. Trans. by Ellie Schleussner (1913). Short Story Index Reprint Ser. *Bks. for Libraries* $11.25

HISTORICAL MINIATURES, Vol. 1. Trans. by Ellie Schleussner (1913). Short Story Index Reprint Ser. *Bks. for Libraries* $15.25

ZONES OF THE SPIRIT. *Haskell* 1974 $14.95

LEGENDS: Autobiographical Setches. 1898. 1912. *Haskell* 1972 $12.95

LETTERS OF STRINDBERG TO HARRIET BOSSE. 1932. Trans. and ed by Arvid Paulson. *Grosset* 1961 pap. $1.45

Books about Strindberg

August Strindberg: The Bedeviled Viking. 1930. By V. J. McGill. *Russell & Russell* 1960 $10.00

Strindberg's Dramatic Expressionism. 1930. By Carl E. Dahlström. *Blom* 1968 $12.50. The authoritative treatment of Strindberg's post-Inferno, expressionist plays.

Strindberg and the Historical Drama. By Walter G. Johnson. *Univ. of Washington Press* 1963 $6.50

August Strindberg. 1968. By Martin Lamm. Trans. by Harry G. Carlson. *Blom* 1971 $17.50. The essential biography of Strindberg.

The Novels of August Strindberg: A Study in Theme and Structure. By Eric O. Johannesson. *Univ. of California Press* 1968 $11.00

Strindberg: A Collection of Critical Essays. Ed. by Otto Reinert. Twentieth Century Views Ser. *Prentice-Hall* 1971 $6.95 pap. $1.95

August Strindberg. By Gunnar Ollén. World Dramatists Ser. *Ungar* 1972 $8.50

Greatest Fire: A Study of August Strindberg. By Birgitta Steene. *Southern Illinois Univ. Press* Crosscurrents–Modern Critiques Ser. 1972 $6.95

LAGERLÖF, SELMA (OTTILIANA LOVISA).   1858–1940.   (Nobel Prize 1909)

Selma Lagerlöf, winner of the Nobel Prize in 1909, was the first woman to be elected a member of the Swedish Academy. Her first novel, "The Story of Gösta Berling" (1891, o.p.), assured her position as Sweden's greatest storyteller. She retold the folk tales of her native province, Varmland, in an original and poetic prose. She wrote steadily, but her work is uneven in quality. It "tended to be unashamedly subjective, its characters are moved by impulse and by inner vision, [and] its style often favors rhetorical effects"—(Gustafson). "The Wonderful Adventures of Nils" is a delightful fantasy for children. Her charming autobiography, "Marbacka," is a trilogy ("Marbacka" 1926; "Memories of My Childhood" 1934; "The Diary of Selma Lagerlöf"). Her correspondence with the Nobel prizewinner Nelly Sachs, whom she assisted and encouraged, will not be released until 1990.

FROM A SWEDISH HOMESTEAD. 1899. Trans. by Jessie Brochner 1901. *Bks. for Libraries* $14.75. A modern version of the theme "la belle et la bête," with a concern for the psychology of the split personality.

JERUSALEM. 1901. Trans. by Jessie Brochner. 1903. *Greenwood* $16.95

THE WONDERFUL ADVENTURES OF NILS. 1913. *Pantheon* 1947 $7.19

MARBACKA. 1922. Trans. by Velma S. Howard. 1926. *Finch Press* $12.00; *Gale Research Col.* $12.00

MEMORIES OF MY CHILDHOOD: Further Years at Marbacka. 1930. Trans. by Velma S. Howard. 1934. *Kraus* 1975 $17.00

THE DIARY OF SELMA LAGERLÖF. Trans. by Hanna A. Larsen. 1936. *Kraus* 1975 $13.00

Books about Selma Lagerlöf

Selma Lagerlöf. 1936. By Hanna A. Larsen. *Kraus* 1975 $13.00

LAGERKVIST, PÄR (FABIAN).   1891–1974.   (Nobel Prize 1951)

In 1913 Pär Lagerkvist described his goals as a writer: to achieve classical simplicity and dignity as seen in the models of Homer, classical tragedy, the Old Testament, and the Icelandic saga. In the following 60 years Lagerkvist realized his early goal in dramas and prose of great beauty and terrible immediacy. Man the eternal questioner, man the victim and victimizer, man the pilgrim whose baggage is anxiety and uncertainty, these are just a few of the chords struck by Lagerkvist in his internationally recognized work. What was said of "The Holy Land" is true of all of Lagerkvist's work: " 'The Holy Land' rejects all needless words, compels toward a hidden momentous goal, disturbs with cruel symbols, satisfies with symbols. People and things are symbols yet clear to sight and clearly relevant to man"—(*Choice*). For many readers, Lagerkvist's most compelling personification is that of "The Dwarf," who is the evil that lives in all men. There are no easy answers to the urgent questions Lagerkvist poses. His uncertainty concerning the nature of God is expressed in "The Sibyl," a mystical work that found a particularly enthusiastic audience in the United States.

MODERN THEATRE: Seven Plays and an Essay. Trans. by Thomas R. Buckman. *Univ. of Nebraska Press* 1966 $6.50. Includes The Difficult Hour I; The Difficult Hour II; The Difficult Hour III; The Secret of Heaven; The King; The Hangman; and The Philosopher's Stone.

THE ETERNAL SMILE: Three Stories. Trans. by Erik Mesterton, Denys W. Harding, and David O'Gorman. *Farrar, Straus* (Hill & Wang) 1971 $5.95 pap. $2.95. Includes The Eternal Smile 1920; The Guest of Reality 1925; and The Executioner 1933.

THE MAN WHO LIVED HIS LIFE OVER. 1928. Trans. by Walter Gustafson. (In "Five Modern Scandinavian Plays") introd. by Henry W. Wells. *Twayne* 1971 $8.50

THE DWARF. 1944. Trans. by Alexandra Dick. *Farrar, Straus* (Hill & Wang) 1958 pap. $2.45

BARABBAS. 1950. Trans. by Alan Blair. *Random* Vintage Bks. pap. $1.65; *Bantam* 1968 pap. $.95

EVENING LAND. 1953. Trans. by W. H. Auden and Leif Sjöberg. *Wayne State Univ. Press* 1975 $12.95. Poetry.

THE SIBYL. 1956. Trans. by Naomi Walford. *Random* Vintage Bks. pap. $1.65; *Melvin McCosh Bookseller* 1958 $10.00

THE DEATH OF AHASUERUS. 1960. Trans. by Naomi Walford. *Random* 1962 $6.95

THE HOLY LAND. 1964. Trans. by Naomi Walford. 1966 o.p. The last of five novels, begun in 1950 with "Barabbas," about the significance of Christ's crucifixion. Each novel is a response to the theme, and each must be viewed in relation to the others.

HEROD AND MARIAMNE. 1967. Trans. by Naomi Walford. 1968 o.p.

THE MARRIAGE FEAST. Trans. by Alan Blair and Carl E. Lindin. *Farrar, Straus* (Hill & Wang) 1974 $6.95 pap. $2.75. Nineteen stories.

Books about Lagerkvist

Pär Lagerkvist. By Robert Donald Spector. World Authors Ser. *Twayne* 1973 $7.50

BENGTSSON, FRANS GUNNAR. 1894–1954.

This "gentleman scholar with remarkably sensitive and highly developed literary talents" was best known in his own country as an informal essayist in the great English tradition of Lamb (*q.v.*) and Hazlitt (*q.v.*). He was also a lyric poet, biographer, translator, and, more recently, historical novelist. His prose is "a marvelously virile, precise and flexible medium of expression for a vigorous, many-faceted, and astonishingly learned mind." (Quotations are from the *Columbia Dictionary of Modern European Literature*.) "The Long Ships" is his novel of the tenth-century Vikings. "Under the merriment and the fighting there is a great deal of scholarship as sound as it is imperceptible. Reading this marvelously good-humored ale-broth of a book you say: this is how it must have been to be a Viking chief a thousand years ago"—(*N.Y. Times*). "The Sword Does Not Jest" (1935, U.S. 1960, o.p.) is a "biography of the great Swedish military leader Charles XII." "The picture is as rich in detail as a Brueghel, and we are thus given not only the tragic story of a great man surrounded by mental midgets and clever foes but the story of his times as well"—(*SR*).

THE LONG SHIPS: A Saga of the Viking Age. 1941. Trans. by Michael Meyer. *Knopf* 1954 $6.95

MOBERG, (CARL ARTUR) VILHELM. 1898–1973.

"Emigrants" and "Unto a Good Land" provide the first volumes of Moberg's internationally famous tetralogy describing the lives of Swedish emigrants in the nineteenth century. "The Last Letter Home" (1959, U.S. 1961, o.p.) completes this psychologically penetrating and historically accurate treatment of Swedish settlement in Chisago County, Minnesota. Moberg's strident individualism and enduring empathy with the common man are also seen in "A Time on Earth," in which the old Swedish-American Albert Carlson assesses his life as death approaches. In Scandinavia, Moberg is famous as an historian and dramatist as well as novelist. His "History of the Swedish People," of which two volumes were completed when he died in 1973, depicts in characteristically virile language the life of common people—in sharp contrast to kings and nobility—throughout Sweden's history. One regrets that relatively few of Moberg's some 80 works are currently available to the English-speaking reader.

EMIGRANTS. 1949. Trans. by Gustaf Lannestock. *Popular Lib.* 1971 pap. $1.25

UNTO A GOOD LAND. 1952. 1956. Trans. by Gustaf Lannestock. Eagle Books Ser. *Popular Lib.* 1971 pap. $1.25

A TIME ON EARTH. 1963. Trans. by Naomi Walford. *Simon & Schuster* 1965 $4.50

A HISTORY OF THE SWEDISH PEOPLE. Trans. by Paul Britten Austin. *Pantheon* 2 vols. Vol. 1 From Oden to Engelbrecht 1973 Vol. 2 From Renaissance to Revolution 1974 each $6.95

BOYE, KARIN. 1900–1941.

Karin Boye's poetry and prose from the 1920s and 1930s express her intense search for an understanding of herself in an essentially absurd world. Turning from the emotionally charged Christianity of her youth, Boye never overcame serious periods of depression when she later tried to find coherence through a radical Marxist and psychoanalytic view of man's nature. Loneliness and guilt contended with love of life and belief in religious truth in her later expressionistic poetry. "Kallocain," her most important work of prose, reflects Boye's travels in totalitarian Germany and the Soviet Union. A society is described in which all human activity is harnessed to serve the state, and complete enslavement of the individual is assured by the drug kallocain. The drug forces one to reveal all thoughts. In this novel, which is comparable in some respects to Kafka's (*q.v.*) work and to Aldous Huxley's "Brave New World," the sanctity of the human spirit is threatened to the utmost by the fascist-collective state. Karin Boye took her own life in 1941.

KALLOCAIN. 1940. Trans. by Gustaf Lannestock; introd. by Richard B. Vowles. Nordic Translation Ser. *Univ. of Wisconsin Press* 1966 $8.00

JOHNSON, EYVIND (OLOF VERNER). 1900– (Nobel Prize 1974)

"The Days of His Grace" is one of three powerful historical novels Eyvind Johnson wrote between 1949 and 1964. In this book the American reader has access to a small but important fraction of a literary career that began in 1924. Johnson combines urgent concern for the psychology of the individual with an interest in historical development; he has always been a politically engaged writer. "The Days of His Grace" is set in the empire of Charlemagne; young Italians in their longing for personal and national freedom are overwhelmed by the superior, ruthless force of the totalitarian machine instituted by Charlemagne. Irony, understatement, appropriate variations in language style, and sound research in the historical background of the period make this a fine novel whose message, however, is timeless. Writing for his contemporaries—who know a great deal about oppression and tragedy—Johnson shows that "while the concepts of freedom and independence can be preserved there is hope; the oppressors will never sleep easy at night"—(Orton).

THE DAYS OF HIS GRACE. 1960. Trans. by Elspeth Harley Schubert. *Vanguard* 1970 $8.95

Books about Johnson

Eyvind Johnson. By Gavin Orton. World Authors Ser. *Twayne* 1972 $6.95

EKELÖF, GUNNAR. 1907–1968.

"Ekelöf is a poet of surpassing stature, one of the masters of modern poetry, yet little known in America"—(*LJ*). Few writers of his eminence are more difficult to characterize, for the poetry that began to appear in 1932 is Ekelöf's extremely personal and evolving investigation of human consciousness and culture. For Ekelöf, a twentieth-century mystic, all things, people, and ideas form a complex interdependent unity; the past is in the present and reality for the poet is the changing visions he may find in himself. In their introduction to selections of Ekelöf's work before 1965, Rukeyser and Sjöberg provide fascinating glimpses of a poet whose love of nature and music join with profound loneliness in inimitable lyrical poetry. The strength and genuineness of his often bleak voice won him immense popularity in Sweden as well as almost all the literary awards a Scandinavian poet may receive. The second selection, made by W. H. Auden and Sjöberg, is taken from two of Ekelöf's last volumes: "Diwan over the Prince of Emgión," 1965, and "The Tale of Fatuhmeh," 1966. Here Ekelöf expertly draws from medieval Greek and Middle Eastern literature and spirit to create a mystical and visionary search, through and while suffering, for essential human experience.

FRIENDS, YOU DRANK SOME DARKNESS: Three Swedish Poets. Chosen and trans. by Robert Bly. Bilingual ed. *Beacon* 1975 $8.95 pap. $3.95. Includes poems by Harry Martinson, Gunnar Ekelöf, and Tomas Tranströmer.

SELECTED POEMS OF GUNNAR EKELÖF. Trans. by Muriel Rukeyser and Leif Sjöberg. Fwd. by Rukeyser; introd. by Sjöberg. *Twayne* 1966 $4.00

SELECTED POEMS BY GUNNAR EKELÖF. Trans. with fwd. by W. H. Auden and Leif Sjöberg; introd. by Göran Printz-Påhlson. *Pantheon* 1972 $5.95

Books about Ekelöf

A Reader's Guide to Gunnar Ekelöf's "A Mölna Elegy." By Leif Sjöberg. *Twayne* 1973 $6.00. An essential aid for students of Ekelöf.

BERGMAN, INGMAR. 1918– *See Chapter 10, The Lively Arts and Communications, Reader's Adviser, Vol. 3.*

DAGERMAN, STIG. 1923–1954.

Regarded as the most talented young writer of the Swedish postwar generation, this playwright, novelist, and short story writer, who committed suicide at the age of 31, had published four novels, a collection of short stories, a book of travel sketches, and four full-length plays by the time he was 26. "In its bulk and its overall quality this production by such a young author during a brief span of less than ten years is without a Swedish parallel and is the more astonishing because of the originality of its conception and the variety and range of its form"—(Gustafson). "Dagerman wrote with beautiful objectivity," Graham Green (*q.v.*) has said. "Instead of emotive phrases, he uses a choice of facts, like bricks, to construct an emotion. If it had not been for his early tragic death we might be comparing his work with Gorki's."

THE GAMES OF NIGHT: Ten Stories and an Autobiographical Piece. 1947. Trans. by
  Naomi Walford; introd. by Michael Meyer. 1961 o.p.

TRANSTRÖMER, TOMAS. 1931–

Tranströmer, an occupational psychologist by profession, has regularly published his influential poetry since 1954. His poetic language—admirably reconstructed in the English translations currently available—is the syntax of normal prose bearing strong, often symbolic imagery
from a world the reader recognizes as his own as well as the poet's. Basically simple images are
wonderfully charged with the power to describe human perceptions of nature and of self.
Tranströmer "wants to see the poetic language act as a new communication between experiences,
as a catalyst that liberates man instead of restricting him"—(Sjöberg). Some of his poems are in the
collection by Robert Bly, "Friends, You Drank Some Darkness" (*Beacon Press* 1975 $8.95 pap.
$3.95).

NIGHT VISION. 1970. Trans. by Robert Bly. 1971 o.p.

WINDOWS AND STONES: Selected Poems. Trans. by May Swenson with Leif Sjöberg. Pitt
  Poetry Ser. *Univ. of Pittsburg Press* 1972 $6.95 pap. $2.95

BALTICS. *Oyez* (dist. by Serendipity) 1975 $5.00 pap. $2.50

—D.K.W.

Chapter 14

Russian Literature

"One word of truth outweighs the world."
—ALEKSANDR SOLZHENITSYN

Russian literature begins in the tenth century, with the conversion to Christianity of the Kievan Great-Prince Vladimir Sviatoslavich. Since the Kievan ruler opted for the Greek Orthodox Church, the literature of medieval Rus' is based on the heritage of Byzantium and the cultural achievements of those Slavic lands which had earlier embraced Eastern Christianity (Serbia, Bulgaria, Moravia). The most significant cultural borrowing by Rus' from its neighbors was a literary language (Old Church Slavonic) which could serve as a medium of communication between the various Slavic peoples; the intelligibility of this idiom to the Eastern Slavs ensured a ready transmission of earlier works.

Both religious and secular literary genres are found in medieval Russian culture, which, while concerned with the written word, was equally, if not more, oriented towards other arts (painting, architecture). Original works appear rather early: among the most significant are the "Life of SS. Boris and Gleb," "The Life of Theodosius," Metropolitan Hilarion's "Sermon on Law and Grace," the "Testament" of Vladimir Monomakh, and the various chronicles (especially the first great chronicle, the "Tale of Bygone Years"). Somewhat later, towards the end of the twelfth century, comes "The Tale of Igor's Campaign," the greatest Russian medieval monument. (Portions of these texts are available in the anthology by Zenkovsky, listed below.)

A sharp turning in Russian history occurred during the years 1237–1240, when the independent Russian principalities fell beneath the wave of Mongol expansion. For almost two centuries a component part of the great "empire of the steppes," Russia underwent profound changes which culminated in the creation of a new Russian state dominated by Moscow and by its Great Princes. In literature, however, no fundamental generic transformations took place, and the old forms continued to flourish. A renewal of the literary language in the direction of Greek models and of greater ornamentalism occurred in the fourteenth and fifteenth centuries under the guidance of refugee scholars from the South Slavic states (newly occupied by Turkey). By the middle of the sixteenth century Moscow regarded itself as the chosen successor to the fallen Byzantium (expressed in the doctrine of "Moscow—the third Rome"); its role was celebrated in a series of monumental literary compilations which mirrored the conservatism and self-assurance of Muscovite culture: the "Book of a Hundred Chapters" ("*Stoglav*"), the "Menologion" ("*Chet'i-Minei*"), the "Book of Degrees of Imperial Genealogy" ("*Stepennaia kniga*"), etc.

Changes began to occur in Russian literature as a result of extra-literary events: at the beginning of the seventeenth century, the country passed through a "Time of Troubles" (dynastic struggle, internal revolts, foreign intervention) which gravely undermined its self-satisfied world view. Though a new dynasty, the Romanovs, restored centralized political authority, the literature of the period which follows, be it purely historical or overtly fictional, reveals a considerable uncertainty not only about contemporary historical events, but also about spiritual and moral values. Added turmoil arose as a result of the schism within the Russian Church; the dissatisfied and defeated minority, the Old Believers, found an extremely versatile and brilliant polemicist and stylist in its leader, the Archpriest Avvakum.

During the seventeenth century Russian literature was for the first time seriously exposed to Western influence, through the medium of Polish and Ukrainian culture. An important result of this is the appearance of syllabic poetry, influenced by Polish versification.

A decisive shift in Russian culture, and with it in literature, was brought about by the reforms of Peter the Great, who turned his country towards the West, encouraging the introduction not only of European political, economic, and social ideas, but also of Western European culture. Under the impact of French, German, Dutch, English, and Latin the lexicon of Russian was greatly enlarged, and new terms found their way into a secular imaginative literature. Similarly, under the influence of German and French literatures, a hitherto largely clerical theater became secularized; though rather weak in quality, a native repertoire began to take shape thanks to the labors of Mikhail Lomonosov (1711–1765), Alexander Sumarokov (q.v.), Denis Fonvizin (1745–1792), and others. There was a fundamental change in poetry: Lomonosov, Vasily Trediakovsky (1703–1769) and Sumarokov established a syllabo-tonic system of versification as the basis for most later Russian poetry.

Eighteenth-century Russian literature (dated from approximately the second quarter of the century) was dominated by Classicism. Writers distinguished between different stylistic levels of language and worked within a sharply defined hierarchy of genres. There was little prose; only towards the end of the century did Karamzin (q.v.), a representative of Sentimentalism, make fiction a viable possibility for a writer. The high poetic genres—the ode, the tragedy, the epic—dominated. Of their practitioners, Lomonosov and Gavriil Romanovich Derzhavin (1743–1816), the two outstanding poets of the eighteenth century, must be mentioned.

Classicism, albeit in less strict a form, continued into the nineteenth century. The beginning decades of the new age saw a remarkable coexistence of literary schools and world views: Classicism is still present, Romanticism makes its appearance, and there are the beginnings of the great flowering of Realism. The first forty years of the nineteenth century are known as the Golden Age of Russian poetry. Pushkin (q.v.) not only had remarkable predecessors, but was surrounded by a pleiad of poets of the first magnitude. On his death in 1837 a new major figure, Lermontov (q.v.), made his public appearance; there is also Fyodor Tyutchev (1803–1873), with his marvelous but less well known metaphysical poetry.

The forties saw the emergence of prose. For the next fifty years (until approximately 1890), poetry took a back seat as the literary scene was dominated by a succession of writers who made Russian prose fiction a major component of European literature as a whole: Gogol (q.v.), Dostoevsky (q.v.), Tolstoy (q.v.), Turgenev (q.v.), and others. Their work is tremendously varied, but it possesses a universality: it tackles fundamental human dilemmas, and these qualities make it enduringly appealing to a broader world audience.

Around 1890, a new swing of the pendulum, coinciding with similar developments in Western Europe, once again brought poetry into the foreground. Although prose of major importance continued to be written, the public, weary of the various brands of realistic writing, turned to Symbolism, to a literary movement which attempted to probe beneath the everyday world and claimed to make its art a bridge to the transcendent. Symbolism initiated a second Golden Age of poetry; the great figures of the turn of the century were Zinaida Hippius (q.v.), Fyodor Sologub (q.v.), Andrey Bely (q.v.) and Alexander Blok (q.v.). Their reign lasted a relatively short time; they were joined, rather than replaced, by new poetic groups, the most important of which were the Acmeists (Akhmatova [q.v.] and Mandel'shtam [q.v.]) and the Futurists (Mayakovsky [q.v.] and Khlebnikov [q.v.]). Thanks to the efforts of the various schools, a renewal of poetic language took place—new rhythms were added, the boundaries of the lexicon were greatly expanded, and there was an acceptance of radically different means of composition.

As in the time of Peter, major political events caused Russian literature to set out on a sharply different course. The revolution of October 1917 did not immediately affect literature at the deepest level; however, many writers either died or emigrated during and immediately after the civil war. The vibrant literary bohemia of pre-revolutionary St. Petersburg and Moscow was shattered irrevocably, although during the twenties a rather remarkable revival of prose took place.

In spite of the official censorship, the twenties were a time of relative freedom, of real polemic between literary schools. The Communist Party adopted a generally neutral attitude; at the same time, the emergent patterns of political control over literature began to take shape. The subordination of literature to the Party was decreed in 1934 at the First Congress of the Union of Soviet Writers.

The Congress saw the proclamation of "socialist realism" as the accepted mode of Soviet literature. In spite of alternating periods of political relaxation and control, this doctrine, which requires a writer to portray Soviet reality in an optimistic light, is still the dominant form of politically orthodox literature in the Soviet Union.

The terror of the purges in the 1930s did not leave literature unscathed. Writers and poets of all persuasions, those who had supported the official line as well as those who had fallen silent long before, were imprisoned or executed. Among the victims were such men as Mandel'shtam (q.v.), Isaac Babel (q.v.), and Boris Pilnyak (q.v.). Many writers were driven to silence, while others, like Boris Pasternak (q.v.) and Mikhail Bulgakov (q.v.), created prose masterpieces without any real hopes of seeing them published.

The situation changed somewhat after Stalin's death in 1953. The liberal "thaw" which followed was relatively short-lived, but for the first time in over fifty years certain issues were raised openly in print. A new generation appeared (Yevtushenko [q.v.], Voznesensky [q.v.], and others); although they are perhaps less gifted than the great figures of the past, their message of the need for honesty and freedom in literature found a responsive audience. During the late fifties and sixties some major works, originally destined "for the drawer," were published; perhaps the strongest reaction came in response to Aleksandr Solzhenitsyn's (q.v.) "One Day in the Life of Ivan Denisovich" (1962).

From the late sixties up to the present, Russian literature has become increasingly conservative. Trials of writers such as Sinyavsky (q.v.), Daniel (q.v.), Brodsky (q.v.) and others have been used as an instrument for stifling dissent. In response to these and other pressures, opposition groups within the Soviet Union created "samizdat"—the extraordinary pre-Gutenberg practice of copying and circulating privately texts of works not approved by the authorities. The opposition has been, however, considerably weakened during the seventies, when a number of writers either have been exiled or have left voluntarily for the West; in spite of their departure from their native land, these writers continue to create for an audience both abroad and in the Soviet Union.

The current outlook for Russian literature in the Soviet Union is one of continued controls. As in other areas of Soviet society, Stalinist terror is unlikely to again envelop literature, but open deviation will undoubtedly be repressed. At the same time, one cannot doubt that talented writers will continue to follow the dictates of their conscience, and we may look forward to the appearance of at least some of their work in print in the West.

BACKGROUND

Billington, James. THE ICON AND THE AXE: An Interpretive History of Russian Culture. *Knopf* 1966 $15.00; *Random* Vintage Bks. 1970 pap. $3.95

"This brilliantly written and comprehensive history of Russian culture, an artistic achievement in its own right, is a major contribution to Western understanding of the wellsprings of the Russian—which today means also Soviet—spirit. Rarely is a great body of important information presented as charmingly and interestingly"—(*N.Y. Times*). It was a runner-up for the 1967 National Book Award.

Conquest, Robert. THE GREAT TERROR: Stalin's Purge of the Thirties. *Macmillan* 1973 rev. ed. $4.95. A very readable, highly informative and reliable study of the tragic events which have so profoundly affected Soviet society and culture.

Ginzburg, Eugenia Semyonovna. JOURNEY INTO THE WHIRLWIND. Trans. by Paul Stevenson and Max Hayward, ed. by Helen Wolff. *Harcourt* 1967 pap. 1974 $4.95. A moving autobiographical account by a victim of Stalin's purges (the mother of the writer Aksyonov).

Gorchakov, Nikolai Aleksandrovich. THE THEATER IN SOVIET RUSSIA. Trans. by Edgar Lehrman. 1957 *Bks. for Libraries* 1972 $29.50

Covers the period of Soviet theater's flowering, between 1921 and 1937, and its decline since that year. "A must for all serious students of the twentieth century stage"—*(N.Y. Times)*.

Johnson, Priscilla. KHRUSHCHEV AND THE ARTS: The Politics of Soviet Culture, 1962–1964. Documents sel. and ed. by Priscilla Johnson and Leopold Labedz. *MIT Press* 1965 $12.50

Covers an important moment in the movement of modern Soviet culture. "Rewarding and informative"—*(Choice)*.

Mandelstam, Nadezhda Y. HOPE AGAINST HOPE: A Memoir. Trans. by Max Hayward. *Atheneum* 1970 $10.00. A profound account not only of the fate of the author and her husband, the poet Osip Mandel'shtam *(q.v.)*, but of Russian society during the period of the purges.

Masaryk, Tomáš Garrigue. THE SPIRIT OF RUSSIA: Studies in History, Literature and Philosophy. 1913. Trans. from the German by Eden and Cedar Paul; 2nd ed. with additional chapters and a bibliography by Jan Slavík, trans. by W. R. Lee and Z. Lee. *Harper* (Barnes & Noble) 3 vols. Vols. 1 and 2 1961 set $35.00 Vol. 3 trans. by Robert Bass, ed. by George Gibian 1967 $12.50. A very welcome and valuable reprint of the late president of Czechoslovakia's greatest book.

Medvedev, Roy A. LET HISTORY JUDGE: The Origins and Consequences of Stalinism. Ed. by David Joravsky and Georges Haupt. *Knopf* 1971 $12.50; *Random* Vintage $2.95. A Soviet Marxist's perspective on the Stalin period. This major study complements (without replacing) Conquest's book on the same subject.

Mihajlov, Mihajlo. MOSCOW SUMMER. Introd. by Andrew Field. *Farrar, Straus* Noonday 1965 $4.50

"*Moscow Summer* is the best travelogue ever written on Soviet intellectual life and one of the best on Russian life in general. As reward for this considerable achievement, the Yugoslav government first jailed him, then deprived Mihajlov of his professorship [for] disturbing neighborly relations with the USSR"—(Peter Viereck, in *SR*).

Nemirovitch-Dantchenko, Vladimir. MY LIFE IN THE RUSSIAN THEATER. 1936. Trans. by John Cournos. *Theater Arts* $9.50

Pipes, Richard E. RUSSIA UNDER THE OLD REGIME. *Scribner* 1975 $17.50 pap. $6.95

(Ed.) THE RUSSIAN INTELLIGENTSIA. *Columbia* 1961 $12.50. Ten essays, first published in the Summer 1960 *Daedalus*, on the intellectuals' role in Czarist and Soviet Russia.

Raeff, Marc. ORIGINS OF THE RUSSIAN INTELLIGENTSIA: The Eighteenth-Century Nobility. *Harcourt* Harbinger Bks. 1966 $2.45

Rothberg, Abraham. HEIRS OF STALIN: Dissidence and the Soviet Regime, 1953–1970. *Cornell Univ. Press* 1972 $14.50

Tairov, Alexander. NOTES OF A DIRECTOR. Trans. with introd. by William Kuhlke. *Univ. of Miami Press* 1969 $6.50

Walicki, Andrzej. THE SLAVOPHILE CONTROVERSY: History of a Conservative Utopia in Nineteenth Century Russian Thought. Trans. by Hilda Andrews. *Oxford* 1975 $45.00. A Polish scholar's thorough discussion of a major dichotomy in Russian intellectual thought during the nineteenth century.

HISTORY AND CRITICISM

Alexandrova, Vera. A HISTORY OF SOVIET LITERATURE: 1917–1962. Trans. by Mirra Ginsburg. 1963. *Greenwood* 1971 $17.75. This history covers writers from Gorky to Yevtushenko, with an epilogue on Solzhenitsyn's landmark, "One Day in the Life of Ivan Denisovich." The book is divided into two chronological sections (1917–1939 and 1941–1962), each prefaced by a general comment on literary trends and followed by critical sketches, almost exclusively of fiction writers.

Bann, Stephen, and John E. Bowlt, Eds. RUSSIAN FORMALISM: A Collection of Articles and Texts in Translation. *Harper* (Barnes & Noble) 1973 $7.50. A collection of Russia's most interesting critical school of the early twentieth century.

Baring, Maurice. LANDMARKS IN RUSSIAN LITERATURE. 1910. *Harper* (Barnes & Noble) 1960 pap. $2.50; *Richard West* $10.00

AN OUTLINE OF RUSSIAN LITERATURE. 1915. *Greenwood* $12.25; *Richard West* 1973 $10.75

Borland, Harriet. SOVIET LITERARY THEORY AND PRACTICE DURING THE FIRST FIVE-YEAR PLAN, 1928–1932. 1950. *Greenwood* $13.50

Boyd, A. F. ASPECTS OF THE RUSSIAN NOVEL. *Rowman* 1972 $6.50

Brandes, George. IMPRESSIONS OF RUSSIA. *Apollo* 1968 pap. $1.95; *Peter Smith* $5.00

Brodsky, Joseph, Ed. RUSSIAN POETS ON MODERN POETRY: Akhmatova, Mandelshtam, Pasternak, Mayakovsky, Gumilev, Tsvetaeva. *Ardis* 1975 $13.95 pap. $3.95. This collection contains a number of extremely useful pieces.

Brown, Edward J., Ed. MAJOR SOVIET WRITERS: Essays in Criticism. *Oxford* 1973 pap. $3.95. A very fine critical anthology.

PROLETARIAN EPISODE IN RUSSIAN LITERATURE, 1928–1932. *Octagon* 1971 $11.50

RUSSIAN LITERATURE SINCE THE REVOLUTION. *Macmillan* Collier Bks. 1963 rev. ed. 1969 pap. $2.95. Very readable, quite thorough. The author is a distinguished scholar, a specialist in twentieth-century Russian literature.

Chizhevski, Dmitri. HISTORY OF NINETEENTH-CENTURY RUSSIAN LITERATURE. Trans. by Richard Porter; ed. by Serge Zenkovsky. *Vanderbilt Univ. Press* 1974 2 vols. Vol. 1 The Romantic Period Vol. 2 The Realistic Period each $15.00 pap. each $5.95. An excellent history by a prominent Slavic scholar.

HISTORY OF RUSSIAN LITERATURE. *Humanities Press* 1972 $16.00

Clive, Geoffrey. THE BROKEN ICON: Intuitive Existentialism in Classical Russian Fiction. *Macmillan* 1972 $7.95. A provocative book, written by a thoughtful and original philosopher-critic.

Davie, Donald, Ed. RUSSIAN LITERATURE AND MODERN ENGLISH FICTION. *Univ. of Chicago Press* 1965 $6.75 pap. $1.95

Debreczeny, Paul, and Jesse Zeldin, Eds. LITERATURE AND NATIONAL IDENTITY: Nine-teenth-Century Russian Critical Essays. *Univ. of Nebraska Press* 1970 $8.50

De Vogue, Eugene M. THE RUSSIAN NOVELISTS. Trans. by Jane L. Edmands. 1887. Studies in Russian Literature *Haskell* 1974 $14.95; Essay Index Reprint Ser. *Bks. for Libraries* $11.50

Erlich, Victor, Ed. TWENTIETH CENTURY RUSSIAN LITERARY CRITICISM. *Yale Univ. Press* 1975 $15.00. A recent collection of very important articles.

Fennell, John, and Antony Stokes. EARLY RUSSIAN LITERATURE. *Univ. of California Press* 1974 $18.50. An uneven work, but it contains a great deal of useful information and provocative discussion.

Fennell, John, Ed. NINETEENTH-CENTURY RUSSIAN LITERATURE: Studies of Ten Russian Writers. *Univ. of California Press* 1973 $15.00

Folejewski, Zbigniew, and others, Eds. STUDIES IN RUSSIAN AND POLISH LITERATURE IN HONOR OF WACLAW LEDNICKI. *Mouton* (dist. by Humanities Press) 1962 $19.25. *See the comment in "Polish Literature" Section, this Chapter.*

Freeborn, Richard. THE RISE OF THE RUSSIAN NOVEL: Studies in the Russian Novel from "Eugene Onegin" to "War and Peace." *Cambridge* 1973 $18.50 pap. $8.95

Gasiorowska, Xenia. WOMEN IN SOVIET FICTION, 1917–1964. *Univ. of Wisconsin Press* 1968 $12.50

Gibian, George. INTERVAL OF FREEDOM: Soviet Literature during the Thaw, 1954–1957. *Univ. of Minnesota Press* 1960 $5.50. Examines the period that produced "Dr. Zhivago" in relation to the major literary works of this interval of comparative freedom.

Gifford, Henry. THE NOVEL IN RUSSIA: From Pushkin to Pasternak. *Hillary House* Hutchinson Univ. Library 1964 $3.00

Gifford's purpose is to "investigate the kinds of experience that the Russian novel was called upon to treat, and the qualities of imagination and language that it brought to bear on them." "His appraisal . . . is judicious and interesting, and he often points out the ties between the Russian and Western novel"—(*Choice*).

Gudzii, Nikolai K. HISTORY OF EARLY RUSSIAN LITERATURE. *Octagon* 1970 $21.00. Translation of a standard, exhaustive Soviet textbook on Russian literature from its beginnings to the end of the seventeenth century.

Hapgood, Isabel. RUSSIAN RAMBLES. 1895. *Richard West* 1973 $15.00

SURVEY OF RUSSIAN LITERATURE: With Selections. 1902. *Richard West* 1973 $20.00

Hare, Richard. RUSSIAN LITERATURE FROM PUSHKIN TO THE PRESENT DAY. Select Bibliographies Reprint Ser. *Bks. for Libraries* 1947 $9.75

Hingley, Ronald. RUSSIAN WRITERS AND SOCIETY 1825–1904. *McGraw-Hill* 1967 $4.95 pap. (orig.) $2.95

Holthusen, Johannes. TWENTIETH CENTURY RUSSIAN LITERATURE 1890–1967: A Critical Study. Trans. by Theodore Huebener. *Ungar* 1971 $9.50

Jakobson, R., and E. J. Simmons. RUSSIAN EPIC STUDIES. 1949. *Kraus* 1975 $10.00

James, C. Vaughan. SOVIET SOCIALIST REALISM. *St. Martin's* 1973 $9.95

Junger, Harri, Ed. LITERATURE OF THE SOVIET PEOPLES: A Historical and Biographical Survey. *Ungar* 1971 $12.50

Kern, Gary. THE SERAPION BROTHERS: A Critical Anthology. *Ardis* 1974 $12.95 pap. $3.25. A selection of writings by a group of innovative and interesting authors from the 1920s.

Konovalov, S., Ed. RUSSIAN CRITICAL ESSAYS: Twentieth Century. *Oxford* 1971 $10.25 pap. $5.00

(With D. J. Richards, Eds.) RUSSIAN CRITICAL ESSAYS: Nineteenth Century. *Oxford* 1972 $13.75

Kropotkin, Peter. IDEALS AND REALITIES IN RUSSIAN LITERATURE. 1916. *Greenwood* $14.75; *Richard West* 1973 $13.00

RUSSIAN LITERATURE. 1905. *Blom* 1967 $12.50; *Richard West* 1973 $12.50

Lavrin, Janko. FROM PUSHKIN TO MAYAKOVSKY: A Study in the Evolution of a Literature. 1948. *Folcroft* 1973 $11.95; *Greenwood* 1971 $12.00

AN INTRODUCTION TO THE RUSSIAN NOVEL. 1947. *Greenwood* 1974 $12.25

PANORAMA OF RUSSIAN LITERATURE. *Harper* (Barnes & Noble) 1973 $17.50

PUSHKIN AND RUSSIAN LITERATURE. *Folcroft* 1973 $8.95

RUSSIAN LITERATURE. 1927. *Folcroft* 1975 $10.00

Lednicki, Waclaw. RUSSIA, POLAND AND THE WEST: Essays in Literary and Cultural History. 1954. *Kennikat* 1975 $13.50

Legters, Lyman H., Ed. RUSSIA: Essays in History and Literature. *Humanities Press* 1972 $13.75

Lindstrom, Thais. A CONCISE HISTORY OF RUSSIAN LITERATURE. Vol. 1 From the Beginnings to Chekhov. *New York Univ. Press* 1966 $9.00 pap. $2.95

> The author "has attempted primarily to establish a running connection between Russian literature and its historical environment. . . . She has a firm command of her subject matter. The section on Tolstoy . . . is especially pertinent"—(*LJ*).

Line, Maurice B., and others. BIBLIOGRAPHY OF RUSSIAN LITERATURE IN ENGLISH TRANSLATION TO 1945. 1963. *Rowman* 1972 $7.50

Lord, Robert. RUSSIAN AND SOVIET LITERATURE. *Humanities Press* 1974 $7.50

Luckyj, George S. BETWEEN GOGOL AND SHEVCHENKO. *Libraries Unlimited* 1972 $15.00. (*See Chapter 15, Other European Literature, Section on Ukrainian Literature, this Vol.*)

Magidoff, Robert. GUIDE TO RUSSIAN LITERATURE. *New York Univ. Press* 1965 (orig.) pap. $1.00

Maguire, Robert A. RED VIRGIN SOIL: Soviet Literature in the Late 1920's. Studies of the Russian Institute, Columbia University *Princeton Univ. Press* 1968 $14.50

Mandelstam, Nadezhda. MOZART AND SALIERI. Trans. by Robert MacLean. *Ardis* 1972 $6.95 pap. $2.95. An essay by the widow of the poet Osip Mandelstam (*q.v.*).

Markov, Vladimir. RUSSIAN FUTURISM: A History. *Univ. of California Press* 1968 $15.75. Written by a distinguished specialist, this is the only available survey of a major twentieth-century poetic group. Highly readable and informative.

Massie, Suzanne. THE LIVING MIRROR: Five Young Poets from Leningrad. *Doubleday* 1973 $3.95

Mathewson, Rufus W., Jr. THE POSITIVE HERO IN RUSSIAN LITERATURE. *Stanford Univ. Press* 1975 $14.95

Mersereau, John, Jr. BARON DELVIG'S NORTHERN FLOWERS 1825–1832: Literary Almanac of the Pushkin Pleiad. *Illinois Univ. Press* 1967 $8.50

Mihajlov, Mihajlo. RUSSIAN THEMES. Trans. by his sister and Christopher Bird. *Farrar, Straus* 1968 $6.95; *Noonday* 1968 pap. $2.45. By the well-known Yugoslav thinker and writer.

Miliukov, Paul. LITERATURE IN RUSSIA. Outlines of Russian Culture, Vol. 2. *Peter Smith* 1975 $4.75

> LITERATURE IN RUSSIA, PART 2. *A. S. Barnes* 1975 pap. $1.45

Mirskii, D. S. CONTEMPORARY RUSSIAN LITERATURE, 1881–1925. 1926. *Kraus* 1975 $18.00. A superb survey of the period, it still has not been equalled by any other work in English.

> HISTORY OF RUSSIAN LITERATURE: From Its Beginnings to 1900. Ed. by Francis J. Whitfield. 1926. *Knopf* 1949 $10.00; *Random* 1958 pap. $1.95. The best available history of Russian literature: accurate, insightful, and very readable. Contains abridged versions of Mirskii's "History of Russian Literature" and "Contemporary Russian Literature."

Moore, Harry T., and Albert Parry. TWENTIETH-CENTURY RUSSIAN LITERATURE. Crosscurrents—Modern Critiques Ser. *Univ. of Illinois Press* 1974 $6.95

Muchnic, Helen. AN INTRODUCTION TO RUSSIAN LITERATURE. *Dutton* rev. ed. 1964 pap. $1.95

> RUSSIAN WRITERS: Notes and Essays. *Random* 1971 $10.00

Oulanoff, Hongor. SERAPION BROTHERS: Theory and Practice. *Mouton* (dist. by Humanities Press) 1966 $13.50

Patrick, George Z. POPULAR POETRY IN SOVIET RUSSIA. 1929 *Mouton* (dist. by Humanities Press) 1968 $9.25

Persky, Serge M. CONTEMPORARY RUSSIAN NOVELISTS. Trans. by Frederick Eisemann. 1913. Essay Index Reprint Ser. *Bks. for Libraries* $10.00

Pomorska, Krystyna. RUSSIAN FORMALIST THEORY AND THE POETIC AMBIENCE. *Humanities Press* (Mouton) 1968 $9.25. A very fine examination of the relationship between Russian Futurism and Formalism.

Reavey, George. SOVIET LITERATURE TODAY. 1947. *Greenwood* 1975 $9.50

Roberts, Spencer, Trans. and ed. ESSAYS IN RUSSIAN LITERATURE: The Conservative View. *Ohio Univ. Press* 1968 $10.50

Rogers, Thomas F. SUPERFLUOUS MEN AND THE POST-STALIN THAW: The Alienated Hero in Soviet Prose during the Decade 1953–1963. *Mouton* 1972 $34.25

Salaman, Esther. GREAT CONFESSION: From Aksakov and DeQuincey to Tolstoy and Proust. *Allen Lane* (dist. by Penguin) 1973 $8.75

Shestov, Lev. CHEKHOV AND OTHER ESSAYS. *Univ. of Michigan Press* 1966 $4.40 Ann Arbor Bks. pap. $1.95

By the remarkable philosopher. "Less concerned with the writer, he seeks the idea behind the work—in the case of Chekhov, the imponderable hopelessness of the Russian hero"—*(SR)*.

Shneidman, N. N. LITERATURE AND IDEOLOGY IN SOVIET EDUCATION. *Lexington Bks.* (dist. by Heath) 1973 $13.50

Simmons, Ernest J. INTRODUCTION TO RUSSIAN REALISM: Pushkin, Gogol, Dostoevsky;, Tolstoy, Chekhov, Sholokhov. *Peter Smith* 1975 $5.25

OUTLINE OF MODERN RUSSIAN LITERATURE: 1880–1940. 1943. *Greenwood* 1971 $8.50

THROUGH THE GLASS OF SOVIET LITERATURE. Studies of the Russian Institute of Columbia University *Columbia* 1963 pap. $1.95; *Peter Smith* 1975 $5.00

Slonim, Marc L'vovich. THE EPIC OF RUSSIAN LITERATURE FROM ITS ORIGINS THROUGH TOLSTOY. *Oxford* 1950 Galaxy Bks. pap. $3.95

FROM CHEKHOV TO THE REVOLUTION: Russian Literature 1900–1953. *Oxford* Galaxy Bks. 1962 pap. $2.95

AN OUTLINE OF RUSSIAN LITERATURE. *Oxford* 1958 $6.95

"No better introduction to the giants of the past age could be found."

THE RUSSIAN THEATER: From the Empire to the Soviets. *Macmillan* Collier Bks. pap. $1.50

"This is far and away the most comprehensive single volume dealing with the Russian drama and stage. . . . It is a well-balanced account of what has transpired over the last decades"—*(LJ)*.

SOVIET RUSSIAN LITERATURE: Writers and Problems. 1953. *Oxford* 1964 $10.95, updated ed. (1917–1967) Galaxy Bks. 1967 pap. (orig.) $2.95

These volumes are a good guide to Russian literature as a whole. "He is equally good in discussing ideas and literary values and in relating them to the social background. A detailed treatment of major literary figures is combined with summary but adequate sketches of secondary writers, typical of the various literary trends. All these features, together with the author's lucid and lively presentation, make of his two books an important and welcome contribution"—*(LJ)*.

Spector, Ivar. GOLDEN AGE OF RUSSIAN LITERATURE. 1939. Essay Index Reprint Ser. *Bks. for Libraries* 1975 $11.25

Stacy, Robert H. RUSSIAN LITERARY CRITICISM: A Short History. *Syracuse Univ. Press* 1974 $15.00

Struve, Gleb. RUSSIAN LITERATURE UNDER LENIN AND STALIN 1917–1953. *Univ. of Oklahoma Press* 1971 $9.95 pap. $4.95. The most authoritative Western book on the subject.

Swayze, Harold. POLITICAL CONTROL OF LITERATURE IN THE USSR, 1946–1959. *Harvard Univ. Press* 1962 $10.00

In this solid, well-documented literary, social and political study, Dr. Swayze "painstakingly analyzes the political aims of Soviet literary policy and traces their acceptance (and rejection, during the 1956 'thaw')."

Terras, Victor. BELINSKII AND RUSSIAN LITERARY CRITICISM: The Heritage of Organic Aesthetics. *Univ. of Wisconsin Press* 1973 $17.50

Trotsky, Leon. LITERATURE AND REVOLUTION. *Univ. of Michigan Press* 1960 $6.95 Ann Arbor Bks. pap. $4.95. An interesting, historically important book.

Waliszewski, Kazimierz. A HISTORY OF RUSSIAN LITERATURE. 1910. *Kennikat* 1969 $15.00; *Richard West* 1969 $15.00 1973 repr. of 1910 ed. $25.00

Wilson, Edmund. A WINDOW ON RUSSIA. *Farrar, Straus* 1974 pap. $2.95

Yarmolinsky, Avrahm. ASPECTS OF THE RUSSIAN IMAGINATION. *T. Y. Crowell* (Funk & Wagnalls) 1969 $8.95

 LITERATURE UNDER COMMUNISM. Select Bibliographies Reprint Ser. *Bks. for Libraries* 1960 $10.00

Zavalishin, Vaicheslav. EARLY SOVIET WRITERS. Essay Index Reprint Ser. *Bks. for Libraries* 1958 $17.25

COLLECTIONS

Bakshy, Alexander, Ed. SOVIET SCENE. 1946. *Bks. for Libraries* $18.50

Barratt, G. PUSHKIN PLEIAD. *Hakkert* (forthcoming) $14.00

Blake, Ben, Ed. FOUR SOVIET PLAYS. 1937 *Blom* $13.50

Blake, Patricia, and Max Hayward, Eds. HALF-WAY TO THE MOON: New Writing from Russia. 1965. *Doubleday* Anchor Bks. pap. $1.45
 "Beyond doubt the best single volume of post-Stalin Russian writing available in English"—(*SR*).

Chadwick, Nora Kershaw. RUSSIAN HEROIC POETRY. 1932. *Russell & Russell* 1964 $12.50

Corrigan, Robert W., Ed. MASTERPIECES OF MODERN RUSSIAN THEATER. *Macmillan* Collier Bks. 1967 pap. $1.50. Includes Month in the Country by Turgenev; Uncle Vanya by Chekhov; The Cherry Orchard by Chekhov; Lower Depths by Gorky; and Bedbug by Mayakovsky.

Cournos, John, Ed. A TREASURY OF CLASSIC RUSSIAN LITERATURE: Russian Literature to 1917. *Putnam* Capricorn Bks. 1962 pap. $2.45; *Peter Smith* $4.50

Daniels, Guy, Ed. RUSSIAN COMIC FICTION. *New Am. Lib.* Signet 1970 pap. $1.25

Downing, Charles. RUSSIAN TALES AND LEGENDS. *Walck* (dist. by McKay) 1957 $6.75

Dukas, Vytas, Trans. NINE CONTEMPORARY RUSSIAN STORIES. *Fairleigh Dickinson Univ. Press* $10.00

Esenwein, Joseph B., Ed. SHORT STORY MASTERPIECES: Vol. 3 Russian. Trans. by John Cournos. 1913. *Bks. for Libraries* $9.00

FOUR GREAT RUSSIAN SHORT NOVELS. *Dell* pap. $.75. Includes First Love by Turgenev; The Gambler by Dostoevsky; Master and Man by Tolstoy; and The Duel by Chekhov.

Ginsburg, Mirra, Trans. and ed. THE FATAL EGGS AND OTHER SOVIET STORIES. 1965. *Grove* Evergreen Bks. 1968 pap. $3.95

 LAST DOOR TO AIYA: A Selection of the Best New Science Fiction from the Soviet Union. *S. G. Phillips* 1968 1969 $5.95

Goldberg, Isaac, Trans. MODERN RUSSIAN CLASSICS. *Branden* pap. $.95. Includes Silence by Andreyev; White Dog by Sologub; Father by Chekhov; Her Lover by Gorky; and Letter by Babel.

Guerney, Bernard Guilbert, Ed. A TREASURY OF RUSSIAN LITERATURE. *Vanguard* 1943 $10.00 text ed. $7.50. Many new translations; biographical and critical notes.

 (Trans. and ed.). AN ANTHOLOGY OF RUSSIAN LITERATURE IN THE SOVIET PERIOD FROM GORKI TO PASTERNAK. 1960. *Random* Vintage Bks. pap. $1.95. New translations with biographical and critical notes.

Hamalian, Leo, and Vera Von Wiren-Garczynski, Eds. SEVEN RUSSIAN SHORT NOVEL MASTERPIECES. *Popular Lib.* Living Class. Lib. (orig.) 1967 pap. $.95. Pasternak's The

Childhood of Zhenya Luvers, Dostoyevsky's The Gambler, Leo Tolstoy's Father Sergius, Chekhov's Ward No. 6, Turgenev's The Duelist, Gogol's The Story of How Ivan Ivanovich Quarreled with Ivan Nikiforovich, and Andreyev's The Dilemma.

Hodgetts, E. M. TALES AND LEGENDS FROM THE LAND OF THE TZAR. 1892. *Kraus* $19.00

Hollo, Anselm, Trans. and ed. RED CATS: Yevtushenko, Voznesensky, and Kirsanov. *City Lights* 1961 pap. (orig.) $1.00

Houghton, Norris, Ed. GREAT RUSSIAN PLAYS. *Dell* Laurel Leaf Lib. 1960 pap. $1.25. Includes Gogol's The Inspector General, Turgenev's A Month in the Country, Tolstoy's The Power of Darkness, Chekhov's The Cherry Orchard, Andreyev's He Who Gets Slapped, and Gorky's The Lower Depths.

GREAT RUSSIAN SHORT STORIES. *Dell* pap. $1.25

Iwanik, John, Ed. RUSSIAN SHORT STORIES. *Heath* 1962 pap. text ed. $5.95

Ivanov, Y., Ed. A TREASURY OF RUSSIAN AND SOVIET SHORT STORIES. *Fawcett* 1971 (orig.) pap. $.95

Johnson, D. Barton, and others, Eds. EYEWITNESS: Selections from Russian Memoirs. *Harcourt* 1971 pap. text ed. $6.50

Karlinsky, Simon, and Alfred Appel, Jr., Eds. BITTER AIR OF EXILE: Russian Writers in the West, 1922–1972. *Univ. of California Press* 1975 $15.00 pap. $5.95

Kern, Gary, and Christopher Collins, Eds. THE SERAPION BROTHERS: A Critical Anthology. *Ardis* 1975 $15.95 pap. $3.45

Lyons, Eugene, Ed. SIX SOVIET PLAYS. 1934. *Greenwood* $18.75

Magarshack, David, Trans. and ed. THE STORM AND OTHER RUSSIAN PLAYS. *Farrar, Straus* (Hill & Wang) 1960 $4.50 Mermaid Dramabks. pap. $2.95. Includes Gogol's The Government Inspector, Ostrovsky's The Storm, Tolstoy's The Power of Darkness, Chekhov's Uncle Vanya, and Gorky's Lower Depths.

Magidoff, Robert, Ed. RUSSIAN SCIENCE FICTION. 1969. *New York Univ. Press* 1969 $6.95

Magnus, L. A., Ed. HEROIC BALLADS OF RUSSIA. 1921. *Kennikat* 1967 $8.00

Markov, Vladimir, and Merrill Sparks, Trans. and eds. MODERN RUSSIAN POETRY: An Anthology. *Bobbs* bilingual ed. 1967 $12.50 pap. $5.95

The most comprehensive and up-to-date collection of the Russian poetry of this century. "The number of poems included for each author is remarkably generous, and usually so well chosen that one is really given a true conception of the poetic individuality and particular contribution . . . of a given author"—(*Times,* London)

Newnham, Richard, Ed. SOVIET SHORT STORIES. Various translators. (1929–1961). *Penguin* bilingual ed. (orig.) 1963 pap. $1.25

Noyes, George Rapall, Ed. MASTERPIECES OF THE RUSSIAN DRAMA. 1933. *Dover* 1960 pap. 2 vols. each $3.00; *Peter Smith* 1962 2 vols. set $12.50. Vol. 1 Fonvizin's "The Young Hopeful," Griboyedov's "Wit Works Woe," Gogol's "The Inspector General," Turgenev's "A Month in the Country," Ostrovsky's "The Poor Bride," Pisemsky's "A Bitter Fate" Vol. 2 Alexei Tolstoy's "The Death of Ivan the Terrible," Leo Tolstoy's "Power of Darkness," Gorky's "The Lower Depths," Andreyev's "Professor Storitsyn," Mayakovsky's "Mystery-Bouffe," Chekhov's "The Cherry Orchard."

Pargment, Lila, Ed. GIRL FROM MOSCOW AND OTHER STORIES. *Ungar* bilingual ed. 1968 $5.00

Pomorska, Krystyna. FIFTY YEARS OF RUSSIAN PROSE: From Pasternak to Solzhenitsyn. *M.I.T. Press* 1971 2 vols. each $12.50 pap. each $3.95

Proffer, Carl R., Ed. FROM KARAMZIN TO BUNIN: An Anthology of Russian Short Stories. *Indiana Univ. Press* 1969 $10.95 pap. $4.95

(With Ellendea Proffer, Eds.) THE ARDIS ANTHOLOGY OF CONTEMPORARY RUSSIAN LITERATURE. *Ardis* 1975 $15.00 pap. $5.00

Reavey, George, and Marc Slonim, Trans. and eds. SOVIET LITERATURE. 1934. *Greenwood* 1972 $18.00

Reeve, F. D., Trans. CONTEMPORARY RUSSIAN DRAMA (orig. title: "Recent Russian Plays"). *Pegasus* 1968 $7.50 pap. $2.95. Includes Rozov's Alive Forever, Pogodin's Petrachian Sonnet, Shvarts' Naked King, Panova's It's Been Ages, Zorin's Warsaw Melody.

GREAT SOVIET SHORT STORIES. *Dell* Laurel Leaf Lib. 1962 pap. $.75

(Trans. and ed.) NINETEENTH-CENTURY RUSSIAN PLAYS (orig. title "An Anthology of Russian Plays, Vol. 1, 1790–1890"). *Norton* Norton Lib. 1973 pap. $3.95

TWENTIETH-CENTURY RUSSIAN PLAYS: An Anthology (orig. title "Anthology of Russian Plays, Vol. 2"). *Norton* Norton Lib. 1973 pap. $3.95

Rus, Vladimir, Trans. and ed. SELECTIONS FROM RUSSIAN POETRY AND PROSE. Ill. by Elizabeth Korolkoff. *Harvey House Pubs.* Bilingual ed. 1966 $5.35 lib. bdg. $4.29

Schweikert, Harry C., Ed. RUSSIAN SHORT STORIES, Vol. 1. 1919. Short Story Index Repr. Ser. *Bks. for Libraries* $14.50

Segel, Harold B., Trans. and ed. THE LITERATURE OF 18TH-CENTURY RUSSIA. *Dutton* 1967 2 vols. pap. each $2.95

"A blockbuster of a major work on a subject on which not much is available in English! The editor . . . has done a marvelous job of selecting and translating that century in Russia to bring it alive"—(*PW*).

Seifulina, and others. FLYING OSIP: Stories of New Russia. 1925. Short Story Index Repr. Ser. *Bks. for Libraries* $9.50

Townsend, Rochelle, Ed. RUSSIAN SHORT STORIES. *Dutton* Everyman's 1961 pap. $1.35

Ullstein Verlag Publ. CONTINENT: New Writings by Russian and Eastern European Writers. *Doubleday* 1976 (orig.) pap. $3.95

Whitney, Thomas P., Trans. and ed. THE NEW WRITING IN RUSSIA. *Univ. of Michigan Press* 1964 $6.95 pap. $4.95

A collection of short stories. Mr. Whitney is "one of our foremost experts on modern Russia. . . . His introduction and comments on individual authors are highly knowledgeable and generally sound. . . . His taste in authors is impeccable"—(*LJ*).

Wiener, Leo, Ed. ANTHOLOGY OF RUSSIAN LITERATURE FROM THE EARLIEST PERIOD TO THE PRESENT. 1902. *Blom* 1966 2 vols. set $25.00

Yarmolinsky, Avrahm, Ed. RUSSIANS, THEN AND NOW: Selected Writings from Early Times to the Present. *Macmillan* 1963 $8.50

A TREASURY OF GREAT RUSSIAN SHORT STORIES: Pushkin to Gorky. *Macmillan* 1944 $9.75; *Bks. for Libraries* repr. of 1949 ed. $14.50

Zenkovsky, Serge A., Trans. and ed. MEDIEVAL RUSSIA'S EPICS, CHRONICLES, AND TALES. *Dutton* 1963, 1974 rev. and enlarged ed. pap. $6.50. An extremely inclusive anthology of Old Russian literature (eleventh through seventeenth centuries).

THE IGOR TALE (*"Slovo o Polku Igoreve"*). 1187?.

This twelfth-century monument is an extraordinarily complex and rich text. Its principal focus is an unsuccessful expedition by a minor prince of Rus' against the nomadic Polovtsy; this event moves the author to consider historical events of the past and to appeal for united action against the nomads by the various Rus' princes. The text shows a heavy influence of non-Christian Slavic culture. The manuscript of the *Igor Tale*, discovered in 1795, perished in the Moscow fire of 1812. The work has been the subject of a great deal of scholarly analysis, both in Russia and in the West.

THE TALE OF THE CAMPAIGN OF IGOR; A Russian Epic Poem of the Twelfth Century. Trans. by Robert C. Howes. *Norton* 1973 $6.95

SONG OF IGOR'S CAMPAIGN. Trans. by Vladimir Nabokov. *Random* Vintage Bks. 1960 pap. $1.95

SUMAROKOV, ALEKSANDR PETROVICH. 1718–1777.

As Mirsky rightly puts it, Sumarokov was "the father of the Russian literary profession . . . the first gentleman in Russia to choose the profession of letters." A prolific writer of poetry, plays, and criticism, he was a follower of Voltaire and rather unjustifiedly considered himself a Russian Racine and Voltaire. Historically his major contribution lay in the theater; he was the author of "*Khorev*" (1749), the first Russian tragedy, and of a number of other tragedies and comedies written on classical models. Other genres to which he contributed were the fable, the satire, and the song.

SELECTED TRAGEDIES OF A. P. SUMAROKOV. Trans. by Richard and Raymond Fortune. *Northwestern Univ. Press* 1970 $8.50

KARAMZIN, NIKOLAI MIKHAILOVICH. 1766–1826.

At the age of 22 Karamzin toured Germany, Switzerland, France, and England, and published his travel notes in the form of letters. Already known as a poet and short-story writer, he was well received by literary groups and celebrities in the countries he visited. The letters were originally published in the Moscow *Journal*, 1790–1792; an English translation from the German appeared in 1803.

Karamzin had great influence on the development of Russian language and literature, introducing many Gallicisms to supplant Slavonic words and idioms. He also founded *The Messenger of Europe*, a monthly review which was among the most important in Russia until 1917. He was appointed Court Historian by Alexander I in 1803 and wrote a "History of the Russian State" that covered up to the accession of the Romanovs in 1613, in 12 volumes (1816–1829; 12th vol. unfinished).

SELECTED PROSE. Trans. by Henry M. Nebel. Publications of 18th-Century Russian Lit. Ser. *Northwestern Univ. Press* 1969 $7.50

KARAMZIN'S MEMOIR ON ANCIENT AND MODERN RUSSIA. Written 1811; published posthumously. Trans. by Richard Pipes. *Atheneum* 1966 pap. $2.95

Books about Karamzin

Karamzin: A Russian Sentimentalist. By Henry M. Nebel. Slavistic Printing and Reprints Vol. 60 *Mouton* (Dist. by Humanities Press) 1967 $13.25

N. M. Karamzin: A Study of His Literary Career. By A. G. Cross. *Illinois Univ. Press* 1971 $12.50

Nikolay Karamzin. By Natalya Kochetkova. World Authors Ser. *Twayne* new ed. 1974 $7.95

KRYLOV, IVAN ANDREYEVICH. 1769–1844.

Krylov is considered the greatest of the many writers of fables found at the end of the eighteenth and the beginning of the nineteenth century. He began his literary career as a journalist, and some of his satirical essays are still extremely effective. The sharpness of his pieces led to government reaction; Krylov, in response, disappeared from literature for a long time. He reentered it in 1809 with the publication of some of his fables in book form. From then on until 1844, he continued to produce additional fables and to enjoy enormous success both in the salons of St. Petersburg and among a wider reading public.

In his fables, mostly written between 1810 and 1820, Krylov criticizes human stupidity, arrogance, ineptitude, and other vices. His success is at least partially due to his mastery of "live" language; many of his epigrammatic formulations are so apt and so pithy that they have solidly entered the corpus of Russian idiomatic expressions. For this very reason, he is extremely difficult to translate.

KRYLOFF AND HIS FABLES. Trans. by C. Fillingham Coxwell. 1869. *Scholarly Press* 1970 $9.50

Books about Krylov

Ivan Krylov. By N. L. Stepanov. World Authors Ser. *Twayne* $6.95

AKSAKOV, SERGEI TIMOFEYEVICH. 1791–1859.

A close friend of Gogol (*q.v.*), Aksakov came from the old landholding nobility. His family background becomes the subject for his most important works, "The Family Chronicle" (1856) and "Years of Childhood of Bagrov-Grandson" (1858). Their objectivity and precision of description, as well as their event-filled contents, have made them enduring classics of nineteenth-century prose.

THE FAMILY CHRONICLE. 1856. *Dutton* 1961 pap. $1.55

PUSHKIN, ALEKSANDR SERGEYEVICH. 1799–1837.

   Pushkin is acknowledged as the greatest Russian poet, unsurpassed either in his mastery of diverse literary forms or in the perfection of the blend of form and content which is found in his works. Born in a gentry family, he received a superb education in the Lyceum at Tsarskoe Selo, and there made his literary debut. He was quickly received in St. Petersburg literary society, becoming an intimate of its leading figures. A wild life in the capital ended abruptly in 1820, when some of Pushkin's political verses came to the attention of Emperor Alexander I; the poet was banished to the south of Russia.

   The years of Pushkin's exile were very productive. The Caucasus, the Crimea, and Moldavia, with their strong Oriental elements, moved him to create major works. Equally beneficial to his art was the poet's subsequent restriction to his mother's estate of Mikhaylovskoye (1824–1826); his confinement also kept Pushkin from active involvement with the unsuccessful Decembrist revolt in 1825.

   A new phase in Pushkin's life began in September 1826, when he was summoned by Emperor Nicholas I, granted a pardon for former offenses, and promised special protection. Unfortunately, the poet's existence under the eye of his Imperial patron proved increasingly restrictive: "his inner freedom was forfeited, for he was made to understand that his amnesty was such a signal display of mercy that he could never do too much to live up to it"—(Mirsky). In addition, although his literary genius was in full flower, his personal life was far from happy. In 1831, after a long courtship, the poet married the beautiful but frivolous Nathalie Goncharova, with whom he had little in common. His wife's beauty made her a success in court circles, and Pushkin found himself constantly in the company of men whom he knew scorned him. The final crisis was provoked by Nathalie's friendship with a French loyalist in Russian service, Baron D'Anthes. A series of incidents culminated in a duel between Pushkin and his wife's admirer in January 1837. Pushkin was wounded in the encounter. His death followed two days later. At the orders of the authorities, who feared public demonstrations, he was buried hastily under guard.

   Pushkin demonstrated his genius in short lyrics, long narrative poems, plays, and prose works. His lyrics, especially those of his mature period, are extraordinary in their ease, seeming simplicity, and universality of thought and emotion. His long poems are of various types. Some, such as "The Prisoner of the Caucasus" ("*Kavkazsky plennik*," 1820–1821) and "The Fountain of Bakhchisaray" ("*Bakhchisaraysky fontan*," 1822), are Romantic stories modelled on Byron's Eastern tales. "Eugene Onegin" (1823–1831), the brilliant, psychologically subtle "novel in verse" about a St. Petersburg dandy, helped create the tradition of Russian realism. His final long poem, "The Bronze Horseman" ("*Medny vsadnik*," 1833), centers on the opposition between the rights of the individual and the demands of the state; the conflict is never resolved in this dramatic and majestic work.

   Particularly striking are Pushkin's plays. The Shakespearean "Boris Godunov" (1825) is better known in the West, but it yields in merit to the extraordinarily concentrated "Little Tragedies" (written in the 1830s). The poet's prose, which includes the "Tales of Belkin" ("*Povesti Belkina*," 1831) and "The Queen of Spades" ("*Pikovaya dama*," 1834), is also extremely important; its great artistic merit is shown, in particular, by the fact that it has had an impact on both Dostoevsky and Tolstoy.

   For several decades after his death Pushkin was not sufficiently understood or acknowledged. The situation changed during the 1890s, and since then Pushkin's supreme role in Russian literature has been clarified and accepted by writers, critics, and the reading public at large.

POEMS, PROSE AND PLAYS. Sel. and ed. with introd. by Avrahm Yarmolinsky. *Random* Modern Library Giants 1943 $4.95

PROSE TALES. Trans. by T. Keane. 1914. *Bks. for Libraries* $14.50

COMPLETE PROSE TALES. Trans. by Gillon R. Aitken. *Norton* 1967 $6.95 Norton Lib. pap. $3.95

POEMS. Ed. by H. Jones. *Citadel Press* 1964 pap. $1.25

SELECTED VERSE. Ed. by John Fennell. 1964. *Peter Smith* $3.50

LITTLE TRAGEDIES. Trans. in verse by Eugene M. Kayden; ill. by Vladimir Favorsky. *Antioch Press* (dist. by Kent State Univ. Press) $3.50. Includes The Covetous Knight, Mozart and Salieri, The Stone Guest, and A Feast during the Plague.

RUSLAN AND LUDMILLA. 1820. Trans. by Walter Arndt. *Ardis* 1974 $8.95 pap. $2.95

TALES OF BELKIN. 1830. Trans. and ed. by Jan van der Eng, Jan M. Meijer, and A. G. F. van Holk. *Humanities Press* 1968 pap. $9.50

EUGENE ONEGIN. 1823–1831. Trans. by Eugene M. Kayden *Antioch Press* (dist. by Kent State University Press) 1965 $5.50; trans. in verse and ed. by Vladimir Nabokov Bollingen Ser. *Princeton Univ. Press* 4 vols. Vol. 4 includes photographic reproduction of the 1837 Russian text, other vols. contain elaborate commentary by Nabokov 1964 rev. ed. 1974 boxed set $45.00; trans. in verse by Walter Arndt *Dutton* 1963 pap. $1.75; trans. by E. J. Dent *Oxford* 1946 $2.50; trans. by Babette Deutsch *Penguin* 1975 pap. $2.95. A novel in verse.

THE GOLDEN COCKEREL. 1833. Trans. by Elizabeth C. Hulick. *Astor-Honor* 1962 $3.95; trans. by Patricia Lowe *T. Y. Crowell* 1975 $5.95

THE QUEEN OF SPADES. 1834. (And "and Other Tales") trans. by Ivy Litvinov *New Am. Lib.* 1961 pap. $.60; ("and Other Stories") trans. by Rosemary Edmonds *Penguin* 1962 pap. $.95

A JOURNEY TO ARZRUM. 1836. Trans. by Birgitta Ingemanson. *Ardis* 1974 $6.95 pap. $2.50

THE CAPTAIN'S DAUGHTER. 1836. Trans. by Walter Arndt *Dutton* 1972 pap. $2.25 ("and Other Tales") trans. by Natalie Duddington Everyman's 1961 $3.95 pap. $1.95; ("and Other Great Stories") trans. by N. Duddington and T. Keane *Random* Vintage Bks. 1957 pap. $1.95; *Peter Smith* $4.25

Books about Pushkin

Pushkin. By D. S. Mirsky. 1926. *Dutton* 1963 pap. $1.65; *Folcroft* 1972 $20.00; Studies in Russian Lit. *Haskell* 1974 $13.95
Prelude to Parnassus: Scenes from the Life of Alexander Sergeyvich Pushkin. By James Cleugh. 1936. *Richard West* 1973 $20.00
Pushkin. By Martha W. Beckwith, and others. 1937. *Bks. for Libraries* Black Heritage Library Collection $12.00
Pushkin. By Ernest J. Simmons. 1937. *Peter Smith* $7.50
Centennial Essays for Pushkin. Ed. by Samuel H. Cross and Ernest J. Simmons. 1937. *Russell & Russell* $8.50
Pushkin and Russian Literature. By Janko Lavrin. 1947 *Russell & Russell* 1969 $9.00
Notes on Prosody. By Vladimir Nabokov. *Princeton Univ. Press* Bollingen Ser. 1964 pap. $2.95. Appendix II of his commentary on his translation of "Eugene Onegin."
Pushkin. By David Magarshack. *Grove* 1968 pap. $2.95
Pushkin: Death of a Poet. By Walter N. Vickery. *Indiana Univ. Press* 1968 $6.50
Pushkin: A Comparative Commentary. By John Bayley. Major European Authors Ser. *Cambridge* 1971 $16.50
Pushkin on Literature. By Tatiana Wolff *Harper* (Barnes & Noble) 1973 pap. $10.00
The Pushkin Pleiad: A Primer. By G. Barratt. *Hakkert* (forthcoming) $14.00
Alexander Pushkin. By Walter N. Vickery. World Authors Ser. *Twayne* $6.95

GOGOL, NIKOLAI VASILIEVICH. 1809–1852.

A Ukrainian by background, Gogol is one of Russia's greatest writers, creator of works unsurpassed in imagination and comic wit. Born in the province of Poltava, he came to Petersburg in 1828, already the author of a very weak poem ("Hanz Kuchelgarten") which was severely criticized upon publication. After attempts at establishing himself in several different professions, Gogol achieved a major success with his first volume of stories, "Evenings on a Farm near Dikanka" ("*Vecherana khutore bliz Dikanki*," 1831). Two additional volumes were equally successful—"Mirgorod" (1832) and "Arabesques" (1835).

During this early period, Gogol was in close contact with various groups in Russian intellectual and literary society: with the circle of Pushkin (*q.v.*), with the young idealists led by the critic Belinsky, and with the Slavophiles. Over the years, he drew ever closer to this last group, becoming particularly intimate with the Aksakov family.

His next great literary success came in 1836, with the staging of his comedy "The Inspector-General" ("*Revizor*"). Although its satirical presentation of provincial bureaucracy raised a storm of official protest, the play established its author as a writer of genius. Soon afterwards Gogol left Russia; from 1836 to 1848 he lived almost entirely abroad. During this period, he produced several new works, among them the celebrated story "The Overcoat" ("*Shinel'* ") and the great prose epic "Dead Souls," Part I ("*Mertvye dushi*," 1842).

The last period of Gogol's life (after 1848), was progressively more troubled and gloomy. Certain negative character traits began to dominate the rest of his personality: a belief in a personal mission to save Russia, which was present very faintly in some of his earlier writings, now bloomed fully. This belief took concrete form in the book "Selected Passages from a Correspondence with Friends" (*"Izbrannye mesta iz perepiski s druzyami,"* 1847), in which Gogol offered reactionary and extremely shallow solutions to various types of social problems. The sharply negative reception the book met with in Russia was a bitter blow to its author; partially in response to it he turned towards a simplistic and fanatical brand of Christianity. Under the disastrous influence of Father Matthew Konstantinovsky, he embraced ascetic practices which ruined his physical health and upset his mental balance; one tragic result of this condition was his burning of most of the second part of "Dead Souls." Shortly afterwards, the combination of mental and physical deterioration led to Gogol's death on February 21, 1852.

It is impossible to categorize Gogol with ease. He has been claimed as the founder of Realism in Russia, but has also been considered a Romantic and was an object of special interest for the Symbolists. His early collections ("Evenings," "Mirgorod") are infused with Ukrainian folklore, with its lyrical and comic stories of devils, witches, and young lovers; subsequently, the fantastic is transferred to an urban setting, to the cold world of St. Petersburg, where the demonic assumes a more serious form ("Arabesques"). He is a social critic ("The Overcoat," "The Inspector-General"), yet at the same time he is the creator of powerful grotesque images which are far removed from objective reality. Past generations of readers, writers, and critics have looked at him from widely differing points of view, and future ones will undoubtedly continue to do the same.

THE OVERCOAT (1842) AND OTHER TALES OF GOOD AND EVIL (orig. "Tales of Good and Evil"). Trans. by David Magarshack *Dufour* 1961 $3.50; *Norton* Norton Lib. 1965 pap. $1.95

DEAD SOULS. 1842. *Assoc. Booksellers* Airmont Bks. pap. $.75; *Dutton* Everyman's $2.25; trans. by B. G. Guerney, ed. by René Wellek *Holt* Rinehart Eds. 1948 pap. $1.50; trans. by B. G. Guerney *Random* Modern Lib. pap. $1.35; trans. by Andrew MacAndrew *New Am. Lib.* Signet 1961 pap. $.60; trans. by George Reavey *Oxford* World's Class. 1957 $2.75; trans. by David Magarshack *Penguin* 1961 pap. $1.65; trans. by George Reavey *Norton* Norton Lib. 1971 pap. $1.95

TARAS BULBA. 1842. (And "and Other Tales") *Dutton* Everyman's $3.95 pap. $1.50

THE INSPECTOR-GENERAL. 1836. Acting version by John Anderson *Baker* 1937 $1.25; acting version by John Anderson *French* $1.25; ed. by D. Bondar *Pitman* 2nd ed. 1945 pap. $1.75; (with title "The Government Inspector") trans. by Leonid Ignatieff, adapt. by Peter Raby, introd. by Michael Langham *Univ. of Minnesota Press* 1972 $5.75 pap. $1.95

MIRGOROD. 1835. Trans. by David Magarshack *T. Y. Crowell* (Funk & Wagnalls) Minerva Bks. 1969 pap. $2.50. The title of one of four stories originally published as The Old-World Landowners. (Also: Taras Bulba; Viy; The Story of How Ivan Ivanovich Quarrelled with Ivan Nikiforovich.)

THE COLLECTED TALES AND PLAYS. Trans. by Constance Garnett with introd. by Leonard Kent. *Pantheon* 1964 $10.00. Includes all of his fiction except "Dead Souls."

OLD RUSSIAN STORIES. *A. S. Barnes* Perpetua Bks. 1960 pap. $1.65

THE MANTLE AND OTHER STORIES. Trans. by Claud Field. 1916. *Bks. for Libraries* $9.00

ST. JOHN'S EVE AND OTHER STORIES. Trans. by Isabel F. Hapgood. 1886. *Bks. for Libraries* $12.50

EVENINGS NEAR THE VILLAGE OF DIKANKA. 1831–32. *Ungar* 1960 $4.50. Stories of Ukrainian life.

THE DIARY OF A MADMAN (1835) AND OTHER STORIES. Trans. by Andrew MacAndrew *New Am. Lib.* 1961 Signet pap. $1.25; trans. by R. Wilks *Penguin* 1973 pap. $1.75

LETTERS. Trans. by Carl R. Proffer and Vera Krivoshein; sel. and ed. by Carl R. Proffer. *Univ. of Michigan Press* 1967 $8.00

SELECTED PASSAGES FROM CORRESPONDENCE WITH FRIENDS. Trans. by Jesse Zeldin. *Vanderbilt Univ. Press* 1969 $5.95

Books about Gogol

Gogol. By Janko Lavrin. 1926. *Haskell* 1972 $13.95

Nikolai Gogol. By Vladimir Nabokov. 1944. *New Directions* pap. $2.25

Nikolai Gogol, 1809–1852: A Centenary Survey. By Janko Lavrin. 1951. *Russell & Russell* 1968 $6.50

Gogol: His Life and Works. By Vsevolod Setchkarev. 1953. Trans. by R. Kramer. *New York Univ. Press* 1965 $7.95 pap. $2.25

Gogol as a Short-Story Writer. By F. C. Driessen; trans. by Ian F. Finlay. *Mouton* (dist. by Humanities Press) 1965 $16.50

Dostoevsky and Romantic Realism: A Study of Dostoevsky in Relation to Balzac, Dickens, Gogol. By Donald Fanger. *Harvard Univ. Press* 1965 $8.50; *Univ. of Chicago Press* 1965 pap. $2.45

Nikolay Gogol and His Contemporary Critics. By Paul Debreczeny. *American Philosophical Soc.* 1966 pap. $2.00

Gogol. By Victor Erlich. Russian and East European Studies Ser. *Yale Univ. Press* 1969 $10.00

Gogol: A Life. By David Magarshack. *Grove* 1969 pap. $2.95

Dostoevsky and the Legend of the Grand Inquisitor. By Vasily Rozanov; trans. by Spencer E. Roberts. *Cornell Univ. Press* 1972 $9.50

Divided Soul: The Life of Gogol. By Henri Troyat; trans. by Nancy Amphoux. *Doubleday* 1973 $12.95

Nikolay Gogol. By Thais Lindstrom. World Authors Ser. *Twayne* 1974 $6.95

Gogol from the Twentieth Century: Eleven Essays. Ed. by Robert A. Maguire. *Princteon Univ. Press* 1974 $17.50

ANNENKOV, PAVEL VASILIEVICH. 1812–1887.

A major critic of the nineteenth century, Annenkov was for a time Gogol's secretary and was later a close friend of Turgenev. He exercised a great influence on Russian literary life; his intimate knowledge of his contemporaries makes his memoirs a must for anyone interested in nineteenth-century Russian literature.

EXTRAORDINARY DECADE: Literary Memoirs. Ed. by Arthur P. Mendel. *Univ. of Michigan Press* 1968 $8.50

GONCHAROV, IVAN ALEKSANDROVICH. 1812–1891.

One of Russia's major nineteenth-century novelists, Goncharov came from a family of wealthy merchants. Educated at the University of Moscow, he pursued a career in the civil service, first in the Ministry of Finance, and later, during the more liberal times after 1856, as a censor. His existence was extraordinarily placid; it was troubled only once by an extended sea-voyage to Japan. Goncharov's life did take an unfortunate turn in his later years: he became obsessed with the idea that Turgenev (*q.v.*), as well as the latter's foreign friends (Auerbach, Flaubert), had stolen key themes of his novel "The Precipice" and had used them in their own works.

The corpus of Goncharov's writings includes three novels: "A Common Story" (1847), "Oblomov" (1859) and "The Precipice" (1869), as well as the account of his trip to Japan ("The Frigate 'Pallas,' " 1855–1857), and a number of short stories and essays. "Oblomov" is the best known: its fame rests solidly on the author's sublime celebration of man's slothfulness and boredom, qualities incarnated in Oblomov, the novel's hero (he has since become a literary and psychological byword). Goncharov's other novels have been rather unjustly slighted by the critics. "A Common Story" is a well-constructed, sharply satirical account of a young man's disillusionment with his early ideals. "The Precipice," on which Goncharov worked for almost twenty years, is a massive portrayal of country life which contains a gallery of striking social and psychological types: particularly memorable are the novel's women.

OBLOMOV. 1859. Trans. by Natalie Duddington. *Dutton* Everyman's 1932 pap. $2.25; trans. by Ann Dunnigan *New Am. Lib.* Signet pap. $.95

THE PRECIPICE. 1869. Trans. by M. Bryant. 1915. *Howard Fertig* 1975 $13.75

Books about Goncharov

Oblomov and His Creator: The Life and Art of Ivan Goncharov. By Milton Ehre. Studies of the Russian Institute, Columbia Univ. Ser. *Princeton Univ. Press* 1974 $14.50

Ivan Goncharov: His Life and His Works. By Vsevolod Setchkarev. *Humanities Press* 1974 pap. $24.00

Ivan Goncharov. By A. Lyngstad and S. Lyngstad. World Authors Ser. *Twayne* $6.95

HERZEN, ALEXANDER IVANOVICH. 1812–1870.

Herzen occupies an important place in Russian literature; even more important are his contributions to Russian intellectual and political history. An illegitimate son of a rich nobleman, he was able to lead a rather comfortable life both in Russia and in Western Europe (where he lived from 1847 on). In the thirties, while at the university, together with N. P. Ogaryov, Herzen became the center of a circle whose members were actively interested in politics and socialist ideals. In the 1840s he helped shape the major ideas of Russian Westernism; he also wrote fiction (short stories and the novel "Who Is to Blame?").

After leaving Russia, Herzen became actively involved in European revolutionary movements. Their failure produced one of his masterpieces, the book "From the Other Shore," a series of essays and dialogues dealing with historical subjects. Another triumph is his autobiography "My Past and Thoughts" (written mainly in 1852–1855), which presents a most penetrating view of Russian society in the first half of the nineteenth century. Yet another achievement was *The Bell* (*Kolokol*), a weekly which Herzen published from 1857 on, and which had an enormous influence on both official and unofficial circles in Russia during 1857–1861.

Like the many radical critics (Belinsky, Chernyshevsky, and others), Herzen is characterized by a combination of political and literary interests. Unlike them, however, he never loses an enormous sensitivity of feeling and style, and preserves his humanity through an irony which he directs not only at his ideological adversaries, but also at his allies. In this he is unique in Russian nineteenth-century thought.

THE MEMOIRS OF ALEXANDER HERZEN. 1923. Trans. by J. D. Duff. *Russell & Russell* 2 pts. in 1 vol. 1967 $10.00. Part 1 Nursery and University, 1812–1834; Part 2 Prison and Exile, 1834–1838.

MY PAST AND THOUGHTS. *Knopf* 4 vols. 1968 $30.00; *Random* pap. $4.95; *Gordon Press* 6 vols. $200.00

LERMONTOV, MIKHAIL YUREVICH. 1814–1841.

One of Russia's greatest nineteenth-century poets, Lermontov was at first an officer in the Guards. Because of the views expressed in his poem on the death of Pushkin (*q.v.*) he was transferred to the Caucasus. He was greatly influenced by Byron (*q.v.*). Like Pushkin, he was killed in a duel—at 27.

"A Hero of Our Time," Russia's first psychological novel, is largely autobiographical. Tolstoy called "Taman," one of the five stories of which it is made up, "artistically the most perfect work in Russian literature." As a lyricist Lermontov is second only to Pushkin, and his poetry has attained lasting popularity. Chekhov (*q.v.*) once advised a writer: "I know of no language better than that of Lermontov . . . I should take his tale and analyze it. . . . That's how I would learn to write."

A LERMONTOV READER. Trans. and ed. with introd. by Guy Daniels. *Grosset* Univ. Lib. pap. $2.45

THE DEMON AND OTHER POEMS. Trans. by Eugene M. Kayden. *Antioch Press* (dist. by Kent State Univ. Press) 1965 $4.50

A HERO OF OUR TIME. 1840. Trans. by Vladimir Nabokov with Dimitri Nabokov. *Doubleday* Anchor Bks. 1958 pap. $1.95; trans. by Paul Foote *Penguin* pap. $1.95

Books about Lermontov

Lermontov. By Janko Lavrin. *Hillary House* $2.75
Mikhail Lermontov. By John Mersereau, Jr. Crosscurrents/Modern Critiques Ser. *Southern Illinois Univ. Press* 1962 $4.50

SUKHOVO-KOBYLIN, ALEKSANDR VASILIEVICH. 1817–1903.

Aleksandr Sukhovo-Kobylin is the author of three excellent comedies, "Krechinsky's Wedding," "The Affair," and "The Death of Tarelkin," without which Russian theater would be very much poorer. A nobleman by birth, Sukhovo-Kobylin underwent a traumatic experience when he was accused of murdering his mistress in 1850. After seven years of judicial proceedings, he was finally cleared, but the horror of the accusation and of the pernicious court system left him extremely bitter. All three of his plays contain considerable amounts of satire and the grotesque; the judicial system comes under special attack in the later two works. The first play, a somewhat lighter comedy about a likeable scoundrel, is a staple of the Russian repertoire.

TRILOGY OF ALEXANDER SUKHOVO-KOBYLIN. Trans. by Harold B. Segel. *Dutton* 1969 $6.95

KRECHINSKY'S WEDDING. Trans. by Robert Magidoff. *Univ. of Michigan Press* 1961 $4.50

TOLSTOY, ALEKSEY KONSTANTINOVICH. 1817–1875.

A cousin of Lev Tolstoy (*q.v.*), Count Alexey Konstantinovich Tolstoy is best known as a poet. His verse is highly eclectic; his most important contributions were made in the genres of the historical ballad, the lyric, and satirical verse. As a satirist, in addition to the many fine pieces he wrote under his own name, Tolstoy is also remembered as one of the creators of Koz'ma Prutkov—the fictitious author whose writings devastatingly reflect a quintessence of self-satisfied arrogance and naivete.

Tolstoy's short stories belong to the time of his youth; the first, "The Vampire," dates from 1841. While pleasant reading, they are not particularly significant. Of far greater importance is Tolstoy's splendid trilogy of historical plays about Russia in the sixteenth century: "The Death of Ivan the Terrible" (1866), "Tsar Fyodor Ioannovich" (1868) and "Tsar Boris" (1870).

VAMPIRES: Stories of the Supernatural. Trans. by Fedor Nikanor. *Hawthorn* 1969 $5.95

TURGENEV, IVAN SERGEYEVICH. 1818–1883.

Turgenev was the first great Russian novelist to be popular abroad. He traveled and lived in Europe and received honors not only in Russia, but also in France and England (Henry James included him in a survey of French novelists, and Turgenev is buried in France). His realistic sketches, published first in *The Contemporary*, a literary journal, and later in book form (1852) as "The Hunting Sketches," were immediately successful. They depicted the sufferings of the serfs and helped to achieve their emancipation in 1861.

"The novels of Turgenev cover a period of more than thirty years. They are all short. Each [is] a succession of scenes—some of them of the most exquisite beauty"—(Kropotkin). "He is particularly a favorite with people of cultivated taste; and nothing, in our opinion, cultivates the taste more than to read him." ". . . We move in an atmosphere of unrelieved sadness. We go from one tale to the other in the hope of finding something cheerful, but we only wander into fresh agglomerations of gloom"—(Henry James). Turgenev was popular in Russia, but after the publication of "Fathers and Sons," he received "congratulations, insults, and even some threats from unexpected quarters: the revolutionaries called him an enemy of the people while the reactionaries labeled him the obedient flunky of the Nihilists"—(Slonim). He worked six years on his last novel, "Virgin Soil," a best seller abroad but "a failure in Russia. [It] portrayed the aristocratic class which did not perceive itself in the process of dissolution; it also predicted with a high degree of accuracy the course that future events were to take in the writer's unhappy country"—(*Cyclopedia of World Authors*).

NOVELS. Trans. by Constance Garnett. 1894. *AMS Press* 15 vols. each $12.50 set $185.00; *Scholarly Press* each $12.50 set $185.00

DREAM TALES AND PROSE POEMS. Trans. by Constance Garnett. 1897. *Bks. for Libraries* $11.50

THE BRIGADIER AND OTHER STORIES. Trans. by Isabel F. Hapgood. 1904. *Bks. for Libraries* $19.50

DESPERATE CHARACTER AND OTHER STORIES. Trans. by Constance Garnett. 1917. *Bks. for Libraries* $9.75 *Macmillan* Collier Bks. pap. $.95; trans. by Bernard G. Guerney *Random* Modern Lib. pap. $1.95; trans. by George Reavey *New Am. Lib.* Signet pap. $.75; trans. by Constance Garnett, rev. and ed. by R. Matlaw *Norton* Critical Eds. 1966 $5.50 pap. $2.25 lib. bdg. $4.07; rev. ed. *Penguin* Class. 1975 pap. $1.95; ed. by Neal Burroughs *Simon & Schuster* (Washington Square) 1962 Enrich. Class. pap. $.95

SMOKE. 1867. Trans. by N. Duddington. *Dutton* Everyman's 1949 $3.95 pap. $1.95

THE TORRENTS OF SPRING (also trans. "Spring Torrents"). 1871. Trans. by Constance Garnett. 1916. *Bks. for Libraries* $12.50

VIRGIN SOIL. 1877. Trans. by Rochelle S. Townsend. *Dutton* Everyman's 1955 $3.95 pap. $1.95

LITERARY REMINISCENCES. Trans. by David Magarshack; pref. by Edmund Wilson. 1958. *T. Y. Crowell* (Funk & Wagnalls) Minerva Bks. 1968 pap. $2.45. Contains reminiscences and autobiographical fragments.

LETTERS: A Selection. Ed. by Edgar H. Lehrman. *Knopf* 1961 $5.00. English translation of letters to Tolstoy, Henry James, and others.

THE DISTRICT DOCTOR AND OTHER STORIES. Ill. by Mervin Bileck. *A. S. Barnes* Perpetua Bks. 1951 pap. $1.45

DIARY OF A SUPERFLUOUS MAN (1850) AND OTHER STORIES. Trans. by Isabel F. Hapgood. 1904. *Bks. for Libraries* $11.00

FIRST LOVE (1860) AND OTHER TALES (orig. "Selected Tales"). Trans. by David Magar-shack. *Norton* Norton Lib. 1968 pap. $2.25

LIZA. *Dutton* Everyman's $3.95

THE PORTRAIT GAME: The Game Played with Imaginary Sketches. Trans. and ed. with introd. by Marion Mainwaring. *Horizon Press* 1973 $5.95

THREE NOVELLAS. Trans. by Marion Mainwaring. *Farrar, Straus* 1969 $5.95

A MONTH IN THE COUNTRY. 1850. Adapted into English by Emlyn Williams. *French* acting ed. rev. 1957 $1.25. A comedy in two acts.

THE HUNTING SKETCHES. 1852. (With title "Sketches from a Hunter's Album") trans. and sel. by Richard Freeborn *Penguin* Class. 1967 pap. $1.75; (with title "A Sports-man's Notebook") trans. by Charles and Natasha Hepburn *Viking* Compass Bks. 1957 pap. $1.65

RUDIN. 1856. Ed. by Galina Stilman. *Columbia* 1962 pap. $2.95; *Penguin* Class. Ser. 1975 pap. $2.25

HOME OF THE GENTRY. 1859. Trans. by Richard Freeborn. *Penguin* 1970 pap. $1.65; *Gannon* lib. bdg. $5.00

HAMLET AND DON QUIXOTE. 1860. 1930. *Folcroft* $5.50. An essay.

ON THE EVE. 1860. Trans. by Moura Budberg. *Dufour* 1948 $3.95; trans. by Gilbert Gardiner *Penguin* 1967 pap. $1.50

FATHERS AND SONS (also trans. "Fathers and Children"). 1862. *Amsco School Pubns.* 1970 pap. $1.50; trans. by Constance Garnett *Assoc. Booksellers* Airmont Bks. 1967 pap. $.60; trans. by Barbara Makanowitsky *Bantam* 1960 pap. $.95; trans. by Avril Pyman *Dutton* Everyman's $3.95; trans. by Richard Hare, with introd. by E. J. Simmons *Holt* (Rinehart) 1949 pap. $2.95

Books about Turgenev

Two Masters, Browning and Turgenief. By Philip S. Moxom. 1912. *Folcroft* $8.50
Turgenev: A Critical Study. By Edward Garnett. 1924. *Folcroft* $20.00; *Haskell* 1974 $12.95
Turgenev: The Man, His Art and His Age. By Avrahm Yarmolinsky. 1926. *Macmillan* Collier Bks. pap. $1.50
Democratic Ideas in Turgenev's Works. By Harry Hershkowitz. 1932. *AMS Press* $6.50
Turgenev. By J. A. Lloyd. 1942. *Folcroft* $9.45; *Kennikat* 1971 $9.50
Two Russian Performers: Turgenieff and Tolstoy. By J. A. Lloyd. Studies in Russian Lit. Ser. *Haskell* 1974 $16.95
The Turgenev Family. By Mme V. Zhitova. 1947. *Richard West* $10.00
Turgenev, the Novelist's Novelist: A Study. By Richard Freeborn. *Oxford* 1960 $6.00
Turgenev in English: A Checklist of Works by or about Him. By Rissa Yachnin and David H. Stam. *N.Y. Public Lib.* 1963 $2.50
Ivan Turgenev. By Charles Moser. Essays on Modern Writers Ser. *Columbia* 1972 pap. $1.00
Monarch Literature Notes on Turgenev's Fathers and Sons. By Jane Wexford. *Simon & Schuster* (Monarch) pap. $1.00
The Other Turgenev: From Romanticism to Symbolism. By Marina Ledkovsky. *Humanities Press* 1974 $11.00

PISEMSKY, ALEKSEI FEOFILAKTOVICH.   1820–1881.

"[Pisemsky is] a most interesting interpreter of the slavophile and nationalist spirit in the Russian realistic novel. Whoever wants to have an adequate idea of the latter and, moreover, of the Russian mentality should not miss [him]"—(Marc Slonim, in the *N.Y. Times*). A provincial, Pisemsky was educated in Moscow and spent 20 years in government service. He opposed foreign fashions and European ideas. "One Thousand Souls," a novel, was a favorite with the general public.

ONE THOUSAND SOULS. 1858. Trans. by Ivy Litvinov. 1959. *Greenwood* $18.50

A BITTER FATE. 1859. (In "Masterpieces of Russian Drama," Vol. 1) ed. by George R. Noyes *Dover* pap. $3.00; *Peter Smith* 2 vol. set $10.00

Books About Pisemsky

Pisemsky: A Provincial Realist. By Charles A. Moser. *Harvard Univ. Press* 1969 text ed. $11.00

DOSTOEVSKY, FYODOR MIKHAILOVICH (also Dostoievsky, Dostoevskii, Dostoevski, Dostoyevsky; also Feodor, Fedor). 1821–1881.

Dostoevsky is not only a great Russian novelist, but also one of the most significant figures in modern European letters. The son of a surgeon, he was exposed at an early age to the sight of human suffering, a theme which assumes great significance in his fiction. He was educated as an engineer and worked briefly for the army, but his interests in literature led him to abandon the military and become a professional writer. He made his debut with "Poor Folk" ("*Bednye lyudi,*" 1846), a subtle novel about the psychology of the poor and socially insignificant, which was received enthusiastically by the public and the critics. The instant success was not sustained, however. Dostoevsky's next work, "The Double" ("*Dvoinik,*" 1846) in which fantastic motifs enter the world of bureaucratic Petersburg, met with puzzlement and hostility.

By 1847 Dostoevsky had begun to frequent the meetings of the mildly socialist Petrashevsky circle. In 1849, members of this group were arrested and charged with political crimes; they were eventually sentenced to terms of prison and army service in the ranks, but first all underwent a shattering mock public execution.

The period 1850–1853, which Dostoevsky spent in the Siberian prison at Omsk, produced a profound change in his views. He entered it not only a socialist, but a potential regicide (as twentieth century studies have shown); he emerged, under the influence of the Bible and his fellow prisoners, a deeply devoted Christian and believer in Russia and the Russian state. The views produced by this transformation are reflected in his most celebrated works: "Notes from the Underground" (1864), "Crime and Punishment" (1866), "The Idiot" (1868), "The Devils" (1871–1872), "The Adolescent" (1875) and "The Brothers Karamazov" (1879–1880).

Dostoevsky's private professional life after his return to Petersburg in 1859 was filled with vicissitudes. During the sixties, he witnessed the deaths of his wife, Maria, and his brother, Michael (both of these experiences had a profound effect on him). He was constantly involved with creditors, whose demands forced him to agree to vastly unfair terms offered by publishers, and to write at a very high speed. For several years, he was a passionate and uncontrolled gambler; some of these bouts coincided with a particularly unhappy love affair.

The change for the better in Dostoevsky's life came with his second marriage to Anna Snitkina, a much younger woman who, while not quite able to appreciate her husband's views in full, successfully created an environment in which he could find peace and be able to work. Beginning with the seventies, Dostoevsky's financial affairs were put in order and he and his wife returned to Russia after a four-year stay in Western Europe. Dostoevsky drew close to religious figures and to highly conservative governmental circles; in spite of this, he was read by an ever wider, often very radical, public. At the 1880 Pushkin Celebrations in Moscow, Dostoevsky's public speech was greeted with enthusiasm; the same public display of affection was manifested by thousands at his funeral in 1881.

Dostoevsky's role in modern literature is manifold. He is a profound innovator in the realm of prose, the creator of the so-called "polyphonic novel." In his writings, he examines the most profound philosophical questions, dealing with them by examining the depths of the human psyche (such concerns have made him a precursor of the Existentialists). Finally, he is a religious thinker, and his works have had a broad impact on people's religious consciousness. He is and will certainly continue to be one of the most universal of Russian writers.

GREAT SHORT WORKS OF DOSTOEVSKY. Trans. by George Bird and others; ed. by Ronald Hingley. *Harper* 1968 pap. $1.95

THREE SHORT NOVELS. Trans. by Constance Garnett, rev. and ed. by Avrahm Yarmolinsky. *Doubleday* Anchor 1960 $3.50. Includes The Double, Notes from the Underground, The Eternal Husband.

THE SHORT STORIES OF DOSTOEVSKY. Ed. by William Phillips. *Dial* 1946 $7.50

THE BEST SHORT STORIES. Trans. by David Magarshack. *Random* Modern Lib. 1955 pap. $2.95. Includes Notes from the Underground and The Honest Thief.

NOTES FROM THE UNDERGROUND and THE DOUBLE. Trans. by Jessie Coulson. *Penguin* Class. 1972 pap. $2.50

NOTES FROM THE UNDERGROUND. (And "Poor People," "The Friend of the Family") trans. by Constance Garnett. *Dell* pap. $1.50

NOTES FROM THE UNDERGROUND. (And "The Grand Inquisitor") *Dutton* pap. $1.95

NOTES FROM UNDERGROUND: Short Stories. Trans. by Andrew R. MacAndrew. *New Am. Lib.* Signet pap. $.95

THE GAMBLER, BOBOK, A NASTY STORY. Trans. by Jessie Coulson. *Penguin* Class. pap.
$1.45

THE DREAM OF A QUEER FELLOW. (And "The Pushkin Speech") trans. by S. Koteliansky
and J. M. Murray. *Humanities Press* 1960 pap. text ed. $2.50

STAVROGIN'S CONFESSION and THE PLAN OF THE LIFE OF A GREAT SINNER. 1922 *Haskell*
Studies in Fiction 1972 lib. bdg. $11.95

THE DIARY OF A WRITER. Trans. by Boris Brasol. 1947. *Octagon* 1973 2 vols. lib. bdg.
$47.50. A collection of Dostoevsky's essays and stories on a variety of topics which
reveal many aspects of his thought and clarify the key role of journalistic activity in
his art.

POOR FOLK. 1846. (And "The Gambler") trans. by C. J. Hogarth. *Dutton* Everymans
$3.95 1972 pap. $2.95

POOR PEOPLE (also trans. "Poor Folk"). (And "A Little Hero") trans. with introd. by
David Magarshack. *Doubleday* Anchor pap. $1.95; *Peter Smith* $4.25

THE DOUBLE: A Poem of St. Petersburg. 1846. Trans. by George Bird. *Indiana Univ.
Press* Midland Bks. 1958 pap. $2.45

NETOCHKA NEZVANOVA. 1849. Trans. by Ann Dunnigan. *Prentice-Hall* Spectrum 1971
pap. $2.45

THE FRIEND OF THE FAMILY. 1859. (And "The Eternal Husband," 1870) ed. by Philip
Rahv. *Holt* Rinehart Eds. 1963 pap. $1.25

THE INSULTED AND THE INJURED. 1861. Trans. by Constance Garnett. 1955. *Greenwood*
1975 lib. bdg. $17.25

THE HOUSE OF THE DEAD. 1861–1862. Trans. by Constance Garnett. *Dell* Laurel Leaf
Lib. pap. $1.25; trans. by H. Sutherland Edwards, with introd. by Nicholay Andreyev
Dutton Everyman's $3.95 pap. $2.25

MEMOIRS FROM THE HOUSE OF THE DEAD (also trans. "House of the Dead"). Trans. by
Jessie Coulson. *Oxford* World's Class. 1956 1965 $5.00

WINTER NOTES ON SUMMER IMPRESSIONS. 1863. *McGraw-Hill* 1965 $4.95 pap. $1.95

NOTES FROM UNDERGROUND. 1864. Trans. by Mirra Ginsburg. *Bantam* 1974 $1.25;
trans. by Serge Shishkoff, ed. by Robert G. Durgy *T. Y. Crowell* 1970 pap. $2.95

LETTERS FROM THE UNDERWORLD (also trans. "Notes from Underground"). Trans. with
introd. by C. J. Hogarth. *Dutton* Everyman's $3.95

CRIME AND PUNISHMENT. 1865–1866. Introd. by Raymond R. Canon. *Assoc. Booksellers*
Airmont Classics Ser. pap. $.95; *Bantam* pap. $1.25; *Dell* pap. $1.25; trans. by
Constance Garnett, with introd. by Nikolay Andreyev *Dutton* Everyman's 1972 $3.95
pap. $2.95; *Grosset* Univ. Lib. pap. $2.50; trans. by Constance Garnett, with introd. by
Avrahm Yarmolinsky *Harper* Mod. Class. 1951 $2.80; trans. by Constance Garnett
Heritage Conn. linen bound $11.95 (in prep.); trans. by Constance Garnett *Random*
Modern Lib. $3.95 pap. $2.95; trans. by Sidney Monas *New Am. Lib.* $.95; trans. by J.
Coulson, ed. by George Gibian *Norton* Critical Eds. 1964 text ed. $8.50 pap. text ed.
$2.95; (in 6 Parts and an Epilogue) trans. by Jessie Coulson *Oxford* World's Class.
$5.00; trans. with introd. by David Magarshack *Penguin* Class. 1952 pap. $1.95; trans.
by Constance Garnett *Random* Vintage Bks. pap. $1.95; *Scholastic Bk. Services* pap.
$.75; ed. by M. Scammell *Simon & Schuster* (Washington Square) Enriched Class. 1963
pap. $.95

THE NOTEBOOKS FOR CRIME AND PUNISHMENT. Trans. and ed. by E. Wasiolek *Univ. of
Chicago Press* 1967 $9.50 1974 pap. $3.95

"These notebooks are extraordinarily interesting. They are also wholly necessary to any study
of the complicated development and functioning of Dostoevsky's art"—(*N.Y. Times*).

THE GAMBLER. 1866. (And "The Diary of Polina Suslova") trans. by Victor Terras; ed. by Edward Wasiolek. *Univ. of Chicago Press* 1972 $9.95 pap. $2.95. A very useful edition, especially for its biographical materials.

THE IDIOT. 1868. Trans. by Constance Garnett. *Bantam* pap. $.95; *Dell* Laurel Eds. pap. $1.75; trans. by Eva M. Martin, with introd. by Richard Curle *Dutton* Everyman's $3.95 1972 pap. $2.50; *New Am. Lib.* 1969 pap. $1.50; trans. by David Magarshack *Penguin* pap. $2.95; trans. by J. W. Strahan *Simon & Schuster* (Washington Square) pap. $1.25

THE NOTEBOOKS FOR THE IDIOT. Trans. by Katherine Strelsky, ed. by Edward Wasiolek. *Univ. of Chicago Press* 1967 $9.50 1973 pap. $2.95

THE DEVILS. 1871–1872. Trans. by David Magarshack. *Penguin* Class. 1954 pap. $2.30

THE POSSESSED (also trans. "The Devils"). Trans. by Constance Garnett, with introd. by Nikolay Andreyev. *Dutton* Everyman's 2 vols. each $3.95; trans. by Constance Garnett with a chapter trans. by Avrahm Yarmolinsky *Random* Modern Lib. 1936 $3.95; trans. by Andrew MacAndrew *New American Library* Signet 1962 $1.50

THE NOTEBOOKS FOR THE POSSESSED. Trans. by Victor Terras; ed. by Edward Wasiolek *Univ. of Chicago Press* 1968 $12.50

THE ADOLESCENT (also trans. "A Raw Youth"). 1875. Trans. by Andrew R. MacAndrew. *Doubleday* 1972 pap. $3.50

THE NOTEBOOKS FOR A RAW YOUTH. Trans. by Victor Terras; ed. by Edward Wasiolek. *Univ. of Chicago Press* 1969 $15.00

THE BROTHERS KARAMAZOV. 1879–1880. *Assoc. Booksellers* Airmont Class. pap. $1.25; trans. by Andrew R. MacAndrew *Bantam* 1970 pap. $1.45; abr. ed. by Edmund Fuller *Dell* 1956 pap. $1.50; trans. by Constance Garnett, with introd. by Edward Garnett *Dutton* Everyman's 2 vols. each $3.95; trans. by Constance Garnett *Random* Modern Lib. $5.95 pap. $2.95; ed. by Manuel Komroff-Hill *New. Am Lib.* Signet pap. $1.25; trans. by David Magarshack *Penguin* 2 vols. Vol. 1 pap. $2.25 Vol. 2 pap. $1.95; *Random* Vintage Bks. pap. $2.45

THE NOTEBOOKS FOR THE BROTHERS KARAMAZOV. Ed. by Edward Wasiolek. *Univ. of Chicago Press* 1971 $9.50

THE GRAND INQUISITOR. Trans. by Constance Garnett. *Bobbs* Lib. Arts 1948 pap. $.95; trans. by Constance Garnett Milestones of Thought *Ungar* $1.25

THE UNPUBLISHED DOSTOEVSKY, VOL. ONE: Diaries and Notebooks (1860–1871). Trans. by Berczynski, Boyer, Proffer, Monter; ed. by C. R. Proffer; with introd. by Robert L. Belknap. *Ardis* 1973 $10.95

"The hitherto unpublished notebooks ... brought out in 1971 by the Soviet Academy of Sciences ... most interesting for the general reader will probably be the development of his long-standing polemic with the leading liberal journals and publicists of the day"—(*Choice*).

THE UNPUBLISHED DOSTOEVSKY, VOL. TWO: Diaries and Notebooks (1872–1876). Trans. by Boyer, Proffer; ed. by C. R. Proffer. *Ardis* 1975 $12.95

"The range of material is as varied and fascinating as in Volume 1. . . . By far the most interesting entries are the long fulminating diatribes against Turgenev, ... liberals, Roman Catholicism, etc."—(*LJ*).

LETTERS OF DOSTOIEVSKY TO HIS WIFE. Studies in Dostoyevsky *Haskell* 1974 lib. bdg. $18.95

DOSTOEVSKY: Letters and Reminiscences. Trans. by S. S. Koteliansky and J. Middleton Murray. 1923. Select Bibliographies Reprint Ser. *Bks. for Libraries* $16.50

LETTERS OF FYODOR MICHAILOVITCH DOSTOEVSKY TO HIS FAMILY AND FRIENDS. Trans. by Ethel C. Mayne. *Richard West* $25.00

NEW DOSTOEVSKY LETTERS. Trans. by S. Koteliansky. Studies in Dostoevsky *Haskell* 1974 lib. bdg. $9.95

Books about Dostoevsky

Fyodor Dostoevsky: A Critical Study. By John Middleton Murry. 1916. *Russell & Russell* $8.50

Dostoevsky. By Nicholas Berdyaev. 1934. *New Am. Lib.* Meridian Bks. pap. $2.95

Dostoevsky: The Making of a Novelist. By Ernest J. Simmons. 1940. *Peter Smith* $5.50

Dostoevsky. By André Gide; introd. by Arnold Bennett. *New Directions* new. ed. 1949 pap. $2.25

Tolstoy or Dostoevsky: An Essay in the Old Criticism. By George Steiner. *Knopf* 1959 $8.95; *Dutton* pap. $2.25. A study of two fundamentally opposed views of human life.

Dostoevsky: A Human Portrait. By Robert Payne. *Knopf* 1961 $8.95

Dostoevsky: A Collection of Critical Essays. Ed. by René Wellek. *Prentice-Hall* 1962 $6.50 Spectrum Bks. pap. $1.95

A Study in Dostoevsky. By Vyacheslav Ivanov. *Farrar, Straus* Noonday 1963 pap. $1.95

Dostoevsky and Romantic Realism: A Study of Dostoevsky in Relation to Balzac, Dickens, and Gogol. By Donald Fanger. Studies in Comp. Lit. *Harvard Univ. Press* 1965 $8.50

"This searching and formidably erudite study . . . is a significant contribution to comparative literature, and will be of interest to the literate reader and to the scholar. . . . A worthy addition to a distinguished series"—(*LJ*).

Dostoievsky. By A. Steinberg. *Hillary House* 1966 $2.75. Dostoyevsky's works as autobiography.

"Though short and concise, this is an original and profoundly interesting book. The general reader should be warned that it presupposes an extensive and detailed acquaintance with both the life and the works of its subject"—(*TLS*, London).

Dostoevsky: His Life and Work. By Konstantin Mochulsky. Trans. by Michael A. Minihan. *Princeton Univ. Press* 1967 $17.50 pap. $3.95

First English translation of "the best single work in any language about Dostoevsky's work as a whole"—(George Gibian).

The Structure of the Brothers Karamazov. By Robert L. Belknap. *Mouton* (dist. by Humanities Press) 1967 $10.00

Young Dostoyevsky, 1846–1849: A Critical Study. By Victor Terras. *Mouton* (dist. by Humanities Press) 1969 $18.50

Dostoevsky, Tolstoy, and Nietzsche. By Lev Shestov. Trans. by Bernard Martin and Spencer E. Roberts *Ohio Univ. Press* 1970 $11.00.

Dostoevsky and the Legend of the Grand Inquisitor. By Vasily Rozanov. Trans. by Spencer E. Roberts. *Cornell Univ. Press* 1972 $9.50

Balzac and Dostoevsky. By Leonid Grossman. (And "Composition in Dostoevsky's Novels") trans. by Lena Karpov. *Ardis* 1973 $6.95 pap. $2.95

Dostoevsky and Dickens: A Study of Literary Influence. By N. M. Lary. *Routledge & Kegan Paul* 1973 $11.85

Dostoevsky: His Life and Work. By Leonid Grossman. Trans. by Mary Mackler. *Bobbs* 1975 $12.50

Dostoevsky: Reminiscences. By Anna Dostoevsky. Trans. and ed. by Beatrice Stillman. *Liveright* (dist. by Van Nostrand–Reinhold) 1975 $12.50

NEKRASOV, NIKOLAI ALEXANDROVICH.   1821–1878.

Son of a brutal hunting squire, Nekrasov entered literature at an early age after his father's lack of support forced him to abandon his university studies. A very considerable business ability brought him success in the world of publishing; by 1845, he was the main publisher of the new wave of young writers. From 1846 to 1866 he was the owner and editor of *The Contemporary* (*Sovremennik*), and in his hands the journal became the leading Russian literary organ. Later he achieved a similar success with the journal *Notes of the Fatherland* (*Otechestvennye zapiski*).

Aside from his role as publisher, Nekrasov's principal achievement lies in the realm of poetry. Rightly regarded as a major figure of the nineteenth century, he is at his strongest as a satirist (his masterpiece is the vast poem "Who Is Happy in Russia?"). Not only satire, but also his lyrical and narrative poems are deeply influenced by folk songs; perhaps his most important work which shows the folklore element is the long poem "The Pedlars" ("*Korobeyniki*," 1861), the beginning of which has in turn become a popular folk song.

POEMS BY NICHOLAS NEKRASOV. Trans. by Juliet M. Sockice. *Scholarly Resources, Inc.* 1974 $12.95

WHO CAN BE HAPPY AND FREE IN RUSSIA? 1917. *AMS Press* $12.50

Books about Nekrasov

Nikolai Nekrasov. By Murray B. Peppard. World Authors Ser. *Twayne* 1967 $6.95

Nikolaj Nekrasov. His Life and Poetic Art. By Sigmund S. Birkenmayer. *Mouton* (dist. by Humanities Press) 1968 $14.75

OSTROVSKY, ALEXANDER NIKOLAYEVICH. 1823–1886.

Ostrovsky is the major figure in nineteenth-century Russian theater thanks to the large number of his plays (about fifty, mostly in prose) and to their generally high artistic merit. His work falls into two periods, with 1861 serving as an approximate dividing point. The first period includes dramas which deal mostly with an area of Russian life Ostrovsky knew quite intimately—the society of merchants and of the lower levels of the government bureaucracy. The treatment this social sphere receives at Ostrovsky's hands is quite varied; in spite of Soviet critics, who generally view the playwright as an accusing chronicler of social evil, Ostrovsky clearly exhibits both an attraction and a disgust for certain attitudes and human types he depicts. Among the most famous plays of this group are "Among Friends One Always Comes to Terms" ("*Svoi lyudi—sochtemsya,*" 1850), and "Poverty Is No Crime" ("*Bednost' ne porok,*" 1854). His masterpiece is "The Storm" ("*Groza,*" 1860), in which social themes provide the background and the motivation for a tragic love story.

Ostrovsky's writing after 1861 is rather different from what he did earlier. He devotes himself in part to historical drama and to folkloric themes: his achievement in the latter area is "The Snow Maiden" ("*Snegurochka*"). Other plays deal with realistic subjects; some of them have become staples of Russian repertoire.

PLAYS. Ed. by George R. Noyes. 1917 *AMS Press* 1969 $11.50

FIVE PLAYS OF ALEXANDER OSTROVSKY. (orig. "Other Plays by Ostrovsky") trans. and ed. by Eugene K. Bristow. *Pegasus* 1969 pap. $2.95. Includes It's A Family Affair, We'll Settle It Ourselves; Poor Bride; Storm; Scoundrel; Forest.

EASY MONEY AND TWO OTHER PLAYS: Even a Wise Man Stumbles and Wolves and Sheep. Trans. by David Magarshack. 1944. *Greenwood* $11.75; *Verry* $2.50

ARTISTS AND ADMIRERS: A Comedy in Four Acts. Trans. by E. Hanson. *Harper* (Barnes & Noble) 1970 pap. $2.75

SALTYKOV-SHCHEDRIN, MIKHAIL (pseud. of Mikhail Yevgrafovich Saltykov). 1826–1889.

The satirist Mikhail Yevgrafovich Saltykov published much of his work under the pseudonym Shchedrin, and "according to the custom of Russian literary history, he has been immortalized under the dual name of Saltykov-Shchedrin"—(Harkins). He served as a government official until 1868, when he resigned to devote himself to writing. A liberal, interested in Western literature generally, he and his writings suffered the political ups and downs of changing times. In later life he enjoyed immense popularity, but his short stories and sketches were too journalistic and topical to have survived. His major work, a realistic novel, was "The Golovlyov Family," a dark depiction of the animal cruelties of the serf-owning landed class. D. S. Mirsky calls it "one of the most terrible visions of ultimately dehumanized humanity ever conceived by a major writer." To Arnold Bennett (*q.v.*) it ranked "among the very greatest novels in the world."

THE GOLOVLYOV FAMILY. 1872–1876. Trans. by Natalie Duddington, with introd. by Edward Garnett. *Dutton* Everyman's $3.95

CHERNYSHEVSKY, NIKOLAI GAVRILOVICH. 1828–1889.

Son of a priest, Chernyshevsky became, together with N. Dobrolyubov (1836–1961) and D. Pisarev (1840–1868), one of the leading radical thinkers of mid-nineteenth-century Russia. His views were fanatical: he championed utilitarianism and a rather naively construed idea of progress. His first work was his doctoral dissertation, "The Aesthetic Relation of Art to Reality" (1855). His most famous book is "What Is to Be Done?" ("*Chto delat'*"), which he wrote while imprisoned for revolutionary activity in the Peter and Paul Fortress in St. Petersburg. Almost devoid of artistic merit, this novel had an enormous impact on Russian intelligentsia because of its ideas, and it is still regarded as a major classic in the Soviet Union.

WHAT IS TO BE DONE? 1863. Abr. ed. by I. B. Turkevich. Russian Library Ser. *Random* 1961 pap. $1.95

Books about Chernyshevsky

Sons against Fathers: Studies in Russian Radicalism and Revolution. By E. Lampert. *Oxford* 1965 $12.75

N. G. Chernyshevskii. By Francis B. Randall. World Authors Ser. *Twayne* 1967 $6.95

Chernyshevskii: The Man and the Journalist. By William F. Woehrlin. Russian Research Center Studies *Harvard Univ. Press* 1971

The Thought and Teachings of N. G. Černyševskij. By N. G. Pereira. Slavistic Printings and Reprintings Ser. *Mouton* (dist. by Humanities Press) 1975 pap. text ed. $13.00

TOLSTOY, COUNT LEO (NIKOLAYEVICH) (also Tolstoi).   1828–1910.

Tolstoy's life and literary career were characterized by moral and artistic seeking, and by conflict with himself and his surroundings. Of old nobility, he began by living the rather normal, dissipated life of a man of his class; however, his inner compulsion for moral self-justification led him to a different set of experiences. In 1851 he became a soldier in the Caucasus, and began to publish while stationed there. Even more significant were his experiences during the Crimean War; the siege of Sevastopol provides the background for his analyses of human behavior in battle in the "Sevastopol Stories" ("*Sevastopol'skie rasskazy*," 1855–1856).

After the war, Tolstoy mixed for a time with St. Petersburg literary society, an experience which he did not find satisfactory. From 1856 to 1861 he travelled extensively abroad. In 1862 he married Sophie Andreyevna Behrs: this union proved extremely happy for a long time, but his conversion in 1879 led to increasing unhappiness and bitter conflict.

Tolstoy's life after his marriage was centered on his family. He accepted and gloried in this happy, satisfied existence, and celebrated it in the final section of "War and Peace." A different note emerged in "Anna Karenina"; a process was beginning which culminated in Tolstoy's conversion to a special, rational form of Christianity in which moral behavior was of supreme importance. The conversion is powerfully described in "The Confession" ("*Ispoved*" 1880).

Following his inner transformation, Tolstoy began to proselytize his new faith. A supreme polemicist, he actively participated in debates on a large number of political and social issues, generally finding himself at odds with the government. His teaching of nonresistance, which later so profoundly influenced Mahatma Gandhi, attracted many followers; his stature was enormous both within Russia and abroad, and his excommunication by the Orthodox Church resulted in the celebrated cartoon which showed the great writer disproportionately larger in stature than his ecclesiastical judges.

The story of his final years is one of increasing inner torment leading to final tragedy. Living as he did on a luxurious estate, Tolstoy felt himself to be at odds with his own teachings. He adopted an increasingly simple style of life, came into conflict with his wife over the disposition of his property (which she wished to safeguard for their children), but could never really justify himself in his own eyes. In 1910, surrounded by world adulation but desperately unhappy at home, Tolstoy ran away. His health did not permit him to go far; he caught pneumonia and died at the railway station of Astapovo on November 7. His death was headline news throughout the world.

Tolstoy's art evolved significantly in the course of his life, but at the same time possesses a certain inner unity. From the beginning, Tolstoy concentrated on man's inner life. However, an important difference between early and late works lies in the fact that where at first his focus is on the gulf between superficial behavior and subconscious motivation, he subsequently puts this motivation to the test of moral standards and uses it for didactic purposes.

The body of Tolstoy's writings is enormous, encompassing not only pure fiction, but also a vast amount of publicistic material. His three great novels are "War and Peace," "Anna Karenina" and "Resurrection" ("*Voskresen'e*"). Many of his short works are of equally great artistic value; among them, "The Death of Ivan Ilyich" is a philosophical text of the first order, while "Hadji-Murat" is a gem of narration and plot construction.

COMPLETE WORKS. Trans. and ed. by Leo Wiener. 1904–1905. *AMS Press* 24 vols. each $21.00 set $490.00

GREAT SHORT WORKS. Trans. by Louise and Aylmer Maude; ed. with introd. by John Bayley. *Harper* Perennial Lib. 1967 $1.75. Includes The Cossacks, Family Happiness, The Death of Ivan Ilyich, Father Sergius, The Devil, The Kreutzer Sonata, Master and Man, Hadji Murad, Alyosha the Pot.

TWENTY-THREE TALES. Trans. by Aylmer and Louise Maude. *Oxford* World's Class. $7.50

RUSSIAN STORIES AND LEGENDS. Trans. by Louise and Aylmer Maude. *Pantheon* 1967 lib. bdg. $5.89

SIX SHORT MASTERPIECES. Ed. by F. D. Reeve. *Dell* Laurel Eds. pap. $.75. Includes Two Hussars, A Happy Married Life, Yardstick, The Death of Ivan Ilyich, The Kreutzer Sonata, After the Ball.

TALES OF ARMY LIFE. Trans. by Louise and Aylmer Maude. *Oxford* World's Class. $5.75

THE COSSACKS, SEVASTOPOL, THE INVADERS AND OTHER STORIES. 1899. *Bks. for Libraries* 3 vols. in 1 $20.50

THE DEATH OF IVAN ILYCH AND OTHER STORIES. Trans. by Aylmer Maude. *New Am. Library* Signet 1960 pap. $1.25; *Oxford* World's Class. $4.75

ESARHADDON AND OTHER TALES. 1903. *Bks. for Libraries* $8.00

FATHER SERGIUS AND OTHER STORIES AND PLAYS. 1911. *Bks. for Libraries* $13.00

THE KREUTZER SONATA AND OTHER STORIES. Trans. by Benjamin R. Tucker. 1890. *Bks. for Libraries* $13.75

THE KREUTZER SONATA, THE DEVIL AND OTHER TALES. Trans. by J. D. Duff and Aylmer Maude. *Oxford* World's Class. 1940 $5.50

MASTER AND MAN AND OTHER PARABLES. Introd. by Nikolay Andreyev. *Dutton* Everyman's $3.95 pap. $1.95

THE RUSSIAN PROPRIETOR AND OTHER STORIES. Trans. by Nathan H. Dole. 1887. *Bks. for Libraries* $13.75

THE SNOW STORM AND OTHER STORIES. Trans. by Louise and Aylmer Maude. *Oxford* World's Class. $5.00

THE COSSACKS. (And "The Death of Ivan Ilyich" and "Happy Ever After") trans. by Rosemary Edmonds. *Gannon* lib. bdg. $5.00; *Penguin* Classics Ser. $1.25

THE COSSACKS AND THE RAID. Trans. by Andrew MacAndrew. *New Am. Lib.* Signet 1961 pap. $1.25

FABLES AND FAIRY TALES. *New Am. Lib.* Plume 1962 pap. $1.25

TWENTY-TWO RUSSIAN TALES FOR YOUNG CHILDREN. Trans. by Miriam Morton. *Simon & Schuster* 1969 lib. bdg. $4.50

LITTLE STORIES. *Aurora* 1971 $1.95

SEBASTOPOL: Tales. 1855–56. Trans. by Frank D. Millet, with introd. by Philip Rahv. *Univ. of Michigan Press* 1961 pap. $2.45

CHILDHOOD (1852), BOYHOOD (1854), and YOUTH (1857). Trans. by Louise and Aylmer Maude. *Oxford* World's Class. $5.75; trans. by Rosemary Edmonds *Penguin* Class. 1964 pap. $1.45; *Simon & Schuster* (Washington Square) 1968 pap. $.95

WAR AND PEACE. 1865–1869. *Avon* 1973 pap. $3.95; anonymous translation (1886) *Dutton* Everyman's 2 vols. each $3.95; trans. by Ann Dunigan *New Am. Lib.* Signet 1968 pap. $1.95; trans. by L. and A. Maude; ed. by George Gibian *Norton* Critical Eds. 1966 pap. $5.95; trans. by L. and A. Maude *Oxford* World's Class. 1922–23 $11.50; trans. by Rosemary Edmonds *Penguin* Class. 2 vols. pap. each $2.50; introd. by Clifton Fadiman *Simon & Schuster* Inner Sanctum Ed. 1942 $12.95

WAR AND PEACE. Trans. by Constance Garnett; ed. by Manuel Komroff *Bantam* abr. ed. 1955 pap. $1.50; ed. by Edmund Fuller *Dell* pap. $.75; ed. for the modern reader in a trans. rev. by Princess Alexandra Kropotkin *Grosset* 1956 $3.95; trans. by Constance Garnett *Random* Modern Lib. Giants 1931 $5.95; trans. by L. and A. Maude, ed. by E. J. Simmons *Simon & Schuster* (Washington Square) pap. $1.25 rev. ed. Enriched Class. Ser. 1972 pap. $1.25

ANNA KARENINA. 1873–1877. *Assoc. Booksellers* Airmont Class. pap. $1.25; abr. ed. by Edmund Fuller *Dell* Laurel Leaf Lib. $.75 *Dodd* Great Ill. Class. 1966 $5.95; trans. by Constance Garnett, ed. by L. J. Kent and N. Berberova *Random* Modern Library 1930 pap. $2.95; trans. by David Magarshack *New Am Lib.* Signet pap. $1.25; trans. by Louise and Aylmer Maude, ed. by George Gibian *Norton* Critical Eds. 1970 text ed. $9.00 pap. text ed. $4.25; trans. by L. and A. Maude *Oxford* World's Class. 1950 $7.50; trans. by Rosemary Edmonds *Penguin* pap. $2.95

WHAT MEN LIVE BY. 1882. Ill. by Jeff Hill. *Peter Pauper Press* 1954 $1.95

RESURRECTION. 1889–1900. Trans. by Vera Traill *New Am. Lib.* Signet pap. $1.25; trans. by Louise Maude *Oxford* World's Class. 1952 $5.75; trans. by Rosemary Edmonds *Penguin* Class. 1966 pap. $2.45

MASTER AND MAN. 1895. Ed. by Eleanor Aitken. *Cambridge* 1969 text ed. $2.95. Short story.

TOLSTOY ON EDUCATION. Trans. by Leo Wiener. *Univ. of Chicago Press* 1967 $8.50
Phoenix Bks. 1968 pap. $2.95

CONFESSION (1879), THE GOSPEL IN BRIEF (1881), and WHAT I BELIEVE (1882). Trans.
by Aylmer Maude. *Oxford* World's Class. $4.25

WHAT IS ART? 1897–98. Trans. by Aylmer Maude. *Bobbs* Lib. Arts 1960 pap. $2.25;
(and "Essays on Art") *Oxford* World's Class. 1962 $7.50; *Somerset Pub.* repr. of 1959 ed.
$15.50

THE KINGDOM OF GOD IS WITHIN YOU. 1905. Trans. by Leo Wiener; introd. by Kenneth
Rexroth. *Farrar, Straus* Noonday pap. $3.95

THE KINGDOM OF GOD AND PEACE ESSAYS. Trans. with introd. by Aylmer Maude. *Oxford*
World's Class. 1947 $6.00

THE LAW OF LOVE AND THE LAW OF VIOLENCE. Trans. by Mary Koutouzow Tolstoy. *Holt*
1970 $3.95 pap. $1.75

WRITINGS ON CIVIL DISOBEDIENCE AND NONVIOLENCE. *New Am. Lib.* Signet pap. $1.25

WAR, PATRIOTISM, PEACE. *Garland Pub.* lib. bdg. $12.00

WHAT THEN MUST WE DO? (And "A Letter to Engelhardt") trans. by Aylmer Maude.
Oxford World's Class. 1975 $7.25

WHY DO MEN STUPEFY THEMSELVES? *East Ridge Press* 1975 pap. $2.50

GUY DE MAUPASSANT. Studies in French Literature *Haskell* 1974 lib. bdg. $7.95

THE PRIVATE DIARY OF LEO TOLSTOY: 1853–1857. 1927. *Kraus* $13.00

TOLSTOY; LITERARY FRAGMENTS, LETTERS AND REMINISCENCES. Trans. by Paul England,
ed. by René Füllöp-Miller. 1931 *AMS Press* $9.25

ESSAYS AND LETTERS. Trans. by Aylmer Maude. 1909. *Bks. for Libraries* 1973 $16.75

Books about Tolstoy

Tolstoi as Man and Artist with an Essay on Dostoievsky. By D. S. Merezhkovsky. 1902. *Scholarly Press* 1970 $19.50. A study by an early Symbolist writer and critic.

The Last Days of Tolstoy. By Vladimir G. Chertkov. Trans. by Nathalie A. Duddington. *Kraus* 1973 $14.00. By one of Tolstoy's closest intimates in the final period of his life.

Reminiscences of Tolstoi. By Count Ilya Tolstoy. 1914. *Haskell* 1974 lib. bdg. $18.95

Reminiscences of Tolstoy, Chekhov and Andreyev. By Maxim Gorky. 1920. Trans. by Leonard Woolf and others, introd. by Mark Van Doren. *Hillary House* 1968 $4.50; *Folcroft* $20.00

The Countess Tolstoy's Later Diary, 1891–1897. By Sofia Tolstaia. Trans. by Alexander Werth. 1929. Select Bibliographies Reprint Ser. *Bks. for Libraries* facsimile ed. $12.25

The Final Struggle: Being Countess Tolstoy's Diary for 1910. By S. Tolstoy. *Octagon* 1972 lib. bdg. $15.00

Leo Tolstoy. By Ernest J. Simmons. 1945. *Peter Smith* 2 vols. Vol. 1 The Years of Development Vol. 2 The Years of Maturity set $12.00; *Routledge & Kegan Paul* 1973 $13.25 pap. $6.00

The Hedgehog and the Fox: An Essay on Tolstoy's View of History. By Isaiah Berlin. *Simon & Schuster* Touchstone 1953 pap. $1.50

An erudite and ingenious essay on history in "War and Peace." The author "has chosen to subject these historical passages to careful attention. In this brilliant essay he not only succeeds in making very good sense out of Tolstoy's historical theory but also finds in it an indispensable key to the complex and divided personality of the great Russian novelist"—*(N.Y. Times)*.

Tolstoy: A Life of My Father. By Alexandra L. Tolstoy. 1953 *Octagon* lib. bdg. $11.50

Tolstoy or Dostoevsky: An Essay in the Old Criticism. By George Steiner. *Dutton* 1971 pap. $2.25; *Knopf* 1959 $8.95

Literature and Aesthetics: Tolstoy and the Critics. By Holley G. Duffield and M. Bilsky. *Scott, Foresman* 1965 pap. $4.35

Tolstoy between War and Peace. By Waclaw Lednicki. *Mouton* (dist. by Humanities Press) 1965 $11.50. A distinguished Slavist traces Tolstoy's attitude toward Poland through his writings.

Tolstoy and the Novel. By John Bayley. *Viking* Compass Bks. 1968 pap. $1.95

Bayley's judgments "are overwhelming in their insights and rightness. [He] is superbly the 'good reader' for whom Tolstoy longed, sympathetic and stimulating. . . . But the attempt to place Tolstoy within 19th century Russian literature is disappointing as criticism and inadequate as literary history"—*(N.Y. Times)*.

Introduction to Tolstoy's Writings. By Ernest J. Simmons. *Univ. of Chicago Press* 1968 $7.50
1969 pap. $1.95

Tolstoy. By Henri Troyat. Trans. by Nancy Amphoux. *Dell* Laurel Ed. 1969 pap. $1.65

An excellent, highly readable work. "The biographer's method has been to let all the characters
in his work speak for themselves whenever possible, and one feels that he has scoured in his
work the uttermost reaches. . . . Henri Troyat has drawn up a definitive version of the balance
sheet. No man . . . can consider it and fail to be moved by awe, humility and exaltation"—(James
Lord, in the *N.Y. Times*).

Tolstoy: A Collection of Critical Essays. Ed. by Ralph E. Matlaw. *Prentice-Hall* Spectrum Bks.
1967 $5.95 pap. $1.95

"What is especially interesting and really quite important to the study of Tolstoy is the emphasis
in this collection on his conscious artistry"—(*LJ*).

Tolstoy the Rebel. By Leo Hecht. *Revisionist Press* 1975 lib. bdg. $29.95

LESKOV, NIKOLAI SEMYONOVICH. 1831–1895.

"Leskov is a delicate psychologist," writes V. S. Pritchett. "He is robustly comical, extravagantly
grotesque . . . a writer of great vitality who does not suffer from boredom. His voice is the voice of
the discoverer and traveler whose stories have the dust and jolts of the journey on them. . . . Leskov's
natural successor was Gorky, whose university was the Russian people and who recognized
in Leskov a master." He is one of the few nineteenth-century Russian writers who did not come
from the aristocracy. The son of a minor civil servant, he was brought up by his aunt, an English
Quaker, after his parents died. His early employment with an Englishman, the estate manager
of a Russian landowner, took him all over Russia and required the writing of long reports. His
employer noted Leskov's ability with words and suggested that he become a journalist.

He is mainly known in this country for his story "Lady Macbeth of the Mtsensk District" (1865),
which was made into an opera by the composer Shostakovich. At the time of its first performance
it was attacked by Stalin for modernist and romantic tendencies. In spite of other attacks and
critical hostility Leskov has always been widely read in Russia and is considered one of its greatest
storytellers.

SELECTED TALES. Trans. by David Magarshack; introd. by V. S. Pritchett. *Farrar, Straus*
Noonday 1961 pap. $3.45

THE SATIRICAL STORIES. Trans. and ed. by William B. Edgerton. *Pegasus* 1969 $7.50
pap. $2.95

THE CATHEDRAL FOLK. 1872. Trans. by Isabel F. Hapgood. 1924. *Greenwood* lib. bdg.
$17.75. A moving narrative of Russian provincial clergy.

THE WILD BEAST. Trans. by Guy Daniels. *T. Y. Crowell* (Funk & Wagnalls) 1968 $3.95

POMYALOVSKY, NIKOLAI GERASIMOVICH. 1835–1863.

Pomyalovsky's twenty-eight year life was tragic. Educated at a brutal clerical seminary, he then
had to struggle hard for existence, became a drunkard, and died of delirium tremens. His most
famous work, "Seminary Sketches" (1862–1863), is based on his own experiences in school and its
strong impact results from a vivid and detailed accumulation of horrors undergone by the chief
protagonist. Pomyalovsky's other novels include "Bourgeois Happiness" and "Molotov."

SEMINARY SKETCHES. 1862–1863. Trans. by Alfred R. Kuhn. *Cornell Univ. Press* 1973
$8.75

KOROLENKO, VLADIMIR GALAKTIONOVICH. 1853–1921.

Korolenko ranks among the most important writers of late nineteenth-century Russian literature. Of mixed Russian-Polish parentage, he grew up in semi-Polish territories, and oriented
himself towards Russia only after 1863. A student in Petersburg and later in Moscow, he was
expelled for secret political activity; between 1879 and 1885 he was exiled in Siberia. From 1885 to
1895 he lived in the provincial city of Nizhny Novgorod, where he produced most of his best work.
In 1895 he returned to the capital and was elected a member of the Academy in 1900.

A major figure among the Populists, Korolenko fought actively against social and political
injustice. After October 1917, he was hostile to the Bolsheviks, and he maintained this attitude until
his death in December 1921.

Korolenko's stories are distinguished by many characteristics: a charming lyricism, an appreciation both of nature and of man, and a wonderful humor. His "History of My Contemporary"
(1910–1922), an autobiography which shows the life in his native region of Volhynia, reveals many
of these qualities, and is perhaps his best work.

MAKAR'S DREAM AND OTHER STORIES. Trans. by Marian Fell. 1916. Short Story Index
   Reprint Ser. *Bks. for Libraries* $12.25

BIRDS OF HEAVEN AND OTHER STORIES. Trans. by Clarence A. Manning. 1919. Short
   Story Index Reprint Ser. *Bks. for Libraries* $10.25

SIBERIA: Three Short Stories. *Saifer* $5.00

THE BLIND MUSICIAN. 1890. *Gordon Press* $9.00; *Greenwood* lib. bdg. $9.00

HISTORY OF MY CONTEMPORARY. 1910–1922. Trans. by Neil Parsons. *Oxford* 1972
   $12.00

GARSHIN, VSEVOLOD MIKHAILOVICH. 1855–1888.

Although his total literary output was extremely small—about twenty short stories—Garshin is
rightly regarded as a very talented writer. Of gentry origin, he possessed an extraordinary moral
sensitivity and a spirit of compassion for humanity and its suffering. These qualities were given a
special stimulus by his experiences during the war with Turkey (1877), when he enlisted as a
private, fought well, and was finally wounded and invalided. The war was reflected in "Four Days"
(1877), a popular story about a wounded soldier who for four days remains on the battlefield next
to the putrefying corpse of a Turk.

In spite of the reputation brought him by "Four Days," Garshin's subsequent life was unhappy.
In his last years he grew increasingly morbid, passed over the brink of madness, and finally
committed suicide by throwing himself down a staircase.

Among Garshin's stories, the best known are "Attalea Princeps" (a fable about a palm tree) and
"The Red Flower" (about an inmate of a lunatic asylum—a theme later taken up by Chekhov in
"Ward No. 6").

THE SIGNAL AND OTHER STORIES. Trans. by Rowland Smith. 1915. *Books for Libraries*
   facsimile ed. $12.00

THE TRAVELLING FROG. *McGraw-Hill* 1966 $3.95

CHEKHOV, ANTON PAVLOVICH (also Tchekhov, Tchekov, Tchekhoff, Chekhov). 1860–1904.

The greatest of Russian dramatists, Chekhov was also a major writer of short stories—he wrote
over 500. Most of the latter are less than ten pages long, and many have never been translated.
The "Oxford Chekhov," edited by Ronald Hingley, proposes to remedy this. Chekhov, says Thais S.
Lindstrom (in *SR*), "revolutionized the short story [and] created its modern form . . . a new kind of
short fiction which lacking beginning or end, was 'all middle' . . . streaked with seemingly
irrelevant realistic detail that was made to carry a heavy burden of meaning. . . . The one thematic
factor which is a constant in the stories . . . is the depiction of life in all its grubbiness." "Chekhov
concentrated on the reality of man alone, of man unsupported by the comfort of false hopes"—
(*N.Y. Review of Books*). British and American critics are fascinated by Chekhov: "[His reputation]
has grown steadily and quietly, like the man himself, until today there is scarcely a critic who would
not place those brief stories—by a man who always regarded himself as a minor writer and never
attempted to emulate his famous contemporaries in the writing of long novels—among the major
achievements of Russian literature"—(Frank O'Connor). "I assume there is something unique
about Chekhov. I think it is this: There was in this profane saint so much of what one seeks in
human beings that mere admiration does not encompass one's response to him. Only love does"—
(Charles Simmons).

THE OXFORD CHEKHOV. Trans. and ed. by Ronald Hingley. 5 vols. available. Vol. 1
   Short Plays 1968 $8.50 Vol. 2 Platonov, Ivanov, The Seagull 1967 $12.00 Vol. 5
   Stories, 1889–1891 1970 $10.25 Vol. 6 Stories, 1892–1893 1971 $17.00 Vol. 8 Stories,
   1895–1897 1965 $8.50

"If ever a series deserved popular and scholarly success at the same time, this is it. . . . *The Oxford
Chekhov* is a landmark in our Russian studies. May the woolly, mannered, picturesquely-Slav
Chekhov of previous translators vanish for ever, and Dr. Hingley's sharp-edged, disconcertingly
modern Chekhov flourish"—(*TLS*, London).

THE PORTABLE CHEKHOV. Ed. with introd. by Avrahm Yarmolinsky. *Viking* 1947 $6.25
   1955 pap. $3.25

PLAYS AND STORIES. Trans. by S. S. Koteliansky. *Dutton* Everyman's 1937 $3.95 pap.
   $1.35

BEST KNOWN WORKS. 1929. *Bks. for Libraries* $22.50

Stories

THE SHORT STORIES. Various translators. *Random* Modern Lib. 1932 $2.95. Twenty-two tales.

GREAT STORIES. Ed. by David Greene. *Dell* pap. $.95

SELECTED STORIES. Trans. by Ann Dunnigan. *New Am. Lib.* Signet (orig.) 1960 pap. $.95

SELECTED STORIES. Trans. by Jessie Coulson. *Oxford* World's Class. 1963 $3.00

SELECTED SHORT STORIES. Ed. by G. A. Birkett and Gleb Struve. *Oxford* 1951 $3.50

SELECT TALES. Trans. by Constance Garnett. 1949. *Harper* (Barnes & Noble) 2 vols. 1961 1963 each $8.50

SEVEN SHORT STORIES. Trans. with introd. by Ronald Hingley. *Oxford* 1974 pap. $3.95

SEVEN SHORT NOVELS. Trans. by Barbara Makanowitzky. *Norton* Norton Lib. pap. 1971 $2.45

NINE HUMOROUS TALES. 1918. *Bks. for Libraries* $6.50

RUSSIAN SILHOUETTES. Trans. by Marian Fen. 1915. *Bks. for Libraries* $12.50

THE STEPPE AND OTHER STORIES. Trans. by Adeline Kaye. 1915. *Bks. for Libraries* $10.00

THE GRASSHOPPER AND OTHER STORIES. Trans. by A. E. Chamot. 1926. *Bks. for Libraries* $10.50

THE SINNER FROM TOLEDO AND OTHER STORIES. Trans. by Arnold Hinchliffe. *Fairleigh Dickinson Univ. Press* 1972 $8.00

THE KISS (1887) AND OTHER STORIES. Trans. by R. E. Long. 1915. *Bks. for Libraries* $11.50

MY LIFE AND OTHER STORIES. Trans. by S. S. Koteliansky and Gilbert Cannan. 1920. *Bks. for Libraries* $10.00

THE BLACK MONK AND OTHER STORIES. Trans. by R. E. Long. 1903. *Bks. for Libraries* $11.00

THE WOLF AND THE MUTT. Trans. by Guy Daniels. *McGraw-Hill* 1971 $3.83

THE IMAGE OF CHEKHOV. Trans. with introd. by Robert Payne. *Knopf* 1963 $6.95. Forty stories in the order in which they were written.

WARD SIX (1892) AND OTHER SHORT NOVELS. *New Am. Lib.* 1965 Signet pap. $.95

THE LADY WITH THE LAPDOG (1898) AND OTHER TALES. Trans. by David Magarshack. *Penguin* 1964 pap. $1.45

UNKNOWN CHEKHOV: Stories and Other Writings. Trans. by Avrahm Yarmolinsky. *T. Y. Crowell* (Funk & Wagnalls) 1968 $6.95 pap. $2.95

Plays

BEST PLAYS: The Seagull, Uncle Vanya, The Three Sisters, The Cherry Orchard. Trans. with introd. by Stark Young. *Random* Modern Lib. 1930 1956 $3.95

FOUR GREAT PLAYS: The Cherry Orchard, The Seagull, The Three Sisters, Uncle Vanya. *Bantam* 1968 pap. $1.25

SIX FAMOUS PLAYS: The Cherry Orchard, The Bear, The Proposal, The Three Sisters, Uncle Vanya, The Seagull. Trans. by Marian Fell. *Hillary House* 1959 pap. $2.25

SIX PLAYS. Trans. by Robert W. Corrigan. *Holt* 1962 pap. $1.95

THE MAJOR PLAYS: Ivanov, The Seagull, Uncle Vanya, The Three Sisters, The Cherry Orchard. Trans. by Ann Dunnigan. *New Am. Lib.* Signet 1964 pap. $.75

SHORT PLAYS. Trans. by Ronald Hingley. *Oxford* 1969 pap. $1.85. Contains all the short dramatic works.

PLAYS: Ivanov, The Seagull, Uncle Vanya, The Three Sisters, The Cherry Orchard, The Bear, The Marriage Proposal, Jubilee. Trans. by Marian Fen. *Penguin* Class. Ser. 1951 1959 pap. $2.50

IVANOV, THE SEAGULL, AND THREE SISTERS. Trans. by Ronald Hingley. *Oxford* 1967 pap. $2.25

PLATONOV. Trans. with introd. by David Magarshack. *Farrar, Straus* (Hill & Wang) 1964 Mermaid Dramabks. pap. $1.75

IVANOV. 1886. English version by John Gielgud based on trans. by Ariadne Nicolaeff. *Theater Arts* 1966 $1.85

THE SEAGULL. 1896. Trans. by Stark Young *French* 1950 $1.25

UNCLE VANYA. 1899. Ed. by Jacques Chwat *Avon* Bard Bks. 1974 pap. $.75; trans. by Stark Young *French* pap. $1.25; (and "The Cherry Orchard") trans. by Ronald Hingley *Oxford* 1965 pap. $1.95; trans. by Tyrone Guthrie and Leonid Kipnis *Univ. of Minnesota Press* Drama Eds. 1969 $5.00 pap. $1.25

THE THREE SISTERS. 1901. *Avon Bks.* 1965 pap. $.60; trans. by Stark Young *French* 1941 $1.25; trans. by Randall Jarrell *Macmillan* 1969 $5.95

THE CHERRY ORCHARD. 1904. *Avon* Bard Bks. pap. $.60; trans. by Stark Young *Baker* pap. $1.25; trans. by Stark Young *French* 1947 pap. $1.25; adapted by John Gielgud *Theater Arts* 1963 pap. $1.95

Journal

LITERARY AND THEATRICAL REMINISCENCES. Trans. and ed. by S. S. Koteliansky. 1927 *Blom* 1965 $11.75; *Haskell* 1974 $13.95

Letters

LETTERS *Blom* 3 vols. Vol. 1 The Life and Letters of Anton Tchekhov (1925) trans. and ed. by S. S. Koteliansky and Philip Tomlinson $10.75 Vol. 2 Letters to Olga Knipper (1925) trans. and ed. by Constance Garnett $12.50 Vol. 3 Letters on the Short Story, the Drama, and Other Literary Topics (1924) ed. by Louis S. Friedland, introd. by Ernest J. Simmons $11.75 (*see next entry*).

LETTERS ON THE SHORT STORY, THE DRAMA AND OTHER LITERARY TOPICS. 1924. Sel. and ed. by Louis Friedland. *Dover* 1966 pap. $2.50; *Peter Smith* $4.50

A "very useful, exciting, interesting, and highly informative collection"—(*Choice*).

Books about Chekhov

Anton Chekhov. By Nina Toumanova. *Columbia* 1960 $8.00 pap. $1.50

Chekhov: A Biography. By Ernest J. Simmons. 1962 *Univ. of Chicago Press* Phoenix Bks. 1970 pap. $3.95

The Breaking String: The Plays of Anton Chekhov. By Maurice Valency. *Oxford* 1966 $8.50

Valency "traces Chekhov's development as a playwright, interweaving biographical data and analysis of his other writing. . . . The discussion goes far beyond mere analysis of the plays; it is a comprehensive study of the writer"—(*N.Y. Times*).

Chekhov and Other Essays. By Lev Shestov. *Univ. of Michigan Press* 1966 Ann Arbor Bks. pap. $1.95

The Chekhov essay of the Soviet philosopher Shestov, "an original thinker and an eloquent writer, . . . is penetrating, controversial, and very moving. . . . He sees Chekhov as 'the poet of hopelessness' "—(*N.Y. Review of Books*).

Chekhov: A Collection of Critical Essays. Ed. by Robert Louis Jackson. *Prentice-Hall* 1967 $6.50 Spectrum Bks. pap. $1.95. Most of the essays are by Russian writers.

Chekhov, the Man. By Korney Chukovsky. *Haskell* 1974 $8.95

SOLOGUB, FYODOR (pseud. of Fyodor Kuzmich Teternikov). 1863–1927.

Sologub, poet and novelist, was a leading Russian decadent and symbolist who after 1917 became one of the "inner exiles" of revolutionary Russia. He died in 1927 and has been denounced in official Soviet circles as a decadent exponent of erotic and fantastic symbolism. His work, a far cry from "socialist realism," is pessimistic, relieved by occasional sardonic humor. The *Saturday Review* said of "The Petty Demon": "Technically speaking, this is a typically Russian novel in that it leaves the reader's imagination ablaze. Sologub is a literary craftsman of stature. . . . 'The Petty Demon' is a work of art that may be regarded as complementary to Dostoevsky's 'The Possessed' and 'The Brothers Karamazov.' "

THE PETTY DEMON. 1907. Trans. with pref. and notes by Andrew Field; introd. by Ernest J. Simmons. 1962 *Indiana Univ. Press* Midland Bks. 1970 pap. $2.95

THE CREATED LEGEND. 1908–1912. 1916. *Greenwood* 1975 $15.25

THE WHITE DOG (in "Modern Russian Classics"). Trans. by Isaac Goldberg. *Branden* pap. $.95

SHESTOV, LEV. 1866–1938.   *See Chapter 5, Philosophy,* Reader's Adviser, *Vol. 3.*

BAL'MONT, KONSTANTIN DMITRIEVICH.   1867–1942.

Bal'mont, born into a landed family, attended Moscow University, from which he was expelled for taking part in a student movement. In 1905 he went to Paris. In his poetry he attempts to capture fleeting moods in highly fluent, musical, carefully measured verse. For this reason he has been called "the Russian Swinburne"—after the English poet (*q.v.*) who, like Bal'mont, was influenced by Baudelaire and Shelley.

Bal'mont translated the complete works of Shelley into Russian; also works of Calderón, Whitman, Poe, Verlaine, Baudelaire (*qq.v.*), and many others. His own works have been extensively translated into English. They include: "Gift to the Earth" (1921), "Haze" (1922), "Mine—To Her: Poems about Russia" (1923), "The Northern Lights" (1923), "In the Parted Distance" (1930), "The Blue Horseshoe" (1937), and two autobiographical works in prose, "Under the New Sickle" (1923), and "Air Path" (1923).

SELECTED POEMS. (In "Modern Russian Poetry: An Anthology") trans. and ed. by Vladimir Markov and Merrill Sparks. *Bobbs* 1967 $12.50 pap. $5.95

VERESAYEV, VIKENTI (pseud. of Vikenty Vikentievich Smidowicz).   1867–1946.

Veresayev, a physician by profession, was initially associated with the *Znanie* (Knowledge) group founded by Gorky. His basic orientation was realistic. In 1901, he published his nonfictional "Memoirs of a Physician," which became extremely successful. His subsequent works deal with the intelligentsia in its confrontation with the revolution. His two novels on this subject are "In a Blind Alley" *("V Tupike,"* 1922), and "The Sisters" (1933).

In addition to work in fiction, Veresayev made important contributions to the study of Pushkin and Gogol. He also translated a significant amount of Greek poetry into Russian.

THE DEADLOCK. 1922. Trans. by Nina Wissotzky and Camilla Coventry. *Hyperion* 1973 $15.75

THE SISTERS. 1933. Trans. by Juliet Soskice. *Hyperion* 1974 $16.50

GORKY, MAXIM (also Gorki—pseud. of Aleksei Maksimovich Peshkov).   1868–1936.

The man who renamed himself Gorky (Bitter) was an ardent Communist and his books are better known to the masses than the works of any other Russian. His formal education totaled only five months, and "what he later called ironically 'my universities' were his experiences along the banks of the Volga river as a docker, cobbler's apprentice, baker, errand boy, and handyman"— (Slonim). He played "an equally important part in his country before and after the Revolution"— the events of his life were interwoven with those of Russian history and with his literary expression. "Mother" was the "first portrayal in Russian Literature of the factory proletariat as a nascent force destined to break down the existing order." Gorky is the "poet of the barefoot brigade, of the vagabonds who eternally wander from one end of Russia to the other. . . . He is a student of sensational effect, and the short story is peculiarly adapted to his natural talent"— (Persky). Gorky's play "The Lower Depths" is his work best known in America. This famous proletarian drama was a formative influence on Eugene O'Neill's (*q.v.*) "The Iceman Cometh" in its depiction of the dregs of modern society. His autobiography shows his great faith in man and courage in the midst of sordidness and misery.

Nondramatic Works

A BOOK OF SHORT STORIES. Ed. by Avrahm Yarmolinsky and Moura Budberg. 1930 *Octagon* 1972 $13.50

SELECTED SHORT STORIES. Introd. by Stefan Zweig. *Ungar* 1959 $8.00

SELECTED SHORT STORIES. *Beekman Pub.* 1975 $10.00

FOMA GORDEYEV. 1899. 1956. *Greenwood* 1974 $13.25

ORLOFF AND HIS WIFE: Tales of the Barefoot Brigade. Trans. by Isabel F. Hapgood. 1901. *Bks. for Libraries* 1973 $19.75

TWENTY-SIX AND ONE AND OTHER STORIES. 1902. *Bks. for Libraries* 1973 $12.75

THE OUTCASTS AND OTHER STORIES. 1905. *Bks for Libraries* $10.00

TALES FROM GORKY. Trans. by Nisbet R. Bain. 1902. *Folcroft* $15.00

TALES OF TWO COUNTRIES. 1914. *Bks. for Libraries* $10.25

STORIES OF THE STEPPE. 1918. *Bks. for Libraries* $7.00

THROUGH RUSSIA. Trans. by C. J. Hogarth. *Dutton* Everyman's 1922 $3.95 pap. $1.75. Short stories.

DECADENCE. 1925. Trans. by Veronica Dewey. 1927. *Folcroft* $12.50

THE BYSTANDER. Trans. by Bernard Gilbert Guerney. 1930. *Folcroft* $10.00; *Oriole Eds.* 1974 $14.50. Vol. I of "The Life of Klim Sangin" (1927–1936).

THE MAGNET. Trans. by Alexander Bakshy. 1931. *Oriole Eds.* 1974 $16.50. Vol. 2 of "The Life of Klim Sangin."

OTHER FIRES. Trans. by Alexander Bakshy. 1933 *Oriole Eds.* 1974 $12.50 Vol. 3 of "The Life of Klim Sangin."

CULTURE AND THE PEOPLE. 1939. *Bks. for Libraries* $12.25

ON LITERATURE. *Univ. of Washington Press* 1974 $10.00; *Beekman Pub.* 1975 $8.95. Selected articles.

LITERATURE AND LIFE. Trans. by Edith Bone. 1946. *Folcroft* $15.00

THE LIFE OF A USELESS MAN. Trans. by Moura Budberg. *Doubleday* Anchor Bks. 1972 pap. $1.95

Plays

THE LOWER DEPTHS AND OTHER PLAYS. Trans. by Alexander Bakshy and Paul S. Nathan. *Yale Univ. Press* 1945 1959 pap. $2.75. Includes The Lower Depths (1902); Barbarians; Enemies (1906); Queer People; Vassa Zheleznova (1910); The Zykovs; Yegor Bulychov (1932).

THE LOWER DEPTHS. 1902. Trans. by Jacques Chwat. *Avon* Bard Bks. 1974 pap. $.75; trans. by Edwin Hopkins *Branden* pap. $.95; trans. by Kitty Hunter-Blair and Jeremy Brooks *Viking* 1974 $5.95 Compass Bks. pap. $2.25

ENEMIES. 1906. Trans. by Jeremy Brooks and Kitty Hunter-Blair. *Viking* 1974 $4.95 Compass Bks. pap. $2.25

MOTHER. 1907. Trans. by Isidore Schneider *Citadel Press* 1972 pap. $3.95; trans. by Margaret Wettlin *Macmillan* Collier Bks. 1962 pap. $.95

Journals and Letters

REMINISCENCES OF TOLSTOY, CHEKHOV AND ANDREYEV. Trans. by S. S. Koteliansky and Leonard Woolf. 1920. *Folcroft* $20.00; *Hillary House* 1968 $4.50; *Richard West* $12.50

AUTOBIOGRAPHY. 1913–1923. Trans. by Isidore Schneider *Citadel Press* 1969 pap. $3.95; *Macmillan* Collier Bks. 1962 pap. $1.50; *Peter Smith* $6.75. Includes: My Childhood (1913); In the World (1915); My Universities (1923).

MY CHILDHOOD. 1913. *Beekman* 1975 $7.50; trans. by Margaret Wettlin *Oxford* World's Class. 1961 $2.95; trans. by R. Wilks *Penguin* $1.75. Pt. I of his Autobiography.

MY APPRENTICESHIP. 1923. Trans. by Ronald Wilks. *Beekman Pub.* 1975 $12.50; *Penguin* 1974 $2.25

UNTIMELY THOUGHTS: Essays on Revolution, Culture and the Bolsheviks, 1917–1918. Trans. with introd. by Herman Ermolaev. *Eriksson* (dist. by Independent Publishers Group, c/o David White, 60 E. 55 St., New York, N.Y. 10022)

FRAGMENTS FROM MY DIARY. 1924. Trans. by Moura Budberg. *Folcroft* 1974 $20.00; *Haskell* 1974 $14.95; *Penguin* $2.95; *Praeger* 1972 $8.95

Books about Gorky

Maxim Gorky. By Hans Ostwald. 1950. *Richard West* $15.00

Maxim Gorky and His Russia. By Alexander S. Kaun. 1931. *Blom* 1968 $12.50

Maxim Gorky, Romantic Realist and Conservative Revolutionary. By Richard Hare. *Oxford* 1962 $5.00

Gorky: His Literary Development and Influence on Soviet Intellectual Life. By Irwin Weil. *Random* 1966 pap. $2.95; *Peter Smith* $5.00

Maxim Gorky, the Writer: An Interpretation. By F. M. Borras. *Oxford* 1967 $6.00

Bridge and the Abyss: The Troubled Friendship of Maxim Gorky and V. I. Lenin. By Bertram D. Wolfe. *Praeger* 1967 $15.00

Maksim Gorki. By Gerhard Habermann; trans. by E. Schlant. Modern Literature Monographs Ser. *Ungar* 1971 $6.00 pap. $1.75

HIPPIUS, ZINAIDA NIKOLAEVNA. 1869–1945.

Wife of the writer Merezhkovsky, Hippius is considered one of the "older" Symbolist poets. Her verses are striking both in execution and in content: "from the very beginning she made her verse a wonderfully refined and well-tempered instrument for the expression of her thought"— (Mirsky).

In addition to poetry, Hippius published several volumes of short stories and two novels, "The Devil's Doll" (1911) and "Román-Tsarevich" (1914). In 1917, she and her husband became anti-Bolshevik and subsequently emigrated from Russia.

SELECTED WORKS OF ZINAIDA HIPPIUS. Trans. and ed. by Temira Pachmuss. *Univ. of Illinois Press* 1972 $10.00

BETWEEN PARIS AND ST. PETERSBURG: Selected Diaries of Zinaida Hippius. Ed. by Temira Pachmuss. *Univ. of Illinois Press* 1975 $12.50

Books about Hippius

Zinaida Hippius: An Intellectual Profile. By Temira Pachmuss. *S. Illinois Univ. Press* 1970 $12.50

BUNIN, IVAN ALEKSEYEVICH. 1870–1953. (Nobel Prize 1933)

Bunin was little known in this country until he won the Nobel Prize in 1933, the only Russian writer to achieve this honor until it was offered to Pasternak (*q.v.*) in 1958. "The Gentleman from San Francisco," his remarkable symbolic story, was translated first by D. H. Lawrence, S. S. Koteliansky, and Leonard Woolf in 1923. Bunin began as a poet but abandoned poetry for the short story. His tales, preoccupied with love and death, are among the best in any language and are notable for what Edmond Jaloux called their "magic realism." Bunin translated Longfellow's (*q.v.*) "Hiawatha" and much of Tennyson (*q.v.*) and Byron (*q.v.*) into Russian. An anti-Bolshevik, Bunin lived in exile in Paris after 1919, enduring great poverty until he won the Nobel Prize. He later lived in the United States. He left unfinished a manuscript study of his great friend Chekhov (*q.v.*).

THE GENTLEMAN FROM SAN FRANCISCO (1916) AND OTHER SHORT STORIES. Trans. by Olga Shartse with introd. by Thompson Bradley. *Simon & Schuster* (Washington Square) 1962 pap. $.45

ELAGHIN AFFAIR AND OTHER STORIES. Trans. by Bernard G. Guerney. *T. Y. Crowell* (Funk & Wagnalls) 1968 $5.95 Minerva Press pap. $2.50

THE VILLAGE. 1910. Trans. by Isabel F. Hapgood. 1923. *Howard Fertig* 1975 $12.50

THE WELL OF DAYS. Trans. by Gleb Struve and H. Miles. 1933. *Howard Fertig* 1975 $12.50

VOLGA. Trans. by Guy Daniels. *S. G. Phillips* 1970 $4.95

MEMOIRS AND PORTRAITS. 1951. *Greenwood* 1968 $12.00

CHAPYGIN, ALEKSEY PAVLOVICH. 1870–1937.

Of peasant background, Chapygin attracted attention with "White Hermitage" (1915), a novel thought of very highly by Gorky. "Stepan Razin" is a great historical novel about the seventeenth-century Cossack rebel and brigand.

STEPAN RAZIN. Trans. by Paul Cedar. 1946 *Hyperion* 1973 $18.50

KUPRIN, ALEXANDER IVANOVICH. 1870–1938.

Kuprin began as a member of the *Znanie* group *(see entry for Veresayev)*. His education in a cadet school and subsequent army service provided him with material for many of his early works. The most important of these is "The Duel" (1905), which deals critically with Russian army life. The subject matter and high literary qualities of his novel made it very popular; however, Kuprin's other works do not measure up to this early achievement. "The Pit" *("Yama")* is the best known of his later works because of its subject matter—the life of prostitutes.

Kuprin's pre-Revolutionary writings have been well explored by the critics. His works in emigration after the Revolution are less well known; although numerous, they appear to be less viable artistically.

RIVER OF LIFE AND OTHER STORIES. 1916. *Bks. for Libraries* $9.75

SENTIMENTAL ROMANCE AND OTHER STORIES. Trans. by S. E. Berkenbilt. *Pageant-Poseidon* $5.95

SLAV SOUL AND OTHER STORIES. 1916. *Bks. for Libraries* $8.75

GAMBRINUS AND OTHER STORIES. Trans. by Bernard G. Guerney. 1925. *Bks. for Libraries* $6.50

ANDREYEV, LEONID NIKOLAYEVICH (also Andreev). 1871–1919.

Andreyev, pessimistic and mystical, spoke for the average intellectual of broad political and cultural interests which he expressed in his many short stories, novels, and plays. He and his friend Gorky *(q.v.)* were briefly imprisoned in 1905 for anti-Czarist activities, but he later supported Kerensky and rejected Gorky's communism. Unhappy with developments after the 1917 Revolution, he died in exile in Finland.

LITTLE ANGEL AND OTHER STORIES. 1915. *Bks. for Libraries* $11.00

WHEN THE KING LOSES HIS HEAD AND OTHER STORIES. Trans. by Archibald J. Wolfe. 1919. *Bks. for Libraries* $12.25

THE SEVEN THAT WERE HANGED (1909) AND OTHER STORIES. 1958. *Random* Vintage Bks. pap. $1.25

HE WHO GETS SLAPPED. 1916. *French* $1.50; trans. by Gregory Zilboorg 1922. *Greenwood* 1975 $12.25. Play.

Books about Andreyev

Leonid Andreyev. By Alexander Kaun. 1924. *Bks. for Libraries* $15.50; *Blom.* 1969 $12.50
Reminiscences of Tolstoy, Chekhov and Andreyev. By Maxim Gorky. Trans. by Leonard Woolf and others. 1934. *Hillary House* 1968 $4.50
Dostoyevsky and Andreyev: Gazers upon the Abyss. by H. H. King. 1936. *Kraus* $8.75
Leonid Andreyev: A Study. By James B. Woodward. *Oxford* 1969 $12.00
Leonid Andreyev: A Critical Study. By Alexander S. Kaun. *AMS Press* 1970 $9.50
Leonid Andreyev. By Josephine M. Newcombe. Modern Literature Monographs *Ungar* 1973 $6.00

PRISHVIN, MIKHAIL MIKHAILOVICH. 1873–1954.

By training Prishvin was a specialist in agriculture; he published his first work, "In the Land of Unscared Birds" *("V krayu nepugannykh ptits")* in 1907. The emphasis on nature themes found in this book is characteristic of much of Prishvin's subsequent prose. Prishvin, whose style links him with the symbolist master of prose, A. Remizov (1877–1957), is also distinguished by his rich, colorful use of the Russian language.

JEN SHENG: The Root of Life. Trans. by George Walton and Philip Gibbons. 1936. *Hyperion* 1973 $10.00

TREASURE TROVE OF THE SUN. Trans. by T. Balkoff-Drowne. *Viking* 1952 1967 $4.50

SHISHKOV, VYACHESLAV YAKOVLEVICH. 1873–1945.

An engineer by profession, Shishkov lived most of his life in Siberia, and many of his works are set in that region. One of his more interesting books is a historical novel about the eighteenth-century Cossack rebel Pugachev ("Pugachev," 1943–1944, left uncompleted).

CHILDREN OF DARKNESS. 1931. *Hyperion* 1973 $13.00

BERDYAEV, NICHOLAS (also Berdiav, Berdiaev). 1874–1948. *See Chapter 5, Philosophy,* Reader's Adviser, *Vol. 3.*

KUZMIN, MIKHAIL ALEXEYEVICH. 1875–1936.

Although almost unknown to most Soviet readers, Kuzmin nonetheless occupies an important place in the history of modern Russian literature. For a long time, he was an intimate of the symbolist poet Vyacheslav Ivanov and lived in Ivanov's celebrated "Tower." In spite of this, Kuzmin's aesthetic credo was very distinct from that of the symbolists; he advocated an abandonment of their reliance on multilayered "forests of symbols" and a return to an appreciation of the material world for its own sake. He put these views into practice in his poems and prose works.

In general, Kuzmin's literary production shows a strong influence of European literature from various periods. This is reflected, for example, in the historical and legendary subject matter of his works, such as "The Deed of Alexander of Macedon" and "The Comedy of St. Alexis." Kuzmin is also unique in Russian literature in treating the theme of homosexuality quite freely in a number of his poetic and prose pieces.

WINGS: Prose and Poetry of Mikhail Kuzmin. Trans. and ed. by Michael Green and N. Granoien; introd. by Vladimir Markov. *Ardis* 1972 $6.95 pap. $2.95

"One could ask for no better introductions to his [Kuzmin's] work than these fine translations, with Vladimir Markov's concise and informative preface"—(*The Russian Review*, 1972).

SERGEYEV-TSENSKY, SERGEY NIKOLAYEVICH. 1876–1959.

A representative of the Neo-Realist movement, Sergeyev-Tsensky is the author of a series of novels whose overall title is "Transfiguration." "Valya" (1923), highly regarded by Gorky, is the first of the series. Other novels in this set were published during World War II.

TRANSFIGURATION. 1923. Trans. by Marie Budberg; ed. by Maxim Gorky. 1926 *Hyperion* 1973 $13.25

ARTSYBASHEV, MIKHAIL PETROVICH. 1878–1927.

Artsybashev is best remembered as the author of "Sanin" (1907), a work which preached the freedom of man's natural inclinations. The author's contempt for conventional morality provoked the wrath of many critics, but at the same time made his novel extraordinarily popular among Russian schoolchildren.

Expelled in 1923 from Russia by the Soviet government, Artsybashev and his writings are generally a taboo subject in Soviet literary history.

THE MILLIONAIRE. Trans. by Percy Pinkerton. 1915. *Bks. for Libraries* $9.25

TALES OF THE REVOLUTION. 1905–1906. Trans. by Percy Pinkerton. 1917. *Bks. for Libraries* 1972 $11.25

BELY, ANDREY (also Biely—pseud. of Boris Nikolayevich Bugayev). 1880–1934.

Andrey Bely was one of the major Symbolist poets of the "younger" generation and, at the same time, is considered to be one of the most important figures in twentieth-century Russian prose. He was born into the family of a famous mathematician and initially devoted himself to the physical sciences. Influenced by the philosopher Vladimir Solovyov, he began to celebrate in his poetry the coming of the Divine Wisdom, Sophia (in this belief he joined Alexander Blok, q.v.). Although he was influenced by the 1905 revolution, a more serious development was his falling under the spell of the German "anthropologist" Rudolf Steiner. His belief in anthroposophy continued after the 1917 upheavals; it was combined with shifting attitudes for and against the Bolshevik Revolution. In 1922 Bely went to live in Berlin, but returned to Russia in 1923 and lived there quietly until his death in 1934.

Bely's prose is brilliantly innovative in language, composition, and subject matter; not surprisingly, it had a great impact on early Soviet literature. Two of his novels, "St. Petersburg" and "The Silver Dove" were influenced by Gogol (whom Bely studied in great detail). Their subject is Russian history taken from a broad perspective. This theme is not found in "Kotik Letaev" (1917), a work which focuses instead on the psychology of a developing infant.

Other particularly notable works by Bely include the four "Symphonies," "The Memoirs of a Crank" (o.p.), "The Crime of Nicholas Letaev," and several volumes of memoirs and literary essays.

THE SILVER DOVE. 1909. Trans. by George Reavey. *Grove* 1974 $8.95 1975 pap. $4.95

ST. PETERSBURG. 1913. Trans. with introd. by John Cournos. *Grove* 1959 Evergreen Bks. 1962 pap. $2.95

KOTIK LETAEV. 1922. Trans. by Gerald Janecek. *Ardis* 1971 $6.95 pap. $2.95

Books about Bely
> Frenzied Poet: Andrey Biely and the Russian Symbolists. Trans. by Oleg Maslenikov. 1952.
> *Greenwood* 1968 $13.00
> Apocalyptic Symbolism of Andrej Belyj. By D. Cioran. *Mouton* (dist. by Humanities Press) 1973
> $24.00

BLOK, ALEKSANDR ALEKSANDROVICH (also Alexander).   1880–1921.

Blok was one of the greatest of modern poets, a symbolist representing the most cultivated of the Russian intelligentsia. His work expressed the mystical yearning of the Russian people and man's eternal spiritual conflict. He welcomed the 1917 Revolution with his poems "The Twelve" (1918) and "The Scythians" (1918), but enthusiasm soon gave way to "silence and growing disillusionment"—(Gleb Struve). In a famous address delivered six months before his death, Blok declared the poet's need for "peace and freedom": "The poet dies because he can no longer breathe: life has lost its meaning."

SELECTED POEMS OF ALEKSANDR BLOK. Ed. by James Woodward. *Oxford* 1968 $6.50 pap. $3.25

THE PUPPET SHOW. (In "Twentieth Century Russian Plays: An Anthology," orig. "Anthology of Russian Plays," Vol. 2) trans. and ed. by F. D. Reeve. *Norton* 1973 pap. $3.95; *Random* Vintage Bks. (orig.) pap. $1.95

THE TWELVE (1918) AND OTHER POEMS. Trans. by Jon Stallworthy and Peter France. *Oxford* 1970 $5.75

THE SPIRIT OF MUSIC. Trans. by I. Freiman. 1946. *Hyperion* 1973 $7.00

Books about Blok
> Alexander Blok, Prophet of Revolution: A Study of His Life and Work Illustrated by Translations from His poems and Other Writings. By Sir Cecil Kisch. *Roy Pubs.* 1961 $5.50. This well-written and readable book is not a biography but rather a critical assessment of Blok's work, showing how his poetry was influenced by his life.
> Aleksandr Blok: Between Image and Idea. By Franklin D. Reeve. *Columbia* 1962 $10.00. This is "a formidably academic, exhaustive explication" for the student rather than the general reader. Blok's poems are here "scrupulously analyzed and interpreted in chronological sequence." Both Russian and literal English versions are provided.
> Alexander Blok: A Study in Rhythm and Metre. By Robin Kemball. *Mouton* (dist. by Humanities Press) 1965 $36.75
> Aleksandr Blok: The Journey to Italy. By Lucy E. Vogel. *Cornell Univ. Press* 1973 $15.00

CHUKOVSKY, KORNEY IVANOVICH.   1882–1969.

Chukovsky's literary activity, which began early, encompassed various fields. He is best known for his "From Two to Five," a highly readable, thoughtful, and knowledgeable book about the verbal behaviour of young children. Among children he is well-known for a collection of poems which has become a classic and which is constantly being reprinted. Chukovsky has also been an active literary critic and scholar.

TELEPHONE. *Bobbs* 1971 $4.50. Children's verses.

FROM TWO TO FIVE. Trans. and ed. by Miriam Morton. *Univ. of California Press* 1963 $7.50 pap. $2.45

GLADKOV, FYODOR VASILYEVICH.   1883–1958.

Born into a poor peasant family, Gladkov had a difficult early life. He was involved in revolutionary activities in 1905 and, with the success of the October Revolution, engaged once again in political work.

Gladkov's literary activity began early, but developed only after 1922, when he participated in various proletarian literary organizations. "Cement," his most famous novel, was published in 1925. Although it later underwent several revisions, each of which reflected Gladkov's subordination to shifting political-literary trends, the earliest version is the most interesting. The novel deals with the transition from the Civil War period to the postwar reconstruction of industry and society. Its heroes, cement worker Gleb Chumalov, his wife Dasha, Party leader Badin, engineer Kleist, and others are portrayed vigorously and objectively; their internal problems and contradictions exist side by side with their accomplishments.

In subsequent years, Gladkov moved away from the romaticism of "Cement." His later works include a "5-year plan" novel, "Power" (*"Energiya"*), and a three-volume autobiography (1949–1954).

CEMENT: A Novel. 1925. Trans. by A. S. Arthur and C. Ashleigh. *Ungar* $6.50 pap. $3.50

ROMANOV, PANTELEIMON SERGEYEVICH. 1884–1938.

Romanov's novels and stories "deal with Soviet youth, with love and marriage, and with the problem of reconciling the romantic impulses of human nature with the new morals and the stern demands of Communist ideology"—(Struve). He was particularly interested in problems of sex, in the new morality of the early period after the revolution. The best-known of his works, widely read in the West, is "Three Pairs of Silk Stockings" (actual title "Comrade Kislyakov").

WITHOUT CHERRY BLOSSOMS. Trans. by Leonide Zarine; ed. by Stephen Graham. 1932 *Bks. for Libraries* $9.00; 1930 *Hyperion* 1973 $13.00

DIARY OF A SOVIET MARRIAGE. Trans. by J. Furnivall and R. Parmenter. 1936 *Hyperion* 1974 $11.00

THREE PAIRS OF SILK STOCKINGS. 1930. Trans. by Leonide Zarine; ed. by Stephen Graham. 1931. *Hyperion* 1973 $14.75

ZAMYATIN, YEVGENY IVANOVICH (also Zamiatin, Eugene). 1884–1937.

Zamyatin was born in Central Russia, studied at the Polytechnic Institute in St. Petersburg, and became a naval engineer. His first story appeared in 1908, and he became serious about writing by 1913, when his story "A Tale of Provincial Life" ("*Uezdnoye*") was published. In 1916 he supervised the construction of icebreakers for the Russian government in England; after his return to Russia, he published two satirical stories about English life: "The Islanders" ("*Ostrovityane*," 1918), and "The Fisher of Men" ("*Lovets chelovekov*," 1922).

During the civil war and the early twenties Zamyatin published prose and theatrical works. He himself characterized his writing as "Neorealist": based on a microscopic examination of objects, leading to a grotesque view of the world. A very fine craftsman, Zamyatin influenced a number of young writers, such as Olesha (*q.v.*) and Ivanov (*q.v.*).

His best-known work is "We" ("*My*"). Written in 1920–1921, this satirical tale of a future anti-utopia, which directly influenced George Orwell's (*q.v.*) "1984," was published abroad in several translations during the twenties. In 1929 a shortened Russian version appeared in Prague; the violent press campaign which followed led to Zamyatin's resignation from the All-Russian Writers' Association. The continuation of attacks on him by the so-called "proletarian poets" led Zamyatin to write directly to Stalin, requesting permission to leave the Soviet Union. This being granted, he settled in Paris, where he continued to work until his death in 1937.

THE DRAGON: Fifteen Stories. Trans. and ed. with introd. by Mirra Ginsburg. *Random* 1967 $5.95

WE. 1920. *Bantam* 1972 pap. $1.75; trans. by Gregory Zilboorg, introd. by Peter Rudy, pref. by Marc Slonim *Dutton* 1959 pap. $1.75; trans. by Mirra Ginsburg *Viking* 1972 $6.95; *Gregg* repr. of 1934 ed. 1975 $13.00

A SOVIET HERETIC: Selected Essays by Yevgeny Zamyatin. Trans. and ed. by Mirra Ginsburg. *Univ. of Chicago Press* 1970 $9.50 Phoenix Bks. 1974 pap. $4.95

Books about Zamyatin

Zamyatin: A Soviet Heretic. By David J. Richards. *Hillary* 1962 $2.75
The Life and Work of Evgenij Zamiatin. By Alex M. Shane. *Univ. of California Press* 1968 $11.50
Brave New World and We, 1984: An Essay on Anti-Utopia. By Edward J. Brown. Essay Ser. *Ardis* 1974 $6.95 pap. $2.50

KHLEBNIKOV, VELIMIR (Viktor Valdimirovich). 1885–1922.

Khlebnikov, who together with Mayakovsky formed the core of genius within the Futurist group, was a poet and utopian thinker. He is celebrated for his extraordinary attempts at linguistic experimentation. His work, however, is very complex and rich in meaning and he remains as one of the most misunderstood Russian poets.

Among his writings we find a large number of long poems, stories, theoretical articles, and especially large-scale cyclical texts which he termed "supertales."

Khlebnikov is famed not only for the difficulty of his works, but also for his extraordinarily idealistic and pilgrim-like life.

SNAKE TRAIN: Poetry and Prose. Trans. and ed. by Gary Kern; introd. by Edward J. Brown. *Ardis* 1976 $12.95

TARASOV-RODIONOV, ALEXANDER IGNATYEVICH. 1885–1937?

Although he was the author of a number of prose works, Tarasov-Rodionov is best remembered for his 1922 novel "Chocolate." Written after his demobilization from the Red Army, "Chocolate" presented the story of a local Soviet security police (*Cheka*) chief, who because of a series of accidents, is condemned to death by his comrades. The novel, which revealed quite a bit about the operation of the Cheka, was both popular and controversial; its theme—that a good Party man must be sacrificed to appease popular prejudice—provoked attacks accusing the author of ideological error.

Tarasov-Rodionov's planned trilogy, "Heavy Steps" ("*Tyazhelye shagi*"), about the 1917 Revolution, was never completed; only the first two volumes appeared.

CHOCOLATE. 1922. Trans. by Charles Malamuth. 1932. *Hyperion* 1973 $13.50

FEBRUARY 1917. 1928. Trans. by William A. Drake. 1931. *Hyperion* 1973 $16.00

NEVEROV, ALEXANDER (pseud. of Alexander Sergeyevich Skobelev). 1886–1923.

Before the revolution, Neverov, who came from a peasant family, wrote stories of village life. "City of Bread," his best known work, is based on his experiences in Tashkent during the famine of 1920–1921.

CITY OF BREAD. 1923. Trans. anonymous. 1927. *Hyperion* 1973 $13.00

MAKARENKO, ANTON SEMYONOVICH. 1888–1939.

Makarenko's "Road to Life" is a semifictional Soviet classic about the author's experiences in Maxim Gorky's colony for waifs and strays produced by the revolution. The author was a noted pedagogue and his account remains quite interesting for a student of the period.

THE ROAD TO LIFE. 1934. Trans. by I. Litvinov and T. Litvinov. 1951 *Oriole Editions* 1973 $12.50

OGNYOV, NIKOLAY (pseud. of Mikhail Grigoryevich Rozanov). 1888–1938.

Ognyov's early works were written under the strong influence of Boris Pilnyak (*q.v.*). "Diary of a Communist Schoolboy" (translation of Russian title is "Diary of Kostya Ryabtsev") is much simpler in form. Its interest lies in its subject: the life of a schoolboy (presented through his eyes) in the revolutionized Soviet schools. Ognyov's thorough knowledge of Soviet education makes the book particularly interesting for a historian of the subject.

DIARY OF A COMMUNIST SCHOOLBOY. 1926–1927. Trans. by Alexander Werth. 1928. *Hyperion* 1973 $13.00

SOBOL, ANDREY MIKHAYLOVICH. 1888–1926.

Sobol began his literary career shortly before the revolution. His first novel, "Dust" (1915) was met very favorably by the critics. His post-revolutionary stories are realistic (they frequently deal with revolutionaries and counterrevolutionaries who no longer believe in their respective causes), but his manner has a fantastic, nightmarish quality. He committed suicide in Moscow.

FREAK SHOW. Trans. by Jenny Cowan. 1930. *Hyperion* 1973 $17.00

AKHMATOVA, ANNA ANDREYEVNA. 1889–1966.

Akhmatova began as an Acmeist (she was first married to another Acmeist poet, Nikolay Gumilev), a creator of simple, yet psychologically deep, lyric poems with which she achieved an extraordinary popularity. During the Stalin years, she was almost completely barred from literature; her son, the historian Lev Gumilev, became the victim of repeated arrests and prison terms. In 1946, together with Mikhail Zoshchenko, Akhmatova became the object of a public campaign by Zhdanov, at that time cultural "boss" and one of Stalin's closest associates. She reappeared for the broad Soviet public in the sixties, when her works once again began to be published (a collection appeared in 1965). Awarded the Taormina prize, she was permitted to travel to the West, where she received an honorary doctorate from Oxford.

Akhmatova is one of the major figures of twentieth-century Russian poetry. In addition to her lyric poems, she is particularly celebrated for the cycle "Requiem," prompted by her son's arrest, and for the "Poem without a Hero," the product of a twenty-year effort.

POEMS OF AKHMATOVA. Trans., sel., and introd. by Stanley Kunitz with Max Hayward. Bilingual ed. *Little-Atlantic* 1973 $7.95 pap. $3.95

SELECTED POEMS OF ANNA AKHMATOVA. Trans. by Richard McKane. *Oxford* 1969 $4.50

A POEM WITHOUT A HERO. 1940–1960. Trans. by Carl R. Proffer and Assya Humesky. *Ardis* 1973 $5.95 pap. $2.25

Books about Akhmatova

Anna Akhmatova. By Sam N. Driver. World Authors Ser. *Twayne* $6.95

PLATONOV, ANDREY PLATONOVICH. 1889–1951.

Until comparatively recently, Platonov was remembered primarily as a member of the Pereval group of the twenties and early thirties (Pereval was a gathering of writers who were influenced by the basically humanistic and cultivated ideas of the critic Voronsky). A very fine prose stylist, at the end of the twenties Platonov was vehemently attacked for his ideological "mistakes" by the more extreme "proletarian" writers, and such assaults eventually forced him to stop publishing. He resurfaced during the war, but new attacks once again reduced him to silence.

As a result of these persecutions, only a portion of Platonov's real output has been known. Within the last few years, however, publication of more of his works has shown him to be an important figure in twentieth-century Russian prose.

THE FOUNDATION PIT. Trans. by Thomas Whitney, preface by Joseph Brodsky. *Ardis* bilingual ed. 1974 $10.00 pap. $3.95; *Dutton* 1975 $7.50

THE BARREL ORGAN. Trans. by Carl R. Proffer. *Ardis* 1974 $6.95

FIERCE AND BEAUTIFUL WORLD. Trans. by Joseph Barnes, introd. by Y. Yevtushenko. *Dutton* 1971 $6.95 pap. $1.95. A collection of short stories.

Books about Platonov

Andrei Platonov: A Complete Bibliography. Ed. by Pranas Sveikauskas. Bibliography Ser. *Ardis* 1975 $8.95

PASTERNAK, BORIS LEONIDOVICH. 1890–1960. (Nobel Prize refused 1958)

Pasternak was acclaimed as the greatest Russian poet of the post-revolutionary era some 30 years before "Dr. Zhivago" made him world famous. "In the Twenties Pasternak became known as an innovator who had absorbed and fused the elements of futurism and symbolism. He used fresh, highly personal poetic language, created a new diction within the framework of relatively simple meters and captivated his readers by the dynamism of his verse, the dazzling fire of his metaphors and his passionate approach to life and art . . . . Unlike most of the symbolists and expressionists of his time, Pasternak was a poet in a major key; he affirmed the triumph of the principle of life"—(Marc Slonim). But he was a difficult writer whose works puzzled the public. Between 1923 and 1936 he was allowed to publish, in very small printings. Two thin booklets appeared in 1943 and 1945, but long after World War II no original works were allowed to come out in book form in Russia.

"Dr. Zhivago," after being rejected by the journal *Novy Mir*, was published in Italy in 1957. (The Italian publisher ignored Pasternak's request to return the manuscript to him for revision.)

Pasternak won the Nobel Prize for Literature on October 23, 1958, the first Soviet citizen to do so. (Bunin [*q.v.*] was so honored in 1933, but he was living in France.) It was not until three days after the announcement that *Pravda* heaped abuse on the writer, declaring that he should reject the prize. Pasternak was then formally read out of the Soviet Union of Authors. Shortly afterward he declined the award.

Pasternak's works are published here in the original Russian: "*Sochinenia*" (ed. by Gleb Struve and Boris Filipoff. *Univ. of Michigan Press* 4 vols. Vol. 1 Early Poetry, 1912–1932 1961 $10.00 Vol. 2 Short Prose, 1915–1958 1961 $8.50 Vol. 3 Later Poetry and Miscellaneous Writings 1961 $9.00 Vol. 4 Doctor Zhivago 1959 $7.50).

SAFE CONDUCT. Various translators; introd. by Babette Deutsch. *New Directions* 1958 pap. $2.25. An early autobiography (1931), three short stories, and poems.

POEMS. 1916–1959. Trans. by Eugene M. Kayden. *Antioch Press* (dist. by Kent State Univ. Press) 2nd rev. ed. 1964 $5.50. A selection of 185 poems, including one on Pasternak's Nobel Prize nomination. The poet was pleased with these translations.

IN THE INTERLUDE: Poems. 1945–1960. Trans. by Henry Kamen; fwd. by Sir Maurice Bowra; notes by George Katkov. *Oxford* bilingual ed. 1962 $8.00 pap. $1.75

An "excellent" translation insofar as poetry can be translated at all: "all such enterprise is basically futile. Pasternak is one of the very few great Russian poets of the last three decades and the appearance of his poems in the original will be welcomed by all who know the Russian language"—(*LJ*).

DOCTOR ZHIVAGO. 1957 (pub. in Italy). Trans. by Max Hayward and Manya Harari. *Pantheon* 1958 $7.95 ill. ed. 1960 $12.50; trans. by Frederick Manfred *New Am. Lib.* Signet 1960 pap. $1.50

I REMEMBER: Sketch for an Autobiography. 1957. Trans. with introd. and notes by
David Magarshack. 1960. *Peter Smith* $5.00. Includes an essay on "Translating
Shakespeare" translated by Manya Harari. Covers some of the same ground as "Safe
Conduct" (*see above*) from a later viewpoint.

SEVEN POEMS. Trans. by George L. Kline. *Unicorn Press* 1970 $6.00 pap. $3.00

Books about Pasternak

The Three Worlds of Boris Pasternak. By Robert Payne. *Coward* 1961 $5.00; *Indiana Univ. Press*
Midland Bks. 1963 pap. $1.95
   This is a combined biographical and critical study of the writer, whose "three worlds" are
   those of poet, novelist, and political figure. "An elaborate account is given of the international
   incident created by 'Dr. Zhivago,' and the critical analyses of the short stories and the verse
   are sometimes very illuminating. The volume contains many pieces translated by Mr.
   Payne"—(*LJ*).
Pasternak's Lyric: A Study of Sound and Imagery. By Dale L. Plank. *Mouton* (dist. by
Humanities Press) 1966 $9.00
Pasternak's "Doctor Zhivago." By Mary F. and Paul Rowland. *Southern Illinois Univ. Press* 1967
$4.95 pap. $2.25
The Poetic World of Boris Pasternak. By Olga R. Hughes. Princeton Essays in Lit. Ser. *Princeton
Univ. Press* 1974 $9.00
Boris Pasternak. By J. W. Dyck. World Authors Ser. *Twayne* $6.95

BULGAKOV, MIKHAIL AFANASYEVICH. 1891–1940.

   Mikhail Bulgakov was a playwright and novelist who enjoyed a high reputation as a satirist of
Soviet life in the comparatively free air of the 1920s, when Ernest J. Simmons (in *SR*) recalls seeing
both him and one of his plays in Moscow. "The Days of the Turbins," a play based on his first novel
"The White Guard" (1925), was a serious drama on the dilemma of White officers caught between
the old regime and the Revolution; "The Purple Island" (1928), a satirical play on government
theater censorship, already rearing its head at that time. Then Bulgakov himself fell victim to
censorship in the 1930s and was denied publication and performance of his original work.
Stanislavsky, says Simmons, "appointed him to the staff of the Moscow Art Theater as a kind of
literary consultant, a position he held until his death in 1940 at the age of forty-eight. In the last
ten years of his life Bulgakov was virtually forgotten as a creative writer. His dramatizations of the
novels of others were performed . . . and he wrote a play based on the life and works of Molière.
But during all that time he did what some Soviet authors do today—he 'wrote for the drawer.' "
   He has only recently been "discovered" again in the Soviet Union. His "Theatrical Novel"
(1936–1937), published here as "Black Snow," a satire on the Moscow Art Theater and its
personalities, delighted readers who first encountered it in the 1960s, and "The Master and
Margarita," on its appearance in the Soviet magazine, *Moskva*, even more so. It is a fantasy which
may be read on several levels—as a satire on Soviet life and "more profoundly, as a vast allegory of
the struggle between the powers of darkness and the powers of light, with universal implications."
Satan and his crew are at large in Moscow, and the "most brilliant and certainly the most serious
theme" is that of Pontius Pilate vs. Christ. "The Heart of a Dog," which was published here in
different translations of the same text, "firmly establishes Bulgakov as one of the few truly great
writers produced by the Soviet Union during the half-century of its existence and also as that
nation's most accomplished satirist"—(Maurice Friedberg, in *SR*). It deals with a scientist who
creates a man from a dog. The man becomes a Soviet bureaucrat and the scientist, exasperated by
the behavior of his creation, turns him back into canine form. This novel has not, as of this writing,
been published in the Soviet Union; it was written in 1925.

THE EARLY PLAYS. Trans. and ed. by Ellendea Proffer. *Indiana Univ. Press* 1972 $12.50
Midland Bks. pap. $3.95

THE DIABOLIAD AND OTHER STORIES. Trans. by Carl R. Proffer; ed. by Carl R. and
Ellendea Proffer. *Indiana Univ. Press* 1972 $6.95 Midland Bks. pap. $2.95

WHITE GUARD. 1924. *McGraw-Hill* 1971 $7.95 pap. 1975 $3.95

THE HEART OF A DOG. Trans. by Mirra Ginsburg *Grove* 1968 Black Cat Bks. pap. $1.95;
trans. by Michael Glenny *Harcourt* 1968 Harvest Bks. pap. $1.45

FLIGHT: A Play in Eight Dreams and Four Acts. Trans. by Mirra Ginsburg. *Grove* Evergreen pap. 1969 $2.25

BLACK SNOW. 1936–1937. Trans. by Michael Glenny. *Simon & Schuster* 1968 $4.50

THE MASTER AND MARGARITA. Trans. by Mirra Ginsburg *Grove* 1967 (abr. ed.) $5.95 Black Cat Bks. 1967 (abr. ed.) pap. $1.95; trans. by Michael Glenny *Harper* 1967 $6.95

A COUNTRY DOCTOR'S NOTEBOOK. Trans. by Michael Glenny. *Bantam* 1975 $1.50

EHRENBURG, ILYA GRIGORIEVICH (also Ehrenbourg). 1891–1967.

"Poet, journalist, novelist and propagandist, Ehrenburg stands almost alone among modern Russian writers in his cosmopolitan background and outlook. Nearly a decade of exile in pre-1917 Paris introduced him to . . . artists and writers, among them Modigliani, Picasso, Léger, and Diego Rivera. [The first volume of his autobiography] takes him from an orthodox Jewish childhood in Kiev, through the Paris years to the outbreak of the October Revolution, his return to Russia and the Civil War"—(*LJ*). In "Memoirs: 1921–1941," the spokesman for the Soviet "Thaw" wrote about literary figures of the twenties and thirties, the Spanish Civil War and the Stalin purges. In "The War: 1941–1945," with "deep sensitiveness to human suffering" (*SR*), he re-creates the hard war years in Russia and his own role as anti-German propagandist. "Post-War Years: 1945–1954" deals with the end of the Stalinist period. Malcolm Muggeridge has described Ehrenburg as then "a dictatorial regime's tame intellectual," who "toed the line when it was necessary [and] averted his eyes when his friends were struck down," in order to survive; but he became the most outspoken of the "survivors" who remained politically acceptable.

"The Thaw," a series of vignettes about ordinary people in a provincial town of modern Soviet Russia, was attacked as a "bourgeois deviation," but not suppressed. As a novel it has been called "colorless and undistinguished," but it is valuable as social commentary. This book gave its name to the immediately post-Stalin literary era, and as the recent intellectual atmosphere wavered between freeze and thaw, so did Ehrenburg's acceptability.

JULIO JURENITO. 1922. Trans. by Anna Bostock and Yvonne Kapp. *Dufour* 1963 $3.95. A satirical novel, not published in the U.S.S.R. until 1964 (in a censored version).

THE LOVE OF JEANNE NEY. 1923. Trans. by Helen C. Mathewson. 1930. *Greenwood* 1968 $17.00

OUT OF CHAOS. Trans. by A. Bakshy. 1934. *Octagon* 1972 $15.00

THE NINTH WAVE. 1953. Trans. by Tatania Shebunina and Joseph Castle. 1955. *Greenwood* 1974 $33.00

MEMOIRS: 1921–1941. Trans. by Tatania Shebunina and Yvonne Kapp. *Grosset* Univ. Lib. pap. $2.95. Includes Vol. 3 Truce: 1921–1933, Vol. 4 Eve of War: 1933–1941, and part of his autobiography, "People, Years, Lives."

FURMANOV, DMITRY ANDREYEVICH. 1891–1926.

Furmanov earned a place for himself in Soviet literature as the author of "Chapaev" (1923). This work, in part a novel, in part documentary literature, is based on Furmanov's experiences as a political commissar with the forces of Chapaev, a guerrilla leader in the Urals. Furmanov successfully depicts Chapaev's psychology and his political "development." The work achieved enormous popularity in the Soviet Union and was subsequently made into a successful film.

CHAPAYEV. 1923. Trans. by George and Jeanette Kittell, ed. by O. Gorchakov. 1935 *Hyperion* 1973 $17.00

MANDELSTAM, OSIP EMILIEVICH (also Mandel'shtam, Mandelstamm). 1891– 1938.

An Acmeist, Mandelstam is one of the greatest twentieth-century Russian poets. "All the ideologically 'correct' poets, who seem to hold the pen between their hobnailed boots, shrink to mere ranters in the face of this most delicate and inspired of verbal artists, Russian inheritor of the best of French symbolism, even surrealism, wonderful chronicler of an age of transition and pain"—(Anthony Burgess). "The cascades of Mandelstam's glittering or tranquil images leaping out of one another, the historical, psychological, syntactical, verbal allusions, contrasts, collisions, whirling at lightning speed, dazzle the imagination and the intellect"—(Sir Isaiah Berlin, in the *N.Y. Review of Books*).

Mandelstam reached the height of his reputation in 1928, when both his collected verse and his prose vignettes were published. Soon after his arrest in 1934 he was brought before Stalin himself for questioning, "in its own sinister way perhaps the profoundest tribute ever paid by the Soviet Union to the power of Mandelstam's pen"—(Clarence Brown). In 1937, on the plea of Mandelstam's wife, his close friend Boris Pasternak was able to intervene personally with Stalin on the poet's behalf. As a result of this (telephone) interview Mandelstam was released for a year only to be arrested again in 1938. He suffered periods of insanity before his death in the winter he had dreaded at the Vladivostok camp.

THE COMPLETE POETRY OF OSIP MANDELSTAM. Trans. by Burton Raffel and Alla Burago. Russian Lit. in Translation Ser. *State Univ. of New York Press* 1973 $15.00 microfiche $7.50

STONE AND OTHER POEMS. Trans. by S. Fehsenfeid. *Ardis* 1974 $6.95 pap. $2.50

SELECTED POEMS. Trans. by David McDuff. *Farrar, Straus* 1975 $10.00 pap. $3.95

THE COMPLETE CRITICAL PROSE AND LETTERS: With Selected Memoirs and Fictional Prose. Trans. and ed. by Jane Gary Harris and Constance Anthony. *Ardis* $15.00

THE PROSE OF OSIP MANDELSTAM. (Orig. "The Egyptian Stamp" in the U.S.S.R., 1928.) Trans. with a critical essay by Clarence Brown. *Princeton Univ. Press* 1965 $8.50 pap. $2.95

Books about Mandelstam

Hope against Hope: A Memoir. By Nadezhda Y. Mandelstam. Trans. by Max Hayward. *Atheneum* 1970 $10.00

Mozart and Salieri. By Nadezhda Mandelstam. Trans. by Robert McLean. *Ardis* 1972 $6.95 pap. $2.95

Hope Abandoned, Vol. 2. By Nadezhda Mandelstam. Trans. by Max Hayward. *Atheneum* 1974 $13.95

Mandelstam. By Clarence Brown. *Cambridge Univ. Press* 1973 $13.95

Osip Emilievich Mandelstam: An Essay in Antiphon. By Arthur A. Choen. *Ardis* 1974 $6.95 pap. $2.50

FEDIN, KONSTANTIN ALEKSANDROVICH. 1892–

Gleb Struve called the publication of "Early Joys" and "No Ordinary Summer" "perhaps, the most outstanding literary event of the postwar period." They are written in a broad realistic manner, with the inevitable homage to Stalin, and were awarded the Stalin Prize. Born into a family of mixed aristocratic and peasant descent, Fedin in his early stories expressed nostalgic regret for the passing of the prerevolutionary way of life. He is president of the Writers' Union and, as such, a strong conservative in battles over censorship.

CITIES AND YEARS. 1924. Trans. by Michael Scammell. 1962. *Greenwood* 1975 lib. bdg. $19.50

Books about Fedin

Konstantin Fedin. By Julius M. Blum. *Mouton* (dist. by Humanities Press) 1967 $13.25

PAUSTOVSKY, KONSTANTIN. 1892–1968.

Paustovsky, the "moral catalyst [and] personified conscience of the thaw" (*SR*), participated in the revolutionary street demonstrations of 1905 and saw a classmate assassinate the Czar's Prime Minister, Stolypin. He was a medical orderly in World War I and later a newspaper reporter. He was for many of his last years head of the Gorky Institute for Literature in Moscow and "the writer most respected in Russia by intellectuals as well as the general reader"—(*SR*). He was among the signers of Solzhenitsyn's (*q.v.*) letter attacking censorship, and in 1966 he made an appeal for clemency for the convicted writers Daniel and Sinyavsky (*q.v.*) and continued to plead thereafter for other persecuted literary figures. He was awarded the Order of Lenin in 1967.

He is known in the U.S.S.R. for his short stories, which "combine his dreams with an exceptionally sharp eye and ear for realistic detail and an unfailing memory"—(*LJ*). In his autobiography the "prose is deceptively simple; but it captures superbly the emotional atmosphere of a situation and of an era"—(*N.Y. Times*).

THE STORY OF A LIFE. 1947–1960. Trans. by Joseph Barnes. *Pantheon* 1964 $12.95

YEARS OF HOPE. Trans. by Manya Harari and Andrew Thomson. *Pantheon* 1969 $4.95

THE MAGIC RINGLET. Trans. by Thomas P. Whitney. *Addison-Wesley* Young Scott Bks. 1974 $4.75

TSVETAYEVA, MARINA IVANOVNA. 1892–1941.

Tsvetayeva, whose first book appeared in 1911, ranks among the major twentieth-century Russian poets. She is the author of numerous lyric poems and of a number of long poems. Her work is distinguished by great vigor and passion, which are combined with an astonishing mastery of technical aspects of verse (she is one of the great Russian poetic innovators). Particularly striking in this regard are her "Poem of the Mountain" (*"Poema gory"*) and "Poem of the End" (*"Poema konca"*).

During the Civil War, Tsvetayeva's sympathies were explicitly on the side of the Whites. She emigrated in 1922 and led a difficult and isolated existence in Prague and Paris during the twenties and thirties. Her eventual return to the Soviet Union, largely for family reasons, ended in tragedy; isolation and humiliation on part of official Soviet literary figures brought her to suicide in 1941.

SELECTED POEMS. Trans. by Elaine Feinstein. *Oxford* 1971 $8.00

MAYAKOVSKY, VLADIMIR VLADIMIROVICH.   1893–1930.

Mayakovsky is one of Russia's greatest twentieth-century poets (a Futurist). His penchant for exaggeration produced original, explosive poetry and plays and a flamboyant, passionate life. "The Bedbug," his famous comedy, is an antibourgeois satiric vision of the year 1978. His poems are uneven in quality; "laconic and grotesque, whatever their themes, they are always distortions. . . . He wanted, above all, to wipe out sentimentality from both the sense and shape of poetry"— (Helen Muchnic, in *N.Y. Review of Books*). "His metaphors are deliberately offensive to the conventional taste, his diction is peppered with vulgar vernacular, his rhymes are a clownish play with language and thought. Yet the total effect is one of singular beauty"—(Edward J. Brown).

After the Bolshevik Revolution, Mayakovsky flung himself into the production of government propaganda posters, which he illustrated with cartoons. An exhibitionist given to odd forms of dress, he became a public figure through his "public poetry" as well. But he apparently knew great inner conflicts. His private self, expressed in intensely personal verse, remained restless and unhappy, and at 36 he committed suicide.

POEMS. Ed. by H. Marshall. *Farrar, Straus* (Hill & Wang) 1964 $10.00

THE BEDBUG AND SELECTED POETRY. Sel. and ed. with introd. by Patricia Blake; trans. by Max Hayward and George Reavey (bilingual). *Indiana Univ. Press* 1975 $10.50 Midland Bks. pap. $2.95

MYSTERY-BOUFFE. 1921. (In "Masterpieces of the Russian Drama," Vol. 2, ed. by George Rapall Noyes). *Dover* pap. $3.00. Drama in verse.

THE BEDBUG. 1928. (In "Masterpieces of the Modern Russian Theatre," ed. by Robert W. Corrigan). *Macmillan* Collier Bks. (orig.) pap. $1.50; (in "Twentieth Century Russian Plays," orig. title "Anthology of Russian Plays," Vol. 2 ed. by F. D. Reeve) *Norton* 1973 pap. $3.95. Satirical comedy.

ELECTRIC IRON. Trans. by Jack Hirschman and Victor Erlich. *Maya* 1971 pap. $2.00

TIMOTHY'S HORSE. Trans. by Guy Daniels. *Pantheon* 1950 $4.25 lib. bdg. $5.19

COMPLETE PLAYS. Trans. by Guy Daniels. *Simon & Schuster* Touchstone 1971 pap. $2.95

HOW ARE VERSES MADE? *Grossman* (dist. by Viking) Cape Eds. 1970 $3.95 pap. $1.50

Books about Mayakovsky

Mayakovsky and His Circle. By Victor Shklovsky. Trans. & ed. by Lily Feiler. *Dodd* 1972 $8.95

SHKLOVSKY, VICTOR BORISOVICH.   1893–

Shklovsky is known primarily as a theoretician of literature. His most important contributions in this area were made from about 1914 until about 1920—a period during which he was a leading figure in the St. Petersburg OPOJAZ (Society for the Study of Poetic Language), one of the two main groups of the so-called Formalist critics. Shklovsky's main achievements were in the study of prose: in his many articles (a collection of which, "On the Theory of Prose," appeared in the twenties) he brought out the nature of basic devices common to prose literary compositions.

Shklovsky's most interesting nontheoretical works date principally from 1923, during his quite brief emigration from Russia. Their originality and complexity reflect his critical concerns, insofar as their author himself makes use of devices he discusses in his theoretical articles. The first of these, structured in imitation of the works of Laurence Sterne, is the autobiographical "Sentimental Journey" (*"Sentimental 'noye puteshestvie"*). Another, also highly personal, is "200, or Letters Not about Love" (*"200, ili pis'ma ne o lyubvi"*). Other works belonging to this group are: "Knight's Move" (*"Khod konya,"* 1923), "The Third Factory" (*"Tretya fabrika,"* 1926), and "The Hamburg Count" (*"Gamburgsky schet,"* 1928).

SENTIMENTAL JOURNEY: Memoirs, 1917–1922. 1923. Trans. by Richard Sheldon. *Cornell Univ. Press* 1970 $10.00

200, or Letters Not about Love. 1923. Ed. by Richard Sheldon. *Cornell Univ. Press* 1971 $8.50

THIRD FACTORY. 1926. Trans. and ed. by Richard Sheldon. *Ardis* $10.00

Books about Shklovsky

Victor Shklovsky: A Complete Bibliography of Works by and about Him. Ed. by Richard Sheldon. Bibliography Ser. *Ardis* $12.95

BABEL, ISAAC EMMANUILOVICH (also Isaak).   1894–1941?

Babel, a Jewish short story writer born in Odessa, won early success writing of the sufferings of Odessa Jews and of the exploits of the Red cavalry with whom he had fought in the Polish campaign of 1921–1922. The stories of this period were published in "Red Cavalry." Gorky (*q.v.*) was the first to encourage him by printing two of his stories in his magazine *Letopis*. Babel is noted for his precise construction, his use of sharp paradox and his mastery of dialect. His stories are mostly autobiographical. "None of his contemporaries," writes Babette Deutsch, "can match him for vigor, speed, for the taut, strained character of his prose, for his lyricism. His style is as terse as algebra, and yet packed with poetry." He failed to hold his first brilliant success, perhaps because of his unwillingness to submit to Soviet dictation, and his name has not been mentioned in Soviet publications since 1936. He was known to have been in a concentration camp and to have "disappeared" after 1937. The official record of his death, recently disclosed, gives the year as 1941, specifying neither place nor cause.

THE COLLECTED STORIES: Red Cavalry (1926), Tales of Odessa (1924), and Other Stories. Trans. and ed. by Walter Morison; introd. by Lionel Trilling. 1955. *New Am. Lib.* Meridian 1960 pap. $3.95

BENYA KRIK, THE GANGSTER (1927) AND OTHER STORIES. Ed. by Avrahm Yarmolinsky. *Schocken* 1948 $6.00 pap. $1.75

LYUBKA, THE COSSACK AND OTHER STORIES. Trans. by Andrew MacAndrew. *New Am. Lib.* Signet 1964 pap. $.75

A LETTER. 1923. (In "Modern Russian Classics") ed. by Isaac Goldberg. *Branden* pap. $.95

ISAAC BABEL: The Lonely Years, 1925–1939. Trans. by Andrew MacAndrew; ed. with introd. by Nathalie Babel, his daughter. *Farrar, Straus* 1964 $6.75 Noonday pap. $2.75

YOU MUST KNOW EVERYTHING. *Dell* Delta Bks. pap. $2.25

BENIA KRIK: A Film Novel. Trans. by Ivor Montagu and Sergei Nalbandov. *Hyperion* 1973 $7.50

Books about Babel

The Art of Isaac Babel. By Patricia Carden. *Cornell University Press* 1972 $8.50
Isaac Babel. By R. W. Hallett. Modern Literature Monographs *Ungar* 1973 $6.00
Isaac Babel, Russian Master of the Short Story. By James E. Falen. *Univ. of Tennessee Press* 1974 text ed. $9.75

LIDIN, VLADIMIR (pseud. of Vladimir Germanovich Gomberg).   1894–

Lidin, who began to write before the revolution, later wrote several novels and many stories in which he dealt with the new bourgeoisie of the NEP (New Economic Policy) period. "The Price of Life" portrays Soviet students; its hero passes from murder through a series of moral trials to an ultimate regeneration.

THE PRICE OF LIFE. 1928. Trans. by Helen C. Matheson. 1932. *Hyperion* 1973 $14.00

PILNYAK, BORIS (pseud. of Boris Andreyevich Wogau).   1894–1937.

Pilnyak was one of the leading prose writers of the twenties. He became extremely popular after the publication of "The Naked Year" ("*Goly god,*" 1922), his first major work, which dealt with the Revolution and its impact on Russia. His subsequent career was distinguished by several scandals. A 1927 story, "The Tale of the Unextinguished Moon" ("*Povest' o nepogashennoy lune*"), which presented the death of a high Soviet military leader in terms similar to the actual death of the celebrated Army Commander Frunze, brought him into serious difficulties; all issues of the magazine in which the story appeared were confiscated and Pilnyak was forced to admit his "error." A more dangerous situation arose because of the publication of the novel "Mahogany" (*"Krasnoye derevo,"* 1929) in Germany; some of the book's themes provoked very sharp attacks and led to Pilnyak's expulsion from the Association of Soviet Writers. In the thirties, the writer slowly faded from public view, and he disappeared during the purges.

Pilnyak's great impact on Soviet literature comes largely from his style. Continuing the ornamental tradition of Andrey Bely (*q.v.*), he created a literary language which combined epic solemnity with lyricism, which drew on folklore, and which freely created complex, often highly striking or shocking constructions. The attraction of such techniques was so strong that Soviet authorities leveled the charge of "Pilnyakism" against many writers who worked in a similar idiom.

TALES OF THE WILDERNESS. Trans. by F. O'Dempsey. 1925 *Hyperion* 1973 $12.00

THE NAKED YEAR. 1922. Trans. by A. Brown. (abr. ed) 1928. *AMS Press* 1972 $9.50; trans. by Alexander Tulloch *Ardis* 1975 $13.95 pap. $3.95. The 1928 Brown translation is abridged; a full text of the novel is found in the new Tulloch translation.

IVAN MOSCOW. 1927. Trans. by A. Schwartzman. 1935. *Hyperion* 1973 $7.50

VOLGA FALLS TO THE CASPIAN SEA. 1930. 1931. *AMS Press* 1970 $9.00

Books about Pilnyak

Boris Pil'niak: A Soviet Writer in Conflict with the State. By Vera T. Reck. *McGill-Queens Univ. Press* $12.50 pap. $6.00

TYNYANOV, YURY NIKOLAYEVICH. 1894–1943.

Although he is the author of a number of short stories and novels, Tynyanov's major achievements lie in the area of the theory and history of literature. Initially a member of the Formalist group of critics, he moved beyond narrowly Formalist theories to a structuralist approach to the literary work and to literary evolution. He has made lasting contribution to the study of Pushkin, to the theory of poetic language, and other subjects.

Tynyanov's novels not only tend to embody his theoretical views, but are at the same time valuable examples of good historical fiction. His best work is "Death and Diplomacy in Persia" (a direct translation is "The Death of Wazir-Mukhtar") (1929), a biographical novel about the celebrated nineteenth-century satirist Griboyedov. Other novels include *"Kyukhlya"* (1925), a work about the poet Wilhelm Kuchelbecker, and "Pushkin" (1936–1937), which deals with the life of the great poet (*q.v.*). Of Tynyanov's short stories, "Sublieutenant Kizhe" has achieved the greatest renown in the Soviet Union.

DEATH AND DIPLOMACY IN PERSIA. 1929. Trans. by A. Brown. 1938 *Hyperion* 1974 $19.00

ESENIN, SERGEI ALEKSANDROVICH. 1895–1925.

Sergei Esenin achieved world-wide notoriety because of his marriage in 1922 to the dancer Isadora Duncan. His reputation in Russian literature has a more substantive basis in his poetry. The inheritor of peasant traditions, thanks to his birth and upbringing, Esenin was initially influenced by the Symbolists, especially Blok (*q.v.*) and Bely (*q.v.*). His early works, as befits a "peasant poet," are filled with folk and religious themes. After the Revolution, Esenin's hopes for a new Russia brought to his writing strong messianic expectations. He became leader of the Imaginist group, which emphasized striking images as the key element of poetry. His works of this period are rough in both language and imagery, and their contents directly reflect the poet's own taboo-breaking life-style; two famous pieces are "Confession of a Hooligan" (*"Ispoved' khuligana"*) and "Tavern Moscow" (*"Moskva kabatskaya"*).

During the Civil War Esenin was extraordinarily popular. In spite of this, he was subjected to harsh criticism by the authorities and by many writers and critics. A combination of personal difficulties and disillusionment with the Revolution led to the final tragedy: Esenin committed suicide in a room in Leningrad's Hotel Angleterre. He continues to be regarded as a major poet of the twentieth century.

CONFESSIONS OF A HOOLIGAN. *Dufour* pap. $3.50

Books about Esenin

Sergei Esenin: A Biographical Sketch. By Frances De Graaf. *Mouton* (dist. by Humanities Press) 1966 $16.00
Esenin: A Life. By Gordon McVay. *Ardis* 1975 $10.00 pap. $3.95

IVANOV, VSEVOLOD VYACHESLAVOVICH. 1895–1963.

Ivanov, one of the most interesting of Soviet prose writers, began writing before the revolution; his first efforts were encouraged by Gorky. His well-known novel "Armored Train No. 14-69," which appeared in 1922 along with several other works, deals with incidents during the civil war. A very prolific writer, he was at first a member of the Serapion Brothers. Subsequently, his highly "ornamental" style gave way to the sober practices of Socialist Realism.

"Adventures of a Fakir" is autobiographical and very colorful and readable.

THE ADVENTURES OF A FAKIR. 1935. *Hyperion* 1974 $18.50

ZOSHCHENKO, MIKHAIL MIKHAILOVICH. 1895–1958.

"In Soviet literature there is only one name that invariably evokes . . . the image of a 'gay writer,' a 'king of laughter': Mikhail Zoshchenko"—(Vera Alexandrova). He was "perhaps one of the most effective satirists of modern Russia, and certainly one of its most politically obscured talents." He called himself a "naturalist" and his subjects were the "little people" of Russian cities.

Briefly a detective, the author was also successively a carpenter, telephone operator, shoemaker's assistant, militiaman, gambler, and actor. In 1946 he was denounced for not following the line of socialist realism and was expelled from the Writers' Union. "Accused of writing works devoid of political and ideological content and of demoralizing Soviet youth by [his] pessimism, . . . Zoshchenko died in 1958, apparently unforgiven, unrepentant, and unhonored. [His] collected works, however, [were] published in Leningrad in 1960 in an edition of 150,000 copies"— ("Dissonant Voices in Soviet Literature").

NERVOUS PEOPLE AND OTHER SATIRES. Trans. by Maria Gordon and Hugh McLean. *Pantheon* 1963 $5.95; *Greenwood* 1975 lib. bdg. $21.50; *Indiana Univ. Press* 1975 pap. $4.95

SCENES FROM THE BATH HOUSE AND OTHER STORIES OF COMMUNIST RUSSIA. Trans. with introd. by Sidney Monas; sel. by Marc Slonim. *Univ. of Michigan Press* 1961 $5.95 Ann Arbor Bks. pap. $2.95

THE WOMAN WHO COULD NOT READ AND OTHER TALES. Trans. by E. Fen. 1940 *Hyperion* 1973 $10.00

THE WONDERFUL DOG AND OTHER TALES. Trans. by E. Fen. 1942. *Hyperion* 1973 $10.50

BEFORE SUNRISE. 1943. Trans. by Gary Kern. *Ardis* 1974 $12.95 pap. $3.25

ILF, ILYA (pseud. of Ilya Arnoldovich Feinsilberg), 1897–1937, and PETROV, YEVGENY (pseud. of Yevgeny Petrovich Katayev), 1903–1942.

The famous collaboration of Ilf and Petrov created the inimitable Russian rogue and confidence man, Ostap Bender, whose adventures have become classics of Soviet satiric humor. In two novels, Ostap Bender cavorts around the Soviet Union searching for a hoard of jewels concealed in a set of dining chairs ("The Twelve Chairs") and later attempts to unmask an unscrupulous Soviet speculator ("The Golden Calf"). The partners also wrote short stories and contributed to *Pravda* until Ilf's untimely death from tuberculosis. Petrov was killed while working as a reporter during the siege of Sevastopol in World War II.

THE TWELVE CHAIRS (also trans. as "Diamonds to Sit On"). 1928. Trans. by John H. Richardson. *Pyramid Bks.* 1973 pap. $1.25

THE GOLDEN CALF (also trans. as "The Little Golden Calf"). 1931. *Random* 1962 $4.95; trans. by John H. Richardson *Pyramid Bks.* 1973 pap. $1.25; trans. by Charles Malamuth *Ungar* 1961 $8.00 pap. $2.45

LITTLE GOLDEN AMERICA. Trans. by Charles Malamuth. *Arno* 1974 $20.00

KATAYEV, VALENTIN PETROVICH. 1897–

Katayev, brother of Yevgeny Petrov (*q.v.*), was a popular novelist in the 1920s. He "stuck out the black Stalinist period with as little yielding as he could manage [and], as editor of the liberal magazine *Yunost'* (*Youth*), has published some of the ready-to-burst young talent of the last decade"—(*Chicago Tribune*).

Katayev in the twenties produced an outstanding comic novel, "The Embezzlers," and the satirical play "Squaring the Circle" (o.p.). "Both are Soviet classics"—(Max Hayward). In 1933 he wrote "Time Forward," the "most significant," says Marc Slonim, of the "industrial" novels of that period of required socialist realism. *Yunost'* under Katayev's editorship has often provided an outlet for writers temporarily at least unable to publish elsewhere.

THE EMBEZZLERS. 1927. Trans. by Leonide Zarine. *Hyperion* 1973 $13.25; (with Yury Olesha's "Envy") trans. by C. Rougle and T. Berczynski *Ardis* 1975 $13.95 pap. $3.25

THE GRASS OF OBLIVION. 1967. Trans. by Robert Daglish. *McGraw-Hill* 1970 $5.95

MOSAIC OF LIFE: Memoirs of a Russian Childhood. *J. Philip O'Hara* 1975 $20.00

LIBEDINSKY, YURY NIKOLAYEVICH. 1898–1959.

Libedinsky, who spent his childhood in Urals factories, engaged in active political work for the Red Army. He was an active member of groups of "proletarian" writers. "A Week," his first novel, is set during the civil war and deals with problems of Communist administrators of a town: "The novel is interesting as an illustration of the inner workings of the Communist party and as a gallery of lifelike portraits of Communists. . . . Its weakest point is its style"—(Struve). In one of his later novels, "Tomorrow" (1924), Libedinsky expressed his disapproval of the New Economic Policy. The novel came under strong attack and its author later admitted it was an ideological failure.

A WEEK. 1922. 1923 *Hyperion* 1973 $12.00

SOBOLEV, LEONID SERGEYEVICH. 1898–

Sobolev is known for a number of stories and novels. In 1933, he wrote a long novel about the Russian Navy before the revolution ("Capital Refitting"). During World War II, he published a number of short stories about Soviet sailors ("Soul of the Sea," 1942).

ROMANOFF. 1933. Trans. by Alfred Freemantle. 1935. *Hyperion* 1974 $17.50

LEONOV, LEONID MAKSIMOVICH. 1899–

Leonov revived the psychological realistic novel of Dostoyevsky (q.v.) and is known abroad for "Chariot of Wrath" (1946, o.p.), an important novel of World War II. A member of the Praesidium of the Soviet Writers, he twice received the Stalin Prize for literature. In 1960 he published a revised post-Stalin version of his novel of the Moscow underworld, "The Thief," and in 1964 he told Yugoslav author Mihajlo Mihajlov, "Now I can write freely, that's why I am rewriting my old works." In his dramas and novels Leonov's language is, as observed by Yevgeny Zamyatin (q.v.), "crimson, elastic, very Russian, but without slang." He "holds his focus steadily on the human creatures in the foreground, on the riddle of life as it is lived, which has always been the subject matter, after all, of good Russian novels"—(R. W. Mathewson, Jr.).

THE BADGERS. 1925. 1946 *Hyperion* 1973 $14.00

SKUTAREVSKY. 1932. Trans. by Alec Brown. 1936. *Greenwood* 1971 $18.25

SOVIET RIVER. 1931. Trans. by Ivor Montagu and Sergei Nalbanov. 1931 *Hyperion* 1973 $16.00

NABOKOV, VLADIMIR VLADIMIROVICH. 1899–

Nabokov, novelist, poet, and short-story writer, writes in Russian, French, and English, and his novels in English are often translations from the language in which he originally wrote them—by him or made under his supervision. The *Saturday Review* called his analysis and translation into English of Pushkin's (q.v.) "Eugene Onegin" (*see entry under Pushkin*) "the most detailed and rewarding to appear in any language." For Nabokov it was a labor of love, the "great work of my life." He has recently settled in Switzerland, where he is translating his English works into Russian against the day when the Soviet government lifts its present ban on them.

Nabokov's "style, wit, imagery and irony" are apparent in all his works—his "perfectly chiseled" stories, his nostalgic poems and autobiographical sketches, his remarkable novels.

NABOKOV'S DOZEN. *Avon Bard Bks.* 1973 pap. $1.65; *Bks. for Libraries* repr. of 1958 ed. $12.25. Short stories.

NABOKOV'S QUARTET: An Affair of Honor, The Vane Sisters, Lik, Visit to a Museum. 1966. *Pyramid Pubns.* pap. $1.25

"Intelligent, inventive and diverting"—(*LJ*).

THE PORTABLE NABOKOV. Ed. by Page Stegner. *Viking* 1971 $5.75 pap. $3.50

A RUSSIAN BEAUTY AND OTHER STORIES. Trans. by Dmitri Nabokov and Simon Karlinsky. *McGraw-Hill* 1973 $7.95 pap. $3.95

THE DEFENSE. 1930. Trans. by Michael Scammell with the author. *Putnam* 1964 Capricorn Bks. pap. $2.65. A novel about a man destroyed by his addiction to chess.

DESPAIR. 1936. *Putnam* 1966 $6.95 Capricorn Bks. 1970 pap. $2.25
A novel. "A cool, intellectual, witty, and extremely well done tale"—*(LJ)*.

THE GIFT. 1937–38. Trans. by Michael Scammell with the author. *Putnam* 1963 Capricorn Bks. 1970 pap. $2.95. An early novel written in Berlin.

INVITATION TO A BEHEADING. 1938. Trans. by Dmitri Nabokov with the author. *Putnam* 1959 $6.95 Capricorn Bks. 1965 pap. $2.65. Novel.

LAUGHTER IN THE DARK. 1938. *New Directions* 1960 $12.50; *Berkley* pap. $1.25. Novel.

THE REAL LIFE OF SEBASTIAN KNIGHT. 1941. *New Directions* 1959 $9.25. Novel.

NIKOLAI GOGOL. 1944. *New Directions* 1944 pap. $2.25. A critical biography.

LOLITA. 1955. *Berkley* 1975 pap. $1.75; *Putnam* 1958 Capricorn Bks. 1972 pap. $2.95; (screenplay) *McGraw-Hill* 1974 $7.95. A novel.

THE ANNOTATED LOLITA. Ed. by Alfred Appel. *McGraw-Hill* 1970 $15.00 pap. $5.95

PNIN. 1957. *Avon* Bard Bks. 1973 pap. $1.65. Novel.

KING, QUEEN, KNAVE. Trans. by Dmitri Nabokov. *McGraw-Hill* 1968 $5.95; *Fawcett* Crest Bks. 1974 pap. $1.25

ADA, or Ardor. *McGraw-Hill* 1969 $8.95; *Fawcett* Crest Bks. 1974 pap. $1.50

POEMS AND PROBLEMS. *McGraw-Hill* 1970 $7.95

MARY. *McGraw-Hill* 1970 $6.95; *Fawcett* Crest Bks. 1971 pap. $.95

GLORY: A Novel. *McGraw-Hill* 1971 $6.95; *Fawcett* Crest Bks. 1973 pap. $.95

TRANSPARENT THINGS. *McGraw-Hill* 1972 $5.95; *Fawcett* Crest Bks. 1974 pap. $1.25

BEND SINISTER. *McGraw-Hill* 1973 $7.95 pap. $3.95

LOOK AT THE HARLEQUINS. *McGraw-Hill* 1974 $7.95

TYRANTS DESTROYED. Trans. by Dmitri Nabokov. *McGraw-Hill* 1975 $8.95

SPEAK, MEMORY: An Autobiography Revisited. 1951, rev. 1966. *Putnam* 1966 $7.95 Capricorn Bks. 1970 pap. $2.95; *Pyramid Pubns.* pap. $1.25
The autobiography, originally published by *Harper* in 1951 as "Conclusive Evidence" (which sounded like a mystery story), covers Nabokov's boyhood in Russia, his college years in England and his life on the Continent between two world wars. Gilbert Highet calls it "one of the most charming autobiographies written in our time." Philip Toynbee, who sees a touch of the devil in most of Nabokov's writing, describes "Speak, Memory" as "not only a very good book; it is also a devilish pleasant one." According to the author, the 1966 edition is a "re-Englishing of a Russian reversion of what had been an English re-telling of Russian memories in the first place." In the course of these doings he expands, and "lush incrustation piles on incrustation as Nabokov switches from one language to the other"—(Ronald Hingley).

STRONG OPINIONS. *McGraw-Hill* 1973 $8.95

Books about Nabokov

Escape into Aesthetics: The Art of Vladimir Nabokov. By Page Stegner. 1966. *Apollo* 1969 pap. $1.95
"A sound critical study . . . the only thorough-going critique of so much of Nabokov's work as is available in English"—(Howard Mumford Jones).
Nabokov: His Life in Art. By Andrew Field. *Little* 1967 pap. $2.95
Field analyzes all of Nabokov's works—English, Russian, and French—including pre-revolutionary juvenilia he found in the Lenin Library in Moscow. The book is "magnificently sympathetic to Nabokov, and written in part with his cooperation"—(*PW*).
Keys to Lolita. By Carl R. Proffer. *Indiana Univ. Press* 1968 $6.50
Nabokov. By Alfred Appel, Jr. and Charles Newman. *Northwestern Univ. Press* 1970 $12.00; *Simon & Schuster* 1970 Touchstone Bks. pap. $2.95
Vladimir Nabokov. By Julian Moynahan. *Univ. of Minnesota Press* 1971 pap. $1.25
Nabokov's Deceptive World. By William W. Rowe. *New York Univ. Press* 1971 $8.50
Nabokov: A Biography. By Andrew Field. *McGraw-Hill* 1973 $15.00
A Book of Things about Vladimir Nabokov. Ed. by Carl R. Proffer. *Ardis* 1974 pap. $3.50
The Literature of Exhaustion: Borges, Nabokov and Barth. By John O. Stark. *Duke Univ. Press* 1974 $7.95

Vladimir Nabokov. By Donald E. Morton. *Ungar* 1974 $6.00
Reading Nabokov. By Douglas Fowler. *Cornell Univ. Press* 1974 $9.50

OLYESHA, YURY KARLOVICH (also Olesha). 1899–1960.

"Despite the modest volume of his literary output, Olesha will be remembered in the history of contemporary Soviet literature as one of the small band of gifted writers who remained faithful to the end to the ideas for which they had fought when they first entered upon their literary paths"— (Vera Alexandrova). His work was suppressed for many years because, he explained at the first All-Union Congress of Writers in 1934, "The First Five-Year Plan was not my theme." Both "Envy," a novel, and "A List of Assets" focus on the "debate of the intellectual with himself over 'accepting' or 'not accepting' the Soviet regime"—(Edward J. Brown). In his last decade Olyesha published articles, memoirs and essays, characteristically reflecting a "love of freedom and man's creative spirit"—(Alexandrova).

ENVY (1927) AND OTHER WORKS. Trans. by Andrew MacAndrew. *Doubleday* Anchor Bks. (orig.) 1967 $1.95

Books about Olyesha

Invisible Land: A Study of the Artistic Imagination of Iurii Olesha. By Elizabeth K. Beaujour. *Columbia* 1970 $8.00

FADEYEV, ALEXANDER ALEXANDROVICH. 1901–1956.

Fadeyev's career spans the period from the beginning of proletarian literature to the initial stages of destalinization. "The Nineteen" (actual title, "The Rout," 1927), the story of a Red guerrilla unit in the Far East during the Civil War, was extremely well received by the public; the critics noted its debt to Tolstoy's style and method. An ambitious later work, a multivolume novel dealing with a Siberian tribe, "The Last of the Udege," was never actually completed. Fadeyev was more successful with "The Young Guard" (1946), which described the heroic activities of a teenage anti-German resistance group.

Throughout his literary career, Fadeyev was heavily involved in political struggles and debates. From 1939 to 1954 he was one of the leaders of the Union of Soviet Writers, but was removed from the leadership after Stalin's death. He committed suicide in 1956.

THE NINETEEN. 1927. Trans. by R. D. Charques. 1929. *Hyperion* 1973 $13.50

KAVERIN, VENIAMIN (pseud. of Veniamin Alexandrovich Zilberg). 1902–

Since 1922, Veniamin Kaverin has made a number of contributions to Soviet literature. He began as a member of the Serapion Brotherhood, a loose association of writers unified by a common belief in the autonomy of art and the freedom of the writer. He was strongly influenced by Western traditions; his first book, "Craftsmen and Apprentices" (*"Mastera i podmasterya,"* 1923), was influenced by E. T. A. Hoffman and Edgar Allan Poe. Similarly, Kaverin's "The End of a Gang" (*"Konets khazy,"* 1926) was influenced by R. L. Stevenson.

Two of his other novels are of particular note. The first, "The Troublemaker, or The Evenings on Vasilyevsky Island" (*"Skandalist, ili vechera na vasilyevskom ostrove,"* 1928) portrays the Leningrad literary milieu, in particular parodying the activities of the Formalists. The second, "The Unknown Artist" (*"Khudozhnik neizvesten,"* 1931) deals with the problem of the artist in the new society. Of Kaverin's remaining works, "Two Captains" (*"Dva kapitana,"* 1939), a sea adventure story, is noted for its charm and readability.

THE UNKNOWN ARTIST. 1931. Trans. by P. Ross. 1947. *Hyperion* 1973 $9.00

ZABOLOTSKY, NIKOLAI ALEKSEYEVICH. 1903–1958.

Zabolotsky is considered one of the more interesting poets of the Soviet period. His first volume, "Columns" (*"Stolbtsy"*), appeared in 1929. Both the language and the contents of the poems showed a strong influence of Khlebnikov. The parodistic, grotesque reality of this collection provoked a sharp reaction and the volume was withdrawn.

In the thirties, Zabolotsky was subjected to harsh political attacks. He disappeared from literature, briefly returned in 1937 with a collection of much simpler poems, and then vanished again for about ten years. Arrested and exiled, he apparently lived in Siberia and the Caucasus. In 1947–1948 some of his poems began to reappear in print. They were followed by numerous translations. Zabolotsky's own original poems again appeared in 1953 and a volume, "Poems," was published in 1957. In this final collection, little is left of the startling and bizarre world of Zabolotsky's initial volume.

SCROLLS. 1929. Trans. by Daniel Weisbert. *Grossman* (dist. by Viking) 1971 $3.95 pap. $1.50

OSTROVSKY, NIKOLAY ALEKSEYEVICH. 1904–1936.

Ostrovsky is the author of the celebrated inspirational classic "How Steel Was Tempered" (or "Born of the Storm"). Autobiographical in its material, the novel deals with the formation and growth of its Communist hero, Pavel Korchagin. A special aura surrounds the work: its author was blind and bedridden when he wrote it.

BORN OF THE STORM. Trans. by Louise L. Hiler. 1939. *Hyperion* 1974 $15.00

PANOVA, VERA FEDOROVNA. 1905–1973.

Panova's first novel, "The Train" (trans. by Marie Budberg, o.p.), about a hospital train in World War II, won the Stalin Prize in 1946. She later received three Stalin awards for short novels, but her "detachment" and "objectivity" have been criticized by the Soviet's politico-literary authorities as "incompatible with Socialist realism." "She must be credited with having introduced and insisted upon some of the most important themes of the immediate post-Stalin 'thaw' "—(Edward J. Brown).

A SUMMER TO REMEMBER. Trans. from the Russian novel *"Serioja"* and first published in England as "Time Walked" (1959). *A. S. Barnes* (Yoseloff) 1965 $5.95

ON FARAWAY STREET. Trans. by Rya Gabel. *Braziller* 1968 $3.95

IT'S BEEN AGES. (In "Contemporary Russian Drama," orig. title "Recent Russian Plays") trans. by Franklin D. Reeves. *Bobbs* Pegasus 1968 $7.50 pap. $2.95

SHOLOKHOV, MIKHAIL ALEKSANDROVICH. 1905– (Nobel Prize 1965)

A Cossack who still lives in his native village, Sholokhov is the great epic recorder of the Don Cossacks. "It is hard for us in the West even to imagine [his] fame in the USSR. Russian writers are lionized and he is the best-known novelist in the country"—(Olga Carlisle). In 1965 he was awarded the Nobel Prize for Literature. He has also received the Stalin Prize and the Order of Lenin and is a deputy to the Supreme Soviet.

On the question of the authorship and composition of "And Quiet Flows the Don," see the thought-provoking article by Alexander Solzhenitsyn, "Sholokov and the Riddle of the Quiet Don" (*Times Literary Supplement,* London, 1974, p. 1056, and correspondence on pp. 1126, 1197, 1260).

TALES OF THE DON. Trans. by H. C. Stevens. *Knopf* 1962 $5.95. Sixteen short stories written in 1925–1926 which were later developed at greater length in "And Quiet Flows the Don".

THE SILENT DON. 1928–1940. Trans. by Stephen Garry *Knopf* 2 vols. Vol. 1 And Quiet Flows the Don 1934 1959 Vol. 2 The Don Flows Home to the Sea 1940 each $7.95 one vol. ed. $10.75; trans. by H. C. Stevens *Random* Vintage Bks. 2 vols. pap. each $2.95

HARVEST ON THE DON. 1960. Trans. by H. C. Stevens. *Knopf* 1960 $6.95

Books about Sholokhov

World of Young Sholokhov. By Michael Klimenko. *Chris Mass.* $9.95
Mikhail Sholokhov: A Critical Introduction. By D. H. Stewart. *Univ. of Michigan Press* 1967 $8.00
Mixail Soloxov in Yugoslavia: Reception and Literary Impact. By Robert F. Price. East European Monographs *Columbia Univ. Press* 1973 $10.00

TARSIS, VALERIY YAKOVLEVICH. 1906–

Valeriy Tarsis was, until 1960, a prominent member of the Soviet Writers' Union. His studies on Western literature earned him a considerable reputation in his country as a critic; yet, in secret, over 20 years he wrote poems and novels which he knew could never be published in Russia. The manuscript of "The Bluebottle" (o.p.), with several other works of fiction, was smuggled out and published in England. Shortly after the book's appearance in London, Tarsis was officially declared insane and committed to a mental institution. In 1963 the Western press and a number of Soviet writers campaigned successfully for his release. Tarsis was allowed to go to London, but while there, in 1966, he was notified that he was being deprived of his citizenship "for actions discrediting a Soviet citizen."

THE PLEASURE FACTORY. Trans. by Michael Glenny. *T. Y. Crowell* (John Day) 1968 $4.95

KRYMOV, YURY (pseud. of Yury Solomonovich Beklemishev). 1908–1941.

Krymov's career as a writer was rather short (he was killed in battle in 1941). "Tanker Derbent" was his first novel and was extremely successful. Its action is set in a Caspian Sea port, on board an oil tanker. The hero is presented in an original and interesting way; adding to the readability of the novel is its careful interweaving of personal and social problems.

TANKER DERBENT. 1938. Trans. by B. Kagan. 1940. *Hyperion* 1974 $16.50

POLEVOY, BORIS (pseud. of Boris Nikolayevich Kampov). 1908–

Polevoy became extremely famous in the Soviet Union for his "Story about a Real Man," which recounted the adventures of a heroic flier who lost his legs in a forced landing, escaped the enemy, and later rejoined the air force. True-life stories from the war also formed the basis for a subsequent volume of his stories.

Edward Brown, who met Polevoy in person sometime after the XXth Party Congress, describes him as a liberal and "a combination of Jack London (his favorite writer) and a proletarian Jim Tully"—(E. Brown, "Russian Literature since the Revolution").

STORY ABOUT A REAL MAN. 1947. 1952 *Greenwood* $23.00

HERMAN, YURY PAVLOVICH. 1910–1968.

Herman began publishing during the first years of implementation of Socialist Realism. His first novel, "Our Friends" ("*Nashi znakomye*," 1936) was quite old-fashioned in construction, but enjoyed an immediate success. "Alexei the Gangster" is the story of an escaped criminal who is tracked down by a police official.

Herman was also associated with the ill-fated Leningrad magazine *Zvezda,* which in 1946 was purged by A. Zhdanov.

ALEXEI THE GANGSTER. Trans. by Stephen Gary. 1940 *Hyperion* 1974 $16.00

SIMONOV, KONSTANTIN MIKHAILOVICH. 1915–

Simonov has had a long career in Soviet literature as a poet, playwright, and novelist. His poetry includes many love poems as well as pieces dealing with historical subjects; in addition, there are his war poems, some of which became popular both in the Soviet Union and abroad. His plays tend to reflect prevailing political attitudes: "Someone Else's Shadow" ("*Chuzhaya ten'* " 1949), which deals with the battle of Stalingrad, is particularly well-known.

LIVING AND THE DEAD. Trans. by R. Ainsztein. 1962 *Greenwood* 1968 $21.00

SOLZHENITSYN, ALEKSANDR ISAYEVICH. 1918–   (Nobel Prize 1970)

A physicist and mathematician by training, Solzhenitsyn studied at Rostov University. During the war he first served as a private, but eventually rose to the rank of captain and won several medals. In February 1945, in East Prussia, he was arrested by the secret police, who had been intercepting letters critical of Stalin which he and a friend had been exchanging. He was sentenced to eight years in a concentration camp; he served these in various jobs, including that of mathematician in a *sharashka*, a prison research-institute (such an institute is the setting of his novel "The First Circle" ['*V kruge pervom*," 1968]). Exiled "in perpetuity" in 1953, he taught in various secondary schools in Central Asia, where he also successfully overcame a stomach cancer (Solzhenitsyn's experiences in an oncological clinic are reflected in "Cancer Ward" ["*Rakovy korpus*," 1968]). He was freed in 1956 and rehabilitated in 1957, at which point he returned to central Russia.

The early period of Solzhenitsyn's life has shaped the major part of his work to date: he has made himself an unmatched chronicler of the gigantic Soviet system of prisons and concentration camps (the so-called "Gulag Archipelago"). His first published work on this subject was "One Day in the Life of Ivan Denisovich" ("*Odin den' Ivana Denisovicha*," 1962), which appeared during Khrushchev's anti-Stalin campaign in the early sixties. This book, the first to deal honestly with a hitherto unmentionable topic, described the existence of a prisoner in a post-war "special camp," and made Solzhenitsyn immediately famous in Russia and the West.

For a rather brief period, Solzhenitsyn enjoyed a degree of official approbation, and some of his work appeared in the literary magazine *Novy Mir* (*New World*). The situation changed for the worse by the middle of the sixties, when neo-Stalinist forces took the upper hand in Soviet government and society. In effect, Solzhenitsyn was prevented from publishing at home, and was subjected to both official and covert abuse. His response to such attacks was a public letter to the fourth Congress of Soviet Writers (1967), in which he protested not only his own situation, but also the general oppression of Russian literature by the censorship.

In 1968, after a rather complex series of events, "Cancer Ward" and "The First Circle" were published in the West. This led to new attacks and to his expulsion from the Writers' Union in 1969. The awarding to Solzhenitsyn of the 1970 Nobel Prize for literature was viewed by Soviet official circles as all the more of an insult; however, in spite of the ensuing vilification, Solzhenit-syn did not decline the award. A new storm broke out in 1971, after the publication of "August 1914" (*"Avgust chetyrnadtsatogo"*), the first of a projected cycle of "fascicles" dealing with World War I and the Revolution.

The final episode in Solzhenitsyn's duel with Soviet authorities came in December 1973, when the first volume of "The Gulag Archipelago" (*"Arkhipelag GULag"*) was published in Paris. The appearance of this vast chronicle of institutionalized Soviet terror resulted in a dramatic series of events, which culminated in February 1974 with the writer's arrest and subsequent banishment from the Soviet Union.

At present, Solzhenitsyn lives in Switzerland and continues to write and publish. The remainder of "The Gulag Archipelago" (Volumes 2 and 3) appeared in 1975–1976. He has also deliberately assumed a public role as critic of Western attitudes towards and relations with the Eastern bloc, and has lectured widely on this subject. His views on Russia and the West have met with a mixed reception; nonetheless, he continues to be acknowledged as the greatest living Russian writer and one of the great figures of Russian literature as a whole.

WE NEVER MAKE MISTAKES. 1963. Trans. with introd. by Paul W. Blackstock. *Univ. of South Carolina Press* 1963 $5.95; *Norton* Norton Lib. pap. $1.55

Includes "Incident at Krechetovka Station" and "Matryona's House." Two "artful, moving" novellas—*(LJ)*.

STORIES AND PROSE POEMS. Trans. by Michael Glenny. *Farrar, Straus* 1971 $8.95 Noonday pap. $3.25; *Bantam* 1972 pap. $1.50

ONE DAY IN THE LIFE OF IVAN DENISOVICH. 1962. *Bantam* 1970 pap. $.95; trans. by Ralph Parker, introd. by Marvin L. Kalb, fwd. by A. Tvardovsky *Dutton* 1963 $4.95; trans. by Aitken Gillon *Farrar, Straus* 1971 $7.95; *New Am. Lib.* Signet 1963 pap. $.95; trans. by Max Hayward and Ronald Hingley, introd. by Max Hayward and Leopold Labedz *Praeger* 1963 $5.50 pap. $1.95

THE CANCER WARD. 1968. *Bantam* 1969 pap. $1.75; trans. by Rebecca Frank *Dell* 1974 pap. $1.95; trans. by Rebecca Frank *Dial* 1968 $12.95; trans. by Nicholas Bethell and David Burg *Farrar, Straus* 1969 $10.00 Noonday pap. $4.95

THE FIRST CIRCLE. 1968. Trans. by Thomas P. Whitney. *Harper* 1968 $11.95 *Bantam* 1969 pap. $1.50

THE LOVE GIRL AND THE INNOCENT. 1969. *Bantam* pap. $.95; trans. by Nicholas Bethell and David Burg *Farrar, Straus* 1970 $5.95 Noonday pap. $2.95

AUGUST 1914. 1971. Trans. by Michael Glenny *Farrar, Straus* 1972 $10.00 *Bantam* pap. $2.25

A LENTEN LETTER TO PIMEN, PATRIARCH OF ALL RUSSIA. 1972. Trans. by Keith Armes, ed. by Theofanis Stavrous. *Burgess* pap. $1.50

THE NOBEL LECTURE ON LITERATURE. Trans. by Franklin D. Reeve *Farrar, Straus* bilingual ed. 1972 $4.00 Noonday pap. $1.50; trans. by Thomas P. Whitney *Harper* 1972 $4.00

CANDLE IN THE WIND. Trans. by Keith Armes and Arthur Hudgins *Univ. of Minnesota Press* 1973 $6.95; *Bantam* 1974 pap. $1.65

LETTER TO THE SOVIET LEADERS. 1973. Trans. by Hilary Sternberg *Harper* 1974 $3.50 new ed. 1975 pap. $1.50

THE GULAG ARCHIPELAGO, Vol. 1, 1918–1956: An Experiment in Literary Investigation. Trans. by Thomas P. Whitney. *Harper* 1974 $12.50 Perenn. Lib. pap. $1.95

THE GULAG ARCHIPELAGO, Vol. 2: The Soul behind the Barbed Wire. Trans. by Thomas P. Whitney. *Harper* 1975 $15.00 pap. $2.50

(And others) FROM UNDER THE RUBBLE. *Little* 1975 $8.95

Books about Solzhenitsyn

Aleksandr Solzhenitsyn: The Major Novels. By Abraham Rothberg. *Cornell Univ. Press* 1971 $8.50

Solzhenitsyn: A Documentary Record. Ed. by Leopold Labedz. *Harper* 1971 $8.95; enl. ed. with the Nobel Prize Lecture *Indiana Univ. Press* 1973 pap. $3.50

Solzhenitsyn. By David Burg and George Feifer. Illus. *Stein & Day* 1972 $10.00 pap. $3.95

Aleksandr Solzhenitsyn; A Biography. By Hans Bjorkegren. Trans. by K. Eneberg. *Third Press* 1972 $7.95 pap. 1973 $2.95

Alexander Solzhenitsyn: An International Bibliography of Works by and about Him, 1962–73. By Donald Fiene. *Ardis* 1973 $8.95 pap. $3.50

Aleksandr Solzhenitsyn, Beleaguered Literary Giant of the U.S.S.R. By Blythe F. Finke; ed. by D. Steve Rahmas. *SamHar Press* 1973 lib. bdg. $1.98 pap. $.98

Ten Years after Ivan Denisovich. By Zhores Medvedev. *Knopf* 1973 $6.95

Solzhenitsyn. By Christopher Moody. Modern Writers Ser. *Harper* (Barnes & Noble) 1973 $5.75

Solzhenitsyn: A Pictorial Autobiography. Illus. *Farrar, Straus* 1974 $8.96 pap. $2.95

Aleksandr Solzhenitsyn: Critical Essays and Biographical Materials. Ed. by John B. Dunlop and others. *Nordland Pub.* 1975 $15.00

Solzhenitsyn and the Future. By Joseph Vilner. *Exposition* 1975 $4.00

Sanya: My Life with Aleksandr Solzhenitsyn. By Natalya Reshetovskaya. *Bobbs* 1975 $8.95

Solzhenitsyn. Ed. by Kathryn B. Feuer. *Prentice-Hall* Spectrum 1975 (in prep.)

TERTZ, ABRAM (pseud. of Andrei Sinyavsky).   1925–

In February, 1966, Andrei Sinyavsky and Yuli Daniel (pseud. of Nikolai Arzhak) were tried in a closed court, convicted of maligning the Soviet Union through "hostile" and "slanderous" writings published illegally abroad. They received sentences of seven and five years, respectively, in forced-labor camps. Writers in Russia and the West were outraged, and commentators called the trial "a real witch hunt"—(*SR*) and "a scandal, not merely by our own bourgeois notions of justice, but, much more important, in terms of previous opinions expressed by Soviet jurists on the proper handling of such cases"—(*N.Y. Times*). In vain attempts to aid their colleagues, three Soviet writers, including Konstantin Paustovsky (*q.v.*), offered to testify in their behalf, but were rejected by the court. Many writers refused to testify for the prosecution. Ten letters signed by 95 leading Soviet writers protested the trial, and when it was over 63 writers offered themselves as "surety" to gain release for the two. (Only Mikhail Sholokhov [*q.v.*] complained that the sentences were too lenient. In an angry letter to him, Lidiya Chukovskaya, a literary critic, replied that "ideas should be fought with ideas, not with camps and prisons.")

The work of "Abram Tertz," whose identity was long a mystery, first became known in the United States with the publication of "The Trial Begins," called by *Time* "perhaps the most remarkable novel to have come out of the Soviet Union since the Revolution." His books, as well as Daniel's four short stories—his only work to be printed abroad—were first published in Paris.

"Lyubimov" ("The Makepeace Experiment"), Sinyavsky's masterpiece, is the fantastic story of a town by that name—derived, said its author, from the Russian word for "beloved" and indicating his own benevolent approach.

"Fantastic Stories" contains a "strange mélange of surrealist dreams, weird imagery, and extraordinary happenings. Symbol, allegory, and straightforward narrative are interwoven"—(*LJ*). Sinyavsky's critical essay "On Socialist Realism" was described by Arthur Schlesinger, Jr. (*q.v.*) as "the most illuminating diagnosis I have seen of the predicament of the writer in Soviet society."

On Socialist Realism. 1959. Trans. by George Dennis. *Pantheon* 1961 $4.95

The Trial Begins. 1960. Trans. by Max Hayward. *Pantheon* 1960 $2.95; (and "On Socialist Realism") *Random* Vintage Bks. pap. $1.95

The Makepeace Experiment (*Lyubimov*). 1964. Trans. by Manya Harari. *Pantheon* 1965 $3.95; *Random* Vintage Bks. pap. $1.65

A Voice from the Chorus. Trans. by Kyril FitzLyon. *Farrar, Straus* (in prep.)

For Freedom of Imagination. *Holt* 1971 $6.95

KAZAKOV, YURI PAVLOVICH.   1927–

In his 22 short stories, Kazakov explores the life of the unexceptional individual. He is "young, prolific, idiosyncratic, and certainly one of the most significant of contemporary Soviet writers"—(*LJ*). Peter Viereck (in *SR*) notes his "uncanny resemblance to Salinger and Anderson. . . . The concrete individual is paramount: very human and unheroic. . . . The subject matter is the inner private life, especially love and loneliness." Kazakov was born in Moscow and pursued a musical career until 1957, when he began to be published. He is much translated throughout Europe.

Going to Town and Other Stories. Trans. by Gabriella Azrael. *Houghton* 1964 $4.95

KUZNETSOV, ANATOLY.   1929–

Kuznetsov was born in Kiev; he was 12 years old when the Nazis occupied the city in 1941. Babi

Yar ("Old Wives' Gully") is a ravine near Kiev where he witnessed the extermination by the Nazis of 200,000 people—including the entire Jewish population of Kiev—during the two-year occupation. He began writing his impressions at 14 and later expanded them into a "remarkable book that is as much a historical document and a heartfelt cry for peace as it is a novel"—(*PW*). The subject was a forbidden one in the Soviet Union until Yevtushenko (*q.v.*) published his poem "Babi Yar" in 1961 and the government acknowledged the tragedy (denying, however, that the primary victims had been Jews).

BABI YAR: A Documentary Novel. Trans. by Jacob Guralsky; ill. by S. Brodsky. *Dell* Laurel Eds. 1967 pap. $.95

AKSYONOV, VASILIY PAVLOVICH. 1932–

Aksyonov made his debut during the late fifties and early sixties, when he was closely associated with the popular journal *Yunost'* (*Youth*). He is one of the most original and most interesting of contemporary Russian prose writers. His work is distinguished by language which owes much to an ear for contemporary Russian, especially the idiom of the young people. Similarly, his stories concentrate on both the psychology and social problems of Soviet youth—themes which Aksyonov treats honestly and with subtlety, in a way which has earned him repeated official reprimands. His most famous story is "Half-way to the Moon" (*"Na polputi k lune,"* 1962).

IT'S TIME, MY LOVE, IT'S TIME. 1964. *Aurora* 1974 $3.95

VOZNESENSKY, ANDREI ANDREYEVICH. 1933–

Born in Moscow, Voznesensky at first studied architecture, although "poetry was flowing in me like a river under the ice." He studied in the Moscow Architectural Institute during the fifties, but abandoned architecture when the institute burned down in 1957. His first poems were published in *Literaturnaya gazeta* in 1958; however, his first real success was the long poem "Master Craftsmen" (*"Mastera,"* 1959). In 1960, his first two books appeared; these were "Mosaic" and "Parabola." Both of them showed the verbal virtuosity, the inventiveness in all aspects of verse, which have subsequently become a hallmark of Voznesensky's writing.

During the 1960s, Voznesensky made many trips abroad (to the United States, Britain, France, and Italy) and achieved wide international recognition. He became enormously popular in the Soviet Union, thanks in part to his appearances at public poetry readings, many of which were held in the early sixties. He published several important books, among them "Antiworlds" (*"Antimiry,"* 1964) and "The Achilles' Heart" (*"Akhilessovo serdtse,"* 1965).

Voznesensky has been in and out of trouble with the Soviet authorities. A particularly celebrated incident took place when he published a letter (in several Western journals) in which he angrily protested being prevented from attending the Lincoln Center Arts Festival in New York. In spite of this and other incidents, Voznesensky appears to have made a successful adjustment to contemporary Soviet reality.

SELECTED POEMS. Trans. and ed. with introd. by Anselm Hollo. *Grove* 1964 Evergreen Bks. 1966 pap. $2.45; trans. with introd. by Herbert Marshall *Farrar, Straus* Hill & Wang 1966 $4.50 pap. $1.75

ANTIWORLDS AND THE FIFTH ACE. Trans. by W. H. Auden, Jean Garrigue, Max Hayward, Stanley Kunitz, Stanley Moss, William Jay Smith, and Richard Wilbur; ed. by Patricia Blake and Max Hayward. *Schocken* bilingual ed. 1973 pap. $3.95

WALKING ON THE WATER. *Doubleday* $10.00 (in prep.)

YEVTUSHENKO, YEVGENY ALEKSANDROVICH. 1933–

Yevtushenko was born in Zima, a small junction on the Trans-Siberian Railway (and the subject of his long poem "Zima Junction" (*"Stantsia Zima,"* 1956). Although he devoted himself to literature during the early fifties, he emerged as an important poet only after Stalin's death in 1953; his three books—"The Third Snow" (*"Trety sneg,"* 1955), "The Highway of Enthusiasts" (*"Shosse entuziastov,"* 1956), and "The Promise" (*"Obeshchanie,"* 1957)—made him a spokesman for the younger generation.

In 1961, Yevtushenko came out with the poem "Babi Yar," which dealt with the wartime massacre of ninety-six thousand Jews in a ravine near Kiev. The work made Yevtushenko internationally famous and was enormously popular at home; nonetheless, the poet's acknowledgement of the existence of a Soviet anti-Semitism aroused a storm of official opposition.

During the sixties and seventies, Yevtushenko travelled extensively abroad (to the United States, Europe, and Africa). His trips inspired many poetic works, such as "Tenderness," (*"Nezhnost'"*), the 1962 collection of 22 poems on Cuba. In his works, he has been both topical and generally autobiographical; on the whole, however, his writing lacks true depth.

Yevtushenko's early reputation as a defender of artistic freedom in the Soviet Union has generally been dispelled during the seventies. On the whole, the poet has openly shifted towards a more official position, though on occasion he has uttered liberal views.

SELECTED POEMS. Trans. with introd. by Robin Milner-Gulland and Peter Levi. *Dutton* 1962 $5.50; *Penguin* 1963 pap. $.90

YEVGENII YEVTUSHENKO: Selected Poetry. Ed. by R. Milner-Gulland. *Pergamon* 1964 $4.00 pap. $3.00

POETRY, 1953–1965. Trans., sel., and ed. by George Reavey. *October House* bilingual ed. 1964 $6.50 pap. $2.95

YEVTUSHENKO: Poems. Trans. by Herbert Marshall. *Dutton* bilingual ed. 1966 $4.95

YEVTUSHENKO'S READER: The Spirit of Elbe, A Precocious Autobiography, Poems. *Dutton* 1966 $5.95 pap. $2.65; *Avon* Bard Bks. 1973 pap. $1.45

BRATSK STATION (1966) AND OTHER NEW POEMS. Trans. by T. Tupikina-Glaessner, G. Dutton, and I. Mezhakoff-Koriakin; introd. by Rosh Ireland. *Doubleday* Anchor Bks. (orig.) 1967 pap. $1.95; *Praeger* 1967 $4.95

YEVGENY YEVTUSHENKO: Poems Chosen by the Author. Trans. by Peter Levi and Robin Milner-Gulland. *Farrar, Straus* (Hill & Wang) bilingual ed. 1967 $3.95 pap. $1.95

STOLEN APPLES. Trans. by noted American poets; ill. by Ray Davidson. *Doubleday* $8.95 limited ed. $25.00; Anchor Bks. pap. $3.95

FROM DESIRE TO DESIRE. *Doubleday* 1976 $6.95

A PRECOCIOUS AUTOBIOGRAPHY. 1963. Trans. by Andrew R. MacAndrew. *Dutton* 1963 pap. $1.25

AKHMADULINA, BELLA. 1937–

Formerly married to Yevtushenko (*q.v.*), Akhmadulina is one of the most important contemporary Russian poets. Her first collection of poems was published in 1962. She is distinguished by a command of striking imagery and language: "... it is her purpose, in part achieved, that every line be an unobtrusive *bon mot*"—(E. Brown, *Russian Literature since the Revolution*).

FEVER AND OTHER NEW POEMS. Trans. by Geoffrey Dutton and others. *Morrow* 1969 $5.50; *T. Y. Crowell* (Apollo Eds.) 1969 pap. $1.50

BRODSKY, JOSEPH ALEXANDROVICH. 1940–

Brodsky's first poems appeared mainly in *Sintaksis* (*Syntax*), an underground Leningrad literary magazine. In 1964, he became the object of international concern after being tried and sentenced to five years of forced labor for "parasitism." Thanks to the intervention of prominent cultural figures in the Soviet Union, he was freed after 18 months. In 1972 he emigrated to the United States, where he is now Poet in Residence at the University of Michigan (Ann Arbor).

Brodsky's work is distinguished, among other features, by a strong interest in religious themes. His best-known work is "Elegy to John Donne" (1963).

JOSEPH BRODSKY: Selected Poems. Trans. by George Kline. *Harper* 1974 $5.95 *Penguin* pap. $2.95

TENDRYAKOV, VLADIMIR F. 1943–

Tendryakov is one of a number of young prose writers who attracted considerable attention during the sixties by going beyond the conventions of socialist realism. His forte has been the short story; his pieces generally have been set in remote Soviet backwoods villages and he has concerned himself with problems of individual morality.

THREE, SEVEN, ACE AND OTHER STORIES. Trans. by David Alger and others. *Harper* 1973 $6.95

—H.B.

Chapter 15

Other European Literature

"Litera scripta manet"—*"the written word endures."*

ALBANIAN LITERATURE

The first works of Albanian literature, published over a period of about two centuries, were mainly of a religious and didactic character. This period extends from the mid-sixteenth century to roughly the mid-eighteenth century, and includes works by Albanians in Albania and by Albanian authors in southern Italy and Sicily. It began with the publication in 1555 of Bishop Gjon Buzuku's *"Meshari"* (Liturgy), the earliest known book in the Albanian language. The single extant copy of the book is in the Vatican Library. In 1592, Fr. Llukë Matranga, an Italo-Albanian from Sicily, published his *"E mbusame e krështërë"* (Christian Doctrine). The work is a translation of Fr. Ledesma's catechism, *"Dottrina Christiana."* A noted work of this period is *"Gjella e Shën Mëriis Virgjër"* (Life of the Virgin Mary) by Jul (Giulio) Variboba, another Italo-Albanian. It was published in Rome in 1762.

Ecclesiastical and didactic literature continued to be written through the eighteenth and nineteenth centuries. By this time, however, the range of Albanian literature was broadened with the publication of dictionaries, folklore, and works of a romantic and patriotic character. The outstanding writer of this epoch was the Italo-Albanian Jeronim (Girolamo) de Rada (1814–1903), whose romantic and patriotic works conferred upon him the stature of national poet of the Albanian people. According to critic Arshi Pipa, de Rada's *"Milosao"* (1836) marks "the birth of Albanian romantic literature," and "remains the jewel of Albanian poetry to this day." Two significant contemporaries of de Rada's were Kostandin Kristoforidhi (1827–1895), a pioneer lexicographer, and Thimi (Efthim) Mitko (1820–1890), whose *"Bëlietta Shqipëtare"* (The Albanian Bee), which he published in 1878 in Alexandria, Egypt, was the first comprehensive collection of the folklore of southern Albania.

The founding of the League of Prizren in 1878 marked the beginning of Albania's national awakening, which culminated in the country's independence in 1912. The movement for independence was paralleled by intense literary activity. Among the writers of the national awakening, the most influential was Naim Frashëri (1846–1900), author of *"Bagëti e Bujqësi"* (Cattle and Crops) (1886), a moving poem about pastoral society; and *"Istori e Skënderbeut"* (History of Scanderbeg) (1898), an epic poem depicting the life of Albania's medieval national hero.

The turn of the century marked the appearance of a realistic literary trend, combined with cynicism, that was best exemplified in the work of Andon Çako ("Çajupi") (1866–1930), especially in his anthology entitled, *"Baba Tomorri"* (Father Tomorri) (1902). Unlike Catholic clergymen of earlier periods, Fr. Gjergj Fishta (1871–1940), a Franciscan friar, is celebrated for his *"Lahuta e Malcis"* (The Lute of the Highlands) (1937), a poem in 30 cantos, which praises the valor and virtues of northern Albanians in their struggles against the neighboring Slavs, the Serbs and Montenegrins. Many consider Fishta's epic poem to be the finest flower in Albanian poetic literature. Another clergyman, Bishop Fan (Theofan) S. Noli (1882–1965) holds an honored place in Albanian letters for his book of poems, *"Albumi"* (1948), and the excellence of the critical essays that accompanied his translations of Shakespeare, Ibsen, Cervantes, and other classic authors.

By the 1930s, Albanian literature began to show increasingly the influence of socialist and radical ideas. The best representative of this trend by far is Migjeni, an acronym for Millosh Gjergj Nikolla (1911–1938). His works, *"Luli i Vocërr"* (Little Luli), and *"Kanga*

Lirije" (Songs of Freedom), have as their main theme an outright condemnation of the social injustices of his time. Migjeni thus stands at the threshhold of the literature of "socialist realism," which has characterized the postwar era in Albania.

Drizari, Nelo. FOUR SEAS TO DREAMLAND. *The National Press* 1969 $5.00. The adventures of a boy are traced from his native land of Albania to his new life in America—the dreamland of his aspirations. (Available from The Free Albania Organization, 397B W. Broadway, S. Boston, Mass. 02127.)

Frashëri, Naim. SKANDERBEG'S RETURN AND OTHER POEMS. *Naim Frashëri* 1970 pap. $0.40. Selections from the poetic writings of the most popular poet of Albania's national awakening. The work includes the complete text of *"Bagëti e Bujqësi"* (Cattle and Crops), a passionate tribute to rural life. Translated by Ali Cungu. (Available from Albania Report, P.O. Box 912, New York, N.Y. 10008.)

Kadare, Ismail. THE GENERAL OF THE DEAD ARMY. *Grossman* (dist. by Viking) 1972 $7.95. The best-known novel in recent Albanian literature has been published in some two dozen foreign countries since its appearance in Albania in 1963. "Not just a revelation of Albanian literature—a revelation in any terms"—*(L'Express,* Paris). (Available from Albania Report at discount rate.)

Skendi, Stavro. ALBANIAN AND SOUTH SLAVIC ORAL EPIC POETRY. American Folklore Society Memoirs Ser. 1954. *Kraus* 1975 $12.00

ALBANIAN NATIONAL AWAKENING 1878–1912. *Princeton Univ. Press* 1967 $17.50

SPECIMENS OF ALBANIAN CONTEMPORARY PROSE. Trans. by Ali Cungu. *Naim Frashëri* 1969 pap. $.70. An anthology of six short stories, most of them based on actual events, and all of them reflecting the principle of "socialist realism." (Available from Albania Report.)

—P.R.P.

BULGARIAN LITERATURE

Bulgaria has a long literary history. The Golden Age of old Bulgarian literature occurred in the late ninth and early tenth centuries, following the country's official Christianization. At that time Bulgaria transmitted Byzantine Christian traditions to all those Slavs who would become Eastern Orthodox Christians, including the Russians. Then, after a substantial interval, the Silver Age of old Bulgarian literature took place during the late fourteenth century, when the country was on the verge of falling (as it did in 1393) before the Turkish armies on their victorious path to Constantinople.

For nearly four centuries thereafter Bulgarian literature and culture scarcely existed, until in 1762 the monk Paisii of the Hilendar Monastery on Mount Athos summoned his countrymen to a rebirth of national consciousness in his major historical work, which circulated only in manuscript for several decades. By 1825, slowly and uncertainly, Bulgarian literature had begun to recover from the isolation imposed upon it by Turkish political rule and Greek cultural hegemony. The few intellectuals and writers of whom Bulgaria could boast from 1825 to about 1875 had to devote much of their energy to the liberation of their homeland. The most striking union of art and revolution in this period was the life of the poet Khristo Botev. Botev composed a small number of nearly perfect lyrics in which he expressed his revolutionary convictions; then, when the hour struck, he led a band of followers from Rumanian exile into Bulgaria in support of the April 1876 uprising. But his movements were traced by the Turkish authorities, and he was felled by a Turkish bullet when the rebellion had already been quelled.

Political liberation came to Bulgaria only after the Russo-Turkish War of 1877–1878, when the newly independent Bulgarians had to set about learning to govern themselves. The process was not an easy one. Ivan Vazov (he would later become the national

Bulgarian writer) chronicled the heroic events of the Liberation, through which he had lived, in prose and poetry, but he later wrote with satire and sorrow of the independent Bulgarian citizen, who in too many ways seemed unworthy of the liberty bought with so much sacrifice. The prose writer Aleko Konstantinov, likewise sorely disappointed by the political machinations of the Bulgarian elite, created the immortal fictional image of Bay Ganyu, the quintessential bumbling Bulgarian philistine. In addition, he was one of the first of his countrymen to describe the United States, after a visit to the Chicago World's Fair of 1893. In the end, Konstantinov fell victim to an assassin's bullet.

By the end of the nineteenth century the task of instilling a national consciousness in the ordinary Bulgarian was sufficiently well in hand to permit the rising generation of writers to preach a new consciousness of the achievements of western and world culture. Prominent among these writers was the poet Pencho Slaveykov, who in such works as "Epic Sonos" hymned the gigantic cultural contributions of men like Shelley and Beethoven. Slaveykov, the only Bulgarian author ever nominated for a Nobel Prize, died in political exile in 1912.

After the catastrophes of the two Balkan wars and the First World War, Bulgarian literature and culture truly came of age between the two global conflicts. Bulgarian literature attained its greatest successes in the shorter forms of the short story and the lyric poem. Yordan Yovkov and Elin Pelin contributed sensitive stories drawn from the Bulgarian countryside, stories deeply embedded in a specific milieu, but not a milieu so particular that the western reader cannot appreciate the stories' universal human significance. Poets wrote in abundance during these two decades, everyone from several belated Symbolists, to revolutionary communists, to the modernist Elisaveta Bagryana, the finest woman poet Bulgaria has yet produced. The novel and the drama also blossomed, although they could not fully match the energies of the short story and the lyric; and literary criticism and literary journalism came of age with the appearance of such publications as Vladimir Vasilev's *Zlatoroq* (Golden Horn), which numbered the majority of the worthwhile Bulgarian writers during the interwar years among its contributors.

The communist seizure of power in Bulgaria (1944) had profound effects upon Bulgarian literature. Regimented in such organizations as the Union of Bulgarian Writers, authors were pressured to produce works useful for the building of a communist society. During the worst years of Bulgarian Stalinism, any independent literature virtually ceased to exist, and even such classics as Vazov were in danger of ceasing to be reprinted. But with the thaw of 1956 and ensuing years in the communist bloc, it became possible once again to write more freely. During the 1960s and 1970s limited literary experimentation has been permitted, and Bulgaria can now boast a considerable group of young poets of substantial technical proficiency ready to deal with unapproved topics when given the opportunity. Some have risked writing prose satire on contemporary reality, but only a few, for satires can have unfortunate consequences for their authors. Others have chosen to retreat from the present to historical novels, in which universal human problems may be treated with more objectivity. Among the historical novelists are Dimitur Talev, whose great historical trilogy, published in the early 1950s, depicts the struggle for independence against the Turks; and Anton Donchev, whose novel "Time of Parting"—describing the agony of Bulgarians who, under Turkish occupation in the seventeenth century, chose death rather than deny their Christian faith—appeared in English translation in the United States in 1968, to critical approval.

A brief anthology of contemporary Bulgarian prose and poetry, edited by Charles A. Moser, was issued as the Winter 1972–1973 number of *The Literary Review*, published by Fairleigh-Dickinson University.

For all its vicissitudes—including especially official pressures—Bulgarian literature continues to grow and develop. In the past it has made modest but distinctive contributions to the store of European culture, and one may hope that in the future it will continue to do so.

Kirilov, Nikolai, and Frank Kirk. INTRODUCTION TO MODERN BULGARIAN LITERATURE. *Twayne* 1969 $7.95. A large anthology of short stories by various authors from the late nineteenth century to the present. Though arranged in somewhat haphazard fashion, provides some notion of the character of modern Bulgarian literature. Includes a brief introduction.

Manning, Clarence, and Roman Smal-Stocki. THE HISTORY OF MODERN BULGARIAN LITERATURE. 1960. *Greenwood* 1974 $9.75. A brief account of Bulgarian literature from earliest times to the modern day. A convenient reference, but too often factually unreliable.

Moser, Charles A. A HISTORY OF BULGARIAN LITERATURE, 865–1944. *Mouton* (dist. by Humanities Press) 1972 $25.75. A more detailed treatment of Bulgarian literature from earliest times to 1944 than the preceding; gives relatively greater weight to the literature of the twentieth century. Extensive bibliography.

VAZOV, IVAN. 1850–1921.

Poet, dramatist, short-story writer, and novelist, Vazov entirely dominated the literary scene in Bulgaria at the close of the nineteenth century. By the time of his death he was generally recognized as the patriarch of Bulgarian letters, and has since become the national writer. He lived through the heroic period of his country's history, its liberation through the Russo-Turkish War of 1877–1878. He chronicled the events of his times, glorified his countrymen's achievements, and agonized over their shortcomings. He also took a lively interest in the distant past of his country. Through the power of his pen he succeeded in stimulating a sense of nationhood in his fellow Bulgarians, and now lies buried in the center of his country's capital.

UNDER THE YOKE. International Studies and Translations Program *Twayne* $8.50. The classic Bulgarian novel and Vazov's finest work. Describes the abortive April uprising of 1876, when the Bulgarians rose against hopeless odds in an attempt to drive their Turkish oppressors from their homeland. A central document for an understanding of the Bulgarian historical viewpoint.

ELIN PELIN (pseud. of Dimitur Ivanov). 1877–1949.

An excellent short-story writer, Elin Pelin came from the village to the city to earn his living through literature. The two principal collections of his stories appeared in 1904 and 1911, and brought him fame as the bard of the peasants inhabiting the region around Sofia. He also gained renown as a humorist and satirist, and promoter of progressive ideals. After 1922 he wrote very little; following the 1944 revolution he wrote primarily for children.

SHORT STORIES. International Studies and Translations Program *Twayne* $6.50. Brief works set in the Bulgarian countryside, exploring the intimate human problems of the peasant in his ordinary life.

YOVKOV, YORDAN. 1880–1937.

The best prose craftsman in modern Bulgarian literature, Yovkov deserves wider renown than he presently enjoys. A withdrawn and solitary individual, Yovkov filtered the materials provided by real life through his memory to produce extraordinarily delicate small masterpieces. Even when he treated the sharpest of human conflicts—as he did in his stories of the First World War— his reader emerged with the conviction that life is essentially good, despite all the horror it contains. Yovkov's most characteristic hero is the impractical daydreamer, incapable of dealing with the real world; but the gallery of his literary creations is very extensive. In the 1930s he turned to writing for the stage. Like Elin Pelin, Yovkov was most at home in the rural world of the peasant.

SHORT STORIES. International Studies and Translations Program *Twayne* $6.00. Ultimately affirmative stories of the trials and tragedies of life in the Bulgarian countryside.

TALEV, DIMITUR. 1898–1965.

A native of Macedonia, Talev gained prominence in Bulgarian literature in the 1950s, especially with his historical trilogy "The Iron Candlestick" (1952), "St. Elijah's Day" (1953), and "The Bells of Prespa" (1954), in which he chronicled the struggle for Bulgarian cultural and intellectual independence against the Greeks and Turks from the early nineteenth century to the early twentieth century. Later, with the publication of "The Monk of Hilendar" (1962), Talev moved even further back in history to the eighteenth-century beginnings of the movement for cultural revival. Talev displays a great capacity for understanding the character of his people in historical context.

THE IRON CANDLESTICK. 1952. International Studies and Translations Program *Twayne* $6.95. The first novel of his great trilogy, dealing with the history of a family starting in the 1830s.

—C.A.M.

BYELORUSSIAN LITERATURE

Early Byelorussian literature traces its origin to the eleventh and twelfth centuries when various chronicles and religious works appeared. Among the most prominent authors of this period are St. Cyril of Turaŭ, Klim Smalacič, and Abraham of Smolensk.

The sixteenth century is considered the Golden Age of Old Byelorussian literature. The leading role here belongs to Dr. Francišak Skaryna (1480?–1540), a prominent writer, scholar, and humanist. The most important of his achievements was the publication of his translation (with commentary) of the Bible into the old Byelorussian language. (For most complete bibliography on Dr. Francišak Skaryna see: Scoriniana, 1517–1967, *Annals*, Byelorussian Institute of Arts and Sciences, Vol. 5, New York, 1970. pp. 181–268.) Among other prominent writers of this period are Vasil Ciapinski (1540–1603), Symon Budny (1530–1593), Todar Jeŭlašeŭski (1546–1604), and towards the end of the sixteenth century the brothers Zizanii, Laŭren and Sciapan.

Literary activity during the seventeenth and eighteenth centuries was limited both in quantity and type. However, the romantic movement of the first half of the nineteenth century brought about a revival of interest in the language and ethnography of the Byelorussian people. The revival of Byelorussian literature followed. Nineteenth-century authors included Jan Čačot (1796–1847), Vincuk Dunin-Marcinkievič (1807–1884), Alherd Abuchovič (1840–1898), and Francišak Bahusevič (1840–1900), the father of modern Byelorussian literature.

The beginning of the twentieth century marks a very rapid growth and flowering of Byelorussian literature: poetry, belles-lettres, and drama. The literature, mostly lyrical at the beginning, gradually encompassed national feelings of the Byelorussians and helped to promote the national revival. The protagonists of the revival were Janka Kupala, Jakub Kolas, Maksim Bahdanovič, Zmitrok Biadula, Aloiza Ciotka, and many others from the group around the newspaper *Naša Niva*, Vilna 1906–1915. The literary situation after World War I became quite complex. Byelorussia was divided into two parts: the eastern part, later known as Byelorussian SSR, came under Soviet rule, and western Byelorussia became Polish until 1939. Western Byelorussia produced many talented writers, mainly in Vilna, and in Soviet Byelorussia literature reached high standards. The nationally minded group of writers originated a monthly literary–political journal, *Polymia* (*Flame*), and a strictly literary journal, *Uzvyšša* (*Excelsior*). The magazine *Maladniak* (*Saplings*) was the publication of the left wing group. This situation existed until the early 1930s when *Polymia* was extensively purged, *Uzvyšša* was closed, and literary development in Soviet Byelorussia became entirely controlled by the Party.

The post-World War II period in Byelorussian literature largely reflects the general political climate—i.e., Stalin era and post-Stalin years. During this time many writers of the 1920s and 1930s were rehabilitated and hundreds of new talented ones appeared. Authors such as Ivan Shamiakin, Vasil Bykaŭ, Ivan Melež, Maksim Tank, Kandrat Krapiva, Piatro Hlebka, Mikhas Lynkoŭ, Andrej Makajenak, and many others became well known in the Soviet Union and abroad. The Union of Soviet Byelorussia's Writers counts over 300 members, and two literary journals in Byelorussian, *Polymia* (*Flame*) and *Maladosc* (*Youth*) are published today.

Detailed information on studies on Byelorussian literature may be found in current articles in the following periodicals: *Belorussian Review* (Munich), *Journal of Byelorussian Studies* (London), and *Soviet Literature* (Moscow).

History and Criticism

Adamovich, Anthony. OPPOSITION TO SOVIETIZATION IN BELORUSSIAN LITERATURE (1917–1957). Fwd. by Alexander Dallin. *Scarecrow Press* (for the Institute for the Study of the USSR, Munich) 1958 $12.00

The best-known Byelorussian literary critic in the professional field since the middle of 1920s surveys and analyzes one of the most complex periods in the development of Byelorussian literature. The author bases his study largely on his personal knowledge and experience of the literature and of the epoch considered. He divides the period into the following sections: ciphers and deciphers; 1917–1918 revolutions; counter currents 1919–1920; escape inward 1920–1922; reorientation and revival 1922–1925; national progressive rise 1925–1926; reaction renewed 1927; under fire 1928; communist nationalists join in 1927–1929; climax 1929; beginning of the end 1929; end and exile, post–1929; today. Includes comprehensive bibliography, notes, a few translations and original Byelorussian texts; provides biographical data and brief listings of works for over 40 writers.

McMillin, Arnold B. A HISTORY OF BYELORUSSIAN LITERATURE: From Its Origins to the Present Day. *W. Schmitz Verlag* (Pestalozzistr. 1–3, Postfach 21108, D-6300 Giessen, West Germany) 1976

This is the most complete and authoritative survey of Byelorussian literature. There are 19 chapters and a short introduction. The volume covers the following: spiritual writing of the 12th–15th centuries; chronicle and memoir writing; Skaryna; prose-writing in the 16th–17th centuries; poetry from Skaryna to Polacki; the 18th century; the rebirth of Byelorussian literature, first half of the 19th century; Dunin-Marcinkievič; Bahusevič; Bahusevič's contemporaries; the age of *Naša Niva*; Bahdanovič; Harun; Kupala; Kolas; from revolution to war, 1917–1945; Biadula; Čorny; and post-war developments.

Provides very extensive bibliography, footnotes, indexes of names and literary works. The author, the leading authority in Byelorussian literature, is presently with the University of London, School of Slavonic and East European Studies.

MODERN BYELORUSSIAN WRITING: Essays and Documents. Ed. by Thomas E. Bird. Queens Slavic Papers, Vol. 3 *Queens College Press* 1976 $10.00

A thorough and illuminating survey by a dozen scholars. The best over-all compendium dealing with Byelorussian writing in the emigration available in a western language. Attention is given in separate chapters to prose, poetry, drama, and the religious press, and to Byelorussian holdings in western-hemisphere libraries. Contains individual essays on N. Arsennieva, Ul. Hlybinny, R. Krushyna, and M. Siadnioŭ, together with useful bibliographies of their works. Provides an account of the history and fate of such journals as *Byelorussian Youth, Bayavaya Uskalos, Kryvič, Moladz, Napierad, Sakavik, Konadni*, and *Vici*. Several documents are appended dealing with the literary groups: Bayavaya Uskalos, Šypšyna, and Uzvyšša.

Stankevich, Stanislaŭ. BELORUSSIAN LITERATURE. (In "Discordant Voices: The Non-Russian Soviet Literatures, 1953–1973") ed. by G. S. N. Luckyi. *Mosaic Press* (Oakville, Ontario, Canada) 1975 $9.95 pap. $4.95. An authoritative analysis, by a well-known Byelorussian literary critic, of dissident political voices in Soviet Byelorussian literature.

Collections

COLOURS OF THE NATIVE COUNTRY: Stories of Byelorussian Writers. Ed. by Ninel Volk-Levanovic. *Bielarus Publishers* (Minsk; order from Four Continent Book Corp., 156 Fifth Ave., New York, N.Y. 10010) 1972 $5.00

Eighteen writers are represented in this collection by as many short stories covering the period 1927–1964. The eighteen stories have been rendered into smooth, colloquial English by R. Lipatov, M. Mintz, and A. Weise. The preface is written by Aleh Loyka who traces the glories of Byelorussia from references in the "Tale of the Host of Igor" in the 12th century through the post-World War II period. The volume includes Jakub Kolas, Kuzma Čorny, Kichas Lynkoŭ, Ivan Shamiakin, Ivan Mielež, Janka Bryl, Pilip Piastrak, Alaksei Kulakoŭski, Vasil Bykaŭ, Janka

Skryhan, Ivan Navumenka, Mikola Lupsiakoŭ, Uladzimir Karatkievič, Alena Vasilevič, Ivan Ptasnikaŭ, Mihas Stralcoŭ, Ivan, Cyhrynaŭ, and Barys Sačanka.

LIKE WATER, LIKE FIRE: An Anthology of Byelorussian Poetry from 1828 to the Present Day. Ed. and trans. by Vera Rich. *Crane-Russak* 1971 $16.00

Vera Rich, well-known translator and authority in Slavonic literatures, accomplished her best in putting out this pioneering volume of Byelorussian poetry. The book presents a large selection of modern Byelorussian poetry from its beginning in the early part of the nineteenth century through *Naša Niva*, the years of World War I and the poetry of Soviet Byelorussia up to and including the poets of today. It is divided into the following parts: the early period (1828–1905); the *Naša Niva* period (1906–1914); the years of adjustment (1917–1939); interlude—western Byelorussia (1921–1939); unification and war (1939–1945); the years of reconstruction (1945–1953); the thaw and after (1954–   ); provides notes, biographical data on authors, index of poems. With the anthology, the first in the English language, Vera Rich aims "to make the water and fire of Byelorussian poetry—the limpid waters of lyricism, the patriotic fire of an emerging nation—flow and burn again in their original rhythms and patterns."

Books with Byelorussian Themes

Akula, Kastus. TOMORROW IS YESTERDAY. *Pannonia Pubs.* (2 Spadina Rd. Toronto 179, Ontario, Canada) 1968 $10.00. A story of a widow who lives with her mother and two children in northeastern Byelorussia. The author depicts the almost insurmountable hardships of life during the changes of political powers during World War II. Akula is a widely known Byelorussian journalist and an active contributor to Canadian periodicals and newspapers covering literary and political aspects of Byelorussian life in America.

Obukhova, Lydia. A TALE OF POLESIE. *Foreign Languages Pub. House* (Moscow; order from Four Continent Book Corp., 156 Fifth Ave., New York, N.Y. 10010) 1965 $8.00. Colorful description of life in the villages among the forests and marshes of Byelorussian Palessie.

Richardson, Anthony. NO PLACE TO LAY MY HEAD. *Odhams Press* (dist. by British Bk. Centre, 996 Lexington Ave., New York, N.Y. 10021) 1957 $8.00. Richardson, the author of "Wingless Victory," "Nick of the River," and other stories, tells in this novel of two brothers, Byelorussians, who find themselves fighting on opposite sides during the war. The events and descriptions accurately portray life in Byelorussia at that time. The story ends with one of the brothers, Sasha Nioman, settled in Great Britain.

SHAMYAKIN, IVAN. 1921–

Shamyakin was born in the village of Karma, near Gormel, in Byelorussia. He studied in a vocational-technical school in Gormel, and served in the army during World War II. His novel "Deep Current" made his fame in the late 1940s, and brought him popularity throughout the USSR. He is especially good at describing everyday life in Byelorussian villages. In 1958 he was awarded the Jakub Kolas award. His numerous works have been translated into German, Bulgarian, and many of the languages of the Soviet Union.

SNOWTIME. Trans. by Olga Shartse. *Progress Publishers* (Moscow; order from Four Continent Book Corp., 156 Fifth Ave., New York, N.Y. 10010) 1973 $6.00. A popular and arresting novel, which focuses on a former partisan detachment commander and his family and the varied threads of their lives as they are unwoven in a novel of intrigue, careerism, and moral dilemmas.

BYKAŬ, VASIL. 1924–

Bykaŭ was born in a small village called Byčki, near the Byelorussian city of Lepel. He served in the army during World War II, and is now on the editorial staff of a newspaper in Grodno, Byelorussia. He has studied sculpture at the Vitebsk Arts Institute. His novels are notable for their impressive psychological descriptions of soldiers under stress. Some of his works, like "Third Rocket" and "Alpine Ballad," have been made into motion pictures by Belarus Film. He is a frequent contributor to the Byelorussian and Soviet journals; his many works have appeared in translations into Chinese, Uzbek, and other languages, as well as into Russian and Italian.

ALPINE BALLAD. *Foreign Languages Pub. House* (Moscow; order from Four Continent Book Corp., 156 Fifth Ave., New York, N.Y. 10010) 1967. A story of the love between a Byelorussian prisoner of war and an Italian girl.

THE ORDEAL. *Dutton* 1972 $5.95. A story of guerrilla warfare in Byelorussia.

—V.K.

CZECHOSLOVAK LITERATURE

Czech literature has always had stronger ties with Western Europe than with the Slavic East. The flowering of Czech poetry in the fourteenth century already reflected strong western influence. This flowering was interrupted by the Hussite Wars which diverted literature into the struggle against Roman Catholicism. The literature of this period is confined to religious and moralistic tracts.

In the sixteenth century the Moravian Bishop Jan Blahoslav and the historian Veleslavín furthered the development of the Czech literary language. The height of Czech prose in the late sixteenth century is the translation of the Bible made for the Bohemian Brethren. The Thirty Years' War (1618–1648) marked the end of Old Bohemia and its incorporation into the Hapsburg empire. The Hapsburgs reimposed Catholicism on the country by force, and literature in the Czech language almost entirely ceased. A notable exception was the Protestant J. A. Comenius (1592–1670), who became famous throughout Europe for pedagogical works.

Czech literature began to revive toward the end of the eighteenth century, and contacts with the West were re-established. Josef Dobrovsky (1753–1829) and Josef Jungmann (1773–1847) contributed to the renewal of the literary language. This first stage of the literary revival was followed by a resurgence of poetry in the works of Jan Kollar and K. H. Macha (1810–1836). Macha's romantic epic poem "*Maj*" marks the beginning of modern Czech poetry. Literature in the second half of the nineteenth century gave expression to the growing national consciousness and the desire for independence from Austria. Božena Němcová (1820–1862), in her novel *Grandmother* (1855), gave a realistic depiction of country life with strong national overtones. The journalist and satirist Karel Havlíček Borovský (1821–1856) satirized the Austrian government in his poems. Jan Neruda (1834–1891) wrote poetry, short stories, and feuilletons. The poet and novelist Svatopluk Čech (1846–1908) and the historical novelist Alois Jirásek (1851–1930) devoted themselves to national themes. The poet Jaroslav Vrchlický (1853–1912) and the neo-romantic Julius Zeyer, although leaders of a more esthetically oriented group of writers, were also associated with the upsurge of national consciousness.

In the 1890s, the reaction against romanticism and optimistic liberalism found expression in the writings of Tomáš G. Masaryk and in the poetry of J. S. Machar (1864–1942) and Petr Bezruč (1867–1958). The major poets at the turn of the century are symbolists and lyric poets: Otakar Březiná, Antonin Sova, Fráňa Šrámek, and S. K. Neumann. In the post-World War I period some poets like Jiří Wolker and Josef Hora took their inspiration from the Bolshevik Revolution, while others like Vítězslav Nezval were influenced by Surrealism. The social novel and short story developed during the early twentieth century with the works of Marie Majerova, Vladislav Vancura, and Ivan Obracht. Jaroslav Hašek portrayed the dissolution of the Austrian empire in his comic novel "The Good Soldier Schweik." Karel Čapek wrote plays, novels, and short stories expressing a humanist, pragmatic philosophy. His best work is the trilogy of philosophical novels "Hordubal" (1933), "The Meteor" (1934), and "An Ordinary Life" (1934).

In communist Czechoslovakia, a new generation of writers emerged after the easing of government controls on literature in the 1960s. These contemporary writers include the novelists Milan Kundera, Josef Škvorecký, and Ludvík Vaculík; the poet Miroslav Holub; and the playwright Háclav Havel. Since the fall of the Dubček regime, government control has been re-established and many of these writers' works are banned.

Busch, Marie, and Otto Pick, Trans. SELECTED CZECH TALES. 1925. *Bks. for Libraries* $8.50

Chudoba, F. SHORT HISTORY OF CZECH LITERATURE. 1924. *Kraus* $15.00

French, Alfred. POETS OF PRAGUE: Czech Poetry between the Wars. *Oxford* 1969 $7.75

   (Ed.). ANTHOLOGY OF CZECH POETRY: A Bilingual Anthology. Vol. 1 Introd. by René Wellek. *Michigan Slavic Translations* (Department of Slavic Languages and Literatures, Univ. of Michigan, Ann Arbor, Michigan 48104) 1973 $4.50 pap. $2.00

Harkins, William E. RUSSIAN FOLK EPOS IN CZECH LITERATURE: 1800–1900. 1951. *Greenwood* $13.75

Hughes, Ted, and Daniel Weisbort, Eds. MODERN POETRY IN TRANSLATION, No. 5: The Czech Poets. 1969 *Grossman* $3.00 pap. $1.25

Liehm, Antonin J. THE POLITICS OF CULTURE. Trans. by Peter Kussi, ill. by Adolf Hoffmeister. *Grove* 1972 $10.00. An important collection of interviews with writers who were involved in the "Prague Spring."

Lutzow, Count. A HISTORY OF BOHEMIAN LITERATURE. *Folcroft* 1973 $12.50

Nemcova, Jeanne W., Sel. and trans. with introd. CZECH AND SLOVAK SHORT STORIES. *Oxford* World's Class. 1967 $3.75

   Twenty representative stories of the past century. "This excellent sampler should be welcomed by any public or academic library"—(*LJ*).

Selver, Paul. CZECHOSLOVAK LITERATURE: An Outline. *Gordon Press* $29.95.

   (Trans.) ANTHOLOGY OF CZECHOSLOVAK LITERATURE. 1929. *Kraus* $12.00

Součková, Milada. CZECH ROMANTICS. 1958. *Humanities Press* $9.00

   LITERARY SATELLITE: Czechoslovak-Russian Literary Relations. *Univ. of Chicago Press* 1970 $8.95

RILKE, RAINER MARIA. 1875–1926. *See Chapter 12, German Literature, this Volume.*

HAŠEK, JAROSLAV. 1883–1923.

   In his satirical novel "The Good Soldier Schweik," Jaroslav Hašek created the fat and cowardly dogcatcher-gone-to-war who personified Czech bitterness toward Austria in World War I. The book roused the Czechs to resistance and made Hašek famous. The humorous complications in which Schweik becomes involved derive from Hašek's own experience: his work as a journalist was interrupted by the war and, like Schweik, he became a soldier. Eventually he was taken prisoner by the Russians. Later he returned to Prague to work as a free-lance writer. At his death he had completed only four "Schweik" novels of a projected six. Martin Esslin has said, "Schweik is more than a mere character; he represents a basic human attitude. Schweik defeats the powers that be, the whole universe in all its absurdity, not by opposing but by complying with them. . . . In the end the stupidity of the authorities, the idiocy of the law are ruthlessly exposed." The character of Schweik made a tremendous impression on Bertolt Brecht (*q.v.*), who transformed his name to use him afresh in the play "Schweyk in the Second World War."

   THE GOOD SOLDIER SCHWEIK. 1920–1923. Trans. by Cecil Parrott. *T. Y. Crowell* 1974 $10.00 pap. $3.95; *New Am. Lib.* Signet pap. $1.25; *Ungar* $8.50 pap. $2.95

KAFKA, FRANZ. 1883–1924. *See Chapter 12, German Literature, this Volume.*

ČAPEK, KAREL. 1890–1938.

   The plays of Karel Čapek presage the Theater of the Absurd. "R.U.R." (Rossum's Universal Robots) was a satire on the machine age. He created the word "robot" (from the Czech noun *robota*, meaning work) for the man-made automatons who in that play took over the world, leaving only one human being alive. "The Insect Comedy," whose characters *are* insects, was written in collaboration with his brother Josef and is an ironic fantasy on human weakness. "The Makropoulos Secret," later used as the basis for Janacek's opera, was an experimental piece which questioned whether immortality is really desirable. All the plays have been given successfully in New York. Most deal satirically with the modern machine age or war. He is best known internationally as a dramatist, but he was also an accomplished novelist, essayist and writer of political articles. His bitingly satirical novel "The War with the Newts" (1936, *Berkley* pap. $.75) reveals Čapek's apprehension over the possible consequences of scientific advance. Čapek is also the author of "Apocryphal Stories" (U.S. 1949, trans. by D. Round o.p.) and "The Gardener's Year" (trans. by M. and R. Weatherall o.p.), humorous essays about gardening.

(With Josef Čapek) R.U.R. and THE INSECT PLAY. *Oxford* 1961 pap. $2.50

R.U.R. 1920. *French* $1.25; *Baker* $1.25; *Simon & Schuster* (Washington Square) 1969 pap. $.75

(With Josef Čapek; adapted by Owen Davis) THE WORLD WE LIVE IN (The Insect Comedy). 1921. *French* $1.25

THE MAKROPOULOS SECRET. 1923. Adapted by Randal C. Burrell; introd. by H. T. Parker. *Branden* pap. $.95

MONEY AND OTHER STORIES. 1930. Short Story Index Reprint Ser. *Bks. for Libraries* $9.75

PRESIDENT MASARYK TELLS HIS STORY. 1935. Eastern Europe Collection Ser. *Arno* 1970 $12.00

INTIMATE THINGS. 1936. Essay Index Reprint Ser. *Bks. for Libraries* $7.75

THE ABSOLUTE AT LARGE. *Hyperion Press* 1973 $8.50 pap. $3.50

Books about Čapek

On Thought and Life: Conversations with Karel Čapek. By Thomas G. Masaryk. Trans. by M. and R. Weatherall. 1938. *Bks. for Libraries* $9.75

Karel Čapek. By William E. Harkins. *Columbia* 1962 $7.50

Karel Čapek: An Essay. By A. Matuska. *Vanous* pap. $2.40. A critical examination of his works. Bibliography, index.

WERFEL, FRANZ. 1890–1945. *See Chapter 12, German Literature, this Volume.*

HRABAL, BOHUMIL. 1914–

Hrabal worked as a lawyer, clerk, railwayman, traveling salesman, steelworker, and laborer before turning to literature in 1962. In his tragic-comic novels and short stories he concentrates on the everyday lives of ordinary people. Thomas Lask says, "Hrabal shows an offbeat, original mind, a fey imagination and a sure hand in constructing his tales"—(*N.Y. Times Book Review*). Hrabal's novel "Closely Watched Trains" (1965) was made into an internationally successful movie.

THE DEATH OF MR. BALTISBERGER. Trans. by Michael Henry Heim. *Doubleday* 1975 $6.95

Thomas Lask says of this collection of short stories: "The conversation at a bar, at a family picnic, even on a lover's walk reveals a design essentially patternless and, when juxtaposed to events of some weight or significance, results in a series of weird, grotesque tales. . . . The key to Hrabal is that though the details are always realistic, the uses he puts them to are not"—(*N.Y. Times Book Review*).

MNACKO, LADISLAV. 1919–

This leading Communist writer and journalist, who had known the highest literary honors his country could bestow, received much publicity both for his satirical novel about Czech Communist leadership and for his criticism of Czech anti-Semitism and of the Czech pro-Arab position on the Arab-Israeli war. On the book's American publication, in August 1967, he was stripped of his citizenship and the honors he had won and expelled from the Communist Party. "The Taste of Power," praised by *Library Journal* as "a work of major significance," exposes "the ironic discrepancies between the public conduct and private motives of . . . [a thinly disguised head of state], a far from attractive yet curiously human figure for whom the taste of power had slowly turned into the taste of gall"—(*SR*).

THE TASTE OF POWER. Trans. by Paul Stevenson. *Praeger* 1967 $5.95

HOLUB, MIROSLAV. 1923–

A distinguished scientist as well as a poet, Holub writes verse no less experimental than his research in clinical pathology. The noted British critic A. Alvarez, in his introduction to this collection, sees Holub's main concern as "the way in which private responses, private anxieties, connect up with the public world of science, technology and machines."

ALTHOUGH. *Grossman* Cape Editions 1971 $3.50 pap. $1.50

ŠKVORECKÝ, JOSEF. 1924–

One of the foremost Czech writers of the postwar generation, Škvorecký is the author of five novels, many film scripts, and the translator into Czech of Faulkner, Hemingway, and Dashiell Hammett. His first novel, "The Cowards," published in 1958 (o.p.), took an unorthodox look at the events of May 1945 when Czechoslovakia was liberated from the Nazis. The novel was, in its author's words, a "*succès scandal.*" In spite of a ban by the Party, "The Cowards" circulated underground and exerted a powerful influence on young Czech writers before the political thaw set in. Škvorecký was fired from his job as an editor of *World Literature* and was unable to publish under his own name until 1963. "Miss Silver's Past" was the last of his books to appear in Czechoslovakia, where it was published in 1969. Another novel, "The Tank Corps," which should have appeared the same year was banned. Škvorecký left Czechoslovakia in 1968 and now teaches at the University of Toronto.

Miss Silver's Past. Trans. by Peter Kussi. *Grove* 1974 $8.95

This novel "tells a spellbinding story of moral corruption and political cynicism in the guise of a love story that turns into a murder mystery. But beyond a diverting thriller, this novel also offers a remarkable account of life among the privileged few in a Communist society, the first book to give us a glimpse of the underworld of intellectual pimp and literary prostitute that rules the cultural establishment"—(Publisher's note).

VACULÍK, LUDVÍK. 1926–

One of the outstanding Czech novelists of the post-war generation, Vaculík has been a shoemaker, teacher, soldier, and journalist. His first novel, "The Busy House," appeared in 1963. He edited *Literarni Listy* from 1966 until 1968 when it was suppressed by the government. His novel "The Axe," published in 1966, made Vaculík famous in Czechoslovakia. He was among the writers who criticized the Novotny régime at the Writers' Union Congress in 1967. He was expelled from the Party but was readmitted during the "Prague Spring" of 1968. At this time Vaculík wrote the "Two Thousand Word Manifesto" which was signed by thousands and which some believe contributed to the Soviet leaders' decision to intervene militarily. He was expelled from the Party a second time and his writings are now banned in Czechoslovakia.

The Axe. Trans. by Marian Sling. 1966. *Harper* 1973 $6.95

Neal Ascherson describes this novel as "the story of a lonely farmer who deliberately destroys his own family relationships and friendships to bring socialist collectivization to his village in Moravia and who—through the very challenge that his own integrity offers to the corrupt Stalinist bureaucracy of the new order—is himself destroyed."

The Guinea Pigs. Trans. by Káča Poláčková. *Third Press* 1973 $7.95; introd. by Neal Ascherson *Penguin* 1975 pap. $3.50

In his introduction to this novel, Neal Ascherson writes: "One could try to discuss *The Guinea Pigs* without bringing up Franz Kafka, but it would be a useless exercise. This is the same world of meaningless, menacing activity broken into by strokes of atrocity delivered by an authority never named or identified. . . . Vaculík has invented a world in which guinea pigs are human, like children and women, but men who go out of doors are metamorphosed into creatures. Their last human trait to survive is inquisitiveness, and those who are too inquisitive disappear. There is no more horrible fable of alienation than this."

KUNDERA, MILAN. 1929–

One of the foremost contemporary Czech writers, Kundera is a novelist, poet, and playwright. His play, "The Keeper of the Keys," produced in Czechoslovakia in 1962, has been performed in more than a dozen countries. His first novel, "The Joke" (1967, o.p.), is a biting satire on the political atmosphere in Czechoslovakia in the 1950s. It tells the story of a young Communist whose life is ruined because of a minor indiscretion: writing a postcard to his girl-friend in which he mocks her political fervor. "The Joke" has been translated into a dozen languages and was made into a film which Kundera wrote and directed. His novel "Life Is Elsewhere" won the 1973 Prix Médicis for the best foreign novel. His books are no longer published in Czechoslovakia.

Laughable Loves. Trans. by Suzanne Rappaport. *Knopf* 1974 $6.95; introd. by Philip Roth *Penguin* 1975 pap. $3.50

"These are stories of the ways in which people respond—stunned or energized, frightened or amused—when their own buried erotic impulses are suddenly released; stories told with subtle grace and an astonishing psychological precision"—(Publisher's note).

Life Is Elsewhere. Trans. by Peter Kussi. *Knopf* 1974 $6.95

This internationally acclaimed novel has not been published in Czechoslovakia or anywhere else, for that matter, in the original Czech. It has been described as a "brilliant, unsparing, and high-comic novel—a portrait of the self-deluded poet defining himself through abstract cliché yet determined to stand out as Hero, whose naive and frenzied venture into the real blood and guts of

politics preordains his emergence as fool and informer, setting in motion a tragedy of errors. . . .
Life Is Elsewhere demonstrates the gifts that have won for Kundera the praise of such diverse
writers as Sartre, Aragon and Philip Roth."

—G.K.

ESTONIAN LITERATURE

The Estonian language belongs to the Baltic-Fennic branch of the Finno-Ugrian sub-family of the Uralic languages.

Estonia has a record of literary distinction most remarkable in relation to the size of its population; challenged, indeed, in this respect only by Iceland. Estonia possesses the richest treasury of folklore of any European country. Its mere million inhabitants have produced over 400,000 folk songs. These poems were sung by peasants and fishermen primarily before the nineteenth century; their preservation is the work of Estonian and Finnish scholars who recorded their words and music. Almost all Estonian popular poetry has a stylistic unity based on certain formal characteristics which, it is believed, were acquired toward the end of the pagan era (about 1200 A.D.). A major characteristic of Estonian folk poetry is its quantitative meter—that is, the length of the pronunciation of each syllable in each word is rigidly defined, both for phonetic correctness and for determining the meaning of the word. The language itself contains an immense vocabulary for expressing the varied sounds of such natural phenomena as wind and water, and is therefore particularly suited for onomatopoeia. Its richness in vowels is surpassed only by the Hawaiian language. The resulting musicality of Estonian fascinated the first poets to use it. The German poet Otto von Taube described it as being simultaneously "the song of a lark and the flight of a butterfly."

No warrior songs from the Viking era nor texts in the Estonian language prior to the late thirteenth century have been preserved. Like many European authors, Estonians wrote predominantly in Latin during the Medieval, Renaissance, and Baroque periods, until the reformed church replaced Latin with Estonian. The first books in Estonian were published in 1525. Although Estonian literary poetry finds its roots early in the seventeenth century, there was little significant literature until the beginning of the nineteenth century. One of the aims of the leaders of the nineteenth-century nationalist movement was to enlarge Estonian literature, and with this object the Estonian Learned Society was founded in 1819. Its success was largely due to the publication in 1857–1861 of the "*Kalevipoeg*." Composed by Friedrich Reinhold Kreutzwald (1803–1882) from diverse songs and fragments of longer poems originating between the tenth and thirteenth centuries, it is one of the great epic works of world literature. Its publication was an inspiration to Estonian writers and critics, and gave the language a new prestige both at home and abroad. It has been translated into many European languages, as well as into Hebrew. Unlike the Finnish epic poem, "*Kalevala*," "*Kalevipoeg*" has a unified plot. The principal story is of the struggle between the legendary King Kalevipoeg and the German and Danish invaders in the thirteenth century. Characteristic of the entire poem is a feeling for the organic unity of men and nature whereby nature is no mere background to a story, but an essential part of it. So waters, trees, animals, and stars may converse with men, not by a flight of fancy, but simply and naturally. Though such a concept of natural phenomena has its origin in the magical beliefs of the ancient Estonians, it has persisted and pervades Estonian literature even today.

The most important Estonian writers of the nineteenth century were the poets Kristjan Jaak Peterson (1801–1822), Lydia Koidula (1843–1886), and Juhan Liiv (1864–1913). All three were organically talented, although only Liiv achieved a certain universality of vision. His most substantial works were created in the first decade of the twentieth century. With him began the symbolist movement in Estonia. Leaders of this movement were Villem Ridala (1885–1942), whose quiet-toned lyrics introduced quantitative meter into Estonian literary poetry, and the fiery Gustav Suits (1883–1956) (*q.v.*), who, in seeking an all-European kind of Estonian-ness, dominated the literary scene from 1905 to about 1930. A unique figure of the symbolist group was Ernst Enno (1875–1934), a metaphysical, vocal poet. In symbolist prose Aleksander Tassa (1882–1955) and Friedebert Tuglas (1886–1971) excelled in short stories. The latter was also the first important literary critic of Estonia. The symbolist poets were followed by the expressionists: Jaan Oks (1884–1918), also an experimental prose writer; August Alle (1890–1952); Henrik Visnapuu (1889–1951), the "Walt Whitman of Estonian poetry"; and Marie Under (1883–) (*q.v.*), Estonia's greatest poet, and one of the most significant lyricists of modern Western literature. Sensual and strong-minded, her work is of rare immediacy and power. The symbolist tradition however did not die out, and the neo-symbolists Heiti Talvik (1904–1947?) (*q.v.*) and Betti Alver (1906–) (*q.v.*) achieved in their poetry a new perfection. Some of their contemporaries and younger poets, writing in different styles, display a remarkable versatility and depth of modernist perception. These include the highly original mystical visionary Uku Masing (*q.v.*); the animist Bernard Kangro (*q.v.*); the surrealist Ilmar Laaban (1921–); the passionately individual symbolizer Arno Vihalemm (1911–); and the intellectualists Ivar Grünthal (1924–), Ain Kaalep (1926–), and Jaan Kaplinski (1941–).

In general, Estonian prose has not matched the accomplishments of Estonian poetry. A number of Estonian prose writers have, nonetheless, produced work of international quality. Among them are the realists Eduard Vilde (1865–1933) and Anton Hansen Tammsaare (1878–1940). The latter in his monumental five-volume novel, "Truth and Justice," gave a panoramic view of modern Estonian rural and urban society. The realists are succeeded by the experimentalists Karl August Hindrey (1875–1949), Peet Vallak (1893–1959), Bernard Kangro, and Karl Ristikivi (1912–). Kangro's and Ristikivi's introspective novels combine consummate craftsmanship with subtle allegorization and symbolism. Similar qualities joined with the psychology of a shy, lonely person are displayed in Katrin Jakobi's (1909–) sole collection of short stories, "Summer's Homeland," probably the most refined work of Estonian prose.

The development of modern Estonian poetry and prose would have been impossible without the contributions of two men: the linguist and translator Johannes Aavik (1880–1973), who by drastic reform successfully modernized the Estonian tongue; and Ants Oras (1900–) (*q.v.*), foremost Estonian poet–translator, as well as the most significant literary historian and critic. They have greatly influenced the linguistic and stylistic maturation of Estonian letters.

ESTONIAN POETRY AND LANGUAGE: Studies in Honor of Ants Oras. Ed. by Viktor Kõressaar and Aleksis Rannit. *Estonian Learned Society in America* (dist. by Estonian Publishing Co., Estonian House, 958 Broadview Ave., Toronto, Ontario, Canada M4K ZR6) 1965 $8.00

Kurman, George. THE DEVELOPMENT OF WRITTEN ESTONIAN. Uralic and Altaic Ser. No. 90 *Indiana Univ. Research Center* pap. $6.00

Maas, Selve. THE MOON PAINTERS AND OTHER ESTONIAN FOLK TALES. *Viking* 1971 $4.95

Mägi, Arvo. ESTONIAN LITERATURE: An Outline. *The Baltic Humanitarian Association* (dist. by Eesti Kirjanike Kooperativ; publisher's rep.: Evald Rink, 1420 Oak Hill Dr., Wilmington, Del. 19805) $6.00

Nirk, Endel. ESTONIAN LITERATURE: Historical Survey with Biobibliographical Appendix. *Kirjastus Eesti Raamat* (Issued by the Institute of Language and Literature, Academy of Sciences of the Estonian SSR; publisher's rep.: Hellar Grabbi, 3602 Albee Lane, Alexandria, Va. 22309) $8.00

Oras, Ants, and Bernard Kangro. ESTONIAN LITERATURE IN EXILE. *Estonian PEN Club and Eesti Kirjanike Kooperativ* (publisher's rep.: Evald Rink, 1428 Oak Hill Drive, Wilmington, Del. 19805) 1967 $5.00

Parming, Marju Rink, and Tönu Parming, Comps. BIBLIOGRAPHY OF ENGLISH-LANGUAGE SOURCES ON ESTONIA. *Estonian Learned Society in America* (dist. by Estonian House, 243 East 34 St., New York, N. Y. 10016) 1974 $5.50. In this work, items that were in print at the time of its compilation are marked with a star.

Raun, Alo, and Andrus Saareste. INTRODUCTION TO ESTONIAN LINGUISTICS. 1965 *Int. Pubns. Service* $15.00

Rubulis, Aleksis. BALTIC LITERATURE: A Survey of Finnish, Estonian, Latvian and Lithuanian Literatures. *Univ. of Notre Dame Press* 1970 $8.50

Ziedonis, Arvids Jr., and others, Eds. BALTIC LITERATURE AND LINGUISTICS. *Association for the Advancement of Baltic Studies* (366 86 St., Brooklyn, N. Y. 11209) $8.50 pap. $3.95

SUITS, GUSTAV. 1883–1956.

This Estonian poet, translator, and literary historian studied at the University of Tartu, Estonia, and Helsinki, Finland. He was professor of Estonian and Comparative Literature at the University of Tartu, 1919–1944. He fled to Finland and Sweden and worked until his death at the Nobel Institute in Stockholm. In his search for Symbolist perfection of form Suits enriched modern Estonian verse technically and intellectually. His collections of poetry are: *"Elu tuli"* (The Fire of Life, 1905); *"Tuulemaa"* (The Land of Winds, or The Land of Tuule [Thule], 1913); *"Kõik on kokku unenägu"* (Everything Is But a Dream, 1922); *"Lapsesünd"* (Childbirth, 1922); and *"Tuli ja tuul"* (Flame and Wind, 1950).

FLAMES ON WINDS. Trans. by W. K. Matthews. *Boreas Pub. Co.* (London) 1953 (dist. by Estonian House, 243 East 34 St., New York, N. Y. 10016) $2.50. Selected poetry in English translation.

UNDER, MARIE. 1883–

A poet and translator, she took her secondary education in a German school in Tallinn, Estonia. She worked mostly as a free-lance writer. She fled to Stockholm in 1944 and still lives there. Under is considered Estonia's greatest lyrical poet. She is the author of 13 collections of verse, of which the following ones are especially outstanding: *"Hääl varjust"* (Voice from the Shadow, 1927); *"Rõõm ühest ilusast päevast"* (Delight in a Beautiful Day, 1928); *"Kivi südamelt"* (A Stone off the Heart, 1935) *"Ääremail"* (On the Brink, 1963). Under was several times nominated for the Nobel Prize.

CHILD OF MAN. Trans. by W. K. Matthews. *Boreas Pub. Co.* (London) 1955 (dist. by Estonian House, 243 East 34 St., New York, N. Y. 10016) $2.50. Selected poetry in English translation.

ORAS, ANTS. 1900–

Oras is Estonia's leading poet–translator (into Estonian, English, and German), literary historian, and critic. He was educated at the Universities of Tartu (Estonia), Leipzig, and Oxford, and served as professor of English in Tartu from 1934 to 1943. In 1943 he fled to Sweden and was professor of English at the University of Florida in Gainesville from 1949 until 1974. Known in the West primarily as a critic of English Renaissance and modernist poetry and as a publicist, he has exercised a remarkable and still-growing influence among Estonian poets and also among some prose writers who have a similar love for stylistic purity and an ethically earnest philosophy of life. His books in English dealing with Estonia include "Baltic Eclipse," "Estonian Literary Reader," and "Estonian Literature in Exile." Of his many longer essays, see "Marie Under and Estonian Poetry" in *The Sewanee Review* (Vol. 78, No. 1, Winter 1970, pp. 247–268; also published separately in revised form in 1975 by the Foundation of Estonian Arts, New York, for the 40th International P.E.N. Congress). (*For the bibliography of Oras' work until 1965, "Estonian Poetry and Language: Studies in Honor of Ants Oras," see the general list above.*) He has translated many books from their original language into Estonian, including Goethe's "Faust" Parts 1 and 2, plays and poems of Shakespeare, works of Pope, Molière, Tasso, Pushkin, and Heine, the "Bucolics" of Virgil, and numerous modern prose works. Most recently he has published an impressive translation of Virgil's *"Aeneis"* into Estonian quantitative dactylic hexameters (*Eesti Kirjanike Kooperativ*, Lund, Sweden, 1975).

MILTON'S EDITORS AND COMMENTATORS FROM PATRICK HUME TO HENRY JOHN TODD 1695–1801: A Study in Critical Views and Methods. *Oxford* 1931 $15.25; *Haskell* 1969 $16.95

CRITICAL IDEAS OF T. S. ELIOT. 1932 *Folcroft* $10.00

NOTES ON SOME MILTONIC USAGES: Their Background and Later Development. 1938. *Folcroft* $8.50

ON SOME ASPECTS OF SHELLEY'S POETIC IMAGERY. 1938. *Folcroft* $8.50

BALTIC ECLIPSE. (1948, o.p.)

PAUSE PATTERNS IN ELIZABETHAN AND JACOBEAN DRAMA. Humanities Monographs Ser. *Univ. Presses of Florida* 1960 pap. $3.00

ESTONIAN LITERARY READER. (1963, o.p.). Contains a survey of Estonian literature (in English), Estonian texts, and the complete glossary.

BLANK VERSE AND CHRONOLOGY IN MILTON. Humanities Monographs Ser. *Univ. Presses of Florida* 1966 pap. $2.50

(With Bernard Kangro) ESTONIAN LITERATURE IN EXILE. *Estonian PEN Club and Eesti Kirjanike Kooperativ* (publisher's rep.: Evald Rink, 1428 Oak Hill Drive, Wilmington, Del. 19805) 1967 $5.00

TALVIK, HEITI. 1904–c. 1947.

Talvik was a poet-prophet and a Baudelairean kind of existentialist of considerable passion and precise verse structure. He wrote two books of poems: *"Palavik"* (The Fever, 1934); and *"Kohtupäev"* (Doomsday, 1937). He died in a Soviet concentration camp around 1947. Seven of Talvik's poems, translated by W. K. Matthews, appear in the latter's "Anthology of Modern Estonian Poetry" (1953, o.p.). See also Aleksis Rannit's "Heiti Talvik, an Estonian Poet: From Decadent Dream to Martyrdom" in *The American Pen*, No. 2, 1975, pp. 10–19, with translations by Matthews and Ants Oras.

ALVER, BETTI. 1906–

An Estonian poet writing in a framework of neosymbolist and neoclassicist tradition, Alver now lives in Estonia. Her most significant books are: *"Tolm ja tuli"* (Dust and Fire, 1936)—eight poems from this collection appear in W. K. Matthews' "Anthology of Modern Estonian Poetry," (1953, o.p.)—and *Tähetund* (Siderial Hour, 1966). She achieved considerable plasticity, lightness, and virtuosity of form but became in her late work a tragic existentialist and sibylline poet. She is famous also for her masterful metrical translation of Pushkin's "Eugene Onegin," on which she worked for about two decades.

KALMUS, AIN (pseud. of Evald Mänd). 1906–

A writer and theologian, Kalmus was educated at the Baptist Theological Seminary, Tallinn, Estonia, and at Andover Newton Theological School, Newton Center, Massachusetts. He came to the United States in 1946, and was chaplain of the First Baptist Church of Rockport, Massachusetts from 1947 to 1954. From 1954 to 1975 he was pastor for students of Amherst College. A poetical realist, Kalmus is the author of religious and historical novels of which the *"Prohvet"* (Vadstena, Sweden, 1950; trans. by the author into English as "The Unfaithful," 1954, o.p.) is his best achievement. The translation, however, does not do justice to this fine, biblically stylized work.

MASING, UKU. 1909–

A poet, translator, linguist, theologian, and orientalist, Masing was educated at the University of Tartu, Estonia. While somewhat influenced by the religious philosophy of the East and oriental poetic diction, Masing is at the same time a highly original *poeta doctus*, innovative both in his hermetic symbolization and in his verse structure. Of his four collections of poems, two are of true international significance: *"Neemed vihmade lahte"* (Promontories into the Gulf of Rains, Tartu, 1935) and *"Džunglilaulud"* (Jungle Songs, Stockholm, 1965). Masing's Estonian originals are primarily convincing as musically intervening works of prophecy and are full of hallucinatory beauty. Five of his poems, one of them a longer work, appear in English translation by W. K. Matthews in his "Anthology of Modern Estonian Poetry," (1953, o.p.). See also Vincent B. Leitch, "Religious Vision in Modern Poetry: Uku Masing Compared with Hopkins and Eliot," in *Journal of Baltic Studies*, Vol. 4, No. 4, Winter 1975, pp. 281–294.

KANGRO, BERNARD. 1910–

A poet, prose writer, playwright, literary historian, and critic, Kangro was educated at the University of Tartu, Estonia. In 1944 he fled to Sweden where he now lives, editing and publishing the literary periodical *Tulimuld*. Kangro's publications include fourteen collections of poems and six novels of the Tartu cycle. Kangro's poetry, with its rich language, musicality, and animist ideas, is predominantly elegiac and delusory. Kangro's novels of the Tartu cycle, which unfortunately are not yet rendered into English, are among the boldest structural experiments and most brilliant psychological achievements in modern fiction.

EARTHBOUND. Trans. by W. K. Matthews. *Tulimuld* (Lund) 1951 (dist. by Estonian House, 243 East 34 St., New York, N.Y. 10016) $3.00. Selected poems in English translation.

EKBAUM, SALME. 1912–

A novelist and poet, Ekbaum was educated as a pharmacist at the University of Tartu, Estonia. At present he lives in Toronto, Canada. He is the author of thirteen novels and three collections of poems. Of the novels written in the style of intuitive realism, *"Ilmapõllu inimesed"* (The Folk of Ilmapõllu, Gothenberg, 1948, translated into English by Leida Krass as "Farm in the Forest," Gothenburg, Orto, 1949); and *"Külaliseks on ootus"* (The Guest Is Expectation, Toronto, 1952) are outstanding. Ekbaum's most mature book of lyrical poems is *"Ajatar"* (Goddess of Time) available in Estonian from *Estoprint Ltd.* (548 Front St. W., Toronto, Ontario, Canada 1974 $4.00).

RANNIT, ALEKSIS. 1914–

Musical fluidity as well as terseness of structure and power of introspection distinguish the poetry of Aleksis Rannit. He studied both art and literature at the universities of Tartu (Estonia) and Vilnius (Lithuania) and esthetics and classical archaeology at Freiburg, in Germany. He made the acquaintance of Braque, Matisse, Morandi, and other painters, whose art has influenced his poetry. Since 1960 he has been curator of Russian and East European Studies at Yale. In 1962 he was elected a member of the International Academy of Arts and Letters in Paris. His work has appeared in book form in translations into German, Russian, Lithuanian, and Hungarian, and is now, through critical studies and numerous English translations, becoming known to an increasing audience in America. His books of poetry include, in addition to those listed below: *"Akna raamistuses"* (Framed by the Window, 1937), *"Käesurve"* (A Grip of the Hand, 1945), *"Suletud avarust"* (The Enclosed Expanse, 1956), *"Kuiv hiilgus"* (Dry Radiance, 1963), *"Kaljud"* (Cliffs, 1969), and *"Sõrmus"* (The Ring, 1972).

He defines poetry as a "dance of syllables, . . . the consensually pulsating expression of our spirit, . . . a kind of sorcery in which metaphorical thinking blends with authentic reality to create a mythical order." The poems themselves are filled with sharp apprehensions and vivid realizations of the congruence of sound-symbolization and meaning.

DRY RADIANCE: Selected Poems. 1963. Trans. by Henry Lyman, with a critical, biographical, and bibliographical introd. (in "New Directions: An International Anthology of Prose and Poetry") *New Directions* Vol. 25 1972 $9.25 pap. $3.75; for other poems, see also Vol. 24 1972 $8.95 pap. $3.45 and Vol. 32 1976 $8.95 pap. $2.95

. . . LINE. Trans. from the Estonian by Henry Lyman. Four original woodcuts by Gottfried Honegger. *Adolph Hürlimann* (Rindermarkt 17, Zürich, Switzerland) 1970 $60.00

DONUM ESTONICUM: Poems in Translation. Trans. by H. W. Tjalsma and Cid Corman. *The Elizabeth Press* (103 Van Etten Blvd., New Rochelle, N.Y. 10804) bilingual ed. 1976 $16.00 pap. $8.00. The English versions appear with Estonian originals *en face*.

Books about Rannit

Aleksis Rannit: Lühimonograafia (Aleksis Rannit: A Short Monograph). By Viktor Terras. *Eesti Kirjanike Kooperativ* 1975 (dist. by Estonian House. 243 East 34 St., New York, N.Y. 10016) $7.00 pap. $3.00. In Estonian.

Note: The biographical note on Rannit was written by the general editor of this volume.

VIIRLAID, ARVED. 1922–

A novelist and poet, Viirlaid was educated at the Tallinn State College of Art. He served as an officer in the Finnish army from 1943 to 1944; since 1954 he has lived in Toronto, Canada. He began as a poet and has produced four collections of civic and lyrical verse, of which *Jäätanud peegel* (Frozen Mirror, Lund, 1962) is perhaps the best. In his poems as well as his prose he is a politically engaged writer. Of his novels, *Sadu jõkke* (Rain for the River, 1964) and *Ristideta Hauad* (Graves without Crosses, 1952) are masterworks of critical realism and have met with considerable international attention.

GRAVES WITHOUT CROSSES. 1952. Trans. by Ilse Lehiste. *Clarke, Irwin* (791 St. Clair Ave. W., Toronto, Ontario, Canada 1972) $9.50

RAIN FOR THE RIVER. 1964. Trans. by Martin Puhvel. *Tafelberg-Uitgewers* (1 Dorp St., P.O.B. 879, Cape Town 8000, South Africa) 1964 price on request

—A.R.

GREEK LITERATURE

For Ancient Greece see Chapter 7, Classical Greek Literature, this Volume.

Modern Greece, a designation commonly used to refer to the Greek nation from the War of Independence (1821–1833) to the present, is something of a cultural phenomenon. The accomplishments of the ancient Greeks had been mostly forgotten during the four centuries of Turkish domination, but with the War of Independence came a consciousness of the past and a renaissance, which combined elements of ancient Greece and the Byzantine empire with modern elements to produce a unique literature. This consciousness of the past, amounting almost to an obsession with some authors, pervades modern Greek literature.

The vigorous cultural life of modern Greece—which has recently produced a Nobel prize-winner, George Seferis—was in 1967 being stifled by the severities of a military "reform" dictatorship which had set the usual paraphernalia in motion: books were banned, and writers, musicians, artists and editors arrested and jailed, or deprived of their citizenship. The arrest of the 58-year-old poet Yannis Ritzos was vigorously protested by 100 French writers of all political complexions in the summer of 1967, and Stanley Kauffmann wrote bitterly in the *New Republic* of the failure of American government, as well as its traveling performers and artists, to show effective disapproval.

The literary journal *Greek Heritage,* the American quarterly of Greek culture edited by Kimon Friar, publishes modern Greek writers in translation (address inquiries to The Athenian Corp., 360 N. Michigan Ave., Chicago, Ill. 60601). A good selection of poetry can be found in "Modern European Poetry" edited by Willis Barnstone and others (*Bantam* 1966 pap. $1.95).

With the restoration of the democracy in 1974 conditions in Greece have once again returned to normal, and the Greek government has shown its interest in the arts by appointing a scholar of international renown, Mr. Constantine Trypanis, himself a poet, to the post of Minister of Culture.

Barnstone, Willis, Ed. EIGHTEEN TEXTS: Writing by Contemporary Greek Authors. *Harvard Univ. Press* 1972 $7.95. Published during the rule of the Junta.

Dalven, Rae, Trans. and ed. MODERN GREEK POETRY. 1949. *Russell & Russell* 1971 $27.50

Dimaras, C. T. A HISTORY OF MODERN GREEK LITERATURE. 1948. Trans. by Mary P. Gianos. *State Univ. of N.Y. Press* 1972 $15.00 pap. $4.95. Originally published in 1948 and a classic study, but the translation is flawed.

Friar, Kimon, Trans. and ed. MODERN GREEK POETRY. *Simon & Schuster* 1973 $20.00. Includes a full introduction and essay on translating modern Greek.

Gianos, Mary P., and Kimon Friar, Trans. and eds. INTRODUCTION TO MODERN GREEK LITERATURE: An Anthology of Fiction, Drama, and Poetry. *Twayne* 1969 $6.95. Limited to authors born between the years 1850 and 1914. Fiction and drama translated by Gianos, poetry by Friar.

Keeley, Edmund, and Peter Bien, Eds. MODERN GREEK WRITERS. Essays in Literature *Princeton* 1972 $10.00

Keeley, Edmund, and Philip Sherrard, Trans. and eds. SIX POETS OF MODERN GREECE. *Knopf* 1961 $6.00

   "The selections stress the burning consciousness these poets share of their heritage. Something almost Delphic broods over the six who project their own personal visions": Cavafy, Sikelianos, Seferis, Antoniou, Elytis, Gatsos.

Kulukundis, Elias. THE FEASTS OF MEMORY: A Journey to a Greek Island. *Holt* 1967 $5.95

    An American's return to Kasos, home of his seagoing forebears. "A book that enriches our memories, enlightens our quests"—(Harry Mark Petrakis, in *SR*).

Merchant, Paul, Ed. MODERN POETRY IN TRANSLATION: No. 4. The Greek Poets. *Grossman* 1968 $3.00 pap. $1.25

Miller, Henry. COLOSSUS OF MAROUSI. *New Directions* pap. $1.75. Travels with Miller and Katsimbalis (the Colossus). The romantic view of Greece.

Politis, Linos. A HISTORY OF MODERN GREEK LITERATURE. Trans. by Robert Liddell. *Oxford* 1973 $17.75. More up-to-date than the history of Dimaras, but lacking some of the elegance of the earlier study.

Sherrard, Philip. THE MARBLE THRESHING FLOOR. 1956. *Bks. for Libraries* $13.25

Spencer, Terence. FAIR GREECE, SAD RELIC: Literary Philhellenism from Shakespeare to Byron. 1954. *Octagon* 1971 $17.00

Trypanis, Constantine A., Trans. and ed. THE PENGUIN BOOK OF GREEK VERSE. *Penguin* $5.25; *Peter Smith* 1971 $7.50

MAKRIYANNIS, JOHN. 1797–1864.

    A hero in the War of Independence, Makriyannis is also one of the greatest figures in modern Greek demotic literature. When he was 32 years old he taught himself to write in order to record his memoirs, by which he hoped to justify his life and politics in the early years of the new nation. The result was a document of great artistic importance. Makriyannis' manuscript was not published until 1907, 43 years after his death, and the effect on the Greek literary world was enormous. Seferis, for example, regarded Makriyannis as the "humblest and also the steadiest" of his teachers.

MAKRIYANNIS: The Memoirs of General Makriyannis, 1797–1864. Trans. by H. A. Lidderdale. *Oxford* 1966 $8.50

PALAMAS, KOSTES. 1859–1943.

    Palamas is the central figure of the New School of Athens and "is a milestone in the history of Greek literature, for his works are the outburst, the catharsis of the long drama of more than 2,000 years, which from the days when the Alexandrian poets ceased to sing had not found the great personality who would give voice to the national sufferings and aspirations, agonies and glories, in works of full magnitude"—(Trypanis, in "Medieval and Modern Greek Poetry").

THE TWELVE WORDS OF THE GYPSY. Trans. by Frederic Will. *Univ. of Nebraska Press* 1964 $4.50

    An epico-lyric poem of a gypsy musician, who as a "symbol of freedom and art," "develops into the Greek patriot," and finally into the "Hellene, citizen of the world"—(Trypanis).

Books about Palamas

Kostis Palamas. By Thanasis Maskaleris. *Twayne* 1972 $5.95

CAVAFY, CONSTANTIN P. (Kabaphēs, Konstantinos Petrou). 1863–1933.

    Cavafy was born in Alexandria where he lived his whole life. He has always been closely associated with that city. During his lifetime he was considered *the* poet of Alexandria, and today his name is identified primarily with Lawrence Durrell's (*q.v.*) characterization of him in the "Alexandria Quartet." "As a writer he starts with the ordinary life of his own city, which he knew at all levels from the most to the least reputable. From this, with its complex mixture of West and East, ... he formed his own outlook on life and sense of values.... As a result, his indulgent cynicism, his understanding disillusion, can often bring historical subjects right home today.... Cavafy's subtle use of language, his mixture of common speech, officialese and self-deflating formalisms to produce complex overtones of immediacy, irony and detachment, are not more than hinted at in the existing translations; but his awareness of life, and his attitudes to it, have a rich place in the modern world"—("Modern World Literature"). Cavafy's verse is discussed in C. M. Bowra's "The Creative Experiment" (1958, o.p.). Some of his poems are included in Keeley and Sherrard's "Six Poets of Modern Greece" (*see above*).

THE COMPLETE POEMS OF CAVAFY. Trans. by Rae Dalven; introd. by W. H. Auden. *Harcourt* 1961 1966 pap. $1.95

This volume presents new translations. "They make genuine poetry, supple, sensitive and civil, as Cavafy's Greek required, and they often catch something of his characteristic 'demotic' touches. The translator has added useful notes on the poet's life and style and on some of the historical allusions"—(*Guardian,* Manchester, England). Auden's introduction is excellent.

COLLECTED POEMS. Trans. by Edmund Keeley and Philip Sherrard; ed. by George Savidis. *Princeton Univ. Press* 1974 $18.50

SELECTED POEMS. Trans. by Edmund Keeley and Philip Sherrard. *Princeton Univ. Press* 1972 $7.50 pap. $1.75. A selection, regarded by the translators as Cavafy's "most significant and characteristic poems."

PASSIONS AND ANCIENT DAYS: New Poems. Trans. by Edmund Keeley and George Savidis. *Dial* 1971 $5.00 pap. $1.95

Books about Cavafy

Constantine Cavafy. By Peter Bien. Essays on Modern Writers *Columbia* 1964 $1.00

KAZANTZAKIS, NIKOS.   1885–1957.

The distinguished novelist, poet and translator was born in Crete and educated in Athens, Germany, Italy—and Paris, where he studied under Henri Bergson. He found time to write some 30 novels, plays, and books on philosophy, to serve his government, and to travel widely. He ran the Greek Ministry of Welfare from 1919–1921 and was Minister of State briefly in 1945.

Kazantzakis "has created in Zorba one of the great characters of modern fiction. The novel reflects Greek exhilaration at its best"—(*TLS*, London). A film version of 1965, starring Anthony Quinn, made Kazantzakis widely known in this country and he became a particular interest of American young people. Intensely religious, he imbued his novels with the passion of his own restless spirit, "torn between the active and the contemplative, between the sensual and the aesthetic, between nihilism and commitment"—(*Columbia Encyclopedia*). Judas, the hero of "The Last Temptation of Christ," is asked by Christ to betray Him so that He can fulfill His mission through the Crucifixion. For this book Kazantzakis was excommunicated from the Greek Orthodox Church. John Ciardi (in *SR*) called the "Odyssey: A Modern Sequel"—Odysseus transformed to a revolutionary saint—"a monument of the age." The reverent fictional biography "Saint Francis," which follows the historical account closely, is told simply and with a cumulative emotional impact. "The Fratricides," Kazantzakis' last novel, portrays yet another religious hero, a priest caught between Communists and Royalists in the Greek Civil War. "A searing but poetic work"—(*LJ*), it illustrates his conviction that "Christ—and Greece—will be resurrected only when fearless men witness and die for love; only when man somehow surpasses man"—(Peter Bien, in *SR*). "Report to Greco," described by Kimon Friar (in *SR*) as "among the world's great *apologia vita*," is a loosely constructed autobiography addressed to the Cretan master painter El Greco, who Kazantzakis felt shared his own tormented quest for God. Marc Slonim says (in the *N.Y. Times*): "Throughout his work Kazantzakis remained true to the Hellenic tradition: his heroes are harmoniously developed individuals who feel a strong bond with their physical environment; the author's poetic imagination is of the kind that created legends and myths to explain man and the universe."

"Journeying: Travels in Italy, Egypt, Sinai, Jerusalem and Cyprus" (trans. by Themi Vasils and Theodora Vasils *Little* 1975 $7.50 pap. $3.95), "Spain" (trans. by Amy Sims *Simon & Schuster* 1963 $5.00), "Journey to the Morea" (trans. by F. A. Reed *Simon & Schuster* 1965 $4.95), and "England: A Travel Journal" (1940. *Simon & Schuster* 1966 $5.00) record his impressions of these lands.

THREE PLAYS: Kouros, Melissa, Christopher Columbus. *Simon & Schuster* 1969 $7.50

THE ROCK GARDEN. 1936. Trans. from the French by Richard Howard. *Simon & Schuster* 1963 $5.95 pap. $2.25. One of his earliest novels, it tells of a European caught in the Sino-Japanese wars of the 1930s.

THE ODYSSEY: A Modern Sequel. 1938. Trans. into English verse by Kimon Friar. *Simon & Schuster* 1958 $14.95 1962 pap. $4.95

This takes up the story of Odysseus where Homer left off and "is a major achievement"—(Moses Hadas, in *N.Y. Herald Tribune*).

THE GREEK PASSION. 1938. Trans. by Jonathan Griffin. *Simon & Schuster* 1954 1959 $7.95 pap. $2.95

ZORBA THE GREEK. 1946. Trans. by Carl Wildman. *Simon & Schuster* 1953 1959 $8.95 pap. $2.95

THE LAST TEMPTATION OF CHRIST. 1951. *Simon & Schuster* 1960 $9.95 pap. $3.45; *Bantam* pap. $1.45

SAINT FRANCIS. 1953. Trans. from the Greek by Peter A. Bien. *Simon & Schuster* 1962 $7.50 1964 pap. $2.95. A novel.

FREEDOM OR DEATH. Trans. by Jonathan Griffin; pref. by A. den Doolaard. *Simon & Schuster* 1955 1961 $6.00 pap. $2.95

THE SAVIORS OF GOD. Trans. by Kimon Friar. *Simon & Schuster* 1960 $5.95 1969 pap. $1.95

THE FRATRICIDES. Trans. by Athena G. Dallas. *Simon & Schuster* 1964 $5.00 pap. $1.95. A novel.

REPORT TO GRECO. Trans. by Peter A. Bien. *Simon & Schuster* 1965 $7.50; *Bantam* pap. $1.65

REFLECTIONS ON GREECE. *Walker & Co.* 1971 $30.00

SYMPOSIUM. Trans. by Theodora Vasilis and Themi Vasilis. *T. Y. Crowell* 1975 $5.95

Books about Kazantzakis

Nikos Kazantzakis and his Odyssey: A Study of the Poet and the Poem. By Pandelis Prevelakis. Trans. by Philip Sherrard; pref. by Kimon Friar. *Simon & Schuster* 1961 $5.00

Nikos Kazantzakis: A Biography Based on His Letters. By Helen Kazantzakis. *Simon & Schuster* 1968 $12.00

"The intimate and moving account of the life, the work, the thoughts, the loves of this major literary figure, author of 'Zorba the Greek' and other works of fiction and nonfiction. His wife has woven into her text hundreds of his unpublished letters, from those of his school days to the last notes he wrote on his deathbed"—(*PW*).

Nikos Kazantzakis. By Helen Kazantzakis. *Simon & Schuster* 1970 pap. $3.95

Kazantzakis and the Linguistic Revolution in Greek Literature. By Peter Bien. *Princeton Univ. Press* 1972 $9.00

Nikos Kazantzakis. By Peter Bien. *Columbia* 1972 pap. $1.00

SEFERIS, GEORGE (Sepheriadēs, Georgios). 1900–1971. (Nobel Prize 1963)

Seferis, in 1961 Greece's ambassador to London, has done much to "unite the distinctive heritage of Greek tradition with the *avant-garde* developments in European poetry." He is regarded as one of the greatest poets of his time. He was born in Smyrna and moved to Athens when he was 14. He studied in Paris at the end of the First World War and afterward joined the Greek diplomatic service. "Eminent as he is as a European poet," wrote Rex Warner, "Seferis is preeminently a Greek poet, conscious of the Greek tradition which shaped, and indeed created the tradition of Europe. Throughout the poetry of Seferis one will notice his profound consciousness of the presences of the past and its weight." His themes show a constant awareness of both the dignity and inevitable sorrow of man. His images, the voyage, the search and the ruins which become alive and yet suggest death, are universal, his treatment of them contemporary. His language has a disciplined power and simplicity. In addition to the "Poems," selections from his poetry appear in Keeley and Sherrard's "Six Poets of Modern Greece" (*see above*). "The 18-member Royal Swedish Literary Academy said Mr. Seferis was awarded the $51,158 [Nobel] prize 'for his eminent lyrical writing, inspired by a deep feeling for the Hellenic world of culture' "—(*N.Y. Journal American*).

COLLECTED POEMS, 1924–1955. Trans. and ed. with introd. by Edmund Keeley and Philip Sherrard. *Princeton Univ. Press* 1967 $15.00 pap. $3.95. Bibliography, notes.

POEMS. Trans. by Rex Warner. *Little* 1961 pap. $1.95

"These beautiful, disturbing poems are reports on a journey that never ends, through a landscape that is half modern Greece and half the darkest recesses of the human mind"—(*Atlantic*). Drawing on the richness of mythology, Seferis "expresses most powerfully the eternally tragic in the living present. . . . Most persistent of his themes is the Odyssey myth, stemming no doubt from his own personal experience of exile."

THREE SECRET POEMS. Trans. by Walter Kaiser. *Harvard Univ. Press* 1969 $5.95

A POET'S JOURNAL: Days of 1945–1951. Trans. by Athan Angnostopoulos. *Harvard Univ. Press* Belknap Press 1974 $7.95

VENEZIS, ILIAS (Elias Mellos). 1904–

Born in Asia Minor, Venezis escaped to Athens in 1923 after the Asia Minor disaster. He is the author of numerous books, many of which have been translated into English.

BEYOND THE AEGEAN. Trans. by E. D. Scott-Kilvert. *Vanguard* 1955 $3.50

"The dominant quality of this book is its sheer exotic and lyric beauty. . . . Placed beside the more turbulent works of Nikos Kazantzakis, this lovely novel of Venezis' shows us that there is a rich vein of contemporary Greek writing"—(*N.Y. Times*).

Books about Venezis

Elias Venezis. By Alexander Karanikas and Helen Karanikas. *Twayne* 1969 $6.95

RITSOS, YANNIS. 1909–

Ritsos, imprisoned by the recent regime, has repeatedly suffered from his strong revolutionary sentiments. "Haunted by death, driven at times to the edge of madness and suicide, Ritsos throughout his life has been upheld by his obstinate faith in poetry as redemption, and in the revolutionary ideal"—(Friar, "Modern Greek Poetry").

ROMIOSSINI. *Dustbooks* 1970 pap. $1.50

GESTURES AND OTHER POEMS, 1968–1970. Trans. by Nikos Stangos. *Grossman* 1971 $7.50 pap. $4.50

SELECTED POEMS. Trans. by Nikos Stangos; introd. by Peter Bien *Penguin* 1974 $3.50. Ritsos' most recent poems. The earliest in the volume dates from 1957.

EIGHTEEN SHORT SONGS OF THE BITTER MOTHERLAND. Trans. by Amy Mims; ed. with introd. by Theofanis G. Stavrou; ill. by the poet. *North Central Pub. Co.* 1974

ELYTIS, ODYSSEUS (Odhiseas Alepoudhellis). 1911–

Odysseus Elytis, poet, painter, and translator, was born in Crete and was educated in Athens and Paris. As a young poet he "turned away from the poetry of the damned . . . the nostalgia of autumnal landscapes foreign to Greece, and embraced the tenets of surrealism as a liberating force" —(Friar in "Modern Greek Poetry").

THE AXION ESTI. Trans. by Edmund Keeley and George Savidis. *Univ. of Pittsburgh Press* bilingual ed. 1974 $7.50 pap. $3.50

Greek and English on facing pages. "The Axion Esti" "has been named by poets and Greek scholars alike as one of the major Greek poems of this century."

THE SOVEREIGN SUN: Selected Poems. Trans. by Kimon Friar. *Temple Univ. Press* 1974 $10.00

VASSILIKOS, VASSILIS. 1934–

"Undoubtedly the best young prose writer in Greece today," says Kimon Friar (in *SR*), Vassilikos had his first novel, "Jason" (1952), published when he was only 19. He has also written "Victims of Peace" (1956), a novel, and a book based on his United States tour under grant from the Ford Foundation called "The Mythology of America."

PHOTOGRAPHS. *Harcourt* 1970 $5.95

Z. Trans. by Marilyn Calmann. *Ballantine Bks.* 1971 pap. $.95; *Farrar, Straus* 1968 $6.95

OUTSIDE THE WALLS. *Harcourt* 1973 $6.95

THE HARPOON GUN. *Harcourt* 1973 $6.95

—P.W.W.

HUNGARIAN LITERATURE

Religious literature and translations of the Bible predominate in Hungarian literature from its beginnings in the thirteenth century until the seventeenth century. The polemical works of Pazmany, the leader of the Counter-Reformation in Hungary, represent the pinnacle of this religious literature. The emergence of a national literature begins in the late eighteenth century with the novels of Dugonics and the poetry of Gvadanyi. Kazinczy (1759–1831) reformed the literary language, promoted literary criticism, and tried to raise Hungarian literature to the level of German classicism. Karoly Kisfaludy's almanac

"Aurora" marked the reaction against classicism and the beginning of Romantic poetry and of the short story. The novel developed with the works of Josika and Eotvös. National aspirations found expression in the lyric poetry of Petöfi (1823–1849) and the epic poems of Arany (1817–1882).

In the twentieth century a growing Western influence in literature is reflected in the works of Babits and Kosztolanyi, both of whom published in the leading literary journal *Nyugat (The West)*. The novel flourished in the works of Mikszath, Gardonyi, Herczeg, and Molnár. Kosztolanyi and Karinthy introduced the theme of urban life into literature. The novels of Z. Moricz focus on the grim life of the peasantry. *Nyugat* remained the leading literary periodical between the two world wars. Its contributors during this period included the novelist and poet Gyula Illyes and the poet Attila Jozsef. The Second World War saw the end of *Nyugat* and the death of most of its contributors. Under the Communist regime, in spite of the government's attempt to impose its conception of literature, creative writing has shown renewed vigor and richness in the works of Gyula Illyes, Aron Tomasi, Jozsef Lengyel, George Faludy, Ferenc Juhasz, and others.

Cushing, G. F., Ed. HUNGARIAN PROSE AND VERSE. Trans. by Ibsen. 1956. *Humanities Press* $4.25

Duczynszka, Ilona, Ed. THE PLOUGH AND THE PEN: Writings from Hungary, 1930–1956. *Dufour* $8.95

Horanyi, Mátyás. THE MAGNIFICENCE OF ESTERHÁZA. Trans. by András Deák. *Dufour* 1963 $12.95

"Research in the Esterháza documents, available at the National Széchényi Library only since 1949, is gradually yielding a full picture of 18th- and early 19th-century life at that fabulous palace near Vienna." With the publication of several studies in Hungarian and German, a fairly clear idea of Joseph Haydn's life there as opera conductor has emerged. This valuable volume, the first in English on the subject, includes also all manner of stage entertainment from puppet shows on, at both Esterháza and Kismarton, the other family seat of the aristocratic Esterhazy family.

Klaniczay, Tibor, and others. HISTORY OF HUNGARIAN LITERATURE. *Ungar* $7.50

This Marxist-oriented study lays "strong emphasis on the relations between literature and the social background, especially when dealing with this century"—*(LJ)*.

Ray, David, Ed. FROM THE HUNGARIAN REVOLUTION: A Collection of Poems. *Cornell Univ. Press* 1966 $6.50

Poems inspired by the Hungarian Revolution, some written by refugees, some by political prisoners, some by concerned Americans. *Choice* recommends this collection, "not only as another selection of Hungarian poems, but also as a deeply moving document of human suffering, and of the indestructibility of the human spirit." Biographical sketches and background notes.

Reményi, Joseph. HUNGARIAN WRITERS AND LITERATURE. Ed. by August J. Molnar. *Rutgers Univ. Press* 1964 $12.00

The late Hungarian-American author and teacher examines the literature of the 19th and 20th centuries (1790–1955). Included are articles on the humor and tragic sense in Hungarian writing. "These brilliant essays" are recommended by *Library Journal* for "all sizable libraries." *Choice* says, "Each study is a literary gem. . . . In Reményi's skillful hands many Hungarian writers . . . become comprehensible" as part of Hungarian and world literature. Bibliography and index.

Szabó, Tamas (pseud.). BOY ON THE ROOFTOP. Trans. from the French by David Hughes. 1958. *Peter Smith* $4.50

"Few who read this simple indescribably graphic account of a Hungarian schoolboy in action will easily rub out the memory of the Hungarian uprising. There isn't a false note in the book"— *(N.Y. Herald Tribune)*. "Boy on the Rooftop" is the personal account of the Hungarian Revolution by a 15-year-old boy who commanded a group of teenagers during the street fighting in Budapest. This is an altogether moving and remarkable document.

Szabolcsi, Miklos, Ed. LANDMARK: Hungarian Writers on Thirty Years of History. *Vanous* $5.75

Tezla, Albert. INTRODUCTORY BIBLIOGRAPHY TO THE STUDY OF HUNGARIAN LITERATURE. *Harvard Univ. Press* 1964 $10.00

MADÁCH, IMRE.   1823–1864.

Madách's drama in verse, "The Tragedy of Man," is Faustlike in theme. It begins and ends in heaven, and Adam and Eve are its protagonists, with Lucifer battling God for the possession of their souls. The tribulations of the two human beings on earth—in various guises—lead them in the end to a "nonsentimental philosophy of fortitude." "Struggle . . . is faith in action" (says Reményi) is the play's message.

Madách's own life was beset with difficulties and personal sorrows. Early in his career he held public office, and just before his early death from heart failure he was a member of Parliament; but political imprisonment and an unhappy marriage in the intervening period had strengthened his own strong tendency to melancholy. "The Tragedy of Man" is still performed on the Hungarian stage as one of its great classics.

THE TRAGEDY OF MAN. 1861. Trans. by J. C. W. Horne. *Heinman* 3rd ed. 1957 $5.00; *Vanous* $2.25; *Gordon Press* $28.00

PETŐFI, SANDOR.   1823–1849.

Considered the greatest lyric poet of nineteenth-century Hungary, Petőfi takes as the subject for most of his poems the life of the Hungarian peasantry. The main themes of his poetry are love and patriotism. He is best known for his poem about peasant life "Janos the Hero" and for the "Talpra Magyar," known as the Hungarian "Marseillaise," written during the Hungarian struggle for independence in 1848. Petőfi enlisted in the army in order to take part in this struggle and is believed to have died during the battle of Segesvar in 1849, at the age of 26.

WORKS. *Hungarian Cultural Foundation* 1971 $9.80

SIXTY POEMS. Trans. by Emil Delmar. 1948 *Kraus* $5.00

Books about Petőfi

Tribute to Sandor Petőfi on the 150th Anniversary of his Birth. *Int. Pubns. Service* 1974 $5.00

JÓKAI, MÓR (also Móricz, Maurice).   1825–1904.

Mór Jókai, an author of romances who enjoyed great popularity in his day, was a sort of Jules Verne of Hungary who became known throughout Europe. He wrote more than a hundred novels. "As a storyteller par excellence he had a place second to none in Hungarian literature. [Within limitations] he was a major writer and the core of his art was the expression of an astonishingly rich imagination"—(Reményi). Though weak in characterization, Jókai was a master of suspense and fantastic—sometimes "scientific"—adventure, which took place in exotic settings and was colored by his own exuberant optimism. From the age of 20 he was able to devote himself successfully to literature. "Black Diamonds" (1870) and "The Man with the Golden Touch" (sometimes translated "A Modern Midas") are his two outstanding tales.

TALES FROM JÓKAI. Trans. by R. Nisbet. 3rd ed. 1904 *Bks. for Libraries* $11.75

THE MAN WITH THE GOLDEN TOUCH. 1872. Trans. by Mrs. H. Kennard; rev. by Elizabeth West. *Ungar* $5.00. A novel.

THE DARK DIAMONDS. Trans. by Frances Gerard. *Vanous* $3.75

MIKSZÁTH, KÁLMÁN.   1847–1910.

With Mikszáth, the Hungarian novel became more socially concerned again after Jókai's "escapism," through Mikszáth was far from revolutionary. He was, rather, a liberal who took part in politics and described the foibles of his society with gentle cynicism and mocking humor—not unlike our own Mark Twain. He was adept at characterization and made use of the anecdotal vignette in portraying the Hungarian ruling class as well as its peasants. "St. Peter's Umbrella" (1895) is perhaps his finest work. He wrote enchanting books for children and in 1907 a critical study of Mór Jókai (*q.v.*) in two volumes.

ST. PETER'S UMBRELLA. Trans. by B. W. Worswick. *Vanous* $2.50

STRANGE MARRIAGE. Trans. by Istvan Farkas, rev. by Elizabeth West. *Vanous* $3.75

GARDONYI, GEZA.   1863–1922.

Gardonyi is known for his historical novels containing idyllic pictures of peasant life and for his conventional lyric poetry.

SLAVE OF THE HUNS. *Bobbs* 1969 $5.00

ADY, ENDRE.   1877–1919.

Considered the greatest Hungarian lyric poet of the twentieth century, Ady introduced new vigor into the stagnant, conventional poetry of the turn of the century. His early poetry was revolutionary in both language and content and offended literary and political conservatives. In his later writings, from before and during World War I, he voices his anguish at social injustice and the carnage of war. Ady wrote poetry dealing with love and religion as well as with social and political themes.

POEMS OF ENDRE ADY. *Hungarian Cultural Foundation* 1969 $9.80

MOLNÁR, FERENC. 1878–1952.

In "Liliom" Molnár wrote with imagination and beauty a play which shows the inarticulate courage, faith, and humanity of a sideshow barker. The success of the play in New York first brought Molnár into prominence in America. (It was a flat failure when first produced in Budapest in 1909, but it has been played since all over the world.) Rodgers and Hammerstein (*q.v.*) transplanted "Liliom" to New England and set it to music as "Carousel," a three-year hit (1946, o.p.). "The Guardsman" is a witty treatment of a love triangle. "The Play's the Thing," Molnár's last work of importance, is a play within a play. His skillful one-act plays are so Freudian that one suspects him of quietly ridiculing the cult. He loved royalty, artists, the poor. S. N. Behrman (*q.v.*), writing in the *New Yorker*, says: "Molnár's theme is himself and he has taken his society right along with him over the footlights and confided to it expansively in stage whispers. Unlike the novel, the theatre has rarely been autobiographical: Molnár's plays are the great exception."

As a correspondent in the first World War he came in contact so constantly with death that there is always the intimation of mortality in his stage fantasies. He lived in exile in New York after 1940. "Companion in Exile: Notes for an Autobiography" (trans. by Barrows Mussey 1950, o.p.) is an odd and moving memoir written for the woman who was his secretary and who died in New York in 1947.

LILIOM: A Legend in 7 Scenes and a Prologue. 1909. Eng. text by Benjamin F. Glazer
    French 1944 $1.75; *Baker* $1.25

THE GUARDSMAN. 1910. *French* Mss. (*see publisher's catalog for price information*)

THE PLAY'S THE THING. 1925. Adapted by P. G. Wodehouse. *French* $1.75

MORICZ, SZIGMOND. 1879–1942.

Moricz was a novelist, short story writer, and playwright associated with the literary journal *Nyugat* (*The West*). In his early works, Moricz described the grim reality of the countryside in a stark, naturalistic manner. His later novels about the upper classes are less forceful than the early ones. Among his best known novels are "The Torch" (1917), and his historical novels in the trilogy "Translyvania" (1922–1935). Moricz is generally recognized as Hungary's first modern writer.

BE FAITHFUL UNTO DEATH. Trans. by Susan K. Laszlo. *Vanous* $4.00

BABITS, MIHALY. 1883–1941.

A poet, novelist, essayist, and translator of great stature in the literary life of twentieth century Hungary, along with Ady, Moricz, Kosztolanyi, and other writers, Babits contributed to the leading literary journal *Nyugat* (*The West*). He became editor of *Nyugat* in 1929. Babits' poetry is rarified and difficult to understand. In his later writings, he turned to the depiction of social reality. His outstanding novel "The Children of Death" (1927) gives a sympathetic portrayal of the dissolution of the middle classes. Babits also translated Sophocles, Dante, Shakespeare, and Goethe into Hungarian.

THE NIGHTMARE. Trans. by Eva Racz. *Vanous* $4.00

LUKÁCS, GYÖRGY (also Georg, George). 1885–

George Steiner (*q.v.*) in "Language and Silence" calls Lukács "the one major critical talent to have emerged from the gray servitude of the Marxist world." This well-known writer on European literature combines a Marxist-Hegelian concern for the historical process with great artistic sensitivity. Lukács joined the Hungarian Communist Party in 1918, serving in its first government until the defeat of Bela Kun. He spent many years in exile, first in Berlin and then, (1933–1945) in Moscow, writing and studying. He later became a professor of esthetics in Budapest, but after the 1956 revolution he was stripped of influence because of his too-friendly attitude to non-Marxist literatures. "A communist by conviction, a dialectical materialist by virtue of his critical method, he has nevertheless kept his eyes resolutely on the past. . . . Despite pressure from his Russian hosts, Lukács gave only perfunctory notice to the much heralded achievements of 'Soviet realism.' Instead, he dwelt on the great lineage of eighteeenth and nineteenth-century European poetry and fiction. . . . The critical perspective is rigorously Marxist, but the choice of themes is 'central European' and conservative"—(Steiner). Lukács has concentrated mainly on criticism of Russian, French and German authors, and often writes in German. Robert J. Clements (*SR*, Nov. 4, 1967) found Hungarian young people regarding him as somewhat *passé*.

STUDIES IN EUROPEAN REALISM. 1946. Introd. by Alfred Kazin. *Grosset* Univ. Lib. pap. $1.95

The introduction is "clear, concise and very laudatory"—(*LJ*).

THE HISTORICAL NOVEL. 1955. Trans. by Hannah and Stanley Mitchell. *Humanities Press* 1965 $8.75

REALISM IN OUR TIME: Literature and the Class Struggle. 1962. Trans. by John and Necke Mander; pref. by George Steiner. *Harper* 1964 pap. $1.75; *Peter Smith* $3.75

GOETHE AND HIS AGE. *Grosset* 1969 pap. $2.45

SOLZHENITSYN. Trans. by William D. Graf. *M.I.T. Press* 1971 $5.95 pap. $1.45

WRITER AND CRITIC AND OTHER ESSAYS. Trans. by Arthur D. Kahn. *Grosset* 1971 $6.95 pap. $2.95

THEORY OF THE NOVEL. Trans. by Anna Bostock. *M.I.T. Press* 1972 $5.95 pap. $1.95

Books about Lukács

George Lukács' Marxism, Alienation, Dialectics, Revolution. By Victor Zitta. *Humanities Press* 1964 $9.75

Georg Lukács. By Ehrhard Bahr and Ruth G. Kunzer. Modern Literature Monographs *Ungar* 1972 $6.00

Georg Lukács. Ed. by G. H. Parkinson. *Random* 1970 $7.95

George Lukács. By George Lichtheim. Modern Masters Ser. *Viking* 1970 $5.75 pap. $1.85

Lukács' Concept of Dialectic: With Biography, Bibliography, and Documents. By I. Maszaros. *Humanities Press* 1972 $7.50

KARINTHY, FRIGYES. 1887–1938.

A brilliant writer of parodies, satires, and literary caricatures, Karinthy is the best-known Hungarian humorist. He wrote for the literary journal *Nyugat* (*The West*). He has been called an "optimistic Swift" for his sequels to "Gulliver's Travels": "Voyage to Faremido-Capillaria" (1916, 1921). His best prose work is "Journey around my Skull" (1937), the account of a brain operation he underwent. Karinthy also translated works by Swift, Heine, Mark Twain, and A. A. Milne.

PLEASE SIR. Trans. by Istvan Farkas. *Vanous* $3.00

"A humorous and perceptive picture of the clash between adolescents in school"—("The Penguin Companion to European Literature").

ZILAHY, LAJOS. 1891–

Zilahy is a contemporary short-story writer, novelist, and playwright, well known abroad, whose social and political ideas—particularly his pacifism—permeate his work. At one time Zilahy and his wife donated their wealth to the Hungarian government for the founding of an institute to promote world peace. Anti-Nazi and anticommunist both, they took refuge in the United States in 1947. Zilahy is the finest of Hungarian war novelists; one of his best-known books, "Two Prisoners" (U.S. 1931), the story of a couple whose married life is irrevocably split by World War I, was called "brilliant" by the *Times Literary Supplement*, London. Another is "The Dukays" (U.S. 1931, o.p.), an indictment of the Hungarian nobility presented as a family chronicle.

TWO PRISONERS. 1931. Great Novels and Memoirs of World War I Ser. *Stackpole* 1968 $8.95

LENGYEL, JOZSEF. 1896–

A novelist, memoirist, and short story writer, Lengyel was an active Communist who, in 1937, was arrested and held in Siberia until 1955. In his writings he describes his experiences of this period and tries to understand the debasement of socialism into Stalinism. His writings include "From Beginning to End" (memoirs), "The Judge's Chair" and "Acta Sanctorum" (stories).

CONFRONTATION. Trans. by Anna Novotny. *Citadel Press* 1973 $6.95

TAMASI, ARON. 1897–1966.

A novelist, short story writer, and dramatist, Tamasi described himself as being "closest to realism—not only in describing social relationships, but in trying to comprehend the life of man as a unity of science and poetry." Tamasi, who had deep roots in the rural Szekler region of Hungary, participated in the populist movement. His novel "Titled Nobility" (1931, o.p.) is an indictment of feudalism in the countryside. His short stories and fables appeared in the collections "Paradise Gone Wild" (1956, o.p.) and "Light and Moonlight" (1958, o.p.). His best-known novels are those in the Abel trilogy (1932–1934), the picaresque tale of a resourceful peasant prankster. An autobiographical novel, "Cradle and Owl" (o.p.), appeared in 1949.

ABEL ALONE. Trans. by Mari Kuttna. *Vanous* $3.50

NÉMÉTH, LÁSZLÓ. 1901–

Néméth is known as a brooding philosopher and reformer who has written many books on the situation of Hungary in Europe as well as critical works, journalism, and a number of novels. He has "maintained that 'the Hungarian writer should be ascetic, his voice should be cultured, he should live with the poor and should not fear solitariness.' There is a contrast between the urbane horizon of his critical writings and the folkishness of his imaginative work"—(Reményi). "Revulsion" (1947, o.p.) is an example of the latter. The sensitive story of a young farm girl, set in the Hungary of the late 1930s, it gives a vivid picture of village and rural life. "Written in the tradition of Flaubert and Pasternak by one of Hungary's leading authors and critics . . . this novel can be recommended to every thoughtful person"—(*LJ*).

GUILT. *Dufour* 1966 $8.50

ILLYES, GYULA. 1902–

A poet, dramatist, novelist, essayist, and translator, Illyes published his first volume of poems in 1928. His published works amount to over 35 volumes in Hungarian. He succeeded Mihaly Babits as editor of *Nyugat* (*The West*), the main Hungarian literary periodical in the first four decades of the twentieth century. He was one of the leaders of the populist movement in literature, which attempted to "explore the village" and to write about the squalid condition of the peasantry. His largely autobiographical study of the peasantry, "People of the Puszta," is considered a classic. When *Nyugat* failed, he started a new journal, *Magyar Csillag* (*Hungarian Star*), which was closed down by the Nazis in 1944. He edited a third journal, *Válasz* (*The Answer*), between 1945 and 1948. Illyes has always written in the "daily language of simple people," drawing on the wealth and rhythms of the Hungarian language.

PEOPLE OF THE PUSZTA. Trans. by G. F. Cushing. *Int. Pubns. Service* 1971 $7.50; *Vanous* $4.50

ONCE UPON A TIME. *Branden* 1975 $7.50

Books about Illyes

Tribute to Gyula Illyes: Poems. Ed. by Thomas Kabdebo and Paul Tabori. Trans. by Vernon. *Occidental* 1968 pap. $4.50

JÓZSEF, ATTILA. 1905–1937.

A poet, József was born in poverty and remained poor all his life. In his poetry he protested against the conditions of the working class. He was a contributor to *Nyugat* (*The West*). His first collection of poems was "Beggar of Beauty" (1922). In the last years of his life he became a poet of national and world stature. His best works are the collections of poems "The Bear's Dance" (1934), "There Is No Pardon" (1936–1937), and "Last Poems" (1937). József drew on Hungarian folklore, German expressionism, and French surrealism but integrated these materials into his own powerful poetic style. After being held in disrepute by the Communist regime during the Zhdanov period, József is now considered the greatest Hungarian poet.

WORKS. Ill. *Hungarian Cultural Foundation* 1973 $7.90

SELECTED POEMS AND TEXTS. Ed. by George Gomori. Trans. by John Bakti. *Dufour* 1973 $8.50

KOESTLER, ARTHUR. 1905–

An ex-communist, now a socialist, Koestler "was born a displaced person (in Budapest): half-Hungarian, half-Jew, he was educated in Vienna, worked in Germany and Palestine, lived in France"—(V. S. Pritchett). He was Near East correspondent for a German chain of newspapers and magazines; as a special correspondent for the *London News Chronicle* in the Spanish Civil War, he was captured and sentenced to death, but released through the intervention of the British Government. He escaped from France in 1940, joined the British army, worked with the BBC, and has lived in England since 1941.

His books are powerful, theatrical reports of modern problems. He blends the novelist's and historian's material with furious vitality and force, but with a tendency to try to fit life into his elaborately constructed theories—a dazzling performance and stimulating, if not always convincing. "The Sleepwalkers" turned a spotlight on a dilemma of our time, the split between science and religion. In "The Lotus and the Robot," Koestler sets out to discover for himself whether the West can find answers for its moral and spiritual problems. "He gives his attention in the first half of the book to four contemporary Indian saints and to Yoga; in the second half he analyzes Zen Buddhism and in a brief epilogue gives his conclusions on the East-West relationship"—(*LJ*).

THE GLADIATORS. 1939. Trans. by Edith Simon. *Macmillan* 1967 Danube Eds. $5.95. A historical novel about the rising of the slaves in ancient Rome.

DARKNESS AT NOON. 1941. Trans. by Daphne Hardy. *Bantam* pap. $1.25; *Macmillan* 1941 $7.95; *Random Mod. Lib.* 1946 $2.95. Novel about a political prisoner of the communists.

DIALOGUE WITH DEATH. 1942. Trans. by Trevor and Phyllis Blewitt; new pref. by the author. *Macmillan* 1960 Danube Eds. 1967 $5.95 pap. $1.25. Describes Koestler's prison experiences during the Spanish Civil War.

ARRIVAL AND DEPARTURE. 1943. *Macmillan* 1967 Danube Eds. $5.95. Psychological novel about a European communist.

THE YOGI AND THE COMMISSAR, AND OTHER ESSAYS. 1945. (With new pref. by the author) *Macmillan* Danube Eds. 1967 $5.95

THIEVES IN THE NIGHT: The Chronicle of an Experiment. 1946. New postscript by the author. *Macmillan* Danube Eds. 1967 $5.95. A novel of Palestine, 1937–1939.

INSIGHT AND OUTLOOK: An Inquiry into the Common Foundations of Science, Art and Social Ethics. 1949. *Peter Smith* $4.50

THE AGE OF LONGING. (1951, o.p.) Novel of the Paris international intelligentsia.

THE SLEEPWALKERS: A History of Man's Changing Vision of the Universe. 1959. *Grosset* 1963 Univ. Lib. pap. $3.45

"It is a whale of a book—more than six hundred pages—close packed with unhackneyed facts, striking generalizations, bold paradoxes, and passionately propounded theories"—(*N.Y. Herald Tribune*).

THE LOTUS AND THE ROBOT. 1960. *Harper* pap. $2.25

THE WATERSHED: A Biography of Johannes Kepler. *Doubleday* 1960 pap. $2.50

THE ACT OF CREATION. *Macmillan* 1964 $7.95; *Dell* 1966 pap. $1.95

A "beautifully readable . . . immensely ranging" explanation of the creative process—(*N.Y. Review of Books*).

(Ed.) SUICIDE OF A NATION? *Macmillan* 1964 $4.95. An inquiry into the state of Britain today.

THE GHOST IN THE MACHINE. *Macmillan* 1968 $6.95; *Regnery* pap. $3.45

SCUM OF THE EARTH. *Macmillan* 1968 $7.95

DRINKERS OF INFINITY: Essays Nineteen Fifty Five to Nineteen Sixty Seven. *Macmillan* 1969 $7.95

(With J. R. Smythies, Eds.) BEYOND REDUCTIONISM: New Perspectives on the Life of Sciences. *Macmillan* 1970 $8.95; *Beacon* 1971 pap. $3.95

THE ROOTS OF COINCIDENCE. *Random* 1972 $5.95 pap. $1.95

THE CASE OF THE MIDWIFE TOAD. *Random* 1972 $5.95 1973 pap. $1.65

THE CALL GIRLS. *Random* 1973 $5.95; *Dell* 1974 pap. $1.25

ARROW IN THE BLUE: An Autobiography. *Macmillan* 1952 $7.95. From his birth in Budapest to his alliance with the Communist Party in 1931.

THE INVISIBLE WRITING. A continuation of "Arrow in the Blue." *Macmillan* 1954 $8.95. His seven years, 1931–1938, "as an embattled member of the Communist Party."

Books about Koestler

Chronicles of Conscience: A Study of George Orwell and Arthur Koestler. By Jenni Calder. Critical Essays in Mod. Lit. Ser. *Univ. of Pittsburgh Press* 1969 pap. $2.95

Arthur Koestler. By Wolfe Mays. Makers of Modern Thought Ser. *Judson* 1973 pap. $1.50

JUHÁSZ, FERENC. 1928–

Juhász's first book of poems, *The Winged Colt* (1947, o.p.), made his reputation before he was 20. After several works glorifying the new Communist regime, Juhász in the early 1950s began to move away from politics and to develop his own original poetic style. The large epic poem "The Prodigal Country" (o.p.), according to Gomori, introduced a "new epoch in modern Hungarian poetry." Juhász's collection of poems "Battling the White Lamb" (1957, o.p.) contains "The Boy Changed into a Stag Cries Out at the Gate of Secrets," which W. H. Auden called "one of the greatest poems written in my time." After being in official disfavor in the late 1950s and early 1960s, Juhász is now tolerated by the regime and allowed to travel abroad. Hungarians consider him the greatest poet of his generation and the heir to Attila József.

Boy Changed into a Stag: Selected Poems. 1949–1967. Trans. by Kenneth McRobbie and Ilona Duczynska. *Oxford* 1970 $3.95

ARNOTHY, CHRISTINE. 1929–

Christine Arnothy was only 15 when she endured the siege of Budapest in 1944. She did not escape from Hungary until five years later. "By that time she was old enough to understand the nature of life under the communist terror and to study its functioning with precocious maturity of judgment." *The Christian Herald* called her first book, "I Am Fifteen—and I Don't Want to Die," "a small but terrible classic . . . a veritable masterpiece of mental and physical torture that moves steadily towards spiritual fulfillment." "God Is Late" (U.S. 1957, o.p.) and "It Is Not So Easy to Live" (U.S. 1960, o.p.) continue her vivid descriptions of Hungarian life under the communist regime through the story of her escape to a new life in Paris. "The Charlatans" (U.S. 1959, o.p.) is a novel about a bourgeois family in Paris.

I Am Fifteen—and I Don't Want to Die. 1956. *Scholastic Bk. Service* pap. $.75

—G.K.

LATVIAN LITERATURE

Indigenous Latvian literature, primarily in the form of folk songs (*dainas*) and fairy tales, was preserved in oral form well into the nineteenth and even the twentieth century when it was gradually recorded for posterity. The folk songs, mostly terse lyric quatrains, are the most original part of the literary heritage; at present the recorded collection well exceeds one million songs.

The earliest written literary texts in Latvian, dating from the sixteenth century, were mainly religious or moralizing in nature; their authors were German clergymen who belonged to the ruling class in what is now Latvia.

The beginnings of modern Latvian literature written by Latvians coincided with the "National Awakening" of Latvians in the second half of the nineteenth century. Early literary efforts were directed primarily toward the establishment of the language as a viable medium for modern literature and toward the creation of a romanticized picture of the unexplored era before foreign rule. Around the turn of the century, Latvian writers became more directly influenced by contemporary literary and political developments abroad. At this time, especially in the wake of the 1905 revolution, ideological divisions between the literary nationalists and Marxists developed. A literary group exiled itself to Soviet Russia after the founding of independent Latvia in 1918 and published until Stalin's purges decimated it. But most writers—including some figures later prominent in Soviet Latvia—stayed in the newly founded state.

Soviet occupation in 1940, World War II, and the re-establishment of a Soviet regime in 1944–1945 split the writers once again. The literary exile in the West, now primarily in the United States, Canada, Australia, Sweden, Germany, and England, originally included some of the prominent names of the literature of independent Latvia. Now entering its third generation, this group is fighting the dual problems of a deteriorating idiom and a dwindling readership. In Soviet Latvia, the postwar "socialist realism" with its emphasis on the glorification of the heroic struggle against fascism and of the communist system, has given way to freer forms of expression by a younger generation of writers, although their work, too, is closely monitored by party and state ideologues. Their forte is especially a versatile use of the linguistic and folkloristic idiom, and many of them enjoy tremendous popularity. Both in Soviet Latvia and in exile, lyric poetry has flourished.

Translations into English have been rather sporadic, and little is available in print. The advent of new official and social attitudes toward ethnic heritage in the United States and Canada and the efforts of such organizations as the Association for the Advancement of Baltic Studies may, however, lead to a more systematic program of making Latvian literature accessible to the English-speaking public. The activities of the AABS have already helped in the creation of a respectable body of secondary literature about Latvian literature. See *Books Abroad*, Vol. 47, No. 4 (Autumn 1973), devoted to Baltic literatures, and all other issues with regular reviews of recent Latvian books; Arvīds Ziedonis and others, Eds., "Baltic Literature and Linguistics" (*AABS* 1973 $8.50 pap. $3.95), proceedings of the Third Conference on Baltic Studies in Toronto 1972; *Journal of Baltic Studies*, all issues, but particularly Vol. 6, No. 2–3 (Summer/Fall 1975, annual subscription $20.00 institutional, $15.00 individual, $7.50 student) devoted to a selection of literary papers from the Fourth Conference on Baltic Studies in Chicago, 1974. The AABS publications, including *Journal of Baltic Studies*, are available from the Executive Office, 366 86 Street, Brooklyn, N.Y. 11209. Books listed below may be ordered from: Latvian Bookshop, Leons Rumaks, 27 Miller Place, Hempstead, N.Y. 11550.

Andrups, Jānis, and Vitauts Kalve. LATVIAN LITERATURE. Trans. by Ruth Speirs. Ill. *Zelta Ābele* 1954 $9.00. Essays covering Latvian literature from folklore to the immediate post-World War II period. No coverage of Soviet Latvian writing.

Rubulis, Aleksis, Ed. LATVIAN LITERATURE. *Daugavas Vanags* 1964 $4.00. An uneven selection of uneven translations of prose fiction, containing, among others, samples of acknowledged past and present masters of Latvian prose: Rūdolfs Blaumanis, Jānis Akurāters, Kārlis Skalbe, Jānis Jaunsudrabiņš, Edvards Virza, Jānis Veselis, Ēriks Ādamsons, Anšlāvs Eglītis, Jānis Klīdzējs, Guntis Zariņš, Ilze Šķipsna, Andrejs Irbe.

Speirs, Ruth, Trans. LET US GET ACQUAINTED. *Zvaigzne* 1973 $5.00. Nine Soviet Latvian poets. Translations of A. Čaks, J. Grots, A. Grigulis, B. Saulītis, O. Vācietis, I. Ziedonis, I. Auziņš, V. Līvzemnieks, M. Čaklais.

TRANSLATIONS FROM THE LATVIAN. *Exeter Book* 1968 $2.00. Selections from two exiled authors of the New York Hell's Kitchen group, Linards Tauns and Gunars Saliņš.

WINDOWS: Latvian Poems. *Exeter Book* 1972 $2.00. Selections from five Soviet Latvian poets: A. Čaks, I. Ziedonis, O. Vācietis, V. Līvzemnieks, M. Čaklais.

Straumanis, Alfreds, Ed. CONFRONTATIONS WITH TYRANNY. *Southern Illinois Univ. Press* 1976 $15.00. First in a projected series of volumes of drama translations. This volume contains two each of Estonian, Latvian, and Lithuanian plays dealing with a common theme.

RAINIS, JĀNIS (pseud. of Pliekšāns, Jānis). 1865–1929.

The acknowledged grand master of Latvian literature, Rainis wrote both drama and verse. His symbolic–philosophic dramas strive for a synthesis of national and human, social and individual concerns. His philosophy of humanity is best expressed in "Joseph and His Brothers," a drama written in blank verse. See Arvids Ziedonis, Jr., "The Religious Philosophy of Jānis Rainis" *Latvju grāmata* 1969 $6.80.

JOSEPH AND HIS BROTHERS. Trans. by Grace Reese. *Ziemeļblazma* 1965 $5.50. Play.

ZĪVERTS, MĀRTIŅŠ. 1903–

The best and most prolific Latvian dramatist (his plays number about 50), Zīverts resides in Sweden and writes for the less-than-ideal exile stage which forces him to employ classic simplicity. A minimum of characters, and a tightly constructed stage action are characteristic. External action is held to a minimum and grows out of adroitly used dialogue. "The Ore" is based on an anecdote about the discoverer of iron ore in northern Sweden.

THE ORE. Trans. by Alfred Straumanis. *Sala Press* 1968 $3.00. Play.

EGLĪTIS, ANŠLĀVS. 1906–

Eglītis, now residing in California, was first schooled in the pictorial arts. His prolific output of prose reveals this schooling. His characters are drawn sharply with a predilection for sketch and caricature; his adroitly developed plots abound in the unexpected, adventuresome, and even fantastic; he has a penchant for the portrayal of the grotesque and exotic (the novel "Ajurjonga" takes place in Mongolia). Eglītis is also an accomplished dramatist.

AJURJONGA. Trans. by L. Parks. *Daugava* 1955 $3.00. '

EGLĪTIS, ANDREJS. 1912–

Much of Eglītis' poetry is shaped by the experiences of World War II and the loss of Latvia's independence thereafter. Some of his most powerful verse evokes doomsday imagery and is carried by intense patriotic and religious mysticism. "Here, however, his work is represented by a small handful of patriotic poems together with a larger number which combine the simplicity of the folk song with the elegance of fashioned lyric"—(Derek Stanford). Eglītis lives in Sweden.

No SUCH PLACE LASTS SUMMERLONG. *International Poetry Society,* and *HUB Publications* 1974 $3.00. An anthology of poems by Eglītis and Velta Sniķere, who did the translation.

SNIĶERE, VELTA. 1920–

"Many of her poems seek to locate inner states in an outward language. . . . Sometimes her lines sound like proverbs heard in a dream, maxims enunciated in folk-song"—(Derek Stanford). Sniķere resides in England.

No SUCH PLACE LASTS SUMMERLONG. *See Andrejs Eglītis above.*

JAUNZEMIS, AUSMA.

Jaunzemis belongs to the younger generation of American–Latvian poets who are equally at ease in Latvian and English. Jaunzemis has already developed her characteristic style. The volume below was written while she was recovering from an auto accident in 1968.

MORPHIUM DREAMS/MORFIJA SAPŅI. Trans. by the author. *Echo Pub.* 1975 $4.00. A bilingual volume with studio photographs by H. Hofmane.

—V.N.

LITHUANIAN LITERATURE

Lithuanian literature in the native tongue began late, in the eighteenth century. Bucolic poetry by Kristijonas Donelaitis (1714–1780) and Antanas Baranauskas (1835–1902) came first, followed by late nineteenth-century winds of romantic nationalism. Jonas Maironis (1862–1932) was the outstanding bard of national awakening, but later poets sought inspiration in all trends and corners of literary Europe. Vincas Mykolaitis-Putinas (1893–1966), a poet, playwright, and novelist, was influenced by Russian Symbolism; Jonas Aistis (1904–1973) developed a highly individualized blend of French-influenced modernistic idiom and national folklore heritage, and Bernardas Brazdžionis (1907–) sought the Lithuanian soul across the landscapes of Catholic mysticism. In prose, Vincas Krėvė-Mickevičius (1882–1954) established a wide frame, from lyrical-mythological dream language to folksy realism. Mykolaitis-Putinas developed the psychological novel with autobiographical overtones. Antanas Vienuolis (1882–1957) became the chronicler of Lithuanian life between the wars, while Petras Cvirka (1909–1947) turned his eyes to issues of social justice. Antanas Vaičiulaitis (1906–) created poetic, impressionistic prose. Lithuanian drama during the independence period was mostly concerned with heroic deeds of the past and petty-bourgeois misdeeds of the present.

The return of Soviet power in 1944 forced Lithuanian literature into two frames of existence: exodus abroad and tyranny at home. The first decades after the war were marked by considerable vitality and high literary achievement among the exiles. The foremost emigré poet is Henrikas Radauskas (1910–1970), an intellectual, a visionary, and an amused player with multiple dimensions of reality. Kazys Bradūnas (1917–) dwells on the mystique of the native soil, and Alfonsas Nyka-Niliūnas (1919–) writes complex, thoughtful poetry tinged with philosophical existentialism. In prose, Antanas Škėma (1911–1961), novelist and playwright, probed deeply into the soul-destroying experience of exile and war. Lithuanian drama was enriched by two young playwrights, Algirdas Landsbergis (1924–   ), who also writes prose, and Kostas Ostrauskas (1928–   ). Both are modernistic writers, mixing humor, dreams, and death on a palette depicting the ironies of the human condition.

In the Soviet Union, inspiration regained its wings sometime around 1956, the "liberal" Khrushchev era. Searching, careful writers, balancing truth and pretense on the knife edge of political pressure, have been growing in numbers and talent in recent years. The oldest of them, Juozas Grušas (1901–   ) creates subtle moral encounters with conscience in his plays and prose. Justinas Marcinkevičius (1930–   ) experiments with style and plays with man's conscience in search of faith in Communism. Mykolas Sluckis (1929–   ) is a detailed, realistic novelist of the daily run of life. At the opposite end, Icchokas Meras (1934–   ), who now resides in Israel, depicts the dramatic situation of mankind *in extremis* by means of intensely symbolic, experimental prose. Sigitas Geda (1943–   ) and Antanas Venclova (1937–   ) are two extremely talented young poets of modernistic, pantheistic, and philosophical bent.

Of the authors mentioned above, some works by Vincas Krėvė-Mickevičius, Kristijonas Donelaitis, Antanas Baranauskas, Antanas Vaičiulaitis, Antanas Škėma, Algirdas Landsbergis, and Kostas Ostrauskas have been translated into English.

General Studies

Rubulis, Aleksis. BALTIC LITERATURE. *Univ. of Notre Dame Press* 1970 $8.50. A survey of the Finnish, Estonian, Latvian, and Lithuanian literatures, including a generous selection of translations.

Šilbajoris, Rimvydas. PERFECTION OF EXILE. *Oklahoma Univ. Press* 1970 $8.50. Fourteen essays describing fourteen different Lithuanian authors writing in exile. The book contains a historical survey of Lithuanian literature.

Ziedonis, Arvids, and others, Eds. BALTIC LITERATURE AND LINGUISTICS. *Association for the Advancement of Baltic Studies* (366 86 St., Brooklyn, N.Y. 11209) $8.50 pap. $3.95. A collection of papers read at the 1972 conference, held at the University of Toronto, of the Association for the Advancement of Baltic Studies.

Zobarskas, Stepas. THE LITHUANIAN SHORT STORY: Fifty Years. *Manyland* 1975 $4.50

Collections

Zorbarskas, Stepas, Ed. LITHUANIAN FOLK TALES. *Manyland* 1959 $4.50

LITHUANIAN QUARTET. *Manyland* 1962 $4.95. A novel, a novella, and four short stories by Aloyzas Baronas, Marius Katiliškis, Algridas Landsbergis, and Ignas Šeinius.

THE MAKER OF THE GODS. *Voyages Press* 1961 $3.00. Ten Lithuanian stories translated by Zorbarskas, a short story writer who has lived in the United States since 1947.

SELECTED LITHUANIAN SHORT STORIES. *Manyland* 1963 $5.00. Representative selections by some 18 Lithuanian authors.

Periodicals

JOURNAL OF BALTIC STUDIES. A publication of the Association for the Advancement of Baltic Studies, containing articles discussing various aspects of Baltic cultures, including literature.

LITUANUS. A Lithuanian cultural quarterly, published in Chicago by the Lithuanian Foundation, Inc.

DONELAITIS, KRISTIJONAS. 1714–1780.

Author of the first important literary work in Lithuanian, Donelaitis, a village pastor, wrote very little else. "The Seasons" grew out of his efforts to enlist the services of art in his pastoral work. The long narrative poem surveys the course of the seasons in the life of eighteenth-century

Lithuanian peasants "plodding the treadmill of time toward a hoped-for eternity in which their plain country virtue is to meet its just reward"—("Perfection of Exile").

THE SEASONS. Trans. by Nadas Rastenis. *Lithuanian Days Publishers* 1967 $4.00

BARANAUSKAS, ANATANAS. 1835–1902.

A Roman Catholic bishop, Baranauskas included creative writing among his other hobbies. "The Forest of Anykščiai" was written in response to the challenge to produce poetry in the Lithuanian language which would measure up to the standards of written Polish. This idyllic work, tracing the history and the demise of a small forest grove, met the challenge in exquisite syllabic verse, melodious and expressive to mirror the complex emotional experience of man living in an instinctive harmony with nature.

THE FOREST OF ANYKŠČIAI. Trans. by Nadas Rastenis. *Lithuanian Days Publishers* 1970 $3.00. A narrative poem.

KUDIRKA, VINCAS. 1858–1899.

One of the most important Lithuanian figures in that country's period of combined enlightenment and national awakening, Kudirka wrote with fierce patriotism and unyielding national pride, urging his countrymen to respect their own nation and to struggle for its liberation from the foreign yoke. The "Memoirs" is a bitter political satire against the Russian rule in Lithuania in late nineteenth century.

MEMOIRS OF A LITHUANIAN BRIDGE. Trans. by Nola M. Zobarskas. *Manyland* 1961 $2.00

KRĖVĖ, VINCAS (MICKEVIČIUS). 1882–1954.

The grand old man of Lithuanian letters, Vincas Krėvė laid the foundations for many levels and styles of Lithuanian prose and drama, greatly extending the powers of spoken Lithuanian to function as an effective written medium. *"Dainavos šalies senų žmonių padavimai"* (Legends of the Old People of Dainava, 1912) elevated the heroic Lithuanian past in irridescent beauty of quasi-folkloristic language approaching high poetry. The historical plays "Šarūnas," 1912, and "Skirgaila," 1925, depict Lithuanian rulers confronted with tremendous moral and intellectual challenges as they struggle to create and then to defend a unified Lithuanian nation. "The Herdsman and the Linden Tree" presents some of the best realistic village stories Krėvė wrote. They tell of men in tune with Nature whose souls, close to the God of their own understanding, are unable to make peace with the accepted social norms of morality.

THE HERDSMAN AND THE LINDEN TREE. Trans. by Albinas Baranauskas. *Manyland* 1961 $2.00

ŠEINIUS, IGNAS (JURKŪNAS). 1889–1959.

At the beginning of the nineteenth century, significant contributions to the development of Lithuanian prose style came from the influence of impressionism, often of the Scandinavian variety. Šeinius is one such impressionistic writer, intensely emotional but highly controlled in his finely tuned language. His most important novel, *"Kuprelis"* (The Hunchback), written in 1911, depicts a lonely dreamer, crippled physically in his body and emotionally by the philistine world in which he must live. "Siegfried Immerselbe" is quite different in tone, being a sparkling satire against racism: an aging Nazi is rejuvenated and much improved by the infusion of Jewish blood.

REJUVENATION OF SIEGFRIED IMMERSELBE. Trans. by Albinas Baranauskas. *Manyland* 1965 $5.00

RAMONAS, VINCAS. 1905–

An educator by profession, Ramonas made his mark in Lithuanian literature with two novels dealing with the psychological and moral traumas brought about by the first Soviet occupation of Lithuania in 1941. The first novel, *"Dulkės raudonam saulėleidy"* (Dust in the Red Sunset) was serialized in 1943. The second, "Crosses," describes with painful intensity the moral and ideological conflict among poor and rich Lithuanian farmers who were deceived and destroyed by the Soviet regime. Ramonas has also written a number of delicately chiselled short stories. "At its best, Ramonas' prose blends precise realistic observation with subtle symbolic allusion"—(*Encyclopedia Lituanica*).

CROSSES. *Lithuanian Days Publishers* 1954 $4.00

GLIAUDA, JURGIS. 1906–

When the exigencies of exile deprived Gliauda of his profession as a lawyer, he turned to *belles lettres* and rapidly developed into a prolific novelist, conservative in terms of moral and ethnic values but often experimental in the structure and language of his work. First written in 1945,

"House upon the Sand" pictures the "crime and punishment" of a German landowner just before Hitler's empire crumbled. "Understatement and simplicity of style reveal an ordinary German infected by the dread disease of Nazism and its consequences."

House upon the Sand. Trans. by Raphael Sealey and Milton Stark. *Manyland* 1963 $3.95

VAIČIULAITIS, ANTANAS. 1906–

Educator, diplomat, and writer, Vaičiulaitis stands among the best Lithuanian prose stylists. He is able to register barely perceptible nuances of feeling and to control complex, brooding mental processes in a language which is lucid, elegant and appears deceptively simple on the surface. A gentle lyrical touch, an eye for miniature patterns in nature and in human experience, are blended with a quiet, refined sense of irony and humor. His main novel, "Valentina," 1936, portrays the unfulfilled love of two fragile souls under a dreamy summer sky filled with dark forebodings. "Noon at a Country Inn" contains a number of Vaičiulaitis' best short stories, in which human foibles are depicted with loving wit, and human tragedy with restrained candor.

Noon at a Country Inn. Trans. by Albinas Baranauskas. *Manyland* 1965 $3.95

BARONAS, ALOYZAS. 1917–

One of the most prolific Lithuanian prose writers in exile, Baronas has written eight novels and two collections of short stories. His frequent theme is the paradoxical predicament of humanity, possessing exalted religious and moral values and traditions, yet unable to stop its recurrent paroxysms of self-destruction, or even to take meaningful action in the small dilemmas of everyday life. "Footbridges and Abyssess" describes the day-to-day existence of a slave laborer forced to dig trenches for the retreating German army amidst fantastic cruelty and stupidity which mocks both hope and despair.

Footbridges and Abysses. Trans. by J. Žemkalnis. *Manyland* 1966 $5.00

The Third Woman. Trans. by Nola M. Zobarskas. *Manyland* 1968 $5.00. Love, conscience, and exile in a triangular intrigue of marriage and romance.

LANDSBERGIS, ALGIRDAS. 1924–

Landsbergis began writing in exile, in Germany. His novel *"Kelione"* (The Journey, 1954) "not so much reflects as refracts the realities of wartime existence as a slave laborer in Germany, passing them through the prism of a young man's consciousness"—(*Encyclopedia Lituanica*) which is itself shattered by the loss of home and by the traumatic realization that the entire edifice of civilized Europe is crumbling before his eyes. *"Vejas Gluosniuose"* (Wind in the Willows, 1958), a mystery play, turns to a legend about Saint Casimir, the patron saint of Lithuania, who was said to have inspired the Lithuanian troops to victory against the Russians by his miraculous appearance on a white horse. The play shows us the saint learning of further possibilities of human perfection from the language of the mortals, fragile and evanescent like their own souls. "Five Posts" is a soul-searing play about hopeless guerilla resistance imposing crushing burdens of grim heroics upon gentle, creative people for whom peace and freedom have become dreams beyond possibility.

Five Posts in a Market Place; A Play. *Manyland* 1968 $4.00

(With Clark Mills, Eds.) The Green Oak. *Voyages Press* 1962 1963 $5.00. Selected Lithuanian poetry, including folksongs (dainos), some of which are very old, and signed poems written since the early eighteenth century.

(Ed.) The Green Linden. *Voyages Press* 1963 $5.00. Selected Lithuanian folk songs.

—R.S.

NETHERLANDIC LITERATURE

Netherlandic literature consists of the writing from several geographic areas that have little more than their language in common. They include the kingdom of the Netherlands and the northern part of Belgium. In some former colonies certain social strata are involved. In earlier days there was also some literary activity in the Netherlandic language in the American settlement of New Amsterdam. In the course of time the language has of course undergone many changes. Much older writing can no longer be understood without some knowledge of linguistic developments. There are also marked regional distinctions in usage, vocabulary, and pronunciation. But the basic linguistic structure is everywhere the same and except for a word here or there all Netherlandic writing is intelligible throughout its range. As this implies, South African writing is not usually considered as forming part of Netherlandic literature. Afrikaans has evolved out of seventeenth-century Netherlandic but over the centuries has come to deviate drastically from the mother tongue.

Netherlandic belongs to the West Germanic family of languages. In keeping with the geographic position of the Low Countries it takes up a position about halfway between German and English. The vocabulary resembles that of German while the grammar is more like that of English. But the literature is in spirit not really close to that either of Germany or of England. Ever since the Middle Ages historical circumstance has tended to link the Netherlands culturally to the Latin sphere. The great lasting impact of the Renaissance strengthened this trend. Throughout most of its history Netherlandic literature has in substance been oriented toward France.

In religion the Netherlands did not follow the lead of the Roman Catholic countries of southern Europe. Since the turn of the seventeenth century most of the Dutch have been protestants while the Flemish were catholics. This distinction has been of some importance in the literary development of the respective regions. From the turn of the seventeenth till the middle of the nineteenth century there existed a corresponding economic difference. Holland thrived on its far-flung business enterprises after it gained independence from Spain. Flanders remained in the Hapsburg realm and languished until Belgium emerged as an autonomous state. But in both areas civilization has almost from the beginning been middle-class oriented. There was an absence of courtly pomp and circumstance to stimulate aristocratic art forms. The characteristic businesslike tone of public life in the Low Countries stimulated down-to-earth realism.

This orientation made the novel the genre of preference. More than any other literary form, it permits close observation and description of things and people. The novel also allows for digressions. This suited the didactic character of the Netherlandic people, who seldom miss an opportunity to deliver a lecture or sermon. A widespread tendency toward pietistic introspection found its literary counterpart in a fascination with the workings of the human mind. This interest culminated in the psychological novel that has flourished ever since the middle of the nineteenth century. But while the epic genre appealed to the ethnic character of the Netherlandic authors, the drama was not congenial to their creative stance. Only during the seventeenth-century "Golden Age" were plays of significance and merit written in Netherlandic.

Although at first sight it may not seem to fit in with the rather sober nature of the people, poetry has through the centuries played an important part in Netherlandic writing. The scenery and the age-old battle against the sea had the effect of stressing man's dependence on the elements. This awareness of an essential unity with the universe constitutes a genuinely lyric impulse. The language itself is abundantly capable of the subtle nuances that lend effectiveness to verse. In this genre the synthesis of Latin-oriented style and vision with a Germanic linguistic medium has resulted in highly original and valuable work.

The history of Netherlandic literature follows broadly the phases and movements of western European writing generally. The earliest preserved texts are from the second half of the twelfth century. They are obviously the products of a well-established tradition. With one or two exceptions the subjects are derived from French or Latin sources. In the case of the thirteenth-century animal epic "Reynard the Fox," this borrowed topic was sublimated into a creatively autonomous text. Most of the usual medieval genres are represented: saint's lives, pre-courtly and courtly or Arthurian tales, mystic and didactic texts. In the Renaissance era literary activity was centered in the Chambers of Rhetoricians which promoted a manneristic style. Much of the humanistic writing was of course cosmopolitan in nature and couched in Latin. The Dutchman Desiderius Erasmus represented this movement at its finest.

In the first half of the seventeenth century Netherlandic literature reached its peak. National independence had just been won by the northern part of the Low Countries and Holland was an oasis of peace, prosperity, and culture in a Europe racked by war. But although the South had at this time begun its long period of decline, the Flemish continued to play a part in Netherlandic writing. In fact the parents of dramatist Joost van den Vondel, the greatest figure of this "Golden Age," hailed from the city of Antwerp. In this period writers worked closely together with scholars who in the spirit of humanism studied and interpreted the poetics of antiquity. Both the theory and practice of literature exerted great influence on the developing literature in the vernacular that was emerging in Germany. This was virtually the only time when Netherlandic literature exerted influence on a European level.

After this period of unequaled flowering Netherlandic writing settled into a rut of complacency and provincialism that lasted for two and a half centuries. The dominant role of the middle class and its crass materialism are reflected in the unrelenting mediocrity of the literature. It was not until the end of the nineteenth century that the vicious circle of smugness and pedestrianism was broken. Characteristically, it was the developments in France that triggered a renewal in Netherlandic literary life. It took the form of the "Movement of 'Eighty," which as of the year 1880 introduced a new spirit of artistry and sophistication into Netherlandic literature. But promising though this fresh start was, the impulse was not strong enough to bring about a lasting change in literary atmosphere.

The decisive breakthrough did not come until around the time of the First World War. At this time a new reform movement started—again with a renewal of lyric writing. It led to the low-key verism of the thirties, which is a monument to the staunch anti-fascism of the Dutch intellectuals. But Netherlandic literature came close to total obliteration as Hitler launched his campaign of conquest. Essayist Menno ter Braak committed suicide as the Germans invaded Holland in May 1940. It was the only remaining way in which he could register his protest against the spirit of barbarity that was engulfing European civilization. Novelist Eduard du Perron on the same day died of a heart attack in a German bombing raid. Lyric poet Hendrik Marsman tried to escape the country and the advancing German army but the ship on which he tried to make his way to England was sunk in the Channel and he died. These three had been the leaders of Netherlandic literature in the period between the two world wars.

Their deaths meant that Netherlandic writing after 1945 had to start from scratch. In the following phase on the whole the important western European currents were echoed across the full range from existentialism to eroticism. But right through the sixties there was a peculiar morbidness of theme and tone that had its roots in the traumatic wartime experiences of the leading authors. One of the most interesting developments was the emergence of a very strong Flemish novel. In the first decade after World War II Dutch novelist Simon Vestdijk had dominated the field. Since then, however, Flemish authors like Louis Paul Boon have established their supremacy. But outstanding though some of their works are, on the whole Netherlandic literature is most interesting for its past achievements as a vital link in Western European writing.

The amount of Netherlandic literature in English translation is relatively small, and the amount of material available from American publishers smaller still. Therefore, we have included in the list below a number of works (in print) published in English in the Netherlands or in Great Britain. Books published in the Netherlands may be ordered through W. S. Heinman, 1966 Broadway, New York, N.Y. 10023. British books, indicated by (London) or another British place-name after the name of the publisher, may be ordered from the British Book Centre, 153 East 78 Street, New York, N.Y. 10021.

Background

There are a number of older works about aspects of the civilization and history of the Low Countries, both by English-speaking authors such as J. L. Motley ("The Rise of the Dutch

Republic." 1900. *AMS Press* 6 vols. each $17.50) and native scholars like Pieter Geyl ("The Revolt of the Netherlands" *Benn* London), G. J. Renier ("The Dutch Nation: An Historical Study," *o.p.*), and Johan Huizinga ("The Waning of the Middle Ages: A Study of the Forms of Life, Thought and Art in France and the Netherlands in the XIVth and XVth Centuries" *St. Martin's* 1924 $12.95; *Doubleday* pap. $2.50). A more recent work is the following brief but useful essayistic survey: "The Pillars of Society: Six Centuries of Civilization in the Netherlands" by William Z. Shetter *James H. Heineman* 1971 pap. $7.50. Other relevant works are: "Dutch Society" by Johan Goudsblom *Random* 1967 pap. $2.95; *Peter Smith* $4.25, and "The Dutch Republic and the Civilization of the Seventeenth Century" by Charles Wilson *McGraw-Hill* 1968 pap. $2.45.

Literary Studies

ESSAYS ON DRAMA AND THEATRE. LIBER AMICORUM BENJAMIN HUNNINGHER. *Moussault/ Standaard* (Netherlands) 1973. Studies presented to Dr. B. Hunningher on the occasion of his retirement from the chair of drama and theater arts at the University of Amsterdam.

Fens, Kees. TWENTY YEARS OF DUTCH LITERATURE. Some Trends and Central Figures. *Ministry of Cultural Affairs, Recreation and Social Welfare* (address: Steenvoordelaan No. 370, Ryswyk, Netherlands) gratis. A small brochure.

Meijer, Reinder P. LITERATURE OF THE LOW COUNTRIES: A Short History of Dutch Literature in the Netherlands and Belgium. *Twayne* (Van Gorcum) 1971 $15.00. The best available literary history of Netherlandic literature from its beginnings to the modern era.

Romein-Verschoor, Anna H. M. SILT AND SKY: Men and Movements in Modern Dutch Literature. 1950. *Kennikat* 1969 $6.00

Twayne Publishers, a division of G. K. Hall & Co. (Boston), publishes a continuing series of monographs about leading literary figures from all parts of the globe. So far, eight volumes have appeared in the Netherlandic section of *Twayne*'s World Authors Series. These concise monographs deal with the life and work of the authors concerned with special consideration of their importance in an international context. Each volume also contains a chronological table and a selected bibliography.

DESIDERIUS ERASMUS. By J. Kelley Sowards. World Authors Ser. *Twayne* 1975 $7.95

FRANÇOIS HEMSTERHUIS. By Heinz Moenkemeyer. World Authors Ser. *Twayne* 1975 $9.95

JEAN LECLERC. By Samuel A. Golden. World Authors Ser. *Twayne* 1972 $6.95

MACROPEDIUS. By Thomas W. Best. World Authors Ser. *Twayne* 1972 $6.95

MULTATULI. By Peter King. World Authors Ser. *Twayne* 1972 $6.95

JACQUES PERK. By Rene Breugelmans. World Authors Ser. *Twayne* 1974 $8.50

BENEDICT DE SPINOZA. By Henry E. Allison. World Authors Ser. *Twayne* 1975 $8.50

HENRIK VAN VELDEKE. By John R. Sinnema. World Authors Ser. *Twayne* 1972 $6.95

Collections

Angoff, Charles, Ed. STORIES FROM THE *Literary Review. Fairleigh Dickinson Univ. Press* 1969 $8.00. Prose by A. Albers, translated by A. Brotherton; prose by Styn Streuvels, translated by Flemish novelist Marniz Gijsen.

FROM THE GREEN ANTILLES. Introd. by Barbara Howes. 1966 *Panther Bks.* (London); pap. *Souvenir Press* (London). Works by four Netherlandic authors from the West Indies.

Holmes, James S., Trans. A QUARTER CENTURY OF POETRY FROM BELGIUM. Introd. by Eugene van Itterbeek. *A. Manteau* (Netherlands) 1970. Netherlandic originals and English translations of texts by almost 50 poets from the post-World War II era.

King, Peter K., Trans. DAWN POETRY IN THE NETHERLANDS. *Polak and van Gennep* (Netherlands) 1971. Netherlandic texts and English translations of poetry on the day-break theme from the Middle Ages to the twentieth century.

Koningsberger, Hans, Trans. and ed. MODERN DUTCH POETRY. *Netherlands Information Service* o.p. Selections from the works of 36 twentieth-century poets, edited and translated by an established American author of Dutch origin.

Krispyn, Egbert, Ed. MODERN STORIES FROM HOLLAND AND FLANDERS: An Anthology. *Twayne* 1973 $8.50. Short prose by leading writers from the fifties and sixties, rendered into English by various translators.

Mallinson, Vernon, Trans. and ed. MODERN BELGIAN LITERATURE (1830–1960). *Heinemann* (London) 1967. Anthology of prose from the time when Belgium became an independent kingdom until its present period of literary prominence.

Murphy, Henry C., Ed. ANTHOLOGY OF NEW NETHERLAND, or Translations from the Early Dutch Poets of New York with Memoirs of Their Lives. 1865. *Friedman* $6.00; *Kennikat* $6.00; *Mss Information Corp.* $14.95; *Somerset Pubs.* $9.50. Annotated edition of memoirs and poems by Jacob Steendam, Henricus Selyns, and Nicasius de Sillè, who during the seventeenth century lived and worked in New Amsterdam.

Rich, Adrienne, Ed. NECESSITIES OF LIFE: Poems 1962–1965. *Norton* 1966 $4.50 pap. $1.95. A bilingual collection of works by a half dozen of this century's leading poets, several of whom had died before the period indicated in the title.

Wolf, Manfred, Trans. CHANGE OF SCENE: Contemporary Dutch and Flemish Poems in English Translation. *Twowindows Press* (dist. by Serendipity) 1969 pap. $2.50. A small but good selection of texts by a baker's dozen of poets who made their name in the fifties.

THE SHAPE OF HOUSES: Women's Voices from Holland and Flanders. *Twowindows Press* (dist. by Serendipity) 1974 pap. $3.50. Texts by five women poets.

(Trans. and ed.) TEN FLEMISH POEMS. *Twowindows Press* (dist. by Serendipity) 1972 pap. $2.25. A slender volume containing work by five poets.

REYNARD THE FOX.   12th century.

The well-known main actors in the collection of stories known as the Reynard cycle are a clever, smooth-talking, unprincipled fox, and his constant adversary, a stupid, coarse-mannered, equally unprincipled wolf, named Ysengrim. The tales appear to have originated in the Netherlands, where they became the vehicle for lively comic scenes and sharp satires of the Church and the Court. Their influence has been world-wide, and parallel versions of the tales may be found in the literature of nations far removed from the Low Countries. There are many other versions of the Reynard cycle than those listed below. Perhaps the most brilliant of them all is the Latin poem "Ysengrimus" by Nivardus of Ghent, whose keen-witted verse has been translated into Dutch and German, but not yet into English.

THE HISTORY OF REYNARD THE FOX. Trans. from the Dutch by William Caxton (1422–1491). Ed. by N. F. Blake. Early English Text Society *Oxford* 1970 $9.75; ed. by A. Arber 1878 *Richard West* $20.00. The first of these is an illustrated edition of the text, which became an English classic in hands of its translator and publisher, the man who brought the art of printing to England.

REYNARD THE FOX AND OTHER MEDIEVAL NETHERLANDS SECULAR LITERATURE. Ed. and introd. by E. Colledge; trans. by Adriaan J. Barnouw and E. Colledge. *Sijthoff* (Netherlands) Bibliotheca Neerlandica 1 $8.75. Aside from the famous beast epic this volume contains "The Fight with the Dragon: The King of Faerie's Castle" from *"Walewein,"* as well as "Charles and Elegast," "Lancelot of Denmark," and the farce "Say That Again."

ERASMUS, DESIDERIUS.   1469–1536.   *See Chapter 4, World Religions*, Reader's Adviser, *Vol. 3.*

EVERYMAN. c. 1475.

The Dutch version of this famous mystery play is called *"Elckerlyc."* According to the most recent scholarship, this is the original text from which were derived the English "Everyman" (ed. by A. C. Cawley *Harper* (Barnes & Noble) 1970 pap. $3.25), the German *"Jedermann"* and the Latin *"Homulus," "Hecastus."* The play vividly dramatizes an allegory of man's need for salvation when faced with death. Salvation comes not from money, friends, or family, but from good deeds and the Church. The play is still often performed, with great effect.

THE MIRROR OF SALVATION: A Moral Play for Everyman. Trans. by Adriaan J. Barnouw. *Martinus Nijhoff* (Netherlands) Bibliotheca Neerlandica 2 1971.

REVIUS, JACOBUS. 1586–1658.

This strongly Calvinist poet is noted for his synthesis of the traditions of popular Netherlandic poetry with the forms and conventions developed in Renaissance Italy.

SELECTED POEMS. Trans. with introd. by Henrietta ten Harmsel. *Wayne State Univ. Press* 1968 $8.95

SPINOZA, BARUCH (or BENEDICTUS DE). 1632–1677. *See Chapter 5, Philosophy, Reader's Adviser, Vol. 3.*

MULTATULI (pseud. of Eduard Douwes Dekker). 1820–1887.

Multatuli is the most important Netherlandic novelist of the nineteenth century. His best-known work is "Max Havelaar," which was based upon his experiences as a government official in the Dutch East Indies. In it, he lambasts the colonial regime for its alleged exploitation and maltreatment of the native population. The book's documentary value is open to question, but in literary and esthetic terms it was far ahead of its time.

MAX HAVELAAR, or The Coffee Auctions of the Dutch Trading Company. 1860. Trans. and ed. by Roy Edwards. *British Bk. Centre* 1967 $10.00

THE OYSTER AND THE EAGLE: Selected Aphorisms and Parables. Trans. and ed. with annotations and introd. by E. M. Beekman. *Univ. of Mass. Press* 1974 $8.00. A collection of some of Multatuli's minor writings.

Books about Multatuli

Multatuli. By Peter King. World Authors Ser. *Twayne* 1972 $6.95

GEZELLE, GUIDO. 1830–1899.

The great original talent of this poet–priest re-established Flemish literature in the second half of the nineteenth century.

POEMS/GEDICHTEN. Trans. by Christine d'Haen. Pref. by Bernard Kemp. *Colebrant* (Netherlands) bilingual ed. 1972.

EMANTS, MARCELLUS. 1848–1923.

Emants' "A Posthumous Confession" is the first-person account of a social misfit who murders his wife. In spite of Emants' awkward style it created a sensation when it appeared in 1894. To the author's dismay, the public tended to identify him with the protagonist.

A POSTHUMOUS CONFESSION. Trans. by J. M. Coetzee. Lib. of Netherlandic Lit., *Twayne* 1975 price not set

EEDEN, FREDERIK VAN. 1860–1932.

In his turn-of-the-century novel about a woman's sexual urges, the author's handling of the topics of erotic passion, drug abuse, and prostitution reveals his training as a psychiatrist.

THE DEEPS OF DELIVERANCE. Trans. by Margaret Robinson. Lib. of Netherlandic Lit. *Twayne* 1975 $8.95

ELSSCHOT, WILLEM. 1882–1960.

Elsschot was a Flemish advertising agent who wrote in his spare time. The two novels "Soft Soap" and "The Leg" (of the twenties and thirties) are hard-bitten, cynical accounts of the seamier side of business life. The third text in the volume listed below, "Will-o'the-Wisp," is a novella rather than a novel. It evokes the melancholy mood of a rainy evening in Antwerp as experienced by some foreign sailors.

THREE NOVELS. Trans. by A. Brotherton. *British Bk. Centre* 1965 $5.95

BORDEWIJK, FERDINAND.   1884–1965.

The major work of this unorthodox novelist, "Character," appeared in 1938; it deals with the psychological interdependence of father and son and the tragic conflicts that result.

CHARACTER. Trans. by E. M. Prince. *Dufour* Council of Europe Bks. 1966 $6.75

CLAES, ERNEST.   1885–1968.

"Whitey," which first appeared in 1920, is the author's best work. It is a largely autobiographical novel of Claes's boyhood in the Flemish countryside.

WHITEY. 1920. Trans. by Charles Dowsett. *Oxford* 1970 $2.00

TIMMERMANS, FELIX.   1886–1947.

Timmermans' writings were both voluminous and various, although uneven. He dominated Flemish prose in the early years of this century. His book about St. Francis is a romanticized hagiography.

THE PERFECT JOY OF ST. FRANCIS. 1932. Trans. by Raphael Brown. 1952. *Doubleday* 1974 pap. $1.95

OSTAIJEN, PAUL VAN.   1896–1928.

Ostaijen was a Flemish avant-garde writer who led the expressionist movement in Flemish literature. He wrote not only stories, but also poems and criticism.

PATRIOTISM, INC. AND OTHER TALES. Trans. and ed. by E. M. Beekman. *Univ. of Mass. Press* 1971 $9.50 pap. $4.00

VESTDIJK, SIMON.   1898–1971.

Vestdijk has the distinction of having tried his hand, with respectable results, at nearly every genre of literature. He published 50 novels, 7 volumes of short stories, 22 volumes of poetry, and 33 collections of essays and critical prose. Furthermore, he distinguished himself as a translator of American and British writers into Dutch.

RUM ISLAND. 1940. Trans. by B. K. Bowes. 1963 *Calder & Boyars* (London) 1966

GARDEN WHERE THE BRASS BAND PLAYED. 1950. Trans. by A. Brotherton. 1965 *British Bk. Centre* $6.75

WALSCHAP, GERARD.   1898–

This novelist, born in Flanders, has always been a highly controversial writer, not least because of his strong social-critical impulse. "The Man Who Meant Well" concerns man's yearning for justice.

THE MAN WHO MEANT WELL. 1936. Trans. by Adrienne Dixon. *Panther Bks.* (London) 1975

MARRIAGE and ORDEAL. *British Bk. Centre* 1963 $6.25

GIJSEN, MARNIX (pseud. of J. A. Goris).   1899–

"Lament for Agnes" is a slight tale of youthful love ending in the girl's sickness and death, set in Belgium during the First World War and the years thereafter. Autobiographical elements mingle with allusions to the Orpheus and Eurydice myth.

LAMENT FOR AGNES. 1951. Trans. by W. James-Gerth. Lib. of Netherlandic Lit. *Twayne* 1975 $6.95

ACHTERBERG, GERRIT.   1905–1962.

Gerrit is an important poet whose often difficult verse from the thirties, forties, and fifties reflects a morbid fascination with death.

A TOURIST DOES GOLGOTHA AND OTHER POEMS. Selected, trans. and explicated by Stan Wiersma. *Being Publications* (P.O. Box 1269, Grand Rapids, Mich. 49501) 1972

BLAMAN, ANNA (pseud. of Johanna P. Vrugt).   1906–1960.

The pessimistic views on life, love, and death of this prize-winning author in some respects anticipated the wave of literary eroticism of the late sixties.

A MATTER OF LIFE AND DEATH. 1954. Trans. by Adrienne Dixon. Lib. of Netherlandic Lit. *Twayne* 1974 $7.95

COHEN, ELIE A. 1909–

This survivor of a Nazi death camp put his experiences into a soul-searching memoir. The excellent English version is by a top translator.

THE ABYSS: A Confession. Trans. with introd. by James Brockway. *Norton* 1973 $5.95

BOON, LOUIS PAUL. 1912–

Boon is the foremost Flemish novelist of the post-World War II period. A major theme of his significant, structurally complex work, "Chapel Road," is the rise and fall of socialism in Flanders. Boon is considered a candidate for the Nobel Prize for Literature.

CHAPEL ROAD. Trans. by Adrienne Dixon. Lib. of Netherlandic Lit. *Twayne* 1972 $7.95; *Hippocrene Bks.* 1972 pap. $3.95

MORRIËN, ADRIAAN. 1912–

Morriën is one of the more prominent figures in the early post-World War II years.

THE USE OF A WALL-MIRROR. Trans. by Ria Leigh-Loohuizen. *Twowindows Press* (dist. by Serendipity) 1970 pap. $2.85

CARMIGGELT, SIMON. 1913–

Carmiggelt is a writer of short, whimsical pieces about contemporary daily life in Holland. The pieces in the collections listed below first appeared in the daily press.

A DUTCHMAN'S SLIGHT ADVENTURES. Trans. by Elizabeth Willems-Treeman. *De Arbeiderspers* (Netherlands) 1966 (price available upon request)

I'M JUST KIDDING: More of a Dutchman's Slight Adventures. Trans. by Elizabeth Willems-Treeman. *De Arbeiderspers* (Netherlands) 1972 (price available upon request)

LAMPO, HUBERT. 1920–

Lampo's novel, "The Coming of Joachim Stiller," first published in 1958–1959, is an interesting variation on the Christ theme. The author is the major Flemish exponent of "magic realism."

THE COMING OF JOACHIM STILLER. Trans. by Marga Emlyn-Jones. Lib. of Netherlandic Lit. *Twayne* 1974 $7.95

WOLKERS, JAN. 1925–

Especially through the film version of "Turkish Delight" Wolkers has received much publicity and critical attention. He is a very typical representative of the explicit eroticism of the sixties, but there are also subtle and compassionate tones in his work that set it apart from the run-of-the-mill literary titillations.

A ROSE OF FLESH. Trans. by John Scott. *Braziller* 1963 $4.50

THE HORRIBLE TANGO. Trans. by R. R. Symonds. (1970, o.p.)

TURKISH DELIGHT. Trans. by Greta Kilburn. *Delacorte* 1974 1976 $6.95

CAMPERT, REMCO. 1929–

Campert is one of the leading figures in the post-World War II experimental movement in poetry.

IN THE YEAR OF THE STRIKE: Poems. Trans. by John Scott and Graham Martin. *Swallow* 1969 $4.95

CLAUS, HUGO. 1929–

This versatile Flemish author has published novels, stories, and poetry, as well as a dozen stage and screenplays. He has also made a name as a translator of Dylan Thomas, and as a film and stage director. The original version of his play "Friday" appeared in 1969.

FRIDAY. 1969. Trans. by the author and Christopher Logue. *Broadwick House/Davis-Poynter* (London) A Davis-Poynter Playscript 1972

SISTER OF EARTH. Trans. by George Libaire. (1966, o.p.). One of Claus's major novels.

FRANK, ANNE. 1929–1945.

Anne Frank was a Jewish girl who, during the German occupation of Holland (from 1940 to 1945), hid from the Gestapo in a back room of an old house in Amsterdam. She and her family were eventually discovered by the Germans. Anne Frank died in a concentration camp. Her diary has become a widely known classic of modern literature.

THE DIARY. Trans. by M. M. Doubleday-Mooyaart; introd. by Eleanor Roosevelt. *Doubleday* 1967 $7.95; *Random* Modern Lib. $3.95; *Simon & Schuster* (Washington Square) 1972 pap. $1.50

THE DIARY. Dramatized by Frances Goodrich and Albert Hackett. Ed. by Michael Marland. *Random* 1956 $5.50

TALES FROM THE HOUSE BEHIND. Trans. by H. H. B. Mosberg and Michael Mok. Ill. by Peter Spier. *Pan Bks.* (London) A Piccolo Book 1971

Books about Anne Frank

A Tribute to Anne Frank. Ed. by Anna G. Steenmeijer in collaboration with Otto Frank and Henri van Praag. *Doubleday* 1971 $8.95

RUYSLINCK, WARD (pseud. of R. K. M. de Belser). 1929–

The title of this author's first novel, "The Deadbeats," sums up the theme. His fifth novel, "Golden Ophelia," deals with the fate of the sensitive outsider in our mechanized society.

THE DEADBEATS. 1957. Trans. by R. B. Powell. Council of Europe Translations *Peter Owen* (London) 1968 $3.00

GOLDEN OPHELIA. 1966. Trans. by David Smith. *Peter Owen* (London) 1975

GEERAERTS, JEF. 1930–

In "Gangrene," a Belgian official looks back on his experiences in the former Congo colony. The book wallows in decay and putrefaction and pays extensive tribute to the protagonist's amazing virility. Critical opinion on the English edition has been sharply divided.

GANGRENE. Trans. by Jon Swan. *Viking* Richard Seaver Bks. 1975 $7.95

HEERESMA, HEERE. 1932–

Heeresma is a prolific and versatile Dutch writer. "A Day at the Beach" is one of his best stories.

A DAY AT THE BEACH. 1962. Trans. by James Brockway. *London Magazine Editions* (London) No. 10 1967

INSINGEL, MARK. 1935–

This author's "Reflections," first published in 1968, is an extremely "experimental" novel, without recognizable narrative.

REFLECTIONS: A Novel. Trans. by Adrienne Dixon. *Red Dust* 1972 $4.75

CREMER, JAN. 1940–

Cremer is the author of a controversial, shocking best-seller of the sixties.

I JAN CREMER. Trans. by R. E. Wijngaard and Alexander Trocchi. *Panther Bks.* (London) 1968 pap. $1.00

JAN CREMER 2. Trans. by Jon Lubius. *Panther Bks.* (London) 1970 pap. $1.00

—E.K.

POLISH LITERATURE

Polish literature, while largely unknown in the English-speaking world, has been both rich and artistically vital. Highly responsive to European literary trends, it has been profoundly affected by specific Polish developments.

The initial development of Polish literature was largely determined by the adoption of Catholicism as the official religion of the newly created medieval Polish state (tenth century). As elsewhere in Western Europe, Latin, used in the liturgy and religious literature, also served as the medium in which secular themes and ideas were expressed. During the period from the tenth through the fifteenth centuries, the dominant genres were those of religious literature (homiletic, hagiographic, etc.). Significantly enough, two of the most important early texts in the vernacular are collections of sermons ("*Kazania świętokrzyskie*" and "*Kazania gnieźnieńskie*").

Notwithstanding the paucity of vernacular texts, the end of the fifteenth century saw the creation of a rich, subtle, and adaptable Polish literary language which made possible the brilliant flowering of literature during the sixteenth century. In this period Poland's political, economic, and military strength, which made her a major power in Central Europe, created the climate for a vital Renaissance culture in which literature played a major part. The initial phase of that culture, commonly thought to span the years 1506–1543, includes the growth of literature and the rapid spread of printed works against the background of an interaction between the remnants of medieval thought and the new Renaissance humanism. The second, mature phase covers the years 1543–1584. Its glory is the work of Jan Kochanowski (1530–1584), the first great Polish poet, author of, among others, Latin elegies, a translation of the Psalter ("*Psalterz Dawidów*"), a collection of lyrical songs ("*Pieśni*"), a collection of short poems ("*Fraszki*"), and a cycle of laments devoted to the death of his daughter. Other notable writers of this period include the prolific poet and polemicist, Mikolaj Rej (1505–1569), the brilliant thinker Andrzej Frycz Modrzewski (1503–1572) (author of the Latin treatise "*Commentarii de Republica emendanda*," 1551–1554), the superb publicist of the Counter-Reformation Piotr Skarga (1536–1612) (author of the treatise "*Kazania sejmowe*," which was structured as a cycle of sermons, and others). The final phase of the Renaissance, which may be thought of as lasting until 1620, is already transitional: it is marked by a change from the optimistic, tolerant humanism of the sixteenth century to the pessimistic culture of the seventeenth century Baroque, troubled by both political uncertainties and religious conflict. Among the literary figures of this period we find Szymon Szymonowicz (1558–1629), the author of a superb collection of idylls, and Piotr Kochanowski (1566–1620), translator of Ariosto's "*Orlando Furioso*" and Tasso's "*Gerusalemme Liberata*" (the latter, published in 1618, was particularly influential).

The next major period in Polish literature and culture is the Baroque, thought to extend from 1620 to 1763. Still far from understood and properly evaluated, Baroque culture developed in an age of political and economic decline, of external threats and increasing internal anarchy. The decline of cities and of trade was accompanied by a turning inward on the part of large masses of the gentry (*szlachta*). The intellectual and cultural horizons of this group, educated largely in Jesuit schools, were quite narrow; the principal foreign elements that shape it are Ukrainian (a result of the Cossack wars) and Oriental (a product of successive wars with Turkey). The latter influence leads to the creation of a popularly based phenomenon termed the "Sarmatian Baroque," which coexists along with a more elevated tradition, based on Western models.

The Baroque period is noted for a flowering of lyrical poetry, which based itself on the principle "unity in multiplicity," and which sought to embody this idea by using unexpected rhetorical effects, rich imagery and "conceits" ("*concetti*") (the same style was known as "marinism" in Italy). Use of elaborate formal devices characterizes the work of such poets as Jan Andrzej Morsztyn (1613–1693) and Szymon Zimorowicz (d. 1629).

Another genre which comes into its own during this period is that of the historical epic. The many wars in which seventeenth-century Poland found itself constantly engaged provide ample materials. Thus, the Cossack rebellion of Chmielnicki is reflected in the "*Wojna domowa z Kozaki i Tatary*" (1681) of Samuel Twatdowski (1600–1661). Similarly, one of the wars with Turkey is described in the "*Wojna chocimska*" of Wacław Potocki (1621–1696).

Yet another genre of this period which we must mention is that of historical memoirs. Of its numerous practitioners, the most prominent is Jan Chryzostom Pasek (1630–1701) (*q.v.*).

The next major period in Polish literary history is that of the Enlightenment (1763–1818). Coinciding with the loss of Polish independence as a result of the third partition (1795), Enlightenment culture is characterized by energetic political, scientific, and cultural activity, and especially by the influence of the Encyclopedists and, later, the

French Revolution. The general emphasis on the dissemination of new ideas is relevant, in particular, in the development of a press on the European model. It is also manifested in the publicistic activities of such figures as Adam Naruszewicz (1733–1796), Stanisław Staszic (1755–1826), and Hugo Kollątaj (1750–1812). It is also seen in the establishment and development of public theater (1765), which is supported with material (mainly comedies) by such men as Franciszek Bohomolec (1720–1784) and Wojciech Bogusławski (1757–1829) (an actor, director, and prolific writer). As for the poetry of the Enlightenment, it is principally either sentimental lyrics, or satire and fable. The great practitioner of the latter two genres is Bishop Ignacy Krasicki (1735–1801) (q.v.).

Romanticism, which falls between 1818 and 1863, is shaped by the presence of common European political, intellectual, psychological, and literary conceptions, as well as by specifically Polish developments. Among the latter, the leading role attaches to the unsuccessful 1831 uprising and the resulting emigration of the political and artistic intelligentsia to Western Europe, especially to France. While the political aspirations of this numerous group were not realized, its members included leading literary figures who produced in the West (especially in Paris) a brilliant literature which had a profound impact not only in partitioned Poland, but elsewhere in Europe as well. A special contribution of Polish Romanticism to European thought was a conception of national messianism which proved particularly attractive during a period of continuous revolutionary ferment.

Poets are the giants of the Romantic period. The three principal figures are Adam Mickiewicz (1798–1855) (q.v.), Juliusz Słowacki (1809–1849), and Cyprian Norwid (1821–1883) (q.v.). They are the creators not only of lyric and epic poems, but also of dramas and treatises in which contemporary events and historical plots are frequently illuminated by a political and religious vision.

The Romantic period is also characterized by the activity of many other poets, playwrights, and writers. A major contributor to the theater is Zygmunt Krasiński (1812–1859) (q.v.). Mention must also be made of Józef Kraszewski (1812–1887), whose prolific activity created the historical novel.

As was already noted, the literary and political thought of the Romantic emigrés exercised great influence in Poland proper. This influence ended after 1863, in reaction to the failure of a major uprising in Russian-occupied Poland. The new intellectual current based itself on the philosophy of Comte and the English utilitarians: its proponents emphasized practical work in the economic and social spheres.

Positivism may be thought of as spanning the period 1863–1890. The term commonly designates the culture of this period as a whole; the literary manifestation of the new ideology is known as "critical realism." At the same time, the new tradition in literature cannot claim exclusivity; it coexists with numerous remnants of Romanticism.

Although the literature of the period includes a number of poets, it is dominated by prose which finds many of its themes in history, especially ancient history. Polish masters of the short story, novella, and novel, such as Eliza Orzeszkowa (1841–1910), Henryk Sienkiewicz (1846–1916), and Bolesław Prus (1847–1912), acquire reknown both in their own country and in Europe and the United States.

Positivist writers continue to flourish well into the second decade of the twentieth century. At the same time, the literary scene grows increasingly complex. From 1890 on, new currents are felt which lead to a rebirth of poetry and to the transformation of fiction and theater. The changes are carried out by the "Young Poland" ("Młoda Polska"). Like their contemporaries elsewhere in Europe, members of this literary generation rejected the concrete, program-oriented ideology of positivism and replaced it with a return to Romantic traditions, with a focus on the individual psyche and a wide-scale use of symbols. Among the most brilliant poets of "Young Poland" we find Kazimierz Tetmajer (1865–1940), who introduced into Polish lyric poetry pessimistic and sensual themes characteristic of the "decadence," and Jan Kasprowicz (1860–1926), who moved from the lyrical poetry of his youth to hymns dealing on a titanic scale with the problem of good and evil. Other remarkable poets are Leopold Staff (1878–1957) and Bolesław Leśmian (1878–1937) (*q.v.*). Another major figure of "Young Poland" is Stanisław Wyspiański (1869–1907), gifted visionary playwright and painter. Finally, the new trend is reflected in prose, especially in the writings of Stefan Żeromski (1864–1925) and Władysław Reymont (1867–1925) (*q.v.*).

The interwar period is a particularly diverse one in Polish literary history. Writers of earlier generations continue to be active; simultaneously, many other groups arise. Poetry once again plays a major role. The dominant group is that of the "Skamandrites," led by Julian Tuwim (1894–1953), whose experiments significantly enrich the repertoire of Polish poetry. Another significant group is the Cracow avant-garde, characteristically represented by Jan Przyboś (b. 1901).

Prose is also highly viable at this time. Among major writers we find Julian Kaden Bandrowski (1885–1944), Zofia Nałkowska (1884–1954), Maria Dąbrowska (1889–1965) (*q.v.*), Brunon Schultz (1892–1942) (*q.v.*) and Witold Gombrowicz (b. 1904) (*q.v.*).

The Nazi occupation brought with it a systematic destruction of the Polish literary intelligentsia. Notwithstanding this massacre, and the continuous peril of arrest and death, an active clandestine literature was created within the ranks of the resistance movement.

Postwar literature has found itself split into two streams, the domestic and the emigré. The former, as expected, has passed through stages roughly analogous to Soviet developments (Socialist Realism, Stalinism, the "thaw," de-Stalinization, etc.). The latter, created by refugees from the Nazi invasion and the postwar Polish state, continues to develop to this day. Its centers are found in Western Europe and the United States. Of its cultural organs, the Parisian monthly *Kultura* deserves special attention. The boundaries of the two camps, the domestic and the "foreign," have sometimes become quite blurred. Writers on both sides have changed their allegiance, and each side pays attention to the activities of its ideological and, in part, artistic competitor. Such a process of interaction provides some justification for regarding the two components not as inexorably fixed apart, but as individual stages of a potentially larger entity.

History and Criticism

Bird, Thomas E., Ed. QUEENS SLAVIC PAPERS: Modern Polish Writings, Vol. 1. *Queens College Press* Vol. 1 1973 pap. $4.00

Ehrlich, Victor, and others, Eds. FOR WIKTOR WEINTRAUB: Essays in Polish Literature, Language and History Presented on the Occasion of His 65th Birthday. *Humanities Press* (Mouton) 1975 $77.50. A distinguished collection of scholarly contributions on diverse topics.

Folejewski, Zbigniew, and others, Ed. STUDIES IN RUSSIAN AND POLISH LITERATURE IN HONOR OF WACLAW LEDNICKI. *Humanities Press* (Mouton) 1962 $19.25

Gömöri, George. POLISH AND HUNGARIAN POETRY, 1945–1956. Trans. by Ibsen. *Oxford* 1966 $7.20. Criticism.

Guergelewicz, Mieczyslaw. INTRODUCTION TO POLISH VERSIFICATION. *Univ. of Pennsylvania Press* 1970 $10.00. A useful introductory study.

Kridl, Manfred. A SURVEY OF POLISH LITERATURE AND CULTURE. Trans. by O. Scherer-Virski. *Columbia* 1956 $17.50. A discussion of Polish literature up to 1939 by a distinguished literary historian.

Krzyzanowski, Julian. POLISH ROMANTIC LITERATURE. 1931. Essay Index Reprint Ser. *Bks. for Libraries* facs. ed. $11.50. An eminent Polish scholar's fundamental examination of a major literary period.

Lednicki, Waclaw. RUSSIA, POLAND AND THE WEST: Essays in Literary and Cultural History. 1954. *Kennikat* $13.50. Erudite and provocative essays by a distinguished scholar.

Maciuszko, Jerzy J. POLISH SHORT STORY IN ENGLISH: A Guide and Critical Bibliography. *Wayne State Univ. Press* 1968 $17.50

Milosz, Czeslaw. HISTORY OF POLISH LITERATURE. *Macmillan* 1969 $14.95. An excellent survey by a distinguished poet and scholar, which covers Polish literature from its beginnings to 1965.

Scherer-Virski, Olga. THE MODERN POLISH SHORT STORY. *Humanities Press* (Mouton) 1955 $14.25

Collections

Coleman, Marion M. THE POLISH LAND. *Cherry Hill Bks.* rev. ed. 1974 pap. $5.00

Gillon, Adam, and Ludwik Krzyzanowski, Eds. INTRODUCTION TO MODERN POLISH LITERATURE: An Anthology of Fiction and Poetry. Various translators. *Twayne* 1963 $7.95

> "This is a volume to be welcomed ... To work one's way through it and through ... 'The Modern Polish Mind' [*see below*] means to possess a knowledge in depth of the Polish imagination in our time"—(*SR*).

Kuncewicz, Maria, Ed. THE MODERN POLISH MIND: An Anthology. *Grosset* Univ. Lib. 1963 pap. $2.95. An excellent collection of stories and essays by modern Polish writers.

Ordon, Edmund. TEN CONTEMPORARY POLISH STORIES. 1958. *Greenwood* 1974 $12.75

Peterkiewicz, Jerzy, and Burns Singer, Eds. FIVE CENTURIES OF POLISH POETRY. *Oxford* 2nd ed. 1970 $5.00. A good, representative selection.

Tyrmand, Leopold, Ed. EXPLORATIONS IN FREEDOM: Prose, Narrative, and Poetry from *Kultura*. *Macmillan* (Free Press) 1970 $8.95

PASEK, JAN CHRYZOSTOM. 1630–1701.

> Pasek was an adventurer, soldier, and politician. His many activities, typical of a man of his troubled times, provided him with a wealth of materials for his memoirs. Pasek's love and mastery of detail, displayed in a rich, witty, and racy colloquial language, have given his writings not only lasting artistic value, but have also made them a source of ideas and idiom for subsequent poets and writers (Słowacki, Sienkiewicz, and others).

MEMOIRS OF THE POLISH BAROQUE: The Writings of Jan Chryzostom Pasek. Trans. and ed. with introd. and notes by Catherine S. Leach. Fwd. by Wiktor Weintraub. *Univ. of California Press* 1976 $20.00

KRASICKI, IGNACY. 1735–1801.

> The best poet of the Enlightenment, Krasicki conbined literary activity with a brilliant ecclesiastical career. Scion of an impoverished aristocratic family, he became Bishop of Warmia and, towards the end of his life, Archbishop of Gniezno. A courtier and a lover of life, he was a typical representative of the Enlightenment culture. Krasicki's literary fame rests principally on satirical-humorous works. These include two mock-heroic epics. "The Mousiad" (*Myszeis*, 1775) and "Monachomachia, or the War of the Monks" (*Monachomachia albo wojna mnichów*, 1778). They also include two superb collections of poems, "Fables" (*Baśnie i przypowieści*, 1779) and "Satires" (*Satyry*, 1779).

Books about Krasicki

Ignacy Krasicki. By David Welsh. World Authors Ser. *Twayne* 1969 $6.95

FREDRO, ALEXANDER. 1793–1876.

> Son of a rich landowner, Fredro participated in the 1812 French campaign against Russia as aide-de-camp to Napoleon. Subsequently, disillusioned with the Emperor, he departs from the contemporary Romantic tradition by consistently debunking the Napoleonic myth. A prolific comedy writer with a Classicist outlook, he spent most of his life quietly on his estate. His most productive period was from 1821 to 1835. In his plays, which have become a fixture of Polish theater, he exhibits a keen interest in and sensitivity to human beings. "Maidens' Vows" (*Śluby*

panieńskie) and "Vengeance" (*Zemsta*) are among his most amusing works. In another, "Mr. Jowialski" (*Pan Jowialski*), Fredro created a memorable figure of a teller of fables and proverbs.

THE MAJOR COMEDIES OF ALEXANDER FREDRO. Trans. by Harold B. Segel. Columbia Slavic Studies Ser. *Princeton Univ. Press* 1969 $14.50

MICKIEWICZ, ADAM BERNARD. 1798–1855.

Mickiewicz was born in Lithuania in the family of a landless lawyer. He received a solid classical education at Wilno University, then the best in Poland. Arrested in 1823 for suspected revolutionary activities, he was exiled to Russia in 1825. His four and a half years there were a period of poetical and social success: he became a friend of Pushkin and a welcome figure in aristocratic salons. In 1829, Mickiewicz left Russia. During the 1831 uprising, he appeared briefly in Prussian Poland and subsequently joined the Great Emigration in Paris, where he was viewed as a spiritual leader of the exiles. In 1840, he assumed the newly created chair of Slavic literatures at the Collège de France, which he held until 1844. During the early forties, Mickiewicz became a follower of the Lithuanian mystic Towiański, a move which finished him as a poet and made him unpopular with most of his fellow exiles. After the outbreak of the Crimean War, his anti-Russian activities brought the poet to Turkey, where he died in late 1855. His remains were transferred to a crypt in Wawel Castle in Cracow in 1890.

Although his education in classical literature left a perceptible trace on his poetic diction, Mickiewicz was both the initiator of the Romantic movement and one of its great figures. His literary position was established in 1822 with the publication of a short but striking anthology of poems. His subsequent ballads and historical poems were even finer; however, he reached special heights in his dramatic cycle "Forefathers' Eve" (*Dziady*, 1823). Mickiewicz's Russian period is distinguished by the creation of sonnets (especially the "Crimean Sonnets" cycle) and of the poem "Konrad Wallenrod" (1826–1827).

A period of relative poetic sterility which began after "Konrad Wallenrod" ended in 1832, when Mickiewicz published his "Books of the Polish Nation" (*Księgi narodu i pielgrzymstwa polskiego*), a work in Biblical prose which aspired to be the gospel of the emigrés, and which is the clearest expression of Polish national messianism. In 1832 Mickiewicz also wrote "Forefathers' Eve, Part III," which he loosely connected with the earlier dramatic cycle, and in which he considered Poland's relationship with Russia through the prism of an intense personal vision.

Mickiewicz's last masterpiece is *"Pan Tadeusz"* (1834). This work, which continues the traditions of the epic, to a degree represents a turning away on the poet's part from Romanticism. The poem deals with life in Lithuania in 1811 to 1812. A large number of characters, all of whom are basically good, and a wealth of lovingly described details of nature and the country society, combine to make *"Pan Tadeusz"* an extraordinary, if idealized, canvas of gentry life.

POEMS. Ed. by George R. Noyes. Various translators. *Polish Institute of Arts and Sciences in America* 1944 $2.50

KONRAD WALLENROD AND OTHER WRITINGS. Trans. by Parish and others, ed. by George R. Noyes. 1925. *Greenwood* 1975 lib. bdg. $12.25

PAN TADEUSZ. 1834. Trans. by Watson Kirkconnell. 1962. *Polish Institute of Arts and Sciences in America* 1968 $6.50

Books about Mickiewicz

Adam Mickiewicz: The National Poet of Poland. By Monica M. Gardner. 1911. Eastern Europe Collection Ser. *Arno* 1970 $13.50

Adam Mickiewicz: Poet of Poland: A Symposium. Ed. by Manfred Kridl. 1951. *Greenwood* $13.00

The Poetry of Adam Mickiewicz. By Wiktor Weintraub. *Humanities Press* (Mouton) 1954 $16.00. An excellent, readable survey by an eminent scholar.

Literature as Prophecy: Scholarship and Martinist Poetics in Mickiewicz's Parisian Lectures. By Wiktor Weintraub. *Humanities Press* (Mouton) 1959 $6.50

Adam Mickiewicz. By David Welsh. World Authors Ser. *Twayne* 1966 $6.95

KRASIŃSKI, ZYGMUNT. 1812–1859.

Until World War One, Krasiński was considered, together with Mickiewicz and Slowacki, a national "poet-seer." At present his reputation has been significantly diminished, but he is rightly viewed as a major figure of the Romantic period. Son of a Napoleonic general and subsequent adherent of the Russian czar, Krasiński declined to pursue a career in St. Petersburg and went abroad, where his background enabled him to live the life of a great aristocrat. His best work, the poetic drama "The Undivine Comedy" (*Nieboska Komedia*, 1835) deals with the problem of a poet's moral responsibility in a social framework (an important Romantic dilemma) and with the problem of revolution. *"Iridion"* (*Irydion*, 1836), another poetic drama, is set in third-century A.D. Rome. On one level, the play's action centers on a major political struggle; on another, it deals with the problem of Christianity in the world.

IRIDION. 1836. Trans. by Florence Noyes; ed. by George R. Noyes. 1926. *Greenwood* 1975 lib. bdg. $14.25

Books about Krasiński

Zygmunt Krasiński, Romantic Universalist: An International Tribute. Ed. by Waclaw Lednicki. *Polish Institute of Arts and Sciences* 1964 $3.00

NORWID, CYPRIAN. 1821–1883.

Norwid's life was basically tragic; it was marked by exile (in Western Europe, and for some time in America), poverty, and a lack of recognition from his contemporaries. His work was "discovered" around the turn of the century; recent editions of his writings have brought out the depth of his literary achievement. His greatest work is the *"Vade-Mecum,"* a collection of poems which was completed in 1865, but which was first published as a unit in 1947. His "Letters" and "Twelve Poems" (in English translation) have appeared in the international poetic almanac *Botteghe Oscure*, XXII (1958).

Books about Norwid

Cyprian Norwid. By George Gömöri. World Authors Ser. *Twayne* 1974 $7.95

PRUS, BOLESŁAW (pseud. of Aleksander Głowacki). 1845–1912.

Prus was by profession an extremely productive and highly influential journalist, who won fame with his *Weekly Chronicles* (*Kroniki tygodniowe*), short pieces on diverse subjects. His work in fiction began with short stories, usually about the Warsaw poor. His first novel, "The Outpost" (*Placówka*, 1886), dealt with village life, focussing in particular on the mechanism of German settlement in Polish lands. In "The Doll" (*Lalka*), Prus creates an enormous, rich canvas of Warsaw life, into which he weaves the story of his hero Wokulski and his doomed passion for the aristocratic Isabella. His third major novel, "The Pharaoh" (*Faraon*, 1895–1896), is set in eleventh-century B.C. Egypt, and deals with the unsuccessful struggle of a young pharaoh against the dominant priestly class.

THE DOLL. 1890. Trans. by David Welsh. *Hippocrene Bks.* 1972 pap. $5.95; *Twayne* 1972 $9.50

SIENKIEWICZ, HENRYK. 1846–1916. (Nobel Prize 1905)

Far more celebrated than any of his Positivist contemporaries, Sienkiewicz began as a journalist and achieved considerable reknown with his account of a two-year journey to the United States. Between 1882 and 1888 he wrote three historical novels dealing with political and military events in seventeenth-century Poland: "With Fire and Sword" (*Ogniem i mieczem*, 1884), "The Deluge" (*Potop*, 1886), and "Pan Michael" (*Pan Wołodyjowski*, 1887–1888). In creating these works, Sienkiewicz spoke explicitly of his desire to "comfort the hearts" of his compatriots. Although superficial in its analysis of historical events, the trilogy gained enormous popularity both in Poland and in other Slavic countries thanks to Sienkiewicz's masterful use of epic techniques and of the seventeenth-century colloquial idiom. Even more popular, if artistically far weaker, was his *"Quo Vadis?"* (1896), a novel about Rome in the age of Nero (Sienkiewicz's fame in the West is chiefly based on this work). Another historical novel, "The Teutonic Knights" (*Krzyżacy*, 1900), deals with the fifteenth-century struggle between Poland-Lithuania and the Teutonic Order. Among his other works we must mention "The Połaniecki Family" (*Rodzina Połanieckich*, 1895), a work which extolled the virtues of philistinism and which was sharply attacked by the progressive intelligentsia.

TALES. Ed. by M. M. Gardner. *Dutton* Everyman's 1928 $2.25

WESTERN SEPTET: Seven Stories of the American West. Trans. by Marion M. Coleman. *Cherry Hill* 1973 pap. $5.00

HANIA. 1876. Trans. by Jeremiah Curtin. 1897. *Bks. for Libraries* 1973 $14.50

THE DELUGE. 1886. Trans. by Jeremiah Curtin. 1898. *AMS Press* 2 vols. set $19.00; *Scholarly Press* repr. of 1891 ed. 2 vols. set $19.00

PAN MICHAEL. 1887–1888. Trans. by Jeremiah Curtin. 1898. *Greenwood* 1968 $24.00

QUO VADIS? A Narrative of the Time of Nero. 1896. *Assoc. Booksellers* Airmont Bks. 1968 pap. $.95; trans. by C. J. Hogarth *Dutton* Everyman's 1941 1960 pap. $1.75; trans. by Jeremiah Curtin *Little* new ed. 1943 $6.95

Books about Sienkiewicz

Henryk Sienkiewicz. By Waclaw Lednicki. *Humanities Press* (Mouton) 1960 pap. text ed. $8.00. A very good survey.

Wanderers Twain: Exploratory Memoir on Helen Modjeska and Henryk Sienkiewicz. By Arthur P. and Marion M. Coleman. *Cherry Hill* 1964 $5.00

Henryk Sienkiewicz. By Mieczyslaw Giergielewicz. World Authors Ser. *Twayne* 1968 $6.95

REYMONT, WŁADYSŁAW STANISŁAW. 1867–1925. (Nobel Prize 1924)

Reymont's literary career was preceded by a variety of jobs. He began to write while working as a railroad switchman near the city of Lodz. His knowledge of this major textile center is reflected in the novel "The Promised Land" (*Ziemia obiecana*, 1899), in which he dissected the corruption of the city's industrial elite. Reymont's major accomplishment, which brought him the Nobel Prize, is the four-volume novel "The Peasants" (*Chłopi*, 1904–1909), in which he presents the life of a village community in epic terms.

Books about Reymont

Wladyslaw Stanislaw Reymont. By Jerzy Krzyzanowski. World Authors Ser. *Twayne* $6.95

LEŚMIAN, BOLESŁAW. 1878–1937.

Educated as a lawyer, Leśmian (pseudonym) initially wrote poems in Russian as well as Polish. A linguistic experimenter, he drew deeply on Polish and world folklore to create an exotic poetic world distinguished by sensuality, a focus on minute elements of nature, and a constant awareness of death.

Books about Leśmian

Bolesław Leśmian. The Poet and His Poetry. By Rochelle Stone. *Univ. of California Press* 1976 $15.96

WITKIEWICZ, STANISŁAW IGNACY (WITKACY). 1885–1939.

Son of an eminent Warsaw art critic, Witkiewicz went through traumatic experiences in Russia during World War I (he served in the Russian army) and the beginning of the Revolution. A prolific writer, he also painted and wrote papers on philosophy. His creative writings consist mainly of novels and dramas (at least 36, of which only 22 have survived). In his plays, Witkiewicz deals with profound social and philosophical problems in a way which makes him a forerunner of the "theater of the absurd."

THE MADMAN AND THE NUN AND OTHER PLAYS. Trans. by Daniel C. Gerould and C. S. Durer. *Univ. of Washington Press* 1968 deluxe ed. $12.50 pap. $4.95

TROPICAL MADNESS: Four Plays. Trans. by Daniel C. Gerould *Drama Bk. Specialists* 1973 $7.95 pap. $2.95

DĄBROWSKA, MARIA. 1892–1965.

Dąbrowska, who was educated in both the natural and social sciences, was highly dedicated to the cause of social and national progress. Author of a great many articles and some fiction, she made an artistic breakthrough in 1926 with a volume of stories about agricultural workers, who are presented as complex human beings, without condescension or sentimentality. Her major work is "Nights and Days" (*Noce i dnie*, 1932–1934), an epic narrative which, focussing on a gentry family, describes the progression and transformation of separate generations.

Books about Dąbrowska

Maria Dąbrowska. By Zbigniew Folejewski. World Authors Ser. *Twayne* 1967 $6.95

TUWIM, JULIAN. 1894–1953.

A Jew by birth, Tuwim was the major figure of the "Skamander" school and a leading poet of interwar Poland. A marvelous innovator of poetic language, he published not only numerous collections of poetry, but also several encyclopedic works on folklore. His best poem is "Ball at the Opera" (*Bal w operze*, 1936), in which he presents an apocalyptic vision of a dictatorship. His most ambitious work, "Polish Flowers" (*Kwiaty polskie*), was written mainly during World War II, in exile in Brazil and the United States.

THE DANCING SOCRATES AND OTHER POEMS. Int. Studies and Trans. Ser. *Twayne* 1971 $5.00

WIERZYŃSKI, KAZIMIERZ (CASIMIR). 1894–

Another of the "Skamander" poets, Wierzyński began with joyful, vigorous volumes of verse. Later he turned to public issues and his poetry became more serious and bitter. Subsequently he became a bard of the Piłsudzki regime. After the outbreak of the war, he left Poland and eventually settled in the United States, where he wrote his best poems. "The Life and Death of Chopin," first published in New York, became a best-seller and has been translated into many languages.

THE LIFE AND DEATH OF CHOPIN. 1949. *Simon & Schuster* Touchstone 1971 pap. $3.95

PARANDOWSKI, JAN. 1895–

Parandowski, whose literary career began in Lwow and continued in Warsaw, has been president of the Polish P.E.N. Club. A classicist by education, he has concentrated on ancient Greece and Rome in his fiction and essays. His first published novel, "King of Life" (*Król życia*, 1921), was about Oscar Wilde. His series on classical subjects, among which "The Olympic Discus" is particularly outstanding, is distinguished by an exquisite style which continues Roman, French, and Polish Renaissance traditions in prose. After the war, Parandowski achieved a great success with a prose translation of the "Odyssey."

THE OLYMPIC DISCUS. 1933. Trans. by A. M. Malecka and S. A. Walewski; introd. by George Harjan. *Ungar* $5.00 pap. $1.75

Books about Parandowski

Jan Parandowski. By George Harjan. World Authors Ser. *Twayne* $6.95

WITTLIN, JOZEF. 1896–

Wittlin's best-known work is "Salt of the Earth" (*Sól ziemi*, 1936). Its hero is a draftee into the Austrian army during World War I who goes through the war without understanding its causes or the mechanisms which control his fate. Originally intended as the first volume of a larger cycle, it has been translated into a number of languages. Wittlin currently lives in the United States.

Books about Wittlin

Joseph Wittlin. By Zoya Yurieff. World Authors Ser. *Twayne* $6.95

GOMBROWICZ, WITOLD. 1904–1969.

Gombrowicz, son of a wealthy lawyer, studied law at Warsaw University and philosophy and economics in Paris. His first novel, *"Ferdydurke"* (1937), with its treatment of existential themes and a daring use of surrealist techniques, became a literary sensation in Warsaw. "Yvonne, Princess of Burgundia" (1935), which anticipated many themes of the theater of the absurd, was also enormously successful; together with another of his plays, "The Marriage" (1953), it has been staged throughout the world.

During the war, Gombrowicz lived in Argentina. In the post-war period, *"Ferdydurke"* was at first banned by the Polish authorities (continuing a ban imposed by the Nazis). During the "thaw," it was published in Warsaw in 1957 and its author was hailed as the "greatest living Polish writer" by the critic Sandauer. The ban on Gombrowicz's works was reimposed in 1958. By this time, however, Gombrowicz had achieved a wide reputation in Western Europe and the United States. In the sixties, he settled in France.

YVONNE, PRINCESS OF BURGUNDIA. 1935. Trans. by K. G. Jones and C. Robbins. *Grove* Evergreen pap. $1.95

FERDYDURKE. 1937. Trans. by Erick Mosbacher. *Grove* Evergreen pap. $2.95

THE MARRIAGE. 1953. Trans. by Louis Iribarne. *Grove* Evergreen 1969 pap. $1.95

PORNOGRAFIA. 1960. Trans. from the French by Alastair Hamilton. *Grove* Evergreen 1967 pap. $2.45

COSMOS. 1965. Trans. by Eric Mosbacher. *Grove* Evergreen 1969 pap. $2.95. Won the International Literary Prize in 1965.

A KIND OF TESTAMENT. Trans. by Alastair Hamilton. *Temple Univ. Press* 1973 $7.00

LEC, STANISŁAW JERZY. 1909–1966.

Lec published his first book (poetry) in 1933, the year he received his law degree from the University of Lwow. His career as poet, satirist, and epigrammatist was only temporarily broken by the war, during which he served in the underground after escaping from a concentration camp. After the war he rose high in the ranks of Polish writers.

UNKEMPT THOUGHTS. 1959. Trans. by Jacek Galazka. *T. Y. Crowell* (Funk & Wagnalls) 1967 Minerva Bks. pap. $1.50

"This collection of his aphorisms, skillfully translated, reveals in addition to the sharp, tart, witty, insightful characteristics of the classical aphorism a chilling, piercing quality that reflects the harsh reality of his life"—*(LJ)*.

MORE UNKEMPT THOUGHTS. Trans. by Jacek Galazka. *T. Y. Crowell* (Funk & Wagnalls) 1968 $.95

MIŁOSZ, CZESŁAW. 1911–

Born in Lithuania, Miłosz published his first volume of poetry in 1933. His next, "Three Winters" (*Trzy zimy*, 1936), expressed very strongly the "catastrophic" themes current among a number of poets. During the war, he continued his literary activities underground, In 1951, he emigrated from Poland. Miłosz is the author of several prose works, one of which, the well-known study "The Captive Mind" (1953), analyzes East European intellectuals' relationship to Stalinism. He presently teaches at the University of California at Berkeley.

SELECTED POEMS. Various translators. Introd. by Kenneth Rexroth. *Seabury Press* Continuum 1973 $5.95

"His poetry . . . has a subtlety and a profundity that come from an intensely humane literary sensibility, a remarkable understanding of the complexity of the human mind and its speech and a breadth of experience unusual in contemporary writers"—(Rexroth).

DYGAT, STANISŁAW. 1914–

Dygat began to publish before 1939. During the war, he was interned for a time in a German concentration camp near Bodensee, an experience which provided him with material for a subsequent antiheroic novel (1946). Among his other novels, "Journey" (*Podróż*, 1958), and "Disneyland" (1965), have been particularly successful.

CLOAK OF ILLUSION. Trans. by David Welsh *M.I.T. Press* 1970 $12.95

HERLING, GUSTAW (Herling-Grudziński). 1919–

Herling (Herling-Grudziński) became known as a literary critic shortly before 1939. During the war, he was imprisoned for a time in a labor camp in the north of Russia. After the war, he lived in England and finally settled in Naples. "A World Apart" is an excellent work on Stalinist camps. A collection of his short stories has appeared in English under the title "The Island" (1967).

A WORLD APART. 1951. Trans. by Joseph Marek. *Greenwood* 1951 1974 lib. bdg. $12.75

TYRMAND, LEOPOLD. 1920–

Tyrmand is one of the leading figures in Poland's recent literary renaissance. He was a student at the Academie des Beaux Arts in Paris when the war broke out, and after the Germans captured the city he was deported back to Poland. In 1944, he escaped to Norway, and during the remainder of the war he worked with the Norwegian underground and Red Cross. He returned to Warsaw in 1946 and became a journalist, writing novels and short stories as well.

KULTURA ESSAYS. *Macmillan* Free Press 1970 $9.95

ROSA LUXEMBERG CONTRACEPTIVES COOPERATIVE: A Primer of Communist Civilization. *Macmillan* 1972 $5.95

(Ed.) EXPLORATIONS IN FREEDOM: Prose, Narrative and Poetry from *Kultura*. *Macmillan* (Free Press) 1970 $8.95

LEM, STANISŁAW. 1921–

Lem is not only Poland's best science fiction writer, but he has also acquired a solid world reputation. A medical graduate of Cracow University, he is at home both in the sciences and in philosophy, and this broad erudition gives his writings genuine depth. He has published extensively, not only fiction, but also theoretical studies. A trend towards increasingly serious philosophical speculation is found in his later works, such as "Solaris" (1961) (made into an excellent Soviet film).

THE CYBERIAD: Fables for the Cybernetic Age. Trans. by Michael Kandel. *Seabury Press* Continuum $8.95

THE FUTUROLOGICAL CONGRESS. Trans. by Michael Kandel. *Seabury Press* Continuum 1974 $6.95

THE INVESTIGATION. *Seabury Press* Continuum 1974 $7.95

THE INVINCIBLE. *Seabury Press* Continuum $6.95; trans. from the German by Wendayne Ackerman *Ace Bks.* pap. $1.25

MEMOIRS FOUND IN A BATHTUB. Trans. by Michael Kandel and Christine Rose. *Seabury Press* Continuum 1973 $6.95

SOLARIS. *Berkley Pub.* 1971 pap. $.75

RÓŻEWICZ, TADEUSZ. 1921–

A soldier in the underground Home Army during the Nazi occupation, Różewicz began to publish immediately after 1945. His first volumes of poetry, "Anxiety" (1947) and "The Red Glove" (1948), made wide use of war material and deliberately sought to destory literary conventions. In focusing on man as essentially alone in the universe, the poet approached the conceptions of the French existentialists. After 1956, Różewicz turned his attention to the stage, writing plays which basically belong to the theater of the absurd.

THE CARD INDEX AND OTHER PLAYS. Trans. by Adam Czerniawski. *Grove* 1970 pap. $1.95. Includes The Interrupted Act and Gone Out.

BIAŁOSZEWSKI, MIRON. 1922–

Białoszewski's first volume of poems, "Turns of Things" (*Obroty rzeczy*), appeared in 1956. Deliberately provocative in its use of grotesque imagery, it has a considerable impact. His next book, "Erroneous Emotions" (*Mylne wzruszenia*, 1961), was radically antipoetic in its choice and use of words and sounds.

THE REVOLUTION OF THINGS. Trans. by Bogdan Czaykowski and Andrzej Busza. *Charioteer Press* 1974 $5.00

BOROWSKI, TADEUSZ. 1922–1951.

Borowski finished his secondary schooling in the underground school system of occupied Warsaw and then began to study at the underground Warsaw University. He published a mimeographed volume of poems in 1942. Subsequently, he was arrested by the Gestapo and sent to Auschwitz. After liberation (from another camp—Dachau), Borowski wrote a series of powerful and grotesque short stories about Auschwitz. Although initially he reacted with skepticism to Marxist ideology, he later became a convert and an ardent champion of socialist realism. A combination of personal and ideological factors apparently led to his suicide in 1951.

THIS WAY FOR THE GAS, LADIES AND GENTLEMEN. *Penguin* 1976 pap. $2.95

MROZEK, SLAWOMIR. 1930–

Mrozek's plays are well known in Eastern Europe, and "Tango" has been performed throughout the world. It is the story of an intellectual who wants to reform his own family but falls prey to his ruthless brother, who establishes a dictatorship. The work of a playwright who is "unquestionably the leading Polish dramatist ... 'Tango' is lively enough and witty enough to command attention in any circumstances, but, apart from its intrinsic attractiveness, it must also be seen as a parable of modern history and belongs to Mrozek's continuing war against power's savage parody of logic. [In theme and technique] Mrozek best embodies the present spirit of the Polish theatre"— (*Tulane Drama Review*). "Tango" was recently performed in St. Paul, Minn., by the Minnesota Theater Company. Clive Barnes said (in the *N.Y. Times*), "The play is as full of faults as a piece of Swiss cheese is of holes. But ... it sends one out into the street upon a whirl of speculation, and during its course it stings your wits into laughter."

"The Elephant" (trans. by Konrad Syrop *Grove* 1963 $3.95 Black Cat Bks. pap. $.95), is a collection of savage and satiric short stories. "They are all fantastic, yet they reflect, bitterly and wittily, the realities of life behind the Iron Curtain"—(*Times*, London). He "has employed the techniques of Orwell and Kafka to present contemporary man as terrified and ludicrous. Mrozek's brief fables are grotesque, scathing comments on the new bureaucrats of the People's Democracies." It must be pointed out that these are the comments of Westerners; Mrozek is still performed in Poland, where "Tango" had its sensational first showing in Warsaw in 1966. Mrozek now lives and works, however, in Genoa, Italy.

SIX PLAYS. Trans. by Nicholas Bethell. *Grove* Evergreen Bks. 1967 $2.45. Includes The Police, The Martyrdom of Peter Ohey, Out at Sea, Charlie, The Party, Enchanted Night.

THREE PLAYS. Trans. by Teresa Dzieduszycka, Lola Gruenthal, and Ralph Manheim *Grove* 1973 $6.95 Evergreen Bks. pap. $2.45. Includes Striptease, Repeat Performance, and The Prophets.

THE ELEPHANT. Trans. by Konrad Syrop 1963. *Greenwood* lib. bdg. $10.75

TANGO. Trans. by Ralph Manheim and Teresa Dzieduszycka. *Grove* Evergreen Bks. 1969 pap. $1.95. A play.

VATZLAV. Trans. by Ralph Manheim. *Grove* Evergreen Bks. 1970 pap. $1.95

HLASKO, MAREK.   1934–1969.

> Hlasko began his literary career as a correspondent among workers. His first stories were published in 1955 in literary periodicals; their publication as a single collection under the title "First Step in the Clouds" (*Pierwszy krok w chmurach,* 1956) met with a very favorable reception. He followed up his success with a novella, "The Eighth Day of the Week" (1956, U.S. 1958, o.p.). While Hlasko's popularity grew during the Polish "thaw," he faced increasing difficulties with the authorities, and defected to the West in 1958. In emigration, his portrayal of life under communism grew harsher; the publication of "The Graveyard" increased the Polish authorities' hostility towards him. He died in Wiesbaden, Germany, at the age of 35.

THE GRAVEYARD. 1958. Trans. by Norbert Guterman. 1959 *Greenwood* 1975 lib. bdg. $9.25

—H. B.

PORTUGUESE LITERATURE

When nearly 50 years of censorship by an outwardly prudish, ultra-rightist government ended with the "Carnation Revolution" of April 25, 1974, the presses and bookstores of Portugal experienced a new awakening of publication and trade. Hitherto forbidden works, by nationals and foreigners alike, of political, social, religious, and moral import were openly advertised, displayed, purchased, and read throughout the country.

The Salazar-Caetano era was highly allergic to all writing that challenged the Portuguese status quo. Two books were, if not responsible for, at least significantly concomitant with the downfall of the old regime. General António de Spínola's *"Portugal e o futuro"* (Portugal and the Future) expressed a war hero's perception of the futility of further colonial war and advocated a loose federation of Portuguese-speaking countries in which Portugal would become an African satellite (to Mozambique and Angola).

More literary and more renowned was the case of "The Three Marias: New Portuguese Letters" by Maria Isabel Barreno, Maria Teresa Horta, and Maria Velho da Costa (*qq.v.*). Even though there is an erotic tradition dating back to the Middle Ages in Portuguese literature, the twentieth-century "guardians of morality" were offended when these women, in 1972, published a collection of mildly erotic letters, sketches, and verse in which they depicted and protested the plight of modern woman discovering herself in a male-dominated society. In the earliest Portuguese compositions, *cantigas de escárnio* and *cantigas de maldizer,* of the goliards and travelling bards (as well as in those of Dom Dinis, King of Portugal from 1279–1325, and of his father, Alphonse The Wise of León), the modern reader can find shockingly explicit sexuality, yet these poems, written by men, have found their way into courses in medieval literature and the national literary heritage.

Perhaps to avoid censorship, perhaps to drive home the fact that women in Portugal were as much men's captives in 1972 as in 1650, the "three Marias" modelled their work on a "Portuguese" classic of the seventeenth century, *"Lettres Portugaises,"* written in French, supposedly by Mariana Alcoforado, a nun in Beja, a work claimed as national patrimony by both France and Portugal.

While the women acknowledged joint authorship, individual entries in the book remained anonymous, hiding under variations of the ubiquitous feminine name, Maria.

Despite the reluctance of publishers, typesetters, and retailers to handle such material (a law had been passed which held all parties responsible for "offensive" literature published without prior government approval), *"Novas Cartas Portuguesas"* was published in the spring of 1972, but was confiscated a few days later—after nearly selling out. The authors were imprisoned, brought to trial in the fall of 1973, and acquitted on May 7, 1974 by a judge who had delayed sentencing and ended up praising the work and the authors' literary talents. (Some suggest that before April 25 the judge was well aware that political change was afoot, and he simply wanted to remain in favor with the new order.)

With their imprisonment, trial, and acquittal the authors have been victims, martyrs, and, finally, heroes of the feminist movement. Their book has been reprinted in Portugal and translated into French, English, Italian, Spanish, German, and Swedish. While "The Three Marias: New Portuguese Letters" has had mixed reviews in this country, the authors have become international celebrities and sought-after feminist speakers.

Atkinson, William C. HISTORY OF SPAIN AND PORTUGAL. *Penguin* Pelican Bks. pap. $1.95; *Gannon* $5.00

Bruce, Neil. PORTUGAL: The Last Empire. *Halsted Press* 1975 $8.95

Consigliere Pedroso, Zophimo. PORTUGUESE FOLK TALES. Trans. by Henriqueta Monteiro. 1882. *Blom* 1969 $8.50. A pleasing collection of fairy tales common to Europe but recorded in Portugal.

Cunhal, Alvaro. PORTUGAL: The Democratic and National Revolution. Trans. by Ted Slade. *Int. Pubs.* 1974 pap. $3.95

Feinstein, Alan S. FOLK TALES FROM PORTUGAL. *A. S. Barnes* 1972 $4.95

This is an "adequate collection . . . cover[ing] a variety of situations and a spectrum of human vices and virtues . . . comfortably pared . . . interest is sustained . . . enjoyable"—(*LJ*).

Livermore, H. V. NEW HISTORY OF PORTUGAL. *Cambridge* 1966 $14.50 pap. $4.95. Perhaps the best history of Portugal in any language.

Longland, Jean R., Trans. and ed. SELECTIONS FROM CONTEMPORARY PORTUGUESE POETRY. Fwd. by Ernesto Guerra Da Cal. *Harvey House Pubs.* (E. M. Hale & Co.) 1966 $4.89

Reviewers considered the 43 poems by 28 modern poets a good introduction to Portuguese poetry, "a quiet delight . . . faithfully translated . . . [and] finely designed"—(*LJ*). Its poetry is "well chosen and will appeal to both teenagers and adults"—(*Commonweal*).

Soares, Mário. PORTUGAL'S STRUGGLE FOR LIBERTY. Trans. by Mary Felton. *Int. Pubns. Service* 1975 $21.00

CAMÕES, LUIZ VAZ DE (also Luís de Camoëns).   1524–1580.

The most famous work of Portuguese literature at the time of the Renaissance, this epic treats the chief episodes of Portuguese history in *ottava rima*. Camões also wrote sonnets and comedies. He is notable for developing the Portuguese lyric to its highest point and for his influence on national drama. As a soldier (nicknamed "Swashbuckler") he led a picaresque life, dying in Lisbon of the plague.

THE LUSIADS. 1572. Trans. with introd. and notes by Leonard Bacon. *Hispanic Society* 1950 $4.50; trans. by W. C. Atkinson. *Penguin* 1952 1973 pap. $2.25

This "admirable translation . . . shed[s] new light on many obscure passages. [It was done] by a scholar deeply versed in Camonian criticism"—(*Bulletin of Hispanic Studies*).

THE LUSIADS. Trans. by Sir Richard Fanshawe, ed. with introd. by Geoffrey Bullough. *Southern Illinois Univ. Press.* Centaur Class. 1964 $19.50

Books about Camões

Luis de Camoëns and the Epic of the Lusiads. By Henry H. Hart. *Univ. of Oklahoma Press* 1962 $7.95. This book of research about the poet-soldier relates his story in detail, presents translations of his lyrics in a chronological arrangement, and includes descriptive information on the poet's era and the places where he spent his life; it is enjoyable as well as informative.

Camoëns and His Epic. By William Freitas. *California Institute of Intl. Studies* 1963 pap. $2.50

QUENTAL, ANTERO DE. 1842–1891.

The poet, of Azorian origin, was the high priest and mentor of the rebellious "Generation of 1870" which attacked the reigning romantics in the Coimbra Uproar and in the Democratic Speeches at the Lisbon Casino (*see Eça de Queiroz below*). His poetic creation spanned three decades and encompassed romanticism, socialism, rationalism, metaphysical pessimism, and mysticism.

SONNETS AND POEMS OF ANTERO DE QUENTAL. Trans. by Griswald Morley. 1922. *Univ. of California Press* 1973 $8.50

When Morley's translation first appeared in English it was hailed as "the best translation to date from this important Portuguese poet"—(*Nation*). Morley accomplished this by "not lapsing into the impossible, . . . [yet] retain[ing] the sonnet form"—(*New Statesman*).

EÇA DE QUEIROZ, JOSÉ MARIA (also Queirós). 1843–1900.

Eça de Queiroz is unquestionably Portugal's greatest novelist. He was a constant innovator in the Portuguese literary world of his day, beginning his career in the 1860s writing for newspapers and magazines. He participated in the realist-naturalist revolt against the romantics who were headed by the poet António Feliciano de Castilho and who dominated the era. The two main manifestations of this revolt were the "Coimbra Uproar" of 1865 (*A Questão Coimbrã*) and the Democratic Speeches at the Lisbon Casino in 1871.

With "The Sin of Father Amaro" Eça introduced realistic and naturalistic techniques into Portuguese fiction. This is a long, tedious novel about provincial life, pettiness, ignorance, and corrupt clergy. Much of its detail comes from Eça's experience as a low-level bureaucrat in Leiria, the locale of the novel. His second novel, "Cousin Bazílio," is "Madame Bovary" set in Lisbon. It is much quicker reading than "The Sin" and lends itself to dramatization. Of Eça's works in translation, "The Maias" follows in the realistic-naturalistic vein of Queirosian prose. It is Eça's greatest work, a final attempt to create a Portuguese "Human Comedy." It is an "undeniable masterpiece, a chronicle of the decay which [has] affected Portuguese society in [read "since"] the last quarter of the nineteenth century"—(*N.Y. Herald Tribune*). While critics have refered to the work of Eça de Queiroz in terms of social criticism and protest, he is, instead, an "imaginative, critical, and witty observer of people"—(Guerra Da Cal). Of course faithful portrayals of late nineteenth-century types were, in themselves, literary indictments of the society and of the times.

Another side of Eça de Queiroz appears in "The Mandarin," "The Relic," "The Illustrious House of Ramires," and "The City and the Mountains." All but the third have humor, fantasy, wit, social criticism, and didactic purpose in common. Eça, in his preface to "The Mandarin," maintains that fantasy is the true nature of the Iberian temperament. The first two books tell the reader that honesty, frankness, hard work, and courage are the keys to happiness and success. "The City and the Mountains" advocates a return of the educated upper class to the soil, to regenerate, in a paternalistic fashion, a national dynamic among the folk. The protagonist of "The Illustrious House of Ramires" ransoms his family's prestige through colonial enterprise. It must be remembered that the last two novels were written after the humiliating Ultimatum delivered by Great Britain in 1890, which forced Portugal to give up its claim to the central African territory between Angola and Mozambique.

THE SIN OF FATHER AMARO. 1876. Trans. by Nan Flanagan. 1963 o.p.

COUSIN BAZÍLIO. 1878. Trans. by Roy Campbell. 1954 o.p., (with title "The Dragon's Teeth" trans. by Mary J. Serrano) 1889. *Greenwood* 1972 $17.75

THE MANDARIN. 1880. Trans. by Richard Franko Goldman. *Ohio Univ. Press* 1965 $7.95. A novella and three short stories.

THE RELIC. 1886. Trans. by Aubrey Bell. 1930 o.p.

THE MAIAS. 1888. Trans. by Patricia McGowan Pinheiro and Ann Stevens *St. Martin's* 1965 $7.95

A "good translation"—(*N.Y. Herald Tribune*).

THE ILLUSTRIOUS HOUSE OF RAMIRES. 1897. Trans. by B. Head. *Ohio Univ. Press* 1968 $7.00

THE CITY AND THE MOUNTAINS. 1901. Trans. by Roy Campbell. *Ohio Univ. Press* 1967 $6.50

"Admirably translated"—(*New Republic*).

LETTERS FROM ENGLAND. Trans. by Ann Stevens. *Ohio Univ. Press* 1970 $7.00. This is a collection of Eça's correspondence with Brazilian and Portuguese newspapers during his stay in England as consul, 1874–1888.

RIBEIRO, AQUILINO.   1885–1963.

Ribeiro was an enemy of totalitarianism both under the monarchy (ending 1910) and under the Salazar government, from 1926 until the time of his death. He was imprisoned and exiled by both regimes. "When the Wolves Howl" (o.p.) is a novel which indicts the indifference and intransigence of the Salazar government concerning the plights of Portugal's rural poor. In the mountains of the Beira region a group of peasants resists the government but ends up in a patricidal conflict. The translation has been described as "serviceable but uneven."

PESSOA, FERNANDO.   1888–1935.

Pessoa is the poetic genius of twentieth-century Portugal. His creation is such that he is ranked among the world-wide greats of this century: Picasso, Stravinsky, Joyce, Braque, and Le Corbusier—(N.Y. Review of Books). He is unusual within the Portuguese context for having received a British education in Durban, South Africa where he excelled as a student and as a young English-language poet. He received the Queen Victoria Prize for his entrance exam at the University of Cape Town. Never graduating from a university (he enrolled at the University of Lisbon), he worked for various commercial concerns in Lisbon as a "foreign correspondent" until his death in 1935.

Pessoa's British education gave him direct access to poets normally ignored or only known in translation by the Portuguese literary community of the time: Milton, Byron, Shelley, Keats, Tennyson, and Wordsworth. These poets' influence is evident in much of his creation, e.g., "Ela Canta a Pobre Cefeira" inspired by Wordsworth's "The Solitary Reaper."

Pessoa is singular in the history of poetics for having written verse not only in terms of his own poetic outlook, but also in terms of the outlooks of fictitious poets he created. His heteronyms, not to be confused with pseudonyms, are Ricardo Reis, Alberto Caeiro, and Álvaro de Campos. Each poet has a separate life history, and each writes from a separate philosophical and aesthetic point of view.

SELECTED POEMS BY FERNANDO PESSOA. Trans. by Edwin Honig; introd. by Octavio Paz. *Swallow* 1971 $8.00. Includes poems by his heteronyms as well as some of his English sonnets and selections from his letters. This collection is valuable because it makes Pessoa's letters explaining his reasons for creating heteronymic poets available to English readers. The translations, both of the poetry and Paz's introduction (in Spanish), have been criticized as awkward.

SELECTED POEMS. Trans. by Peter Rickard. *Univ. of Texas Press* 1971 $4.75; pap. $2.25

This collection places undue emphasis on the heteronyms—perhaps because they are easier to translate. Nonetheless, it provides an "ideal first acquaintance with Pessoa, [since] the selection is broad and sensible [even though] Rickard . . . is . . . too cautious [and] Pessoa is made to sound more Victorian than he is"—(N.Y. Review of Books). In addition, the "prefatory study is a model of thoroughness and lucidity."

SIXTY PORTUGUESE POEMS. Trans. by F. E. G. Quintanilha. 1971. *Verry* 1973 $11.00

This collection is considered "informative rather than interpretive [but], of the three, the most faithful to Pessoa"—(Bulletin of Hispanic Studies).

NAMORA, FERNANDO.   1919–

FIELDS OF FATE. 1954. Trans. by Dorothy Ball. *Crown* 1970 $5.95

This novel, set in the Alentejo region of Portugal, portrays the rural Portuguese's relationship to the land, animals, and to fellow human beings. It has had mixed reviews: "[an] engrossing pastoral . . . of memorable beauty"—(N.Y. Times Book Review) which "failed to survive the choppy, awkward, British translation . . . [and] is barely readable"—(Book World). Alternately, *Library Journal* describes it as "an unpretentious delight . . . well served . . . by an always felicitous translation."

BARRENO, MARIA ISABEL, 1939– , MARIA TERESA HORTA, and MARIA VELHO DA COSTA.

THE THREE MARIAS: New Portuguese Letters. Trans. by Helen R. Lane. 1972. *Doubleday* 1975 $10.00

American reviewers have been divided in their opinions about "The Three Marias." Some have called the book "tedious" or "maddeningly imprecise, self indulgent." Others have praised it as an "extraordinary contribution to feminist literature." Clearly the volume touches upon a controversial subject, and prompts its readers to speak of feminism, Portugal, politics, and repression, rather than of the strictly literary merits of the work itself. One of the most valuable features of the

English version is Donald Ericson's translation of the original "Portuguese Letters," not included in the Portuguese edition *(for further comment see introduction, this Chapter, above)*.

—C.A.B.

RUMANIAN LITERATURE

Cultural life in Rumania was extremely lively, open, and cosmopolitan during the first four decades of this century, when Bucharest was nicknamed the "little Paris." Although Western influences were opposed by some intellectually traditionalist and politically conservative circles, the Rumanian intelligentsia was, by and large, so Westernized that it could participate quite naturally in all the significant Western European cultural movements. Sometimes Rumanians were even—and literally so—in the avant-garde: Brancusi, for instance, who started revolutionizing modern sculpture around 1910, or Tristan Tzara and Marcel Janco, who launched Dada in Zurich in 1916.

The interbellum certainly was one of the richest periods in the history of Rumanian literature. With poets as powerful and diverse as Tudor Arghezi, Lucian Blaga, Ion Barbu, Tristan Tzara, B. Fundoianu (Benjamin Fondane), Ilarie Voronca, and Ion Vinea or prose writers such as Liviu Rebreanu, Panait Istrati, Mihail Sadoveanu, Mircea Eliade, Camil Petrescu, and M. Blecher, Rumanian literature was not aesthetically inferior to any one of the major literatures of the West, in spite of the fact that, written in a minor language, it enjoyed little circulation outside the country. The Rumanians who chose to write in French (from Tzara during World War I to Eugène Ionesco and E. M. Cioran after World War II) have illustrated, in a congenial major language, some of the hidden potentialities of Rumanian literary genius.

After World War II, as a consequence of the Communist takeover, the writers who for one reason or another did not or could not emigrate had to choose between remaining silent or complying with the theoretical and practical requirements of "socialist realism," as these had been defined by the cultural censors of Stalinism. After Stalin's death in 1953 an utterly unpredictable rhythm of ideological freezes and thaws emerged. A more serious attempt at de-Stalinization started only in 1964, when Rumania embarked upon its maverick foreign policy within the Soviet bloc. The cautiously, half-heartedly liberalizing trend was apparently not destined to last long and ended abruptly in 1971, when the Rumanian Communists saw fit to promote what some Western observers have called a "mini-cultural revolution." The Chinese suggestions of this label are apt: they point to the fact that the Rumanian Communist Party opposes the "hegemony" of Moscow not from a liberal but, on the contrary, from an extreme leftist point of view.

During the years of "liberalization," a number of very interesting writers appeared. Ion Caraion, St. A. Doinas, I. Negoitescu, Alex Ivasiuc, and many others were forgiven their political sins and released from prison; they were given the right to publish. How free they actually were became evident a few years later when Paul Goma, also a former political prisoner, tried to publish an autobiographical novel. The censorship said no. In the meantime, however, Goma's manuscript had been smuggled out of the country, and the book finally appeared in German and French. Western European critics readily labeled Goma "the Rumanian Solzhenitsyn"; if he has not been forced out of the country like the author of "Gulag," this seems due to the fact that the authorities have been able to silence and isolate Goma completely.

In spite of many restrictions and difficulties, between 1964 and 1971—and in certain rare cases after that date—Rumanian literature has enriched itself with a number of solid and sometimes courageous works (with luck and ambiguity one could evade the censor) signed by poets such as Nichita Stanescu, Leonid Dimov, Marin Sorescu, Ion Alexandru, Ana Blandiana, Mircea Ivanescu or by fiction writers such as Nicolae Breban (whose last novel, however, was rejected by the censor), Marin Preda, St. Banulescu, Fanus Neagu, and Augustin Buzura. The overall picture of contemporary Rumanian literature would be not only incomplete but seriously distorted if the contribution of numerous émigré writers were not taken into account. Among these writers are Mircea Eliade, Vintila Horia, Petru Dumitriu, Virgil Ierunca and, more recently, D. Tsepeneag, Toma Pavel, Petru Popescu, to mention just a few names.

Byng, Lucy M., Trans. ROUMANIAN STORIES. 1921. Short Story Index Reprint Ser. *Bks. for Libraries* $11.75

MacGregor-Hastie, Roy, Trans. and ed. with introd. ANTHOLOGY OF CONTEMPORARY ROMANIAN POETRY. 1969 *Dufour* $7.95

This volume is part of the UNESCO Collection of Representative Works, European Series. It is the first anthology in English of contemporary Rumanian poetry and as such it is obviously useful. The editor and translator, however, "fails to distinguish between those poets who have made an important contribution to Rumanian literature and those who are little more than acolytes and imitators"—(*The Modern Language Journal*).

Manning, Olivia, Ed. ROMANIAN SHORT STORIES. *Oxford* World's Class. 1971 $5.50

Steinberg, Jacob, Ed. INTRODUCTION TO RUMANIAN LITERATURE. Fwd. by Demostene Botez, member of the Rumanian Academy. *Twayne* 1966 $7.95

"A collection of competent examples from a literature that deserves . . . to be better known among English-speaking readers"—(*SR*). This anthology contains only fiction. (Both the fiction and the editing are heavily colored by ideology.)

EMINESCU, MIHAIL. 1850–1889.

Rumanians regard Eminescu as their greatest poet. The richness and suggestive verbal power of his poetry have prompted some to compare him to Keats. His influence was so profound that Rumanian poetry and poetic diction have developed along lines that would have been impossible to predict on the basis of their traditions and achievements up to the mid-nineteenth century. "His use of archaisms, dialectal words, and neologisms, together with skillful metaphor, simile and alliteration, enhanced the expressive power of Rumanian and endowed it with a great richness, while the philosophical nature and profundity of his work gave Rumanian poetry a maturity it hitherto lacked"—("*Cassell's Encyclopaedia of World Literature*," 2nd ed., 1973). The complexity of Eminescu's stylistic imagination makes his poetry extremely hard to translate. Among the several attempts to translate Eminescu into English, the most notable one was the collection of Sylvia Pankhurst published in 1930, to which George Bernard Shaw contributed a preface. The new translations are superior at least insofar as they reflect the great changes in poetic taste that have occurred since the late 1920s, when Miss Pankhurst discovered Eminescu.

THE LAST ROMANTIC: Mihail Eminescu. English versions and introd. by Roy MacGregor-Hastie. *Univ. of Iowa Press* 1972 $7.50. Part of the European Series of the Translations Collection of UNESCO.

ARGHEZI, TUDOR. 1880–1967.

Arghezi is widely considered Rumania's most important poet after Eminescu. Influenced by French *Symbolisme*, Arghezi developed as a modernist but at the same time as a poet of tradition and ancestral continuity, reconciling in his work the most contradictory spiritual and aesthetic tendencies of his age. One of the great writers of this century, it was only after World War II that a series of more or less successful translations won him a belated recognition in the West. He has been translated into Italian by Nobel Prize winner Salvatore Quasimodo and into Spanish by Rafael Alberti and Pablo Neruda.

SELECTED POEMS. Trans. by Michael Impey and Brian Swann, introd. by Michael Impey. Lockert Lib. of Poetry in Translation *Princeton Univ. Press* 1976 $16.50 pap. $3.95. While some English translations of Arghezi have appeared in journals or anthologies, this is the first time the English-speaking public is offered a representative selection of his poetry in book form.

SADOVEANU, MIHAIL. 1880–1961.

Sadoveanu, who produced over 120 books, is generally considered to be Rumania's greatest prose writer. His fiction is being published for the first time in this country under a U.S.-Rumanian cultural exchange program. "Tales of War" was inspired by the War of Independence (1877) against Turkey. "Although this is a youthful work and some of the tales are scarcely more than anecdotes, it does constitute an authentic record of an heroic people fighting to liberate their country from the tyranny of Ottoman rule." In "Evening Tales" he writes "mostly of simple folk, of innkeepers and bailiffs, highwaymen and gypsies, fishermen and hunters, with the inevitable boyar or landowner supplying an element of conflict." In "The Mud-Hut Dwellers," "vivid descriptions of peasant life in 19th-century Rumania charm and captivate the reader. . . . The novel is an affirmation of man, of the joy and love which can be his in spite of his condition"—(*Choice*). His novel "The Hatchet" (1930), translated by E. Farca, is currently o.p.

TALES OF WAR. 1905. *Twayne* 1961 $3.95

THE MUD-HUT DWELLERS. 1912. *Twayne* 1964 $3.95

"The anonymous translator deserves gratitude for rendering the novella into smooth, idiomatic English"—(*SR*).

EVENING TALES. Trans. by E. Farca and others. *Twayne* 1962 $4.95

ISTRATI, PANAIT. 1884–1935.

Romain Rolland, who discovered and enthusiastically recommended Istrati's writings to the French, called him "a Balkan Gorki." Istrati wrote all his major works in French, translating them into Rumanian himself. "Kyra Kyralina" and "Bandits" belong to a cycle of novels in which Istrati "describes with the vividness of a wandering minstrel a primitive, oriental Rumania"—(*Encyclopedia of World Literature in the Twentieth Century*). "Russia Unveiled" is a translation of *La Russie nue*, Istrati's indictment of communism after a trip to Russia in 1927. Istrati had been a revolutionary and a sympathizer of the Soviet Union, but firsthand knowledge of the grim realities of Soviet life made him an outspoken opponent of communism. His disenchantment with the Soviet regime anticipates a similar reaction on the part of other interbellum revolutionary writers, including André Gide with his famous "Back from the USSR" (1937).

KYRA KYRALINA. 1924. Trans. from the French by James Whitall. 1926. Short Story Index Reprint Ser. *Bks. for Libraries* $10.00

BANDITS. 1925. Trans. from the French by William A. Drake. 1929. Short Story Index Reprint Ser. *Bks. for Libraries* $12.25

RUSSIA UNVEILED. 1929. Trans. from the French by R. J. Curtis. 1931. *Hyperion Press* $17.00

REBREANU, LIVIU. 1885–1944.

The eminent novelist, theater critic, playwright, and essayist Liviu Rebreanu was at the height of his influence in the years between the two World Wars. An innovator in Rumanian literature, he is remembered particularly for his portrayals of Rumanian villagers living under hardship, and for his treatment of war and revolution. He wrote many short stories before turning to longer fiction. Of the novels, "Ion," a vast panorama of Transylvanian village life before World War I, is a "landmark in the history of the Rumanian novel"—(*Cassell's Encyclopaedia of World Literature*). "The Forest of the Hanged," about that war, and "Uprising," about a peasants' revolt, are his two other important novels.

ION. 1920. Ed. by Ralph M. Aderman. *Dufour* 1965 $9.75; *Twayne* 1967 $6.95

UPRISING. 1932. *Dufour* 1964 $9.75

TZARA, TRISTAN. 1896–1963.

Tzara published his first Rumanian poems while he was a high-school student in Bucharest (1912). In 1915 he went to Switzerland, where a year later, together with a group of friends including Hans Arp, Hugo Ball, and his compatriot Marcel Janco, he established "what was to be the grandfather of all 20th century avant-garde movements: dadaism"—(*Encyclopedia of World Literature in the Twentieth Century*). From 1916 on, Tzara wrote exclusively in French but authorized publication of his earlier poetic manuscripts in various Rumanian avant-garde periodicals during the interbellum period. The first poems of Tristan Tzara were collected in 1934 by his Rumanian friend Sasa Pana; they were translated into French by Claude Sernet in 1965 and are now also available in English.

SELECTED POEMS. *Trigram Press* 1975 $10.50 pap. $6.00

APPROXIMATE MAN AND OTHER WRITINGS. Trans. from the French with introd. by Mary Ann Caws. *Wayne State Univ. Press* 1973 $11.75

FIRST POEMS. Trans. from the Rumanian by Michael Impey and Brian Swann; introd. by Michael Impey. *New Rivers Press* (dist. by Serendipity Bks.) 1976 pap. $1.25

Books about Tzara

Tristan Tzara: Dada and Surrational Theorist. By Elmer Peterson. *Rutgers Univ. Press* 1971 $9.00

STANCU, ZAHARIA. 1902–1974.

Stancu began his literary career as a poet. During the 1930s he was active as a journalist and edited such periodicals as *Azi* (*Today*) and *Lumea romaneasca* (*Rumanian World*). After the Second World War he published a cycle of novels which won him official recognition. He was president of the Rumanian Writers' Union from 1965 until his death.

BAREFOOT. *Twayne* 1968 $8.50

THE GYPSY TRIBE. *Abelard* 1973 $10.25

ELIADE, MIRCEA. 1907–

Born in Bucharest, Rumania, Mircea Eliade studied at the University of Bucharest and, from 1928 to 1932, at the University of Calcutta with Professor Surendranath Dasgupta. After taking his doctorate in 1933 with a dissertation on Yoga, he taught at the University of Bucharest and, after the war, at the Sorbonne in Paris. Eliade has been a professor of the history of religions at the University of Chicago since 1957. He is "by nearly unanimous consent the most influential student of religion in the world today"—(*N.Y. Times Book Review*). He is at the same time a writer of fiction, known and appreciated especially in Western Europe where several of his novels and volumes of short stories have appeared in French, German, Spanish, and Portuguese. "Two Tales of the Occult" is the first volume of Eliade's rich literary *oeuvre* to appear in English. The English-speaking reader can now discover the "other side" of this outstanding scholar and philosopher of religion. The two tales included in the recent volume try "to relate some yogic techniques, and particularly yogic folklore, to a series of events narrated in the genre of a mystery story." Both "Nights at Serampore" and "The Secret of Dr. Honigberger" evoke the mythical geography and time of India. Moreover, as the author himself confesses, in both novelettes a number of characters are real—"the Tibetan scholar, Johan van Manen, and the learned Islamicist, Lucian Bogdanoff . . . ; and, as for Swami Shivananda, I lived near him for six months of my stay in the Himalayan ashram at Rishi Kesh." Mythology, fantasy, and autobiography are skillfully combined in Eliade's tales.

TWO TALES OF THE OCCULT. Trans. by William Ames Coates. *McGraw-Hill* (Herder & Herder) 1970 currently o.p.

For Eliade's studies of mythology and religion see Chapter 4, World Religions, Reader's Adviser, Vol. 3.

CIORAN, EMILE M. 1911–   *See Chapter 5, Philosophy, Reader's Adviser, Vol. 3*

IONESCO, EUGENE. 1912–   *See Chapter 9, French Literature, this Volume.*

DUMITRIU, PETRU. 1924–

This author is the Rumanian novelist best known to Americans. Dumitriu's successful early literary career in Rumania included writing for magazines in Bucharest, winning the Rumanian State Prize for Literature three times, and serving as director of the State Publishing House. In 1960, however, he left Rumania to live in the West, escaping through East Berlin. "Meeting at the Last Judgment" (U.S. 1962, o.p.), based on his own experiences, presents a revealing picture of the fear-ridden lives of the Rumanian communist elite. "Incognito" "re-emphasizes the author's earlier theme: the awesome power with which the Communists are able to take over a country once the will of its people has been demoralized"—(*LJ*). Its sequel, "The Extreme Occident" (U.S. 1964, o.p.), shows "the whole of present-day Western Europe as one vast cesspool of aimlessness, desperation, and lost or corrupted values," said the *Saturday Review*, which criticized Dumitriu for his "tone of self-righteous lecturing" and for (in "The Extreme Occident") his "unblushing imitation of Dostoevsky." Dumitriu's books are alive with melodramatic cloak-and-dagger activities, as well as the ideological overtones noted above. Having fled the East to discover (perhaps with some literary exaggeration) that the West is not all he had imagined, he has generally encountered there either high praise ("fascinating," "brilliant") or censure ("heavy going," with dialogue "stilted and literary") for the same works. Dumitriu now lives in West Germany.

INCOGNITO. 1962. Trans. from the French by Norman Denny. 1964 *Melvin McCosh Bookseller* $8.50

—M.C.

UKRAINIAN LITERATURE

For our purposes here, Ukrainian literature is defined as literature written in the Ukrainian language and excluding writings in other languages on Ukrainian themes, or writings composed within the boundaries of the Ukrainian ethnic territory, but written in languages other than Ukrainian. Therefore, excluded from our list are works by such Soviet writers as Viktor Nekrasov (a Russian writing in Kiev) or Wanda Wasilewska (wife of the prominent Soviet Ukrainian playwright O. Kornijčuk) who wrote in Polish, or Mykola Hohol (Nikolai Gogol), V. G. Korolenko, and their eighteenth-century predecessors—I. Bohdanovyč, V. Kapnist, and V. Narižny.

Brief but excellent resumés of Ukrainian literary history are available in George S. N. Luckyj's article in the *Encyclopedia of World Literature in the Twentieth Century*, ed. by Wolfgang Bernard Fleischman (*Ungar* 1971 4 vols. $107.00), and in the "Penguin Companion to Literature," Vol. 2, ed. by Anthony Thorlby (*Penguin* rev. ed. 1971 pap. $4.95)—the latter article is by Victor Swoboda. See also Luckyj's essay on Ukrainian Literature in his edition of "Discordant Voices: The Non-Russian Soviet Literatures 1953–1973" (*Mosaic Press*, P.O.B. 1032, Oakville, Ontario. pap. $4.95). I have taken extensively from both of these essays. I am much indebted to Marta Tarnawsky (University of Pennsylvania Library), Svitlana Lutzky-Andrushkiv (New York Public Library), and Basil Nadraga (Library of Congress) for their assistance in preparing this essay.

The beginnings of Ukrainian literature might well be traced to the period of the Kievan Rus' (eleventh to thirteenth centuries). These early centuries witnessed the creation of a rich literature of *vitae*, chronicles, and epics. Some of the surviving momuments such as the great epic of the twelfth century, the "*Slovo o polku Ihorevě*" (The Tale of Ihor's Campaign, *q.v.*) and the important chronicle "Tale of Bygone Years" (*Pověst Vremennyx Lět*) are singular witnesses to the achievements of Kievan culture and have been much translated. Equally impressive are the *Dumy* or Cossack lyric-epic songs of the middle period of Ukrainian literature of the sixteenth and seventeenth centuries. It is indisputable, however, that modern Ukrainian literature in the vernacular is dated from the publication of the first portion of the "*Eneyida*" (1798) by Ivan Kotljarevs'kyj (1769–1838), a long syllabo-tonic verse travesty of Virgil. The important story, "Marusia," by Hryhorij Kvitka-Osnov"janenko (1777–1843), is o.p. (English translation, 1940).

Despite the many censorship restrictions imposed in the eighteenth and especially in the nineteenth century on the Ukrainian printed word (e.g., the Ems decree of 1876), Ukrainian literature manifested its strength in the writings of the poet Taras Ševčenko (1814–1861) and the Galician Ukrainian writer and scholar Ivan Franko (1856–1916). While the figures of Ševčenko, Franko, and P. Kuliš (1819–1897) have been studied to a significant degree in English and their works translated (with uneven degrees of skill), other important Ukrainian fiction writers and dramatists still await their translators.

Uneven too is our knowledge of the figures of the Modernist movement in Ukrainian literature of the early twentieth century. Thus, while figures such as the prose writers Kocjubyns'kyj and Stefanyk and the dramatist Lesja Ukrajinka have gained considerable notice in the West (Kocjubyns'kyj's story, "Tini zabutyx predkiv," 1913 serving as the basis of the highly acclaimed motion picture "Shadows of Forgotten Ancestors"), other members of this movement remain untranslated, or are available to the English-speaking reader only in brief extracts in anthologies.

The rich literature of the first decade of the Soviet Ukrainian literature, and especially the VAPLITE (National Communists) exemplified by Mykola Xvyl'ovyj (1893–1933), the novelist Valerian Pidmohyl'nyj (1901–1941), and the playwright Mykola Kuliš (1892–1942) have been extensively studied and translated by Professor George S. N. Luckyj (University of Toronto). Sadly, other writers are less well-known to Western audiences, although a reminiscence and critical study exists of the Neo-classicist poet, Myxaijlo Drai-

Xmara (1889–1935), written by his daughter, Oksana Asher ("A Ukrainian Poet in the Soviet Union," 1959, o.p.).

The period between 1928 and 1932 saw terrible purges sweep across the Ukraine, and led to the silencing, death, or intellectual reformation of many of the major figures of the Ukrainian literary renascence of the twenties. After the creation of the Ukrainian Writers' Union (1934), only socialist realism would serve as a permissible literary style. Several of the figures who best typify this school have been extensively translated into English by the Foreign Languages Publishing House in Moscow, as well as in the Ukraine. See, for example, the work of: Oleksandr Hončar (1918–   ; "Standard Bearers: A Novel," 1948, o.p.; "Short Stories," 1954, o.p.); Ivan Kočerha (1881–1952); Oleksandr Kornijcuk (1905–   ); Vadym Sobko (1912–   ); Volodymyr Sosjura (1898–1965; "Poems of the Soviet Ukraine," 1939, o.p.; "Ukrainian Poem," 1952, o.p.; "Love Ukraine," 1954, o.p.); and Myxaijlo Stel'max (1912–   ; "Guarantee of Peace", 1951, o.p.; "Let the Blood of Man Not Flow," 1957, o.p.).

Only with the death of Stalin were political conditions impinging upon Ukrainian literature sufficiently lightened to permit a rebirth in Ukrainian poetry and prose as represented by the Šestydesjatnyky ("People of the Sixties") and the new literature of dissent symbolized in literary criticism by Jevhen Sverstjuk (1928–   ).

After the establishment of Soviet rule in the eastern Ukraine, several centers of Ukrainian creative writing existed outside the borders of the Ukrainian RSR. In the western Ukraine (Galicia), which during the interwar period remained under Polish rule, a number of poets and prose writers were active. Other centers of the Ukrainian emigration were in Warsaw, Prague (Czechoslovakia), and, in the years after the Second World War, in the United States and Canada.

After the Second World War such individuals as Viktor Domontovyč, Dokija Humenna (1904–   ), and Vasyl' Barka (1908–   ), as well as the literati associated with the so-called New York Group—Bohdan Bojčuk, Bohdan Rubčak, Jurij Tarnavs'kyj, Emma Andijevs'ka, and Jevhenja Vasyl'kivs'ka—reached prominence within the Ukrainian community. There is no single bibliography covering all works in English translation, nor do the traditional concepts of "o.p." apply easily to Ukrainian translations of belle-lettristic works or the critical literature dealing with them. Works published in emigration, for example, were often inadequately advertised and distributed, and therefore it would be improper to consider older works still stockpiled in warehouses as o.p. Since this is but a *selected in print* list we have listed with few exceptions only separate (monographic or pamphlet-size) translations and criticism of Ukrainian belles lettres. Their number is rather small in proportion to those which appeared in serial publications (and more frequently in newspapers rather than periodicals) and chrestomathies. For example, a significant number of translations appeared in such serial publications as the *Ukrainian Weekly* (Jersey City, N.J.), the *Ukrainian Review* (London, 1954–   ), *International Literature* (1933–1945, continued as *Soviet Literature*, Moscow), the *Ukrainian Quarterly* (New York, 1944–   ), *Ukrainian Life* (Scranton, Pa., 1940–1942), as well as such publications as *Slavonic and East European Review* (London, 1922–   ), *Horizons* (New York, 1956–   ), *Ukrainian Canadian*, and *Svoboda*.

The number of individuals in the West who worked as translators of Ukrainian literature are relatively few. Here we might mention such pioneers of translations as Wladymyr Semenyna, Honoré Ewach (see his "Ukrainian Songs and Lyrics: A Short Anthology of Ukrainian Poetry," *Ukrainian Publishing Co.* c. 1933 o.p.). Ewach—in Ukrainian, Onufrij Ivakh (1900–1964)—was a prolific poet in his own right. Other translators include Stepan Shumeyko, Volodymyr Deržavyn (1899–1964), Clarence Manning, the prolific Florence Randal Livesay (1874–1954), a Canadian poetess, the Presbyterian minister Percival Cundy (1881–1949), Rev. Alexander Jardine Hunter (1868–1940), and Professor Watson Kirkconnell.

History and Criticism

Čyževs'kyj, Dmytro. A HISTORY OF UKRAINIAN LITERATURE: From the 11th to the End of the 19th Century. Trans. by Dolly Ferguson, Doreen Gorsline, and Ulana Petyk. Ed. with fwd. by George S. N. Luckyj. *Ukrainian Academic Press* 1975 $25.00. A revised and enlarged edition of the work published in Ukrainian in 1956. Sure to become a classic study. The author is one of the most distinguished of living Slavists.

Gudzii, Nikolai K. HISTORY OF EARLY RUSSIAN LITERATURE. Trans. from the 2nd Russian ed. by Susan Wilbur Jones. Introd. by Gleb Struve. 1949. *Octagon* 1970 $21.00. A text prepared by a distinguished Soviet Ukrainian scholar of the literature of Kievan Rus' (old Ukrainian literature of the eleventh to thirteenth centuries) and Muscovy. Contains much factual information on old Ukrainian literature of the eleventh to seventeenth centuries.

Luckyj, George S. N. BETWEEN GOGOL' AND ŠEVČENKO: Polarity in the Literary Ukraine, 1798–1847. Harvard Series in Ukrainian Studies *Adler's* 1971 $19.00; *Libraries Unlimited* 1972 $15.00. An important study of early nineteenth-century Ukrainian history and literature in the vernacular by the single most prolific Western scholar of Ukrainian literature.

LITERARY POLITICS IN THE SOVIET UKRAINE, 1917–1934. 1956. *Bks. for Libraries* $14.25. Deals with literary organizations, their histories and conflicts; revised from a doctoral dissertation at Columbia University, New York.

Mandryka, M. I. HISTORY OF UKRAINIAN LITERATURE IN CANADA. *Ukrainian Free Academy of Sciences*, Winnipeg (order from: Ukrainian Book Store, P.O. Box 1640, 10207 97 St., Edmonton, Alberta, Canada T5J 2N9) 1968 $7.50 pap. $6.00. A useful critical study by a prolific Canadian-American scholar and poet; with extensive bio-bibliographies.

Manning, Clarence A. UKRAINIAN LITERATURE: Studies of the Leading Authors. Fwd. by Watson Kirkconnell. 1944. *Bks. for Libraries* 1971 $9.50. A series of cameos of the major modern figures by a prolific American student and translator of Ukrainian literature.

Shabliovs'kyi, Jevhen Stepanovych. UKRAINIAN LITERATURE THROUGH THE AGES. Trans. by Abraham Mistetsky, Andrew Marko, and Anatole Bilenko; verses trans. by John Weir; ed. by Anatole Bilenko. *Mistetstvo* 1970 (order from: Ukrainian Book Store, P.O. Box 1640—10207 97 St., Edmonton, Alberta, Canada T5J 2N9) $3.75. A brief study by an important Soviet Ukrainian scholar of modern Ukrainian literature.

UKRAINE: A Concise Encyclopaedia. Prepared by Shevchenko Scientific Society. Ed. by Volodymyr Kubijovyč; fwd. by Ernest J. Simmons. *Univ. of Toronto Press* (published for the Ukrainian National Association) Vol. 1 1963 $45.00 Vol. 2 1971 $60.00 set $94.50. The best reference work available in English that deals exclusively with Ukrainian affairs. Chapter VIII, pp. 960–1097, contains an extensive section dealing with literature.

Collections

Andrusyshen, C. H., and Watson Kirkconnell, Trans. THE UKRAINIAN POETS, 1189–1962. *Univ. of Toronto Press* (published for the Ukrainian Canadian Committee) 1963 $12.50. The single best anthology of Ukrainian poetry from the twelfth century to the modern period; contains almost a hundred figures with critical introductions.

FOUR UKRAINIAN POETS: Drach, Korotych, Kostenko, Symonenko. Trans. by Martha Bohachevsky-Chomiak and Danylo S. Struk; ed. with introd. by George S. N. Luckyj. *Quixote* (dist. by Morningside Bks., New York) 1969 (address orders to Ukrainian Book Store, P.O. Box 1640—10207 97 St., Edmonton, Alberta, Canada T5J 2N9). Ivan Drač (1936–   ), Vitalii Korotyč (1936–   ), Lina Kostenko (1930–   ), and

Vasyl' Symonenko (1935–1963), together with Mykola Vinhranovsky (1936–   )
and others, were members of a group of poets known as the *Šestydesjatnyky* or poets of
the 1960s. They protested in voices fresh with new images and poetics.

Luchkovich, Michael, Ed. THEIR LAND: An Anthology of Ukrainian Short Stories. Pref.
by Clarence A. Manning; introd. by Luke Luciw; biographical sketches by Bohdan
Krawciw. *Svoboda* (81–83 Grand St., Jersey City, N.J. 07303) 1964 $3.00. A well-
annotated, wide-ranging anthology of 21 modern Ukrainian short stories.

Luckyj, G. S. N., Ed. MODERN UKRAINIAN SHORT STORIES. *Ukrainian Academic Press*
bilingual ed. 1973 $8.50. A useful reader with parallel texts containing short stories
by 11 modern authors.

Slavutych, Yar. THE MUSE IN PRISON: Eleven Sketches of Ukrainian Poets Killed by
Communists, and Twenty-two Translations of Their Poems. Fwd. by Clarence A.
Manning. *Svoboda* (81–83 Grand St., Jersey City, N.J. 07303) pap. $1.00

STORIES OF THE SOVIET UKRAINE. *Progress Publishers*, Moscow (order from Four Continents
Book Corp., 156 Fifth Ave., New York, N.Y. 10010) 1970. Twenty-six Ukrainian
stories translated into English from Russian versions of the original Ukrainian texts;
with an introduction by the poet–physician Vitalij Korotyč.

Zenkovsky, Serge A., Trans. and ed. MEDIEVAL RUSSIA'S EPICS, CHRONICLES, AND TALES.
1963 *Dutton* pap. $2.95; rev., enl. ed. 1974 $6.50. A useful anthology containing
excerpts from some of the major monuments of Kievan Rus'.

Folk Literature

FOLK HEROES OF UKRAINE. Trans. and adapted by Mary Skrypnyk; ill. by O. Danchenko.
Ukrainian Canadian 1966 $.50 (order from: Ukrainian Book Store, see above for
address). Selections from a series in the magazine *Ukraine*, published in Kiev. English
translations first appeared serially in *Ukrainian Canadian*, 1963–1964.

THE POOR LAD AND THE CRUEL PRINCESS: Ukrainian Folk Tale. Trans. by John Weir; ill.
by Yuli Kriha. *Mistetstvo* 1969 (order from Ukrainian Book Store, see above for
address)

THE STRAW BULL-CALF: Ukrainian Folk Tale. Trans. by John Weir; ill. by Yevhen
Solovyov. *Mistetstvo* 1969 (order from Ukrainian Book Store, see above for address)

TELESIK: Ukrainian Folk Tale. Trans. by John Weir; ill. by Nina Denisova. *Mistetstvo* 1969
(order from Ukrainian Book Store, see above for address)

TUSYA AND THE POT OF GOLD, FROM AN OLD UKRAINIAN FOLKTALE. Retold and ill. by
Yaroslava. 1971. *Atheneum* $4.75

UKRAINIAN FOLK TALES: Tales about Animals. Trans. by Irina Zheleznova. *Foreign
Languages Publishing House*, Moscow (order from Four Continents Book Corp. 156
Fifth Ave. New York, N.Y. 10010) 1957?

UKRAINIAN FOLK TALES. Sel. and trans. by Anatole Bilenko; ed. by Olga Shartse; ill. and
designed by Roman Adamovich. *Dnipro* (Kiev) (order from: Ukrainian Book Store,
P.O. Box 1640—10207 97 St., Edmonton, Alberta, Canada T5J 2N9)

ŠEVČENKO, TARAS (also Shevchenko). 1814–1861.

Ševčenko is the outstanding Ukrainian romantic poet, creator of the Ukrainian literary
language and symbol of the national movement. He was born a serf and educated in St.
Petersburg to serve as a portraitist and artist. His freedom was purchased in 1838 by several of his
admirers. Ševčenko's first eight poems were collected in the *"Kobzar"* ("The Bandura Player,"
1840). The publication of this collection created a literary sensation. This collection was followed
in the next three years by *"Haidamaky"* ("The Haidamaks," 1841) and a series of poems based
strongly on folksong rhythms. The writings composed after his return to the Ukraine in 1843
included strong invectives against serfdom and the baneful role that Russians had played in
Ukrainian history.

For a decade after 1847 Ševčenko was exiled to Central Asia for his participation in the Sts.
Cyril and Methodius Society. This clandestine organization advocated the union of all Slavs on the

basis of independence and equality. During his exile he wrote several lyrics and novelettes. The poems of the last four years of his life, including *"Neofity"* and "Mariya" (1859), are built on strongly religious themes.

THE POETICAL WORKS OF TARAS SHEVCHENKO: The Kobzar. Trans. by C. H. Andrusyshen and Watson Kirkconnell. Published for the Ukrainian Canadian Committee by the *University of Toronto Press* 1964 $12.50. A good collection by two veteran interpreters of Ukrainian poetry.

SHEVCHENKO'S TESTAMENT. Annotated commentaries by John Panchuk. *Svoboda Press* (81–83 Grand Street, Jersey City, N.J. 07303) 1965 $3.00. Contains a list of published English translations of Shevchenko's "Testament."

KATERINA: A Poem. Trans. by John Weir. *Dnipro* (order from Ukrainian Book Store, P.O. Box 1640—10207 97 St., Edmonton, Alberta, Canada T5J 2N9) 1972

Books about Ševčenko

> Taras Shevchenko: Bard of the Ukraine. By D. Doroshenko. Pref. by Clarence A. Manning. *United Ukrainian Organizations of the United States* 1936 o.p. Despite its age, a still useful and erudite interpretation by an outstanding Ukrainian statesman and historian.
>
> Taras Shevchenko; A Biographical Sketch. By Maksim Rylsky and Alexander Deutch. Trans. from Russian by John Weir. *Progress Publishers* (order from Ukrainian Book Store, see above for address) $.20
>
> Taras Ševčenko: The Man and the Symbol. *Association of Ukrainians in Great Britain* (order from Ukrainian Book Store, see above for address) 1951 $.30
>
> The Humanism of Shevchenko and our Time. By Yevhen Shabliovsky. Trans. by Mary Skrypnyk with participation of Petro Kravchuk. *Naukova Dumka* (order from Four Continents Book Corp., 156 Fifth Ave., New York, N.Y. 10011) 1971

KULIŠ, PANTELEJMON (also Kulish). 1819–1897.

Kuliš, a scholar as well as a novelist, in "The Black Council" gives a vivid picture of the different levels of society in 17th-century Ukraine. His theme is the need for people to be motivated by high ideals as they engage in the "struggle of truth with injustice."

THE BLACK COUNCIL. Trans. and abr. by George Luckyj and Moira Luckyj with an introd. by Romana Bahrij Pikulyk. Ukrainian Class. in Translation *Ukrainian Academic Press* 1973 $7.50

FRANKO, IVAN. 1856–1916.

Franko, a prolific Galician Ukrainian writer, scholar, and journalist, was a master of several genres; his works also show an extraordinary variety of themes. His earliest published works include a series of romantic historical novels and a group of naturalistic portrayals of the conflict of nascent industrialism and labor in the Ukraine. Other works depict the social disintegration of the gentry and the attempts of the new intelligentsia to supplant it. He is perhaps best known for his epic verses, especially the great epic *"Moisei"* (Moses), 1905, in which he expounds his philosophy of the nation and the role of the charismatic personality.

IVAN FRANKO: The Poet of Western Ukraine—Selected Poems. Trans. with biographical introd. by Percival Cundy; ed. by Clarence A. Manning. 1948. *Greenwood* 1968 $14.25

MOSES AND OTHER POEMS. Trans. by Vera Rich and Percival Cundy. *Shevchenko Scientific Society* (order from Svoboda Bookstore, 81-83 Grand St., Jersey City, N.J. 07303) 1973 $7.00

POEMS AND STORIES. Trans. by John Weir. *Ukrainska Knyha* (order from Ukrainian Book Store, P.O. Box 1640—10207 97 St., Edmonton, Alberta, Canada T5J 2N9) 1956 $3.50

STORIES. Trans. by John Weir and Cecilia Dalway; ed. by A. Bilenko; comp. with introd. by Yevhen Kirilyuk. *Mistetstvo* (order from Ukrainian Book Store, see above) 1972 $1.70

KOCIUBYNSKY, MYXAJLO. 1864–1913.

In his earliest work, Kociubynsky introduced impressionistic devices under the influence of Western European writers. Later works dealt with the theme of the 1905 Revolution, its suppression, and its consequences on the human psyche.

THE BIRTHDAY PRESENT (1911) AND OTHER STORIES. Trans. by Abraham Mistetsky; ed. by Richard Dixon. *Dnipro Publishers* (order from Ukrainian Book Store, P.O. Box 1640—10207 97 St., Edmonton, Alberta, Canada T5J 2N9) 1973

STEFANYK, VASYL'.   1871–1936.

Stefanyk, from Galicia, is known for his short stories in dialect. Real voices come through his tragic tales in urgent, laconic dialogue or monologue. "As in the 'tragic' stories of Kotsiubynsky, hard external circumstances (misery, family catastrophe, drunkenness, painful parting with one's native village, and the like) served in Stefanyk's stories only as a pretext for the unfolding of the theme of tragedy in the life of a human being"—*(Ukraine: A Concise Encyclopedia)*. "The Stone Cross" is a collection of 32 stories in translation.

THE STONE CROSS. Trans. by Joseph Wiznuk in collaboration with C. H. Andrusyshyn. Published for the Stefanyk Centennial Committee by *McClelland & Stewart* (order from Ukrainian Book Store, P.O. Box 1640—10207 97 St., Edmonton, Alberta, Canada T5J 2N9) $5.95

Books about Stefanyk

Wasyl Stefanyk: Articles and Selections. By Peter Prokop and others. *Kobzar Pub. Co. Ltd.* (order from Ukrainian Book Store, see above) 1971. Reprints from the journal, *The Ukrainian Canadian.*
A Study of Vasyl' Stefanyk: The Pain at the Heart of Existence. By D. S. Struk. Fwd. by G. S. Luckyj. *Ukrainian Academic Press* 1973 $8.50. Contains 13 novellas in translation: Loss, A Stone Cross, Suicide, Sons, Children's Adventure, All Alone, The Agony, The Thief, Sin, Les' Family, News, Mother, The Pious Woman.

UKRAJINKA, LESJA (pseud. of Larysa Petrivna Kvitka, *née* Kosač).   1871–1913.

The earliest works of Lesja Ukrajinka were lyric poems with exotic themes and motifs borrowed from remote times and places. After experimenting in prose drama, she wrote a great number of dramatic poems, the genre for which she is most famous.

SPIRIT OF FLAME: A Collection of the Works of Lesya Ukrainka. Trans. by Percival Cundy; fwd. by Clarence A. Manning. *Bookman Associates* (order from Ukrainian Book Store, P.O. Box 1640—10207 97 St., Edmonton, Alberta, Canada T5J 2N9) 1950 $7.50; 1950. *Greenwood* 1971 $14.75. A posthumous publication by a prolific amateur translator of Franko and Lesja Ukrajinka.

IN THE CATACOMBS: Dramatic Poem. Trans. by John Weir. *Mistetstvo* (order from Ukrainian Book Store, see above) 1971

Books about Lesja Ukrajinka

Lesya Ukrainka: Life and Work. By Constantine Bida. Published for the Women's Council of the Ukrainian Canadian Committee by the *Univ. of Toronto Press* 1968 $12.50. Contains selections from her work translated by Vera Rich.

KULIŠ, MYKOLA.   1892–1942.

Kuliš was an outstanding Soviet Ukrainian dramatist. He first wrote in the vein of ethnographic realism, but went on to compose highly original expressionistic plays. *"Patetychna Sonata"* (The Sonata Pathetique, 1931) is a vivid representation of the Revolution of 1917, which is allegorically presented as an expressive and profoundly tragic sonata. The play was staged by the two leading theaters in Russia, but its presentation was not allowed on the Ukrainian stage.

SONATA PATHETIQUE. Trans. by George S. N. Luckij and Moira Luckij with an introd. by Professor Ralph Lindheim. Ukrainian Classics in Translations *Ukrainian Academic Press* 1975 $7.50

XVYL'OVYJ, MYKOLA (also Khvyl'ovyi; pseud. of Mykola Fitil'ov).   1893–1933.

Xvyl'ovyj began his career as a poet, but achieved greatest fame as a short story writer. Politically and culturally he was at first a national Communist, but soon became disillusioned with Stalin's nationality policy towards Ukraine and committed suicide in 1933. In the great literary debates of the twenties he advocated orientation towards Europe, a policy rejected by the Communist party. He was one of the founders of VAPLITE (*Vil'na Akademiia Proletars'koi Literatury*), the Free Academy of Proletarian Literature, dissolved in 1928.

STORIES FROM THE UKRAINE. Trans. with introd. by George S. N. Luckyj. 1960 *Citadel Press* pap. $1.65

DOVZHENKO, OLEKSANDR. 1894–1956.

A Soviet Ukrainian writer and filmmaker best known for "his motion picture stories, such as *'Povist' polumianykh lit'* (Tale of the Flaming Years, 1944–1945) and *'Antarktyda'* (Antarctic, 1952), and especially his autobiographical novel, *'Zacharovana Desna'* (The Bewitched Desna, 1954–1955), and *'Poema pro more'* (Poem about the Sea)"—(*Ukraine: A Concise Encyclopedia*), p. 1074.

THE POET AS FILMMAKER: Selected Writings. Ed., trans., with introd. by Marco Carynnyk. *M.I.T. Press* 1973 $12.50 1975 pap. $5.95

PIDMOHYLNY, VALERIAN. 1901–1941.

Pidmohylny's last novel, *"Nevelychka drama"* (A Little Drama), published in 1930, shows the influence of French writers such as Maupassant. In his earlier works he experimented with impressionistic psychological stories and with literary expressionism.

A LITTLE TOUCH OF DRAMA. 1930. Trans. by George S. N. Luckyj and Moira Luckyj, with introd. by George Shevelov. Ukrainian Class. in Translation *Ukrainian Academic Press* 1972 $7.50

HONCHAR, OLEKSANDER. 1918–

Honchar's novels deal with events of World War II, and with aspects of life in the Soviet Union. He is adept at descriptions of nature and is a precise stylist in the Ukrainian literary language.

THE CYCLONE. Soviet Novel Ser. *Progress Publishers* (order from Four Continent Book Corp., 156 Fifth Ave., New York, N.Y. 10011) 1972

SVERSTIUK, JEVHEN. 1928–

Sverstiuk's essays touch upon many subjects, but all bear upon the national spirit of the Ukraine. In his long defence of Honchar's novel *"Sobor"* (Cathedral), he combines his concern for the Ukraine "with more universal themes of concern for ecology, education, and an attack on the modern dehumanization of society." The most recent essay in the collection listed below, "Ivan Kotliarevsky Is Laughing," 1969, is an attempt to "reinterpret the beginnings of modern Ukrainian literature. To him Kotliarevsky's *"Eneida"* (1798), the Ukrainian travesty of Vergil, appears more complex in its allegory than scholars have thought up to now"—(George Luckyj).

CLANDESTINE ESSAYS. Trans. and ed. by George S. N. Luckyj. Harvard Ukrainian Research Institute Monograph Ser. *Ukrainian Academic Press* 1976 $7.50 pap. $5.00

HUTSALO, JEVHEN. 1937–

Hutsalo (or Gutsalo) is a talented writer of short stories. In his recent volume, *"Peredchuttia radosti"* (Prevision of Happiness), he touches upon problems of religion and of collaboration with the Germans in World War II. Most of his work presents pictures of village life as seen and lived by the characters in the stories.

A PREVISION OF HAPPINESS AND OTHER STORIES. Trans. by Eve Manning. Soviet Short Stories Ser. *Progress Publishers* (order from Four Continent Book Corp., 156 Fifth Avenue, New York, N.Y. 10011) 1974

—E.K.

YIDDISH LITERATURE

Yiddish literature by individual authors, in the modern sense, has existed for only about 150 years; the popular language, derived from German, has been spoken for nearly a thousand years (see the article "Yiddish Language" in the *Encyclopedia Judaica*, Vol. 16, pp. 789 ff). Numerous works in Yiddish have been translated into English, especially in recent years. The importance of this growing field of research is evident in many ways. For example, the Yivo Institute for Jewish Research, in New York, issues publications in Yiddish and in English, arranges exhibitions, and sponsors academic courses under the name of "The Max Weinreich Center for Advanced Jewish Studies." Yiddish courses are taught for credit at over 20 colleges and universities throughout the United States and Canada, and annual conferences are held by teachers of Yiddish. A new journal called *Yiddish* is published by Queens College Press; its issues are devoted to articles on Yiddish language and culture. Isaac Bashevis Singer's play "Yentl" is now being produced at the Eugene O'Neill Theater. A successful motion picture, "Hester Street," based on a novel by Abraham Cahan, founder and editor of the famous New York newspaper, the *Jewish Daily Forward*, has played with success. Yiddish literary and folklore material has appeared on television and records, and adult study groups engaged in the study of Yiddish testify to the continuing vitality of the subject.

Active translation of Yiddish works into English began at the end of the past century and proceeded with the growing numbers of eastern European Jewish immigrants to America, and with the contemporaneous developing and maturing of Yiddish literature. Many masters, and some minor figures, have been translated, but the field is still an open territory in need of competent and talented hands to explore all its riches. Many of the older translations have gone out of print, and are available now only in libraries. But several other older translations have appeared in reprint editions.

Historical Studies

Yiddish language and literature developed under the impact of various historical, geographical, and sociological factors. The conditions of Jewish life in Eastern Europe, the revivalist dynamism of the Hasidic movement, the ethnic survival of immigrants in the New World are some of the factors which shaped the Jewish experience and its literary expression. The books listed below (which include pictorial representations) are a selection of studies available in this vast field.

Buber, Martin. HASIDISM AND MODERN MAN. Trans. by Maurice Friedman. *Harper* Torchbks. pap. $2.50. Exposition of a movement which left an indelible mark on the development of modern Yiddish literature.

LEGEND OF THE BAAL-SHEM. Trans. from the German by Maurice Friedman. *Schocken* 1969 $6.50 pap. $2.95. On the founder of Hasidism, Israel Baal-Shem-Tov, who lived in the eighteenth century.

THE ORIGIN AND MEANING OF HASIDISM. *Horizon Press* 1972 $6.95 pap. $3.45

Cahan, Abraham. THE EDUCATION OF ABRAHAM CAHAN. Trans. from the Yiddish "*Bleter fun Mein Leben*," Vols. 1 and 2. Introd. by Leon Stein. *Jewish Publication Society* 1969 $7.50. Memoirs of an important personality in American-Jewish literature, the founder and editor of the *Jewish Daily Forward*.

Doroshkin, Milton. YIDDISH IN AMERICA: Social and Cultural Foundations. *Fairleigh Dickinson Univ. Press* 1970 $12.50. Covers the period 1880–1920 and concentrates on two major institutions of Eastern European Jewry: the Yiddish press and the "*landsmanshaftn*," or fraternal organizations.

Dubnow, Simon. HISTORY OF THE JEWS IN RUSSIA AND POLAND FROM THE EARLIEST TIMES UNTIL THE PRESENT DAY. Trans. from the Russian by I. Friedlaender. With a biographical essay, new introd. and outline of the history of Russian and Soviet Jewry 1917–1974, by Leon Shapiro. *KTAV* 1975 3 vols. in 2 $35.00. Classic survey of the history of Eastern European Jewry by one of its pioneer historians. Reprinted from the 1916 edition by the Jewish Publication Society of America.

Fishman, Joshua. YIDDISH IN AMERICA: Socio-Linguistic Description and Analysis. *Indiana Univ. Press* 1965 pap. $3.00. (Indiana Univ. Research Center in Anthropology, Folklore and Linguistics, Publication no. 36, and International Journal of American Linguistics, Vol. 31, No. 2, Pt. 2). Socio-cultural background, periodization, and statistical data on Yiddish in America.

Hapgood, Hutchins. THE SPIRIT OF THE GHETTO. Ed. with introd. and notes by Moses Rischin; ill. by Jacob Epstein. *Harvard Univ. Press* Belknap Press 1967 $12.50; 1968 *House of Collectibles* $7.95; with pref. and notes by Harry Golden *Schocken* 1966 pap. $2.95. Classic study of early immigrant Jews on New York's Lower East Side.

Heschel, Abraham Joshua. THE EARTH IS THE LORD'S: The Inner World of the Jew in Eastern Europe. Ill. by Ilya Schor. *Harper* 1968 Torchbks. pap. $2.25. Eloquent exposition of spiritual values, goals, and aspirations of traditional East European Jewry.

A PASSION FOR TRUTH. *Farrar, Straus* 1973 $8.95. Presentation of the philosophical system of Reb Mendl of Kotzk, a Hasidic figure whose personality and ideas found their reflection in Yiddish literature.

Howe, Irving. THE WORLD OF OUR FATHERS. *Harcourt* $14.95. The story of East European Jews in America, their struggles, achievements, and contributions to American life are presented here by a literary and social historian who based his work on first-hand research and combines a thorough knowledge of the American scene with intimate knowledge of American Jewish life and letters.

Metzker, Isaac, Ed. A BINTEL BRIEF: Sixty Years of Letters from the Lower East Side to the *Jewish Daily Forward.* Fwd. and notes by Harry Golden. *Doubleday* 1971 $6.95. The letters reflect the life and problems of Yiddish-speaking immigrants from Eastern Europe.

Rabinowicz, Harry M. THE WORLD OF HASIDISM. *Hortmore House* 1970 $6.95. History of the movement by a competent scholar in the field.

Roskies, Diane K., and David G. Roskies. THE SHTETL BOOK. *KTAV* 1975 $10.00 pap. $5.95. Anthology of source materials on a little town in Eastern Europe selected as a typical example of similar Jewish communities in pre-war Eastern Europe.

Shazar, Zalman. MORNING STARS. Trans. from the Hebrew *"Kochvei Boker"* by Sulamith Schwartz Nardi. *Jewish Publication Society* 1967 $4.50. Excellently written reminiscences of a childhood in Eastern Europe by the third President of Israel. Revealing as an intellectual history of a generation which reached from traditional small-town Jewish life in Eastern Europe to the modern nationalist movements and the state of Israel.

Soltes, Mordecai. THE YIDDISH PRESS: An Americanizing Agency. 1925. American Education: Its Men, Institutions and Ideas *Arno* 1969 $8.50. Thorough study based on an analysis of primary sources.

Tcherikower, Elias, Ed. THE EARLY JEWISH LABOR MOVEMENT IN THE UNITED STATES. Trans. from the Yiddish and rev. by Aaron Antonovsky. *YIVO Institute for Jewish Research* 1961 $12.00. Documented study of Jewish mass migration and its European background.

Warembud, Norman. GREAT SONGS OF THE YIDDISH THEATER. *Quadrangle-N.Y. Times* $12.50. Collection of songs from "Second Avenue," arranged for piano, guitar, and voice. Lyrics are transcribed in Roman characters.

Weinryb, Bernard D. THE JEWS OF POLAND: A Social and Economic History of the Jewish Community in Poland from 1100 to 1800. *Jewish Publication Society* 1973 $10.00

"Polish Jewry became the bedrock of Ashkenazic Jewry. . . . The book records the development of this Jewish community, it attempts to capture [its] uniqueness"—(Publisher's note).

Wirth, Louis. THE GHETTO. *Univ. of Chicago Press* 1928 $11.50; *Phoenix Bks.* 1956 pap. $3.95

"A famous and highly readable sociological study of American Jewish immigrants, with special reference to Chicago and in relation to their European roots"—(Feinsilver).

Zborowski, Mark, and Elizabeth Herzog. LIFE IS WITH PEOPLE: The Culture of the Shtetl. *Schocken* 1962 pap. $3.95

"This monograph can be regarded as a primary source on Eastern European Jewish culture"—(Margaret Mead in the introduction).

Albums

Filmus, Tully. SELECTED DRAWINGS. With an Essay by Isaac Bashevis Singer. Introd. by George Albert Perret. *Jewish Publication Society* 1971 $12.50. Realistic technique applied to sketches of Jewish traditional life. The essay by Bashevis Singer is on "Hasidism and Its Origins."

A PEOPLE APART: Hasidism in America. Photographs by Philip Garvin; text by Arthur A. Cohen. *Dutton* 1970 $20.00. Over 130 prints with an introduction entitled "An Essay in Praise of Hasidism."

Reiss, Lionel S. A WORLD AT TWILIGHT: A Portrait of the Jewish Communities of Eastern Europe before the Holocaust. Art by Lionel S. Reiss. Text by Milton Hindus. Pref. by Isaac Bashevis Singer. *Macmillan* 1971 $17.95

"L. S. Reiss . . . had the power and the courage to tell visually the story of a people . . . Prof. Milton Hindus presents a historical background to Mr. Reiss' work"—(Isaac Bashevis Singer in the preface).

Shulman, Abraham. THE OLD COUNTRY. Fwd. by Isaac Bashevis Singer. *Scribner* 1974 $12.95. Photographs selected from the illustrated supplements to the *Jewish Daily Forward.*

Vishniac, Roman. POLISH JEWS: A Pictorial Record. *Schocken* 1947 pap. $2.95. Some 31 black-and-white photographs by a famous artist-photographer; with an introductory essay by Abraham Joshua Heschel.

Literary Studies

Scholarship in the field of Yiddish started in Germany and Eastern Europe at the turn of the century. It was conducted in Russian, German, and Yiddish and in the period between the two world wars was pursued mainly by two groups of scholars: one centered around the Yiddish Scientific Institute (now Yivo Institute for Jewish Research) in Vilna, the other around the government-sponsored chairs for Yiddish linguistics and literature in Minsk (Byelorussian SSR) and Kiev (Ukrainian SSR). With the annihilation of Jewish centers in Eastern Europe by the Nazis in World War II, the center of Yiddish scholarship shifted to the United States, where the Yivo Institute for Jewish Research was reestablished in 1940. The books already published are listed below. In preparation is the English translation of the monumental "History of the Yiddish Language," by Max Weinreich, which appeared in the original Yiddish in New York in 1973.

Beck, Evelyn Torton. KAFKA AND THE YIDDISH THEATER: Its Impact on His Work. *Univ. of Wisconsin Press* 1971 $12.50. Study of Kafka's relationship to the Yiddish theater which performed in Prague in the theatrical season of 1910–1911.

Biletzky, Israel Ch. ESSAYS ON YIDDISH POETRY AND PROSE WRITERS OF THE TWENTIETH CENTURY. Trans. from the Hebrew by Yirmiyahu Haggi. *I. L. Peretz Library* (order from *Keter*) 1969

Goldsmith, Emanuel S. ARCHITECTS OF YIDDISHISM AT THE BEGINNING OF THE TWENTIETH CENTURY. *Fairleigh Dickinson Univ. Press* 1976 $15.00. The Yiddish language and culture movement and its significance for Jewish life.

Feinsilver, Lillian Mermin. TASTE OF YIDDISH. *A. S. Barnes* Yoseloff 1970 $10.00. Includes observations on the general characteristics of the language, a list of idiomatic expressions with their translations, and a study of mutual influences between Yiddish and English.

FOR MAX WEINREICH ON HIS SEVENTIETH BIRTHDAY: Studies in Jewish Languages, Literature and Society. *Mouton* (dist. by Humanities Press) 1964 $44.75. Contributions to Yiddish linguistics, literature, and Jewish sociology by scholars paying tribute to a major figure in Yiddish studies.

Herzog, Marvin I. THE FIELD OF YIDDISH: Studies in Language, Folklore and Literature. 3rd collection, ed. by Marvin I. Herzog, Wita Ravid, and Uriel Weinreich. *Mouton* (dist. by Humanities Press) 1969 $13.75. Scholarly contributions dealing with Yiddish language in its historical development, its dialects, onomastics, as well as with Yiddish literature and folklore. The first two collections, which appeared in 1954 and 1965, are out of print. A fourth is in preparation.

YIDDISH LANGUAGE IN NORTHERN POLAND. General Publications *Indiana Univ. Research Center* 1965 pap. $5.00

Lifson, David S. THE YIDDISH THEATER IN AMERICA. 1965 o.p. Study of the origin, rise, and decline of the Yiddish theater in America.

Liptzin, Sol. ELIAKUM ZUNSER: Poet of His People. *Behrman House* 1950 $3.00. Definitive biography of a Yiddish folk poet who lived 1840–1913. A critical edition of his works, prepared by Dr. Morkhe Schaechter, was published by *Yivo* in 1964.

A HISTORY OF YIDDISH LITERATURE. *Jonathan David* 1972 $10.00

". . . one-volume historical presentation that surveys the vast range of Yiddish creativity since its medieval beginnings. . . . Special emphasis has been placed on the contemporary period"— (Publisher's note).

THE MATURING OF YIDDISH LITERATURE. *Jonathan David* 1970 $6.95

Sequel to "Flowering of Yiddish Literature," discusses "Yiddish writers and poets who rose to prominence during the period of 1914–1939"—(Publisher's note).

Madison, Charles A. YIDDISH LITERATURE, ITS SCOPE AND MAJOR WRITERS. *Ungar* 1968 $10.00; *Schocken* pap. $4.50

After a historical survey of the development from the beginning to Mendele "the book . . . treats individually the work of fourteen major writers . . . major novels, plays and poems are outlined and discussed critically"—(Publisher's note).

Matenko, Percy. TWO STUDIES IN YIDDISH CULTURE: The Aqedath Jishaq—A Sixteenth Century Yiddish Epic (introd. and notes by Percy Matenko and Samuel Sloan) and Job and Faust—A Study and Translation of C. Zhitlowsky's Essay. *E. J. Brill* (order from W. S. Heinman, Imported Books, 1966 Broadway, New York, N.Y. 10023) 1968 price on request

The first study includes the full transliterated Yiddish text of the poem; the second is a translation from an author who is described as "a transitional figure straddling the ghetto world and the world of Western Enlightenment"—(Preface).

Miller, James. THE DETROIT YIDDISH THEATER 1920–1937. *Wayne State Univ. Press* 1967 $8.95

Miron, Dan A. A TRAVELER DISGUISED: A Study in the Rise of Modern Yiddish Fiction in the 19th Century. *Schocken* 1973 $10.95. About the contribution of Mendele Mocher Sforim to the development of Yiddish fiction.

Pinsker, Sanford. THE SCHLEMIEL AS METAPHOR: Studies in the Yiddish and American Jewish Novel. *Southern Illinois Univ. Press* 1971 $5.45. A study of a comic figure who is conceived as a metaphor of the Jewish and human condition. The works of Mendele, Sholem Aleykhem, Bashevis Singer, and American-Jewish writers are analyzed.

Rayfield, J. R. LANGUAGES IN A BILINGUAL COMMUNITY. *Mouton* (dist. by Humanities Press) 1970 pap. $10.50. Study of usage of English and Yiddish in an American Jewish community.

Roback, A. A. THE STORY OF YIDDISH LITERATURE. 1940. *Gordon Press* 1974 $34.95. The first comprehensive survey in English since 1900. Includes a bibliography of translations and other works in English on the subject.

Rosten, Leo. THE JOYS OF YIDDISH: A Relaxed Lexicon of Yiddish . . . often Encountered in English. *McGraw-Hill* 1968 $10.00; *Simon & Schuster* Pocket Bks. pap. $1.95

"Leo Rosten has wedded scholarship to humor and gives the reader . . . a new kind of dictionary. It ranges across the whole . . . realm of Jewish culture, thought, history, religion, customs, wit"—(Publisher's note).

Rubin, Ruth. VOICES OF A PEOPLE: The Story of Yiddish Folksong. *McGraw-Hill* 2nd ed. 1973 $9.95. Covers historical development from the sixteenth century to the present; provides content analysis and music to selected songs.

Samuel, Maurice. IN PRAISE OF YIDDISH. *Regnery* (Cowles) 1975 $5.95

> The purpose of the book is "to convey the spirit of Yiddish . . . its unique interweave of the homey and the historic"—(Publisher's note).

Schwarzbaum, Haim. STUDIES IN JEWISH AND WORLD FOLKLORE. *Walter de Gruyter* (order from W. S. Heinman, Imported Books, 1966 Broadway, New York, N.Y. 10023) 1968 (Supplement-Serie zu *Fabula*, Zeitschrift für Erzählforschung, Reihe B, Unter-suchungen, Band 3)

> "Comprehensive work based on a collection of 540 Yiddish folktales and fables, '*Ma'aselech un Mesholim*' by Naftoli Gross . . . providing an authoritative outline of many common *motifs* in Jewish and international folk-narrative"—(Preface).

Weinreich, Uriel, and Beatrice Weinreich. YIDDISH LANGUAGE AND FOLKLORE: A Selective Bibliography for Research. *Humanities Press* pap. $2.50. Includes works both in English and Yiddish, and covers books as well as contributions to journals.

Wiener, Leo. THE HISTORY OF YIDDISH LITERATURE IN THE NINETEENTH CENTURY. With a new introd. by Elias Shulman. *Hermon Press* 1972. $14.50

> Originally published in 1899, the book was "the first introduction to Yiddish literature for the English reader . . . though now slightly dated [it] remains a classic handbook. . . . Dr. Elias Shulman . . . provides an exhaustive introduction"—(Publisher's note).

Wisse, Ruth R. THE SHLEMIEL AS MODERN HERO. *Univ. of Chicago Press* 1971 $5.45. Study of a representative character in modern Yiddish fiction who reappears in a different disguise in contemporary American literature.

Yiddish: A Quarterly Journal Devoted to Yiddish and Yiddish Literature. Vol. 1, Nos. 1–4, 1973–1975 *Queens College Press* in prep.

Zinberg, Israel. A HISTORY OF JEWISH LITERATURE. Vol. 7 Old Yiddish Literature from Its Origins to the Haskalah Period. Trans. and ed. by Bernard Martin. *Hebrew Union College Press* (dist. by *KTAV*) 1975 $17.50

> ". . . an account of the rich literature produced in this language from its origins in the eleventh century to the dawn of the era of Enlightenment"—(Publisher's note). With valuable bibliographi-cal notes edited and supplemented with newest contributions by the translator, a glossary of Hebrew and other terms, and an index.

Collections

The anthologies available in the field of Yiddish are arranged by literary genres, or by subjects. Along with collections of stories, poetry, essays, drama or mixed genres, there are others dedicated to reflecting areas of Jewish life, such as intellectual history, the Hasidic heritage, the American scene, the Holocaust period, or the rich and popular field of Jewish folklore. A valuable feature of the anthologies are introductory essays on the chosen subjects.

Ausubel, Nathan, Ed. A TREASURY OF JEWISH FOLKLORE: Stories, Traditions, Legends, Humor, Wisdom and Folk Songs of the Jewish People. *Crown* 1948 $5.95

> A TREASURY OF JEWISH HUMOR. *Doubleday* 1951 $8.95. Both anthologies contain a rich selection of material from Yiddish sources.

Ayalti, Hanan J., Ed. YIDDISH PROVERBS. *Schocken* 1949 $3.00 1963 pap. $1.25. Bilingual with the Yiddish transliterated.

Betsky, Sarah Zweig, Trans. and ed. ONIONS AND CUCUMBERS AND PLUMS: 46 Yiddish Poems in English. 1958. Granger Index Ser. *Bks. for Libraries* $9.50. Selection from modern Yiddish poets, with Yiddish and English on opposite pages.

Buber, Martin. TALES OF RABBI NACHMAN. Trans. by Maurice Friedman. *Schocken* 1968 pap. $2.45. Collections of folk tales ascribed to Hasidic leaders culled from various sources and edited by a highly articulate interpreter of the Hasidic movement.

> TALES OF THE HASIDIM. Trans. by Olga Marx. *Schocken* 2 vols. 1947 1948 Vol. 1 The Early Masters $7.50 pap. $3.45 Vol. 2 The Later Masters $7.50 pap. $2.95

Cooperman, Jehiel B., and Sarah H. Cooperman, Trans. AMERICA IN YIDDISH POETRY: An Anthology. *Exposition Press* 1967 $10.00. Poems about America and American life.

Dawidowicz, Lucy S., Ed. THE GOLDEN TRADITION: Jewish Life and Thought in Eastern Europe. 1967. *Beacon Press* pap. $3.45. An anthology of writings representing the major movements and personalities of Eastern European Jewry from the Enlightenment period to 1939. An extensive introduction by the compiler summarizes the rich intellectual heritage in which the Yiddish component played a major part. Includes bibliography and index.

Frank, Helen A., Trans. and comp. YIDDISH TALES: The Modern Jewish Experience. *Arno* 1975 $36.00. Reprint of the edition published by the Jewish Publication Society of America, Philadelphia, 1912.

Glatstein, Jacob, Israel Knox, and Samuel Margoshes, Eds. ANTHOLOGY OF HOLOCAUST LITERATURE. Associate eds.: Mordecai Bernstein, Adah B. Fogel. *Atheneum* Temple Bks. pap. $4.95; *Jewish Publication Society of America* 1969 $10.00. Most of the materials included are translations from the Yiddish.

Goodman, Henry, Ed. THE NEW COUNTRY: Stories from the Yiddish about Life in America. *Yiddisher Kultur Farband* (80 Fifth Ave., New York, N.Y.) 1961 $4.75. Excellent selection from representative American-Yiddish writers, arranged topically in six chapters. Biographical notes about the authors included.

Howe, Irving, and Eliezer Greenberg. A TREASURY OF YIDDISH POETRY. *Holt* 1972 pap. $4.95. An important effort making outstanding Yiddish poets available to the English reader for the first time.

A TREASURY OF YIDDISH STORIES. *Schocken* 1970 pap. $4.50. Comprehensive selection covering Yiddish writers of the nineteenth and twentieth centuries, with a valuable introduction by Irving Howe.

VOICES FROM THE YIDDISH: Essays, Memoirs, Diaries. *Univ. of Michigan Press* 1972 $8.95. An anthology arranged by topics such as The Founding Fathers, East European Scene, A Few Central Themes and Figures, Jewishness in America, The Holocaust, Yiddish: Language and Literature, with an introduction by Irving Howe.

Jaffe, Marie B., Trans. and comp. TEN FOR POSTERITY: An Anthology of Yiddish Poems. *Exposition* 1972 $6.00. Included are poems by Itzik Manger, Mani Leib, Yehoash, Aaron Zeitlin, H. Leivick, Rachell Weprinsky, Meyer Ziml Tkatch, Hinde Zaretsky, I. J. Schwartz, and Raizel Zychlinska.

Landis, Joseph C., Trans. and ed. THE GREAT JEWISH PLAYS. *Avon* 1974 pap. $3.95; *Horizon Press* 1972 $7.95. Includes The Dybbuk by S. Anski, God of Vengeance by Sholem Asch, Green Fields by P. Hirshbein, King David and his Wives by David Pinsky, and The Golem by H. Leivick.

Leftwich, Joseph, Trans., comp. and ed. AN ANTHOLOGY OF MODERN YIDDISH LITERATURE. *Mouton* (dist. by Humanities Press) 1974 $10.00. Includes stories, essays, plays, and poems of 42 Yiddish writers of the pre- and post-1939 period. With an introduction, biographical notes, glossary, and bibliography.

THE GOLDEN PEACOCK: A Worldwide Treasury of Yiddish Poetry. *A. S. Barnes* (Yoseloff) 2nd rev. ed. 1961. A comprehensive anthology with an introduction by the compiler.

THE WAY WE THINK: A Collection of Essays from the Yiddish. *A. S. Barnes* (Yoseloff) 1969 2 vols. $20.00. Selection of essays by older and modern writers dealing with issues of Jewish life and Yiddish literature.

Levin, Meyer. CLASSIC HASSIDIC TALES: Marvellous Tales of Rabbi Israel Baal Shem and his Great-Grand-Son, Rabbi Nachman. Retold from Hebrew, Yiddish and German Sources. *Citadel Press* 1966

Lifson, David S., Trans. and ed. Epic and Folk Plays of the Yiddish Theater. *Fairleigh Dickinson Univ. Press* 1975 $14.50. Includes the following five plays of which the first four have been performed on the Yiddish stage: Farvorfen vinkel, by Peretz Hirshbein, Hirsh Lekert by H. Leivick, Yankel Boyla by Leon Kobrin, Recruits by Axenfeld-Reznik, and Haman's Downfall by Chaim Sloves.

Mintz, Jerome R. Legends of the Hasidim: An Introduction to Hasidic Culture and Oral Tradition in the New World. Photog. by the author. *Univ. of Chicago Press* 1968. The introduction provides an insight into the historic roots and present-day culture of the Hasidic community, followed by a collection of tales and legends recorded by the author from the mouths of the informants. A great deal of the material was translated from the original Yiddish.

Neugroschel, Joachim, Trans. and comp. Yenne Velt: The Great Works of Jewish Fantasy and Occult. With introd. by Neugroshel. *Stonehill* 1976. $25.00. Described as a "definitive collection," the anthology includes works from the medieval "*Mayse-Bukh*" to the stories of Isaac Bashevis Singer. Included are works by I. B. Gotlober, Mendele Mocher Seforim, I. L. Peretz, S. Ansky, the Soviet-Yiddish writers Der Nister, M. Kulbak, and D. Bergelson, as well as the tales of Rabbi Nakhman of Bratslav.

Rosenfeld, Max, Comp. Pushcarts and Dreamers: Stories of Jewish Life in America by Sholem Asch [and others] *A. S. Barnes* (Yoseloff) 1969 $4.95

Rubin, Ruth. A Treasury of Jewish Folksongs. Piano settings by Ruth Post; drawings by T. Herzl Rome; poetry adaptations by Isaac Schwartz, Jacob Sloan, and the editor. *Schocken* 1950 $7.50 pap. $3.50. Yiddish texts in transcription are provided along with English translations.

White, Bessie F., Trans. Nine One-Act Plays from the Yiddish. 1932. *Branden* $3.75. Includes works by Sholom Aleichem, I. L. Peretz, David Pinski, Jacob Gordin, I. D. Berkowitz, Z. Libin, Z. Levin, and Samuel Daixel.

Whitman, Ruth, Trans. and comp. An Anthology of Modern Yiddish Poetry. *October House* bilingual ed. 1966 $7.50 pap. $2.95

"An expertly prepared collection . . . valuable, highly readable"—(*LJ*).

Wisse, Ruth R., Ed. with introds. and notes. A Shtetl and Other Yiddish Novellas. *Behrman House* 1973 $12.50. Includes five novels by masters of Yiddish letters: Mendele Mocher Sforim, S. Lansky, David Bergelson, I. M. Weissenberg, and Joseph Opatoshu, translated for the first time into English, with an introduction tracing the development of modern Yiddish literature in the late nineteenth and early twentieth centuries.

Juvenile Literature

Yiddish literature for children developed in Eastern Europe at the end of the nineteenth century. The great Yiddish author Sholom Aleichem wrote a number of moving stories about Jewish children, their sorrows arising from poverty and rigid norms of religious education, and their joys experienced in the circle of tightly knit families and in direct contact with nature in their rural or small-town environment. The stories of I. L. Peretz based on Jewish folklore and tradition were another source of Yiddish children's literature which introduced the Jewish child to the world of the remote past and miraculous events. Younger writers, especially Mani Leib and Kadye Molodovsky, created beautiful poetry for children which sparkled with humor and playfulness expressed in a truly masterful children's idiom, often combined with an undercurrent of lyricism and nostalgia for the lost world of a blissful childhood. Yiddish juvenile literature developed also in America, where it displayed both elements of fantasy and realism. The list below will bring out some positive developments in the field of translations, such as the existence of two anthologies compiled by competent writers and educators and some works of

individual writers of established reputation. On the other hand, it is to be regretted that
Sholom Aleichem's collection "Jewish Children" (1920) was allowed to go out of print and
that such talented juvenile poets as the two mentioned above and many others have never
been adapted into the English idiom.

Einhorn, David. THE SEVENTH CANDLE AND OTHER FOLK TALES OF EASTERN EUROPE.
  Trans. by G. Pashin. Ill. by the author. *KTAV* 1968 $3.50
    "Some allegories, some fantasies, but all 27 stories deal with Jewish ethics and values in the shtetl
    of Eastern Europe"—("A Book List for the Jewish Child").

Goldberg, Itche, Comp. and Ed. YIDDISH STORIES FOR YOUNG PEOPLE. *Kinderbuch* 1966.
  Includes stories by Mendele Mocher Seforim, Sholom Aleichem, I. L. Peretz, Sholem
  Asch, Abraham Reisen, Yehuda Steinberg, Chaver Paver, and folk tales.

Hirsh, Marilyn. COULD ANYTHING BE WORSE? A Yiddish Tale Retold and Illustrated by
  Marilyn Hirsh. *Holiday House* 1974 $4.95. Convinced nothing could be worse than the
  noise and confusion of his home, a man consults his rabbi who has some very wise
  advice.

Howe, Irving, and Eliezer Greenberg, Eds. YIDDISH STORIES OLD AND NEW. Introd. by
  Irving Howe. *Holiday House* 1974 $5.95. Selection of stories by Sholom Aleichem,
  I. L. Peretz, Abraham Reisen, I. D. Berkowitz, I. Metzker, I. Manger, Joseph
  Opatoshu, and I. B. Singer.

Peretz, I. L. THE CASE AGAINST THE WIND AND OTHER STORIES. Trans. and adapted by
  Esther Hautzig. Ill. by Leon Steinmets. *Macmillan* 1975 $6.95

  SELECTED STORIES. Ed. by Irving Howe and Eliezer Greenberg. *Schocken* 1974 $6.95

Rothchild, Sylvia. I. L. PERETZ: Keys to a Magic Door. *Jewish Publication Society* 1973 $3.50
    "Few Jewish story-tellers of the past century have been more beloved than I. L. Peretz. The
    development of his talents, the personal and social problems which he had to face in a society
    altogether different from our own are here narrated with pathos and understanding"—("JPS
    Members' Catalog").

Rudashevski, Yitskhok. THE DIARY OF THE VILNA GHETTO, June 1941–April 1943. Trans.
  from the Yiddish manuscript . . . by Percy Matenko. *Ghetto Fighters House* (order from
  Keter) 1973. A moving diary of an adolescent who was doomed to death in Eastern
  Europe under Nazi rule.

Sholem Aleichem. TEVYE, A MIRACLE. *Fleet* 1972 $3.95. An adaptation of the famous
  Tevye stories.

Shulevitz, Uri. THE MAGICIAN: An Adaptation from the Yiddish of I. L. Peretz. *Macmillan*
  1973 $3.95
    "An old couple, with neither food nor candles to celebrate Passover, receive a mysterious visitor
    who supplies everything they need"—(Library of Congress card).

Simon, Solomon. THE WANDERING BEGGAR, or The Adventures of Simple Shmerel.
  Trans. by the author and his son, David Simon. Ill. by Lilian Fischel. *Behrman House*
  1955 (c. 1942) $3.50. Fantastic adventures of a simpleton who outsmarts wise men.

THE WISE MEN OF HELM AND THEIR MERRY TALES. Trans. by Ben Bengal and Solomon
  Simon; illus. by Lillian Fischel. *Behrman House* 1945 $4.50

MORE WISE MEN OF HELM AND THEIR MERRY TALES. Ed. by Hannah Goodman, ill. by
  Stephen Kraft. *Behrman House* 1965 $4.50. Stories about incredibly foolish people.

Singer, Isaac B. ALONE IN THE WILD FOREST. Ill. by Margot Zemach. *Farrar, Straus* 1971
  $4.50
    "A young orphan's life is changed when the angel he meets in the forest gives him an amulet
    that will fulfill every wish"—(Library of Congress card).

A DAY OF PLEASURE: Stories of a Boy Growing up in Warsaw. Photos by Roman
  Vishniac. *Farrar, Straus* 1969 $4.50. Episodes from the author's childhood.

ELIJAH THE SLAVE. Ill. by Ezra J. Keats. *Farrar, Straus* 1970 $4.95
    "Tale of a beautiful act of charity"—("A Book List for the Jewish Child, 1972").

FEARSOME INN. Trans. by the author and Elizabeth Shub. Ill. by Nonny Hogrogian. *Scribner* 1967 $4.50

"Three beautiful maidens held captive by the witches of the Fearsome Inn are liberated by three youths through the superior mystical powers of the Cabala and all live happily ever after"—("A Book List for the Jewish Child").

THE FOOLS OF CHELM AND THEIR HISTORY. Trans. by Elizabeth Shub. Ill. by Uri Shulevitz. *Farrar, Straus* 1973 $4.95

"Even though they were poor, the people of Chelm were content with their lives until the council of sages made them aware of their problems"—(Library of Congress card).

JOSEPH AND KOZA, or The Sacrifice to the Vistula. Trans. by the author and Elizabeth Shub. Ill. by Symeon Shimin. *Farrar, Straus* 1970 $4.50

"A tale of Joseph, a wandering Jew and goldsmith, who rescues his damsel from death and teaches the concept of one God all in one fell swoop. Winner of 1970 National Book Award for children's literature"—("A Book List for the Jewish Child").

MAZEL AND SHLIMAZEL, or The Milk of a Lioness. Trans. by the author and Elizabeth Shub. Ill. by Margot Zemach. *Farrar, Straus* 1967 $6.95

"A typical folktale of a peasant lad and his experiences with good luck and bad. Splendid, colorful artwork enhances the literary style of the author"—("A Book List for the Jewish Child").

THE TOPSY-TURVEY EMPEROR OF CHINA. Trans. by the author and Elizabeth Shub. Ill. by William Pene du Bois. *Harper* 1971 $3.50 lib. bdg. $3.79

WHEN SHLEMIEL WENT TO WARSAW AND OTHER STORIES. Trans. by the author and Elizabeth Shub. Ill. by Margot Zemach. *Farrar, Straus* 1967 $4.50

"Written for a wide audience, these stories have a 'Chelmish' flavor"—("Book List for the Jewish Child").

WHY NOAH CHOSE THE DOVE. Trans. by Elizabeth Shub. Ill. by Eric Carle. *Farrar, Straus* 1968 $4.95

"As each animal boasts of the qualities he feels make him especially worthy to go on Noah's Ark, Noah takes a particular liking to the dove"—(Library of Congress card).

THE WICKED CITY. Trans. by the author and Elizabeth Shub. Ill. by Everett Fisher. *Farrar, Straus* 1972 $4.50

"Retells the Old Testament tale of the destruction of Sodom"—(Library of Congress card).

ZLATEH THE GOAT AND OTHER STORIES. Trans. by the author and Elizabeth Shub. Ill. by Maurice Sendak. *Harper* 1966. $4.50

"Seven short stories coming out of the author's background as a young Jewish boy in Poland before World War I"—(Library of Congress card).

JACOB BEN ISAAC, of JANOW. d. 1620?

Very little is known about the author of the seventeenth-century "best seller" which has had over 200 editions since its first known appearance in 1622. The book is a collection of rabbinical commentaries and legends on the Bible and was meant for women and uneducated folk as a source of information, edification, and entertainment. It reflects charmingly the Jewish folk psyche, its naive piety, its absolute identification with the word of God as transmitted in the Bible, and its stern adherence to the moral principles of its religious tradition.

TZEENAH U-REENAH: A Jewish Commentary of the *Book of Exodus*. Trans. by Norman C. Gore. *KTAV* 1965 $7.50

GLUCKEL OF HAMELN. 1645–1724.

A writer who lived in Hamburg, Germany in the seventeenth century, her memoirs were first published by her family in 1896 and are considered a classic of older Yiddish literature. The thoughts, feelings, and way of life of her period are charmingly reflected in her book.

THE LIFE OF GLUCKEL OF HAMELN, 1646–1724. Trans. by Beth-Zion Abrahams. 1963 o.p.

MENDELE MOCHER SEFORIM (pseud. of Shalom Jacob Abramowitz). 1836–1917.

This writer, known as "the grandfather of Yiddish literature," first won fame under the pen-name of Mendele the Book Peddler. "The Nag" (1873, U.S. 1954, o.p.) a satirical allegory, tells of the adventures of an impoverished scholar and an undernourished and battered work horse, symbol of the Jewish people. The novelist and essayist, whose influence has been great upon younger European writers, was reared in a small town in the province of Minsk, Russia, and received a traditional orthodox Jewish education. After his father's death, when he was 14, he set out as a wandering scholar and, with another wanderer, gained a great fund of experience and insight into Jewish and Russian folkways. His first essays were in Hebrew, but for his popular tales he turned to Yiddish as a more suitable vehicle. He has been called the creator of classical Yiddish. Benjamin III, the hero of the story listed below, has been called the Jewish Don Quijote, setting out—in company of Senderl, the counterpart of Sancho Panza—on a fantastic journey to find the Lost Ten Tribes and save the people of Israel.

THE TRAVELS AND ADVENTURES OF BENJAMIN THE THIRD. 1878. Trans. by Moshe Spiegel. *Schocken* 1949 1968 pap. $1.50

LINETSKI, ISAAC JOEL. 1839–1915.

The author, a contemporary of the great Yiddish classic writer, Mendele Mocher Seforim, earned his fame by a single book, *"Dos Poylishe Yingl"* (The Polish Lad), which first appeared in 1867. Based on first-hand experience, it was a biting satire on the backwardness, fanaticism, ignorance, and superstitions of Jewish small town life of the mid-nineteenth century. However, the author criticized constructively; his aim was to expose in order to bring change and improvement.

THE POLISH LAD. Trans. by Moshe Spiegel. Introd. by Milton Hindus. *Jewish Publication Society* $7.95

PERETZ, I[SAAC] L[OEB]. 1852–1915.

One of the three "founding fathers" of Yiddish literature, "I. L. Peretz stands at the intellectual center of Yiddish culture and literature. Born in Poland he was exposed . . . to that conflict of ideas and impulses which was to dominate his . . . life as a writer and intellectual leader: the conflict between traditionalism as embodied in a powerful Hasidic inheritance, and modernism, the new trend of secular-progressivist thought that was beginning to sweep through the world of East European Jewry"—(Irving Howe in "A Treasury of Yiddish Stories," *Viking* 1954). Peretz wrote short stories, plays, and essays. His collected works appeared in several editions, the latest by "CYCO" in New York in 11 volumes, 1947–1948. A bibliography of translations from Peretz into English was compiled by Uriel Weinreich and appeared in the *Field of Yiddish*, 1954, Vol. 1.

BONTSHE THE SILENT. Trans. by A. S. Rappoport. 1927. *Bks. for Libraries* $11.25

PERETZ. Trans. and ed. by Sol Liptzin. 1947. *Bks. for Libraries* 1972 $19.00

STORIES AND PICTURES. Trans. by Helena Frank. 1906. *Bks. for Libraries* $13.75; *Gordon Press* $29.95

Books about Peretz

Y. L. P., Prince of the Ghetto. By Maurice Samuel. *Schocken* 1973 pap. $2.45
"Maurice Samuel retells the folk and Hasidic tales of Peretz . . . [he] weaves a continuous commentary on the man Peretz and on the world he epitomized"—(Publisher's note).

SHOLOM ALEICHEM (pseud. of Sholem Rabinowitz). 1859–1916.

Sholom Aleichem (Hebrew greeting meaning "Peace be unto you!") was born in Kiev, Russia, and settled in the United States in 1914. He wrote with humor and tenderness about the Yiddish-speaking Jews of Eastern Europe and won the title "the Jewish Mark Twain." (Mark Twain, on meeting him, referred to himself as "the American Sholom Aleichem.") "He is the passer-by, the informal correspondent, the post office into which Jews drop their communications to the world. All he does, you understand, is to write down stories people bring him. He invents nothing"—(Alfred Kazin in "Contemporaries"). The highly successful Broadway musical "Fiddler on the Roof" (by Joseph Stein, *Simon and Schuster* Pocket Bks. 1971 pap. $.95) is based on the tales about Tevye the dairyman. In the winter of 1966 the Folksbiene, a Yiddish drama company, presented an adaptation of Sholom Aleichem's novel "Wandering Stars" (U.S. 1952, o.p.) in New York. Bel Kaufman, author of "Up the Down Staircase," wrote in the *Saturday Review* of Oct. 1, 1966, an affectionate memoir of her grandfather, whose works are still immensely popular.

STORIES AND SATIRES. Trans. by Curt Leviant. *Macmillan* (Collier) 1970 pap. $1.75

OLD COUNTRY. Trans. by Julius and Frances Butwin. *Crown* 1956 pap. $1.98

TEVYE'S DAUGHTERS. Trans. by Frances Butwin. *Crown* 1959 pap. $1.98

ADVENTURES OF MOTTEL, THE CANTOR'S SON. Trans. by Tamara Kahana. *Macmillan* (Collier) 1961 pap. $1.25

INSIDE KASRILEVKE. Trans. by Isidore Goldstick. *Schocken* 1965 pap. $2.25

GREAT FAIR: Scenes from My Childhood. Trans. by Tamara Kahana. *Macmillan* (Collier) 1970 pap. $1.50

Books about Sholom Aleichem

    The World of Sholom Aleichem. By Maurice Samuel. *Knopf* $5.95; *Random House* Vintage 1973 pap. $2.45
    "A pilgrimage through ... the townlets and villages of the famous Pale of Settlement, recounting the adventures of the chief characters in the works of Sholom Aleichem and recreating the folklore, the outlook and the memories which were in part transplanted to America"—(Pub. note).
    The World of Sholom Aleichem. By Arnold Perl. *Dramatists* 1953 pap. $1.85. Contains three short plays: A Tale of Chelm, Bontche Schweig (based on a story by I. L. Peretz) and The High School (based on a story by Sholom Aleichem).
    Tevye and His Daughters. Based on the Tevye Stories of Sholom Aleichem. By Arnold Perl. *Dramatists* 1958 pap. $1.85
    My Father, Sholom Aleichem: A Memoir by Marie Waife-Goldberg. *Schocken* 1971 pap. $3.45; *Simon & Schuster* 1968 $7.50
    "A warm, captivating book"—(*LJ*).
    The Man Who Loved Laughter, The Story of Sholom Aleichem. By Louis Falstein. *Jewish Publication Society* 1968 $3.50
    Sholom Aleichem: Person, Persona, Presence. By Dan A. Miron. Uriel Weinreich Memorial Lecture, I *Yivo Institute for Jewish Research* 1972 pap. $1.50. About Sholom Aleichem's pseudonyms and their meaning in his work.
    Sholom Aleichem: A Non-Critical Introduction. By Sol Gittleman. *Mouton* (dist. by Humanities Press) 1974 $8.75
    "The book is intended to serve as an introductory overview for the non-specialist in search of a brief description of the origins of the Yiddish language and its literature, as well as a consideration of Sholom Aleichem's writings and their meaning within the world of both the East European *shtetl* and New York's East Side"—(Publisher's note).

ROSENFELD, MORRIS. 1862–1923.

    Born in Russia, Rosenfeld settled in the United States in 1886. His famous collection of poems from the sweatshop made him the poetic champion of the immigrant working masses. It was the first Yiddish book to be translated into English. Its translator, Leo Weiner, was Professor of Slavic Languages at Harvard and author of a history of Yiddish literature in English. This first translation rendered Yiddish verse into English prose. Later translations of Rosenfeld's poetry were much more successful, but are currently out of print.

SONGS FROM THE GHETTO. 1898. Trans. by Leo Weiner. *Gregg* 1970 $8.00

ANSKY, S. (pseud. of Solomon Zeinvil Rapoport). 1863–1920.

    Born in a small town in White Russia, Ansky obtained his education in traditional Jewish schools of the period, and by self-study. His democratic ideas and love for the poor and underprivileged prompted his interest in folk psychology and its artistic reflection—folklore. His famous play "The Dybbuk" is based on a popular belief in possessed souls to which Ansky gave a highly poetic and symbolic interpretation.

THE DYBBUK. Trans. with introd. by S. Morris Engel. *Nash Pub. Corp.* 1974 $6.95

PINSKY, DAVID. 1872–1959.

    Born in Russia, Pinsky became involved early in labor Zionist activities. In 1898 he emigrated to the United States. His works include novels, short stories, and plays. According to a critic, ". . . it is the earliest stories that seem most fresh ... the young Pinsky was able to communicate compassionate tenderness in writing about the Jewish poor"—(Irving Howe, "Treasury of Yiddish Stories," *Viking* 1954).

TEMPTATIONS: A Book of Short Stories. Trans. by Isaac Goldberg. 1919. *Bks. for Libraries* $11.75

ADLER, JACOB. 1877–1974.

    The author, popular with the readers of the Yiddish press, was born in Dynow, Galicia, and emigrated to the United States in 1890. He wrote humorous prose and verse and published his works in the periodical press, as well as in book form. One of his popular characters was known as Yente Telebende. Some of his works appeared under the pseudonym B. Kovner.

LAUGH, JEW, LAUGH: Short Humorous Stories. Trans. by Abraham London. 1934. *Bks. for Libraries Press* 1970 $8.75

SHAPIRO, LAMED. 1878–1948.

Lamed Shapiro was born in the Ukraine, visited the United States in 1905, and returned in 1911. Considered a master of the twentieth-century Yiddish story, he was "a successor to the first generation of Yiddish writers . . . but after some early influence he departed radically from their style and subject matter. . . ." He is "an exacting craftsman with a sophisticated artistic sensibility, carefully attuned to the modes of Western fiction . . ."—(Publisher's note).

THE JEWISH GOVERNMENT AND OTHER STORIES. Trans. and ed. with introd. by Curt Leviant. *Twayne* 1971 $7.00

ASCH, SHALOM (also Sholem). 1880–1957.

The author, one of the major figures in Yiddish letters, was born in Kutno, near Warsaw, Poland. Educated in the orthodox Hebrew schools, he began writing in 1901, first in Hebrew, then in Yiddish. His early, quietly humorous stories of Jewish small-town life brought Yiddish literature to international notice. His epic novels and plays dealt with the contemporary scene and the Jewish experience on a world-wide scale from Poland, Germany, and Soviet Russia to Palestine and the United States. He portrayed the Jewish historic past in all its moral grandeur and beauty. The range and reach of his talent were wide; his collected works appeared in Yiddish in 29 volumes. A great deal was translated into English, but some of the translations are now out of print. A bibliography of English translations from his works was compiled by Libby Okun-Cohen and appeared in the *Bulletin of Bibliography* (Vol. 22, No. 5, Jan./Apr. 1958).

IN THE BEGINNING: Stories from the Bible. 1914. Trans. by Caroline Cunningham. *Shocken* 1966 $4.95

MOTTKE THE THIEF. 1916. Trans. by Willa and Edwin Muir. *Greenwood* $13.00

MOTHER. 1925. Trans. by Nathan Ausubel. *AMS Press* 1970 $8.75

SALVATION. 1934. Trans. by Willa and Edwin Muir. *Schocken* 1968 2nd ed. pap. $2.45

CHILDREN OF ABRAHAM: The Short Stories of Sholem Asch. Trans. by Maurice Samuel. 1942. *Bks. for Libraries* $14.50

TALES OF MY PEOPLE. Trans. by Meyer Levin. 1948. *Bks. for Libraries* $9.50

RABOY, ISAAC. 1882–1944.

Born in the Ukraine, the author emigrated to the United States in 1904. He acquired first-hand knowledge of Jewish immigrant life in this country by working in sweatshops, in factories, and on farms. His novels depict the encounter of the Jewish immigrant with American life, his failures, disappointments and successes.

NINE BROTHERS: A Novel. Trans. by Max Rosenfeld. Fwd. by Itche Goldberg. *Yiddisher Kultur Farband* (80 Fifth Ave. N.Y.C.) 1968 $5.00. The Yiddish original was published in 1936.

OPATOSHU, JOSEPH. 1886–1954.

One of the great Yiddish novelists, Opatoshu was born in Poland and came to the United States in 1907. His first writings were naturalistic stories of contemporary life. He was especially interested in "lower strata" and underworld characters, and described life of the "New York Ghetto." Later he concentrated on historical subjects. Several of his historical novels have been translated into English, but are now out of print. The latest to be translated, the collection listed below, bears the title of the first novella dealing with Jewish life in the sixteenth century. It describes "the wedding that unites two important Jewish families. The medieval Regensburg Ghetto is brilliantly depicted through the celebrants: beggars, minstrels, yeshiva students, dancers, a young duke, wealthy merchants, an innkeeper and his wife, and a host of others. The mood is one of gaiety and gusto"—(Publisher's note).

A DAY IN REGENSBURG: Short Stories. Trans. by Jacob Sloan. 1968, o.p.

ESSELIN, ALTER (adapted name of Ore Serebrenik). 1889–1974.

Born in the Ukraine, in a working class family, the author came to the United States in 1908. His poetry appeared in numerous journals and in book form. In 1955 he received the Kovner Award for Yiddish poetry, distributed by the Jewish Book Council of America.

POEMS. Trans. by Joseph Esselin. *Interface* 1968

GREENBERG, HAYIM. 1889–1953.

Greenberg was born in Bessarabia and acquired his extensive education in Hebrew, Yiddish, and Russian letters by self-study. He was active in the Zionist movement from his early youth and became one of the leading figures in the Zionist movement in Europe and America, especially in the cultural field. In 1924 he settled in the United States, where he contributed articles and edited several important journals in Hebrew, Yiddish, and English. His main interest centered around the idea of Jewish cultural survival in the Diaspora. Besides the book listed below, two volumes of his essays under the title "The Inner Eye" were published by the Jewish Frontier Association between 1953 and 1964.

HAYIM GREENBERG ANTHOLOGY. Sel. with introd. by Marie Syrkin. *Wayne State Univ. Press* Waynbook 1968 $8.95

SHAZAR, SHNEUR ZALMAN. 1889–

The author, third President of the State of Israel, is a scholar and writer who uses both Hebrew and Yiddish in his work. The Yiddish collection of his poetry, edited by Abraham Sutzkever, appeared in 1973 as an expression of his feelings in the period of both tragic and hopeful events in Jewish history. The English version was undertaken at the suggestion of the translator and was warmly welcomed by the author.

POEMS. Trans. by Joseph Leftwich. *A. S. Barnes* 1974 $4.95

GOTTESFELD, CHONE. 1890–1964.

Born in a small town of eastern Galicia, the author came to the United States in 1908. He had a difficult life; from being an errand boy for a newspaper he rose to become a very popular columnist and writer for the stage. The collection cited below contains sketches written in a humorous vein and reminiscences.

TALES OF THE OLD WORLD AND THE NEW. Trans. by Jacob Richman. *A. S. Barnes* Yoseloff 1964

SINGER, ISRAEL JOSHUA. 1893–1944.

I. J. Singer, brother of Isaac Bashevis Singer, was born in Poland, came to the United States in 1934 and was naturalized in 1939. His works include novels, short stories, and plays. Philip Rahv called his most notable book, "The Brothers Ashkenazi," "the most important novel of Jewish life so far published in English." The strength of Singer's work lies in his "extraordinary knowledge of varieties of human beings, and that ability to seize upon significant traits in character and to present them with a minimum of strokes and a maximum of power"—(Milton Rugoff). "Yoshe Kalb" "is [a] story . . . of mistaken ideals, of purity and youth imposed upon and corrupted, of superstition, intolerance, and worldly striving gilded with piety. . . . Told with great exuberance, and a kind of ironic high spirits"—(SR). "There are fine things in the book: a wonderfully satiric portrait of a narrow and superstitious *shtetl* life that is a good antidote to current sentimentalization of that life, while still doing justice to its Brueghel-like vitality"—(*New Republic*). It was first serialized in the *Jewish Daily Forward* and has been dramatized.

STEEL AND IRON. 1927. Trans. by Joseph Singer. *T. Y. Crowell* (Funk & Wagnalls) 1969 $6.95. The impact of World War I and the Russian Revolution on Jewish life.

YOSHE KALB. 1932. Trans. by Maurice Samuel; introd. by Isaac Bashevis Singer. 1965 *Lancer* 1972 pap. $1.25; *Vanguard* 1974 $7.95. A portrayal of Hasidic life in nineteenth-century Galicia (a province of eastern Poland under Austrian rule).

THE BROTHERS ASHKENAZI. 1936. Trans. by Maurice Samuel. *Knopf* 1936 1939 $8.95 A "panoramic novel"—(*PW*) of Jewish life in Poland before Hitler.

THE RIVER BREAKS UP. Trans. by Maurice Samuel. 1938. *Vanguard* 1974 $6.95. Collection of short stories.

EAST OF EDEN. 1938. Trans. by Maurice Samuel. 1939. *Vanguard* 1974 $7.95. The deceived hopes and expectations of Jewish Communists in Soviet Russia.

THE FAMILY CARNOVSKY. 1943. Trans. by Joseph Singer. *Harper* Harrow Bks. 1973 pap. $1.50; *Vanguard* 1969 $6.95. Tragedy of assimilated Jewish families in Nazi Germany.

OF A WORLD THAT IS NO MORE. 1946. *Vanguard* 1970 $6.95. Memories of childhood.

ALQUIT, B. (pseud. of Eliezer Blum).   1896–1963.

Short story writer and poet, Alquit was a member of the avant-garde literary group *"In Zikh,"* and also contributed to dailies and periodicals. His short stories are realistic and contemporary, his poetry in a modern mood. He was born in Chełm, Poland, and came to the United States in 1914. His literary activity developed on American soil.

REVOLT OF THE APPRENTICES AND OTHER STORIES. 1958. Trans. by Etta Blum. *A. S. Barnes* Yoseloff 1969

GLATSTEIN, JACOB.   1896–1971.

Born in Lublin, Glatstein died in the United States where he had lived since 1914. One of the major figures in modern Yiddish poetry, Glatstein cultivated free verse and poetry closely related to the reality of contemporary events and social environment. A master of Yiddish language, forceful and blunt in its use, he created poems which became classic expressions of Jewish attitudes and reactions to the tragic events of the Holocaust. He also wrote brilliant prose; especially remarkable are two accounts of his trip to Europe on the eve of World War II.

POEMS. Sel. and trans. by Etta Blum. *I. L. Peretz Publishing* 1970

THE SELECTED POEMS OF JACOB GLATSTEIN. Trans. with introd. by Ruth Whitman. 1972 o.p.

HOMEWARD BOUND. 1938. Trans. by Abraham Goldstein. *A. S. Barnes* Yoseloff 1960 $4.95

HOMECOMING AT TWILIGHT. 1940. Trans. by Norbert Guterman; fwd. by Maurice Samuel. *A. S. Barnes* Yoseloff 1962

CHAVER PAVER (pseud. of Gershon Einbinder).   1900–1964

Born in Bershad, the Ukraine, the author came to the United States in 1923. His stories portray in a realistic and humorous vein Jewish immigrant life in the Depression era. He was also a prolific juvenile writer.

CLINTON STREET AND OTHER STORIES. Trans. by Henry Goodman. *Yiddisher Kultur Farband* (80 Fifth Ave., N.Y.C.) 1974

SINGER, ISAAC BASHEVIS.   1904–

Isaac Bashevis Singer is I. J. Singer's (*q.v.*) younger brother. Born in Radzymin, Poland, he had a traditional Jewish education and attended a rabbinical seminary in Warsaw. His first fiction was written in Hebrew, the more recent in Yiddish. His work was not translated into English until he was 46. Since coming to the United States in 1935, he has been on the staff of the *Jewish Daily Forward*, in which "The Manor" was serialized. "The Family Moskat," his lengthy first novel, is unlike Singer's other works in that it does not involve fantasy. This history of a Polish-Jewish family, from the early 1900s to World War II, "is crowded with incidents, conversations and descriptions [and] is notably free of introspection"—(*SR*). It was a selection of the Book Find Club and was awarded the Louis Lamed Prize. "In My Father's Court," Singer's memoir of his childhood in Poland, offers a glimpse of Hassidic life. *Library Journal* called it "well written and thoroughly enjoyable. It is filled with pathos and humor and gives the reader much insight into [his] other writings." In 1964 Singer was elected to the National Institute of Arts and Letters. Edmund Wilson has said of Singer: "Though steeped into the rabbinical tradition, he requires less effort of adjustment on the part of the non-Jewish reader than the relentlessly rabbinical Agnon. I recommend him, by the way, to the Swedes if they want to give any more prizes to the highest representatives of a culture which stems straight from the sacred books upon which we have all been brought up"—(in *Commentary*). In 1975 Singer received an honorary doctoral degree from the Hebrew University of Jerusalem and the S. J. Agnon Golden Medal Award from the American Friends of the Hebrew University.

"Satan in Goray," a story of religious hysteria among persecuted Jews in a small Polish town in the seventeenth century, is "a remarkable book, brilliant, enigmatic." The *N.Y. Times* said of it: "This black-mirror narrative of miracles and cabala, of a hamlet in seventeenth-century Poland and a false Messiah, is in the tradition of such classics as 'The Dybbuk' and 'The Golem.' Poetically conceived, it captures the fever of longing, the folk-frenzy for salvation, that possessed the Jewish population of central Europe after the dark decade of the Chmielnickl massacres, three centuries before Hitler." In "The Slave" Singer once again has taken seventeenth-century Poland for his setting. "The plot is simple and exciting, the characters successfully developed. But the book is even more remarkable for its brilliant evocation of the mystique of these primitive times and for the beautiful double parallel drawn between this Jacob and his Biblical counterpart and between the plight of these Polish Jews and the plight of their modern counterpart, the Polish Jews of World War II"—(*LJ*). Singer has written a number of books for children, some of which are listed in the section on juvenile literature.

AN ISAAC BASHEVIS SINGER READER. *Farrar, Straus* 1971 $10.00; *Sunburst* 1971 pap. $5.95

SELECTED SHORT STORIES. *Random* Modern Lib. $2.45

GIMPEL THE FOOL AND OTHER STORIES. Trans. by Saul Bellow and others. *Farrar, Straus* 1957 $6.95 Noonday pap. $1.45; *Avon Bks.* 1965 pap. $.75

"Among the most heart-piercing, penetrating, unforgettable stories ever written"—(Kenneth Rexroth).

THE SPINOZA OF MARKET STREET. Trans. by Elaine Gottlieb and others. *Farrar, Straus* 1961 $6.95; *Avon Bks.* $1.25. An anthology of 11 short stories.

SHORT FRIDAY AND OTHER STORIES. *Farrar, Straus* 1964 $5.95

Sixteen tales which "penetrate life, death, reality, the supernatural, and have an earthy quality that makes for enjoyable reading"—(*LJ*).

ISAAC BASHEVIS SINGER READING HIS STORIES. *Cardmon* TC 1200 $5.95. A recording. The author reads "Gimpel the Fool" and "A Piece of Advice" (from "The Spinoza of Market Street").

SATAN IN GORAY. 1935. Trans. by J. Sloan. *Farrar, Straus* 1955 $7.95; *Avon Bks.* 1964 1966 pap. $1.25

THE FAMILY MOSKAT. 1950. Trans. by A. H. Gross. *Farrar, Straus* 1965 $7.95 Noonday pap. $3.95

THE MAGICIAN OF LUBLIN. *Farrar, Straus* 1960 $5.95. A novel of nineteenth-century Poland.

THE SLAVE. Trans. by the author and Cecil Hemley. *Farrar, Straus* 1962 $6.95; *Avon Bks.* 1964 1971 pap. $1.25

THE MANOR. *Farrar, Straus* 1967 $6.95; *Dell* 1969 pap. $1.25. This first volume of a planned trilogy is set in nineteenth-century Poland. Calman Jacoby and his family are the protagonists through whom Singer examines the effects of a changing society upon Jewish life.

IN MY FATHER'S COURT. Trans. by Channah Kleinerman-Goldstein, Elaine Gottlieb, and Joseph Singer. *Farrar, Straus* 1966 $5.95 Noonday pap. $1.95

"One of the truly outstanding books in its genre"—(*SR*).

THE SÉANCE AND OTHER STORIES. *Farrar, Straus* 1968 $5.95 Noonday 1969 pap. $2.25; *Avon* pap. $.95

THE ESTATE. *Farrar, Straus* 1969 $6.95; *Dell* 1971 pap. $1.25

A FRIEND OF KAFKA AND OTHER STORIES. *Farrar, Straus* 1970 $6.95; *Dell* Delta 1972 pap. $2.65

A CROWN OF FEATHERS. *Farrar, Straus* 1973 $8.95; *Fawcett* Crest pap. $1.50. Winner of a National Book Award.

ENEMIES: A Love Story. *Farrar, Straus* 1972 $6.95; *Fawcett* Crest 1973 pap. $1.25

(With Ira Moskowitz). THE HASIDIM. Paintings, drawings, and etchings by Ira Moskowitz. Text by Isaac Bashevis Singer and the artist. *Crown* 1973 $10.00

PASSIONS AND OTHER STORIES. Trans. by the author and others. *Farrar, Straus* 1975 $8.95

See also under Juvenile Literature above.

Books about Singer

Isaac Bashevis Singer and the Eternal Past. By Irving Buchen. *New York Univ. Press* Gotham Lib. 1968 $8.95 pap. $2.45

Isaac Bashevis Singer. By Ben Siegal. Pamphlets on American Writers Ser. *Univ. of Minnesota Press* 1969 pap. $1.25

Critical Views of Isaac Bashevis Singer. Ed. by Irving Malin. *New York Univ. Press* Gotham Lib. $8.95 pap. $2.45

The Achievement of Isaac Bashevis Singer. Ed. by Marcia Allentuck. Modern Critiques Ser. *Southern Illinois Univ. Press* 1970 $4.95

Isaac Bashevis Singer. By Irving Malin. Mod. Lit. Monographs *Ungar* 1972 $6.00

KATZ, MENKE. 1906–

Katz is a prolific poet writing mostly free verse in a modernistic vein. Many of his motifs and images deal with his childhood in a small town in pre-war Lithuania. He is fluent in both Yiddish and English and translates his own work.

BURNING VILLAGE. *The Smith* 1972 $5.00

ROCKROSE. *Horizon Press* $4.50

EMIOT, ISRAEL GOLDVASSER (pseud. of Melech Janovski). 1909–

Born in Poland, in an Orthodox family, Emiot became interested in modern Yiddish literature and joined the ranks of Yiddish writers in the mid-twenties. During World War II he was a refugee in Soviet Russia. He has published several collections of poetry, fiction, and memoirs in Yiddish, and contributes to Yiddish and English periodicals. He lives in Rochester, New York.

MY YESTERDAYS: (Short Stories). Trans. by Byrna Weir and the author. *Jewish Community Center of Greater Rochester* 1973

GRADE, CHAIM. 1910–

One of the greatest living Yiddish writers, Chaim Grade was born in Vilna, where he received a thorough education in the Talmudic academies of the region thanks to the efforts of his mother, who dedicated her life to giving her son adequate support for uninterrupted study. Grade started to write poetry in 1932 and very soon won the recognition of the literary world. He escaped the onslaught of the Nazis as a refugee in the Soviet Union only to return and find his mother and wife killed and his home town destroyed. His later work, both poetry and prose, is dedicated to the tragic theme of the Holocaust and to the re-creation of a world which is no more. His prose is sculpturesque in its portrayal of life and characters deeply rooted in Jewish tradition and the lore of his native land; his poetry is forceful and dramatic with the pathos of national and personal tragedy. Only a small part of his work has been translated into English.

THE SEVEN LITTLE LANES. Trans. by Curt Leviant. *Bergen Belsen Memorial Press of the World Federation of Bergen-Belsen Assns.* 1972 (Remembrance Award Library)

THE WELL: A Novel. Trans. by Ruth Wisse. 1967 o.p.

BRYKS, RACHMIL. 1912–1964.

Born in a small town near Łodz, Poland, the author lived through the terrible experience of the ghetto in Łodz and the concentration camp Auschwitz. His work deals almost exclusively with this experience.

A CAT IN THE GHETTO: Four Novelettes. Trans. by S. Morris Engel; introd. by Sol Liptzin; pref. by Irving Howe. *Bloch Pub. Co.* 1959

SUTZKEVER, ABRAHAM. 1913–

Sutzkever is one of the greatest living Yiddish poets. He started to write in his native city of Vilna in the 1930s, and lived in the ghetto of Vilna under Nazi occupation. He joined the partisans in 1943, and was called as a witness to the Nuremberg trials of 1946. Now he lives in Israel where he edits the Yiddish quarterly *Di Goldene Keyt* (*The Golden Chain*). His collected works in two volumes were published in Israel in 1963. Since then he has published three more collections of poems. A great master of word and image, he found his own way of extracting beauty from the somber realities of Jewish life and expressing the tragedy and heroism of the holocaust period.

SIBERIA: a Poem. Trans. and introd. by Jacob Sonntag. With a letter on the poem and drawings by Marc Chagall. 1961 o.p.

Books about Sutzkever

Abraham Sutzkever, Partisan Poet. By Joseph Leftwich. *A. S. Barnes* Yoseloff 1971 $5.50

KA-TZETNIK 135633 (pseud.). 1917–

The author chose not to appear under his real name and adapted as his pen-name a Yiddish word meaning an anonymous inmate of a concentration camp. Himself a survivor of one of the worst of those camps, Auschwitz, he describes the underworld created by the Nazis for their victims in a manner which tries to convey the nightmarish quality of the experience.

ATROCITY. *Lyle Stuart* 1963 $4.95

—D. A.

YUGOSLAV LITERATURE

Yugoslavia is a land of exceptional diversity. There are three standard literary languages—Slovenian, Serbo-Croatian and, of late, Macedonian—and three major religious traditions, Catholic, Orthodox, and Moslem, of which the latter does not entirely coincide with the lines of linguistic cleavage. In the past, literary activity was carried on in a number of divergent social-linguistic zones, each focused on a large town such as Dubrovnik, Zagreb, or Belgrade, and each more or less isolated from the others, drawing inspiration and support from larger centers beyond the borders: Budapest and Vienna, Moscow, Rome, Paris, or Istanbul.

The primary literatures, historically, are those of Croatia and Serbia. Both the current traditions date back only to the 1760s, and by contrast with the West are characterized by their lack of continuity with earlier centuries. The rich ecclesiastical writing of medieval Serbia was throttled by the Turkish invasions and subsequent domination during the fourteenth to nineteenth centuries. Verse drama and the literary epic were cultivated along the Dalmatian coast in the sixteenth and seventeenth centuries, centered in Dubrovnik and influenced by the Italian Renaissance. But that tradition too died away, leaving no legacy. Yugoslav literature as it exists today is a modern development.

As has so often been true of national literatures, the reasons have to do with the adoption of a common vernacular acceptable to Orthodox Serb and Catholic Croat alike. What is distinctive about the Yugoslav case is that this process was accelerated by the collection and publication of a living oral folk tradition. The first four volumes of Vuk Karadžić's epochal collection appeared between 1823 and 1833. Vuk was a Serb of peasant origin who was the first to gather the heroic epic systematically, on a broad scale, and with fair regard for the authentic voice of illiterate singers. The impact was overwhelming and lasting, and the heroic epic became the pride of Yugoslav literature, especially coinciding as it did with a dynamic turn in Balkan history occasioned by the receding of Turkish influence. The region was alive with nationalist awakenings which fed on such autocthonous creation. To those educated on the classics of Greece and Rome it was natural to assume that history and folk epic are one, that folk tradition preserves and ought to preserve great historical events such as the Serbian risings of 1804–1817, to use what was found for purposes of national propaganda as if mistaking the "Iliad" (an oral composition), teleologically, for the "Aeneid" (a literary work), and to seek modern Homers in every back-country village. Only in the 1930s was such a person found in Avdo Međedović. The fact that it was Americans who "discovered" him, and who understood the significance of this a century and more after Goethe and other Romantic folklorists first drew the world's attention to the possibility that an oral epic tradition had survived in the Balkans unbroken since classical times, testifies to the persistence of an international interest in what Yugoslavia has to contribute to world literature. Forceful, unaffected prose translations into English are now making this unique contribution better known.

These literatures have shared general European developments over the past century and a half. Serbo-Croatian has had its romantic dramas, heavily influenced by Shakespeare (known in German translations), or based, for example, on the folk epics about Marko Kraljević, Marko the King's Son. It has had its realistic prose portrayals of village or small-town life, with due allowance for local color and psychological verisimilitude, and its modernist experiments with form and symbol around the turn of the century. If well translated, which it has not been, some of this writing could take its place alongside other such period productions in the West; the Slovenes, to take just one instance, had a gifted

Romantic poet in France Prešeren. But much of what was produced before the advent, at the end of World War I, of the two giants of modern Serbian and Croatian literature, Andrić and Krleža, is now of interest only for internal development. Following the national liberation there was, predictably, a body of stories and novels based on war themes, often brutally presented, under the flag of socialist realism. Since the mid-1950s, however, when that doctrine was compelled to compete on equal terms with other stylistic modes and thematic interests, the literary scene in Belgrade, Zagreb, and the other centers has been increasingly lively. Such writers as Bulatović and Vasko Popa show the presence of purely literary concerns in an ideological society. Others, like the Bosnian Meša Selimović, are yet to be heard in translation to the degree they deserve.

History and Criticism

Barac, Antun. A HISTORY OF YUGOSLAV LITERATURE. Trans. by Petar Mijusković. 1955. *Michigan Slavic Publications* $3.50 pap. $2.00

> The only general survey available in English which covers literary developments from the medieval Serbian state through the interwar period in all the present Yugoslav republics. Facts are comprehensive and reliable, but succinct to the point of often being mere lists, and critical judgement is limited to generalization. Barac's approach is Marxist.

Despalatović, Elinor M. LJUDEVIT GAJ AND THE ILLYRIAN MOVEMENT. *Columbia* 1975 $12.00. Although Gaj himself was at most tangential to literature, the pan-South-Slavist Illyrian group of which he was a founder and leader in the 1830s and 1840s played the major role in the resurgence of Croatian letters at that time.

Kadić, Ante. CONTEMPORARY CROATIAN LITERATURE. *Humanities Press* 1960 pap. $5.75

CONTEMPORARY SERBIAN LITERATURE. *Humanities Press* 1964 pap. $5.25

FROM CROATIAN RENAISSANCE TO YUGOSLAV SOCIALISM. *Humanities Press* 1969 $22.00

> The first two books are useful surveys of twentieth-century developments in the literatures of the two major republics, similar to that of Barac in the emphasis on lists of authors and their works but carrying the story into the 1960s and providing as well some account of ideological groupings and organs of publication. The third work consists of essays on a variety of authors, including Andrić and Krleža; as criticism, it is much more stimulating than the two handbooks.

Kimball, Stanley B. THE AUSTRO-SLAV REVIVAL: A Study of Nineteenth-Century Literary Foundations. *The American Philosophical Soc.* New Series—Vol. 63, Pt. 4 1973 $4.00

> This is a brief monograph on the pioneering era (1826–1879) of the patriotic literary foundations known as *maticas* which played a key role in national revivals under the Hapsburgs. Their most characteristic activity, publishing, was aimed at broadening access to good literature and raising popular standards. Development of the Serbian, Croatian, and Slovenian *maticas* are covered in separate chapters, as well as their Czech, Slovak, and Moravian sister societies.

Lord, Albert B. THE SINGER OF TALES. *Atheneum* 1965 pap. $3.95; Studies in Comparative Literature *Harvard Univ. Press* 1960 $10.00. The classic exposition, based on field-collected South Slavic texts, of the oral theory of epic composition and transmission within a living tradition. Part Two applies the theory to Homer and to medieval oral epics (Beowulf, Chanson de Roland, Digenis Akritas).

Low, David H., Trans. THE BALLADS OF MARKO KRALJEVIĆ. 1922. *Greenwood* 1968 $11.75. A good starting point in acquainting oneself with the tradition of Christian epic in Serbia and Montenegro. The "ballads" have been culled from Vuk's nineteenth-century collections and arranged by Low as a cycle. A brief, useful introduction and some background notes enhance his slightly stylized prose translations.

Lukić, Sveta. CONTEMPORARY YUGOSLAV LITERATURE: A Sociopolitical Approach. Trans. by Pola Triandis; ed. by Gertrude J. Robinson. *Univ. of Illinois Press* 1972 $11.95. A critical and stimulating analysis by a Marxist revisionist thinker of what we would term the literary scene, 1945–1968, in Yugoslavia and its impact on the formation of literary standards. Valuable for its integral perspective on the literatures of that country, as opposed to the standard multi-regional treatment.

Mihajlov, Mihajlo. MOSCOW SUMMER. Introd. by Andrew Field; fwd. by Myron Kolatch.
   Farrar, Straus 1965 $4.50

   RUSSIAN THEMES. Trans. by Marija Mihajlov. *Farrar, Straus* 1968 $6.95 Noonday pap.
   $2.45

   Mihajlov exemplifies a strong critical tradition in those countries of Eastern Europe where
   freedom of conscience and speech are suppressed and where as a consequence criticism of
   literature tends to serve broader ends than the narrowly aesthetic. By profession a teacher and
   writer on Russian literature, Mihajlov, like some of the authors he most admires, writes out of
   conviction and has not hesitated to publish. For his efforts, he has gone to jail. He belongs to a
   stubbornly growing number of intellectuals in Eastern Europe who have been willing to endure
   persecution for their ideas; one thinks of his own countryman, Milovan Djilas, and of Solzhenitsyn. There are many others, relatively unknown here. Mihajlov first came to attention for his
   "Moscow Summer," an investigation of the Russian cultural atmosphere of 1964. "Russian
   Themes" continues this vein but also includes lengthy essays on authors more or less taboo in the
   Soviet Union—Pasternak, Zamyatin, Solzhenitsyn, and Tertz.

Price, Robert F. MIKHAIL SHOLOKHOV IN YUGOSLAVIA: Reception and Literary Impact.
   Columbia (East European Quarterly) 1973 $12.50

   This is a published dissertation, and not one of very high quality at that. It is, though, of interest
   to the general reader for its synopses and discussion of popular but untranslated war novels by
   half a dozen Yugoslav writers of realistic prose. Lacking the novelty of stylistic experiment or the
   charm of forbidden content, these novels by Branko Ćopić, Dobrica Ćosić, Mirko Božić, and
   others are unlikely ever to be published in English. Thematically, the works chosen for analysis by
   Price have in common local peasant resistance to the partisans' efforts to unite the country against
   its fascist occupiers, in the name of Communist ideals (as the comparison with Sholokhov implies),
   and the savage fratricidal conflicts that resulted.

SERBOCROATIAN HEROIC SONGS COLLECTED BY MILMAN PARRY. *Harvard Univ. Press* 1954
   Vol. 1 Novi Pazar: English Translations trans. and ed. by Albert Bates Lord 1954
   $14.50 (Vol. 2 contains the original Serbocroatian text); Vol. 3 The Wedding of
   Smailagić Meho by Avdo Međedović trans. and ed. by Albert Bates Lord and David
   E. Bynum 1974 $17.50 (Vol. 4 contains the original Serbocroatian text).

   Volume 1 contains examples of the heroic epic as it was sung in the 1930s by South Slavs whose
   forebears had converted to Islam. Parry found these Moslem areas of Yugoslavia—Bosnia and
   parts of Montenegro—the best testing ground for his ideas about orality, because the singers there
   were essentially uncontaminated by printed song books. A number of the songs found here in fine
   prose translations are multiforms of widely distributed tales about the capture of cities, or the
   captivity, rescue, or return of heroes, and bear comparison with the "Iliad" and the "Odyssey" of
   Homer.
   Vol. 3 contains the "Smailagić Meho," dictated in July 1935 in the Montenegrin market town of
   Bijelo Polje by an illiterate Moslem Yugoslav butcher and epic singer, Avdo Međedović. The poem
   bears the distinction of being the longest published oral epic collected in Europe in modern times
   and is, therefore, a prime source for the comparative study of epic traditions. It is also an
   exceptionally fine and engrossing tale in its own right, marked by human insight and delicate
   characterization. The volume includes translated conversations with Avdo the singer; essays by
   Professor Lord on the other known multiforms of the song, and on Avdo's originality; and
   compendious background notes to the period dealt with by Avdo, when Sulejman's conquests had
   broadened the Empire to its greatest limits in the Balkans, notes which not infrequently vie with
   the song itself in their interest for the historian or folklorist.

Subotić, Dragutin. YUGOSLAV POPULAR BALLADS: Their Origin and Development. 1932.
   Norwood Editions $27.50. Of special interest is the lengthy section in this book on
   Yugoslav traditional poetry in German, French, and English literature.

Collections

Johnson's anthology of 36 writers, most of whom were in their thirties during the decade
of the 1960s, attempts to convey something of the literary currents of that time. Its stories,
lyric verse, and fragments of novels are arranged not only by genre but by stylistic and
thematic affinities, rather than by linguistic-cultural region. Similarly, Lenski focuses on
recent prose fiction. Complementary, in a sense, to these are the two other collections
currently in print, in which the works chosen for translation are divided more or less

equally in bulk by the watershed of World War I. Koljević begins in the last quarter of the nineteenth century with the period of the realistic, regional short story; the editors of the *Twayne* anthology go back to the roots of the modern period at the end of the eighteenth century. Readers should be advised that a good deal of the *Twayne* anthology consists of short prose extracts or brief poems, and that many of the translations are outdated.

Authors of particular interest who are not included in the list of individual authors, but whose works are available in anthologies, are: Laza K. Lazerević (1851–1891), Simo Matavulj (1852–1908), Antun Gastav Matoš (1873–1914), Borisav Stanković (1875–1927), Vladan Desnica (1905–1967), Branko Ćopić (1915–   ), Kole I. Čašule (1921–   ), and Živko Čingo (1935–   ).

Holton, Milne, Ed., THE BIG HORSE AND OTHER STORIES OF MODERN MACEDONIA. *Univ. of Missouri Press* 1974 $9.50

Twelfth and last of the Slavic languages to be codified, newly enriched lexically, Macedonian has rapidly developed a literature of its own in the postwar decades. A little space was assigned in the *Twayne* anthology to this brand new literature's established figures. Holton's collection of 20 stories attempts, as he says, "to represent as selectively as possible something of the range of matter and manner in Macedonian fiction today," and concentrates on the younger generation of writers. Regionalism, lyrically felt and expressed, in one way or another unites all of them. Another common denominator, Holton notes in his introduction, is their exploration of the shifting attitudes of newly urbanized villagers.

Johnson, Bernard, Ed. NEW WRITING IN YUGOSLAVIA. 1970 *Peter Smith* $5.25

Koljević, Svetozar, Trans. and ed. YUGOSLAV SHORT STORIES. *Oxford* World's Class. 1966 $6.00

Lenski, Branko, Ed. DEATH OF A SIMPLE GIANT AND OTHER MODERN YUGOSLAV STORIES. *Vanguard* 1965 $7.95

Mikasinovich, Branko, Dragan Milivojević, and Vasa Mihailovich, Eds. INTRODUCTION TO YUGOSLAV LITERATURE: An Anthology of Fiction and Poetry. *Twayne* 1973 $6.95

KARADŽIĆ, VUK STEFANOVIĆ.   1787–1864.

Serbia's great linguist, ethnographer, and collector-publisher of oral traditional materials, Vuk, as he is known, played as important a role in the cultural development of nineteenth-century Yugoslavia as perhaps any single individual can play. A largely self-made scholar from the peasantry, his defining and championing of the Serbian popular language at a time when there was confusion as to what "Serbian" was or should be, as a language, determined its further development well into the twentieth century. His orthographic simplifications and other reforms underlie today's single Serbo-Croatian language. Vuk's encyclopedic dictionary (1818), in its expanded 1852 edition, is still a treasury of useful information on the southern Slavs in the eighteenth and early nineteenth centuries, and one which is absorbingly presented—scholarship without pedantry. If the dictionary is comparable, in a large sense, to Samuel Johnson's, then Vuk's translation of the New Testament resembles Luther's in its conception and impact. Vuk is considered the most reliable historian of the Serbia of his day. His connoisseur's descriptions of national life and customs founded Serbian ethnography. He corresponded with all the leading literary and scientific figures of his time (two letters appear in the *Twayne* anthology, *see above, Section on Collections*) and was a member of all the national cultural societies of western and eastern Europe. In sum, Vuk exercised an unrivalled influence on the development of national self-consciousness in Yugoslavia through original publications, folklore collections, and correspondence. Some of his writings can be found translated in Duncan Wilson's fine general biography, the only one in English.

Books about Vuk Karadžić

The Life and Times of Vuk Stefanović Karadžić, 1787–1864: Literacy, Literature, and National Independence in Serbia. By Duncan Wilson. *Oxford* 1970 $17.00

NJEGOŠ, PETAR II PETROVIĆ, Prince-Bishop of Montenegro.   1813–1851.

A revered figure in the Serbian literary heritage, Njegoš combined forcefulness and statecraft of a high order with great originality as a poet. "The Mountain Wreath" (1847), his most widely known and quoted work, is a dramatic poem modeled on the South Slavic decasyllabic oral epic. Its subject is the fratricidal conflict of Montenegro's Orthodox Christians with renegades who had accepted Islam, culminating in a legendary massacre of the latter toward the beginning of the eighteenth century. The only English translation, in any case dated, is now out of print apart from brief excerpts. Of greater interest and access to the Western reader is Njegoš' philosophic, Miltonian epic "The Ray of the Microcosm" (1845), an allegory built around the soul's journey back to outer space. Until recently this remarkable work has been available in the translation of Anica Savic-Rebac (Harvard Slavic Studies, No. 3), with a most stimulating and informative introduction. Milovan Djilas' biography of Njegoš devotes about a third of the book to these literary epics and other, minor, poems by Montenegro's poet-ruler.

THE MOUNTAIN WREATH. 1847. Trans. by James W. Wiles 1925. *Greenwood* $12.00 (Excerpts in Mikasinovich, "Introduction to Yugoslav Literature," *see above, Section on Collections.*)

Books about Njegoš

Njegoš: Poet, Prince, Bishop. By Milovan Djilas. Trans. by Michael B. Petrovich. *Harcourt* 1966 $10.00

MEÐEDOVIĆ, AVDO. 1875–1955. *See above, Section on History and Criticism, entry for* "Serbocroatian Heroic Songs Collected by Milman Parry."

ANDRIĆ, IVO. 1892–1975. (Nobel Prize 1961)

Few Yugoslav writers are more deeply identified with a particular locale than is Andrić with Bosnia, and none has more consummately endowed his chosen milieu with philosophic overtones: the world of matter and desire, evil by nature, is ineluctable; man's urge toward self-transcendence, enduring; his aspiration, illusory. Andrić used and reused the deceptively simple building blocks which were his native land's legacy: rocks, aridity, steep hills, narrow horizons, thirst. At the same time he created a stunning variety of action and character, again reflecting the ethnic and religious color, the historic schisms, of this westernmost frontier of the Ottoman Empire. Though each of his works has essentially the same thing to say, one never is aware of sameness in reading Andrić; a superb story-teller, on that level he does not repeat himself. Yugoslavs like to refer to him as "classic," by which more is meant than general esteem: the psychological realism of his narrative mode (more apparent than real, it should be observed), the harmoniously balanced restraint and parsimony of his verbal art, and above all that tone of "epic" detachment which, even in translation, belongs unmistakably to Andrić. The Nobel Prize in literature (1961) only confirmed a long series of awards and honors bestowed on Andrić by his own country in the decades which led up to it. He is Yugoslavia's most distinguished twentieth-century author.

Because of his international stature, Andrić has been a little better served in translation than most other Yugoslav writers. The two collections of stories now in print contain several of his best and also longest in the genre, and give some notion of both his pre- and postwar work. Eighteen stories, however, out of about one hundred and fifty do not adequately represent Andrić— preeminently a short story writer. "Devil's Yard," set in an Istanbul holding depot for criminals and the politically suspect, is a long novella which, in its compression and suggestive prison-frame construction, is arguably Andrić's best single work. Of his three novels, written in seclusion in Belgrade during World War II and published immediately thereafter, "The Bridge on the Drina" is best known. It chronicles 350 years of history in an out-of-the-way town of eastern Bosnia, Višegrad, where the author spent his own childhood. The events of history, ever bloody and violent, the "shifting dust" of human desires (as the Moslem youth Bahtijarević thinks in a particularly memorable nighttime scene on the bridge), are counterpoised by serene moments at the center, or *kapia*, of this finely proportioned, Turkish-built structure, where the townspeople are wont to rest and where exceptionally they experience an ecstatic inner transcendence of their time and place. "Bosnian Chronicle" (in the original "A Chronicle of Travnik") concerns another small provincial town during the brief years of Napoleon's influence in the Balkans, 1807–1814. Based solidly on diplomatic correspondence and personal memoirs, it is the most realistic and historical of Andrić's writings. "Woman from Sarajevo" ("Miss" in the original), his slightest and most slighted novel, is the story of a spinster's obsessive avarice, a psychological study whose heroine slowly retreats into an inner world richer, more complete, and more satisfying than the world of reality. Typical of Andrić but overshadowed by the other two novels, this work has received less attention than it deserves.

THE PASHA'S CONCUBINE AND OTHER TALES. Trans. by Joseph Hitrec. *Knopf* 1968 $6.95. Includes The Bridge on the Žepa (1925), The Journey of Ali Djerzelez (1920), Confession (1928), By the Brandy Still (1930), Mustapha Magyar (1923), In the Camp (1922), The Pasha's Concubine (1926), Thirst (1934), The Snake (1948), The Scythe (1951), Woman on the Rock (1958), Bar Titanic (1951), and A Summer in the South (1960).

THE VIZIER'S ELEPHANT: Three Novellas. Trans. by Drenka Willen. *Regnery* 1970 pap. $2.45. Includes The Vizier's Elephant (1947), Anika's Times (1931), and Zeko (1948).

THE BRIDGE ON THE DRINA. 1945. Trans. by Lovett F. Edwards. 1959 o.p. This important novel is currently in print in the United Kingdom. *Allen & Unwin* (order from British Bk. Centre) 1959 $5.50

BOSNIAN CHRONICLE. 1945. Trans. by Joseph Hitrec. 1963 o.p.

NEIGHBORS. 1946. (In Lenski, "Death of a Simple Giant," *see above, Section on Collections.*)

THE CLIMBERS. 1958. (In Koljević, "Yugoslav Short Stories," *see above, Section on Collections.*)

THE WOMAN FROM SARAJEVO. Trans. by Joseph Hitrec. 1965 o.p. Andrić's third novel is currently in print in the United Kingdom. *Calderbooks* (order from British Bk. Centre) 1973 pap. $2.00

DEVIL'S YARD. Trans. by Kenneth Johnstone. *Greenwood* 1975 $9.75

KRLEŽA, MIROSLAV. 1893–

Widely read, deeply admired, protean in his many-sided activity, Krleža has far greater potential to interest the Western reader than the meager listing below might suggest. Among living Yugoslav writers he is unquestionably the most eminent.

Krleža is so much the antithesis of Andrić that the two have been treated recently at book length as "antipodes," much as Tolstoy and Dostoevsky seem fated to be juxtaposed in Russian criticism. Like Andrić, Krleža's career has spanned more than six decades of publication; likewise his intellectual and artistic leadership, early established, has been maintained without lapse. While Andrić entered his country's foreign service and pursued literature on the side for 20 years, Krleža espoused Marxism soon after World War I, was noted for his admiration of Lenin and Bolshevism and for anticipating Stalinism (1925), and until late in the 1930s was a leading spokesman for the Left. Krleža was the responsible editor, or a major contributor, for four significant literary journals in the interwar years, participating in memorable polemics on ideological and aesthetic issues such as the proper role of tendency in literature. An exceptional blend of scepticism with commitment, he is a classic instance of the *écrivain engagé* and a true polymath of letters, prodigiously active in the political essay, the memoir, the travelogue, the literary polemic, and finally scholarship, as well as imaginative literature. Indeed, there is hardly a species of the written word which Krleža has not distinguished by his strong personal stamp; in drama and the critical essay he raised Yugoslav literature to its highest pinnacle of achievement. In and out of controversy over his long career, and for some time after the war under a cloud with Tito, he now occupies an unchallenged position of cultural leadership.

A collected edition of Krleža has been appearing since the early 1960s and now runs to about thirty volumes, of which eight are essays and memoirs. His work, which lacks the cohesion of thought and style of Ivo Andrić, has passed through several phases, of which only one is represented in English in a handful of the best-known stories dating back to 1919 and two novels from the 1930s. Krleža made of Zagreb and the surrounding small towns of the Croatian plain a distinctive literary domain: Pannonia. (He revived an ancient Roman appelative for the region.) In an excellent introduction to the volume of translations he has edited (*see below*), Branko Lenski with reason calls it Krleža's own Yoknapatawpha County, evocative of a complex and many-layered way of life. It is fecund and richly manured, swarms with livestock large and small, is steeped in timeless routine and superstition, its denizens themselves a flock of cud-chewing ruminants, vegetally unaware and contributing mightily to a staple Krležan theme, death-in-life. His heroes are psychological misfits, often artists of some kind, heirs of the romantic visionaries and culture heroes of Krleža's early symbolic dramas, for whom knowledge was a metaphysical quantum, Adam's curse and painful to bear. These oversensitive protestors have courage up to a point, their weapons are usually ineffective words, and they are in the end unable to shake the Pannonian mud from their feet. In "The Cricket beneath the Waterfall" (1937), the West generally is smeared with this mud, and its cast-off material and spiritual detritus pollutes the biosphere in a brilliantly extended, controlling metaphor (typical of Krleža's technique) which starts with civilization as a digestive process.

In the late twenties Krleža created a notorious Zagreb family, the Glembays, complete with genealogy and intricate family history spanning six generations. Three stories about them appear in the Lenski collection. The longest, "A Funeral in Teresienburg," typifies one side of Krleža, who is past master at mocking the Austro-Hungarian establishment in all its functions and malfunctions. The complex of eleven stories and three plays as a whole, though, is about the moral decline and dissolution of the wealthy, widely entrenched Glembay clan behind its patrician facade, a theme perhaps most powerfully set forth in the dramatic trilogy "Messieurs the Glembays," "In the Throes of Death," and "Leda"; nothing of this has yet appeared in translation.

The similarly tainted world of Catholic canons ensconced in smug comfort is the setting of "The First Mass of Aloyz Tiček" (1921). Krleža's anticlericalism, robust and scathing, leaves room for poetry and touches of humor as he portrays the life of the Kaptol section of Zagreb, its ecclesiastical nerve-center; he is far from being merely a satirist. He writes in a baroque, even gaudy, highly charged and expressionist style. As his best-known hero, Philip Latinowicz, remarks, "the only creative reality is what initially shocks our senses: man really sees only what he notices for the first time." Philip is a painter with distintegrating nerves, back in the environs of Zagreb with his aging mother Regina after a career in the West. Engaged in putting all "Pannonia" on canvas, obsessed by the elusive world of his childhood, he is haunted by the peculiar sensation of being many men in one, all his possible fathers. "The First Mass of Aloyz Tiček," counted among the best prose of Yugoslav literature, is the most complete example yet available in translation of Krleža's beloved death-in-life theme, as it is also of the author's deep culture, his sense of historical convergence. The past of whatever age, remote and Roman, medieval, recently imperial, is never more than lightly buried in the rich loam and marshland of Pannonia. Eternally recurrent, it ferments in the present. For Philip, beset by werewolves and vampires, by half-forgotten pagan practices, return to his own past is a journey punctuated by unsettling shocks of *déjà vu*, the sudden awareness of atavistic throwbacks—reality, as he thinks, infernalized.

THE FIRST MASS OF ALOJZ TIČEK. 1921. (In Koljević, "Yugoslav Short Stories," *see above, Section on Collections.*)

THE RETURN OF PHILIP LATINOWICZ. 1932. Trans. by Zora Depolo. *Vanguard* 1968 $8.95

ON THE EDGE OF REASON. 1938. Trans. by Zora Depolo. *Vanguard* 1975 $8.95

THE CRICKET BENEATH THE WATERFALL AND OTHER STORIES. Ed. by Branko Lenski. *Vanguard* 1972 $8.95. Includes Dr. Gregor and the Evil One, A Funeral in Teresien-burg, The Love of Marcel Faber-Fabriczy for Miss Laura Warronigg (all 1926–1930), The Cricket beneath the Waterfall (1937), Devil's Island (1923), and Hodorlahomor the Great (1919).

KOSMAĆ, CYRIL. 1910–

Kosmać is a leading Slovenian writer of realistic, but evocative and lyrically colored prose depicting village life in the Adriatic coastal region of that republic under Italian occupation and after the liberation. Some of his work reflects Kosmać's personal experience of Italian jails before the war. Characteristic of his writing is a "fusion of realism with fantastic incident, combining an occasionally grotesque conception of reality with the symbolic power of a rude yearning for beauty, love, and—death"—("Yugoslav Literary Lexicon"). His semi-autobiographic novel "A Day in Spring" (1953, U.S. 1959) is currently o.p. Anthologized stories in English are listed below.

THE CATERPILLAR. (In Koljević, "Yugoslav Short Stories"; also in Mikasinovich, "In-troduction to Yugoslav Literature," *see both above, Section on Collections.*)

DEATH OF A SIMPLE GIANT; LUCK. (Both in Lenski, "Death of a Simple Giant and Other Modern Yugoslav Stories," *see above, Section on Collections.*)

SELIMOVIĆ, MEŠA. 1910–

Selimović is the most admired writer, after Andrić, to emerge from Bosnia, and "Death and the Dervish" is his acknowledged masterpiece. It stands out as one of the most individual and personal books published in postwar Yugoslavia. "Here is the fate of a man 'flung into life,' whose entire philosophy of living, structured by an oriental and Islamic view of the world and manner of thought, is imparted in precise phrases from within, from the center of a world which is only in appearance set in the framework of history, while in reality it is contemporary to the core. The novel is written multi-dimensionally, in a complex, modern manner and with an attentive ear for all that threatens man amidst the great worlds and evil imperatives of unrighteous power. Selimović's message is deeply and consummately human"—(Draško Ređep, in "Yugoslav Literary Lexicon").

DEATH AND THE DERVISH. 1966. (Excerpt, trans. by Svetozar Koljević, in Johnson, "New Writing in Yugoslavia," *see above, Section on Collections.*)

DJILAS, MILOVAN. 1911–

Milovan Djilas is one of this century's most gifted and famous Communist apostates. Having risen to the position of a major leader and theoretician of the Yugoslav Communist Party in the first postwar decade, one of Marshall Tito's closest collaborators and friends, Djilas in a notorious series of journal articles subjected the practice of Communism in his own country to vitriolic, highly embarrassing criticism which went home with the thrust of an insider's knowledge. Shortly thereafter, as if adding insult to injury, in his treatise "The New Class" (English translation 1957) Djilas challenged Communism's doctrinal foundations. Even then no stranger to jail (he had been imprisoned at Sremska Mitrovica from 1933 to 1936), during the next postwar decade Djilas spent another eight years in the same prison. There he worked intermittently on many of the manuscripts later to be published by his friend William Jovánovich in English translation. Since 1966 he has lived quietly in retirement in Belgrade, able to receive visitors but, as before, restricted to publication abroad and only in translation.

For Djilas' political writings, see Chapter 9, History, Government and Politics, *Reader's Adviser*, Vol. 3. His other work includes a fine biography of Njegoš (*q.v.*), Prince-Bishop of Montenegro in the 1830s and 1840s and that republic's most distinguished poet; stories based on various incidents in the partisan struggles during the war, some of which are undoubtedly fictionalized memoirs; an autobiography of his youth (to 1929), "Land without Justice"; and two novels, of which "Montenegro" focuses on the fate of this small country in World War I, while "Under the Colors" explores the contrasting styles of life and thought among Christian and Moslem Montenegrins living along the southern border with Albania in the late 1870s. A chronological pattern has now begun to emerge which suggests that it is the author's intention to treat his country at certain juncture points over a hundred-year span. He himself considers that the work on Njegoš and on his own early years, together with the novel "Montenegro," form a trilogy.

Djilas at his best conveys a strong sense of time and place. Typical themes, all part and parcel of the legendary heroic ethos of his homeland, are the cult of family and clan honor (dramatized in the blood vendetta), the cult of stoic fortitude and personal sacrifice to the point of willing martyrdom, and the degeneration—one could say the inversion—of these ideals in savage, mindless violence. Such is the burden of "Land without Justice," which has disappointed some as lacking in the details of personal development one expects from autobiography and would wish particularly from a Milovan Djilas. The book is actually about Montenegro as a locale in the conscience and the consciousness of a child, a child shaped by a strongly traditional, rural, small-group society. Characteristic of Djilas is a fluent and brilliant flow of ideas too often unchecked for true artistic consistency. He is an uneven writer, certainly no first-rate novelist. Plots are developed with aggravating sluggishness ("epic" is the affirmative label critics like to use). He often seems unaware of when enough is enough, as in Anto Radak's tortures at the hands of the Turks, to which he devoted the first 90 pages of "Under the Colors." Though Djilas is capable of fine passages, poetic and moving, his style tends to be turgid and sometimes bombastic, and he is much given to the sort of pithy aphorism which stems from oral tradition but translates, unfortunately, into platitude. "Land without Justice" and the biography of Njegoš are Djilas' best literary work to date.

LAND WITHOUT JUSTICE. 1958. Tran. anonymous. *Harcourt* pap. $2.85

MONTENEGRO. Trans. by Kenneth Johnstone. *Harcourt* 1963 $5.75

THE LEPER AND OTHER STORIES. Trans. by Lovett Edwards. *Harcourt* 1964 $5.95

NJEGOŠ: Poet, Prince, Bishop. Trans. by Michael B. Petrovich. *Harcourt* 1966 $10.00

UNDER THE COLORS. Trans. by Lovett Edwards. *Harcourt* 1971 $9.75

THE STONE AND THE VIOLETS. Trans. by Lovett Edwards. *Harcourt* 1972 $6.95

LALIĆ, MIHAILO. 1914–

Lalić, a Montenegrin, has published half a dozen novels and several story collections, and is widely judged to be one of the most gifted writers in Serbian today. His reputation was established on the strength of his third novel, "Leleja Mountain" (published as "Wailing Mountain"), which in its second and expanded version published in 1962 won the prestigious Njegoš Award. It is the story of a partisan fighter caught behind the lines. Constructed as a chain of highly dramatic episodes, the work incorporates among them an inner world of fantasy and feverish, hallucinatory reverie (sometimes difficult to follow) which makes it essentially a study of the brutalizing effects of hunting and being hunted in loneliness and self-imposed solitude.

THE SHEPHERDESS. 1948. (In Lenski, "Death of a Simple Giant," *see above, Section on Collections.*)

WAILING MOUNTAIN. 1957, 1962. Trans. by Drenka Willen. *Harcourt* 1965 $4.75. Willen's translation appears to be from the earlier version. For the *Twayne* anthology (Mikasinovich and others, Eds., *see above, Section on Collections*), Petar Mijušković translated two brief but potent scenes.

KONESKI, BLAŽE. 1921–

Koneski is an exceptional figure in the vigorous flowering of postwar Macedonian culture. In the world of scholarship and education he is undisputed dean of Macedonian letters, a prime moving spirit behind the codification of this youngest in the Slavic family of standard literary languages, an outstanding linguist and lexicographer, editor-in-chief of the first Macedonian dictionary (3 vols., 1965–1966), holder of the highest posts in the university at Skoplje and in the Yugoslav writers' union. His translations of Heine, Shakespeare ("Othello"), and especially Njegoš have contributed significantly to shaping modern Macedonian as a literary vehicle by creating suitable stylistic structures and expressive vocabulary. As if all this were not enough, Koneski the creative writer is also a living classic in his own land, first as a poet (several collections in the late forties and fifties) with his own lyric voice, "simple and severe"–("Yugoslav Literary Lexicon"), then as a teller of unpretentious, short tales with a realistic, carefully observed Macedonian backdrop.

THE RYE: THE TREE TRUNK (lyrics); THE EXHIBITION (story). (In Mikasinovich, "Introduction to Yugoslav Literature," *see above, Section on Collections*.)

THE FINAL MOVE. (In Holton, "The Big Horse," *see above, Section on Collections*.)

POPA, VASKO. 1922–

The most translated modern Serbian poet, "Popa combines elements of the grotesque stemming from the powerful surrealist tradition in Serbian poetry with an elliptical, aphoristic manner of expression which goes back to oral tradition"–("Yugoslav Literary Lexicon"). Selected poems are in Mikasinovich, "Introduction to Yugoslav Literature," and Johnson, "New Writing in Yugoslavia," above in the Section on Collections.

THE LITTLE BOX. Trans. and introd. by Charles Simic. 1970 *Charioteer Press* 1973 $5.00

EARTH ERECT. Trans. by Anne Pennington. *Anvil Press* (order from British Bk. Centre) $10.00

MIHAILOVIĆ, DRAGOSLAV. 1928–

As of 1971, Mihailović's published work consisted of a book of stories, "Goodnight, Fred" (1967) and the novel below. Written in a jaunty, highly colloquial style, it is the story of a young boxer, as told by himself, in the underworld of Belgrade's gangland in the late forties and early fifties. With his gift for discourse and ear for urban slang, Mihailović has been considered to be one of the most promising prose writers of the middle generation.

WHEN PUMPKINS BLOSSOMED. 1969. Trans. by Drenka Willen. *Harcourt* 1971 $5.95

BULATOVIĆ, MIODRAG. 1930–

Stylistically one of the more original of the younger Yugoslav writers, Bulatović employs a technique of distortion, warps his imagery and perspective, and injects the bizarre into his narrative in a manner which has disconcerted many readers. His typical subjects are vagabonds and derelicts. The effect of his general perception of life, dark and pessimistic, is deflected by the unusual style and leavened by his grotesque humor. Bulatović's first novel, which brought him wide attention outside Yugoslavia, in now o.p. except for the brief excerpts noted below. His second, with a Montenegrin background much like his other work, reads, to quote Joseph Hitrec (in *SR*), "like an extended pornographic allegory on war and man's tendency to self-destruction."

THE RED COCK FLIES TO HEAVEN. 1959. Trans. by E. D. Goy. 1962 o.p. (Excerpts in Mikasinovich, "Introduction to Yugoslav Literature," *see above, Section on Collections*.)

THE LOVERS. 1960. (Trans. by E. D. Goy in Lenski, "Death of a Simple Giant," *see above, Section on Collections*.)

HERO ON A DONKEY. 1964. *New Am. Lib.* 1969 $6.50 Plume pap. $2.75

A FABLE. (In Johnson, "New Writing in Yugoslavia," *see above, Section on Collections*.)

KIŠ, DANILO. 1935–

Kiš is a novelist (three novels published in the early 1960s), essayist, and translator (Hungarian, French) who works and lives in Belgrade. He "writes in a distinctly personal, lyrical style with a special knack for evoking childhood, or for suggesting the atmosphere of wartime. In modern Serbian literature his novels are conspicuous for their naturalness of expression and purity of inspiration. Close to the latest currents among the youngest generation of European novelists, Kiš is at the same time faithful to the classic ideals of simplicity and balance"–("Yugoslav Literary Lexicon").

GARDEN, ASHES. 1965. Trans. by Mary Stansfield-Popović. *Harcourt* 1975 $7.95

—J. F. L.

Chapter 16

Latin American Literature

> *"Spanish American literature, which is rootless and cosmopolitan, is both a return to and a search for the tradition. . . . A desire for incarnation, a literature of foundations."*
>
> —OCTAVIO PAZ

SPANISH AMERICAN LITERATURE

Latin America's long period of domination by European powers, lasting until the early nineteenth century, created close ties with and dependence on the mother countries of Spain and Portugal until the mid-twentieth century. The first writings to come from the New World are the chronicles of explorers such as Christopher Columbus, Hernán Cortés, Bernal Díaz del Castillo, and Pedro Cieza de León (*see Chapter 9, History, Government and Politics: The Americas,* Reader's Adviser, *Vol. 3*). The first literary work concerning the Americas was *"La Araucana,"* published in three volumes in 1569, 1578, and 1589 (trans. as "The Araucaniad" 1945, o.p.), an epic poem on the campaign against the fierce Araucanian Indians of southern Chile. Although the author, Alonso de Ercilla, a Spaniard, exalts the bravery and dignity of the Indian chieftain Caupolicán, the viewpoint is nevertheless Spanish since in the poem the young chief converts to Christianity. One of the first native writers was Garcilaso de la Vega, born of a Spanish father and an Inca princess, who after years of unsuccessful attempts to claim his inheritance in Spain spent the rest of his life writing histories of the Incas and of Peru.

The seventeenth and eighteenth centuries are relatively barren of original literary work. Most writers cultivated an extremely mannered and artificial Baroque style derivative of European models. One exception is the lyric poet Sor Juana Inés de la Cruz, born in Mexico of Spanish and Creole parentage, who took religious vows to devote herself to books and writing. Ultimately, she was frustrated by the intellectual poverty of colonial life in Mexico, as was Carlos Sigüenza y Góngora, a poet, scholar, and author of Mexico's first novel, *"Los Infortunios de Alonso Ramírez"* (1690) (trans. as "The Misadventures of Alonso Ramírez" 1962, o.p.). The South American continent developed intellectual autonomy more slowly than did Mexico, with Juan de Espinosa Medrano in Peru still writing in the culteranist style (*see Chapter 11, Spanish Literature*) and an apology for Luis de Góngora (*q.v.*) in 1662, ten years after Góngora's death.

In spite of the fact that nearly three centuries had elapsed since the discovery, Spanish America was still culturally dependent on Europe at the beginning of the nineteenth century. At the same time, however, a uniquely Latin American culture was silently being created through the mixture of races, confrontation with an immense and unique landscape, and development of native traditions, some of which are only now gaining expression. The literature of the early nineteenth century is quite naturally preoccpied with the subjects of revolution and patriotism. For example, José Joaquín Olmedo's "The Victory of Junín: Song to Bolívar" (1825) celebrates one of Latin America's great liberators, Simón Bolívar. The end of Spanish domination, however, brought to many countries dictatorships almost as oppressive as European rule. The literary figures of the mid-nineteenth century were concerned almost exclusively with political and social problems, such as the plight of the gaucho—José Hernández (*q.v.*)—while others, such as José Mármol of Argentina, were exiled for their outspoken defense of liberty or political beliefs. At the same time some writers were beginning to recognize as a problem the growing United States imperialism which had replaced European colonialism. Possibly due to the need for expressing such ideas, the literature of this period tends to the essay, diary, realistic novel, and *"costumbrismo"* or the sketch of local customs.

This history of dependence and preoccupation with everyday realities accords even more significance to the fact that modernism, the aesthetic movement which revolutionized twentieth-century Spanish letters, had its origin in South America. With his volume "Azure" (1888), Rubén Darío (*q.v.*) introduced modernism to Spain (*see Chapter 11, Spanish Literature*). With this event, Spanish American literature may be said to have achieved true independence.

Social and political conditions of the early twentieth century, symbolized by the Mexican Revolution (1910–1920), brought an end to the modernist style of "art for art's sake." Upon the overthrow of dictator Porfirio Díaz, Mexico effectively freed herself, and consequently her literature, particularly the novel, flourished. Also effective in wrenching Latin America from European arms were the two world wars, which brought both alliance with and dependence on the United States, and the Spanish Civil War (1936–1939), which severed the sentimental attachment to Spain that still remained. The result has been a period of innovation and creativity unparalleled in any world literature at this time. In the field of poetry both Gabriela Mistral (*q.v.*), a member of the postmodernist movement concered with simplicity and spontaneity, and Pablo Neruda (*q.v.*), in the succeeding generation sometimes called the vanguard, won the Nobel Prize for Literature. In fiction the regional novel dealing with, for example, the gaucho, Indian, landscape, and customs, has experienced tremendous development as writers endeavor to understand their unique traditions and to reinterpret their history. These novels often angrily protest social conditions. At the same time an original style best described as magic realism or suprarealism, the integration of the real and the fantastic, has renewed the novel, making it a viable form here at a time when it appears to have been exhausted in Europe. Gabriel García Márquez's (*q.v.*) "One Hundred Years of Solitude" and the Nobel Prize winning *"El Señor Presidente"* by Miguel Ángel Asturias (*q.v.*) demonstrate the possibilities of novelistic creation realized in Latin America. In the theater too a resurgence has occurred, although it has been slower to develop and until recently has been sponsored primarily by universities.

Latin American writers, for reasons of financial necessity, political beliefs, or personal ambition, have traditionally been actively involved in public life, and this continues to be true. Many are ambassadors representing their nations abroad, while numerous others hold posts as directors of national libraries, in ministries of education, or in civil service. As a group their political views may be categorized as leftist, and their primary concern is securing social justice and economic equality within their own countries as well as the world's recognition of their unique history and culture.

The number of translations of Latin American works is burgeoning at this time, and it is impossible to list all of them. The Latin American Studies Association was formed in 1966 and will join *University Microfilms* in reprinting important works. The *Southern Illinois University Press* has undertaken the Contemporary Latin American Classics Series and the *University of Texas Press* its Pan-American Series. Soon after the publication of this volume two new bibliographies of Latin American literature will be available: "Latin American Literature in English Translation: An Annotated Bibliography" by Shaw Bradley will be published by *New York University Press*, and the *Center for Inter-American Relations* will release an updated version of its 1970 bibliography.

Literary Criticism and History

Adams, M. Ian. THREE AUTHORS OF ALIENATION: Bombal, Onetti, Carpentier. *Univ. of Texas Press* 1975 $7.65

Aldrich, Earl M., Jr. THE MODERN SHORT STORY IN PERU. *Univ. of Wisconsin Press* 1966 $10.00. The first study of a rapidly evolving literature; includes short excerpts in English and Spanish.

Anderson Imbert, Enrique. SPANISH AMERICAN LITERATURE: A History. Trans. by John V. Falconieri. *Wayne State Univ. Press* 2nd ed. rev. and enl. 2 vols. Vol. 1 1492 to 1910 Vol. 2 1910 to 1963 pap. $3.95 each

An extraordinarily complete study by an Argentine writer of "keen critical abilities"—*(LJ)*.

Arciniegas, German. LATIN AMERICA: A Cultural History. Trans. by Joan MacLean *Knopf* 1966 $10.00 text ed. $7.95

Brushwood, John S. MEXICO IN ITS NOVEL: A Nation's Search for Identity. Pan American Ser. *Univ. of Texas Press* 1966 $9.75 pap. $2.45

"A revealing analysis for academic and large public libraries"—*(LJ)*. Includes an extensive list of novels by date.

THE SPANISH AMERICAN NOVEL: A Twentieth Century Survey. Pan American Ser. *Univ. of Texas Press* 1975 $15.95

Carrera Andrade, Jorge. REFLECTIONS OF SPANISH AMERICAN POETRY. Trans. by Don C. Bliss and Gabriela C. Bliss. *State Univ. of New York Press* 1973 $6.00. Essays on the authentic voice and original spirit of Latin American poetry by a well-known Ecuadorian poet.

Coester, Alfred. THE LITERARY HISTORY OF SPANISH AMERICA. 1919. *Cooper* rep. of 2nd 1928 ed. 1971 $15.00

Englekirk, John E., and others. AN OUTLINE HISTORY OF SPANISH AMERICAN LITERATURE. *Irvington Bks.* 1965 3rd ed. pap. $3.65. A useful introductory guide with extensive bibliographies of suggested reading, editions, translations, and critical references for each author.

Fein, John M. MODERNISM IN CHILEAN LITERATURE: The Second Period. *Duke Univ. Press* 1965 $7.75. A historical account of the development of the theoretical bases of modernism.

Foster, David W. CURRENTS IN THE CONTEMPORARY ARGENTINE NOVEL: Arlt, Mallea, Sábato, Cortázar. *Univ. of Missouri Press* 1975 $10.00. Chapter 1 outlines the history of the Argentine novel prior to the authors discussed, and the final chapter discusses more recent novels; includes a substantial bibliography.

Franco, Jean. INTRODUCTION TO SPANISH AMERICAN LITERATURE. *Cambridge* 1969 $13.95 pap. $4.95. A comprehensive, relatively difficult history of Spanish American Literature beginning with colonial times.

THE MODERN CULTURE OF LATIN AMERICA: Society and the Artist. 1967. *Penguin* 1970 pap. $2.95

"A judicious and illuminating account of the chief movements" *(LJ)* since 1888 by a lecturer in Spanish at the University of London.

SPANISH AMERICAN LITERATURE SINCE INDEPENDENCE. *Harper* (Barnes and Noble) 1973 $10.00 pap $5.95

Gallagher, David P. MODERN LATIN AMERICAN LITERATURE. *Oxford* 1973 pap. $1.95

Goldberg, Isaac. STUDIES IN SPANISH AMERICAN LITERATURE. 1920. *Folcroft* 1973 lib. bdg. $25.00; *Richard West* $25.00

Gonzáles Peña, Carlos. HISTORY OF MEXICAN LITERATURE. 1960. Ed. by Gusta Barfield Nance and Florence J. Dustan. *Southern Methodist Univ. Press* 3rd ed. 1968 $8.50 pap. $3.45

Guibert, Rita, Ed. SEVEN VOICES: Seven Latin American Writers Talk to Rita Guibert. Trans. by Frances Partridge. *Knopf* 1975 pap. $2.95. Interviews with Pablo Neruda, Jorge Luis Borges, Miguel Ángel Asturias, Octavio Paz, Julio Cortázar, Gabriel García Márquez, and Guillermo Cabrene Infante.

HANDBOOK OF LATIN AMERICAN STUDIES. Various eds. *Univ. Presses of Florida* Vols. 1–35 1935–1974 each $15.00 to $25.00

This comprehensive bibliography, begun in 1935 by *Harvard University Press* and edited by noted Latin American scholars, has now been reorganized into two volumes—social sciences and humanities—to be published in alternate years, starting with Vol. 26, on the humanities.

Harmon, Mary. EFRÉN HERNÁNDEZ: A Poet Discovered. *Univ. Press of Mississippi* pap. $2.95. A study of the Mexican poet.

Harss, Luis, and Barbara Dohmann. INTO THE MAINSTREAM: Conversations with Latin American Writers. *Harper* 1967 $7.95 1969 pap. $2.95

This "most valuable work now available in English on . . . present-day writing in Latin America [despite] a sometimes over-excited and always humorless prose" (*N.Y. Times*) discusses Carpentier, Asturias, Borges, Cortázar, Rosa, Onetti, Rulfo, Fuentes, García Márquez and Vargas Llosa.

Langford, Walter M. THE MEXICAN NOVEL COMES OF AGE. *Univ. of Notre Dame Press* 1971 $8.95 pap. $3.95. A useful study of modern Mexican novelists.

Menton, Seymour. PROSE FICTION OF THE CUBAN REVOLUTION. Latin American Monographs *Univ. of Texas Press* 1975 $12.50. The author's purpose in this extensive study is to record and classify the more than 200 volumes of novels and short stories published in Cuba since 1959.

Pearson, Lon. NICOMEDES GUZMÁN: Proletarian Author in Chile's Literary Generation of 1938. *Univ. of Missouri Press* 1976 (in prep.)

Picón-Salas, Mariano. A CULTURAL HISTORY OF SPANISH AMERICA: From Conquest to Independence. Trans. by Irving A. Leonard. *Univ. of California Press* 1962 pap. $2.45. A standard work.

Ramos, Samuel. PROFILE OF MAN AND CULTURE IN MEXICO. Trans. by Peter G. Earle. *Univ. of Texas Press* 1962 $7.50 pap. $1.95. In this Mexican classic a philosopher, critic, and professor attempts to explore Mexican culture through the use of Adlerian psychoanalysis.

Schwartz, Kessel. THE MEANING OF EXISTENCE IN CONTEMPORARY HISPANIC LITERATURE. Hispanic-American Studies *Univ. of Miami Press* 1969 $8.95

A NEW HISTORY OF SPANISH AMERICAN FICTION. *Univ. of Miami Press* 1972 2 vols. Vol. 1 From Colonial Times to the Mexican Revolution and Beyond Vol. 2 Social Concern, Universalism, and the New Novel each $10.00

Spell, Jefferson Rea. CONTEMPORARY SPANISH AMERICAN FICTION. 1944 *Univ. of North Carolina Press* 1968 $10.00. Includes a bibliography of the novels and collections of short stories discussed along with lists of English translations and reviews.

Terry, Edward Davis, Ed. ARTISTS AND WRITERS IN THE EVOLUTION OF LATIN AMERICA. *Univ. of Alabama Press* 1969 $4.95. Critical essays on Miguel Ángel Asturias, Euclides da Cunha, social protest in the Spanish American novel, art and life in Mexico, José Vasconcelos, José Mariátegui, Chilean politics.

Torres-Ríoseco, Arturo. ASPECTS OF SPANISH-AMERICAN LITERATURE. *Univ. of Washington Press* 1963 $3.50

These four essays are "rewarding reading on the whole. . . . His excellent discussion of such present-day novelists as Jorge Luis Borges, Alejo Carpenter and Carlos Fuentes will probably be of most interest"—(*LJ*).

THE EPIC OF LATIN AMERICAN LITERATURE. 1942. *Peter Smith* 1957 $4.25; *Univ. of California Press* 1959 1963 pap. $2.25. Scholarly, detailed guide covering the sixteenth century to the present; excellent choice of representative passages.

Zea, Leopoldo. THE LATIN AMERICAN MIND. Trans. by James H. Abbott and Lowell Dunham. *Univ. of Oklahoma Press* 1963 1970 $6.95. An eminent Mexican philosopher traces the rise of positivism as the aftermath of Romanticism; an important work.

Collections

Ahern, Maureen, and David Tipton. PERU: The New Poetry. *Dufour* 1970 $7.95. Peruvian poetry from the 1960s.

Babín, María Teresa, and Stan Steiner. BORINQUÉN: An Anthology of Puerto Rican Literature. *Random* 1974 pap. $3.75. A comprehensive anthology including an introductory history of Puerto Rican literature and critical and biographical sketches of each author.

Blackwell, Alice Stone, Trans. SOME SPANISH-AMERICAN POETS. 1929. Introd. by Isaac Goldberg. *Greenwood* (repr. of 1937 ed.) bilingual 1968 $12.50. Selections by poets from 19 Spanish-American countries.

Carpentier, Hortense, and Janet Brof, Eds. DOORS AND MIRRORS: Fiction and Poetry from Spanish America 1920–1970. *Grossman* 1972 $3.50. An extensive selection of fiction and poetry; various translators.

Coester, Alfred, and W. E. Bailey. PLAYS OF THE SOUTHERN AMERICAS. 1942. Play Anthology Reprint Ser. *Bks. for Libraries* $12.75. The Foreign Girl by F. Sanchez, My Poor Nerves by L. Vargas Tejeda, Cabrerita by Acevedo Hernández.

Cohen, John M., Ed. LATIN AMERICAN WRITING TODAY. *Peter Smith* 1967 $3.50. Selections from 32 authors.

WRITERS IN THE NEW CUBA: An Anthology. Introd. by ed. *Peter Smith* 1967 $4.25. Selections from 21 authors currently living in Cuba with an excerpt from Fidel Castro's 1961 speech "Words to Intellectuals."

Colecchia, Francesca, and Julio Matas, Trans. and eds. SELECTED LATIN AMERICAN ONE ACT PLAYS. *Univ. of Pittsburgh Press* 1974 $9.95 pap. $3.95. Ten plays with an excellent introduction.

Craig, George Dundas, Trans. and comp. THE MODERNIST TREND IN SPANISH AMERICAN POETRY: A Collection of Representative Poems of the Modernist Movement and the Reaction. 1934. *Gordian* 1971 $9.00

Cranfill, Thomas M., Ed., and George D. Schade, Translations ed. THE MUSE IN MEXICO: A Mid-Century Miscellany. *Univ. of Texas Press* 1958 $6.95. Poetry, fiction, photographs, and drawings.

Donoso, Jose, and others, Eds. TriQUARTERLY ANTHOLOGY OF CONTEMPORARY LATIN AMERICAN LITERATURE. *Dutton* 1969 $8.95 pap. $3.95. An extensive collection of essays, fiction, and poetry.

Flores, Angel, and Harriet Anderson. MASTERPIECES OF LATIN AMERICAN LITERATURE. *Macmillan* 2 vols. Vol. 1 $10.95 Vol. 2 $9.95. Excellent introductions to each author and bibliographies.

Foster, David William, and Virginia Ramos Foster, Eds. MODERN LATIN AMERICAN LITERATURE. *Ungar* 2 vols. 1975 set $30.00. Selections from reviews and critical articles on works by twentieth-century Latin American authors, including Brazilian; an excellent reference work.

Franco, Jean, Ed. SHORT STORIES IN SPANISH. *Penguin* 1966 pap. $1.95. The majority of these stories are by Spanish American writers: Onetti, Rulfo, Martínez, Moreno, Benedetti, and others.

Frank, Waldo, Ed. TALES FROM THE ARGENTINE. Trans. by Anita Brenner. Short Story Index Reprint Ser. 1930 *Bks. for Libraries* $8.75. Stories by Ricardo Güiraldes, Lucio Vicente López, Leopoldo Lugones, Robert J. Payró, Horacio Quiroga, and Domingo Faustino Sarmiento.

Hays, Hoffman Reynolds, Ed. TWELVE SPANISH AMERICAN POETS, An Anthology. *Beacon Press* bilingual ed. 1972 $12.50 pap. $3.95

Howes, Barbara, Ed. THE EYE OF THE HEART: Short Stories from Latin America. *Bobbs* $10.95 pap. $5.95; *Avon* 1975 pap. $2.25. An excellent selection of 42 short stories by Latin American writers; includes six Brazilian writers.

Jones, Willis Knapp. LATIN AMERICAN WRITERS IN ENGLISH TRANSLATION: A Classified Bibliography. 1944. *Blaine Ethridge* 1972 $8.00

SPANISH-AMERICAN LITERATURE IN TRANSLATION. *Ungar* 2 vols. Vol. 1 A Selection of Prose, Poetry, and Drama before 1888 Vol. 2 A Selection of Poetry, Fiction, and Drama since 1888. Vol 1 $8.50 Vol. 2 $9.50. An extensive collection.

(Trans) MEN AND ANGELS: Three South American Comedies. *Southern Illinois Univ. Press* 1970 $7.95. The Quack Doctor by J. F. C. Barthes and C. S. Damel, The Fate of Chipí Gonzalez by J. M. Rivarola Matto, and The Man of the Century by M. Frank.

Levine, Suzanne Jill. LATIN AMERICAN FICTION AND POETRY IN TRANSLATION. *Interbook* 1970 pap. $1.25. A bibliographical reference work.

(With Hallie D. Taylor, Trans.) TRIPLE CROSS. *Dutton* 1972 $8.95. Holy Place by Carlos Fuentes, Hell Has No Limits by José Donoso, From Cuba with a Song by Severo Sarduy.

Oliver, William I., Trans. and ed. VOICES OF CHANGE IN THE SPANISH AMERICAN THEATER: An Anthology. Pan American Ser. *Univ. of Texas Press* 1971 $8.00. Loose the Lions by E. Carballido, The Camp by G. Gambaro, The Library by C. Maggi, In the Right Hand of God the Father by E. Buenaventura, The Mulatto's Orgy by L. S. Hernández, Viña and Three Beach Plays by S. Vodanovic.

Onís, Harriet de, Ed. GOLDEN LAND: An Anthology of Latin American Folklore in Literature. *Knopf* 1961 $6.95. Latin American myths and legends as sources for its literature from colonial times to the present.

Paz, Octavio, Ed. AN ANTHOLOGY OF MEXICAN POETRY. Trans. by Samuel Beckett; pref. by C. M. Bowra. Poetry Paperback Ser. *Indiana Univ. Press* $6.95 pap. $2.45. Paz chose the poems and wrote a historical introduction for this important collection.

Williams, Miller, Ed. CHILE: An Anthology of New Writing. *Kent State Univ. Press* 1968 pap. $1.95. Twelve authors, including Pablo Neruda.

CIEZA DE LEÓN, PEDRO DE. 1518?–1560. *See Chapter 12, Travel and Adventure, Reader's Adviser, Vol. 3.*

SARMIENTO, DOMINGO FAUSTINO. 1811–1888.   Argentina

Born into a lower-class family, Sarmiento became President of the Argentine Republic in 1868. His reputation in literature is based on "Civilization and Barbarism: Life of Juan Facundo Quiroga," a combination of essay, history, and novel. Demonstrating the actions of both Juan Manuel de Rosas, the dictatorial governor of Argentina, and the gaucho Facundo, Tiger of the Pampas, to be barbaric, Sarmiento advocates the civilizing influences of education and economic progress. His romantic view of the gaucho led him to create a legendary character rather than a historical figure. The narratives and sketches in "Travels" have been described as "a virtual novel" (Anderson Imbert) for their imaginative quality.

LIFE IN THE ARGENTINE REPUBLIC IN THE DAYS OF THE TYRANTS, or Civilization and Barbarism. 1845. Trans. by Mary T. Main. Library of Classics *Macmillan* (Hafner) pap. $3.95; *Macmillan* 1961 pap. $1.50; *Gordon Press* $29.95

TRAVELS: A Selection. 1845–1847. Trans. by Ines Muñoz *Organization of American States* 1963 $1.50

SARMIENTO ANTHOLOGY. Trans. by Stuart E. Grummon; ed. by Allison Bunkley. 1948. *Kennikat* 1971 $12.50

Books about Sarmiento

Life of Sarmiento. By Allison W. Bunkley. 1952. *Greenwood* lib. bdg. $22.00
Domingo Faustino Sarmiento. By Frances G. Crowley. World Authors Ser. *Twayne* 1972 $6.95

HERNÁNDEZ, JOSÉ. 1834–1866.   Argentina

"Martín Fierro" is a lyrical epic poem written in praise of gaucho culture at a time when gauchos were looked upon as curiosities or nuisances by the European-dominated Buenos Aires society and were being swallowed up by industrial and agricultural progress. Hernández's purpose was twofold: to educate people about the vanishing culture of the gaucho and to educate the gauchos themselves. This poem became the voice of the gaucho people and a part of their tradition. One of its translators wrote that the "artistic value most notable throughout the poem is Hernández's ability to create striking metaphors and similes in concise, primitive language that accurately captures the loneliness of the vast pampas and the inner feelings of its inhabitants—the gauchos. . . ." The gaucho Martín Fierro, an outlaw, relates his own misfortunes at the hands of a society which degrades and abuses him. In the second part Fierro engages in a song contest and through their singing, the suffering of the gaucho and his black rival gains universal significance.

THE GAUCHO MARTÍN FIERRO. Pt. I The Depart 1872; Pt. 2 The Return 1879. Trans. by Frank Carrino and others *Scholars Facsimiles* (reprint of 1872 edition) 1970 $10.00; trans. by Catherine E. Ward *State Univ. of New York Press* 1967 $10.00 1974 pap. $1.45

MARTÍ, JOSÉ. 1853–1895.   Cuba

Martí is a symbol of Cuban independence, for he campaigned throughout his life for its liberation and finally died in the war against Spain. Rejecting aestheticism, he wrote simple, sincere verses in a romantic style, as in *"Ismaelillo"* (1882) and *"Versos sensillos"* (1891). The articles in the collections here were published in newspapers during his lifetime, primarily in *La nación* of Buenos Aires.

MARTÍ ON THE U.S.A. Ed. by Luis Baralt. Latin American Classics Ser. *Southern Illinois Univ. Press* 1966 $5.95

INSIDE THE MONSTER: Writings on the United States and American Imperialism. Trans. by Elinor Randall; ed. by Philip Foner. *Monthly Review* 1975 $16.50

Books about Martí

Martí, Martyr of Cuban Independence. By Felix Lizaso. 1953. *Greenwood* lib. bdg. $12.00
José Martí: Cuban Patriot. By Richard B. Gray. *Univ. Presses of Florida* 1962 $8.50

DARÍO, RUBÉN (pseud. of Félix Rubén García Sarmiento). 1867–1916.   Nicaragua

Darío, a Nicaraguan who traveled widely in the Spanish-speaking world, initiated the "modernism" movement in twentieth-century Spanish poetry with *"Azul"* (Azure) (1888), a volume in three parts consisting of stories, poetic prose, and poetry. Influenced by the French symbolists and Parnassianism, he strove for renovation of language, artistic refinement, and elegant expression. His was a world of swans, centaurs, and doves, of art for art's sake. With his "Profane Prose" (1896) he distinguished himself as the true leader of the modernist movement. The title itself reveals his desire to alter the use of language, for the contents are neither prose nor profane, but rather elegant, aristocratic verse. Here Darío experimented with combinations of rhythms, sounds, accents, and meter, treating exotic themes such as peacocks and princesses with erotic and pagan tones. His next volume, "Songs of Life and Hope" (1905), which contains some of his best verses, shows a turn away from evasion of reality toward a meditative introspection on life and death, as well as a note of preoccupation about the power of the United States, as revealed in "To Roosevelt." His subsequent volumes become more melancholy and profound.

SELECTED POEMS. Trans. by Lysander Kemp; prologue by Octavio Paz; epilogue by Federico García Lorca and Pablo Neruda; ill. by John Guerin. *Univ. of Texas Press* 1965 $5.95

Books about Darío

Critical Approaches to Rubén Darío. By Keith Ellis. Romance Ser. *Univ. of Toronto Press* 1975 $12.50

AZUELA, MARIANO. 1873–1952.   Mexico

After receiving his degree in medicine, Azuela returned to poor districts to practice, a manifestation of his lifelong concern for the *pueblo* of Mexico. During the Mexican Revolution, Azuela openly joined Francisco Villa, becoming Director of Public Education in Jalisco under the Villa government. When that government fell, he served as doctor to Villa's men during their retreat northward. From these experiences came his novel "The Underdogs," which he published in installments in a newspaper upon fleeing to Texas in 1915. That novel, which has been called an "epic poem in prose of the Mexican revolution"—(Torres-Rioseco), deals with the revolution from the point of view of lower-class characters, examining the circumstances which keep them in poverty and depicting the brutality of the fighting. An admirer of Zola, Azuela stressed the effect of environment on character in many of his novels. "The Flies" concerns the defeat of Villa, the "flies" being those followers who abandon him in his moment of weakness. It reveals Azuela's basic pessimism about human nature.

THE UNDERDOGS. 1916. Trans. by E. Munguia, Jr.; fwd. by Harriet de Onís. *New Am. Lib.* Signet pap. $.95

TWO NOVELS OF MEXICO: The Flies (1918) and The Bosses (1917). Trans. by Lesley Byrd Simpson. *Univ. of California Press* 1956 pap. $2.25

Books about Azuela

Mariano Azuela. By Luis Leal. World Authors Ser. *Twayne* 1971 $6.95

VASCONCELOS, JOSÉ. 1882–1959.   Mexico

Vasconcelos was prominent in Mexican life as a politician, essayist, statesman, and minister of education. His five-volume memoirs, abridged in the edition below, are a combination of autobiography, essay, and novel. Vasconcelos' subject is the whole of twentieth-century Mexican history and particularly his role in it. His account is personal, revealing his resentment of the United States, his inside view of the revolution, his unsuccessful campaign for the presidency, and his travels abroad after his defeat. "His private life was as turbulent as his public one: the abridgment skillfully balances the two. . . . The volume serves as an excellent introduction to his thought and times"—(*LJ*).

A MEXICAN ULYSSES: The Autobiography of José Vasconcelos. 1935–1959. Trans. and abr. by W. Rex Crawford. 1963. *Greenwood* 1972 $13.00

Books about Vasconcelos

Vasconcelos of Mexico: Philosopher and Prophet. By John H. Haddox. Pan American Ser. *Univ. of Texas Press* 1967 $5.95

RIVERA, JOSÉ EUSTASIO. 1888–1928.   Colombia

After the publication of a book of romantic sonnets entitled "The Promised Land" (1921), Rivera wrote his only novel, "The Vortex," prototype of the Latin American jungle novel. Tearing down the romantic view of the jungle as magnificent landscape peopled by innocent natives, Rivera presents a man-eating, terrifying green trap which closes upon the protagonists. The narrator is Arturo Cova, a *persona* of Rivera, whose memoirs relate his seduction of a young girl, their escape into the jungle, crime and corruption in the rubber industry, and the extreme violence which results when man's instincts are unchecked by civilization. Based on historical data, personal observation, and travel logs, "The Vortex" grew out of the conflict Rivera saw between literary presentations of the jungle and his own experience of it. Rivera died of diseases contracted in the jungle in the course of his work as a member of a commission appointed to settle a boundary dispute between Colombia and Venezuela.

THE VORTEX. 1924. Trans. by James K. Earl. *T V R T* 1976 (in prep.)

MISTRAL, GABRIELA (pseud. of Lucilia Godoy y Alcayaga). 1889–1957.   Chile

Gabriela Mistral's pen name was formed from those of Frédéric Mistral, a Provençal poet, and Gabriel D'Annunzio, the Italian patriot. Her first major collection of poetry was published in the United States in 1922 under the title *"Desolación."* The sonnets of this volume are a tender evocation of her passion for a young lover and her anguish at his suicide. Critics consider her collection *"Tala"* (Felling of Trees), published in Buenos Aires in 1938, her best work. Her poetry, as revealed in "Selected Poems," is "carefully restrained, shaped with the skillful craft of an artist who knows that the only way to real intensity of emotion in a poem is by creating an intense language and form"—(*Chicago Sunday Tribune*).

Love—physical, religious, humanitarian, and maternal—is the primary subject of Gabriela Mistral, whose unhappy love affairs provided the source of much of her poetic drive. Remaining single, she fulfilled her maternal instincts by teaching school and adopting a nephew, who died before he reached maturity. Among the ideas expressed in her poetry are anti-imperialism and a feminist rebellion against a masculine society.

On the invitation of the Mexican government, she reorganized that country's school system in the 1920s. She represented Chile in various posts at the League of Nations, the United Nations, and Chilean cousulates.

SELECTED POEMS. Trans. by Langston Hughes. *Indiana Univ. Press* 1957 pap. $1.75

Books about Mistral

Gabriela Mistral: The Poet and Her Work. By Margot Arce de Vásquez. 1958. *New York Univ. Press* 1964 $4.00 pap. $1.75

"This excellent study, . . . written in a pure and sympathetic style with admirable clarity and continuity, . . . will help vastly in understanding Mistral's poetry"—(*LJ*).

Gabriela Mistral's Religious Sensibility. By Martin C. Taylor. Publications in Modern Philology *Univ. of California Press* 1968 $7.00

TRAVEN, B. (pseud. of Berick Traven Torsvan). 1890–1969. Mexico

The mystery of the identity of B. Traven, a novelist who lived in anonymity in Mexico for over 30 years, has been cleared up by his widow. Several of the legends which surrounded him—that he was a World War I Bavarian revolutionary, a U.S. citizen of Swedish parentage, and a translator named Hal Croves who appeared on the set of "Treasure of the Sierra Madre"—proved to be true. Traven was born in Chicago in 1890 and moved to England and Germany with his parents. Under the name of Ret Marut he founded a socialist newspaper, *Der Zeigelbrenner*, and was involved in the Bavarian Socialist Republic. At its overthrow in 1919 he fled, wandering across Europe and the seas without papers. Upon reaching Mexico in 1922 he changed his identity to avoid being extradited. In his nearly successful attempt to maintain his privacy, he once wrote, "I have a country and that, sir, is called *Myself*. . . . *I* am my country and *I* am its government."

Traven's multiple identities make placing him in a national literature difficult. While he was an American by birth, and the majority of his novels were first published in German, many Mexican critics have claimed him as a Mexican novelist. The "Dictionary of Mexican Writers" classifies him as a Mexican author "through the depth with which he has treated and dramatized a most important aspect of the social reality of the country," while another critic (Luis Alberto Sánchez) labels him *the* novelist of the Mexican Revolution. "The Bridge in the Jungle," "The Rebellion of the Hanged," and "The White Rose" (in print in Great Britain) deal with the Mexican revolution from the viewpoint of the common man, of whom Traven was always the champion. "The Bridge in the Jungle," considered his best work, demonstrates the clash of cultures as an Indian boy slips on his new American shoes and falls to his death from a bridge built by an American oil company which did not think handrails necessary for the agile, barefoot natives. Traven is best known in the United States for "The Treasure of the Sierra Madre," made into a film starring Humphrey Bogart.

THE NIGHT VISITOR AND OTHER STORIES. Introd. by Charles Miller. *Farrar, Straus* (Hill & Wang) 1967 pap. $2.95

THE KIDNAPPED SAINT AND OTHER STORIES. Ed. by Mina C. Klein and H. Arthur Klein. *Lawrence Hill* 1974 $6.95

THE DEATH SHIP. 1926. *Lawrence Hill* 1973 $8.50; *Macmillan* 1962 pap. $1.25

THE TREASURE OF THE SIERRA MADRE. 1927. *Lanewood* 1972 $9.00 pap. $6.50; *New Am. Lib.* pap. $.95

THE COTTON PICKERS. 1929. *Farrar, Straus* (Hill & Wang) 1969 $5.00 pap. $2.65

CARRETA. 1930. *Farrar, Straus* (Hill & Wang) 1970 $5.95 pap. $2.95

GOVERNMENT. 1931. *Farrar, Straus* (Hill & Wang) 1971 $5.95

MARCH TO THE MONTERIA. 1933. *Farrar, Straus* (Hill & Wang) 1971 $5.95

THE GENERAL FROM THE JUNGLE. 1936. *Farrar, Straus* (Hill & Wang) 1973 $8.95 pap. $2.95

CREATION OF THE SUN AND THE MOON. 1936. *Farrar, Straus* (Hill & Wang) 1968 $3.95

THE REBELLION OF THE HANGED. 1938. *Farrar, Straus* (Hill & Wang) 1974 pap. $2.95

THE BRIDGE IN THE JUNGLE. 1938. *Farrar, Straus* (Hill & Wang) 1967 $5.00

VALLEJO, CÉSAR. 1892–1938. Peru

Vallejo's status as a *mestizo*, of part Indian blood, produced the tremendous psychological conflicts and alienation from society which mark his work. In his first volume, "The Black Heralds" (1918), he mixes French symbolism with the Indian spirit, expressing bitterness at his suffering and condition of isolation. "Trilce" is a literary rebellion in twisted syntax and absurd structure which nevertheless expresses deep emotions of solitude and the helplessness of oppressed peoples. After the publication of "Trilce," Vallejo moved to Paris, where he became a Communist. His posthumously published "Human Poems" and "Spain, Let This Cup Pass from

Me" reveal his anguish over the Spanish Civil War and express the idea that the proletarian fight will bring immortality to the combatants.

TRILCE. 1922. Trans. by David Smith. *Grossman* 1974 $20.00 pap. $5.95

SPAIN, LET THIS CUP PASS FROM ME. 1939. Trans. by Alvaro Cardoña-Hine *Red Hill* 1972 pap. $2.50; (with title "Spain, Take This Cup from Me") trans. by Clayton Eshelman and José R. Barcia *Grove* 1974 $10.00 Evergreen pap. $2.95; (with title "Spain, Take This Bitter Cup Away from Me") trans. by Jim Bradford *Grasshopper Press* 1974 pap. $4.00

POEMAS HUMANOS: Human Poems. 1939. Trans. by Clayton Eshelman. *Grove* bilingual ed. 1969 $8.50 pap. $3.45

ASTURIAS, MIGUEL ÁNGEL. 1899–   (Nobel Prize 1967)   Guatemala

This Guatemalan novelist, playwright, poet, translator, and diplomat won the 1967 Nobel Prize for Literature "for his highly colored writings rooted in a national individuality and Indian tradition." His first novel, *"El Señor Presidente,"* a fictional account of the sordid, terror-ridden period of violence and human degradation under the Guatemalan dictator Estrada Cabrera, was completed in 1932 but not published until 1946 for political reasons. Thomas Lask described Asturia's novelistic technique as follows: "In both books ['*El Señor Presidente*" and "*Mulata,*" o.p.] the reader, even through the translations, is aware of a writer with a free-wheeling imagination in the use of words and images, a bold, surrealistic dreamer who feels compelled to follow the oblique, lurid course of his imagination rather than in keeping his characters—and his readers— within conventional bounds"—*(New York Times)*.

Asturias, who during his first stay in Paris associated with surrealists André Breton and Paul Eluard, describes his process of writing as "automatic." "What I obtain from automatic writing is the mating or juxtaposition of words which, as the Indians say, have never met before," he has stated. In 1966, Asturias received the Lenin Peace Prize for writings that "expose American intervention against the Guatemalan people." His collection of short stories, "Weekend in Guatemala," concerns the overthrow in 1954 of President Jacobo Arbenz Guzmán, now generally acknowledged to have been accomplished with the aid of the U.S. Central Intelligence Agency. A trilogy of novels, "Strong Wind" (1950), "The Green Pope" (1954), and "Eyes of the Interred" (1960), is a powerful indictment of American economic domination in Guatemala as symbolized by the United Fruit Company.

Following the 1954 uprising, Asturias lived in exile for eight years. In 1967, on the election of President Julio César Méndez Montenegro, he was restored to his country's diplomatic service as its Ambassador to Paris. "My work," he says, "will continue to reflect the voice of the peoples, gathering their myths and popular beliefs and at the same time seeking to give birth to a universal consciousness of Latin American problems."

EL SEÑOR PRESIDENTE. 1946. Trans. by Francis Partridge. *Atheneum* 1964 $6.95

STRONG WIND. 1950. Trans. by Gregory Rabassa. *Delacorte* 1961 $6.95

THE GREEN POPE. 1954. Trans. by Gregory Rabassa. *Delacorte* 1971 $8.95

EYES OF THE INTERRED. 1960. Trans. by Gregory Rabassa. *Delacorte* 1973 $15.00

BORGES, JORGE LUIS. 1899–   Argentina

Borges regards all of man's endeavors to understand an incomprehensible world as a fiction; hence, his fiction is metaphysical and based on an "esthetics of the intellect," in his words. Also a prolific writer of essays, Borges' voice is clearest in his stories, which Jean Franco has described as follows: "Each of the stories to which he gave the name 'ficciones' ["*Ficciones*", "*El Aleph,*" "Dreamtigers"] is a small masterpiece, whose deceptively limpid surface constantly knots the reader into problems. Saturated with literary references, often as near to essay as to the conventional idea of the short story, the 'ficciones' nevertheless challenge print culture at a very deep level and perhaps even suggest its impossibility." A central image in Borges' work is the labyrinth, a mental and poetic construct, "a universe in miniature" which man builds and therefore believes he controls but which nevertheless traps him. In spite of Borges' belief that man cannot understand the chaotic world, in his fiction he continually attempts to do so.

Born in Buenos Aires, Borges was educated by an English governess and studied in Europe. He returned to Argentina in 1921, where he helped to found several avant-garde literary periodicals. After the fall of Juan Perón, whom he vigorously opposed, in 1955, he was appointed director of the Argentine National Library. With Samuel Beckett he won the $10,000 International Publishers Prize in 1961, thus establishing himself as one of the most prominent writers in the world. In 1967 he held the Charles Eliot Norton professorship at Harvard.

LABYRINTHS: Selected Stories and Other Writings. Ed. by Donald A. Yates and James E. Irby; trans. by Harriet de Onís, Anthony Kerrigan and others; pref. by André Maurois. *New Directions* 1961 pap. $1.95

This contains 22 "fictions," 10 essays, and 8 parables. Among the essays are: "The Argentine Writer and Tradition," "The Fearful Sphere of Pascal," "Valéry as Symbol," "Kafka and His Precursors." The parables concern such subjects as Dante's "Divine Comedy," "Cervantes and the Quixote," and various philosophical problems.

SELECTED POEMS: 1923–1967. Ed. with introd. by Norman Thomas di Giovanni. *Delacorte* bilingual ed. 1972 $12.50

THE ALEPH AND OTHER STORIES: 1933–1969. Trans. by Norman Thomas di Giovanni. *Dutton* 1970 $7.95; *Bantam* 1971 pap. $1.95

THE UNIVERSAL HISTORY OF INFAMY. 1935. Trans. by Norman Thomas di Giovanni. *Dutton* 1972 $6.95. Short story collection.

BOOK OF IMAGINARY BEINGS. 1944. Trans. by Norman Thomas di Giovanni. *Dutton* 1969 $7.95; *Avon* 1970 pap. $1.45. A modern bestiary of fantastic monsters and mythical beasts.

FICCIONES. 1944. Trans., ed., and with introd. by Anthony Kerrigan. *Grove* Evergreen Bks. 1962 $2.45

OTHER INQUISITIONS. 1952. Trans. by Ruth L. C. Simms; introd. by James E. Irby. *Univ. of Texas Press* 1964 $4.75; *Simon & Schuster* (Washington Square) 1968 pap. $1.95. Essays.

DREAMTIGERS. Trans. by Mildred Boyer and Harold Morland from "*El Hacedor*" ("The Maker," 1960); introd. by Miguel Enguidaros; woodcuts by Antonio Frasconi. *Univ. of Texas Press* 1963 $4.00; *Dutton* pap. $2.25

"A collection of miscellaneous poems, stories, anecdotes, essays, and vignettes, all of which add up to a psychic portrait of the author"—(*LJ*).

A PERSONAL ANTHOLOGY. 1961. Various translators. Ed. with fwd. by Anthony Kerrigan. *Grove* 1967 $5.00 pap. $1.95

"Composed of twenty-eight prose pieces (stories, essays, parables) and twenty poems, ["A Personal Anthology"] has been translated admirably into English"—(*SR*). "The book is both a delight for Borges fans and an introduction for Borges tyros. It splendidly displays the various facets of a remarkable, original literary personality—gravity, skepticism, wit, fantasy, playfulness, and an affectionate, sorrowfull concern for the human race"—(*New Yorker*).

AN INTRODUCTION TO AMERICAN LITERATURE. 1967. Trans. and ed. by Robert O. Evans and L. Clark Keating. *Univ. Press of Kentucky* 1971 $5.95

AN INTRODUCTION TO ENGLISH LITERATURE. 1967. Trans. and ed. by Robert O. Evans and L. Clark Keating. *Univ. Press of Kentucky* 1974 $6.95

IN PRAISE OF DARKNESS. 1969. Trans. by Norman Thomas di Giovanni. *Dutton* bilingual ed. 1974 $8.95 pap. $3.95

DOCTOR BRODIE'S REPORT. 1970. Trans. by Norman Thomas di Giovanni. *Dutton* 1972 $5.95; *Bantam* pap. $1.95. Short stories.

THE CONGRESS. 1971. Trans. by the author and Norman Thomas di Giovanni. *Enitharmon Press* 1973 limited ed. $8.50 limited signed ed. $22.50. Short story; includes a chronological table of Borges' works.

BORGES ON WRITING. Ed. by Norman Thomas di Giovanni and others. *Dutton* 1973 $6.95. Based on transcripts of Borges' discussions in a graduate writing program at Columbia University in 1971.

Books about Borges

Conversations with Jorge Luis Borges. By Richard Burgin. *Holt* 1968 $3.95. Informal interviews with Borges during his years at Harvard conducted by a student who, as Borges puts it in the introduction, helped him to know himself.

The Cyclical Night: Irony in James Joyce and Jorge Luis Borges. By Louis A. Murillo. *Harvard Univ. Press* 1968 $6.95. Detailed analyses of "The Garden of Forking Paths," "Death and the Forking Compass," "Emma Zunz," "The God's Script," and "The Immortal."

The Narrow Act: Borges' Art of Allusion. By Ronald Christ. *New York Univ. Press* 1969 $9.50 pap. $3.50. Focuses on Borges' literary device of allusion; a useful critical work with an introduction by Borges.

Mythmaker: A Study of Motif and Symbol in the Short Stories of Jorge Luis Borges. By Carter Wheelock. Pan American Ser. *Univ. of Texas Press* 1969 $7.50

Jorge Luis Borges. By Martin S. Stabb. World Authors Ser. *Twayne* 1970 $6.95

Jorge Luis Borges. By Jaime Alazraki. Essays on Modern Writers *Columbia Univ. Press* 1971 pap. $1.00

Cardinal Points of Jorge Luis Borges. By Lowell Dunham and Ivar Ivask. *Univ. of Oklahoma Press* 1972 $5.95 pap. $2.95

Jorge Luis Borges. By John M. Cohen. *Harper* Barnes & Noble 1974 $5.75

GOROSTIZA, JOSÉ. 1901–   Mexico

"Death without End," an abstract, metaphysical volume, has been called "the most important Mexican poem to appear up to that time in his generation" by Enrique Anderson Imbert. The central metaphor of this large, ambitious work is the glass of water, a symbol of the poet and of mankind, which momentarily is given form by the glass (intelligence and language), but which may be spilled and run into nothingness and chaos.

DEATH WITHOUT END. 1939. Trans. by Laura Villaseñor. Humanities Research Literary Ser. *Univ. of Texas Press* 1969 $10.00

GUILLÉN, NICOLÁS. 1902–   Cuba

Guillén, leader of the Afro-Cuban school, writes a poetry inspired by African dance, Cuban ballads, song rhythms, and speech patterns. In his first volumes, "Motives of Sound" (1930) and "*Sóngoro Cosongo*" (1931), meaning is communicated primarily through sound, and some poems are in Afro-Spanish dialect. Much of his subsequent poetry was politically motivated: "West Indies Ltd." (1934) by anti-imperialist views and "Spain" (1937) by his support for the Republic during the Spanish Civil War. In some of his recent volumes he has successfully combined lyricism with political and social protest. Poems in "*Tengo*" deal with the Cuban revolution.

TENGO. 1964. Trans. by Richard J. Carr; introd. by José Antonio Portuondo. *Broadside* 1974 $7.25

PATRIA O MUERTE: The Great Zoo (1967) and Other Poems, 1925–1969. Trans. by Robert Márquez. *Monthly Review* 1972 $8.50 pap. $3.25

MAN-MAKING WORDS. Trans. by Robert Márquez and David Arthur McMurray. *Univ. of Massachusetts Press* 1972 pap. $3.25

DÍAZ SÁNCHEZ, RAMÓN. 1903–1968.   Venezuela

"Cumboto" won the William Faulkner Foundation prize for the best novel published in Ibero-America between 1945 and 1962. Díaz Sánchez's subject in many of his works is black and white relationships, and in "Cumboto" he explores the soul of the Negro and the psychology of interracial mixing. After working as a proofreader, newspaperman, and municipal judge, Díaz Sánchez became co-director of the newspaper *El Tiempo* in Caracas and director of Culture and Fine Arts of the Ministry of Education in Venezuela.

CUMBOTO. 1950. Trans. by John Upton; ill. by Kermit Olliver Pan American Ser. *Univ. of Texas Press* 1969 $6.50

MALLEA, EDUARDO. 1903–   Argentina

Mallea has been associated with Argentina's avant-garde since the late 1920s and for 15 years greatly influenced Argentine letters from his position as literary director of the progressive newspaper *La Nación*. His view of the world basically existentialist, Mallea's concerns are man's loneliness, lack of communication, and alienation. He names as literary influences Blake, Rimbaud, Kierkegaard, Unamuno, Kafka, Joyce, and Proust, and he was the first to introduce European novelistic techniques to Argentina. "Fiesta in November" portrays in fragmentary counterpoint scenes a 24-hour period during which upper-class Argentine society enjoys its luxury and talks politics while a poet is assassinated for his political views. The novel has been interpreted as a reference to the murder of García Lorca. "All Green Shall Perish" is an allegorical narrative in which the spiritual life of Agata, a woman seeking love who ends in solitude and self-destruction, parallels the life of an Argentine province. He utilizes stream of consciousness techniques and disjunctures of chronological time to portray inner realities. Mallea won the Buenos Aires Municipal Prize for prose in 1935 and the National Prize for Literature in 1937.

ALL GREEN SHALL PERISH AND OTHER NOVELLAS AND STORIES. Ed. and introd. by John B. Hughes. *Knopf* 1966 $7.95

"Seven works of this distinguished Argentine writer, including two novellas, "Fiesta in November" (1938) and "All Green Shall Perish" (1941), are presented in this anthology.... The translations, each by a different person, are excellent. The introduction is long and incisive. Highly recommended"—(*LJ*).

CARPENTIER, ALEJO.   1904–   Cuba

A composer and musicologist, Carpentier consciously applied the principles of musical composition to his novels. Imprisoned for political activity in 1928, he escaped with the aid of Robert Desnos, a French surrealist poet, to Paris, where he joined the literary circles of surrealist Louis Aragon, Tristan Tzara, and Paul Eluard. Surrealism influenced his style and, according to Carpentier, helped him to see "aspects of American life he had not previously seen, in their telluric, epic, and poetic contexts." "Lost Steps" takes the form of the diary of a Cuban musician and intellectual who seeks escape from civilization during his trip to a remote Amazon village in search of native musical instruments. In his introduction, Priestley writes, "In this tale of a search and how it ended, so magnificent and memorable in its descriptive power, so rich in its poetic symbolism, Carpentier is both enchanting us and making us face a piercing and profound criticism of our modern society." The three short stories "The Road to Santiago," "Journey to the Seed," and "Similar to Night," and the novel "The Pursuit," in "The War of Time" (the title is an allusion to a line from Lope de Vega defining man as "a soldier in the war of time") demonstrate a preoccupation with historical and subjective time. Of the style of the novel Enrique Anderson Imbert has written, " 'The Pursuit' is a puzzle with its pieces carefully mixed: the reader apprehends, little by little, in each fragment the total design."

Carpentier has been director of Cuba's National Press, which published many millions of volumes in an ambitious program. At present he is Cuba's ambassador to France.

KINGDOM OF THIS WORLD. 1941. Trans. by Harriet de Onís. *Macmillan* 1971 pap. $1.50

THE LOST STEPS. 1953. Trans. by Harriet de Onís; introd. by J. B. Priestley. *Knopf* 1956 rev. ed. 1967 $5.95

WAR OF TIME. 1958. Trans. by Frances Partridge. *Knopf* 1971 $4.95

NERUDA, PABLO (pseud. of Neftalí Ricardo Reyes).   1904–1973.   Chile
(Nobel Prize 1971)

Neruda's poetry has moved through a variety of periods and styles, beginning as romantic in "Crepusculary" (1923), which in its treatment of the lower classes shows the roots of his later communism. In "Twenty Poems of Love and A Song of Despair," one poem for each year of his life plus one, his tone becomes more despairing, a mood amplified in "The Attempt of Infinite Man," a painful confrontation with man's limits. His three volumes of "Residence on Earth" are surrealist in style and subject matter, characterized by twisted syntax, audacious metaphors, and truncated phrases which express the chaos of the modern mind and an ontological despair. In 1927 Neruda entered Chile's diplomatic corps, and after an unpleasant tour in the Orient he became Consul in Barcelona and then moved to Madrid in 1935. He devoted himself to the cause of the Spanish Republic, and its destruction by Franco's forces led him into political activism and a conversion to communism. In volumes such as "Spain in the Heart" and "Intimate Letter to Millions" his verse becomes less hermetic, more accessible, and particularly more political. He saw as his mission the education of the proletariat, and the pessimism of his early period changed to an optimism about man's solidarity and the future of communism.

Neruda remained an international figure throughout his life, traveling to Russia and supporting Fidel Castro, as well as an important force in Chilean politics. His extraordinary poetic talent and his active social role made him a legendary and symbolic figure for intellectuals, students, and artists from all of Latin America. "The tension, the repression, the drama of our position in Latin America doesn't permit us the luxury of being uncommitted," he said. Neruda won the Nobel Prize in 1971 "for poetry that, with the action of an elemental force, brings alive a continent's destiny and dreams." He died in Chile shortly after the *coup d'état* which deposed President Allende in 1973.

SELECTED POEMS. Trans. and ed. by Ben Belitt; introd. by Luis Monguio. *Grove* bilingual ed. 1961 pap. $2.95

TWENTY LOVE POEMS AND A SONG OF DESPAIR. 1924. Trans. by W. S. Merwin. *Grossman* Cape Editions 1970 $3.50 pap. $1.95

RESIDENCE ON EARTH AND OTHER POEMS. Trans. by Donald Walsh *New Directions* $10.00; trans. by Angel Flores *Gordian* bilingual ed. 1974 $9.00. Residence I 1925–1931; Residence II 1931–1935; Residence III 1935–1945; Meeting under New Flags.

FIVE DECADES: Poems 1925–1970. Trans. by Ben Belitt. *Grove* pap. $3.95

THE HEIGHTS OF MACCHU PICCHU. 1950. Trans. by Nathaniel Tarn; pref. by Robert Pring-Mill. *Farrar, Straus* bilingual ed. 1967 $4.95 Noonday pap. $2.25

THE CAPTAIN'S VERSES. 1952. Trans. by Donald D. Walsh. *New Directions* 1972 pap. $1.95

EXTRAVAGARIA. 1958. Trans. by Alastair Reid. *Farrar, Straus* 1974 $8.95

THE SPLENDOR AND DEATH OF JOAQUÍN MURIETA. 1966. Trans. by Ben Belitt. *Farrar Straus* bilingual ed. 1972 $7.95 pap. $2.95. A play on "a Chilean bandit done injustice in California on July 23, 1853."

NEW POEMS: 1968–1970. Trans. by Ben Belitt. *Grove* 1972 $5.95 pap. $2.95

WE ARE MANY. Trans. by Alastair Reid; photos by Hans Ehrmann. *Grossman* 1968 $5.00 pap. $2.95

TOWARD THE SPLENDID CITY: Nobel Lecture. *Farrar, Straus* bilingual ed. 1974 $4.95 Noonday pap. $1.95

Books about Neruda

The Word and the Stone: Language and Imagery in Neruda's "Canto General." By Frank Russ. Modern Language and Literature Monographs *Oxford* 1972 $11.25

YAÑEZ, AUGUSTÍN. 1904–   Mexico

An important figure in Mexican public life, Yañez has served as governor of his state of Jalisco, a professor at the National University, and Secretary of Public Education. At the same time he is an important novelist, and his "The Edge of the Storm," published in 1947, has been termed by Walter M. Langford the single most important work in the history of the Mexican novel. Influenced by Dos Passos, Aldous Huxley, and James Joyce, Yañez brought the Mexican novel into the twentieth century in the areas of narrative technique and psychological penetration. "The Edge of the Storm" is the first of a trilogy, now including "The Prodigal Land" (1960) and "The Lean Lands" (1962). In the latter novel, a peasant family must make a choice between surrendering their land, traditionally the symbol of power, or a sewing machine, symbol of the new industrial age, to the greedy, oppressive boss of the territory. His technique here is characterized by an abundance of proverbs, estimated by one critic, Carballo, to make up nearly one-third of the text.

LEAN LANDS. 1962. Trans. by Ethel Brinton. Pan American Ser. *Univ. of Texas Press* 1968 $6.50

ICAZA, JORGE. 1906–   Ecuador

"The Villagers" (*"Huasipungo"*), originally published in 1934 and substantially revised and expanded in 1951, is a powerful condemnation of the exploitation of the Indians in Latin America. The title is Quechua for the plot of land worked by the Indians as tenant farmers, land which American companies want for roads, lumber, and oil. Landowners, the priest, and the police conspire with capitalistic enterprise to force the Indians from territory they have held for generations. Sometimes compared to "Tobacco Road" and "Grapes of Wrath," *"Huasipungo"* has been called "the most ferocious painting of one of the more painful realities of our America"— (Luis Durand). The novel has been translated into numerous languages. Icaza's novel "In the Streets" won a national prize in 1953.

THE VILLAGERS (*Huasipungo*). 1934. Trans. with introd. by Bernard Dulsey; ed. by J. Cary Davis; pref. by the author. Contemporary Latin American Classics Ser. *Southern Illinois Univ. Press* 1964 pap. 1974 $2.85

AGUILERA MALTA, DEMETRIO. 1909–   Ecuador

"Manuela" is the first in Aguilera Malta's projected ten-volume series of historical novels on famous Latin Americans. This novel deals with Simón Bolívar and Manuela Sáenz, his mistress and political adviser. She was awarded the title "Caballeresca del Sol," the Peruvian government's

Knight of the Sun decoration, for her assistance to San Martín in obtaining the independence of Peru. "Manuela" "is dramatically and poetically told, in modern stream of consciousness technique, and the historical figures assume reality"—(*Book World*). Aguilera Malta first came to prominence in 1930 for his contribution to a collection of naturalistic short stories, "Those Who Go Away," which marked a break with Romanticism in Ecuadorian literature.

MANUELA: La Caballeresca del Sol. 1964. Trans. with introd. by Willis Knapp Jones; fwd. by J. Cary Davis. Contemporary Latin American Classics Ser. *Southern Illinois Univ. Press* 1967 $6.95

ONETTI, JUAN CARLOS. 1909– Uruguay

Onetti excels at fantastic, surrealistic narrative and a dense, indirect prose style. His subject is the decay and materialism of the modern world. The narrator of "Brief Life" creates a number of other existences for himself to escape the boredom and limits, symbolized by his wife's mastectomy, of his own. "The Shipyard" (trans. by Rachel Caffyn 1968, o.p.), generally considered his best novel and the winner of the Faulkner Prize for the best Latin American novel of the year in 1961, demonstrates the central character's inability to control his life in an absurd existence. Onetti's works are not thoroughly pessimistic, however, for his characters never cease trying to create meaning.

BRIEF LIFE. 1950. Trans. by Hortense Carpentier. *Grossman* 1975 $10.00

ANDERSON IMBERT, ENRIQUE. 1910– Argentina

A well-known critic and professor of Latin American literature at Harvard University, Enrique Anderson Imbert is also a writer of short stories and novels. "The Other Side of the Mirror" contains both the stories published in "Proofs of Chaos" (1946) and a score of additional stories. The title in Spanish, "*El grimorio*," means "book of magic," and in these charming stories Anderson Imbert presents a magical, fantastic world on the other side of Alice in Wonderland's mirror under a realistic guise. The translator, who worked in collaboration with the author, writes, "The real world vanishes and we are in a world of magic, the distorting mirror image of our own."

THE OTHER SIDE OF THE MIRROR. 1961. Trans. by Isabel Reade. Contemporary Latin American Class. *Southern Illinois Univ. Press* 1966 $5.95 pap. continental ed. $3.00

MUJICA LÁINEZ, MANUEL. 1910– Argentina

"Bomarzo," an unusual novel which Alberto Ginastera adapted into an opera, is a fantastic reconstruction of the Italian Renaissance through the confessions of Pier Francesco Orsini, Duke of Bomarzo. Through the consciousness of the Duke, who becomes a black magician in his quest for immortality, the author demonstrates the flaws in the Renaissance humanistic tradition from which modern Western civilization originates.

BOMARZO. 1962. Trans. by Gregory Rabassa. *Simon & Schuster* 1969 $10.00

BENÍTEZ, FERNANDO. 1911– Mexico

A historian, the author of several studies of Mexico's Indians, and a member of the National Institute of Indigenous Affairs, Benítez has also written short stories and novels on Mexican cultural and historical themes. "The Poisoned Water," based on a true incident, takes the form of a priest's letters regarding the murder of the *cacique*, boss of the village, and the brutal revenge taken by military authorities. The traditions and symbols of the Mexican pueblo and his concern for the Indians, whom he regards as oppressed and exploited, are the bases of all Benítez's works.

THE POISONED WATER. 1961. Trans. by Mary E. Ellsworth. Contemporary Latin American Classics Ser. *Southern Illinois Univ. Press* 1973 $7.95

BIOY CASARES, ADOLFO. 1914– Argentina

Bioy Casares has collaborated with Borges (*q.v.*) on a number of works, including their "Anthology of Fantastic Literature" (1940), a documentation of the development of Spanish American suprarealism. "The Invention of Morel," about which Borges states in his prologue that Bioy Casares has disproven Ortega's theory that there exists no new subject matter for the novel, concerns a scientist's illusions of immortality, while in "Diary of the War of the Pig" the author pits young and old against each other in a war of generations.

THE INVENTION OF MOREL (1953) and Other Stories from *La Trama Celeste* (1948). Trans. by Ruth L. Simms; prologue by Jorge Luis Borges. *Univ. of Texas Press* 1964 $6.50

DIARY OF THE WAR OF THE PIG. 1969. Trans. by Gregory Woodruff and Donald A. Yates. *McGraw-Hill* 1972 $5.99

CORTÁZAR, JULIO. 1914–   Argentina

Cortázar's view that fantasy and reality, the rational and the irrational exist on both intersecting and identical planes has produced his formal experiments with the novel, experiments always in the spirit of philosophical and literary play. The stories in "Blow-up and Other Stories" explore from fresh perspectives the nature of time, space, and reality—in "The End of the Game" a woman embraces a beggar to find that they have exchanged identities; "Blow-up" provided Antonioni with the point of departure for his film of that title. A reviewer in *Nation* wrote of the techniques of the stories, "Their effects come off, both as technical feats and as reverberating ideas." In "Cronopios and Famas" he created a world filled with fantastic beings. Cronopios are green creatures representing the magic in everyday life, while famas are those seeing only conventional reality. In "All Fires the Fire," a collection of eight stories, his consolation for the despair of modern life is that finally "all fires burn together as one." The protagonist of "Hopscotch," in quest of reality (the Heaven or Home of a hopscotch game), tries to liberate himself from the restrictions imposed by time, language, and social conventions. "I was trying," the author writes, "to break the habits of readers—not just for the sake of breaking them, but to make the reader free . . . space and time are left completely by the wayside. There are moments in it when the reader will not know where or when the action is taking place." "Sixty-two: A Model Kit" (literally translated, A Novel to Put Together) continues the theoretical lines developed in "Hopscotch," giving the reader an opportunity to build the novel as he would a model airplane by selecting the parts he will read.

BLOW-UP AND OTHER STORIES (orig. "End of the Game and Other Stories"). Trans. by Paul Blackburn. *Macmillan* 1968 $1.50

These 15 stories were selected from *"Bestiario"* (1951), *"Las Armas Secretas"* (1959), and *"Final del Juego"* (1956). "Beautifully translated"—(*N.Y. Times*).

CRONOPIOS AND FAMAS. 1962. Trans. by Paul Blackburn. *Pantheon* 1969 $4.95

HOPSCOTCH. 1963. Trans. by Gregory Rabassa *Pantheon* 1966 $8.95; *New Am. Lib.* pap. $3.95; *Avon* 1974 pap. $1.95

ALL FIRES THE FIRE AND OTHER STORIES. 1966. Trans. by Suzanne J. Levine. *Pantheon* 1973 $5.95

SIXTY-TWO: A Model Kit. 1968. Trans. by Gregory Rabassa *Pantheon* 1972 $6.95; *Avon* 1973 pap. $1.65

PARRA, NICANOR. 1914–   Chile

In an effort to transform poetry, Parra has invented what he calls the "antipoem," which, he says, "returns poetry to its roots." His work is comparable to that of the American Beat poets of the 1950s in its nonpoetic flat tone, direct statement, black humor, and violence. He intends his poetry as an affront to society, and indeed he has scandalized some. Parra is a professor of theoretical physics at the University of Chile and an accomplished folk musician. Pablo Neruda (*q.v.*) called him "one of the great names in the literature of our language."

POEMS AND ANTIPOEMS. 1954. Trans. by Allen Ginsberg, William Carlos Williams, Denise Levertov, and others. *New Directions* bilingual ed. 1967 $5.50 pap. $1.95

EMERGENCY POEMS. Trans. with introd. by Miller Williams. *New Directions* 1972 $8.75 pap. $2.75

PAZ, OCTAVIO. 1914–   Mexico

Octavio Paz conceives of poetry as a way of transcending barriers of world, time, and individual self. Through poetry he seeks to achieve a state of innocence and a euphoria of the senses, and he expresses anguish when language fails him. Much of Paz's poetry is erotic, with woman being the vehicle across the abyss to "the other side of the river" where union with a universal consciousness is possible. Poetry for Paz is necessarily in conflict with society because of its potential for transmuting and reforming it. Some consider his essays, as in "Labyrinth of Solitude," studies of Mexican character and traditions, and "The Bow and the Lyre," statements of aesthetics and poetics, to be superior to his poetry.

Paz served as Mexico's ambassador to India from 1962 to 1968, when he resigned to protest the government's treatment of students demonstrating prior to the Olympic Games in Mexico City.

THE LABYRINTH OF SOLITUDE: Life and Thought in Mexico. Trans. by Lysander Kemp. *Grove* Evergreen Bks. 1962 pap. $3.95. A collection of essays.

EARLY POEMS, 1935–1955. (Orig. "Selected Poems") trans. by Muriel Rukeyser and others. *Indiana Univ. Press* rev. ed. 1973 $7.95; *New Directions* pap. $2.50

THE BOW AND THE LYRE. 1956. Trans. by Ruth C. Simms. Pan American Ser. *Univ. of Texas Press* 1973 $8.50. The author explains his poetic theory.

ALTERNATING CURRENT. 1961–1967. Trans. by Helen R. Lane. *Viking* 1973 $7.95 pap. $1.95. Essays on poetry, fiction, and philosophy.

CONFIGURATIONS. 1965. Trans. by the author and others. *New Directions* bilingual ed. 1971 $6.50 pap. $2.75. Includes Sun Stone (1957) and Blanco (1967).

THE OTHER MEXICO: Critique of the Pyramid. Trans. by Lysander Kemp. *Grove* 1972 pap. $1.95. Lectures on Mexican history and culture given at the University of Texas in 1969.

CONJUNCTIONS AND DISJUNCTIONS. 1969. Trans. by Helen R. Lane. *Viking* 1974 $7.95

RENGA: A Chain of Poems. Trans. by Charles Tomlinson; fwd. by Claude Roy. *Braziller* 1972 $5.95 pap. $2.45. Poems by Octavio Paz and others translated from Spanish, French, and Italian.

CHILDREN OF THE MIRE: Modern Poetry from Romanticism to the Avant-Garde. *Harvard Univ. Press* 1974 $7.95. The Charles Eliot Norton Lectures for 1971–1972.

Books about Paz

The Poetic Modes of Octavio Paz. By Rachel Phillips. *Oxford* 1972 $12.00

ARREOLA, JUAN JOSÉ. 1918–   Mexico

"Confabulario and Other Inventions" is a collection of Arreola's short stories, satiric sketches, and fables published from 1941 to 1961 in several separate volumes. One section comprises his "Bestiary," 26 fables and allegories, each developing the human qualities and foibles of a particular beast. No subject escapes his pointed satirical pen in his witty, compact, phantasmagorical stories, which are reminiscent of the works of Borges (*q.v.*) and Quevedo (*q.v.*).

CONFABULARIO AND OTHER INVENTIONS: 1941–1961. Trans. by George D. Schade; ill. by Kelly Fearing. Pan American Ser. *Univ. of Texas Press* 1974 $10.00 pap. $2.95

RULFO, JUAN. 1918–   Mexico

Rulfo's collection of short stories, "The Burning Plain," deals with the Mexican poor, specifically Jalisco peasants—their traditions, problems, and passions. His first novel, "Pedro Páramo," also based on rural life, treats the theme of the *cacique* or boss of a town. Juan Preciado's mother on her deathbed sends him on a journey back to the town of Comala, which she remembers as verdant and vital, but Juan finds instead a village of dead souls. The structure of the novel, influenced in part by Faulkner, involves the juxtaposition and transposition of pieces of narrative, monologue, dialogue, and poetic prose. Enrique Anderson Imbert has written of the work, "The reader is chilled with horror, as if he were dreaming an absurd nightmare; the images, which occasionally are of great poetic force, tragically evoke the annihilation of a whole Mexican town."

THE BURNING PLAIN AND OTHER STORIES. 1953. Trans. by George D. Schade. *Univ. of Texas Press* 1967 $5.00 pap. $2.25

PEDRO PÁRAMO: A Novel of Mexico. 1955. Trans. by Lysander Kemp. *Grove* 1959 Black Cat Bks. pap. $1.25

MARQUÉS, RENÉ. 1919–   Puerto Rico

"The Oxcart" is one of many works by Puerto Rican authors in the 1950s and 1960s that reveal a surge in Puerto Rican pride and ethnic identity. The play involves the difficulties of a Puerto Rican immigrant to the United States and advocates a return to the land and culture of Puerto Rico. The play was widely performed in both Spanish and English by traveling companies on the streets of New York City in the summer of 1967. Marqués studied at Columbia University.

THE OXCART. 1951. Trans. by Charles Pilditch. *Scribner* 1969 pap. text ed. $1.96

GARRO, ELENA. 1920–   Mexico

Best known as a dramatist, Elena Garro won the important Premio Xavier Villaurrutia in 1963 for the novel "Recollections of Things to Come." The interior world of the characters' memories of life in Ixtepec during the Cristero rebellion is narrated dramatically in poetic prose. The translator writes of the work, "The town tells its own story against a variegated background of political change, religious persecution, and social unrest." A choreographer, script writer, and journalist, Elena Garro was at one time married to the Mexican poet Octavio Paz.

RECOLLECTIONS OF THINGS TO COME. 1962. Trans. by Ruth L. C. Simms. Pan American
   Ser. *Univ. of Texas Press* 1969 $6.50

CARBALLIDO, EMILIO.   1925–   Mexico

Carballido is known primarily as a playwright and one of the leaders of a movement which has
revitalized Mexican theater during the 1950s and 1960s. Previously, Mexican theater had been
derivative of European models. Carballido is responsible for breaking from the traditional realistic
drama and introducing a surrealistic, fantastic world, one to which the Mexican novel had already
turned, into the theater. The translator writes, "He [Carballido] is the first Mexican playwright
who consistently creates plays that transcend the specifically realistic and restrictively Mexican to
achieve a theater that can be called modern, contemporary, and universal." At the same time,
Carballido probes the nature of reality and of man's responsibility to himself and others. The play
"Theseus," included in the volume "The Golden Thread," is a twentieth-century version of the
Greek myth, in which Theseus takes full responsibility for his actions, willfully neglecting to put
up the white sail of victory upon his return from killing the minotaur on Crete so that his father
will hurl himself from the Parthenon and he will become king. "The Norther" is a short novel.

THE GOLDEN THREAD (1957) AND OTHER PLAYS. Trans. by Margaret Sayers Peden. Pan
   American Ser. *Univ. of Texas Press* 1970 $6.50. The Mirror, The Time and the Place,
   The Intermediate Zone, The Clockmaker from Cordoba, Theseus.

THE NORTHER. 1958. Trans. by Margaret Sayers Peden. Pan American Ser. *Univ. of
   Texas Press* 1968 $4.95

CASTELLANOS, ROSARIO.   1925–   Mexico

Rosario Castellanos is one of the first Mexican novelists to deal with Indian characters as
complete human beings rather than as stereotypes or political causes. A European child raised by
an Indian nurse narrates a portion of the novel "Nine Guardians" (*Balún Canán*), and through
the eyes of this seven-year-old girl Castellanos reveals the mystery and excitement of Indian life.
The novel represents the first of her Chiapas cycle of four novels, all humanizing the Indian.

NINE GUARDIANS. 1957. Trans. by Irene Nicholson. *Vanguard* 1960 $3.95

DONOSO, JOSÉ.   1925–   Chile

Donoso has been compared to Henry James for his psychological penetration of characters and
to William Faulkner for novelistic technique. In "This Sunday" he focuses on a family's activities
on Sundays to view the boredom, passions, and misery of Chilean bourgeois society and its
servants. "Obscene Bird of Night" deals with the decline of feudal society through the story of a
land-holding family whose daughter's head is transformed into that of a bird. While the family
regards her as a child-saint, the peasants see her as a child-witch. The male secretary charged with
her education tells his story of the decay of the family from an old people's home.

THIS SUNDAY. Trans. by Lorraine O'Grady Freeman. 1966. *Knopf* 1967 $5.95

THE OBSCENE BIRD OF NIGHT. 1970. Trans. by Hardie St. Martin and Leonard Mades.
   Knopf 1973 $7.95

WOLFF, EGON.   1926–   Chile

After working as a chemical engineer, Wolff began writing plays in 1958. He is one of a group
of playwrights who developed with the support of Chilean university theaters. His plays most
often deal with the demise of the guilt-ridden middle class, as does "Paper Flowers," which, in the
translator's words, portrays the "destruction of a bourgeoisie indifferent to its surrounding social
problems."

PAPER FLOWERS: A Play in Six Scenes. Trans. by Margaret Sayers Peden. *Univ. of
   Missouri Press* Breakthrough Bks. 1971 $4.50 pap. $3.00

GARCÍA MÁRQUEZ, GABRIEL.   1928–   Colombia

García Márquez has created a fictional world in a town named Macondo, which is the setting for
all of his novels. "One Hundred Years of Solitude," his epic novel covering a one-hundred-year
cycle of the town's existence, traces its founding by José Arcadio Buendía with an incestuous relationship through its destruction by cyclone. Aureliano, one of the final survivors, discovers a manuscript predicting his final solitude and his death at the moment he finishes reading it. The magical
style mingles the fantastic, mythical, and commonplace on multiple levels. The novel has an Old
Testament tone and structure. Although much of the novel is comic, its characters are finally
tragic for their self-imposed isolation and destruction. Of the translation listed below *Book World*
wrote, "Rabassa's translation is a triumph of fluent, gravid momentum, all stylishness and common-

sensical virtuosity." With this work García Márquez established himself as a novelist of great importance.

LEAF STORM AND OTHER STORIES. 1955. Trans. by Gregory Rabassa. *Harper* 1972 $6.50; *Avon* 1973 pap. $1.65

NO ONE WRITES TO THE COLONEL AND OTHER STORIES. 1961. Trans. by J. S. Bernstein. *Harper* 1968 $6.95; *Avon* 1973 pap. $1.50

ONE HUNDRED YEARS OF SOLITUDE. 1967. Trans. by Gregory Rabassa. *Harper* 1970 $10.00; *Avon* 1971 pap. $1.95

CABRERA INFANTE, GUILLERMO. 1929– Cuba

"Three Trapped Tigers," winner of the Barcelona Seix Barral Prize in 1964, makes Havana night life before the revolution a symbol of the decadence of the Batista regime. The protagonists are singers, musicians, aristocrats, and intellectuals who live off an American-supported and dominated entertainment world. The triumph of the novel is its language, a combination of "Spanglish" and "cubano," the language of the lowest classes. In his puns and word play (the title in Spanish is a tongue twister) Cabrera Infante demonstrates debts to his acknowledged masters: Lewis Carroll, Nabokov, and Joyce. At the same time, however, he attempts to free Cuban language and literature from constricting foreign influence. In 1965, he defected from Cuba to England, where he now resides.

THREE TRAPPED TIGERS. 1964. Trans. by Donald Gardner and Suzanne Jill Levine in collaboration with the author. *Harper* 1971 $8.95

FUENTES, CARLOS. 1929– Mexico

The most famous Mexican novelist of the century is probably Carlos Fuentes, also an essayist, journalist, film writer, and diplomat. Fuentes has provoked a great deal of controversy, some rivals claiming that he does not deserve the recognition accorded him, while others, most notably the U.S. State Department, have objected to his political activity, in particular his open support of Fidel Castro.

All of Fuentes's works demonstrate his primary concern, the interpretation of Mexican culture and history. He finds Mexico's search for identity particularly difficult due to its beginning with the annihilation of the Indians: "The nostalgia for the past in Mexico is a direct result of the original defeat, of the fact that Mexico was a country that lost its tongue, its customs, its power, everything." The protagonist of "Where the Air Is Clear," described by Fuentes as "a synthesis of the Mexican present," is the whole of Mexico City, and a panorama of postrevolutionary Mexican life is presented through a wide range of characters from various classes and professions. "The Death of Artemio Cruz," which made an international reputation for Fuentes, narrates a dying man's reflections on the crucial decisions of his life as vitality and energy drain from him. At the appearance of "A Change of Skin" in English, Robert J. Clements described it as a "great book . . . incorporating every technique of the contemporary novel . . . bursting in energy, capacious in content, gripping in evocation, and humanitarian in its universal tolerance"—(*SR*). Although his subsequent novels are of interest, none yet surpasses these in significance. In 1975 Fuentes was appointed Mexico's ambassador to France.

WHERE THE AIR IS CLEAR (*La Región Más Transparente*). 1959. Trans. by Sam Hileman. *Farrar, Straus* 1971 pap. $2.95

GOOD CONSCIENCE. 1959. Trans. by Sam Hileman. *Farrar, Straus* 1961 1964 pap. $2.25

THE DEATH OF ARTEMIO CRUZ. 1962. Trans. by Sam Hileman. *Farrar, Straus* 1964 $4.95 Noonday pap. $2.25

A CHANGE OF SKIN. 1967. Trans. by Sam Hileman. *Farrar, Straus* 1968 $6.95; *Putnam* 1970 pap. $3.25

PUIG, MANUEL. 1932– Argentina

"Betrayed by Rita Hayworth" is an innovative novel narrating through a variety of techniques the story of a young Argentine boy who lives vicariously through the movies. Puig uses the phenomenon of compulsive movie-going as a symbol for alienation and escape from reality. The characters' emotions and responses to life are conditioned by the movies, primarily American movies, and limited by them. Alexander Coleman wrote of the novel's style, "Puig does camp up in a fabulous way, full of literary allure, magnetic glower, smouldering good looks and plenty of panache and strut"—(*N.Y. Times*). "Heartbreak Tango" is a soap opera of a novel evoking the spiritual emptiness of the 1930s and the vulgarity of popular art. Puig has worked as a scriptwriter and film director.

BETRAYED BY RITA HAYWORTH. 1968. Trans. by Suzanne Jill Levine. *Dutton* 1973 $6.95; *Avon* pap. $1.65

HEARTBREAK TANGO. 1969. Trans. by Suzanne Jill Levine. *Dutton* 1973 $6.95

VARGAS LLOSA, MARIO. 1936–   Peru

Vargas Llosa's first novel, "The City and the Dogs" (translated as "The Time of the Hero" 1966, o.p.), brought both scandal and fame to its author. A thousand copies were ceremoniously burned in Peru, where Vargas Llosa was denounced as an enemy of the state, but it was published in Spain to high critical acclaim. Vargas Llosa spent two years at the boys' military academy scathingly depicted here. "Vargas Llosa skillfully depicts the corruption within the academy, never permitting us to forget that it is an inevitable reflection of the hypocrisy without. . . . What he possesses in abundance is the novelist's willingness to live with complexity and to magnify every minor crack in the world's surface so that we can see what it hides"—(*Nation*).

"The Green House," based on his memories of experiences in the jungle, contains five interrelated stories fragmented through the five parts of the novel and covering a span of 45 years. Space, time, character, and action are broken and juxtaposed in a marvelous display of novelistic technique. Implicit are critiques of Peru's religious and military establishments. In "Conversations in the Cathedral," *la Catedral* being a bar, Vargas Llosa uses the conversation between the son of a wealthy man and his father's mulatto chauffeur as a base for a series of juxtaposed pieces of other conversations, again exposing a corrupt society and revealing man's weaknesses and desperate condition.

Vargas Llosa, who received his doctorate from the University of Madrid and has lived in London and Paris, now lives in Peru.

THE GREEN HOUSE. 1966. Trans. by Gregory Rabassa. *Harper* 1961 $7.95; *Avon* 1973 pap. $1.65

CONVERSATIONS IN THE CATHEDRAL. 1969. Trans. by Gregory Rabassa. *Harper* 1975 $12.50

ARENAS, REINALDO. 1943–   Cuba

The novel "Hallucinations" recreates the life of Fray Servando Teresa de Mier, a Mexican priest (1765–1827) famous for his hatred of the Spaniards who denied even that they had brought Christianity to the New World, in a poetic style in which time, space, and character move on multiple planes of fantasy and reality. Arenas begins with a letter to the friar: "Ever since I discovered in you an execrable history of Spanish literature, described as 'the friar who had traveled over the whole of Europe on foot having improbable adventures,' I have tried to find out more about you." He discovers that he and Servando are the same person, and hence author and character become one.

HALLUCINATIONS: Being an Account of the Life and Adventures of Friar Servando Teresa de Mier. 1969. Trans. by Gordon Brotherston. *Harper* 1971 $6.50

BRAZILIAN LITERATURE

Brazil's bonds to Europe were even more durable than those of the Spanish American countries. King John VI, then Prince Regent of Portugal, fled to Brazil in 1807 just prior to the Napoleonic invasion and established a court in Rio de Janeiro. When he returned to Portugal in 1820 due to a Brazilian rebellion, he left his son Pedro I as Regent. Pedro I declared Brazil's independence in 1822, and he and his son Pedro II reigned until 1889. Brazil was thus effectively governed by the Portuguese almost up to the twentieth century. The result of this long domination is that Brazilian literature developed its own voice even more slowly than the rest of South American literature.

Literature in Brazil begins in the sixteenth century with the narratives of explorers and missionaries, as, for example, the Jesuit priest Jose de Anchieta (1534–1597), who wrote dramas to educate the Indians and lyric poetry. It was only in 1668 that Portugal herself gained recognition of her independence from Spain, and Brazil's writers of the seventeenth century, usually either born or educated in Europe, imitated both Spanish and Portuguese gongorist poets. The eighteenth century saw the establishment of academies which sponsored the writing of histories, and the transplantation of some of the worst aspects of Neoclassicism.

Romanticism dominated Brazilian literature from 1836, the date of a manifesto published in Paris by a group of Brazilians, to the 1880s. The Romantic movement helped Brazil toward a consciousness of her identity by freeing literature from European forms and subjects and admitting the expression of Brazilian themes. Many writers, such as the poet Antônio Gonçalves Dias (1823–1864), turned to Indian themes. José Martiniano de Alencar's novel *"O Guarani"* ("The Guarani Indian") (1857) was significant not only for its focus on the Indians but also for its portrayal of landscape and its stylistic achievements. These innovations and others were gathered and perfected by Brazil's greatest novelist, Machado de Assis (*q.v.*). Reactions against Romanticism took the form of Parnassianism in poetry and the realistic novel in fiction.

The modernist movement, connoting in Brazilian letters the literary and linguistic renovation which began in the 1920s rather than the Spanish and Spanish American aestheticism, started with Modern Art Week in 1922, a week-long presentation of modern painting, sculpture, and music which was organized by Mário de Andrade (*q.v.*) and others. The modernists' purpose was to free the Brazilian language from classical Portuguese rules and syntax and to create a uniquely Brazilian language and literature. With the modernists Brazil finally achieved literary autonomy, and no subsequent writer discussed here is without a debt to this nationalistic literary movement.

Literary Criticism and History

Azevedo, Fernando de. BRAZILIAN CULTURE: An Introduction to the Study of Culture in Brazil. 1950. Trans. by William R. Crawford. *Macmillan* (Hafner) 1971 $32.50

Coutinho, Alfrânio. INTRODUCTION TO LITERATURE IN BRAZIL. Trans. by Gregory Rabassa. *Columbia* 1969 $15.00

Goldberg, Isaac. BRAZILIAN LITERATURE. 1922. *Bks. for Libraries* $16.00; *Gordon Press* $34.95

Hulet, Claude L. BRAZILIAN LITERATURE. *Georgetown School of Languages* 1974 3 vols. Vol. 1 1500–1800 Vol. 2 1880–1920 Vol. 3 Since 1920 each $10.50 pap. each $6.50

Jesus, Carolina Maria de. CHILD OF THE DARK: The Diary of Carolina Maria de Jesus. Trans. by David St. Clair. *New Am. Lib.* Signet 1964 pap. $1.25. Moving journal of a Brazilian Negro slum dweller, it became a best seller in Brazil and took its author out of the slums.

Livermore, H. V., and W. J. Entwistle, Eds. PORTUGAL AND BRAZIL. *Oxford* 1953 $12.00. Articles on history and culture, including literature.

Martins, Wilson. THE MODERNIST IDEA: A Critical Survey of Brazilian Writing in the Twentieth Century. Trans. by Jack Tomlins. *New York Univ. Press* 1970 $12.00

Moog, Clodomor V. AN INTERPRETATION OF BRAZILIAN LITERATURE. Trans. by John Knox. 1951. *Greenwood* $7.00

Nist, John A. THE MODERNIST MOVEMENT IN BRAZIL: A Literary Study. *Univ. of Texas Press* 1967 $8.25

This study considers both individual modernist poets (with many well-translated examples of their verse) and the Brazilian literary scene of the early 1920s. It is "directed primarily toward the student and scholar; but samplings from authors like Bandeira, Drummond de Andrade and Jorge de Lima should interest most readers"—(*LJ*).

Putnam, Samuel. MARVELOUS JOURNEY: A Survey of Four Centuries of Brazilian Writing. 1948. *Octagon* 1971 $12.50

Veríssimo, Érico. BRAZILIAN LITERATURE: An Outline. 1945. *Greenwood* $10.50. Lectures delivered at the University of California, Berkeley, in 1944.

Collections

Bishop, Elizabeth, and Emanuel Brasil, Eds. AN ANTHOLOGY OF TWENTIETH-CENTURY BRAZILIAN POETRY. Trans. by Paul Blackburn and others. *Wesleyan Univ. Press* 1972 pap. $3.94. Selections with biographical introductions from 14 poets.

Grossman, William L., Trans. MODERN BRAZILIAN SHORT STORIES. *Univ. of California Press* 1967 $8.95 pap. 1974 $2.25. Short stories written during Brazil's modernist period, a literary revival beginning in 1922.

Jong, Gerrit de, Jr. FOUR HUNDRED YEARS OF BRAZILIAN LITERATURE: Outline and Anthology. *Brigham Young Univ. Press* 1969 pap. $5.95

Nist, John A., Trans. and ed. MODERN BRAZILIAN POETRY: An Anthology. 1962. *Kraus* 1968 $11.00

ASSIS, JOACHIM MARIA MACHADO DE (Machado de Assis, J. M.).   1839–1908.

Machado de Assis' achievements in both the novel and poetry make him Brazil's paradigm of a writer. His novels are characterized "by a psychological insight as well as a broad view of social conditions in Brazil and the world. The seriousness of the realistic view is high-lighted with ironic humor"—(*SR*). Beginning as a romantic, Assis developed a style which embraced realism, naturalism, and symbolism. "Epitaph for a Small Winner" reveals his essential pessimism, as the only consolation for Brás Cubas is that he has not passed on his misery to any offspring. "Esau and Jacob," the story of rival twin brothers in the time of the establishment of the Brazilian Republic, has been termed "a brilliantly peopled novel of manners, a romance, an arsenal of aphoristic wit and wry sermonizing, and a psychological study of considerable penetration"—(*N.Y. Times*). His final novel, "Counselor Ayres' Memorial," consists of the protagonist's diary and dialogue with himself.

Born in the slums of Rio de Janeiro, Assis was orphaned early in life. He advanced from typesetter to proofreader and finally to journalist before entering the Brazilian civil service. He is the author of nine novels, over 200 short stories, opera libretti, drama, and lyric poetry. His wife Carolina was a constant companion and secretary, and one of his most famous poems is an elegiac sonnet "To Carolina."

THE PSYCHIATRIST AND OTHER STORIES. Trans. by William L. Grossman and Helen Caldwell. *Univ. of California Press* 1963 $6.00 pap. $2.35. Twelve short stories written between 1881 and 1905.

THE HAND AND THE GLOVE. 1874. Trans. by Albert I. Bagby, Jr. Studies in Romance Languages *Univ. Press of Kentucky* 1970 $4.95

EPITAPH OF A SMALL WINNER. 1881. Trans. by William L. Grossman. *Farrar, Straus* 1952 Noonday 1955 pap. $2.45

DOM CASMURRO. 1900. Trans. by Helen Caldwell. *Univ. of California Press* 1966 $6.50 pap. $2.85

ESAU AND JACOB. 1904. Trans. with introd. by Helen Caldwell. *Univ. of California Press* 1965 $8.50

COUNSELOR AYRES' MEMORIAL. 1908. Trans. by Helen Caldwell. *Univ. of California Press* 1973 $8.95

Books about Assis

The Brazilian Othello of Machado de Assis: A Study of Dom Casmurro. By Helen Caldwell. *Univ. of California Press* 1960 $6.50

Machado de Assis: The Brazilian Master and His Novels. By Helen Caldwell. *Univ. of California Press* 1970 $10.00

CUNHA, EUCLYDES DA.   1866–1909.

Cunha accompanied Brazilian government forces on a series of four military expeditions in 1896–1897 to put down a rebellion started by a religious fanatic, Antonio the Counsellor, who had proclaimed himself the Messiah. This account of the battles, originally published as newspaper stories, is an inquiry into the condition of the Brazilian people embellished with descriptions of landscape and living conditions. The work has been described as "the first literary work in Brazil . . . to face Brazilian social problems adequately and with imagination"—(Seymour-Smith). The book may be marred for the modern reader by its doctrine of racial superiority and an overly complex style.

REBELLION IN THE BACKLANDS. 1902. Eng. trans. 1944; abr. Eng. trans. 1947. Trans. from *Os Sertões* with introd. and notes by Samuel Putnam. *Univ. of Chicago Press* 1957 pap. $5.25

RAMOS, GRACILIANO. 1892–1953.

"Anguish," considered "a major novel of the contemporary literary movement of Latin America" (SR) narrates through interior monologue the psychic breakdown of a frustrated intellectual who fails at love. The novel reveals Ramos' introspective quality and his pessimistic view of the emptiness of modern life, perhaps due in part to his writing it while in prison. Ramos was one of many leftist intellectuals purged by President Getúlio Vargas' government during the 1930s. "Barren Lives" examines the psychology of poverty during the drought in the interior of northeastern Brazil. The novel is narrated through the minds of several members of a family who due to their lack of education and primitive natures rarely communicate verbally. Of his technical accomplishments Morton Dauwen Zabel wrote in *Nation*, "Graciliano Ramos is notable among contemporary Brazilian writers for a severity of style, an accuracy of social and moral observation, and an intensity of tragic sensibility which derive as much from a fidelity to native experience as from the stylists—Proust [q.v.], Joyce [q.v.], and, more relevantly, Céline [q.v.]—whom his American publisher mentions as models."

Anguish. 1936. Trans. by L. C. Kaplan. 1946. *Greenwood* $11.25

Barren Lives. 1938. Trans. by Ralph E. Dimmick. *Univ. of Texas Press* 1965 $5.75

ANDRADE, MÁRIO de. 1893–1945.

Mário de Andrade was born in San Paulo of Indian-Negro-Portuguese ancestry. One of the leaders of the Brazilian modernist movement, Andrade's purpose was to review the Brazilian language and to awaken his countrymen to the need for social change. He published "Hallucinated City" upon discovering "that my poetry had the power to irritate the bourgeois." Leland H. Chambers writes of that volume, "With their rebelliousness, their scorn of normality, their disparate imagery, and their sense of the integrity of the alienated and dissociated personality, these 22 poems shocked Brazilian poetry into the twentieth century in 1922." Andrade's fictional (most notably his folk novel "Macunaíma" of 1928, o.p.) and poetic experiments with Brazilian dialects of Portuguese and his essays on Brazilian culture paved the way for the development of the regional prose fiction of the 1930s.

Hallucinated City. 1922. Trans. by Jack E. Tomlins *Vanderbilt Univ. Press* 1968 $5.00

FREYRE, GILBERTO de MELLO. 1900–

Dr. Gilberto Freyre, winner of the 1967 Aspen Award for Outstanding Contribution to the Humanities, has been influential is changing the way Brazilians see themselves and their country. By relating Brazilian history to modern life and by demonstrating how Portuguese, Negro, and Indian have intermingled to form a unique culture and a great nation, Freyre has destroyed the nation's inferiority complex. Alexander Coleman writes of "The Masters and the Slaves," "His is a Proustian history, a rich web of counterpoint between formative cultural factors and psychological and biological predisposition, all made living once again within the reconstituted 'tone' of the period." Freyre, whose sociohistorical writings have had a pervasive influence on modern Brazilian fiction, terms his "Mother and Son" a "semi-novel." The political and social currents of late nineteenth-century Brazil move against the portrait in the foreground of an overbearing mother and her effeminate son destined for the priesthood: "There is a special charm in this book, in its combination of the earthy and the spiritual, of warmth and intellectuality"—(SR).

A popular public figure in Brazil, Freyre is affectionately known as Gilberto. He has served as a member of Brazil's U.N. delegation and in its Chamber of Deputies. In 1967, Columbia University, where he once taught, appointed him to a panel to consider the problems of cities and city planning.

The Masters and the Slaves: A Study in the Development of Brazilian Civilization. 1933. Trans. by Samuel Putnam. *Knopf* 1964 $12.50 abr. ed. pap. $3.50

The Mansions and the Shanties: The Making of Modern Brazil. 1936. Trans. by Harriet de Onís. *Knopf* 1963 $12.50

New World in the Tropics: The Culture of Modern Brazil. Written in English. *Knopf* 1959 $7.95

Portuguese in the Tropics. Trans. by H. M. D'O Matthew and F. de Mello Moser. *Hafner Service Agency* 1961 $8.50

Mother and Son: A Brazilian Tale (*Dona Sinhá e o Filho Padre*). 1966. Trans. by Barbara Shelby. *Knopf* 1967 $4.95

Order and Progress: Brazil from Monarchy to Republic. Trans. by Rod W. Horton. *Knopf* 1970 $12.50

VERÍSSIMO, ÉRICO. 1905–

Veríssimo is a novelist of manners with "a sociologist's eye, a bemused and tolerant mind and a caricaturist's skill with words"—(*N.Y. Times*). "Crossroads" and "The Rest Is Silence," explorations of the intertwining of individual and family lives, lead stylistically and thematically toward his central work, "Time and the Wind," a fictional epic biography of a family of Rio Grande do Sul. The work is in two volumes: Volume 1, "The Continent 1745–1895," and Volume 2, "The Portrait 1898–1945." From 1953 to 1956 Veríssimo was director of the Department of Cultural Affairs for the Pan American Union in Washington, and the novel "His Excellency, the Ambassador" provides a glimpse of the hypocrisies of diplomatic life and an insight into the phenomenon of revolutionaries who, after gaining victory, become as unscrupulous as those they replace. Veríssimo's work is generally optimistic. Of his general philosophical stance Richard A. Mazzara writes, "The form of the works varies considerably, but the moral expressed by his chief spokesmen remains essentially the same: one should live life to the fullest, profiting by all experience, and art must reflect and encourage this continuing search for plenitude"—(*PMLA*).

CROSSROADS. 1935. Trans. by L. C. Kaplan. 1943. *Greenwood* $14.25

CONSIDER THE LILIES OF THE FIELD. 1939. Trans. by Jean N. Karnoff. 1947. *Greenwood* $14.25

THE REST IS SILENCE. 1943. Trans. by L. C. Kaplan. 1947. *Greenwood* $17.25

TIME AND THE WIND. 1949 1951. Trans. by Linton L. Barrett. 1951. *Greenwood* $20.50

HIS EXCELLENCY, THE AMBASSADOR. 1965. Trans. by Linton L. and Marie M. Barrett. 1967 *Melvin McCosh Bookseller* $9.50

ROSA, JOÃO GUIMARÃES. 1908–1967.

Many critics consider João Guimarães Rosa to be the best Brazilian novelist since Machado de Assis (*q.v.*). "The Devil to Pay in the Backlands" is a Faustian quest for self-knowledge and identity with a northeastern bandit, Riobaldo, as protagonist. "But," as Emir Rodríguez Monegal points out, "this is a modern morality tale, and therefore not a simple one, so Rosa's angel and his devil are not always clearly distinguishable." The devil in fact turns out to be Riobaldo's unconscious and submerged instincts. A *New York Times* reviewer wrote of the novel, "He entrances the readers with the beauty and grandeur of these backlands. But his descriptions of outer nature are always subordinate to a poignant inner realism, which remains local in flavor while presenting the elemental contrasts of human nature everywhere." In the *Times Literary Supplement* the artistic achievement of the novel was defined: "To the Brazilian public 'Big Backlands: Narrow Paths' [the literal translation of the title] was remarkable above all because it signified a linguistic revolution. The language was compounded from archaic Portuguese, from dialects and neologisms."

Rosa was a country doctor in his native state. He took part in the revolution and civil war of 1930–1932, then embarked on a diplomatic career, serving in Hamburg, Bogotá, and Paris. He was elected to the Brazilian Academy of Letters in 1963 but had himself postponed his investiture—"because he feared 'the emotion of the moment' " (*N.Y. Times*)—until a few days before his unexpected death from a heart attack in November, 1967.

THE DEVIL TO PAY IN THE BACKLANDS. 1956. Trans. by James L. Taylor and Harriet de Onís. *Knopf* 1963 $6.95

QUEIRÓS, RAQUEL DE. 1910–

Raquel de Queirós gained national recognition at the age of 20 with her first novel, "The Year Fifteen" (1930), which won the Graça Aranha Foundation Prize. A realistic account of the 1915 drought in the Brazilian northeast, the novel also reveals the immaturity of the author as an artist. In "The Three Marias," however, she triumphed artistically. While demonstrating women's subordinate and degrading roles in an unsympathic society the novel at the same time reveals her compassion for men's predicaments as well. Fred P. Ellison writes of her work, "Simplicity, sobriety, and directness are characteristic of all her writing, but are most highly refined in 'The Three Marias.' . . . And as an artist, one of the most gifted of the present generation, she has been able to give beautiful form to her tragic but inspiring vision."

THE THREE MARIAS. 1939. Trans. by Fred P. Ellison. Pan American Ser. *Univ. of Texas Press* 1963 $5.00

AMADO, JORGE. 1912–

Elected to the Brazilian Academy of Letters, Jorge Amado possesses a talent for storytelling as well as a deep concern for social and economic justice. For some critics, his early works suffer from his politics: Fred Ellison writes, "He reacted violently to his times, and some of his books have been marred by extreme partisanship to the left." In the works represented in English translation, however, his literary merits prevail. "The Violent Land" chronicles the development of Brazilian territory and struggles for its resources, memorializing the deeds of those who built the country. "Gabriela: Clove and Cinnamon," which achieved critical and popular success in both Brazil and the United States, is still more artistic, relating a sensual love story of a Syrian bar owner and his beautiful cook whose skin is the color of the spices which enliven her food. "Home Is the Sailor" concerns Captain Vasco Moscoso de Aragão, a comic figure in the tradition of Don Quijote, who poses as a retired sea captain and must suddenly command a ship in an emergency. In "Doña Flor" Amado introduces the folk culture of shamans and Yoruba gods who resuscitate Doña Flor's first husband amid her marriage to the second. The protagonists of "The Shepherds of the Night" are Bahia's poor, and "Amado has given us a deeply moving and funny picture of life in the slums" —(*Nation*).

THE VIOLENT LAND. 1942. Trans. by S. Putnam; fwd. by the author. *Knopf* 1945 rev. ed. 1965 $6.95

GABRIELA: Clove and Cinnamon. 1958. Trans. by James L. Taylor and William L. Grossman. *Knopf* 1962 $6.95; *Avon* 1974 pap. $1.95

HOME IS THE SAILOR: The Whole Truth Concerning the Redoubtful Adventures of Captain Vasco Moscoso de Aragão, Master Mariner. 1962. Trans. by Harriet de Onís. *Knopf* 1964 $5.95

SHEPHERDS OF THE NIGHT. 1964. Trans. by Harriet de Onís. *Knopf* 1966 $7.95
"An exhuberant sentimental trio of novellas."

DOÑA FLOR AND HER TWO HUSBANDS. 1966. Trans. by Harriet de Onís. *Knopf* 1969 $6.95

TENT OF MIRACLES. 1969. Trans. by Barbara Shelby. *Knopf* 1971 $7.95

TEREZA BATISTA: Home from the Wars. *Knopf* 1975 $10.00

ADONIAS FILHO (pseud. of Adonias Aguiar). 1915–

"Memories of Lazarus" is the central novel of a trilogy including "Servants of Death" (1946) and "Body Alive" (1962). Adonias Filho, along with Lispector (*q.v.*) and Rosa (*q.v.*), was a leader of the vanguardist movement of 1945, whose members were influenced by Joyce, Proust, Kafka, Faulkner (*qq.v.*) and the *nouveau roman*. Adonias Filho has progressively moved away from realism: "I continue to believe too much in man, and in the possibilities of his intelligence, to accept reality as the life blood of the novel." Thus, the translator comments about this novel set in the Ouro Valley, "Alexandre's narration quickly transcends the local; time becomes a function of his hallucinations." Oliveiros Litrento has written of the trilogy, "The diabolic surrealist and the Christian novelist joined hands in 'The Servants of Death,' 'Memories of Lazarus' and 'Body Alive,' a trilogy woven from the fabric of damnation and despair. . . . The novels are only circumstantially stories of Bahia. They are essentially histories of the collective hallucination of a world in panic, stories of ancestral blemish, narrated impressionistically."

MEMORIES OF LAZARUS. 1952. Trans. by Fred P. Ellison. Pan American Ser. *Univ. of Texas Press* 1961 $5.00
"Ellison does an admirable job of recreating the novel's nightmare imagery"—(*LJ*).

LISPECTOR, CLARICE. 1924–

"Family Ties" is a collection of short stories revealing Lispector's existentialist view of life and demonstrating that even family ties and social relationships are temporary. Although tied to each other and to the outside world, the characters are finally totally alone and separate. She received praise from American critics for "The Apple in the Dark" (1967, o.p.), a novel about a guilt-ridden man's vain search for the ultimate knowledge (Eve's apple) which he believes will bring him hope: "Miss Lispector is a superb writer, an artist of vivid imagination and sensitivity, with a glorious feeling for language and its uses"—(*SR*).

Clarice Lispector was born in the Ukraine. Law student, editor, translator, and newswriter, she has traveled widely, spending eight years in the United States.

FAMILY TIES. 1960. Trans. by Giovanni Pontiero. *Univ. of Texas Press* 1972 $5.75

SUASSUNA, ARIANO. 1927–

THE ROGUE'S TRIAL. 1959. Trans. by Dillwyn F. Ratcliff. *Univ. of California Press* 1963 $5.00 pap. $1.50. Play.

One of Brazil's leading modern playwrights takes aim here at race prejudice, legal quibblings, landowners and hypocritical and avaricious members of the clergy. It is a modern "miracle play" and satire based on ballads and folk tales of northeastern Brazil. This prizewinning drama has been translated into four languages.

—C. S.

Chapter 17

African Literature

". . . African literature has its roots in Africa and is neither an appendage to French or British literature nor yet an African replica of popular western authors."

—ERNEST EMENYONU

There are more books being written today about Africa and by African authors than at any previous time. Colleges and universities all over the world are offering courses on African literature, and prominent African authors such as Chinua Achebe, Wole Soyinka, and Leopold Senghor are assured a place in literary history along with other internationally acclaimed authors. The Eurocentric view of African writing is no longer valid. It is being judged on its own merits and by an increasing number of African scholars.

People in the book world are having difficulty keeping abreast of the new books being published in Africa. At the international conference on publishing and book development held at the University of Ife, Nigeria, in 1973, it was proposed that a comprehensive listing of books published in Africa be established. As a result, Part I of "African Books in Print" (ABIP) was published in July 1975. It lists by author, title, and subject books published in Africa, written in English as well as several African languages. Well over 400 pages, it sells for $37.50 and is available in the United States from: International Scholarly Book Services, Inc., c/o Blackwell's, Beaverton, Oregon 97005. "African Book Publishing Record" (ABPR) is a quarterly supplement to ABIP. In the past, because of an almost complete absence of publishing companies on the continent, African authors have had to look to publishing companies outside the continent, mainly in England and France, to publish their works. In the last decade a number of publishing companies have been established on the continent that publish works not only in the language of the former colonists, that only the educated elite can read, but also in several of the indigenous African languages. In this way the masses are also exposed to the literary achievements of their fellow Africans. The East African Publishing House, a pioneer in the field, is the largest of the indigenous publishers. Located in Nairobi, it has over 400 titles to its credit. Undoubtedly African publishers have acted as a catalyst in encouraging aspiring young Africans to write, knowing they have more of an opportunity now than in the past to have their works published.

The majority of African literature is written in either French or English, the languages of the ex-colonists. In examining the beginning of francophone African writing we can direct our attention to the novel *"Batouala"* by the West Indian writer René Maran. This was one of the early African novels to receive international attention. Originally published in French in 1921, it caused quite a stir in France because of its candid attack on French colonialism. The novel is based on Maran's personal impressions while serving in the French Colonial Service in Central Africa. Despite the controversy, Maran received the prestigious Prix Goncourt in 1922 for the best novel written in French. Fifty years later, in 1972, the first English edition of *"Batouala"* was published by Black Orpheus Press, translated by Barbara Beck and Alexandre Mboukou.

The decade of the 1930s marked a new era in African literature—the birth of négritude. This term grew out of the intellectual environs of three black literary artists, Léon Damas, Aimé Césaire, and Léopold Senghor. The word was actually coined by Césaire, but the credit is usually given to Senghor, for it is he who was and still is its prime exponent. In a *N.Y. Times* article (September 11, 1975) entitled "Négritude and the U.S.," Senghor writes: "Négritude is, on the one hand, the sum of the qualities of the 'values,' as they are called today, that characterize the civilization of the black people like the sense of Communion and that of Rhythm; it is, on the other hand, the way in which every black lives or understands the living of those values." One of Senghor's more succinct definitions is, "the sum total of cultural values of the Negro-African world." At the time of its birth négritude was a rebuke to the negative African images created by the colonists, and it was towards this end that many black French intellectuals geared their works.

Négritude was looked at more critically during the 1960s. Pan-Africanists especially denounced it as being passé and urged African writers to look towards more uniting themes that would also involve the masses.

Much of Africa's literature stems from its oral tradition and consists of the handing down of folk tales by word of mouth from one generation to another. For centuries Africans have verbalized their "literature" mainly in the form of folk tales and proverbs. Every village had its favorite storyteller whose main duty was to relate the numerous myths and tales associated with the village. Many times the listening audience and story teller would collaborate and together they would dramatize these narratives. This type of writing is especially evident in the works of West African authors. Many have transmitted these tales into written form without losing the rich and colorful flavor associated with them. A prime example is "The Palm-Wine Drinkard" by Amos Tutuola. The publication of this novel, in 1952, is generally taken as a starting point of contemporary African-English literature—(Hans M. Zell). "The Palm-Wine Drinkard" is based on the author's Sunday-night visits to a palm plantation where he would listen to an old man who sat around drinking palm wine and telling tales. Tutuola uses a type of pidgin English which greatly enhances the "folkishness" of his tales. The book has been translated into six different languages.

What we have tried to do in this section on African literature is present a representative cross-sectional listing of books relative to the subject. A myth held by many concerning Africa is that it is one homogeneous country. Quite the contrary, Africa is a vast continent consisting of over 35 independent nations comprising a kaleidoscope of diverse ethnic and cultural backgrounds. The books we have selected by no means represent a totality, but rather what we consider among the most representative in the field.

The material is divided into three broad categories: journals relating to African literature; background books, consisting of bibliographies, anthologies, and critiques; and creative writing arranged alphabetically by author. These are followed by main author listings for several of the more prominent authors.

JOURNALS

AFRICANA JOURNAL: A Bibliographic and Review Quarterly. *Holmes & Meier* (Africana Pub. Corp.) (by subscription) individuals $20.00 per yr.; institutions $35.00. Formerly entitled *Africana Library Journal*, this is an excellent bibliographic source for African material. It includes bibliographic articles, book reviews, and a current listing of recently published books concerning Africa divided into subject and geographic headings.

OKIKE: An African Journal of New Writing. $9.00 per yr. (Okike, P.O. Box 597, Amherst, Mass. 01002). *Okike* was first published in 1971 in Enugu, Nigeria, but has since moved to Amherst, Massachusetts. Edited by the noted novelist Chinua Achebe, this popular journal consists of essays, book reviews, and poetry by noted authors.

RESEARCH IN AFRICAN LITERATURES. $6.00 per yr. (Research in African Literatures, Box 7457, Univ. of Texas, Austin, Tex. 78712). A very informative journal in the field of African literature. Published biannually, it consists of essays, bibliographies, new publications and book reviews. It is edited by Bernth Lindfors.

BACKGROUND BOOKS AND COLLECTIONS

Awoonor, Kofi. THE BREAST OF THE EARTH: A Survey of the History, Culture and Literature of Africa, South of the Sahara. *Doubleday* 1975 $15.00

Beier, Ulli, Comp. and ed. AFRICAN POETRY: An Anthology of Traditional African Poems. *Cambridge* 1966 $4.95 pap. $2.65

A "genuine, fine collection" from all parts of the continent—*(LJ)*.

Dathorne, O. R. THE BLACK MIND: A History of African Literature. *Univ. of Minnesota Press* 1971 $22.50. A history of African literature from the oral tradition to contemporary writings.

Diop, Birago. TALES OF AMADOU KOUMBA. *Oxford* 1966 $4.50

Diop's rendition of West African folktales. "He is a fabulist of a high order and tells these tales of man and beast with extraordinary humor"—*(Choice)*.

Dorson, Richard M., Ed. AFRICAN FOLKLORE. *Indiana Univ. Press* 1972 $15.00 Anchor Bks. pap. $3.50. The first part of this book includes an essay by the author; Part 2 consists of the papers presented at the African Folklore Conference held at Indiana University in 1970, and Part 3 includes African verbal texts.

Ganz, David L. A CRITICAL GUIDE TO ANTHOLOGIES OF AFRICAN LITERATURE. *African Studies Assn.* (Waltham, Mass. 02215) 1973 $5.00. Review of 59 anthologies of African literature, plus a bibliography of 155 titles.

Gerard, Albert S. FOUR AFRICAN LITERATURES: Xhosa, Sotho, Zulu, Amharic. *Univ. of California Press* 1971 $17.50. An analysis of the origin and growth of modern literature produced in the African languages named in the subtitle.

Gleason, Judith Illsley. THIS AFRICA: Novels by West Africans in English and French. *Northwestern Univ. Press* 1967 $6.50. This study discusses African literary history and the modern African novel in its social and political context. Included are essays on Chinua Achebe, Cyprian Ekwensi, and Mongo Beti, among others.

Herdeck, Donald E. AFRICAN AUTHORS: A Companion to Black African Writing, 1300–1973. *Inscape Corp.* 1973 $27.50. Bio-bibliographic sketches of over 500 African authors, including a discussion of their works.

Hughes, Langston, Ed. AN AFRICAN TREASURY. *Crown* 1960 $4.00. Thirty stories, articles, and other writings by African authors.

POEMS FROM BLACK AFRICA. *Indiana Univ. Press* 1963 $6.50 pap. $1.75. Work of 36 poets of contemporary Africa and some translations from the Yoruba (Nigeria) by Ulli Beier.

Jablow, Alta. YES AND NO: The Intimate Folklore of Africa. Introd. by Paul Goodman. *Greenwood* 1973 $10.00

"Particularly delightful, and relatively little known to non-Africans, are the dilemma stories, which pose ethical and moral . . . problems . . . Mrs. Jablow has selected excellent examples from the oral traditions of many peoples of African's western bulge. Her book will not only instruct scholars and specialists but also entertain general readers"—*(LJ)*.

Jones, Eldred, Ed. AFRICAN LITERATURE TODAY. *Holmes & Meier* (Africana Pub. Corp.) Nos. 1–4 each $8.95 No. 5 The Novel in Africa 1971 pap. $7.95 No. 6 Poetry in Africa 1973 $10.00 No. 7 Focus on Criticism 1975 $10.50. This is a critical review, published annually, of major African authors and their works. The editor is from Sierra Leone and is at present professor of English at the University of Sierra Leone.

Jordan, A. C. TALES FROM SOUTHERN AFRICA. Perspectives on Southern Africa *Univ. of California Press* 1973 $10.00

TOWARDS AN AFRICAN LITERATURE: The Emergence of Literary Form in Xhosa. Perspectives on Southern Africa *Univ. of California Press* 1973 $6.00. Companion volumes presenting and examining Xhosa literature from preliterate times to the present. The author, a Xhosa himself, died in 1968. He was an expert on Xhosa literature.

Killam, G. D., Ed. AFRICAN WRITERS ON AFRICAN WRITING. *Northwestern Univ. Press* 1973 $5.00 pap. $2.50. A collection of essays by 14 well-known African authors. African literature in the form of drama, novels, and poetry is discussed in relation to cultural content, nationalistic themes, teaching methods, and language forms. Biographical sketches are included.

Litto, Frederic M., Ed. PLAYS FROM BLACK AFRICA. *Farrar, Straus* (Hill & Wang) 1968 pap. $4.50. John Pepper Clark's Song of a Goat and Efua Sutherland's Edufa are among the works included.

Markward, Edris, and Leslie Lacy, Eds. CONTEMPORARY AFRICAN LITERATURE. *Random* 1972 pap. $5.95. An anthology of various forms of African literature.

Moore, Gerald. SEVEN AFRICAN WRITERS. *Oxford* Three Crown Books 1962 $1.50. Critical analysis of the works of Senghor, Mphahlele, David Diop, Laye, Tutuola, Achebe, and Beti.

Obiechina, Emmanuel. AN AFRICAN POPULAR LITERATURE. *Cambridge* 1973 $14.95 pap. $5.95

ONITSHA MARKET LITERATURE. *Holmes & Meier* (Africana Pub. Corp.) 1972 $5.95

Onitsha market literature sprang up in Onitsha, Nigeria at the close of World War II. This pamphlet form of literature is extremely popular among the masses. Romance and morals are two of the most popular themes. "Dr. Obiechina's study of the Onitsha pamphlet phenomenon is the fullest and the most serious so far. It relates the literature appropriately to the social ferment of the times, and is as delightful to read as the pamphlets themselves"—(Achebe).

Olney, James. TELL ME AFRICA: An Approach to African Literature. *Princeton Univ. Press* 1974 $15.00 pap. $3.45

"After an introductory chapter the book is substantially the study of about six well-known books. The chapter headings are peculiar in that Achebe is discussed as "Love, Sex and Procreation" and the controversial "Duty of Violence" is seen as "Pornography, Philosophy and History." The book concludes with an "Anti-conclusion"—(*Choice*).

Palmer, Eustace. AN INTRODUCTION TO THE AFRICAN NOVEL. *Holmes & Meier* (Africana Pub. Corp.) 1972 $10.00. Critical study of 12 books by Chinua Achebe, James Ngugi, Camara Laye, Elechi Amadi, Ayi Kwei Armah, Mongo Beti, and Gabriel Okara.

Pieterse, Cosmo, and Dennis Duerden, Eds. AFRICAN WRITERS TALKING. *Holmes & Meier* (Africana Pub. Corp.) 1972 $12.50 pap. $5.50. A series of radio interviews, taped in London, with major English-speaking African writers, covering the period 1962–1969.

PROTEST AND CONFLICT IN AFRICAN LITERATURE. *Holmes & Meier Pubs.* 1969 $6.50 pap. $3.00

Rutherford, Peggy, Ed. AFRICAN VOICES: An Anthology of Native African Writing. *Vanguard* 1959 $6.95. This collection of African writing contains stories ranging from folktales to modern sketches. Some poetry is included.

Schmidt, Nancy J. CHILDREN'S BOOKS ON AFRICA AND THEIR AUTHORS: An Annotated Bibliography. *Holmes & Meier* (Africana Pub. Corp.) 1975 $15.00

Sergeant, Howard, Ed. AFRICAN VOICES. *Lawrence Hill* 1974 $7.50. A collection of the writings of 45 African poets.

Tucker, Martin. AFRICA IN MODERN LITERATURE: A Survey of Contemporary Writing in English. *Ungar* 1967 $7.50. This study provides illuminating insights on British, American, and African attitudes as expressed in fiction, drama, and poetry concerned with Africa.

Walker, Barbara K., and Warren S. Walker, Eds. NIGERIAN FOLK TALES. *Rutgers Univ. Press* 1961 $9.00. Nigeria still has a strong oral tradition and there remains a great reservoir of folklore and storytelling in spite of the influence of Western culture and education. These stories were recorded by Professor and Mrs. Walker almost entirely verbatim from an oral rendition by two Nigerians, Olawale Idewu and Omotayo Adu.

Zell, Hans M., and Helene Silver, Comps. and eds. A READER'S GUIDE TO AFRICAN LITERATURE. *Holmes & Meier Pubs.* 1972 $12.50 pap. $4.95. One of the most comprehensive reference books on African literature. An annotated bibliographic listing of over 800 books, with biographical sketches and portraits of over 50 African authors in addition to information concerning journals and publishers in the field.

WORKS BY AFRICAN AUTHORS

More works of interest are available than we have space to treat in main entries.

Abraham, W. E. THE MIND OF AFRICA. 1962. *Univ. of Chicago Press* 1963 $7.50 Phoenix Bks. pap. $3.25

> The author has taught philosophy at the University of Ghana and was the first African ever to be elected to a fellowship at All Souls, Oxford. His book has a double interest—"as an intellectual self-portrait of the present young generation of educated Africans and as a very important contribution in its own right to the problems of culture and nationality, of politics, morals, and social continuity at a place and time of rapid and crucial change."

Ahmad, Nassir bin Juma Bhalo. POEMS FROM KENYA: Gnomic Verses in Swahili. Trans. and ed. with introd. by Lyndon Harries (bilingual). *Univ. of Wisconsin Press* 1966 $10.00. The verse of a young Kenyan in the didactic tradition of Kenyan gnomic poetry.

Bebey, Francis. AGATHA MOUDIO'S SON. 1971. Trans. by Joyce Hutchinson. *Lawrence Hill* 1973 $5.95 pap. $2.95. Translation of "*Le fils d'Agatha Moudio*," which was written by the Cameroonian author. This book won the Grand Prix Litteraire de l'Afrique Noire in 1968.

Beti, Mongo. POOR CHRIST OF BOMBA. 1956. Trans. by Gerald Moore. African Writers Ser. *Humanities Press* 1972 $5.50 pap. $2.50. A novel that deals with the church and France in the Cameroons.

Brutus, Dennis. LETTERS TO MARTHA AND OTHER POEMS FROM A SOUTH AFRICAN PRISON. African Writers Ser. *Humanities Press* 1968 pap. $1.75

A SIMPLE LUST. *Farrar, Straus* (Hill & Wang) 1973 $7.95 pap. $3.45

> Dennis Brutus has risked everything in his fight against South African apartheid—in the fields of sports (he founded a committee to bring about interracial South African Olympic teams), poetry, and politics. He has been arrested many times in South Africa and served 18 months at hard labor (1963–65) on Robben Island. He is now an exile, living in London. He visited the United States early in 1967, lecturing to raise funds for South Africa's apartheid victims. His impressionistic poetry, says Ezekiel Mphahlele, "seems to ooze out of a blistered soul."

Charhadi, Driss Ben Hamid. A LIFE FULL OF HOLES. Rendered from the Maghribi into English by Paul Bowles. *Grove* 1964 Black Cat Bks. 1966 pap. $.95. A unique work of autobiographical fiction by an illiterate young Moroccan, who dictated this story into a tape recorder.

Clark, John Pepper. AMERICA, THEIR AMERICA. *Holmes & Meier Pubs.* (Africana Pub. Corp.) 1969 pap. $3.50

CASUALTIES, POEMS 1966–1968. *Holmes & Meier Pubs.* (Africana Pub. Corp.) 1970 $5.00 pap. $2.75

THE EXAMPLE OF SHAKESPEARE. *Northwestern Univ. Press* 1971 $5.25 1971 pap. $2.95

> The Nigerian poet and playwright, of "free spirit and abundant talent," (Moore and Beier, "Modern Poetry from Africa"), is an African writing primarily for Africans. His poetry and plays, which "make no attempt to explain ritual and customs for the non-African reader" (*Africa Report*), are rooted in myth and tribal custom. His plays are often tragic.

OZIDI: A Play. *Oxford* 1966 pap. $1.90

A REED IN THE TIDE: A Selection of Poems. *Humanities Press* 1970 pap. $2.00

THREE PLAYS: Song of a Goat; The Masquerade; The Raft. *Oxford* 1964 pap. $2.75

Diop, David Mandessi. HAMMERBLOWS AND OTHER WRITINGS. Trans. and ed. by Simon Mpondo and Frank Jones. *Indiana Univ. Press* 1973 $5.00. Diop died in a plane crash in 1960. This work includes some of his writings translated into English, accompanied by the French text.

Emecheta, Buchi. SECOND-CLASS CITIZEN. *Braziller* 1975 $6.95. A first novel by a young Nigerian woman writer, it explores the racism and frustration encountered by a Nigerian couple living in London.

Fuja, Abayomi. FOURTEEN HUNDRED COWRIES AND OTHER AFRICAN TALES. *Simon & Schuster* (Washington Square) 1962 pap. $1.25. Stories for children written by a Nigerian author.

Gatheru, R. Mugo. CHILD OF TWO WORLDS: A Kikuyu's Story. *Praeger* 1964 $6.50; *New Am. Lib.* Mentor Bks. 1972 pap. $1.25

The unsophisticated autobiography of an African born in 1925, who struggled to get an education in Kenya, India, the United States, and England—where he became a lawyer. "This simple, straightforward and immensely *human* document reveals to us what it means to one individual to be a Kikuyu, a Kenyan and an African amid the complexities of the modern world"—(St. Clair Drake).

Jabavu, Noni. DRAWN IN COLOR: African Contrasts. *Int. Pubns. Service* 1960

This is an "honest, quiet, perceptive and real" book of personal experiences. The author, "Xhosa by birth, daughter of a distinguished scholar, comes from a well-known South African family . . . She herself, educated in England and married to an Englishman, returned to her old home." The second half of her book describes her visit to her sister in Uganda and her disillusionment in East Africa.

Kane, Cheikh Hamidou. AMBIGUOUS ADVENTURE. Trans. by Katherine Woods. *Macmillan* Collier Bks. 1969 pap. $1.25

Winner of the 1962 Grand Prix for French-Speaking Black Africa, the author is a Sengalese political leader. His novel tells of Samba Diallo, son of a tribal chieftain, and his search for creed and identity. Kane provides literary impetus for the Muslim revival now occurring in Africa—where Christianity has often appeared to be the supporter and shield of colonialism.

Kaunda, Kenneth. AFTER MULUNGUSHI: The Economics of Humanism. Ed. by Bastiaaen De Gaay Fortman. *Int. Pubns. Service* 1969 $7.50

LETTER TO MY CHILDREN. *Longman* 1974 $6.00 pap. $2.25

ZAMBIA SHALL BE FREE: An Autobiography. 1963. *Humanities Press* 1969 pap. $2.00

(With Colin Morris) HUMANIST IN AFRICA. *Abingdon* $3.50

Now President of Zambia (the former Northern Rhodesia), Kaunda has an intellect and strength of character—he is a Christian with pacifist leanings—which have won him international respect. This is the story of his early years: "boyhood in a Protestant mission; work as a teacher, cooperative farmer, and used clothes salesman; development of his interest in politics; and career as an important figure in the African independence movement. The style is simple, sincere, and readable." He reveals himself as "an eager, hearty, dedicated, and idealistic yet practical politician."

For further study see "Zambia's President: Kenneth Kaunda" by Florence T. Polatnick and Alberta L. Saletan (Biography Ser. *Simon & Schuster* [Messner] 1972 $4.50 text ed. $4.29).

Kennedy, Scott. IN SEARCH OF AFRICAN THEATRE. *Scribner* 1973 $10.95. A personal account of the African theater by an American black who has been both observer and participant.

Kgositsile, Keoraptse. MY NAME IS AFRIKA. *Doubleday* 1971 $4.95 pap. $1.95. Poetry by a noted South African-born author.

La Guma, Alex. A WALK IN THE NIGHT AND OTHER STORIES. *Northwestern Univ. Press* 1967 $4.95 pap. $2.50. A novel by a South African writer.

(Ed.) APARTHEID: A Collection of Writings on South African Racism. *International Pub. Co.* 1972 pap. $1.65

IN THE FOG OF THE SEASONS' END. *Third Press* 1973 $6.95

Laye, Camara. DARK CHILD. 1954. Trans. by James Kirkup and others. *Farrar, Straus* 1969 $5.95 pap. $1.95. An autobiographical novel that was first published in Paris under the title *"L'enfant noir."* This first novel established Laye's reputation as one of Africa's leading novelists.

Luthuli, Albert. LET MY PEOPLE GO. 1962. *New Am. Lib.* Mentor Bks. 1969 pap. $3.95

Autobiography of the outstanding South African chieftain who, after many years of teaching and of nonviolent struggle in the African National Congress for the freedom of his people, found himself silenced and confined to the area near his farm, where he was killed by a train in 1967. He won the Nobel Peace Prize in 1961. For further study see "Portraits of Destiny" by Melville Harcourt (*Sheed & Ward* [Twin Circle] 1966 $5.50).

Mandela, Nelson. NO EASY WALK TO FREEDOM. Ed. by Ruth First. African Writers Ser. *Humanities Press* 1974 $2.25

Selections from the autobiographical writings, speeches, and trial transcriptions of the leader whom Dr. Verwoerd considered the arch enemy of white South Africa, now enduring life imprisonment on Robben Island. "Reading his wise and civilized words, one can only wonder at the stupidity of a government which forces men like Mr. Mandela to resort to sabotage. . . . The miracle is that this man is no preacher of hate"—(*TLS*, London).

Ngugi, James. WEEP NOT CHILD. 1964. *Macmillan* 1969 Collier Bks. pap. $1.25. This noted Kenyan author now publishes under the name Wa Thiong'o Ngugi (*see below*). "Weep Not Child" is a novel set during the Mau-Mau uprising in Kenya.

Ngugi, Wa Thiong'o. SECRET LIVES AND OTHER STORIES. *Lawrence Hill* 1975 $6.95. A collection of short stories, all with an African setting.

Nicol, Abioseh. THE TRULY MARRIED WOMAN AND OTHER STORIES. *Oxford* 1965 pap. $1.30

Nicol won the (British) Margaret Wrong Prize and Medal for Literature in Africa in 1952. His poetry is "quietly moving and deeply personal"—(Langston Hughes). The *Oxford* story collection centers around the experiences of African civil servants in the colonial period.

Two AFRICAN TALES. *Cambridge* 1965 $2.75 pap. $1.75

Nkosi, Lewis. RHYTHM OF VIOLENCE. *Oxford* 1964 pap. $1.30

A play about race relations. Lewis Nkosi, born in 1938, is a South African journalist and critic of neo-African literature now living in exile in London, where he is literary editor of "The New African." *Africa Report* compares his concern with "the meaning of being Negro" to that of a James Baldwin with a sense of humor: "Like Baldwin, he has an eagle eye for chinks in the white man's armor." In 1964 he conducted a series of American television interviews with African writers which was broadcast on National Educational Television in 35 states. He has also published short stories.

Plaatje, Solomon. MHUDI: An Epic of South African Native Life a Hundred Years Ago. 1930. *Greenwood* (Negro Univ. Press) 1970 $11.00

Sellassie, Sahle. AFERSATA. African Writers Ser. *Humanities Press* 1968 pap. $1.75

SHINEGA'S VILLAGE: Scenes of Ethiopian Life. Trans. by Wolf Leslau. *Univ. of California Press* 1964 $5.95

The first Ethiopian novel to be translated into English treats village life. A "pleasant tale"—(*LJ*).

Selormey, Francis. THE NARROW PATH: An African Childhood. *Praeger* 1966 $4.95

In this autobiographical novel "African life and its customs intermingled with Western influence in education make an enlightening view of Ghana"—(*LJ*).

Tolson, Melvin. HARLEM GALLERY. *Macmillan* Collier Bks. 1969 pap. $1.50

HARLEM GALLERY: Book One, the Curator. *Twayne* 1971 $6.00

LIBRETTO FOR THE REPUBLIC OF LIBERIA. *Twayne* 1953 1971 $4.50; *Macmillan* Collier Bks. 1970 pap. $1.50

Dr. Tolson, at his death the poet laureate of Liberia, died in 1966 in the United States, where he had spent much of his life in university teaching. On first publication the "Libretto" was praised by Seldon Rodman in the *N.Y. Times* as "by all odds the most considerable poem written by an American Negro, but a work of poetic synthesis in a symbolic vein not unworthy to be discussed in the company of . . . 'The Wasteland,' 'The Bridge' and 'Paterson.' " He wrote several volumes of verse and was awarded the Hokin Prize by *Poetry* Magazine in 1951.

U'Tamsi, Felix T. Selected Poems: Tchicaya U'Tam'si. Trans. by Gerald Moore. African Writers Ser. *Humanities Press* 1970 $1.75

U'Tamsi is a Congolese poet and novelist who lives and works in Paris. Little influenced by the concept of "Négritude" (*see Introduction to this Chapter*), he "seems to have a distinctively Congolese passion and intensity"—(Moore and Beier, "Modern Poetry from Africa").

CLOETE, (EDWARD FAIRLY) STUART (GRAHAM).   1897–

After a period of farming in his native South Africa. Stuart Cloete made his reputation with his first book, "The Turning Wheels" (1937, o.p.), a novel about the Great Boer Trek which was a choice of the American Book-of-the-Month Club and the English Book Society. He has lived in many parts of the world and written on South African affairs from a somewhat conservative point of view. In his 15 later novels he "has told more of the world about more of South Africa than any other modern writer"—(*LJ*). *Library Journal* called "Rags of Glory"—650 pages about the Boer War—"a rousing, lusty story full of violence [and] sex, handsome hussars, and beautiful women. . . . A fine novel." "The Thousand and One Nights of Jean Macaque" (1965, o.p.) is "a succession of fabliaux in prose, set forth by a totally unillusioned and fairly abject petty journalist, who is also a votary of profane love. . . . It is also a collection of *pensées*. . . . Call these sardonic chiselings the work of a profounder, wittier, more human J. P. Donleavy"—(*N.Y. Times*). "The Abductors" describes the fictional career of an aristocratic British procurer in the white-slave traffic. "Halfway through the story we meet reform in the person of the Victorian journalist, W. T. Stead. At this point the book becomes a documentary, for Stead was a real-life crusader who fought vice in the newspapers and through the courts"—(John Barkham, in *SR*). Cloete concludes with 18 pages (after the novel's end) describing the facts of white slavery today.

Rags of Glory. *Avon* 1964 1973 pap. $1.50

The Abductors. *Simon & Schuster* (Trident) 1966 $5.95

How Young They Die. *Simon & Schuster* (Trident) 1970 $6.95

A Victorian Son. *T. Y. Crowell* (John Day) 1973 $7.95

PATON, ALAN.   1903–

Paton, the eldest son of English settlers, was born in Pietermaritzburg, South Africa, and spent 25 years as an educator and public official. In 1935 he became principal of Diepkloof Reformatory for African boys in Johannesburg and became known as South Africa's expert on penal reform. In 1946 he started on what was to have been a tour of penal institutions in Scandinavia, Great Britain, the United States, and Canada. On the train from Stockholm to Trondheim he began work on the novel "Cry, the Beloved Country" but continued to study penal practice during his travels. The manuscript was completed in December 1947 in San Francisco and was published almost a year later. "No novel of the present has more successfully stated the social problems of a nation"—(*N.Y. Times*). It has sold more copies in South Africa than any other book with the exception of the Bible, was a best seller here and has been translated into 12 languages. "Too Late the Phalarope" is his second sociological story of South Africa, written in the same simple, cadenced prose.

Because of his outspoken criticism of current policies in South Africa, Paton's passport was revoked in an effort to stifle or at least soften his protest. "Tales from a Troubled Land" prove that he is not easily silenced. The theme of these beautifully written simple stories is still the spiritual damage caused by the apartheid policy in South Africa. Three nonfiction studies of his country are "The Land and People of South Africa" (*Lippincott* 1955 rev. ed. 1964 1972 $4.95), "South Africa in Transition" (U.S. 1956, o.p.) and "Hope for South Africa" (1959, o.p.). "South African Tragedy: The Life and Times of Jan Hofmeyr" describes the rise to power and subsequent defeat of the courageous Afrikaner statesman who dared to oppose the color bar. "The tragedy of the book is South Africa's rather than Hofmeyr's"—(*LJ*).

"Sponono" (written with Krishna Shah, 1965, o.p.), which appeared briefly on Broadway in 1964, and is based on three of the "Tales from a Troubled Land," reflects Paton's experience as head of an African boys' reformatory. Its theme is the difficulty of communication between the headmaster and an attractive but incorrigible pupil.

Cry, the Beloved Country. *Scribner* 1948 $4.95 introd. by Lewis Gannett Mod. Stand. Authors 1950 $3.60 pap. 1960 $1.95; *Franklin Watts* lg.-type ed. 1966 $9.95. A story of comfort in desolation.

Too Late the Phalarope. *Scribner* 1953 1963 pap. $1.65

Tales from a Troubled Land. *Scribner* 1961 $3.95 pap. $2.25. Ten short stories.

South African Tragedy: The Life and Times of Jan Hofmeyr. *Scribner* 1965 $2.95

INSTRUMENT OF THY PEACE. *Seabury Press* 1967 $3.95

"A series of meditations and observations inspired by a prayer of St. Francis." The author's "attempt to formulate his own thought . . . on the deep meaning of the Gospels"; with discussion of contemporary problems.

THE LONG VIEW. Ed. by Edward Callan. *Praeger* 1967 $6.95

(With others) CREATIVE SUFFERING: The Ripple of Hope. *United Church* Pilgrim Press 1970 pap. $2.25

APARTHEID AND THE ARCHBISHOP. 1974. *Scribner* $10.00

Books about Paton

Alan Paton. By Edward Callan. World Authors Ser. *Twayne* 1968 $6.95

SENGHOR, LÉOPOLD SÉDAR.   1906–

Along with Aimé Césaire, his close friend, Senghor is the personification of the ideals of black artists of French expression. Born of a *Sérère* father and a *peul* mother, he received his elementary education with the Fathers of the Holy Spirit just north of his birthplace in Joal. In 1922, he entered the seminary in Dakar with the intention of preparing himself for a religious career. Momentarily disappointed when it became clear that he did not have a calling to that life, he distinguished himself at the lycée of Dakar. In 1928 he continued his studies in Paris. The geographical and social displacement left its mark on him. In 1929 he began his long friendship with Césaire, newly arrived from Martinique. His classmates at the Lycée Louis-le-Grand included Pompidou, Queffelec, and Thierry Maulnier.

In 1934, with Césaire and others, he organized a little review, *L'Étudiant noir*, where for the first time these young poets invented and gave meaning and expression to the concept of négritude. A teacher in the lycées until the Second World War, he served in the French forces and experienced prison life under the Germans.

In 1945 his first collection of poems, *"Chants d'ombre,"* appeared. In the same year, he was elected as deputy from Senegal to the Constituent Assembly, and from thenceforth the careers of poet and administrator remained closely mingled. These years mark the beginning of the important review *Présence africaine* (under the aegis of Gide, Camus, and others) which has remained the life center of black literature of French expression. The year 1948 saw the all-important *"Anthologie de la nouvelle poésie nègre et malgache,"* prefaced by Jean-Paul Sartre.

In 1959 Senghor was named counselor to the President of the French Community and in 1960 he was elected the first president of the independent Republic of Senegal, a position he has continued to hold. With all his political commitments and his constant action for the advancement of all ex-colonial peoples, he has continued to write, in both prose and poetry, to persistent critical acclaim. Surely, he is the dean of all African as well as of all Caribbean writers in French. His collection of poems in 1961, *"Nocturnes,"* contains the following verse that is at once the mark of the political leader and the poet:

> The splendor of honors is like the Sahara
> An immense void.

SELECTED POEMS. Trans. by John Reed and Clive Wake. *Atheneum* 1964 $5.95

ETHIOPIQUES. 1956. Trans. by Jessica Harris. *Third Press* 1975 $6.95 pap. $3.95

NOCTURNES. 1961 Trans. by John Reed and Clive Wake. *Third Press* 1971 $5.95 pap. $1.95

ON AFRICAN SOCIALISM. Trans. with introd. by Mercer Cook. *Praeger* 1964 $4.95 pap. $1.95

NATIONHOOD AND THE AFRICAN ROAD TO SOCIALISM. *French & European* 1971 $5.50; *Panther House* 1971 $4.50

NÉGRITUDE AND HUMANISM. Trans. by Wendell A. Jeanpierre. *Third Press* 1975 $10.00

THE FOUNDATIONS OF "AFRICANITÉ", or "Négritude" and "Arabité." *French & European* pap. $3.50

Books about Senghor

African Image in the Work of Senghor. By Barend Van Niekerk. *Verry* 1970 pap. $10.00

Léopold Sédar Senghor. By Jacques L. Hymans. *Edinburgh Univ. Press* (dist. by Aldine) 1972 $8.75

The Concept of Négritude in the Poetry of Léopold Sédar Senghor. By Sylvia Ba. *Princeton Univ. Press* 1973 $11.00

The Poetry of Léopold Sédar Senghor. By Okechukuv S. Mezu. *Fairleigh Dickinson Univ. Press* 1973 $6.75

ABRAHAMS, PETER. 1919–

A leading African writer from South Africa, Peter Abrahams was born in Johannesburg. At the age of 20 he emigrated to England, a refugee from apartheid—the point to which he brings us in "Tell Freedom," one of the earliest of books by Africans to be published in English. It was followed by "Mine Boy," a vivid picture of the life of an African miner who finally stood up to his white boss and became a man. Other important novels were "Wild Conquest," a story of the African resistance to the great Boer trek, and "A Wreath for Udomo," a *roman à clef*, in which Abrahams foretold with sophisticated narrative skill the downfall of a hero not unlike Kwame Nkrumah. His most recent book, "This Island, Now," the story of a Caribbean revolution, continues Abrahams' fictional study of the races in conflict, which he has already explored in a variety of settings and periods. "Do new tyrannies inevitably replace old ones? Can a decadent power structure, centuries old, be radically changed overnight, and at what sacrifice? Do the idealistic aims of a revolution justify the sordid means? These are the novel's timely concerns"—(*PW*). "This is a novel of major importance"—(*LJ*).

Abrahams, like most African intellectuals in South Africa, is the product of an urban environment, and his novels are polished in the manner of his white compatriots Alan Paton (*q.v.*) or Nadine Gordimer (*q.v.*). Claude Wauthier calls him "in many ways the Richard Wright of Southern Africa," though he lacks Wright's (*q.v.*) great bitterness of tone. Abrahams has recently settled with his family in the island of Jamaica.

WILD CONQUEST. 1950. Africana Ser. *Doubleday* 1971 Anchor Bks. pap. $1.95

MINE BOY. 1955. *Macmillan* Collier Bks. 1970 pap. $1.50

A WREATH FOR UDOMO. 1956. *Macmillan* Collier Bks. African-American Lib. 1971 pap. $1.95

THIS ISLAND, NOW. 1967. *Macmillan* Collier Bks. 1971 pap. $1.95. A novel.

TELL FREEDOM. *Knopf* 1954 $5.95; *Macmillan* Collier Bks. 1969 pap. $1.50. His autobiography, describing life in South Africa under apartheid. It has been called "the mirror of life in a tragic lane."

MPHAHLELE, EZEKIEL. 1919–

Born in a South African slum in 1919 and banned from his teaching career for encouraging organized protest against government educational policies, Mphahlele has lived since 1957 in Nigeria, Paris, Kenya, and the United States. His autobiography, "Down Second Avenue," published in London in 1959, first brought him to the attention of an international public; it has since been translated into eight Mbari languages. He was one of the founders of the Mbari Writers and Artists Club at Ibadan, Nigeria, in 1962.

Mphahlele has written—and continues to write—short stories, of which several volumes have been published abroad, and he frequently analyzes intellectual and social developments in contemporary Africa for journals here and overseas. He has taught English at the University of Ibadan and African Literature at the University of Colorado and the University of Denver. Commenting on the future of African writing he had this to say to an interviewer (*Africa Report*, July, 1964): "We African writers will have to come to terms with the meaning of literature as a criticism of life. . . . We have to realize that just giving anthropological information or sociological information is not good enough. When we've got our focus on our own society and criticize it, we shall then know that we are doing it for our immediate audience, which is in Africa, and not necessarily playing up to the gallery in order to please the British publisher. . . . We should be able to experiment with style . . . give English a new and fresh ring. . . . We shan't care a damn whether we are published abroad or not. But this also means that we must have publishing houses in Africa." In *Africa Today* (Dec. 1966), he wrote: "As we learn to laugh at ourselves, we shall also, I think, create a literature that echoes our laughter."

DOWN SECOND AVENUE: Growing up in a South African Ghetto. 1959. *Doubleday* Anchor Bks. 1971 pap. $1.95; *Peter Smith* $4.00

THE AFRICAN IMAGE. *Praeger* 1962 1974 $8.50 pap. $2.95. Essays on the African as he has been regarded and portrayed by the white man.

(Ed.) AFRICAN WRITING TODAY. *Penguin* 1967 pap. $3.50. An anthology.

IN CORNER B. *Northwestern Univ. Press* 1967 $2.00

WANDERERS. Ed. by Malcolm McPherson. *Macmillan* 1971 $6.95

VOICES IN THE WHIRLWIND AND OTHER ESSAYS. *Farrar, Straus* (Hill & Wang) 1972 $6.95
pap. $2.65

TUTUOLA, AMOS. 1920–

Tutuola is a native of Abookuta, Nigeria. He received his elementary education at a Salvation
Army School and later went to Lagos High School. His novels, written in a strange pidgin English,
are "wholly African, wholly outside our Western-European culture-range." This very different
English is "lively, simple, vigorous, sometimes outrageously 'quaint' "—when he uses such terms as
"drinkard," "ghostesses," "ultra-beautiful ladies."

Claude Wauthier writes of him: "Tutuola is both a Grimm and an Edgar Allan Poe to Africa.
The world of fantasy in which this Nigerian moves so easily is also that of the legends and myths of
the Yoruba country. In his *The Palm-Wine Drinkard* there is a journey into the land of the dead
where everything is topsy-turvy—a sort of African *Alice through the Looking Glass.*" Lewis Nkosi
described the controversy around Tutuola's writing in *Africa Report*: "Europeans were fascinated
by Tutuola's very personal use of the English language. But . . . in Nigeria [readers] argued that
Tutuola's ungrammatical use of English was not experimental and that he simply did not know
any other way to write. Some Africans asked why the English publishers had not properly edited
Tutuola's manuscript." Behind this criticism seems to have lain the fear that Tutuola's "primitive"
quaintness was playing up to European stereotypes of the ignorant, childlike, happy African. He
has, however, continued to write in the same manner—some seven books or more, published in
England, none of which, he says, have taken him over a month, and "The Palm-Wine Drinkard"
only three days!

THE PALM-WINE DRINKARD. 1952. *Grove* Evergreen Bks. 1962 pap. $1.95; *Greenwood*
$9.25. A novel.

MY LIFE IN THE BUSH OF GHOSTS. *Grove* Evergreen Bks. 1962 $1.95

BRAVE AFRICAN HUNTRESS. *Grove* Evergreen Bks. 1970 pap. $1.95

Books about Tutuola

Amos Tutuola. By Harold R. Collins. World Authors Ser. *Twayne* 1969 $6.95

EKWENSI, CYPRIAN. 1921–

Born in Minna, Nigeria, Ekwensi received his primary education in Nigeria and Ghana. He
began writing while he was a student at London University, Chelsea School of Pharmacy. His first
full-length novel, "People of the City," is a portrayal of the newly urbanized Africans' adjustment
to a complex and impersonal environment. In contrast, "Burning Grass" is a novel about the
cattlemen of the Northern Savannah. "Ekwensi is one of the earliest and most prolific of the
socially realistic Nigerian novelists who presents the conflict between personal desire and group
duty as the major problem of his country"—(Martin Tucker). He is concerned with the corruption
of the new African city, compared to which the outworn traditional life may offer a kind of peace
to those who return to it with knowledge of the broader world.

THE DRUMMER BOY. *Cambridge* 1960 $1.25

THE PASSPORT OF MALLAM ILIA. *Cambridge* 1960 $1.25

TROUBLE IN FORM SIX. *Cambridge* 1966 $1.25

BURNING GRASS: A Story of the Fulani of Northern Nigeria. African Writers Ser.
Humanities Press 1966 pap. $1.75

LOKOTOWN AND OTHER STORIES. African Writers Ser. *Humanities Press* 1966 pap. $1.75

JAGUA NANA. *Fawcett* Premier Bks. 1969 pap. $.75

PEOPLE OF THE CITY. *Fawcett* Premier Bks. 1969 pap. $.75

JACOBSON, DAN. 1929–

Dan Jacobson was born in Johannesburg. After graduating from the University of Witwaters-
rand in 1949, he lived for a brief period in Israel. Shortly thereafter he went to England, where,
except for two years spent at American universities, he has lived ever since. Peter Abrahams (*q.v.*)
said of his first novel, "The Trap" (1955, o.p.): "At its best the writing has a cool, unhurried clarity
that is wholly admirable. But it is Dan Jacobson's re-creation of the feel and smell and mood of a
Boer farm on the African veld that is the most distinguished feature of this impressive short
novel." "The Zulu and the Zeide" (1959, o.p.) is the warmhearted tale of a young Zulu hired by a
Jewish family to look after their old *zeide*, or grandfather. It was adapted as a musical, "The Zulu

and the Zayda," by Howard da Silva and Felix Leon and ran successfully on Broadway for most of the 1965–1966 season, with Ossie Davis and Menasha Skulnik in the title roles. "No Further West" (1961, o.p.) contains Jacobson's sympathetic and perceptive observations on California life after a year's stay here. "The Beginners" (1968, o.p.), Jacobson's fifth novel, traces the lives of a South African Jewish family over four generations. "Subtleties of character and the Jewish psyche in relation to its environment are given more importance than local color"—(*LJ*). The *N.Y. Times* has described Jacobson as a "major figure in South African literature since World War II."

THROUGH THE WILDERNESS AND OTHER STORIES. *Macmillan* 1968 $5.95

THE RAPE OF TAMAR. Ed. by Robert Markel. *Macmillan* 1970 $5.95; *Avon Bks.* 1973 pap. $.95

THE WONDER-WORKER. *Little-Atlantic* 1974 $5.95

ACHEBE, CHINUA. 1930–

"Achebe's skill is now so recognized that he is required reading in Nigerian schools and part of the syllabus in many comparative literature courses in colleges in Africa, Europe and the United States"—(Martin Tucker). "One of Nigeria's finest writers" (Eliot Fremont-Smith), he writes of the Nigeria of the Ibos and the city of Lagos. "Things Fall Apart," his first novel, won him an international readership. It describes African tribal life, whose traditional ways are threatened and begin to deteriorate with the coming of the white man. In "No Longer at Ease" (the title is taken from T. S. Eliot) a young man from these tribal beginnings is sent to England to be educated and returns to take a position in the British civil service. "The phrase that recurs . . . and that can be heard behind all the other music of its pages is 'Our people have a long way to go' "—(Tucker). His third novel, "Arrow of God," with an African priest as its hero, is in part "an excellent satire of Joyce Cary's 'Mister Johnson' " (*Africa Report*). The London *Sunday Times* said of it, "The telling is polished; images effortlessly light up the pages; the ear is faultless." In 1965 it won the first *New Statesman* Award (London).

"A Man of the People," a political novel set in an imaginary country like modern Nigeria, was hailed as prophetic in 1966, when its publication nearly coincided with the overthrow of the Nigerian government of Prime Minister Balewa. Achebe comes from the Eastern Region, which seceded as the state of Biafra in 1967. The book contains the often quoted passage: "The trouble with our new nation was that none of us had been indoors long enough. . . . We had all been in the rain together until yesterday. Then a handful of us—the smart and the lucky and hardly ever the best—had scrambled for the one shelter our former rulers had left and had taken it over and barricaded themselves in. . . ."

Eliot Fremont-Smith says, "[Chinua Achebe] writes in a decidedly Western or Anglo-American style" but Willie Abraham (African author of "The Mind of Africa") finds that "he is one of those novelists who, in my opinion, comes nearest to being an African novelist"—(*Africa Report*). "Mr. Achebe's evocation of atmosphere and his presentation of the way Africans speak and of their often utterly alien thought processes are both fascinating and convincing"—(*TLS*, London).

Chinua Achebe received his B.A. degree from the University of Ibadan and pursued a career in broadcasting (with the BBC in Africa) from 1954 on, becoming First Director of External Broadcasting for Nigeria in 1961. He has visited the United States. His first two novels were translated into German, Italian and Spanish.

THINGS FALL APART. 1959. *Astor-Honor* $5.95 pap. $1.95. Novel.

NO LONGER AT EASE. 1961. *Astor-Honor* $5.95 pap. $1.95; *Fawcett* Premier Bks. 1970 pap. $1.45. Novel.

ARROW OF GOD. 1964. *Doubleday* Anchor Bks. 1969 pap. $1.45. Novel.

CHIKE AND THE RIVER. *Cambridge* 1966 $.95. Short stories.

A MAN OF THE PEOPLE. 1966. *Doubleday* 1967 Anchor Bks. pap. $1.45

CHRISTMAS IN BIAFRA AND OTHER POEMS. *Doubleday* 1973 $5.95 Anchor Bks. pap. $2.50

GIRLS AT WAR AND OTHER STORIES. *Doubleday* 1973 $5.95; *Fawcett* Premier Bks. 1974 pap. $1.25

(With John Iroaganachi) How THE LEOPARD GOT HIS CLAWS. *Third Press* 1973 $4.95

Books about Achebe

The Novels of Chinua Achebe. By G. D. Killam. *Holmes & Meier Pubs.* 1969 $5.50 pap. $2.50

Chinua Achebe. By Arthur Ravenscroft. Writers and Their Work Ser. *British Bk. Centre* $2.95 pap. $1.20

Chinua Achebe. By David Carroll. World Authors Ser. *Twayne* $6.95

FUGARD, ATHOL. 1932–

Athol Fugard was born in Meddelburg, South Africa, of European parentage. He was educated at Port Elizabeth Technical College and majored in philosophy at the University of Cape Town. An internationally acclaimed playwright (and foe of apartheid), his plays have been produced both here and abroad. For the past ten years he has been working in South Africa with a group of young black actors called the Serpent Players. In 1974 two members of this group, John Kani and Winston Ntshona, appeared on Broadway in two plays written by Fugard, "The Island" and "Sizwe Banzi Is Dead." Kani and Ntshona shared the Tony Award for best actor for their performances in these two plays.

PEOPLE ARE LIVING THERE: A Play in Two Acts. *Oxford* 1970 pap. $1.30

THREE PORT ELIZABETH PLAYS. *Viking* 1974 $7.95

OKIGBO, CHRISTOPHER. 1932–1967.

An Ibo, strongly committed to the Biafran cause, this promising young poet, who had already distinguished himself as one of Nigeria's leading poets during his brief literary career, was killed in action during the Biafran war. His biographer, Dr. Anozie, says of him, "Okigbo's poetry is difficult. You feel that a final comprehension is just round the corner, but it's a corner you never reach. . . . Okigbo's poetry is constantly exploring two irregular dimensions of myth . . . myth as a privileged mode of cognition . . . myth and totem are seen as not merely cognitive but affective and even evaluative in a given cultural context—that for example, of the Ibo-speaking people of Nigeria."

Okigbo was indeed a complex individual, not one who readily gave in to tradition and conformity. He was awarded the first prize for poetry in 1966 at the First Festival of Negro Arts held in Dakar. Okigbo rejected the award on the grounds that he did not subscribe to the terms "Negro art" or "African literature." There is a spiritual vein in much of his poetry. "He himself said that 'Heavensgate' was originally conceived as an Easter sequence and that the various sections of the poem represent the various stations of the traveller's Cross"—(*Présence Africaine*).

LABYRINTHS WITH PATH OF THUNDER. *Holmes & Meier Pubs.* (Africana Pub. Corp.) 1971 $5.00

Books about Okigbo

The Trial of Christopher Okigbo. By Ali Al'Amin Mazrui. 1971. *Third Press* 1972 $5.95
Christopher Okigbo: Creative Rhetoric. By S. O. Anozie. Modern African Writers Ser. *Holmes & Meier Pubs.* 1972 $8.00 pap. $3.75

SOYINKA, WOLE. 1934–

At a time when most African writers are taking the world and themselves very seriously, the foremost playwright of Nigeria, who is poet and novelist as well, is a satirist with a sense of humor and perhaps the most mature of African writers—one who can convey universal truths in terms of the local Nigerian scene. An indication of his stature, says Martin Tucker (in *Africa Today*), is that "of all the contemporary African writers, Soyinka is the one who makes the least pretense of social instruction," a feature "that has until recently made African writers [in English or French] seem more interested in nationalism than in literature. . . . Soyinka's plays are concerned with the mystery and fascination of devouring countryside. His characters either return to the vital land or else leave it, finding in its voraciousness their necessary fulfillment. Often enough that fulfillment is doom, but Soyinka's plays are so powerful . . . that no sense of depression accompanies his work."

Wole Soyinka (his first name is pronounced "Wally") attended Ibadan University and then, in England, the University of Leeds, from which he received his B.A. with honors in English. During this sojourn he was able to work in London at the experimental Royal Court Theatre, which produced "The Lion and the Jewel" before his return to Nigeria in 1960. Of "The Lion and the Jewel," on its revival in 1966, the *Observer* (London) said, "Soyinka's parable of progress is the most sophisticated spectacle in town." The story of the struggle within a Nigerian tribe of today between the western-educated schoolmaster and the more-or-less feudal and elderly chief to win the village belle allows Soyinka to satirize both the paraphernalia of western civilization, as absorbed or yearned after by the schoolteacher, and the paradoxes of tribal custom and superstition. "Wisdom lies somewhere between: neither in tradition nor modernism, but in the foxiness which knows what to take from both"—(*Observer*). The chief triumphs as the lady shrewdly eyes her best bargain. "The Road," another play, was, says the *Observer* (of Dec. 18, 1966), "one of the most powerful and original works seen in London last year."

Soyinka has written one novel, "The Interpreters," "the most complex novel yet to emerge from Nigeria, [one remarkable for its] quick pace . . . cleverly manipulated action . . . brilliant dialogue . . . dazzling images and darting metaphors"—(*Africa Report*). The writer came to the United States in the summer of 1967 to discuss, with Ossie Davis and others, the formation of a Nigerian film-producing company which will make motion pictures of some of Soyinka's own works. "The Trials of Brother Jero" and "The Strong Breed" opened at the Greenwich Mews Theater in New York Nov. 10, 1967. The former is "a slight play," a "very funny curtain raiser" (*N.Y. Times*), about a charlatan posing as a prophet, the latter a "parable about a young, educated Nigerian who is forced to become the . . . ritual scapegoat for the town where he is selflessly serving as a teacher." On the strength of these, said Dan Sullivan, Soyinka is "one of the continent's leading artistic national resources." "Kongi's Harvest" was produced off Broadway in the same season by the Negro Ensemble Company of New York.

Ironically the plays opened as Mr. Soyinka lay in prison charged with treason in the revolt of the region of Nigeria known as Biafra at the time of its attempted secession. A *N.Y. Times* editorial described the appeal on his behalf to the Nigerian government by American and British members of P.E.N. "Apart from writing in favor of reconciliation, he has not taken sides in this war," said the *Times*, a report confirmed by the playwright himself in a smuggled statement which reached the *Times* of Nov. 9, 1967. Fears for his life were expressed. In a most interesting article published in the East Africa English-Language journal *Transition*, June/July 1967, Soyinka has written sadly of the lot of the African writer since independence: "The African writer found that he could not deny his society; he could, however, temporarily at least, deny himself. . . . If he has not already arrived at this discovery, the writer from East or West African states is coming closer to the terrible understanding that it is not his South African comrade who is the creature of compassion. Already he has begun to shrink from the bewildered stare of the South African, knowing that he, the supposedly free mind . . . has himself become the creature of despair." Where the African writer should *lead*, he has had to conform in the birth pangs of the new states, unable to exercise his prophetic calling "in the very collapse of humanity. Nevertheless the African writer has done nothing to vindicate his existence, nothing to indicate he is even aware this awful collapse has taken place. For he has been generally without vision."

COLLECTED PLAYS. *Oxford* Vol. 1 new ed. 1973 pap. $3.95; Vol. 2 1974 pap. $4.50

THREE SHORT PLAYS. *Oxford* 1969 pap. $1.75

THE LION AND THE JEWEL. *Oxford* 1963 $1.50. A play.

A DANCE OF THE FORESTS. *Oxford* 1963 $1.50

THE ROAD. *Oxford* 1965 $1.50. Play.

THE INTERPRETERS. 1965. African American Lib. Ser. *Macmillan* Collier Bks. 1970 pap. $1.50; *Holmes & Meier Pubs.* (Africana Pub. Corp.) 1972 $9.00

KONGI'S HARVEST. *Oxford* 1967 $1.50. Play.

IDANRE AND OTHER POEMS. *Farrar, Straus* (Hill & Wang) 1968 $3.95

(With D. O. Fagunwa) FOREST OF A THOUSAND DEMONS. *Humanities Press* 1969 $1.75

MADMEN AND SPECIALISTS. *Farrar, Straus* (Hill & Wang) Mermaid Dramabks. 1972 $6.95 pap. $2.45

A SHUTTLE IN THE CRYPT. *Farrar, Straus* (Hill & Wang) 1972 $6.95 pap. $2.65

THE MAN DIED. *Harper* 1973 $8.95

CAMWOOD ON THE LEAVES and BEFORE THE BLACK-OUT. *Third Press* 1974 $5.95 pap. $2.95

THE BACCHAE OF EURIPIDES: A Communion Rite. *Norton* 1974 $6.95

SEASON OF ANOMY. *Technomic Pub.* 1974 $8.95

Books about Soyinka

Wole Soyinka. By Eldred D. Jones. World Authors Ser. *Twayne* 1971 $6.95
Wole Soyinka. By Gerald Moore. *Holmes & Meier Pubs.* 1972 $6.00 pap. $3.00

HEAD, BESSIE. 1937–

This author was born in Pietermaritzburg, South Africa. She is one of the handful of African women novelists. In 1964 she left South Africa and now resides in Botswana. There is only a sparse amount of biographical information available on her. In the November 1975 issue of *Ms.* magazine her short story entitled "Witchcraft" was published. The author says of herself, "I forcefully created for myself, under extremely hostile conditions, my ideal life. I took an obscure and almost unknown village in the Southern African bush and made it my own hallowed ground. My work was always tentative because it was always so completely new: it created new worlds out of nothing; it battled with problems of food production in a tough semidesert land; it brought all kinds of people, both literate and semiliterate together, and it did not really qualify who was who. . . . But nothing can take away the fact that I have never had a country; not in South Africa or in Botswana where I now live as a stateless person." In addition to writing novels Ms. Head works as a journalist in Botswana.

Her most recent novel, "A Question of Power," "is about the 'inner journey' of a young colored woman in Botswana, South Africa. In her quest for sanity, she is prey to voices and 'appearances' by several characters who speak of the search for power—physical, sexual and political—in modern Africa. The kind of power dealt with transcends the usual category of white and black; ultimately the dimension of the novel is spiritual. This is an intriguing novel in that it represents a change from the traditional (i.e., social/realistic) novel that characterizes the work of most African novelists today"—(*Choice*).

WHEN RAIN CLOUDS GATHER. *Simon & Schuster* 1969 $5.95

A QUESTION OF POWER. *Pantheon* 1974 $6.95

AIDOO, AMA ATA.   1942–

One of the most popular African women writers, Ms. Aidoo was born in Abeadzi Kyiakor, Ghana. Known mainly as a short-story writer, she has also written poetry and plays. Her first play, "The Dilemma of a Ghost," was written during her student days at the University of Ghana. It has since been performed in Ghana and Nigeria and received high acclaim. "Miss Aidoo displays a gift—very useful to a social dramatist—of showing both sides of the coin at the same time. She shows the reverence of African village society towards motherhood while at the same time exposing the inherent cruelty of a system which makes the childless woman utterly miserable"—(Eldred Jones).

"No Sweetness Here" is a collection of 11 short stories depicting the life of African women in both rural and urban settings. "There is in all of them a quality which makes the reader feel he is being nudged gently toward a more profound understanding of modern Africa"—(*N.Y. Times*).

Her poems and short stories have appeared in many of the major African journals: *Black Orpheus, Présence Africaine*, and *Zuka*.

DILEMMA OF A GHOST. 1965 *Macmillan* 1971 Collier Bks. pap. $1.25

NO SWEETNESS HERE. 1969. *Doubleday* Anchor Bks. 1972 pap. $1.95

—G.J.

Chapter 18

Middle Eastern Literature

"The sanctuaried East"

—F. THOMPSON

ANCIENT NEAR EASTERN LITERATURE

Ancient Near Eastern literature comprises works from at least seven major cultures which thrived some three thousand years before the time of Christ in the lands bordering upon the Eastern Mediterranean. For convenience they may be spoken of as belonging to three dominant cultural streams: (a) the *Mesopotamian-Anatolian*, which includes productions written in cuneiform (wedge-shaped) characters on clay tablets, as well as on stone stelae or prepared rock surfaces, by the Sumerians (Lower Iraq, c. 3000–2000 B.C.), the Babylonians (Lower Iraq, c. 2000–539 B.C.), the Assyrians (Upper Iraq, c. 2000–612 B.C.) and the Hittites (Central Turkey, c. 1750–1200 B.C.); (b) the *Syro-Palestinian*, which is characterized chiefly by Canaanite literature from Ras Shamra (ancient Ugarit) on the Syrian coast, written in a cuneiform alphabetic script on clay tablets, and dating to about 1400 B.C., and by the Bible (*q.v.*), the sacred book of the Hebrews, which contains materials that begin to appear in written form some five hundred years later in the Hebrew script on papyrus and other soft materials; and (c) the *Egyptian*, which contains works inscribed on stone (such as pyramid, temple, and tomb inscriptions), and on papyrus, the whole extant body covering a time period from c. 2500–330 B.C. A small corpus of royal inscriptions emanating from Achaemenid kings (c. 539–330 B.C.), produced in cuneiform on stone stelae and on prepared rock faces, when added to the limited number of clay tablets emanating from Elamite culture (c. 3000 B.C. *et seq.*), represents the chief written materials of the oldest classical Iranian culture.

Since the totality of the literatures just delineated comes from an area where the three continents of Europe, Western Asia, and Africa meet, it is characterized by works in a number of both related and unrelated languages. The chief language subdivisions represented are Semitic, Indo-European, Indo-Iranian, and Hamito-Semitic. The classical representatives of the eastern branch of the Semitic languages are Babylonian and Assyrian; of the Western, Canaanite (Ugaritic), Hebrew, Phoenician, Aramaic, and Syriac. Indo-European is represented by Hittite, Indo-Iranian by Old Persian, and Hamito-Semitic by ancient Egyptian. The major unclassified languages include Sumerian, upon whose literary heritage of themes and forms much of Assyrian and Babylonian literature is founded; Hurrian (the Biblical Horite), which contributed much to Hittite religion and literature; and Kassite and Elamite, each of which remains little known.

It should be appreciated then that ancient Near Eastern literature is the result of a process of continual transmission of themes and forms between cultures of vastly different origins and modes of life, and of different degrees of sophistication, all interacting for almost three millennia in a single geographical arena. What facilitated this transmission throughout the region were the two dominant writing systems—the cuneiform, developed by the Sumerians, which became the normative form of expressing the many different languages of peoples inhabiting the northern tier of regions in the Near East, and the hieroglyphic, which although limited for the most part to Egypt, gave the impetus for the development of experiments in cursive writing within the Syro-Palestinian corridor. But what most allows us to speak of ancient Near Eastern literature as a category, in addition to the circumstance that it comes from a definable time period and a circumscribed area, and that it is expressed in a few common writing systems (although in different languages), is the characteristic that it has been elaborated from some half dozen major genres, and but a slightly larger number of lesser genres. For the former we have myth, epic, historical narrative, wisdom literature (i.e., theodicies, instructions, meditations, proverbs, and sayings), hymns and prayers, and incantations and omens. For the latter we may add fables, folktales and legends, lamentations, songs, dialogue-debates, autobiography, satire, riddles, and the like. This nucleus was already established in the earliest times by the Sumerian and the Egyptian "core" civilizations, and was continually favored in all subsequent phases of society in Mesopotamia and Egypt, as well as by new societies of the intermediate and the fringe areas. The traditionalist bent of ancient Near Eastern peoples, in particular of the ruling cadres which controlled the production of literature (*see below*), fostered continual copying and recopying of ancient works (as much to train new scribes in the art of writing as to preserve the outstanding works), so that where fresh themes appear, they do so most often within recognizably older literary forms.

Accordingly one may experience a sense of an underlying pervasive spirit of common cosmic awareness on the part of ancient Near Eastern cultures which is reflected, despite regional variations, in the literature from all parts of the area. The one outstanding exception to this statement is the religious vision of the Hebrews and Christians as presented in the Bible, but even here, despite the appearance of new genres reflecting that vision (such as the books of prophecy in the Old Testament, and the gospel, the epistle, and the apocalyptic of the New), there is constant use of traditional genres developed by the older, non-Biblical societies.

It is well to issue a few cautions before passing on to a presentation of guides to understanding the literature here discussed. For the contemporary Western reader, "literature" means *"belles-lettres,"* but in the ancient Near East works such as myths, epics, and the various forms of short imaginative literature that we would include under the term are but a very small minority of the written materials produced by a representative society. Far more important were what we would call "scholarly" texts, and religious texts of everyday use. The excavation of Assurbanipal's library (c. 650 B.C.) at Ninevah in the last century disclosed that in this great repository (the ancient Near Eastern equivalent to the noted Library of Alexandria) the majority of works comprised omen literature, magical formulae and instructions, lexical materials of all types, and lists of objects belonging to both the natural and the human spheres of activity. Even historical texts and legal codes were minimal in number by comparison with the others. In Egypt the situation was not much different, highest priority in all periods being reserved for funerary texts, then to the myriad of textual materials relating to priestly training and activity, to charms, omens, amulets, and the like. The great medical and mathematical texts also represent practical compendia. It might be well to remind ourselves that writing was not necessarily invented to preserve the great thoughts and feelings of mankind; the evidence too frequently suggests that this precious intellectual tool was most often applied to the purposes of political and religious administration. Accordingly, the listings below will also offer some guides to materials which are non-bellelettristic.

Furthermore, the Western reader thinks of literature as being predominantly produced by private persons, with the assistance of independent publishing houses. By contrast, however much the single literary creator lies behind a work which has become known to us from the ancient Near East, the work is preserved and continually recopied in what the late A. L. Oppenheim of the University of Chicago has called "the stream of tradition." The original writer fades into obscurity and the work enters the public realm to serve a social purpose. Too often we are completely ignorant of the essential background details of any particular piece of literature. We do know that the greater and lesser works both served to train scribes and to form a corpus of consultative materials for the king's benefit. Of course the great myths and epics may have entertained the public through being declaimed by accomplished readers; certainly they existed in oral form. We simply do not know very much about the creation of, and audience for, a good many of the non-scholarly and non-liturgical works we encounter. The only really "private" materials in the ancient Near East are the thousands of business documents and letters which have been excavated; of the imaginative writings, perhaps some anonymous love poems, which have gained great popularity.

Finally, two additional points must influence our approach to the literature of the ancient Near East. Because this literature was produced long before the time of Aristotle and the invention of literary theory, it defies classification into neat and precisely defined genres, although "genre" as used above is a generally useful term. There are examples of historical writing which approach the epic in style and intent, while such a composition as the famous "Law Code of Hammurabi" is today recognized less as a document giving an accurate reflection of the legal usage of its time than as a calculated laudation of Hammurabi the king, as "Law Giver," something which its highly florid prologue and epilogue, and its idealistic tone, confirm. One of the urgent tasks for present and future scholars is to propose principles of literary theory and criticism which are valid in terms of the evidence available in the absence of any such aids produced internally by the societies in question. The second point worth emphasizing is that the line between religious, or more properly, sacred, literature, and secular literature is by no means clear. It is truly difficult to accept any such distinction for societies in which religious perspectives were as totally pervasive as they were in each of the societies of the ancient Near East. We forget that most societies in the history of the world have been what we should call "religious societies," and their literatures, unlike that of Greece (where individual mental and aesthetic activity was not influenced by the existence of a restrictive religious outlook), usually reflect the dominant sacred viewpoints of the tradition. Consequently one must be as careful not to read Western secular viewpoints into ancient Near Eastern literature as one normally would in not interpreting ancient actions and institutions by contemporary standards of motivation and accomplishment.

General Background

Until the post-World War II era there were relatively few comprehensive and up-to-date surveys of ancient Near Eastern history, culture, and society in English. Within the last two decades a number of excellent and inexpensive volumes have appeared. The following list presents a convenient introductory nucleus providing the necessary background to the literatures:

Chiera, E. THEY WROTE ON CLAY. Ed. by George G. Cameron. *Univ. of Chicago Press* 1938 $7.50 pap. $2.95. A sensitive introduction to the world of clay tablets and the environment from which they emanate. For the general reader.

Contenau, G. EVERYDAY LIFE IN BABYLON AND ASSYRIA. 1950. *Norton* 1966 $3.95

Ferm, V., Ed. FORGOTTEN RELIGIONS. 1950 Essay Index Reprint Ser. *Bks for Libraries* $16.00. Excellent summary articles on Egyptian, Sumerian, Assyro-Babylonian, Hittite, and Canaanite religions, among others, by S. Mercer, S. N. Kramer, A. L. Oppenheim, H. G. Güterbock, and T. Gaster, respectively.

Gurney, O. R. THE HITTITES. *Penguin* Pelican 2nd ed. 1954 pap. $2.25
"An attempt to present a balanced picture of what is known of the Hittites and in the chapter on literature to give some impression of the more important types of documents found among their archives."

Jacobsen, T., with Henri Frankfort and John Wilson. THE INTELLECTUAL ADVENTURE OF ANCIENT MAN. *Univ. of Chicago Press* 1946 $12.00. Not to be overlooked. The single comprehensive book in English which attempts to penetrate through to the intellectual first principles of ancient Near Eastern thought, especially Egyptian and Babylonian. This book is an indispensable adjunct to literary study.

Kirk, G. S. MYTH: Its Meaning and Functions in Ancient and Other Cultures. *Univ. of California Press* 1970 $9.50 pap. $3.85. A wide-ranging, nonconventional exploration of the nature and meaning of myth by a Hellenist who can see beyond the limits of the intellectual borders of ancient Greece; especially interesting in its chapters on ancient Mesopotamia, and Greek-Hurrian-Hittite connections.

Kramer, Samuel Noah, Ed. MYTHOLOGIES OF THE ANCIENT WORLD. *Doubleday* Anchor Bks. 1961 pap. $1.95

"Using the most up-to-date translations, ten leading scholars take a fresh look at ancient mythologies in a work that can be read with pleasure and profit by both the specialist and the general reader." This is an absolutely essential volume, with each essay being of the highest quality. Of special notice is Rudolf Anthes' essay on mythology in Ancient Egypt, which is a little masterpiece in itself. Other cultures treated are Sumeria, Babylonia and Assyria by S. N. Kramer, Hittite by H. Güterbock, Canaanite by C. Gordon, Iran by M. J. Dresden, and Greece by Michael H. Jameson, along with several from the non-Near Eastern arena.

THE SUMERIANS: Their History, Culture, and Character. *Univ. of Chicago Press* 1963 $10.00 Phoenix Bks. pap. 1971 $2.95

"An uncontested authority on the civilization of Sumer, Professor Kramer writes with grace and urbanity"—(*LJ*).

Montet, P. ETERNAL EGYPT. 1964, o.p. An excellent and handy cultural survey of Egypt by an outstanding French Egyptologist.

Moscati, Sabatino. THE FACE OF THE ANCIENT ORIENT: A Panorama of Near Eastern Civilizations in Pre-Classical Times. *Doubleday* Anchor Bks. 1962 pap. $2.50. Intelligent summation of important aspects of ancient Near Eastern history and culture, written in a style which is attractive to the general reader.

Oppenheim, A. L. ANCIENT MESOPOTAMIA. *Univ. of Chicago Press* 1964 $12.00 Phoenix Bks. 1968 pap. $4.95

"This splendid work of scholarship . . . sums up with economy and power all that the written record so far deciphered has to tell about the ancient and complementary civilizations of Babylon and Assyria"—(Edward B. Garside in the *N.Y. Times Book Review*). A careful reading of this book will provide the serious reader and the student with the firmest foundation to the study of Mesopotamia from the sources that is available anywhere.

Orlin, Louis L. ANCIENT NEAR EASTERN LITERATURE: A Bibliography of One Thousand Items on the Cuneiform Literatures of the Ancient World. *Campus Pubs.* 1969 pap. $5.00

Saggs, H. W. F. THE GREATNESS THAT WAS BABYLON. *Praeger* 1969 $13.00; *New Am. Lib.* Mentor Bks. pap. $2.25. A wide-ranging survey of Babylonian civilization.

Wilson, John. THE CULTURE OF ANCIENT EGYPT. 1951. (Orig. title: "The Burden of Egypt: An Interpretation of Ancient Egyptian Culture") *Univ. of Chicago Press* 1956 pap. $3.45

A beautifully written and sustained essay on the processes of ancient Egyptian history and culture. The author writes, "This is not a history of ancient Egypt, but rather a book about ancient Egyptian history." What Professor Wilson has produced is "scholarship in its finest form, concerned with the humanity that has preceded us, and finding in man's past grandeur and failure much meaning for men of today."

Collections

Breasted, James H., Trans. and ed. ANCIENT RECORDS OF EGYPT. 5 vols. in 3 1906–1907 *Russell & Russell* 1962 $65.00. Although long out-of-date, these recently reissued volumes still serve as a useful introduction to Egyptian historical writing.

Erman, Adolf, Ed. THE ANCIENT EGYPTIANS: A Sourcebook of Their Writings. Introd. by William K. Simpson. 1927. *Harper* Torchbks. 1966 pap. $3.25

"Remains by far the best selection and translation of Egyptian belles-lettres which has appeared so far. Erman, who was the real creator of modern scientific Egyptology, also possessed a rare understanding of Egyptian mentality and a profound appreciation of ancient Egyptian psychology. It is fair to say that the book will long continue to hold its high position among anthologies of the kind, and there will be few who are not charmed by it"—(William F. Albright). The translations employ archaic English which occasionally makes the Old Egyptians sound like Old Englishmen, but this should be no impairment to the reader's enjoyment. Simpson has provided an up-to-date introductory essay.

Faulkner, R. O., Trans. THE ANCIENT EGYPTIAN PYRAMID TEXTS. *Oxford* 1969 $12.00. A very recent translation incorporating the fruits of Egyptological linguistic research in the 60 years since the standard edition of Sethe was published. The book is designed to be used both by philologists and students of ancient religion.

Gaster, T. THE OLDEST STORIES IN THE WORLD. *Beacon* 1958 pap. $3.95. A very elementary retelling of a number of myths and legends designed for the general reader but probably more appropriate to the young. A useful index of motifs appears at the end.

(Ed.) THESPIS: Ritual, Myth and Drama in the Ancient Near East. 2nd rev. ed. 1961. *Gordian* 1975 $15.00. Lively, imaginative, but controversial in the field.

Grayson, A. Kirk, and Donald B. Redford, Eds. PAPYRUS AND TABLET. *Prentice-Hall* 1973 Spectrum pap. $2.45. A varied collection of fresh translations.

Kramer, Samuel Noah. HISTORY BEGINS AT SUMER: Twenty-Seven Firsts in Man's Recorded History. *Doubleday* Anchor Bks. 1959 pap. $2.50

Lambert, W. G. BABYLONIAN WISDOM LITERATURE. *Oxford* 1960 $20.50. Although specifically limited to wisdom literature, the volume offers translations of many texts.

Luckenbill, D. D. ANCIENT RECORDS OF ASSYRIA AND BABYLONIA. 2 vols. 1926–1927. *Greenwood* 1969 $37.00. Though half a century old, these volumes are still useful as a basic introduction to Assyro-Babylonian historical writing. The translations are seriously in need of modernization in accordance with the progress of Assyriological research. The volume by J. B. Pritchard, listed below, contains some more recent translations of the Assyrian materials.

Pritchard, James B., Ed. ANCIENT NEAR EASTERN TEXTS RELATING TO THE OLD TESTAMENT. *Princeton Univ. Press* 1950 2nd ed. 1955 3rd ed. 1969 $37.50

Although the intent of the volume is to provide texts bearing upon the Old Testament, the contents represent most of the major works of ancient Near Eastern civilization. It is a collection of translations by major scholars, ranges widely into all periods, and covers all of the principal genres and many of the lesser. It is the best all-round collection in English, and absolutely indispensable for the reader who wants to encounter the originals in a scholarly, yet readable form. The paperback abridgement of this work ("The Ancient Near East," Vol. 2 *Princeton Univ. Press* 1973 pap. $3.95) is disappointing because of its many omissions.

Simpson, William K., Ed. THE LITERATURE OF ANCIENT EGYPT: An Anthology of Stories, Instructions and Poetry. *Yale Univ. Press* 1973 $15.00 pap. $3.95. Modern translations by foremost Egyptologists.

Some Individual Texts

In addition to James B. Pritchard's collection, "Ancient Near Eastern Texts," the reader should consult appreciations and criticisms of regional ancient Near Eastern literature cited above. In this section only easily procurable translations and studies of a few well-known individual works will be noted.

ATRA-HASIS: The Babylonian Story of the Flood. Trans. and ed. by W. G. Lambert and A. R. Millard. (And "The Sumerian Flood Story," trans. by M. Civil) *Oxford* 1969 $13.00

"Ever since the original decipherment of fragments of Babylonian literature some 90 years ago, wide interest has been taken in the flood story, which is related in some way to the Hebrew account in Genesis. Hitherto the only complete Babylonian version has been a digest incorporated in the 'Gilgamesh Epic.' Over the past five years large portions of the full Babylonian account have come to light in which the hero is called Atra-Hasis. This book offers the first edition and translation of the new material, along with improved forms of the 'Sumerian Flood' story (by M. Civil) and the other Babylonian fragments."

THE BABYLONIAN GENESIS. Trans. by A. Heidel. *Univ. of Chicago Press* 2nd ed. 1951 Phoenix pap. $2.45

"A careful . . . translation and interpretation of the 'Enuma-Elish' [Babylonian Creation Story] and related texts. The book also contains a long chapter on the Old Testament parallels found in the Akkadian [Assyro-Babylonian] 'creation' texts, which is quite detailed and informative. . . ."

THE BOOK OF THE DEAD: The Papyrus of Ani in the British Museum, The Egyptian Text with Interlinear Transliteration and Translation, a Running Translation, Introduction, Etc. Trans. and ed. by E. A. Wallis Budge. 1895. *Dover* 1967 $4.95. Although three quarters of a century old, and technically improved upon by philological research since its date of publication, Budge's book remains an accessible introduction to the burial ritual texts of the Middle Kingdom Egyptians and their successors.

THE EPIC OF GILGAMESH. Trans. by N. K. Sandars. *Penguin* 1960 pap. $1.25. A prose version which may serve as an introduction, but which is aesthetically less satisfying than the translation into poetry in Pritchard's "Ancient Near Eastern Texts," cited above under Collections.

THE GILGAMESH EPIC AND OLD TESTAMENT PARALLELS. Ed. by A. Heidel. *Univ. of Chicago Press* 1946 $7.50 Phoenix pap. $3.75

"Chapters 1 and 2 of the book contain translations, fully annotated, of the Gilgamesh Epic, the Sumerian version of the deluge from Nippur, the Atrahasis Epic, Berossus' account of the deluge, the story of Ishtar's descent to the underworld, the myth about Nergal and Ereshkigal, and an Assyrian prince's vision of the underworld." More recent and scientific translations of the "Enuma Elish" appear in Pritchard's "Ancient Near Eastern Texts," cited above under "Collections," but Heidel's works evoke wide-ranging insights into the enigmatic connections between Mesopotamian and Hebrew ideas.

—L. L. O.

ARABIC LITERATURE

Arabic is the major living Semitic language. As the language of Muhammad the Prophet (d. 632) (*q.v.*) and of Islam, it was carried by conquest and spread by civilization over a vast area stretching from Morocco and Spain in the west through India to Indonesia in the east. Today it is the primary language of the Arabs in Arabia, of the inhabitants of the North African countries, and of Egypt, Jordan, Syria, Iraq, and Lebanon. It has also been the language of religious education wherever Islam prevailed—Turkey, Iran, Afghanistan, Pakistan, parts of India, and Indonesia.

There is a marked divergence between the "classical" language of literature and the spoken language of the people. The classical language of the past, due largely to the influence of the *Qur'ān* (*q.v.*), and the present-day standard literary Arabic exhibit a marked uniformity regardless of locale; the vernacular dialects, however, differ greatly from place to place. The written language, therefore, has been and is a unifying element in the Arab world and in Islamic civilization.

Under the term "Arabic literature" orientalist scholars include all the corpus of Arabic writing. For this brief account, however, notice can be taken only of belles-lettres, with some attention to the *Qur'ān* and a few of the sciences, because Arabic literature by any count of authors and titles is virtually unparalled in extent.

The study of Arabic literature is usually divided into broad periods corresponding to political chronology as follows: (1) the pre-Islamic, or *Jāhilīyah* era (to A.D. 622); (2) the time of Muhammad and his successors (622–661); (3) the Umayyad period (661–750); (4) the 'Abbāsid period (750–1055), and the time of 'Abbāsid decline or Turkish hegemony in Baghdad (1055–1258); (5) the Mamluk era (1258–1800); and (6) the modern age (1800–   ). As a rule, literature has flourished when and where political power and wealth have combined.

The pre-Islamic era of *Jāhilīyah* (to A.D. 622) is important in Arabic literary history. *Jāhilīyah* means "ignorance" and refers to the state of the Arabs before the revelation came to Muhammad. While the earliest known Arabic literature was rhymed prose (*saj'*) used by sorcerers, it is poetry that characterizes the *Jāhilīyah* era. Poets occupied an important place in Arabian tribal society for they served as recorders of glorious deeds, revilers of enemy tribes, and inspirers in battle. The great literary form was the *qaṣīdah*, which corresponds roughly to the ode.

The *qaṣīdah* is a poem of varying length (often over 100 lines) with a single rhyme, and using one of several meters. The *qaṣīdah's* historical development is unknown; it seems to have suddenly appeared in its perfected form to establish itself in the sixth century as the preeminent Arab verse form, setting the standards for subsequent poets.

Each *qaṣīdah* has an invariable sequence of three sections: (1) the *nasīb*, in which the poet expresses his emotions upon finding the traces of a deserted encampment, usually of his or his lover's tribe; (2) the body of the poem, which usually is filled with acute descriptions of the poet's travels, or of his mount, the terrain, or a hunt; and (3) the conclusion, in which the poet praises himself, his tribe, or a benefactor—or reviles his enemies.

The themes of the *Jāhilīyah qaṣīdah* were limited. It is in the use of language within the restrictions of form and technique that the poets excelled. Great poets came from both the desert and the settled areas along the Syrian and Persian borders. To a large degree, these *qaṣīdah* poets created a commonly held, high standard of literary language that down through time has created one of the bases of Arab nationalism. Their poetry is also important as a source of information on pre-Islamic life.

Among the "desert" poets one can mention al-Shanfarā al-Azdī, who was famed for persistence in revenge and for his poem entitled "*Lāmīyat al-'Arab*" (because the rhyming consonant is the *lām*). Another, interestingly the son of a black Ethiopian woman, was the valorous 'Antara ibn Shaddād who has become the legendary center of a romance cycle ("*Qiṣṣat 'Antara*") of continuing popularity among Arab readers.

Among the "court" poets of settled areas, the engaging "vagabond king" Imru' al-Qays ibn Hujr (d. c. 540) is often regarded as the best of poets. Not only pagan, but also Jewish and Christian Arab poets gained fame in the deserts of Arabia. The Jew al-Samaw'al ibn 'Ādiyā, whose loyalty became an Arab proverb, and the Christian 'Adī ibn Zayd (d. 604?), whose drinking songs earned him a lasting reputation, are the best known. Women, too, swelled the ranks of poets and were especially apt in composing elegies. The most famous was al-Khansā, whose odes on the deaths of her brothers are among the most stirring examples of Arabic expression.

Certain of the greatest *qaṣīdahs* are called *mu'allaqah* (the suspended), perhaps because they were exhibited at an annual poetic competition. The plural term *mu'allaqāt* is applied to a famous collection of the masterpieces of seven poets—or, sometimes, ten poets.

Besides the ode, other verse forms flourished in the *Jāhilīyah*. Much of this poetry survived via oral transmission and was collected in anthologies such as the two that were titled "*Dīwān al-Hamāsah*" by Abū Tammām and by al-Buhturī in the tenth century. A vast quantity of early poetry is also found in the 21 volumes of the "*Kitāb al-Aghānī*" ("Book of Songs") by al-Iṣfahānī (d. 967).

The possibilities in two or three centuries of oral transmission by the *rāwis* for error or corruption have led a few modern critics to doubt the genuineness of much pre-Islamic poetry. Nevertheless, most critics still accept as genuine the poems ascribed to the great poets of the sixth century.

The Age of Ignorance ended for the Arabs with the revelation of the *Qur'ān* to the prophet Muḥammad. The *Qur'ān*, which literally means the "recitation," embodies the eternal word of God in a language and style that profoundly affected Arabic literature to the present day.

The revelations are in rhymed prose. The earlier, or Meccan, revelations preach the imminence of Judgment Day and the awesome power of God by words of truly inspiring poetic beauty; the latter, or Medinan, revelations by and large are prosaic statements on the needs of the Islamic community.

The Prophet died in 632. Twenty years later the revelations were collected from the minds of men and then edited and arranged in 114 chapters in order of decreasing length.

The style of the *Qur'ān* is unique and almost inimitable, and translations have never conveyed the qualities that distinguish it and endear it to the Arabic speaker. It has been of incalculable influence, and studies necessary for its comprehension have helped create various branches of Arabic science, such as philology, law, and theology. As the Book of Islam, it was the instrument by which Arabic became an international language of civilization.

The forms of pre-Islamic poetry were continued throughout the era of Muḥammad and his four successors, called the *Rāshidūn* (rightly guided) Caliphs, by a number of poets of no great merit. However, the new Islamic morality drastically changed what was regarded as acceptable. Certain types of poetry were suppressed, such as the wine song; others, such as the *fakhrīyāt* (praising one's tribe) or the *rithā'īyāt* (elegies) were directed to serve Islam. Ḥassan ibn Thābit became the Prophet's panegyrist; but Ka'b ibn Zuhayr's panegyric, known as the *"Bānat Su'ād,"* is still highly regarded among pious Muslims. Most of the verse of this first Islamic period is below the technical and aesthetic levels of *Jāhilīyah* poetry.

After the death of Muḥammad, affairs of state and military expansion were led by a succession of four elected Caliphs until in 750 the secular Umayyad dynasty was established in Damascus. The Umayyads carried on the old Arab spirit and generally were heedless of Islam.

Poetry flourished under the Umayyads, especially in 'Iraq, to which many of the Arabian tribes had emigrated in the first years of Arab conquest. The *qaṣīdah* maintained its position as the vehicle of elegant expression par excellence, and several poets revived and carried on the good old traditions of *Jāhilīyah* poetry. The Christian al-Akhtal (d. 710/11) is equal in skill to the *Jāhilīyah* poets and, with his contemporaries al-Farazdaq (d. 732/3) and Jarīr ibn 'Aṭiyah (d. 732/3) engaged in a famous poetic competition of *hijā'* (sarcastic satire) the results of which, regarded as the best of Umayyad era verse, are recorded in the book *"al-Naqā'id."*

The *qaṣīdah* was not the only form. During the Umayyad era the luxurious living conditions, especially in Mecca and Medinah, favored the development of the love poem, or *ghazal*, which allowed a more direct and simpler expression of feeling than the *qaṣīdah*. An older Syrian or Persian tradition may have influenced the *ghazal*. The most accomplished composer of these love songs for voice was 'Umar ibn Abī Rabī'ah (d. 720?). The deeds of two other love poets are legendary: Jamīl is celebrated for the purity of his passion for Buthaynah, and Majnūn provides the classic example of a man driven mad (*majnūn*) by unconsummated love for Laylā. The story of Laylā and Majnūn provided inspiration for a number of later Persian and Turkish poets.

The Umayyad period gave rise to philological studies, for with changing social conditions (from nomadism to settled life) it was necessary to collect and study the literary remains of the *Jāhilīyah* era. Thus there are collections of historical traditions (*akhbār*) dealing mainly with the feuds of the tribes; proverbs (*amthāl*) in which the Arab people are rich; and anthologies (*dīwāns*) of individual poets or of a tribe's poets. Certain collections of poetry were arranged by topic or theme. This activity of collecting and classifying continued for centuries.

The assumption of power by the 'Abbāsid dynasty in 750 both reflected and accelerated tendencies changing the Arab Empire into an Islamic empire in which non-Arab peoples, especially those representing the Hellenistic tradition, were to become the dominant creative force. Virtually all the arts and sciences known to man flourished to an extent hitherto unequalled, and the 'Abbāsid era may justly be termed the "golden era" of Arabic literature in its broadest sense.

Prodigious efforts were applied to the religious sciences of Islam such as *Qur'ān* interpretation, and to jurisprudence and theology. In support of these, advances were made in philology. The natural sciences stemmed from a well-organized activity of translating from Greek sources, and soon Muslim savants were making original contributions in all areas.

The "Arabs" thus preserved much of Greek science and philosophy that eventually found its way to Europe. This survey, however, must leave aside those areas and confine its attention to literature in the narrower sense.

The *qaṣīdah* continued to be written even though the conditions of life from which it developed had long since vanished. Ibn al-Walīd al-Ansārī (d. 823/4) wrote traditional *qaṣīdahs*, along with panegyrics and love poems. But the new Arab literature was the literature of the court and of highly developed city life, not the desert camp. The virtues of the desert were replaced by an interest in all the vices of luxurious society, and this new spirit found expression in a number of stylistic embellishments.

The greatest early example of the new spirit in Arabic poetry is provided by Abū Nuwās (d. 810?). While his work is not a true example of the new style, he forsook the formal *qaṣīdah* and composed in all the other verse forms, especially drinking songs (*khamrīyāt*) and the *ghazal*, showing generally irreverent and immoral preferences in choice of theme and language.

In contrast to Abū Nuwās and the "licentious" poets of the new style, there stands the poet Abū al-ʿAtāhīyah (748–820) who in direct and simple language contrasting with the complex embellishments favored by most Arabic writers dealt with religious and philosophical matters in a spirit of melancholy or despair, urging the good life against the coming of Judgment Day.

As the ʿAbbāsid caliphs lost direct control over outlying areas of the empire, Arabic literature received an impetus from new centers of wealth and patronage. Foremost among these principalities was the Hamdanid dynasty of Aleppo and Mawsil, especially with patronage from the amir Ṣayf al-Dawlah. The poet al-Mutanabbī (915/6–965) was the leading literary light in Ṣayf al-Dawlah's entourage. Some regard him as the greatest Arabic poet. Along with him we must cite the Hamdanid prince-poet Abū Firās al-Hamdānī (d. 967/8).

Abū al-ʿAlā al-Maʿarrī (d. 1057/8) stands to one side of the mainstream of ʿAbbāsid society both as an individual and as a poet. In an early collection of poems, the "*Saqt al-Zand*," he imitated al-Mutanabbī. But this blind poet bravely put forth his own criticism of contemporary social conditions and general human frailities in a remarkable collection of later poems under the title "*Luzūm Mā Lam Yalzam*." While the content is profound, the form exhibits complicated literary devices that detract from the modern reader's enjoyment.

Another aspect of ʿAbbāsid poetry is seen in the work of ʿUmar ibn al-Fāriḍ. This poet devoted his live to mysticism, and his poems are allegories treating the union of man and God. His greatest poem, the "*Nazm al-Sulūk*," describes his spiritual progress towards God.

Arabic prose literature developed for the first time under the ʿAbbāsids from the stimulus of translations from Persian, Syriac, and Greek texts. Ibn al-Muqaffaʿ (d. 758/9), who was born a Persian, translated from the Pahlavi language the work known in Arabic as "*Kalīlah wa-Dimnah*" in a language of exemplary clarity. A century later, al-Jāḥiẓ (d. 868/9) gained fame as the most versatile of prose writers in Arabic. Aside from erudite contributions to philological and legal studies, al-Jāḥiẓ poured into his numerous prose works an immense store of both useful and otiose information. His seven-volume masterpiece, the "*Kitāb al-Ḥayawān*" ("Book of Animals"), is usually seen as the first great example of what is called an *adab* work—one in which the information necessary for the general education of a gentleman of culture is put forward in a kind of encyclopedic anthology of prose and poetry with interpretive commentary. It is one of the distinctive and most popular types of classical Arabic literature.

Adab literature was further developed by Ibn Qutaybah (d. 889/90), a man of widely diverse interests and publications, in his *"Adab al-Kātib"* ("Culture of the Scribe"), his *"Kitāb al-Ma'ārif"* ("Book of Knowledge"), and most notably in his *" 'Uyūn al-Akhbār"* ("Sources of Information"). A more organized and encyclopedic treatment of *adab* topics is found in the *" 'Iqd al-Farīd"* ("Unique String of Pearls") by Ibn 'Abd Rabbih (d. 939/40), a native of Cordoba.

Within Arabic prose literature, the form known as the *maqāmah* (assembly, station, or situation) occupies a unique place in the application of *adab* to a narrative. The *maqāmah* (pl. *maqāmāt*) was seemingly created and brought to perfection by Badī' al-Zamān al-Hamadhānī (969–1008), a Persian who is one of the most famous Arabic prose stylists. In al-Hamadhānī's *"Maqāmāt,"* a wily intelligent rogue travels around tricking people. Each episode is one *maqāmah*, and these are strung together in a narrative of rhymed prose by a friend of the rogue who is a good, honest person. The *maqāmah* form reached its greatest stylistic development at the hands of al-Ḥarīrī (d. 1121/2). A vast storehouse of *adab* is applied by al-Ḥarīrī to each of the 50 "situations" in which the picaresque rogue, Abū Zayd, pulls off a trick to deceive or get money from people, while the good bourgeois Arab narrator, Ḥārith, offers ineffective remonstrance. The work of al-Ḥarīrī was very popular, as is shown by the number of extant manuscripts. His *"Maqāmāt"* quickly became the most illustrated of texts; these illustrations are only now becoming recognized as an important source for interpreting social conditions in the twelfth-century Arab world.

Yet another area of artistic prose is chancellery documents. In these writings (*Inshā'*) the most ornate style was utilized. The letters (*"Rasā'il"*) of Ibn Hilāl al-Ṣābī (d. 994/5) led the move to an "official" style which reached its peak in the embellished epistles of al-Qāḍī al-Fāḍil (d. 1199/1200), secretary to Saladdin. Examples of official prose are preserved in textbooks, of which a fine specimen is Ḍiyā al-Dīn Ibn al-Athīr's *"al-Mathal al-Sā'ir."*

In addition to written literature, the Arabic language is rich in verbal expression. The early romances from pre-Islamic times were put into writing during the 'Abbāsid era. The fact that the Arab gift for story-telling is appreciated in the Western world is due entirely to translations of the "Arabian Nights," known in Arabic as *"Alf Laylah wa-Laylah"* ("One Thousand Nights and One"). Actually, Arab critics do not regard the "Nights" as literature. The "Nights" consist, at least partially, of stories derived from India and Persia that, after centuries of reworking, finally were set down in writing in the era of the Bahrī Mamluks of thirteenth- and fourteenth-century Cairo. The most recent research indicates that the translations into Western languages are *not* based on authenticated texts.

The western reaches of the Islamic Empire comprised what is now Algeria, Morocco, Sicily, and Spain. The political history of this area, the Maghrib, is of no concern here, except to note that it was independent of the eastern rulers. Just as the Umayyads of Cordoba (756–1071) provided liberal patronage to authors, so too were the small principalities that decorated the political landscape avid in their support of culture.

Poetry among the Spanish Arabs saw not only a continuation of transferred classical Arabian modes of expression and the later style of the 'Abbāsid court, but interesting new forms of stanzaic poems appeared, due most likely to the influence of native Romance poetry in Andalusia. The *muwashshaḥah* (girdled) became a favorite form. It consists of stanzas of four to six strophes allowing various rhyme schemes. Love was the usual theme. The most famous composer of *muwashshaḥah* was the blind poet of Toledo, al-Ṭūtilī (d. 1126).

The popular idiom was utilized in another of the strophic forms, namely the *zajal* (melody). These remained mostly in the realm of oral literature, but their highest literary development was attained by the Cordoban troubadour, Ibn al-Quzmān (d. 1160).

All educated men—and literacy was common in Muslim Spain due to state-supported education—were expected to be competent poets. No exception was the statesman Ibn

Zaydūn (d. 1071/2) of Cordoba who, after fleeing to Seville, addressed eloquent love poems to the princess Wallādah. Even the most acerbic proponent of the narrowest, most fundamentalist theology in Islam, namely Ibn Hazm (994–1064), produced a collection of love poems. His "*Ṭawq al-Ḥamāmah*" ("Dove's Neckband") is one of the few works in Arabic to gain appreciation in the West.

In 1258 the Mongols sacked Baghdad and destroyed the centers of Arabic learning in Iraq and Iran, starting the period of several centuries of "decadence" in Arabic literature. Henceforth, Persian literature would dominate the Iranian areas of Islam. Only Syria, Egypt, and the western lands of Islam remained to Arabic civilization; but due to changed economic conditions and complicated spiritual factors, it is superficially apparent that the vital flame of Arabic civilization was dampened, or one can argue that Islamic civilization had reached its ultimate stage of self-fulfillment and had no need of further innovation. This period of what is fashionable to call "decline" is usefully labeled the "Age of the Mamluks" because Cairo under those slave (*mamlūk*) dynasties became the principal Arab city.

In terms of quantity, a great many titles in Arabic were written in this period of decline. New titles are continually being discovered, and until systematic research has progressed further, only tentative conclusions are in order. In the Arabic linguistic sciences and in the Islamic sciences, the tendency was toward encyclopedic summations of branches of learning, or toward commentaries or glosses on particular works of earlier authors. Exemplary among encyclopedias is the "*Miftāḥ al-Saʿādah*" of the Turkish polygraph Tāshköprüzādah (d. 1560/1), while another Turk, Ḥājjī Khalīfah (also known as Kātib Çelebī, d. 1657/8), produced the most complete survey of Arabic literature in his systematic "*Kashf al-Zunūn fī Asāmī al-Kutub wa-al-Funūn.*"

Work in the natural sciences virtually stopped. History, on the contrary, was vigorously pursued. No summary of the era can avoid mentioning that unique individual, the Tunisian Ibn Khaldūn (1332–1406) who, during an adventurous public life, wrote the "*al-ʿIbar . . . ,*" whose introduction (*al-Muqaddimah*) set forth his systematic theory of historical development that gained him the recent appellation "founder of sociology."

The qualitative decline of Arabic poetry is signaled by the work of Ṣafī al-Dīn al-Ḥillī (d. 1349/50) who was the court poet at Mardin in Anatolia. He is criticized today because of excessive use of various artifices and lack of spontaneity—judgments that may reflect more the tastes of Western orientalists than of his contemporary Arab critics. Other notable poets of the fourteenth century, both from Spain, were Ibn al-Wardī and Ibn Nubātah.

Ibn ʿArabshāh (d. 1450/1) was a prominent prose stylist and is known for his "*Fākihat al-Khulafāʾ* " ("Fruit of the Caliphs"); and the genre of chancellery writings is best represented by the "*Ṣubḥ al-Aʿshā*" of al-Qalqashandī (d. 1418), which also contains valuable historical information.

The history of Arabic literature prior to its modern renaissance traditionally closes with the conquest of Egypt by the Ottoman Turks in 1517. After that date the channeling of Arab wealth to Istanbul and the alteration of world trade patterns effectively destroyed the economic support needed for a flourishing literature.

Modern Arabic literature has its origins in political and social changes resulting from the impact of Western ideas upon the Arab world. This impact began early in the nineteenth century and continues today. These developments were most important in Syria (which included Lebanon) and Egypt. In Syria the active agents were at first Protestant and Catholic missionaries whose schools trained generations of westernized Arabs, primarily Christians. In Egypt, after the startling invasion by Napoleon in 1798 that marked a new era in East-West confrontation, it was the educational reforms introduced by the ruler Muḥammad ʿAlī and the consequent translations of European texts that provided the base for the nineteenth-century revival, or renaissance.

In both Syria and Egypt two tendencies in thought and in literature were apparent in the nineteenth century. There was a modernism that emulated Western models, and there was a return to classical Arabic forms. The two tendencies had to do not only with the type of literary expression, i.e., the prevalent European forms of the novel, short-story, drama, and verse against the traditional forms of *qaṣīdah* and *maqāmah*, but more especially with the movement away from classical Arabic language towards a new language capable of expressing new ideas. It is partly true that the history of modern Arabic literature is the history of changes in the written language. The conflict between the "old" and the "new" continues: poets of traditional Islamic and Arabic education are still following the old poetic forms, observing the rules of rhyme, meter, and end consonant, while the avant-garde apply the latest European or American techniques.

In Syria, the Christian Nāṣif al-Yāzijī (1800–1871) through a number of works employing traditional themes sought to restore the primacy of classical Arabic. But Syrian leadership in the nineteenth century was due not only to the revival of classical Arabic, but also to an appreciation of the values of Western literature and a deprecation of the Islamic past. In Beirut Buṭrus al-Bustānī (1819–1883), who produced an innovative dictionary and a vast encyclopedia, is typical of a number of prose writers whose use of a simple style in a wide range of publications helped bring about the literary revival.

The Syrians led also in the all-important rise of journalism that was a formative factor in the later emergence of the short story or short novel as the preferred type of narrative prose. After 1860 Ottoman oppression caused a large-scale emigration of the educated classes from Syria and Lebanon. Many went to Egypt and continued their journalistic and literary careers. A notable transplant was Ya 'qūb Ṣarrūf (1852–1927) and his important journal *al-Muqtaṭaf*. Thousands went to the New World where, under radically different social conditions, a distinct Syro-American school of Arabic literature sprang up for a few decades of glory.

Egypt, after the first two decades of the twentieth century, has been the home of new trends in literature. This is due in some measure to the influx of educated and talented Syrians; also, Egypt enjoyed a time of relative prosperity and some measure of freedom under the British occupation. There was also a growing, literate middle class. But most scholars point to the writings of the religious reformer Muḥammad 'Abduh (1849–1905) that created the intellectual system within which Islam and social progress could combine. 'Abduh's writings, along with those of various nationalist leaders, especially Muṣṭafā Kāmil (1874–1908) in his journal *al-Liwā*, and Qāsim Amīn (1865–1908), assisted the emergence of a simplified prose style able to convey new ideas in an appropriate vocabulary. The essays of Muṣṭafā Luṭfī al-Manfalūṭī (1876–1924) stand out in two regards: first, they are the most complete expression of the European and Egyptian intellectual currents that flooded Egypt; and second, their use of classical language in a manner that handled new thoughts with clarity marked the progression of the language towards a new flexibility.

By 1930 an "Egyptian School" was emerging that combined the Muslim and the Arabic heritages with national feeling. Muḥammad Ḥusayn Haykal (1888–1956) by numerous essays and articles led this school's efforts to assist the growth of both a new prose and nationalism. He is also the creator (in 1914) of *"Zaynab,"* a story about an Egyptian peasant girl that is the earliest imaginative prose work in Arabic that combines the necessary ingredients of the Western novel.

Ṭāhā Ḥusayn (1889–1973) is the Egyptian author best known in the West. In addition to his long and controversial career, the blind, Sorbonne-educated professor of literature is famous for his autobiographical *"al-Ayyām"* ("The Days"), the subject and style of which influenced the development of the Egyptian novel.

The short story is the most popular form of literary expression in many Arab countries. The most respected figure in its history is the Egyptian Maḥmūd Taymūr (1894–) because of his great output over several decades and his high literary ability. Leading writers today are Yūsuf Idrīs (1927–   ), Najīb Maḥfūẓ (1911–   ), and Iḥsān ʿAbd al-Qaddūs (1919–   ). Both novel and short story share a perplexing problem, namely how best to render dialogue. Because the spoken language differs from region to region, conversation in an ʿIrāqī novel might not be readily intelligible to Egyptian readers, and the gradual development of "modern standard Arabic" has not completely solved this problem.

Drama has not been part of the history of classical Arabic literature. In Egypt, however, there has been a variety of vulgar or folk theatrical forms—perhaps with roots in Pharonic times. The shadow play was well developed, and a few texts have survived from the thirteenth century.

Modern Arabic drama had its inception in 1848 when Mārūn al-Naqqāsh (1817–1855) staged a play in Beirut modeled on Molière's *"l'Avare"* (*q.v.*). The roots of modern drama in Egypt were placed by Ya ʿqūb Ṣanūʿ (1839–1912), who wrote and staged plays that, although European in structure, drew upon folk theater. Apart from Ṣanūʿ''s efforts, much of the drama produced in Egypt up to World War I was of the musical comedy variety in which the singing was more important than the drama.

Serious theater has been vigorously pursued in Egypt since World War II, and the role of television in stimulating the most recent theater can not be overemphasized. Tawfīq al-Ḥakīm (1898–   ) is perhaps the most significant dramatist. In his long literary career during which he has written over 70 plays, much experimentation and development can be traced. Social and political issues increasingly occupy serious Egyptian dramatists. Yūsuf Idrīs is currently the most popular playwright. There still is controversy over the extent to which Arabic dramatists should follow European models; but in the question of language, the use of colloquial speech when required by the situation is fully accepted.

Modern Arabic poetry has developed out of the same social and political changes as prose literature. Chronologically, poetry has lagged behind—perhaps because of the weight of the legacy of classical verse. Maḥmūd Sāmī al-Bārūdī (1839–1904) is credited with the earliest efforts to revive classical Arabic poetry and thus is called the founder of the "neo-classical" school which, simply stated, retained old poetic techniques, used a purer language, but treated new themes and ideas. The ʿIrāqī al-Jawāhirī (1900–   ) is a prominent member of the neo-classical tradition.

Among the Syrians who moved to Egypt, Khalīl Maṭrān (1872–1949) led a new movement in Arabic poetry in which the influence of the French Romanticists dominates. Maṭrān's main contribution was the successful use of forms and techniques beyond those of the neo-classicists. These changes were adopted and extended most notably by the Egyptians Abū Shādī (1892–1955), ʿAbd al-Raḥmān Shukrī (1886–1958), ʿAbbās al-ʿAqqād (1889–1964), and Ibrāhīm al-Māzinī (1889–1949). Abū Shādī and Shukrī, obviously influenced by the English Romantics, emphasized the emotional approach of the poet to his theme over the formal rules of prosody.

The New World also contributed, briefly but strongly, to the modernizing tendency through the *Mahjar* (emigrant) school of Syrians who settled mainly in New York and São Paulo. Affected by Western education and a freer social environment, those in America responded to Transcendentalism and to Whitman. One Syro-American, Gibrān Khalīl Gibrān (1883–1931), has reached a new crest of popularity in the last decade; another, Amīn al-Rīhānī (1876–1940), introduced the prose poem into Arabic literature. Ilīyā Abū Mādī (1889–1957) is probably the best of *Mahjar* poets.

The present trends in Arabic poetry arose after World War II. To some extent, the anti-Western sentiment that prevailed as a consequence of the Palestine disaster led to a conscious discarding of Western themes. Romanticism is all but gone; and the younger poets, beginning with the Lebanese, have turned increasingly to "free verse" to convey their concern with social issues. The move to free verse is attributed to the poems and essays of Luwīs ʿAwaḍ (1915–   ) and associated with the highly regarded ʿIrāqī poetess Nāzik al-Malāʾikah (1923–   ). The poets of the Resistance (i.e., against Israel) have especially favored free verse. The influence of T. S. Eliot and his "Wasteland" (*q.v.*) on contemporary poets is axiomatic. Current practitioners of the art have dropped all the technical restraints of prosody and express themselves in prose poetry. Tawfīg al-Sāyigh (1923–1971) led the way in many of these innovations.

Abdel, Wahab, Farouk. MODERN EGYPTIAN DRAMA: An Anthology. Studies in Middle Eastern Literatures *Bibliotheca Islamica* 1974 $12.50. The author has provided a good 40-page introduction to the subject; translations follow from The Sultan's Dilemma by Tawfiq al-Hakim, The New Arrival by Mikhail Roman, A Journey Outside the Wall by Rashad Rushdi, and The Farfoors by Yusuf Idris.

Altoma, Salih J. MODERN ARABIC LITERATURE: A Bibliography of Articles, Books, Dissertations and Translations in English. Occasional Papers *Asian Studies Research Institute* (Goodbody Hall 101, Indiana University, Bloomington, Indiana 47401) 1975 $4.00. This useful bibliography lists 850 items. There are no annotations, but the work is essential as a starting point for researchers.

ARAB AUTHORS SERIES. *Heinemann* (London) (direct inquiries to the British Bk. Centre)

    A series of English translations of Arabic authors. Four volumes have appeared to date: Midaq Alley by Najib Mahfuz, Season of Migration to the North by Tayyib Salih, Fate of a Cockroach by Tawfiq al-Hakim, and Modern Arabic Short Stories trans. and ed. by Denys Johnson-Davies (*see main entry below*).

    Forthcoming volumes (late 1976) are: Death of the Morning by Tawfiq Yusuf Awwad, Modern Egyptian Short Stories trans. and ed. by Denys Johnson-Davies, Anthology of Modern Arabic Verse trans. and ed. by Issa J. Boulatta, and The Man Who Lost His Shadow by Fathi Ghanim.

BIRDS THROUGH A CEILING OF ALABASTER: Three Abbasid Poets—Arab Poetry of the Abbasid Period. Trans. with introd. by G. B. H. Wightman and A. Y. al-Udhari. Classics Ser. *Penguin* 1975 pap. $1.95. This has a brief but interesting introduction on Arabic poetry and the difficulties of translating it. The translators deliberately use present-day English in an attempt to convey the tone of poems by Ibn al-Ahnaf, Ibn al-Mu'tazz, and al-Ma'arri. For popular, nonscholarly reading.

Gibb, H. A. R. ARABIC LITERATURE: An Introduction. *Oxford* 1926 1974 pap. $2.50. H. A. R. Gibb was perhaps the outstanding English Arabist of the twentieth century, and this book, although dated in some respects, remains the best account in small compass of Arabic literature from pre-Islamic times through the 'Abbāsid era. Modern literature is not included.

Goldziher, Ignace. A SHORT HISTORY OF CLASSICAL ARABIC LITERATURE. Trans., rev., and enl. by Joseph Desomogyi. *Georg Olms* (Dammstr. 50, Hildesheim, Germany) 1966. Goldziher (1850–1921) was one of the greatest figures in European Islamic studies. This book is recommended because it is the best brief account in English of the whole body of medieval Arabic literature and scholarship.

Hamori, Andras. ON THE ART OF MEDIEVAL ARABIC LITERATURE. Princeton Essays in Literature *Princeton Univ. Press* 1974 $10.00. The author applies modern literary criticism to three main subjects. He starts by tracing the changes that occurred in poetic genres from pre-Islamic times through the tenth century; in the second section he analyzes the techniques used to provide coherence in poetry; and in the third he examines the structure of two tales from the "Arabian Nights." The sections on poetry are innovative and should be useful to advanced students of Arabic.

Haywood, John A. MODERN ARABIC LITERATURE 1800–1970: An Introduction, with Extracts in Translation. 1971. *St. Martin* 1973 $10.95

Johnson-Davies, Denys. MODERN ARABIC SHORT STORIES. *Oxford* 1967 $7.25. Includes 20 short stories.

JOURNAL OF ARABIC LITERATURE. E. J. Brill (Oude Rijn 33a, Leiden, Netherlands) Vol. 1– 1970– . This is the most important scholarly journal for modern and classical Arabic literature. Translations are included.

Khouri, Mounah A., and Hamid Algar. AN ANTHOLOGY OF MODERN ARABIC POETRY. *Univ. of California Press* 1974 $12.00. This work contains a short but excellent introduction on the development of modern poetry. Selections (text and translation) from poets are carefully arranged in chronological order. Short biographical sketches are given. This work is essential for tracing, understanding, and appreciating modern poetry.

Khouri, Mounah A. POETRY AND THE MAKING OF MODERN EGYPT, 1882–1922. *E. J. Brill* (Oude Rijn 33a, Leiden, Netherlands). Studies in Arabic Literature: Supplements to the *Journal of Arabic Literature*, Vol. 1. 1971. The author has made an interesting, scholarly, and successful effort to use poetry as a source of social and political information. The work is valuable because of its wealth of information on poets and poetry.

Kilpatrick, Hilary. THE MODERN EGYPTIAN NOVEL: A Study in Social Criticism. *Ithaca Press* (12 Southwark St., London SE1 1RQ, England) 1974. The author studies and traces specific topics in Egyptian prose from Haykal's *"Zaynab"* up to 1968. The book can serve as a reference work for biographical and bibliographical information.

Le Gassick, Trevor J. "Literature in Translation: Modern Arabic." Middle East Studies Association *Bulletin*, Vol. 5, No. 1, Feb. 1, 1971 pp. 26–38. A good, brief account of the history, trends, and problems of translating modern Arabic fiction by one of the best of translators.

Maḥfūẓ, Najīb. GOD'S WORLD: An Anthology of Short Stories. Trans. with introd. by Akef Abadir and Roger Allen. Studies in Middle Eastern Literatures *Bibliotheca Islamica* 1973 pap. $6.75. Translations of 20 stories by one of the leading Egyptian authors. For information about the author, see: "The Changing Rhythm: A Study of Najib Mahfuz's Novels" by Sasson Somekh. *E. J. Brill* (Oude Rijn 33a, Leiden, Netherlands) Studies in Arabic Literature, No. 2, 1973. This is a thorough study by an Israeli student of modern Arabic literature. The work also contains a fine account of the development of the modern Arabic novel.

Manzalaoui, Mahmoud, Ed. ARABIC WRITING TODAY: The Short Story. *Univ. of California Press* 1970 $8.50. First issued in 1968 by the American Research Center in Cairo, this work contains translations of representative stories from 30 authors.

Monroe, James T. HISPANO-ARABIC POETRY: A Student Anthology. *Univ. of California Press* 1975 $20.00

al-Muwaylihī, Muhammad. A STUDY OF HADĪTH 'ĪSĀ IBN HISHĀM, MUHAMMAD AL-MUWAYLIHĪ'S VIEW OF EGYPTIAN SOCIETY DURING THE BRITISH OCCUPATION. Trans. and introd. by Roger M. A. Allen. *State Univ. of New York Press* 1974 $42.00 (microfiche ed.)

The translator presents this work as an accurate description of nineteenth-century Egyptian society during the dynamic period of modernization and westernization. He places the work within the traditions of Arabic literature, and points out its role as the first modern Arabic novel. Allen adds a biography of the author, and provides evidence from Cairo newspapers to check the authenticity of Muhammad al-Muwaylihī's description of Egyptian life and institutions.

Nicholson, R. A. A LITERARY HISTORY OF THE ARABS. *Cambridge* 1907 new ed. 1969 $17.50 pap. $5.75. This is the standard in-depth English-language work on classical Arabic belles-lettres up to the fall of Baghdad in 1258. It contains a wealth of information not found in the smaller surveys.

—D. H. P.

ARMENIAN LITERATURE

Armenian literature is one of the most distinctive of all the literatures of the Middle East. Beginning as the independent expression of a nation newly converted to Christianity, it flourishes today in such different environments as the Soviet Union, the Middle East, and the United States.

A native script was invented by the monk Mashtots c. 400; by making the liturgy, the Bible (*q.v.*) and other ecclesiastical texts available in the vernacular, he put a seal on the missionary work begun by St. Gregory the Illuminator a century before. An original literature developed surprisingly rapidly. Young men in Mashtots' circle were sent to Syria, Asia Minor, and Constantinople in order to study Greek and Syriac and to translate the works of major Christian writers into Armenian. Some of these same men in their maturer years produced original compositions, primarily in the fields of history, philosophy, and theology. Ecclesiastical interests tended to dominate classical Armenian literature, and unfortunately only a few fragments of the earlier oral pagan poetry have survived. Nor has any of the written pre-Christian literature, composed in Greek, been preserved.

By the late sixth century, Armenian scholarly interests had spread to secular themes, especially to the grammatical, rhetorical, and philosophical studies pursued in the schools of Constantinople. Many Armenians went there to study despite the schism between the Greek and Armenian churches that became irrevocable after the mid-sixth century. Scientific learning had its greatest exponent in the seventh century Ananias of Shirak, who wrote on many subjects including mathematics, astronomy, and geography.

The principal branches of classical Armenian literature, however, were history, theology, and poetry. Although some Armenian historical works are more in the style of chronicles, the major works show sophistication and finesse. Agathangelos, who describes the conversion of King Tiridates a century or so after the event, is in the tradition of the literary hagiographer. But Elishē, who describes the conflict between Christian Armenia and Zoroastrian Persia in the fifth century, is a master of the classical tradition; his complex narrative is enlivened with speeches and letters reflecting the historian's view of what would have been appropriate to the occasion as he describes the interplay of patriotism and opportunism, of Christian principles and pagan impiety. Moses Khorenatsi (variously ascribed to the fifth or eighth centuries) paints a larger canvas. He traces the history of his people from the days of Noah's descendants to the time of Mashtots. His prime interest is to elucidate (sometimes in fanciful ways) the origins and pedigrees of the various noble families, and in so doing he has preserved snatches of ancient epic songs that were still being sung in his own day in remoter parts of Armenia. The tradition of Armenian historiography flourished right down to the seventeenth century. The "History" of Arakel of Tabriz, for example, is valuable for its description of the Persian-Ottoman conflict, and is also noteworthy as the first Armenian historical work to be printed (in Amsterdam, 1669), though Armenian printing dates back to 1512.

But such works, and also the extensive religious poetic literature (notably by the tenth-century Gregory of Narek and the twelfth-century Nerses Shnorhali) were written in the classical tongue, not the vernacular of the common man. Of more popular secular interest were the collections of fables, and the songs and poems of the lyric bards. The most famous of the latter is Sayat-Nova (1712–1795). Born in Tiflis, he sang and wrote in Georgian and Azeri as well as Armenian. Mention must also be made of the oral folk-epic commonly known as "David of Sassoun" which was popular in the Armenian countryside but not recorded in writing until late in the nineteenth century. The epic consists of four cycles in rhythmic prose, each telling of the exploits of a succeeding generation of legendary heroes from the wild region of Sassoun, southwest of Lake Van, who defend their homeland from foreign tyrants. "David" is the hero of the third generation and has become, especially in Soviet Armenia, a symbol of patriotic valor.

It is a significant result of the dispersion of the Armenian people over many centuries that literature in the modern tongue developed outside the native homeland—in Constantinople, the political and cultural center for Armenians of the Ottoman empire, and in Tiflis, the equivalent for Armenians of the Caucasus. Despite the great efforts of the Mekhitarists (a religious order founded by Mekhitar in 1701 that was devoted to education and scholarship) to raise the level of Armenian culture, they could not touch the masses, for they used the classical tongue in their translations of Western books, ancient and modern, into Armenian. Not only was the old language incomprehensible to the public, but new political and nationalistic ideas of secular origin were penetrating to Armenians in the Ottoman and Russian empires. The task of nineteenth-century writers was thus twofold: to fashion a literary medium out of the dialectical vernaculars that were heavily overladen with Turkish and Persian, and to give literary expression to ideas of freedom and patriotism and to disseminate them among their fellow Armenians. Here, especially in Constantinople, the newly burgeoning press played a major role.

Modern Armenian literature thus reflects concerns that found little echo in the classical writers; the novel, satiric and realistic prose stories, the theater, and lyric poetry of secular inspiration are the forms typical of modern writing through which national aspirations were expressed.

In Western Armenian, that is the literary Armenian of Constantinople, the following are the most typical of a large galaxy of writers. In the development of mid-nineteenth century theater, which extolled the glories and heroes of the Armenian past—with the only too obvious comparison of contemporary servitude—the lead was taken by Mgrdich Beshiktashlian (1828–1868). The comic theater is represented by the satirist Hagop Baronian (1843–1891). Among the romantic novelists, Joseph Shishmanian (who used the pen-name Dzerents) is outstanding (1822–1888); while in the medium of the short story Arpiar Arpiarian (1852–1908) is famous for his sketches of Constantinople life, and Grigor Zohrab (1861–1915) for the vigor of his ironic attacks on decadent morality. In poetry Bedros Turian (1851–1872) is the greatest lyric exponent of love for his people and anguish at their present sufferings; he is known as the "nightingale of Uskudar." His sentiments were echoed by Daniel Varuzhan and Siamanto (pen-name for Atom Yarjanian), both of whom were killed in the massacres of 1915.

The founder of Eastern Armenian literature is Khachatur Abovian (1809–1848), renowned for his romantic novel "Wounds of Armenia" (o.p.) which describes the tragic situation of his homeland. A similar patriotic spirit inspired the poetry of Gamar-Katiba (pen name for Raphael Patkanian, 1830–1892). The most famous playwright in Eastern Armenian was Gabriel Sundukian (1825–1912), who drew penetrating sketches of Armenian life in Tiflis. In prose the most influential writer was Raffi (pen name for Hakob Melik-Hakobian, 1835–1888); his historical novels stress the theme of Armenian independence. Also noteworthy are the novels and plays descriptive of Armenian life at the turn of the century by Shirvanzadé (pen name for Alexander Movsessian, 1858–1925) and the prose works of Avetis Aharonian (1866–1947). Aharonian played an important role in the short-lived Armenian republic (1918–1920), and his novels reflect the terrible sufferings of the Armenians in the preceding years.

The most outstanding poets in Eastern Armenian are Hovhannes Toumanian (1869–1923)—perhaps best known for his tragic narrative love poem "Anush," (o.p. in separate ed.) based on village life in his native Lori, which was later set as an opera—and Avetik Issahakian (1875–1957), lyric poet of love and humanity.

The list of translations that follows is necessarily misleading, for few of the major Armenian writers have been rendered into English. More is available in French, though often only in books long out of print. Only in Russian is there a representative sampling of Armenian works in translation.

The only complete survey of Armenian literature is that by V. Inglisian in "*Handbuch der Orientalistik*," Erste Abteilung, Siebenter Band, "*Armenisch und Kaukasische Sprachen*," Leiden/Köln, *E. J. Brill*, 1963, pp. 156–250. This book also contains a valuable survey of Georgian literature by G. Deeters, pp. 129–155. Very sketchy is the chapter on Armenian and Georgian Literature by D. M. Lang in "A Guide to Eastern Literatures," edited by David Marshall Lang, (1971, o.p.). Brief surveys of the classical literature may be found in S. Der Nersessian, "The Armenians" (Volume 68 of "Ancient Peoples and Places," General Editor: Glyn Daniel, 1970, o.p.); C. J. F. Dowsett, "Armenian Historiography" in "Historians of the Middle East," edited by Bernard Lewis and P. M. Holt (1962, o.p.); and Karekin Sarkissian, "A Brief Introduction to Armenian Christian Literature," *Faith Press*, 1960 reprinted 1974 (order from British Bk. Centre). For modern Western Armenian literature see James Etmekjian, "The French Influence on the Western Armenian Renaissance, 1843–1915," (1964, o.p.).

Collections

Boyajian, Zabelle C., Comp and ill. ARMENIAN LEGENDS AND POEMS. *Columbia* 1916; reissued by the *Armenian General Benevolent Union* 1958 o.p. This volume includes selections of early legends in prose and a wide range of translations in verse of medieval and modern poetry, some being traditional folk songs, others by known authors. Pages 125–191 contain a valuable essay on Armenian epics, folk songs, and medieval poetry by Aram Raffi (son of the famous novelist).

Hoogasian-Villa, Suzie, Comp. and ed. ONE HUNDRED ARMENIAN TALES AND THEIR FOLKLORISTIC SIGNIFICANCE. *Wayne State Univ. Press* 1966 $9.95. A valuable collection of folktales as told by Armenian immigrants to the United States.

KORIUN.   c. 450.

Koriun was one of the many pupils of the monk and scholar Mashtots, who invented the Armenian alphabet c. 400. The biography listed below is one of the earliest compositions in Armenian. Norehad's translation is based on the modern Armenian translation by Manuk Abeghian, published in Erevan in 1941.

THE LIFE OF MASHTOTS. Trans. by Bedros Norehad. *Armenian General Benevolent Union* (628 Second Ave., New York, N.Y. 10016) 1964 $3.00 pap. $2.00.

AGATHANGELOS.   late fifth century.

Agathangelos is the pseudonym of the unknown historian who gave final form to the story of the conversion of Armenia and the work of St. Gregory the Illuminator. "The Teaching of Saint Gregory" is the longest part of his "History." It is in the form of a sermon supposedly preached by St. Gregory the Illuminator over a period of 60 days to King Tiridates before his conversion.

THE TEACHING OF SAINT GREGORY. An Early Armenian Catechism. Trans. with commentary by Robert W. Thomson. *Harvard Univ. Press* 1970 $8.00

YEGHISHEH (ELISHĒ).   late fifth or sixth century.

Elishē's history tells of the unsuccessful revolt by the Armenians in the fifth century against Zoroastrian Iran. It is the classic exposition of the Armenian attitude toward religion and patriotism.

THE HISTORY OF VARTANANK. Trans. into English by Dickran H. Boyajian; trans. into modern Western Armenian by Hovhannes Zovickian. *The Delphic Press* (New York) Published by the Knights of Vartan Inc. on the occasion of the 1500th anniversary of the battle of Avarair 1952 2nd ed. 1975 (order from the National Association for Armenian Studies and Research, 175 Mt. Auburn St., Cambridge, Mass. 02138)

MOVSES DASXURANÇI.   early tenth century.

The history of Movses is a valuable source for the history of the Caucasus from the fourth to the tenth centuries. But Movses does not compare as a literary artist with Elishē (see above).

MOVSES DASXURANÇI. The History of the Caucasian Albanians. Trans. by C. J. F. Dowsett. 1961 o.p.

DAVID OF SASSOUN.   late medieval period.

The deeds of David of Sassoun were repeated orally in the Armenian countryside, but not written down until the late nineteenth century. (For additional details, see the introductory essay above.)

DAVID OF SASSOUN: The Armenian Folk Epic in Four Cycles. Trans. and ed. by Artin K. Shalian. *Ohio Univ. Press* 1964 $12.00. A translation of the Armenian edition, Erevan 1939. This is a synthetic edition put together from more than 50 variant versions in different dialects.

DAREDEVILS OF SASSOUN: The Armenian National Epic. By Leon Surmelian. *Swallow Press* 1966 $5.00. This is a retelling of the epic compiled from the dialectical variants in the author's own fashion, a more individual rendering than that of Shalian.

DAVID OF SASSOUN: Armenian Folk Epic. Trans. by Aram Tolegian. *Twayne* (order from the National Association for Armenian Studies and Research, 175 Mt. Auburn St., Cambridge, Mass. 02138) 1961. This is a translation of the Armenian text by the poet Hovhannes Toumanian and covers the third cycle only (the cycle of which David is the hero).

TOUMANIAN, HOVHANNES. 1869–1923.

THE BARD OF LOREE: Selected Works of Hovhannes Toumanian. Trans. and comp. by Mischa Kudian. *Mashtots Press* (order from Armenian General Benevolent Union, 628 Second Ave., New York, N.Y. 10016) 1970 $4.00

HOVHANNES TOUMANIAN: A Selection of Stories, Lyrics and Epic Poems. Trans. by Dorian Rottenberg and Brian Bean. *T and T Publishers* (order from the National Association for Armenian Studies and Research, 175 Mt. Auburn St., Cambridge, Mass. 02138) 1971 $5.95

TOTOVENTS, VAHAN. 1889–1937.

Totovents' most famous work is his "Scenes from an Armenian Childhood," reminiscences of his earliest years in the Anatolian province of Harput. The original Armenian (published in 1930) was entitled "Life on the Old Roman Road." His "Tell Me, Bella" is a collection of stories of Armenian life in the first quarter of this century.

SCENES FROM AN ARMENIAN CHILDHOOD. Trans. by Mischa Kudian. 1962 o.p.

TELL ME, BELLA. Trans. and comp. by Mischa Kudian. *Mastots Press* (order from Armenian General Benevolent Union, 628 Second Ave., New York, N.Y. 10016) 1972 $5.50. The selection was made by the translator.

—R. W. T.

HEBREW LITERATURE

Background reading in Jewish history and cultural development is requisite and illuminating for understanding both the conditions which gave rise to modern Hebrew literature and the thematic content of the literature. Prepared under the auspices of UNESCO, "Jewish Society through the Ages" ed. by H. H. Ben-Sasson and S. Ettinger (*Schocken* 1975 $12.50 pap. $3.95) contains essays on a variety of topics concerning Jewish life from ancient to modern times. There is also Cecil Roth's social, cultural, and religious history in "A History of the Jews" (*Schocken* 1975 pap. $3.95), and the highly valuable collection of essays by leading scholars of Jewish history, literature, and philosophy is again available in the 4th edition of the 3-volume "The Jews" ed. by Louis Finkelstein (*Schocken* 1975 pap. Vol. 1 $4.95 Vol. 2. $4.50 Vol. 3 $5.95). The Israel Pocket Library series of 16 volumes edited by G. Wigoder (1975 *Keter* pap. 14 vols. $2.50 ea., 2 vols. $1.95 ea.) is a guide to many aspects of Israel and the Jewish people, from archeology to religious values to Zionism. The tragic experience of European Jews from 1933 to 1945 is one of the major themes in modern Hebrew literature; it is also one of the sources for the spiritual struggles encountered by Israeli writers both of the generation that witnessed and experienced the horror and those who came after it. Two works by Lucy S. Dawidowicz "The War against the Jews, 1933–1945" (*Holt* 1975 $15.00) and "A Holocaust Reader" (*Behrman* 1975 $12.50 pap. $4.95), and Nora Levin's "The Holocaust: The Destruction of European Jewry, 1933–1945" (*Schocken* 1975 pap. $6.95) are carefully researched studies of the events. Primary source materials which shed light on twentieth-century Jewish history may be found in "Modern Jewish History: A Source Reader" ed. by Robert Chazan and Marc Lee Raphael (*Schocken* 1975 $20.00 pap. $7.95).

For reading in the history of Zionism one may consult the reprint of "The Zionist Idea" ed. by Arthur Hertzberg (*Jewish Publication Society*, 1975 $18.50 pap. $2.95). Aryeh Rubinstein's "The Return to Zion" (*Leon Amiel* 1975 $3.95) is a brief history of Jewish settlement in Israel. A study of the position of the land of Israel and religion in the thinking of Jews by an American rabbi and scholar is presented "Jews, Judaism and the State of Israel" by Ben Zion Bokser (*Herzl* 1975 $6.95). Two works helpful in summarizing the political life, including ideology and institutional or bureaucratic functions, of the State of Israel are "Israel: Its Politics and Philosophy" ed. by Israel T. Naamani and others (*Behrman* 1975 pap. $4.95) and "State and Society in Israel" ed. by Daniel J. Elazar (*Behrman* 1976). A major problem which penetrates much contemporary literary work in Israel is discussed in "The Rift in Israel: Religious Authority and Secular Democracy" by Leslie S. Clement (*Schocken* 1975 $7.50).

Recent works on the political and military dilemma of Arab-Israeli relations include: Isaia Friedman's "The Question of Palestine 1914–1918: British-Jewish-Arab Relations" (*Schocken* 1975 $12.00); Frank Gervasi's "Thunder over the Mediterranean" (*McKay* 1975 $8.95); Yehoshefat Harkabi's "Palestinians and Israel" (*Halsted* 1975 $9.95); Netanel Lorch's "The Jewish-Arab War 1920–1974" (*Keter* 1976); John N. Moore, Ed., "The Arab-Israeli Conflict" (*Princeton Univ.* 1975 3 vol. set $95.00 pap. Vol. 1 abr. $12.50); James Parkes' "Whose Land? A History of the Peoples of Palestine" (*Peter Smith* 1975 $4.00); and "The Yom Kippur War" (*Doubleday* 1975 $10.00). On kibbutz life see Y. Criden's and S. Gelb's "The Kibbutz Experience" (*Herzl* 1975 $7.95) which is based on a taped dialogue between the two authors, Americans, who settled on a kibbutz in Israel. L. Tiger's and J. Shepher's "Women in the Kibbutz" (*Harcourt* 1975 $10.00) uses sociometric apparatus to investigate one of the early frontiers in the liberation of women in Israel.

The intellectual and religious movements in modern Jewish life that provide the framework within which writers of Hebrew literature grope with the spiritual, cultural, and psychological challenges that are their heritage may be summarily examined in two works by Jacob B. Agus: "The Evolution of Jewish Thought" (*Arno* 1975 $22.00), and "Modern Philosophies of Judaism" (*Behrman* 1975 pap. $3.25). Also helpful are Gershon Greenberg's "Modern Jewish Philosophies" (*Behrman* 1976), and David Rudavsky's "Modern Jewish Religious Movements" (*Behrman* 1975 $6.95 pap. $3.95).

For a history of the Hebrew language and the Hebrew book see, respectively, William Chomsky's "Hebrew; The Eternal Language" (*Jewish Publication Society* 1975 pap. $3.95) and R. Posner's and I. Ta-Shema's "The Hebrew Book: An Historical Survey" (*Keter* 1975 $30.00). "A History of Jewish Literature" ed. and trans. by B. Martin (*Ktav* 1975 Vols. 1–5 each $15.00. Vols. 6–9 each $17.50) was written originally in Yiddish by Israel Zinberg (1873–1939). It is a monumental work which traces the development of Jewish literature from tenth-century Spain to nineteenth-century Russia. It deals with major Jewish writers of poetry, fiction, and drama, as well as contributors to other fields such as philosophy, history, the Bible, religious law, folklore, and legend. Simon Halkin's "Modern Hebrew Literature: From the Enlightenment to the Birth of Israel" (*Schocken* 1975 $6.00 pap. $2.95), originally published in 1950, is an excellent guide to trends and values in Hebrew literature during the first 50 years of our century. "Escape into Siege" by Leon I. Yudkin (*Routledge & Kegan Paul* 1975 $11.75) is a survey of contemporary Israeli literature. Josephine Z. Knopp's "The Contemporary Jewish Novel: Judaism on Trial" (*Univ. of Illinois Press* 1975 $7.95) deals with how modern writers are concerned with ancient beliefs in describing modern life.

"Bibliography of Modern Hebrew Literature in English Translation" comp. by Yohai Goell in 1968 is again available (*Keter* 1975 $8.95). This is a comprehensive listing of 7,500 items that have been translated from Hebrew into English, including general anthologies, poetry, prose and drama, essays, criticism, and children's literature. It is an excellent reference work, containing indexes of authors and translators, and a list of periodicals. Unfortunately, it has not been updated since 1968. (Books published by *Keter*

Publishing House, Jerusalem, are available in the U.S. from Keter, Inc., 440 Park Avenue South, New York, N.Y. 10016.)

Since there are more books of interest than we have room for in the main author entries, a number of literary works are included in the following general list.

Alter, Robert, Ed. MODERN HEBREW LITERATURE. *Behrman* 1975 $12.50 pap. $4.95. An anthology of short stories of contemporary writers, including M. Z. Feierberg, H. N. Bialik, J. H. Brenner, A. Barash, H. Hazaz, S. Y. Agnon, S. Yizhar, A. B. Yehoshua, Y. Amichai, and A. Oz. Professor Alter provides an introduction, together with critical and explanatory comments on the works included.

Baron, Dvora. THE THORNY PATH AND OTHER STORIES. Trans. by Joseph Schacter. *Keter* 1975 $5.00. Dvora Baron was a winner of the Bialik Prize (1934) and other awards for her literary work. Her stories are based upon Jewish life in Eastern Europe and her own experiences while exiled in Egypt during World War I (many Jews who had come to Palestine were in Egyptian exile during the war).

Bartov, Hanoch. WHOSE ARE YOU, SON? *Holt* 1971 $6.95. A recent work by the author whose novel "The Brigade" (1965, o.p.) won the Shlonsky Prize in 1965.

Ben Zion, Raphael, Trans. ANTHOLOGY OF JEWISH MYSTICISM. *Yesod* 1975 $5.00

Berechiah ben Natronai Ha-Nakdan. FABLES OF A JEWISH AESOP. Trans. by Moses Hadas. *Columbia* 1967 1975 $12.50. Called "Ha-Nakdan" because he punctuated many manuscripts, this copyist, translator, grammarian, and writer of fables lived in the thirteenth century, in France and England. He translated fables of Aesop mostly from a French collection titled *"Ysopet"* that had been written down by Marie de France (c. 1170), from a lost Latin translation of *"Romulus,"* and from other collections of the medieval East. In his preface, Berechiah mentions the low moral state of Jews in England in his day.

Bin-Gorion, Emanuel, Ed. MIMEKOR ISRAEL: Classical Jewish Folktales. Trans. by I. M. Lask. *Indiana Univ. Press* 3 vols. 1975 set $42.50. Over a thousand tales.

Blocker, Joel, Ed. ISRAELI STORIES: A Selection of the Best Contemporary Hebrew Writing. Introd. by Robert Alter. *Schocken* 1975 $6.00 pap. $2.45. Nine stories by S. Y. Agnon, H. Hazaz, A. Megged, Y. Kaniuk, B. Tammuz, S. Yizhar, M. Shamir, and Y. Amichai.

Braude, William G., and Israel J. Kapstein, Trans. PESIKTA DE-RAB KAHANA. *Jewish Publication Society* 1975 $15.00. Midrash, rabbinic discourse to extract and explicate the underlying significance of the Bible, was composed in Palestinian schools during the first five centuries of our era.

Brenner, Yosef Haim. BREAKDOWN AND BEREAVEMENT. Trans. by Hillel Halkin. *Jewish Publication Society* 1975 $7.50. This is the last novel by Brenner (1881–1921). It tells the story of Hefez, who searches for a spiritual homeland in Palestine. The setting is an agricultural settlement prior to World War I, where many of Brenner's uprooted generation attempted to create a new life from themselves, having left their European ties behind.

Burnshaw, Stanley, and others, Eds. THE MODERN HEBREW POEM ITSELF: From the Beginnings to the Present, 69 Poems in a New Presentation. *Schocken* 1975 pap. $5.95. This anthology contains transliterated Hebrew poems and their English translations together with commentaries.

Dan, Joseph, Ed. JEWISH HASIDIC THOUGHT. *Behrman* 1976 pap. $3.95. An anthology of the doctrinal and anecdotal sources of the mystic movement of the eighteenth century. Presents spiritual and social values of Hasidism, inherent in Hasidic notions of God, man, the world and the *tzaddik* (holy man).

Davis, Eli. WHO HEALETH ALL THY DISEASES. *Rubin Mass* 1975. Dr. Davis was a founder of the physician's organization of Hadassah and the medical center in Jerusalem. His novel is a love story set against the background of the lives of physicians and their patients from 1949 to 1955. Some of the problems concerning medical care in Israel are touched upon.

Dayan, Moshe. DIARY OF THE SINAI CAMPAIGN. Trans. by George Weidenfield. *Schocken* 1975 pap. $1.95. General Dayan commanded the Israeli forces that swept through the Sinai desert in 1956 and 1967, and has served as Minister of Defense for the State of Israel.

Eisenberg, Azriel, and Leah Ain-Globe. HOME AT LAST. *Bloch* 1975 $6.95. An anthology of stories about some immigrants to Israel.

Feierberg, Mordecai Zeev. WHITHER? AND OTHER STORIES. Trans. with introd. by Hillel Halkin. *Jewish Publication Society* 1975 $4.95. Relates the story of the struggles of Eastern European Jewish youths who are disappointed with the Enlightenment, yet not content with being traditional Jews. Feierberg (1874–1899) had firsthand knowledge of such youths.

Glatstein, Jacob, and others, Eds. AN ANTHOLOGY OF HOLOCAUST LITERATURE. *Jewish Publication Society* 1975 $10.00 pap. $4.95. A collection of articles by people who were either victims or eyewitnesses of the tragedy during World War II.

Glatzer, Nahum N., Ed. A JEWISH READER. Trans. by Olga Marx and others. *Schocken* 1975 pap. $2.95. Formerly titled "In Time and Eternity," this source book contains items of prayer, theology, philosophy, folklore, law, and mysticism.

Goitein, S. D., Ed. FROM THE LAND OF SHEBA: Tales of the Jews of Yemen. *Schocken* 1975 $7.50. Published originally in German in the 1930s, this volume contains folktales and proverbs of the Jews of Yemen, one of the oldest Jewish communities in the world. The tales portray the ethical and religious traditions of generations of Jews whose attitudes and values were greatly shaped by Oriental traditions and life styles.

(Ed.) JEWS AND ARABS: Their Contacts through the Ages. *Schocken* 1975 $10.00 pap. $2.95. Explores social and intellectual relations between Jews and Arabs living under Islamic hegemony, particularly as the relations affected the development of Jewish philosophy, law, literature, and ritual. Professor Goitein's scholarly presentation lends historical perspective to contemporary views of Jews and Arabs.

Goldin, Judah, Trans. THE FATHERS ACCORDING TO RABBI NATHAN. *Schocken* 1975 pap. $4.95. Rabbi Nathan Ha-Bavli lived in the second century A.D., when the Mishnah was being compiled. "*Avot De-Rabbi Nathan*" is a commentary on an early form of the Mishnah, "*Avot*." It is devoted to aggadic subjects (not strictly legal matter in rabbinic literature).

Hertz, Joseph H., Trans. PIRKE ABOTH: Sayings of the Fathers. *Behrman* 1975 $2.95. Hebrew text and translation of one of the best-known portions of the Mishnah, compiled around 200 A.D.

Ibn Daud, Abraham. SEFER HA-QABBALAH: Book of Tradition. Ed. with introd. by Gershon D. Cohen. *Jewish Publication Society* 1975 $8.50. Abraham ibn Daud (c. 1110–1180) wrote this work to uphold the rabbinic tradition against those who denied the legitimacy of rabbinic exegesis and the "oral law." The text, in Hebrew with English translation, traces the historical roots of Golden Age Andalusian Jews to the times of Alexander the Great in order to ground the Spanish tradition in early rabbinic origins dating from the time of the second Temple (destroyed in 70 A.D.).

Ibn Gabirol, Solomon. SOLOMON IBN GABIROL: Selected Religious Poems. Ed. with introd. by Israel Davidson. *Jewish Publication Society* 1975 pap. $3.95. Known among Europeans as the philosopher Avicebron, and as author of "The Fountain of Life," a Neo-Platonic work, Solomon ibn Gabirol (c. 1021–1053 or 1058) was better known among his Jewish contemporaries in Spain as a poet. His poetry included secular as well as religious themes. Indeed, as did many of his fellow Jewish poets at the time, Gabirol used the forms and material of Arabic poetics masterfully in his Hebrew poetry. Later generations of Jews particularly revered him for his religious sensitivity in those poems which bordered on mysticism and prayer.

Jacobs, Louis, Trans. and ed. THE CHAIN OF TRADITION SERIES. *Behrman* 1975 Vols. 1–3 each $3.95 Vol. 4 $4.50 Vol. 5 $4.95. Selections and commentaries on Jewish literary works from Mishnaic to modern times.

Kahn, Shalom J., Ed. A WHOLE LOAF: Stories from Israel. *Vanguard* 1975 $7.95. A collection of 15 stories.

Lamm, Norman. A HASIDISM READER. *Ktav* 1976 $12.50 pap. $4.95. A presentation of Hasidic works with an introduction to the history of this religious movement.

Leviant, Curt, Ed. KING ARTUS. *Ktav* 1975 $10.00. The Hebrew text and translation of the King Arthur tale as found in Hebrew literature, and a general study of the Arthurian motif in Hebrew literature.

(Ed.) MASTERPIECES OF HEBREW LITERATURE: A Treasury of Two Thousand Years of Jewish Creativity. *Ktav* 1975 pap. $5.95

Meir, Golda. A LAND OF OUR OWN: An Oral Autobiography. *Jewish Publication Society* 1975 $6.95

MY LIFE. *Putnam* 1975 $12.50. The former Prime Minister of Israel discusses aspects of her life, one integrally involved with the movement for the independence and well-being of Israel.

Memmi, Albert. JEWS AND ARABS. *J. Philip O'Hara* 1975 $7.95 pap. $4.95

Albert Memmi is both a Jew and an Arab. In former books he pleaded for justice for colonized Arabs; in this book he pleads for Jews and appeals for a dialogue between both peoples. The essays collected in this volume, written over a 20-year period, are particularly illuminating, since they have been written from the point of view of a Jew who grew up in Tunisia, and who therefore considers Zionism in a Middle Eastern perspective rather than the usual view of it as European in origin, Herzlian in scope, and post-Holocaust in realization.

Michener, James A. FIRSTFRUITS: A Harvest of New Israeli Writing. Fwd. by Chaim Potok. *Jewish Publication Society* 1975 $6.95. Fifteen tales representing the first 25 years of Israel's existence as a state, including stories by A. Barash, H. Hazaz, S. Y. Agnon, A. Oz, and A. Megged.

Nahmad, H. M., Trans. and ed. A PORTION IN PARADISE: And Other Jewish Folktales. *Schocken* 1975 pap. $2.95. Contains over 40 stories, legends, and folktales from biblical and secular sources and from all over the world.

Neugroschel, Joachim, Ed. YENNE VELT: The Great Works of Jewish Fantasy and Occult. *Stonehill* 1975 $25.00

Oren, Uri. LOVING STRANGERS. *Avon* 1975 pap. $1.50. Love story of an Israeli officer and an Arab woman.

Oz, Amos. ELSEWHERE PERHAPS. Trans. by Nicholas de Lange. *Bantam* 1975 $1.50. One of Israel's foremost novelists tells about human relationships on a kibbutz.

MY MICHAEL. Trans. by Nicholas de Lange. *Random* 1975 $6.95

TOUCH THE WATER, TOUCH THE WIND. Trans. by Nicholas de Lange. *Harcourt* 1975 $5.95. Novel about a husband and wife who leave Stalin's Russia for Israel and join a kibbutz.

UNTO DEATH: Two Novellas. Trans. by Nicholas de Lange. *Harcourt* 1975 $6.95

Penueli, S. Y., and A. Ukhmani, Eds. ANTHOLOGY OF MODERN HEBREW POETRY. Various trans. *Keter* 1975 2 vols. pap. set $10.00. A fine selection, made under the auspices of the Institute for the Translation of Hebrew Literature.

Reichert, Victor E., Trans. THE TAHKEMONI OF JUDAH AL-HARIZI. *Bloch* 1975 $14.95. Al-Harizi was a Golden Age Jewish poet in medieval Spain.

Shahar, David. THE PALACE OF SHATTERED VESSELS. Trans. by Dalya Bilu. *Houghton* 1975 $7.95. The story of the spiritual search of Gabriel Jonathan Luria (a descendant of the kabbalist, Rabbi Yitzhaq Luria). The setting for the story is the enchanting and unique world of the mystic in Jerusalem.

Shazar, Rachel Katznelson, Ed. THE PLOUGH WOMAN. Trans. by Maurice Samuel. *Herzl Press* 1975 $7.95 pap. $3.95. Rachel Shazar (1888–), leader of the working women's movement in Israel and wife of the third president of the State of Israel, is the editor of this collection of memoirs of young pioneer women in early twentieth-century agricultural settlements. The collection indicates the position of women in the early kibbutz movement and their social and cultural contributions to building a new Jewish society in Israel.

Vilnay, Zev. THE SACRED LAND. *Jewish Publication Society* 1975 Vol. 1 $6.95 Vol. 2 $7.50. These illustrated volumes contain tales about holy places, ancient fortresses, wildernesses, legendary waterplaces, cities and their inhabitants. The stories are drawn from the Bible, Talmud, Midrash, and writings of pilgrims of all religions. The first volume is concerned with legends of Jerusalem; the second volume with those of Judaea and Samaria.

Weizmann, Chaim. TRIAL AND ERROR: The Autobiography of Chaim Weizmann. Introd. by Abba Eban. *Schocken* 1975 $3.95. Chaim Weizmann (1874–1952) was the first president of the State of Israel and a leader of the Zionist movement.

Yizhar, S. MIDNIGHT CONVOY AND OTHER STORIES. Trans. by M. Arad and others. *Keter* 1975 $5.00. Yizhar, or Yizhar Smilansky (1916–), writes stories involving conflicts between the individual and society and the struggle for survival and peace.

Zim, Jacob, Ed. MY SHALOM, MY PEACE. Trans. by Dov Vardi. *McGraw-Hill* 1975 $9.95. Jewish and Arab children in Israel express their longing for peace in words and pictures.

See also Chapter 4, World Religions: Judaism, and Chapter 9, History, Government and Politics: Mid-East—Jewish History, Reader's Adviser, Vol. 3. In this Volume, see Chapter 15, Other European Literature: Yiddish Literature.

THE TALMUD. second–sixth centuries A.D. *See Chapter 4, World Religions: Judaism, Reader's Adviser, Vol. 3.*

HALEVI, JUDAH. c. 1075–1141.

Judah Halevi was born in Toledo, Spain, about 15 years before the Arab Almoravide penetration into southern Spain; about 50 years later the Almohades penetrated further north. Jewish communities in southern Spain had developed in a sophisticated manner while under Moslem rule (in contradistinction to northern, Christian Spain), and an aristocratic courtly life thrived among the politically and economically successful Jews. Golden Age poets were attached to courtiers and reflected the lifestyle and literary refinement that was so typical of Arab courts throughout the Islamic world. It is not surprising that Halevi received his education in southern Spain where the high culture of the Golden Age Jewish aristocracy flourished. Indeed, with the Christian Reconquest of Spain that brought tragic destruction to the Jewish communities, and brought an end to the Golden Age, Halevi shifted the thematic content of his work and charted a new genre in Hebrew poetry. In his philosophical work "The Kuzari" and in many of his religious poems Halevi urged a turning away from the secular roots of "high culture" as found in Aristotelianism, Neo-Platonism, and the polished refinement of love and wine poetry that was typical of Golden Age poems (and his own early poems). Instead he passionately pressed for renewed dedication to ardent hope in the return to Zion and the national revitalization of the Jewish people's ancestral relationship with God.

"The Kuzari" was originally written in Arabic, and translated into Hebrew in the twelfth century. It is largely an apologetic argument for Jewish ancestral beliefs and a rejection of the philosopher's rationalistic pursuits. The thrust of Halevi's critique of philosophy is directed to Jewish intellectuals of his time who seek to ground their religion in reasoned propositions; Halevi's objective is to assert the historicity of Judaism as a divinely revealed religion which cannot be reduced to the principles of philosophic discourse. The book is a rare item among medieval philosophical works in its anti-rationalist stance.

SELECTED POEMS. Trans. with introd. by Nina Salaman. 1923. *Arno* $22.50; *Gordon Press* $35.00; *Jewish Publication Society* 1975 pap. $3.95

THE KUZARI: An Argument for the Faith of Israel. Introd. by Henry Slonimsky. 1905. *Schocken* 1964 1975 pap. $3.45; *Shalom* $15.00

MAIMONIDES (Rabbi Moses ben Maimon). 1135–1204.   *See Chapter 4, World Religions: Judaism*, Reader's Adviser, *Vol. 3*.

HA-AM, AHAD (Asher Hirsch Ginzberg). 1856–1927.

One of the leading members of the Hibbat Zion movement in Russia, Ahad Ha-Am developed an idea of Zionism which was not rooted in completely political ideals. While he did agree with those who urged the establishment of a national Jewish homeland for the sake of obtaining the survival of many desperate Jews who suffered under the severity of Czarist Russia, Ahad Ha-Am placed more emphasis on the need to create a national consciousness by cultural preparation. "Cultural Zionism" developed around the idea of a Jewish state as the "spiritual center" for all Jews. After he settled in Palestine, Ahad Ha-Am continued to expound his ideas of cultural and spiritual revitalization, and many individuals of his generation and after him have been influenced by these ideas.

SELECTED ESSAYS OF AHAD HA-AM. 1962. Trans. and ed. with introd. by Leon Simon. *Jewish Publication Society* 1975 pap. $3.95

TEN ESSAYS ON ZIONISM AND JUDAISM. 1922. *Arno* $15.00

BIALIK, CHAIM NACHMAN (also Hayyim). 1873–1934.

Born of humble parentage in the Ukraine, Bialik went to Odessa in 1891, where he was a teacher and publisher. He was influenced by early Zionist ideas, particularly those of Ahad Ha-Am, and lived in various places in Europe, writing and teaching. By the time he settled in Tel Aviv, in 1924, his fame had become legendary. Bialik brought about a revolution in Hebrew poetry, avoiding European trends and drawing inspiration from early Hebrew literature. In prophetic, rhetorical poems of national revival, Bialik identified himself with the fate of his people and called upon Jews to express pride in their heritage and to resist the Russian pogroms. The crises of his generation were not his only themes, however; he wrote many lyrical poems of a personal character and songs of nature. He also wrote short stories, translated works of such authors as Cervantes, Shakespeare, Heine, and others into Hebrew, and he wrote a variety of essays on Hebrew literature, language, style, and culture. Israel's highest literary prize and an Israeli publishing house are named for him.

SELECTED POEMS. Ed. by I. Efros. *Bloch* 1965 $5.50

AND IT CAME TO PASS. Trans. by Herbert Danby. *Hebrew Publishing Co.* 1975 $4.00. A collection of retold legends and stories of kings David and Solomon.

Books about Bialik

H. N. Bialik: In the Paths of his Poetry. By Zusha Shapira. *Emesh* (Tel Aviv; not available in U.S.) 1974. A study of Bialik's poetry.

BUBER, MARTIN. 1878–1965.

Martin Buber was born in Vienna and educated at various European universities. His early interest in Zionism was one of culture and education. At the age of 25, he took up the study of Hasidism and began a long career of retelling many Hasidic stories in an adaptive form. He was a professor of Jewish religion and ethics at the University of Frankfort, and after settling in Palestine in 1938, he served as professor of social philosophy at the Hebrew University in Jerusalem. Buber has a world-wide reputation as a leading philosopher of the twentieth century.

THE WAY OF RESPONSE: Selections from the Writings of Martin Buber. Ed. by Nahum N. Glatzer. 1966 *Schocken* 1975 $6.50 pap. $2.95

POINTING THE WAY. Ed. by Maurice S. Friedman. *Schocken* 1975 pap. $2.95. A collection of essays.

TALES OF THE HASIDIM. 1947. 1948. *Schocken* 2 vols. Vol. 1 The Early Masters Vol. 2 The Later Masters 1975 each $7.50 pap. Vol. 1 $3.45 Vol. 2 $2.95

ISRAEL AND THE WORLD: Essays in a Time of Crises. 1948. *Schocken* 1975 pap. $2.45

ON ZION: The History of an Idea. 1952. Trans. by Stanley Godman. *Schocken* 1973 $7.00

THE LEGEND OF THE BAAL-SHEM. *Schocken* 1975 pap. $1.95. Twenty-five stories about the life of the Baal-Shem Tov, founder of the Hasidic movement. Buber's narration is based on Hasidic pamphlets, notebooks, and collections of folktales. He also presents an account of the ecstatic and mystic themes in Hasidism.

TEN RUNGS: Hasidic Sayings. *Schocken* 1975 pap. $1.75

Books about Buber

Martin Buber: Prophet of Religious Secularism. By Donald J. Moore. *Jewish Publication Society* 1975 $6.00. A Jesuit priest explores the religious thought of Martin Buber.

See also Chapter 4, World Religions, Section on Religious Leaders, Reader's Adviser, *Vol. 3.*

BEN GURION, DAVID.   1886–1973.

Statesman and minister of defense, David Ben Gurion began his early career as a political leader in the pioneer labor movement and struggle for Jewish independence. He was born in Russian Poland and was involved there with Zionist groups. In 1906 he settled in Palestine as an agricultural worker. Convinced of the importance of Jewish settlement in Palestine, he embarked on a series of preparatory steps which included the study of law in Turkey. He was one of those arrested by the Ottoman administration in Palestine, accused of spying, and sent into exile in Egypt. His contribution to the organization of the Histadrut labor union helped bring about Jewish involvement in agricultural and industrial occupations. His first coalition government of the State of Israel established patterns for future governments. He resigned from his position as prime minister in 1963.

ISRAEL: Years of Challenge. *Holt* 1963 $5.00

ISRAEL: A Personal History. 1971. *T. Y. Crowell* (Funk & Wagnalls) 1975 $20.00

BEN-GURION LOOKS AT THE BIBLE. Trans. by Jonathan Kolatch. *Jonathan David* 1972 $12.50

THE JEWS IN THEIR LAND. *Doubleday* 1974 $9.95

MY TALKS WITH ARAB LEADERS. *Keter* 1975 $12.00. An account, often verbatim, of secret talks between Ben Gurion and Arab leaders from 1933 through 1963.

DAVID BEN GURION: In His Own Words. *Fleet* 1968 $5.95

LETTERS TO PAULA. Trans. by Aubrey Hodes. *Univ. of Pittsburgh Press* 1972 $6.95

Books about Ben Gurion

Fighter of Goliaths: The Story of David Ben-Gurion. By Gertrude Samuels. *T. Y. Crowell* 1961 $5.50

David: The Story of Ben Gurion. By Maurice Edelman. *Putnam* 1965 $6.50

Ben Gurion State-Builder. By Avraham Avi-Hai. *Halstead Press* 1974 $12.50. Professor Avi-Hai traces Ben Gurion's rise to power, his role in building the State of Israel, his impact on defense and foreign policies, relations with the Arabs, and the conflict in his political party which led to his resignation.

BURLA, YEHUDA.   1887–1969.

Yehuda Burla was born in Jerusalem to a family that had lived in the city for three centuries. During World War I he served as an interpreter in the Turkish army. He was also the director of Hebrew schools in Damascus for five years, head of the Arab Department of the Histadrut, and Director of Arab Affairs in the Ministry of Minorities. As a writer, Burla was dedicated to depicting the lives of Middle Eastern Jews, the Sephardim. His works describe life among Jews in the Balkans and Arab lands.

IN DARKNESS STRIVING. 1968. Trans. by Joseph Schacter. *Keter* 1975 $4.50. This is the novel of a Jew, married and a father, living in Damascus, and involved with a young Moslem divorcee. Inner growth in the face of personal suffering is the scope of the book, as the reader sees the hero traveling through Arab villages selling his merchandise.

AGNON, SHMUEL YOSEF. 1888– (Nobel Prize 1966)

Born in Galicia (now part of Poland), into a home typically influenced by rabbinic and Hasidic traditions and the reviving spirit of European culture, Agnon began writing in Hebrew and Yiddish at the age of eight. He contributed poetry and prose to periodicals, such as *Ha-Mizpeh* and *Der Juedische Wecker*. After he left his hometown of Buczacz, he no longer wrote in Yiddish. He arrived in Palestine in 1907, and except for ten years spent in Germany, he remained in Israel. When, in 1914, he met Salman Schocken, then owner of a department store in Berlin, it was the start of both a lifelong friendship and a highly successful business venture, for Agnon convinced Schocken that someone should undertake the publishing of Hebrew books. Many years later four volumes of Agnon's collected works in Hebrew were published by the Berlin *Schocken Verlag* in 1931. Agnon was awarded the Bialik Prize for Literature in 1934, and in 1936 he was made an honorary Doctor of Hebrew Letters by the Jewish Theological Seminary of America. Other honors followed, culminating in the Nobel Prize.

Agnon often deals with philosophical and psychological problems in a miraculous or supernatural manner. Reality is colored in a dream-like atmosphere. Agnon is concerned with contemporary problems of a spiritual nature: the disintegration of traditional life, loss of faith and identity, and loneliness.

Almost medieval in style, his works evoke a former time, though they have universal appeal to the modern reader. Agnon himself has said: "I am not a modern writer. I am astounded that I have even one reader. I don't see the reader before me. . . . No, I see before me only the Hebrew letter saying 'write me thus and not thus.' I, to my regret, am like the wicked Balaam. It is written of him that 'the word that God putteth in my mouth, that shall I speak' "—(quoted in the *N.Y. Times*).

THE BRIDAL CANOPY. 1931. Trans. by I. M. Lask. *Schocken* 1975 $5.95 pap. $3.95. A novel set in nineteenth-century Galicia, the story of a poor and pious Hasid who seeks to provide his three eligible daughters with dowries so that they may marry and fulfill the commandment of being fruitful.

IN THE HEART OF THE SEAS. 1947. Trans. by I. M. Lask. *Schocken* 1975 $3.95. The story of the pilgrimage to Palestine of Polish Jews in the early nineteenth century.

DAYS OF AWE. 1948. Introd. by Judah Goldin. *Schocken* 1975 $7.50 pap. $2.95. A collection of traditions, legends, and learned commentaries pertaining to the Jewish High Holy Days.

TWO TALES: Betrothed; Edo and Enam. 1965. Trans. by Walter Lever. *Schocken* 1975 $4.95

A GUEST FOR THE NIGHT. 1968. Trans. by Misha Louvish. *Schocken* 1975 $6.95. Written after the author revisited his home town in Galicia. Agnon has the narrator describe the desolation time has wrought.

TWENTY-ONE STORIES. 1970. Ed. by Nahum N. Glatzer. *Schocken* 1975 $6.50 pap. $2.95

Books about Agnon

Nostalgia and Nightmare: A Study in the Fiction of S. Y. Agnon. By Arnold J. Band. 1968. *Univ. of California Press* 1974 $18.50. Includes list of works and bibliography.
The Fiction of S. Y. Agnon. By Baruch Hochman. *Cornell Univ. Press* 1970 $8.50
S. Y. Agnon. By Harold Fisch. Modern Literature Monographs *Ungar* 1975 $7.00. An overview and informative critique of some of Agnon's work.

HAZAZ, HAIM. 1898–

Born in Kiev, Russia, Haim Hazaz moved to Palestine in 1931. His early works are based on themes of village life among European Jews. However, he is not restricted in era or location; his fiction encompasses wide geographic, historical, and ethnographic variations.

GATES OF BRONZE. Trans. by S. Gershon Levi. *Jewish Publication Society* 1975 $7.95. A novel set in a fictional village in Russia, during the crisis faced by Jews who experienced the Bolshevik Revolution.

SHAMIR, MOSHE. 1921–

Born in Safed, Israel, Shamir is a writer of novels, plays, short stories, and contemporary comment. His writings reflect psychological and social problems among Israelis.

MY LIFE WITH ISHMAEL. 1970. Trans. by Rose Kirson. *International Scholarly Bk. Services* 1975 $9.50

WITH HIS OWN HANDS. 1970. Trans. by Joseph Schacter. *Keter* 1975 $5.00. The story of a youth coming of age in Israel who faces the harsh realities which are inevitable in a country at war.

AMICHAI, YEHUDA. 1924–

Yehuda Amichai was born in Germany and emigrated to Palestine in 1936. His novels and poetry are innovative in their use of Hebrew terms. During World War II and Israel's War of Independence in 1948 Amichai began to introduce new words of technical, legal and administrative meaning into his poetry to replace sacral phrases. His poetry reflects the modernizing of the Hebrew language within the last 40 years.

POEMS. Trans. by Assia Gutman. *Harper* 1969 $6.95

SONGS OF JERUSALEM AND MYSELF. 1973. Trans. by Harold Schimmel. *Harper* 1975 $5.95. The translator received the Jewish Book Council's Kovner Award for this book.

—N. F. P. and L. H. S.

PERSIAN LITERATURE

Persian, or *Farsi*, is a member of the Iranian branch of the Indo-European languages. From the time of Cyrus the Great (ruled 559–529 B.C.), who founded the Achaemenid dynasty, the Persians have had an effect on world political history by contesting with the Greeks, Romans, Byzantines, Arabs, and the Ottoman Turks for hegemony in the Middle East and, more importantly, have made brilliant contributions to world civilization in religion and the arts and sciences. Their attainments in lyric poetry, epic narrative, and mystical imagery are unsurpassed in world literature.

Persian literary history is usually divided into eras that correspond to major political epochs. These are the time of the Achaemenid dynasty (539–330 B.C.); the Sassanian dynasty (A.D. 225?–651); the 'Abbasid Caliphate (750–1258); the Mongol domination, including the Il-Khanid and Timurid periods (1258–1500); and the modern period from the commencement of the Safavids (1501) to the present day, with subdivisions for the nineteenth century, the Constitutional era, and the post-World War II period. The term "Persian literature" is usually restricted to the prose and poetry written after the Islamic conquest of Iran in the seventh century.

Little is known about Achaemenid literature. Its major monument is the impressive Behistun rock inscriptions in cuneiform of Darius the Great (ruled 521–485 B.C.) which record the deeds of that great king in Old Persian. In religious literature, the "*Avesta*" (*q.v.*) of Zoroastrianism was produced at an unknown date, perhaps around 1000 B.C., but only portions of the original texts have survived. These, too, are written in Old Persian.

After the destruction of the Achaemenids in 331 B.C. by Alexander the Great, a long time of troubles was followed by a glorious revival of Persian power and a renewed Zoroastrianism under the Sassanian dynasty. The language of this era is called *Pahlavi*, or "middle Persian," and it was written in a script derived from Aramaic. In *Pahlavi* there is a religious literature consisting of commentaries, called the "*Zand*," on the "*Avesta*"; and there is a secular literature that is of importance in Persian literary history, for in prose works such as the "*Yatkār-i Zarīrān*" (called often the "*Shāh-nāmah-i Gushtāsp*") and the "*Karnāmak-i Artakhshīr-i Pāpakān*" are found many of the legends that persist in later Persian literature.

The Arab conquest of Iran and the country's consequent Islamization caused profound changes in Persian language and literature. The new language, sometimes called *Dari*, is "modern Persian," and it has maintained an unusual uniformity for the past 1,000 years. Arabic script replaced the Pahlavi, countless borrowings of Arabic words occurred, especially for religious, scientific, and technical concepts, and certain literary forms were modified. The most far-reaching and penetrating change, however, was the defeat of Zoroastrianism and the adoption of Islam. Largely due to political reasons, Iran in time came to be identified with the Shi'ite branch of Islam as an expression of Persian "nationalism." And as a corollary of this change, the gifted Persians played a large role in the process of converting Arab civilization, which was based on the Arabic language and the Arabic *Qur'ān* (*q.v.*), into Muslim or Islamic civilization in which virtually all of the arts and sciences of mankind flourished and advanced.

As the central authority of the Arabs in the 'Abbasid Caliphate at Baghdad weakened, various petty dynasties in Iran became independent. These dynasties, through patronage, fostered the development of Persian literature—as well as, it should be said, of philosophic and scientific work in the universal language of Arabic. Under the Samanids (874–999), a cluster of poets and prose-writers flourished whose clear, simple, yet fluent style (so much in contrast with the ornately embellished work of the later Safavid era) is sometimes called *Khurasani*, after the name of the Samanid territory.

Rūdakī (d. 954?) developed into the earliest of the great classical poets, and al-Bal'amī at the same court, in his adaptation of the Persian Ṭabarī's great history in Arabic, created the oldest surviving prose in the modern Persian language, with a style that is regarded as a model of fluent expression. The poet Daqīqī commenced a long epic that, after his death, was taken up and completed by Firdawsī.

Greater yet as patrons of literature were the rulers of what is today Afghanistan, the Ghaznavids, especially the conqueror Mahmud of Ghazna (d. 1030). The Ghaznavids' conquests resulted in a significant cultural exchange between India and the Islamic world. Persian became the court language of much of India until the period of British rule.

At the Ghaznavid court, panegyric poets flourished, such as 'Unṣūrī, Farrukhī, 'Asjadī, and Manūchihrī Dāmghānī. 'Asjadī was an original poet. The greatest figure, however, was Firdawsī (934?–1020?) whose "*Shāhnāmah*" (Book of Kings) is accepted without question as *the* Iranian epic. Retelling at great length the stories of early Iranian heroes, Firdawsī carries his epic verse down through the Sassanian rulers.

The Iranian world in the eleventh century was dominated by the Saljuk Turks who, although they conquered and ruled a vast domain previously held by numerous princes, still maintained the fiction of the Arab Caliphate. Like the Ghaznavids, who had been pushed into India where they continued to patronize Persian literature, the Saljuks were quick to accept Persian as the language of the court, and under their patronage so many great authors flourished that their period can be called the golden age of Persian literature.

The Saljuk vizir Niẓām al-Mulk is remembered for the "*Siyāsat-nāmah*," a treatise on practical government. A comparable work was written by Kay Kā'ūs ibn Iskandar. His "*Qābūs-nāmah*" has some of the aspects of the "Mirror for Princes" literature. A contemporary, the traveller-philosopher and statesman for both Ghaznavid and Saljuk, as well as Ismā'īlī propagandist, Nāṣir-i Khusraw (1004–1077?) wrote several of the best works to come from Persian writers in India. Recording his travel observations in the "*Safar-nāmah*," Nāṣir-i Khusraw left an invaluable fund of observations on contemporary conditions, especially in Egypt. His poems, which are relatively straightforward in style, contain his philosophy and Ismā'īlī beliefs.

By the end of the tenth century, Persian poetry had been colored with the tenets and images of Islamic mysticism known as sufism. Sufism provided the background and imagery of the greatest Persian poets of the twelfth century. The poets, in brief, describe the striving of men (each of whom has a particle of the divine spirit) for unity with God, usually with images drawn from profane love.

Sanā'ī (d. 1130 or 1131) was one of the great Islamic mystics and a skilled poet. He was the first to combine the *masnavī* form of rhymed couplets with sufi poetry. His major work, the "*Ḥadīqat al-Ḥaqīqah*," is an early effort to cast the sufi spell over several daily life concerns in a kind of anecdotal essay. The mathematician 'Umar Khayyām (d. 1132) produced a number of quatrains that express a deep scepticism of established religion and the world in general, the refuge from which seems to be intoxication. These quatrains, once regarded as mediocre by Persian critics, were redone by FitzGerald and strung together into a poem of almost epochal impact for ninteenth-century English readers that made the name Omar a household word. A greater author was Niẓamī 'Arūẓī of Samarqand (fl. 1155). His *"Chahār Maqālah"* (Four Treatises) is a prose work arranged in sections on writing, poetry, astrology, and medicine. In poetic skill he was surpassed by Niẓāmī Ganjavī (1141?–1209), who mastered the romantic epic in masnavi form and who is considered to be among the greatest of Persian poets. His *"Khusraw u Shīrīn"* and *"Laylā u Majnūn"* retell the old stories in superior masnavi form. Another work, the *"Haft Paykar"* (Seven Effigies), contains seven stories told to the Sassanian king Bahrām Gur by his seven wives. The *"Haft Paykar,"* according to the profound Islamicist G. E. von Grunebaum, is "one of the most sophisticated works of world literature, unrivaled in harmony of word and thought." His *"Iskandar-nāmah"* treats the legend of Alexander the Great. These four romances plus the *"Makhzan al-Asrār"* (Treasury of Secrets), which is a collection of 20 ethical discourses, make up his so-called *"Khamsah"* (Quintet) which has inspired emulation by later writers and visual depiction by miniaturists.

The Saljuk era with its patronage produced many panegyrists. Their work was generally cast in the *qaṣīdah,* which is a form borrowed from the Arabs, relatively short, with each line having the same rhyme. Anvarī is the best of the class, with Khāqānī close behind. The panegyrics of both are characterized by obscure allusions and hyperbole that frequently cloud the meaning.

The mainstream of the sufi current in Persian poetry had as its chief ornament at the close of the Saljuk era one Farīd al-Dīn 'Aṭṭār (1142?–1229?) who after years of travel settled in Nishapur. He set forth in a famous, extended allegory in *masnavi* form named the *"Manṭiq al-Ṭayr"* (Conference of the Birds) the seven stages of the mystics' search for truth. He also composed a biographical work named the *"Tazkirat al-Awliyā',"* which is still a source of value.

The Mongol attack by Chingiz Khan (d. 1227) and his successors wrought many changes in the Muslim world. In the Iranian areas, the Mongol dynasties of the Il Khāns gave way to the Turcoman onslaught of Tamerlane (d. 1405) at the end of the fourteenth century. The internal political situation of Iran was chaotic for 200 years; in that troubled time sufism gained over orthodoxy in the struggle for mens' minds and affected deeply most of the great Persian poets. It has been observed, however, that the Mongol period by reducing the influence of Arabic may have stimulated a reversion in prose to a clearer, simpler Persian style.

The greatest sufi poet is Jalāl al-Dīn Rūmī (1207–1273) who, though born in Balkh (and thus sometimes referred to al Balkhī), settled in Qonya in Anatolia (Rūm) after years of travel. There, under the influence of one Shams of Tabriz, a wandering dervish, Rūmī turned out much lyrical poetry that was assembled under the title of the "Dīvān of Shams-i Tabrīzī." But Rūmī's major work is the *"Masnavī-i Ma'navī"* (Spiritual Masnavi), known simply as "The Masnavi." Its 26,000 couplets stand as one of the great, complete expressions of Islamic mysticism.

Other sufi poets, lesser in the volume of their work than Rūmī but not in terms of quality, ornamented Persian literature under the Mongols. 'Irāqī (d. 1288) is known for his *"Lama'āt"* (Flashes) on mystical love and for his divan whose *ghazels* frequently depict spiritual love in compelling, erotically physical terms. Mahmūd Shabistarī (d. 1320) wrote the long-popular *masnavi* poem entitled *"Gulshān-i Rāz,"* a sort of manual of sufism.

One of the most popular, beloved, and well-known of Persian authors, especially in Europe, is Sa'dī of Shiraz (1213?–1292). His work is noted for its human and ethical content. Like many another poet, he travelled widely for several years, gaining experiences to be drawn upon in his prolific literary life. His *"Būstān"* (Orchard) contains poetic essays and anecdotes of ethical import, on such topics as love, government, happiness, and various virtues. A work similar in content but expressed for the most part in unencumbered prose is his *"Gulistān"* (Rose Garden). This is composed of numerous stories of an anecdotal nature designed to point out a moral or an ethical situation. The *"Gulistān"* is often cited as the finest Persian prose.

The master poet of the Persian language is fully within the sufi tradition. That poet is Ḥāfiẓ of Shiraz (d. 1389 or 1390) whose poems on the traditional themes of love and beauty may not be original or profound—merely the most beautiful. Ḥāfiẓ wrote in various forms, but he is best known for his lyrical odes.

The final author of emminence to appear in the Timurid era and to flourish under the patronage of the noted vizir and litterateur Mīr 'Alī Shīr Navā'ī (d. 1501) was Jāmī (1414–1492) who excelled in both prose and poetry. Under the title of *"Haft Awrang"* (Seven Thrones) are grouped seven of Jāmī's *masnavi* poems. These treat familiar themes such as the old story of *"Yūsuf u Zulaykhā."* Jāmī also wrote a large biographical dictionary of Islamic mystics under the title of *"Nafaḥāt al-Uns."* His *"Bahāristān"* is a very popular imitation in prose and poetry of Sa'dī's *"Gulistān."*

In addition to sufi poetry, the Mongol era produced much prose writing on various topics. The philosopher and scientist Nāṣir al-Dīn Ṭūsī (1201–1274) wrote one of the great ethical treatises within the Islamic tradition in his book the *"Akhlāq-i Nāṣirī."* History was well represented, for historians were utilized to perpetuate the glories of the Mongol princes. In the Ghaznavid court, Abū al-Faḍl Bayhaqī (996–1077) had turned out a long work, now only partially preserved, on the history of the Ghaznavids, combining a clear style with historically valid information. 'Atā Malik Juvaynī (d. 1283) accompanied Hulagu on various expeditions. His *"Tārīkh-i Jahān-gushā"* (History of the World's Conqueror) covers Mongol history, Chingiz Khan, and the Ismā'īlis. An even greater historian was the statesman Rashīd al-Dīn Faẓl Allāh (d. 1318). His *"Jāmi' al-Tavārīkh"* is a universal history of high quality, useful for its information on the Mongols and Turks. The *"Tārīkh-i Guzīda"* by Ḥamd Allāh Mustawfī is another history of note, as it deals with events up to the author's own time, especially the Islamic era of Persia. Mustawfī also produced in his *"Ẓafar-nāmah"* a sort of continuation of Firdawsī's *"Shāhnāmah."* The last notable historian of the Mongol era was Mīrkhwānd, whose *"Rawẓat al-Ṣafā"* (Garden of Purity) is a universal history of great popularity. The author carries the account down to the time of Mīr 'Alī Shīr Navā'ī.

Persian literature in the early modern period (sixteenth and seventeenth centuries) differed in no essential way, save quality, from the previous era. Patronage was less lavish under the Safavids (1502–1796) who made Shi'ite Islam the established religion. Hātifī (d. 1521) pursued the genre of romantic epic with works on the familiar themes of *"Laylā u Majnūn"* and *"Khusraw u Shīrīn."* Panegyric continued in the *qaṣīdahs* of Ahli Shīrāzī (d. 1536) for Shāh Ismā'īl. Ahli's *"Sham' u Parvānah"* (The Candle and the Moth) is fully mystical in theme and imagery. 'Urfī Shīrāzī (d. 1590 or 1591), who lived mostly in India, was the most famous of the sixteenth-century poets.

Most of the poets of Safavid Iran clustered at the court of Shāh 'Abbās (ruled 1587–1629) at Isfahan. Faṣīhī (d. 1639) was a skilled panegyrist, and Shifā'ī (d. 1628) turned out a number of *masnavi* poems in the sufi style. Probably the best representative of Persian literature was Zulālī Khwānsārī (d. 1615 or 1616) whose seven typical *masnavis*, collectively termed the *"Sab' Sayyārah,"* include his highly regarded version of *"Mahmūd va Ayāz."*

Shi'ism did not encourage sufi poetry; rather a more religious verse celebrating the virtues of the imams and the martyrdom of Ḥusayn was fostered by the Safavids. Muhtasham Kāshānī (d. 1588) led this movement by his *haft-bands* (poems based on units of seven lines) of simple, direct, and sincere eloquence. *Marthiyas* or elegies on Ḥusayn were common, and they had a vulgar counterpart in popular literature in the *"Rawẓa-Khwānī"* which were recited during the month of Muharram. The martydom of Ḥusayn on the tenth of that month became the occasion for the *"Ta'ziyah,"* a dramatic representation (frequently with bloody self-wounding) that is known in the West as the "Persian

Passion Play." The *"Ta'ziyah"* is quintessential poetic-dramatic expression of the peoples' identification with the heroes of Shi'ism.

During the late seventeenth and eighteenth centuries—the weakest period in the history of Persian literature—the principal authors were Ṣā'ib Isfahānī (d. 1677), a poet of skill in all forms; Fayyāẓ, who, typifying the new spirit in Iran, poeticized the Shi'ite martyrs; and ʿAlī Ḥazīn (d. 1766), who was prolific in divans and *masnavis*. The 18th century was crowned by Luṭf ʿAlī Āzar (1711–1780/81) who, after many years of political life, became a mystic. While best known for his biographical dictionary of poets (*"Ātash-kada"*), his poetic skill is amply evident in his divan and the rendition of *"Yūsuf u Zulaykhā."*

The nineteenth century witnessed a quickening tempo of changes in society. Accurate generalizations about the literature of the time are difficult. European powers contested for hegemony and the country was opened to Western influences. Printing, or rather lithography, spread after 1816. Newspapers were started, but had no deep effect until the first decade of the twentieth century. In 1852 the *Dār al-Funūn* ("College") was established in Teheran and acted as a channel for European ideas and influences, directly stimulating translations, especially from the French, which replaced the rhetoric of traditional Persian prose by a simple expository style.

Through the nineteenth century panegyric poetry in the traditional form flourished at the Qajar court. Ṣabā (1795–1822/3) wrote excellent *qasīdahs*, and his epic modeled on Firdawsī's *"Shāh-nāmah"* was well received at the time. Critics agree that Qā'ānī (1808–1854) is the most complete and versatile poet of the century. His themes sometimes were concerned with the social issues of Qajar Iran. But only one poet of rank cried out against the evils of society, and that was Yaghmā (1782–1859), who tried in some of his work to use the common language. He was the forerunner of many poets of the later nineteenth century and of the Constitutional Period.

As the nineteenth century progressed, political events led to a demand for reforms such as had been achieved in Turkey and Egypt. The journals and newspapers became important vehicles of political criticism and agents in the creation of new literary style or direction that has been described as a literary renaissance. Many of the journals existed outside of Iran. One such journal was Malkum Khān's *Qānūn*, founded in London in 1890. In Iran the period of influential journalism ended in 1910 when a time of repression set in. *Kava*, founded in Berlin in 1916, and its successor, *Iranshahr*, aided both the political and literary movements of reform.

The literary revival had to do mostly with increased realism, the treatment of social themes, nationalism, and the use of a more natural common speech. The major poets of the literary revival were often journalists. ʿĀrif Qazvīnī (1882–1934), Bahar (1880–1951), Yaḥyā Dawlatābādī (1864–1939), Aḥmad Adīb Pīshāvarī (1844–1930), Adīb al-Mamālik (d. 1917), and Abū al-Qāsim Lāhūtī (1887–1957) all wrote poetry in which satire was used to criticize social or political conditions and in which national feeling is clearly present.

Persian prose had declined in quality during the Safavid period, but a revival occurred in Qajar Iran of the nineteenth century. A manifestation of this is seen in the stylistic reforms introduced in official correspondence by the statesman and author Qā'im Maqām Farāhānī (1779–1835) and by Mīrzā Taqī Khān, the Amīr-i Kabīr (d. 1852). Malkum Khān (1833–1905), who is known as a constitutional reformist, influenced many younger authors with his prose style in numerous essays dealing with political and social topics.

The beginnings of modern prose are seen in the work of Zayn al-ʿĀbidīn (1837–1910). His *"Siyāḥat-nāmah-i Ibrāhīm Beg"* (Travels of Ibrahim Beg) seems to have first appeared in print in 1888 in Istanbul. It is the earliest novel, and the first of its three volumes achieves a telling effect through sharply drawn portraits of the subject conditions of life in Iran. The book was very popular, and its use of the spoken language of the people impressed other authors.

Another book of import was the Persian translation of James Morier's "The Adventures of Hajji Bābā of Ispahan" made by Mīrzā Ḥabīb of Isfahan who bitterly opposed Qajar despotism and the stultifying conservatism of the *mullahs*. Even today, the book's style is highly regarded in Iran.

Early in the twentieth century, the trends of the nineteenth century accelerated and concentrated. The Constitutional Period of Iran (1905–1921) saw a widening national concern for social political reform expressed in the press. The great Iranian scholar 'Alī Akbar Dihkhudā (1879–1956) used the journals for his many satirical essays attacking the establishment in a style still regarded as exemplary, using the common idiom. The era of journalistic impact lasted until about 1910.

Stylistic reforms for prose led in two directions: conservatives tended towards the models of the Samanid era, and modernists wanted a Western style, particularly the style of the later French Romantics. Translation activities accelerated also, and the translators (who were also creators of prose and poetry) had to give up the usual rhetorical embellishments of Persian prose and create a new and simple style. The Pahlavi era (1921–   ), while its political oppression discomfited many liberals and authors, did by its strong nationalism foster research in Persian folklore, opening up new avenues of work and inspiration based on the verbal heritage of the Iranians. There were numerous novelists during the rule of Riza Shah (1921–1941), but they avoided political criticism and tended to turn their attention to moral issues of women and prostitution in a rather superficial way.

The literary scene after World War II is largely concerned with the social problems arising from a medieval society struggling to succeed in a twentieth century Westernized world. The short story in this "age of prose" has become the dominant and most advanced vehicle of prose expression. Journals maintain their importance for literature. The principal journals are *Armaghān, Mihr,* and *Sukhan*.

The most significant authors are involved with social themes. Muḥammad Mas'ūd Dihatī, who was assassinated in 1948, is typical in his pessimistic appraisals of urban life in Iran. The position of woman is a common concern of prose writers. The best recent example, perhaps, is 'Alī Muḥammad Afghānī's *"Shawhar-i Āhū-Khanum"* (1961), which is a long "social history" novel about a traditional middle-class Iranian family.

Muḥammad 'Alī Jamāl-Zādah (1899–   ) is the principal postwar innovative writer, whose work is significant for prose development as well as social criticism. In numerous works he stresses the inability of the European-educated Persian youth to find a place in society. Another persistent theme is the futility of honesty versus the corruption in the bureaucracy. He satirizes the ignorant and reactionary mullahs. An early (1921) collection of stories, *"Yakī Būd Yakī Na-būd,"* established his reputation as a realist and influenced subsequent writers.

Ṣādiq Hidāyat (1903–1951) is regarded as the outstanding creator of short stories or novellas, not only for his artistic style and deep insight into human motivation, but also as a model emulated by the latest authors. Deciding upon a literary career, Hidāyat prepared himself by serious study of Iranian and nineteenth-century French literature. A major interest of his was Sassanian civilization, and he burrowed deeply into Pahlavi language and Zoroastrianism. He became an authority in folklore. Striking features of Hidāyat's work are the unusual characters he invents and depicts with verisimilitude as he explores human motivation. Deeply pessimistic pictures emerge from most of his work.

Other contemporary figures are Ṣādiq Chubak (1918–   ) who seems most comparable to Hidāyat in using psychological insight; Sa'īd Nafīsī (1897–1966), perhaps best known as a scholar of literature, but also a highly regarded novelist; Buzurg 'Alavī (1904–   ) whose socialism clearly emerges in his famous novel *"Chashmhāyash"* (Her Eyes) about a socialist artist and his wealthy girlfriend; and the scholar and journalist 'Alī Dashtī, who in many short stories has treated the identity problems of the educated, modern Iranian woman.

Persian literature has been a vehicle of expression by a uniquely gifted people and is one of the outstanding artistic achievements of mankind. While prose has dominated in recent years, poetry in traditional and modern forms is not neglected. The Persian genius for literature continues undiminished in the modern world.

Browne, Edward Granville. A LITERARY HISTORY OF PERSIA. 1902–1929. *Cambridge* 4 vols. 1969 each $14.50

This is the most valuable work in English on the subject. Browne had a deep love of Iran and its people and was the most sensitive interpreter of Persian life and literature among nineteenth- and early twentieth-century orientalists. Browne includes numerous texts and translations and carries his narrative down to 1924. The Islamic era, however, receives the most attention.

Hekmat, Forough, and Yann Lovelock. FOLK TALES OF ANCIENT PERSIA. Ill. by Muhammad Bahrami. Persian Heritage Ser. *Caravan Bks.* (dist. by Scholars' Facsimiles) 1974 $9.00. This volume one of the UNESCO Collection of Representative Works, Asian Series, contains eight folktales from ancient Persia, preserving part of the oral storytelling tradition of present-day Iran.

Kamshad, Hassan. MODERN PERSIAN PROSE LITERATURE. *Cambridge* 1966 $11.95

This work contains the best discussion in English of contemporary Persian prose literature. Kamshad gives a good historical background, settles the question of the identity of the Persian translator of Morier's "Hajji Baba," and analyzes the principal authors of the twentieth century. The second part of the book provides an analysis of the life and work of Şādiq Hidāyat. There is an excellent general bibliography and an extensive list of Hidāyat's work.

Levy, Reuben. PERSIAN LITERATURE; An Introduction. 1923. *Folcroft* 1974 $6.50; *Greenwood* 1974 $8.75; *Richard West* 1973 $6.50. This is a still-useful survey (excellent for its small compass) of the principal authors and main features of the subject up to the modern period, where the coverage is weak. Several brief translations are given.

Morier, James. ADVENTURES OF HAJJI BABA OF ISPAHAN. 1824. *Dufour* 1960 $4.95; *Oxford* World's Class. $5.00. This English novel, a best-seller in its day, and still known to a wide readership, created a sensation when it was translated into Persian; readers were astounded that an English writer could capture the Persian atmosphere so accurately.

Rypka, Jan, and others. HISTORY OF IRANIAN LITERATURE. Trans. by P. van Popta-Hope; ed. by Karl Jahn. *D. Reidel Pub. Co.* $55.00

Done with the collaboration of many scholars, this was originally written in Czech by one of the most accomplished of Iranologists. The present English edition was translated from the German, with revisions. It is an excellent, in-depth account of the subject that uses the results of Russian researches not usually available to English readers. In addition to Persian literature, it covers Tajik Literature, folk literature, Persian literature in India, and Judeo-Persian literature. Occasionally its style is heavy. A good index and bibliographies increase the book's value as a reference tool. A useful list of translations and articles in English may be found in an article by Gernot L. Windfuhr and John R. Workman, "Literature in Translation—Iranian into English," in the Middle Eastern Studies Association *Bulletin* Vol. 7 (1973), No. 1, pp. 9–41.

Storey, Charles Ambrose. PERSIAN LITERATURE: A Bio-Bibliographical Survey. 1935 1953 *Verry* 2 vols. 1970 1973 Vol. 1, pt. 1 $27.50 pt. 2 $27.50 Vol. 2, pt. 1 pap. $17.50. This monumental work was not completed by the time of Storey's death. Intended to be the essential reference work for advanced researchers, the work is to be continued by G. M. Meridith-Owens. So far, only the sections on Qur'ānic literature, history and biography; astronomy and astrology; geography; and medicine have been printed.

Yohannan, John D. PERSIAN POETRY IN ENGLAND AND AMERICA: A 200-Year History. Persian Studies Ser. *Caravan Bks.* (dist. by Scholars' Facsimiles) 1975 $30.00. A detailed study of the interpenetration of Persian and English literatures.

FIRDAWSI. 934?–1020?

Firdawsī gained immortality through his *"Shāhnāmah,"* an epic of unique literary and historical importance in Iran. Containing upwards of 50,000 couplets (editions vary) the poem is a vast collection of Indo-European and Iranian legends and history strung together and terminating in the year 641 A.D. Much attention is given to the hero Rustam and his battles, and many of the partial translations into various languages treat his exploits. Matthew Arnold's (*q.v.*) "Sohrab and Rustum" is based on the tragic encounter of the hero and his son. The Persian text was printed first in Calcutta in 1811; the most exact edition is that of E. Bertel's (Moscow, 1960–). Levy's prose translation is the most accessible English rendition.

THE EPIC OF THE KINGS: Shah-nama, the National Epic of Persia. Trans. by Reuben Levy. 1967. *Routledge & Kegan Paul* 1973 $16.75

SUHRAB AND RUSTAM: A Poem from the Shah-namah of Firdausi. Trans. by James Atkinson. *Scholars' Facsimiles* 1972 $10.00. Facsimile reproduction, with an introduction by Leonard R. N. Ashley, of the Calcutta 1814 edition.

GURGĀNĪ, FAKHR AL-DĪN AS'AD.   eleventh century.

"*Vīs u Rāmīn,*" one of the earliest romantic epics in Persian, was written about 1054. The popular story concerns the love of Vīs, who is wife to the elderly king Mūbad Manīkān, and Rāmīn, the king's young and handsome brother. Gurgānī's work is based on an older Pahlavi story.

VĪS AND RĀMĪN. Trans. by George Morrison. *Columbia* 1972 $15.00

MANŪCHIHRĪ DĀMGHĀNĪ.   eleventh century.

Manūchihrī was one of the leading court poets at Ghazna and has left a modest divan consisting mostly of panegyrics. Currently available on his work is "The Divan of Manūchihrī Dāmghānī, A Critical Study" by Jerome W. Clinton (*Bibliotheca Islamica* Studies in Middle Eastern Literatures, 1 1972 $8.00). This is a work of literary criticism on the fine points of Manūchihrī's style and of the poetry at the Ghaznavid court.

NĀṢIR-I KHUSRAW.   1004–1077?

Nāṣir-i Khusraw is one of the most enigmatic of the great figures in Persian literature. Part of the difficulty in gaining a full understanding of the man and his work comes from the fact that many of his texts have been modified by later editors or copyists. The "*Safarnāmah,*" at least, which is an account of a seven-year journey to Egypt, is valuable for its contemporary observations.

DIARY OF A JOURNEY THROUGH SYRIA AND PALESTINE. Trans. by Guy Le Strange. 1893. 1971 o.p.

OMAR KHAYYAM.   1021?–1122.

Known in Iran as a leading mathematician, Omar gained a literary importance through certain quatrains that were translated by Edward FitzGerald. The "*Rubā'iyāt*" are justly famous in English translation. Others besides FitzGerald have tried their hand at translating it. Bowen's is a good example of competent and pleasing work. Robert Graves' effort caused well-founded adverse comment by orientalist scholars.

RUBAIYAT OF OMAR KHAYYAM. Trans. by Edward FitzGerald. 1859. Numerous paperback editions are available. For close students of FitzGerald's poem, which justly ranks as an important contribution to English literature, the best of the in-print editions is "Rubaiyat of Omar Khayyam: A Comparative Printing of the First Four Quaritch Editions of Edward FitzGerald's Renderings into English Verse with Notes Showing the Variants in the Fifth Wright Edition." 1915. *Folcroft* $45.00

A NEW SELECTION FROM THE RUBAIYAT OF OMAR KHAYYAM. Rendered into English verse by John Charles Edward Bowen. With a literal translation of each Persian quatrain by A. J. Arberry. *Dufour* 1961 $4.75

THE RUBAIYAT OF OMAR KHAYYAM: A New Translation with Critical Commentaries by Robert Graves and Omar Ali-Shah. 3rd ed. 1968 o.p.

Books about Omar

In Search of Omar Khayyam. By 'Alī Dashtī. Trans. from the Persian by L. P. Elwell-Sutton. Persian Studies Monographs *Columbia* 1971 $13.50. Dashtī is a man of many parts and is thoroughly versed in the literature of his native Iran. This work, beautifully translated by the noted scholar Elwell-Sutton, is essential reading for those who want an accurate understanding of the many problems of Khayyam and of his quatrains.

SANĀ'Ī GHAZNAVĪ.   d. 1130 or 1131.

Sanā'ī is the first poet to utilize the *masnavi* form as a vehicle of mystic or sufi thought. The "Garden of Truth" is his longest work, having about 10,000 couplets (editions vary), and was well regarded by later poets. Stephanson's partial translation first appeared in Calcutta.

THE FIRST BOOK OF THE HADĪQATU'L-L-HAQĪQAT, or The Enclosed Garden of the Truth. Trans. and ed. by J. Stephanson. 1911. *S. Weiser* 1970 1975 $12.50

'AṬṬĀR, FARĪD AL-DĪN.   1142?–1229?

Little accurate information is known about 'Aṭṭār, who is one of the great sufi poets of Iran. An apothecary and physician, 'Aṭṭār has had many works attributed to him. Probably the *"Manṭiq al-Ṭayr"* is his most notable composition. It is an allegory in rhymed couplets in which birds on a pilgrimage go through the seven stages of the mystics' path to the truth.

THE CONFERENCE OF THE BIRDS. Trans. by C. S. Nott. 1917 1954 *Shambhala Pubns.* 1971 pap. $2.95; *S. Weiser* $3.95

MUSLIM SAINTS AND MYSTICS: Episodes from the Tadhkirat al-Awliya. Trans. by A. J. Arberry. 1966. UNESCO Collection of Representative Works: Persian Heritage Ser. *Routledge & Kegan Paul* 1973 $13.25

NIZĀMĪ GANJAVĪ.   1141?–1209.

Nizāmī is poorly represented by English translations: the *"Makhzan al-Asrār"* (The Treasury of Mysteries) was done by G. H. Darab in London, 1945; The *"Haft Paykar"* (The Seven Portraits) by C. E. Wilson, London 1924; The *"Iskandar-nāmah"* by H. Wilberforce Clarke in London, 1881. The least important of his works is probably "The story of Laylā and Majnūn."

THE STORY OF LAYLĀ AND MAJNŪN. Trans. by R. Gelpke; English version in collaboration with E. Mattin and G. Hill. 1966. *Verry* $11.00

RŪMĪ, JALĀL AL-DĪN.   1207–1273.

Rūmī, the greatest sufi poet, was born in Balkh, and settled in Anatolia after years of travel. His major work, the *"Masnavi,"* stands as one of the great, complete expressions of Islamic mysticism.

DISCOURSES OF RUMI. Trans. by A. J. Arberry. *S. Weiser* 1972 $3.50. This is Rūmī's poetical treatise on sufism, the *"Fihi Ma Fihi."*

MYSTICAL POEMS OF RUMI: First Selection, Poems 1–200. Trans. by A. J. Arberry. UNESCO Collection of Representative Works: Persian Heritage Ser. *Univ. of Chicago Press* 1968 $12.50 Phoenix Bks. 1974 pap. $2.95

SA'DĪ.   1213?–1292.

Sa'dī's anecdotes of a moral or ethical nature have had a wide appeal down through the centuries, and they have been frequently translated into European languages.

MORALS POINTED AND TALES ADORNED: The Bustan of Sa'di. Trans. by G. M. Wickens. *Univ. of Toronto Press* 1975 $20.00

RASHĪD AL-DĪN, FAZL ALLĀH.   1247?–1318.

This scholar and man of politics was the author of a valuable world history, *"Jāmi' al-Tavārīkh,"* which is particularly useful for information on the Mongol period.

THE SUCCESSORS OF GENGHIS KHAN. Trans. by John Andrew Boyle. UNESCO Collection of Representative Works: Persian Heritage Ser. *Columbia* 1971 $15.00. This is a translation of a portion of the history.

ḤĀFIẒ.   d. 1389 or 1390.

In the course of a long career as a court poet, Hāfiz achieved mastery of the lyric form known as the *ghazal*. His subtlety and excellence of phrasing place him in the highest ranks of Persian poetry, and his work has been read and translated widely outside his native land.

THE DIVAN. Trans. into English prose by H. Wilberforce Clarke. 1891. 2 vols. *S. Weiser* 1970 $45.00. This is a reprint of the Calcutta edition. Most of the Divan, or collection of poems, consists of *ghazals*. Clarke's translation was made before the scientific study of the texts began. Even today the chronology of the *ghazals* is not completely settled, nor is there agreement on the fundamental question of literal versus allegorical interpretations of the poetry.

HIDĀYAT, ṢĀDIQ. 1903–1951.

Critics regard Ṣādiq Hidāyat among the outstanding writers of the twentieth century. Known primarily for his short stories, he was influenced by Poe and Kafka. His stories plumb the depths of human motivation and seek out the meaning of life. In his work a deep pessimism emerges, which he himself could not overcome and which led him to suicide.

THE BLIND OWL. Trans. by D. P. Costello. *Grove* 1958 1969 pap. $1.95. "The Blind Owl" (*"Būf-i Kūr"*) was published first in India in 1937. Most readers find this translation morbid and depressing, but most agree that this work of self-analysis is Hidāyat's masterpiece. Costello's translation appeared first in 1958.

Books about Hidāyat

Hidayat's Ivory Tower: Structural Analysis of The Blind Owl. By Iraj Bashiri. *Manor House* 1974. The author stresses the importance of the covert details of Hidāyat's life in this detailed and penetrating study. He also provides his own, new, translation of the *"Būf-i Kūr,"* and points out Hidāyat's debt to ancient Indian sources as well as to Rilke.

ĀL AḤMAD, JALĀL. 1923 or 1924–1963.

THE SCHOOL PRINCIPAL: A Novel. Trans. by John K. Newton. Introd. and notes by Michael C. Hillman. Studies in Middle Eastern Literatures *Bibliotheca Islamica* 1974 pap. $5.00. The original title is *"Mudīr-i Madrasah."*

—D. H. P.

TURKISH LITERATURE

Turkish is one of the widely dispersed Turkic languages that are found from Sinkiang to the Balkans. By convention, the word "Turkish" is applied most properly to the language and literature of the Ottoman Turks and their descendants in modern Turkey. Thus one may speak of Ottoman Turkish literature (c. 1400–1920) and modern Turkish literature from 1920 to the present.

The Ottoman Turks formed one of a number of principalities in Anatolia (Asia Minor) that arose in the late thirteenth century and contended for dominance following the collapse, due to the Mongol incursions, of the Saljuk Turkish empire. By 1453, with the capture of Constantinople, the Ottomans were well on the way to establishing the last great Islamic empire, a world power that succumbed during World War I.

Just as their predecessors, the Great Saljuks, had derived their civilization from Iran using Persian as the court language, the Ottomans, lacking a strong literary tradition, took Persian as their model. The literature of the Ottomans, well into the nineteenth century when European influence prevailed, is largely based on the themes and techniques of Persian literature. The Ottoman poets took over completely the mystical-philosophical system known as sufism and the whole corpus of its symbolism.

The numerous verse forms used in Ottoman poetry were likewise borrowed. One of the favorite forms, the *mesnevi* (rhymed couplets), might have been an indigenous form, as used in the eleventh-century Uighur *"Qutadqu Biliğ,"* but innumerable Persian models were available for imitation. The *mesnevi* was used primarily for long narrative poems. The *ghazel* was a short poem, generally in five or ten couplets (called *beyts*) in which the first two hemistiches rhyme and that rhyme is continued in the second line of each succeeding *beyt*. The *ghazel* was the most popular of Ottoman poetic forms. The third form is the *qasidah*, which was used usually for panegyric odes. It is longer than the *ghazel* and employs the same rhyme throughout.

The meters used in Ottoman poetry came originally from the Arabo-Persian system. The names of the most popular are the Hejez, the Rejez, Remel, and Khafif.

As in form and meter, so too in rhetoric: the Turks dipped into the treasury of this Arabo-Persian art that gives Ottoman poetry its artificial and ornate flavor so much at variance with modern taste.

The history of Turkish literature can be divided as follows: the early period to 1453; the classic era from 1453 to 1600; the post-classic era of decline; the nineteenth and early twentieth centuries; and the contemporary period following World War I.

Important authors of the early period were Gülşehri (fl. 1300) who produced a long *mesnevi* type poem based on the Persian poet 'Aṭṭâr's "*Manṭiq al-ṭâ'ir*"; Aşik Paşa (1271–1332) whose "*Garib-name*" sets forth the tenets of philosophical mysticism; Ahmedi (1334–1413), a lyric poet with encyclopedic erudition, whose long poem "*Iskender-name*" continued the tradition of the Alexander romance of the Persian poet Niẓâmî; and Şeyhi (d. 1325?) whose poems by and large exemplify the full use of mystical symbolism and whose style was further developed than that of his predecessors.

In addition to the literature of mystic symbolism, other types from this early era deserve mention. One is the legendary romance typically built upon the heroic exploits of Seyyid Baṭṭal, the model *ghazi* or warrior against the infidel Byzantium. The other is the literary celebration of the Prophet's birth. The most famous of this genre was the *mevlid* of Süleyman Çelebi (d. 1421?).

The second era is usually regarded as the classic era of Ottoman poetry and corresponds in time with the "golden age" of the Ottoman Empire. It is known also as the age of the Turkish lyric. Ahmed Paşa (d. 1496/7) was the foremost poet during the time of the conquests and is mentioned as the real founder of Ottoman poetry. His principal source of inspiration was the Chagatay poetry of Alî Shîr Nevâ'î (1441–1501). Necatî (d. 1509) was even more skilled in the lyric mode. But without question the greatest lyrics were the *ghazels* of Bâkî (1526–1600). A court poet and a member of the academic elite of Istanbul, Bâkî skillfully entwined themes of homosexual love and mystical allegory expressed in elaborate images and ornate language.

The *mesnevi* remained popular, as well. Here the best representative is Hamdi (d. 1509) whose "*Yusuf o Zelikha*," an elaboration of the long-popular story of Joseph and Potiphar's wife as told by the Persian poets Firdawsī and Jāmī, shows a real advance in the technical treatment of the theme.

This golden age of Turkish poetry, in the words of E. G. Browne, "is marked by no essential change from that which goes before; it proceeds along the old familiar Persian lines . . . the principal object . . . being . . . not so much the expression of true feeling as grace of diction and faultless manipulation of language."

The post-classic era is characterized by an increasing devotion and adherence to Persian models, often of an Indo-Persian style. Nef'i (1572?–1635), the consummate panegyrist and scurrilous satirist, achieved perfection in the *qasidah*. Others of renown in this era were 'Aṭâ'î (d. 1634), whose "*Sâkî-name*" was deprecated for obscenity and praised for originality; Sabit (d. 1712), whose work is typically neo-Persian; Nedim (1681–1730), many of whose poems achieved a naturalness heretofore lacking, especially in the type called *şarki*; and Şeyh Gâlip (1757–1799), known chiefly for his "*Hüsn ü 'Işq*," an allegory of beauty and love. The most renowned poet of the age was Nâbî (1642?–1712), who took the seventeenth-century Persian poet Sâ'ib as his model. But despite being the most Persianized of poets, Nâbî produced a masterpiece in his "*Haireyye*," a didactic *mesnevi* poem of good counsel for his son in a language that is more Turkish than Persian. Nâbî, then, is usually regarded as both the culmination of the classic period of dependence of the Persian muse and the harbinger of the era of transition.

The modern era of Turkish literature was dependent on European influences that swept across Turkey during the nineteenth century and profoundly affected most aspects of life. Numerous Turks were sent to Europe for education and, upon their return, became proponents of change. A flood of translations, largely of French authors, poured over Turkey. Ibrahim Şinasi (1826–1871), who founded literary journals and translated French poets, is regarded as the major precursor of the new movement. Ziya Paşa (1825–1880) pursued a political career and supported the reforms of the Young Turks: in literature he urged the use of a simple Turkish style. A Romantic School arose, following mostly the inspiration of Victor Hugo. It used new Western types of expression, the novel and theatrical drama, and often found inspiration in themes from common life. Namik Kemal (1840–1888) wrote the first modern Turkish novel, "*Intibah*" (The Awakening) in 1876. He is also known for several plays, often of political intent. The other prominent figure among the Romantics was 'Abdülhak Hamit Tarhan—usually referred to as Hamit (1851–1937)—who wrote numerous plays and several poems.

A distinct school is seen among the authors who clustered around Reca'i-zade's journal *Servet-i Funun*. These authors imitated late nineteenth-century French themes and style, yet preferred to use rather archaic Persian and Arabic vocabulary instead of the living Turkish of Istanbul. The poet Tevfik Fikret (1867?–1915) successfully adapted the techniques and style of Western authors in his verse, which often treated themes from lower-class life. The prolific novelist and short-story writer Halit Ziya Uşakligil (1869?–1945), whose best work is probably the novel "*Işq-i Memnu*'" (Forbidden Love), successfully adopted French narrative style and is, consequently, the first modern prose writer.

Strong nationalist tendencies characterize the work of Mehmet Emin (1869–1944). He glorified the virtues of the Turks and used a largely Turkish vocabulary in many of his poems. However, it is probable that the style of Ziya Gökalp (1875–1924), who established the "sociological" basis of Turkish or Pan-Turanian nationalism, had a more profound effect in forming a nationalist school. His poem "*Turan*," and others, approached the style of popular Turkish poetry. Gökalp influenced a number of authors collectively called the "new pens" after his journal *Genç kalemler*, and their work increasingly used a purer Turkish vocabulary. Ömer Seyfeddin (1884–1920) is the foremost of those earlier writers of a true vernacular literature.

The establishment of the Republic of Turkey with its program of reform under the leadership of Mustafa Kemal Atatürk created a new environment for the development of Turkish literature. Of the numerous authors spawned by the new Turkey, perhaps the outstanding are Ahmet Haşim Alusi (1884/5–1933), Yahya Kemal Beyatli (1884–1958), Halide Edib Adivar (1885–1964), and Yakup Kadri Karaosmanoğlu (1888–1975). Haşim and Kemal were primarily poets; Edib and Kadri were novelists. Part of the interest in Edib's novels arises from her position as Turkey's leading female activist. Yakup Kadri's work can be regarded as opening up an interest in rural, specifically Anatolian, subjects. Many of the most recent authors of Turkey have come from villages and have exploited the subject matter of their experiences. Mahmut Makal's "*Bizim Köy*" (Our Village) is one of the best known works of the Anatolian School.

No recital of Turkish literature would be complete without mention of folk literature. In addition to folk poetry, which was beneath the contempt of the Ottoman stylists, folk tales flourished and are still alive in Anatolia. One special type of tale is attached to the figure of Nasreddin Hoca (or Hodja), a clownish character whose rural wit usually gets the better of his opponents. Still another type of folk literature is the Turkish shadow theater known as *karagöz* which had its origin in the Far East, developed in Turkey, and had an influence on the growth of drama in Turkey.

In summation, Turkish literature for centuries adhered to Persian models. These were swept aside by a tide of European influences in the latter half of the nineteenth century, and today Turkish authors find inspiration for a vigorous and realistic prose and poetry in their native soil.

And, Metin. DANCES OF ANATOLIAN TURKEY. 1959. *Johnson Reprint* pap. $5.50

KARAGÖZ: Turkish Shadow Theatre. 1975 (order from the publisher: *Dost Yayinlari*, Izmir Caddesi 22/9, Yenişehir—Ankara, Turkey). The most recent of several scholarly investigations by a life-long student of *karagöz*, this work has much information on traditional Turkish folk-theater and is embellished with good illustrations.

Bombaci, Alessio. HISTOIRE DE LA LITTÉRATURE TURQUE. Trans. from the Italian by I. Mélikoff. *Klincksieck* Institut d'Études Turques de l'Université de Paris 1968. This is the only reliable, detailed survey of Turkish literature up to World War II. An enlarged, English edition is under preparation by Kathleen Burrill for *Columbia University*'s Publications in Near and Middle East Studies.

Gibb, E. J. W. A HISTORY OF OTTOMAN POETRY. 1900–1907. *Luzac & Co.* (P.O. Box 157, 46 Gt. Russell St., London WC1B 3PE) 1958–1967. 6 vols. $50.00. Gibb lived to finish only volume 1; the remaining volumes are the work of Edward B. Browne, an outstanding English orientalist of the late nineteenth and early twentieth centuries. This is the only comprehensive work on the subject. It contains numerous translations from the major poets and a detailed commentary and criticism in late nineteenth-century terms. Volume 1 has an excellent account of Turkish prosody.

Rathbun, Carole. THE VILLAGE IN THE TURKISH NOVEL AND SHORT STORY 1920 TO 1955. *Humanities Press* (Mouton) 1972 $23.50. A scholarly but readable analysis of a most important theme in recent fiction. The work of ten Turkish authors forms the basis of this excellent study.

TALES OF NASRETTIN HODJA. Ed. by E. C. Parnwell. Ill. *Oxford* $1.00. A collection of witty tales surrounding the comic figure of Hodja (or Hoca).

Walker, Warren S., and Ahmet E. Uysal. TALES ALIVE IN TURKEY. 1966 o.p. Two thorough scholars made this fine collection of Turkish tales still current in Anatolia. However, "objectionable" themes have been deleted. With useful notes, bibliography, and index.

ADIVAR, HALIDE EDIP.   1884–1964.

Halide Edip was born in Istanbul and educated at the American Girls' College. She taught in various capacities from 1903 to 1917 and entered into political and cultural affairs during World War I. She was an active participant in the Struggle for National Independence.

After a long sojourn in England (1936–1939) Miss Edip returned to Turkey and served as professor of English literature at Istanbul University from 1940 to 1950. She was the first Turkish woman to hold professorial rank. From 1950 to 1954 she was a member of the National Assembly.

Edip, the outstanding Turkish woman of the twentieth century, is known primarily for her novels and memoirs. Of her 20-odd volumes, the most popular deal with the events of the War for Independence. Several have been translated into foreign languages and some have been the basis of motion pictures.

MEMOIRS OF HALIDE EDIP. 1926. *Arno Press* World Affairs: National and International Viewpoints 1972 $24.00. Essential reading because so much of twentieth-century Turkey is reflected in the life of this leading female personality.

TURKEY FACES WEST. 1930. *Arno Pess* $15.00

HIKMET, NAZIM.   1902–1963.

Nazım Hikmet was born in Salonika. After participating in the Struggle for National Independence, he taught school for a brief period and then studied economics and sociology in Moscow (1922–1934). Upon returning to Turkey he worked as a journalist and in a film studio. He was in continual trouble with the Turkish authorities during the thirties because of his adherence to communism, and in 1938 he was sentenced to a 20-year term in prison. Released in 1950—partly because of world opinion—he left Turkey and lived in exile until his death in 1963.

Hikmet's poetry (he also wrote plays) represents a complete break with the traditional heritage and a full acceptance of occidental models. Much of his work was inspired outside of Turkey and reached a universal dimension; nevertheless, the land and people of Turkey figure prominently as sources of inspiration. He has been especially well received in France via translation. Ironically, most of his work has appeared in Turkey only since his death.

SELECTED POEMS. Trans. by Taner Baybars. *Grossman* 1967 pap. $1.50. A representative selection from his work.

DAĞLARCA, FAZIL HÜSNÜ. 1914–

Born in Istanbul and educated in military schools, Dağlarca pursued a military career until 1950. He then worked in various ministries through 1959 when he left government service to found a publishing house and devote himself to literature.

Dağlarca's poems have appeared in all the leading Turkish journals, and he has published over 40 books, including at least 27 volumes of poetry. His poems are distinguished by a skillful and unusual use of language. His style seems to be genuinely Turkish, not revealing direct foreign influences. His style and themes have gradually evolved, but since 1950 with the work *"Toprak Ana"* (Mother Earth) he has pursued social realism.

SELECTED POEMS: *Seçme Şiirler*. Trans. by Talât Sait Halman. Pitt Poetry Ser. *Univ. of Pittsburgh Press* 1969 pap. $2.95. These are good translations.

KEMAL, YAŞAR. 1922–

Yaşar Kemal was born in the Turkish village of Gökçeli. After finishing his secondary education he worked in various jobs in southern Anatolia, gaining a deep knowledge of the folklore of the region.

Kemal's first volume of short stories was issued in 1952 and since then over 15 volumes have appeared. His novels, short stories, and *reportage* deal with Anatolian themes.

MEMED, MY HAWK. Trans. by Edouard Roditi. *Pantheon* (order from British Bk. Centre) 1961 $3.50. Probably his most popular novel; it has been translated into at least 23 languages. This is a translation of Vol. 1 of the original (1955) edition, titled *"Ince Memed"* (They Burn the Thistles) (*see entry below*).

ANATOLIAN TALES. Trans. by Thilda Kemal. *Collins* (order from British Bk. Centre) 1969 $2.10

THEY BURN THE THISTLES. Trans. by Margaret E. Platon. *Harvill Press* (order from British Bk. Centre) 1973 $6.00. A translation of Vol. 2 of *"Ince Memed."*

IRON EARTH, COPPER SKY. Trans. by Thilda Kemal. *Harvill Press* (order from British Bk. Centre) 1974 $5.50. A prize-winning drama, originally titled *"Yer Demir, Gök Bakır."*

—D. H. P.

Chapter 19

Asian Literature

"*Asia is not going to be civilized after the methods of the West. There is too much Asia and she is too old.*"

—KIPLING, "The Man Who Was"

History has often shown us that a renaissance of learning and artistic creation follows the discovery or rediscovery of an alien culture. The glories of Asian civilization have for too long been neglected in the West by most of those not involved in the scholarly examination of Asia's history, philosophy, religion, technology, or arts. The literatures of the Orient are both numerous and rich and, in general, their relatively recent discovery has only followed Western attention to Asia's history and civilization. The great divergences which exist between occidental and oriental civilizations are perhaps best reflected in the literary tradition which, in Asia, has always been closely related to cultural developments. Forms of expression differ markedly from those most prevalent in the West, with historical chronicles, unique poetic styles, and folk tradition among the most striking features. The themes prominent in Eastern literature have developed as a result of the importance of religion in society and of imperial and court institutions in the case of classical literature, and from the impact of contacts with the West and of political revolution in the case of modern literature. While these may be considered characteristics typical of the continent, the important variations in the literary works of each Asian nation should not be ignored. Although even the best translation can only convey a part of the meaning of the original, especially when the reader is only slightly aware of the traditions and ideals of the culture of which that literature is a part, to study Asian literature is to greatly expand one's intellectual and aesthetic horizons and to begin to reach an understanding of the heritage of an endlessly fascinating area of our world.

SOUTH ASIA: LITERATURE OF INDIA AND PAKISTAN

The vast extent of the Indian subcontinent, which includes the modern nations of India, Pakistan, and Bangladesh, is indicated by the existence of more than a dozen languages in which literary efforts have been pursued. The major traditional literary languages of the region before the tenth century were Sanskrit in the north and Tamil in the south. Other spoken languages, including Bengali, Marathi, Kanarese, Malayalam, Urdu, and Telugu appeared in literature by the seventeenth century. With the Muslim incursions and the establishment of Muslim rule in nearly the whole of the subcontinent between the tenth and sixteenth centuries, Islamic influence joined that of Hinduism and Buddhism as the major cultural strains of the region. As a result of the British Raj, a great deal of modern and contemporary writing has been in English, which for a long period was the *lingua franca* of the area. With independence came partition, making Urdu the language of Pakistan while Hindi is replacing English as the only viable interstate language of India.

The main types of literature in the early period were folktales, verse, and versions of the Sanskrit classics, and after 1500, *bhakti* devotional lyrics, primarily to Krishna and Rama. Nearly all the literature until modern times was poetic in form, derived either from Sanskrit or, in the case of Urdu, from Persian verse. With Western influence came the adoption of Western forms, such as novels and short stories, and the rediscovery of the Sanskrit dramatic tradition.

Good background reading on the subcontinent can be found in several books. Percival Spear's "India: A Modern History" (*Univ. of Michigan Press* 1961 new rev. ed. 1972 $10.00) has been split into two volumes by *Penguin*, of which Volume 2, covering the sixteenth to mid-twentieth centuries, has been published (1966 pap. $1.45). *Choice* "strongly recommends" the *Penguin* for advanced students: "Its value certainly exceeds its price." "India: A World in Transition" (*Praeger* 1963 rev. ed. 1966 3rd ed. 1968 $8.50 pap. $3.95) is by Beatrice Pitney Lamb, a former editor of the *United Nations News.* "After a brief and skillful analysis of the pivotal historical developments which have left their imprint upon the character of today's India, she discusses the importance of Hinduism, the religious minority groups, caste, cultural links, and language barriers as they are affected by or affect social change." Kusum Nair, an Indian newspaperwoman, spent a year visiting Indian villages. Her "Blossoms in the Dust: The Human Factor in Indian Development" (*Praeger* 1962 pap. $2.25) supplies "grass-roots evidence much needed by Indian planners, economists and social psychologists." "India, India," by Lisa Hobbs of the *San Francisco Examiner* (*McGraw-Hill* 1967 $4.95) is a "controversial" account of her return to India after an absence of 20 years, which "should rank as one of the most accurate and sensitive evocations of contemporary India available"—(*PW*). "The Cambridge Shorter History of India" by John Allan, Sir T. Wolseley Haig, and H. H. Dodwell (*Verry* 1964 1969 $12.00) is a standard historical treatment of India. Arthur L. Basham's "The Wonder That Was India: A Survey of the History and Culture of the Indian Subcontinent before the Coming of the Muslims" (1954 *Taplinger* 3rd ed. 1968 $13.50; *Grove* Evergreen Bks. 1959 pap. $6.95) includes bibliographical material on the literary history of pre-Muslim India and on translations into English of Sanskrit and early Tamil works. "India: A Critical Bibliography" by Michael J. Mahar (*Univ. of Arizona Press* 1964 pap. $3.50) "contains about 2,000 topically arranged entries . . . mainly books published since 1940. . . . The annotations are descriptive rather than critical. A basic reference work"—(*LJ*). It is indexed.

Alexander, Horace. CONSIDER INDIA: An Essay in Values. *Asia Pub. House* 1961 $4.50

> An English Quaker "buttresses his philosophy of universal brotherhood with liberal . . . interpretations of Hinduism and Buddhism. In considering India, his strong affinity is for Buddhism reborn, the Bhagavad Gita, Gandhi, Gandhi's successor Vinoba Bhave, and non-violence . . . he pays tribute to other Indians like . . . Tagore who have contributed to what he suggests may be 'a new world culture.' Indians as well as philosophical and religious-minded Westerners will be interested"—(*LJ*).

Ali, Ahmed, Trans. and ed. THE GOLDEN TRADITION. Studies in Oriental Culture Ser. *Columbia* 1973 $15.00 pap. $4.95. Translations from the Urdu of works by eighteenth- and nineteenth-century writers, with commentary by the editor. This period saw the zenith of Urdu literature.

Alphonso-Karkala, J. B. ANTHOLOGY OF INDIAN LITERATURE. *Penguin* Pelican 1971 pap. $2.95

INDO-ENGLISH LITERATURE IN THE NINETEENTH CENTURY. 1970. *Paragon Reprint* 1971 $5.00

Asher, R. E., and R. Radharkrishnan. TAMIL PROSE READER. *Cambridge* 1971 $8.50

Bhattacharya, Deben, Trans. SONGS OF THE BARDS OF BENGAL. *Grove* Evergreen 1970 pap. $2.95

Birla, L. N. FOLK TALES FROM RAJASTHAN. *Asia Pub. House* 1964 $4.75

Chaitanya, Krishna. A HISTORY OF MALAYALAM LITERATURE. *Kennikat* 1971 $17.50

Chavarria-Agular, O. L., Ed. TRADITIONAL INDIA. *Prentice-Hall* 1964 pap. $1.95. Excerpts from outstanding works on the India of the pre-Christian period, linked by commentary.

Coomaraswamy, A. THE DANCE OF SHIVA. *Farrar, Straus* rev. ed. 1957 pap. $2.45; *Gordon Press* $11.00

Dimock, Edward C., Trans. and ed. THE THIEF OF LOVE: Bengali Tales from Court and Village. *Univ. of Chicago Press* 1963 $9.50

(Ed.) THE LITERATURES OF INDIA: An Introduction. *Univ. of Chicago Press* 1974 $12.00

(With Denise Levertov, Trans.) IN PRAISE OF KRISHNA: Songs from the Bengali Cycle. *Doubleday* (UNESCO) 1967 Anchor Bks. $1.25. Sixteenth- and seventeenth-century allegorical poems on the love of Radha and Krishna. With commentary.

Dutt, Rhomesh C. CULTURAL HERITAGE OF BENGAL: A Biographical and Critical History from Earliest Times. *Verry* 3rd rev. ed. 1962 $6.50. An excellent work whose scope includes the rich literature in Bengali, a major language of northern India and present-day Bangladesh.

Faridi, Shah N. HINDU HISTORY OF URDU LITERATURE. *Verry* 1966 $4.50

Gargi, Balwant. FOLK THEATRE OF INDIA. Fwd. by Millard B. Rogers. *Univ. of Washington Press* 1966 $8.95

"An excellent study [and] a brilliant combination of art and literature"—*(LJ)*.

George, K. M. SURVEY OF MALAYALAM LITERATURE. *Asia Pub. House* $8.50. Malayalam is the language of part of southern India.

WESTERN INFLUENCE ON MALAYALAM LANGUAGE AND LITERATURE. *South Asia Bks.* 1972 $7.50

Ghose, Sudhin N. FOLK TALES AND FAIRY STORIES FROM INDIA. *Golden Cockerel Press* 1962 (standard) $20.00 (special) $40.00

Gorekar, N. S. GLIMPSES OF URDU LITERATURE. *Inter-Culture Assocs.* 1961 $4.00

Government of India. THE NATIONAL BIBLIOGRAPHY OF INDIAN LITERATURE 1901–1953. Comp. by B. S. Kesavan, Director of the Indian National Scientific Documentation Center, New Delhi, and Y. M. Mulay, Librarian of the National Library, Calcutta. 3 vols. *Verry* each $25.00

For the first time in history, an accurate and exhaustive record of all Indian publications in English and the following languages is available in roman script: Assamese, Bengali, Gujerati, Kannada, Malayalam, Hindi, Marathi, Oriya, Punjabi, Sanskrit, Tamil, Telugu, and Urdu.

Gowen, Herbert. A HISTORY OF INDIAN LITERATURE. 1931. *Richard West* 1973 $21.25

Guha-Thakurta, P. BENGALI DRAMA. 1930. *Greenwood* 1974 $11.75

Humayun Kabir, Ed. GREEN AND GOLD: Stories and Poems from Bengal. 1958. *Greenwood* 1970 $13.00. An anthology devoted to contemporary Bengali works.

Ingalls, Daniel H. H., Trans. and ed. AN ANTHOLOGY OF SANSKRIT COURT POETRY: Vidyakara's Subhasitaratnakosa. *Harvard Univ. Press* 1965 $17.50

Short specimens from the works of over 200 poets of the eighth to eleventh centuries. Even the neophyte will enjoy these "glowing, fresh sense-evoking epigrams and lyric passages"—*(LJ)*.

Jussawalla, Adil, Ed. NEW WRITING IN INDIA. *Penguin* 1974 pap. $2.25

Karan Singh, Y., Trans. and ed. SHADOW AND SUNLIGHT: An Anthology of Dogra-Pahari Songs. *Asia Pub. House* 1963 $7.50

Musical notations and translations into Hindi. This selection was made by His Highness Maharaja Karan Singh, Head of the State of Jammu and Kashmir, poet, philosopher, musicologist, and Ph.D., Delhi University. "The editor, a poet in both Dogri and English, has wisely made his English translations close to the original rather than aiming at English poetry. The Hindi translations will be useful to students of that language."

Kripalani, Krishna. MODERN INDIAN LITERATURE: A Panoramic Glimpse. *Humanities Press* 1968 $4.50; *Tuttle* 1971 $3.50

Krishna-Rao, A. V. THE INDO-ANGLIAN NOVEL AND THE CHANGING TRADITION. *Int. Pubns. Service* 1974 $10.50

Lal, P. THE CONCEPT OF AN INDIAN LITERATURE: Six Essays. *South Asia Bks.* 1972 $8.50; *Inter-Culture Assocs.* 1973 $4.00

(Trans. and ed.) GREAT SANSKRIT PLAYS IN MODERN TRANSLATION. With introd. and commentary. *New Directions* 1963 $10.00 pap. $4.45

Plays from the fourth century B.C. to the ninth century A.D. translated in a "precise, flexible modern idiom"—*(LJ)*.

Matthews, D. J., and C. Schackle. AN ANTHOLOGY OF CLASSICAL URDU LOVE LYRICS. *Oxford* 1972 $19.25

Misra, Vidya Niwas, Ed. MODERN HINDI POETRY: An Anthology. Trans. by Leonard Nathan and others. Pref. by Josephine Miles; introd. by S. H. Vatsyayan. *Indiana Univ. Press* 1965 $6.50

> A collection of about 40 young poets. "What makes this anthology unique is the fact that the original poems have been translated, 'trans-created' and adapted from Hindi into English by Americans, all accomplished and gifted poets in their own right. It is an imaginative and pleasing experiment"—(K. Natwar-Singh, in the *N.Y. Times*).

Natwar-Singh, K. TALES FROM MODERN INDIA. *Macmillan* 1966 Collier Bks. 1973 pap. $2.95

> Short stories by 13 twentieth-century Indian writers, from Tagore to Rama Rau, including some not yet known to the West. "A notable achievement"—(Nancy Wilson Ross, in the *N.Y. Times*). "Surpasses any previous, modern English language collection"—(*Choice*).

Panter-Downs, Mollie. OOTY PRESERVED: A Victorian Hill Station in India. *Farrar, Straus* 1967 $4.95. From the pages of the *New Yorker* comes this charming description of a once-flourishing British resort as it is in the late 1960s.

Peeradina, S., Ed. CONTEMPORARY INDIAN POETRY IN ENGLISH. *Verry* 1973 $7.00

Prabhavananda, Swami, and Frederick Manchester. THE SPIRITUAL HERITAGE OF INDIA. *Vedanta Press* 1963 pap. $1.95. A compact yet comprehensive chronological survey with ample quotations and comments illustrating the great works of Indian thought (the *Vedas*, the *Gita*, Jainism, Buddhism, the six systems of Hindu thought) and of the expounders of Vedanta, including Sri Ramakrishna.

Rahbar, Muhammad Daud. CUP OF JAMSHID: A Collection of Original Ghazal Poetry. *Claude Stark* 1974 $7.00. *Ghazal* poetry is lyrical verse dominated by themes of sexual love which also serve as the vehicle for the poet's expression of his devotion to his God. Ghalib (*q.v.*) and Mir (c. 1723–1810) are the outstanding exponents of this verse form written in classical Urdu.

Ramaunjan, A. K., Trans. THE INTERIOR LANDSCAPE: Love Poems from a Classical Tamil Anthology. *Indiana Univ. Press* 1967 pap. $1.95

> "Although this poetry is unfamiliar, it is delightful reading"—(*LJ*).

Sadiq, Muhammad. A HISTORY OF URDU LITERATURE. 1964 o.p. This valuable history is unfortunately no longer available.

Sen, Sukumar. HISTORY OF BENGALI LITERATURE. 2nd ed. *South Asia Bks.* 1971 $4.75

Sharda, S. R. SUFI THOUGHT: Its Development in Panjab and Its Effects on Panjabi Literature from Baba Farid to 1850 A.D. *South Asia Bks.* 1974 $11.50

Spencer, Dorothy M. INDIAN FICTION IN ENGLISH: An Annotated Bibliography. *Univ. of Pennsylvania Press* 1960 $4.50. Comprehensive guide to fiction and autobiography and a good introduction to Indian culture with some 300 selected and annotated items, arranged alphabetically by author; introductory essay on "Indian Society, Culture and Fiction."

Srinivasa, Iyengar, K. R. INDIAN WRITING IN ENGLISH. *Asia Pub. House* 1962 2nd ed. 1973 pap. $11.00. A useful and readable survey, covering 150 years of "Indo-Anglian literature," up to 1961. Single chapters deal with major figures such as Gandhi, Nehru, Raja Rao, Tagore, Sri Aurobindo and Narayan, with survey chapters on journalism, poetry, drama and the novel. Selected bibliographies are supplied for each chapter.

Thani Nagayam, S. X. LANDSCAPE AND POETRY: A Study of Nature in Classical Tamil Poetry. *Asia Pub. House* 1967 $4.25. Tamil, with Sanskrit, is the major language of India.

TAMIL CULTURE AND CIVILIZATION: Readings, The Classical Period. *Asia Pub. House* 1971 $7.95

Van Buitenen, J. A. B., Trans. TALES OF ANCIENT INDIA. *Univ. of Chicago Press* 1959 $7.00 pap. 1969 $2.45. Fourteen robust tales, several of the major ones appearing for the first time in English, and all of them newly translated from the Sanskrit into clear, readable and entertaining English.

Vidyapati, Thakura. LOVE SONGS OF VIDYAPATI. Trans. by Deben Bhattacharya. Ed. with introd. and notes by W. G. Archer. 1965 *Inter-Culture Assocs.* 1970 pap. $1.20; *Grove* 1970 pap. $2.95
Fine translation of classic of Indian erotic literature. "Worthy and delightful"—*(Choice)*.

Weaver, Albrecht. THE HISTORY OF INDIAN LITERATURE. *Folcroft* 1973 $35.00

Williams, Haydn M., Ed. STUDIES IN MODERN INDIAN FICTION IN ENGLISH. 2 vols. *Inter-Culture Assocs.* Greybird Bks. 1975 $24.00 pap. $8.00

See also Chapter 4, World Religions—Hinduism, Reader's Adviser, *Vol. 3.*

THE VEDAS. c. 1300–1000 B.C. *See Chapter 4, World Religions—Hinduism*, Reader's Adviser, *Vol. 3.*

THE UPANISHADS. c. 600 B.C. *See Chapter 4, World Religions—Hinduism*, Reader's Adviser, *Vol. 3.*

THE RAMAYANA (The Lay of Rama). c. 500 B.C.–c. 200 A.D.
The Sanskrit epic, begun about 500 B.C., was probably the work of many writers but its reputed author was the poet Valmiki (fl. third century B.C.). In its present form, of which there are three versions, it contains about 24,000 couplets, divided into seven books. Books II–VI contain a two-part story: the realistic first part about Prince Rama and his half-brother and their succession to the throne; the second about Rama's supernatural adventures with gods, demons, and talking animals and birds. Books I and VII, added as a religious framework, have made the work a sacred text for millions of Hindus, who strive to emulate Prince Rama as a reincarnation of Vishnu and his wife, Sita.

THE RAMAYANA OF VALMIKI. Trans. by Ralph T. H. Griffith. 1870–1874 3rd ed. *Int. Pubns. Service* 1963 $9.00. A good verse translation which preserves much of the flavor of the original.

THE RAMAYANA: The Story of Rama. *Inter-Culture Assocs.* 1974 $9.50 pap. $4.95

THE RAMAYANA. Trans. by C. Rajagopalachari. *Orientalia* 1968 pap. $1.95

THE RAMAYANA (and "Mahabharata"). Trans. and ed. by Romesh C. Dutt. *Dutton* Everyman's $3.95 pap. 1972 $1.75; (without "Mahabharata") *Inter-Culture Assocs.* 1966 pap. $2.40. A fairly good metrical translation of the main narrative elements; a useful abridgment.

QUEST FOR SITA. Sel. from The Ramayana and ed. by Maurice Collis. *Putnam* Capricorn Bks. 1965 pap. $1.95

THE RAMAYANA: As Told by Aubrey Menon. 1954 *Greenwood* $1.75. A satirical recreation of the epic featuring originality of interpretation rather than fidelity to tradition.

THE RAMAYANA OF R. K. NARAYAN: A Shortened Modern Prose Version of the Indian Epic, Suggested by the Tamil Version of Kamban. *Viking* 1972 $7.95. An Indian novelist's recreation of the Tamil epic which was based on Valmiki's.

THE RAMAYANA OF GOSWAMI TULSIDAS (Rama Charit Manas Tulsidas). Trans. by S. P. Bahadur. *Inter-Culture Assocs.* 1973 $7.50

Books about the Ramayana
Indian Epic Poetry: An Analysis of Ramayana. By M. Monier-Williams. 1893. *Krishna Press* $25.95. An excellent account of the epic with comparative references to Western literature.

Ramayana: Myth or Reality? By H. D. Sankalia. *South Asia Bks.* 1973 $6.50

Ramayana in Telugu and Tamil: A Comparative Study. By C. R. Sarma. *Verry* $5.00

ASOKA, King of Magadha. fl. 259 B.C.

THE EDICTS OF ASOKA. Trans. and ed. by N. A. Nikam and R. P. McKeon. *Univ. of Chicago Press* 1958 $4.00 Phoenix Bks. pap. $1.50

ASOKAN INSCRIPTIONS. Trans. and ed. by R. Basak. *Verry* 1959 $5.50

Books about Asoka

Asoka Maurya. By Balkrishna Gokhale. Rulers and Statesmen of the World Ser. *Twayne* 1966 $6.95

Asoka. By Radhakumud Mookerji. 1962 *South Asia Bks.* 1972 $7.00

MAHABHARATA, BHAGAVADGITA. 200 B.C.–200 A.D. *See Chapter 4, World Religions—Hinduism*, Reader's Adviser, *Vol. 3*.

VĀTSYĀYANA. c. 300 A.D.

The famous Hindu classic was first translated into English from the Sanskrit by Sir Richard Burton in 1883 for the Kama Sastra Society of London and Benares. "Vātsyāyana made it clear that he drew on earlier Kāma Sutras, none of which, it seems, survived except in references in other works. 'Kama' in sanskrit means desire, affection, love, lust, sensual pleasure; it is also one of the four goals of life, and it may refer to the god of love. 'Sutra' indicates a style of writing composed of aphorisms, precepts, and the like. Vātsyāyana's treatise has seven parts: general observations on social life, classes of women, and so on; on sexual union and various practices . . .; on acquisition of a wife; conduct of a wife; about wives of other men; about courtesans; on how to be attractive, adornment, and so forth. The style is dry, matter of fact, highly technical, at times [unintentionally] hilarious, very readable. As Professor A. L. Basham, University of London, comments: 'It cannot be said to support promiscuity or to encourage perversion. . . . There is no trace of romantic embroidery or false glamour.' . . . Unquestionably the text has value as it throws considerable light on secular life of ancient India"—(*LJ*). The "Kāma Sutra" had a great influence of Kālidāsa (*q.v.*) and other writers of Sanskrit poetry.

THE KAMA SUTRA OF VĀTSYĀYANA: The Classic Hindu Treatise on Love and Social Conduct. Trans. by Sir Richard Burton and F. F. Arbuthnot *Berkley* pap. $1.25; trans. by Sir Richard F. Burton, introd. by John W. Spellman, fwd. by Santha Rama Rau *Dutton* 1962 1964 pap. $1.45; trans. by Sir Richard Burton and F. F. Arbuthnot, ed. with introd. by W. G. Archer *Putnam* Capricorn Bks. 1963 pap. $.95

KĀLIDĀSA. 376–454?

The Indian dramatist and poet Kālidāsa is often regarded as one of the most remarkable figures in classic Sanskrit literature.

SHAKUNTALĀ: A Play and Other Writings. Trans. with introd. by Arthur W. Ryder. *Dutton* Everyman's 1959 pap. $1.35. Ryder made his free translation in 1912. "Sakuntalā" is a play in verse, a fanciful tale of lovers who are separated by adversity and later reunited by happy chance.

SHAKUNTALĀ. Trans. by Bagishwar Vidhalankar. *Inter-Culture Assocs*. pap. $1.10

THE CLOUD MESSENGER. Trans. from the Sanskrit "*Meghaduta*" by Franklin and Eleanor Edgerton. *Univ. of Michigan Press* 1964 $4.40 pap. $1.75

"The Cloud Messenger," a new and beautiful translation of a 110-stanza lyric, is "an exquisite love poem, simple, powerful, and rich in imagery, recommended to all subject and poetry collections"—(*LJ*). There is a roman transcription of the Sanskrit text.

MEGHDOOT. Trans. by Bagavatsharan Upadhyaya. *Inter-Culture Assocs.* pap. $1.10

THE DIVINE MARRIAGE. Trans. by George Bosworth Burch. *Verry* 1970 $4.50

DYNASTY OF RAGHU. Trans. by Robert Antoine. *Inter-Culture Assocs.* 1975 $6.00

Books about Kālidāsa

Kālidāsa. By Krishnamoorthy. World Authors Ser. *Twayne* $6.95

Kālidāsa: His Style and His Times. By S. A. Sabnis. *Int. Pubns. Service* 1966 $9.00

BHARTRIHARI. fl. 600 A.D.

The work of this poet, who traditionally is thought to have flourished at the end of the sixth and beginning of the seventh centuries, is now considered to be that of a group of poets. The translation into free verse by a University Fellow in Oriental Studies at the University of Pennsylvania is based on the Sanskrit of D. D. Kosambi's edition, published in India in 1948. "The *Satakatrayam* contains 200 poems and is divided into three sections—on man and his worldly gains, erotic emotion, and renunciation. . . . Though translated with scholarly care, this edition is aimed at the general reader. . . . The spirit and sonority of the poems make it indispensable for poetry collections, and its place in the history of secular Indian literature makes it important for more general collections"—(*LJ*).

POEMS. Trans. by Barbara Stoler Miller; fwd. by William Theodore de Bary. With the transliterated Sanskrit text of the "Satakatrayam: Niti, Sringara, Vairagya." UNESCO Collection of Representative Works, Indian Ser. *Columbia* 1967 $12.00 pap. $2.25

VAIRAGYA-SATAKAM: The Hundred Verses on Renunciation. *Vedanta Press* pap. $.75

GHĀLIB, MIRZĀ ASADULLĀH KHĀN. 1797–1869.

A poet and writer who was born in Agra and spent most of his life in Delhi, he began writing Urdu and Persian verse as a child and compiled his first Urdu collection in 1821. For the next 30 years, however, he wrote almost solely in Persian. He was one of the greatest writers of Urdu lyric poetry, the *ghazal*.

THE LETTERS OF GHALIB, SHAKESPEARE OF THE INDIAN MUSLIM WORLD. Trans. and ed. by Muhammad Daud Rahbar. *Claude Stark* 2 vols. 1976 set $24.00 pap. set $15.00

GHALIB, 1797–1869: Vol. 1 Life and Letters. Ed. by Ralph Russell and Khurshidul Islam. *Harvard Univ. Press* 1969 $15.00

TAGORE, SIR RABINDRANATH (also Ravindranatha Thakura). 1861–1941. (Nobel Prize 1913)

The Hindu poet-philosopher was on a lecture tour in the United States when he was awarded the Nobel Prize in 1913. Harriet Monroe had published in *Poetry* his first work in English, translations he had made himself of his Bengálese poems. He used the £8,000 prize money for the upkeep of the school which he had established in 1901 at Santiniketan, Bolpur, Bengal, and which later developed into an international university called Visva-Bharati. He was knighted in 1915 but surrendered the title four years later in protest against British suppression of the Punjab riots; later he permitted it to be used again. He was the author of about 60 volumes of poetry in addition to novels, plays, short stories, and essays. His verse, even in English, is full of music and color, and its lofty spirit assures its survival.

Late in life he took up painting and set over 3,000 poems to music. His paintings were little known here until the publication of "Drawings and Paintings of Rabindranath Tagore: Centenary, 1860–1961" (introd. by Prithwish Neogy *Heinman* 1961 $15.00). Selected by Monroe Wheeler of New York's Museum of Modern Art and Kshitis Roy, the work offers a good introduction to one aspect of a many-sided man. Other sides are now being revealed. Interested in science, a founder of three schools in which there is more than a trace of modern educational theories, Tagore was "an Asian philosopher who believed that the West had an important contribution to make to the East, a man who believed in world unity long before the days of the League of Nations." A lifelong friend of Gandhi (*q.v.*), he was one of the earlier prophets of One World.

COLLECTED WORKS. *Gordon Press* $190.00

COLLECTED POEMS AND PLAYS. *Macmillan* 1937 1966 $7.00

COLLECTED STORIES. *Verry* pap. $2.75

A TAGORE READER. Ed. by Amiya Chakravarty. 1961. *Beacon* 1966 pap. $3.95. A new collection of whole pieces and excerpts: letters, travel notes, drama, short stories, poems, criticism, and philosophy.

A TAGORE TESTAMENT. Trans. by Indu Dutt. *Inter-Culture Assocs.* 1969 pap. $1.60

TOWARDS UNIVERSAL MAN. *Asia Pub. House* 1961 1969 $6.50

This anthology of 18 essays, newly translated by Indian scholars and little known outside Bengal, was prepared by the Tagore Commemorative Volume Society in honor of the centenary of his birth. Written between 1892 and 1941, these essays "illuminate an aspect of Tagore's mind not well known in the West—his intense interest in the social conditions from which the rising tide of nationalism developed."

THE GOLDEN BOAT. 1893. Trans. by Bhabani Bhattacharya. *Inter-Culture Assocs.* 4th ed. 1970 pap. $1.80

CHITRA: A Play. 1895. *Verry* pap. $1.75. A lyrical drama based on a story from the Mahabharata.

SACRIFICE (1901) AND OTHER PLAYS. *Verry* $2.75

BINODINI. 1902. Trans. by Krishna Kripalani. *Univ. Press of Hawaii* 1965 $5.00. First English translation of Tagore's novel "Chokner."

GORA. 1908. *Verry* pap. $3.75. A social and psychological novel reflecting Tagore's view of the untenability of orthodox Hinduism in the modern world and the weakness, as well, of narrow, modern sectarianism.

KING OF THE DARK CHAMBER. 1910. *Verry* pap. $3.50. An expression in dramatic form of the concern of much of Tagore's poetry—the mystery of the relationship between God and man.

GITANJALI (Song Offerings). 1912. Introd. by W. B. Yeats. 1935 1952 *Branden* gift ed. $2.00 pap. $.95; *Verry* pap. $2.25. A collection of prose translations by the author from the original Bengali.

THE POST OFFICE. 1912. Trans. by Devabrata Mukerjee. *Cuala Press* (dist. by Irish Univ. Presses) 1971 $9.60; *Verry* $2.75

CRESCENT MOON: Child-Poems. 1913. *Verry* $2.00

THE GARDENER—LYRICS. 1913. *Verry* pap. $2.00. Lyrics of love and life translated from the original Bengali by the author.

SADHANA: Realization of Life. 1914. *Verry* $3.00; *Omen Press* 1972 pap. $3.25

FRUIT GATHERING: Sequel to Gitanjali. 1916. *Verry* $2.75

HOME AND THE WORLD. 1916. *Verry* $3.75. A novel reflecting Bengali political atmosphere and struggles during the first decades of this century.

HUNGRY STONES AND OTHER STORIES. 1916. *AMS Press* 1970 $10.00; *Verry* $4.50

STRAY BIRDS. 1916. *Verry* $2.50

NATIONALISM. 1917. *Greenwood* 1973 $9.50

PERSONALITY: Lectures Delivered in America. 1917. *Verry* pap. $3.25

MASHI AND OTHER STORIES. 1918. Short Story Index Reprint Ser. *Bks. for Libraries* $10.25

THE WRECK. 1921 *Verry* pap. $4.00

CREATIVE UNITY. 1922. *Gordon Press* $35.00; *Verry* pap. $2.75

RED OLEANDERS. 1924. *Verry* $2.75. A drama in one act.

BROKEN TIES AND OTHER STORIES. 1925. *Bks. for Libraries* $10.25. Includes the stories Broken Ties, In the Night, The Fugitive Gold, The Editor, Giribala, The Lost Jewels, and Emancipation.

FIREFLIES. 1928. *Macmillan* 1951 $6.00

THE RELIGION OF MAN. 1931 1950 *Beacon* 1961 pap. $2.45; *Hillary House* 1970 pap. $2.00. The Hibbert lectures delivered in London, 1930.

SHEAVES: Poems and Songs. 1932. Trans. by Nagendranath Gupta. 2nd ed. 1950. *Greenwood* 1971 $9.00

MY REMINISCENCES. 1912. *Gordon Press* $35.00. Gives the background of Tagore's early life.

GLIMPSES OF BENGAL: Selected from the Letters of Sir Rabindranath Tagore, 1885–1895. 1921. *Verry* pap. $2.25

Books about Tagore

The Philosophy of Rabindranath Tagore. By S. Rhadakrishnan. 1918. Studies in Asiatic Literature *Haskell* 1974 $14.95

Rabindranath Tagore: Poet and Dramatist. By Edward J. Thompson. 1926. Studies in Asiatic Literature *Haskell* 1974 $15.95; *Richard West* $15.00

Rabindranath Tagore: A Centenary Volume, 1861–1961. *Int. Pubns. Service* 1961 $15.00. Studies on the many aspects of his personality and genius contributed by writers from many parts of the world. A publication of the Sahitya Akademi (National Academy of Letters), Rabindra Bhavan, New Delhi, India.

Rabindranath Tagore: A Biography. By Krishna Kripalani. *Oxford* 1962 $8.50. One of the best studies of the poet's life by Tagore's granddaughter's husband.

The Social Thinking of Rabindranath Tagore. By Sasadhar Sinha. *Asia Pub. House* 1962 $4.50. Although lacking in unity and consistency, and marred by typographical errors, the book does give some idea of this little-known side of a great man.

Asian Ideas of East and West: Tagore and His Critics in Japan, China and India. By Stephen N. Hay. East Asian Ser. *Harvard Univ. Press* 1970 $15.00

GOKHALE, GOPAL KRISHNA.   1866–1915.

Historian and economist, Gokhale "was one of the leading pre-World War I Indian politicians, also a professor and a member of various legislative bodies. Already as a young man he was called Mahatma (Great Spirit) by Gandhi"—*(LJ)*.

THE SPEECHES AND WRITINGS OF GOPAL KRISHNA GOKHALE: Vol. 1, Economics. Ed. by R. P. Patwardham, L.E.S. and D. V. Ambekar. *Asia Pub. House* 1963 1968 $7.75

"This new edition, of which Volume 1 deals with economic subjects, is the first comprehensive compilation of his work. . . . Numerous footnotes by the editors provide helpful brief biographical information about many English and Indian personalities mentioned by Gokhale. . . . Naturally, interest will be limited to students of India's economic history, but for them this is valuable source material"—*(LJ)*.

ANCIENT INDIA. *Asia Pub. House* 4th ed. 1960 $5.00

ASOKA MAURYA. *Twayne* 1966 $6.95

(Ed.) ASIAN STUDIES: No. 2, Images of India. *Humanities Press* 1971 $6.50

SAMUDRA GUPTA. *Asia Pub. House* $6.50

Books about Gokhale

Gokhale: The Man and his Mission. By C. P. Aiyar and others. *Asia Pub. House* $1.75

GANDHI, MOHANDAS K(ARAMCHAND).   1869–1948. *See Chapter 4, World Religions*, Reader's Adviser, *Vol. 3.*

IQBAL, SIR MUHAMMAD.   c. 1873–1938.

Iqbal is the most popular Urdu poet of this century. He studied law and philosophy at Cambridge and took a Ph.D. from Munich. In 1930, he declared his belief in the necessity of a Muslim state in northwest India, what is now the core of Pakistan. He was also a philosopher and wrote in Persian as well as Urdu. He is acclaimed as Pakistan's national poet.

SIX LECTURES ON THE RECONSTRUCTION OF RELIGIOUS THOUGHT IN ISLAM. 1930. *Scholarly Resources, Inc.* $14.00. A theoretical and political discussion and a part of his corpus concerned with awakening contemporary Muslims from spiritual slumber.

THE NEW ROSE GARDEN OF MYSTERY and THE BOOK OF SLAVES. Versified English trans. by M. Hadi Hussain. Introd. by S. A. Vahid. *Orientalia* 1969 pap. $1.95

IQBAL: Poet-Philosopher of Pakistan. Ed. by Hafeez Malik. Studies in Oriental Culture Ser. *Columbia* 1971 $13.50

TILAK, LAKSHIMIBAI (Gokhale).   1873–1936.

I FOLLOW AFTER: An Autobiography. 1934–37. Trans. by E. Josephine Inkster. *Oxford* 1950 $2.40

The original is in Marathi, the language of southern Bombay State. The author was the wife of Narayan Waman Tilak, well-known Indian Christian, poet and writer of hymns, who became converted after his marriage. His wife eventually "follows after." "Her autobiography contains much information on life in the latter part of the nineteenth century among Maratha Brahmans as well as material on Indian Christians at this period"—(Spencer's "Indian Fiction in English").

RADHAKRISHNAN, SIR SARVEPALLI.   1888–   *See Chapter 4, World Religions*, Reader's Adviser, *Vol. 3.*

CHAUDHURI, NIRAD C(HANDRA).   1897–

Mr. Chaudhuri is a learned and controversial Indian journalist, "the most widely read Indian writer of today, and deservedly so"—(Khushwant Singh, in the *N.Y. Times*). In "The Continent of Circe: Being an Essay on the Peoples of India" (o.p.), the first of a series he plans to write on the peoples of India, he reexamines Indian history and development from the Aryan invasion to the present to illustrate his thesis that the Indian environment has devitalized and dehumanized its inhabitants. "Nonetheless, the final impression is not that of an iconoclast but a positive thinker, a man deeply identified with his country and with the Hindu faith. Not in 50 years have I read anything more irritating, thought-provoking, witty, beautifully worded and exhilarating"— (Singh). "A Passage to England" (U.S. 1960, o.p.) is an account of the author's first trip outside India. The *New Yorker* called it "miraculously perceptive and charmingly written. . . . Though Mr. Chaudhuri stresses the differences between East and West, his book will help the reader toward an unsentimental appreciation of both."

THE AUTOBIOGRAPHY OF AN UNKNOWN INDIAN. *Univ. of California Press* 1968 $10.00

Contains much information on life in East Bengal at the beginning of this century. "It is invaluable for its pictures of life in Calcutta, where the author lived from 1910–1942"—(Spencer's "Indian Fiction in English").

To LIVE OR NOT TO LIVE. *South Asia Bks.* 1971 pap. $2.50; *Inter-Culture Assocs.* pap. $1.60

INTELLECTUAL IN INDIA. *Verry* 1970 $3.50

NEHRU, JAWAHARLAL.   1899–1964. *See Chapter 9, History, Government and Politics, Reader's Adviser, Vol. 3.*

NARAYAN, R. K.   1906–

R. K. Narayan writes enchanting and deceptively simple stories in English about the south Indian town of Malgudi and its people. He "is one of the few writers of fiction who does not falsify his picture of Indian society in order to excite false pathos or point a moral." He was introduced to British readers by Graham Greene (*q.v.*) and he has stated that he owes his literary career to the English author. "Narayan's comedy . . . is classical art, profound and delicate art"—(*N.Y. Times*). Santha Rama Rau has said, "Narayan is unquestionably India's finest novelist, and his wonderful world of Malgudi is one of the great fictional creations of our time."

SWAMI AND FRIENDS (1935) and THE BACHELOR OF ARTS (1937): Two Novels of Malgudi. *Michigan State Univ. Press* 1954 $3.95; Swami and Friends *Fawcett* 1970 pap. $.75; The Bachelor of Arts *Inter-Culture Assocs.* 1970 pap. $2.25. The first novel pictures episodes in the life of a small boy, the second depicts the hero at college.

THE DARK ROOM. 1938. Orient Paperback Ser. *Inter-Culture Assocs.* 1972 pap. $1.60'

GRATEFUL TO LIFE AND DEATH. (Orig. "The English Teacher.") 1945. *Michigan State Univ. Press* 1953 1961 $3.00; *Pyramid Bks.* 1972 pap. $1.75

AN ASTROLOGER'S DAY AND OTHER STORIES. 1947. *Inter-Culture Assocs.* 1964 pap. $2.25

THE PRINTER OF MALGUDI. 1949. *Michigan State Univ. Press* 1957 $3.50

THE FINANCIAL EXPERT. 1952. *Michigan State Univ. Press* 1953 $4.00; *Farrar, Straus Noonday* 1959 pap. $2.50. The life of a moneylender—his trials and tribulations.

WAITING FOR THE MAHATMA. *Michigan State Univ. Press* 1955 $6.00; *Farrar, Straus Noonday* 1975 $2.45. The love story of an innocent who is caught up in the Quit India movement.

NEXT SUNDAY. 1955. Orient Paperback Ser. *Inter-Culture Assocs.* 1973 pap. $1.80

LAWLEY ROAD AND OTHER STORIES. 1956. *Inter-Culture Assocs.* 1969 pap. $1.00

THE GUIDE. 1958. *Inter-Culture Assocs.* 1975 pap. $2.50. The story of Raju's rise from shopkeeper to holy man.

THE VENDOR OF SWEETS. *Viking* 1967 1969 lge.-type ed. $6.95; *Avon Bks.* pap. $1.45. The story of an old man's problems with his Americanized son.

A HORSE AND TWO GOATS. *Viking* Studio Bks. 1970 $5.75

RELUCTANT GURU. *Inter-Culture Assocs.* 1975 pap. $2.00

THE RAMAYANA OF R. K. NARAYAN: A Shortened Modern Prose Version of the Indian Epic, Suggested by the Tamil Version of Kamban. *Viking* 1972 $7.95

MY DAYS: A Memoir. *Viking* 1974 $8.95

Books about Marayan

R. K. Narayan. By William Walsh. Writers and Their Work Ser. *British Book Centre* 1972 $2.95 pap. $1.20

R. K. Narayan. By P. S. Sundaran. *Humanities Press* 1973 pap. $2.50

The Novels of R. K. Narayan. By Lakshmi Holmstrong. *Inter-Culture Assocs.* 1975 $6.00

RAO, RAJA.   1909–

The novelist was born into a very old Brahmin family of Mysore. He took his degree in English and history at Madras University and went to Europe at the age of 19, researching in literature at the University of Montpelier and at the Sorbonne. He spent the war years in India searching for the spiritual tradition of India, traveling on his quest from the Himalayas to Cape Comorin.

KANTHAPURA: A Novel. 1937. *New Directions* 1967 pap. $2.75. E. M. Forster (*q.v.*) has referred to "Kanthapura" as perhaps the best novel in English to come from India. It is the story of how Gandhi's struggle for independence from the British came to a typical village, Kanthapura, in South India.

THE SERPENT AND THE ROPE. 1960. *Inter-Culture Assocs.* 1968 pap. $3.50

Of this novel, the British *Observer* said, "Raja Rao has developed an original English style, in which poetry, philosophy and laughter delightfully mingle. It is about the whole nature of the contrasts between India and Europe, East and West. It is witty and lively." "In this beautiful semi-autobiographical novel, Raja Rao presents a new and different kind of Hindu sage, a Brahmin who is equally attracted to East and West, commutes frequently between the two, and dramatizes in his own person their irreconcilable conflict"—(*N.Y. Times*). For the same book he was praised by Lawrence Durrell and André Malraux.

THE CAT AND SHAKESPEARE: A Tale of Modern India. 1963. Orient Paperback Ser. *Inter-Culture Assocs.* 1975 pap. $1.40

"The Cat and Shakespeare" is a difficult, sometimes puzzling fable—" 'a metaphysical comedy' on the Hindu theme that a soul must depend upon God as a kitten depends upon its mother. . . . The book requires multiple readings; one is not enough to follow the thought and at the same time to obtain a sufficient reward from Raja Rao's graceful and austere English and his striking and witty imagery"—(*SR*).

Books about Rao

Raja Rao. By M. S. Naik. World Authors Ser. *Twayne* 1972 $6.95

LALL, ANAND (Arthur Samuel Lall).   1911–

Anand Lall, a former permanent representative of India to the United Nations, has held many important administrative appointments in the government of India, among them that of consul general of India in New York, 1951–1954. Born in Lahore, in what is now Pakistan, he was educated both at Lahore University and at Oxford. He has published numerous articles, poems and stories. In "The House at Adampur," his first novel, he wrote of "the wealthy industrialists and the intelligentsia of India (primarily Delhi) in the tense period that preceded Indian independence. He writes with the understanding and warmth of one who knows the best and the worst of both the East and the West and of the brutal, as well as the intellectual, conflicts of those critical years"—(*N.Y. Times*). His later writings on international relations include "Modern International Negotiation" (*Columbia* 1966 $14.00) and "How Communist China Negotiates" (*Columbia* 1968 $13.50 pap. $2.95).

SEASONS OF JUPITER: A Novel of India. 1958 *Greenwood* $12.00

FAIZ, AHMAD FAIZ.   1912–

Faiz studied in Lahore, lectured in Amritsar, participated in the Indian Labour Movement, and served in the Indian Army during World War II. A revolutionary, he writes classical *ghazal* love poetry, often altering traditional themes to express his ideas. He is a Lenin Prize winner and has written some of the most popular Urdu verse in recent years.

POEMS BY FAIZ. Trans. by Victor Kiernan. 1962. UNESCO Collection of Representative Works: Indian Ser. *Crane-Russak* 1971 $11.75

MALGONKAR, MANOHAR. 1913–

Malgonkar is an English-language novelist and story writer, sometime army officer, big game hunter, and the grandson of a former prime minister of an Indian state.

DISTANT DRUM. 1960. Orient Paperback Ser. *Inter-Culture Assocs.* 1974 pap. $2.75

COMBAT OF SHADOWS. 1962. *Inter-Culture Assocs.* 1968 pap. $1.80. The earliest of his novels published in the West; the author writes of British tea planters in the last years of the British Raj.

THE PRINCES. *Viking* 1963 $4.95

" 'The Princes' is an unusual novel in that it is anti-Congress in tone, but then, a novel written from inside about the Indian regal tradition and its final collapse must reflect the nostalgia of the vanquished and offer some defense of a way of life that has passed. . . . His personal experience gives the early pages of the novel such verisimilitude as to lead one to forget that the medium is fiction"—(*LJ*).

A BEND IN THE GANGES. 1964. *Inter-Culture Assocs.* 1975 pap. $3.20. A tale of intrigue and adventure in India during World War II.

SPY IN AMBER. *Inter-Culture Assocs.* 1971 pap. $1.80. A screenplay.

THE DEVIL'S WIND: Nana Saheb's Story. *Viking* 1972 $7.95. A presentation, in the form of a novel, of the so-called Indian mutiny of a century ago.

A TOAST IN WARM WINE. *Inter-Culture Assocs.* 1975 pap. $2.00

Books about Malgonkar

Manohar Malgonkar. By G. S. Amur. Indian Writer's Ser. *Humanities Press* 1973 pap. $2.75

SIVASANKARA PILLAI, THAKAZHI. 1914–

The writer is a lawyer, born in the state of Kerala on the southwest coast of India, the setting for many of his novels and short stories.

CHEMMEEN: A Novel. Trans. by Narayana Menon; introd. by Santha Rama Rau. 1962 *Inter-Culture Assocs.* 1964 pap. $2.40

"By rare good fortune, one occasionally comes upon a novel that is truly haunting, remaining in the mind to be turned over and over and revealing its inner light anew with each examination. Such a work is this novel, the first best seller to be acclaimed in India, winner of the highly-coveted President's Award, India's top literary honor. . . . Skillfully interweaving realism and legend, psychology and superstition, [the author] has created a subtle, brilliant picture of life among the fisherfolk of South India"—(*N.Y. Herald Tribune*).

TWO MEASURES OF RISE. *Inter-Culture Assocs.* 1967 pap. $2.00

THE UNCHASTE. Trans. by M. K. Bhaskaran. *Inter-Culture Assocs.* 1971 pap. $1.60

THE IRON ROD. *Inter-Culture Assocs.* 1974 pap. $2.00

SINGH, KHUSHWANT. 1915–

Born and bred in India, the novelist has recently been a specialist on Indian affairs for UNESCO in Paris.

THE TRAIN TO PAKISTAN (*Mano Majra*). 1955. *Greenwood* 1975 $11.50; *Grove* Black Cat Bks. 1961 pap. $1.95

"*Mano Majra*" was chosen by the publishers from 250 entries as the winner of the $1,000 award contest for manuscripts from India. The author, who is known also in India for a distinguished book of short stories, "The Mark of Vishnu," "brings to this novel both . . . an ability to tell a compelling story and a deep knowledge of the Sikhs in particular and of the life of the Punjab in general. . . . It is a short, powerful, ugly story about one of the most tormented episodes in Indian history"—(*N.Y. Times*). Mano Majra, a small Punjabi village in a remote section of what was to become the frontier between India and Pakistan, was caught in the terrible summer of 1947 in the violence and killings that accompanied the great movement of ten million refugees.

I SHALL NOT HEAR THE NIGHTINGALE. 1959. *Greenwood* 1968 $13.00; *Inter-Culture Assocs.* 1970 pap. $2.00. Singh's second novel is about the ancient Sikhs who are about to throw off the yoke of foreign rule.

HISTORY OF THE SIKHS. *Princeton Univ. Press* Vol. I 1469–1839 1963, o.p. Vol. 2 1839–1964 1966 $15.00

This is a comprehensive study of the religious movement, founded in the fifteenth century, which tried unsuccessfully to reconcile Islam and Hinduism and whose Indian adherents are still numerous, identifiable by their turbans and beards—and by the typical surname "Singh." "Based on original documentation in English, Persian and Gurmukhi [it] is the first modern history of the Sikhs and should find a place in all specialized libraries"—(LJ).

A BRIDE FOR THE SAHIB AND OTHER STORIES. *Inter-Culture Assocs.* 1967 pap. $1.60

BLACK JASMINE. *Inter-Culture Assocs.* 1971 pap. $1.80

GURUS, GODMEN AND GOOD PEOPLE. *South Asia Bks.* Orient Longman 1975 $9.00

KHUSHWANT SINGH'S INDIA: A Mirror for Its Monsters and Monstrosities. Ed. by Rahul Singh. 1969. *Inter-Culture Assocs.* 1975 pap. $2.20. Fifteen polemical essays originally contributed to British and American journals.

KHUSHWANT SINGH'S VIEW OF INDIA: Lectures on India's People, Religions, History and Contemporary Affairs. Ed. by Rahul Singh. *Inter-Culture Assocs.* 1975 pap. $3.95

(With Suneet B. Singh) HOMAGE TO GURU GOBIND SINGH. *Inter-Culture Assocs.* 1970 pap. $1.60

(Ed.) I BELIEVE. *Inter-Culture Assocs.* 1971 pap. $1.60

(Ed.) LOVE AND FRIENDSHIP. *Inter-Culture Assocs.* 1974 $1.80

(With Jaya Thadani, Eds.) LAND OF THE FIVE RIVERS: Stories from the Punjab. *Inter-Culture Assocs.* 1965 pap. $2.00

RAJAN, BALACHANDRA. 1920–

The author, a professor of English at the University of Delhi, was a Cambridge Don in the 1940s and later a United Nations delegate and Indian representative to the International Atomic Energy Agency. In addition to his novels, he has written a number of studies in the field of English literary criticism, including "Paradise Lost and the Seventeenth Century Reader" (1947. *Harper* [Barnes and Noble] 1962 $3.50; *Univ. of Michigan Press* Ann Arbor Bks. 1967 pap. $1.95) and "W. B. Yeats: A Critical Introduction" (*Hillary House* 1965 $4.50 pap. $2.25). He has edited "T. S. Eliot: A Study of His Writings by Several Hands" (1947 *Russell and Russell* 1966 $10.95) and, with A. C. George, "Makers of Literary Criticism" (*Asia Pub. House* Vol. 1 1965 $13.00).

THE DARK DANCER. 1958. *Greenwood* $14.25

Of the author's first novel, the *Yale Review* has said, it "is the first Indian novel . . . that employs the full resources of the Impressionist school whose great masters in English are Conrad and James. . . . Here at last is a novel that honestly confronts the dilemma of the Indian intellectual, caught between East and West."

TOO LONG IN THE WEST. *Inter-Culture Assocs.* 1961 pap. $1.00

The splendidly comic story of a lively daughter of an Indian university professor, who after taking her degree at Columbia, returns to a tiny, remote, and eccentric Indian village to acquire a bridegroom in the traditional way. "New Yorkers will find an additional bonus in the friendly yet honest portrait of their city, one of the best we have had from a foreign hand"—(LJ).

RAMA RAU, SANTHA. 1923–

She is the daughter of the diplomat and statesman, Sir Benegal Rama Rau, and Lady Rama Rau, the leader in women's political and social welfare movements in India.

HOME TO INDIA. *Harper* 1945 $4.50 lib. bdg. $4.43

THIS IS INDIA. *Harper* 1954 lib. bdg. $6.29. An excellent introduction to her native country.

REMEMBER THE HOUSE. *Harper* 1956 $7.95. Novel.

"Remember the House" is Santha Rama Rau's first novel. In this as in her other books she has done much to make "the myriad faces of India plainer to the Western eye." Her word pictures of the Indian background are vivid and she gives us some idea of the "inner and permanent realities of Indian modes of thinking" in her own circle.

THE SURVIVOR. *Harper* 1968 $4.95

VIEW TO THE SOUTHEAST. 1957 o.p. A delightful report on her return visit to the romantic and crucial countries of her "East of Home."

My Russian Journey. *Harper* 1959 $5.95. Candid scenes of Russian life based on her three-month stay in Leningrad, Moscow, and Uzbekistan.

Gifts of Passage. *Harper* 1961 $5.95

Of "Gifts of Passage," the *Christian Science Monitor* has written: "Santha Rama Rau ... seems quite able to see herself and events as other peoples see them. Consequently, her outlook upon the customs, habits, talents, and peculiarities of many peoples is distinctly cosmopolitan. But it has none of the tinge of boredom or overurbanity that word often conveys. Her reports of her travels make engrossing reading, because they are both subjective and objective. And because they are humane."

MARKANDAYA, KAMALA (pseud. of Kamala Purnaiya Taylor). 1924–

Kamala Markandaya is a Brahmin woman now residing in London with her English husband. She "writes with narrative power, with flashes of somewhat grim humor and with deep compassion"—*(N.Y. Times)*. She fashions "a remarkable prose of extreme clarity and calm ... and suggests the spiritual terrors of our time"—*(LJ)*.

Nectar in a Sieve. *T. Y. Crowell* (John Day) 1955 $4.95; *New Am. Lib.* Signet pap. $1.25

"A simple, unaffected story of human suffering, which does more than a shelf of books on history and economics to explain the people of India"—*(Time)*. It is a story about a gentle peasant couple of southern India.

Possession. 1963. *Inter-Culture Assocs.* 1967 pap. $1.20. In this novel, rich in wit and human fascination, two worlds and two remarkable individuals—a titled English woman and a penniless Indian boy—meet, collide, and learn from one another.

A Handful of Rice. *T. Y. Crowell* (John Day) 1966 $7.95; *Inter-Culture Assocs.* 1969 pap. $1.10; *Fawcett* Premier Bks. 1971 pap. $.75. A realistic portrayal of lower-class life in a modern Indian city.

The Coffer Dams. *T. Y. Crowell* (John Day) 1969 $6.95; *Fawcett* Premier Bks. 1971 pap. $.75. An examination of the activities of a British engineering firm invited to build a dam in India.

The Nowhere Man. *T. Y. Crowell* (John Day) 1972 $8.95

Two Virgins. *T. Y. Crowell* (John Day) 1973 $7.95; *New Am. Lib.* 1975 pap. $1.25

JHABVALA, RUTH PRAWER. 1927–

The *Saturday Review* calls Mrs. Jhabvala "one of India's best novelists writing in English." Unfortunately, most of her books are presently out of print. She was born in Germany of Polish parents and educated in London. Married to a Parsee architect, she lived in Delhi, the setting of all her novels, for many years. "Seeming to take root the day she arrived on Indian soil, ... she has completely grasped the workings of the Indian mind. ... She misses very little that goes on anywhere, at any level"—*(SR)*. "Amarita" (U.S. 1956, o.p.) and "The Nature of Passion" (U.S. 1957, o.p.) are two witty and charming novels about life in modern India, "adroitly well-written and thoroughly enjoyable." Santha Rama Rau, in the *N.Y. Times,* said that "The Nature of Passion" has "the richly human texture of life as it is really lived in an Indian city." "Get Ready for Battle" (U.S. 1963, o.p.), a tale of tangled marital relationships, is "a subtle comedy of manners tempered with understanding and filled with unexpected delights." "A Backward Place" (U.S. 1965, o.p.) is an "occasionally malicious portrait of a society that Mrs. Jhabvala views with compassion, amusement and insight"—*(SR)*.

A Stronger Climate. *Norton* 1969 $4.95. Nine Stories.

An Experience of India. *Norton* 1972 $6.95

Travelers. *Harper* 1973 $6.95

SAHGAL, NAYANTARA (PANDIT). 1927–

Prison and Chocolate Cake. *Knopf* 1954 $5.95

"Prison and Chocolate Cake" is the autobiography of the young daughter of Mme. Pandit and the niece of Nehru, who was educated in part in the United States. In this book she has "given us in the most simple, charming and generous terms the spirit of the Indian struggle for freedom, and the idealism and dignity of her parents, her illustrious uncle and their associates as she knew them as a child"—*(N.Y. Herald Tribune)*.

A TIME TO BE HAPPY. 1958. *Inter-Culture Assocs.* 1963 pap. $1.60. This is her first novel, "a series of deftly sketched portraits," in which she "recaptures the atmosphere of upper-class India in the period just before and just after independence."

FROM FEAR SET FREE. 1962. *Inter-Culture Assocs.* 1970 pap. $1.60

"From Fear Set Free" continues her autobiography and "relates her return from Wellesley College to a partition-ravaged India in 1947 and shows an acute awareness of the strength and weaknesses of her country.... The book is personal and highly intimate, not only giving the reader insight and understanding into the family life of a changing India, but also delineating the personalities of the author's mother and uncle (Nehru) with the sympathy and detail born of kinship"—(*LJ*).

THIS TIME OF MORNING. 1965. *Inter-Culture Assocs.* 1969 pap. $1.60. This novel is concerned with Indian bureaucracy in the 1950s.

THE DAY IN SHADOW. *Norton* 1972 $6.95

VAID, KRISHNA BALDEV. 1927–

The author received his Ph.D. from New York University and then returned to India to teach.

STEPS IN DARKNESS: A Novel. *Grossman* 1962 $3.50; *Inter-Culture Assocs.* 1973 pap. $1.60

Written by a young Indian professor, and translated by him from its original Hindi, this drab, naturalistic novelette about India's urban poor has had varying reviews. It is the story of a young boy's search for happiness. Yet the model his family sets before him is one of constant bickering, poverty and hate. He needs the kindness and love which "a house divided against itself" cannot give him. Perhaps in this one small Hindu household, one critic suggests, Krishna Vaid has written a parable of modern India.

TECHNIQUE IN THE TALES OF HENRY JAMES. *Harvard Univ. Press* 1964 $8.00

SILENCE AND OTHER STORIES. Writers Workshop Greenbird Ser. *Inter-Culture Assocs.* 1975 $10.00 pap. $4.00

MEHTA, VED (PARKASH). 1934?–

The author, blind since the age of three, came from a cultured but not wealthy Hindu family in the Punjab and grew up in Simla and Bombay. "Walking the Indian Streets" (1960, o.p.) is his account of his endeavor to reidentify himself with his family and his country after ten years' absence. "Fly and the Fly-Bottle" (1963, o.p.) is a collection of conversations with and about contemporary British philosophers and historians, which first appeared in the *New Yorker*. Ved Mehta has also written "The New Theologian" (1966, o.p.), a report on current trends in the theology of such eminent Christian thinkers as Paul Tillich, Karl Barth, Bishop John Robinson, Reinhold Niebuhr and Dietrich Bonhoeffer. Mehta's style is elegant, lucid, and conversational—that of the indefatigably curious, but knowledgeable, dilettante. In a different vein altogether is the novel "Delinquent Chacha" (1967, o.p.), a "featherweight piece" (*LJ*) about the antics of an irrepressible, ne'er-do-well *chacha* (Hindustani for uncle) who is determined to enter his dream world of British high society. Mr. Mehta now lives and works in New York. (*See also Dom Moraes, following.*)

FACE TO FACE. *Little* 1957 $7.50; *Peter Smith* $5.00. An autobiographical piece about the author's early years in India and his high school and college education in the United States.

PORTRAIT OF INDIA. *Farrar, Straus* 1970 $12.95; *Penguin* 1973 pap. $3.25

JOHN IS EASY TO PLEASE: Encounters with the Written and Spoken World. *Farrar, Straus* 1971 $7.50

DADDYJI. *Farrar, Straus* 1972 $6.95

MORAES, DOM. 1938–

Dom Moraes grew up in India and was educated at Oxford. He has spent much of his life in England, where he won the Hawthornden Prize with his first book of poems, "A Beginning" (1957). A British "Poems" (1960) was a choice of the (English) Poetry Book Society. "John Nobody" (1965) was his third poetry volume, and the present "Poems" is selected from all three. M. L. Rosenthal (in the *N.Y. Times*) finds Moraes derivative, "yet a finely grained personality does emerge despite the many easy expansive effects and the uncertainty of voice." Professor John M. Willingham, however, says of Moraes (in *LJ*) that "the sense of a clearly defined speaker sharpens and describes the meticulously ordered utterance" in a "distinguished collection." "The poems speak of alienation, loss, discovery, and love—in short the whole range of mid-century lyricism." Mr. Moraes has also published, in England, a book about his return to India at the time his friend Ved Mehta (q.v.) also returned. Mehta wrote a humorous article in the *New Yorker* (1967) lightly accusing his friend of frivolous embroidery in recounting quite differently some of the same events Mehta wrote about in "Walking the Indian Streets." Moraes has also translated Indian poetry into English.

POEMS, 1955–1965. *Macmillan* 1966 $4.95

FROM EAST AND WEST: A Collection of Essays. *International Scholarly Bk. Services* (Vikas) 1971 $7.50; *Int. Pubns. Service* 1972 $9.00

THE TEMPEST WITHIN: An Account of East Pakistan. *Harper* (Barnes & Noble) 1971 $5.50

VOICES FOR LIFE: Reflections on the Human Condition. *Praeger* 1975 $7.95 pap. $3.95

SOUTHEAST ASIA: LITERATURE OF BURMA, THAILAND, INDONESIA, MALAYSIA, VIETNAM, AND THE PHILIPPINES

Although Southeast Asia is considered to be a distinct geographical region, the civilizations, languages, and literatures of each country in the area have developed as a result of different influences, both in the premodern and modern periods. Buddhism, Hinduism, and Islam, adapted in varying ways to indigenous beliefs, customs, and settings, are reflected in the classical literature of each state in the region.

With the exception of Thailand, colonization of the Southeast Asian countries by various Western powers in the nineteenth and twentieth centuries directly affected official languages of instruction and indirectly the literary languages. Indeed, the common bond among the Southeast Asian nations can be said to be the predominance of external influences on the historical, political, and cultural lives of each.

Although the region has received much political attention in recent years, translation of its literature into English has not kept pace. Much that exists is scattered in journals and unpublished manuscripts or is available only abroad. The colonial heritage is again reflected in the concentration of translations in the languages of the former colonial powers, especially in the cases of Cambodia and Laos. To attempt to bridge this gap for the English reader, and by way of introduction to the literature, a number of bibliographies and anthologies have been published. The most outstanding are given below.

Brandon, James R. THEATER IN SOUTHEAST ASIA. *Harvard Univ. Press* 1967 $15.00 pap. 1974 $4.95

> Including bibliographies, resumés of major genres, and extracts, this first survey of contemporary Southeast Asian theater "discusses four distinct but interrelated aspects of theater in eight Southeast Asian countries: the cultural setting and development of theater genres; the performing arts and production methods; the theater as a social institution; and the theater as a communication medium"—(*LJ*).

Embree, John F., and Lillian Ota Dotson. BIBLIOGRAPHY OF THE PEOPLES AND CULTURES OF MAINLAND SOUTHEAST ASIA. 1950. *Russell & Russell* 1972 $37.50. Despite its age, this bibliography, until recently o.p., is the best such work available, with excellent sections on folklore, language, and literature.

Hanrahan, Gene Z., Ed. 50 GREAT ORIENTAL STORIES. 1965 o.p. Originally published by *Bantam* and currently o.p., the volume includes an outstanding selection of short stories and tales from Southeast Asia.

Jenner, Philip N. SOUTHEAST ASIAN LITERATURES IN TRANSLATION: A Preliminary Bibliography. Asian Studies at Hawaii *Univ. Press of Hawaii* 1973 pap. $3.50. An invaluable reference source which draws together bibliographical information on the diverse and scattered literature of all the Southeast Asian nations. All languages into which the literature has been translated are covered.

José, F. Sionil, Ed. ASIAN PEN ANTHOLOGY. Introd. by Norman Cousins. *Taplinger* 1967 $7.50

The 27 stories and 31 poems by over 40 authors included in this collection "give an excellent indication of the contemporary literary scene"—(*Choice*).

Shimer, Dorothy Blair, Ed. THE MENTOR BOOK OF MODERN ASIAN LITERATURE: From the Khyber Pass to Fuji. *New Am. Lib.* Mentor Bks. 1969 pap. $1.75. A valuable anthology, including critical commentary and biographical notes on the authors.

Burmese Literature

Although linguistically and ethnically linked to China, from the eleventh-century founding of the first powerful Burmese kingdom at Pagan until the colonial period of the nineteenth and twentieth centuries, the cultural life of Burma was dominated by India. Burma's classical literature was in great part an expression of the religious and philosophical concepts of Indian Buddhism. Popular animist beliefs in spirits (*nat*) and other supernatural beings are barely visible in the written literature. The earliest surviving records are twelfth-century stone inscriptions, and the earliest literary texts date from the mid-fifteenth century. Poetry was the principal genre until the eighteenth century, taking the form of the *pyo*, long religious poems on Buddhist themes written by Buddhist monks. It was not until the late eighteenth century, under Thai influence, that literature of entertainment, popular dramas (*pya-zat*), and long poems (*yagan*) on increasingly secular themes began to appear. Prose remained at the service of the court and the cloister, primarily because printing did not become widespread until the late nineteenth century.

"The Great Chronicle" ("*Maha Ya-zawin-gyi*") by U Kala (1678?–1738?) was the first full-scale historical work in Burmese prose, and it was incorporated into "The Glass Palace Chronicle" ("*Hmannān Ya-zawin-gyi*"), the official history compiled in 1830 by a group of royal scholars. By the time of British annexation in 1886, court dominance had lost sway in literature for the public, and new forms in verse, drama, and the short story had been introduced.

Translations of Burmese literary works remain, in general, scattered; the *Journal of the Burma Research Society* and *The Guardian Magazine*, both published in Rangoon, have over the years included articles and translations of works by many twentieth-century authors, such as Ma Ma Lei, Dagon Taya, and Theip-pan Maung Wa. Godfrey E. Harvey's "History of Burma" (1925. *Octagon* 1967 $13.00) includes information on literature. "Old Burma—Early Pagan" by Gordon H. Luce and others (U.S. 1969–1970, o.p.) is the definitive work on the archeology and art of Pagan, with many references to Hindu-Buddhist literature. John F. Cady's "History of Modern Burma" (*Cornell Univ. Press* 1958 $25.00) is an excellent treatment of the modern period.

THE GLASS PALACE CHRONICLE OF THE KINGS OF BURMA. Trans. by Pe Maung Tin and Gordon H. Luce. 1923. *AMS Press* 1975 $9.00

Htin, Aung Maung, Trans. and ed. BURMESE DRAMA: A Study with Translations of Burmese Plays. *Oxford* 1937 $4.25. A good general survey with full translations of "The Water Carrier" by U Pon-nya and three other dramas and extracts from several other plays. Htin has also edited "Burmese Folk Tales" (U.S. 1948, o.p.) and "Burmese Law Tales: The Legal Element in Burmese Folklore" (U.S. 1962, o.p.).

BURMESE MONK'S TALES. *Columbia* 1966 $10.00. A Burmese writer, dramatist, and translator, Htin has served as a correspondent of *The Times*, London. These tales are modern didactic stories, forming a new sub-genre of Burmese literature.

Lustig, R. F., Ed. BURMESE CLASSICAL POEMS. *Paragon Reprint* 1968 pap. $2.50. An excellent collection originally published in 1966 by the *Rangoon Gazette*.

Nu, U. THE PEOPLE WIN THROUGH: A Play. Introd. by Edward Hunter. 1952. *Melvin McCosh Bkseller*. 1957 $9.50. An anticommunist propaganda play written by the first prime minister of the Union of Burma, 1948–1961. His "Man, the Wolf of Man" is a prewar novel about life in prison under the British.

Pe, U Hla, Ed. BURMESE PROVERBS. 1962. Wisdom of the East Ser. *Paragon Reprint* $3.50. Originally published in London in the UNESCO Collection of Representative Works: Burmese Series, this is the best available work on the subject.

Thein, Pe Myint. SELECTED SHORT STORIES. Trans. by Patricia M. Milne. Southeast Asian Studies Data Paper *Cornell Univ.* 1973 pap. $4.00. A Burmese politician, writer, and journalist, many of whose short stories chronicle his own life.

Thai Literature

The classical literature of Thailand, like its culture, is a synthesis of Hindu and Buddhist influences and native attitudes and settings. The earliest Siamese literature dates from the mid-thirteenth century and takes the form of historical inscriptions, didactic poetry, and moral sayings. During the classical period, which extended to the nineteenth century, the play, including court and popular drama, shadow plays of various types, and stories based on the Rāma legend, coexisted with more secular lengthy historical poems and epic romances concerned with Thai heroes. The seventeenth-century love poetry by Si Prat is particularly noteworthy. As the output of traditional poetic literature declined, prose became the dominant literary medium in the post-1850 period; popular forms of elegies, lyrics, folksongs, and tales continue to the present day.

Although English translations in Thailand are increasing in recent years, little of the work of outstanding Thai writers such as Si Prat, Kukrit Pramoj, and Sunthorn Bhu has been published in the United States. As background to Thai civilization, in addition to the popular "Anna and the King of Siam" by Margaret Landon (*T. Y. Crowell* [John Day] 1944 $6.27; *Simon & Schuster* Pocket Books pap. $.95), several more scholarly treatises are worthy of mention. "Thailand: The New Siam" by Virginia Thompson (1941. 2nd ed. *Paragon Reprint* 1967 $17.50 pap. $7.50) includes a section on literary development. The modern period is well treated in "Politics in Thailand" by David A. Wilson (*Cornell Univ. Press* 1962 $13.50 pap. $1.95) and in "Thailand: The Modernization of a Bureaucratic Polity" by Fred W. Riggs (*Univ. Press of Hawaii* East West Center 1966 $10.00).

Cadet, J. M., Trans. THE RAMAKIEN: The Thai Epic Myth. *Kodansha International* (dist. by Harper) 1971 $16.50. Based on the Indian "Rāmāyana" but probably patterned after a Javanese version, the "Rāmakien" is the longest and most famous epic of premodern Thailand.

Draskau, Jennifer, Trans. and ed. TAW AND OTHER THAI STORIES. Writing in Asia Ser. *Humanities Press* 1974 pap. $2.75

Jumsai, M. L. Manich. HISTORY OF THAI LITERATURE: Including Laos, Shans, Khanti, Ahom and Yunnan-nanchao. *Int. Pubns. Service* 1974 pap. $7.50; *Paragon Reprint* 1975 pap. $5.50. The best history of Thai literature available, written by the author of several histories of Thailand.

Manuet Banhān, Phya, Ed. SIAMESE TALES OLD AND NEW: The Four Riddles, and Other Stories. Trans. by Reginald LeMay. 1930. *Folcroft* 1974 $25.00. These tales express the Thai outlook on life, their capacity for humor, philosophical values, and the place of magic and superstition in their lives. The translator was formerly judge of the International Court in Bangkok.

Paribatra, Mon Dusdi, Ed. THE RELUCTANT PRINCESS: A Legend of Love in Siam. Ill. by Sukit Chuthama. *Tuttle* 1963 $5.00

Rama, King, 2nd. SANG THONG: A Dance-Drama from Thailand. Trans. by Fern S. Ingersoll. *Tuttle* 1972 $6.00

Soonsawad, Thong-In, Trans. Thai Poets. *Paragon Reprint* 1968 pap. $1.50

Srinawk, Khamsing. The Politician and Other Stories. Trans. by Domnern Garden; introd. by Michael Smithies. *Oxford* 1973 pap. $4.75

Toth, Marion Davies, Trans. and ed. Tales from Thailand. Ill. by Supee Pasutanavin. *Tuttle* 1971 $7.15

Wray, Elizabeth, and others, Trans. and eds. Ten Lives of the Buddha: Siamese Temple Paintings and Jataka Tales. *John Weatherhill* 1972 $15.00. *Jataka* tales are stories based on the births of Buddha.

Indonesian and Malaysian Literature

Malaysia and Indonesia comprise what has been traditionally referred to in the West as the Malay Peninsula and Archipelago. Although over 200 languages, most with no written literature, are spoken in the area, Malay, now called *Bahasa Malaysia* and *Bahasa Indonesia*, is the *lingua franca* in both nations, and taking precedence over Javanese, Sundanese, and Balinese, is the dominant literary language. The spread of Islam into the region between the fourteenth and sixteenth centuries lent the classical version of the Malay language (written in Arabic script) and its literature (rhymical, long-winded, and well suited to religion and romance) its distinctive character. There is a considerable Hindu-derived, although Muslim-influenced, literature, due to Hindu influence in early Java, the Malacca Straits, and still today in Bali. This influence is reflected in versions of the *"Rāmāyāna,"* the *"Mahābhārata,"* and romance cycles which have provided the plots of the Javanese *wayang* shadow plays. Together with folk literature, of which the *pantun*, a quatrain adapted to love poetry and song, has long been the most popular verse form, histories and picaresque novels and the Persian-derived *sha'ir* verse form were the major literary genres of pre-modern Malay.

Nationalist sentiments, first in the Netherlands East Indies and later in Malaya, led to the founding of a teachers' training college in Minangkabau, Sumatra, which undertook the development of a modern literary language based on classical Malay and influenced by Dutch grammar and vocabulary, and to the establishment in Batavia of the *Balai Pustaka* (Hall of Books) which sponsored the publication of Malay translations of European works. These events spurred the development of a new literary language. The modernization of the language has today reached a point where *Bahasa Malaysia* and *Bahasa Indonesia* have few essential differences except in the area of spelling; adoption of uniform spelling is a stated goal of the two nations. Among many outstanding monographs on the history and culture of the Malay world are "The Golden Chersonese and the Way Thither," by Isabella L. Bird (1883. Oxford in Asia Historical Reprint Ser. *Oxford* 1968 $7.15), a perceptive popular history; "The Malays: A Cultural History," by Richard O. Winstedt (6th ed. *Routledge & Kegan Paul* 1961 $5.00); and "The Story of the Dutch East Indies," by Bernard H. Vlekke (1945. *AMS Press* $14.00), both standard historical treatments.

Indonesian Literature

Anwar, Chairil. The Complete Poetry and Prose of Chairil Anwar. Trans. and ed. by Burton Raffel. *State Univ. of New York Press* bilingual ed. 1970 $12.50 pap. $6.50. Anwar, who died in 1949, lived only 27 years but is still regarded as modern Indonesia's most outstanding writer. The corpus of his work includes some 75 original poems and several dozen translations or adaptations.

Aveling, Harry. A Thematic History of Indonesian Poetry, 1920 to 1974. *Northern Illinois Univ. Center for Southeast Asian Studies* (dist. by Cellar Book Shop, 18090 Wyoming, Detroit, Mich. 48221) 1974 pap. $4.00

Brandon, James R., Ed. On Thrones of Gold: Three Javenese Shadow Plays. *Harvard Univ. Press* 1970 $15.00

Echols, John M., Ed. INDONESIAN WRITING IN TRANSLATION. 1956 o.p. Compiled primarily for a course on Southeast Asian literature in translation at Cornell University, this anthology brings together poetry, short stories, and essays and includes biographical sketches of the writers.

Jaspan, M. FOLK LITERATURE OF SOUTH SUMATRA. *International Scholarly Bk. Services* 1964 pap. $6.90

Kartini, Raden Adjeng. LETTERS OF A JAVANESE PRINCESS. Trans. by Agnes Louise Symmers; ed. with an introd. by Hilda Geertz. UNESCO Collection of Representative Works: Indonesian Ser. *Norton* 1964 pap. $1.95

Koutsoukis, A., Trans. INDONESIAN FOLK TALES. *Verry* 1970 $5.50

Lubis, Mochtar. A ROAD WITH NO END. Trans. by Anthony H. Johns. *Regnery* 1970 $4.95

TWILIGHT IN DJAKARTA. Trans. by Claire Holt. *Vanguard* 1964 $4.50. Lubis, one of Indonesia's outstanding modern novelists, is also a political journalist.

McVey, Ruth T., Ed. INDONESIA. Survey of World Cultures Ser. *Human Relations Area File Press* 1962 $12.00. Particularly good is the chapter "Genesis of a Modern Literature," by Anthony Johns.

Multatuli. MAX HAVELAAR, or The Coffee Auctions of the Dutch Trading Center. *British Bk. Centre* 1967 $10.00. A historical novel.

Peacock, James L. RITES OF MODERNIZATION: Symbolic and Social Aspects of Indonesian Proletarian Drama. *Univ. of Chicago Press* 1968 $12.75

Raffel, Burton. THE DEVELOPMENT OF MODERN INDONESIAN POETRY. *State Univ. of New York Press* 1967 $17.00

(Ed.) ANTHOLOGY OF MODERN INDONESIAN POETRY. *State Univ. of New York Press* 1964 2nd ed. 1968 pap. $4.95

Rendra, W. S. BALLADS AND BLUES: Poems Translated from Indonesia. Trans. by Harry Aveling and others. Oxford in Asia Historical Reprint Ser. *Oxford* 1974 $12.75

Simatupang, Iwan. THE PILGRIM. Trans. by Harry Aveling. Writing in Asia Ser. *Humanities Press* 1976 pap. price not set

Simatupang, T. B. REPORT FROM BANARAN: The Story of the Experiences of a Soldier during the War of Independence. Trans. by Benedict R. Anderson and Elizabeth Graves. Modern Indonesian Project Translation Ser. *Cornell Univ. Press* 1972 pap. $6.50

Toer, Pramoedya Ananta. THE FUGITIVE. Trans. by Harry Aveling. Writing in Asia Ser. *Humanities Press* 1976 price not set. One of the greatest of Indonesian writers, Toer was born in Java in 1925 and is a writer of revolution. The majority of his themes are related to the revolutionary fight against the Dutch, British, and Japanese.

Ward, Philip. INDONESIAN TRADITIONAL POETRY. *Oleander Press* 1975 $6.95

Malaysian Literature

Abdullah, Bin Abdul Kadir. HIKAYAT ABDULLAH. Ed. by A. H. Hill. Oxford in Asia Historical Reprint Ser. *Oxford* 1970 $16.75. Abdullah, who was clerk to Sir Stamford Raffles, broke with tradition in this, his autobiography, by writing about current conditions in Malaya, in particular Malay contacts with Europeans. This can be said to be the first modern book published in Malaya.

Bastin, John, and R. Roolvink, Eds. MALAYAN AND INDONESIAN STUDIES. *Oxford* 1964 $17.50. This volume, dedicated to Sir Richard Winstedt, includes a few essays on the literature.

Geddes, W. R. NINE DAYAK NIGHTS. *Oxford* 1957 pap. $1.95. This volume of translations includes the epic "The Story of Kichapi."

Rice, Oliver, and Majid, Abdullah, Eds. MODERN MALAY VERSE, 1946–61. Trans. by Abdullah Majid Asraf and Oliver Rice with the assistance of James Kirkup and the poets. Introd. by James Kirkup. *Oxford* 1963 pap. $1.75. This is the best available anthology of contemporary Malaysian poetry.

SEJARAH MELAYU, or Malay Annals. Trans. and ed. by C. C. Brown. Introd. by C. C. Roolvink. 1952 Oxford in Asia Historical Reprint Ser. *Oxford* 1970 $10.50. One of the finest of all Malay classics, and one of the most important historical works concerned with Malaya.

Skeat, Walter W. FABLES AND FOLK-TALES FROM AN EASTERN FOREST. Ill. by F. H. Townsend. 1901. Folklore Ser. *Norwood Editions* $7.50. Includes twenty-six tales from the Malay peninsula.

Starweather, Chauncey C., Trans. and ed. MALAYAN LITERATURE. 1901. *Richard West* $25.00. An anthology which includes romantic tales, epic poetry, and royal chronicles.

Wilkinson, R. J., Ed. PAPERS ON MALAY SUBJECTS: A Selection. 1900. Oxford in Asia Historical Reprint Ser. *Oxford* 1971 $16.75. A systematic account of the Malays of the Malay Peninsula, their society, cultural traditions and history.

Winstedt, Richard O. A HISTORY OF CLASSICAL MALAY LITERATURE. 1961. *Oxford* 2nd ed. 1969 $12.00 pap. $9.00. This outstanding work includes a good bibliography.

Vietnamese Literature

In Vietnam, where the tradition of writing prose and verse in Chinese characters and according to Chinese rules and conventions persisted until the nineteenth century, the influence of Chinese culture in Southeast Asia was most strongly felt. By the thirteenth century there developed a system of writing Vietnamese in Chinese-style characters called *chu nom*. Nom literature gradually assumed a manner distinctive from Chinese forms and reached its height of excellence at the beginning of the nineteenth century. Its decline thereafter is in part attributable to the development, by seventeenth-century Christian missionaries, of a romanized script, *quoc ngu*, which spread after French colonization, and is now universally used. Among the poetic genres most common in both the classic and folk literatures of Vietnam are the *luc bat* (six- and eight-syllable lines alternating), and the *truyen*, which was normally in the form of verse novels or verse romances and which was especially popular in the eighteenth century. Although studies and translations of Vietnamese literature have been primarily published in French, American involvement has produced many historical and political monographs—two by Joseph Buttinger, "Vietnam: A Dragon Embattled" (*Praeger* 2 vols. 1967 $18.50) and "A Dragon Defiant: A Short History of Vietnam" (*Praeger* 1972 $6.50 pap. $2.50) and a number by the late Bernard B. Fall.

Balaban, John T., Trans. and ed. VIETNAMESE FOLK POETRY. Keepsake Ser. *Unicorn Press* 1974 $5.00

Ly-Qui-Chung, Ed. BETWEEN TWO FIRES: The Unheard Voices of Vietnam. Introd. by Frances FitzGerald. *Praeger* 1970 $5.95 pap. $1.95

"These nine previously unpublished short stories by South Vietnamese citizens, collected through a public writing contest, describe death, pain, loss, destruction, and bewilderment, but almost never mention politics"—(*Atlantic*).

Monigold, Glen W., Trans. and ed. FOLKTALES FROM VIETNAM. *Peter Pauper Press* (dist. by Van Nostrand-Reinhold) 1964 $1.95

Nguyen, Du. TALE OF KIEU: The Classic Vietnamese Verse Novel. Trans. and ed. by Huynh Sanh Thong. With pref. by Gloria Emerson and historical background by Alexander Woodside. *Random* Vintage Bks. pap. $1.95. In the *truyen* form, this long narrative poem is considered the greatest in the Vietnamese language. Nguyen Du was a poet and son of a high government official; this, his major work, was completed in 1820, the year of his death.

Nguyen, Ngoc Bich, and others, Trans. and eds. A THOUSAND YEARS OF VIETNAMESE POETRY. *Knopf* 1975 $8.95 pap. $4.95

Nhat-Hanh, Thich. CRY OF VIETNAM. Trans. by Helen Coutant. *Unicorn Press* 1971 $6.00 pap. $2.00. An example of the work of a modern Vietnamese poet.

Nielsen, Kay, and Jon Nielsen, Eds. THE WISHING POND AND OTHER TALES OF VIETNAM. Trans. by Lam Chan Quan. *Harvey House Pubs.* (dist. by Hale) 1969 $6.00

Raffel, Burton, Trans. FROM THE VIETNAMESE: Ten Centuries of Poetry. 1968 o.p. A recently published anthology of representative poetic works.

Sun, Ruth Q., Trans. and ed. LAND OF THE SEAGULL AND FOX. *Tuttle* 1967 $5.00

Weiss, Peter. NOTES ON THE CULTURAL LIFE OF THE DEMOCRATIC REPUBLIC OF VIETNAM. *Dell* Delta 1970 $2.25. Translated from the German, this volume includes chapters on "Beginnings of a Modern Literature," "Conversations with Authors," "Tradition, Ceremonials, Poetics," and "Literature in South Vietnam."

Philippine Literature

The various migrations to and occupations of the Philippine archipelago throughout its history have led to a diversity of languages and cultural influences in its literature. The migration of the Malayo-Polynesian peoples introduced Tagalog, Ilokano, and Binisaya as major indigenous languages. Unfortunately, few examples remain today of the poetry, usually oral, proverbs, love songs, and ballads of the period prior to the Spanish conquest in the mid-sixteenth century. The Spaniards introduced a new language and a romanized alphabet and also new literary forms and themes. Spanish chivalric tales were freely adapted, in particular by the Tagalog poet Francisco Balagtas in his *"Florante at Laura"* first published in 1838 (trans. in 1950 by G. St. Clair, o.p.). Roman Catholic liturgy was the basis for indigenous Biblical stories and choral chanting. The popular *moro-moro* plays were based on Spanish models, their most common plot being the conflict between Christians and Moors. The American occupation of the Philippines from 1898 to 1946 saw the adoption of English as the official medium of instruction and therefore as the literary language of a number of modern writers. One of the most prominent of these is José Garcia Villa, a novelist, short story writer, and poet.

Translations of Philippine literature into English have to date appeared mostly under Filippino imprint. These include, among others, "PEN Short Stories" edited by Francisco Arcellona (1962 o.p.) and "The Authentic Voice of Poetry" edited by Ricaredo Demetillo (1962 o.p.). "Brown Heritage: Essays on Philippine Cultural Tradition and Literature," compiled by Antonio G. Manuud (1967 o.p.), is a massive collection of critical and historical essays on the subject. American involvement in the Philippines has produced many studies of the islands, including an excellent recent one by Peter W. Stanley, "A Nation in the Making: The Philippines and the United States, 1899–1921" (Harvard Studies in American-East Asian Relations Ser. *Harvard Univ. Press* 1974 $12.00).

Agcaoilli, T. D., Ed. PHILIPPINE WRITING: An Anthology. 1953 *Greenwood* 1971 $16.00

Casper, Leonard. NEW WRITING FROM THE PHILIPPINES: A Critique. *Syracuse Univ. Press* 1966 $10.00. Mr. Casper is also the author of "The Wounded Diamond: Studies in Modern Philippine Literature," published in Manila in 1964.

Fansler, Dean Spruill, Ed. FILIPPINO POPULAR TALES: With Comparative Notes. 1921. *Kraus* 1969 $22.00

González, Nestor Vicente Madali. THE BAMBOO DANCERS. 1960. *Swallow* $3.95. Filippino writer and poet writing in English and currently teaching at the University of the Philippines. Other novels by González include "The Winds of April" (1940) and "A Season of Grace" (1956) not currently available in the United States.

Hosillos, Lucila V. Philippine-American Literary Relations, 1898–1941. *Oriole Eds.* 1969 $10.00

Joaquin, Nick. Tropical Gothic. Asian and Pacific Writing Ser. *Univ. of Queensland Press* (order from Technical Impex Corp.) 1972 $7.00 pap. $3.50. A Filippino poet, essayist and journalist, Joaquin is considered one of the giants of modern Filippino literature. Made famous by his short story "Three Generations" (1940), he writes essays for the Philippines Free Press under the name of Quijano de Manila. A great deal of his writing is scattered among periodical publications.

Rizal, José y Alonso. Lost Eden: *Noli Me Tangere*. 1887. Trans. by Leon M. Guerrero. 1961. *Greenwood* 1968 $15.25. Rizal, Filippino national hero and writer who wrote in Spanish, died in 1896. Both his poetic and prose works, including *"Noli Me Tangere,"* his first novel, express the rising nationalistic feeling of the Philippine middle class of the late nineteenth century. *"Noli Me Tangere"* was prohibited by the censor when it was published and any copies found in the Philippines were burned.

Subversive. 1891. Trans. by Leon M. Guerrero. *Norton* 1968 pap. $1.95; *Peter Smith* $4.75. Originally published in London under the title *"El Filibusterismo,"* this sequel to *"Noli Me Tangere"* is sharply critical of the Spanish colonizers, but less successful as writing.

San Juan, E., Jr. Introduction to Modern Filippino Literature. *Twayne* 1974 $6.95

Yabes, Leopoldo y. Philippine Literature in English. *Krishna Press* $35.95

EAST ASIA: LITERATURE OF CHINA, JAPAN, KOREA, MONGOLIA, AND TIBET

Chinese Literature

China possesses one of the major literary traditions in the world, with a history of over three thousand years. The primary reasons for its preservation over so long a period are threefold: the use of printing from the twelfth century onwards, the practice of collecting and reproducing libraries, and, most importantly, an unbroken cultural tradition based above all on the Chinese script as a language medium independent of dialectal differences. As the literary language became increasingly removed from the spoken and thus less vital, literature had a natural impulse toward imitation. Indeed, after the formative classical period beginning with Confucius, the literary history of China becomes one of imitation of different models, especially in the prose form. In poetry, vernacular folksongs often exerted strong influence on literary form. Fiction and spoken drama were the only forms of literary prose in which the vernacular language was employed until recent times. It was to this *pai-hua* that the twentieth-century literary revolutionaries turned.

The three kingdoms and six dynasties from the third through the sixth centuries were a period of preparation for the great literary ages of T'ang and Sung. Confucianism lost much of its earlier intellectual sway to philosophical Taoism. The most famous writers of the period are remembered for their poetry, which began to show the elaborate and circumscribed forms culminating in the *lü-shih*, the regulated poem of the T'ang period. The short story, which was also to find perfection during the T'ang, began to develop in its two major categories, the supernatural and the historical tale. Prose and verse literature as developed during the T'ang, Five Dynasties, and Sung periods of the seventh through twelfth centuries remained the models until the twentieth century. In the characteristic short poetry of the period, there was a tendency toward an allusive style, intellectualism and erudition. The *tz'u* form, a song lyric written in irregular meter to conform to the rhythm of a particular tune, first appeared during the T'ang Dynasty, was extended during the Sung, and was later a major element of the great Yüan dramas. In the prose writing of the time, there was a movement toward a simpler style, a turning back to the "old" style (*ku-wên*) of the classical and Han periods, used particularly in T'ang short stories, which were to become the chief thematic sources of the Yüan drama. The novel appeared in complete form during the Ming and Ch'ing dynasties, including "The Romance of the Three Kingdoms" (*q.v.*), "The Golden Lotus" (*q.v.*), "The Dream of the Red Chamber" (*q.v.*), and "Water Margin" (*q.v.*). Contacts with the West during the nineteenth and twentieth centuries influenced cultural and literary trends as well as political events. Changes in language, style, and theme during this period have been more violent than at any earlier time of political change in China. Since the turn of the century, Chinese literature has been written with consistently close attention to social and political relevance.

During the last 25 years, there have been many studies both of Chinese literature and of Chinese history and civilization, too numerous to mention here. The following will give the reader only the highlights of the more general treatises, most of which have bibliographies appended for further reading: "A History of East Asian Civilization," Vol. 1: "East Asia—The Great Tradition," by John K. Fairbank and Edwin O. Reischauer and Vol. 2: "East Asia—The Modern Transformation" by John K. Fairbank, Edwin O. Reischauer, and Albert M. Craig (*Houghton* Vol. 1 1960 Vol. 2 1965 each $13.95); "China: A Short Cultural History" by Charles P. Fitzgerald (*Praeger* 1954 3rd. ed. pap. $4.95); "The Chinese: Their History and Culture" by Kenneth S. Latourette (2 Vols. in 1 4th rev. ed. *Macmillan* 1964 $12.50); "Chinese Thought and Institutions" by John K. Fairbank (*Univ. of Chicago Press* 1957 $8.50 pap. $3.25); and John Meskill's "An Introduction to Chinese Civilization" (*Columbia* 1973 $17.50).

Arlington, Lewis C., Ed. CHINESE DRAMA. *Blom* $32.50

  (With Harold Acton, Eds.) FAMOUS CHINESE PLAYS. 1937 *Russell & Russell* 1963 $17.50

Asia Society and Roger B. Bailey. GUIDE TO CHINESE POETRY AND DRAMA. Asian Literature Bibliography Ser. *Hall* 1973 $9.50

Asia Society and Jordan D. Paper. GUIDE TO CHINESE PROSE. Asian Literature Bibliography Ser. *Hall* 1973 $9.50. This volume and the one above serve as introductions to Chinese prose, poetry, and drama, summarizing and evaluating selected works available in English translation.

Ayling, Alan, and Duncan Mackintosh, Eds. and trans. A COLLECTION OF CHINESE LYRICS. Bilingual with Chinese calligraphy by Lee Yim. Ill. by Fei Ch'eng Wu. *Vanderbilt Univ. Press* 1967 $7.50

  "A conscientious labour of love and a pioneering venture in a neglected field"—(*TLS*, London).

  FURTHER COLLECTION OF CHINESE LYRICS. *Vanderbilt Univ. Press* 1970 $7.50

Bauer, Wolfgang, and Herbert Franke, Trans. and eds. THE GOLDEN CASKET: Chinese Novellas of Two Millennia. Trans. from the German by Christopher Levenson. 1964 o.p. Illustrates the development of the novella in China from its origins to its decline in the nineteenth century. Slightly abridged.

Birch, Cyril, Trans. STORIES FROM A MING COLLECTION: Chinese Short Stories Published in the Seventeenth Century. *Grove* Evergreen pap. $2.25. Six diverse examples from the period when storytelling art reached its peak.

  (Ed.) AN ANTHOLOGY OF CHINESE LITERATURE. *Grove* Evergreen Vol. 1 From Earliest Times to the Fourteenth Century. Assoc. ed., Donald Keene. 1965 pap. $3.95. Vol. 2 From the Fourteenth Century to the Present. 1972 pap. $3.95

  "The first true anthology in English of Chinese literature. [It] is enjoyable, informative and ... readable to the student and the general reader alike"—(*LJ*). With historical and literary commentary.

  (Ed.) STUDIES IN CHINESE LITERARY GENRES. *Univ. of California Press* 1974 $12.50

Bishop, John Lyman, Ed. STUDIES IN CHINESE LITERATURE. Harvard-Yenching Institute Studies *Harvard Univ. Press* 1965 pap. $4.50

Bynner, Witter, and Kang-hu Kiang, Eds. THE JADE MOUNTAIN: A Chinese Anthology, Being Three Hundred Poems of the T'ang Dynasty, 618–906. 1929 *Knopf* 1939 $4.95; *Random* Vintage Bks. pap. $1.95

Chai, Ch'u, and Winberg Chai, Trans. and eds. A TREASURY OF CHINESE LITERATURE: A New Prose Anthology Including Fiction and Drama. 1965 *Hawthorn* $8.95; *Apollo* 1975 pap. $4.25. Selected pieces connected by commentary, offering details not easily found elsewhere. The section on drama is especially valuable.

Chang, H. C., Ed. CHINESE LITERATURE: Popular Fiction and Drama. (Orig. "Literature of China") *Edinburgh Univ. Press* (dist. by Aldine) 1973 $8.75. An anthology of short stories and excerpts from the best-known plays and novels. Each selection is well translated and fully annotated.

Ch'en Shou-yi. CHINESE LITERATURE: A Historical Introduction. *Ronald* 1961 $10.95

Chow, Tse-tsung. THE MAY FOURTH MOVEMENT: Intellectual Revolution in Modern China. 1960 Harvard East Asian Ser. *Stanford Univ. Press* 1967 pap. $3.95. A detailed analysis of the main intellectual currents in China during the 1915–1923 period. Chapter 11, "The Literary Revolution," discusses the development of twentieth-century Chinese prose writing.

de Bary, William Theodore, Wing-tsit Chan, and Burton Watson, Comps. SOURCES OF CHINESE TRADITION. *Columbia* 1960 $17.50 2 vols. 1964 pap. Vol. 1 $4.00 Vol. 2 $3.00. Chinese classics well translated, with chronological charts and helpful introductory notes.

Fletcher, W. J. B., Trans. and ed. GEMS OF CHINESE VERSE and MORE GEMS OF CHINESE POETRY. 1919. *Paragon Reprint* 1966 2 vols. in 1 $12.50. Bilingual. Includes well-known masterpieces of the T'ang dynasty.

Gibbs, Donald A., and Yun-chen Li, with the assistance of Christopher Rand. A BIBLIOGRAPHY OF STUDIES AND TRANSLATION OF MODERN CHINESE LITERATURE, 1918–1942, Harvard East Asian Monographs *Harvard Univ. Press* 1975 $8.50. A comprehensive guide to nearly all English translations of modern Chinese literature with identification of the Chinese original from which the translation was made. Includes references to studies of each author.

Giles, Herbert A. A HISTORY OF CHINESE LITERATURE. 1901. With a supplement on the modern period by Liu Wu-chi. *Ungar* 1967 $7.50; 1923 ed. *Richard West* 1973 $15.00

A popular history for many years. "Professor Liu's account of modern Chinese drama is the first in any Western language. . . . A valuable handbook"—(*LJ*). "The prose volume remains to this day the only one of its kind"—(*Choice*).

(Ed.) GEMS OF CHINESE LITERATURE. 1923. *Dover* 2nd rev. ed. $2.50; *Paragon Reprint* 2 vols. in 1 1965 $12.50; *Richard West* $45.00

Goldman, Merle. LITERARY DISSENT IN COMMUNIST CHINA. Harvard East Asian Ser. *Harvard Univ. Press* 1967 $10.00; *Atheneum* 1971 pap. $3.75

An investigation of the conflict between the Chinese Communist party and China's writers in the 1940s and 1950s. "It sheds much light on one aspect of the Chinese situation that has been largely neglected"—(*N.Y. Times*).

Graham, Angus Charles, Trans. and ed. POEMS OF THE LATE T'ANG. *Penguin* 1965 pap. $1.25

"Recommended for undergraduate students of poetry, comparative literature, and Far Eastern studies"—(*Choice*).

Hawkes, David, Trans. and ed. CH'U TZ'U: The Songs of the South. 1959 1962 o.p. An ancient Chinese anthology. Compilation ascribed to Liu Hsiang.

Hightower, James Robert. TOPICS IN CHINESE LITERATURE: Outlines and Bibliographies. Harvard-Yenching Institute Studies Ser. *Harvard Univ. Press* 3rd rev. ed. 1962 pap. $3.50. A concise and authoritative guide.

Hsia, Chih-tsing. A HISTORY OF MODERN CHINESE FICTION. *Yale Univ. Press* 1961 2nd rev. ed. 1971 $25.00 pap. $5.95. The first serious study in English, providing a practical acquaintance with the writing itself by means of copious passages of translations from representative novels. The author is a native of China with a Ph.D. from Yale.

Hsu, Kai-yu. THE CHINESE LITERARY SCENE: A Writer's Visit to the People's Republic. *Random* Vintage Bks. 1975 pap. $3.95

(Trans. and ed.) TWENTIETH CENTURY CHINESE POETRY: An Anthology. 1963 *Cornell Univ. Press* 1970 pap. $3.45

"Easily the best work in English concerning China since the end of World War II, this is an indispensable book for all libraries"—(*LJ*). The work of over 50 poets has been beautifully translated. The editor gives dates of both poets and poems wherever possible, together with excellent biographical and critical introductions.

Huang, Joe C. HEROES AND VILLAINS IN COMMUNIST CHINA: The Contemporary Chinese Novel as a Reflection of Life. *Universe Bks.* Pica Press 1974 $15.00. The first full-fledged study of the Communist Chinese novel.

Isaacs, Harold Robert, Ed. STRAW SANDALS: Chinese Short Stories, 1918–1933. Foreword by Lu Hsün. *M. I. T. Press* 1974 $10.00. A collection of 23 short stories, a play and a poem, assembled in 1934 with the guidance of two outstanding modern Chinese writers, Lu Hsün and Mao Tun. Well translated, with biographical information on 16 chosen authors.

Jenner, William John Francis, and Gladys Yang, Trans. and eds. MODERN CHINESE STORIES. *Oxford* 1974 pap. $2.95

Klemer, D. J., Ed. CHINESE LOVE POEMS. *Doubleday* 1959 $3.95

Lee, Leo Ou-fan. THE ROMANTIC GENERATION OF MODERN CHINESE WRITERS. Harvard East Asian Ser. *Harvard Univ. Press* 1973 $15.00

Lewis, Richard, Ed. THE MOMENT OF WONDER: A Collection of Chinese and Japanese Poetry. *Dial* 1964 $5.95

"An anthology from anthologies but well-selected"—(*LJ*).

Liang, Ch'i-ch'ao. INTELLECTUAL TRENDS IN THE CH'ING PERIOD. Trans. with introd. and notes by Immanuel C. Y. Hsu. *Harvard Univ. Press* 1959 $7.00

A lively portrayal of the intellectual developments in China under the Ch'ing (or Manchu) dynasty, which ruled from 1644–1912. J. R. Levenson has written a biography of the Chinese journalist, scholar and political figure, "Liang Ch'i-ch'ao and the Mind of Modern China" (*Harvard Univ. Press* 1953 2nd ed. 1959 $5.00) which gives also an account of his contribution to the history of his country.

Lin, Julia C. MODERN CHINESE POETRY: An Introduction. Publications on Asia of the Institute for Comparative and Foreign Area Studies *Univ. of Washington Press* 1973 $10.00 pap. $2.95. Translations of twentieth-century poetry with extensive commentary by the author.

Liu, James J. Y. THE ART OF CHINESE POETRY. *Univ. of Chicago Press* 1962 Phoenix Bks. pap. $2.75. A careful study by a professor of Chinese at Stanford University.

Liu Wu-chi. AN INTRODUCTION TO CHINESE LITERATURE. *Univ. of Indiana Press* 1966 $12.50 pap. $3.95

"Poetry in different forms is the main topic of the first part of the book. The popular novel of the Yuan and the Ming dynasties is treated extensively. The contemporary literary scene is given selective coverage. . . . On the whole . . . a valuable contribution"—(*LJ*).

(With Irving Lo, Trans. and eds.) SUNFLOWER SPLENDOR: Three Thousand Years of Chinese Poetry. *Doubleday* Anchor Bks. 1975 $5.95

McNaughton, William, Ed. CHINESE LITERATURE: An Anthology from the Earliest Times to the Present Day. *Tuttle* 1974 $15.00

Meserve, Walter Joseph, and Ruth Ingeborg Meserve, Trans. and eds. MODERN LITERATURE FROM CHINA. *New York Univ. Press* 1974 $15.00 pap. $3.95. Translations of twentieth-century Chinese short stories, poetry, drama, and essays, including a number difficult to obtain in English translation elsewhere such as Mao Tun's "Spring Silkworms" and Tsao Yu's "Thunderstorm."

Palandri, Angela C. Y. Jung, Trans. and ed. MODERN VERSE FROM TAIWAN. *Univ. of California Press* 1972 $9.50

Payne, Robert, Ed. THE WHITE PONY: An Anthology of Chinese Poetry from the Earliest Times to the Present Day. 1974. *New Am. Lib.* Mentor pap. $1.25. Newly translated; comprehensive and authoritative.

Prusek, Jaroslav. CHINESE HISTORY AND LITERATURE: Collection of Studies. *Reidel* 1970 $26.50; *Humanities Press* 1970 $26.50

Rexroth, Kenneth, Trans. ONE HUNDRED POEMS FROM THE CHINESE. *New Directions* 1956 $6.00 pap. $1.75

(With Ling Chung, Trans. and eds.) THE ORCHID BOAT: Women Poets of China. *Seabury Press* Continuum Bks. 1972 $6.95

Scott, A. C. AN INTRODUCTION TO THE CHINESE THEATRE. 1959 o.p.

LITERATURE AND THE ARTS IN TWENTIETH CENTURY CHINA. *Int. Pubns. Service* 1963 $7.00; *Peter Smith* $5.00

(Trans. and annot.) TRADITIONAL CHINESE PLAYS. *Univ. of Wisconsin Press* Vol. 1 1967 pap. $2.50 Vol. 2 1969 $10.00 pap. $2.50 Vol. 3 1974 $10.00

Tsien, Tsuen-hsuin. WRITTEN ON BAMBOO AND SILK: The Beginnings of Chinese Books and Inscriptions. *Univ. of Chicago Press* 1962 $9.50. How Chinese writing developed and how it was used from ancient times to the emergence of the age of printing; an indispensable book.

Waley, Arthur. THREE WAYS OF THOUGHT IN ANCIENT CHINA. 1939 *Harper* (Barnes & Noble) 1953 $8.50; *Doubleday* Anchor Bks. 1956 pap. $1.95

TRANSLATIONS FROM THE CHINESE. Ill. by Cyrus LeRoy Baldridge. 1941 1955 *Random* Vintage 1971 pap. $1.95. Includes "170 Chinese Poems" and "More Translations from the Chinese."

Wang, Chi-chen. Trans. TRADITIONAL CHINESE TALES. 1944. *Greenwood* 1969 $13.00. A collection of 20 Chinese stories from the sixth to the sixteenth centuries, covering most aspects of this genre in China.

Watson, Burton D., Trans. BASIC WRITINGS OF MO TZU, HSUN TZU AND HAN FEI TSU. *Columbia* 1967 $12.00

New translations of the teachings of three philosophers from China's classical age, the fifth to third centuries B.C. The English renderings are "of consistently high quality" (*SR*), the texts well chosen and introductions helpful.

EARLY CHINESE LITERATURE. Companions to Asian Studies Ser. *Columbia* 1962 $11.00 pap. $2.95. A capable survey of the formative stages of Chinese history, philosophy, and poetry (covering the approximate period 1000 B.C.–100 A.D.).

RECORDS OF THE GRAND HISTORIAN OF CHINA. *Columbia* 1961 2 vols. Vol. 1 Early Years of the Han Dynasty Vol. 2 The Age of Emperor Wu trans. from the "Shih Chi" of Ssu-ma Ch'ien each $15.00

Wylie, A. NOTES ON CHINESE LITERATURE. *Paragon Reprint* 1964 $12.50

Yoshikawa, Kōjirō. AN INTRODUCTION TO SUNG POETRY. Trans. by Burton Watson. Harvard-Yenching Institute Monograph Ser. *Harvard Univ. Press* 1967 $7.00. Well-written discussion of an important period.

Zung, Cecilia S. L. SECRETS OF THE CHINESE DRAMA. 1937. *Blom.* $15.00

See also Chapter 4, World Religions—Buddhism, Confucianism, Taoism, Reader's Adviser, *Vol. 3.*

LIU HSIEH. c. 465–522 A.D.

Liu Hsieh was a literary critic and artist "whose most delightfully titled book is a fitting text for those who would reflect upon the history of Chinese literary thought"—(*LJ*).

THE LITERARY MIND AND THE CARVING OF DRAGONS: A Study of Thought and Pattern in Chinese Literature. 501–502. Trans. with introd. and notes by Vincent Yu-chung Shih. o.p.

HAN-SHAN. fl. 627–649.

Han-shan holds an important place in Chinese literature as the author of great poetry on Buddhist themes. Our only source of information, except the poems themselves, about the impecunious scholar who lived at a place called Cold Mountain, is an undated preface to the poetry of Han-shan and Shih-te written by Lü-ch'iu Yin, an official of the T'ang dynasty.

COLD MOUNTAIN: 100 Poems by the T'ang Poet Han-Shan. Trans. by Burton Watson. 1962 *Columbia* 1970 $7.50 pap. $2.45. *LJ* quotes Arthur Waley, who wrote in the introduction to his own translation of the poems: " 'Cold Mountain' is often the name of a state of mind rather than a locality. It is on this conception, as well as on that of the 'hidden treasure,' . . . that the mysticism of the poems is based."

LI PO (also Li T'ai-po, Li Tai-Peh, Le Pih, Ly Pé, etc.). 701–762.

China's greatest lyric poet, known throughout the Orient for over 1,000 years, is famous for his exquisite imagery, allusions, and richness of language. He lived a dissipated life at the court of the T'ang emperor and was one of a band known as the "Eight Immortals of the Wine Cup." He is supposed to have drowned while boating, in a drunken attempt to embrace the reflected moon.

THE WORKS OF LI PO THE CHINESE POET. 1922. Trans. by Shigeyoshi Obata. *Paragon Reprint* 1966 $6.00

Books about Li Po

The Poetry and Career of Li Po, 701–762 A.D. By Arthur Waley. *Hillary House* 1949 1958 $4.50. A biography of the poet, which includes translations of many of his poems.
On Li Po. By Elling Eide. (In "Perspectives on the T'ang," ed. by Arthur F. Wright and Denis Twitchett.) *Yale Univ. Press* 1973 $15.00. Eide gives a detailed analysis of three important poems by Li Po.

WANG WEI. c. 701–761.

"Wang Wei was a famous poet, [physician,] calligrapher, musician, and painter of 8th-century China at the height of the brilliant T'ang Dynasty. His poetry is intense, brilliant, and moving"— (*Kirkus*). Wang Wei wrote almost exclusively in quatrains, which delicately portray quiet scenes like those depicted in his few surviving paintings, some of which have been reproduced in books of his poetry. "His love of meditation, of scenic beauty, and of pictorial art is thoroughly reflected in his poetry, thus founding the school of nature poets"—(Che'en Shou-Yi). A devout Buddhist, he entered a Buddhist monastery after his wife's death.

HIDING THE UNIVERSE. Trans. by Yip Wai-lim. *Grossman* Mushinsha Bks. 1972 $12.50 pap. $4.95

POEMS OF WANG WEI. Trans. by G. W. Robinson. Classics Ser. *Penguin* 1974 pap. $1.85

Books about Wang Wei

Wang Wei, the Painter-Poet. By Lewis C. Walmsley and Dorothy W. Walmsley. *Tuttle* 1968 $6.60
Chinese Lyricism: Shih Poetry from the Second to the Twelfth Centuries, with Translations. By Burton Watson. *Columbia* 1971 $9.00 pap. $3.45. Burton Watson provides a thoughtful analysis of Wang Wei's poetry in comparison with that of Li Po, Tu Fu, and others.

TU FU. 712–770.

This Chinese poet of the brilliant T'ang dynasty, born in Shensi province, was second only to Li Po in fame. Tu Fu had "such a high opinion of his own poetry that he prescribed it as a cure for malarial fever"—(Herbert A. Giles). He was especially admired for his beautiful lyrics.

SELECTED POEMS. Trans. by Rewi Alley. China's Poems and Plays Ser. *Great Wall Press* 1973 $4.50

A LITTLE PRIMER OF TU FU. By David Hawkes. *Oxford* 1967 $10.25

Books about Tu Fu

Tu Fu, China's Greatest Poet. By William Hung. *Russell & Russell* 1969 $15.00; supplementary vol. of notes Harvard-Yenching Institute Publication Ser. *Harvard Univ. Press* 1952 $4.25. Includes translations of 374 poems, chosen to illustrate the poet's life and times.

Tu Fu. By A. R. Davis. World Authors Ser. *Twayne* 1971 $6.95

PO CHÜ-I (also Po Chü-yi, Pai Chü-i).   772–846.

This Chinese poet, author of more than 70 books, was known especially for his fine lyrics. He was a government official under the T'ang dynasty.

COLLECTED WORKS. Trans. by Howard S. Levy. *Paragon Reprint* 1971 2 vols. Vol. 1. The Old Style Poems $10.00 Vol. 2 The Regular Poems $8.00

LAMENT EVERLASTING: The Death of Yang Kuei fei. Trans. by Howard S. Levy. *Paragon Reprint* 1962 $2.00. An able translation of one of Po Chü-i's most memorable poems.

PO CHÜ-I AS A CENSOR: His Memorials Presented to Emperor Hsien-tsung during the Years 808–810. Trans. by E. Feifel. 1961 o.p.

WANG SHIH-FU.   fl. thirteenth century.

The life story of this famous Chinese playwright, a native of Peking, is unknown. It is thought that he wrote 14 plays, of which only three have survived.

ROMANCE OF THE WESTERN CHAMBER. Trans. by S. I. Hsiung. 1935 Translations from the Oriental Classics Ser. *Columbia* 1968 $12.00 pap. $4.00; trans. by T. C. Lai and Ed Gamarekian. Writing in Asia Ser. *Humanities Press* 1974 pap. $2.25. This is the most famous Chinese play of all times, and has entered the repertoire of Western theaters. Its theme of the tragic lovers has been repeated in numerous Chinese ballads and plays from the fourteenth century to the present.

LO KUAN-CHUNG.   c. 1330–1400.

Very little is known of this writer, author of one of China's most famous novels. "The Romance of the Three Kingdoms" (trans. by C. H. Brewitt-Taylor, U.S. 1925 1959 *Tuttle* 1969 2 vols. set $15.00) is a fictional account of historical events of the third century. The main plot is divided into short chapter plots, which makes the whole work easily adaptable to the opera, storyteller, and marionette forms, in which it is widely known in Chinese. "It consists mainly of stirring scenes of warfare, of cunning plans by skillful generals, and of doughty deeds by bloodstained warriors"— (Herbert Giles).

SHIH NAI-AN.   fl. before 1400.

A Chinese writer who is traditionally assumed to be the author of the romance *"Shui-hu chuan,"* and one of the greatest writers of Chinese popular literature. Nearly all that is known of his life is that he lived at the turn of the Mongol-Ming periods, in or near Hangchow.

WATER MARGIN. Trans. by J. H. Jackson. 1937 *Paragon Reprint* 1968 $17.50 pap. $12.50; (with title "All Men Are Brothers") trans. by Pearl S. Buck. 1933 *T. Y. Crowell* (John Day) 1968 2 vols. $20.00. Shih Nai-an in his own introduction says that he wrote the 70 chapters of the *"Shui-hu chuan"* for his own pleasure. Furthermore, he mentions, "Life is so short that I shall not even know what the reader thinks about it, but still I shall be satisfied if a few of my friends will read it and be interested."

Books about Shih Nai-an

The Evolution of a Chinese Novel; Shih-hu-chuan. By Richard G. Irwin. Harvard-Yenching Institute Studies Ser. *Harvard Univ. Press* 1953 pap. $4.00

WU CH'ENG-EN.   1500–1582.

A novelist and poet from Kiangsu province, Wu spent part of his life as district governor and master of ceremonies in the regent's palace in Nanking before returning to his home and his writing.

MONKEY. Trans. by Arthur Waley. 1942 *Grove* Evergreen 1958 pap. $2.95. This translation of Wu Ch'eng-en's best-known work, the *"Hsi-yu chi,"* or "Record of a

Journey to the West," is the foremost example of a Chinese novel on a supernatural theme. It is theoretically based on the travels of Hsüan-tsang, a Chinese Buddhist monk who journeyed to India between 629 and 645.

Books about Wu Ch'eng-en

The Hsi-yu Chi: A Study of Antecedents to the Sixteenth Century Chinese Novel. By G. Dudbridge. Studies in Chinese History, Literature and Institutions *Cambridge* 1970 $25.00

WANG SHIH-CHÊNG. 1526–1590.

Many novels were written during the Ming Dynasty (1368–1644), but the names of their authors have rarely been preserved. "The Golden Lotus" has been attributed to Wang Shih-chêng, although some scholars believe that it was written later, in the closing years of the Ming Dynasty. Pearl Buck (*q.v.*) calls it "the greatest novel of physical love which China has produced." The *Saturday Review* has said: "This extraordinary book . . . plunges the reader into the midst of Chinese society as it existed during the first quarter of the twelfth century . . . when official corruption was rampant and political chaos imminent. It records the amorous exploits and grisly end of a wealthy merchant . . . and the criminal exploits and ghastly death of Golden Lotus, the merchant's Fifth Lady. . . . It records much besides, with a wealth of detail that makes the pages bustle with life; much that will seem strange to today's readers, and much that will seem strangely familiar to them." "Flower Shadows behind the Curtain" (trans. by Vladimir Kean U.S. 1959, o.p.) is considered by some to be the sequel written perhaps 20 years later either by the same author or by one whose command of his medium equals that of the original novelist. Some of the same characters appear, some appear in reincarnations.

THE GOLDEN LOTUS. Trans. by Clement Egerton. 1954 *Routledge & Kegan Paul* 1972 4 vols. set $35.00

LI YÜ. 1611–1680.

Li Yü, a playwright, novelist, poet, and essayist born in Kiangsu province, can be considered representative of the intellectual world of the late Ming period. His work reflects his unorthodox views and bohemian way of life.

JOU PU TUAN (Ju-p'u-t'uan), THE PRAYER MAT OF FLESH: A 17th Century Erotic Moral Novel. Trans. by Richard Martin from the German version by Franz Kuhn. 1963 1967 *Grove* Evergreen Bks. pap. $1.95

R. H. Van Gulik, the Dutch authority on Chinese Ming erotic literature, had this to say about the story of the sensual adventures of a student in seventeenth century China: "From the literary point of view, this book is, after the Chin-p'ing-mei, the best Ming erotic novel. It is written in a fluent, elegant style, interspersed with good poetry, witty dialogues, and clever character sketches. Although it abounds in obscene passages, they are often combined with philosophical disquisitions on the frailty of human nature; this tends to soften the stark realism of the erotic scene."

TS'AO CHAN (also Ts'ao Hsüeh-ch'in). c. 1717–1764.

THE DREAM OF THE RED CHAMBER. 1792. Trans. by Chi-chen Wang. 1929. *Twayne* 1958 $7.00; *Doubleday* Anchor Bks. pap. $2.50; *Grosset* $3.45

This is an abridged version of a great Chinese classic, attributed to Ts'ao Chan, which chronicles several generations of men and women, their trials and tribulations, the pathos and the comedy of their existence. For three generations Ts'ao Chan's family were superintendents of the imperial textile factory at Nanking and became very wealthy. In 1728 all their property was confiscated so that the family lived in great poverty in the one house in Peking which was returned to them. The story of the decline of a great house in "The Dream of the Red Chamber" may be based on the vicissitudes of his own family. It is remarkable for the masterly portraiture of the 50 or more major characters. The first printed edition contained 120 chapters, but it is thought that 40 were added by Kao O, who wrote the preface. A Chinese scholar has said: "If you wish to understand China at all, you must read her poetry and 'Dream of the Red Chamber.'" For further information *see* "The Dream of the Red Chamber; A Critical Study" by Jeanne Knoerle (*Indiana Univ. Press* East Asian Ser. 1973 $6.95).

LIU T'IEH-YÜN (also Liu Ngo, Liu E, Liu O). 1857–1909.

TRAVELS OF LAO TS'AN. Trans. and annot. by Harold Shadick. *Cornell Univ. Press* 1952 $8.50 pap. $2.95

"Since the novel translated here may justly be characterized as one of the great novels in the Chinese literary tradition, it is fortunate that it has been put into English by so competent a hand as the professor of Chinese literature at Cornell University. Written in the years 1904–1907 by a

Chinese scholar and official of unusual versatility and skill, these Travels throw a powerful light on both the dark and bright aspects of Chinese officialdom in the closing years of the Manchu dynasty"—(*U.S. Quarterly Book Review*).

LU HSÜN (also Lusin, Lu Xun; pseud. of Chou Shu-jen).   1881–1936.

A writer, essayist, translator, poet, and literary theorist and critic, Lu Hsün was born in Chekiang province of an educated family. A participant in the May Fourth (1919) Movement, he was a founding member of the League of Left-Wing Writers in 1930. He translated a number of European works of literature and theoretical studies on art and literature into Chinese, and helped to introduce modern art to China. The extent of his work and its high standards laid the foundation for modern Chinese literature.

A BRIEF HISTORY OF CHINESE FICTION. Trans. by Yang Hsien-yi and Gladys Yang. 1920 1924 1959 *Hyperion Press* 1973 $18.50. An able translation of Lu Hsün's most important scholarly work and the first of its kind to be published in China.

AH Q AND OTHERS: Selected Stories of Lusin. Trans. by Wang Chi-chen. 1941. *Bks. for Libraries* 1971 $9.00; *China Bks.* 1974 pap. $.75; *Greenwood* 1971 $12.25. Eleven of Lu Hsün's best stories, including his most famous, "The True Story of Ah Q."

SELECTED STORIES. 3rd ed. Trans. by Hsien-yi and Gladys Yang. *Oriole Eds.* 1973 $8.50; *China Bks.* 1972 $2.50 pap. $1.75

SILENT CHINA: Selected Writings of Lu Xun. Trans. and ed. by Gladys Yang. *Oxford* 1974 pap. $2.95

WILD GRASS. 1927. *China Bks.* 1974 $1.00. A collection of all of Lu Hsün's prose poems.

HU SHIH.   1891–1962.

This scholar was educated at Cornell and Columbia universities and taught for many years at the Peking National University. He served as Chinese Ambassador to the United States from 1938 to 1942, and from 1958 until his death was president of the Academia Sinica. He was a strong promoter of the use of the vernacular in Chinese literature, and was one of the literary reformers of the May Fourth Movement.

(With Lin Yutang) CHINA'S OWN CRITICS: A Selection of Essays. 1931 *Paragon Reprint* 1969 $7.00

CHINESE RENAISSANCE. *Paragon Reprint* 2nd ed. 1963 $8.50

DEVELOPMENT OF THE LOGICAL METHOD IN ANCIENT CHINA. *Paragon Reprint* 2nd ed. 1963 $8.50; *Krishna Press* (div. of Gordon Press) $29.95

Books about Hu Shih

Hu Shih and the Chinese Renaissance: Liberalism in the Chinese Revolution, 1917–1937. By Jerome Grieder. Harvard East Asian Ser. *Harvard Univ. Press* 1970 $12.50

MAO TSE-TUNG.   1893–1976.

Born into a prosperous peasant family in Hunan province, Mao first came into contact with revolutionary writings in the decade of the 1910s. Mao was present at the founding of the Communist Party in 1921 and has been the most influential leader in China since 1935. President of the People's Republic from 1949 to 1959, he is now chairman of the Communist Party. As a result of his education, he has a great command of classical Chinese; this, together with his sense of history, casts his poetry in the traditional style.

QUOTATIONS FROM CHAIRMAN MAO TSE-TUNG. Ed. by Stuart R. Schram, with introd. by A. Doak Barnett. *Bantam* 1966 pap. $1.25; 2nd ed. 1967 *China Bks.* $.60. This "little red book" is the Bible of Chinese Maoists and required reading for the student of contemporary China.

MAO PAPERS: Anthology and Bibliography. Ed. by Jerome Ch'en. *Oxford* 1970 $10.00

MAO TSE-TUNG: An Anthology of His Writings. Ed. by Anne Freemantle. *New Am. Lib.* Mentor Bks. 1971 pap. $1.25

THE POEMS OF CHAIRMAN MAO. Trans. by Willis Barnstone and Ko Ching-po. *Harper* Torchbks. 1972 pap. $6.50

POEMS OF MAO TSE TUNG. Trans. and ed. by Hua-ling Nieh Engle and Paul Engle. *Dell* Delta 1973 pap. $2.45

TEN POEMS AND LYRICS. Trans. with woodcuts by Wang Hui-ming. *Univ. of Mass. Press* 1975 $7.00 pap. $3.50

TALKS AT THE YENAN FORUM ON LITERATURE AND ART. 1942 *China Bks.* 1965 $.50. Mao gives his definition of the cultural policies of the Communist Party, summing up at the same time Chinese discussions of the revolutionary literature of the preceeding 20 years. He states that literature and art must support other revolutionary activities.

Books about Mao Tse-Tung

Mao and the Chinese Revolution. By Jerome Ch'en. With 37 poems by Mao Tse-tung trans. by Michael Bullock and Jerome Ch'en. *Oxford* Galaxy Bks. 1965 pap. $3.50
This book is one of the three standard biographies of Mao. "The poems are translated with an unusual degree of sensitivity for the nuances and subtleties that are characteristic of Chinese poetry"—(C. T. Hu, in *SR*).
Mao Tse-tung. By Stuart R. Schram. *Simon & Schuster* 1967 $7.95; *Penguin* Pelican 1968 pap. $1.65
Mao. Ed. by Jerome Ch'en. Great Lives Observed Ser. *Prentice-Hall* 1969 $5.95 pap. $1.95

See also Chapter 2, General Biography and Autobiography Reader's Adviser, *Vol. 3*.

LIN YUTANG. 1895–1976.

Dr. Lin, born in China, lived in New York, then in Cannes, France, with his wife and three daughters. Early in 1954 he was appointed chancellor of the new Chinese University in Singapore but because of a disagreement with the trustees on policy, he and his staff left early in 1955 before the university opened its doors. He has helped immeasurably in an understanding between East and West. A product of an ancient civilization, with both a classical and a modern educational background, he writes an idiomatic, sparkling English in the best essay tradition. The earlier books are notable for their wisdom, wit and humor. Unfortunately, "My Country and My People" (1935 rev. and enl. ed. 1939) is now o.p. He has edited "The Wisdom of India" (1942 o.p.) and edited and translated "The Importance of Understanding" (1960 o.p.).

(With Hu Shih) CHINA'S OWN CRITICS: A Selection of Essays. 1931. *Paragon Reprint* 1969 $7.00

PRESS AND PUBLIC OPINION IN CHINA. 1936. *Greenwood* 1968 $11.25

THE IMPORTANCE OF LIVING. T. Y. *Crowell* (John Day) 1937 $10.95; *Putnam* pap. $3.25

MOMENT IN PEKING: A Novel of Contemporary Chinese Life. 1939 *Popular Lib.* 1968 pap. $1.25. This and "A Leaf in the Storm" (1942 o.p.), are Lin Yutang's best-known novels.

BETWEEN TEARS AND LAUGHTER. 1943. Essay Index Reprint Ser. *Bks. for Libraries* 1972 $9.50

GAY GENIUS: The Life and Times of Su Tungpo. 1947. *Greenwood* 1971 $15.00. A biography of Su Shih, 1036–1101.

THE VERMILION GATE: A Novel of a Fair Land. 1953. *Greenwood* 1971 $18.25

(Trans. and adapted) WIDOW, NUN AND COURTESAN: Three Novelettes from the Chinese. 1951. *Greenwood* 1971 $12.50

IMPERIAL PEKING: Seven Centuries of China. 1961. *Dufour* $17.50; *Int. Pubns. Service* $14.00. With an essay on the art of Peking by Peter C. Swann. A gracefully written account of the 1000-year history and the near-mythical beauty of the great city.

MAO TUN (pseud. of Shen Yen-ping). 1896–

One of modern China's best and most representative novelists, Mao Tun is an active member of the Literary Research Organization, a writers' group founded in 1920 to foster a "literature of humanity," depicting society and its ills. He was Minister of Culture for the People's Republic of China from 1949 to 1966. His novels protesting exploitation of workers and peasants and advocating change by revolution have established him as a prominent literary figure in Communist China. "Among all the novelists sympathetic to the extreme left Mao Tun was artistically outstanding"—(A. C. Scott).

MIDNIGHT. Trans. by Hsu Meng-hsiung. Currently o.p., this novel written in 1930–1931 is Mao Tun's greatest work, a picture of life in Shanghai in 1930.

SPRING SILKWORMS AND OTHER STORIES. Trans. by Sidney Shapiro. o.p. Thirteen short stories, dealing with life in the countryside and written between 1930 and 1936. Originally published in English translation in 1956.

LAO SHE (also Lao Sheh, Lau Shaw, S. Y. Shu; pseud. for Shu Ch'ing-ch'un). 1899– 1966.

Born in Peking of Manchu descent, he was the only major twentieth century writer from North China. He resided in England and later in the United States, and was heavily influenced by Western writing, especially that by Dickens. Two of his best-known works, "The Drum Singers" trans. by Helena Kuo, and "Rickshaw Boy" trans. by Evan King, are now o.p.

CAT COUNTRY: A Satirical Novel of China in the 1930's. Trans. by William A. Lyell, Jr. *Ohio State Univ. Press* 1970 $8.00

Books about Lao She

Lao She and the Chinese Revolution. By Ranbir Vohra. Harvard East Asian Monographs *Harvard Univ. Press* 1974 $8.50

CHIANG YEE. 1903– *See Chapter 12, Travel and Adventure, Reader's Adviser, Vol. 3.*

PA CHIN (pseud. of Li Fei-kan). 1905–

Pa Chin, a novelist, short story writer, and translator, spent the years 1927–1929 in France. His novels, for which he is best-known, express two major themes: an attack on the traditional patriarchal family such as the one into which he was born, and a defense of young revolutionaries fighting for a better future for mankind. He has been criticized since 1949, most recently during the Cultural Revolution.

FAMILY. Trans. by Sidney Shapiro with suppl. pts. trans. by Lu Kuang-huan; introd. by Olga Lang. 1931. *Doubleday* Anchor Bks. 1972 pap. $2.95; *Peter Smith* 1972 $4.75. Pa Chin's most popular novel, which forms a trilogy with two succeeding novels, "Spring" ("*Ch'un*") 1937 and "Autumn" ("*Ch'iu*") 1940.

Books about Pa Chin

Pa Chin and His Writings: Chinese Youth between Two Revolutions. By Olga Lang. Harvard East Asian Ser. *Harvard Univ. Press* 1967 $11.00

HAN SUYIN (pseud. of Dr. Elizabeth Comber). 1917–

Han Suyin, whose name means "the Chinese gamble" (with the added phrase "for liberty" understood), is "a doctor, a writer, a speaker, a pamphleteer, a wife and mother, a formidable intellect and very much a woman." She was born in Peking, the daughter of a Chinese scholar and engineer named Chow and his Belgian wife. After graduation from Yenching University in Peking, she went to London to study medicine.

A colorful life took her back to China and then to Hong Kong. Her second husband, a British foreign correspondent, was killed covering the Korean war. "A Many-Splendored Thing," filmed as "Love Is a Many-Splendored Thing" with Jennifer Jones and William Holden in 1955, is the memoir of this love affair. "And the Rain My Drink (1956, o.p.) is a novel of modern-day Malaya. "The Mountain Is Young" (1958, o.p.) is set in the Himalayan kingdom of Nepal. The gateway of the ancient and magnificent ruins at Angkor Vat and Angkor Thom—an enormous staring four-faced head—provides the title for the popular tale of intrigue and suspense, "The Four Faces" (1963, o.p.). "The Crippled Tree" (1965, o.p.) and "A Mortal Flower" are two volumes of autobiography describing Miss Han's experiences and attitudes as a Eurasian. "*The Crippled Tree* is written by a woman who does not like and admire us [Americans] as we want to be liked . . . [but] Han Suyin writes with elegance and style"—(*SR*). Passionately anti-American and anticolonialist, "over and over again Han Suyin takes a slice of childhood memory and slaps it between two great hunks of political sermon before serving it up"—(Emily Hahn).

She has recently lived in Singapore with her third husband, Leonard Comber, formerly a British police officer, now a student of Oriental cultures. Of her writing about Asia for the West, she says: "I write as an Asian with all the pent-up emotions of my people. What I say will annoy many people who prefer the more conventional myths brought back by writers on the Orient. All I can say is that I try to tell the truth. Truth, like surgery, may hurt, but it cures."

A MANY-SPLENDORED THING. *Little* 1952 $6.95

A MORTAL FLOWER: China Autobiography, History. *Putnam* 1966 $6.95

CHINA IN THE YEAR 2001. 1967 o.p.

"Not an apologia for Communist China [but] something much stronger, a dogmatic assertion of China's growing power and revolutionary Force"—(*PW*). Based on the author's 11 visits to China.

THE MORNING DELUGE: Mao Tse Tung and the Chinese Revolution, 1893–1954. *Little* 1972 $12.50

Japanese Literature

Ivan Morris writes, in the *N.Y. Times*: "No country as remote from the West as Japan—geographically, culturally, and above all linguistically—has ever been so richly represented here by translated fiction." With Japan's emergence as a world power during the past decade, interest in Japanese literature, especially that of the contemporary period, has increased in the West as one means of better understanding our Eastern neighbor. Morris finds that the subjects of Japan's fiction are "depressingly familiar" to us in the West. "Except for a few remaining pockets of traditionalism (the geisha and kabuki worlds, for example) modern Japan is little wedded to ceremony and ritual." In its novels elders are not respected but tormented; materialism reigns. Yet there remains a characteristic "type of sensuous awareness, a delight in the details of sound and feel and smell, that appears far more strongly in Japan and in much Japanese literature, than in the modern West."

Japanese writers, unlike the Germans, are still strangely silent on the subject of the war years. "In the Japanese view, the atomic bomb was an expiation of their war guilt. With the two explosions over Hiroshima and Nagasaki, Japan was transformed from aggressor into victim. . . . Since V-J day, only a handful of novels have seriously dealt with the war. Even those tended to put all the blame on the militarists"—(*Time*, April 5, 1963). The classic description of the A-bomb's immediate effect on Japan is John Hersey's (*q.v.*) "Hiroshima" (*Knopf* 1946 $4.00; *Random* Modern Lib. $2.95; *Bantam* pap. $.75). A recent excellent summary of what has happened to the victims is Rafael Steinburg's "Postscript from Hiroshima" (*Random* 1967 $5.95). (*See also Chapter 9, History, Government and Politics, Section on Modern World at War,* Reader's Adviser, *Vol. 3*.)

A good short history is Edwin O. Reischauer's "Japan: The Story of a Nation" (*Knopf* 1970 rev. ed. 1974 $7.95) which is based on his "Japan, Past and Present," first published in 1946. Both the early and modern periods of Japanese history are excellently treated in the standard work "A History of East Asian Civilization," Vol. 1: "East Asia—The Great Tradition" by John K. Fairbank and Edwin O. Reischauer and Vol. 2: "East Asia—The Modern Transformation" by John K. Fairbank, Edwin O. Reischauer, and Albert M. Craig (*Houghton* Vol. 1 1960 Vol. 2 1965 each $13.95). W. G. Beasley's "The Modern History of Japan" (*Praeger* 1974 $10.00 pap. $4.95), currently in its second edition, is another standard history. "Tradition and Modernization in Japanese Culture," edited by Donald H. Shively of Harvard University (Studies in the Modernization of Japan *Princeton Univ. Press* 1971 $14.50) is a collection of papers covering changes in Japanese government, the arts, literature, philosophy, religion, and language during the Meiji and early Taishō periods of the late nineteenth century. A good introduction to Japanese civilization is Arthur E. Tiedemann, ed., "An Introduction to Japanese Civilization" (Companions to Asian Studies *Columbia* 1974 $17.50).

Four words frequently encountered in discussions of Japanese literature are *haiku*, the traditional 17-syllable three-line lyric poem; *tanka*, that of 31 syllables and five lines; *kabuki*, a stylized popular or comic drama; and *No* or *Noh*, drama classical in form, noble or tragic in theme. Both the latter employ music, dancing, and stylized gesture. Japanese postwar theater is more impressive for its classical than for its modern productions; acting, setting, and direction are generally excellent. *Haiku* and *tanka* are still composed in abundance, according to strict rule; the *haiku* form has become a literary vogue in the United States.

Asia Society, Alfred H. Marks, and Barry D. Bort. GUIDE TO JAPANESE PROSE. Asian Bibliography Ser. *Hall* 1975 $12.00

Asia Society and Leonard C. Pronko. GUIDE TO JAPANESE DRAMA. Asian Bibliography Ser. *Hall* 1973 $9.50

Asia Society, J. Thomas Rimer, and Robert E. Merrill. GUIDE TO JAPANESE POETRY. Asian Bibliography Ser. *Hall* 1976 $12.00. This volume and the two preceding serve as introductions to Japanese poetry, prose, and drama, summarizing and evaluating selected works available in English translation.

Blyth, Reginald H., Trans. and ed. HAIKU. *Japan* 4 vols. 1949–52 Vol. 1 Eastern Culture Vol. 2 Spring Vol. 3 Summer-Autumn Vol. 4 Autumn-Winter each $11.00

   HISTORY OF HAIKU. *Japan* 2 vols. Vol. 1 From the Beginning up to Issa 1963 Vol. 2 From Issa up the Present 1946 each $11.00

Bowers, Faubion. JAPANESE THEATRE. Fwd. by Joshua Logan. 1952 o.p.

Bownas, Geoffrey, and Anthony Thwaite, Trans. and comps. THE PENGUIN BOOK OF JAPANESE VERSE. *Penguin* bilingual ed. 1964 pap. $1.75

Brandon, James Rodger, Trans. and ed. KABUKI: Five Classic Plays. UNESCO Collection of Representative Works: Japanese Ser. *Harvard Univ. Press* 1975 $20.00

Elliot, William, and Noah Brannen, Trans. and eds. FESTIVE WINE: Ancient Japanese Poems from the Kinkafu. *Weatherhill* 1969 $6.95

Ernst, Earle. KABUKI THEATRE. 1956 1959. *Univ. Press of Hawaii* East West Center 1974 pap. $4.95

Halford, Aubrey S. and Giovanna M. THE KABUKI HANDBOOK: A Guide to Understanding and Appreciation, with Summaries of Favorite Plays, Explanatory Notes, and Illustrations. *Tuttle* 1957 $4.25

Hearn, Lafcadio. JAPAN: AN INTERPRETATION. 1904. *Tuttle* 1955 1963 $4.95 pap. $3.75

   A JAPANESE MISCELLANY. 1901. *Tuttle* 1954 pap. $2.20

   See Chapter 15, Essays and Criticism, Reader's Adviser, Vol. 1, for Hearn's other works.

Henderson, Harold G., Trans. and comp. AN INTRODUCTION TO HAIKU: An Anthology of Poems and Poets from Basho to Shiki. *Doubleday* 1958 $5.50 Anchor Bks. pap. $1.95

Hibbett, Howard Scott. THE FLOATING WORLD IN JAPANESE FICTION. 1959. Select Bibliographies Ser. *Bks. for Libraries* 1970 $11.50; *Tuttle* 1974 pap. $3.95

Japanese Classics Translation Committee. THE NOH DRAMA: Ten Plays from the Japanese. *Tuttle* 1960 $6.50

Kagawa, Toyohiko, and other Japanese poets. SONGS FROM THE LAND OF DAWN. Interpretation by Lois J. Erikson; decorations by Henry Y. Sugimoto. 1949. Granger Index Reprint Ser. *Bks. for Libraries* $7.50

Keene, Donald, Comp. and ed. ANTHOLOGY OF JAPANESE LITERATURE. Various translators. Earliest Era to 1868 *Grove* Evergreen Bks. 1956 1960 pap. $3.95; Modern Japanese Literature: An Anthology 1869 to Present *Grove* 1956 1960 Evergreen Bks. pap. $3.95

   "Japanese literature has about as long a history as English literature and contains works in as wide a variety of genres as may be found in any country. It includes some of the world's longest novels and shortest poems, plays which are miracles of muted suggestion and others filled with the most extravagant bombast. It is, in short, a rich literature which deserves better understanding and recognition"—(Introd.).

   JAPANESE LITERATURE: An Introduction for Western Readers. 1953. *Grove* 1955 Evergreen Bks. pap. $1.45. A brief work, very selective; beautifully written by an outstanding scholar and translator who is eminently successful at whetting the neophyte's appetite for more.

   (Trans.) THE BATTLES OF COXINGA. 1956. *Cambridge* $12.50 The most popular Japanese play ever written for the puppet theater; good explanatory introduction.

   MODERN JAPANESE NOVELS AND THE WEST. *Univ. Press of Virginia* 1961 $3.75

   No: The Classical Theatre of Japan. *Kodansha International* 1966 $35.00 pap. $4.95

"The most comprehensive book of No drama ever published in English. A beautiful book"—(*LJ*). Includes photographs by Hiroshi Kaneko, lists of plays currently performed, drawings of costumes and a phono-sheet of music.

(With Royall Tyler, Trans. and eds.) TWENTY PLAYS OF THE NO THEATRE. *Columbia* 1970 $15.00 pap. $4.95

Kokusai Bunka Shinkokai, Ed. INTRODUCTION TO CLASSIC JAPANESE LITERATURE. 1948. *Greenwood* 1970 $20.00

Lewis, Richard, Ed. THE MOMENT OF WONDER: A Collection of Chinese and Japanese Poetry. *Dial* 1964 $5.95

Miner, Earl. THE JAPANESE TRADITION IN BRITISH AND AMERICAN LITERATURE. *Princeton Univ. Press* 1958 pap. $2.95. Valuable study of Japanese influence on such poets as Yeats and Pound.

(With Robert H. Brower, Trans. and eds.) ANTHOLOGY OF JAPANESE COURT POETRY. *Stanford Univ. Press* 1961 $12.50. Analysis and criticism with new translations of more than 600 poems from 550 A.D. through 1433.

Miyamori, Asataro, Ed. MASTERPIECES OF JAPANESE POETRY, ANCIENT AND MODERN. 1936. *Greenwood* 2 vols. 1970 $41.00

Miyoshi, Masao. ACCOMPLICES OF SILENCE: The Modern Japanese Novel. *Univ. of California Press* 1974 $7.95 pap. 1975 $3.25

Morris, Ivan. THE WORLD OF THE SHINING PRINCE: Court Life in Ancient Japan. *Knopf* 1964 $7.95
A study of the age of Genji, the "Shining Prince." "This volume gives verve and color to a unique way of life which has rarely been recaptured"—(*LJ*).

(Ed.) DICTIONARY OF SELECTED FORMS IN CLASSICAL JAPANESE LITERATURE. *Columbia* 1966 $10.00

MODERN JAPANESE STORIES: An Anthology. Trans. by Edward Seidensticker and others. *Tuttle* 1961 $7.75. A remarkable and important collection of 25 stories written between 1910 and 1954.

Nihon Gakujutsu Shinkōkai, Trans. THE MAN'YŌSHŪ: One Thousand Poems. 1940 Records of Civilization Ser. *Columbia* 1965 1969 $17.50 pap. $6.00. A collection in 20 books, compiled during the eighth century, the "*Man'yōshū*" is the earliest extant anthology of Japanese poetry.

Putzar, Edward D., Trans. JAPANESE LITERATURE: A Historical Outline. (Adapted from "*Nihon bungaku*," Hisamatsu Sen'ichi, gen. ed.) *Univ. of Arizona Press* 1973 pap. $6.50. This translation of the work of Japanese scholars is a balanced comprehensive history of Japanese literature.

Reischauer, Edwin O., and J. K. Yamagiwa, Trans. and eds. TRANSLATIONS FROM EARLY JAPANESE LITERATURE. Harvard-Yenching Institute Studies *Harvard Univ. Press* 1951 2nd abr. ed. 1972 pap. $9.00. The first edition includes translations of *The Izayoi nikki*, *The Tsutsumi Chūnagon monogatari*, *The Heije monogatari*, and *The Ōkagami*; the second abridged edition excludes the latter title. Each of these works is representative of a major type of Japanese writing from the eleventh to the thirteenth century.

Rexroth, Kenneth, Trans. and ed. ONE HUNDRED POEMS FROM THE JAPANESE. *New Directions* 1955 $5.00 pap. $1.75. The poems are translated with beauty and subtlety by a poet; helpful introduction, biographical notes, and bibliography.

Sakanishi, Shio, Trans. THE INK SMEARED LADY AND OTHER KYOGEN. *Tuttle* 1960 pap. $2.95. Folk plays.

Scott, Adolphe C. KABUKI THEATRE OF JAPAN. *Macmillan* 1966 pap. $2.95

Shiffert, Edith, and Yuki Sawa, Trans. ANTHOLOGY OF MODERN JAPANESE POETRY. *Tuttle* 1972 $6.25

Smith, Robert J., and Richard A. Beardsley, Eds. JAPANESE CULTURE: Its Development and Characteristics. 1963 *Johnson Reprint* pap. $14.00. Of the 18 contributors, 8 were native Japanese scholars; a symposium of high quality.

Waley, Arthur. THE NŌ PLAYS OF JAPAN. 1921. *Grove* Evergreen Bks. 1957 pap. $3.95. Translations of 20 of the most famous ones and summaries of many others by the foremost Western translator of modern times.

(Trans.) JAPANESE POETRY: The Uta. 1946 o.p.

Yasuda, Kenneth. THE JAPANESE HAIKU: Its Essential Nature, History and Possibilities in English, with Examples. *Tuttle* 1957 $3.00

(Trans.) LAND OF THE REED PLAINS: Ancient Japanese Lyrics from the Manyoshu. *Tuttle* bilingual ed. 1972 pap. $3.00

(Trans.) A PEPPER-POD. *Tuttle* 1974 $4.75. Succinct translations of selected *haiku* with an introductory essay on the nature and development of the *haiku* form.

Recently Published Translations of Works by Japanese Authors

More works of interest, old and new, have appeared recently than we have space to treat in main entries. Here is a brief selection.

Fukuzawa, Yukichi. AUTOBIOGRAPHY. 1897. Trans. and rev. by Eiichi Kiyooka; fwd. by Carmen Blacker. *Columbia* (UNESCO) rev. ed. 1966 $12.50

By a 19th-century scholar who was also a popular writer and traveler to the West, his "unusual personality [comes] alive" here—(*LJ*).

Ishihara, Shintaro. SEASON OF VIOLENCE AND OTHER STORIES. Trans. by John G. Mills and others. *Tuttle* 1966 $3.85

Winner of the Akutagawa Literary Prize. The stories concern unfettered postwar Japanese youth. "Recommended . . . as a documentation of a real current social problem"—(*LJ*).

Kenko. ESSAYS IN IDLENESS: The Tsurezuregusa of Kenko. Trans. by Donald Keene. *Columbia* (UNESCO) 1967) $10.00 pap. $2.95

"The first complete English translation in 50 years. . . . Miscellaneous essays and anecdotes written by a Buddhist recluse in the 14th century. . . . A classic . . . one of the earliest and most influential statements of Japanese aesthetic theory"—(*LJ*).

Kobayashi, Takiji. THE FACTORY SHIP and THE ABSENTEE LANDLORD. Trans. by Frank Motofuji. *Univ. of Washington Press* 1973 $6.95. These two newly translated novelettes represent some of the best work of one of the best-known writers of Japan's proletarian literature school.

Mushakoji, Saneatsu. THE PASSION AND THREE OTHER JAPANESE PLAYS. Trans. by Noboru Hidaka. 1933. *Greenwood* 1971 $10.50. Mushakoji, an early twentieth-century novelist and playwright, presents in "The Passion" a clear illustration of his liberal and humanitarian views. The volume also includes Kunio Kishida's "The Roof Garden" and Sensabura Suzuki's "Living Koheiji."

Nakanoin Masatada no musume. THE CONFESSIONS OF LADY NIJO. Trans. by Karen Brazell. *Doubleday* Anchor Bks. 1973 pap. $2.95; (with title "Lady Nijo's Own Story [*Towazugatari*]: The Candid Diary of a 13th Century Japanese Imperial Concubine," trans. by Wilfred Whitehouse and Eizo Yanagisawa) *Tuttle* 1974 $10.00

An autobiographical narrative of 36 years, 1271–1306, in the life of Lady Nijo, starting when she became the concubine of a retired emperor in Kyoto at the age of 14 and ending with an account of her new life as a wandering Buddhist nun. In comparing the two translations, K. L. Richard states that the Whitehouse translation "creates a mood apart from the intent of the original text. . . . The Brazell translation, while retaining the poems in verse form had better sacrificed poesy for clarity"—(*Pacific Affairs*).

Naoe, Kinoshita. PILLAR OF FIRE. Trans. by Kenneth Strong. UNESCO Asián Fiction Ser. *Crane-Russak* 1972 $9.75. A novel of peace and social justice.

Ooka, Shobei. FIRES ON THE PLAIN: A Novel. Trans. by Ivan Morris. *Penguin* 1957 pap. $1.75. One of the most important novels published in Japan since World War II.

Osaragi, Jiro. THE JOURNEY. Trans. by Ivan Morris. *Knopf* 1960 $5.95. One of the first contemporary novels to be translated into English, it is an extraordinary story of postwar Japan. Osaragi began his career in the Japanese Foreign Office. He has written plays, travel books, and novels, many of which have been bestsellers in Japan.

Shimei, Futabatei (pseud.). JAPAN'S FIRST MODERN NOVEL: Ukigumo of Futabatei Shimei. Trans. with critical commentary by Marleigh Grayer Ryan. *Columbia* 1967 $12.00 pap. $3.95. A brief and readable love story of the 1880s, with biographical and critical notes.

Takeda, Taijun. THIS OUTCAST GENERATION and LUMINOUS MOSS. Trans. by Yusaburo Shibuya and Sanford Goldstein. *Tuttle* 1967 $3.25

"Moral studies in the best sense of the phrase, these novellas deserve wide circulation"—(*LJ*). "Sordid" themes of the aftermath of World War II are transformed into "true works of art" by a perceptive and distinguished nodern novelist.

Takeyama, Michio. HARP OF BURMA. Trans. by Howard Hibbett. *Tuttle* (UNESCO) 1966 pap. $2.95

A simple, prizewinning story of "a Japanese soldier of World War II caught in Burma after the cease fire and a vivid and moving insight into the soldier as a man"—(*Choice*).

TALE OF HEIKE: Heike Monogatari. Trans. by Hiroshi Kitagawa and Bruce T. Tsuchida. Fwd. by Edward G. Seidensticker. *International Scholarly Bk. Service* (Univ. of Tokyo Press) 1975 $47.00. The author of this epic depicts in 12 books and an epilogue the rise and fall of the House of Taira (the Heike clan) and its defeat at the hands of the powerful Minamoto (Genji clan). Original authorship is attributed to Nakayama Yukinari, born c. 1164. The "*Heike monogatari*" has inspired hundreds of later works and has acted as a major support of the warrior ethos in Japan.

Teika, Fujiwara. POEMS OF OUR TIME. Trans. with introd. by Robert H. Brower and Earl Miner. *Stanford Univ. Press* bilingual 1967 $6.00

"This first complete translation of the 13th-century *Kineai Shuka* is another of the most valuable Japanese literary offerings that Professors Brower and Miner have given us. . . . Highly recommended"—(*LJ*).

YOSHITSUNE: A Fifteenth-Century Japanese Chronicle. Trans. with introd. by Helen Craig McCullough. *Stanford Univ. Press* 1966 $8.50

The legend of Yoshitsune, a twelfth-century Japanese warrior, has long been a source for No plays and other Japanese literary works. "The translation reads easily and often delightfully. . . . Belongs in any library" with an interest in Japanese history or literature—(*Choice*).

MURASAKI, SHIKIBU (pseud.) c. 978–1025.

Murasaki Shikibu, a lady of the Fujiwara clan, is generally acknowledged to be the author of most if not all of the "*Genji monogatari*," the finest of the Japanese prose romances. Little is known of her personal life; even her name is in doubt. Her sobriquet derives from an office held by her father and probably from the name of an important character in the book itself. She is also the author of the "*Murasaki Shikibu nikki*" (Diary of Murasaki Shikibu), a memoir of her life at court in the service of the Fujiwara Chancellor Michinaga from 1008 to 1010.

THE TALE OF GENJI. Trans. by Arthur Waley. *Random* (Modern Lib.) $4.95; *Doubleday* Anchor Bks. 1955, 1959 Part 1 pap. $2.95 Part 2 o.p. Contains The Tale of Genji; The Sacred Tree; A Wreath of Cloud; Blue Trousers; The Lady of the Boat; The Bridge of Dreams.

GENJI MONOGATARI. Trans. by Kencho Suematsu. Introd. by Terence Barrow. *Tuttle* 1974 pap. $3.75

SEI SHŌNAGON. fl. c. 980.

"The *Makura no sōshi* is a classical Japanese text ascribed to a 10th-century author known as 'Sei Shōnagon'; the original is part literary miscellany, part diary, and part poetaster's commonplace book, with over three hundred sections arranged in more or less random order, without respect to subject matter. In its present form (and that now translated with great distinction and sensitivity by Ivan Morris) the text is an accumulation from many different times and hands, a mountain of accretions which has built up around what was probably a fairly small late-10th-century nucleus.

"There is some slight reason for attributing that nucleus to a Heian court lady, but little or nothing is really known about her, and her name has not survived. ('Sei' is an abbreviation for an aristocratic clan name; 'Shōnagon' is a court title; but we know the actual names of very few of the Heian literary ladies.)"—(Roy Andrew Miller, in the *Nation*). "The 'Sei Shōnagon' of [Morris's] translation," he goes on, "who charms us by her insistence upon what 'I enjoy,' what 'I like to see,' and 'what I find unattractive,' is essentially a human figure . . . from our own . . . world." The second volume consists of scholarly notes and comment upon the text of Volume 1.

THE PILLOW BOOK OF SEI SHŌNAGON. Trans. and ed. by Ivan Morris. *Columbia* 1967 2 vols. Vol. 1 $12.50 Vol. 2 $15.00 set $25.00; *Penguin* 1971 pap. $2.25

IHARA, SAIKAKU (pseud. of Hirayama Togo; also Ibara Saikaku).   1642–1693.

Ihara, born of a humble family, became a well-to-do merchant. He began his literary career as a prolific poet. He was an outstanding and influential novelist and *haiku* poet.

THE LIFE OF AN AMOROUS WOMAN AND OTHER WRITINGS. Trans. and ed. by Ivan Morris. *New Directions* 1963 $7.50 pap. $3.95

COMRADE LOVES OF THE SAMURAI and SONGS OF THE GEISHAS. Trans. by Edward P. Mathers. *Tuttle* 1972 $2.95. "Comrade Loves of the Samurai" is a story of homosexual love between samurai, and "Songs of the Geisha" is a collection of geisha folksongs.

THE LIFE OF AN AMOROUS MAN. 1682. Trans. by Kengi Hamada. *Tuttle* 1963 pap. $2.95. A frank account of the adventures of a Japanese man-about-town. It provides interesting insights into the life of the rising merchant class in seventeenth-century Tokyo.

FIVE WOMEN WHO LOVED LOVE. 1686. Trans. by Wm. Theodore De Bary; with a background essay by Richard Lane and 17th-century ill. by Yoshida Hambei. *Tuttle* 1955 pap. $3.50. A collection of fine stories each dealing with the love affair of a different woman; among the last of Saikaku's erotic tales.

THE JAPANESE FAMILY STOREHOUSE, or The Millionaires' Gospel Modernised. 1688. Trans. by G. W. Sargent. 1959 o.p. A collection of 30 anecdotes of success and failure in business and an exploration of merchant morality.

THIS SCHEMING WORLD. 1694. Trans. by M. Takatsuka and D. C. Stubbs. *Tuttle* 1965 1973 $3.85 pap. $2.95. Debtors and creditors and their tricks.

BASHŌ (pseud. of Matsuo Munefusa; also Bashō Matsuo).   1644–1694.

A Japanese poet and the most influential writer of *haiku* and *haibun* in the formative years of these genres. In the early 1680s, he became a recognized *haiku* teacher and spent much of his later life in travels through Japan; his travel sketches make up the core of his literary work.

BACK ROADS TO FAR TOWNS: Bashō's Oku-no- hosomichi. Trans. by Cid Corman and Kamaike Susumu. *Grossman* Mushinsha Bks. 1968 $8.50

MONKEY'S RAINCOAT. Trans. by Maeda Cana. *Grossman* Mushinsha Bks. 1973 $20.00 pap. $5.95

THE NARROW ROAD TO THE DEEP NORTH AND OTHER TRAVEL SKETCHES. Trans. by Nobuyuki Yuasa. *Gannon* $5.00; Classics Ser. *Penguin* 1974 pap. $1.85

WAY OF SILENCE: The Prose and Poetry of Basho. Ed. by Richard Lewis. *Dial* 1970 $4.95

Books about Bashō

Matsuo Bashō. By Makoto Ueda. World Authors Ser. *Twayne* 1970 $6.95

ISSA, KOBAYASHI (pseud. of Kobayashi Nobuyuki).   1763–1827.

Issa was a master of *haiku* and *haibun*, a prose equivalent of *haiku*. His poetry is greatly admired for its clarity and humanity.

OF THIS WORLD: A Poet's Life in Poetry. Ed. by Richard Lewis. *Dial* 1968 $4.95 text ed. $4.58

Don't Tell the Scarecrow and Other Japanese Poems. *Scholastic Bk. Services* Four Winds 1970 $5.62 Starline 1974 pap. $.75

The Autumn Wind. Trans. and ed. by L. Mackenzie. o.p.

The Year of My Life: A Translation of Issa's "Oraga Haru." Trans. by Nobuyuki Yuasa. 1960 *Univ. of California Press* rev. ed. 1973 $8.50 pap. $2.45. An autobiographical record of the year 1819 translated into poetry and prose.

MORI ŌGAI (pseud. of Mori Rintarō). 1862–1922.

A novelist, playwright, literary critic, and prolific translator from German and Scandinavian, Mori played a key role in the development of modern Japanese drama and poetry.

Vita Sexualis. 1909. Trans. by Kazuji Ninomiya and Sanford Goldstein. *Tuttle* 1972 $5.00. This autobiographical novel, which first appeared in 1909, is an important forerunner of modern fiction in its candid treatment of human sexuality.

The Wild Geese. 1911–1913. Trans. by Kingo Ochiai and Sanford Goldstein. *Tuttle* 1958 1974 pap. $3.50. This romantic novella of unfulfilled love, set against a background of social change, was written in 1911. It was filmed, and shown abroad as "The Mistress."

OKAKURA, KAKUZO. 1862–1913.

Okakura was born in Yokohama and like many other merchants' sons of the time was raised with an orientation towards the West. He entered Tokyo Imperial University in 1877, where he undertook his study of Oriental arts. He travelled extensively in India, China, and Europe and finally found his niche, first as Advisor and later as Curator of Oriental Art at the Boston Museum of Fine Arts.

"The Book of Tea," written in English, has been translated into innumerable languages including Japanese. Okakura wrote it soon after he arrived in America and before publication read it aloud "in the artistic gathering that centered around Mrs. Gardner, the 'Queen of Boston,' who ruled an aesthetic kingdom in her palatial home at Fenway Court." The volume has come to be read as a key to Western understanding of Eastern ideas. "Okakura's insight and compassion, his irony and his power of self-observation, and the piquant lyricism of his style have won the book a far greater audience than he could ever have imagined"—(Quotations are from Elise Grilli's Foreword).

The Book of Tea. 1906. Fwd. and biographical sketch by Elise Grilli. *Tuttle* 1957 $5.95; ed. with introd. by Everett F. Bleiler *Dover* 1962 pap. $1.00; *Gannon* $4.50

Ideals of the East with Special Reference to the Art of Japan. *Tuttle* 1970 $2.95

Books about Okakura

The Life of Kakuzo. By Y. Horioka. 1963 o.p.

NATSUME, SŌSEKI (pseud. of Natsume Kinnosuke). 1867–1916.

The leading novelist of the late Meiji and early Taishō periods, Sōseki studied English at Tokyo Imperial University and spent the years 1900–1903 in England. He succeeded Lafcadio Hearn as lecturer in English literature at the University and resigned in 1907 to become the literary editor of the newspaper *Asahi Shimbun*. As part of his duties, he agreed to publish serially one novel each year, a commitment which, with few lapses, he was able to meet for the rest of his career.

I Am a Cat. 1906. Trans. by Aiko Ito and Graeme Wilson. *Tuttle* 1972 $5.00. A satire, from a feline point of view, of Japanese life and attitudes.

Botchan. 1906. Trans. by Alan Turney. *Tuttle* 1968 $4.75; *Kodansha International* 1972 $6.50. The tragicomic record of a young Tokyo schoolteacher's experience in a provincial school.

Kokoro. 1914. Trans. by Edwin McClellan. 1957 *Regnery* 1967 pap. $1.95. Describes the tragic failure of a man who in his youth betrayed his best friend.

Grass on the Wayside (*Michikusa*): A Novel. 1915. Trans. and ed. by Edwin McClellan. UNESCO Collection of Representative Works: Japanese Ser. *Univ. of Chicago Press* 1969 $7.00

LIGHT AND DARKNESS: An Unfinished Novel. 1916. Trans. by V. H. Viglielmo. UNESCO Collection of Representative Works: Japanese Ser. *Univ. Press of Hawaii* 1971 $9.00

TEN NIGHTS OF DREAM, HEARING THINGS, THE HEREDITY OF TASTE. Trans. by Aiko Ito and Graeme Wilson. *Tuttle* 1974 $6.95

Books about Sōseki Natsume

Natsume Sōseki. By Beongcheon Yu. World Authors Ser. *Twayne* 1969 $6.95

Two Japanese Novelists: Sōseki and Toson. By Edwin McClellan. *Univ. of Chicago Press* 1969 $8.95

TANIZAKI, JUNICHIRO (or Jun-Ichiro). 1886–1965.

Tanizaki was born in Tokyo, the son of an old merchant family, and studied Japanese literature at Tokyo Imperial University. In his bohemian youth he was influenced by Poe, Baudelaire, and Oscar Wilde (*qq.v.*). After the earthquake of 1923, he moved from the cosmopolitan Tokyo area to the gentler and more cultured Kyoto region. He then abandoned his Westernization and became deeply absorbed in the Japanese past. Tanizaki translated three versions of "The Tale of Genji" (*q.v.*) into modern Japanese, first between 1939 and 1941, and later between 1951 and 1954 and 1959 and 1960. He received the Imperial Prize in Literature in 1949 and in 1964 was elected an honorary member of the American Academy and the National Institute of Arts and Letters.

SEVEN JAPANESE TALES. Trans. by Howard S. Hibbett. *Knopf* 1963 $6.95; *Berkley* pap. $.95. Includes shorter works such as Tattoo (1910), A Blind Man's Tale (1931), A Portrait of Shunkin (1933), and The Bridge of Dreams (1959).

SOME PREFER NETTLES. 1928. Trans. by Edward G. Seidensticker. *Berkley* pap. $1.25

The *Atlantic* called "Some Prefer Nettles" "a delicately composed and subtly shaded work of art." It is a significant novel about an unhappy modern marriage. The author divorced his first wife under similar amicable circumstances two years after this novel appeared in Japan, and in 1935 married again.

ASHIKARA AND THE STORY OF SHUNKIN: Modern Japanese Novels. 1936. Trans. by Roy Humpherson and Hajime Okita. *Greenwood* 1970 $9.50

THE MAKIOKA SISTERS. 1946–1949. Trans. by Edward G. Seidensticker. *Knopf* 1957 $7.95; *Grosset* Univ. Lib. 1966 pap. $3.50; *Berkley* 1975 pap. $2.95

The *New Yorker* found "The Makioka Sisters" "an extraordinary book, which can truly be said to break new ground." Published between 1946 and 1949, it is one of the most important novels of the immediate postwar years.

THE KEY. 1956. Trans. by Howard S. Hibbett. *Knopf* 1961 $5.95; *Berkley* 1971 pap. $.95. A study of the impact of the fear of impotence on a middle-aged man.

DIARY OF A MAD OLD MAN. 1961. Trans. by Howard S. Hibbett. *Knopf* 1965 $4.95; *Berkley* 1971 pap. $.95

Tanizaki, in his later writing, became increasingly preoccupied with sexuality. "The Diary of a Mad Old Man" is the story of a dying man not yet feeble enough to cease desiring his attractive young daughter-in-law. "In examining the fantasies, schemes and 'outrageous' behavior of Utsugi, Tanizaki explores the edges of 'absolute need' and its effect upon established notions of morality.... Tanizaki was a pro, and he was never more so than in this lean, taut book"—(*SR*). Howard Hibbett's translation is, as usual, excellent.

KAGAWA, TOYOHIKO. 1888–1960.

This Christian mystic and social worker wrote poetry, philosophical and religious essays, and books for children, as well as novels. One of the best-known novels was "A Grain of Wheat" (1936, o.p.). His autobiographical novel "Before the Dawn" (1924, o.p.) sold 250,000 copies.

LOVE, THE LAW OF LIFE. Rev. by Glenn Clark. 1951 o.p.

(With others) SONGS FROM THE LAND OF DAWN. *Bks. for Libraries* Granger Index Reprint 1949 $7.50

Books about Kagawa

Saint in the Slums: Kagawa of Japan. By Cyril J. Davey. 1961 *Christian Literature* 1968 pap. $1.25. This simple and sympathetic biography, first published in England, gives a vivid picture of Kagawa and his struggles for the education which equipped him for his life's work—combating poverty and disease in the slums of Japan. His poems, quoted throughout, "enrich the subject and deepen one's understanding of the man."

AKUTAGAWA, RYUNOSUKÉ. 1892–1927.

Akutagawa studied English literature at Tokyo Imperial University from 1913 to 1916 and in 1919 became an editor of the newspaper *Osaka Mainichi*. He was a disciple of Natsume Sōseki (*q.v.*) and devoted most of his writing to the short story form. His stories have "little or no contact with reality, dealing in the strange, supernatural and macabre, and are almost plotless in the Western sense—impressionistic rather than narrative"—(*LJ*). He died by suicide.

TALES, GROTESQUE AND CURIOUS. Trans. by Takashi Kojima. 1930. *Japan* 1963 rev. ed. $2.00. Includes "Rashomon" and the author's first story, "The Nose."

HELL SCREEN AND OTHER STORIES. Trans. by W. H. Norman. 1948 *Greenwood* 1971 $10.50. "Hell Screen" (1918) was later made into a film.

RASHOMON AND OTHER STORIES. Trans. by Takashi Kojima; introd. by Howard Hibbett; ill. by M. Kuwata. *Liveright* 1952 enl. ed. 1961 new ed. 1970 $5.95 pap. $1.95. Two stories, "Rashomon" and "In a Grove" (1914), were the source for the Japanese film "Rashomon," which won the grand prize at the twelfth International Film Festival at Venice (1951).

JAPANESE SHORT STORIES. Trans. by Takashi Kojima; introd. by John McVittie. *Liveright* 1961 rev. ed. 1962 1970 $5.95 pap. $2.45

EXOTIC JAPANESE STORIES. Trans. by Takashi Kojima and John McVittie. *Liveright* 1972 $6.95 pap. $3.95. Sixteen unusual tales and unforgettable images.

TU TZE-CHUN. 1920. by Dorothy Britton; introd. by Edward G. Seidensticker; woodcuts by Naoka Matsubara. *Kodansha International* 1965 $7.50

"Tu Tze-chun" is an adaptation of a ninth-century Chinese tale of "a youth who squanders his fortune and . . . eventually finds peace through being human. . . . A delightful story and a beautiful book"—(*LJ*).

KAPPA. Trans. by Geoffrey Bownas; introd. by G. H. Heally. *Tuttle* 1971 pap. $2.95; trans. by Seiichi Shiojiri 1951 new ed., rev. 1970 *Greenwood* $8.75. A satire on Japanese art, society, and morals.

FOOL'S LIFE. Trans. by Will Petersen. *Grossman* Mushinsha Bk. 1970 $10.00

Books about Akutagawa

Akutagawa; An Introduction. By Beongcheon Yu. *Wayne State Univ. Press* 1972 $9.95. An introduction to his life and work.

KAWABATA, YASUNARI. 1899–1972. (Nobel Prize 1968)

This distinguished novelist, literary critic, and former Chairman of the Japanese Center of the PEN Club was born in Osaka. As a boy, he hoped to become a painter, an aspiration reflected in his novels. He was graduated from Tokyo Imperial University in 1924. He is noted for infusing naturalism, imported from France, with a sensual, more Japanese impressionism. He was awarded the Nobel Prize for Literature in 1968 "for his narrative mastership, which with great sensibility expresses the essence of the Japanese mind." He died by suicide in 1972, leaving no note of explanation.

SNOW COUNTRY. 1947. *Berkley* pap. $1.50; (and "The Thousand Cranes") UNESCO Collection of Representative Works: Japanese Ser. *Knopf* 1969 $6.95. C. J. Rolo in the *Atlantic* called "Snow Country" "one of the finest short novels I have read since the war . . . The writing throughout is subtle, delicately moving and full of striking imagery." Serialized between 1935 and 1937, but not published in book form until 1947, it is a beautiful story of a country geisha's love for a Tokyo dilettante.

THE THOUSAND CRANES. 1949–1951. Trans. by Edward G. Seidensticker. *Berkley* pap. $1.50. A poignant yet simple story of ill-fated love.

SOUND OF THE MOUNTAIN. 1949–1953. Trans. by Edward G. Seidensticker. *Knopf* 1970 $6.95; *Berkley* 1971 pap. $1.25. A series of short stories on the domestic life of an elderly Tokyo businessman and his family. Reputed to be the author's favorite work.

JAPAN THE BEAUTIFUL AND MYSELF. 1968. Trans. by Edward G. Seidensticker. *Kodansha International* 1969 $1.50. The lecture the author delivered in Stockholm when he received the Nobel Prize.

HOUSE OF THE SLEEPING BEAUTIES AND OTHER STORIES. Trans. by Edward G. Seidensticker. *Kodansha International* 1969 $6.50. Includes, the stories "One Arm" and "Of Birds and Beasts."

THE MASTER OF GO. Trans. by Edward G. Seidensticker. *Knopf* 1972 $5.95; *Berkley* 1974 pap. $1.75

THE IZU DANCER AND OTHER STORIES. Trans. by Edward G. Seidensticker and Leon Picon. *Tuttle* 1974 pap. $3.75

THE LAKE. Trans. by Reiko Tsukimura. *Kodansha International* 1974 $6.95

BEAUTY AND SADNESS. Trans. by Howard S. Hibbett. *Knopf* 1975 $7.95

DAZAI, OSAMU (pseud. for Tsushima Shūji).   1909–1948.

One of the most accomplished writers to emerge in Japan in the immediate postwar years, Dazai's novels and stories reflect his own mental instability. He has been classified as a "decadent." His death was by suicide.

NO LONGER HUMAN. Trans. by Donald Keene. *New Directions* 1958 1973 pap. $2.25

A short novel that explores with . . . intelligence and delicacy the heart and mind of a young man who feels himself to be 'no longer human,' a creature outside of the human race"—(Gene Baro, in the *N.Y. Herald Tribune*). It purports to be three notebooks left by a young man who has died insane, with a prologue and epilogue by their discoverer. The translation, by an expert, is well done. "The book transcends mere cultural history. . . . It makes plausible that deep impulse in all of us which (in our weakness) we are most resolute to ignore—the wish to die"—(Donald Barr, in the *N.Y. Times*).

THE SETTING SUN. Trans. by Donald Keene. 1947, U.S. 1956 *New Directions* rev. ed. 1968 pap. $1.95

" 'The Setting Sun,' controversial though it seemed, shows so much social insight into contemporary Japan and psychological refinement in the study of its people that it may well be a book of permanent value"—(Gene Baro, in the *N.Y. Herald Tribune*).

ABÉ, KŌBŌ (pseud. for Abé Kimifusa).   1925–

Abé, a writer, dramatist, and essayist, is the leading figure of the *sengoha* postwar school and the most decidedly modernist avant-garde author in Japan today. Influenced by surrealism and dadaism, realism and fantasy are intermingled in his work, which paints a picture of the condition of modern man.

THE WOMAN IN THE DUNES. 1962. Trans. by E. Dale Saunders; ill. by Machi Abé (the author's wife). 1964 *Random* Vintage Bks. 1972 pap. $1.95

"The Woman in the Dunes," a novel later made into a film, expresses Abé's taste for the bizarre. It is the story of an insect-hunter (male) entrapped in a sandpit with a woman who becomes symbolically the spider, he her prey. The author has "combined a Crusoe-like fascination with survival with the larger issues of liberty and obligation"—(Thomas Lask, in the *N.Y. Times*).

THE FACE OF ANOTHER. 1964. Trans. by E. Dale Saunders. 1966 o.p.

"The Face of Another" describes the fortunes of an accidentally mutilated scientist who dons a mask to hide his wounds and seduce his own wife. "The central shaping metaphor of face and facelessness is brilliant, and Abé's relentless pursuit of its every implication is powerful"—(*SR*).

THE RUINED MAP. Trans. by E. Dale Saunders. *Knopf* 1969 $5.95

FRIENDS. Trans. by Donald Keene. *Grove* 1969 $3.95 Evergreen Bk. pap $2.45

INTER ICE AGE FOUR: A Novel of the Future. Trans. by E. Dale Saunders; ill. by Machi Abé. *Knopf* 1970 $5.95. A novel of social criticism using the technique of science fiction.

THE BOX MAN. Trans. by E. Dale Saunders. *Knopf* 1974 $6.95; *Berkley* 1975 pap. $1.95

MISHIMA, YUKIO (pseud. of Kimitake Hiraoka).   1925–1970.

Mishima was born in Tokyo. On graduation from the Peers' School he received a citation from the Emperor as the highest honor student. After graduating from the Tokyo Imperial School of

Jurisprudence in 1947 he began writing—novels, short stories, four successful plays for the Kabuki Theatre, one-act plays and several volumes of essays. Immediately after World War II, he was brought to this country as a guest of the State Department and of *Partisan Review*. His interest in Japanese classics distinguished him from many of his literary contemporaries who felt that the pre-Meiji literary past could never be recovered. His commitment to traditional Japanese culture was consummated on November 25, 1970, when, in an act that created a great sensation, Mishima committed *seppuku* in the traditional manner, shortly after delivering to his agent the final installment of his last novel.

DEATH IN MIDSUMMER AND OTHER STORIES. Trans. by Ivan Morris, Donald Keene and others. *New Directions* 1966 pap. $2.25

Although some of Mishima's works are set in the historical past, he is concerned with questions very relevant to the modern world—amorality, nihilism, man's capacity for evil. Howard Hibbett said (in *SR*) of "Death in Midsummer": "Psychological analysis in the classic French tradition is enhanced by . . . a sensibility fusing passions, meditations, and landscapes in the great tradition of Japanese literature."

CONFESSIONS OF A MASK. 1949. Trans. by Meredith Weatherby. *New Directions* 1958 1968 pap. $2.25. The semiautobiographical record of awakening sexuality in a lonely youth during and after a war.

THIRST FOR LOVE. 1950. Trans. by Alfred H. Marks; introd. by Donald Keene. *Knopf* 1969 $4.95; *Berkley* 1971 pap. $1.50. Concerns a love-deprived woman driven to commit murder.

FORBIDDEN COLORS. 1951. Trans. by Alfred H. Marks. *Knopf* 1968 $6.95; *Berkley* 1974 pap. $1.95. The story of an old man's exploitation of a young man in revenge against life, somewhat disappointing to most critics.

THE SOUND OF WAVES: A Love Story. 1954. Trans. by Meredith Weatherby; ill. by Yoshinori Kinoshita. *Knopf* 1956 $4.95; *Berkley* 1971 pap. $1.50. "The Sound of Waves," a story of first love in a Japanese fishing village, is told with great tenderness and depth of feeling.

THE TEMPLE OF THE GOLDEN PAVILION. 1956. Trans. by Ivan Morris. *Knopf* 1959 $6.95; *Berkley* pap. $1.75. The burning of the 500-year-old Kinkakuji Temple by a neurotic young acolyte is the basis of this complex novel.

FIVE MODERN NŌ PLAYS. Trans. by Donald Keene. 1957 *Random* Vintage Bks. 1973 pap. $1.95. These are experimental combinations of Nō plots with contemporary characters and situations.

AFTER THE BANQUET. 1960. Trans. by Donald Keene. *Knopf* 1963 $6.95; *Berkley* 1971 pap. $1.75

THE SAILOR WHO FELL FROM GRACE WITH THE SEA. 1963. Trans. by John Nathan. *Knopf* 1965 $4.95; *Berkley* 1971 pap. $1.50

"The Sailor Who Fell from Grace with the Sea," the symbolic tale of a young boy's relationship with his mother and her seafaring lover, is "profoundly, even beautifully macabre. . . . In its portrayal of adult passion and its manipulation of narrative points of view it recalls Henry James, while in its picture of childhood, its almost allegorical approach, it reminds one of William Golding in 'Lord of the Flies' "—(*SR*).

MADAME DE SADE. Trans. by Donald Keene. *Grove* 1967 pap. $2.45

The play "Madame de Sade," in which de Sade himself does not appear, concerns his female household, revolving around his wife (in the author's words) "with something like the motions of the planets." He, however, is the center of conversation. "It is in reality a morality play . . . more an intellectual exercise than a dramatic experience (though it had a 'great success' when staged in Tokyo)"—(*LJ*). There is little evidence that it is written by a Japanese. Photographs from the Tokyo production are included in the present edition—the costumes were French rococo.

SUN AND STEEL. Trans. by John Bester. *Kodansha International* 1970 $10.00; *Grove* Evergreen Bks. 1972 pap. $2.45

SPRING SNOW. Trans. by Michael Gallagher. *Knopf* 1972 $7.95; *Simon & Schuster* Pocket Bks. 1975 pap. $1.95

RUNAWAY HORSES. Trans. by Michael Gallagher. *Knopf* 1973 $7.95; *Simon & Schuster* Pocket Bks. 1975 pap. $1.95

THE TEMPLE OF THE DAWN. Trans. by E. Dale Saunders and Cecilia Segawa Seigle. *Knopf* 1973 $7.95; *Simon & Schuster* Pocket Bks. 1975 pap. $1.95

THE DECAY OF THE ANGEL. Trans. by Edward G. Seidensticker. *Knopf* 1974 $6.95; *Simon & Schuster* Pocket Bks. 1975 pap. $1.95. The last four novels comprise Mishima's tetralogy entitled "The Sea of Fertility," vols. 1–4, originally published in Japanese between 1969 and 1971. Thought by the author to be his greatest work, it reflects his view of Japan from the turn of the century into the future.

Books about Mishima

The Life and Death of Yukio Mishima. By Henry Scott-Stokes. *Farrar, Straus* 1974 $10.00. This is the first biography of Mishima to be published in the West.
Mishima: A Biography. By John Nathan. *Little* 1974 $8.95

OË, KENZABURO. 1935–

Kenzaburo Oë is one of Japan's most popular and prolific writers. While he has broken away from the semi-autobiographical novel which characterizes the writing of so many of Japan's modern authors, some of Oë's most successful works use the familiar setting of his native Shikoku. He has been an active political writer for Japan's new left and is said to have an encyclopedic knowledge of current American fiction. Oë's literary and philosophical sources range from Twain and Melville to Sartre and Camus.

A PERSONAL MATTER. 1964. Trans. with introd. by John Nathan. *Grove* Black Cat Bks. pap. $1.95. This novel, his first to be translated into English, describes the maturing of the hero—called Bird—when he is faced with the decision as to whether his brain-damaged baby must live or die. "One of the most affecting and exciting novels of the year, [it] is in part autobiographical (one of the author's children is mentally retarded); but it also reflects the spiritual groping—a search for authenticity—that seems common to our age, not only in Japan but among intelligent, aware people around the world. One of the triumphs of the novel is that Bird himself is convincingly intelligent—a difficult and rare achievement in fiction."

THE SILENT CRY. Trans. by John Bester. *Kodansha International* 1974 $10.00

Korean Literature

No history of Korean literature can be written without acknowledging the strong influence of Chinese culture in pre-modern Korea. Indeed, until the mid-fifteenth century the use of Chinese characters was standard practice in Korean literature. Among the most important examples of early Korean work extant is a group of 45 poems written in Chinese between the seventh and fourteenth centuries. In the 1440s a new Korean alphabet was devised by a group of scholars under royal patronage. The first work published in this new alphabet was the *"Yong Pi Ŏ Ch'ŏn Ka"* ("The Song of the Dragons Flying to Heaven," *q.v.*), a long poem in praise of the founders of the Yi dynasty.

The literature which has received a great amount of critical attention consists of poems from the late sixteenth to the early nineteenth centuries called *sijo,* a form of lyric poem with prescribed versification. Early prose, or *sosŏl,* is generally in the novel form and many of the extant examples are translations and imitations of Chinese works. Foremost are two novels by Kim Man-jung (1637–1692) written in Chinese and later translated into Korean by Kim Ch'unt'aek (1670–1717). One, *"Sa-ssi Namjŏng ki,"* which has recently appeared in English translation in Seoul ("A Korean Classic: The Story of Mrs. Sah's Journey to the South." Trans. by The Creative Writing Group. *English Student Association* 1973), is the tale of a concubine who replaces a wife and brings a husband to ruin. The second, *"Kuun mong"* ("A Nine Cloud Dream"), regarded by some as technically the best of the *sosŏl,* is a highly readable story which gives a vivid picture of Korean Buddhism, Confucianism, and Taoism as they operated in Korean life. This novel is one of three in an excellent collection also published in Seoul ("Virtuous Women: Three Masterpieces of Traditional Korean Fiction." Trans. by Richard Rutt and Kim Chong-un. UNESCO Collection of Representative Works: Korean Ser. *Korean National Commission for UNESCO* 1974). This volume also includes "The True History of Queen Inhyŏn" and "The Song of a Faithful Wife, Ch'unhyang."

Twentieth-century Korean literature is characterized by a movement to break away from classical traditions, both in style and theme. Among the outstanding modern writers are Yi Kwangsu and Kim Tongin, both prodigious producers of novels and short stories, and Kim Sowŏl, author of "The Azaleas," one of the most popular modern Korean poems. It should be noted that, while Korean publishers have issued a number of English translations of Korean literary works, both in the form of anthologies and separate pieces, in particular under the aegis of the Korean National Commission for UNESCO and the Korean Center of the International PEN, materials published in the United States have until quite recently concentrated on Korean history and politics. There are a number of excellent studies in this field, including "Corea: The Hermit Nation" by William E. Griffis (1882 1911 rev. 9th ed. *AMS Press* $25.00); "A History of Korea" by William E. Henthorn (*Macmillan* (Free Press) 1971 $9.95 pap. 1974 $3.95); and "Korea: The Politics of the Vortex" by Gregory Henderson (*Harvard Univ. Press* 1968 $13.50).

Gale, James S., Trans. Korean Folk Tales: Imps, Ghosts and Fairies. *Tuttle* 1963 pap. $2.20

Grigsby, Joan Savell, Trans. and ed. The Orchid Door: Ancient Korean Poems. Ill. by Lilian Miller. 1935 *Paragon Reprint* 1970 $6.00. Free translations of a number of premodern Korean poems.

Ko, Won, Trans. and ed. Contemporary Korean Poetry. Iowa Translation Ser. *Univ. of Iowa Press* 1970 $5.50

Lee, Peter Hacksoo. Korean Literature: Topics and Themes. Association for Asian Studies Monograph Ser. 1965 o.p.

(Trans. and ed.) Poems from Korea: A Historical Anthology. Rev. ed. UNESCO Collection of Representative Works: Korean Ser. *Univ. Press of Hawaii* 1973 $7.50. A revised edition of his "Anthology of Korean Poetry," published in 1964, brought up-to-date to reflect the most recent scholarship.

(Trans. and ed.) Flowers of Fire: Twentieth-Century Korean Stories. *Univ. Press of Hawaii* 1974 $12.00

Pai, Inez Kong, Trans. and ed. The Ever White Mountain: Korean Lyrics in the Classical Sijo Form. Ill. by Tai Shin Kin. 1965 o.p. A well-translated selection of classical Korean poetry with a lengthy introduction and a bibliography.

Pihl, Marshall R., Ed. Listening to Korea: A Korean Anthology. *Praeger* 1973 $9.00. An anthology of modern Korean prose literature.

Rutt, Richard, Trans. and ed. The Bamboo Grove: An Introduction to Sijo. UNESCO Collection of Representative Works: Korean Ser. *Univ. of California Press* 1971 $7.50. An excellent collection of *sijo* poems, with commentary by a leading scholar in the field.

The Songs of Dragons Flying to Heaven: A Korean Epic. Trans. by James Hoyt. UNESCO Collection of Representative Works: Korean Ser. *Univ. of Washington Press* 1971 $7.50. A translation of the classic *"Yong Pi Ŏ Ch'ŏn Ka."*

Songs of Flying Dragons: A Critical Reading. Trans. with critical commentary by Peter Hacksoo Lee. UNESCO Collection of Representative Works: Korean Ser. *Harvard Univ. Press* 1975 $16.95

Zŏng, In-sŏb, Trans. and ed. Folktales from Korea. 1953 *Greenwood* $13.75. Professor Zŏng has also translated two anthologies published in Korea: "Modern Short Stories from Korea" and "Pageant of Korean Poetry," and is the author of "An Introduction to Korean Literature."

Mongolian Literature

European scholars had long thought that Mongolian literature consisted almost entirely of translations, mainly of Buddhist works. Now, however, there is evidence of a rich tradition of oral and written literature as early as the thirteenth century. The earliest work extant, "The Secret History of the Mongols" (*q.v.*) dates from that time and is devoted principally to the life of Genghis Khan. It contains narrative and alliterative verse and is an important source on early Mongolian culture. Historical writing underwent a revival in the seventeenth century and consisted primarily of chronicles written under Lamaist influence. Folktales, fantastic or historical, and lyric poetry, mostly in the form of folk songs, epics, and stories comprised the bulk of the literature of entertainment which developed by the eighteenth century. The Revolution of 1921 saw a break in the literary tradition, with much writing thereafter becoming an instrument of political persuasion. While there are some noteworthy monographic studies of Mongolia, in particular Charles R. Bawden's "The Modern History of Mongolia" (*Praeger* 1968 $13.50) and a number by Owen Lattimore, such as "Nomads and Commissars: Mongolia Revisited" (*Oxford* 1962 $7.95), much of the work on Mongolian literature has taken place abroad, especially by such scholars as Paul Pelliot, Nicholas Poppe, and Walther Heissig. The most important work of the modern period is B. Rintchen's historical novel "Dawn on the Steppes," which is not currently available in English.

Bira, Sh. MONGOLIAN HISTORICAL LITERATURE OF THE SEVENTEENTH–NINETEENTH CEN-TURIES WRITTEN IN TIBETAN. Trans. from the Russian by Stanley N. Frye; ed. by Ts. Damdinsirren. Occasional Papers *Mongolia Society* $4.00

BLo' Bzan Bs Tan' Jin. ALTAN TOBCI: A Brief History of the Mongols. Ed. by Francis W. Cleaves. Harvard-Yenching Institute Scripta Mongolica Ser. *Harvard Univ. Press* 1952 pap. $5.50

Gerasimovich, Ljudmila Konstantinova. HISTORY OF MODERN MONGOLIAN LITERATURE, 1921–1964. 1965. *Mongolia Society* 1969 pap. $8.00

Mongolia Society. MONGOLIAN FOLKTALES, STORIES AND PROVERBS IN ENGLISH TRANS-LATION. 1967 o.p. This volume includes a section on English translation of Mongolian literature.

Poppe, Nicholas. THE DIAMOND SUTRA: Three Mongolian Versions of the Vajracchedika Prajnaparamita. *Int. Pubns. Service* 1971 $27.50

Rasipungsuy. BOLOR ERIKE: Mongolian Chronicle in Five Parts. Ed. by Francis W. Cleaves. Harvard-Yenching Institute Scripta Mongolica Ser. *Harvard Univ. Press* pap. $30.00

Secen, Sayang. ERDENI-YIN TOBCI: Mongolian Chronicles in Four Parts. Harvard-Yenching Institute Scripta Mongolica Ser. *Harvard Univ. Press* 1956 pap. $20.00

Schwartz, Henry G., Trans. and ed. MONGOLIAN SHORT STORIES. Program in East Asian Studies Occasional Papers Ser. *Western Washington State Univ. Press* 1974 pap. $4.00

Waley, Arthur. THE SECRET HISTORY OF THE MONGOLS AND OTHER PIECES. 1964 o.p.

Tibetan Literature

Tibetan was developed as a literary language from the seventh century onwards, its 30-letter syllabary based on an Indian model. Many of the works produced from then until the thirteenth century were translations of Sanskrit Buddhist works, done in close collaboration with Indian scholars in a regularized fashion. These have survived today in the Tibetan Buddhist Canon, the *"Kanjur"* (teachings of Buddha) and the *"Tanjur"* (translated treatises in the form of commentaries by Indian teachers). The indigenous tradition of story-telling relating to doctrines of Buddhist sages developed by the eleventh century and took its best form in what is known as religious biography (*rnam-thar*, or works of salvation); the best known of these is that by Mi-la Ras-pa (*q.v.*). The other native literature that existed, mainly lay poetry, songs, legends, and chronicles, was by the fourteenth century submerged by the dominant Buddhist influence of the many religious houses and orders.

Interest in Tibetan civilization, especially on the part of European scholars, has led to a number of English translations of Tibetan works and of monographs on Tibetan history. Outstanding among the latter are "A Cultural History of Tibet" by David L. Snellgrove and Hugh Richardson (U.S. 1968, o.p.) and "Tibetan Civilization" by R. A. Stein, a prominent French Tibetanist (trans. by J. E. S. Driver; ill. by Lobsang Tendzin. rev. ed. *Stanford Univ. Press* 1972 $10.00). "Tibet" by Thubten Jigme Norbu and Colin Turnbull (*Simon & Schuster* 1968 $7.50 pap. 1970 $2.95) is a highly readable portrait of the people, religions, and customs of Tibet.

General Studies and Collections

DeLattre, Pierre. TALES OF THE DALAI LAMA. *Ballantine Bks.* 1973 pap. $1.25

Francke, A. H. ANTIQUITIES OF INDIAN TIBET. Ed. by F. W. Thomas. 2 vols. *South Asia Bks.* 1972 $30.00. Includes personal narratives and chronicles, translated with commentary.

Karmey, Samten G., Trans. and ed. THE TREASURY OF GOOD SAYINGS: A Tibetan History of Bon. London Oriental Ser. *Oxford* 1972 $32.00. A reassembly of scriptures from the pre-Buddhist Tibetan religion known as *bon* and a history of that religion.

Snellgrove, David L. THE HEVAJRA TANTRA: A Critical Study. *Oxford* 1959 $22.50

Von Schiefner, F. A., and W. R. Ralston. TIBETAN TALES. Norwood Folklore Ser. *Norwood Editions* $22.50

Vostrikov, A. I. TIBETAN HISTORICAL LITERATURE. Trans. by H. C. Gupta; ed. by D. Chattopadhyaya. 1970. Soviet Indology Ser. *Verry* 1972 $14.00

Willis, Janice Dean, Ed. THE DIAMOND LIGHT OF THE EASTERN DAWN: An Introduction to Tibetan Buddhist Meditations. *Simon & Schuster* 1972 $6.95 pap. 1973 $2.45

Individual Authors and Works

B Lo' bZàn ye-śes. THE YOUNGER BROTHER DON YOD: A Tibetan Play, Being the Secret Biography from the Words of the Glorius Lama, The Holy Reverend Blo bZang Ye Sttes. Trans. by Thubten Jigme Norbu and Robert B. Ekvall. Asian Studies Research Institute Oriental Ser. *Indiana Univ. Press* 1968 $6.50. The author lived between 1663 and 1737.

Mi-la Ras-pa. THE HUNDRED THOUSAND SONGS OF MILAREPA. Trans. by Carma C. C. Chang. *Harper* 1962 1970 $1.95; *University Bks.* 1970 $25.00. Revered as a great hermit and mystic and famed as the author of many religous and didactic songs which were worked by his followers into cycles of biographical anecdotes. He lived between 1040 and 1123.

sGam-po-pa. THE JEWEL ORNAMENT OF LIBERATION. Trans. by H. V. Guenther. Clear Light Ser. *Shambhala Pubns.* 1971 $4.95. An important philosophical and mystical writer and one of the chief disciples of Mi-la Ras-pa, sGam-po-pa lived between 1079 and 1153.

THE TIBETAN BOOK OF THE DEAD, or The After-death Experiences on the Bardo Plane, according to Lama Kazi Dawa-Samdup's English Rendering by W. Y. Evans-Wentz. *Oxford* 1936 1957 $12.50 pap. 1960 $2.95; *Peter Pauper* $1.95; *Causeway Bks.* 1973 $8.95; trans. by Francesca Fremantle and Chogyam Trungpa Clear Light Ser. *Shambhala* 1975 $12.50 pap. $3.95

THE TIBETAN BOOK OF THE GREAT LIBERATION. Ed. by W. Y. Evans-Wentz. *Oxford* 1954 $11.50 pap. 1968 $3.95

Yongden, Lama. MIPAM: A Tibetan Novel. Trans. by Percy Lloyd and Bernard Miall. *Mudra* (dist by Book People) 1972 pap. $3.95

—J. K. K.

Author Index

This index includes all authors mentioned in connection with titles of books they have written, whether they appear in introductory essays, general bibliographies at the beginnings of chapters, discussions under the main author headings, or "Books about" sections under main authors. Authors mentioned in passing—to indicate friendships, relationships, etc.—are generally not indexed. Exceptions to this have been made in chapters on foreign literatures little translated into English in an effort to aid the user in understanding the position of important writers in the historical progress of the literature. Editors are not indexed unless there is no specific author to be named; such books include anthologies, bibliographies, yearbooks, and the like. Translators are not indexed except in those rare cases in which the translator seems as closely attached to a title as the real author, for example Fitzgerald's translation of the "Rubáiyát of Omar Khayyám." Only last names and initials are listed. If two or more persons with the same surname and initials appear, first names are given in full. Chinese names are also given in full, e.g. Mao Tse-tung. Page numbers for main author headings are given in boldface.

Title Index

Titles of all books discussed in any section of "The Reader's Adviser" are indexed here, except broad generic titles such as "Complete Works," "Selections," "Poems," "Correspondence," etc. The Viking "Portable . . ." series is not indexed if the author's name is included in the title. In-print volumes of this series will be found under the main heading of the author concerned. In general subtitles are omitted. When two or more identical titles by different authors appear, the last name of the author is given in parentheses following the title. Subject headings are not indexed. We refer the reader to the detailed table of contents for this information.